An Introduction to Health Psychology

Second edition

Val Morrison and Paul Bennett

PEARSON

Prentice
Hall

Harlow, England • London • New York • Boston • San Francisco • Toronto
Sydney • Tokyo • Singapore • Hong Kong • Seoul • Taipei • New Delhi
Cape Town • Madrid • Mexico City • Amsterdam • Munich • Paris • Milan

Pearson Education Limited
Edinburgh Gate
Harlow
Essex CM20 2JE
England

and Associated Companies throughout the world

Visit us on the World Wide Web at:
www.pearsoned.co.uk

First published 2006
Second edition published 2009

© Pearson Education Limited 2006, 2009

ISBN: 978-0-273-71835-2

British Library Cataloguing-in-Publication Data
A catalogue record for this book is available from the British Library

Library of Congress Cataloging-in-Publication Data
A catalog record for this book is available from the Library of Congress

10 9 8 7 6 5 4 3
11 10

Typeset in 10.25/12.5pt Sabon by 35
Printed and bound by Graficas Estella, Navarra, Spain

CONTENTS

Supporting resources

Visit **www.pearsoned.co.uk/morrison** to find valuable online resources

Companion Website for students
- Multiple choice questions for self-testing
- Links to useful, up-to-date websites
- Searchable glossary to explain key terms
- Flashcards to test knowledge of key terms and definitions

For instructors
- A printable testbank of multiple choice questions for use in a classroom setting
- Tutorial ideas
- Downloadable PowerPoint slides
- Suggestions for essay questions to test deeper understanding of the subject

Also: The Companion Website provides the following features:
- Search tool to help locate specific items of content
- E-mail results and profile tools to send results of quizzes to instructors
- Online help and support to assist with website usage and troubleshooting

For more information please contact your local Pearson Education sales representative or visit **www.pearsoned.co.uk/morrison**

LIST OF FIGURES

LIST OF TABLES

LIST OF PLATES

PREFACE

Background to this book

Health psychology is a growth discipline at both undergraduate and post-graduate level; it is also an exciting, challenging and rewarding subject to study, with career opportunities developing within health care as well as within academic settings. We wrote this book because we believed that a comprehensive European-focused textbook was required that didn't pre-dominantly focus on health behaviours, but which gave equal attention to issues in health, in illness, and in health-care practice and intervention. Someone must have read our first edition because we have been asked to produce this second one! We have maintained our comprehensive coverage of health, illness and health care, while updating and including reference to significant new studies, refining some sections, restructuring others, and basically we have worked towards making this new edition distinctive and (even) stronger than the first!

At the outset of writing in 2005, we believed that for psychologists textbooks should be led by psychological theory and the evidence, as opposed to being led by behaviour or by disease. Diseases may vary clinically, but, psychologically speaking, they share many things in common – for example, potential for life or behaviour change, distress, challenges to coping, potential for recovery, involvement in health care and involvement with health professionals. We still believe this, reviewers of the first edition seemed to concur, and so we have stuck to this format in this second edition. We very much hope that you enjoy what we have put together.

Aims of this textbook

The overall aim of this textbook is to provide a balanced, informed and comprehensive UK/European textbook with sufficient breadth of material for introductory students, but which also provides sufficient research depth to benefit final year students or those conducting a health psychology project. In addition to covering mainstream health psychology topics such as health and illness beliefs, behaviour and outcomes, we include topics such as socio-economic influences on health, biological bases, individual and cultural differences and psychological interventions in health, illness and health care, as these are all essential to the study of health psychology.

In this edition, as in the first, we have constructed chapters which followed the general principle of issue first, theory second, research evidence third, and finally the application of that theory and, where appropriate, the effectiveness of any intervention. We first examine factors that contribute to health, including societal and behavioural factors, and how psychologists and others can improve or maintain individuals' health. We then examine the process of becoming ill: the physiological systems that may fail in illness, psychological factors that may contribute to the development of illness, how we cope with illness, and how the medical system copes with us when we become ill. Finally, we examine a number of psychological interventions that can improve the wellbeing and perhaps even health of those who experience health problems. For example, in Chapter 3 we describe associations between illness and behaviour such as smoking; in Chapter 5 we examine the empirical evidence of psychosocial explanations of smoking behaviour based on general theories such as social learning theory and specific models such as the Theory of Planned Behaviour, then in Chapter 6 and Chapter 7 we show how this evidence can be put to use in both individual and group-targeted interventions. Describing, predicting and then intervening are primary goals of health psychologists.

This text is intended to provide comprehensive coverage of the core themes in current health psychology but it also addresses the fact that many individuals neither stay healthy, nor live with illness, in isolation. The role of family is crucial and therefore while acknowledging the role of significant others in many chapters, for example in relation to influencing dietary or smoking behaviour, or in providing support during times of stress, we also devote a large part of a specific chapter to the impact of illness on significant others. Another goal of ours in writing this textbook was to acknowledge that Western theorists should not assume cross-cultural similarity of health and illness perceptions or behaviours. Therefore from the first edition to this current edition we have integrated examples of theory and research from non-Westernised countries wherever possible. Throughout this text runs the theme of differentials, whether culture, gender, age/developmental stage, or socio-economic, and as acknowledged by reviewers and readers of the first edition, our commitment to this is clearly seen in the inclusion of a whole chapter devoted to socio-economic differentials in health.

Structure of this textbook

We have made no sweeping structural changes to this second edition. The textbook continues to be structured into three broad sections. The first, *Being and Staying Healthy*, contains seven chapters, which first examine factors that contribute to health, including societal and behavioural factors, and then describe how psychologists and others can improve or maintain individuals' health. Chapter 1 considers what we actually mean when we talk about 'health' or 'being healthy' and presents a brief history to the mind–body debate which underpins much of our research. In this edition we consider more fully the influence of ageing and of culture on health, and in doing so illustrate better the biopsychosocial model which underpins health psychology. Chapter 2 describes how factors such as social class, income and even postcode can affect one's health, behaviour and access to health care. Indeed, the health of the general population is influenced by the socio-economic environment in which we live and which differs both within and across countries and cultures. We have tried to reflect more of this diversity in the present volume.

Many of today's 'killer' illnesses, such as some cancers, heart disease and stroke, have a behavioural component. Chapters 3 and 4 describe how certain behaviours such as exercise have health-enhancing effects whereas others, such as poor diet or smoking behaviour, have health-damaging effects. Evidence of lifespan, cultural and gender differentials in health behaviours is presented to an even greater degree than in our first edition. These behaviours have been examined by health and social psychologists over several decades, drawing on several key theories such as social learning theory and socio-cognitive theory. In Chapter 5 we describe several models which have been rigorously tested in an effort to identify which beliefs, expectancies, attitudes and normative factors contribute to health or risk behaviour. This chapter has been reworked for the second edition to include more consideration of personality and its influence on behaviour, and on motivational theories of health behaviour. This section, therefore, presents evidence of the link between behaviour and health and illness, and highlights an area where health psychologists have much to offer in terms of understanding or advising on individual factors to target in interventions. We therefore end with two chapters on intervention. Chapter 6 presents evidence of successful and less successful approaches to changing individual behaviours that increase risk for disease, while Chapter 7 applies the same review and critique to population approaches such as health education and promotion.

The second section, *Becoming Ill*, contains six chapters which take the reader through the process of becoming ill: the physiological systems that _____ in illness, the psychological factors that may contribute to the development of illness, how _____ with illness, and how the medical system copes with us when we become ill. We start ___ ____ ____ with a whole chapter dedicated to describing biological and bodily processes relevant to the physical experience of health and illness (Chapter 8). In this second edition, this chapter covers a broader range of illnesses as well as some individual CASE STUDY examples and more signposts to relevant psychological content to be found elsewhere in the book. Chapter 9 describes how we perceive, interpret and respond to symptoms, highlighting individual, cultural and contextual factors that influence these processes, and has seen slight restructuring in the current edition in order that illness perception is more clearly distinguished from symptom perception. Also in this second edition you will find expanded coverage of children and illness, in terms of their illness perceptions and responses, and throughout this chapter, as elsewhere in the textbook, we have drawn increasingly from qualitative studies, and also from good quality longitudinal studies. In Chapter 10 presenting to, and communicating with, health professionals is reviewed with illustrations of 'good' and 'not so good' practice. The role of patient involvement in decision making is an important one in current health policy and practice and the evidence as to the benefits of patient involvement is reviewed here. In this second edition we have introduced some case studies, and in this chapter, those introduced are then reflected on in Chapter 17 when describing interventions to enhance quality of life. The second edition has improved and expanded consideration of health-care policy and guidance as these highlight whether (or not) psychological theory and practice has 'made a difference': for example, we have considered guidelines for treatment related to specific health problems, such as those produced by NICE in the UK. Chapters 11 and 12 take us into the realm of stress, something that very few of us escape experiencing from time to time! We present an overview of stress theories, where stress is defined either as an event, a response or series of responses to an event, or as a transaction between the individual experiencing and appraising the event, and its actual characteristics. We describe in some detail a field of study known as psychoneuroimmunology, involving the study of how the mind influences the body via alterations in immunological functioning, which influence health status. Chapter 12 presents the research evidence pertaining to factors shown to 'moderate' the potentially negative effect of seemingly stressful events (for example, aspects of personality, coping styles and strategies, social support, optimism). These two chapters highlight the complexity of the relationship between stress and illness. Chapter 13 turns to methods of alleviating stress, where it becomes clear that there is not one therapeutic 'hat' to fit all, as we describe a range of cognitive, behavioural and cognitive-behavioural approaches.

In the third section, *Being Ill*, we turn our attention to the impact of illness on the individual and their families across two chapters. In the first of these (Chapter 14), we define and describe what is meant by 'quality of life' and how research has shown it to be challenged or altered by illness. In Chapter 15 we address other illness outcomes such as depression, and acknowledge the importance of family and significant others in patient outcomes. As stated earlier, perhaps unique to this textbook, there is a large section devoted to the impact of providing care for a sick person within the family and how differing beliefs and expectations of illness between the caregiver and the care-receiver can play a role in predicting health outcomes for both individuals. One of the many new RESEARCH FOCUS sections found in this second edition highlights this area of study. Chapter 16 addresses a phenomenon that accounts for the majority of visits to a health professional – pain – which has been shown to be much more than a physical experience. This chapter is the only disease-specific chapter in our text, but we chose to contain a chapter on pain and place it at this point towards the end of our book because, by illustrating the multidimensional nature of pain, we draw together much of what has preceded (in terms of predictors and correlates of illness, health-care processes etc.). Pain illustrates extremely well the biopsychosocial approach health psychologists endeavour to uphold. In a similarly holistic manner Chapter 17 looks at ways of improving health-related quality of life by means of interventions such as stress management training, the use of social support, and illness management programmes.

Finally, we close the second edition of this text in the same way as we closed the first, with Chapter 18, which we have called Futures. This chapter has changed significantly in that it now has three key foci: (i) how a number of psychological theories can be integrated to guide psychological interventions, (ii) how the profession of health psychology is developing in a variety of countries and the differing ways it is achieving growth, and (iii) how psychologists can foster the use of psychological interventions or psychologically informed practice in areas (both geographical and medical) where they are unused. This ends our book therefore by highlighting areas where health psychology research has or can perhaps in the future, 'make a difference'.

Hence this second edition contains much of what will be familiar to readers of the first, but rather than simply update our material (actually updating is not that simple!), we have, with an eye on the extremely constructive feedback from several excellent European reviewers, in summary, done the following:

- kept the same basic structure;
- continued to construct sections and chapters within them on the basic principle of issue first, theory second, research evidence third, and where appropriate, interventions fourth;
- increased our emphasis on critical psychology, in terms of casting a more macro-eye over social, environmental and cultural influences on health and illness;
- increased use of qualitative studies and personal experiences in an attempt to make the experiences of trying to maintain health or becoming ill more personal and accessible, for example, through the use of case studies in some chapters;
- added more features where they proved popular with readers and reviewers (e.g. What do YOU think?, RESEARCH FOCUS) and removed some where opinion was mixed (e.g. our cartoons . . . do let us know if you want them back!);
- provided internet websites at the end of most chapters that link to both academic and health-care-related sites, providing an easy link to a wide range of resources and interesting issues beyond the present text.

We hope you enjoy reading the book and learn from it as much as we learned while writing it. Enjoy!

Acknowledgements

This project has been a major one which has required the reading of literally thousands of empirical and review papers published by health, social and clinical psychologists around the globe, many books and book chapters, and many newspapers to help identify some hot health issues. The researchers behind all this work are thanked for their contribution to the field.

On a more personal level, several key researchers and senior academics also acted as reviewers for our chapters, firstly for chapters being prepared for the first edition, and for some, also reviewing the first edition in order to help us prepare the second! At each stage they have provided honest and constructive feedback. They provided informed suggestions which really have made this a better book than it might otherwise have been! They also spotted errors and inconsistencies that are inevitable with such a large project, and took their role seriously.

Many thanks also to the indomitable editorial team at Pearson Education, with several development editors having taken their turn at the helm and guided us through a few bad patches where academic demands and our own research prevented us from spending time on 'the book': originally Morten Fuglevand, the Acquisitions Editor; Jane Powell; the wonderfully supportive Paula Parish, and David Cox, and for the second edition Catherine Morrissey and Janey Webb. They have pushed, pulled, advised and cajoled us up to this point where we hand over to the production team. We owe continued thanks to Morten who secured Pearson's agreement to 'go colour'; we think it makes a difference and hope you do too. To those more hidden to us, the design team, photo acquisitions people, cartoonist and publicist, thanks for enhancing our text with some excellent features. We are grateful to you all.

Finally, to those that have made the coffee in the wee small hours, brought us wine, or otherwise kept us going while we hammered away at our computers in the North and the South of Wales, heartfelt thanks. To Dave, who unexpectedly died in December 2006 and so never had to put up with me during this second edition process, thank you for the memories. To Tanya who took on the role of coffee-maker, my unending love and immense pride. To Gill who stoically coped with my absences during both day and night . . . I think you noticed them! Love and thanks for looking after me.

Val Morrison and Paul Bennett

August 2008

GUIDED TOUR

CHAPTER 15

The impact of illness on patients and their families

Learning outcomes

By the end of this chapter, you should have an understanding of:

- typical models of adjustment to illness
- the negative emotional consequences of physical illness, for both the person with illness and those around them
- the evidence that benefits can be derived from being ill or providing care to an ill relative or friend
- the diverse nature of coping responses in the face of illness or caregiving
- how some forms of caregiving can be detrimental to the recipient
- why research should consider the perceptions and responses of the ill person and their informal caregivers when trying to predict psychosocial outcomes

Learning Outcomes at the start of each chapter introduce key topics that are covered, and summarise what is to be learnt.

Whatever the impact of this discussion on PB's career, the discussion held a key truth. Psychologists and others can develop many and complex interventions, but unless they are implementable within the context of a busy, and tightly resourced health-care service (as they all are), they will not be taken up by health-care professionals, and managers will not fund them. Interventions such as the Recurrent Coronary Prevention Program (which worked) and the ENRICHD study (which didn't) described in Chapter 17 may show the potential impact of complex and extended psychological interventions on health. But even if both had proved enormously successful, neither would be implemented in most existing health services. Interventions such as establishing implementation intentions or using simple distraction techniques to reduce worry may be less glamorous than these hugely expensive multi-factorial studies, but they may ultimately be of more benefit. Health psychologists may usefully concentrate on this type of intervention if they want their interventions to be of value in the health-care system.

RESEARCH FOCUS

Skevington, S.M., Day, R., Chisholm, A. and Trueman, P. (2005). How much do doctors use quality of life information in primary care? Testing the trans-theoretical model of behaviour change. *Quality of Life Research*, 14: 911–22.

The authors note that many quality of life (QoL) scales have been developed in recent years for general (i.e. measuring QoL across a number of health conditions) and specific (measuring QoL for one specific condition) use, and that QoL is acknowledged as an important outcome measure in health care. However, there is little empirical evidence showing whether doctors are actually measuring and using this information in clinical practice. The authors identify three benefits of doctors using generic QoL scales: (i) they can use the same scale over a variety of conditions, (ii) they enable comparisons between groups of patients with many different diagnoses, and can be used for audit purposes, and (iii) norms are available for 'well' people, giving them additional baseline information about the quality of their patients' life. The present study aimed to measure how and why general practitioners (family doctors) used, or did not use, measures of QoL.

Method

Procedure and sample
The study comprised a cross-sectional national postal survey of 800 British GPs using names taken from the UK Medical Directory. A pilot questionnaire was tested on 200 doctors, and then the main sample (n = 600) was derived by taking the first doctor's name on every seventh page of this document. The questionnaire was mailed to each GP, with a stamped addressed envelope in which to return the completed questionnaire. A reminder phone call was made if this was not returned within two weeks. A second reminder was sent in the post two weeks later, if necessary.

Questionnaire
The GP's were asked the following questions:

- the stage of change they were in in relation to the use of QoL measures (pre-contemplation, contemplation, planning, action, maintenance);

Research Focus boxes provide a summary of the aims and outcomes of current empirical papers. They encourage an understanding of methods used to evaluate issues relevant to health psychology and problems associated with those methods.

IN THE SPOTLIGHT

Smoking, drinking and teenage pregnancy

Studies of adolescent girls have pointed to the importance of self-concept (i.e. concept of what one 'is') and self-esteem (i.e. concept of one's 'value' or 'worth') in determining involvement or non-involvement in risk behaviours. Some theorists further suggest that a significant amount of adolescent behaviour is motivated by the need to present oneself to others (primarily peers) in a way that enhances the individual's reputation, their social identity (Emler 1984). In some social groups the 'reputation' that will help the individual 'fit' with that social group will involve risk-taking behaviours (Odgers *et al.* 1996; Snow and Bruce 2003). Snow and Bruce (2003) found female smokers to have less self-confidence, to feel less liked by their families, and to have lower physical and social self-concepts, while their peer self-concept surprisingly did not differ from that of non-smokers. In relation to becoming pregnant as a teenager, low self-esteem and a negative self-concept may again be implicated, as teenage mothers often show a history of dysfunctional relationships and social and financial strain. Alcohol appears to play a significant role in early sexual activity likely to lead to becoming pregnant, rather than being necessarily a problem during pregnancy. For example, alcohol consumption and being 'drunk' or 'stoned' is a commonly cited reason for first having sex when a teenager (e.g. Duncan *et al.* 1999; Wellings *et al.* 2001) and for subsequently having unprotected sex and risking both pregnancy and sexually transmitted diseases (Hingson *et al.* 2003). In contrast, there is some evidence that teenagers are less likely to drink during pregnancy than older mothers, thus placing their unborn child at lower risk of foetal alcohol syndrome (California Department of Health Services 2003). In terms of other behaviours during pregnancy, teenage mothers are more likely to have a poor diet and smoke during pregnancy than older mothers and, combined with their often physical immaturity, these behaviours may contribute to the higher rates of miscarriage, premature birth and low birthweight babies (Department of Health 2003; Horgan and Kenny 2007). Horgan and Kenney further note that the death rate for babies and young children born to teenage mums is 60 per cent higher than that for those born to older mothers, and younger mums are also three times more likely to suffer from post-natal depression.

Teenage substance use therefore has the potential to create significant long-term problems for the individual and potentially their child. However, changing adolescent risk behaviour is often challenging, given the complexity of influences thereon, but there is some evidence that interventions which address self-esteem issues before addressing 'behaviour' problems, including under-age sex, smoking and drinking alcohol, seem to meet with greater success than those which do not (e.g. Health Development Agency Magazine 2005).

Carbon monoxide reduces circulating oxygen in the blood, which effectively reduces the amount of oxygen feeding the heart muscles; nicotine makes the heart work harder by increasing blood pressure and heart rate; and together these substances cause narrowing of the arteries and increase the likelihood of thrombosis (clot formation). Tars impair the respiratory system by congesting the lungs, and this is a major contributor to the highly prevalent chronic obstructive pulmonary disease (COPD: e.g. emphysema) (Julien 1996). Overall, the evidence as to the negative health effects of smoking tobacco is indisputable, and more recently the evidence as to the negative effects of passive smoking has been increasing (Department of Health 1998b).

In The Spotlight boxes present some (often controversial) material – such as issues around smoking and teen pregnancy or ethnicity and pain – to provoke thought.

 What do YOU think? Have you ever experienced something which has challenged your quality of life? If so, in what way did it challenge it, and how did you deal with it? Did you find that one domain of QoL took on greater importance than it had previously? Why was this the case? Have the 'weightings' you attach to the different domains returned to their pre-challenge levels or has the event had a long-lasting impact on how you evaluate life and opportunities?

If you are lucky enough not to have experienced any major challenges to your QoL, consider how the loss of some aspect of health seems to have impacted on someone you know. Consider whether you would respond in the same way were you to lose that same aspect of health.

While being limited in terms of one's activities or roles is commonly a predictor of poorer mental and physical QoL, this is not always the case. Over half of the older people surveyed by Evandrou (2006) who had long-standing limiting illness self-rated their health as good or fairly good, highlighting the fact that quality of life is about more than just physical health and physical function. While a key global aim of interventions to enhance QoL, regardless of disease type, is the improvement and maintenance of physical and role functioning, in old age as at all ages QoL continues to be multidimensional. Even among the 'oldest old' (i.e. 85 or older), QoL encompasses psychological, social and environmental wellbeing (Grundy and Bowling 1999). ISSUES (below) addresses the question of whether or not QoL is attainable at the end of life, as a result of either ageing or terminal illness.

Plate 14.1 Social isolation increases the risk a reduced quality of life.
Source: Jerry Cooke/Corbis

What do YOU think? boxes ask the reader to pause and reflect on their own beliefs, behaviours or experiences. In this way, material can be contextualised within the reader's own life, helping to deepen understanding.

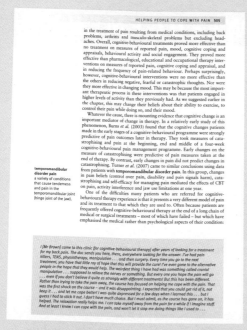

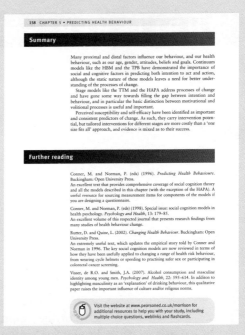

Key terms are defined alongside the text for easy reference and to aid understanding. Some terms are given a further, in-depth definition in the end-of-book **Glossary**.

Case Examples help the reader to grasp how the material applies to real-world outcomes and situations. **Case Studies** giving an insight into potential careers in Health Psychology are included in chapter 18.

Further Reading each chapter is supported by suggested further reading to direct the reader to additional information sources.

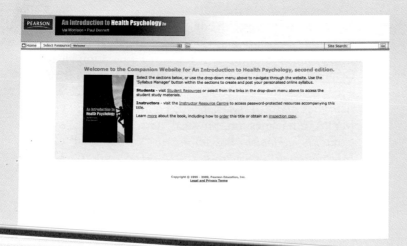

The **Companion Website** at **www.pearsoned.co.uk/morrison** includes resources such as multiple choice questions, weblinks, a searchable glossary and flashcards for students, and PowerPoint slides and tutorials for lecturers.

PUBLISHER'S ACKNOWLEDGEMENTS

We are grateful to the following for permission to reproduce copyright material:

Table 1.1 from National Statistics website: www.statistics.gov.uk, Crown copyright material is reproduced with the permission of the Controller Office of Public Sector Information (OPSI); Figure 2.1 from 'Inequalities in health expectancies in England and Wales: small area analysis from the 2001 Census', *Health Statistics Quarterly* 34 (Rasulo, D., Bajekal, M. and Yar, M. 2007), © Crown copyright 2007, Crown copyright material is reproduced with the permission of the Controller Office of Public Sector Information (OPSI), also reproduced with the permission of the author; Table 2.1 from WHO (2007) www.who.int; Figure 2.2 from *Fair Shares for All: Report of the National Review of Resource Allocation for the NHS in Scotland*, Scottish Executive, Crown copyright material is reproduced with the permission of the Controller of Her Majesty's Stationery Office and the Queen's Printer for Scotland; Table 2.2 from *Independent Inquiry into Inequalities in Health*, HMSO (Acheson, D. 1998), Crown copyright material is reproduced with the permission of the Controller of Her Majesty's Stationery Office and the Queen's Printer for Scotland; Figure 3.1 from 'Overweight and obesity as determinants of cardiovascular risk', *Archives of Internal Medicine*, 162, pp. 1867–1872, American Medical Association (Wilson, P.W.F., D'Agostino, R.B., Sullivan, L., Parise, H. and Kannel, W.B. 2002); Table 3.1 from *Alcohol Policy and the Public Good*, p. 10, Oxford University Press (Edwards, G., Anderson, P., Baboir, T., Casswell, S., Ferrence, N. *et al.* 1994), original source WHO, Geneva; Table 3.2 from *Report 5*, International Center for Alcohol Policies (1998); Figure 3.2 from *A Primer of Drug Action: A Concise, Nontechnical Guide to the Actions, Uses and Side Effects of Psychoactive Drugs*, 7th edn, W.H. Freeman, (Julien, R.M. 1996); Figure 3.3 from BHF coronary heart disease statistics at www.heartstats.org, produced with permission of the British Heart Foundation Health Promotion Research Group, University of Oxford; Figure 3.4 from PHLS Communicable Disease Surveillance Centre (2001); Figure 3.5 from the *National Survey of Sexual Attitudes and Lifestyles*, 1990; Figure 4.1 from 'Young people meeting the MVPA guidelines on physical activity (%)', *Young People's Health in Context – Health Behaviour in School-aged Children (HBSC) Study: International Report from 2001/2002 Survey*, Copenhagen, WHO Regional Office for Europe, 2004 (Health Policy for Children and Adolescents, No. 4), Figure 3.17, p. 94; Figure 5.3 from http://userpage.fu-berlin.de/~health.hapa.htm, reproduced with permission from Professor Dr Ralf Schwarzer of Freie Universität, Berlin; Figures 8.1, 8.2, 8.3 and 8.4 from Carlson, *Foundations of Physiological Psychology*, pp. 69, 76, 78 and 90, © 2005, reproduced by permission of Pearson Education, Inc.; Figure 9.1 from 'A symptom perception approach to common physical symptoms', *Journal of Social Science and Medicine*, 57(12), pp. 2343–2354 (Kolk, A.M., Hanewald, G.J.F.P., Sehagen, S. and Gijsbers van Wijk, C.M.T. 2003), copyright © 2003 with permission from Elsevier; Table 9.2 from 'Seeking medical consultation: perceptual and behavioural characteristics distinguishing consulters and nonconsulters with function dyspepsia', *Psychosomatic Medicine*, 62, pp. 844–852, Lippincott, Williams & Wilkins (Cheng, C. 2000); Figure 9.2 from Radley, A., *Making Sense of Illness: The Social Psychology of Health and Disease*, copyright (© Alan Radley 1994), reproduced by permission of SAGE Publications, London, Los Angeles, New Delhi and Singapore; Figure 9.3 from 'Illness cognition: using common sense to understand treatment adherence and affect cognitive interactions', *Cognitive Therapy and Research*, 16(2), 1992, p. 147 (Leventhal, H., Diefenbach, M. and Leventhal, E.), © Springer, part of Springer Science + Business Media, with kind permission from Springer Science + Business Media; Figure 9.4 from 'Determinants on three stages of delay in seeking care at a medical setting', *Medical Care*, 7, pp. 11–29, Lippincott, Williams & Wilkins (Safer, M.A., Tharps, Q.J., Jackson, T.C. and Leventhal, H. 1979); Figure 10.1 from 'Breaking bad news: a review of the literature', *Journal of the American Medical Association*, 276, pp. 496–502, American Medical Association (Ptacek, J.T.P. and Eberhardt, T.L. 1999); Table 11.1 from 'The social readjustment rating scale', *Journal of Psychomatic Research*, 11, pp. 213–218 (Holmes, T.H. and Rahe, R.H. 1967), © 1967 Elsevier, Inc., with permission from Elsevier; Figure 11.1 from *Stress and Health: Biological and Psychological Interactions* (Lovallo, W.R. 1997) p. 77, copyright 1997 by SAGE Publications, Inc., reprinted by permission of SAGE Publications, Inc.; Figure 11.2 and Table 11.3 from *Stress and Health*, Brooks/Cole (Rice, P.L. 1992), reprinted by permission of the author; Table 11.2 from 'From psychological stress to the emotions: a history of changing outlooks', *Annual Review of Psychology*, 44, pp. 1–21, © Annual Reviews (Lazarus, R.S. 1993); Figure 12.1 from *Stress and Emotion: A New Synthesis* (Lazarus, R.S. 1999), p. 198, reprinted with permission from Free Association Books, London; Figure 12.3 from 'Hardiness and health: a prospective study', *Journal of Personality and Social Psychology*, 42, pp. 168–77 (Kobasa, S.C., Maddi, S. and Kahn, S. 1982), APA, adapted with permission; Figure 14.1 from 'Quality of life: a process view', *Psychology and Health*, 12, pp. 753–767 (Leventhal, H. and Coleman, S. 1997), reproduced with permission from Taylor & Francis, www.tandf.co.uk/journals; Figure 15.1 from 'Positive effects of illness reported by myocardial infarction and breast cancer patients', *Journal of Psychosomatic Research*, 47, pp. 537–543 (Petrie, K.J., Buick, D.L., Weinman, J. and Booth, R.J. 1999), © 1999 with permission from Elsevier; Figure 15.2 from 'Turning the tide: benefit finding after cancer surgery', *Social Science and Medicine*, 59, pp. 653–662 (Schulz, U. and Mahomed, N.E. 2004), © 2004 with permission from Elsevier; Figure 15.3 from R.F. De Vellis, M.A. Lewis and K.R. Sterba (2003) 'Interpersonal emotional processes in adjustment to chronic illness', in J. Suls and K.A. Wallston (eds) *Social Psychological Foundations of Health and Illness*, Blackwell Publishing; Figure 16.1 from *Biological Psychology*, 1st edn, Figure 8.22 p. 274, Sinauer Associates, (Rosenzweig, M.R., Breedlove, S.M. and Watson, N.V. 1996).

We are grateful to the following for permission to reproduce the following photos:

Alamy/Big Cheese Photo (p. 2); Alessandro Bianchi/Reuters/Corbis (Plate 1.1, p. 7); Photofusion Library/David Townend (Plate 1.2, p. 25); Hartmut

Schwarzbach/Still Pictures (p. 33); Photofusion Library/Robert Brook (Plate 2.1, p. 43); Alamy Images/Richard Newton (Plate 3.2, p. 78); University of Bangor, School of Psychology (Plate 4.1, p. 97); Jacob Silberberg/Getty Images (Plate 4.2, p. 118); Rex Features/SUTTON-HIBBERT (Plate 5.1, p. 129); Michael A. Keller/zefa/Corbis (Plate 5.2, p. 154); Getty Images/Natalie Kauffman (p. 159); Alamy/Medical-on-line (Plate 6.1, p. 169); Image 100/Corbis (Plate 6.2, p. 180); © Chris Lisle/Corbis (p. 187); Terrence Higgins Trust (Plate 7.1, p. 195); © Comic Relief UK, courtesy of Comic Relief UK (Plate 7.2, p. 202); AFP/Getty Images (p. 219); Dr Andrejs Liepins/Science Photo Library, (Plate 8.1, p. 228); Eye of Science/Science Photo Library (Plate 8.2, p. 228); Lester V. Bergman/Corbis (p. 253); Alamy Images/Bubbles Photo Library (Plate 9.1, p. 256); Health Screening (UK) Ltd (Plate 9.2, p. 279); Alamy/Image Source (p. 289); Rex Features/TM & 20th Century Fox/Everett (Plate 10.2, p. 305); Alamy Images/Image Broker (Plate 11.1, p. 324); Rex Features/Cameron Laird (Plate 11.2, p. 329); Alamy/Peter Bowater (p. 354); Alamy/Steve Hamblin (Plate 12.1, p. 368); Alamy/David Sanger (p. 389); Alamy/The Hoberman Collection (Plate 13.1, p. 400); John Cole/Science Photo Library (Plate 13.2, p. 409); Alix/Science Photo Library (p. 417); Jerry Cooke/Corbis (Plate 14.1, p. 424); Alamy/Photofusion (p. 444); Reg Charity/Corbis (Plate 15.1, p. 469); David Mack/Science Photo Library (p. 478); David Cannon/Allsport/Getty Images (Plate 16.1, p. 487); Will & Deni McIntyre/Science Photo Library (Plate 16.2, p. 507); Alamy/Sandii McDonald (p. 511); University of Wales Bangor (Plate 18.1, p. 547); Bananastock/Photolibrary.com (Plate 18.2, p. 554).

In some instances we have been unable to trace the owners of copyright material, and we would appreciate any information that would enable us to do so.

PART I

Being and staying healthy

CHAPTER 1

What is health?

Learning outcomes

By the end of this chapter, you should have an understanding of:

- key models of thinking about health and illness: the biomedical and the biopsychosocial
- how health is more than simply the absence of physical disease
- the domains of health considered important by different populations
- the influence of age/lifestage and culture on health concepts
- the role of psychology in understanding health and illness
- the aims and interests of the discipline of health psychology

CHAPTER OUTLINE

What do we mean by health, and do we all mean the same thing when we use the term? This chapter considers the different ways in which people have been found to define and think about health: first, by providing an historical overview of the health concept that introduces the debate over the influence of mind on body; and, second, by illustrating how health belief systems vary according to factors such as age and culture. Evidence is provided from studies of both Western and non-Western populations. We also explore the issue of developmental differences in health perceptions and examine whether children define and think about health differently to a middle-aged or elderly person. Against this backdrop of defining health and describing health belief systems, we then introduce the field of health psychology and outline the field's key areas of interest. What is health psychology, and what questions can it address?

What is health? Changing perspectives

Stone (1979) pointed out that until we can agree on the meaning of health and how it can be measured we are going to be unable to answer questions about how we can protect, enhance and restore health. The root word of health is 'wholeness', and indeed 'holy' and 'healthy' share the same root word in Anglo-Saxon, which is perhaps why so many cultures associate one with the other: e.g. medicine men have both roles. Having its roots in 'wholeness' also suggests the early existence of a broad view of health that included mental and physical aspects. This view has not held dominance throughout history, as the next section illustrates.

Models of health and illness

One needs first to be clear about what health is. Health is a word that most people will use, but without realising that it may hold different meanings for different people, at different times in history, in different cultures, in different social classes, or even within the same family, depending, for example, on age. Some different, but not necessarily oppositional, views of health are described below.

■ Mind–body relationships

Archaeological finds of human skulls from the Stone Age have attributed the small neat holes found in some skulls to the process of 'trephination' (or trepanation), whereby a hole is made in order for evil spirits to leave the ailing body. Disease appeared to be attributed to evil spirits. However, by the time of ancient Greece the association between mind and body was viewed somewhat differently. The ancient Greek physician Hippocrates (*circa* 460–377 BC) considered the mind and body as one unit, but did not attribute illness to evil spirits but to the balance between four circulating bodily fluids (called humours): yellow bile, phlegm, blood and black bile. It was thought that when a person was healthy the four humours were in balance, and when they were ill-balanced due to external 'pathogens', illness occurred. The humours were attached to seasonal variations and to conditions of hot, cold, wet and dry, where phlegm was attached to winter (cold–wet), blood to spring (wet–hot), black bile to autumn (cold–dry), and yellow bile to summer (hot–dry). Furthermore, it was thought that the level of specific bodily humours related to particular personalities: excessive yellow bile was linked to a choleric or angry temperament; black bile was attached to sadness; excessive blood was associated with an optimistic or sanguine personality; and excessive phlegm with a calm or phlegmatic temperament. Interestingly, as far back as Hippocrates, it was suggested that eating healthily would help to preserve the balance of the humours, showing an early awareness of a relationship between nutrition and health (Helman 1978). This humoral **theory** of illness therefore attributed disease states to bodily functions but also acknowledged that bodily factors impacted on the mind.

theory
a general belief or beliefs about some aspect of the world we live in or those in it, which may or may not be supported by evidence. For example, women are worse drivers than men.

This view continued with Galen (*circa* AD 129–199), another influential Greek physician. Galen considered there to be a physical basis for all ill health (physical or mental) and believed not only that the four bodily humours underpinned the four dominant temperaments (the sanguine, the choleric, the phlegmatic and the melancholic) but also that these temperaments could contribute to the experience of specific illnesses. For example, he proposed that melancholic women were more likely to get breast cancer, offering not a psychological explanation but a physical one because melancholia was itself thought to be underpinned by high levels of black bile. This view was therefore that the mind and body were interrelated, but only in terms of physical and mental disturbances both having an underlying physical cause. The mind was not thought to play a role in illness **aetiology**. This view dominated thinking for many centuries to come but lost predominance in the eighteenth century as organic medicine, and in particular cellular pathology, developed and failed to support the humoral underpinnings. However, Galen's descriptions of personality types were still in use in the latter half of the twentieth century (Marks *et al.* 2000: 76–7).

aetiology (etiology): the cause of disease.

In the early Middle Ages (fifth–sixth century), however, Galen's theories lost dominance as health became increasingly tied to faith and spirituality. Illness was at this time seen as God's punishment for misdeeds or, similar to very early views, the result of evil spirits entering one's soul. Individuals were considered to have little control over their health, whereas priests, in their perceived ability to restore health by driving out demons, did. As the Church was at the forefront of society, science developed slowly. The mind and body were generally viewed as working together, or at least in parallel, but because medical understanding was limited in its development through the prohibition of scientific investigation such as dissection, mental and mystical explanations of illness predominated. Such causal explanations therefore called for treatment along the ~~~~~~ of ~~punishment, abstinence from sin, prayer or hard work.

These religious views persisted for many centuries until the early fourteenth and fifteenth centuries when a period of 'rebirth', a Renaissance, began, with individual thinking becoming increasingly dominant and thus a religious perspective became only one among many. The scientific revolution of the early 1600s led to a huge upsurge in scholarly and scientific study and developments in physical medicine; as a result, the understanding of the human body, and therefore the explanations for illness, became increasingly organic and physiological, with little room for psychological explanations.

During the early seventeenth century, the French philosopher René Descartes (1596–1650), like the ancient Greeks, proposed that the mind and body were separate entities. However, Descartes also proposed that inter-action between the two 'domains' was possible, although initially the under-standing of how mind–body interactions could happen was limited. For example, how could a mental thought, with no physical properties, cause a bodily reaction (e.g. a neuron to fire) (Solmes and Turnbull 2002)? This is defined as **dualism**, where the mind is considered to be 'non-material' (i.e. not objective or visible, such as thoughts and feelings) and the body is 'material' (i.e. made up of real 'stuff', physical matter such as our brain, heart and cells). The material and the non-material were considered independent. Physicians acted as guardians of the body, which was viewed as a machine amenable to scientific investigation and explanation. In contrast, theologians acted as guardians of the mind, a place not amenable to scientific investi-gation. The suggested communication between mind and body was thought to be under the control of the pineal gland in the midbrain (see Chapter 8), but the process of this interaction was unclear. Because Descartes believed that the soul left humans at the time of death, dissection and autopsy study now became acceptable to the Church, and the eighteenth and nineteenth centuries witnessed a huge growth in medical understanding. Anatomical research, autopsy work and cellular pathology concluded that disease was located in human cells, not in ill-balanced humours.

Dualists developed the notion of the body as a machine (a **mechanistic** viewpoint), understandable only in terms of its constituent parts (molecular, biological, biochemical, genetic), with illness understood through the study of cellular and physiological processes. Treatment during these centuries became more technical, diagnostic and focused on the body internal, with individuals perhaps more passively involved than previously, when they had been called upon to pray or exorcise their demons in order to return to health. This approach underpins the **biomedical model** of illness.

dualism
the idea that the mind and body are separate entities (cf. Descartes).

mechanistic
a reductionist approach that reduces behaviour to the level of the organ or physical function. Associated with the **biomedical model**.

biomedical model
a view that diseases and symptoms have an underlying physiological explanation.

■ Biomedical model of illness

In this model, a symptom of illness is considered to have an underlying pathology that will hopefully, but not inevitably, be cured through medical intervention. Adhering rigidly to the biomedical model would lead to pro-ponents dealing with objective facts and assuming a direct causal relationship between illness, its symptoms or underlying pathology (disease), and adjust-ment outcomes. The assumption is that removal of the pathology will lead to restored health, i.e. illness results from disease. This relatively mechanistic view of how our bodies and its organs work, fail and can be treated allows little room for subjectivity. The biomedical view has been described as reduc-tionist: i.e. the basic idea that mind, matter (body) and human behaviour can all be reduced to, and explained at, the level of cells, neural activity or biochemical activity. Reductionism tends to ignore evidence that different people respond in different ways to the same underlying disease because of differences, for example, in personality, cognition, social support resources or cultural beliefs (see later chapters).

Plate 1.1 Having a disability does not equate with a lack of health and fitness as Oscar Pistorius has shown the world.

© Alessandro Bianchi/Reuters/Corbis

Biopsychosocial model of illness

What is perhaps getting closer to the 'truth', as we understand it today, is the view of dual-aspect monists: those with this viewpoint would agree that there is one type of 'stuff' (monist) but would suggest that it can be perceived in two different ways: objectively and subjectively. For example, many illnesses have organic underlying causes, but they also elicit uniquely individual responses due to the action of the mind, i.e. subjective responses. So, while aspects of reductionism and dualistic thinking have been useful, for example in furthering our understanding of the aetiology and course of many acute and infectious diseases (Larson 1999) such as coronary heart disease and AIDS, we would propose that the role of the 'mind' in the manifestation of, and response to, illness is crucial to the advancement of our understanding of the complex nature of health and illness. Consider for example the extensive evidence of 'phantom limb pain' in amputees – how can pain exist in an absent limb? Consider the widespread acknowledgement of the placebo effect – how can an inactive (dummy) substance lead to similar levels of reported pain or other symptom reduction in that described by those receiving an active pharmaceutical substance or treatment? (see also Chapter 16). Subjectivity in terms of beliefs, expectations and emotions interact with illness perceptions to play an important role in the illness or stress experience (see Chapter 9 in terms of symptom perception, and Chapter 11 in terms of stress reactivity). This text aims to illustrate that psychological and social factors can add to biological or biomedical explanations and understanding of health and illness experiences. This is known as the **biopsychosocial** model, and it is employed in health psychology as well as in several allied health professions, such as occupational therapy and, to a growing extent, in the medical profession (Turner 2001; Wade and Halligan 2004).

biopsychosocial
a view that diseases and symptoms can be explained by a combination of physical, social, cultural and psychological factors (cf. Engel 1977).

■ Challenging dualism: psychosocial models of health and illness

Evidence of changed thinking is illustrated in an editorial in the *British Medical Journal* (Bracken and Thomas 2002) suggesting that it is time to 'move beyond the mind–body split'. The authors note that simply because neuroscience now enables us to explore the 'mind' and its workings by the use of increasingly sophisticated scanning devices and measurements, this does not mean we are furthering our understanding of the 'mind' – the thoughts, feelings and the like that make up our lives and give it meaning. They comment that 'conceptualising our mental life as some sort of enclosed world living inside our skull does not do justice to the reality of human experience' (p. 1434). The fact that this editorial succeeded in being published in a medical journal with a traditionally biomedical stance suggests that Descartes's 'legacy' is finally weakening.

The tension between those who viewed the mind and body as separate (dualists) and those who saw them as a unit (monists) has lessened as understanding of the bi-directional relationship between mind and body has grown. Psychology has played a significant role in this altering perspective. A key influence was Sigmund Freud in the 1920s and 1930s, who redefined the mind–body problem as one of 'consciousness'. Freud postulated the existence of an 'unconscious mind', following examination of patients with conversion hysteria. Unconscious conflicts were identified, using hypnosis and free association techniques, as the 'cause' of physical disturbances such as the paralysis and loss of sensation seen in some patients, for whom no underlying physical explanation was present (i.e. hysterical paralysis, e.g. Freud and Breuer 1895).

Freud stimulated much work into unconscious conflict, personality and illness, which ultimately led to the development of the field of *psychosomatic medicine* as we now know it (see later section). Psychologists have highlighted the need for medicine to become more holistic and to consider the role played in the aetiology, course and outcomes of illness, by psychological and social factors. The biopsychosocial model signals a broadening of a disease or biomedical model of health to one encompassing and emphasising the interaction between biological processes and psychological and social influences (Engel 1977, 1980). In doing so, it offers a complex and multivariate, but potentially more comprehensive, model with which to examine the human experience of illness. It burgeoned in popularity as a result of the many challenges to the biomedical approach as briefly illustrated above, but it was also due to increasing recognition of the role individual behaviour plays in health and illness. It is to this that we turn attention briefly now, with key behaviours explored more fully in Chapters 3 and 4.

Behaviour and health

The dramatic increases in life expectancy witnessed in Western countries in the twentieth century, partially due to advances in medical technology and treatments, led to a general belief, in Western cultures at least, in the efficacy of traditional medicine and its power to eradicate disease. This was most notable following the introduction of antibiotics in the 1940s; although

Fleming discovered penicillin in 1928, it was some years before it and other antibiotics were generally available. Such drug treatments, alongside increased control of infectious disease through vaccination and improved sanitation, are partial explanations of UK life expectancy at birth increasing from 47 years in 1900 to 74.6 years in 1980 (Whelan 1988). A continued increase is seen in the 2005 figures whereby the life expectancy at birth for females born in UK was 80.7 compared with 85.2 years for women born in Japan. For men the differential is slightly less: 76.1 years for UK-born men compared with 78.3 years for those born in Japan. These cultural variations can be explained to a large extent by differences in lifestyle and diet. In fact, much of the fall in mortality seen in the developed world preceded the major immunisation programmes and therefore it is the wider social and environmental changes, such as developments in education and agriculture, which led to changes in diet, or the development of sewerage and waste disposal systems, which are mainly responsible for improved public health (see also Chapter 2).

One hundred years ago, the ten leading causes of death were infectious diseases such as tuberculosis and pneumonia, with diseases such as diphtheria and tetanus highly common. If people living then had been asked what they thought being healthy meant, they may have replied 'avoiding infections, drinking clean water, living into my 50s/60s'. Death was frequently a result of highly infectious disease becoming epidemic in communities unprotected by immunisation or adequate sanitary conditions. However, in the last century, at least in developed countries, there has been a downturn in deaths resulting from infectious disease, and the 'top killers' make no mention of TB, typhoid or measles but instead list for example cancer, heart, lung and liver disease and accidents. Table 1.1 shows the leading 'physical' causes of mortality as recorded at various points over the past 106 years. It should be noted that the dementias are also attributed as the cause of death in significant numbers, e.g. over 13,000 deaths in 2006 in England and Wales, however the table presents only those causes considered applicable to all ages groups. These diseases have a behavioural component in that they have been linked to behaviour such as smoking, excessive alcohol consumption, increasingly sedentary lifestyles and poor diet. It has been estimated that approximately two-thirds (Doll and Peto 1981) to three-quarters (Peto and Lopez 1990) of cancer deaths are attributable, in part at least, to our behaviour (note that Peto increased this estimate over the nine years between the two publications cited). The upturn in cancer deaths over the last 100 years is in part because people are living longer with illnesses they previously would have died from; thus they are reaching ages where cancer **incidence** is greater. Although such figures are not wholly attributable to the increase in smoking and other cancer-related behaviour, a person's own behaviour does increase such disease risk significantly. By 2006, diabetes is seen to have regained its 1995 position as 8th; this slight rise from 9th position in 2000 obscures the fact that prevalence almost doubled between 1995 and 2006. Perhaps this finding reflects what has been described as the obesity epidemic (see Chapters 3 and 4). As Table 1.1 (overleaf) shows, the leading causes of death have however been relatively stable over the past decade.

Worldwide, the leading causes of death include heart disease, cancer, accidents and respiratory disorders, with AIDS predominating in many African

incidence
the number of new cases of disease occurring during a defined time interval – not to be confused with prevalence, which refers to the number of established cases of a disease in a population at any one time.

Table 1.1 Comparison of leading (physical) causes of death, 1900–2006 (England and Wales)

Rank	1900	1995	2000	2006
1.	Influenza and pneumonia	Cancer	Cancer (all)	Cancer (all)
2.	Tuberculosis, all forms	Heart disease	Heart disease	Heart disease
3.	Gastroenteritis	Stroke	Pneumonia	Pneumonia
4.	Heart disease	Pneumonia	Stroke	Stroke
5.	Stroke	Chronic lung disease	Lung disease	Chronic lung disease
6.	Kidney disease	Accidents	Accidents	Accidents
7.	Accidents	Suicide	Suicide	Liver disease
8.	Cancer	Diabetes mellitus	Liver disease	Diabetes
9.	Diseases of infancy	Liver disease	Diabetes	Suicide

- 1900 data from World Health Organization, www.who.int/countries/gbr
- 1995 and 2000 data from Department of Health, *The Nation's Health*, www.doh.gov.uk
- Only gender difference in 1995 is suicide 7th in males, liver disease 7th in females; in 2000 is reversal of diabetes and suicide ranking in women, i.e. diabetes is 7th.
- 2006 data from Office for National Statistics (2008), HMSO. See also www.statistics.gov.uk

and Asian countries and globally being the fourth leading cause of death. The World Health Organization (2002) has cited life expectancy at birth in sub-Saharan Africa as being 47 years but notes that this would be approximately 62 years if there were no AIDS. Projected worldwide mortality estimates place heart disease, cerebrovascular disease including strokes, chronic lung disease (COPD), lower respiratory infections, and throat and lung cancers as the top five killers (in order as listed) by 2020, with HIV infection entering the global 'top ten' for the first time (Murray and Lopez 1997). These authors also predict, using sophisticated statistical modelling, that worldwide, death from infectious diseases such as measles and malaria, and from perinatal (birth) and nutritional diseases, will significantly decline, whereas tobacco-related diseases will increase almost three-fold. Such links between individual behaviour, health and illness provide a key reason as to why health psychology has grown rapidly, given its focus on personal and social influences on health-related behaviour (see Chapters 3 and 4).

It might be expected, given the changes in what people are dying from, that views of what health is may also have changed over time. We can see this, for example, when comparing eighteenth-century Britain with twentieth-century Britain. In the eighteenth century, health was considered an 'egalitarian ideal', aspired to by all and considered as potentially being under an individual's control. Doctors were available to the wealthy as 'aids' to keeping oneself well. However, by the mid twentieth century this had changed. New laws regarding sickness benefit, and medical and technological advances in diagnostic and treatment procedures are associated with health being inextricably linked to 'fitness to work'. Doctors were required to declare whether individuals were 'fit to work' or whether they could adopt the 'sick role' (see also Chapter 10). Many today continue to see illness in terms of its effects on their working lives, although some also look at work role and conditions and consider the effects it has on illness (see discussion of occupational stress in Chapter 11).

Another change is seen in the challenges to the assumption that traditional medicine can, and will, cure us of all ills. Over recent decades, many more people have acknowledged the potential negative consequences of some treatments, particularly pharmacological ones (consider for example the long-term use of anxiolytics such as Valium), and as a result the 'complementary' and 'alternative' medicine industry has burgeoned.

Individual, cultural and lifespan perspectives on health

Lay theories of health

If a fuller understanding of health and illness is to be attained, it is necessary to find out what people think health, and illness, are. The simplest way of doing this is to ask them. Here we explore lay perceptions of health. An early study by Bauman (1961) asked the question 'What does being healthy mean?' and found that people make three main types of response:

1. that health means a 'general sense of well-being';
2. that health is identified with 'the absence of symptoms of disease';
3. that health can be seen in 'the things that a person who is physically fit is able to do'.

She argued that these three types of response reveal health to be related to:

- feeling
- symptom orientation
- performance.

It is worth noting that respondents in Bauman's study did not answer in discrete categories: nearly half of the sample used two of the above categories, and 12 per cent used all three types of definition, highlighting the fact that the way we think about health is often multifaceted. A word of caution is also needed before generalising from these findings. Bauman's sample consisted of patients with diagnoses of quite serious disease, and it is likely that healthy people will think about health in a different way.

It has been shown that factors such as current health status do influence subjective views of health and reports of what 'health is'. For example, Benyamini *et al.* (2003) asked almost 500 elderly people to rate factors in order of importance to their subjective health judgements, and the most important factors were found to relate to physical functioning and vitality (being able to do what you need/want to do). However, the current health status of the sample (poor/fair; good; very good/excellent) influenced other judgements; for example, those in poor/fair health based their health assessments on symptoms or indicators of poor health, whereas those in good health considered more positive indicators (being able to exercise, being happy). Subjective health judgements were more tied to health behaviour in 'healthier' individuals. Krause and Jay (1994), when examining the frames of reference drawn on by people when asked to evaluate their own health status, found that older respondents were more likely to refer to health *problems* when making their appraisals, whereas younger respondents referred to health behaviour. This raises the issue of health being considered differently when it is no longer present. Health is considered to be good when nothing is

health behaviour
behaviour performed by an individual, regardless of their health status, as a means of protecting, promoting or maintaining health, e.g. diet.

wrong (perhaps more commonly thought in older people) and when a person is behaving in a health-protective manner (perhaps more commonly thought in younger people). It also highlights that other personal and social factors, such as age, influence health perceptions, as described in the next section.

■ Social representations of health

A well-cited, early study by Herzlich (1973) conducted unstructured interviews with a small (n = 80) sample of French adults in order to ascertain the 'social representations' of health and illness (see also Chapter 9) and found that although some people found it hard to distinguish health from an absence of illness, health was generally viewed as a state of equilibrium across various aspects of the person, encompassing physical, psychological, emotional and social wellbeing. Bennett (2000: 67) considers these representations of health to distinguish between health as 'being', i.e. if not ill, then healthy; 'having', i.e. health as a positive resource or reserve; and 'doing', i.e. health as represented by physical fitness or function (as found in Benyamini *et al.*'s study of the elderly referred to above). The similarities between Herzlich's and Bauman's study are noticeable, although Bauman's respondents appear to have focused more on the 'being' healthy and 'doing' aspects, which may be in part because 'having' health as a resource was not prominent in the minds of her patient sample.

A more representative picture of the health concept can be obtained from a large, questionnaire-based survey of 9,000 members of the general public, the *Health and Lifestyles* survey (Blaxter 1990). Her findings suggest that health concepts are perhaps even more complex than the earlier studies had proposed. This survey asked respondents to:

- Think of someone you know who is very healthy.
- Define who you are thinking of (friend/relative etc. – do not need specific name).
- Note how old they are.
- Consider what makes you call them healthy.
- Consider what it is like when you are healthy.

About 15 per cent could not think of *anyone* who was 'very healthy', and about 10 per cent could not describe what it was like for them to 'feel healthy'. This inability to describe what it is like to feel healthy was particularly evident in young males, who believed health to be a norm, a background condition so taken for granted that they could not put it into words. By comparison, a smaller group of mostly older women could not answer for exactly the opposite reason – they had been in poor health for so long that either they could not remember what it was like to feel well or they were expressing a pessimism about their condition to the interviewer (Radley 1994: 39).

The categories of health identified from the survey findings were:

- *Health as not ill*: i.e. no symptoms, no visits to doctor therefore I am healthy.
- *Health as reserve*: i.e. come from strong family; recovered quickly from operation.
- *Health as behaviour*: i.e. usually applied to others rather than self; e.g. they are healthy because they look after themselves, exercise, etc.

- *Health as physical fitness and vitality*: used more often by younger respondents and often in reference to a male – male health concept more commonly tied to 'feeling fit', whereas females had a concept of 'feeling full of energy' and rooted health more in the social world in terms of being lively and having good relationships with others.

- *Health as psychosocial wellbeing*: health defined in terms of a person's mental state; e.g. being in harmony, feeling proud, or more specifically, enjoying others.

- *Health as function*: the idea of health as the ability to perform one's duties; i.e. being able to do what you want when you want without being handicapped in any way by ill health or physical limitation (relates to the World Health Organization's concept of handicap; i.e. an inability to fulfill one's normal social roles, usually resulting from some impairment or disability (WHO 1980)).

These categories confirm the presence of health as something more than physical, i.e. as something encompassing psychosocial wellbeing, and seem to fit with Herzlich's 'being' and 'doing' categorisations (see Bennett 2000: 66) and Bauman's findings of clusters of beliefs in 'health as not ill'. Generally, we can conclude that these dimensions of health are fairly robust (at least in Western culture, see later section for culture differences).

Another important finding is that subjective health evaluations are reached through comparison with others, and in a similar way one's concept of what health is, or is not, can be shaped. For example, Kaplan and Baron-Epel (2003) interviewed 383 Israeli residents and found that young people reporting sub-optimal health did not compare themselves with people of the same age, whereas many older people in sub-optimal health did. When in optimal health, more young people than old compared themselves with people their age. The authors interpret this as evidence that people try to get the best out of their evaluations – a young person will be likely to perceive their peers to be generally healthy, so if they feel that they are not, they will be unwilling to draw this comparison. In contrast, older people when in poorer health are more likely to compare themselves with same-aged peers, who may generally be thought to have normatively poorer health, and therefore their own health status seems less unusual. Asking, as Bauman's study did, a person to consider what it is that they would consider as 'being healthy' inevitably will lead people into making these types of comparison. Health is a relative state of being.

World Health Organization definition of health

The dimensions of health described in the preceding paragraphs are reflected in the WHO (1947) definition of health as a '*state of complete physical, mental and social well-being and . . . not merely the absence of disease or infirmity*'. This definition sees individuals as ideally deserving of a positive state, an overall wellbeing and illness-fully functioning. In 1978, the WHO launched the Global Strategy for Health for All by the Year 2000, with the aim of '*the attainment by all citizens of the world by the year 2000 of a level of health that will permit them to lead a socially and economically productive life*' (WHO 1981). This led to the development of health targets which shaped policy documents in both European and non-European countries. In England, for example, *The Health of the Nation* White Paper (DoH 1992) and the *Saving Lives: Our Healthier Nation* report (Department of

Health 1999b) set out targets for reduction in cancers, heart disease, strokes and AIDS: targets were to reduce cancers by a fifth or more in the under-75 age group, and reduce heart disease and strokes by two-fifths, by 2010. The nature, specificity and time-frame of targets varies from country to country. For example, in Belgium targets were aimed at reducing smokers, fat intake, fatal accidents, infectious diseases (by vaccination programmes) and increasing health screening in the over-50s, by 2002; in The Netherlands (Langer Gezond Leven – 'Towards a Longer and Healthier Life', Ministry of Health, 2003) the targets were to achieve reductions in cardiovascular disease, cancers, alcohol dependency, mental health problems, asthma and lung disease, and movement disorders by 2020. Although the WHO targets were not fully attained by 2000, and the DoH 2010 target is unlikely to be achieved, some progress has been made. For example reductions have been seen in mortality in developed countries from lung, colon and prostate cancers in men, and breast and colorectal cancers in women.

Such targets and policy documents assume a clear relationship between people's behaviour, lifestyle and health. However, what they less clearly acknowledge and what is often not explicitly addressed are the socio-economic and cultural influences on health, illness and health decisions. These important influences on health are addressed in the next chapter. The WHO definition also fails to make explicit mention of the role of the 'psyche' which, as this text will show, plays a major role in the experience of health and illness.

Cross-cultural perspectives on health

What is considered to be 'normal' health varies across cultures and as a result of the economic, political and cultural climate of the era in which a person lives. Think of how pregnancy is treated in most Western civilisations (i.e. medicalised) as opposed to many Third World regions (naturalised). The stigma of physical impairment or disability among South Asian communities may have consequences for the family which would not be considered in Caucasian families: for example, having a sibling with a disability may affect the other siblings' marriage chances or even the social standing of the family (Ahmad 2000). The way in which certain behaviour is viewed also differs across time and between cultures. For example, alcohol dependence has shifted from being seen as a legal and moral problem, with abusers seen as deviant to a disease treated in clinics; and smoking has shifted from being considered as glamorous and even desirable to being socially undesirable and indicative of a weak will. Perhaps reflecting this shift, the prevalence of males over age 16 currently smoking in England has dropped significantly over the past thirty years, although the decline is less pronounced for females (The Health Survey for England (2007), Health and Social Care Information Centre (2008); and see Chapter 3).

What is normal and what is defined as sick in a given culture can have all sorts of consequences. If a particular behaviour is labelled as a sickness, the consequences will differ greatly from those received if the behaviour is labelled as deviant; for example, societal responses to illicit drug use have ranged from prohibition through criminalisation to an illness requiring treatment.

There is growing evidence that Westernised views of health differ in various ways from conceptualisations of health in non-Westernised civilisations. Chalmers (1996) astutely notes that Westerners divide the mind, body and soul in terms of allocation of care between psychologists and psychiatrists, medical professions and the clergy. She observes that this is not the case in some African cultures, where these three 'elements of human nature' are integrated in terms of how a person views them, and in how they are cared for. This holistic view considers the social as well as the biological, the spiritual as well as the interpersonal, and health as an integrated state consisting of all these elements. Until recently, with the development of quality of life research (see Chapter 14), spiritual wellbeing was rarely considered as contributing to a person's perception of health. Furthermore, attributing continued health to a satisfied ancestor would be likely to raise a few eyebrows if stated aloud in a conversation with peers. Spiritual explanations are present in Western reports, if uncommon: for example, supernatural forces such as faith, God's reward, may be perceived as supporting health. Negative supernatural forces such as 'hexes' or the 'evil eye' can also share the blame for illness and disability, as evidenced by cross-cultural studies of illness attributions (e.g. Landrine and Klonoff 1992, 1994) and, as we described above, in earlier historical periods. Among some ethnic groups, Hindus and Sikhs in particular, it has been reported that disability is considered a punishment for past sins within the family (Katbamna *et al.* 2000). These belief systems can have profound effects on living with illness or indeed caring for someone with an illness or disability (see Chapter 15).

In addition to beliefs of spiritual influences on health, studies of some African regions consider that the community or family work together for the wellbeing of all. This **collectivist** approach to staying healthy and avoiding illness is far different to our **individualistic** approach to health (consider how long the passive smoking evidence was ignored). For example, in a study of preventive behaviour to avoid endemic tropical disease in Malawians, the social actions to prevent infection (e.g. clearing reed beds) were adhered to more consistently than the personal preventive actions (e.g. bathing in piped water or taking one's dose of chloroquine) (Morrison *et al.* 1999). Collectivist cultures emphasise group needs to a greater degree than individualistic ones, which emphasise the uniqueness of its members (Matsumoto *et al.* 1996, cited in Marks *et al.* 2000: 56). Several Eastern cultures (Japanese, Chinese) also exhibit **holistic** and collectivist approaches to health. For example, following a comparative study of Canadian and Japanese students, Heine and Lehman (1995) highlighted a need to 'distinguish between cultures that promote and validate "independent selfs", i.e. find meaning through uniqueness and autonomy, and cultures that promote and validate "interdependent selfs", i.e. find meaning through links with others and one's community' (Morrison *et al.* 1999: 367). Cultures that promote an interdependent self are more likely to view health in terms of social functioning rather than simply personal functioning, fitness, etc. Several research studies by George Bishop and colleagues (e.g. Quah and Bishop 1996; Bishop and Teng 1992) have suggested that Chinese Singaporean adults view health as a harmonious state where the internal and external systems are in balance, and on occasions where they become imbalanced, health is compromised. *Yin* – the positive energy – needs to be kept in balance with the *yang* – the negative energy (also considered to be female!). Eastern cultures hold spiritual beliefs about health and illness, with illness or misfortune commonly being attributed to predestination. Obviously, to maximise effectiveness of health promotion efforts, it is important to acknowledge the existence and effects

collectivist

a cultural philosophy that emphasises the individual as part of a wider unit and places emphasis on actions motivated by collective, rather than individual, needs and wants.

individualistic

a cultural philosophy that places responsibility at the feet of the individual; thus behaviour is often driven by individual needs and wants rather than by community needs or wants.

holistic

root word 'wholeness'; holistic approaches are concerned with the whole being and its wellbeing, rather than addressing the purely physical or observable.

of such different underlying belief systems (see Chapters 6 and 7).

In the Western world, there is a growing recognition of the value of alternative remedies for health maintenance or treatment of symptoms, and the alternative medicine and complementary therapy industries have grown enormously. A mixture of Western and non-medical/traditional medicine can be found in many regions of sub-Saharan Africa, where, for example in Malawi, a person may visit a faith healer or a herbalist as well as a local Western clinic for antibiotics (Ager *et al.* 1996). Similarly, among some Aboriginal tribes spiritual beliefs in illness causation coexist with the use of Western medicines for symptom control (Devanesen 2000). The biomedical view is therefore seen to be acknowledged and assimilated within the culture's belief system as both the availability of Western medicine and the population's understanding of its methods and efficacy grows. However, our understanding of culturally relevant cognitions regarding illness and health behaviour is still limited, and further cross-cultural research is required.

As we will discuss in a later chapter (Chapter 9), the use of health care, either traditional or Western, will in part be determined by the nature and strength of an individual's cultural values and beliefs. Illness discourse will reflect the dominant conceptualisations of individual cultures, and it should become clear at various points throughout this text that how people think about health and illness shapes their expectations, health behaviour, and their use of health promotion and health-care resources.

Lifespan, ageing and beliefs about health

Psychological wellbeing, social and emotional health are not only influenced by the ageing process, they are also affected by illness, disability and hospitalisation, all of which can be experienced at any age. Although growing older is associated with decreased functioning and increased disability or dependence, it is not only older people who live with chronic illness. For example, a survey of young people aged 2–24 (using parent proxy reports for those aged under 13) found that approximately a quarter of the young people had a longstanding illness (predominantly respiratory conditions such as asthma) (statistics from the Health Survey for England, www.doh.gov.uk/stats/selfrep.htm).

There are, however, developmental issues which health professionals should be aware of if they are to promote the physical, psychological, social and emotional wellbeing of their patient or client. While the subsequent section considers lifespan issues in relation to health perceptions, it is recommended that interested readers also consult a health psychology text focusing specifically on such issues, e.g, Penny *et al.*'s edited collection (1994).

■ Developmental theories

The developmental process is a function of the interaction between three factors:

1. *Learning*: a relatively permanent change in knowledge, skill or ability as a result of experience.
2. *Experience*: what we do, see, hear, feel, think.

3. *Maturation*: thought, behaviour or physical growth, attributed to a genetically determined sequence of development and ageing rather than to experience.

Erik Erikson (Erikson 1959; Erikson *et al.* 1986) described eight major life stages (five related to childhood development, three related to adult development), which varied across different dimensions, including:

■ cognitive and intellectual functioning;
■ language and communication skills;
■ the understanding of illness;
■ health care and maintenance behaviour.

It is important that each of these dimensions be taken into consideration when examining health and illness perceptions or behaviour. Deficits or limitations in cognitive functioning (due to age, accident or illness) may, for example, influence the extent to which an individual can understand medical instructions, report their emotions or have their health-care needs assessed. Communication deficits or limited language skills can impair a person's willingness to place themselves in social situations, or impede their ability to express their pain or distress to health professionals or family members. The understanding that an individual has of their symptoms or their illness is crucial to health-care-seeking behaviour and to adherence, and individual health behaviour influences one's perceived and/or actual risk of illness and varies hugely across the lifespan. All these aspects are covered in this textbook in the relevant chapters.

Piaget (1930, 1970) was largely responsible for developing a maturational framework for understanding cognitive development, which has also provided a good basis for understanding the developmental course of concepts regarding health, illness and health procedures. Piaget proposed a staged structure to which, he considered, all individuals follow in the sequence described below:

1. *Sensorimotor* (birth–2 years): an infant understands the world through sensations and movement, lacks symbolic thought. Moves from reflexive to voluntary action.

egocentric

self-centred, such as in the pre-operational stage (age 2–7 years) of children, when they see things only from their own perspective (cf. Piaget).

2. *Pre-operational* (2–7 years): symbolic thought develops by around age 2, thereafter simple logical thinking and language develop, generally **egocentric**.

3. *Concrete operational* (7–11 years): abstract thought and logic develop hugely; can perform mental operations (e.g. mental arithmetic) and manipulate objects.

4. *Formal operational* (age 12 to adulthood): abstract thought and imagination develop as does deductive reasoning. Not everyone may attain this level.

work is influential in terms of providing an overarching structure within which to view cognitive development. For example, his work describes how an infant, from birth to 2 years, slowly acquires symbolic thinking and language and the ability to imitate the actions of others, but that it is only in the latter part of the second stage that children begin to develop logical thought (albeit generally very egocentric thought). Of more relevance to a health psychology text, however, is work that has more specifically addressed children's developing beliefs and understanding of health and illness constructs. The subsequent sections describe this work, using Piagetian stages as a broad framework.

■ Sensorimotor and pre-operational stage children

Little work with infants at the sensorimotor stage is possible in terms of identifying health and illness cognitions, as language is very limited until the end of this stage. At the pre-operational stage, children develop linguistically and cognitively, and symbolic thought means that young children develop awareness of how they can affect the external world through imitation and learning, although they remain very **egocentric**. Health and illness are considered in black and white, i.e. as two opposing states rather than as existing on a continuum. Children here are slow to see or adopt other people's viewpoints or perspectives. This ability is crucial if one is to empathise with others, and thus a pre-operational child is not very sympathetic to a family member being ill, not understanding why this means they can no longer expect the same amount of play, for example.

Illness concept

It is important that children learn over time some responsibility for maintaining their own health; however, few studies have examined children's conception of health, which would be likely to influence their behaviour. Research has instead focused more often on generating illness concepts. For example, Bibace and Walsh (1980) suggest, on the basis of asking children aged 3–13 questions about health and illness, that an illness concept develops gradually. The questions were about knowledge – 'What is a cold?'; experience – 'Were you ever sick?'; attributions – 'How does someone get a cold'; and recovery – 'How does someone get better?' They revealed that there is a progression of understanding and attribution for causes of illness and described six developmentally ordered descriptions of how illness is defined, caused and treated.

Under-7s generally explain illness on a 'magical' level – explanations are based on association.

- *Incomprehension*: child gives irrelevant answers or evades question: e.g. sun causes heart attacks.

- *Phenomenonism*: illness is usually a sign or sound that the child has at some time associated with the illness, but with little grasp of cause and effect: e.g. a cold is when you sniff a lot.

- *Contagion*: illness is usually from a person or object that is close by, but not necessarily touching the child; or it can be attributed to an activity that occurred before the illness: e.g: 'You get measles from people'. If asked *how*? 'Just by walking near them'.

■ Concrete operational stage children

Children over 7 are described by Piaget as capable of thinking logically about objects and events, although they are still unable to distinguish between mind and body until around age 11, when adolescence begins.

Illness concept

Bibace and Walsh describe explanations of illness at around 8 to 11 years as being more concrete and based on a causal sequence:

■ *Contamination*: i.e. children at this stage understand that illness can have multiple symptoms, and they recognise that germs, or even their own behaviour, can cause illness: e.g. 'You get a cold if you take your jacket off outside, and it gets into your body'.

■ *Internalisation*: i.e. illness is within the body, but the process by which symptoms occur can be partially understood. The cause of a cold may come from outside germs that are inhaled or swallowed. These children *can* differentiate between body organs and function and can understand specific, simple information about their illness. They can also see the role of treatment and/or personal action as returning them to health.

In this concrete operational stage, medical staff are still seen as having absolute authority, but their actions might be criticised/avoided: e.g. reluctance to give blood, accusations of hurting unnecessarily, etc. Children can, like adults, be encouraged to take some personal control over their illness or treatment at this stage in development, and this can help the child to cope. They also need to be encouraged to express their fears. Parents need to strike a balance between monitoring a sick child's health and behaviour and being overprotective, as this can detrimentally affect a child's social, cognitive and personal development and may encourage feelings of dependency and disability (see Chapter 15 for further discussion of coping with illness in a family).

■ Adolescence and formal operational thought

Adolescence is a socially and culturally created concept only a few generations old. Many primitive societies do not acknowledge adolescence, and children move from childhood to adulthood with a ritual performance, not years of transition as viewed by many Western societies as a distinct period in life. Puberty is a period of both physical and psychosocial change that can influence self-perception; indeed, during early adolescence (11–13 years), as individuals prepare for independence and peers take on more credence than parents, much of life's health-damaging behaviour commences, e.g. smoking (see Chapter 3).

Illness concept

Bibace and Walsh describe illness concepts at this stage as those at an abstract level – explanations based on interactions between the person and their environment:

■ *Physiological*: children from around 11 years reach a stage of physiological understanding, and most can now define illness in terms of specific bodily organs or functions, and with age begin to appreciate multiple physical causes, e.g. germs plus pollution plus behaviour.

■ *Psychophysiological*: in later adolescence (from around 15 years) and adulthood, many people grasp the idea that mind and body interact, and they understand or accept the role of stress, worry, etc. in the exacerbation and even the cause of illness. It is worth noting that many adults may not achieve this level of understanding about illness and may continue to use more cognitively simplistic explanations.

It should be noted that Bibace and Walsh's study focuses predominantly on the issue of illness causality. Other work has shown that children and young people are able to think about health and illness in terms of other dimensions, such as controllability and severity (e.g. Goldman *et al.* 1991; see Chapter 9 for fuller discussion of illness perceptions).

Adolescents perceive themselves as having more control over the onset and cure of illness and are more aware that personal actions can influence outcomes. This means that advice and interventions are understood more and may be acted upon as they can understand complex remedial and therapeutic procedures: e.g. they understand that taking blood can help to monitor the progress of disease.

Childhood is an important period for the development of health and illness concepts, also for the development of attitudes and patterns of health behaviour that will impact on future health status (see Chapter 3). According to these staged theories, a child's ability to understand their condition and associated treatment is determined by the level of cognitive development attained. This level of understanding will subsequently determine how children communicate their symptom experience to parents and health-care staff, their ability to act on health advice, and the level of personal responsibility for disease management that is feasible. These aspects should not be overlooked when care and educational programmes are developed. While cognitive development is important, such staged theories have not met with universal support (e.g. Dimigen and Ferguson 1993, in relation to concepts of cancer). Illness concepts are now thought to derive more from a range of influences, such as experience and knowledge, rather than from relatively fixed stages of cognitive development (see RESEARCH FOCUS).

RESEARCH FOCUS

Children's conceptions of health: how complex are they?

Normandeau, S., Kalnins, I., Jutras, S. *et al.* (1998). A description of 5- to 12-year-old children's conception of health within the context of their daily life, *Psychology and Health*, 13(5): 883–96.

Background
Studies based on stage theories of cognitive development suggest that children move from very concrete and rigid views of illness based on observables to more abstract concepts that understand causality, interior body and mental health. However, cognitive development is not the only influence – experience of health and illness plays a role, as does socialisation; thus it is suggested that studies of children's concepts of health (as well as other concepts) are best studied in relation to context and experience,

Aims
The study aimed to describe 5–12-year-old children's conceptions of health in the context of their daily lives by asking them to consider health in terms of their daily experiences and getting them to generate themselves the features of illness that they consider most important. A further aim was to examine the influence of demographic and socio-economic variables on illness concepts.

continued

Methods

A total of 1,674 children (well balanced for gender – 828 boys, 846 girls) from four different urban areas and three different rural areas in the province of Quebec, Canada, were recruited using sampling methods that generated representative gender and socio-economic back-grounds. The cross-sectional study employed mixed **qualitative** and **quantitative methods**, using structured interviews as well as open-ended questioning. Qualitative data were coded, categorised and sys-tematised using content analysis, and then categories of data were analysed according to gender, age group and social class. Children were assessed in terms of what is described as 'four complementary dimensions': (1) *criteria of good health* – 'Can you tell me the name of two or three friends who are healthy?', 'What do you see [*see note below] as signs of good health in your friends?'; (2) *behaviours necessary to maintain health* – 'Is it necessary to do particular things to be healthy?', if yes, 'Which things are necessary?'; (3) *consequences of being healthy* – 'What does being in good health allow you to do?'; and (4) *threats to health* – 'Can you tell me, in general, what is the most dangerous thing to children's health?' (*The use of 'see' as opposed to 'think' may lead the children to consider visible signs of health, which is perhaps leading.)

qualitative methods aim to describe the 'quality' and nature of experience, beliefs and behaviours, usually of a particular group of individuals.

quantitative methods aim to quantify (count) the frequency or type of experience, beliefs and behaviours, of a generally large, and ideally representative group of people.

Results

Only response categories mentioned by 100 or more children were considered for detailed analysis (thus losing data from those children who had unusual conceptions and beliefs).

Criteria of good health

The children generally identified three main criteria for good health:

1. being functional (practising sports, absence of disease);
2. mental health (wellbeing, looking healthy, feeling good about oneself, good relationships with others);
3. lifestyle health behaviour (healthy diet, good hygiene, sleeping well).

Components of these dimensions showed some age variation: e.g. functionality in older children was more associated with sports participation and physiological functioning, whereas in younger children it was more related to 'going outside'. Older children also considered 'not being sick' as more important; in terms of lifestyle behaviour, older children more often referred to good diet than did younger children; and in terms of mental health older children more often referred to self-concept, whereas younger children referred more to the quality of relationships with others. No effects were found in terms of gender or socio-economic background.

Perception of health behaviour

Lifestyle factors were considered as the key to good health by all ages, but older children were more concerned with undertaking engaging in physical activity and sleeping well, whereas younger children thought eating specific healthy foods or avoiding unhealthy foods was most important.

Socio-economic status influenced the extent to which children thought it was necessary to have healthy behaviour, with those from urban upper-middle-class areas emphasising this

continued

aspect of health most. Age interacted with socio-economic environment. Gender did not influence conceptions regarding health behaviour.

Consequences of being healthy
Mainly children think that the consequence of health is being able to function by doing things one wants to do, and to a lesser extent having good mental health.

Age effects existed in that older children were more likely to mention being functional and being able to do more things including leisure activities, and more often mentioned better physiological functioning to be a consequence of health (relates to Bibace and Walsh's findings in this age group). No effect of socio-economic environment or gender was found in terms of perceived health consequences.

Threats to health
The major threats to health were perceived to be poor lifestyle behaviour such as smoking, doing drugs, drinking and eating unhealthily. Age effects showed that perceptions of threat change significantly with age, particularly between the 5–6 and 8–12 age groups. Taking drugs and smoking was most commonly reported in the 8–9 and 11–12 age groups, whereas eating bad foods was most common in the youngest children (5–6 years). Dangerous behaviour and road safety issues were of greater concern to the younger children. Socio-economic environment interacted with age to affect the extent to which unhealthy eating was an issue. No effects were found for gender in terms of what was perceived as health threats.

Discussion
What this study clearly shows is that children as young as 5 have multidimensional concepts of health that are more complex than simply a change from concrete to abstract thinking as described by Piaget or Bibace and Walsh. Very early on, children's conceptions include a mental health dimension, which is contrary to that found in early research. Perhaps this is due to the methodology of inviting children to talk about their concepts in relation to their own lives and experience. Age differences existed across each of the four domains studied and are perhaps particularly evident in terms of perceived threats to health (although this probably reflects greater experience of smoking, drinking and drug use among the older children). Evidence from this study offers support for widening models of children's health concepts to include the role of personal experience and socialisation. No evidence was found for a gender effect on any of the assessed domains, suggesting perhaps that gender differences either do not exist or possibly do not emerge until later in adolescence.

Strengths and limitations
This is a large study with good sampling that asks young children to express their own views and beliefs, and as such is relatively unique. However, the study does not address actual behavioural practices and therefore there is no check on whether children report conceptions that are inconsistent with their actual behaviour. Examining subgroups of children in terms of, for example, smoking behaviour or diet may well have been informative in terms of early rationalisations of risk behaviour.

■ **Adulthood 17/18+**

Adulthood tends to be divided between early (17–40), middle age (40–60) and elderly (60/65+). Early adulthood blends out of adolescence as the person forges their identity and assumes the roles and responsibility of adulthood – a time of consolidation. Early adulthood has been described as the prime of life, when all sorts of transitions occur, such as graduation, new careers, pregnancy, marriage, childbirth; many will divorce, some will lose a parent. While Piaget did not describe further developments in cognitive processes during adulthood, new perspectives develop from experience, and what is/has been learned is applied with a view to achieving life goals. The shift from acquisition of learning to application of what has been learned means that health education should be more practical in orientation, emphasising application of information. Adults are less likely than adolescents to adopt new health-risk behaviour and are generally more likely to engage in protective behaviour: e.g. screening, exercise, etc. for health reasons (see Chapter 4). Transitions in adulthood do not affect all sectors of the adult population in the same way: for example, marriage has been found to benefit health in men – i.e. they have lower illness scores than men living alone, whereas for women, being married carries no such protection (Blaxter 1987; Macintyre 1986), suggesting differential social support perhaps (see Chapter 12 for a discussion of stress moderators).

In contrast to the generally positive view of early adulthood, middle age has been identified as a period of uncertainty, anxiety and change, where some question their achievements, goals and values, or experience uncertainty of roles when children become adults and leave home themselves.

What do YOU think?

Is middle age a state of mind? Are you 'as young as you feel'?
Think of your parents, aunts and uncles or of family friends in their forties. Do they seem to share outlooks on life, expectancies and behaviours that are significantly different to those of you and your friends? How do you view growing older? Think about how it makes you feel and question these feelings.

◼ Ageing and health

In the UK, as elsewhere in the world, the ageing population (accepting the cut-off age for 'older people' to be 65 or over) has burgeoned, but more particularly the percentage of persons living into their late 70s or 80s has increased (Office for National Statistics, *Social Trends 29*, 1999) and is projected to increase further. The United Nations Secretariat (2002) have predicted an increase in those aged over 60 from 10 per cent of the population to 20 per cent by 2050. The implications for health and social care resources are obvious, given the **epidemiology** of illness: i.e. the fact that the incidence of many diseases increases with longevity. Not all elderly people are ill or infirm, but even among the minority who go on without chronic health problems (physical and/or mental), episodes of acute illness are commonplace. The 2000 Health Survey for England (www.dh.gov.uk/public/healtholderpeople2000pres.htm) reports that of those aged 65 and above, 13 per cent of those living at home (10 per cent of those aged 65–79; 25 per cent of those over 80) have a serious disability, compared with 69 per cent of men and 79 per cent of women living in residential homes. This figure suggests that there is a considerable extent of disability in the community. This was confirmed in the 2005 Health Survey for England where arthritis was found to be the most common chronic condition reported by women

epidemiology
the study of patterns of disease in various populations and the association with other factors such as lifestyle factors. Key concepts include mortality, morbidity, prevalence, incidence, absolute risk and relative risk. Type of question: Who gets this disease? How common is it?

aged over 65 years (47 per cent women, 32 per cent men) and for men, the most common condition was cardiovascular disease (37 per cent men, 31 per cent women). Two-fifths of the older people sampled reported limitations in performing at least one functional activity, usually walking without stopping or discomfort. Does the process of ageing influence how an older person thinks about themselves and their health?

self-concept
those conscious thoughts and beliefs about yourself that allow you to feel are distinct from others and that you exist as a separate person.

Empirical research has shown that **self-concept** is relatively stable through ageing (e.g. Baltes and Baltes 1990) and that changes in self-concept are not an inevitable part of the ageing process. In fact, *ageing is not necessarily a negative experience* (although it may become so because of the ageist attitudes that exist in many industrialised countries). Growing older may present an individual with new challenges, but this should not be seen as implying that ageing is itself a problem (Coleman 1999).

With increasing age, sensory and motor losses are most common, with a large proportion of our elderly being physically impaired in some way. In an ageing society disability is common; 85 per cent may experience some chronic condition (Woods 2008). Elderly people often report expecting to have poor health, which can result in poor health-care checks and maintenance as they regard it as pointless; they may think loss of mobility, poor foot health and poor digestion as an inevitable and unavoidable part of growing old, so they may not respond to symptoms as they should (e.g. Leventhal and Prohaska 1986; Sarkisian *et al.* 2001). Exercise tends to decline in old age as it may be avoided in the belief that it will over-exert the joints, heart, etc.; the elderly tend to underestimate their own physical capacities, yet as we shall see in Chapter 4, exercise is both possible and beneficial. There is growing interest in 'successful ageing' – what it is and how it can be achieved. IN THE SPOTLIGHT below describes some of the models of successful ageing and empirical evidence that supports a multidimensional 'lay model' rather than a biomedical model based on physical and mental functioning, in terms of predicting quality of life.

IN THE SPOTLIGHT

Successful ageing and quality of life

As described in this chapter, health is commonly viewed in terms of how we feel and what we do. With ageing comes the potential for decline in physical and mental functioning and for possible restrictions in social functioning; however, there is significant evidence that such 'decline' does not have to be inevitable for all of us. If we can identify factors associated with 'successful ageing', then health promotion efforts can target the factors associated with this. First, however, 'successful' ageing needs to be defined and different definitions tend to be used by different parties! Bowling and Iliffe (2006) describe 5 'models' of successful ageing and the variables considered within each model. Variables were all categorised or dichotimised, e.g. presence/absence of diagnosis; sense of purpose/no sense of purpose etc., in order for each model to allocate a score of 'successfully aged' or not:

Biomedical model: based on physical and psychiatric functioning – diagnoses and functional ability

Broader biomedical model: as above but includes social engagement and activity

Social functioning model: based on the nature and frequency of social functioning and networks, social support accessed

Psychological resources model: based on personal characteristics of optimism and self-efficacy and on sense of purpose, coping and problem-solving, self-confidence and self-worth (see Chapter 12 for a discussion of many of these positive cognitions)

Lay model: based on the above variables plus socio-economic variables of income and 'perceived social capital' which included, access to resources and facilities, environmental quality and problems (e.g. crime, traffic, pollution, places to walk, feelings of safety).

It is clear that these models become progressively more inclusive. The study assessed all the above variables in a sample of 999 individuals aged over 65 years and assigned them either as successfully aged or not based on achieving the 'good' score on each variable, e.g. no physical conditions versus one or more. The authors then tested which of these models 'best' distinguished those that rated quality of life (QoL) as 'Good' (included 'So good, could not be better, to 'Good') instead of 'Not good' (included 'Alright' to 'so bad, could not be worse'). Successful ageing can then be considered as being made up of the factors contained within the most predictive model.

While each model could independently predict QoL, the strongest prediction was achieved by the Lay model. Those individuals who scored as 'successfully aged' on the basis of lay model variables were more than FIVE times more likely to rate their QoL as 'good' and not 'not good' (Odds ratio (OR) 5.493). The odds of a good QoL rating was next best among those classified on the broader biomedical model (OR 3.252), then the biomedical model (OR 2.598) and then the psychological (OR 2.413) and social models (OR 1.998).

It is not the purpose of this section to provide the statistical detail but more to point to the importance of multidimensional models of health. All models were successful in predicting QoL and so the findings do not suggest that medical or psychological or social variables are not important, but rather that a model addressing all factors is 'better'. A broader model also opens up a range of opportunities for intervention; the challenge now is to use such findings to develop and evaluate health promotion interventions with older populations. One caveat to this, however, is that the sample used by Bowling and Iliffe was 98 per cent white and thus we cannot conclude that the model of successful ageing best associated with QoL would hold for non-white samples.

Plate 1.2   Hiking can be enjoyed by all age groups, including senior citizens.
Source: Photofusion Picture Library/David Townend

This chapter has described what is often meant by 'health'. In focusing on health, we have acknowledged that health is a continuum, not simply a dichotomy of sick versus healthy. Most of us will experience in our lifetime varying degrees of health and wellbeing, with periods of illness at one extreme and optimal wellness at the other. Some may never experience optimal wellness. 'Health refers to a state of being that is largely taken for granted' (Radley 1994: 5) and is often only appreciated when lost through illness. The final section of this chapter introduces what is broadly considered to reflect the discipline of health psychology and the final chapter of this book addresses careers in health psychology.

What is health psychology?

Psychology can be defined as the scientific study of mental and behavioural functioning. Studying mental processes through behaviour is limited, however, in that not all behaviour is observable (for example, is thought not behaviour?) and thus for many aspects of human behaviour we have to rely on self-report, the problems of which are described elsewhere.

Psychology aims to describe, explain, predict and where possible intervene to control or modify behavioural and mental processes, from language, memory, attention and perception to emotions, social behaviour and health behaviour, to name just a few. The key to scientific methods employed by psychologists is the basic principle that the world may be known through observation = **empiricism**. Empirical methods go beyond speculation, inference and reasoning to actual and systematic analysis of data. Scientific research starts with a theory, which can be defined as a general set of assumptions about how things operate in the world. Theories can be vague and poorly defined (e.g. I have a theory about why sports science students generally sit together at the back of lectures) to very specific (e.g. sports science students sit at the back of lectures because they feel like 'outsiders' when placed with the large numbers of psychology majors). Psychologists scientifically test the validity of their hypotheses and theories. On an academic level this can increase understanding about a particular phenomenon, and on an applied level it can provide knowledge useful to the development of interventions.

Psychologists use scientific methods to investigate all kinds of behaviour and mental processes, from the response activity of a single nerve cell to the role adjustments required in old age. Different kinds of psychologist will employ different methods, and this text highlights those that are most commonly employed by health psychologists: for example, the use of questionnaires, interviews and psychometric assessments (such as of personality).

empiricism
arising from a school of thought that all knowledge can be obtained through experience.

What connects psychology to health?

As introduced in this chapter, people have beliefs about health, are often emotional about it and have a behavioural role to play in maintaining their health and coping with illness. Health psychology can address questions such as why some people behave in a healthy way and others do not. Is it all a matter of personality? Does a person who behaves in a healthy manner in one way, e.g. doesn't smoke, also behave healthily in other ways, e.g. attend dental screening? Are we rational and consistent beings? Does gender, age or socio-economic status affect health either directly or indirectly via their effects on other things? Why do some people appear to get ill all the time while others stay healthy? Health psychology integrates many cognitive, developmental and social theories and explanations, but it applies them solely to health, illness and health care. You may want to pick up an introductory psychology text and look at the learning, motivation, social, developmental and cognitive sections in more detail.

The main goals of health psychology, derived from Matarazzo's definition (1982), are to develop our understanding of biopsychosocial factors involved in:

- the promotion and maintenance of health;
- improving health-care systems and health policy;
- the prevention and treatment of illness;
- the causes of illness: e.g. vulnerability/risk factors.

Unlike some other domains of psychology (such as cognitive science), health psychology can be considered as an applied science, although not all health psychology research is predictive. For example, some research aims only to *quantify* (e.g. what percentage of school pupils drink under age?) or *describe* (e.g. what are the basic characteristics of underage drinkers, such as age, sex, socio-economic status). Descriptive research ideally provides the foundation for the generation of more causal questions: e.g. what is it about low socio-economic status that increases the incidence of risky behaviour? By simply measuring health beliefs and attitudes, we can begin to grapple with the issue of predictors (see Chapters 3–5) before developing interventions.

Health psychology and other fields

Health psychology has grown out of many fields within the social sciences. It has adopted and adapted models and theories originally found in social psychology, behaviourism, clinical psychology, cognitive psychology, etc. Health psychology in Europe is, as in the USA, linked with other health and social sciences (e.g. health economics, behavioural medicine, medical sociology) and with medicine and allied therapeutic disciplines. Few academic or practitioner health psychologists work alone; most are involved in an array of inter- and multidisciplinary work (for a discussion of professional health psychology, see Chapter 18).

There are several contrasts with other popular disciplines, as highlighted below, each of which may vary in terms of methods of assessment, research, treatment and intervention.

Medical psychology

This is based upon an essentially mechanistic medical model: i.e. an underlying impairment causes some symptom that requires treatment/cure in order to enable a return to 'normal' (however defined) health. Health psychologists do not dispute the biological basis of health and illness but have aided in the development of a more holistic model. Health psychologists still have to have an understanding of the various body systems (nervous system, endocrine system, immune system mainly), but also relevant to areas studied in the psychology of health are the respiratory and digestive systems (see Chapter 8).

Behavioural medicine

This is an interdisciplinary field drawing on a range of behavioural sciences, including psychology, sociology and health education, in relation to medical conditions (Schwartz and Weiss 1977). Behavioural medicine developed in the 1970s at around the same time as health psychology, and it also provided a challenge to the biomedical model dominant at the time. Behavioural medicine examines the development and integration of behavioural and biomedical knowledge and techniques of relevance to health and illness. As its name suggests, behavioural principles are employed (i.e. that behaviour results from learning through classical or **operant conditioning**). This underlying principle is then applied to techniques of prevention and rehabilitation, and not solely to treatment. Behaviour also includes emotions such as fear and anxiety, although behavioural medicine is not concerned with mental health problems on their own. Behavioural medicine furthered the view that the mind had a direct link to the body (e.g. anxiety can raise blood pressure, fear can elevate heart rate), and some of the therapies proposed, such as biofeedback (see Chapter 13), work on the principle of operant conditioning and feedback.

operant conditioning attributed to Skinner, this theory is based on the assumption that behaviour is directly influenced by its consequences (e.g. rewards, punishments, avoidance of negative outcomes).

> **What do YOU think?**
>
> Think of some health behaviours you think you might have learned and consider the circumstances under which you learned them. What factors influence your maintenance of these behaviours?
>
> Think of any health problem you have experienced and whether you consider a role for your behaviour in either avoiding that problem in the future or in helping recovery from it.

Psychosomatic medicine

This developed in the 1930s and initially was the domain of now well-known psychoanalysts, e.g. Alexander, Freud. Psychosomatic medicine offered an early challenge to biomedicine as discussed earlier in the chapter. 'Psychosomatic' refers to the fact that the mind and body are both involved in illness, and where an organic cause is not easily identified the mind may offer the trigger of a physical response that is detectable and measurable. In other words, mind and body act together, not just the mind. Early work asserted that a certain personality would lead to a certain disease (e.g. Alexander's ulcer-prone personality), and while evidence for direct causality has proved limited, these developments in thinking certainly did set the groundwork for fascinating studies of physiological processes that may link personality type to disease (see Chapter 11's discussion of hostility and heart disease associations, for example). Until the 1960s, psychosomatic research was predominantly psychoanalytical in nature, focusing on psychoanalytic interpretations of illness, such as asthma, ulcers or migraine being triggered by repressed emotions. However, one limitation to result from this work is that among those adhering to a biomedical viewpoint, illnesses with no identifiable organic cause were often considered as nervous disorders or psychosomatic conditions for which medical treatment was often not forthcoming. Illnesses with no physical evidence are known as psychogenic.

Psychosomatic medicine today is more concerned with mixed psychological, social and biological/physiological explanations of illness, and illnesses addressed are often referred to as 'psychophysiological' (e.g. DSM-II) with acceptance that psychological factors can affect any physical condition (DSM-IIIR and DSM-IV).

Medical sociology

Medical sociology exemplifies the close relationship between psychology and sociology, with health and illness being considered in terms of social factors that may influence individuals. It takes a wider (macro) approach to the individual in that they are considered within family, kinship, culture. While health psychology also considers external influences on health and illness, it has traditionally focused more on the individual's cognitions/beliefs and responses to the external world and obviously takes a psychological rather than a sociological perspective. The advent of critical health psychology (see below) may make the boundaries between medical sociology and health psychology more blurred.

Clinical psychology

Health psychology and health psychologists are often confused with clinical psychology and clinical psychologists! Clinical psychology is concerned with mental health and the diagnosis and treatment of mental health problems. Clinical psychologists are typically practitioners working within the health-care setting, delivering assessments, diagnoses and psychological interventions that are derived from behavioural and cognitive principles. Many of these principles inform health psychology research and practice (see the many examples of cognitive-behavioural interventions outlined in this text), but the difference fundamentally comes down to the populations with whom we work and the professional status of our discipline. Different countries differ on this and you are referred to your national psychological associations for more information and also to Chapter 18 where we have described health psychology careers.

Health psychology

Health psychology takes a biopsychosocial approach to health and illness (Engel 1977, 1980) and thus considers biological, social and psychological factors involved in the aetiology, prevention or treatment of physical illness, as well as in the promotion and maintenance of health. Health psychology is changing as it grows and recently it has been suggested (Marks 2002: 3–7) that four approaches to health psychology are developing in parallel:

1. *clinical health psychology*, which merges clinical psychology's focus on assessment and treatment with a broader biopsychosocial approach to ill- and health-care issues and which is generally the domain of clinical psychologist practitioner (e.g. ... and Kennedy 1998);

2. *public health psychology*, with an emphasis on public health ... immunisation programmes, epidemics, and resultant health education and promotion – this area draws from multidisciplinary sources (e.g. social science, economics, politics);

3. *community health psychology*, which employs the methods of action research and aims at the achievement of healthy groups and healthy communities; and

4. *critical health psychology*, which warrants a little more attention here.

Critical health psychology

Health psychology has been criticised (e.g. Eiser 1996; Radley 1996) for being too individualistic in focus, too concerned with individual aspects at the expense of the social. This book hopes to address some of these concerns by addressing wider influences on health and illness such as culture, lifespan and socio-economic variables. Humans do not operate in a vacuum but are interacting social beings shaped, modelled and reinforced in their thoughts, behaviour and emotions by people close to them, by less known people, by politicians, by their culture, and even by the era in which they live. Consider, for example, women and work stress – this was not an issue in the 1900s, when society neither expected nor particularly supported women to work, whereas in the twenty-first century we have a whole new arena of women's health issues that in part may relate to the way women's roles have shifted in society.

Another criticism aimed at health psychology in the early twenty-first century, is that we have focused more on illness than on health (e.g. Marks *et al.* 2000: 22); however, in this text we have successfully balanced these and shown how one can influence responses to the other. Critical health psychologists argue that the biopsychosocial model needs clearer distinction from the biomedical model, particularly in relation to the development of the 'social' component. As Crossley (2000: 6) points out, the biopsychosocial model is more often treated in health psychology research as if the three components are simultaneous influences (but still separate) rather than fully integrated ones. The focus on individual thought, feeling and action, she claims, underplays the role played by society and politics in our human experience of health and illness. Contexts and cultures need more attention: for example, a greater acknowledgement of the rich and growing diversity of cultures in the UK and the rest of Europe. Unlike many undergraduate health psychology texts, we aim to provide you with an understanding of cultural influences on health and the responses to illness.

Criticism is inevitable when a discipline has been evolving for only thirty or so years, and it will continue to evolve by attending to these and other voices. Such a critique of one's own discipline is important and beneficial in opening up debates and discussions so that the discipline and those within it do not become complacent. As potential health psychologists of the future, readers should be aware of the importance of reflection and critique. This text aims to address its critics by addressing cultural and social perspectives on health and illness in an integrated manner, while at the same time providing coverage of mainstream topics, questions and methods. Central to the argument of critical health psychologists is that *understanding* human health and illness should be the central goal. This text will provide you with that crucial understanding.

Summary

This chapter has introduced key areas of interest to health psychologists, including:

- What is health?
  - Health appears to consist broadly of domains of 'having', 'doing' and 'being', where health is a reserve, an absence of illness, a state of psychological and physical wellbeing; is evident in the ability to perform physical acts, as fitness, and is generally something that is taken for granted until it is challenged by illness.

- How has health and illness been viewed over time?
  - Views of health have shifted from fairly holistic views, where mind and body interact, to more dualist views, where the mind and body are thought to act independently of one another. This is shifting back towards holism, with the medical model being challenged by a more biopsychosocial approach.

- What influence does culture have on how health is perceived?
  - Cultures can be grounded in collective or individualistic orientations, and these will influence explanations for health and illness as well as the behaviour of those within the culture.

- What influence might lifespan play on how health is perceived?
  - Children can explain health and illness in complex and multidimensional terms; and human expectations of health change over the lifespan as a function of background and experience as well as of cognitive development.

- What is health psychology?
  - Health psychology is the study of health, illness and health-care practices (professional and personal).
  - Health psychology aims to understand, explain and ideally predict health and illness behaviour in order that effective interventions can be developed to reduce the physical and emotional costs of risky behaviour and illness.
  - Health psychology offers a holistic but fundamentally psychological approach to issues in health, illness and health care.

Further reading

Bowling, A. and Iliffe, S. (2006) Which model of successful ageing should be used? Baseline findings from a British longitudinal survey of ageing. *Age and Ageing*, 35: 607–614.
As described in this chapter, this useful paper outlines both the different models of ageing that exist, as well as data showing support for a broad model.

Marks, D.F., Murray, M., Evans, B. and Willig, C. (2000). *Health Psychology: Theory, Research and Practice*. London: Sage.
This book provides an indepth and critical consideration of the developing (in 2000) field of health psychology with particular focus on health within the broader social, political and cultural context.

Penny, G.N., Bennett, P. and Herbert, M. (eds) (1994) *Health Psychology: A Lifespan Perspective*. Switzerland: Harwood Academic.
In particular, Bibace and Walsh's chapter on children's perceptions of illness. The chapter on adolescent health behaviour by Nutbeam and Booth is interesting in terms of cognitive development, but the chapter on caring for the elderly is more relevant to Chapter 15 on caring, as, sadly, little is said about the health concept either in the elderly or in the middle-aged.

Radley, A. (1994) *Making Sense of Illness: The Social Psychology of Health and Illness*. London: Sage Publications.
This book is well worth a look in order to get a broader perspective than the predominantly psychological one offered here. It is also highly relevant to Chapter 2 in its discussion of social inequalities.

The British Psychology website is useful for defining health psychology as a discipline and as a profession (see also Chapter 18).
www.bps.org.uk

 Visit the website at **www.pearsoned.co.uk/morrison** for additional resources to help you with your study, including multiple choice questions, weblinks and flashcards.

CHAPTER 2

Health inequalities

Learning outcomes

By the end of this chapter, you should have an understanding of:

- the impact of poverty on health
- causes of variations in health between and within countries
- the impact of social deprivation on health and theories of why this occurs
- the health impact of having a minority status in society
- the impact of gender on health
- the relationship between work stress, unemployment and health

CHAPTER OUTLINE

This chapter considers differences in health status that arise not as a result of individual behaviour but from the social context in which we live. Among other things, it considers why better-off people tend to live longer than those who are less well off, why women generally live longer than men, and why people from ethnic minorities are more likely to die earlier than those from majority populations. The greatest killer in the world is poverty, which is associated with poor nutrition, unhealthy water supplies, poor health care, and other factors that directly influence health. Among people who do not experience such poverty, more subtle social and psychological factors influence health. Men's health, for example, may be influenced by a general reluctance to seek medical help following the onset of illness. People who are economically deprived may experience poorer health because of problems of accessing health care, and greater levels of stress than the more economically well off. This chapter examines how social and psychological processes differentially influence health as a result of **socio-economic status** (SES), ethnicity, gender and working environment.

socio-economic status
a measure of the social class of an individual. Different measures use different indicators, including income, job type or years of education. Higher status implies a higher salary or higher job status.

Health differentials

Where we live can impact on our risk for disease as much, if not more, than how we live. The biomedical model and even health psychology have typically focused on individual risk factors such as personality, diet and levels of exercise as risk factors for poor health. We discuss some of these issues in Chapters 3 and 4, and 11. However, there is an emerging body of evidence that environmental and social factors may have an equal, if not greater, influence on our health. The better-off live longer than the less well-off. People who occupy minority roles in society as a result of ethnic or other factors may experience more illness or die earlier than the majority population. Women live longer than men and findings suggest this may be as much a consequence of social and psychological factors as biological ones. Evidence in support of these assertions has only emerged relatively recently, and because of its political implications it has, on occasion, been controversial. Attempts have even been made to suppress relevant data. This is perhaps best illustrated by publication of the Black Report (available as Whitehead *et al.* 1992). This was one of the first British publications to identify poverty as a cause of ill health. Commissioned by a Labour government in 1977, the committee reported in 1980 when a Conservative government was in power. Unable to prevent its publication, their immediate response was to 'bury' the report, publishing a limited number of copies on the August bank holiday, when it received minimal publicity. The only way for most people to access the report was to read the book version published over a decade later (Whitehead *et al.* 1992).

This chapter considers how people in various groups in society may experience differences in health and longevity as a result of their SES, ethnicity, gender and working conditions. It considers each factor separately, although in reality each of them may be intimately intertwined. People in ethnic minorities, for example, still tend to be less well off than the majority population and may suffer adverse health effects as a result of both their ethnicity and SES. Accordingly, although this chapter attempts to identify the specific health gains or risks associated with different social contexts, it should be remembered that many individuals face multiple advantages or disadvantages as a result of occupying several social contexts.

Evidence of health differentials

health differential
a term used to denote differences in health status and life expectancy across different groups.

There are clear **health differentials** between countries. Almost all the countries whose populations experience the shortest number of years in what the World Health Organization (WHO) call 'the equivalent of full health' are in Africa (see Table 2.1). The countries with the best health are scattered around the world, although European and Scandinavian countries predominate. Nearly one-third of deaths in the developing countries occur before the age of 5 years (WHO 1995), while a further third of deaths occur before the age of 65 years. This contrasts with the average two-thirds of deaths that occur after the age of 65 years within the industrialised countries.

The factors that contribute to these differences are economic, environmental and social. They include a lack of safe water, poor sanitation, inadequate diet and poor access to health care which even when accessed is frequently rudimentary and lacking in resources. The WHO (1995) estimated that poverty causes 12 million deaths each year in children under the age of 5 living in the developing world, with the most common causes of

Table 2.1   The average years of 'equivalent of full health' for men in the top and bottom 10 countries of the world in 2002

Top 10	Average years of 'full health'	Bottom 10	Average years of 'full health'
Japan	72	Botswana	36
Iceland	72	Afghanistan	35
Sweden	72	Zambia	35
Australia	71	People's Republic of Congo	35
San Marino	71	Zimbabwe	34
Switzerland	71	Liberia	34
Italy	71		33
Monaco	71	Angola	32
Norway	70	Lesotho	30
Canada	70	Sierra Leone	27

Source: WHO (2007)

death being diarrhoea, dysentery and lower respiratory tract infections. Major killers among the adult population included tuberculosis and malaria. One particular problem now facing many developing countries in Africa is HIV infection and AIDS. Botswana, Zimbabwe and Swaziland have HIV infection rates of 30 per cent or higher (UNAIDS 2008). There are over 11 million AIDS orphans in the region and this number is expected to rise to more than 20 million by the year 2010 (UNAIDS 2008). Of note also is that the richest country in the world, the USA, fared rather badly on this index, at only 26th place in the rankings, with an 'equivalent of good health' expectancy of 67 years. A number of explanations for this apparent anomaly include the following, some of which are considered in more depth later in the chapter:

- Some social groups within the USA, such as Native Americans and the inner-city poor, have extremely poor health – more characteristic of developing countries rather than rich industrialised ones.

- HIV has contributed to a higher proportion of death and disability to young and middle-aged Americans than in most other industrialised countries.

- The USA is one of the leading countries for cancers relating to tobacco use, especially lung cancer and chronic lung disease.

- The USA has high levels of violence, especially of homicides, compared to other industrialised countries.

Even the 'haves' experience health differentials

While the industrialised world may not have the profound levels of poverty and illness found in the developing world, there are gradients of wealth within these countries, and differentials in health that match them. The richer people *within* most industrialised countries are likely to live longer than the less well off (Marmot *et al.* 1991) and be healthier while alive. One example of this can be found in data reported by Rasulo *et al.* (2007). They calculated the expected healthy lifespan of individuals living in 8,797 defined areas of the UK and the level of social deprivation of each area using a measure of deprivation known as the Carstair's deprivation score. This measures levels of household overcrowding, male unemployment, low social class and car ownership. They then calculated the average healthy life expectancy across the range of levels of deprivation and found a linear relationship between deprivation scores and expected healthy life expectancy (see Figure 2.1). They reported a staggering 13.2 years' difference in healthy life expectancy between those in the least and most deprived areas (Figure 2.1).

Similar findings can be found across the industrialised world. It is important to note that the relationship between income and health is *linear*, indicating not just that the very poor die earlier than the very rich. Instead, it indicates that quite modest differences in wealth, or social factors indicative of wealth, impact on health throughout the social groups. This effect can be incredibly subtle. Marmot *et al.* (1991), for example, reported that middle-class UK executives who owned one car were more likely to die earlier than their peers who had two cars.

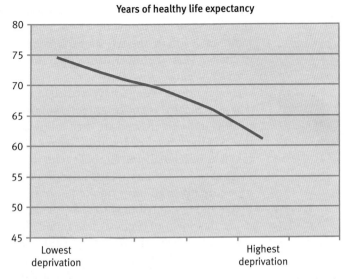

Figure 2.1   Years of healthy life expectancy according to Carstair's deprivation scores in the UK

Source: from 'Inequalities in health expectancies in England and Wales: small area analysis from 2001 Census', *Health Statistics Quarterly*, 34 (Rasulo, D., Bajekal, M. and Yar, M. 2007), © Crown copyright 2007; Crown copyright material is reproduced with the permission of the Controller, Office of Public Sector Information (OPSI), also reproduced with the permission of the author

What do YOU think?

While there is consistent evidence in industrialised countries that the better-off live longer, engage in less health-damaging behaviours, and experience less illness than those who are more economically deprived, this is not always the case in other countries. Singh *et al.* (1997), for example, reported that rates of heart disease were higher among Indian rural middle classes than among the lower social groups. What factors do you think may contribute to these differences? Are they likely to be a transient or permanent phenomenon? Do such findings indicate that we should be cautious in generalising any associations between social class and health across countries and cultures?

Explanations of socio-economic health inequalities

A number of explanations for health inequalities in the industrialised countries have been proposed, some of which attribute responsibility to the individual. Others suggest that something about occupying different social groups itself can directly impact on health. But, the first question that has to be addressed is the causal direction between socio-economic status (SES) and health. Does SES influence health, or does health influence SES?

■ Social causation versus social drift

The first explanation for health differentials pits a social explanation against a more individual one. The first, the social causation model, suggests that low SES 'causes' health problems – that is, there is something about occupying a low socio-economic group that adversely influences the health of individuals.

The opposing view, the social drift model, opposes this view. This suggests that when an individual develops a health problem, they may be unable to maintain a job or the levels of overtime required to maintain their standard of living. They therefore drift down the socio-economic scale: that is, health problems 'cause' low SES.

Longitudinal studies have provided evidence relevant to these hypotheses. These typically identify a representative population of several thousand healthy individuals who are then followed over a number of years to see what diseases they develop and from what causes they die. Differences in measures taken at baseline between those who do and do not develop disease are considered to be risk factors for disease: people who die of cancer, for example, are more likely to have smoked at baseline than those who do not, suggesting smoking contributes to risk for developing cancer. Each of the studies using this form of analysis has found that baseline measures of SES predict subsequent health status, while health status does not predict SES so strongly. Socio-economic status is therefore generally seen as a *cause* of differences in health status rather than a consequence (e.g. Marmot *et al.* 1991). Other data supporting the social causation model show that many people's health deteriorates as they move from employment to unemployment as a result of factors unrelated to individual health, particularly if they experience economic difficulties (e.g. Ferrie *et al.* 2001). Data from Davey-Smith and Philips (1991) are also relevant here. They considered the relative role of childhood versus adult environments on the health of adults. Their analyses indicated that the social context in which we live as an adult has a greater influence on our health than the one that we experienced as a child. These data again suggest that the impact of the environment on our health is not fixed, and that changes in SES throughout the lifespan will affect our health. A cautionary note must be made here, however. Not all studies show a negation of childhood factors on later health. Kittleson *et al.* (2006), for example, reported a longitudinal study involving over a thousand male medical students and found that despite them all becoming doctors, and therefore occupying the same socio-economic group, those who came from economically deprived backgrounds were more than twice as likely to develop **coronary heart disease** (CHD) before the age of 50 years than those from more affluent backgrounds, even after adjusting for risk factors for CHD including body mass index, cholesterol level, amount of exercise, smoking, hypertension, diabetes mellitus and parental history of heart disease.

coronary heart disease a narrowing of the blood vessels that supply blood and oxygen to the heart. Results from a build-up of fatty material and plaque (**atherosclerosis**). Can result in **angina** or **myocardial infarction**.

premature mortality death before the age it is normally expected. Usually set at deaths under the age of 75 years.

Different health behaviours

We identified in Chapter 1 how a number of behaviours influence our health. With this in mind, one obvious potential explanation for the higher levels of ill health and **premature mortality** among people in the lower socio-economic groups is that they engage in more health-damaging and less health-promoting behaviours than those in the higher socio-economic groups. This does seem to be the case. People in the lower socio-economic groups in industrialised countries tend to smoke and drink more alcohol, eat a less healthy diet and take less leisure exercise than the better-off (e.g. Choiniére *et al.* 2000). However, there is consistent evidence that while differences in health-related behaviours account for some of the socio-economic differences in health, they do not provide the full story. In a study of 50,000 Finnish men and women, Kivimäki *et al.* (2007), for example, reported that people from low-income groups were twice as likely to develop CHD before the age of 64 years than those in high-income groups. This risk fell by 29 per cent after statistical adjustment for risk factors including smoking, heavy alcohol consumption, physical inactivity and obesity – but a significant risk due to socio-economic factors remained. Both SES and behaviour appear to independently predict health. What is perhaps worth considering here is *why* people in the lower socio-economic groups engage in more health compromising behaviours. It does not appear to be the result of lack of knowledge (Narevic and Schoenberg 2002). Rather, it may be a deliberate choice based on a calculation of the costs and benefits of such behaviours. Work by Graham (1994), for example, suggested that working-class women smokers were well aware of the adverse health consequences of smoking, but continued to do so as it helped them cope with the day-to-day stresses of running a family with low economic resources. The type of health-behaviour choices we make, and in some cases the availability of such choices, may be constrained by the social context in which we live.

Of particular interest is that socio-economic factors may, on occasion, actually overwhelm the effects of individual behaviour. An example of this can be found in the work of Hein *et al.* (1992), who reported the outcomes of a 17-year prospective study of CHD in Danish men. As predicted, they found that smokers were three-and-half times more likely to develop CHD than non-smokers. However, sub-analyses showed that white-collar smokers were six-and-half times more likely to develop CHD than the equivalent non-smokers, while blue-collar workers experienced no additional risk for CHD as a result of their smoking. These data suggest that the health risks associated with smoking may be worse among those people who were not placed at risk of disease as a result of their socio-economic position. This may come as some relief for the women smokers interviewed by Graham, and has implications for the type of health policy and intervention that may influence the health of such individuals.

■ Access to health care

Access to health care is likely to differ according to both personal characteristics and the health-care system with which the individual is attempting to interact. The majority of studies of this phenomenon have been conducted in the USA, where different health-care systems operate for those with and without health insurance. Here, the less well-off clearly receive poorer health care. Rahimi *et al.* (2007), for example, found that some individuals experienced substantial financial barriers to health care following a myocardial infarction (MI: see Chapter 8). Eighteen per cent of their large sample of patients, the majority of whom had health insurance, reported that financial barriers prevented them from having appropriate care: 13 per cent reported financial barriers to accessing appropriate medication. Poor access to health care or medication was associated with poorer quality of life, more hospitalisation and a higher prevalence of angina.

By contrast, in the UK where there are no economic barriers to health care, people in the lower socio-economic groups access health care more frequently than those in the higher SES groups (see Figure 2.2), suggesting that no such economic division is found in the UK. Unfortunately, what these data

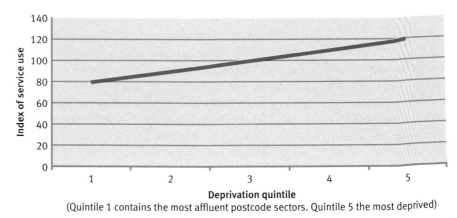

Figure 2.2   Health service use according to level of social deprivation in Scotland in 1999.

Source: Scottish Executive (1999)

coronary artery bypass grafts
surgical procedure in which veins or arteries from elsewhere in the patient's body are grafted from the aorta to the coronary arteries to improve blood flow to the heart muscle.

statins
drugs designed to reduce cholesterol levels.

do not address is whether the increased use of health-care resources is sufficient to counter the additional levels of poor health associated with low economic status. What evidence there is suggests this is not the case. The Scottish Executive's (1999) report on health inequalities, for example, revealed considerable differences between the rates of a number of medical and surgical procedures across the poor and the more affluent areas across Scotland: rates of hip replacements, hernia repairs and varicose vein surgery were much higher per head of population among the better-off than those living in economically deprived areas. In addition, although a higher percentage of the most deprived sections of society received **coronary artery bypass grafts** for CHD than did those in the higher SES groups, the relative difference was not as great as the differences in the prevalence of CHD between the groups. Although more people received surgery, the poorer population remained relatively deprived of health care in comparison to those in the higher SES groups. There is evidence also of consistent differences in the type of treatment people can access in primary care. In an Australian study, Stocks *et al.* (2004) found that patients from high socio-economic groups were more likely to be prescribed **statins** than people with the equivalent levels of cholesterol from low-income groups. People from lower socio-economic groups may also be less likely to seek appropriate medical care even when it is available. Wamala *et al.* (2007) reported that people from lower socio-economic groups were up to twelve times less likely to seek appropriate medical treatment than those in the higher groups.

Environmental factors

A third explanation for differences in health across social groups suggests that people in lower socio-economic groups are exposed to more health-damaging environments, including working in dangerous settings such as building sites, and have more accidents than those in the higher socio-economic groups throughout their working life (Acheson 1998). In addition, they may experience home conditions of low-quality housing, dampness and higher levels of air pollution than those in the higher socio-economic groups

Inequalities of health provision

There is consistent evidence that where we live contributes to the quality of the health care we can potentially receive. Some of these differences may be obvious. In the UK, for example, all medicine prescriptions are free in Wales but cost £6.10 per item in England. Other differences are less obvious, but still very real. The *Daily Telegraph* reported the following in its 26 November 2007 online edition:

> Cancer care in Britain is subject to a postcode lottery, with some health Trusts spending three times more on patients than others. Huge discrepancies in funding mean that the life expectancy of patients can vary from region to region as expensive life-saving drugs are dispensed to only those living in certain areas. Health experts say patients in higher-spending areas could have as much as a 20 per cent better chance of survival than those in areas where the spending is low.

Differences across various health Trusts across England were:

Most spent (per person)	Least spent (per person)
1 Nottingham City £17,028	Oxfordshire £5,182
2 Knowsley £16,819	Dorset £5,259
3 Manchester £14,999	Bedfordshire £5,262
4 Tower Hamlets, London £14,767	Cornwall and Isles of Scilly £5,749
5 Heart of Birmingham £14,511	Harrow, Middlesex £5,800
6 Salford Teaching £14,118	South Gloucester £5,902
7 City and Hackney, London £13,722	Herefordshire £5,967
8 Leicester City £13,217	West Sussex Teaching £6,038
9 Newham, London £12,753	Northumberland £6,108
10 Wakefield £12,454	Yorkshire, East Riding £6,379

Of course, it is possible that high levels of spending on cancer were to the detriment of treatment of other conditions, and may not represent the quality of service actually provided. However, the differences across the country on treatments considered to be a high priority by the national government is of concern, and may need to be addressed at a governmental level.

atheroma
fatty deposit in the intima (inner lining) of an artery.

(Bashir 2002). Environmental factors may also work through social and psychological pathways. One mechanism involves the stress associated with overcrowding. There is clear evidence both from animal and human research that overcrowding is associated with high levels of stress hormones and, in animals, accelerated development of **atheroma** and CHD (Baum *et al.* 1999).

More subtle processes may also be at work. One example of this can be found in research examining the effect of the type of housing we occupy. In Britain, premature mortality rates are about twenty-five per cent higher among tenants than owner-occupiers (Filakti and Kox 1995). Tenants also report higher rates of long-term illness than owner-occupiers. Wood *et al.* (2003), for example, found that after adjusting for age, male renters were one-and-a-half times more at risk of developing CHD than male owner-occupiers; women renters were over twice as likely to develop CHD as their owner-occupier counterparts. There are a number of explanations for these differentials:

- renters may experience more damp, poor ventilation, overcrowding, and so on;
- rented occupation may be further away from amenities, making access to leisure facilities or good quality shops more difficult;
- renters earn less than people who own their house;
- the psychological consequences of living in differing types of accommodation may directly impact on health.

Although the fourth pathway has received little attention, MacIntyre and Ellaway (1998) found that a range of mental and physical health measures were significantly associated with housing tenure even after controlling for the quality of housing, and the age, sex, income and self-esteem of their occupiers. They interpreted these data to suggest that the type of tenure itself is directly associated with health. They suggested, for example, that the degree of control we have over our living environment will differ according to whether or not we own the property in which we live, and may influence mood, levels of stress, and perceived control over a wider set of health behaviours – all of which may contribute to ill health.

Psychosocial factors

The implication of the previous section is that poor housing leads to stress, which in turn leads to ill health. This argument can be widened to suggest that differences in stress experienced as a result of a variety of factors may contribute to differences in health across the social groups. This seems a reasonable hypothesis. There is consistent evidence that people of all ages in the lower socio-economic groups not only experience more stress than their equivalents in the higher socio-economic groups (e.g. Marmot *et al.* 1997), but also frequently have less personal resources to help them cope with them (Finkelstein *et al.* 2007). There is also significant evidence to suggest that stress can adversely impact on health (see Chapter 11).

Some of the stresses (and restrictions in life opportunities) that may be experienced more by people in lower socio-economic groups than by the economically better off are summarised below (see Carroll *et al.* 1996a):

- Childhood: family instability, overcrowding, poor diet, restricted educational opportunities;
- Adolescence: family strife, exposure to others' and own smoking, leaving school with poor qualifications, experiencing unemployment or low-paid and insecure jobs;
- Adulthood: working in hazardous conditions, financial insecurity, periods of unemployment, low levels of control over work or home life, negative social interactions;
- Older age: no or small occupational pension, inadequate heating, food, etc.

Wilkinson (1990) took this argument one stage further. He compared data on income distribution and life expectancy across nine Western countries, and found that while the overall wealth of each country was not associated with life expectancy, the income *distribution* across the various social groups (i.e. the size of the gap between the rich and poor) within each country was. The correlation between the two variables was a remarkable 0.86: the higher the income disparity across the population, the worse its overall health. Longitudinal data also contribute to the strength of his argument. Forwell (1993) tracked average age of mortality and income distribution in Glasgow between the years 1981 and 1989. During this period, there was a significant increase in the income distribution within the population: the income of the richer section of society increased significantly more than that of the people in the lower SES groups. As these income disparities increased over this period, so did rates of premature mortality across the lower-income groups, despite their access to material goods, food, clothing and so on, remaining relatively constant over time, or even improving.

These data lead us back to the stress hypothesis. In his explanation of these phenomena, Wilkinson suggested that the wider the wealth disparities within society, the lower the levels of social cohesion and **social capital** within society. A wide distribution of wealth results in lower social capital: a more even distribution results in higher levels of social capital. Low social capital is associated with both individual distrust and dissatisfaction, and social factors such as high levels of crime. This, Wilkinson contended, is inherently stressful and results in high levels of stress-related illness among those individuals who are (relatively) socially deprived. Data to support this contention have recently been reported by a number of researchers, one of whom (Kawachi *et al.* 1997; see also RESEARCH FOCUS) analysed the association between income inequality and social capital across 39 US states. They asked respondents in each state whether 'Most people can be trusted – or would most people try to take advantage of you if they got the chance?' The percentage of participants who thought that people 'try to take advantage' (suggesting low levels of social capital) was highly correlated with the degree of income inequality in each state. This, in turn, was strongly correlated with overall mortality.

social capital
feelings of social cohesion, solidarity and trust in one's neighbours.

Plate 2.1   Just kids hanging around. But how will their life circumstances affect their health (and perhaps that of others)?

Source: Photofusion Picture Library/Rober Brook

RESEARCH FOCUS

Scheffler, R.M., Brown, T.T., Syme, L. *et al.* (2008). Community-level social capital and recurrence of acute coronary syndrome. *Social Science and Medicine*, 66: 1603–13.

Background

As we noted in the main text, there is increasing evidence that populations living in areas with high levels of social capital have relatively low levels of CHD. The authors of this study suggested that what is not clear, is whether these associations are attributable to social capital or other factors that may co-vary with the geographical variation in social capital. They suggested a number of alternative explanations for the association between social capital and health that need to be discounted before the social capital and health link can be unambiguously claimed.

- Social capital may increase the availability of information on behaviours that influence cardiovascular disease risk such as regular visits to the doctor and not smoking.
- High levels of social capital may lower the effort required to organise politically, which may result in more health resources being brought into a community.
- High levels of community-level capital may be associated with high levels of social support, which is independently associated with better health.

In their analyses, they explored the relationship between social capital and the likelihood of having a further acute coronary event in people who already had CHD, controlling for each of the factors they identified as potentially accounting for the relationship between social capital and disease.

Method

Their data were gathered from a variety of sources:

- *Hospital notes* provided age, gender, race/ethnicity, past medical history and clinical history during the time period of the study.
- *The California Automated Mortality Linkage System* provided evidence of death.
- *The Agency for Health Care Quality and Research* provided Petris Social Capital Index (PSCI) and gini scores. The PSCI is a measure of social capital, measuring the percentage of any population working in voluntary organisations. The gini score is a measure of income distribution.
- *The California Department of Finance* provided data on the Herfindahl index of racial/ethnic concentration.

Statistical analysis

A series of logistical regressions were used to model the association between the PSCI and participants having a further acute cardiac problem requiring them to visit hospital. Their first analysis included the following independent variables: the PSCI, age, gender and race/ethnicity, allowing the assessment of the contribution of individual variables to the risk of a further cardiac event. Their analyses grew in complexity to their final analysis, which included all the potentially contributing variables. The authors then considered the degree to which social capital was still able to independently predict the likelihood of an individual having a further acute coronary event.

Results

Their final sample comprised 34,752 people living in northern California who had been hospitalised and survived an acute coronary event between 1 January 1998 and 31 December

2002. Over this period, 7,916 (23 per cent) of these individuals had a further acute coronary event.

Their first analysis, which just included individual data, showed that high levels of community-level social capital were associated with an 11 per cent reduction in the recurrence of acute coronary events. Their final analysis showed that only those living in areas with median household income below $54,000 appeared to benefit from exposure to community-level social capital. Individuals below this income who lived in areas with high levels of social capital had a 9 per cent reduction in risk of the recurrence of acute coronary syndrome. No statistically significant association was found for those living in areas where the median household income was $54,000 or greater.

Discussion

These data suggest that high levels of social capital will directly reduce the risk of an acute coronary event, but that this influence is limited to those individuals who live in a relatively low-income area. In an attempt to explain this finding, the authors considered some other data they have published from their data set. One crucial finding was that although PSCI scores were associated with a number of health behaviours (low smoking, increased fruit and vegetable consumption), these effects were found throughout the population. However, PSCI scores were negatively associated with psychological distress only among people whose income was below the median. This led them to suggest that the route by which social capital influences risk for disease was by reducing levels of psychological distress within the population.

A further factor related to social capital, that may co-vary with SES, is the social support available to the individual. A large number of positive social relationships and few conflictual ones may buffer individuals against the adverse effects of the stress associated with low economic resources. Conversely, a poor social support system may significantly increase risk for disease (Taylor and Seeman 1999). Sadly, the potentially protective effect of good social support may be less available than previously. In contrast to research conducted in the 1950s, people in the higher social groups now appear to have more social support than those in the lower social groups, particularly where low socio-economic status is combined with high levels of social mobility and frequent changes of address (Chaix *et al.* 2007).

Minority status and health

A second factor that determines an individual's place in society is whether or not they occupy majority or minority status within the general population. This is usually considered in terms of the ethnic or cultural background of the individual, their sexuality, religion, and so on. Perhaps the most obvious minority within any population are people who differ from the majority in terms of skin colour: often considered under the rubric of ethnic minorities. Nazroo (1998) pointed out that ethnicity encompasses a variety of issues, including language, religion, migration, culture, ancestry and forms of identity. Each of these may individually or together contribute to differences between the health of different ethnic groups. He therefore warned about considering all people in all ethnic minority groups as one single entity and thereby failing to recognise the reality of their differing lives. These cautions are perhaps reflected in findings that in the UK, while rates of ill health and premature mortality among people from ethnic minorities are generally higher than those of the indigenous population, people from the Caribbean experience better health (Wild and McKeigue 1997). The prevalence of different diseases also varies across ethnic groups. Rates of heart disease among British men from the Indian sub-continent, for example, are 36 per cent higher than the national average. The Afro-Caribbean population has particularly high rates of **hypertension** (Lane *et al.* 2002) and **strokes**, while levels of diabetes are high among Asians. By contrast, rates of lung cancer are relatively low in people of Caribbean or West African origin (Balarajan and Raleigh 1993).

In searching for explanations of the relatively poor health among people in ethnic minorities, a number of issues have to be borne in mind. Perhaps the most important is that a disproportionate number of them also occupy low socio-economic groups. Before suggesting that being in an ethnic minority *alone* influences health, the effects of these socio-economic factors need to be excluded. This can be done by comparing disease rates between people in ethnic minorities and people from the majority population matched for income or other markers of SES, or by statistically partialling out the effects of SES in comparisons between majority and minority populations. Once these are done, any differences in mortality between the two groups lessen. Haan and Kaplan (1985), for example, found significantly higher rates of disease and premature mortality between American black and white populations (as large as a 30 per cent difference), which disappeared after partialling out the effects of SES. Other studies (e.g. Sorlie *et al.* 1995) have found a reduction, but not negation, of health differentials after partialling out the effects of SES.

Socio-economic status certainly exerts an influence within ethnic minorities. Just as for the majority population, people in the higher socio-economic groups generally live longer and have better health throughout their life than those with less economic resources (Harding and Maxwell 1997; Davey Smith *et al.* 1996). However, again highlighting the dangers of considering people in different ethnic minorities as one single group, there are some exceptions to this rule. In the UK, there appears to be no SES-related differential risk for CHD among men born in the Caribbean or West or South Africa (e.g. Harding and Maxwell 1997). Similarly, while Tobias and Yeh (2006) found a strong relationship between SES and health among New Zealand Maoris, no such gradient was found among Pacific and Asian populations. Despite these cautionary notes, there is a general consensus that ethnicity impacts on health, and a number of explanations for these differences have been proposed. These mirror, to some extent, those associated with SES: differences in health-related behaviours, stress and access to health care.

hypertension
a condition in which blood pressure is significantly above normal levels.

stroke
damage to the brain either as a result of a bleed into the brain tissue or a blockage in an artery, which prevents oxygen and other nutrients reaching parts of the brain. More scientifically known as a cerebro-vascular accident (CVA).

Differential health behaviours

The behavioural hypothesis suggests that variations in health outcomes may be explained by differences in behaviour across ethnic groups. In the UK, for example, many Asian males of Punjabi origin consume high levels of alcohol and develop alcohol-related disorders; levels of consumption among Muslim people are minimal, with total abstinence being common. In a study of immigrants to the UK, Bhopal *et al.* (2002) reported that male Bangladeshi immigrants had a higher fat diet than most other ethnic groups, while Europeans were more physically active than Indians, Pakistanis or Bangladeshis (Hayes *et al.* 2002). Their higher levels of activity were associated with lower body-mass indexes, blood pressure, blood glucose and insulin levels. By contrast, Dundas *et al.* (2001) found that white people living in Newcastle were more likely to smoke and drink excessively than Black Caribbean and Black Africans, with rates of drinking above the recommended limits of 19, 11 and 4 per cent in each group respectively.

Stress

A second explanation for the health disadvantages of people in minority groups focuses on the psychosocial impact of occupying minority status. People from ethnic minorities may experience wider sources of stress than majority populations as a consequence of specific stressors such as discrimination, racial harassment and the demands of maintaining or shifting culture. Two experimental studies conducted by Clark (Clarke 2000; Clark and Gochett 2006) suggest a mechanism through which this may become manifest. In the first of these studies, Clarke found that among a sample of young African American women, the more they reported experiencing racism, the greater their increases in blood pressure during a task in which they talked about their views and feelings about animal rights. Clarke took this to indicate that these women had developed a stronger emotional and physiological reaction to general stress as a result of their long-term responses to racism. In their second study, Clark and Gochett measured blood pressure, perceived racism, and the coping responses a sample of black American adolescents used in response to racism. They found that blood pressure did not vary according to the level of racism the participants reported. However, blood pressure was highest among those individuals who were both subject to racism and whose coping response was not to 'accept it' – individuals who perhaps became angry in response to racist behaviours. Accordingly, one contributor to high blood pressure in young black people may be chronically high arousal as part of a negative emotional or behavioural response to a variety of stressors – including racism – that they experience. A related explanation is known as 'John Henryism'. This suggests that successful black individuals have to push harder than their white equivalents to achieve the same level of success, and that their higher blood pressure reflects the stress of such effort (Merritt *et al.* 2004; see also IN THE SPOTLIGHT in Chapter 8).

Access to health care

A third explanation for the relatively poor health among ethnic minorities may be found in the problems some face in accessing health care. The situation in the USA was succinctly summarised in a report produced by the US Institute of Medicine (Committee on Understanding and Eliminating Racial and Ethnic Disparities in Health Care, Institute of Medicine *et al.* 2002), which noted that:

- African Americans and Hispanics tend to receive lower quality of care across a range of diseases, including cancer, CHD, HIV/AIDS and diabetes.
- African Americans are more likely than whites to receive less desirable services, such as amputation of all or part of a limb.
- Disparities are found even when clinical factors, such as severity of disease, are taken into account.
- Disparities are found across a range of clinical settings, including public and private hospitals, and teaching and non-teaching hospitals.
- Disparities in care are associated with higher mortality among minorities.

These inequalities are by no means restricted to the USA. Other examples can be found across the world. The Health Utilisation Research Alliance (2006) reported that New Zealand Maoris consulted their general practitioners at similar rates or less frequently than people with a European origin, despite having significantly higher rates of disease. In the UK, access to female GPs is lowest in areas with high concentrations of Asian residents (Birmingham Health Authority 1995): a factor that may inhibit Asian women's use of health-care services and, in particular, uptake of screening for cervical cancer (Naish *et al.* 1994). The Illinois Racial and Ethnic Health Disparities Council gave these stark reasons for the disparities in access to health care in the USA:

- **Individual factors**: racial bias, stereotyping and clinical uncertainty affect a physician's interaction with minority patients. Doctors are more likely to ascribe negative racial stereotypes to minority patients. Physicians are more likely to make negative comments about minority patients when discussing their case. Although most physicians claim they do not operate with overt bias, unconscious biases influence their interaction with racial and ethnic patients. Health-care professionals err in decisions about care for racial and ethnic minorities more often than in decisions about health care for whites. Physicians can understand the symptoms of white patients better than those of racial and ethnic minorities. (*Note the implicit assumption that the physician is not from an ethnic minority.*)
- **Organisational-level factors**: Racial and ethnic minorities face discrimination and exclusion from the health-care system. Health-care systems discriminate against racial and ethnic minorities through passive means – stereotyping, patient confusion and exclusion due to financial resources. Health-care systems are not always user-friendly and often confuse people. Individuals' access to health care are complex issues, influenced by health insurance, patients' rights and skyrocketing costs; racial and ethnic minorities' struggles are exacerbated by cultural and language differences.

Gender and health

An average woman's life expectancy in the industrialised countries is significantly greater than that of men. In the UK, for example, women are

risk ratios
compares the probability of a certain event occurring in two groups. A risk ratio of 1 implies that the event is equally likely in both groups. A risk ratio greater than 1 implies that the event is more likely in the first group. A risk ratio less than 1 implies that the event is less likely in the first group.

likely to live six years longer than men, with women dying on average at the age of 80 years and men at 74 years (WHO 2002: www.who.int). A large contributor to this difference is the earlier onset of CHD in men than women. Nearly three-quarters of those who die of an MI before the age of 65 years are men (American Heart Association 1995). However, of those men and women who do survive to the age of 65 years, women are still likely to live longer than men. Okamoto (2006), for example, reported data indicating that Japanese women aged 65 years were likely to live a further 22.5 years; men were likely to live an additional 17.4 years. Reddy *et al.* (1992) identified the following male/female **risk ratios** for dying prematurely from a variety of diseases in the USA:

Table 2.2   Relative risk for men dying prematurely (before the age of 65) from various illnesses in comparison with women

Cause	Male/female ratio
Coronary heart disease	1.89
Cancer	1.47
Stroke	1.16
Accidents	2.04
Chronic lung disease	2.04
Pneumonia/flu	1.77
Diabetes	1.11
Suicide	3.90
Liver disease	2.32
Atherosclerosis	1.28
Renal disease	1.54
Homicide/legal intervention	3.22
Septicaemia	1.36

These data indicate, for example, that men are nearly twice as likely to die before the age of 65 years of heart disease than women, and over three times more likely to die from violence ('legal intervention' is a US euphemism for the death penalty). Despite these differences in disease rates and mortality, men report higher levels of self-rated health, and contact medical services less frequently than women (Reddy *et al.* 1992). By contrast, women report higher levels of physical symptoms and long-standing illnesses than men (Lahelma *et al.* 1999). It is worth noting that while this pattern of mortality is common among industrialised countries, the pattern of health advantage is often different in industrialising countries. Here, differences in the life expectancy of men and women are smaller and in some cases are reversed (WHO 2008): women are more likely to experience higher rates of premature illness and mortality than men as a result of their more frequent experience of pregnancy and its associated health risks, as well as inadequate health

Biological differences

Perhaps the most obvious hypothesis for the health differences between men and women is that they are biologically different – being born female brings with it a natural biological advantage in terms of longevity. Women, for example, appear to have greater resistance to infections than men across the lifespan. Other biological explanations have considered the role of sex hormones. For some years, it was thought that high levels of oestrogen in women delayed the onset of CHD by reducing the tendency of blood to clot and keeping blood cholesterol levels low. However, data from a variety of sources, including Lawlor *et al.* (2002) who reported rates of CHD in women living in the UK and Japan, have found no evidence of any reduction of risk prior to the menopause or increase in risk following it. Instead, the rates of CHD gradually rise as women get older, just as they do in men. Our understanding of the role of testosterone in men has also changed over time. High levels of testosterone were thought to increase risk levels of atheroma, and increase risk for MI. Now, the reverse appears to be true, and high levels of testosterone are considered to be *protective* against CHD, probably as a consequence of its impact on lipids within the blood: high testosterone is associated with low levels of **HDL cholesterol** (Malkin *et al.* 2003).

HDL cholesterol
The so-called 'good cholesterol': see Chapter 8.

A second apparently biological cause of higher levels of disease in men involves their greater physiological response to stress than women. Men typically have greater increases in stress hormones and blood pressure in response to stressors than women, which may place them at more risk for CHD. However, there is increasing evidence these differences may not be the result of innate biological differences between the genders. Sieverding *et al.* (2005) found that blood pressure reactivity of men and women did not differ during a simulated job interview, but did vary according to the degree of stress they reported during the interview. Similarly, Newton *et al.* (2005) found no gender differences between men's and women's blood pressure and heart rate during discussions with previously unknown individuals. Dominance and not gender was consistently associated with blood pressure reactivity, with men who were challenged by a highly dominant male partner experiencing the greatest increase in blood pressure (and probably the most stress). It seems that it is not so much the gender of the individual that drives their physiological reactivity: rather, it is the type of stresses that the person is exposed to or the psychological response they evoke. Accordingly, any gender differences in stress reactivity may be more the result of long-term exposure to different stresses between the genders rather than biologically determined differences.

Behavioural differences

Further evidence that gender differences in health and mortality are not purely biological stems from studies that show clear health-related behavioural differences between men and women. More men than women engaged in all but 3 of 14 non-gender specific health-risk behaviours examined by Powell-Griner *et al.* (1997), including smoking, drinking alcohol, drunk-driving, not using safety belts and not attending health screening. About 6–7 per cent of men drank alcohol heavily – in comparison to 2 per cent of women. In addition, women were more likely than men to eat wholemeal bread, fruit and vegetables at least once per day, and to drink semi-skimmed milk. Finally, although rates of smoking were higher among adolescent girls than adolescent boys, this was only a short-term phenomenon, and more men than women smoked in adulthood.

Not only do men engage in more health-risking behaviours, they are less likely than women to seek medical help when necessary. Men visit their doctor less frequently than do women, even after excluding visits relating to children and 'reproductive care'. Socially disadvantaged women are twice as likely to consult a doctor as their male counterparts when they are ill. High-earning men are even less likely to consult a doctor when ill than their female counterparts (Department of Health and Human Services 1998). The reasons for these behavioural differences may be social in origin. Courtenay (2000) contended that they arise from the different meanings given to health-related behaviours by men and women. According to Courtenay, men show their masculinity and power by engaging in health-risking behaviours and by not showing signs of weakness, even when ill. Traditional masculine beliefs endorse the idea that men are independent, self-reliant, strong and tough. Courtney suggested, for example, that when men say 'I haven't been to a doctor in years', they are both reporting a health practice and making a statement about their masculinity. Charmaz (1994) identified several examples of quite extreme behaviours in which men would engage in order to hide their disabilities, including a wheelchair-bound diabetic man skipping lunch (and risking a coma) rather than embarrassing himself by asking for help in the dining area, and a middle-aged man with CHD declining offers of easier jobs to prove he was still capable of strenuous work. Mahalik et al. (2007) found that masculine beliefs were stronger predictors of risky health behaviours including smoking and alcohol abuse than demographic variables such as education and income. They may be established relatively early in life: adolescents with traditional masculine beliefs are less likely to attend their doctor for a physical examination than those with less traditional beliefs (Marcell et al. 2007). The one health-promoting behaviour that men consistently engage in more than women is leisure exercise (e.g. Steffen et al. 2006). Interestingly, this may also act as a marker of masculinity and power and carry a social message as well as having implications for health.

Unfortunately, inequalities in power between the sexes can adversely impact on women's health. One example of this can be found in the context of sexual behaviours, in which women are frequently less empowered than men. Abbott (1988), for example, found that 40 per cent of a sample of Australian women reported having had sexual intercourse on at least one occasion when they did not want to do so as a result of the pressure from their sexual partner. Similarly, Chacham et al. (2007) found that Brazilian women aged between 15 and 24 years old who had been victims of physical violence by a partner or whose partners restricted their mobility were less likely to use condoms than those with more autonomy and control. Such behaviours clearly place them at risk of a variety of sexually transmitted diseases.

Economic and social factors

The negative impact of adverse socio-economic factors discussed earlier in the chapter does not affect men and women equally. In the UK, for example, nearly 30 per cent of women are economically inactive, and those in work are predominantly employed in clerical, personal and retail sectors in low-paid work. About two-thirds of adults in the poorest households in the UK are women, and women make up 60 per cent of adults in households dependent on Income Support (a marker of a particularly low income: see Acheson 1998). Social isolation is also more frequent among women than men: women are less likely to drive or to have access to a car than men, and older women are more likely than older men to be widowed and to live alone. Women also appear more vulnerable to disrupted or poor social networks than men. Irregular social contact or dissatisfaction with a social network has been associated with both subjective health (Rennemark and Hagberg 1999) and mortality. Iwasaki *et al.* (2002), for example, found that in a population of older Japanese adults, for women only, being single and in irregular or no contact with close relatives were independent risk factors for mortality.

Work and health

Some of the excess mortality among people in lower socio-economic groups may result from the different work environments experienced by people across the socio-economic groups. Part of this difference may reflect the physical risks associated with particular jobs. Although health and safety legislation has improved the working conditions of most workers, there are still environments, such as building sites, that carry a significant risk of injury or disability. Work factors may also influence levels of engagement in health-compromising behaviours. Given the previous discussion on SES and health, it should be of no surprise that blue-collar workers tend to engage in more health-damaging behaviours, such as smoking, than white-collar workers (e.g. Lawrence *et al.* 2007). However, a variety of more subtle work factors may also influence behaviour. Binge drinking, for example, has been associated with job alienation, job stress, inconsistent social controls, and a work drinking culture (e.g. Bacharach *et al.* 2004). Similarly, long work hours, lack of control over work and poor social support have been associated with high levels of smoking among blue-collar workers (Westman *et al.* 1985). Other psychological research has focused on theories which suggest there is something intrinsic to different work environments that impacts directly on health – work stress.

Work stress

One of the first models to systematically consider elements of the work environment that contributed to stress and illness was developed by Karasek and Theorell (1990). Their model identified three key factors that contribute to work stress:

1. the demands of the job
2. the degree of freedom to make decisions about how best to cope with these demands (job autonomy)
3. the degree of available social support.

The model differs markedly from previous concepts of work stress that suggested it was an outcome of the demands placed on the person – the classic 'stressed executive'. Instead, it suggests that only when high levels of demands are combined with low levels of job autonomy, and perhaps low levels of social support (a situation referred to as high job strain), will the individual feel stressed and be at risk for disease. When an individual experiences high levels of demand combined with high levels of autonomy (e.g. being able to choose when and how to tackle a problem) and good social support, they will experience less stress. In contrast to the 'stressed executive' model, those in high-strain jobs are often blue-collar workers or people in relatively low-level supervisory posts (see Figure 2.3).

The majority of studies exploring the health outcomes of differing combinations of these work elements support Karasek's model. Kristensen (1995), for example, reviewed sixteen studies measuring the association between job strain and mental and physical health outcomes. Fourteen reported significant associations between conditions of high job strain and an increased incidence of either CHD or poor mental health. More recently, Nordstrom Dwyer *et al.* (2001) measured the degree of atheroma in the arteries of 467 working men, and found that levels of atheroma were highest among men with the highest job-strain scores. No such association was found among women. Similarly, Clays *et al.* (2007) reported that average **ambulatory blood pressure** at work, home and while asleep was significantly higher in workers with high job strain compared with others. By contrast, there is no evidence that job strain is related to the development of cancer (e.g. Gudbergsson *et al.* 2007).

ambulatory blood pressure
blood pressure measured over a period of time using an automatic blood pressure monitor which can measure blood pressure while the individual wearing it engages in their everyday activities.

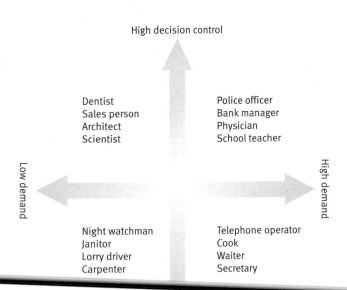

Figure 2.3   Some of the occupations that fit into the four quadrants of the Karasek and Theorell model

What do YOU think?

One sentence in the discussion about job strain has led to a number of key questions: 'Those who are in high-strain jobs are often blue-collar workers or people in relatively low-level supervisory posts.' This has led critics of the Karasek model to question whether job strain is directly related to poor health, or whether the measure of job strain is simply a marker for occupying low SES. Certainly, many of the jobs associated with high job strain are typically those considered to be 'working class'. So, Karaksek and others have begun to explore whether job strain is simply a marker for social class (the third, hidden, variable), whether job strain impacts on health independently of social class, or whether job strain interacts with social class to determine risk of disease. The final model would suggest, for example, that a combination of being from a lower socio-economic group and in a high job-strain occupation would be particularly toxic, while having low-strain occupation would mitigate against the negative effects of being from a lower socio-economic group. How would you set about investigating this phenomenon, and what would you expect to find?

An alternative model of work stress has been proposed by Siegrist *et al.* (1990). They suggested that work stress is the result of an imbalance between perceived efforts and rewards. High effort with high reward is seen as acceptable; high effort with low reward combine to result in emotional distress and adverse health effects. This theory has received less attention than that of Karasek, and most studies of this model (see de Lange *et al.* 2003), have focused on the impact of imbalance on wellbeing rather than physical health. Nevertheless, in a five-year longitudinal study tracking over ten thousand British civil servants (Stansfeld *et al.* 1998) both Karasek and Siegrist theories received some support: lack of autonomy, low levels of social support in work, and effort–reward imbalance each independently predicted poor self-report physical health.

Gender differentials

Reflecting some of the previous discussion, there is consistent evidence that working environments have a different effect on men and women. For men, the experience of work stress and its impact on health is generally a function of the working environment alone. For women, work stress frequently combines with other areas of demand in their lives to influence levels of stress and risk for disease. The term 'work–home spillover' has been used to describe this issue. Women still tend to carry more responsibilities in the home and outside work than men. As a consequence, once they have finished paid work, women are more likely than men to continue working in the home. This argument is perhaps exemplified in the, now rather old, findings of Lundberg *et al.* (1981), who found that female managers' stress hormone levels remained raised following work, while those of male managers typically fell. This effect was particularly marked where the female managers had children. It seems while the men they studied relaxed once they went home, the women continued their efforts – only the context changed. This work–home spillover effect is still widely reported, although there are some exceptions.

Krantz and Lundberg (2006), for example, found that among their sample of Swedish white-collar workers, the women working most hours assumed the least responsibility for household chores. In these circumstances, men and women seemed to share household burdens more evenly, as well as being able to reduce spillover by employing someone to assist in the household. However, they also noted that this effect was limited to the high flyers within their population. For others, this may not be the case.

Where spillover is present, it appears to influence risk for disease. Although having a job appears to improve the health of both men and women – the so-called 'healthy worker effect' – there appears to be a threshold, related to work–home spillover, above which work may have a detrimental effect on health. Haynes and Feinleib (1980), for example, found that working women with three or more children were more likely to develop CHD than those with no children. Adding to this finding, Alfredsson *et al.* (1985) found important gender differences in the impact of working overtime. Working overtime was associated with a *decreased* risk for CHD among men, while it was associated with an *increased* risk in women. For women, working ten hours or more overtime per week was associated with a 30 per cent increase in risk for CHD. It appears that men may have compensated for their increase in working hours by a decrease in demands elsewhere in life. Such compensation may not have been possible for the women they studied, and working overtime simply increased the total demands made on them, resulting in increased rates of stress and ill health. Spillover effects may also influence the health of the wider family. Devine *et al.* (2006) found that mothers experiencing work–home spillover, especially those from lower socio-economic groups, may compromise on things like the quality of food they cook to help cope with the time challenges of their work.

Unemployment

Not having a job appears to have negative effects on both mental and physical health. Ferrie *et al.* (2001), for example, found that not obtaining a secure job or remaining unemployed following redundancy (not due to ill health) were associated with significant increases in minor psychiatric and health complaints – the main cause of which appeared to be the financial insecurity rather than the loss of job *per se*. More recently, Cardano *et al.* (2004) followed a cohort of Italian men and women for a period of 10 years, and found that as people with no health problems left the labour market due to early retirement or unemployment, so their health tended to deteriorate. The threat of unemployment may itself be sufficient to adversely influence health. Dragano *et al.* (2005) found a combination of work stress (based on the effort–reward model) combined with the threat of redundancy was associated with a four-fold higher prevalence of self-reported poor health compared to individuals without their

What do YOU think?

If health is, at least in part, a result of the social and environmental contexts in which we live, then how can society go about reducing them? Most health promotion has focused on changing individual behaviours, such as smoking, lack of exercise, and so on. But is this just tinkering at the edge? Should society work towards changing the health inequalities associated with low SES? Or should we adopt the American model of 'opportunity' to become upwardly economically mobile, and those left behind to fend for themselves? If society does take responsibility for reducing social inequalities, how can it set about doing so? And what about the health disadvantages of people in ethnic minorities and women with children at work? How much should society, and in particular psychologists and others involved in health care, involve itself in improving the health of these groups?

Summary

Poverty is the main cause of ill health throughout the world. However, psychosocial factors may also influence health where the profound effects of poverty are not found.

One broad social factor that has been found to account for significant variations in health within societies is the socio-economic status of different groups. This relationship appears to be the result of a number of factors including:

- differential levels of behaviours, such as smoking and levels of exercise;
- differing levels of stress associated with the living environment, levels of day-to-day stress, and the presence or absence of uplifts;
- differential access to health care and differential uptake of health care that is provided;
- low levels of social capital and its associated stress in some communities.

A second factor that may influence health is being part of a social minority. The experience of prejudice may contribute significantly to levels of stress and disease.

- As many people in minority ethnic groups may also occupy lower socio-economic groups, they may experience further stress as a result of this double inequity.

Gender may influence health, but not only because of biological differences between the sexes. Indeed, many apparent biological differences may result from the different psychosocial experiences of men and women. In addition:

- men engage in more health-compromising behaviours than women;
- men are less likely to seek help following the onset of illness than women;
- many women are economically inactive or in lower paid jobs than men. This makes them vulnerable to the problems associated with low socio-economic status.

The relationship between work and health is complex. Having a job is better for one's health than not having a job. However, if the strain of having a job is combined with significant demands away from the job, this can adversely impact on health. Many women, for example, appear to have high levels of work–home spillover, with its adverse effects on both mental and physical health.

- Jobs with high levels of demand and low levels of autonomy appear to be more stressful and more related to ill health than other types of job.
- The financial uncertainties associated with unemployment also appear to have a negative impact on health.

Further reading

Socio-economic status
Adler, N., Singh-Manoux, A., Schwartz, J. *et al.* (2008). Social status and health: A comparison of British civil servants in Whitehall-II with European- and African-Americans in CARDIA. *Social Science and Medicine*, 66: 1034–45.
This paper provides an interesting contrast between data from one UK study of enormous significance in the exploration of socio-economic risk for coronary heart disease (the Whitehall Study) and a large US study.

Davey Smith, G., Carroll, D., Rankin, S. and Rowan D. (1992). Socioeconomic differentials in mortality: evidence from Glasgow graveyards. *British Medical Journal*, 305: 1554–7.
An intriguing take on the SES–mortality link, in which the authors measured the height of the obelisks in Glasgow graveyards, and found a strong correlation between the height of the obelisks and the age of the individual buried below it. They took this to show that in Victorian times, the richer you were, the longer you lived.

Wilkinson, R. (2006). *The Impact of Inequality: How to Make Sick Societies Healthier*. The New Press.
A five-stars in Amazon books' critique of society and health by the man that introduced the idea of social capital as a key contributor to health.

Gender
Courtenay, W.H. (2000). Constructions of masculinity and their influence on men's wellbeing: a theory of gender and health. *Social Science and Medicine*, 50: 1385–401.
An interesting critique of how men's attitudes towards their masculinity can influence their health-related behaviour and health.

Davidson, K.W., Trudeau, H.A. ... l. (2006). Gender as a health determinant and implications for health education. *Health Education and Behavior*, 33: 731–4.
An interesting review of the impact of gender on health; which factors related to risk for disease associated with gender are modifiable, and suggestions about how to change them.

Payne, S. (2006). *The Health of Men and Women*. Open University Press.
This book examines how gender impacts on our behaviour and health alone, and in interaction with ethnicity and socio-economic disadvantage to impact on our health.

Minority status
Arthur, M., Hedges, J.R., Newgard, C.D. *et al.* (2008). Racial disparities in mortality among adults hospitalized after injury. *Medical Care*, 46: 192–9.
We could have chosen so many papers showing racial disparities in health care. This paper shows that even when admitted to hospital as a consequence of trauma, white patients experience lower levels of mortality than black or Asian people.

Cole, S.W., Kemeny, M.E. and Taylor, S.E. (1997). Social identity and physical health: accelerated HIV progression in rejection-sensitive gay men. *Journal of Personality and Social Psychology*, 72: 20–35.
Although this chapter has focused on the impact of ethnicity on health, other minorities may also experience adverse health. This study examines how HIV-positive gay men who are sensitive to rejection progress more quickly to develop AIDS than those who are less so.

Steffen, P.R., McNeilly, M., Anderson, N. and Sherwood, A. (2003). Effects of perceived racism and anger inhibition on ambulatory blood pressure in African Americans. *Psychosomatic Medicine*, 65: 746–50.
A study, this time of African-American adults, showing a relationship between raised blood pressure and (independently) the degree to which they experience racism and inhibit their anger.

Occupation/gender
Gjerdingen, D., McGovern, P., Bekker, M., *et al.* (2000). Women's work roles and their impact on health, well-being, and career: comparisons between the United States, Sweden, and the Netherlands. *Women's Health*, 31: 1–20.
A useful critique of the impact of gender and occupation on both psychological and physical health.

Lundberg, U. (2005). Stress hormones in health and illness: the roles of work and gender. *Psychoneuroendocrinology*, 30: 1017–21.
A review of studies suggesting that work context and individual responses to stress are more important determinants of health than apparent gender differences.

Steptoe, A. and Willemsen, G. (2004). The influence of low job control on ambulatory blood pressure and perceived stress over the working day in men and women from the Whitehall II cohort. *Journal of Hypertension*, 22: 873–6.
The Whitehall study again, this time showing a relationship between low job control (but not high job demands) and blood pressure during the day.

 Visit the website at **www.pearsoned.co.uk/morrison** for additional resources to help you with your study, including multiple choice questions, weblinks and flashcards.

CHAPTER 3

Health-risk behaviour

Learning outcomes

By the end of this chapter, you should have an understanding of:

- how to define and describe health behaviour
- what health behaviours are associated with elevated disease risk
- the range and complexity of influences upon the uptake and maintenance of health-risk behaviour
- some of the challenges facing health behaviour research

CHAPTER OUTLINE

Behaviour is linked to health. This has been shown over decades of painstaking research that has examined individual lifestyles and behaviour and identified relationships between these and the development of illness. For example, it has been estimated that up to three-quarters of cancer deaths are attributable to a person's behaviour. This chapter provides an overview of the evidence pertaining to an array of behaviour shown to increase an individual's risk of disease, such as unhealthy diet, smoking, excessive alcohol consumption and unprotected sexual behaviour. Evidence regarding the negative health consequences of each type of behaviour is reviewed, and the prevalence of each behaviour considered. Both the health-risk behaviour de-scribed here and the health-enhancing behaviour described in Chapter 4 provide the impetus for many educational and public health initiatives worldwide.

What is health behaviour?

Kasl and Cobb (1966a: 246) defined health behaviour as 'any activity under-taken by a person believing themselves to be healthy for the purposes of pre-venting disease or detecting it at an asymptomatic stage'. This definition was influenced by a medical perspective in that it assumes that healthy people engage in particular behaviour, such as exercise or seeking medical attention, purely to prevent their chance of disease onset. However, this very specific definition should be viewed with caution. Many people engage in a variety of apparently health-related behaviour, such as exercise, for reasons other than disease prevention, including weight control, appearance, as a means of gain-ing social contacts and pleasure. Nevertheless, whether intentional or not, engaging in health behaviour may prevent disease and may also prevent the progression of disease once it is established. This perspective was acknow-ledged by Harris and Guten (1979), who defined health behaviour as 'behaviour performed by an individual, regardless of his/her perceived health status, with the purpose of protecting, promoting or maintaining his/her health'. According to this definition, health behaviour could include the behaviour of 'unhealthy' people. For example, an individual who has heart disease may change their diet to help to limit its progression, just as a healthy person may change their diet in order to reduce their future risk of heart dis-ease. Further elaboration of definitions of health behaviour was provided by Matarazzo (1984), who distinguished between what he termed '**behavioural pathogens**' and '**behavioural immunogens**'. In spite of definitional differences, health behaviour research generally adopts the view that health behaviour is that which is associated with an individual's health status, regardless of current health or motivations.

behavioural pathogen
a behavioural practice thought to be damaging to health, e.g. smoking.

behavioural immunogen
a behavioural practice considered to be health-protective, e.g. exercise.

The World Health Organization (2002) define 'risk' as 'a probability of an adverse outcome, or a factor that raises this probability' (p. 7). As we will see in this chapter in the context of health risk, many of these risks are behavioural, although others are environmental, such as pollution or poverty, and so we address these where possible (see also Chapter 2). It is worth remembering that what is considered health-risk behaviour has changed over the past century as medical understanding has developed; for example, we know now that smoking and excessive exposure to the sun carry significant risks for development of some cancers, whereas our ancestors did not. To further muddy the waters, there is also evidence of health benefits of some behaviours considered generally as 'risky'. Perhaps the best example is sun exposure, receiving growing attention in relation to skin cancer risk, yet in the early twentieth century sun exposure was considered useful in the treatment of skin tuberculosis, and today sunlight therapy may be offered in the treatment of skin disorders. Furthermore there is some tentative evidence relating vitamin D levels (which are raised with sunlight exposure) to reduced cardiovascular risk (Ness *et al.* 1999). Later in this chapter we also raise the issue of beneficial effects of moderate alcohol consumption.

In order to test the nature and extent of associations between behaviour and health, longitudinal studies are necessary. The Alameda County study is notable in this regard (e.g. Belloc and Breslow 1972; Breslow 1983). This study followed 7,000 adults, all of whom were healthy at the beginning of the study, for over fifteen years. By comparing the differences on a variety of baseline measures between those people who developed disease and those who remained healthy, key behavioural factors associated with health and longevity were identified. These have been termed the 'Alameda seven':

- sleeping seven–eight hours a night;
- not smoking;
- consuming no more than one–two alcoholic drinks per day;
- getting regular exercise;
- not eating between meals;
- eating breakfast;
- being no more than 10 per cent overweight.

Fewer than 4 per cent of both females and males who engaged in all seven types of behaviour had died at the fifteen-year follow-up, compared with 7–13 per cent of females and males who reported performing fewer than four of these activities. Also of note was the finding that the benefits of performing these activities were multiplicative: for example, not smoking as well as reporting moderate levels of drinking alcohol, conferred more than twice the benefit of having only one of these 'immunogens'. The relationship between not performing these 'immunogen' behaviours and death was found to increase with age, with marked effects found in those over the age of 65. In other words, the longer we engage in a particular lifestyle, the more it affects our health; that is, the effects of lifestyle behaviour are not only multiplicative but cumulative.

From a health psychology perspective, understanding that behaviour is predictive of mortality is only part of the story. Many epidemiological and the onset of major illnesses such as heart disease or cancer. However, if we are to prevent people from engaging in risk behaviour (which is the goal of health promotion – see Chapters 6 and 7), we also need to understand the psychological and social factors that contribute to the uptake and maintenance of risk behaviour or the avoidance of health-enhancing or preventive behaviour. Such studies are more often conducted by health and social psychologists rather than epidemiologists, and although alluded to in this and the subsequent chapter, are addressed more fully in Chapter 5.

Health-risk behaviour

The message of the Director-General of the World Health Organization (WHO), in the opening to the *World Health Report* (WHO 2002: 3) was stark, but clear. It stated:

> in many ways, the world is a safer place today. Safer from what were once deadly or incurable diseases. Safer from daily hazards of waterborne and food-related illnesses. Safer from dangerous consumer goods, from accidents at home, at work, or in hospitals. But in many other ways the world is becoming more dangerous. Too many of us are living dangerously – whether we are aware of that or not.

This report by the WHO followed massive worldwide research into health risks in developed, developing and underdeveloped countries. Although specific health risks may vary across the world (for example, under-consumption of food in many African nations versus over-consumption in most Western countries), there are many commonalities such as risk conferred by smoking tobacco. The WHO lists the 'top ten' leading risk factors globally, which together account for more than a third of all deaths worldwide, as:

1. being underweight
2. unprotected sexual intercourse
3. high blood pressure
4. tobacco consumption
5. alcohol consumption
6. unsafe water, poor sanitation and hygiene
7. iron deficiency
8. indoor smoke from solid fuels
9. high cholesterol
10. obesity.

For reasons of length, it is impossible to address all ten of these in this chapter, even though the statistics attached to some are horrendous and thought-provoking. Over three million childhood deaths, for example, occur every year in developing countries as a result of being underweight. By contrast, about half a million people die each year in North America and Europe as a result of an obesity-related disease. Behaviour which is associated with high levels of **mortality** in developed countries such as the USA and Europe are highlighted below and discussed in more detail, as they tend also to be the behaviour that has attracted the greatest attention from health psychologists to date:

mortality
death. Generally presented as mortality statistics, i.e. the number of deaths in a given population and/or in a given year ascribed to a given condition (e.g. number of cancer deaths among women in 2000).

- *heart disease*: smoking tobacco, high-cholesterol diet, lack of exercise;
- *cancer*: smoking tobacco, alcohol, diet, sexual behaviour;
- *stroke*: smoking tobacco, high-cholesterol diet, alcohol;
- *pneumonia, influenza*: smoking tobacco, lack of vaccination;
- *HIV/AIDS*: unsafe/unprotected sexual intercourse.

With the exception of HIV/AIDS, these diseases are more common in middle age and beyond than in younger people. Given the worldwide increase in the proportion of the population aged 65 or above, the prevalence of such diseases in our communities will make increasing and significant demands on health-care systems. To illustrate this point further, 5.2 per cent of the world population in 1950 (over 130 million) were aged over 65; by 2005 this percentage had increased to 7.3 per cent (approximately 477 million world-wide). It is estimated that this percentage will increase further to more than one in ten of the population by 2025 (which will amount to 839 million indi-viduals) (United Nations 2006), and that those over 80 years old is likely to increase from 11 per cent in 1940 to 19 per cent of this total by 2050 (United Nations Secretariat 2002). The rates of change vary across different regions of the world: for example, those over 65 has almost doubled in Australia over the past 50 years (10.1 to 19.6 per cent), whereas in the UK it has increased by just over 4 per cent (15.2 per cent to 19.9 per cent). The implications of such statistics for health and social care services are clear, as is the need for health promotion directed at the elderly (see Chapter 7). The next sections take a closer look at some of the major risk behaviours of importance in current times to people of all ages.

Unhealthy diet

What and how we eat plays an important role in our long-term health. Heart disease and some forms of cancer have been directly associated with diet. Our dietary intake and behaviour (e.g. snacking, bingeing) may also confer an indirect risk of disease through its effect on weight and obesity – something we turn to later in the chapter.

The degree of risk for cancer conferred by diet may be surprising. While many cancer deaths (approximately 30 per cent: e.g. Doll and Peto 1981) are attributed to smoking cigarettes, it is perhaps a lesser-known fact that 35 per cent of cancer deaths are attributable, in part, to poor diet. A diet involving significant intake of high-fat foods, high levels of salt and low levels of fibre appears to be particularly implicated (World Cancer Research Fund 1997).

Fat intake and cholesterol

Excessive fat intake has been found to be implicated in disease and death from several serious illnesses, including coronary heart disease. The evidence of a link in cancer remains unclear. (Chapter 8 discusses the biological and chemical processes relevant here). Fatty foods, particularly foods high in sat-urated fats (such as animal products and some vegetable oils), contain sub-stances known as low-density lipoproteins (LDL), which enter our blood. The LDL molecules around the blood-stream and can lead to the formation of plaques in the arteries. Cholesterol carried by LDLs is often called 'bad cholesterol' whereas cholesterol carried by high density lipoproteins is called 'good cholesterol', as it appears to increase the processing and removal of LDLs by the liver. Cholesterol is a lipid (fat) which is present in our own bodily cells but these normal levels can be increased by a fatty diet (and by other factors such as age). Normal circu-lating cholesterol has a purpose in that it is synthesised to produce steroid

atherosclerosis
formation of fatty plaque
in the arteries.

arteriosclerosis
loss of elasticity and
hardening of the
arteries.

hormones and is involved in the production of bile necessary for digestion, but high levels in our bloodstream can reflect high saturated-fat intake which is damaging to our health. Some foods, such as polyunsaturated fats which can be more easily metabolised in the body, or foods such as oily fish which contain Omega-3 fatty acids and which have been found to raise HDL levels, are beneficial to one's health. The health argument is that if fat molecules, a good store of energy in our bodies, are not metabolised during exercise or activity, then their circulating levels become high, and plaques (fatty layers) are laid down on the artery walls (**atherosclerosis**), causing them to thicken and restrict blood flow to the heart. An often related condition, **arterio-sclerosis**, exists when increased blood pressure causes artery walls to lose elasticity and harden, with resulting effects on the ability of the cardiovascular system to adapt to increased blood flow (such as during exercise). These arterial diseases are together referred to as CAD (coronary artery disease) and form a major risk factor for angina pectoris (a painful sign of arterial obstruction restricting oxygen flow) and coronary heart disease (CHD). The 'bad' cholesterols (LDLs) are implicated in this process, although the actual strength of the link between saturated fat intake and blood cholesterol levels is unclear.

Reduced fat intake is a target of health interventions, not solely because of its effects on body weight and, potentially, obesity (see later), but because of the links with CHD. Evidence for this link has come from many studies, including the large prospective MRFIT (multiple risk factor intervention trial) study, which followed over 350,000 adults over six years and found a significant linear relationship between baseline cholesterol level and subsequent heart disease or stroke (Neaton *et al.* 1992). It has been shown that a 10 per cent reduction in serum (blood) cholesterol is associated at five-year follow-up with a 54 per cent reduction in the incidence of coronary heart disease at age 40, a 27 per cent reduction at age 60 and a 19 per cent reduction at age 80 (Law *et al.* 1994; Navas-Nacher *et al.* 2001). Whilst there is some correlational evidence of higher breast cancer death rates in countries where high fat intake is common (e.g. the UK, the Netherlands, the USA) than in countries where dietary fat intake is lower (e.g. Japan, the Philippines), firm causal data is limited, both in terms of breast cancer (e.g. Löf *et al.* 2007) and prostate cancer risk (Crowe *et al.* 2008).

As a result of these and other data, governmental policy documents have been produced in many countries that provide guidelines for healthy eating and dietary targets. In the UK, for example, the Department of Health produced *The Health of the Nation* report (1992), which recommended that a maximum of 35 per cent of food energy (calories) should be derived from fat intake, of which a maximum of only 11 per cent should come from saturated fats. More recently, the recommended percentage fat intake has decreased to 30 per cent (US Department of Health and Human Services 2000; World Health Organization 1999); however, there is evidence that, at least in Europe, average consumption figures appear to remain around 40 per cent. Ethnicity has been shown to have an effect on fat intake, for example, a study of ethnic minority males living in the UK found higher levels of fat intake among Bangladeshi males than among most other ethnic groups (Bhopal *et al.* 1999). It is worth noting that a systematic review (*Cochrane Review*) of evidence derived from four randomised controlled trials concluded that fat-restricted diets were no more effective than calorie-restricted diets in terms of long-term weight loss among overweight or obese individuals

(Pirozzo *et al.* 2003), suggesting that dietary change should not focus solely on fat intake but on total intake. In relation to older populations, however, there is evidence that low rather than high levels of calorific intake are detrimental to health status and cognitive function, and older men living alone seem particularly vulnerable here (Hughes *et al.* 2004).

Salt

systolic blood pressure the maximum pressure of blood on the artery walls, which occurs at the end of the left ventricle output/ contraction (measured in relation to **diastolic blood pressure**).

diastolic blood pressure the minimum pressure of the blood on the walls of the arteries between heart beats (measured in relation to **systolic blood pressure**).

Salt intake is also a target of preventive health measures, with high salt (sodium chloride) intake being implicated in those with persistent high blood pressure, i.e. hypertension. The detrimental effects of high salt intake appear to persist even when levels of physical activity, obesity and other health behaviour are controlled (Law *et al.* 1991).

A recent systematic review and meta-analysis of intervention trials assessed the impact of lowering salt intake in adults who were either normotensive (i.e. 'normal' blood pressure), who had high blood pressure that was not being treated, or who had high blood pressure that was being treated using drug therapy (Hooper *et al.* 2002). Overall, the results of these trials were somewhat mixed in that salt reduction resulted in reduced **systolic** and **diastolic blood pressure**; however, the degree of reduction in blood pressure was not related to the amount of salt reduction. In addition, the trials had no impact on the number of heart disease-related deaths seen in follow-ups lasting from seven months to seven years, with deaths equally distributed across the intervention and control groups. The authors therefore concluded that interventions targeting salt intake provide only limited health benefits.

In spite of mixed findings such as these, guidelines exist as to recommended levels of salt intake. High salt intake is considered to be in excess of 6 g per day for adults, and over 5 g per day for children aged 7 to 14 (British Medical Association 2003a). While it is perhaps difficult to establish the unique health benefits of a reduced-salt diet when examining individuals engaged in more general dietary change behaviour, the BMA guidelines raise awareness of the need to monitor salt intake from early childhood onwards.

Obesity

We include obesity in this section even though it is not a behaviour, because of growing international concern about its increasing prevalence and because it is contributed to by a combination of poor diet and a lack of exercise, both

How is obesity defined?

Obesity is generally measured in terms of an individual's body mass index (BMI), which is calculated as a person's weight in kilograms divided by their height in metres squared (weight/height^2). An individual is considered to be

- 'normal weight' if their BMI is between 20 and 24.9;
- mildly obese (grade 1) if their BMI is between 25 and 29.9 (generally referred to as overweight);
- moderate or clinically obese (grade 2) if their BMI falls between 30 and 39.9;
- severely obese (grade 3) if their BMI is 40 or greater.

Negative health consequences of obesity

As noted at the outset of this chapter, being underweight is the largest global cause of mortality: yet a growing number of people, predominantly in Western or developed countries, are at risk from the opposite problem – obesity. Obesity is a major risk factor in a range of physical illnesses, including hypertension, heart disease, Type 2 diabetes, osteoarthritis and lower back pain. The relative risk of disease appears to increase proportionately in relation to the percentage overweight a person is, although evidence as to this linear relationship remains mixed. The longitudinal Framingham heart study shows a relationship between obesity and mortality which appears over the long term (two–three decades), with the risk of death within twenty-six years being increased by 1 per cent per extra pound in weight in those aged between 30 and 42, and by 2 per cent per extra pound in those aged 50 to 62. The J-shaped curve shown in Figure 3.1 also reminds us of the risk of being underweight, with the lowest mortality in those within the ideal weight range (body mass index 20–24.9).

Obesity is also implicated in psychological ill-health including low self-esteem and social isolation (British Medical Association 2003a; Strauss 2000); among Australian children, for example, it has been associated with poorer health-related quality of life (Williams *et al.* 2005).

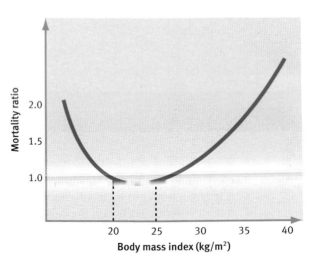

Figure 3.1   The relationship between body mass index and mortality at 23-year follow-up (Framingham heart study).

Source: Wilson, P. *et al.* (2002)

Prevalence of obesity

The European Commission (1999) estimates that 31 per cent of the EU adult population is overweight, with a further 10 per cent reaching weights defined as clinically obese. Alarmingly, excess body weight has recently been identified as the most common child disorder in Europe (International Obesity Taskforce and European Association for the Study of Obesity 2002) and there are particular concerns about the implications of obesity for physical and psychological ill-health.

A 1997 survey of young people aged 16–24 combined interviews about health behaviour with an array of physical measurements, including lung function tests and blood samples. Six per cent of young males and 8 per cent of young females were classified as clinically obese; a further 23 per cent and 19 per cent, respectively, were overweight, and 17 per cent of both genders were underweight (Department of Health 1998a). Social class (lower) was related to increased obesity for young females, but not for males, and as obese children tend to grow up to be obese adults (Magarey *et al.* 2003), interventions need to start early. To be successful, interventions need to first understand the factors associated with the development of obesity.

What causes obesity?

A simple explanation of obesity is that it is a condition that results from an energy intake that grossly exceeds the energy output (Pinel 2003). However, twin studies and studies of adopted children (e.g. Meyer and Stunkard 1993; Price and Gottesman 1991) have also pointed to a genetic component to obesity with genetic explanations. These explanations are generally one of three types:

1. Obese individuals are born with a greater number of fat cells. Evidence of this is limited. For example, the number of fat cells in a person of average weight and in many mildly obese individuals is typically 25–35 million. The number of cells is dramatically increased in a severely obese person, implying the formation of *new* fat cells.

2. Obese individuals inherit lower metabolic rates. However, obese people are not consistently found to have lower metabolic rates than comparable thin persons.

3. Obese individuals may have deficiencies in a hormone responsible for appetite control, or lack of control.

This last explanation has received attention since the 1950s, when a gene mutation was identified in some laboratory mice that had become highly obese (Coleman 1979). Subsequent cloning of this mutated gene found that it was only expressed in fat cells and that it encoded a protein hormone called leptin (Zhang *et al.* 1994). Leptin levels are positively correlated with fat deposits in humans; low levels of injected leptin have been found to reduce eating behaviour and thus body fat in obese mice. This appears to happen due to leptin-signalling receptors in the hypothalamus, which controls functions such as eating (see Chapter 8). However, Pinel (2003) describes how research has not found similar genetic mutation in all obese humans and how injected leptin has not consistently reduced body fat in the obese. However, for the small number of individuals (two children to date) who have been found to hold the gene mutation, leptin therapy has shown some success in reducing food intake and promoting weight loss (Farooqi *et al.* 1999).

Another avenue of research has identified that serotonin, a neurotransmitter (see Chapter 8), is directly involved in producing satiety (the condition where hunger is no longer felt). Early animal experiments investigating the effects on hunger of administering a serotonin **agonist** have had their findings confirmed in humans, where the introduction of serotonin agonists into the body induced satiety, reduced the frequency and quantity of food intake and body weight (Halford and Blundell 2000). This line of research holds promise for future intervention.

agonist
a drug that simulates the effects of neurotransmitters, such as the serotonin agonist fluoxetine, which induces satiety (reduces hunger).

However, the recent upsurge in obesity in developed countries is more plausibly attributed to environmental factors such as lifestyle and behaviour patterns than to an increase in genetic predisposition towards obesity. People of all ages increasingly pass their time indoors, and there is evidence that sedentary activities such as watching television or computing can even reduce a person's metabolic rate, so that their bodies burn up existing calories more slowly. Lack of physical activity in combination with overeating or eating the wrong food types are associated with obesity, and it is unclear which is the primary causal factor. Prediction by epidemiologists of a threefold increase in obesity in the UK between 1980 and 2005 (Department of Health 1995) has been upheld across many parts of the world including parts of North America, Australasia and Eastern Europe, with further growth expected. Effective interventions which aim to make our currently 'obesogenic' environments (BMA 2003a) and behaviour more healthy by addressing healthy eating and, perhaps even more so, exercise behaviour, are therefore high on the public health agenda (see Chapters 6 and 7). Exercise behaviour is discussed more fully in Chapter 4.

■ A final thought on obesity

A word of caution is drawn from the BMA report (2003a) referred to previously: we as individuals, and as a society, must be careful not to over-focus on the weight of individual children – while obesity is on the increase, so too is extreme dietary behaviour and eating disorders; several recent studies point to increasing body dissatisfaction among children and adolescents, particularly females (e.g. Ricciardelli and McCabe 2001; Schur *et al.* 2000). Body dissatisfaction, if taken to extremes in terms of dietary restraint, can potentially have adverse physical and psychological consequences in terms of eating disorders (e.g. Patton *et al.* 1990).

Alcohol consumption

Alcohol (ethanol) is 'the second most widely used psychoactive substance in the world (after caffeine)' (Julien 1996: 101). In Westernised cultures it is also considered an integral part of many life events, such as weddings, birthdays and even funerals, and its social use is widespread. Only a small number of people will, however, become dependent on it to the extent that alcohol will lead to damaging health or social consequences.

Negative health effects of excessive alcohol consumption

Although alcohol is commonly perceived as a stimulant, it is in fact a central nervous system depressant. Low doses cause behavioural disinhibition, while high levels of intoxication lead to a 25-fold increase in the likelihood of an accident, and extremely high doses severely affect respiratory rate, which can cause coma and even death (see Figure 3.2).

It is not only alcohol dependence that causes health problems; so too can acute or prolonged episodes of heavy drinking. Patterns of drinking, as well as the volume consumed, is therefore relevant to health outcomes. Heavy alcohol consumption is implicated in accidents (while driving or operating machinery, for example); in behavioural problems (aggression, suicide, marital disharmony, etc.), and in diseases such as liver cirrhosis, liver and oesophageal cancer, stroke and epilepsy. Hart *et al.* (1999) carried out a 21-year follow-up study among 5,766 Scottish men and found that those who consumed more than 35 units of alcohol a week were at twice the risk of death from stroke than men whose drinking was at light or moderate levels. However, if the amounts of alcohol consumed are low to moderate and the pattern of drinking does not include binges, the World Health Report states that alcohol's relationship to CHD, stroke and diabetes mellitus, is in fact a beneficial one (WHO 2002). (See also IN THE SPOTLIGHT.)

Table 3.1 presents World Health Organization data relating to alcohol-related liver cirrhosis mortality reported across Europe (countries reported

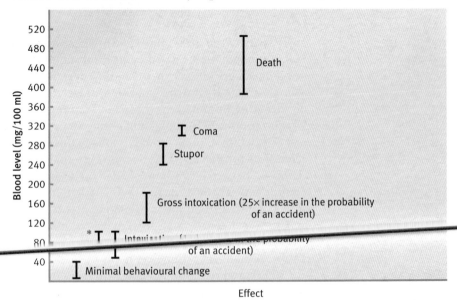

* The legal level of intoxication varies by region, thus the range of values is shown.

Figure 3.2   The particular consequences correlated with different levels of alcohol in a person's bloodstream.

Source: adapted from Julien (1996: 109)

Table 3.1   Deaths in Europe from liver cirrhosis per 100,000 population, ranked highest to lowest with age standardisation

Country	Total	Standardised mortality		M/F ratio
		Males	Females	
Hungary	54.8	79.7	32.6	2.4
Romania	38.1	47.5	28.8	1.6
Germany, former Democratic Republic	33.7	47.9	19.4	2.5
Austria	28.2	41.2	16.4	2.5
Portugal	26.9	39.3	15.1	2.5
Italy	26.8	31.7	18.0	1.8
Czechoslovakia	25.1	38.1	13.4	2.8
Germany, Federal Republic	22.2	30.4	14.6	2.1
Spain	21.0	30.0	12.9	2.3
Luxembourg	18.7	21.9	15.4	1.4
Former Yugoslavia	18.4	27.7	10.2	2.7
France	17.0	23.3	10.6	2.2
Bulgaria	15.0	22.0	7.8	2.8
Poland	13.9	19.1	9.2	2.1
Belgium	11.9	14.4	9.5	1.5
Finland	10.7	15.3	4.2	3.6
Switzerland	9.5	12.9	6.1	2.1
Malta	9.0	14.0	3.9	3.6
Greece	8.9	12.1	5.8	2.1
Israel	8.7	10.3	7.0	2.5
Sweden	6.8	8.8	4.7	1.9
United Kingdom	6.1	6.9	5.3	1.3
Netherlands	5.1	6.3	3.9	1.6
Norway	4.4	5.4	3.3	1.6
Ireland	2.9	3.1	2.7	1.1

Source: adapted from Edwards, G. *et al.* (1994); © Oxford University Press (1994).

any year between 1987 and 1993), where it can be seen that incidence per 100,000 population ranged from a substantial 54.8 in Hungary to a much lower incidence of 2.9 in Ireland. While this seemingly contradicts many a myth about Irish drinkers, interestingly the statistics regarding volumes of alcohol consumed have Ireland among the highest (World Health Organization 2003), thus highlighting the role of other factors in development of cirrhosis. In fact, there is a huge difference within Europe in the percentage of total liver cirrhosis mortality that is attributed to alcoholic liver cirrhosis. Between 1987 and 1995, for example, a massive 90 per cent of Finnish male cirrhosis deaths were attributed to alcohol-related liver cirrhosis, as opposed to 56 per cent among French males, 45 per cent among UK males, 33 per cent among Irish males (a third of a relatively low number as seen above), and 10 per cent among Spanish males. The data presented in Table 3.1 highlight differences in the male–female ratio in different countries.

Culture and social policy are extremely important in predicting drinking behaviour. Consider, for example, Finland, where strict legislation on alcohol sales and consumption was liberalised in the mid-1970s and where cirrhosis deaths showed subsequent increases in the 1980s and 1990s: as reported above, 90 per cent of male deaths were attributed to alcohol, and also 56 per cent of Finnish female cirrhosis deaths.

Liver cirrhosis is not the only cause of death attributed to alcohol. The WHO describe a selection of alcohol-related causes including: cancer of

Table 3.2 Deaths from selected alcohol-related causes per 100,000 (all ages) for selected countries

	Males	Females
UK 1990	91.95	37.61
UK 2000	71.95	30.68
UK 2005	73.51	31.61
Spain 1990	175.23	47.45
Spain 2000	91.89	24.43
Spain 2005	79.82	21.73
Poland 1990	236.18	58.20
Poland 2000	149.19	39.66
Poland 2005	149.64	36.24
Netherlands 1990	79.25	36.35
Netherlands 2000	60.97	27.62
Netherlands 2005	n.a.	n.a.
Finland 1990	221.40	62.75
Finland 2000	139.03	46.08
Finland 2005	143.77	44.39

oesophagus and larynx, alcohol dependence syndrome, chronic liver disease and cirrhosis. Separate data on liver cancer deaths were not available and so the figures should be viewed as rough indicators of alcohol-related deaths. Table 3.2 shows that when examining these data for the years 1990, 2000 and 2005, a decrease in alcohol-related deaths per 100,000 can be seen across the decade between 1990 and 2000; however, this reduction is not maintained in all selected countries and, worryingly, in the UK a slight increase can be seen between 2000 and 2005, among both genders (Leon and McCambridge 2006).

Recommended levels of drinking

Different individuals respond differently to the same amount of alcohol intake, depending on factors such as body weight, food intake and metabolism, the social context in which the drinking occurs, and the individual's cognitions and expectations. It is therefore difficult to determine 'safe' levels of drinking alcohol. While the recommended guidelines on 'safe' levels of alcohol consumption vary from country to country, the UK government's recommended limit for weekly consumption has recently been raised from 21 units of alcohol to 28 units for males, and from 14 to 21 units of alcohol for females (where half a pint of normal-strength lager or a standard single alcohol) = 1 unit). The lower level of these guidelines had been in existence since 1986, and although the move to increase the guidelines to 28 and 21 units for males and females, respectively, came in 1995 (Royal College of Physicians 1995), many health advisers continue to use the 21/14 limits. Some guidelines also recommend one or two alcohol-free days per week.

There is some confusion internationally as to what constitutes a 'standard' measure or 'unit'. Does it mean the strength of the alcohol or the volume? For example, a standard drink in Japan is defined by government guidelines as 19.75 g alcohol, whereas in the UK a standard drink would contain 8 g, and there are many variations in between, as seen in Table 3.3.

Table 3.3   International definitions of what comprises a 'standard' drink (alcohol in g)

Austria	6
Ireland and UK	8
Iceland	9.5
Netherlands	9.9
Italy, Australia, Spain	10
Finland	11
Denmark, France	12
Canada	13.5
Portugal, USA	14
Hungary	17
Japan	19.75

Source: International Center for Alcohol Policies (1998)

Prevalence of drinking alcohol in the young

A survey of over 7,000 English 11–15-year-olds (2000 Survey DoH 2000a, National Centre for Social Research) showed a significant increase in the amount of alcohol consumed in this age group over a ten-year period, from 5.3 units per week in 1990 to 10.4 units in 2000. The authors suggest that the growth in marketing and sale of alcopops (alcoholic drinks with sweetening and flavourings, marketed with a trendy appearance) played a role in the increased consumption pattern of these young people. Twenty-four per cent of this sample had had an alcoholic drink in the previous week: 5 per cent of 11-year-olds and 48 per cent of 15-year-olds. Children in Wales (where both authors of this textbook are based!) top the European league for the numbers who drink weekly and get drunk (Paton 1999).

There is concern about adolescent drinking in many European countries. Sweden, a country with historically high government control over alcohol production and sale, actively campaigns for non-consumption of alcohol among teenagers. However, an impressive survey of nearly 13,000 16-year-olds found that about 80 per cent had consumed alcohol, 25 per cent of whom had drunk illegal, smuggled alcohol, and 40 per cent had drunk home-distilled alcohol. Although levels of consumption are not clear, alcohol is clearly not outwith the grasp of these teenagers (Romelsjo and Branting 2000). Also of concern is the relationship between alcohol consumption and teenage pregnancy (see IN THE SPOTLIGHT in the Smoking section).

Are there positive effects of drinking alcohol?

It is generally accepted that there is a linear relationship between the amount of alcohol consumed over time and the accumulation of alcohol-related illness. However, there are a few question marks around the level of drinking that is damaging. For example, there is some evidence that moderate alcohol consumption may be health-protective, with evidence of a J-shaped relationship between alcohol consumption and CHD risk. Abstinence confers a higher risk than moderate drinking, although not as high as risk conferred by heavy drinking (Doll *et al.* 1994). This surprising finding has emerged from both cross-sectional and prospective studies. The consensus view is that moderate alcohol intake reduces circulating low-density lipoprotein (LDL) levels (high levels are a known risk factor for CHD) (e.g. Shaper *et al.* 1994; see IN THE SPOTLIGHT). However, there are problems in concluding from this, and from studies of non-drinkers where risk of CHD was found to be higher than

IN THE SPOTLIGHT

Is drinking red wine good for your health?

For some time, it has been known that fruit and vegetable consumption is associated with a reduced rate of some cancers, in particular cancer of the gastrointestinal tract (e.g. Potter *et al.* 1993). This has been attributed to the presence of compounds known as 'polyphenols'. Red wine contains many different polyphenolic compounds, and red wine intake has been associated with reduced cardiovascular deaths (e.g. German and Walzem 2000; Wollin and Jones 2001). Early studies identified an association between alcohol ingestion and high-density lipoproteins (HDL – see section on unhealthy diet above) thought to be protective against CHD (e.g. Linn *et al.* 1993). More recently, it has been proposed that red wine poly-

carcinogenesis
the process by which normal cells become cancer cells (i.e. carcinoma).

phenols may also be beneficial in cancer prevention. It is thought that polyphenols inhibit the initiation of **carcinogenesis** due to their antioxidative or anti-inflammatory properties. Additionally, polyphenols may act as suppressing agents by inhibiting the growth of mutated cells or by inducing apoptosis, i.e. cell death. Recent laboratory and animal studies (e.g. Briviba *et al.* 2002) have shown that polyphenols isolated from red wine did in fact inhibit the growth of different colon carcinoma cells, but not breast cancer cells.

Medical authorities and public health officials are wary of announcing health 'benefits' of behaviours usually portrayed as detrimental to health, and results of this nature need to be carefully checked and double-checked. Even the authors of one of the research studies, finding a positive effect of alcohol on HDL level, underplayed the implications of their findings (Linn *et al.* 1993: 811). It is unlikely that many individuals presenting to their GPs with health concerns around a family history of heart disease are told to increase their light alcohol consumption to moderate, and instead will most likely be advised to follow a low-fat diet, yet the protection offered is similar! When the most recent findings relating to cancer reached the attention of the media, it resulted in the kind of headlines that would lead you to believe a cure for cancer had been found! However, there remains a need for further research among human samples, with tight controls over other contributory factors. It will be some years before the evidence as to the effects of red wine drinking on people already with cancer becomes clear. In relation to coronary heart disease, however, the evidence is of longer standing, and it would appear that moderate ingestion of alcohol, and not solely red wine, has health-protective effects (e.g. Nestle 1997).

Things to think about and research yourself

■ Does red wine differ from white wine in terms of its potential effects on health, and if so, how?

■ How might some people interpret these kinds of findings – what beliefs might be reinforced?

average, that not drinking confers increased risk. Non-drinkers may choose not to consume alcohol because they are already in poor health, or because they are members of particular religious or ethnic groups that forbid such use: these factors may hide some other 'cause' of CHD. It is safer to conclude only that heavy drinking has negative effects on health that increase in line with consumption; that moderate levels of drinking may not increase risk and may in fact be protective against CHD (although the protective effects are lost on people who smoke); and that the effects of not drinking at all need further exploration.

Why do some people develop drinking problems?

The reasons why young people start to drink alcohol are, as with most social behaviours, many and varied, with genetics and environment playing important roles. Two commonly cited reasons for having that first drink of alcohol are curiosity and sociability (e.g. Morrison and Plant 1991), but curiosity, unlike sociability, is unlikely to be cited as the reason for continued use. For most people, drinking does not become a problem; much research is conducted to distinguish individuals who maintain safe levels of drinking from those who develop problem drinking. The main aspects considered are:

- Genetics and family history of alcohol abuse: children of problem drinkers are more likely to develop problem drinking than children of non-problem drinkers (e.g. Heather and Robertson 1997). Evidence is inconclusive as parent–child drinking tendencies could also be socialised (see below), although adoptee studies support evidence of heredity to an extent.

predisposition
factors that increase the likelihood of a person engaging in a particular behaviour, such as genetic influences on alcohol consumption.

- The pre-existence of certain psychopathology: mood disorders, anxious **predisposition**, sensation-seeking personality tendencies (e.g. Clark and Sayette 1993; Khantzian 2003; Zuckerman 1979, 1984), although evidence as to personality's role in drinking, or indeed in other substance-use behaviour, remains controversial (Morrison 2003).

- The social learning experience: social learning theory considers alcohol abuse or dependence to be a socially acquired and learned behaviour that has received reinforcement (internal or external, physical, social or emotional rewards). Addiction may result from repeatedly seeking the pleasurable effects of the substance itself (e.g. Wise 1998).

Among older people, evidence points to lower levels of alcohol consumption, and in elderly samples, problem drinking has been shown to be influenced by physical health, access to social opportunities and financial status, with the affluent elderly having higher rates of drinking problems (Livingston and Hinchliffe 1993). For some individuals, however, an increase in alcohol consumption can be attributed in part to loneliness, bereavement or physical symptomatology (e.g. Atkinson 1994).

■ Alcohol dependence

Alcohol problems and how those with such problems are viewed by society have changed over time, from being seen as the immoral behaviour of weak individuals unable to exert personal control over their consumption during

Plate 3.1   The social context is a powerful influence on our eating and drinking behaviour.

the seventeenth–eighteenth centuries, to being the behaviour of passive victims of an evil and powerful substance in the nineteenth century. The earlier 'moral' view considered individuals as responsible for their behaviour and therefore the ethos of treatment was punishment. The latter view considered the individual to have less control over their behaviour, and as such the prohibition of alcohol sales (as seen in the USA) was considered an appropriate societal response, and treatment was offered to those 'victims' who 'succumbed'. The medical treatment of individuals with alcohol problems reflects the beginnings of a disease concept of addiction where the drug was seen as being the problem. However, by the early twentieth century, it was clear that prohibition had failed and the model of alcoholism developed into one that placed responsibility back onto the individual. In 1960, Jellinek described alcoholism as a disease but considered both the nature of the substance and the pre-existing characteristics of the person who used it. While it became accepted that alcohol could be used by the majority without any resulting harm, a minority of individuals developed alcohol dependence, and for these individuals pre-existing genetic and psychological 'weaknesses' were acknowledged. Addiction was seen as an acquired, permanent state of being over which the individual could regain control only by means of abstinence, and treatment reflected this: for example, the self-help organisation, Alcoholics Anonymous, founded in 1935, had the primary goal of helping individuals to achieve lifelong abstinence.

However, in psychology during the early twentieth century, the growth of **behaviourism** brought with it new methods of treatment for those with drinking problems that drew from the principles of social learning theory and conditioning theory. These perspectives consider behaviour to result from learning and from the reinforcement that any behaviour receives. Excessive alcohol consumption, according to these theories, can be 'unlearned' by applying behavioural principles to treatment. Such treatment would aim to identify the cues for an individual's drinking behaviour and the type of

behaviourism
the belief that psychology is the study of observables and therefore that behaviour, not mental processes, is central.

reinforcement individuals receive for their behaviour (see Chapter 6). These approaches therefore consider the individual, their drinking behaviour and the social environment. Nowadays, at least in the UK and elsewhere in Europe, abstinence is considered as one possible treatment outcome among others, such as controlled drinking. In controlled drinking, individuals are encouraged to restrict their consumption to certain occasions/settings/times of day, or to control the alcoholic content of drinks consumed by, for example, switching to low-alcohol alternatives (Heather and Robertson 1997).

Patterns of heavy drinking laid down in late childhood and early adulthood tend to set the pattern for heavy drinking in adulthood, and alcohol-related health problems such as liver cirrhosis tend to accumulate in middle age. Health promotion efforts therefore have two targets: primary prevention in terms of educating children about the risks of heavy drinking and about 'safe' levels of consumption; and secondary prevention in terms of changing the behaviour of those already engaged in heavy drinking. Examples of these are described in Chapters 6 and 7.

Smoking

After caffeine and alcohol, nicotine is the next most commonly used psychoactive drug in society today. While smoking behaviour receives a vast amount of negative publicity arising from the death toll attached to it, nicotine is a legal drug, with sale of nicotine-based substances (cigarettes, cigars) providing many tobacco companies and many governments (as a result of tobacco tax) with a vast income (as does alcohol). A shift in how society views smoking has slowly taken shape, with worksite bans, legislation regarding smoking in public places, and restrictions on tobacco advertising having some effect (e.g. Wakefield *et al.* 2000), but smoking prevalence remains high. Reducing smoking behaviour continues to be a public health target and indeed in developing countries, where smoking prevalence, particularly among men, has increased rather than plateaud or decreased.

Negative health effects of smoking

A 1990 report estimated that approximately three million people worldwide die each year as a result of their use of tobacco cigarettes and, to a lesser degree, cigars (Peto and Lopez 1990). By 2000, smoking-attributable deaths had risen by over one million per year (estimated deaths of 4.9 million; World Health Organization 2002), yet smoking is the key modifiable risk factor for cardiovascular disease across all age groups.

Tobacco products contain carcinogenic tars and carbon monoxide, which are thought to be responsible for approximately 30 per cent of cases of coronary heart disease, 75 per cent of cancers (90 per cent of lung cancer) and 80 per cent of cases of chronic obstructive airways disease. In addition, passive smoking is considered to account for 25 per cent of lung cancer deaths among non-smokers. Passive smoking also carries risks to unborn babies.

IN THE SPOTLIGHT

Smoking, drinking and teenage pregnancy

Studies of adolescent girls have pointed to the importance of self-concept (i.e. concept of what one 'is') and self-esteem (i.e. concept of one's 'value' or 'worth') in determining involvement or non-involvement in risk behaviours. Some theorists further suggest that a significant amount of adolescent behaviour is motivated by the need to present oneself to others (primarily peers) in a way that enhances the individual's reputation, their social identity (Emler 1984). In some social groups the 'reputation' that will help the individual 'fit' with that social group will involve risk-taking behaviours (Odgers *et al.* 1996; Snow and Bruce 2003). Snow and Bruce (2003) found female smokers to have less self-confidence, to feel less liked by their families, and to have lower physical and social self-concepts, while their peer self-concept surprisingly did not differ from that of non-smokers. In relation to becoming pregnant as a teenager, low self-esteem and a negative self-concept may again be implicated, as teenage mothers often show a history of dysfunctional relationships and social and financial strain. Alcohol appears to play a significant role in early sexual activity likely to lead to becoming pregnant, rather than being necessarily a problem during pregnancy. For example, alcohol consumption and being 'drunk' or 'stoned' is a commonly cited reason for first having sex when a teenager (e.g. Duncan *et al.* 1999; Wellings *et al.* 2001) and for subsequently having unprotected sex and risking both pregnancy and sexually transmitted diseases (Hingson *et al.* 2003). In contrast, there is some evidence that teenagers are less likely to drink during pregnancy than older mothers, thus placing their unborn child at lower risk of foetal alcohol syndrome (California Department of Health Services 2003). In terms of other behaviours during pregnancy, teenage mothers are more likely to have a poor diet and smoke during pregnancy than older mothers and, combined with their often physical immaturity, these behaviours may contribute to the higher rates of miscarriage, premature birth and low birthweight babies (Department of Health 2003; Horgan and Kenny 2007). Horgan and Kenney further note that the death rate for babies and young children born to teenage mums is 60 per cent higher than that for those born to older mothers, and younger mums are also three times more likely to suffer from post-natal depression.

Teenage substance use therefore has the potential to create significant long-term problems for the individual and potentially their child. However, changing adolescent risk behaviour is often challenging, given the complexity of influences thereon, but there is some evidence that interventions which address self-esteem issues before addressing 'behaviour' problems, including under-age sex, smoking and drinking alcohol, seem to meet with greater success than those which do not (e.g. Health Development Agency Magazine 2005).

Carbon monoxide reduces circulating oxygen in the blood, which effectively reduces the amount of oxygen feeding the heart muscles; nicotine makes the heart work harder by increasing blood pressure and heart rate; and together these substances cause narrowing of the arteries and increase the likelihood of thrombosis (clot formation). Tars impair the respiratory system by congesting the lungs, and this is a major contributor to the highly prevalent chronic obstructive pulmonary disease (COPD: e.g. emphysema) (Julien 1996). Overall, the evidence as to the negative health effects of smoking tobacco is indisputable, and more recently the evidence as to the negative effects of passive smoking has been increasing (Department of Health 1998b).

Plate 3.2 A young mother smoking with her baby sitting on her lap looking at the cigarette. This is an emotive example of passive smoking.

Source: Alamy Images/Richard Newton

Prevalence of smoking

Worldwide, almost 9 per cent of deaths are attributed to tobacco use and the World Health report points out that between 1990 and 2000 – a relatively short period – there were at least 1 million more deaths attributable to tobacco (WHO 2002). In developed countries tobacco creates the largest disease burden (closely followed by blood pressure, and then alcohol, cholesterol and being overweight). There are some positive signs, however, that at least in developed countries, possibly as a result of growing awareness of the negative health consequences of smoking, changes in the prevalence and uptake of smoking are present. For example, approximately 80 per cent of men and 40 per cent of women smoked in the UK during the 1950s, whereas by 1998 these percentages had declined significantly, to approximately 39 per cent of men and 33 per cent of women (Peto *et al.* 2000). This reduced prevalence has been associated with a decrease in lung cancer rates, but the full benefits of more recent declines in smoking prevalence will only be seen in mortality figures of future decades. A less encouraging finding is that the downturn in the number of men smoking is not reflected among women, who show a slower rate of reduction, and among young girls, who show a greater increase in smoking initiation (Blenkinsop *et al.* 2003; Department of Health 2000; Office for National Statistics 2001). The prevalence of males currently smoking in those aged over 16 in England has dropped from 41 per cent in 1976 to 28 per cent in 1996 (*General Household Survey*: Thomas *et al.* 1998) and further downwards to 24 per cent in 2006. For females, the decline

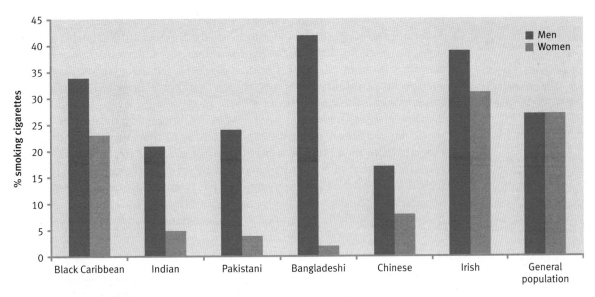

Figure 3.3   Cigarette smoking by gender and ethnic group, England, 1999.
Source: www.heartstats.org

between 1993 and 2006 was less pronounced (26 to 21 per cent) (Health Survey for England, The Information Centre, 2006).

The increased incidence of lung cancer among women over the past two decades is, in part, traceable to the increased prevalence of women smoking since the Second World War, and this worrying upturn is likely to continue if recent survey figures are considered. Ethnic differences in smoking prevalence have also been reported (British Heart Foundation 2004, www. heartstats.org). Bangladeshi men have been found to be at greater risk of coronary heart disease than other groups, due, for example, to their tendency to exercise less and smoke more than their white counterparts (Nazroo 1997; Health Education Authority 1997). To illustrate this further, Figure 3.3 presents data from a survey conducted in 1999, which found that 42 per cent of Bangladeshi males smoked, in comparison with 27 per cent of males across the general population. Also contributing to the higher levels of CHD in this group is the fact that these males also eat less fruit and vegetables and engage in low levels of physical activity in comparison with the general population of males. In contrast, the percentage of Bangladeshi, Indian and Pakistani women smoking is significantly below the general population norm. Aboriginal and Torres Strait islanders have been shown to have one of the highest prevalences of smoking recorded – with 51 per cent of these indigenous populations aged over 15 years smoking (Australian Bureau of Statistics 2005).

As well as culture, there are age differences in smoking prevalence: smoking remains at high levels among the elderly – a population that initiated smoking before the medical evidence as to the health-damaging effects of the behaviour was clear and publicly available. Bratzler et al. (2002) review the impact of smoking on the elderly in terms of increased morbidity, disability and death, and provide a strong argument for the continued need for health promotion efforts to target smoking cessation in order to enhance the quality of life and longevity of older individuals. Evidence of the health gains of smoking cessation have been demonstrated: the American Cancer Society Cancer Prevention Study II, for example, reported a significant decrease in **age-specific mortality** rates for former smokers compared with current smokers, with the benefit being present in those aged over 60, and even in those who ceased smoking aged 70–74. Although elderly groups present particular challenges to health educators, due to the consistent finding that they attribute many health consequences of smoking to the general ageing process, and that they are often highly dependent on the behaviour (psychologically and physically), interventions that combine age-relevant risk information and support are likely to be as effective in achieving smoking cessation as similar interventions in younger populations.

> **age-specific mortality**
> typically presented as the number of deaths per 100,000, per annum, according to certain age groups, for example comparing rates of death from cancer in 2001 between those aged 45–54 with those aged 55–64.

Smoking as an addiction

The addictive potential of smoking arises from the pharmacological substance, nicotine, which acts as a brain stimulant, releases our natural opiates, beta-endorphins, and causes an increased metabolic rate (Julien 1996). Physical dependence arises when an individual develops tolerance to the effects of nicotine and smokes more to attain the same effects or to avoid the withdrawal effects that follow a diminished bloodstream nicotine level (e.g. cravings, insomnia, sweating, increased appetite: e.g. West 1992). In this way, smoking can become self-reinforcing. Psychological symptoms of withdrawal such as anxiety, restlessness and irritability are often so pronounced that individuals may recommence smoking in a deliberate attempt to eliminate these symptoms, which are distressing not only for them but also for those around them! Resuming smoking provides reinforcement in terms of the avoidance of any further withdrawal symptoms.

Why do people smoke?

Smoking behaviour is generally adopted in youth, and there are a significant number of young people smoking and accumulating lung and airway damage that will, for many, create significant health problems in the future (Walker and Townsend 1999). Doll and Peto (1981) reported increased risks of lung cancer in those that initiate smoking in childhood as opposed to adulthood, although only a relatively small proportion of smokers do not start smoking until early adulthood (19+ years).

■ Smoking initiation

As with alcohol, the reasons for smoking initiation are many and varied, and we cover here only the main ones that research has identified.

■ *Modelling, social learning and reinforcement.* Children with peers, elder siblings or parents who smoke are more likely to imitate such behaviour than children with non-smoking significant others (e.g. Biglan *et al.*

1995). Family behaviour and family dynamics are important socialisation processes that inevitably shape the subsequent behaviour of children. Some authors have suggested that smoking parents increase the 'preparedness' of their children towards smoking. That is, parental smoking results in the establishment of positive attitudes towards smoking and possibly reduced perceptions of risk, with the influence of smoking peers resulting in this preparedness turning into action (e.g. Jarvis 2004).

Image and reputation is important during adolescence, and wanting to 'fit' with one's social group is considered important to social functioning (e.g. Tyas and Pederson 1998). Gender differences may exist here. Michell and Amos (1997), for example, found that young males were more ambivalent than females about smoking, as they considered that smoking behaviour conflicted with their desire for physical fitness. Among boys, 'status' in the pecking order appeared to be conferred by fitness, whereas for girls high status was attached to appearing cool and sophisticated or rebellious, and for some, this may be achieved through smoking.

- *Social pressure.* Social or peer pressure, where smoking behaviour is positively encouraged and then reinforced by the responses of significant others, has commonly been cited as a reason for smoking initiation, reflecting either social contagion or influence that a person conforms to. Interestingly, however, Denscombe (2001) reported that young people aged 15–16 years rejected the idea of 'peer pressure' being responsible for smoking initiation, preferring to see the behaviour as something they selected to do themselves. This fits with the notion of smoking initiation being tied up with seeking reputation and status (Snow and Bruce 2003)

- *Weight control.* Weight control has been identified as a motive for smoking initiation and maintenance among young girls but not among young males (e.g. Crisp *et al.* 1999; French *et al.* 1994). Underlying differences in motivation for smoking are crucial to our understanding of why national statistics are showing reducing levels of smoking among boys but less so among girls. It would seem that the greater concern about body image and weight seen among girls needs to be addressed in parallel with perceptions of smoking if smoking behaviour is to be reduced.

- *Risk-taking.* Smoking has been found to be a common feature of those engaged in a larger array of 'risk-taking' or problem behaviour, such as truancy, petty theft or under-age drinking (Sutherland and Shepherd 2001). Low family cohesion has also been associated with higher levels of smoking and drinking among adolescents and young adults aged 12 to 22 (Bourdeaudhuij 1997; Bourdeaudhuij and van Oost 1998), although these studies assessed adolescents and adults at one time point only: thus it is not possible to establish the direction of the effects reported.

- *Health cognitions.* There is evidence that beliefs such as 'unrealistic optimism' regarding the potential of experiencing negative health consequences of smoking (and of other health-risk behaviours) are common: i.e. 'It won't happen to me as I smoke less than other people my age' – see Chapter 5.

- *Stress.* Stress is often cited as a factor which maintains smoking (see below), but there is also evidence of a role for stress in smoking initiation. See RESEARCH FOCUS below.

RESEARCH FOCUS

Does perceived stress influence adolescent smoking?

Byrne, D.G. and Mazanov, J. (2003). Adolescent stress and future smoking behaviour: a prospective investigation. *Journal of Psychosomatic Research*, 54: 313–21.

Smoking behaviour generally commences in adolescence, and research has revealed an array of influences on its uptake, as described above and also in Chapter 2, in terms of socio-economic influences. The experience of stress has been associated with the maintenance of adult smoking, but little work has explored this association in adolescence. Furthermore, if general and specific aspects of stress were found to predict smoking onset in young people, this would have important implications for preventive interventions. Byrne and Mazanov (2003) therefore set out to examine whether stress was a factor in smoking initiation among Australian adolescents. In order to address this causal question, they employed a longitudinal design and hypothesised that adolescent non-smokers at baseline who experienced stress in an intervening year would be more likely to become smokers than non-stressed non-smokers.

Method

Over 2,600 school pupils aged approximately 16 (range 14–18) entered the study having been recruited from 15 Australian schools who agreed to support the study (out of 29 schools invited). Twelve schools remained in the study, and 64 per cent of the sample completed a follow-up (mean age 17, 16 month range 15–19) assessment twelve months later. This resulted in 1419 participants, of whom 21 per cent of boys and 26 per cent of girls were current smokers. In terms of measures employed, participants completed a battery of questionnaires, addressing: socio-demographic variables; smoking behaviour, and patterns and contexts in which smoking took place (for smokers only); sources and intensity of stress using a measure previously developed by the authors which consists of seven sub-scales addressing potential sources of stress (school; family conflict; parental control; school performance; future uncertainty; perceived educational irrelevance; interactions with opposite sex); and a measure of psychological distress, the GHQ12 (Goldberg 1997).

Parental approval had to be given in order for students under 18 years old to participate, but the authors do not note how many failed to obtain this approval and thus were unable to take part. The study was carried out in school time at Time 1, with questionnaires being mailed out only at T2 to participants who were not in school at the time of data collection. The school did not have access to individual data thus student confidentiality was maintained.

Results

The authors present an array of descriptive analyses including data showing that there were significant gender differences in both distress and stress, whereby girls reported higher distress and stress from family conflict, parental control, school performance, future uncertainty and opposite sex interactions. The authors do point out, however, that the actual levels of distress and stress were not likely to be clinically significant in this sample. It would have helped the reader to see this, had maximum possible scores been presented for each of the stress sub-scales, as this is an important finding.

Only a small number of non-smokers at T1 had become smokers by T2 (25 boys, 5.4 per cent; 15 girls, 3.4 per cent) and the percentage of smokers in both genders was less at T2. The authors note that attrition was higher among smokers than non-smokers, and this possibly explains this finding, i.e. smokers did not complete the follow-up. Pupils who failed to complete the follow-up also reported a significantly higher number of friends who smoked at T1 than did those who took part in both phases of the study.

Even though the numbers who became smokers were limited, the authors tested their hypothesis that stress levels would precede smoking onset. Interesting gender differences emerged. For boys, only the stress of attending school distinguished between those who remained non-smokers at both time points, and those who commenced smoking between time points, with smoking uptake being associated with higher stress of attending school. In contrast, reporting higher stress from attending school, family conflict, parental control, and perceived educational irrelevance distinguished those who started smoking from those who remained non-smokers.

Discussion

The authors rightly note that the loss to follow-up of a significant proportion of the sample (47.2 per cent of boys and 44.4 per cent of girls), with evidence of greater incidence of smoking, friends who smoked, and low parental educational levels among those who failed to complete the follow-up, has some bearing on the generalisabiity of their findings. In spite of this, however, the sample size remains large enough to test their main hypothesis. The hypothesis that stress is associated with smoking uptake was not upheld for boys. The weak association with stress of attending school, the authors suggest, may reflect low academic ability or low attainment in the family, both factors associated with smoking uptake generally. Among girls, however, the evidence is stronger, with associations between commencing smoking and all but two of the stress sub-scales (but not the distress measure). More girls in this sample smoked: however, only 3.4 per cent became smokers between T1 and T2 and so these results should perhaps be interpreted with more caution than the authors exhibit. However, the findings reported in this paper are consistent with other surveys of gender and stress, and gender and smoking, and so the authors conclude that the implications of their findings are for the provision of stress management strategies for girls at a stage before smoking has been adopted, in order to potentially prevent smoking uptake.

Curiously, the authors do not consider the role of social background (e.g the child's academic ability or parental educational attainment) in explaining the association between stress and smoking shown for girls as they do when explaining the finding for boys. As we have seen in Chapter 2, socio-economic correlates and predictors of health behaviour exist for both genders (and see Payne (2006) for a review), and therefore is likely to be implicated also on the findings for girls in this paper. Stress is likely to be only one of many possible causes of smoking uptake.

■ Smoking maintenance

Reasons for continuing to smoke are not exclusively the same as reasons given for initiation. In general, people who continue to smoke report:

- pleasure or enjoyment of the behaviour, taste and effects reinforces positive attitudes towards smoking;
- smoking out of habit (psychological and/or physical dependence);
- smoking as a form of stress self-management/coping, anxiety control;
- a lack of belief in their ability to stop smoking.

Psychological dependence is highly complex and depends greatly on the rewards and incentives, motivations and expectations that a person places on their smoking behaviour. For example, Cox and Klinger (2004) describe a motivational model of substance use based on consistent findings that people's decisions about substance use, including tobacco, are not necessarily rational but involve a range of motivational and emotional components. For example, a person considering their smoking behaviour may do so in relation to other aspects of their lives that they may or may not derive satisfaction from. Individuals without commitment to healthy life goals or the motivation to work towards attaining them are less likely to perceive their substance use as a problem and consider themselves as less able to change the behaviour.

■ Stopping smoking

Even people who stop smoking when aged between 50 and 60 can avoid most of their subsequent risk of developing lung cancer or other smoking-related disease or disability (Bratzler *et al.* 2002). Better still, stopping when aged 30 leads to more than 90 per cent of lung cancer risk being avoided (Peto *et al.* 2000). Attempts to help people to stop smoking are viewed positively by the public, and in fact the majority of smokers wish to stop smoking. For example, two-thirds of smokers surveyed in 1996 as part of the UK General Household survey reported wanting to give up (Office for National Statistics 1998). It has been found that stopping smoking is more likely among individuals of a higher socio-economic status (dispelling expectations of significant downturns in smoking among those of lower socio-economic status caused by increases in cigarette prices). For example, in a 6.5-year follow-up study of over 1,300 smokers in the Netherlands, Droomers *et al.* (2002) found that the higher the level of education, the greater the success rates for smoking cessation. Whether this effect is directly attributable to higher levels of knowledge and understanding about potential health consequences, or whether it is confounded by social class (perhaps quitters in higher social classes have fewer smoking acquaintances and friends than non-quitters), remains unclear. Various studies have shown that smoking networks are associated with quitting to a larger degree than health beliefs, whereby not being part of a smoking network facilitates cessation (e.g. Rose *et al.* 1996). Chapters 6 and 7 describe interventions aimed at promoting smoking cessation.

Unprotected sexual behaviour

Negative health consequences of unprotected sexual intercourse

Notwithstanding unwanted pregnancy (see IN THE SPOTLIGHT earlier in the chapter), unprotected sexual intercourse carries with it several risks: infections such as chlamydia and HIV. Sexual behaviour as a risk factor for disease has received growing attention since the 'arrival' of the human immunodeficiency virus (HIV) in the early 1980s and the recognition that AIDS affects heterosexually active populations as well as homosexual populations and injecting drug users who share their injecting equipment. Unlike the other behaviour described in this chapter, sexual practices are not inherently individual behaviour but behaviour that occurs in the context of an interaction between two individuals. Sex is fundamentally 'social' behaviour (although drinking behaviour may also be considered 'social', the actual physical act of drinking is down to the individual). As such, researchers studying sexual practices and the influences upon them, and health educators attempting to promote safer sexual practices such as condom use, face particular challenges.

■ HIV prevalence

The World Health Organization (1999, 2002) has estimated that about forty million people are infected with HIV worldwide, about fourteen million of whom have died. While twenty-eight million (70 per cent) of HIV cases are concentrated in Africa, areas of Europe also have cause for concern. In the UK, for example, there are currently about 42,000 people with HIV, and there have been approximately 14,000 deaths from AIDS. The HIV epidemic in the UK is not dissimilar to that found elsewhere in northern Europe such as in Germany, the Netherlands and Scandinavia; however, the southern European countries of Spain, France, Portugal and Italy have much higher infection figures, attributed in large part to the prevalence of injecting drug use (PHLS Communicable Disease Surveillance Centre 2002).

In many countries, unprotected heterosexual sex has to a large extent taken over from homosexual sex and injecting drug use (IDU) as a route of infection, initially appearing to add weight to research findings of behaviour change among homosexual men (Katz 1997) and offering support to the effectiveness of syringe-exchange schemes for injecting drug users. For example, although needle sharing still occurs, in the UK diagnoses of HIV among IDUs have shown a steady decline over the past sixteen years, from 588 diagnoses in 1985 (or before, but figures were not collated until 1985), to 181 diagnoses in 1995, and 104 new diagnoses among IDUs in 2001 (PHLS Communicable Disease Surveillance Centre 2002) (see Figure 3.4).

However, more recent evidence suggests that the positive changes reported among gay men surveyed from the mid-1980s until the late 1990s are beginning to abate, and an upturn in the practice of unprotected anal sex, sexually transmitted diseases and, inevitably, HIV infection is being witnessed (e.g. Chen et al. 2002; Dodds and Mercey 2002). Part of this downturn in the practice of safer sex may be attributable to the fact that people consider AIDS a disease for which there are a growing number of treatments, and thus the perceived lethality of the disease, and the implicit requirement to practise safer sex, may have been undermined. Additionally, individuals' perceptions of risk may be wrong.

Heterosexual infection has greater implications for women (as the 'receptors' of semen during sexual intercourse) than men, and in the USA this is evidenced in increased female HIV figures (e.g. Wortley and Fleming 1997; Logan et al. 2002). The prevalence of HIV infection in pregnant women is relatively low in Europe, but monitoring has found cases to have risen, suggesting an urgent need for development of further antenatal screening services.

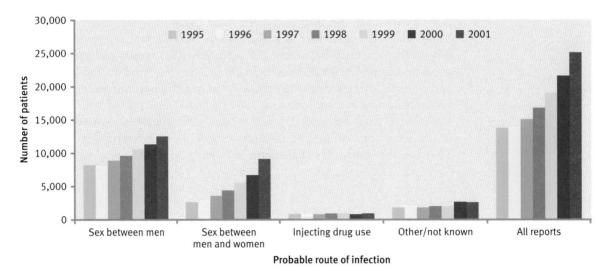

Figure 3.4 Prevalence trends for HIV infection (patients seen for care) by probable route of infection: England, Wales and Northern Ireland, 1995–2001.

Source: PHLS Communicable Disease Surveillance Centre (2001)

■ Chlamydia, HPV and other sexually transmitted diseases

Of growing concern is the upturn in figures relating to the sexually transmitted diseases or infections (STD/STIs) of chlamydia, genital herpes simplex and genital warts, most common among adolescents and young adults. Chlamydia is a curable disease and is also the most preventable cause of infertility: however, a recent national screening survey of prevalence in young people found that 13.8 per cent of those under 16 years old, 10.5 per cent of those aged 16–19 and 7.2 per cent of those aged 20–24 had this infection (Moens *et al.* 2003). Another survey of sexual behaviour, among 11,161 adults aged 16–44, carried out urine testing on half of the sample and found that 10.8 per cent of men and 12.6 per cent of women had had a sexually transmitted infection, 3.6 per cent of men and 4.1 per cent of women had had genital warts, and 1.4 per cent of men and 3.1 per cent of women had chlamydia (Fenton *et al.* 2001). These are worrying figures, given that chlamydia could be avoided through the use of condoms.

A subgroup of a family of viruses known collectively as Human Papilloma Virus (HPV) have been associated with abnormal tissue and cell growth implicated in the development of genital warts and cervical cancer. The high-risk type viruses labelled HPV-16 and HPV-18 together cause over 70 per cent of squamous cell cancers (cancer develops in flat-type cells found on the outer surface of the cervix), and approximately 50 per cent of adenocarcinomas (the cancer develops in the glandular cells which line the cervix). About 95 per cent of cervical cancers are squamous cell type and about 5 per cent are adenocarcinomas. There are also low-risk type of HPV viruses which are associated with the development of genital warts, which do not cause cervical cancer in themselves but which are a sexually transmitted infection which cause significant discomfort. HPV is not contagious as such, but can be transmitted from a single act of sexual intercourse with an infected person.

Whilst condom use reduces the risk of infection, HPV 'lives' on the whole genital area and therefore a condom alone is insufficient to prevent transmission. HPV is startingly prevalent and therefore the discovery of a vaccination against those types of HPV which cause 70 per cent of cervical cancers (but not genital warts) has been billed as a major public health discovery. Clinical trials have found the vaccine to be effective in both adults and children, with 90 per cent effectiveness in those who have not already acquired infection (Lo 2006, 2007; Steinbrook 2006). As a result, from September 2008 the UK government will initiate a vaccination programme targeted at girls aged 12–13 years, on the basis that the vaccination needs to be given before sexual activity commences. Also a 'catch-up' programme in 2009/10 will target 15–17-year-olds, and so by the end of 2010 it is hoped that all girls under 18 will have been offered the vaccine. The vaccination requires three injections over a six-month period and will be made available in secondary schools. Parental permission will of course be required in order for the vaccination to be given.

What do YOU think?

Some US parenting groups have voiced concerns that offering vaccination against a sexually transmitted infection such as this is condoning sexual activity. What do you think? What about sex education more generally? Is offering a vaccination programme through schools the most appropriate way of reaching the population concerned? What young people might be missed?

How might parents react to this vaccination programme? In many states of the USA, adolescents can provide consent for treatments of STIs without that of their parents. Do you think the offering of this vaccine to under-18s is likely to achieve a high uptake? It is likely that we will see a flurry of research into the predictors of uptake and non-uptake of vaccination and therefore, from a health psychology perspective, this is quite an exciting time. Chapter 5 outlines key psychological factors and sociocognitive models of health behaviour and these models are likely to be tested in relation to HPV.

The use of condoms

Prior to HIV and AIDS, sexual behaviour was generally considered to be 'private' behaviour and somewhat under-researched (with the exception of clinical studies of individuals experiencing sexual difficulties). The lack of information as to the sexual practices of the general population made it initially extremely difficult to assess the potential for the spread of HIV infection. One notable survey that was triggered by this need for information was the *National Survey of Sexual Attitudes and Lifestyles*, conducted with nearly 19,000 adults (aged 16–59) living in Britain in 1990–91 (Wellings *et al.* 1994).

Figure 3.5 presents data relating to the percentages of men and women across four age groups who had used condoms during sexual intercourse. It was found that:

■ Young people use condoms more commonly than older people.

■ Females tend to use condoms less often than males.

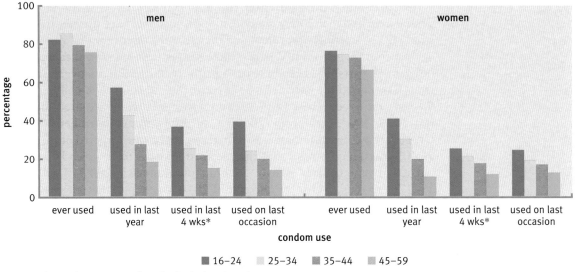

* respondents who were sexually active in the last 4 weeks

Figure 3.5   Condom use by age and gender in the *National Survey of Sexual Attitudes and Lifestyles*.

Source: from the National Survey of Sexual Attitudes and Lifestyles, 1990

- For both males and females condom use was greatest with a 'new' sexual partner (34 and 41 per cent of males and females, respectively, used condoms on all occasions of sex with a single new partner).
- Condom use declined dramatically in those who reported having had multiple new partners (17.5 and 10 per cent, respectively).
- The rate of condom use was lowest in males who had multiple partners who were not new sexual partners (only 5.7 per cent always used a condom).
- Female condom use was less affected by whether multiple partners were 'new' to them or not (14.3 per cent always used a condom with not new multiple partners).

This survey was repeated in 2001 with over 11,000 men and women aged 16–44 years and with a deliberate intention of boosting the cultural mix of the sample which also over-represented London (NATSAL II; Erens *et al.* 2003). Although not as representative a national sample as the first survey, results regarding condom use (any use in the year prior to interview) were encouraging (Cassell *et al.* 2006). A significant increase in usage was reported in both males (from 43.3 per cent in 1990 to 51.4 per cent in 2000) and females (from 30.6 per cent in 1990 to 39.1 per cent in 2000). As in the first survey, condom use was highest among younger respondents and for those for whom the last sexual partner was 'new'. One important finding was the rate of condom use among those with multiple partners – those 'high-risk' individuals were the most likely to report condom use. Non-white ethnicity and being of a non-Christian religion was also found to be associated with greater condom use, highlighting the importance of ensuring representation across differing cultural and religious groupings. Among the heterosexual sample, the prevention of pregnancy was given as the primary reason for condom use, although in the younger sub-sample (16–24-year-olds) prevention of HIV and other STIs was of equal or greater concern. This may reflect increased awareness of HIV and sexual health in the decade between the two surveys, and provide support to those offering health education and health promotion (see Chapters 6 and 7).

Safer sex practices were not influenced solely by concerns about STIs but also by the type, number and length of sexually active relationships a person is engaged in. Condom use commonly begins to decline after six months within any given relationship. Many other factors have been been reported to act as barriers against safer sex behaviour, as we describe in the next section (see also Chapter 5).

■ Barriers to condom use

Alcohol intake has been found to reduce condom use in both younger and older individuals, heterosexuals and homosexuals (e.g. Gillies 1991), an effect sometimes attributed to the disinhibitory effects of alcohol. However, this author notes that alcohol use may simply be an indicator of general risk-taking behaviour (which includes non-use of condoms), and that further research is required to ascertain whether alcohol itself plays a direct causal role.

In terms of women and HIV prevention, many interpersonal, intrapersonal, cultural and contextual factors have been shown to interact and affect whether or not the woman feels able to control the use of condoms in sexual encounters (e.g. Bury *et al.* 1992; Sanderson and Jemmot 1996). In general, surveys of condom use among young women have found that while females share some of the negative attitudes towards condom use found among male samples (such as that condoms reduce spontaneity of behaviour or reduce sexual pleasure), and that they also tend to hold unrealistically optimistic estimates of personal risk of infection with STDs or HIV, women face additional barriers when considering condom use (Bryan *et al.* 1996, 1997; Hobfoll *et al.* 1994). These can include:

- anticipated male objection to a female suggesting condom use (denial of their pleasure);
- difficulty/embarrassment in raising the issue of condom use with a male partner;
- worry that suggesting use to a potential partner implies that either themselves or the partner is HIV-positive or has another STD;
- lack of self-efficacy or mastery in condom use.

These factors are not simply about the individual's own health beliefs and behavioural intentions regarding avoiding pregnancy, STDs or AIDS; they also highlight that sexual behaviour is a complex interpersonal interaction. Safer sexual behaviour perhaps requires multiple-level interventions that target not only individual health beliefs (such as those described in Chapter 5) but also their interpersonal, communication and negotiating skills (see Chapters 6 and 7).

Individual behaviour, where positively or negatively associated with health, can be a sensitive issue, with some people preferring to keep their practices and motivations to themselves. This can create many challenges for those interested in measuring health or risk behaviour with a view to developing understanding of it. While measurement issues are not confined to studies of health behaviour, they are particularly pertinent in this domain (see ISSUES below).

The challenge of measuring health behaviour

The research tradition assumes that the objects of study, e.g. health, illness, or in the context of this chapter, behaviour, remain as fixed entities in people's minds. However, without a researcher actually being present and observing the individual behaving over long periods of time, it is difficult to know whether the behaviour a person reports to the researcher (or clinician) accurately reflects their actual behaviour. Obtaining valid measures of behaviour is made increasingly difficult when one is interested in behaviour that is perhaps considered 'undesirable' (e.g. excessive alcohol or drug use), or when it is private (e.g. sexual behaviour). Researchers also face the challenge of knowing how best to define the behaviours under study, and yet it is only through appropriate definition that measurement becomes possible. For example, rather than defining exercise in terms of organised activity, it could be defined as any physical activity that requires energy expenditure; or in terms of drinking alcohol, whether a 'drink' is defined and counted in terms of standard 'units' (see alcohol section), or size of glass, or strength of alcohol). The definition adopted will influence the questions asked, and furthermore, questions need to address not just the type of behaviour performed but also aspects such as the frequency, duration, intensity, and even social context in which it is performed.

Where direct observation and/or objective measurement (for example, taking blood or urine sample) are not possible, researchers have to rely on *self-report*. When studies are interested in the frequency with which certain behaviour is performed, it is commonplace to ask study participants to complete a diary, for example of cigarettes/alcohol/foods consumed or activities undertaken. Participants in such studies are generally required to either record behaviour daily for a period of a week (any longer places high demand on participants), or to reflect back on the previous week's activity (a retrospective diary – RD). The latter has obvious memory demands – could you accurately recall how many units of alcohol you drank seven days ago? While there is no evidence of a systematic bias towards overestimation or underestimation (Maisto and Connors 1992; Shakeshaft *et al.* 1999), some studies attempt to cross-validate behavioural self-reports by obtaining observer ratings or blood samples. However, observation is not always ethical, and biochemical tests are intrusive and costly. Other studies rely on asking participants about their 'typical or average' behaviour. In such studies, individuals, for example, report the typical amount of alcohol consumed (quantity), and the 'typical or average' number of days on which they consume alcohol (frequency) (e.g. Norman *et al.* 1998). However, this method known as a quantity/frequency index (QFI) may provide over-general information. Shakeshaft and colleagues (1999) compared an RD method with a QFI, and found that the RD method elicited higher reported levels of weekly alcohol consumption than did the QFI. In fact, neither way may be totally accurate.

One way of minimising inaccuracies in reporting is by using continuous *self-monitoring techniques*, such as smoking or food consumption diaries, with short recording periods, e.g. hourly. This can be a useful method of establishing patterns of behaviour and the circumstances in which they occur. For example, smoking or food consumption diaries commonly instruct the person completing them to note not only the time at which each cigarette is smoked or each meal or snack consumed but also the location, whether anyone else was present, whether any particular 'cue' existed and the reasons for consumption. Some studies invite the person to note also whether they are currently experiencing positive or negative emotions. A potential limitation of self-monitoring is that it can be reactive; in other words, it acts as an intervention itself, with participants modifying their consumption on the basis of their increased awareness of their intake. Behaviour that is seen as undesirable is likely to decrease while being monitored, whereas desirable behaviour is likely to increase. This may be useful in a clinical context, where the intention of self-monitoring *is* behaviour change, but in a research context it may be obstructive; for example, it may prevent researchers from obtaining reliable baseline measurement of behaviour against which to evaluate the efficacy of an intervention programme. Reliance on self-monitoring data can also create problems clinically; for example, Warren and Hixenbaugh (1998) reviewed evidence that people with diabetes make up their self-monitored blood glucose levels and found that, in some studies,

social desirability bias the tendency to answer questions about oneself or one's behaviour in a way that is thought likely to meet with social (or interviewer) approval.

individuals did so in order to present a more positive clinical profile to their medical practitioner (i.e. self-presentation bias/**social desirability bias**). This behaviour could potentially disadvantage treatment efficacy or disease management and outcomes.

Self-monitoring techniques are not the only data-collection technique which could potentially elicit self-presentation bias, as there is evidence that collecting data via *face-to-face interviews* can face the same difficulty. Face-to-face interviews enable researchers to seek more explanation for a person's behaviour by using open-ended questions such as 'Think back to your first under-age drink of alcohol. What would you say motivated it? How did you feel afterwards?' Interviews also facilitate the building of rapport with participants, which may be particularly important if the study requires participants to attend follow-up interviews or complete repeated assessments. Rapport may increase commitment to the study and improve retention rates. However, in spite of these advantages, the interview process, content and style may also influence participants' responses. Some people may simply not report their 'risk behaviour' practices (e.g. illicit drug use, unprotected sexual intercourse) or lack of preventive behaviour practices (e.g. toothbrushing, exercising) in the belief they will be judged to be 'deviant', in poor health, or simply as being careless with their health (e.g. Davies and Baker 1987). Impression management is common; i.e. people monitor and control (actively construct) what they say in order to give particular impressions of themselves (or to achieve certain effects) to particular audiences (Allport 1920 first noted this in the domain of social psychology).

So how can you tell whether health behaviour data that are collected provide a true representation of behaviour or simply the outcome of self-presentational processes? It is probably best to assume that they are a bit of both, and when reading statistics regarding the prevalence of particular behaviour, stop to consider the methods used in generating the data and ask yourself what biases, if any, may be present.

Summary

Much of our behaviour has implications for our health and illness status This chapter has defined health behaviour as those behaviours associated with health status, whether or not they are performed with the explicit goal of health protection, promotion or maintenance in mind. The behaviours addressed in this chapter are sometimes referred to as 'behavioural pathogens' or health-damaging behaviour and includes smoking, heavy consumption of alcohol, unprotected sexual behaviour and an unhealthy diet. 'Behavioural immunogens' or health-enhancing behaviours, such as exercise, a balanced diet, health screening and immunisation behaviours are discussed in the next chapter.

This chapter has described behaviours with clear associations with prevalent illnesses, and as such they account for a vast amount of research enquiry within health psychology. A significant body of work has addressed the complexity of social, emotional and cognitive factors that contribute to the uptake and maintenance of health-damaging behaviour, and a range of theories and models of health behaviour which have been developed and tested are described in Chapter 5.

We concluded this chapter by bringing to the reader's attention some of the challenges to effective measurement of health behaviours and, as elsewhere in this text, we encourage readers to stop and think about issues such as self-presentation bias or interviewer effects.

Further reading

Connor, M., Sutherland, E.D., Kennedy, F. *et al.* (2008). Impact of alcohol on sexual decision-making: intentions to have unprotected sex. *Psychology and Health*, 23: 909–34.

This very recent paper is not referred to in the main chapter but is worth a look because it reports three studies where the effects of alcohol intoxication on sexual decision-making depends on gender as well as on behaviourally relevant attitudes and beliefs.

Orford, J. (2001). *Excessive Appetites*: A *Psychological View of Addictions*, 2nd edn. Chichester: John Wiley.

For a thorough exploration of 'appetitive' behaviour including smoking, drinking, eating and sexual behaviour, this book is a classic read. Orford addresses both the changed societal views of health behaviour thought to be addictive and the psychological and physiological explanations of such behaviour.

Snow, P.C. and Bruce, D.D. (2003). Cigarette smoking in teenage girls: exploring the role of peer reputations, self-concept and coping. *Health Education Research*, 18: 439–52.

Given concerns about smoking prevalence amongst young females, this paper provides an interesting account of the crucial influence of self-confidence and self-concept, that may provide a target for health promotion efforts.

For a useful overview of current Department of Health survey statistics pertaining to health behaviour and illness (UK):
www.doh.gov.uk/stats

For a copy of the recent UK survey of adolescent health and health behaviour, including recommendations for interventions:
www.bma/org.uk

For information about the HPV vaccination programme, to commence in the UK in September 2008, look at this website. This website offers a health encyclopedia to members of the public in order to provide up-to-date information about health conditions and their treatments:
http://www.nhsdirect.nhs.uk/articles/article.aspx?articleId=2336

 Visit the website at **www.pearsoned.co.uk/morrison** for additional resources to help you with your study, including multiple choice questions, weblinks and flashcards.

CHAPTER 4

Health-enhancing behaviour

Learning outcomes

By the end of this chapter, you should have an understanding of:

- the behaviour found to have health-enhancing or health-protective effects
- the relevance of healthy diet, exercise, screening and immunisation to health across the lifespan
- the range and complexity of influences upon the uptake and maintenance of health-enhancing behaviour

CHAPTER OUTLINE

As shown in the previous chapter, behaviour is linked to health. However, not all our behaviour has potentially negative effects on our health; much of what we do can benefit our health, and indeed protect against illness. These are sometimes called 'behavioural immunogens'. This chapter provides an overview of the evidence pertaining to an array of such health-protective behaviour, including healthy diet, exercise behaviour, health screening and immunisation. The scientific evidence pertaining to the health benefits of each behaviour is considered, and some national guidelines in relation to the practice of each behaviour are illustrated. A broad array of influences on the uptake or maintenance of specific health-enhancing behaviour is introduced to the reader here in order to provide a foundation for Chapter 5, where psychosocial theories of health behaviour and health behaviour change are explored fully.

The health-enhancing behaviours described in this chapter are common targets of educational and health promotion endeavours worldwide, many examples of which are described in Chapters 6 and 7.

It is important to acknowledge that individual behaviour can both undermine a person's health and act to protect and maintain it. In a society where chronic disease is prevalent and where the population is ageing, it is becoming increasingly important to take positive steps towards healthy living and healthy ageing. Although media coverage and public health campaigns work towards increasing awareness of the beneficial or damaging effect of certain behaviour on our health, it is important to remember that people do not act solely out of a motivation to protect their health or to reduce their risk of illness. As health psychologists, it is important to develop an understanding not only of the consequences of certain behaviour for health but also of the many psychosocial factors that influence health behaviour. The dominant theories applied and tested in this field of health psychology research are described in Chapter 5, and behaviours known to carry a threat to health were described in the previous chapter, so in this chapter we look at some of the behaviours which are considered to benefit health.

Healthy diet

As described in the previous chapter, what we eat plays an important role in our long-term health and illness status. Diet has been found to have both direct and indirect links with illness; for example, fat intake is directly linked to various forms of heart disease by a range of physiological mechanisms, and indirectly related to disease by virtue of its effects on weight control and, in particular, obesity. The World Health Organization (WHO 2002) states that low intake of fruit and vegetables as part of diet is responsible for over three million deaths a year, worldwide, from cancer or cardiovascular disease. Furthermore, 35 per cent of cancer deaths are attributable, in part, to poor diet, particularly high intake of fats and salt and low levels of fibre (World Cancer Research Fund 1997). Given these reports, it is no surprise that government bodies, health ministers and medical authorities are producing guidelines on how to eat healthily, and that health researchers are working towards identifying factors that facilitate the adoption of these guidelines in our daily lives.

The health benefits of fruit and vegetable consumption

antioxidants
oxidation of low-density lipoprotein (LDL or 'bad') cholesterol has been shown to be important in the development of fatty deposits in the arteries; antioxidants are chemical properties (polyphenols) or some substances (e.g. red wine) thought to inhibit the process of oxidation.

meta-analysis
a review and re-analysis of pre-existing quantitative datasets that combines the analysis so as to provide large samples and high statistical power from which to draw reliable conclusions about specific effects.

ischaemic heart disease
a heart disease caused by a restriction of blood flow to the heart.

Fruit and vegetables contain, among other things, vitamins, folic acid, **antioxidants** and fibre, all of which are essential to a healthy body. They may also offer protection against diseases such as some forms of cancer (e.g. of the bowel, digestive system), heart disease and stroke. Block *et al.* (1992) reported that 132 out of 170 studies of the association between fruit and vegetable consumption and all types of cancer, found that fruit and vegetables conferred significant protection against cancer. Evidence to date does not, however, suggest that vegetarianism is protective against all types of cancer, although a large **meta-analysis** of data involving 76,000 men and women did find that vegetarianism reduced the risk of dying of **ischaemic heart disease** (Key *et al.* 1998). However, in this study, vegetarians also reported lower rates of smoking and lower levels of alcohol consumption than non-vegetarians, and although these factors were controlled for in the analyses, other unidentified but important differences may also have existed between the two groups that may further explain the health differences.

Research evidence across individual studies is fairly consistent in finding positive benefits of fruit and vegetable intake (e.g. Ness and Powles 1997; World Health Organization 2003) and a large-scale systematic review (*Cochrane Review*) of all the evidence in relation to cardiovascular morbidity and mortality, as well as all-cause mortality, is underway (Ness *et al.* 2003). The World Health Report (WHO 2002) also attributes between 3.5 and 7.6 per cent of mortality in the year 2000 to low fruit and vegetable intake, with the highest percentage being in the developed world including Europe and America, and the lowest attributable percentage being in high-mortality developing countries including many parts of Africa.

■ Recommended fruit and vegetable intake

Current recommendations are to eat five or more portions of fruit and vegetables a day (one 'portion' is defined as 80 g); however, less than 20 per cent of boys and 15 per cent of girls aged 13 to 15 were found to be doing so recently (Department of Health 1998a; Bajekal *et al.* 2003). There is also substantial evidence that adults are also not following these recommendations, particularly young adults, and males (e.g. Baker and Wardle 2003; Henderson *et al.* 2002).

In RESEARCH FOCUS we describe how changed life circumstances can influence healthy eating, with a particular focus on older men living alone.

Barriers to eating healthily

Hughes G., Bennett, K.M., Hetherington, M. (2004). Old and alone: barriers to healthy eating in older men living on their own. *Appetite*, 43: 269–76.

Background

Much of the research carried out with regards to healthy eating, focuses on young people and their food choices and eating behaviours. While this makes sense in relation to the growing prevalence of obesity (see the previous chapter) and in light of the fact that health behaviours set down in childhoood can contribute towards healthy adulthood, our society is an increasingly ageing one and therefore a greater focus on 'healthy ageing' is also fundamentally required. Loss of appetite and reduced energy is often associated with growing older but it is not an inevitable consequence, and may reflect social factors (such as experiencing a loss of interest in food caused by eating alone), physical factors (access to shops, physical mobility) or personal factors such as lack of skill. Poor nutrition has been associated with cognitive decline and increased risk of certain illnesses, for example anorexia, anaemia, and therefore in order to better support healthy ageing it is important to ascertain what motivates food choice and eating patterns. This study set out to explore these questions among a sample of older men living alone; the choice of men as the focus is justified on the basis that earlier research had shown that women of an older generation were more likely to have been the primary cook and therefore, when widowed, women tended to do better than men in terms of nutrition. Men, on the other hand, may face additional challenges on being widowed – that of learning how to maintain their diet.

Aims

The study aims to identify barriers to eating healthily among a group of men living alone. Healthy eating was investigated in terms of food choice (particularly of fruit and vegetables), energy intake and cooking skills.

Method

Older men were recruited by means of advertising in a range of community settings including sheltered housing, welfare centres, libraries. Both qualitative interviews and quantitative measures (questionnaires, food records) were employed with 39 men aged between 62 and 94 years (mean age 74.8 years). Of the sample 46 per cent were widowed, 36 per cent had never married, 15 per cent were divorced, and one man was married but alone as his wife was in care. None of the sample were currently employed (92 per cent retired). Questionnaires included measures of physical and mental health, wellbeing and mood; two 24-hour food recall questionnaires (one weekday, one weekend day); items regarding smoking and alcohol consumption; and a food frequency questionnaire administered either face-to-face or over the phone. The interviews were all tape-recorded, and questions covered:

- personal factors, i.e. living arrangements, family situation and members, occupation;
- dietary factors, i.e. perceptions of healthy diet and dietary behaviours, appetite changes and patterns (e.g. tendency to skip meals, weight or appetite change);
- diet-related activity, i.e. food and meal planning, shopping and access, use of convenience and fast food, food choices, eating out;
- eating-related activity, i.e. eating alone or not, meal timings and patterns;
- food preparation, i.e. cooking skills, home-growing of foods, domestic help.

The interview also asked the men whether they could offer any advice to other men living alone regarding healthy eating strategies.

Interview data were analysed using a combination of grounded theory (to attempt to develop a 'theory' of healthy eating among older men) and content analysis, and the quantitative data were analysed using SPSS and standard descriptives or nutritional analysis software (to ascertain caloric intake, fat, protein and carbohydrate percentages etc. from the food frequency questionnaire).

Results

The themes under which the data are presented are: health and wellbeing, energy and nutrient intake, cooking skills and fruit and vegetable intake, with all but cooking skill data being extracted from the questionnaire data, and cooking skill data coming from the interviews.

Health and wellbeing: The sample were generally in good health, with those reporting poor subjective health tending to report lowest life satisfaction. Life satisfaction itself positively associated with social engagement.

Energy and nutrient intakes: averages were calculated from the two 24-hour recall datasets. A total of 64 per cent of the men consumed less energy than recommended even when BMI, activity and age were controlled for. Most of the men had low intake of essential nutrients including calcium, magnesium, potassium and zinc; half of them had less than required Vitamin A intake and all of them had less than recommended intake of vitamin D (can be obtained also by exposure to sunshine). Only Vitamin C was about what was required for many (65 per cent of the sample). While almost half (47 per cent) reported not drinking alcohol on the recall days, there was an inevitable association between alcohol intake and energy intake for those that did.

Cooking skills: Based on interview data and on the men's interpretation of whether what they reported reflected 'poor or basic', 'adequate' or 'good' cooking skill, data were grouped and compared with the health measures. Men with 'good' cooking skills consumed more vegetables than those with poor skills, and had better physical health. Energy intake was negatively associated with cooking skills; in other words, those with poorer cooking skills take in more calories (not necessarily a good thing).

Fruit and vegetable intake: As already noted, cooking skill was related to intake of fruit and vegetables: however, only 13 per cent (5 men) consumed the recommended 5-a-day portions. Fruit and vegetable intake was associated also with greater intake of protein, and whether this is in the form of meat, fish or eggs, protein generally requires cooking. It may be therefore that cooking skill is required in order to benefit from protein and vegetable intake.

The interview data are presented in the form of quotations in order to describe participants' views of their cooking skill and food intake, and no consistent patterns emerge other than evidence of divergent knowledge regarding the 5-a-day recommendation and in attitudes to eating fruit and vegetables. The only recommendation seen to emerge is to eat a portion of fruit at breakfast.

Conclusions

This paper provides some evidence of 'unhealthy' eating among older men living alone in that intake of fruit and vegetables and their associated vitamins and minerals is low. In this regard, this paper presents findings consistent with other bodies of evidence. What the paper adds is the findings relating to cooking skills. The suggestion is that, at least in relation to vegetables, intake is low as a result of limited food preparation skills, and that conversely, energy intake is 'better' (in line with recommended daily intake) in those who can cook less well. Those men who cook less well eat more energy-dense foods but less fruit and vegetables.

continued

Somehow interventions need to 'marry' the two things together: i.e. develop cooking skills that provide high energy as well as high nutrient intakes.

While the interview data are used in the final section of the results, it is unclear how the principles of grounded theory were adhered to in that the authors seem to suggest pre-imposing themes on the interview data (where otherwise themes would emerge from the quotation data itself). It would have been interesting to have focused the paper more on the actual qualitative data in order to develop greater understanding of the material gained from the interviews. For a qualitative study (in part) the sample size is in fact very large and it is likely that a vast amount of data has not been reported here. This is frustrating in that we do not really achieve a sense of understanding regarding the motivations towards eating healthily in this population. In spite of these limitations however, this study highlights a need for cooking training in older men.

Why do people not eat sufficient fruit and vegetables?

In spite of growing public awareness of the link between eating and health, fruit and vegetables tend not to be the food of choice of many young people today. For example, the National Diet and Nutrition Survey (Food Standards Agency 2000) found that the foods most frequently consumed by British adolescents were white bread, savoury snacks (e.g. crisps), biscuits, potatoes and confectionery. Although the average vitamin intake was not deficient, intake of some minerals was low. These food preferences can in part be understood by the findings of another recent survey of British young people (Haste 2004), which found that children gave 'It tastes good' (67 per cent) and 'It fills me up' (43 per cent) as the top two reasons for their favourite food choice, above 'Because it is healthy' (22 per cent) and 'It gives me energy' (17 per cent).

Unfortunately, tasting 'good' often appears to correlate with sugar and fat content rather than with healthy food, and preconceptions exist about healthy food that can work against a person making healthy food choices. For example, 37 per cent of Haste's sample agreed with the statement 'Healthy food usually doesn't taste as good as unhealthy food'. Where do these preferences and perceptions come from?

■ Food preferences

Parents play a major role in setting down patterns of eating, food choices and leisure activities inasmuch as they develop the rules and guidelines as to what is considered appropriate behaviour. For example, parental permissiveness was associated with less healthy eating behaviour among adolescents and young adults aged 12 to 22 (Bourdeaudhuij 1997; Bourdeaudhuij and van Oost 1998). Food preferences are generally learned through socialisation within the family, with the food provided by parents to their children often setting the child's future preferences for:

- *cooking methods*: e.g. home-cooked/fresh v. ready-made/processed;
- *products*: e.g. high-fat v. low-fat, organic v. non-organic;
- *tastes*: e.g. seasoned v. bland, sweet v. sour;
- *textures*: e.g. soft–crunchy, tender–chewy;
- *food components*: e.g. red/white meat, vegetables, fruit, grains, pulses and carbohydrates.

Various interventions have targeted the fruit and vegetable intake of young people, such as the Food Dudes programme in North Wales, which targets pre-school and primary-school children (Tapper *et al.* 2003; Horne *et al.* 2004). This programme draws on established learning theory techniques of increased taste exposure to fruit and vegetables, modelling of healthy behaviour through cartoon youth characters, and reinforcement by means of child-friendly rewards (e.g. stickers, crayons) for eating the fruit and vegetables provided at snack and meal times (Lowe *et al.* 2004). Long-term effectiveness of a peer-modelling and rewards-based intervention on the fruit and vegetable consumption of inner-city children was found, with particular gains among those children who ate less fruit and vegetables at the study outset (Horne *et al.* 2004). However, an exposure-only study, a randomised controlled trial of having fruit 'tuck shops' in primary schools, did not find an increase in fruit consumption (Moore *et al.* 2000; Moore 2001), suggesting that availability alone is insufficient to motivate change.

Given the challenge of increasing fruit and vegetable intake, ISSUES below raises the question of whether supplementing a person's diet with antioxidant vitamins (vitamins A, C and E; beta-carotene; folic acid) has benefits in terms of reducing disease risk.

Plate 4.1   'We are what we eat?' The importance of providing positive norms for healthy eating in children.

Source: Bangor University, School of Psychology

Do vitamins protect us from disease?

Research has suggested that a lack of vitamins A, C and E, beta-carotene and folic acid in a person's diet plays a role in blood vessel changes that potentially contribute to heart disease, and low beta-carotene has been linked with the development of cancer. Such associations are attributed to the antioxidant properties of these vitamins (i.e. they reduce the oxidated products of metabolism which would have caused cell damage). Additionally, vitamins C and E have anti-inflammatory effects, and both inflammation and oxidation have been linked with cognitive decline and progression towards dementia. Naturally, such findings stimulate media and public interest, and taking vitamin supplements as a means of protecting one's health has become commonplace, in the USA and more recently across Europe. Vitamin supplements are a growth industry.

However, what is the evidence base as to their effectiveness? Do vitamin supplements work in the same way as vitamins contained in dietary foods do? To address the first question, the United States Preventive Services Task Force (USPSTF: an expert group formed to review research evidence in order to make informed health recommendations) conducted two large-scale reviews of studies of vitamin supplements published between 1966 and 2001. One reviewed the evidence regarding reduced risk of cardiovascular disease (USPSTF 2003) and the other reviewed evidence in relation to reduced risk of breast, lung, colon and prostate cancer (Morris and Carson 2003). They found that even well-designed randomised controlled trials comparing vitamin supplements with an identical-looking placebo pill, in terms of subsequent development of disease, were inconclusive in their findings. Worryingly, they report 'compelling evidence' that beta-carotene supplements were associated with increased lung cancer risk, and subsequent death in smokers. The reviewers noted that it tended to be poorly designed studies that claimed to have found associations between vitamin supplementation and reduced disease risk. For example, observational studies reporting reduced breast cancer risk and vitamin A intake generally failed to control for other aspects of their sample's behaviour, such as their general dietary intake or exercise behaviour. Other evidence, such as reduced risk of colon cancer among those taking folic acid supplements, was based on retrospective reports of those affected/not affected, rather than on long-term prospective follow-up studies of initially healthy individuals. Such findings therefore also need to be interpreted with caution.

In making recommendations for vitamin usage, the USPSTF concluded, with the exception of smokers not taking beta-carotene, there was little evidence of vitamins causing harm, but neither was there conclusive evidence as to their benefits in terms of reduced risk of heart disease or of many cancers, and that eating a healthy diet with these vitamins contained within the foodstuffs was the key factor rather than relying on supplements.

In terms of vitamin C and E supplements and their potential in halting cognitive decline, the evidence is more preliminary. Well-designed randomised controlled trials of those taking vitamins compared with those taking a placebo are still required (Haan 2003). However, what evidence there is has pointed to beneficial effects of vitamins C and E on the verbal fluency and verbal memory scores of healthy elderly women (both the loss of verbal fluency and short-term memory are implicated in the development of dementia). However, the benefits were found only when the vitamins were taken together, and not for either one taken separately (Grodstein *et al.* 2003). These effects are encouraging, and certainly this is an area worthy of further study, given that cognitive decline and dementias are likely to become more widespread in our society with its ageing population.

Overall, therefore, the jury remains out on whether vitamin supplements protect us from disease. Furthermore, and perhaps more importantly, evidence is emerging that some supplements may even be detrimental to the health of a specific subgroup (smokers), and we know little about dose–response effects: i.e. beyond what amount do effects become harmful?

Exercise

The physical health benefits of exercise

Exercise is generally considered as health-protective, reducing an individual's risk of developing diseases such as cardiovascular disease, Type 2 diabetes mellitus and obesity, and with some forms of cancer, including colorectal and breast cancer (Kohl 2001; Kriska 2003; World Health Organization 2002). An early pointer towards the benefits of exercise came from a longitudinal study of the lifestyles of 17,000 former graduates of Harvard University. This study reported 1,413 deaths between 1962 and 1978 and noted that significantly more deaths had occurred among those who had reported leading a sedentary life. In particular, those who exercised the equivalent of 30–35 miles running/walking a week faced half the risk of premature death of those who exercised the equivalent of five miles or less per week. Moderate exercisers were defined as exercising the equivalent of 20 miles per week, and these individuals also showed health benefits in that on average they lived two years longer than the low-exercise group (<5 mile equivalent) (Paffenbarger *et al.* 1986). A similar follow-up study of an elderly male sample (61–81 years) found that the twelve-year death rate was halved in those who walked more than two miles per day compared with those who walked less (Hakim *et al.* 1998). Furthermore, these authors found that the incidence of cancer and heart disease was also lower among those who walked more, and that this effect remained even when other common risk factors such as alcohol consumption and blood pressure were controlled for. All individuals who participated in this study were non-smokers and smoking behaviour therefore did not need to be controlled for; however, this otherwise careful study did not control for an individual's dietary behaviour, which may in part be implicated in the findings.

A review of evidence from several prospective observational studies has suggested that regular physical activity can reduce the risk of coronary heart disease associated with excessive body weight (Blair and Brodney 1999). For example, one study found that overweight individuals – a body mass index (BMI, see Chapter 3) of 25.0 or more – who were active had a lower rate of heart attacks (1.3/1,000 man years) than non-active normal weight (BMI less than 24.9) individuals (heart attack rate 5.5/1,000 man years) (Morris *et al.* 1990). Being 'fat' does not inevitably mean being 'unfit'.

Exercise is also protective against the development of osteoporosis, a disease characterised by a reduction in bone density due to calcium loss, which leads to brittle bones, a loss of bone strength and an increased risk of fractures. It is estimated that, in the UK, someone experiences a bone fracture due to osteoporotic bones every three minutes, and that one in three women and one in twelve men over the age of 50 will have this condition. Regular exercise, particularly low-impact exercise or weight-bearing exercise such as walking and dancing, is not just important to bone development in the young but is also important to the maintenance of peak levels of bone density during adulthood. Additional benefits to muscle strength, coordination and balance can be gained from resistance-strengthening exercise, which in turn can benefit older individuals by reducing the risk of falls and subsequent bone fractures.

In general, therefore, regular exercise is an accepted means of reducing one's risk of developing a range of serious health conditions; furthermore, it is associated with a significant downturn in all-cause mortality among both men (Myers *et al.* 2002) and women (Manson *et al.* 2002). There is also some suggestion that adult health and disease risk is influenced by the level of childhood activity (Hallal *et al.* 2006), although there is need for more longitudinal research to confirm the pathways through which any effects may be achieved (Mattocks *et al.* 2008).

Once a relationship between behaviour and a health outcome has been established, it is important to ask 'how' this relationship operates. In terms of exercise and reduced heart disease risk, it appears that regular performance of exercise strengthens the heart muscle and increases cardiac and respiratory efficiency; it also tends to reduce blood pressure, and people who exercise regularly have a lesser tendency to accumulate body fat (e.g. Pate *et al.* 1995; UK Health Education Authority and UK Sports Council 1992). Exercise therefore helps to maintain the balance between energy intake and energy output and works to protect physical health in a variety of ways; it has also been shown to have benefits on psychological wellbeing.

The psychological benefits of exercise

prosocial behaviour
behavioural acts that are positively valued by society and that may elicit positive social consequences, e.g. offering sympathy, helping others.

Exercise has repeatedly been associated with psychological benefits in terms of elevated mood among clinical populations (e.g. those suffering from depression: Glenister 1996) and decreased risk of anxiety, depression and low self-esteem or body-image among non-clinical populations (Lox *et al.* 2006). It is not simply that regular exercise brings about such long-term benefits to mood as a result of improved body-image or increased physical fitness. Single episodes or limited-frequency aerobic exercise also has benefits, for example upon mood, self-esteem and **prosocial behaviour** (Biddle *et al.* 2000; Lox *et al.* 2006). These psychological benefits of exercise have been attributed to various biological mechanisms, including:

■ exercise-induced release of the body's own natural opiates into the blood stream, which produce a 'natural high' and act as a painkiller;

■ stimulation of the release of **catecholamines** such as **noradrenaline** and **adrenaline**, which counter any stress response and enhance mood (Chapters 8 and 12);

■ muscle relaxation, which reduces feelings of tension.

However, the relationship between exercise and positive mood states is perhaps not as simple as these biological routes suggest. For example, evidence exists of an inverse relationship between exercise intensity and adherence, whereby individuals are less likely to maintain intense exercise than moderate exercise, possibly because it is experienced as adversive (Brewer *et al.* 2000). This suggestion that, beyond a certain level, exercise may in fact be detrimental to mood has been explored further by Hall *et al.* (2002). They examined the affective response of thirty volunteers to increasing levels of exercise intensity and found not only that intense exercise caused negative mood but also that the timing of mood assessments (pre- and post-exercise assessment, compared with repeated assessment during exercise) profoundly changed the nature of the relationship found between exercise and mood. Studies measuring mood before exercise, and again after exercise has ended and the person has recovered, generally report positive affective responses. However, Hall and colleagues' data clearly show considerable mood deterioration as exercise intensity increases, with mood rising to more positive levels only on exercise completion. These authors propose that remembering the negative affective response experienced during exercise is likely to impair an individual's future adherence, and that this may explain why some studies report poor exercise adherence rates. These interesting findings suggest that methodological factors play a role in whether or not exercise is associated with positive mood. Additionally, other factors such as cognitive distraction or actual physical removal from life's problems, or social support gained from exercising with friends, may further combine with biological factors to influence the affective experience reported. Even the exercise environment itself can play a role in mood outcomes, such as room temperature, the presence and type of music, and the presence of mirrors – the latter being associated with negative wellbeing (Martin Ginis *et al.* 2007). Mood is a complex phenomenon!

Moderate regular exercise appears to offer various routes to wellbeing. For some individuals, self-image and self-esteem may be enhanced as a result of exercise contributing to weight loss and control. Rightly or wrongly, we live in a society where trim figures are judged more positively (by others as well as by ourselves) than those that are considered to be overweight. Another potential route to wellbeing may be seen in those who use exercise as a means of coping with stress. Exercise for these individuals may act as a positive distraction from negative and stressful appraisals, or as time out from work or other demands. During exercise, a person may focus on aspects of the physical exertion or on the heart-rate monitor, they may distract themselves by listening to music or planning a holiday, or they may use the time to think through current stressors or demands and plan their coping responses (see Chapter 12). Finally, exercise can have psychological benefits for those experiencing cognitive decline as a result of ageing or dementia. Cotman and Engesser-Cesar (2002) recently reported that physical activity

catecholamines
these chemical substances are brain neurotransmitters and include adrenaline and noradrenaline.

noradrenaline
this catecholamine is a neurotransmitter found in the brain and in the **sympathetic nervous system**. Also known as norepinephrine.

adrenaline
a neurotransmitter and hormone secreted by the adrenal medulla that increases physiological activity in the body, including stimulation of heart action and an increase in blood pressure and metabolic rate. Also known as epinephrine.

was associated with delays in the age-related neuronal dysfunction and degeneration that underlies the types of cognitive decline often associated with Alzheimer's disease, such as memory lapses and not paying attention.

In summary, engaging in regular physical activity is considered to be beneficial for both physical and psychological health, and possibly even for survival, but as with much behaviour, it may be that moderation is required.

The negative consequences of exercise

Paradoxically, excessive reliance on exercise to the extent that exercise becomes a compulsion and produces dependence (evidenced by, for example, experience of withdrawal effects, guilt and irritability when an exercise period is missed) is also an area of investigation by health psychologists (e.g. Hausenblaus and Symons Downs 2002; Ogden et al. 1997). Experimental studies have shown that depriving regular exercisers of exercise can lead to reductions in mood and to irritability (e.g. review by Biddle and Murtrie 1991), with mood restored when exercise is reinstated. The long-term physical consequences of excessive exercising relate to muscle wastage and weight loss rather than to any specific disease; however, these findings are a reminder that moderate levels of behaviour – even behaviour considered health-protective – are better than extreme levels.

Recommendations to exercise

Specific recommendations regarding physical activity suggest at least 30 minutes of moderate intensity exercise on at least 5 days of each week (e.g. Department of Health 2004; US Department of Health and Human Services 1996). The aim of such guidelines is to set activity targets with the potential to reduce blood pressure and the incidence of diabetes, osteoporosis, coronary heart disease and obesity, as well as improving general wellbeing. Guidelines are not intended to be set so high as to be beyond the reach of the average individual, and certainly the advice for a previously inactive individual is to build up their exercise levels gradually, rather than making dramatic changes to both the frequency and intensity of exercise performance. Furthermore, where a pre-existing health complaint exists, plans to become more active should first be discussed with a medical professional.

In spite of obvious health benefits and active campaigning on the part of many health authorities and the media to encourage people of all ages to become more active, exercise levels in some parts of Europe remain low. However, it may be that levels lower than national guidelines can also obtain benefit: for example, a large-scale study of almost 40,000 healthy females aged over 45 concluded that the minimum level of exercise required to reduce heart disease risk may be as little as 20–60 minutes of purposeful walking per week (Lee et al. 2001).

■ Levels of exercise

Only about 45 per cent of the British adult population do some form of exercise at least once a month, and Norman et al. (1998) estimated that only about 25 per cent of this population exercise with sufficient regularity to obtain any protective effects of exercise behaviour. This pattern is not only evident in Britain: for example, a survey conducted across twenty-one European countries found that approximately one-third of 18–30-year-olds did not engage in regular physical activity (Steptoe *et al.* 1997). Gender and age differences have also been reported, with women generally found to be more inactive than men, and older women being less active than younger women (e.g. Stephenson *et al.* 2000). Further evidence of an age effect on participation in regular physical activity was reported by Skelton *et al.* (1999), who found that while 18 per cent of men and 20 per cent of women aged 50–54 were participating in activity at least once a week, only 9 per cent of men and 4 per cent of women aged 80 or more were doing so. The proportions exercising to a level that would be likely to produce health benefits is significantly less again.

Many surveys simply compare people who are under 65 years of age and those over 65, thus data on the behaviour of the 'very old' (i.e. 85+) are limited. Exercise behaviour is likely to be influenced by factors such as current health status and physical functioning, access to facilities, and even personal safety concerns (in terms of walking alone). There is evidence that longevity is predicted by the extent to which a person is physically active. For example, Hakim and colleagues (Hakim *et al.* 1998) followed a cohort of 61–81-year-old men over a period of twelve years and monitored the amount of walking they did. Men who walked more than two miles a day lived significantly longer than those who walked less (21.5 per cent died over the 12 years, compared with 43 per cent).

The prevalence of inactivity is also high in younger samples. For example:

- The National Diet and Nutrition Survey (2000) estimated that 40 per cent of boys and 60 per cent of girls surveyed in the UK were not meeting national recommendations (see above).

- A World Health Organization study of 162,000 young people aged 11, 13 and 15 in thirty-five countries across Europe and North America found that only 35 per cent of 15-year-old boys and only 22 per cent of girls engage in at least one hour of moderate or heavier exercise five days a week, with huge geographical as well as gender differences (www.euro.who.int) (see Figure 4.1).

As illustrated above, many large-scale studies report a gender difference in exercise frequency, with boys generally found to be more active from an early age than girls, and with differences being maintained through adolescence. Cultural differences in the frequency of physical activity have also been reported. For example, the activity levels of Bangladeshi, Indian, Pakistani and Chinese men and women aged over 55 living in the UK was lower than levels reported by white respondents (Joint Health Surveys Unit 2001). Various studies have identified common clusters of reasons for choosing to exercise or not to exercise, although the extent to which this evidence is used to usefully inform intervention programmes has been questioned (e.g. Brunton *et al.* 2003).

Why do people exercise?

People who choose to exercise cite a variety of reasons for doing so, including, most commonly:

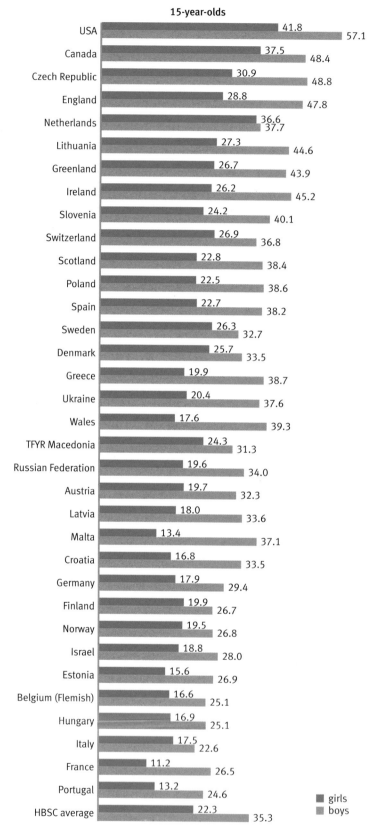

Figure 4.1 Proportion of 15-year-olds across a selection of thirty-five countries who engage in recommended exercise levels (at least one hour of moderate or higher-intensity activity on five or more days per week).

Source: WHO (2004); www.euro.who.int

- desire for physical fitness
- desire to lose weight, change body shape and appearance
- desire to maintain or enhance health status
- desire to improve self-image and mood
- as a means of stress reduction
- as a social activity.

However, it is not to be inferred that choosing *not* to exercise reflects an absence of the types of desire and goals listed above. Many perceived barriers exist that contribute to people's reasons for not exercising, even when they simultaneously report, for example, a desire to lose weight. Barriers commonly mentioned include:

- lack of time
- cost
- lack of access to appropriate facilities and equipment
- embarrassment
- lack of self-belief
- lack of someone to go with to provide support.

Differences have been found in the beliefs and attitudes towards exercise held by those who are active and those who are not active. For example, individuals who exercise regularly are more likely to perceive positive outcomes of exercise than those who do not; perceive fewer barriers to exercising, and believe that exercising is under their own control. These individual health cognitions are discussed in more detail in Chapter 6. There is also some evidence that parental activity during a child's younger years (when child is approximately 2 years old) has a modest effect on increased child activity by the age of 11–12, thus suggesting a role for parental modelling and some scope for parental intervention (Mattocks *et al.* 2008).

Health-screening behaviour

There are two broad purposes of health screening:

1. to detect early asymptomatic signs of disease in order to treat;
2. identification of risk factors for illness to enable behaviour change.

What do YOU think?

What type of health screening behaviour do you engage in? Do you attend dental check-ups? Do you attend even when you have had six months without any symptoms of tooth decay? If not, consider your reasons for not doing so. If you receive a 'clean bill of health', how do you feel? Do you change the way you look after your teeth at all due to feeling reassured that they are 'healthy'?

Do you engage in any form of self-examination (breasts, testes)? If so, what made you start doing this? What would influence whether or not you would go to your doctor if you found something atypical?

Screening for disease detection

Screening for the purpose of disease detection is based on a biomedical model, which states that by identifying abnormalities in cell or organ functioning, treatments can be implemented prior to the onset or advancement of disease symptoms. This is basically secondary prevention in that a specific screening test is offered to individuals identified as being at moderate to high risk of a certain condition on the basis of factors such as family history or age. The best-known examples of this form of screening are:

- screening for breast cancer (mammography);
- screening for cervical cancer (cervical smear or Pap test);
- antenatal screening, e.g. for Down's syndrome or spina bifida;
- bone density screening.

Screening programmes for breast and cervical cancer are based on the fact that incidence of the former is high, and early treatment can reduce 40 per cent of the associated mortality, and although cervical cancer is less common (it is about the eighth most common form of cancer in women), the mortality rate associated with untreated cancer of the cervix is high. Cervical cancer is in fact the top-ranked cancer in females under the age of 35, with regular 'smear tests' (Pap tests) being advocated from early adulthood. Most Western countries have a programme of routine invitation of adult women to cervical screening every five years, with older women (aged 60 or over) being invited every three years in some countries. Antenatal procedures such as amniocentesis also screen for disease by checking whether maternal serum alphafoetoprotein levels are indicative of spina bifida or Down's syndrome. In this instance, screening is routinely offered, at least in the UK, to pregnant women over the age of 30. If screening proves positive, there are no treatment options, but rather decisions to be made regarding continuation or termination of the pregnancy. Another example of screening for disease detection is most common among middle-aged women (and men) and consists of screening to check for signs of bone density deterioration and osteoporosis. In this case, an individual receiving a result indicating early signs of bone disease can take action in terms of increased calcium intake or increased weight-bearing exercise.

Screening for risk factors

The second broad purpose of screening, that of screening for risk factors in those individuals thought to be healthy, is based on the principle of susceptibility. This form of screening aims to identify an individual's personal level of risk for future illness (and in the case of genetic testing, also in their offspring) in order to offer advice and information as to how to minimise further health risk, or to plan further investigation and treatment. Examples of this form of screening include:

- screening for cardiovascular risk (cholesterol and blood pressure assessment and monitoring);
- eye tests to screen for diabetes, glaucoma or myopia;

- genetic testing for carrier status of the Huntington's disease gene, or for breast or colon cancer;
- prenatal genetic testing;
- antenatal screening.

Bearing testimony to the importance of primary prevention, some community or worksite-based programmes offer blood pressure and cholesterol testing, along with an assessment of lifestyle factors and family history of heart disease. These measures and assessments generate an index of general susceptibility, or personal 'risk score' related to potential morbidity. For example, if a person's risk of disease is thought to be moderate or high, preventive measures can be suggested, such as dietary change or smoking cessation. In order for screening to be of public health (societal) benefit as well as benefit to the individual, many of those identified as at risk of future disease would be required to change their behaviour. It will become evident in later chapters that predicting behaviour change is highly complex (Chapter 5), and thus interventions to change individuals' risk behaviour face many challenges (Chapters 6 and 7).

■ Genetic screening

One particular form of risk factor screening deserving of further mention is that of screening for genetic susceptibility. With advances in the diagnostic technology for carrier status of genes predisposing to a range of conditions, such as breast cancer (e.g. genes BRCA1 and BRCA2) (see Sivell *et al.* 2007 for a review) or obesity (e.g. gene MC4R) brought about by programmes of scientific research such as the Human Genome Project, screening has perhaps become more controversial. Stone and Stewart (1996: 4) state: 'the benefits of large-scale genetic screening to individuals, families or society as a whole remain largely theoretical. There is scant evidence to support the view that the public at large perceives a need for carrier screening'. A decade later, and, in contrast, Braithwaite *et al.* (2002) conclude from their review of studies pertaining to specific genetic testing for hereditary cancer that between 60 and 80 per cent of the general population samples studied report high levels of interest in such tests. Family history of cancer generally takes interest levels to around 80 per cent, and, as found with screening generally, interest is frequently found to be higher among more educated samples with greater income (e.g. Lerman *et al.* 1996).

Griffith *et al.* (2008) recently examined whether healthy adults formed an interest in, or intention to seek, genetic testing for breast cancer on the basis of the perceived pros and cons of such testing. Making decisions in this way is sometimes referred to as 'utility maximisation': i.e. it is assumed that a person weighs up the pros and cons of a choice and then selects the option that provides them either with the greatest perceived benefit, or alternatively, the least undesirable consequences. To test whether or not utility maximisation does occur, this study used an experimental design to manipulate the understanding of genetic testing among 142 undergraduate students. Information about testing was provided in three different ways: Positive information only, Positive followed by Negative; Negative follwed by Positive. A fourth group acted as a control and this group received information irrelevant to the genetic-testing decision questions. Pre- and post-manipulation assessments were taken regarding the perceived pros and cons of testing, and the interest in, and likelihood of, testing. The experimental information was found to influence the ratio of pros to cons, although the direction of change was not consistent with the ordering of the information: i.e. provision of positive information only did not increase the weighting of pros in relation to cons. Likewise, the information provision manipulation significantly changed the interest in, and likelihood of, testing reported, but again the ordering did not have the expected effect. Finally, these authors report a non-significant association between the weighted ratio of pros–cons and the post-manipulation interest and likelihood scores. This finding suggests that utility maximisation was *not* occurring and that models of decision making need to look beyond simply the pros and cons of behaviour. This can be seen in the many models of behaviour and health behaviour utilised by health psychologists and these are covered in detail in the next chapter.

What do YOU think?	What does it mean when a person has been tested for carrier status of a particular gene? Do you know? It has been found that the general public commonly do not understand the issues of heritability, recessive genes or gene penetrance. There is an obvious and growing need for education and information about these very issues as more and more genes are identified that predispose us to various diseases.
	What thoughts do you have about genetic testing? Write down a list of pros and cons, for example in relation to breast or prostate cancer testing. Consider what your decision may be if testing were to become more widely available.

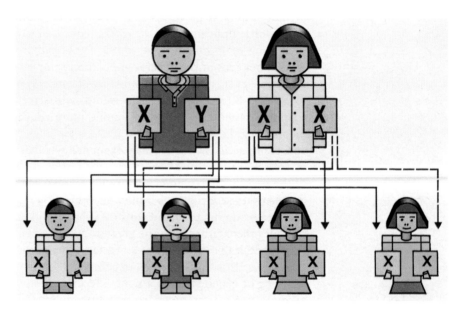

Figure 4.2   A genetic family tree.
Source: © Dorling Kindersley

The costs and benefits of screening

While screening programmes for both disease detection and risk factor status have proliferated, questions remain as to whether there are as many benefits to the individuals undergoing screening as there are to wider society. Furthermore, some findings call into question whether the benefits of screening – in terms of eliciting behaviour change that reduces disease risk to the individual, or in terms of enabling early disease symptoms to be treated and subsequently the threat of disease progression to be reduced or removed – justify the financial costs of implementing large-scale screening programmes.

In order to try to maximise the benefits of screening to both the individual and to society, some researchers have set out what they consider to be necessary criteria for effective screening programmes.

■ Criteria for establishing screening programmes

Austoker (1994: 315) describes several criteria on which the introduction of screening programmes aimed at early detection of prostrate, ovarian and testicular cancer should be based. These criteria can usefully be applied to all forms of screening for disease detection, and many also apply to genetic testing:

- The condition should be an important health problem: i.e. prevalent and/or serious.
- There should be a recognisable early stage to the condition.
- Treatment at an early stage should have clear benefits to the individual (e.g. reduced mortality) compared with treatment at a later stage.
- A suitable test with good **sensitivity** and **specificity** should be available.
- The test should be considered acceptable by the general population.
- Adequate facilities for diagnosis and treatment should be in place.
- Issues of screening frequency and follow-up should be agreed.
- The costs (individual and health care) should be considered in relation to the benefits (individual and public health).
- Any particular subgroups to target should be identified.

sensitivity (of a test) the probability that a test is correctly positive or correctly negative; for example, a sensitive test may have 95 per cent success in detecting a disease among patients known to have that disease, and 95 per cent success in not detecting a disease among disease-free individuals.

specificity (of a test) the likelihood that a test will produce a few false positive results and a few false negatives; i.e. does not produce a positive result for a negative case, and vice versa.

However, it is difficult to conclude whether some screening programmes meet the criteria of benefits outweighing costs, one of Austoker's listed criteria. For example, while public health, disease prevention and detection concerns are being addressed by screening, it is important not to lose sight of the individual. Marteau and Kinmouth (2002: 78) note that:

> a traditional public health approach to screening regards the population benefits of reduced morbidity and mortality as inherent, not to be appraised by individuals before they decide whether or not to participate. In keeping with this, the information accompanying the invitation (to screening) tends to be brief, emphasising the general health benefits of participation.

This suggests that informed choice procedures (where the individual is fully informed prior to making a decision) are not being fully implemented at present. These authors go on to note that providing opportunities for fully informed choice would require informing potential patients about the possible adverse outcomes of screening and the limited prognostic benefits of some treatments (if any are available) for some individuals. This may affect the uptake of screening by some of those who would in fact have benefited from early detection and treatment.

In the case of genetic testing, for example to identify whether an individual carries the gene that predisposes towards the development of Huntington's disease (an adult-onset disease), there is actually nothing that can be done to change the individual's risk, and therefore some question the value of screening other than preparing the individual for their future. In contrast, some individuals, when identified as carrying the BRCA1 or BRCA2 gene for breast cancer, opt for prophylactic surgery (i.e. breast removal) in order that disease cannot manifest itself (Kauff *et al.* 2002; Lerman *et al.* 2000).

It is obviously difficult to control where individuals receive health information from: for example, individuals considering any form of health screening will not approach solely health professionals for information. In the EU, for example, an average of 23 per cent of the population will use the Internet for health information, and in some countries, such as Denmark, that figure doubles (Jørgensen and Gøtzsche 2004). Jørgensen and Gøtzsche undertook a large-scale review of the nature of information about breast cancer screening mammography presented on the websites of international and national organisations. They found that in many cases the information was unbalanced and biased towards screening uptake, and provided limited clear information as to the possibility of false positive and false negative results and as to the adverse effects of screening, such as over-diagnosis and over-treatment. Few websites informed readers of the limited evidence of a reduction in risk of mortality in those screened compared with unscreened individuals (which is in fact only about 0.1 per cent reduction in relative risk of breast cancer over ten years). Overstating the benefits of screening, or understating potential risks or adverse consequences of screening, is not providing the individual with fully informed choice.

If any shift in policy towards shared decision making and fully informed patient choice takes place in the screening domain, it will be essential for the effects of this on the individual (in terms of emotional and behavioural consequences) to be fully evaluated.

In spite of limitations such as those described above, screening is a growing part of preventive medicine across the industrialised world, with genetic testing becoming the 'hot issue' for the twenty-first century. Some types of screening form long-term goals of public health, such as mass screening for the gene for cystic fibrosis among couples during pregnancy (Stone and Stewart 1996). Screening, for whatever risk factor or disease, is not as yet compulsory, and therefore the generally low level of uptake of screening opportunities plays an important part in whether people go on to develop diseases that they may have been able to avoid or reduce their risk of developing.

As shown, health screening covers many conditions across the lifespan, and in relation to the procedures and conditions described above, generally involves an individual attending a screening appointment. However, other forms of health screening exist that rely on an individual performing the screening themselves.

Self-screening behaviour

Self-examination behaviour is most commonly advocated and studied in relation to early detection of breast cancer, although testicular self-examination and skin self-examination are now getting more attention. Among women, breast cancer is the most common cause of cancer death (although the incidence of lung cancer in women is growing), and despite increasing numbers of screening programmes available in health-care settings, up to 90 per cent of all breast cancers are first detected through self-examination. While health campaigns have attempted to promote self-examination behaviour, there has in fact been some controversy over the efficacy of breast self-examination. One study contributing to this controversy is a large, ten-year study carried out in Shanghai, China (Thomas *et al.* 2002), which is described in RESEARCH FOCUS below.

Among men, testicular cancer is the most frequently occurring form of cancer and the second leading cause of death among those aged 15 to 35. Surviving testicular cancer is possible in 95–100 per cent of cases if the disease is detected early; however, over 50 per cent of cases present to health professionals after the early, treatable, stage has passed.

Likewise, skin cancer incidence is also increasing, particularly in those aged 20 to 40, yet early detection of skin lesions through self-examination can lead to high cure rates (McCarthy and Shaw 1989; Eiser *et al.* 1993).

In spite of rising incidence of skin cancer, Ness *et al.* (1999) have noted that 'lay epidemiology' (i.e. the general perception within society) considers sun exposure to be healthy, and that in some instances this may be correct (e.g. positive effect of sun exposure on wellbeing and mood, on vitamin D production and bone strengthening). This presents a challenge to health educators who draw on some evidence of associations between sun exposure and malignant melanoma in an attempt to increase sun protection behaviours (e.g. use of sunscreen, avoidance of sunbeds) from an early age. In Australia, where the majority of studies on skin self-examination and skin protection behaviour have originated, the incidence of skin cancer is high. It might therefore be expected that skin protection behaviour, as well as skin examination, is normative; however, while evidence points to increased prevalence of such behaviours, health education interventions generally have short-lived effects (Aitken *et al.* 2006). There is also some evidence of gender differences in tanning behaviours, with, for example, female British students being more prepared to protect their skin than males while also placing higher value on sun-bathing (Eiser *et al.* 1993). Such differences suggests that any interventions address the value placed on a particular 'risk behaviour', as this will likely affect the effectiveness of intervention (see the previous chapter for the same point in relation to smoking behaviour).

Is self-examination an effective means of disease detection?

Thomas, D.B., Gao, D.L., Ray, R.M. *et al.* (2002). Randomized trial of breast self-examination in Shanghai – final results. *Journal of the National Cancer Institute*, 94: 1445–57.

Background

While breast self-examination (BSE) is acknowledged as increasing the detection of cancerous tissue in the breast at an early, treatable stage, the evidence as to subsequent increases in survival among those who have tumours detected and treated following BSE is mixed. Therefore the aim of this study was to conduct a randomised trial of an intervention where BSE was either taught or not taught, and examine whether reduced breast cancer mortality could be found in those instructed in, and practising, BSE.

Methods

Participants

A total of 289,392 women born between 1925 and 1958 working in textile factories across Shanghai were recruited in 1988 (i.e. aged 30 and over). Over 22,000 were subsequently excluded due to changes in their circumstances, mental or physical illness, refusal, death, omitted baseline questionnaire, or due to having a history of breast cancer (1,336 individuals). The final sample was therefore 266,064.

Design

Factories were randomised to being recruiting centres for either the intervention group (IG) or the control group (CG); in this way, 132,979 participants were allocated to the IG and 133,085 to the CG.

Measures

Proficiency in performing BSE was assessed in a random sample of over 2,400 women in the IG and CG, where the women had to demonstrate breast cancer examination techniques on silicone breast models that had a varying number of lumps to detect. Women also reported the frequency of their own BSE practice.

Procedure

Members of the IG were instructed in when and how best to perform breast self-examination in groups of ten individuals taught by specially trained medical workers. Techniques were demonstrated, practised and discussed. Reinforcement sessions took place after one and three years; actual BSE practice was conducted under medical supervision every three months in Year 1 and then every six months in Years 2–5; and participants received regular reminders at work and at home. In stark contrast, the CG participants received no instruction or information on BSE, but concurrent with the IG's second reinforcement session they received an education session on the prevention of lower back pain (to provide a health focus for these participants that may enhance continued participation).

Follow-up procedures were rigorous, using factory medical workers who collated reports of breast lump detection and referred women with confirmed lumps to hospital surgeons for evaluation. The medical decisions (regarding biopsy, further referrals, diagnosis and treatment) were all recorded. Hospital staff were unaware of which arm of the trial women were in (i.e. blind). The medical records of women with confirmed breast tumours – both benign and malignant – were examined by trained medical staff. Details of the size and spread of malignant tumours, and whether the lymph nodes were implicated (which indicates potential for spread), were recorded.

Deaths up to the end of 2000 were identified from clinical records and regional death registers, and where this failed to provide an up-to-date status, women's homes were visited. Death from breast cancer was defined as one that would not have occurred at the time it did in the absence of the breast cancer.

Results

Analysis took baseline demographic (e.g. age, alcohol and tobacco consumption) and breast cancer risk factors (e.g. number and age of pregnancies, age of menopause, family history of breast cancer) into account and found no differences between those women in the IG and those in the CG. Furthermore, unlike in many other countries, Chinese factory workers are constrained in their choice of hospital – each factory provides primary medical care and refers on, where necessary, to a specific hospital under contract with that factory. There were no effects of hospital in terms of the baseline risk factors of the women in the IG or the CG, and the groups shared affiliations with the same hospitals; thus diagnostic and treatment facilities available to each group were comparable.

Women in the IG had good levels of competence in performing BSE, although it did decline over time. The IG women also found a higher proportion of breast lumps than those in the CG, although the numbers of cancers diagnosed were similar in both groups for each year of the trial after the first year. However, the IG women who detected lumps subsequently found to be malignant did not detect them at a sufficiently less advanced stage to confer an advantage in terms of treatments likely to enhance survival. The study did not find any significant effects of BSE on survival over a 10–11-year period, and an identical percentage of women developed breast cancer and died in each group (0.10 per cent).

Discussion

While the authors report greater detection of lumps in the breast by women in the BSE IG, a higher number of these lumps were found to be benign. The finding of more lumps, which resulted in an increased number of biopsies (many for lumps subsequently found to be benign), has extensive cost implications.

The authors conclude that BSE is unlikely to reduce breast cancer mortality, and as a result of these and similar earlier findings, breast self-examination recommendations have generally been minimised, although some authorities still promote the practice (e.g. the American Cancer Society).

Conclusion

This is a well-conducted, large-scale study that gives ample consideration to factors that may have influenced the results by means of rigorous examination of clinical and contextual data and by impressive follow-up procedures. However, one limitation is that the data pertaining to the frequency of BSE practice are limited and lacking in specificity (most simply reported 'monthly' BSE) and it is therefore unclear just how frequently the IG were in fact performing BSE outwith the actual supervised sessions. Therefore the conclusion is more that the *teaching* of BSE had no survival benefits, and that further study is needed where frequency is more rigorously assessed. For other researchers to obtain such a sample size and such commitment to long-term follow-up as Thomas and colleagues' report will be quite a challenge.

Uptake of screening behaviour

Psychology, particularly health and social psychology, has a large part to play in helping to identify predictors of the uptake of screening programmes, such as individual attitudes and beliefs about illness, about screening, and about preventive behaviour. While the increasing availability of screening programmes for many diseases and disease risk factors seems to have increased uptake, generally uptake remains at a lower level than is considered optimal in terms of disease reduction at a societal level.

■ Factors associated with screening behaviour

A range of factors have been found to be associated with the non-uptake of screening opportunities or self-examination behaviour, including:

- lower levels of education and income;
- age (e.g. younger women tend not to attend risk-factor screening);
- lack of knowledge about the condition;
- lack of knowledge about the purpose of screening;
- lack of knowledge about potential outcomes of screening;
- embarrassment regarding the procedures involved;
- fear that 'something bad' will be detected;
- fear of pain or discomfort during the procedure;
- lack of self-belief (self-efficacy, see Chapter 5) in terms of being able to practise self-examination correctly.

In terms of self-screening behaviour, knowledge of testicular cancer and the practice of self-examination have generally been found to be at a low level. Studies of breast self-examination have found that even among women who do perform it, many do not do so correctly (i.e. it should ideally be carried out mid-menstrual cycle, in an upright position as well as when lying down, and should include examination of all tissue in the breast, nipple and under-arm areas). Worryingly, a recent study (Steadman and Quine 2004) confirmed low levels of knowledge among young adult males about testicular cancer and also found low levels of knowledge regarding the potential benefits of self-examination. This study went on to demonstrate that a simple intervention, which required half of the participants to write down and visualise when, where and how they would self-examine their testes over the forthcoming three weeks, led to a significantly higher proportion of them self-examining than that found in the control group who did not form such plans. This study demonstrates the relative ease with which behaviour can be changed, although a longer-term follow-up would be beneficial to check whether self-examination practices were maintained beyond the study period. This intervention focused specifically on making an individualised plan for action, referred to in health psychology as forming an 'implementation intention'. This construct, and further research supporting its practical utility in developing interventions, is described in the next chapter.

Immunisation behaviour

The purpose of immunisation

antigen
unique process found on the surface of a pathogen that enables the immune system to recognise that pathogen as a foreign substance and therefore produce antibodies to fight it. Vaccinations introduce specially prepared viruses or bacteria into a body, and these have antigens.

Vaccination is the oldest form of immunisation, in which immunity is provided to an individual by introducing a small amount of an **antigen** into their body (either orally, intramuscularly or intradermally (injecting into the skin)), which triggers off the development of antibodies to that specific antigen. Some vaccinations, such as orally administered polio vaccine, measles, mumps and rubella, use live components, while others, such as hepatitis B, use inactivated components. Vaccinations against infectious disease have been credited with the virtual eradication of diseases that in previous centuries caused widespread morbidity and mortality, such as smallpox, diptheria and polio (e.g. Woolf 1996). Public health specialists consider vaccines both safe and successful and at least in developed countries, the incidence of many common, predominantly childhood diseases, such as measles, is low. However, infectious diseases still account for approximately seventeen million deaths in developing countries and half a million deaths in industrialised countries (BMA 2003a). Although immunisation is offered to various subgroups in the population, such as influenza vaccination to the elderly or to those with pre-existing conditions that increase their vulnerability to infection (e.g. asthma), the main emphasis of immunisation is on the prevention of childhood disease. It is policy in the UK to advise parents to immunise their child, as shown in Table 4.1.

Public health policy is to provide vaccinations that provide long-lasting protection against specific disease without adverse consequences to the individual, and with the costs of providing the vaccination being outweighed by the costs of having to treat the disease if no vaccination were to be provided.

Human papillomavirus (HPV)
a family of over 100 viruses, of which 30 types can cause genital warts and be transmitted by sexual contact. While most genital HPV come and go over the course of a few years, some HPV infections may markedly elevate the risk for cancer of the cervix.

Table 4.1   Immunisation policy in the United Kingdom*

Age	Vaccine	Means of administration
2–4 months	polio	by mouth combined injection injection
12–15 months 3–5 years	measles, mumps and rubella (MMR) polio	combined injection by mouth combined injection
10–14 years 15–18 years	measles, mumps and rubella (MMR) rubella (girls) tetanus booster	combined injection injection injection

*HPV: from September 2008 the UK government will initiate a vaccination programme which requires three injections over a 6-month period for girls aged 12–13 years old, on the basis that the vaccinations need to be given before sexual activity commences. A 'catch-up' programme in 2009/10 will target 15–17-year-olds. The vaccination will be made available in secondary schools.

Plate 4.2 Immunisation behaviour is crucial to public health, yet is influenced by many cultural, social, emotional and cognitive factors. Here, a queue of mothers take up the first opportunity of vaccination for their child against measles to be offered in their village.
Source: Jacob Silberberg/Getty

However, immunisation coverage varies in different parts of the world, and even in different regions within countries; there is growing concern that some diseases, such as whooping cough and measles, may re-emerge as uptake has not reached saturation level.

Costs and benefits of immunisation

Over the last century, the widescale benefits of childhood vaccination programmes have become apparent. It is now rare for a child living in the Western world, and increasingly in developing countries where vaccination programmes are being promoted, to die from measles, diphtheria or polio. The World Health Organization had set a target for almost universal vaccination by 2000, and in 1997 there were high hopes of achieving population immunity against measles, at least in Britain, with uptake a reported 97 per cent (Bellaby 2003).

However, widespread publicity following a 1998 study that reported adverse effects of the combined MMR vaccination has largely been 'credited' with the downturn in immunisation uptake, caused by a lack of public confidence. The public debate about vaccine safety has spread generally but has been at its most vociferous in relation to the MMR vaccine, originally introduced in 1988. This is addressed below, IN THE SPOTLIGHT.

While socio-economic variables such as low educational attainment have been found to influence the uptake of vaccination (e.g. New and Senior 1991;

and see Chapter 2) so too do emotional and cognitive variables. For example, Bennett and Smith (1992) studied the vaccination status of 300 children aged 2 to 2½ in Wales and found that those parents who did not have their child vaccinated exhibited anxiety about the risks of vaccination as well as low perceptions of the potential benefits of vaccination. Beliefs such as these and the research evidence as to their utility in explaining health behaviour are examined in Chapter 5.

IN THE SPOTLIGHT

Immunisation debate and the MMR vaccination

In order to achieve population immunity, the required uptake of a measles vaccine is between 92 and 95 per cent (BMA 2003b). The figure for 2001 uptake of the MMR (measles, mumps and rubella combined vaccine) in the UK was below 90 per cent, which signifies a drop of several per cent. In Scotland, MMR coverage dropped from 93.2 per cent in 2000 to 88.5 per cent in 2001, whereas the level of MenC (meningitis C) uptake was 93.7 per cent. Why is one immunisation being taken up less commonly than another? It is likely that this is in part due to differing perceptions of the illnesses concerned (meningitis is almost universally feared, whereas measles may be considered a less serious illness); in part due to the manner in which health professionals advocate the different vaccines (e.g. New and Senior 1991) and in part due to the nature of publicity attracted by the different diseases/vaccines.

Concerns about immunisation and vaccination are not new, but over recent years debate has raged in relation to the suggested link between the measles, mumps and rubella (MMR) vaccine and autism, and to a lesser degree (at least in terms of publicity) inflammatory bowel disease (IBD). Media concerns have a tendency to become public and parental concerns, and as a result a significant decline in the percentage of children immunised against these diseases has been witnessed.

What stimulated the media debate?
Wakefield *et al.* (1998) published a paper in the highly respected medical journal, *The Lancet*, which speculated that there may be a link between MMR vaccine and autism and/or IBD on the basis of their finding that among twelve children referred for gastroenterological investigation, nine manifested varying degrees of behavioural problems that had received autistic spectrum diagnoses. In eight cases, parents attributed the onset of behavioural symptoms to a time following the MMR vaccine. However, this study was seriously limited by its small sample size, and the link was only speculative, but the media did not address these weaknesses. Many other larger-scale studies have followed Wakefield *et al.*'s, such as Peltola *et al.*'s (1998) study, which found no evidence of a link between MMR, autism and inflammatory bowel disease in spite of conducting a fourteen-year prospective study; or Taylor *et al.*'s (1999) study, which reviewed 500 children with autism born between 1979 and 1994 and found no sudden increase in autism cases associated with the introduction of the MMR vaccine in 1988 and no difference in the age of autism diagnosis between those who had been immunised and those who had not (Taylor *et al.* 1999). Taylor and colleagues more recently confirmed these findings in a population study conducted in five health districts in England (Taylor *et al.* 2002).

continued

In spite of ongoing media debate, there is therefore little current evidence to support a link. The current stance of the World Health Organization and thus the medical authorities elsewhere is that there is no link between MMR and autism or IBD as evidenced by methodologically valid studies.

However, parental fears remain, along with some cynicism about the medical profession's statements on the matter. One option proposed to address concerns that the combined vaccine was problematic, was to provide measles, mumps and rubella vaccines singly. However, the World Health Organization advised against this on the grounds that the extended period of time necessary to provide three separate injections increases overall levels of non-adherence to the vaccination programme, which then exposes children to infection and increases the likelihood of epidemics occurring. Concerned parents point to the fact that some countries, such as France, provide the vaccines singly to babies aged 9–12 months (although it is usually given in combined MMR form subsequently) and use this as support for the argument that the MMR vaccine is unsafe.

Things to think about and research yourself

Do you think that you would provide your child(ren) in the future with vaccination protection? Would you consider all vaccines as equally important or would you weigh up the pros and cons for each one independently? Where can people find reliable evidence of the pros and cons of immunisation?

How do you think health professionals could better convince the public as to the benefits of immunisation? Where do policy makers and public health speakers go 'wrong' in communicating the need for immunisation?

Summary

This chapter has provided an overview of a range of behaviour often described as 'behavioural immunogens': behaviour that acts in ways that protect or enhance an individual's health status. A lack or low level of 'immunogens' is also detrimental to health, as is reflected in the rising obesity figures (see Chapter 3) attributed in large part to low levels of physical activity. Given the convincing evidence of a behaviour–disease association reviewed in this chapter and in Chapter 3, we could perhaps be forgiven for expecting that the majority of people would behave in a manner that protects their health. However, this is not borne out by statistics, and it is increasingly evident that there is a complexity of influences on health behaviour practices. Chapter 5 goes on to describe the key psychosocial theories and models of health behaviour that dominate current thinking in health psychology research.

Further reading

Hopwood, P. (1997). Psychological issues in cancer genetics: current issues and future priorities. *Patient Education and Counselling*, 32: 19–31.
This paper offers a clear review of important issues in relation to cancer genetic testing, such as for the BRCA1/2 genes, updated in Sivell's paper below.

Sivell, S., Iredale, R., Gray, J. and Coles, B. (2007). Cancer genetic risk assessment for individuals at risk of familial breast cancer. Cochrane Database of Systematic Reviews: CD003721.
This useful paper provides a review of randomised controlled trials relating to the impact of genetic risk assessment in cancer. Addresses many issues raised a decade earlier by Hopwood and shows how science has progressed.

Department of Health (2004) *Choosing Health: Making healthy choices easier*.
This UK governmental White Paper sets out the key principles for supporting the public to make healthier and more informed choices in regards to their health. The DoH website is a useful site for accessing many such policy and discussion documents. This link will take you to useful downloads including the above:
http://www.dh.gov.uk/en/Publicationsandstatistics/Publications/PublicationsPolicy andGuidance/DH_4094550

Commission of the European Communities (2007). White Paper. *Together for Health: A Strategic Approach for the EU 2008–2013*.
On 23 October 2007 the European Commission adopted a new Health Strategy which aims to provide an overarching strategic framework spanning core issues in health (e.g. in relation to ageing, child health, health behaviours, occupations) at the European level. This and other documents can be downloaded from:
http://ec.europa.eu/health/ph_overview/strategy/health_strategy_en.htm

 Visit the website at **www.pearsoned.co.uk/morrison** for additional resources to help you with your study, including multiple choice questions, weblinks and flashcards.

CHAPTER 5

Predicting health behaviour

Learning outcomes

By the end of this chapter, you should understand and be able to describe:

- how social and cognitive factors influence uptake of health or risk behaviour
- the components of several key psychosocial models of health behaviour
- how 'continuum' or 'static' models differ from 'stage' models in terms of how they consider behaviour change processes
- the research evidence that supports the social and cognitive factors found to be predictive of health behaviour and health behaviour change

CHAPTER OUTLINE

The previous two chapters have described behaviour that is associated with health and illness. This chapter aims to describe the key theoretical models that have been proposed and tested in terms of their ability to explain and predict why people engage in health-risk or health-enhancing behaviour. Personality, beliefs and attitudes play an important role in motivating behaviour, as do our goals and intentions, social circumstances and social norms. The key psychological models and their components are described and critiqued, drawing on evidence from studies of an array of health behaviours. While our understanding of health behaviour remains incomplete due to the complexity of influences upon human behaviour generally, the empirical studies described have identified many significant and modifiable influences upon health and health behaviour that offer potential targets for future health promotion and health education.

Influences on health behaviour

mediate/mediator
some variables may mediate the effects of others upon an outcome: for example, individual beliefs may mediate the effects of gender upon behaviour; thus gender effects would be said to be indirect, rather than direct, and beliefs would be mediator variables.

One way of considering the factors predictive of health behaviour is to view some influences as 'distal', such as socio-economic status, age, ethnicity, gender and personality, and others as 'proximal' in their influence, such as specific beliefs and attitudes towards health-compromising and health-enhancing behaviour. This division is somewhat arbitrary but is intended to reflect the fact that some influences operate on behaviour by means of their effects on other factors, such as a person's attitudes, beliefs or goals. For example, there is reasonably consistent evidence that people in the lower socio-economic groups drink more, smoke more, exercise less and eat less healthy diets than those in the higher socio-economic groups, in both the UK and elsewhere in the European Union (e.g. Cavelaars *et al.* 1997; Choiniére *et al.* 2000), but this finding does not explain 'why' this is the case, (see Chapter 2 for a full discussion of socio-economic inequalities in health). Further explanation can be offered through studies that have found that social class affects perceptions of health (see Chapter 1). These perceptions or beliefs can be considered 'closer' to the behaviour (more proximal) and offer a potentially more changeable target for intervention than would an intervention aimed at altering a person's social class. Beliefs may therefore **mediate** the effects of more distal influences, and this hypothesis can be tested statistically.

In terms of age, the health behaviours that receive the majority of attention from educational, medical and public health specialists (i.e. smoking, alcohol consumption, unprotected sexual activity, exercise and diet) are patterns of behaviour set down in childhood or early adulthood. For example, according to the 1996 General Household Survey in the UK, 82 per cent of smokers took up the habit as teenagers (Thomas *et al.* 1998). However, attitudes also change at this time. Adolescents generally begin to seek autonomy (independence), which may include making health-related decisions for themselves: for example, whether or not to start smoking, whether or not to brush their teeth before bed. Influences on decisional processes, attitudes and behaviour change during these years, with more credence being given to the attitudes, beliefs, values and behaviour of one's peers than to the advice or attitudes of parents or teachers (e.g. Chassin *et al.* 1996; Hendry and Kloep 2002). While establishing a sense of identity among one's peer group, it is perhaps not surprising that, for some adolescents, this will include the initiation of 'risk' behaviour as part of rebelling against authority or because the behaviour is considered to be 'cool' or sophisticated and grown-up (Camp *et al.* 1993; Michell and Amos 1997).

Gender has been shown to exert a significant influence on the nature and performance of healthy or health-risk behaviours, as we have described in the two preceding chapters. What is necessary is better understanding of why this is the case. Perceptions of health and the meanings attached to health and health behaviours offer a partial explanation, with males seeming to engage in risk behaviours such as drinking alcohol as a projection of their masculinity (Visser and Smith 2007). Conversely they may also engage in the health beneficial activity – exercise – for similar reasons (Steffen *et al.* 2006), and they may avoid health care for related reasons, for example to be seen as being 'strong' (Marcell *et al.* 2007). The recent study by Visser and Smith (2007) presents qualitative material which beautifully illustrates the linkages made between health risk behaviour and masculinity, and how other factors, such as sporting success, can 'compensate' for the reduced perceived masculinity assumed from lower levels of drinking. Selected quotes from males aged 18–21 include:

> . . . really icons of masculinity who go out and booze, and get in fights, and get lots of women and stuff like that, they are regarded as . . . the prime kind of, you know, specimens of maleness.

> . . . because I was better than most of the players, they didn't, like, pressure me into drinking, because . . . you know, it was kind of like I could say to them 'Forget it' or whatever. Um . . . that was, that's personally me, but then I have friends who . . . weren't quite as experienced as me at hockey, but just to kind of get into the group I think they felt the need to partake in that [drinking].

However, there were exceptions to this association between masculinity and drinking behaviour, with ethnicity and religion exerting stronger influences on the behaviour of some black and Asian Muslim interviewees than did the need to be seen as 'masculine'.

> I'm a Muslim guy, you know, and if you are a Muslim you are not allowed to drink. And I'm a guy that, you know I pray, you know. I pray and so I don't drink. I never, never tried to drink either.

Many models of health behaviour have been proposed and tested in terms of their ability to explain and predict the practice, or non-practice, of health-risk and health-enhancing behaviour, through the examination of individual attitudes and health beliefs. The attitudinal, social and cognitive components of these models are the main focus of this chapter; however, these broader influences of age, gender and ethnicity need to be acknowledged to a greater extent than is often the case. We also need to address the fact that health and risk behaviours are generally performed for a reason, and so we turn to this first. Ingledew and McDonagh (1998) have shown that health behaviour serves coping functions (which may be considered as short-term goals of the behaviour); for example, for some individuals smoking may serve the function of coping with stress. These authors identified five coping functions attached to health behaviour: problem solving, feeling better, avoidance, time out and prevention. For example, exercise behaviour loaded on to a 'prevention with problem-solving' function, but also on to a 'time out with problem-solving' function. Such findings highlight the often neglected fact that there are many reasons for why individuals behave in the way that they do; in this case, individuals exercised as a means of preventive health behaviour but also as a means of time out or relaxation. The implication of this is that interventions designed to reduce 'unhealthy' behaviour need to take account of the coping functions or goals that individual behaviour serves for each individual – it is these goals that will motivate the behaviour (see later in this chapter and Chapter 6).

Personality

Personality is, generally speaking, what makes individuals different from one another, in that each of us thinks and behaves in a characteristic manner, showing traits that are particularly enduring regardless of situation. Different scientists have proposed different numbers of key traits or dimensions of personality; two of the major examples are presented here.

Eysenck's three-factor model

1. *extroversion* (outgoing social nature): dimensionally opposite to *introversion* (shy, solitary nature);
2. *neuroticism* (anxious, worried, guilt-ridden nature): dimensionally opposite to *emotional stability* (relaxed, contented nature);
3. *psychoticism* (egocentric, aggressive, antisocial nature): dimensionally opposite to *self-control* (kind, considerate, obedient nature).

According to Eysenck (1970, 1991), individual personality is reflected in an individual's scores along these three dimensions; for example, one individual may score positively and high on neuroticism and extroversion but negatively on psychoticism, whereas another may score positively and high on neuroticism, and negatively and high on extroversion and psychoticism. These three factors have received a lot of support from research studies and are considered to be valid and robust personality factors (Kline 1993). However, another model exists, often referred to as the 'big five' (McCrae and Costa 1987, 1990), which identifies five primary dimensions of personality, and in health psychology it is this theory that has received most attention.

McCrae and Costa's five-factor model

1. neuroticism
2. extroversion
3. openness (to experience)
4. agreeableness
5. conscientiousness.

The Big Five traits have been validated in different cultures (with the exception of conscientiousness) and at different points in the lifespan from age 14 to 50+ (McCrae *et al.* 2000), and are considered therefore relatively stable and enduring.

Although the trait approach to personality is limited in its acknowledgement of situational and cognitive factors that also affect personality and behaviour (as acknowledged by Bandura's social learning/social cognitive theory, see Chapter 3), studies have shown that these relatively stable personality factors are associated with health behaviour. There is a reasonable body of evidence pointing to increased risk-taking behaviour among individuals scoring high on extraversion or openness, and less risk-taking among those scoring higher on agreeableness and conscientiousness (e.g. Nicholson *et al.* 2005). Similar directional associations have also been reported with healthy behaviours. For example, Goldberg and Strycker (2002) carried out a large-scale community survey of the associations between personality and dietary behaviour and found that openness predicted a range of dietary behaviour, including low meat fat consumption and high fibre intake. This is consistent with the findings of Steptoe *et al.* (1995), where openness was associated with a willingness to try novel situations, including new food tastes and types. In general, conscientiousness is associated with positive health behaviour (for a meta-analysis see Bogg and Roberts 2004) whereas neuroticism tends to associate with negative health behaviour (Goldberg and Strycker 2002; Booth-Kewley and Vickers 1994), including dietary 'pickiness' (fussiness) and **neophobia** among a sample of 451 Scottish children aged between 11 and 15 (MacNicol *et al.* 2003).

neophobia
a persistent and chronic fear of anything new (places, events, people, objects).

In seeming contradiction to this negative influence of neuroticism, it has also been associated with high levels of health-care use. This is attributed to the tendency of highly neurotic individuals to report greater attention to bodily sensations and to label them as 'symptoms' of disease more than people lower in neuroticism (Jerram and Coleman 1999; and see Chapter 9). However, Friedman (2003) concluded that there is no consistent evidence that people scoring high on neuroticism engage in a greater range or frequency of health-enhancing behaviour or in less damaging health behaviour than those people with low neuroticism, and that 'healthy neurotics' may exist as well as 'unhealthy neurotics'. This suggests therefore that personality traits such as neuroticism offer insufficient explanation for health or risk behaviour. What may add to the predictive utility of personality factors is some exploration of how personality traits effect the motivations for carrying out behaviour. Self-determination theory (Deci and Ryan 2000) distinguishes between intrinsic and extrinsic motivation whereby a person is motivated to behave in a certain way for the inherent personal satisfaction or rewards it produces, such as feelings of competence or autonomy, or because of other externally situated rewards, such as peer approval. Testing this theory in relation to the safer sexual behaviour of students, Ingledew and Ferguson (2007) found that students scoring high on agreeableness or conscientiousness had intrinsic, autonomous or self-determined motivations to perform safer sex (e.g. Personally, I would practise safe sex because . . . I personally believe it is the best thing for my health), rather than extrinsic, external or controlled motivations (e.g. Personally, I would practise safe sex because . . . I feel pressure from others to practise safe sex). Unfortunately this study was cross-sectional and so whether the identified motives predict behaviour over time is not ascertained.

locus of control
a personality trait thought to distinguish between those who attribute responsibility for events to themselves (i.e. internal LoC) or to external factors (external LoC).

Another commonly investigated aspect of personality is generalised **locus of control** (LoC) beliefs (Rotter 1966). Rotter originally considered individuals to have either an internal LoC orientation (i.e. they place responsibility for outcomes on themselves and consider that their actions affect outcomes) or an external orientation, which suggests that they place responsibility for outcomes at the door of external factors such as luck. Subsequent to Rotter's internal–external control scale, Kenneth Wallston and colleagues (Wallston *et al.* 1978) developed a LoC scale specific to health beliefs, the MHLC (multidimensional **health locus of control**) scale, which identified three statistically independent dimensions:

health locus of control
the perception that one's health is under personal control; controlled by powerful others such as health professionals; or under the control of external factors such as fate or luck.

1. *Internal*: strong internal beliefs consider the individual themselves as the prime determinant of their health state. Internal beliefs are theoretically associated with high levels of health-protective behaviour and with Bandura's self-efficacy construct (see below).
2. *External/chance*: strong external beliefs consider that external forces such as luck, fate or chance determine an individual's health state, rather than their own behaviour.
3. *Powerful others*: strong beliefs on this scale consider health state to be determined by the actions of powerful others such as health and medical professionals.

Wallston argued that these dimensions become relevant only if an individual values their health. This reflects the theoretical underpinning to locus of control, that of social learning or social cognitive theory (Bandura 1986), whereby an individual acts on the expectancy of certain valued outcomes. If individuals do not value their health, it is thought that they are unlikely to engage in health-protective behaviour (even if they feel they have control over their health), because health is not a high priority (e.g. Wallston and Smith 1994). Individuals with an internal HLC or a powerful others HLC who also value their health are therefore more likely to behave in a health-protective manner, whether that be, in the case of internal LoC, commencing a healthy eating programme, or in the case of a powerful others HLC, going to a local health clinic for dietary advice. Powerful others beliefs may detract from an individual taking active responsibility for the relevant behaviour, with such individuals being over-reliant on medical 'cures'.

Despite Wallston's refinements to the Rotter internal–external scale, generalised LoC dimensions have proved to be only a modest predictor of behaviour. Norman and Bennett (1996), for example, reviewed studies that investigated the associations between Wallston's three sub-scales and the protective health behaviour of healthy people and concluded that the relationship was a weak one. This weak association was subsequently confirmed in a large-scale survey of over 13,000 healthy individuals. Positive health behaviour was weakly correlated with higher internal control, and even more weakly associated with lower external and powerful others control beliefs (Norman *et al.* 1998). Such findings suggest that a generalised health LoC (such as assessed by the MHLC) has only a modest influence on specific health behaviour, and research attention has in many cases turned to examining more behaviourally proximal constructs, such as **perceived behavioural control** (see theory of planned behaviour below) and **self-efficacy** (see below and also discussion of the health action process approach model). However, Armitage (2003) found that generalised internal control beliefs independently predicted the relationship between perceived behavioural control and intention (in other words, the ability of more specific perceived behavioural

perceived behavioural control
one's belief in personal control over a certain specific action or behaviour.

self-efficacy
the belief that one can perform particular behaviour in a given set of circumstances.

control beliefs to explain intention was strongest among those individuals with high internal LoC). Armitage therefore proposed that research needs to examine further the influence of dispositional control beliefs on proximal control. Although this debate is relatively new, it suggests that interventions aiming to enhance specific perceived behavioural control beliefs may be most effective if targeted at those with an internal locus of control.

dispositional pessimism
having a generally negative outlook on life and a tendency to anticipate negative outcomes (as opposed to dispositional optimism)

Other personality characteristics may also affect proximal predictors of behaviour. Linda Cameron has shown, following a study of beliefs about skin cancer risk, that beliefs in low personal control over cure of the disease were associated with greater risk perception (perceived likelihood of developing skin cancer) and lower intention to engage in prevention (Cameron 2008). She suggested that this association may reflect underlying personality such as **dispositional pessimism** or anxiety, as other studies have found these to influence susceptibility beliefs (e.g. Gerend *et al.* 2004).

Social norms, family and friends

Humans are fundamentally social beings. Our behaviour is a result of many influences: the general culture and environment into which we are born; the day-to-day culture in which we live and work; the groups, subgroups and individuals with whom we interact; and our own personal emotions, beliefs, values and attitudes, all of which are influenced by these wider factors. We learn from our own positive and negative experience, but we also learn 'vicariously' through exposure to, and observation of, other people's behaviour and experiences. The behaviour of people around us creates a perceived 'social norm', which suggests implicit (or explicit) approval for certain behaviour. For example, a four-year follow-up study of nearly 10,000 American high school students found that 37 per cent of non-smokers at high school had started smoking by college follow-up; 25 per cent of original 'experimental' smokers had increased their smoking behaviour; and the remaining students had stayed the same (either non-smokers, experimenting with smoking (none in last month), current smokers or ex-smokers) (Choi *et al.* 2003). Clear differences were found in the factors that explained initiation to smoking from non-smoking (i.e. white, rebellious students who did not like school) and progression from experimental (irregular, social, short-term) smoking to current smoker. Those who progressed in their smoking behaviour perceived peer approval for their smoking and perceived experimental smoking as safe. Additionally, perceived parental approval was a more important influence on starting smoking than on progression.

In relation to health-risk behaviour, there are many sources of information that a person is exposed to: for example, televised advertisements graphically illustrating the negative consequences of smoking; an older sibling or parent appearing to be healthy in spite of regular binge drinking episodes; a classroom workshop on how to 'just say no' to the first offer of a cigarette or other drug; a friend who smokes telling you that smoking is cool. There is consistent evidence to show that the credibility, similarity to self and even the attractiveness of the source of information influences whether or not attitudinal change or behaviour change occurs as a consequence (e.g. Petty and Cacioppo 1986, 1996; see Chapter 7 for further discussion of influences on the effectiveness of health promotion).

Plate 5.1 Social norms have been found to be important predictors of whether or not a person initiates specific health behaviours, in this instance smoking and drinking alcohol.
Source: Rex Features/SUTTON-HIBBERT

Attitudes

Attitudes are thought to be the common-sense representations that individuals hold in relation to objects, people and events (Eagly and Chaiken 1993). Some theorists have described attitudes as a single component based on affective evaluation of an object/event (i.e. you either like something/ someone or you do not; e.g. Thurstone 1928); others have presented a two-component model, where attitude is defined as an unobservable and stable predisposition or state of mental readiness that influences evaluative judgements (e.g. Allport 1935). From the 1960s onwards, there has been growing acceptance of a three-component model of attitude, whereby attitudes are considered as relatively enduring and generalisable and made up of three related parts – thought (cognition), feeling (emotion) and behaviour:

1. *Cognitive*: beliefs about the attitude-object; e.g. cigarette smoking is a good way to relieve stress; cigarette smoking is a sign of weakness.
2. *Emotional*: feelings towards the attitude-object; e.g. cigarette smoking is disgusting/pleasurable.
3. *Behavioural* (or intentional): intended action towards the attitude-object; e.g. I am not going to smoke.

Early attitudinal theorists considered the three components to be generally consistent with each other and likely to predict behaviour; however, the empirical evidence to support a direct association between attitudes and behaviour has proved difficult to find. This is in part because an individual may hold several different, sometimes conflicting, attitudes towards a particular attitude-object, depending on social context and many other factors. I may, for example, enjoy the taste of a cream cake but be worried about the negative health implications of high fat/high calorie intake. Such contradictory thoughts can produce what is known as 'dissonance', which many people will attempt to resolve by bringing their thoughts into line with one another. However, some individuals maintain a dissociation between attitudes and behaviour, for example so-called dissonant smokers, who continue to smoke despite holding a number of negative attitudes towards smoking. This conflict is sometimes referred to as **ambivalence**, where a person's motivation to change could potentially be undermined by the holding of ambivalent attitudes or competing goals, such as believing low-fat food to be a healthy option that they would like to increase intake of while not wanting to appear obsessive about their diet (e.g. Sparks *et al.* 2001). Attitudes alone are insufficient. Many factors can shape, challenge or change initial attitudes, cause them to be ignored, or increase the likelihood of them being acted upon, as can be seen in this chapter.

ambivalence
the simultaneous existence of both positive and negative evaluations of an attitude-object, which could be both cognitive and emotional.

Risk perceptions and unrealistic optimism

People often engage in risky or unhealthy behaviour because they do not consider themselves to be at risk, or at least do not do so accurately, believing for example that 'I do not smoke as much as "person X" and therefore won't be at risk of cancer compared with them'. Weinstein (1984) named this biased risk perception, which he found to be common, '**unrealistic optimism**' – 'unrealistic' because quite obviously not everyone can be at low risk. He noted that individuals engage in forms of social comparison that reflect best on themselves (comparative optimism/optimistic bias) (Weinstein and Klein 1996; Weinstein 2003); for example, in relation to HIV risk: 'I may sometimes forget to use a condom, but at least I use them more than my friends do'. He found that the negative behaviour of peers is focused on more when making these judgements than is the same peers' positive health behaviour. Selective attention in this way leads to unrealistically positive appraisals regarding personal risk.

Weinstein (1987) identified four factors that are associated with unrealistic optimism:

unrealistic optimism
also known as 'optimistic bias', whereby a person considers themselves as being less likely than comparable others to develop an illness or experience a negative event.

1. a lack of personal experience with the behaviour or problem concerned;
2. a belief that their individual actions can prevent the problem;
3. the belief that if the problem has not emerged already, it is unlikely to do so in the future; e.g. 'I have smoked for years and my health is fine, so why would it change now?';
4. the belief that the problem is rare; e.g. 'cancer is quite rare compared with how common smoking is, so it is pretty unlikely I'll develop it'.

There is some evidence that unrealistic optimism is associated with greater belief in control over events (e.g. 'I am at less risk than others because I know when to stop drinking') and that such beliefs are associated with risk-reducing behaviour (Hoorens and Buunk 1993; Weinstein 1987). However, others, for example Schwarzer (1994), refer to unrealistic optimism as 'defensive optimism' and suggest instead that the relationship between such optimism and behaviour is likely to be negative because individuals underestimate their risk and thus do not take precautions against the risk occurrence. There remains a need to explore further the actual relationship between these constructs and health behaviour.

Risk perceptions within health psychology are often defined (and assessed) as individually generated cognitions. However, risk is perhaps better understood as a social construct, given that we make risk judgements based on the current social and cultural context: for example, if I were to perceive my risk of contracting TB (tuberculosis) high while living in North Wales, this would likely be considered as being unrealistically pessimistic, whereas it may be the case that I work with homeless populations where TB is still present, or that I make regular trips to countries where incidence is high.

Goals and self-regulation of behaviour

outcome expectancies
the outcome that is expected to result from behaviour, e.g. exercise will make me fitter.

self-regulation
the process by which individuals monitor and adjust their behaviour, thoughts and emotions in order to maintain a balance or a sense of normal function.

Social cognition theory assumes that behaviour is motivated by **outcome expectancies** and goals (both short- and long-term goals) i.e. behaviour is viewed as being goal-directed (e.g. Fiske and Taylor 1991; Carver and Scheier 1998). Processes of **self-regulation**, the cognitive and behavioural processes by which individuals guide, control, modify or adapt his or her responses, enable an individual to achieve desired outcomes or reduce undesired outcomes, i.e. their goals. Goals focus our attention and direct our efforts, with more valued, and more specific, goals leading to greater and more persistent effort (Locke and Latham 2002). Cognitive regulation is required as well as emotion regulation if we are to successfully organise and execute goal-directed activity. An inability to control thoughts and evaluate decision options and potential outcomes or regulate emotions (for example when drunk!) may increase risk-taking behaviour (Magar *et al.* 2008). Attentional control is also required in order to achieve desired goals. Luszczynska *et al.* (2004) developed a scale to assess attentional control. This aspect of dispositional self-regulation can be defined as the extent to which a person can focus on activities and goals and avoid being distracted by competing goals, demands, or even negative arising emotions, such as anxiety about failure, that might interfere with goal attainment or, at least, return to goal-directed activity after the distraction has passed or been dealt with. As yet there is no available evidence as to the predictive ability of this scale in terms of behaviour change, but it is an important addition to the factors likely to inform behaviour.

In contrast, there is a wealth of evidence supporting the predictive utility of the next construct we introduce, self efficacy.

What do YOU think?

What is important to you in your current life? Think of three aspects of your life that you currently value highly. Why do you value them? What function do they serve?

What goals do you hope to achieve over the next six months? Over the next ten years? If you engage in any specific health or risk behaviour, how does it 'fit' with your current values and your short- and long-term goals?

Now, project your mind ahead to when you reach middle age (or if you have already reached this, think of your post-retirement years). What do you think will be important to you then? Will the areas of importance change, and why do you think this? Do you think your goals and behaviour will change, and if so, in what way and why?

Self-efficacy

The construct of self-efficacy is defined as 'the *belief* in one's capabilities to organize and execute the sources of action required to manage *prospective* situations' (Bandura 1986). For example, believing that a future action (for example, weight loss) is within your capabilities is likely to generate other cognitive and emotional activity, such as the setting of high personal goals (losing a stone rather than half a stone), positive outcome expectancies and reduced anxiety. These cognitions and emotions in turn affect actions, such as dietary change and exercise, in order to achieve the goal. As Bandura (1997: 24) states: 'It is because people see outcomes as contingent on the adequacy of their performance, and care about those outcomes, that they rely on efficacy beliefs in deciding which course of action to pursue and how long to pursue it'. Success in attaining a goal also feeds back in a self-regulatory manner to further a person's sense of self-efficacy (Bandura 1997) and to further their efforts to attain goals (Schwarzer 1992). In situations where competence of one's own performance is unrelated or less closely tied to outcome (for example, the outcome of physical recovery following a head injury will depend to a large degree on the extent of neurological damage), self-efficacy will be less predictive of outcome.

In relation to the outcomes of individual health behaviour change and maintenance of change, personal performance is important and therefore efficacy has unsurprisingly been found to be predictive, as will be seen in the studies reviewed later in this chapter.

Humans are inconsistent

People can be very inconsistent in their practice of health behaviour; for example, many individuals who are keen exercisers also smoke. Not only do individuals differ from one another in terms of justifications or motivations for behaviour, but their own motivations are likely to change over time. Inconsistencies can perhaps be explained by the following findings:

■ Different health behaviour is controlled by different external factors: e.g. smoking may be socially frowned upon, while exercise may be socially supported; however, cigarettes are readily available, but access to exercise facilities or time may be limited.

■ Attitudes towards health behaviour vary within and between individuals.

■ In the same individual, health behaviour may be motivated by different expectations: e.g. they may smoke to relax, exercise to improve appearance and consume alcohol to socialise.

■ Individuals differ in their goals and motivations: e.g. a teenager may diet for fashion reasons, while a middle-aged man may diet to avoid a second heart attack.

■ Motivating factors may change over time: e.g. drinking alcohol when under age may be a form of rebellion but may later be considered essential to social interaction.

■ Triggers and barriers to behaviour are influenced by context: e.g. smoking may be banned in the workplace, and alcohol consumption may be restricted in front of parents or colleagues in comparison with peers.

The next part of the chapter addresses a range of theories and models that have been developed in an attempt to explain and thereby predict health behaviour.

Models of health behaviour

First, it is important to remind the reader that by adopting healthy habits, we are only reducing the statistical risks of ill health, not guaranteeing that we will lead a long, healthy life. Furthermore, we should not expect that by examining human behaviour and the motives for it, we shall ever be able to fully explain the huge variations in people's health. Behaviour is not the only factor that causes disease. We can, at best, offer a partial (social, cognitive and behavioural) explanation of illness, and an evidence-based conclusion as to how to intervene to prevent or reduce the likelihood of illness in some individuals.

Behaviour change

Early theories as to why we changed our behaviour were based on the simplistic assumption that:

information → attitude change → behaviour change

These were found to be naive. Simply providing information, for example about the benefits of stopping smoking or the value of a low-cholesterol diet, may or may not change a person's attitudes towards this behaviour, and even if attitudes do become more negative, it is not inevitable that this will influence behaviour change (e.g. Eagly and Chaiken 1993). Although many past, and sometimes current, health education campaigns still draw upon this simplistic premise, several psychological models have been proposed as explanations for health behaviour and behaviour change. These models focus primarily on the social cognitions of individuals and are described in the following sections.

Social cognitive models of behaviour change

The health belief model

One of the first and best-known models is the health belief model (HBM) (Rosenstock 1974; Becker 1974; Strecher *et al.* 1997). The HBM proposes that the likelihood that a person will engage in particular health behaviour depends on demographic factors: e.g. social class, gender, age and a range of

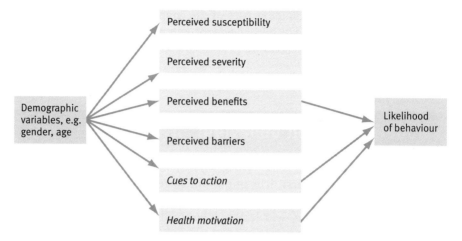

Figure 5.1   The health belief model (original, plus additions in italics).

beliefs that may arise following a particular internal or external cue to action (see Figure 5.1). These beliefs encompass perceptions of threat and evaluation of the behaviour in question, with cues to action and health motivation added at a later date.

In terms of how the various components fit together, this can best be illustrated through specific examples:

■ Perception of threat:
■ I believe that coronary heart disease (CHD) is a serious illness contributed to by being overweight: *perceived severity*.
■ I believe that I am overweight: *perceived susceptibility*.
■ Behavioural evaluation:
■ If I lose weight my health will improve: *perceived benefits* (of change).
■ Changing my cooking and dietary habits when I also have a family to feed will be difficult, and possibly more expensive: *perceived barriers* (to change).
■ Cues to action (added in 1975; Becker and Maiman):
■ That recent television programme on the health risks of obesity worried me (*external*).
■ I am regularly feeling breathless on exertion, so maybe I should really think about dieting (*internal*).
■ Health motivation (added in 1977; Becker *et al.*):
■ It is important to me to maintain my health.

The HBM has been applied to a wide range of behaviour over many years, as illustrated below.

■ The HBM and preventive behaviour

The consensus finding in the breast self-examination (BSE) literature is that many people do not practise it at all, that adherence rates are low and that practice decreases with age, even though the incidence of breast cancer increases with age. The health belief model has been widely used for predicting BSE. Both in terms of predicting intention to perform BSE (e.g. Savage and Clarke 1996) and actual BSE behaviour, it appears that perceiving benefits of self-examination and few barriers to its performance are most consistently and most highly correlated, with perceived seriousness of breast cancer, perceived susceptibility and being motivated towards health (e.g. seeking health information and generally engaging in health-promoting activity) also predictive (e.g. Champion 1990; Ashton *et al.* 2001). In fact, health motivation distinguished between low, medium and high BSE performers, and predicted BSE over a one-year follow-up period (Champion and Miller 1992). This supports the need to assess health motivation rather than assume that all people value health or are motivated to pursue it in the same way.

Studies have shown that different components of the HBM are more or less salient, depending on the behaviour under study. For example, in a review of thirteen studies using the HBM components, Curry and Emmons (1994) found evidence of uptake of breast cancer screening being explained by perceived susceptibility beliefs, low perceived barriers, and cues to action. In contrast, Pakenham *et al.* (2000) did not find susceptibility beliefs to be predictive of mammography uptake. Perceived benefits have been shown to be important predictors of a range of behaviours, including exercise (e.g. Saunders *et al.* 1997) and attendance at antenatal care (Letherman *et al.* 1990), whereas perceiving barriers to performing the required behaviour is perhaps unsurprisingly generally associated with low levels of the behaviour in question, such as dietary adherence among cardiac patients (Koikkalainen *et al.* 1996), and antenatal class attendance (Letherman *et al.* 1990).

■ **The HBM and reducing risk behaviour**

In relation to safer sex practices, Abraham *et al.* (1996) found that HBM variables were not significantly predictive of consistent condom use among sexually active adolescents once a measure of previous condom use had been taken into consideration. This suggests that one of the best predictors of what we do in the future is what we have done in the past. More recent theoretical developments and research studies have acknowledged this by including measures of previous behaviour in their design and analyses (e.g. Yzer *et al.*'s 2001 study of condom use with new sexual partners).

Abraham *et al.* (2002) have also concluded, from a review of the evidence prior to conducting a subsequent study of condom use behaviour, that 'threat perceptions are weaker correlates of condom use than action-specific cognitions, such as attitudes towards condom use, perceived self-efficacy in relation to condom use, the social acceptability of condom use and condom use intentions' (p. 228). These factors are not addressed in the HBM.

■ **Limitations of HBM**

Problems with this model lie in how it has been applied and in its basic content. For example, in terms of application, different authors employ different versions and create questionnaires which can differ: for example, not all HBM studies assess cues to action and health motivation (Harrison *et al.* 1992; Sheeran and Abraham 1996). Further limitations include:

- Rosenstock (1966), in outlining the model, did not specify the manner in which the different variables interact with one another or combine to influence behaviour. He implied that the components operate independently and could usefully be added to each other. Many studies have examined components independently (e.g. Abraham *et al.* 1996).

- Becker *et al.* (1977) suggested that perceived benefits were weighted against perceived barriers, although no guidance was given as to how the combined score was to be calculated (i.e. do you subtract the number of barriers from the number of benefits reported, or vice versa? Can all benefits and barriers carry equal weight to an individual?)

- Strecher and Rosenstock (1997) suggested that adding or multiplying susceptibility scores with severity scores to get an overall 'perceived threat' score may enable greater prediction than using each independently; that cues to action and perceived benefits and barriers may better predict behaviour in situations where perceived threat is high; and that the model may be better tested against intention than actual behaviour. Few of these hypotheses have been tested empirically.

- The HBM is a static model, suggesting that various beliefs occur simultaneously in a 'one-off' assessment. This does not allow for a staged or dynamic process of change in beliefs, as later models show is crucial.

- The HBM assumes that human beings are rational decision makers, which is not necessarily the case.

- The HBM may overestimate the role of 'threat'. Perceived susceptibility has not consistently been found to be a significant predictor of health behaviour change.

- Even if perceived susceptibility is sometimes found to be predictive, it is important that health promotion messages do not overuse fear arousal as this has been shown to be counter-productive to behaviour change by provoking denial (e.g. van der Pligt *et al.* 1993).

- The HBM takes limited account of social influences on behaviour. For example, while young children, who take their cues about health and health behaviour from important adults in their lives, show generally good adherence to medication, adolescent adherence is poorer, reflecting a shift in influence and beliefs about health maintenance (e.g. Bryon 1998).

- The HBM fails to consider whether the individual feels able to initiate the behaviour (or behaviour change) required. Two constructs relate to this: perceived behavioural control and self-efficacy, as exemplified in two of the models discussed next (the theory of planned behaviour and the HAPA).

Given these limitations, it is perhaps not surprising that studies employing the HBM have found that its components account for only a small proportion of variance in behaviour change (see meta-analysis of adult studies by Harrison *et al.* 1992). By initially failing to consider the interactions between its components, the role of social norms and influences, and the factors that can turn beliefs into more proximal (close-up) determinants of behaviour (such as efficacy in carrying out the required behaviour), it provided only a limited account of human action, and more extensive models were developed and adopted.

The theory of reasoned action and the theory of planned behaviour

While the HBM is predominantly a cognitive model of health behaviour derived from subjective expected utility theory (i.e. individuals are active and generally rational decision makers who are influenced by the perceived utility (usefulness to them) of certain actions or behaviour (cf. Edwards 1954), the theory of reasoned action (TRA) and, subsequently, the theory of planned behaviour (TPB) are known as social cognition models (Figure 5.2). These models assume that social behaviour is determined by a person's beliefs about behaviour in given social contexts and by their social perceptions and expectations (cf. social learning theory: Bandura 1986) and not simply by their cognitions or attitudes.

■ The theory of reasoned action

This model (Ajzen and Fishbein 1970; Fishbein 1967) assumes that individuals behave in a goal-directed manner and that the implications of their actions (outcome expectations) are weighed up in a rational manner before the decision is taken whether to engage in the behaviour or not. The model aims to explore and develop the psychological processes involved in making a link between attitude and behaviour by incorporating wider social influences and the necessity of intention formation. IN THE SPOTLIGHT highlights that understanding of factors associated with and predictive of behavioural intention is going to be important in a generation facing new vaccinations for newly publicised conditions.

Behaviour is thought to be proximally determined by intention, which in turn is influenced by a person's attitude towards the object behaviour (*outcome expectancy beliefs*, e.g. positive outcome expectancy: if I stop smoking, exercising will become easier for me; negative outcome expectancy: if I stop smoking, I will perhaps gain weight; and *outcome value*: it is important for me to be healthier) and their perception of social pressure regarding the behaviour (e.g. my friends and parents really want me to stop smoking) (known as a **subjective norm**). The extent to which they wish to comply or fall into line with the preferences or norms of others is known as motivation to comply (I would like to please my parents and friends). The model states that the

subjective norm
a person's beliefs regarding whether important others (referents) would think that they should or should not carry out a particular action. An index of social pressure, weighted generally by the individual's motivation to comply with the wishes of others (see theory of planned behaviour).

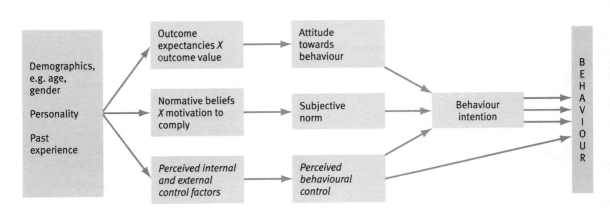

Figure 5.2 The theory of reasoned action and the theory of planned behaviour (TPB additions in italics).

importance of the person's attitudes towards the behaviour is weighted against the subjective norm beliefs, whereby a person holding a negative attitude towards behaviour change (I don't really like dieting) may still develop a positive intention to change in situations where their subjective norm promotes dieting and they wish to comply with their significant others (e.g. all my friends eat more healthily than I do, and I would like to be more like them).

Intention is considered to be the proximal determinant of behaviour, and it reflects both the individual's motivation to behave in a certain manner and how hard they are prepared to try to carry out that behaviour (Ajzen 1991: 199). This compares favourably with the HBM, which simply stated that a combination of motivational beliefs predicted greater or lesser likelihood of action, without a statement of intent ever having been formed.

IN THE SPOTLIGHT

Have you heard of HPV – Human papillomavirus?

Human papillomavirus is a highly prevalent sexually transmitted infection, thought to be present in about 30 per cent of sexually active females at any one time, with an estimated lifetime risk of 75–80 per cent. HPV is implicated in cervical cancer, i.e. it is referred to as a 'necessary cause', although only a small proportion of HPV infections do actually develop into cancer. A preventative vaccine has been developed and licenced in Europe as elsewhere, the USA, Australia for example, and policy has come into place in many countries, including the UK, whereby, from September 2008, vaccination is to be offered to teenage girls aged 12 to 13, with a two-year catch-up programme from 2009 to vaccinate those under 18 missed by the new programme. Parental consent is required, which is controversial, given the implicit acknowledgement of sexual activity. In order to achieve what is known as 'herd immunity', i.e. the whole population is protected, it may be that the vaccination programme will need to be extended to males, but in the first instance teenage girls are to be targeted. This is all quite new and therefore it is important to identify earlier attitudes towards this condition and its prevention. One recent study to report intention to have the HPV vaccination is a Dutch study asking whether a sample of 1,367 adult women would have a '10 year old (grand) daughter' vaccinated. The women were not told that HPV is a sexually transmitted infection. Intention was at a high level with no significant difference between a random sample of women invited for a pap smear test (76 per cent 'yes'), women who had had an abnormal pap smear (81 per cent), women who had survived cervical cancer themselves (77 per cent) and a random group of women not invited for cervical screening within the previous two years (78 per cent). Neither did having children make any difference to hypothetical intention. Intention was however affected by age – those under 50 were significantly more likely to agree to vaccination of their hypothetical '(grand)daughter'. An earlier and smaller study conducted in the UK found a lower level of intention among a sample more directly involved in the decision – 317 parents of 11–12-year-olds. In this study only 38 per cent 'certainly' agreed to vaccination, although a further 43 per cent stated they would probably agree (Brabin et al. 2006).

How do you think you would respond to a similar question were you to have a teenage daughter? While evidence of levels of hypothetical intention are of interest, what is needed now is large studies of actual intention and factors that influence this, along with studies that assess actual behaviour. As this chapter has shown, there are many factors that explain intention, and many more that help translate intention into action. It is a fair bet that the health psychology literature will soon be publishing such studies in relation to HPV vaccination.

The TRA was extended and developed into the more powerful theory of planned behaviour (TPB, see next section) following a vast array of studies (see review and a meta-analysis of eighty-seven studies by Sheppard *et al.* 1988). These studies confirmed the importance of attitudes and subjective norms in explaining intention, and of intention in predicting subsequent behaviour. This meta-analysis reported that the mean correlation of attitudes and social norms with intentions was approximately 0.67, and the correlation between intention and behaviour was between 0.53 and 0.62. This therefore improves significantly on the prediction afforded by the HBM components; however, the model still has limitations. Note also that research evidence supporting a link between intention and subsequent behaviour has been limited by an over-reliance on cross-sectional studies.

Limitations of the TRA

The TRA was initially developed for application to **volitional** behaviour (that under the person's control) and as such does not examine a person's belief in their ability to perform the behaviour in question. However, much behaviour is not completely volitional (for example, addictive behaviours such as smoking, or the negotiation of condom use during sexual encounters). This was addressed in the developed model, the TPB.

volition
action or doing (the post-intentional stage highlighted in the HAPA model of health behaviour change).

■ The theory of planned behaviour

In order to improve the model's ability to address non-volitional behaviour, the TRA was extended to include the concept of perceived behavioural control, becoming known as the theory of planned behaviour (Ajzen 1985, 1991; see Figure 5.2).

Perceived behavioural control (PBC) is defined as a person's belief that they have control over their own behaviour in certain situations, even when facing particular barriers (e.g. I believe it will be easy for me not to smoke even if I go to the pub in the evening). The model also proposed that PBC would directly influence intention and thus, indirectly, behaviour. A direct relationship between PBC and behaviour was also considered possible if perceptions of control were accurate, meaning that if a person believes that they have control over their diet, they may well intend to change it and subsequently do so, but if the preparation of food is in fact under someone else's control, behavioural change is less likely even if a positive intention had been formed) (Rutter and Quine 2002: 12). PBC beliefs themselves are influenced by many factors, including past behaviour and past successes or failures in relation to the behaviour in question, and in this way the PBC construct is very similar to that of self-efficacy. For example, a person who has never tried to stop smoking before may have lower PBC beliefs than a person who has succeeded in stopping previously and who therefore may believe that it will be relatively easy to do so again.

Generally, the TPB has had more success in predicting behavioural change than its predecessor (Sheeran and Orbell 1998). With Ajzen (1991) reporting a mean correlation between PBC and intention of 0.71, it is clear that this construct has been an important addition, although intention remains a stronger predictor of subsequent behaviour than PBC is directly. It has been suggested that PBC may be most powerful when it is considered in interaction with the other components of the model, such as attitudes and motivations (Eagly and Chaiken 1993) and even more dispositional measures of locus of control (e.g. Armitage 2003). However, Armitage *et al.* (1999) compared the predictive utility of *self-efficacy beliefs* with *perceived behavioural control beliefs* in relation to the use of legal and illegal drugs and found that self-efficacy beliefs were more strongly associated with behaviour than were perceived behavioural control beliefs. Self-efficacy is central to the HAPA model described later in this chapter.

In a large-scale meta-analysis of studies employing the TPB, its variables accounted for between 40 and 50 per cent of variance in *intention* and between 19 and 38 per cent of the variance in *behaviour* (Sutton 1998). The TPB has been tested extensively in relation to a range of health behaviour, or behavioural intention, and we can provide only a few examples here.

The TPB and preventive behaviour

Hagger *et al.* (2001) used the TPB to examine children's physical activity intentions and behaviour and found that attitudes, perceived behavioural control and intention were significant influences on exercise behaviour at a one-week follow-up. Perceived behavioural control and attitude both predicted intention, whereas, surprisingly, subjective norm did not. This is in contrast to an earlier study by Godin and Shephard (1986) in exactly the same age group, where subjective norm was predictive. However, various differences exist between the two studies, including for example the fact that Godin's sample was American, where the benefits of exercise – or the risks of obesity – have possibly become more known over the past twenty-five years, hypothetically strengthening the role of personal attitudes and beliefs over social norms.

The TPB has also been used to study physical activity intentions and behaviour among individuals with chronic diseases. For example, Eng and Martin-Ginis (2007) evaluated whether TPB variables explained the actual leisure time physical activity (LPTA) of 80 men and women with chronic kidney disease reassessed one week after their TPB beliefs were assessed. Perceived behavioural control was initially associated with intention to engage in LPTA, and this intention predicted actual behaviour a week later. Among adolescent survivors of cancer, intentions to be physically active on a regular basis were predicted by affective attitudes towards physical activity (e.g. enjoyable–unenjoyable) and instrumental attitudes (useful–useless), but not by any of the other TPB components (34 per cent of variance explained in total). Physical activity itself was explained by intention (19 per cent variance explained) and by self-efficacy (a further 10 per cent variance explained). This study assessed both PBC and SE and it is the latter that emerged significant (Keats *et al.* 2007). That different components of the TPB explain intention and actual exercise behaviour was confirmed in a meta-analysis of exercise behaviour among healthy populations (Hagger 2002).

The uptake of screening opportunities for cervical cancer and breast cancer has been extensively explored, with different TPB variables explaining (or, in cross-sectional studies associating with) intention than explaining actual behaviour. For example, Rutter (2000) found that intention to attend screening was predicted by attitude, perceived behavioural control and subjective norm, although only attitude and subjective norm were predictive of actual uptake of screening. Cross-sectional studies of factors influencing breast screening found subjective norm and perceived behavioural control to be significantly predictive of mammography intention, and attitudes and PBC predictive of intention to undergo a clinical breast examination (Godin *et al.* 2001). Studies of self-screening, in terms of breast or testicular self-examination, report similar differences in predictors of intention compared with predictors of actual behaviour, but more longitudinal studies are crucial if a causal relationship is to be confirmed. A prospective longitudinal study of predictors of mammography uptake is presented in RESEARCH FOCUS.

RESEARCH FOCUS

Belief salience and theory of planned behaviour variables predict breast screening attendance

Steadman, L., Rutter, D.R. and Field, S. (2002). Individually elicited versus modal normative beliefs in predicting attendance at breast screening: examining the role of belief salience in the theory of planned behaviour. *British Journal of Health Psychology*, 7: 317–31.

Background

Subjective norm (SN) beliefs have been found to be partial explanations of intention to act (in addition to attitude and perceived behavioural control) but less often predict behaviour. In many such studies, subjective norm is assessed by asking individuals to state what they believe the norms and expectancies of a range of listed other people are in relation to the behaviour in question. In this method of questioning, an individual is prompted to think of many people or many influences and a 'modal' belief is what is analysed. The same applies to calculations of attitudes, as totals are used rather than examining the strength and **salience** of individual attitudes therein. Steadman and colleagues argue that in modal beliefs, there may be one or more highly salient beliefs that hold high importance to the individual and that prediction of outcomes may be improved if such salient beliefs are analysed rather than modal beliefs.

salience
strength and importance.

Aims of study

To establish both the modal subjective norm beliefs and the individually salient beliefs held by a sample of women who had been invited for breast cancer screening mammography, either as a result of being aged between 50 and 53 and newly eligible for mammography screening, or as older women (54–64) being re-screened as part of the National Health Service (UK) breast screening programme. It was hypothesised that individually generated subjective norm beliefs would have a stronger relationship with intention, and with subsequent uptake of screening, than would modal subjective norm beliefs.

Methods

A total of 1,000 women were randomly assigned to either a condition receiving a questionnaire composed of items assessing TPB constructs, which included a section assessing modal SN beliefs, or to a condition receiving the same core questionnaire but with a section enabling participants to generate individual SN beliefs. The first condition responded to items that asked whether 'My husband or partner/daughter/friends/GP/sister/friends from my religion/experts from the media . . . think that I should have my breasts screened if invited', followed by a further question for each influence acknowledged: 'Generally speaking I want to do what

continued

(the specific normative influence e.g. husband) . . . thinks I should do' (motivation to comply). The scores on each item are then added. In the second condition, women were first invited to name one person 'in particular' who would want them to attend screening, and if they could do this they also identified who it was, and then scored their motivation to comply with this person's wishes. If they could not identify one person in particular (the most salient), they were invited to think of up to six people and score the motivation to comply item for each of these individuals.

Results

A total of 64 per cent of the initial sample completed the study; 15 per cent of women in the individual condition were unable to elicit a normative influence, and 9 per cent of those in the modal condition ticked 'not relevant' to each of the listed potential normative influences. Data from these women were not used further.

The mean number of normative influences elicited in the individual condition was significantly lower than the mean number of influences in the modal condition (mean 2.11, s.d. 1.04) compared with mean 4.17 (s.d. 1.72), but their overall subjective norm rating score was significantly higher (mean 18.12, s.d. 4.14) compared with mean 13.97 (s.d. 5.33). Partners were the most commonly mentioned normative influence in the individual group (74 per cent), whereas in the modal group GPs were the most frequent (88 per cent). No between-group differences were found on the other TPB items, i.e. attitude, perceived behavioural control or intention.

Contrary to the hypothesis, there was not a stronger association between individual SNs and intention than there was between modal SN beliefs and intention. (In both groups, attitudes and PBC also correlated with intention.) However, there was a significant relationship between individual SNs and subsequent attendance (attitude and intention also correlated with attendance), whereas modal SNs were not associated with attendance (and neither were attitude or PBC, although intention was).

These correlations were then tested prospectively. For the condition assessing modal SN beliefs, the TPB model was supported, attitude, SN and PBC predicted 30 per cent variance in intention – but not behaviour, and intention predicted 7 per cent variance in behaviour. In contrast, the condition assessing individual SN beliefs found direct links between attitude, SN, PBC and intention (24 per cent variance explained), but, in addition, SN had a direct effect on actual attendance, adding to the prediction offered by intention (13 per cent variance explained). While these findings suggest better prediction of attendance by assessing individually salient SNs, the difference between the two conditions (modal versus individual SN beliefs) was not actually significant.

Additional analysis examining only the first two normative influences endorsed by those in the individual condition found that these data explained as much as the total SN data, suggesting that the first-named normative influences are the most salient. Similarly, when the normative influences in the modal condition were examined individually, only those pertaining to husband/partner had a significant relationship with intention and behaviour.

Discussion

The results only partially confirmed the authors' hypotheses. There was not a stronger association between individual beliefs and intention or attendance behaviour than between modal beliefs and intention or attendance. However, there was evidence of individual beliefs adding to the prediction of attendance, a result not found in terms of modal SN beliefs. Previous studies have not reported an effect of SN on mammography uptake behaviour, and this may be, as the authors conclude, because 'an individually generated subjective norm is a more sensitive and accurate estimate of the true effect of normative pressure' (p. 327). The hypothesis that the first-mentioned individual influences would be the most salient predictors was confirmed. The finding that, in the modal group, while total SN had no relationship with attendance behaviour, the husband/partner items *did*, is highly important. Such a finding may explain why few studies have previously reported effects of SN on behaviour; i.e. they have been relying on grouped SN data and not considering that different normative influences may be more salient. The implications of this finding alone for how future studies assess TPB components are significant.

It is worth noting that while the removal of data for those who could not identify a normative influence on their behaviour was necessary for this study, this group of women are an interesting group in that their decisions about screening uptake are likely to be made on a very individual basis.

illness representations
beliefs about a particular illness and state of ill health – commonly ascribed to the five domains described by Leventhal: identity, timeline, cause, consequences and control/cure.

Hunter *et al.* (2003) examined the predictors of intention to seek help from a GP for breast cancer symptoms among a general population sample of women. Attitudes towards help seeking (e.g. 'Making an appointment to see my doctor for a symptom that might be cancer would be good/bad, beneficial/harmful, pleasant/unpleasant, wise/foolish, necessary/unnecessary') and perceived behavioural control (e.g. 'There is nothing I could do to make sure I got help for a breast cancer symptom': agree–disagree (seven-point scale)) explained a small but significant amount of variance in intention (7.1 per cent). Subjective norms were not predictive of intention to seek help for such symptoms. It is important to note that the authors also examined participants' perceptions of cancer (**illness representations**; see Chapter 9) and entered these variables into the regression analysis before the TPB variables. Illness representations explained 22 per cent of the variance in intention, and the TPB variables added a further 7.1 per cent thereafter. This highlights the importance of considering individuals' perceptions of the illness that the behaviour in question is related to. For example, when examining smoking behaviour, perhaps perceptions of cancer or COPD should be more fully addressed. Additionally, perceptions of treatment may influence the health behaviour of adherence, as suggested in studies of the beliefs in the necessity of medicine and concerns about taking them (e.g. Clifford *et al.* 2008 and see also Chapter 9).

Ethnic differences in how certain conditions are perceived may also affect help-seeking behaviour, as suggested in a Hawaiian study comparing beliefs about alcoholism and emotional problems held by Caucasian, Philipino, Japanese and native Hawaian adults. Caucasians perceived significantly fewer barriers to disclosing alcohol or emotional problems than the three ethnic minority groups. The perceived barriers showed interesting ethnic differences: for example, ethnic minority groups more often perceived barriers relating to low awareness of where to go for help for alcohol problems, and greater barrier of shame of others finding out about an emotional problem (Takeuchi *et al.* 1988). In our multicultural society it should not be assumed therefore that beliefs about conditions, or about relevant preventative health behaviours, are the same.

The TPB and risk-reducing behaviour

Two different examples of behaviour will be illustrated here: smoking and unprotected sexual intercourse. Smoking is fundamentally an individual behaviour requiring one person only for its performance, whereas unprotected sexual intercourse is a behaviour that involves two people in a social encounter or interaction. Smoking is talked about frequently but as a behaviour is increasingly becoming marginalised, whereas unprotected sexual intercourse is rarely discussed in public, far less performed! A further difference is in the potential for addiction – from high (smoking), through to rare (sexual behaviour) (although sexual addiction does exist; see Orford 2001). There are sufficient differences between these behaviours to perhaps expect that the predictors of each may differ.

Godin *et al.* (1992) reported that the frequency of smoking behaviour over a six-month period among a general population sample could be explained primarily by low perceived behavioural control over quitting beliefs. Norman *et al.* (1999) applied the TPB to smoking cessation and found that the best predictor of intention to quit was not only perceived behavioural control, but also beliefs in one's susceptibility to the negative health consequences of continued smoking. Few studies have actually applied the TPB to smoking cessation, acknowledging that addictive behaviour is subject to different controlling and contributing factors than is behaviour of a more volitional nature. In saying that, however, beliefs in control over the behaviour, and in particular self-efficacy beliefs (as defined in a later model, the HAPA), have been found to be salient.

Sutton *et al.* (1999) compared the TRA and the TPB in predicting the use of condoms and did not find that perceived behavioural control added significantly to the TRA components' explanation of this behaviour. This is in spite of the fact that PBC has been cited as an issue for women regarding the use of condoms in sexual encounters (e.g. Abraham *et al.* 1996; Yzer *et al.* 1998). Factors associated with condom use include previous use of condoms, a positive attitude towards use, subjective norms of use by others, self-efficacy in relation to both the purchase and use of condoms, and intentions (see Sheeran *et al.* (1999) for a meta-analysis of studies). However, many studies have been conducted in educated young adult populations (e.g. students) rather than in more 'chaotic' populations such as injecting drug users, who are at above average risk of HIV infection (e.g. Morrison 1991a) and for whom behaviour change is crucial. It is also important to address whether sexual partners are long-term or casual, as this will also affect real and possibly perceived risk as well as, potentially, attitudes towards the need for, and importance of, 'safe sex'. These factors are likely to influence whether or not the issue of using condoms is raised with a potential partner. It has been suggested that for some individuals the non-use or the use of condoms is less governed by intention (and by implication the cognitive processes that the TPB claims precede intention) than by habit, and, as such, interventions should be targeted very early in a sexual career so as to facilitate the development of 'safer sex' habits (cf. Yzer *et al.* 2001).

Limitations of the TPB

■ The TPB (also true for the TRA) does not acknowledge the potential transaction between the predictor variables (attitudes and subjective norms) and the measured outcomes, i.e. intention or behaviour. Behaviour itself may shape attitudes. This highlights the need for prospective longitudinal studies that examine the changing relationships between variables over time and enable the disentangling of cause–effect relationships.

■ Armitage and Connor (2002) found that the intention to eat or not eat a low-fat diet could be distinguished on the basis of more positive attitudes towards a low-fat diet (higher outcome expectancies and value). However, the subsequent intervention targeting attitudes had a limited effect on actual dietary behaviour, suggesting that translating predictors identified in correlational designs into targets for successful intervention is not straightforward (Michie *et al.* 2007).

■ The prediction of behaviour from the TPB variables is significantly lower than the prediction of intention, providing strong evidence for the need to identify further variables that move an individual from intention to action. Other factors which have emerged include affective (emotional) variables and those that relate to planning processes involved in the initiation of action following intention formation:

  ■ '*Moral norms*': rather than a behaviour being influenced by subjective social norms as in the TPB, it has been recognised that some intentions and behaviour may be partially motivated by moral norms, particularly behaviours that directly involve others such as condom use or drink driving (e.g. Evans and Norman 2002; Armitage and Conner 1998; Manstead 2000).

  ■ *Anticipatory regret* (Triandis 1977; Bell 1982): it has been shown anticipating regret would result if a certain behavioural decision was made which influences both future behavioural intentions and behaviour. For example, anticipatory regret regarding unprotected sexual intercourse increased an individual's intention to use condoms (e.g. Richard *et al.* 1996; van der Pligt and de Vries 1998), although in relation to a single occasion of heavy drinking, anticipating negative affect was not associated with changes in drinking intentions or behaviour (Murgraff *et al.* 1999). The nature of the behaviour and how it is perceived (e.g. risky unprotected sex/less risky drinking occasion) may therefore moderate the effect of anticipatory regret, and further research is needed to explore this. Perugini and Bagozzi (2001) propose that anticipatory emotions (including regret) arise from a person's consideration of the likelihood of attaining or not attaining the desirable outcomes or goals of the behaviour.

  ■ *Self-identity*: how one perceives and labels oneself may influence intention above and beyond the effect of core TPB variables. For example, self-identifying as a 'green consumer' increased intention to eat organic vegetables (Sparks and Shepherd 1992), suggesting that we behave in a manner that is consistent with our self-image.

  ■ *Implementation intention* (II): forming an II is thought to be part of the process involved in turning an intention into action, i.e. filling the intention–behaviour gap highlighted by limitations in behavioural prediction by TPB studies (see below).

Of these possible additions to theories of behaviour change, self-efficacy, anticipatory regret and implementation intentions are currently receiving the most research attention and the most empirical support in terms of adding to the explanation of behaviour.

■ Implementation intentions

One of the reasons why people may not always translate their intentions into action is that they have not made adequate plans as to how, when and where they will implement their intention. Gollwitzer suggests that individuals need to shift from a mindset typical of the motivation (pre-doing) phase towards an implementational mindset, which is found in the volition (doing) phase (Gollwitzer 1993, 1999; Gollwitzer and Oettingen 1998; Gollwitzer and Schaal 1998). Individuals need to make a specific 'when, where and how' plan that commits them to a certain time and place and to using a particular method of action. For example, rather than stating, as is typical in the TPB measures, how strongly I intend to stop smoking, an implementation intention would require me to state that I intend to stop smoking first thing next Sunday morning, at home, using a nicotine replacement patch. Although Ogden (2003) argues that this method of questioning is manipulative rather than descriptive and serves a different purpose to that of simply asking questions about one's attitudes or beliefs (i.e. it has the purpose of intervention and not description), many studies now include a measure of II.

Goal intentions can be distinguished from implementation intentions; for example:

■ goal intention: 'I intend to go on a diet' (motivational, part of TPB);
■ implementation intention: 'I intend to go on a diet on Monday after my party weekend' (planning, not part of TPB).

Implementation intentions have been shown to increase a person's commitment to their decision and the likelihood of their attaining a specified goal by carrying out the intended action. For example, Orbell *et al.* (1997) assessed the attitudes, social norms and intentions of women to perform breast self-examination and then instructed half of the sample to form an II as to when and where they would carry it out. This half of the sample showed a significantly higher rate of subsequent self-examination than the sample that had not formed an II.

Commonly reported barriers to attaining goals or implementing intended behaviour, such as forgetting or being distracted from it, can be overcome by committing the individual to a specific course of action when the environmental conditions specified in their II are encountered (Rutter and Quine 2002: 15). Illustrating this, Gollwitzer and Brandstätter (1997) describe how an II creates a mental link between the specified situation (e.g. next Monday) and the behaviour (e.g. starting a diet). It seems likely that IIs obtain their effects by making action more automatic, i.e. in response to a situational stimuli set down in the II, and in this way enable the person to overcome the 'when will I do this?' type of procrastination that stops many intentions being put into action.

Gollwitzer (1999) also notes that while forming proximal (more immediate) goals leads to better goal attainment than forming distal (long-term) goals, IIs do show persistence over time. For example, forming an II to take vitamin pills persisted over a three-week period in Sheeran and Orbell's (1999) study. This kind of finding could have implications for a range of groups; for example, hospitalised patients could be encouraged to form IIs about their home-based rehabilitation in order to improve exercise adherence and recovery post-discharge. While some people spontaneously form IIs when they form the motivational intention ('I intend to exercise'), many others do not and therefore the encouragement of the formation of IIs offers a fruitful avenue for health education and intervention (see Chapter 6).

Generally, goal attainment is influenced by the value placed on the likely outcome; by the belief that the goal is attainable through the person's actions, i.e. self-efficacy; and by the receipt of feedback on progress made (particularly important where long-term goals, such as weight loss, are involved) (Locke and Latham 2002). It is becoming clear that models of health behaviour change need to address personal goals more effectively.

ISSUES

How the wording and ordering of questions may influence the data obtained

It has been suggested that studies reporting evidence of unrealistic optimism (UO) in a sample may actually be witnessing a measurement artefact; i.e. UO may be appearing as a result of the manner in which the questions are asked (Harris and Middleton 1994). Weinstein originally asked one simple question in an attempt to establish the presence of UO: 'compared with others of my sex/age . . . my chances of developing "disease x" are . . . (great/average/low)'. In other studies, however, two questions have been asked: the first generating a rating for personal risk, the second generating a rating for the risk of similar others (see, for example, Perloff and Fetzer 1986; van der Velde *et al.* 1992), and UO is considered to be present when the second rating is higher than the first. Hoorens and Buunk (1993) manipulated the ordering of these two questions and also the comparison group that their sample of adolescents were required to think of when making their risk judgements. They found significant effects of ordering whereby those rating personal risk first, and then comparative others' risk, exhibited lower levels of UO than those receiving the questions in the opposite order.

To illustrate ordering effects further, Budd (1987) carried out an experiment where the order of theory of reasoned action items was muddled across different versions of a questionnaire. He found that muddling significantly altered the intercorrelations between perceptions of threat, attitude, normative beliefs and intention to either smoke, brush teeth three times per day, or exercise for twenty minutes. Sheeran and Orbell (1996) tried to replicate this using *protection motivation theory* components (see later in the chapter) in relation to different behaviour – that of condom use and dental flossing. While fewer effects of ordering were found, correlation strengths between some key cognitive variables did change. These authors also report that scores on a social desirability scale, along with the perceived salience (relevance and importance to the individual) of the behaviour being addressed, had small but reliable effects on the associations between the health beliefs assessed in the PMT. These types of study highlight the need for researchers to take possible demand effects and questionnaire design factors into consideration when interpreting their findings.

Ogden (2003) further highlights these issues in a review of forty-seven empirical papers that tested the social cognition models outlined in this chapter. She concludes that while social cognition models offered useful tools to guide research, and that research had provided evidence of many of the model components explaining and predicting health behaviour, many findings did not in fact support the theoretically predicted associations. She suggests that part of the 'problem' is that the components of such models are generally assessed using self-completed questionnaires, which may in themselves create beliefs about the behaviour concerned. For

continued

example, a questionnaire with items addressing perceived susceptibility to a particular illness may increase awareness of an issue or may cause the individual to reflect upon their own behaviour and change their belief structure. Potentially, these changed beliefs may alter subsequent behaviour. For example, a study examining beliefs and intentions about future, hypothetical genetic testing uptake for breast cancer (e.g. Morrison *et al.* 2008) asked participants to rate their attitudes towards genetic testing, their outcome expectancies, perceived benefits of, or barriers to testing, and their intention to undertake testing were it to become available. For some individuals, this type of questioning probably caused them to think about something they may not have done previously. The questions provide information to the participant about the behaviour: e.g. 'To what extent do you think that genetic testing will: reduce uncertainty about my long-term risk of breast cancer; enable me to make positive decisions about my future', and this information could potentially change beliefs and attitudes.

Some of health psychology's commonly employed methods of measurement, intended to describe beliefs or behaviour, may actually and unwittingly be operating as cognitive intervention! The direction of change could be manipulated by changing the wording of the questions, in the same way as other studies attempt to change beliefs by manipulating the nature of information provided. While this may be desirable in certain circumstances, this issue of questions as interventions requires greater attention in research designs and greater acknowledgement in the discussion of findings.

So far in this chapter we have reviewed static or continuum models, which describe additive components whereby perceptions or beliefs (or sets of them) are used in combination to try to predict where an individual will lie on an outcome continuum such as an intention or behaviour. We turn our attention now to stage models, i.e. models of behaviour change which consider individuals as being at 'discrete ordered stages', each one denoting a greater inclination to change outcome than the previous stage (Rutter and Quine 2002: 16). According to Weinstein (Weinstein *et al.* 1998; Weinstein and Sandman 2002) a stage theory has four properties:

1. *A classification system to define stages*: it is accepted that the stage classifications are theoretical constructs, and although a prototype is defined for each stage, few people will perfectly match this ideal.

2. *Ordering of stages*: people must pass through all the stages to reach the end point of action or maintenance, but progression to the end point is neither inevitable nor irreversible. For example, a person may decide to quit smoking but not do so; or may quit smoking but lapse back into the habit sometime thereafter.

3. *Common barriers to change facing people within the same stage*: this idea would be helpful in encouraging progression through the stages if people at one stage have to address similar issues, for example if low self-efficacy acted as a common barrier to the initiation of dietary change.

4. *Different barriers to change facing people in different stages*: if the factors producing movement to the next stage were the same regardless of stage (e.g. self-efficacy), the same intervention could be used for all, and the stages would be redundant. Ample evidence exists that barriers are different in the different stages (see below).

The transtheoretical model (TTM)

This model was developed by Prochaska and di Clemente (1984) to address intentional behavioural change. Initially applied mostly to smoking cessation (e.g. di Clemente *et al.* 1991) the existence of 'stages of change' have now been reported in many behaviours (e.g. smoking cessation, cocaine use cessation, taking up exercise, consistent condom use, sunscreen use, weight control, radon testing, reduction of dietary fat intake, mammography screening, and even the modification of delinquent behaviour: Prochaska 1994; Prochaska *et al.* 1994).

The model makes two broad assumptions: that people move through stages of change; and that the processes involved at each stage differ, thus it meets several of the requirements outlined by Weinstein.

■ Stages of change

The stages of change proposed by the TTM are stages of motivational readiness and are outlined below, using dietary behaviour as an illustration:

- *Pre-contemplation*: a person is not currently thinking of dieting, no intention to change dietary intake in next six months, may not consider that they have a weight problem.
- *Contemplation*: e.g. 'I think I need to lose a bit of weight, but not quite yet' reflects awareness of a need to lose weight and consideration of doing so. Generally assessed as planning to change within next six months.
- *Preparation*: a person is ready to change and sets goals such as planning a start date for the diet (within three months). Stage includes thoughts and action, and people make specific plans about change.
- *Action*: for example, a person starts eating fruit instead of biscuits; overt behaviour change.
- *Maintenance*: keeps up with the dietary change, resists temptation.

While the above stages are the five most commonly referred to, there are also:

- *Termination*: where behaviour change has been maintained for adequate time for the person to feel no temptation to lapse and who believe in their total self-efficacy to maintain the change.
- *Relapse*: di Clemente and Velicer (1997) acknowledged that relapse (where a person lapses into their former behaviour pattern and returns to a previous stage) is common and can occur at any stage. This is therefore not an additional stage found at the end of the cycle as an alternative to termination.

People do not necessarily move smoothly from one stage to another. For example, some individuals may go from preparation back to contemplation and stay there for some time, even months or years before re-entering the preparation phase and successfully moving on to action. For others action can fail, maintenance may never be achieved, and relapse is common. The model therefore allows for 'recycling' from one stage to another and is sometimes referred to as a 'spiral' model (e.g. Prochaska *et al.* 1992). The first two stages are generally considered to be defined by intention or motivation; the preparation stage combines intentional and behavioural (volitional) criteria, whereas the action and maintenance stages are purely behavioural (Prochaska and Marcus 1994).

To help to understand factors that influence progression through the stages, the model outlines the psychological processes that are considered to be at play in the different stages (with some being important in more than one stage). These processes include the covert or overt activities that people engage in to help them to progress: for example, seeking social support and avoiding settings that 'trigger' the behaviour, as well as more 'experiential' processes that individuals may go through emotionally and cognitively, such as self re-evaluation or consciousness raising.

These and other processes are the targets of intervention efforts to 'move' individuals through the stages towards effective and maintained behaviour change: for example, motivation-enhancing interventions or self-efficacy training (see Chapter 6).

- In the pre-contemplation stage, individuals are more likely to be using denial and/or may report lower self-efficacy (to change) beliefs and more barriers to change.

- In the contemplation stage, people are more likely to seek information and may report reduced barriers to change and increased benefits, although they may still underestimate their susceptibility to the health threat concerned.

- In the preparation stage, people start to set their goals and priorities, and some will make concrete plans (similar to implementation intentions as described in an earlier section) and small changes in behaviour (e.g. joining a gym). Some may be setting unrealistic goals for success, or underestimating their own ability to succeed. Motivation and self-efficacy are crucial if action is to be elicited.

- In the action stage, realistic goal setting is crucial if action is to be maintained. The use of social support is important in order to receive reinforcement that will help to maintain the lifestyle change.

- Many individuals, for example up to 80 per cent of smokers who quit (Oldenburg *et al.* 1999), will not succeed in maintaining behavioural change and will relapse or 'recycle' back to contemplating a future attempt to change. Maintenance can be enhanced by self-monitoring and reinforcement.

decisional balance
where the costs of behaviour are weighed up against the benefits of that behaviour.

The perception of barriers and benefits, or 'pros and cons', are also found to differ between the stages; for example, an individual in the contemplation stage is likely to focus on both benefits of change and barriers to change, but barriers may be weighted more heavily (e.g. 'even if I get healthier in the long term I am probably going to gain weight if I stop smoking'), whereas someone in the preparation stage is likely to focus more on the benefits of change (e.g. 'even if I gain weight in the short term it will be worth it to start feeling healthier'). The relative weight between pros and cons is referred to as **decisional balance**.

■ The TTM and preventive behaviour

Several interventions aimed at increasing exercise behaviour in middle-aged samples have been based upon the TTM. For example, Cox *et al.* (2003)

conducted a longitudinal trial of an exercise behaviour change programme among sedentary Australian women aged 40–65. The intervention was either exercise centre or home-based and promoted either 'moderate' or 'intense' exercise levels. The study assessed participants' 'stage of change' regarding exercising and also explored the role of self-efficacy and decisional balance in relation to changes in exercise behaviour observed over time. Eighteen months following the intervention the women were reassessed. An increase in the activity levels of those who had received either intervention was found, almost independently of the stage of readiness that women had been in following the intervention. Additionally, the intervention produced increases in self-efficacy in line with the 'stage of change' achieved (i.e. self-efficacy increased as the stage progressed towards action) and appeared to be critical, whereas decisional balance findings were inconclusive. This reflects the findings of Marcus and colleagues (Marcus *et al.* 1992), where regular exercisers (in either the action or maintenance stage) had significantly higher self-efficacy scores than participants in the earlier stages.

■ The TTM and risk-reducing behaviour

In general, the notion of stages of change has received support; however, several studies have questioned whether the change processes outlined by Prochaska and colleagues are in fact useful predictors of change. For example, Segan *et al.* (2002) examined the changes in specific behavioural and experiential processes, self-efficacy and decisional balance among a sample of 193 individuals who were preparing to stop smoking and making the transition to the action stage. Results suggested that some changes in TTM components resulted *from* the transition to action, rather than preceded it: for example, increases in situational confidence and counter-conditioning (where positive behaviour is substituted for smoking). The main findings for the effect of behavioural and experiential processes were not reported, even though the TTM claims that these act as 'catalysts' for change. Furthermore, although self-efficacy was associated with making a quit attempt, it did not predict the success or failure of that attempt. Decisional balance was not predictive of any behaviour change, from quitting to remaining quit or relapsing.

Although a relatively small study, these findings have further questioned the validity of the TTM as a model of change, and they further reinforce the central role of self-efficacy, which is addressed fully in our discussion of a further model, the HAPA, below.

■ Limitations of the TTM

- Prochaska and di Clemente made suggestions for a time-frame within which they distinguish contemplaters from preparers (i.e. thinking of changing but not in the next six months versus thinking of changing within the next three months), but there is little empirical evidence that these are qualitatively different or differ in terms of the attitudes or intentions of stage members (e.g. Godin *et al.* 2004; Kraft *et al.* 1999).

- Past behaviour has subsequently been found to be a powerful predictor of future behaviour change efforts. This has questioned the usefulness of stages, where readiness or intentions to change are assumed to be key

(Sutton 1996). For example, Godin *et al.* (2004) present findings of a model whereby recent past behaviour is combined with future intentions to produce four 'clusters' of individuals with different attributes in terms of current behaviour and future intention to exercise. These authors find that attitudes and perceived behavioural control in relation to readiness for exercise associate more strongly with membership of these staged clusters than with membership of the five stages of change that do not consider past behaviour. Such findings, if replicated longitudinally, would suggest that studies and interventions should be assessing both intentions and current or recent behaviour.

■ Some authors have questioned the validity of five independent stages of 'readiness to change' on the basis of data that did not succeed in allocating all participants to one specific stage (e.g. Budd and Rollnick 1996). Such findings suggest that a continuous variable of 'readiness' may be a better description of this construct than one considered in discrete stages (Sutton 2000).

■ The model may not sufficiently address the social aspects of much health behaviour, such as alcohol consumption (Marks *et al.* 2000).

■ The model does not consider that some people may not have heard of the behaviour or the issue in question. This is likely when a rare or new illness is being considered (such as in the early days of HIV/AIDS or BSE (bovine spongiform encephalopathy)), or when the risk concerned is related to a 'new' behaviour: e.g. mobile phone use, or to newly identified risk factors such as human papillomavirus or HPV (see IN THE SPOTLIGHT above). This is acknowledged in a less commonly employed model, the precaution adoption process model (Weinstein 1988; Weinstein and Sandman 1992) which we illustrate briefly below.

The precaution adoption process model (PAPM)

This stage model (Weinstein 1988; Weinstein and Sandman 1992) was developed as a framework for understanding deliberate actions taken to reduce health risks and was intended to meet the criteria for a stage theory described by Weinstein himself (see above). Weinstein's model has seven stages, and highlights important omissions in the TTM (and indeed omissions in other models) (Table 5.1). The PAPM asserts that people pass through stages in

Table 5.1 Stages in the transtheoretical model and the precaution adoption process model

Stage	Transtheoretical model	Precaution adoption process model
1	pre-contemplation	unaware of issue
2	contemplation	unengaged
3	preparation	considering whether to act
4	action	deciding not to act (and exit the model)
5	maintenance	deciding to act (and proceed to next stage)
6		action
7		maintenance

sequences, but as with the TTM there is no time limit within which to reach the action stage. The major difference between this model and the TTM is that the PAPM has a more sophisticated consideration of the pre-action stages.

- *Stage 1*: a person is basically 'unaware' of the threat to health posed by a certain behaviour; they have no knowledge and therefore are not aware of a risk.

- *Stage 2*: termed 'unengaged', here a person has become aware of the risks attached to a certain behaviour but believes that the levels at which they engage in it is insufficient to pose a threat to their own health (I know smoking can cause various diseases, but I don't smoke enough for them to be a threat). This is seen as an 'optimistic bias' and led to Weinstein's development of the construct of unrealistic optimism (see earlier).

- *Stage 3*: a 'consideration' stage, akin to pre-contemplation. Individuals are deciding about acting on something – so many things compete for our attention that a fair amount can be known about a hazard before it is considered whether to act on this knowledge.

- *Stage 4*: this stage acknowledges that although perceived threat and susceptibility may be high, some people may actively 'decide not to act', which is different from intending to act but then not doing so.

- *Stage 5*: a 'decide to act' stage, similar to intention/preparation. There are important differences between people with a definite stance who have decided to act and those who are undecided (stage 3). Individuals in stage 3 may be more open to information and persuasion than those with a definite stance (decided not to act as in stage 4 or deciding to act as in stage 5). As noted previously, stating an intention to act does not inevitably imply that a person will act. Perceived susceptibility beliefs are considered necessary here to motivate progression to action. Moving from stage 5 to stage 6 relates to moving from motivation to volition.

- *Stage 6*: the action stage, when a person has initiated what is necessary to reduce their risk.

- *Stage 7*: this final stage is not always required. This stage is about maintenance and unlike with smoking cessation, some health behaviour processess are not long-lasting, for example deciding whether or not to have a vaccination or a mammogram.

Weinstein has applied the PAPM to studies of home testing for radon, an invisible odourless radioactive gas produced by the decay of naturally occurring uranium in soil in some geographical areas. It enters homes through cracks in foundations, and although little heard of, it is the second leading cause of lung cancer after smoking (Weinstein and Sandman 2002). Perceived susceptibility (or vulnerability) was found to be crucial in the transition between stage 3 (trying to decide) and stage 5 (deciding to act). However, a stage-matched intervention, as with those based on the TTM, was not as successful in moving 'decided to act' stage 5 participants into action (buying a home radon-testing kit), as it was in shifting the undecided participants into making a decision to act (but not action necessarily).

More research using stage models are needed to more clearly identify the processes that occur within and between stages in order to provide greater justification for stage-matched interventions, which to date have had limited effectiveness and are more costly than 'one size fits all' interventions (see Chapters 6 and 7 for examples).

The health action process approach (HAPA)

The HAPA is a model that has really taken on board the issue of stages and attempts to fill the 'intention–behaviour gap', crucially by highlighting the role of self-efficacy and action plans (Schwarzer 1992).

The HAPA model was developed to apply to all health-compromising and health-enhancing behaviour. It is particularly influential because it suggests that the adoption, initiation and maintenance of health behaviour must be explicitly viewed as a process that consists of at least a pre-intentional motivation phase and a post-intentional volition phase (Figure 5.3). Schwarzer (2001) further divides self-regulatory processes into sequences of planning, initiation, maintenance, relapse management and disengagement; however, we focus here on the first three of these as these are where the model has been best tested.

■ Motivation phase

As we have seen in earlier models such as the TPB, individuals form an intention to either adopt a precautionary measure (e.g. use a condom during sexual intercourse) or change risk behaviour (e.g. stop smoking) as a result of various attitudes, cognitions and social factors. The HAPA proposes that self-efficacy and outcome expectancies are important predictors of goal intention (as found in studies with the TPB and perceived behavioural control). Perceptions of threat severity and personal susceptibility (perceived risk) are considered a distal influence on actual behaviour, playing a role only

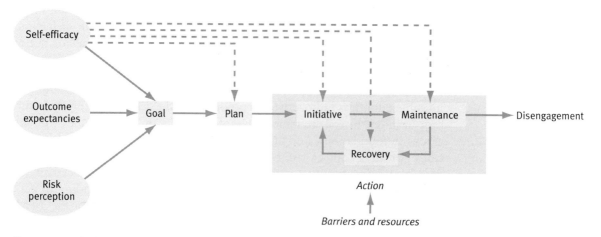

Figure 5.3 The health action process approach model.
Source: Schwarzer (1992); http://userpage.fu-berlin.de/~health/hapa.htm

in the motivation phase. In terms of 'ordering' of self-efficacy and outcome expectancies, the latter may precede the former (e.g. an individual probably thinks of the consequences of their action before working out if they can do what is required). Under conditions where individuals have no previous experience with the behaviour they are contemplating, the authors suggest that outcome expectancies may have a stronger influence on behaviour than efficacy beliefs.

Intention in the motivation phases is considered as a goal intention: e.g. I intend to stop smoking to become healthier. Schwarzer also proposes phase-specific self-efficacy beliefs, with self-efficacy in the motivational stage being referred to as 'task/pre-action self-efficacy': e.g. 'I can succeed in eating a healthy diet even if I have to change my lifestyle a bit'. At this stage, it is important for an individual to imagine successful outcomes and be confident in their ability to achieve them.

■ Volition phase

Once an intention has been formed, the HAPA proposes that in order to turn intention into action, planning has to take place. Here the model incorporates Gollwitzer's (1999; Gollwitzer and Oettingen 2000) concept of implementation intentions, described previously. These 'when, where and how' plans turn the goal intention into a specific plan of action. Schwarzer proposes that at this stage a different kind of self-efficacy is involved, that of *initiative* self-efficacy, whereby an individual believes that they are able to take the initiative when the planned circumstances arise (for example, the morning of the planned smoking cessation arrives and the individual needs to believe that they can then implement their plan).

Once the action has been initiated, the individual then needs to try to maintain the new, healthier behaviour, and at this stage *coping* (or *maintenance*) self-efficacy is considered important to success (e.g. I need to keep going with this diet even if it is hard at first). This form of self-efficacy describes a belief in one's ability to overcome barriers and temptations (such as being faced with a birthday celebration) and is likely to enhance resilience, positive coping (such as drawing upon social support) and greater persistence. If, as many do, the individual suffers a setback and gives in to temptation, the model proposes that *recovery* self-efficacy is necessary to get the individual back on track (Renner and Schwarzer 2003).

While it is a relatively new model, early findings based on the HAPA are encouraging. For example, in a longitudinal study of breast self-examination behaviour among 418 German women, pre-actional self-efficacy and positive outcome expectancies (and not risk perception) were significant predictors of (goal) intention. Self-efficacy beliefs also predicted planning. In terms of actual BSE behaviour by the time of follow-up (twelve–fifteen weeks later) planning was, as hypothesised, highly predictive, with maintenance and recovery self-efficacy also predicting greater frequency of the behaviour (Luszczynska and Schwarzer 2003). These findings support the presence of phase-specific self-efficacy beliefs and provide a possible focus for intervention studies. Although it is perhaps surprising that risk perception was not predictive (given findings of studies using both the HBM and the TPB), it may well be that risk perceptions influenced participants *before* they were

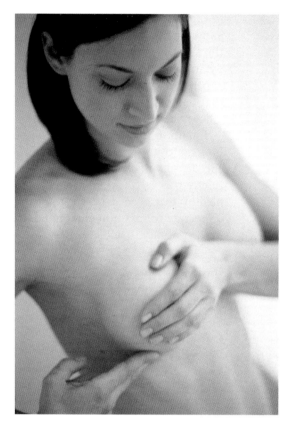

Plate 5.2 Breast self-examination can detect early breast abnormalities, which may be indicative of cancer. Early detection increases the chance of successful treatment.
Source: Corbis/Michael A. Keller/Zefa

assessed for the study and therefore effects on the HAPA variables had passed. It is always hard in research to establish an absolute 'baseline' for measurement, and such results should not be taken as proof that risk perceptions are not important – the body of evidence would prove otherwise. Further evidence of the importance of self-efficacy to recovery from setbacks can be seen in a study of newly unemployed men (Mittag and Schwarzer 1993) where low perceived self-efficacy regarding re-employment and dealing with the challenges of unemployment was associated with heavy drinking behaviour, where high self-efficacy was not.

Are models of health behaviour globally useful?

Health models such as those described in this chapter have brought our understanding of behaviour a long way. However, we are still far from being able to predict all behaviour (perhaps thankfully), and we are further still from successfully developing and implementing interventions that will maximise the adoption or maintenance of healthy lifestyles. While research employing these models has been plentiful, much of it, particularly in relation to the TPB, has been conducted among young healthy populations. The prolific use of student samples, for example, enables theories to be tested and built, and interesting questions to be addressed (such as what influences students' drinking behaviour and given its normative function can it be changed? Or what factors influence non-regular use of condoms, and does drinking alcohol interfere with even the best of intentions?). However, the findings of studies such as these may not translate across to prediction of behaviour among less educated individuals, or to those leading less structured lives, such as the homeless drinker or drug user; or even to those who are attempting to change behaviour as a response to a life-threatening condition, such as dietary change or smoking cessation following a heart attack. Other social, environmental, cognitive and emotional factors are likely to play a role in these diverse populations.

It is often thought that the models described here and used in a great deal of health psychology research focus more on individual cognitions than perhaps is required. Behaviour is influenced hugely by context, by socio-economic resources, by culture and by laws and sanctions. Presented below are some of the criticisms of research based on such models that should be considered if you are planning some research of your own:

- Different factors may be salient in relation to some behaviour but not others (for example, subjective norm may be more important to smoking cessation than to vitamin intake).

- The salience of certain factors may vary by age (attitude may predict intention to adhere to medication in adults, but not in children, where adherence may be influenced more by parental behaviour and beliefs).

- Culture and religion may significantly influence one's beliefs about health and preventive health, thus making the model components hugely diverse and hard to measure in a reliable and valid manner. For example, condom use is considered to be a sin against some religions and therefore health promotion efforts targeting increased susceptibility beliefs about HIV or STDs will face added barriers. Among those of certain faiths, drinking alcohol is banned, thus an individual who is drinking heavily faces very different emotional and normative pressures.

It is important therefore at all times for research to remember the context of behaviour and address such social and cultural factors. Health promotion efforts are likely to have limited success if the health behaviour is treated as though it exists independently of other aspects of human functioning.

Summary

Many proximal and distal factors influence our behaviour, and our health behaviour, such as our age, gender, attitudes, beliefs and goals. Continuum models like the HBM and the TPB have demonstrated the importance of social and cognitive factors in predicting both intention to act and action, although the static nature of these models leaves a need for better understanding of the processes of change.

Stage models like the TTM and the HAPA address processes of change and have gone some way towards filling the gap between intention and behaviour, and in particular the basic distinction between motivational and volitional processes is useful and important.

Perceived susceptibility and self-efficacy have been identified as important and consistent predictors of change. As such, they carry intervention potential, but tailored interventions for different stages are more costly than a 'one size fits all' approach, and evidence is mixed as to their success.

Further reading

Conner, M. and Norman, P. (eds) (1996). *Predicting Health Behaviours*. Buckingham: Open University Press.

An excellent text that provides comprehensive coverage of social cognition theory and all the models described in this chapter (with the exception of the HAPA). A useful resource for sourcing measurement items for components of the models if you are designing a questionnaire.

Conner, M. and Norman, P. (eds) (1998). Special issue: social cognition models in health psychology. *Psychology and Health*, 13: 179–85.

An excellent volume of this respected journal that presents research findings from many studies of health behaviour change.

Rutter, D. and Quine, L. (2002). *Changing Health Behaviour*. Buckingham: Open University Press.

An extremely useful text, which updates the empirical story told by Conner and Norman in 1996. The key social cognition models are now reviewed in terms of how they have been usefully applied to changing a range of health risk behaviour, from wearing cycle helmets or speeding to practising safer sex or participating in colorectal cancer screening.

Visser, de R.O. and Smith, J.A. (2007). Alcohol consumption and masculine identity among young men. *Psychology and Health*, 22: 595–614.

In additon to highlighting masculinity as an 'explanation' of drinking behaviour, this qualitative paper raises the important influence of culture and/or religous norms.

Visit the website at **www.pearsoned.co.uk/morrison** for additional resources to help you with your study, including multiple choice questions, weblinks and flashcards.

CHAPTER 6

Reducing risk of disease – individual approaches

Learning outcomes

By the end of this chapter, you should have an understanding of:

- the costs and benefits of screening programmes for the early detection of risk of disease or disease itself
- the use (and theoretical limitations) of the stages of change model in determining interventions likely to be most effective following detection of risk behaviour
- the process and outcomes of the motivational interview
- the impact of information provision on health-related behaviour following screening for disease risk
- the nature and use of problem-solving approaches and implementation planning to facilitate behavioural change
- how modelling and practice may increase the likelihood of behavioural change
- the use of cognitive-behavioural techniques to facilitate risk factor change

CHAPTER OUTLINE

This chapter considers strategies used to encourage individuals with no evidence of disease to adopt health-enhancing behaviour or stop health-damaging activities. It starts by considering the simplest approach to this issue – screening people for risk of disease as a consequence of either their genetic make-up or their behaviour, and whether this is sufficient to motivate or sustain changes in risk behaviour.

The chapter then considers a number of more complex ways of motivating and maintaining behavioural change based on the degree of motivation an individual may have to achieve change. The first approach we examine is known as motivational interviewing. As its name implies, this has been used particularly with people with low levels of motivation to change their behaviour. The chapter then considers how effective educational programmes are in facilitating change, before examining approaches based on planning and problem-solving techniques, modelling and rehearsing new behaviours, and cognitive-behavioural strategies. The principles of each approach are outlined, and evidence of their effectiveness is considered.

Promoting individual health

How we live our lives has important implications for how long we live, and the degree of physical wellbeing we enjoy while alive (see Chapters 1 and 2). Awareness of these issues, and also the financial consequences of an increasingly elderly population, has led governments across the world to invest significant resources in programmes designed to prevent illness and promote higher levels of fitness and health among the population as a whole. In the 1960s and 1970s, when health promotion became a serious issue for governments and health care, most programmes targeted behaviours known to increase our risk for disease. Fortuitously, perhaps, one of the most widely prevalent diseases, CHD, is also the one most strongly linked to lifestyle factors such as smoking or a sedentary lifestyle. The emerging role of these behaviours in the development of some cancers (see Chapter 3) reinforced the need to promote healthy lifestyles, and was accompanied by an increasing emphasis on encouraging safer sex behaviour following the emergence of HIV infection and AIDS. Biomedical advances have also contributed to the type of preventive services now provided by many health-care services. The ability to identify people at risk of a number of cancers and CHD as a consequence of their genetic make-up has led to programmes designed to identify whether individuals carry the genes that result in increased risk of these diseases, although how that risk is managed once identified is perhaps less clear.

Two broad approaches to facilitating risk factor change can be identified. The first assumes that if we inform people of their risk for certain diseases, this will result in them engaging in long-term preventive behaviour. This model has resulted in screening programmes for risk factors for diseases such as CHD being established throughout the world. More recently, more complex behaviour change technologies have been used to facilitate behavioural change. The next sections of this chapter consider the impact of screening programmes on our physical and psychological health, before considering some of the more complex strategies that have been used to facilitate health-related behavioural change.

Screening programmes

A number of types of screening programme now exist (see Table 6.1). These include testing for genetic risk for breast and ovarian cancer, screening for early detection of breast disease through regular mammography, and screening for the behavioural risk for disease in the case of CHD. Each carries significant implications for those involved and brings particular benefits and challenges:

- Women identified as carrying the gene mutations increasing risk for breast cancer may choose to take preventive action such as breast removal before the onset of disease and will have to live with the knowledge of their risk for many years.
- People identified as hypertensive may be placed on drugs for the rest of their lives.
- Those found to have behavioural risk factors for disease may choose to make lifestyle changes that have implications for both them and their family.

Table 6.1   Some of the common types of screening programme

Type of screening	Example of detection	Possible outcomes of screening
Genetic risk for disease	BRCA1, BRCA2 gene mutations for risk of breast and ovarian cancer	Routine subsequent screening for early detection of disease Preventive surgical procedures
Early detection of disease or its precursors	Cervical screening Mammography Hypertension	Medical or surgical treatment of any abnormalities found Behavioural change
Behavioural risk for disease	Smoking Sedentary lifestyle Poor diet	

Genetic risk of disease

We have now identified the genes linked to a number of significant diseases. Here, we focus on the implications of screening for just one of them – the gene mutations that increase risk of breast and ovarian cancer known as BRCA1 and BRCA2. These gene mutations are responsible for breast and ovarian cancer in approximately 40–45 per cent of individuals with an inherited susceptibility to the disease (Hodgson and Maher 1999). Fortunately, while the risk of cancer associated with them is high, they are relatively rare within the population, and only 4–5 per cent of cases of breast cancer result from these mutations.

The Cancer Genetic Service for Wales (Brain *et al.* 2000) provides an example of how a programme identifying genetic risk of developing breast cancer and BRCA gene mutations can work. In this programme, both men and women whose doctors think they may be at heightened genetic risk for breast cancer are referred to the service. Referral is followed by a letter to the patient from the service asking them to complete and return a family history questionnaire, which would give detailed information about their family history of cancer. Once returned, this is scored by medical geneticists, who identify participants' level of risk for developing cancer: the same as the general population, moderate or high. Patients are informed of their risk level by letter and through telephone contact.

- Women at high risk are invited for further counselling and formal genetic testing involving taking blood and looking for the BRCA gene mutation. They are offered annual mammography to detect breast lumps that may be tumours, or preventive mastectomy.
- Women in the moderate risk level are offered annual mammography.
- Women in the population risk group are discharged from the service.

Knowledge of being at moderate or high risk has significant impact for the individual – and their children, who may also be at genetic risk. With these profound implications, one may expect participation in the testing process to be stressful. However, most people seem to cope with no great anxieties, although about a quarter of those assessed report high levels of distress during their risk assessment (Brain *et al.* 2000). Of particular concern is that this may not be a short-term phenomenon. Brain *et al.* found that while levels of distress typically fell in the period after participants were told their risk level, they rose again over the following months, and one year later they were at the same level as immediately before risk assessment. Nor does being assigned a population risk level necessarily reduce anxiety. Geirdal *et al.* (2005) found that many women found to have no genetic mutations reported higher anxiety and depression levels than women at a higher risk for cancer. It appears that once some people are alerted to their potential risk for cancer, this becomes a long-term worry. We are not sure why this is the case. Perhaps some individuals who are naturally prone to worry find it difficult to tolerate the idea of *any* level of risk. Certainly, the beliefs people hold about the implications of their risk level are associated with anxiety. Bennett *et al.* (2008), for example, found that levels of anxiety following risk provision were associated with feelings of hopelessness about future health and having little control over developing cancer. Family members may also experience significant anxiety in the context of the testing process. Lodder *et al.* (2001) found that 20 per cent of the women found to carry the gene mutation and 35 per cent of their partners reported high anxiety levels. Levels of anxiety were lower but still significant among the couples in which the woman was found not to carry the genetic mutation: 11 per cent of these women and 13 per cent of their partners were clinically anxious. Despite this focus on negative emotions in response to risk assessment, most people do benefit emotionally from the testing process – something we consider IN THE SPOTLIGHT.

A different viewpoint on emotional reactions to health screening

Most studies of the emotional effects of cancer genetic screening have focused on measures of anxiety and depression. Studies with these *outcome* measures include those of Brain *et al.* (2000) described in the main text. An alternative model of anxiety or worry as a *motivator* to engage in testing is exemplified by studies such as Glanz *et al.* (1999), who sent a questionnaire to first-degree relatives of patients diagnosed with colorectal cancer, assessing their willingness or intentions to attend counselling for risk of colorectal cancer. While 45 per cent indicated an interest in taking it up, 26 per cent said they definitely would when testing was available. Strength of intentions was predicted by the degree of cancer worry and perceived risk of cancer.

Despite these and similar studies, the wider emotional responses to cancer genetic screening have been largely ignored. One may go even further to suggest that screening programmes are viewed through a psychopathological perspective – asking what harm we do to people who go through them rather than what benefits people gain. This is clearly a very important issue, but such data present only a partial picture of the emotional response to cancer genetic testing, which may be more positive. Women are unlikely to take part in the testing process unless they have some positive expectation of benefit – evident perhaps through emotional states such as hope or optimism. Similarly, they may feel relief if the testing shows them to be at population risk.

What evidence there is suggests that many individuals with a family history of cancer seek to clarify their genetic risk partly to *reduce* anxiety (Hopwood 1997). Many enter the process with high levels of optimism and hope. In one of the few studies to examine these positive emotional responses to screening, one of the authors (Bennett *et al.* 2008) followed a cohort of women going through genetic risk assessment, measuring their emotions at the beginning of the process and following risk information provision. The overall picture for these women was that although they felt anxious about their test results, they also felt optimistic about the testing process. After being told their risk level, all the women regardless of the genetic risk assigned were more relieved, calm and hopeful and less anxious and sad when they thought about the testing process and their risk for cancer than when they entered the testing process.

Early detection of disease

Breast cancer is the most common cancer in women and the second leading cause of death in women. Mammography provides a means of detecting early cancers before they become obvious to the woman involved. Of those who take part in this type of screening, less than one per cent are found to have an early cancer (Moss *et al.* 2005). Nevertheless, there is good evidence that this detection rate can significantly reduce rates of disease. Sarkeala *et al.* (2008), for example, found a 22 per cent reduction in deaths from breast cancer among Finnish women who were invited to mammography compared to those who had not received such an invitation. In the UK, the age limits of mammography in the absence of any particular risk for disease involve women aged between 50 and 70 years. Screening younger women appears to

ultrasound
the use of ultra-high-frequency sound waves to create images of organs and systems in the body.

fine needle aspiration
entails placing a very thin needle into a mass within the breast and extracting cells for microscopic evaluation. It takes seconds, and the discomfort is comparable with that of a blood test.

biopsy
the removal of a small piece of tissue for microscopic examination and/or culture, usually to help to make a diagnosis.

false positive result
a situation in which an individual is told that they may have a disease or are at risk of disease, but subsequent tests show that they are not at risk or do not have the disease.

be less beneficial, partly because of the lower frequency of tumours in this population, and partly because their higher density of breast tissue makes it difficult to identify small lumps within it.

Despite these benefits, mammography brings a number of concerns and anxieties, particularly for women who consider themselves to be at high risk for breast cancer. Such women frequently report high levels of anxiety both before and after testing – even when their mammogram is found to be normal (Absetz *et al.* 2003). Unfortunately, mammography is not an exact science, and women may be called back for a second mammogram or an **ultrasound** scan, which provides a more accurate view of the breast if the results of the initial mammogram are not clear. Where lumps in the breast *are* found, some women may have a small operation involving a **fine needle aspiration** or a **biopsy** to identify the nature of any lump. Following this procedure, women may be told that the lump is benign (known as a **false positive result**) or that it is cancerous and requires some form of medical or surgical intervention (a true positive). This process is clearly stressful, and while some women may be reassured following these various procedures, others appear to remain anxious for a long time. Austoker and colleagues (e.g. Brett and Austoker 2001), for example, followed a cohort of women who had experienced a false positive result. These women reported higher levels of anxiety than a group of women with an initially clear result for up to a year after their initial assessment. Although their anxiety levels then fell, they rose again in the month before their next routine breast screening was due – presumably as they began to worry about its implications. So strong is this anxiety, it may prevent many women attending subsequent mammography screening, although Brewer *et al.* (2007) reported interesting cross-cultural findings. US women who were given a false positive mammography result were more likely to return for routine screening than those who received normal results; the false positive had no effect on European women's attendance, while Canadian women were less likely to return for routine screening.

A number of studies have tried to find out how best to reduce the stress associated with this type of testing. One approach has involved compressing all the testing procedures into one day rather than over a period of days or even weeks – a process known as 'one-stop testing'. This approach has had mixed results, and the psychological outcomes may depend on the medical outcome. Harcourt *et al.* (1998), for example, found that women found to have no breast problems (about 90 per cent of those referred) appeared to benefit from it emotionally. By contrast, women found to have breast abnormalities did less well than those who took part in a testing and reporting process that took several days. Perhaps a longer time period allowed the affected women to adjust to the possibility of there being problems more than a relatively rushed process that occurred in one day. A different type of intervention targeted at women who were given false positive results was assessed by Bowland *et al.* (2003). They randomly allocated women who had been called back for further investigations and then found to be free of disease into one of three conditions: face-to-face counselling, telephone counselling and usual care. In the counselling sessions, they were encouraged to express their distress, given relevant information and helped to develop solutions to any problems they had. The session took up to one hour. When all the outcome data were analysed, no differences were found between the conditions. However, when the analysis was restricted to just those people who actually took part in the counselling process, these individuals scored better on measures of psychological and physical functioning than those who received the usual care. These results reflect the need to provide counselling not to everybody, just those who need or want it.

■ Increasing uptake

Despite the potential health benefits of mammography, uptake levels remain lower than optimal. In the USA, for example, the percentage of women aged 40 or more who took part in mammography screening rose between 1987 and 1992 (Martin *et al.* 1996), but over 80 per cent of eligible women still did not take part in any screening programme. Many programmes are advertised through television advertisements, leaflets in general practitioner surgeries and so on. More complex interventions to try and increase uptake have also been used. One of the more impressive interventions was reported by Allen *et al.* (2001), who recruited a number of volunteers from the workforces of thirteen US worksites. These women talked about their own positive experiences of screening, gave breast and cancer information to their co-workers and provided social support to women thinking of, or going to, mammography. In addition, they each led a number of small-group discussion sessions, which provided information about screening, how to talk to health-care professionals and how to set goals for health. They also ran two high-profile educational campaigns. Participants in control worksites had no such interventions. Despite these efforts, the percentage of women to have a mammogram increased only marginally in the worksites that ran the intervention over the course of the programme – from 5.6 to 7.2 per cent: a nonsignificant difference. A much simpler approach was followed by Rutter *et al.* (2006) in a study of implementation intentions (Gollwitzer and Schaal 1998, Chapter 5; and later in this chapter). They found that the simple act of inviting women to plan how they would overcome up to three previously identified barriers to attending mammography resulted in a significantly higher uptake than not doing so. Of interest also is that when Australian women were given appropriate information and encouraged to consider both the costs and benefits of mammography by Mathieu *et al.* (2007), this had no effect on mammography uptake.

RESEARCH FOCUS

Rai, T., Clements, A., Bukach, C. *et al.* (2007). What influences men's decision to have a prostate-specific antigen test? A qualitative study. *Family Practice*, 24: 365–71

So far in the chapter we have considered a number of issues surrounding testing for what are mostly health problems of women. But there is now a test that can assess the development of a male cancer – cancer of the prostate. Prostate Specific Antigen (PSA) is a protein produced by the prostate and released into the bloodstream. Levels increase following the onset of prostate cancer. PSA testing involves measuring the levels of PSA circulating in the blood, with the potential of identifying raised levels indicative of the development of prostate cancer.

continued

Unfortunately, there are wide variations in normal levels of PSA; high levels of PSA can occur in the context of other prostate problems, and some men with prostate cancer still have relatively low levels of PSA. The issue is further confounded by the fact that prostate cancer can develop slowly, and many men with prostate cancer will die of other diseases rather than the cancer itself. So, clinical decisions based on PSA results can be complex. Despite these provisos, the UK government has a policy that 'any man who wishes to have a PSA test should have access to the test, provided he has been given full information regarding the possible benefits and limitations associated with receiving [it]'. Full information includes the following:

The PSA test facilitates the early detection of prostate cancer at a stage when potentially curative treatments can be offered.

- There is currently no strong evidence that PSA testing reduces mortality from prostate cancer.
- Not all men with raised PSA will have prostate cancer; the PSA test will not detect all cancers.
- Prostate cancer is diagnosed through a prostate biopsy which can be uncomfortable or painful.
- Prostate biopsies will not detect all prostate cancers.
- Prostate cancers range from aggressive to slow-growing forms – slow-growing tumours may not result in symptoms or shorten life expectancy.
- There is no evidence about the optimum treatment for localised prostate cancer.
- Some treatments for prostate cancer can have significant side effects.

The authors used a qualitative study to investigate why men who had initiated the issue of testing with their GP decided to have the PSA test, whether GPs had given patients this information, and what influence any information they were given had on that decision.

Method
Potential participants were identified from records of their GP's request for a PSA test at a local University Hospital. Referring general practitioners were written to and asked whether they would be willing to forward an invitation to each patient to participate in the study. They were also asked to indicate if the patient had initiated the issue of PSA testing.

A total of 744 questionnaires were sent out to the GPs. The GPs agreed to forward 218 invitations, and 38 men agreed to be interviewed. At interview, 18 of these men had no recollection of PSA testing and/or stated that the issue was initiated by their GP. These men were excluded from the study. The final sample therefore comprised 20 men, all of whom were interviewed within a year of having their PSA test.

Semi-structured interviews were conducted and audio-taped. Participants were asked about their reasons for wanting to be tested, and the nature of any discussion they had with their GP concerning the benefits and limitations of testing. The interviews were subject to thematic analysis, in which the authors first identified key themes from the transcripts, checked the veracity of the themes by discussion, and then marked text within the transcripts illustrating the themes. This text was then examined by all three researchers to check for consistency and accuracy of coding.

Findings
Participants were aged between 45 and 75 years. All had received a 'normal' PSA value. Participants reported having sought testing either because they thought an early diagnosis would increase the chances of successful treatment or they wanted reassurance that they did not have prostate cancer.

. . . every man has a prostrate [*sic*] problem of some kind, some degree and if you can catch it early um you give yourself a damn good chance of getting away with it . . . Whereas if you let it run that's you know can be curtains . . . And I'm not ready for curtains yet. [laughs]

ID6, 58 years

There were several triggers for this. Most had chronic symptoms such as delay when starting to pass urine, combined with factors such as having relatives or friends with prostate cancer, reading about the high rate of mortality from prostate cancer in the media, and worries about their age and potentially declining health. A key trigger was having friends with prostate cancer:

. . . you know when you see friends uh with it who have a pretty healthy life style uh you think 'Oh blimey am I, am I in that bracket?'

ID10, 69 years

At the time of their consultation, most participants had learned about prostate cancer from the media and friends with the disease. Very few had detailed knowledge about the issues surrounding PSA testing described above. And only a minority were much better informed, as was the following individual, after the consultation with his GP.

. . . we talked it through, the pros, the cons, the complications, what would happen if the PSA test proved to be positive, how would I feel, how would I react. . . . the doctor discussed possible treatment . . . and the subsequent consequences of the treatment, incontinence . . . etcetera, etcetera . . . all that was discussed quite openly, in a very relaxed manner. And uh I had no qualms to go for the subsequent PSA test.

ID11, 47 years

The reasons the majority of men were less well informed than this individual may have been, at least in part, because they did not actively seek information – indeed, they may have deliberately blocked information – either because they had already made a decision to have the testing

. . . to be honest I had already made up my mind that I would [have the test] because I had had sufficient outside advice that men over 50 ought to have the test.

ID6, 58 years

. . . it wasn't just like 'Oh I'm walking down the road I'll pop in,' do you know what I mean? . . . I got the information that I wanted from him . . . as much as I needed to make a decision, and I had pretty much made the decision when I went in.

ID5, 47 years

or because they were wary of 'too much' information. They thought that additional information would make them anxious, and they trusted the GP to make the decision for them:

. . . it's nice to have the information but sometimes . . . it's too much information . . . it can put you on the worry, I feel quite happy that uh I had the blood test and if there was anything wrong I have always put my faith in doctors and the Health Service.

ID12, 61 years

Discussion

The authors concluded that the strongest message from this study was that general practitioners struggle to effectively provide men with balanced information regarding the benefits and limitations of PSA testing. They did not always provide men with the required information and many men did not want to be given such information. They had already made the decision to have the test – often on the basis of inadequate information from friends or the media – and did not want to hear potentially confusing or countervailing arguments at this time. Any relevant information needs to be in the public domain far before men seek the test – perhaps in the context of education about general prostate health.

Behavioural risk for disease

body mass index
a measurement of the relative percentages of fat and muscle mass in the human body, in which weight in kilograms is divided by height in metres and the result used as an index of obesity.

Screening programmes targeted at changing health behaviour have generally focused on risk behaviour for CHD: smoking, high-cholesterol diet, low levels of exercise, and so on. Many of the early programmes were established in the UK in the 1990s, the best known of which was developed by the OXCHECK group (OXCHECK Study Group 1994). In this, all adults in participating primary care practices around Oxford who went to their doctor for any reason were invited to attend a 'health check' conducted by a nurse. This involved an interview to identify risk behaviour for CHD as well as measurement of blood pressure and cholesterol levels. Where appropriate, participants were advised to stop smoking, eat a low-cholesterol diet and increase their exercise levels, as well as given medical treatment for hypertension and high cholesterol levels. Unfortunately, the outcome of this procedure was only measured some time after the intervention – at the one- and three-year follow-ups – and we therefore cannot be sure about the short-term effects of the intervention. Nevertheless, at both times there was evidence that some people had benefited from the screening programme. At one-year follow-up, participants' blood pressure levels were lower than those of people who did not take part in the screening programme, as were the cholesterol levels of women, but not men. There were no differences between the groups on measures of smoking or **body mass index**. By the three-year follow-up (OXCHECK Study Group 1995), cholesterol levels, systolic blood pressure and body mass index of both men and women who took part in the programme were lower than those of the controls. Smoking levels remained the same in both groups. It is difficult to disentangle from their results how much any changes in blood pressure and cholesterol were the result of behavioural change, and how much they resulted from the use of medication. However, the lack of change in smoking levels and, to a lesser extent, body mass index suggests that long-term behavioural changes were difficult to achieve. Indeed, the authors concluded that although the programme proved of benefit, changing difficult-to-change behaviours such as smoking may require a more specialised intervention.

More limited interventions have targeted individual risk behaviours such as smoking. A classic study of the impact of the effects of simple advice on smoking levels was reported by Russell *et al.* (1979). In it, general practitioners either gave verbal advice to their patients to stop smoking or combined this with a leaflet giving advice on how to stop smoking. One year after the intervention, 3 per cent of those in the verbal advice and 5 per cent in the advice plus leaflet condition had stopped smoking. Only 0.3 per cent of a comparison group who received no intervention had stopped smoking. Although these quit rates are relatively modest, given the simplicity of both interventions and the number of people attending general practitioners', these were impressive results.

These data were gathered nearly thirty years ago, when levels of smoking were higher and the health messages related to smoking were perhaps less well understood than at the present. It is questionable whether this level of intervention would have such an impact – or even if there is a commitment among health-care workers to working with patients to help them stop smoking. This was certainly the finding of Unrod *et al.* (2007) who found that

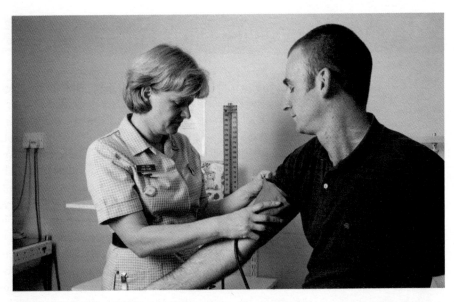

Plate 6.1 The simple process of measuring, identifying and treating high blood pressure can save thousands of lives a year.

Source: Alamy/Medical-on-line

most of their sample of general practitioners were neither actively encouraging their patients to stop smoking nor following simple guidelines on how this may be achieved. However, when these doctors were given specific training in smoking cessation techniques and a one-page leaflet suggesting personalised strategies for how to stop smoking to give to their patients, they found abstinence rates of 12 per cent among the intervention group and 8 per cent among those who received standard physician encounters.

What do YOU think?	Combining genetic counselling and attempts at coronary risk factor change, Audrain *et al.* (1997) fed back participants their level of genetic risk for developing lung cancer in an attempt to motivate smoking cessation. They randomly allocated smokers to either a counselling intervention or counselling combined with level of genetic risk. The risk factor information seemed to increase the motivation of some smokers to change, with almost a doubling of initial cessation rates in this group in comparison with the no-risk information condition. By one-month follow-up, however, any between-condition differences had dissipated, and there were no longer any differences in cessation rates between the groups. The authors noted that those who received the risk information were initially more depressed than those who did not, but these differences also dissipated over time.

Given that high levels of fear typically do not lead to long-term behavioural change (see Chapter 7) and may result in depression and learned helplessness (and may also result in long-term health anxieties), is it fair or ethical to use genetic risk factor information to motivate difficult behaviour change?

Strategies for changing risk behaviour

The evidence reviewed above suggests that while some people will strive to change their behaviour once they are aware of being at risk for an illness such as CHD, many will not, or will not be able to sustain any changes that they make over time. It has become increasingly obvious that making people aware of their risk status may not be enough to foster behavioural change. As a consequence, more sophisticated interventions have been developed to achieve these goals, some of which are considered in this section.

Historically, most one-to-one psychological interventions have been targeted at people who are relatively motivated to change their behaviour. Clinics are held in hospitals, out-patient departments or primary care centres, and the people who take the trouble to attend them are usually motivated to take an active part in any programme of change. However, this is not always the case. The introduction of screening programmes in primary care, for example, has resulted in the identification of many people who are not particularly motivated to change their behaviour. In response to this, efforts have been made to develop interventions that take into account people's differing levels of motivation to change rather than a 'one intervention fits all' approach. This targeted approach has generally been based on a stage model of change developed by Prochaska and di Clemente (1986). Their transtheoretical, or **stages of change model**, identified a series of five stages through which they considered an individual passed when considering change:

stages of change model
developed by Prochaska and di Clemente, this identifies five stages through which an individual passes when considering behavioural change: pre-contemplation, contemplation, preparation, change and maintenance/relapse.

1. *pre-contemplation*: they are not considering change;
2. *contemplation*: they are considering change but have not thought through its exact nature or how it can be achieved;
3. *preparation*: they are planning how to achieve change;
4. *change*: they are actively engaged in change;
5. *maintenance or relapse*: they are maintaining change (for longer than six months) or relapsing.

The model is thought to be applicable to virtually any decision relating to change, from giving up cigarettes to buying a new car. Prochaska and di Clemente noted that the factors that may shift an individual from one stage to another – and they can move back and forth along the change continuum or even skip stages – can differ enormously. As a consequence, the model does not attempt to specify what these factors are – merely that they occur and that they can shift the individual from stage to stage. Accordingly, a smoker may shift from pre-contemplation to contemplation as a result of developing a chest infection, move to preparation and action after seeing a book on giving up smoking in the local library, and relapse after being tempted to smoke while out for a beer with friends.

Other stage models of change have also been developed. Heckhausen (1991), for example, identified four stages of change, each with a different cognitive content:

1. *pre-decisional phase*: thoughts about the desirability and feasibility of change predominate;

2. *decisional phase*: includes consideration of plans about how to change;
3. *change phase*: thoughts about how to initiate and maintain initial change predominate;
4. *evaluative phase*: consideration of how well any outcomes achieved compare with initial goals – leads to regulation of behaviour, maintenance or relapse.

Some studies have found differences in cognitive content in different stages of change. In an examination of incentives and barriers to physical activity for working women, for example, Jaffe *et al.* (1999) found that while precontemplators had few positive expectations regarding exercise, contemplators had positive expectations and a higher number of perceived barriers. Despite this, stage theories of change have been criticised on both theoretical and empirical grounds. Empirical studies have struggled to find a sequential process of change or to be able to consistently place any individual into one stage of change at any one time. Budd and Rollnick (1996), for example, reported that a readiness-to-change questionnaire was able to categorise only 40 per cent of their sample of heavy drinkers as being in one single stage. Many of their responses to the questionnaire suggested that they were in several stages of change – a finding at odds with the idea of differing and exclusive states (or stages) of change. The model has also been found to have mixed predictive utility. While di Clemente *et al.* (1991) found that the stage of change in which smokers began attending a smoking cessation programme was predictive of subsequent levels of smoking, Carlson *et al.* (2003) found that participants' stage of change at baseline was not predictive of smoking status following a cognitive-behavioural smoking cessation group intervention. Of course, in neither case do we know what influence taking part in the intervention had on participants' stage of change. Nevertheless, these data add little to support the stage of change model. These and other data have led critics of the model (e.g. Weinstein *et al.* 1998) to suggest that motivation to change may best be thought of as a continuum, possibly measured as a strength of intention to change (see Chapter 5), rather than a series of steps from one cognitive and behavioural state to a differing one. Interestingly, though, a shift from 'stage of change' to 'motivation' as indicators of likelihood of engagement and completion of therapy may not resolve some of these issues. In their meta-analysis of data relevant to condom use, Noguchi *et al.* (2007) found that populations with intermediate levels of motivation to use condoms were more likely to complete an intervention designed to increase condom use than were those with either low or high levels of motivation.

Despite these criticisms, the stages of change approach has been useful from an intervention perspective in that it has focused consideration on what is the best type of intervention to conduct at each stage of change (or level of motivation to change if it is conceptualised in this way). The most obvious implication of the model is that there is little point in trying to show people *how* to achieve change if they are in the pre-contemplation or possibly the contemplation stage. Such individuals are unlikely to be sufficiently motivated to attempt change, and will benefit little from being shown how to do so. By contrast, an individual in the planning or action stage may benefit from this type of approach.

Motivational interviewing

motivational interview
developed by Miller and Rollnick, a set of procedures designed to increase motivation to change behaviour.

The intervention generally considered most likely to be effective for people who are unmotivated to change their behaviour is known as **motivational interviewing** (Miller and Rollnick 2002). Its goal is to increase an individual's motivation to consider change – not to show them how to change. If the interview succeeds in motivating change, only then can any intervention proceed to considering ways of achieving that change.

Motivational interviewing is designed to help people to explore and resolve any ambivalence they may have about changing their behaviour (Miller and Rollnick 2002). The approach assumes that when an individual is facing the need to change, they may have beliefs and attitudes that both support and counter change. Prior to the interview, thoughts that counter change probably predominate – or else the person would be actively seeking help to achieve change. Nevertheless, the goal of the interview is to elicit both sets of beliefs and attitudes and to bring them into sharp focus ('I know smoking does damage my health', 'I enjoy smoking', and so on). This is thought to place the individual in a state of **cognitive dissonance** (Festinger 1957), which is resolved by rejecting one set of beliefs in favour of the other. These may (or may not) favour behavioural change. If an individual decides to change their behaviour, the intervention will then focus on consideration of how to achieve change. If the individual still rejects the possibility of change, they would typically not continue in any programme of behavioural change.

cognitive dissonance
a state in which conflicting or inconsistent cognitions produce a state of tension or discomfort (dissonance). People are motivated to reduce the dissonance, often by rejecting one set of beliefs in favour of the other.

The motivational interview is deliberately non-confrontational. Miller and Rollnick consider the process of motivational interviewing to be a philosophy of supporting individual change and not attempting to persuade an individual to go against their own wishes, rather than a set of specific techniques. Nevertheless, a few key strategies can be identified. Perhaps the key questions in the interview are:

- What are some of the good things about your present behaviour?
- What are the not so good things about your present behaviour?

The first question is perhaps slightly surprising but important, as it acknowledges that the individual is gaining something from their present behaviour and is intended to reduce the potential for resistance. Once the individual has considered each issue (both for and against change), they are summarised by the counsellor in a way that highlights the dissonance between the two sets of issues. Once this has been fed back to the individual, they are invited to consider how this information makes them feel. Only if they express some interest in change should the interview then go on to consider how to change. Other key elements and strategies include:

empathy
an understanding of the situation from the individual's viewpoint.

- expressing **empathy**;
- avoiding arguments by assuming that the individual is responsible for the decision to change;
- rolling with resistance rather than confronting or opposing it;
- supporting self-efficacy and optimism for change.

What do YOU think?

We all have bad habits or do less of the things we 'ought to do' than we should. Or at least, most of us do. Think of a behaviour you would like to change or could change – to either do more of . . . or less. Then consider the issue in the light of the motivational process . What stage of the motivational process are you in: pre-contemplation, contemplation? Try out a motivational interview on yourself. What are the good things about the status quo? What would you gain if you were to change things? Write down a 'decisional balance sheet', listing the pros and cons of change. Did you expect to write what you did? Did it motivate you to change, or simply accept the status quo? Was it harder to think of reasons for change than reasons to maintain the status quo? It often is!! How did the process feel, and how easy would this be to do with someone else?

drug abuse
involves use of a drug that results in significant social or work-related problems.

Given that the goal of motivational interviewing is to motivate people to consider change, it is perhaps surprising that most outcome studies have not examined this issue at all. Instead, they have focused largely on whether it can alter behaviour in the mid to long term. However, those studies that *have* examined this issue have found the interview to be at least as good if not better at encouraging participation than more direct attempts at persuasion. Carroll, K. *et al.* (2001) found that individuals referred to a treatment programme for **drug abuse** were most likely to continue attending after an initial session that involved a motivational interview: 59 per cent of referrals attended at least one further session following a motivational interview compared with 29 per cent following a standard first session. By contrast, Schneider *et al.* (2000) compared the effectiveness of confrontational with motivational interviewing in persuading substance users to enter treatment for their drug use. At three and nine months into the treatment, an equal percentage of both groups had completed their initial treatment programme – and had made similar gains in terms of reduced drug use. However, the motivational interview was more acceptable and less stressful for both counsellors and clients than the confrontational approach – suggesting that it should be the approach of choice.

Initially, motivational interview techniques were used to help people who presented with substance misuse problems, a context in which it has proven effective (e.g. Hulse and Tait 2002). More recently, the approach has been used with an increasing range of other behaviours. In a simple comparison of advice to stop smoking versus a motivational interview conducted in Spain (Soria *et al.* 2006), smokers were over five times more likely to stop smoking if they received a motivation interview than if simply advised to quit. More complex interventions have also been found to be of benefit. Resnicow *et al.* (2001), for example, examined the impact of the 'Eat for Life' programme conducted among church-attending African Americans. They compared the effect of two interventions in trying to increase fruit and vegetable intake in the target group. These involved either a self-help intervention with a telephone call to encourage use of the programme, or this approach combined with three telephone calls using motivational interviewing techniques. At one-year follow-up, participants in the second group were eating more fruit and vegetables than those in the self-help only group, who in turn were eating more than a no-treatment control group. Whether this was due to the increased attention given to the combined intervention group, or to the motivational elements is not clear. However, when motivational techniques were simply integrated into another therapy, in this case a behavioural weight loss programme, Carels *et al.* (2007) found this led to an increase in weight loss among people experiencing difficulties in achieving significant weight loss.

Problem-solving approaches

problem-focused counselling

a counselling approach developed by Gerard Egan that attempts to foster a collaborative and structured approach between counsellor and client to solving life problems.

Problem-focused interventions provide one form of strategy for considering *how*, rather than *whether*, to change. They are best used for people who are willing to consider changing their behaviour and need help working out how to do this. Perhaps the most clearly described **problem-focused counselling** approach was developed by Egan (e.g. 2006). His form of problem-focused counselling is complex in parts but has an elegantly simple basic framework. It emphasises the importance of appropriate analysis of the problem the individual is facing as a critical element of the counselling process. Only when this has been achieved can an appropriate solution to the problem be identified. A further element of Egan's approach is that the job of the counsellor is not to act as an expert solving the person's problems. Instead, their role is to mobilise the individual's own resources both to identify problems accurately and to arrive at strategies of solution. Counselling is problem-oriented. It is focused specifically on the issues at hand and in the 'here and now', and it has three distinct phases:

1. *problem exploration and clarification*: a detailed and thorough exploration of the problems an individual is facing: breaking 'global insolvable problems' into carefully defined soluble elements

2. *goal setting*: identifying how the individual would like things to be different. Setting clear, behaviourally defined, and achievable goals (or sub-goals)

3. *facilitating action*: developing plans and strategies through which these goals can be achieved.

Some people may not need to work through each stage of the counselling process. Others may be able to work through all the phases in one session. Still others may require several counselling sessions. However, it is important to deal with each stage sequentially and thoroughly. Flitting from stage to stage serves only to confuse both the counsellor and the individual being counselled.

Mrs T provides a good example of how the problem-solving approach may lead to issues and interventions far from those that might be expected. Mrs T took part in a regular screening clinic held at her local GP's surgery, where she was found to be obese and to have a raised serum cholesterol level. Following standard dietary advice, Mrs T agreed to a goal of losing two pounds a week over the following months. She was given a leaflet providing information about the fat and calorific content of a variety of foods and a leaflet describing a number of 'healthy' recipes.

On her follow-up visits, her cholesterol level and weight remained unchanged – so she saw a counsellor to provide her with more help. The counsellor used the problem-focused approach of Egan. In the first session, she explored why Mrs T had not made use of the advice she had previously been given. Mrs T explained that she already knew which were 'healthy' and 'unhealthy' foods. Indeed, she had been on many diets before – without much success. Together, she and the counsellor began to explore why this *was the case. At this point, a number of problems became apparent. One important factor was that she was not receiving support from her family, and in particular her two grown-up sons. Mrs T was the family cook, in a family that often demanded 'fry-ups'. She accepted this role but had difficulty in not nibbling the food as she cooked it. Although she actually ate quite small (and low-fat) meals, her nibbling while cooking significantly increased her calorie and cholesterol intake.*

Mrs T's husband supported her attempts to lose weight and was prepared to change his diet to help her. However, her sons often demanded meals when they got back from the pub, late at night and often the worse for drink. The upshot of this was that Mrs T often started to cook late at night at the end of what may have been a successful day of dieting. She then nibbled high-calorie food while cooking. This had two outcomes. First, she increased her calorie input at a time when she did not need calories. Second, she sometimes catastrophised ('I've eaten so much, I may as well abandon my diet for today') and ate a full meal at this time. It also reduced her motivation to follow her diet the following day.

Once this specific problem had been identified, Mrs T set a goal of not cooking late night fry-ups for her sons. She decided that, in future if her sons wanted this, they could cook it themselves. Once the goal was established, Mrs T felt a little concerned about how her sons would react to her no longer cooking for them, so she and the counsellor explored ways in which she could set about telling them – and sticking to her resolution. She finally decided she would tell them in the coming week, explaining why she felt she could no longer cook for them at that time of night. She even rehearsed how she would say it. This she did, with some effect, as she did start to lose weight.

| What do YOU think? | Think about how you react if a someone asks you for advice. Do you sit and listen to the causes of the problems, invite your friend to consider their options for change, and then decide which one to adopt. Or are you quick to give advice, without really knowing the issues from the perspective of your friend? Most people fit into the latter category, so you are not alone if you came to that conclusion. But how effective is your advice giving likely to be? |

Despite the generally acknowledged effectiveness of the problem-focused counselling approach, there has been surprisingly little empirical examination of its effectiveness. In one of the few studies conducted in a health promotion context, Gomel *et al.* (1993) screened hundreds of factory workers for risk factors for coronary heart disease (CHD), assigning them to one of three groups if at least one risk factor was found:

1. risk factor education
2. problem-focused counselling
3. no intervention control.

Participants in the educational programme received standard advice on the lifestyle changes needed to reduce their risk of CHD (following an information provision model) and some videos showing how to modify these risk factors. Participants in the problem-solving programme first went through an exercise based on motivational interviewing techniques. Following this they identified a number of high-risk situations in which they were likely to engage in CHD-risk behaviour (such as smoking or eating high-fat meals) or which would prevent them from engaging in health-promoting behaviours (such as lack of planning leaving no time for exercise). They were then encouraged to think through how they could minimise their effect. This more complex intervention proved the most effective. Participants in this condition had greater reductions in blood pressure, body mass index and smoking than those in either the education-only intervention or no-intervention control.

In a study targeted more specifically at reducing blood pressure, Elmer *et al.* (1995) also reported the outcome of a programme that incorporated an element of problem solving. Participants were taught to recognise environmental or psychological cues that led to overeating and to plan how to change or cope with them as well as considering how to begin and maintain an exercise programme. They also worked with their partners to develop a joint strategy to support any lifestyle changes they made. One year after the programme started, the intervention appeared to be a success. By this time, 70 per cent of the participants had significantly reduced their alcohol intake and increased their exercise levels. As a consequence, they had achieved significant weight loss over the year, and their blood pressure had fallen significantly.

More sophisticated approaches have integrated motivational interviewing and problem-focused approaches. Steptoe *et al.* (1999) adjusted their intervention to suit the stage of change of participants in a screening programme to identify and reduce risk for CHD. They identified individuals at risk of CHD as a consequence of one or more modifiable risk factors: regular cigarette smoking, high cholesterol levels, and high body mass index combined with low physical activity. Practice nurses then provided brief behavioural counselling on the basis of the stages of change model, using elements of motivational interviews for those who were in pre-contemplation and developing strategies of change for participants who were considering the possibility of change. Compared to no intervention, some benefits were achieved, with modest reductions in dietary fat intake and cigarettes smoked per day, and increased regular exercise at 4- and 12-month follow-up assessments. However, no differences were found between groups on measures of total serum cholesterol concentration, weight, body mass index, or smoking cessation. It seems that more sustained support and counselling may have been necessary to achieve long-term behavioural change with these difficult-to-change behaviours.

■ Smoking cessation as a form of problem solving

Although they may not explicitly state it, many other behavioural change programmes have within them an element of problem identification and resolution. The example of smoking cessation can illustrate this point. Smoking is driven by two processes:

1. a conditioned response to a variety of cues in the environment – picking up the telephone, having a cup of coffee, and so on – the so-called habit cigarette;
2. a physiological need for nicotine – to top up levels of nicotine and prevent the onset of withdrawal symptoms.

acetylcholine
a white crystalline derivative of choline that is released at the ends of nerve fibres in the parasympathetic nervous system and is involved in the transmission of nerve impulses in the body.

Nicotine is an extremely powerful drug. It acts on the **acetylcholine** system, which, in part, mediates levels of attention and activation in the brain and muscle activity in the body. Its activity is bi-phasic: that is, short, sharp inhalations increase activity in this system as the nicotine bonds with the acetylcholine receptors and activates the neurons – resulting in increased alertness. Long inhalations, by contrast, result in the nicotine remaining in the post-synaptic acetylcholine receptors, preventing further uptake of nicotine or acetylcholine by the receptors – leading to feelings of relaxation. Accordingly, when an individual stops smoking, they may have to deal with:

■ the loss of a powerful means of altering mood and level of attention;
■ withdrawal symptoms as a consequence of a biological dependence on nicotine;
■ the urge to smoke triggered by environmental cues.

The best smoking cessation programmes address each of these issues. Following a 'quit day', most call for complete cessation of smoking, following which the individual may have to cope with varying degrees of urges to smoke as a result of withdrawal symptoms or encountering cues that previously were associated with smoking. Any withdrawal symptoms may take up to two or three weeks to subside, and be at their worst in the first two to three days following cessation. Accordingly, there is an acute period of high risk for relapse following cessation that may be driven by the immediate psychological and physiological discomfort associated with quitting.

Many programmes prepare ex-smokers to cope with these problems. Each set of strategies involves a degree of problem solving, as the smoker has to identify both the particular problems they may face and individual solutions to those problems (see Table 6.2). The strategies may involve:

■ how to cope with cues to smoking – this may involve avoiding them completely or working out ways of coping with temptation triggered by smoking cues;
■ how to reduce the possibility of giving in to cravings should they occur;
■ how to cope with any withdrawal symptoms.

Table 6.2 Some strategies that smokers may use to help them to cope in the period immediately following cessation

Avoidant strategies	Coping strategies
Sit with non-smoking friends at coffee breaks	If you feel the urge to smoke, focus attention on things happening around you – *not* on your desire for a cigarette
Drink something different at coffee breaks – to break your routine and not light up automatically	Think distracting thoughts – count backwards in sevens from 100
Go for a walk instead of smoking	Remember your reasons for stopping smoking – carry them on flashcards and look at them if this helps
Chew sugar-free gum or sweets at times you would normally smoke	
Move ashtrays out of sight	
Try to keep busy, so you won't have time to think of cigarettes	

Make it difficult to smoke	Cognitive re-labelling
Don't carry money – so you can't buy cigarettes	These horrible symptoms are signs of recovery
Avoid passing the tobacconist where you usually buy your cigarettes	

nicotine replacement therapy (NRT)
replacement of nicotine to minimise withdrawal symptoms following the cessation of smoking. Delivered in a variety of ways, including a transdermal patch placed against the skin, which produces a measured dose of nicotine over time.

transdermal patch
a method of delivering a drug in a slow release form. The drug is impregnated into a patch, which is stuck to the skin and gradually absorbed into the body.

One strategy for coping with any withdrawal symptoms involves the use of **nicotine replacement therapy (NRT)**, either as a gum or, more recently, as a **transdermal patch**. The development of NRT was initially seen as a major breakthrough that would prevent the need for any psychological intervention to help people to stop smoking. This has not proved to be the case. Indeed, most manufacturers of nicotine replacement products now recommend using a number of problem-solving strategies along with the NRT – a recommendation clearly supported by the outcome of clinical trials of their use. Studies that have examined the use of transdermal nicotine patches, for example, have shown high levels of cessation during their use but high levels of relapse when their use has stopped – or in some cases inappropriately long periods of use of the patches themselves (see Seidman and Covey 1999). Now, most interventions use a combination of nicotine replacement therapy and problem-solving approaches.

Measuring the effectiveness of this approach, Molyneux *et al.* (2003), compared the effectiveness of usual care (no advice) with a problem-solving approach alone or in combination with NRT in 274 hospital patients. The percentage of people who stopped smoking was higher in the combined NRT plus problem-solving group than in the counselling alone or usual care groups. The difference between the groups was significant when the patients were discharged from hospital: 55 per cent, 43 per cent and 37 per cent of each group, respectively, had stopped smoking. By the twelve-month follow-up, the equivalent figures were 17, 6 and 8 per cent. One interesting study took regard of the type of smoker who entered their programme. Hall *et al.* (1985) identified smokers as being primarily nicotine-dependent or primarily habit smokers and assigned half of each type of smoker to either a problem-focused programme, which should be of maximum benefit for habitual smokers, nicotine gum aimed at nicotine-dependent participants, and a combination of both approaches. Each group did indeed fare better from the intervention targeted at their particular problem, although only the nicotine-dependent group benefited from the combined intervention. By the one-year follow-up, 50 per cent of the nicotine-dependent smokers who received the combined programme were still not smoking, compared with 32 per cent who only received the NRT and 11 per cent of those who received the problem-focused intervention. Among the habitual smokers, the equivalent rates were 42, 38 and 47 per cent.

◼ Implementing plans and intentions

A number of interventions have identified the last of Egan's stages as the key therapeutic element. Based on the social cognitive models of the health action process approach (HAPA; Schwarzer and Renner 2000) and implementation intentions (Gollwitzer and Schaal, 1998; see Chapter 5), both of which identified planning as an important determinant of behavioural change, these approaches have simply encouraged individuals to plan how they will engage in their behaviour of choice. Some interventions have targeted relatively simple or short-term behavioural change. De Nooijer *et al.* (2006) found that writing plans to eat an extra serving of fruit per day for one week resulted in a higher intake of fruit than a no-treatment condition. Sheeran and Orbell (2000) found implementation plans resulted in a higher attendance at a cervical screening clinic than a no-treatment condition. Even more impressively,

Armitage (2007) found forming implementation plans resulted in a higher rate of quitting smoking than no intervention, while Luszczynska *et al.* (2007) found that they significantly enhanced the effectiveness of a weight loss programme for obese women. Women who were on a normal commercial weight loss programme achieved a weight loss of 2.1 kilograms over a two-month period, while those given the implementation planning intervention achieved a weight loss of 4.2 kilograms over the same period. Gratton *et al.* (2007) found an intervention based on implementation plans to be equally effective as one designed to enhance motivation in relation to children's fruit and vegetable consumption. On a more cautious note, Michie *et al.* (2004) carried out an experimental study of an intervention aimed at increasing antenatal screening uptake among women who had expressed the intention to do so. Eighty-eight pregnant women were allocated to either standard care or a group asked to write down an action plan for attending or making the screening appointment. No difference in subsequent attendance was found. In the intervention group itself, however, only 63 per cent actually made an action plan, and these women *were* more likely to attend screening (84 per cent of them attended) than the women in this group who had not done so (47 per cent attended). So, a crucial element of any intervention may be to clearly facilitate the planning process.

Modelling change

Problem-focused and 'planning'-based interventions can help individuals to develop strategies of change. However, achieving change can still be difficult, particularly where an individual lacks the skills or confidence in their ability to cope with the demands of change. Egan himself noted that it may be necessary to teach people the skills to achieve any goals they have set or to change the social norms in which such behaviours occur.

vicarious learning
learning from observation of others.

One way that these deficits can be remedied is by learning skills or appropriate attitudes from observation of others performing them – a process known as **vicarious learning**. Bandura's (2001) social cognitive theory (see Chapter 5) suggested that both skills and confidence in the ability to change (self-efficacy) can be increased through a number of simple procedures, including observation of others performing relevant tasks (vicarious learning), practice of tasks in a graded programme of skills development, and active persuasion. The effectiveness of learning from observation of others can be influenced by a number of factors. However, the optimal learning and increases in self-efficacy can generally be achieved through observation of people similar to the learner succeeding in relevant tasks. This may be further enhanced by the use of what Bandura termed coping models, in which those being observed demonstrate a skill or other behaviour in a way that does not leave the observer feeling de-skilled or incapable of gaining the skills. Where complex skills are being taught, behaviour may be shaped by observation of the progressive learning of skills by the models.

One way that this approach can work is through the use of video – an approach that has proven particularly effective in modifying sexual behaviour. Sanderson and Yopyk (2007), for example, found that young sexually active people reported stronger intentions to engage in protected sex, higher self-efficacy in refusing to have unprotected sex, and higher levels of condom use four months after seeing videos providing positive attitudes about condom use and modelling appropriate strategies for negotiating their use. Any behavioural changes may translate into changes in health. O'Donnell *et al.* (1998) monitored over 2,000 people attending sexually transmitted disease (STD) clinics who were randomly allocated to either a control or an intervention group in which they were encouraged and shown how to use safer sex techniques using a video similar to that used by Sanderson and Yopyk. Attendance at further clinics for both groups was tracked for an average of seventeen months following the intervention. By this time, the rate of new infection was significantly lower among those given the video-based education than among controls (23 per cent compared with 27 per cent). Among a subgroup of individuals with a relatively high number of sexual partners, infection rates were 32 per cent among controls and 25 per cent among those who saw the video. Despite these positive findings, the results of Jenkins *et al.* (2000) provide a more cautionary message. They found that watching an interactive video increased their participants' intentions to abstain from sex and to change risky partner behaviour in the short

Plate 6.2   Both watching others, and practice, increases the chances of people purchasing and using a condom.

Source: Royalty-Free/Corbis

term, but that these changes were no longer evident at follow-up. They concluded that risky sexual behaviour was particularly resistant to change but that the single-session intervention had some impact, and could be viewed as a 'priming' effect that could enhance multi-session interventions.

Mathews *et al.* (2002) reported a different, and important, use of video in the context of HIV infection. They used it to teach attenders at an STD clinic in Kwazulu Natal in South Africa how to tell their sexual partners, who they may have infected with HIV, about the need to check their sexual health status. This is important as it would allow these individuals to be treated and to prevent further spread of HIV. As a consequence of the intervention, attenders' confidence in their ability to notify their sexual partners rose, as did the rate of sexual contacts who subsequently attended the clinic.

Behavioural practice

A further addition or alternative to problem-solving or implementation-based strategies involves the actual practice of new behaviour. Here, solutions to problems as well as skills needed to achieve change can be worked out and taught in an educational programme – increasing both skills and self-efficacy. In one study of this approach, again in the context of sexual behaviour, Kelly *et al.* (1994) reported on the effectiveness of an intervention to reduce risky sexual behaviour among women at high risk of HIV infection who had attended an STD clinic. The programme included risk education, training in condom use and practising sexual assertiveness skills such as negotiating the use of a condom. This was compared with a standard education-based programme. The complex intervention proved the most effective. While the women in both groups did not reduce their number of sexual partners, those in the complex intervention reported that more of their partners used condoms on more occasions over the three months following the intervention. Even a simple behavioural element in an intervention can be remarkably effective. As part of an AIDS workshop run for young adults, Weisse *et al.* (1995) asked half the participants to buy a condom from a local shop. Following the workshop, while all participants knew more about HIV infection prevention, only those who took part in the behavioural exercise reported less embarrassment than before while purchasing condoms.

The effectiveness of video intervention can also be enhanced by adding other behavioural change techniques. O'Donnell *et al.* (1995), for example, compared the effectiveness of either a video condition alone or combined with a problem-solving skill-building session with a no-treatment control condition, in attempting to promote safer sexual behaviour among attenders at an STD clinic. One way of directly assessing the impact of their intervention was to provide all of the study participants with a voucher that they could exchange at a local pharmacy for free condoms; 40 per cent of the people who took part in the combined intervention made use of this service, compared with 28 per cent of those in the video condition alone and 21 per cent of the no-intervention control group. It seems that while learning how to do things from a video can be effective, it can still be enhanced by active practice in the skills required to achieve change.

One interesting development of the behavioural practice approach has been on modifying drink driving. 'Fatal Vision goggles' simulate the visual impairment caused by alcohol or other drugs. According to the manufacturers,

'Viewing through the goggles is rather clear, but confusing to the mind. The wearer experiences a loss of equilibrium, which is one of the effects of intoxication'. Different goggles simulate four levels of intoxication. They are now frequently used in drink-driving education programmes in the USA, with wearers using a driving simulator while wearing the goggles. This approach has achieved some modest effects, at least in the short-term (Jewell and Hupp 2005). Unsurprisingly, perhaps, they appear to work best with young people who drink significant amounts of alcohol and who believe that this may impair their driving (Hennessy *et al.* 2006).

Cognitive interventions

The interventions so far considered can be thought of as behavioural interventions, in that they attempt to directly influence behaviour. They may also result in cognitive change – increasing an individual's confidence in their ability to make and maintain any lifestyle changes, and so on – but this is an indirect effect. By contrast, cognitive strategies attempt to change cognitions directly – in particular, those that drive an individual to engage in behaviour that may be harmful to their health or prevent them making appropriate behavioural changes. From a health psychology perspective, various categories of relevant cognitions have been identified, including our attitudes towards the behaviour and any relevant social norms (Ajzen 1985), our beliefs about the costs and benefits of disease prevention and behavioural change (Becker 1974), our self-efficacy expectations (Bandura 2001) and beliefs about an illness or condition and our ability to manage it (Leventhal *et al.* 1984; see Chapter 9). The need to change cognitions is based on the premise that we do not have relevant information or somehow have developed distorted or inappropriate beliefs about a relevant issue, and that changing these beliefs will result in more appropriate (and health promoting) behaviour. The simplest form of intervention may involve the provision of appropriate education – particularly when an individual is facing a new health threat or is unaware of information that may encourage appropriate behavioural change. Such education is likely to be optimal if it targets factors known to influence health-related behaviours. It can educate individuals about the nature of their risk, show them how to change their behaviour, and so on (see the discussion on theory and behavioural change in Chapter 18).

The OXCHECK programme described above provides a good example of a programme based on information provision. Such programmes have frequently been based on the assumption that people will make necessary changes if they are informed of the need to change and the nature of the changes they need to make. Many small-scale health education programmes are still premised on this assumption. However, the relatively low impact of such interventions, as well as an increasing awareness and use of psychological theory, has led to a recognition that any information provision about *what* to change may be significantly enhanced by information about *how* to change and encouraging appropriate planning. A good example of this transition can be found in leaflets on smoking cessation available in the UK, the emphasis of which has shifted from a major emphasis on disease and damaged lungs to consideration of planning and implementing strategies of change. Booklets explaining the need to stop smoking have been added to by step-by-step programmes showing the individual *how* to stop and teaching any skills that may benefit them: e.g. cut down till you smoke about twelve cigarettes a day, choose a quit day, work out strategies to cope with habit cigarettes such as not carrying them with you, and so on. The next chapter considers a number of information-based approaches in the context of health promotion, while Chapter 17 considers their use in individuals who have already developed an illness.

More complex interventions may be required to change inappropriate beliefs that have been developed and reinforced over time. Beliefs that encourage substance use or abuse, for example, may include 'I cannot cope with going to a party without a hit' or 'Drinking makes me a more sociable person'. At the beginning of a history of drug use, positive beliefs such as 'It will be fun to get high' may predominate. As the individual begins to rely on the drug to counteract feelings of distress, more dependent beliefs may predominate: 'I need a drink to get me through the day'. Cognitive interventions may be of benefit where such thoughts interfere with any behavioural change. Key to any intervention is that the beliefs we hold about illnesses, our health, events that have happened or will happen in the future, and so on, are *hypothetical*. Some of these guesses may be correct; some may be wrong. In some cases, because maladaptive beliefs ('I need a shot of whisky to get through this') come readily to mind, they are taken as facts and alternative thoughts ('Well, I might be able to cope without') are not considered. The role of cognitive therapy is to teach the individual to treat their beliefs as hypotheses and not facts, to try out alternative ways of looking at the situation and to have different responses to it based on these new ways of thinking ('Well, I used to cope in this situation before without having a drink. Perhaps I can do the same this time'). One way in which this can be achieved involves a process known as **Socratic dialogue** or guided discovery (Beck 1976). In this, beliefs about particular issues are identified and questioned by the therapist in order to help the individual to identify distorted thinking patterns that are contributing to their problems. It encourages them to consider and evaluate different sources of information that provide evidence of the reality or unreality of the beliefs they hold. Once they can do this in the therapy session, they can be taught to identify and challenge these automatic thoughts in the real world and to replace thoughts that drive inappropriate behaviour with those that support more appropriate behaviour. An example of their use is provided by this extract from a session adapted from Beck *et al.* (1993) using a technique known as the downward arrow technique designed to question the very core of an individual's beliefs – in this case their assumptions about their drinking.

Socratic dialogue
exploration of an individual's beliefs, encouraging them to question their validity.

Therapist	You feel quite strongly that you need to be 'relaxed' by alcohol when you go to a party. What is your concern about being sober?
John	I wouldn't enjoy myself and I wouldn't be much fun to be with.
Therapist	What would be the implications of that?
John	Well, people wouldn't talk to me.
Therapist	And what would be the consequence of that?
John	I need to have people like me. My job depends on it. If I can't entertain people at a party, then I'm no good at my job.
Therapist	So, what happens if that is the case?
John	Well, I guess I lose my job!
Therapist	So, you lose your job because you didn't get drunk at a party?
John	Well, put like that, perhaps I was exaggerating things in my head.

Here, the downward arrow technique has been used both to identify some of the client's core beliefs and to get them to reconsider the accuracy of those beliefs.

A second strategy is to set up homework tasks that directly challenge any inappropriate cognitive beliefs that individuals may hold. An example of this can be found in the case of the individual who believes that they cannot go to a party without drinking, and who may be set the homework task of trying to remain sober at a party – directly challenging their belief that they need to drink alcohol to be socially engaging (and the exaggerated ultimate belief that they will lose their job if they remain sober). Clearly, such challenges should be realistic. If a person attempts a task that is too hard and fails to achieve it, this may maintain or even strengthen the pre-existing beliefs. Accordingly, they have to be chosen with care and mutually agreed by both the individual concerned and the therapist. However, success in these tasks can bring about long-term cognitive and behavioural changes.

The complexities of these types of intervention, which fall under the rubric of cognitive-behavioural therapy, mean that they are used infrequently in the context of primary prevention, and more frequently with people who have already developed health problems (see Chapter 17). However, it can be a useful form of therapy with people who engage in difficult-to-change behaviours such as addiction to alcohol or other drugs that may be harmful to health. In such cases, cognitive-behavioural therapy has proved to be an effective intervention, although whether it is more effective than some alternatives is not clear. Balldin *et al.* (2003) found it to be superior to supportive therapy. However, it may be no more effective than other active interventions. This is perhaps best exemplified by the results of Project MATCH (Project MATCH Research Group 1998). This large study compared three treatment approaches in over 1,500 American problem drinkers:

Alcoholics Anonymous a worldwide self-help organisation for people with alcohol-related problems. Based on the belief that alcoholism is a physical, psychological and spiritual illness and can be controlled by abstinence. The twelve steps provide a framework for achieving this.

- twelve-step facilitation (based around **Alcoholics Anonymous** and involving total abstinence);
- a combination of cognitive and behavioural techniques;
- motivational enhancement therapy (similar to but not the same as motivational interviewing).

By the end of treatment, 41 per cent of people who received the cognitive-behavioural therapy and the same percentage of those in the twelve-step programme were abstinent or drank moderately, while 28 per cent of the motivational enhancement group achieved the same criteria. However, by one- and three-year follow-up, there were few differences between the three groups.

Summary

This chapter has reviewed two broad sets of issues. First, it examined the implications of programmes that set out to identify genetic or behavioural risk factors for disease or, in the case of mammography, to identify diseases at a sufficiently early stage that they can be treated before they became life-threatening. Second, it considered a number of methods by which people found at risk of disease can be encouraged and helped to change any health-compromising behaviour.

The first section considered three kinds of screening programme:

1. screening for genetic risk of disease;
2. screening for the early detection of disease or its precursors;
3. screening for behaviour that places an individual at risk of disease.

Each approach can be particularly stressful, although most people who go through these screening programmes benefit emotionally from them.

One of the outcomes of screening is that an individual may be asked to change any health behaviour that places them at particular risk of disease. A number of approaches to behavioural change in which the health-care professional can work on a one-to-one basis were considered, each of which is likely to be optimally effective in people with differing levels of motivation or ability to change. The approaches considered were:

■ *Motivational interviewing*: a process of increasing motivation when people are not thinking of change or are not strongly motivated to consider change.

■ *Problem-focused counselling*: a structured approach to identifying causes of problems or elements that are preventing change, identifying new goals, and developing strategies through which to achieve those goals. This works best in people who are motivated to address particular issues.

■ *Implementation intentions*: simply encouraging people to plan how they will change can be sufficient to encourage change in some contexts.

■ *Modelling and rehearsal of change*: these can both increase the belief that an individual has in their ability to achieve change (self-efficacy) and provide them with the skills needed to achieve change if they do not have them.

■ *Cognitive-behavioural approaches*: these address cognitions that may be preventing an individual from working on change, and they provide a structured approach to achieving change.

Each of these various approaches can be used either jointly or singly depending on the nature and magnitude of the problems an individual faces.

Further reading

Carlsson, S., Aus, G., Wessman, C. *et al.* (2007). Anxiety associated with prostate cancer screening with special reference to men with a positive screening test (elevated PSA): Results from a prospective, population-based, randomised study. *European Journal of Cancer*, 43: 2109–16.
Men, apparently, don't feel very anxious when they find they have a high PSA score. Or are we not good at measuring their anxiety?

Miles, A. and Wardle, J. (2006). Adverse psychological outcomes in colorectal cancer screening: does health anxiety play a role? *Behaviour Research and Therapy*, 44: 1117–27.
An interesting study further studying the role of psychological factors that may moderate our response to health information following screening – and in particular the role of health anxiety.

Sivell, S., Iredale, R., Gray, J. and Coles, B. (2007). Cancer genetic risk assessment for individuals at risk of familial breast cancer. *Cochrane Database of Systematic Reviews*: CD003721.
A review of the psychological impact of cancer genetic risk assessment. As usual with Cochrane reviews, the review is limited to randomised controlled trials (the authors eliminated 54 of the 58 papers they initially thought relevant), and therefore excludes longitudinal studies of the impact of genetic risk assessment where no-intervention trial was conducted, but it does summarise some of the literature well.

Hettema, J., Steele, J. and Miller, W.R. (2005). Motivational interviewing. *Annual Review of Clinical Psychology*, 1: 91–111.
An excellent critique of where we are at with the practice and theory underlying motivational interviewing.

Miller, W. and Rollnick, S. (2002). *Motivational Interviewing: Preparing People to Change Addictive Behaviour*. New York: Guilford Press.
A guide to motivational interviewing from its originators. The book shows motivational interviewing in its present form, which now synthesises elements of 'pure' motivational interviewing (as described in the chapter) with a problem-focused approach. Later chapters provide evidence of its effectiveness in a variety of settings.

http://www.motivationalinterview.org/
Those wanting to explore the world of MINTies would do worse than going to this page, set up by Miller himself, with the goal of providing resources for clinicians, researchers and trainers in relation to motivational interviewing.

Egan, G. (2001). *The Skilled Helper: A Problem-Management and Opportunity-Development Approach to Helping*. Brooks/Cole: Pacific Grove, CA.
One of the bibles of problem-focused counselling. It shows the process to be rather more complex than the 'Egan-lite' described in the chapter.

Rutter, D. and Quine, L. (2002). *Changing Health Behaviour: Intervention and Research with Social Cognition Models*. Buckingham: Open University Press.
An edited text describing a number of interventions each of which is either derived from or involves measures relevant to a number of social cognition theories, including the health action process and theory of reasoned action, among others.

Van Osch, L., Reubsaet, A., Lechner, L. *et al.* (2008). The formation of specific action plans can enhance sun protection behavior in motivated parents. *Preventive Medicine*, 47: 127–32.
One of the most recent studies of the use of implementation intentions. Published after the chapter was finished, so not included in the main text.

Wilson, R. and Branch, R. (2005). *Cognitive Therapy for Dummies*. Chichester: John Wiley and Sons.
As good an introduction to cognitive-behavioural therapy as you are likely to get (23 five-star reviews in Amazon). Useful as background reading for Chapters 16 and 17 as well.

Visit the website at **www.pearsoned.co.uk/morrison** for additional resources to help you with your study, including multiple choice questions, weblinks and flashcards.

CHAPTER 7

Population approaches to public health

Learning outcomes

By the end of this chapter, you should have an understanding of:

- the benefits and limitations of using the mass media
- the elaboration likelihood model and its use in media campaigns
- how the environment may be used to influence health-related behaviours
- the outcomes of interventions targeting whole populations' heart and sexual health
- the nature and effectiveness of interventions targeted at more specific populations: worksite and school health-promotion initiatives
- the emerging use of the internet as a change agent, and some of the limitations of its present use

CHAPTER OUTLINE

In the last chapter, we considered how we can influence health-related behaviour through individually based interventions. While these may be effective, no government or body involved in public health has the resources to intervene at a one-to-one level with the entire population – nor would people in the population want to be involved in any attempt to do so. So attempts to influence the health-related behaviour of large groups of people or entire populations necessarily involve other approaches. Perhaps the most obvious means through which health promoters attempt to influence our behaviour is through media campaigns. However, there are a number of other potential routes through which our behaviour can be influenced, including economic and environmental influences. This chapter considers the strengths and limits of the use of mass media approaches to health promotion, before considering some of the other approaches that have been used. We look at the effectiveness of influencing behaviour through the use of environmental factors in the workplace and school, and the use of peer education. Finally, we consider the emerging use of the internet as an agent of behavioural change. Theories relating to each approach are considered as well as the effectiveness of interventions based on them.

Promoting population health

In the previous chapter, we considered a number of one-to-one or small-group interventions that have been used to change health-related behaviour. Many proved reasonably effective, so from the viewpoint of their absolute effectiveness, they could generally be considered 'a good thing'. However, they are expensive to provide, and achieve change in relatively few individuals. Accordingly, from a cost-effectiveness perspective, they are perhaps less impressive. They are also impractical to provide on a large-scale basis. As a result of this, a parallel set of theories and studies have considered how to change the behaviour of large groups of individuals. Approaches that target whole populations are likely to be less effective in achieving change in any one individual than one-to-one interventions. Nevertheless, because of the large number of individuals who may be reached through this type of intervention, they may still achieve significant change over an entire population. A one-to-one intervention that achieved change in, say, 1 per cent of those who took part would be considered highly ineffective. A large-scale intervention that targeted hundreds of thousands if not millions of individuals and achieved a similar success rate could be considered highly effective at least in terms of the resources and costs necessary to achieve any changes. That is, such interventions have the potential to be highly cost-effective.

Using the mass media

Perhaps the most obvious contribution of psychology to public health initiatives can be found in the design and implementation of mass media campaigns. The earliest media campaigns adopted a 'hypodermic' model of behavioural change, which assumed a relatively stable link between knowledge, attitudes and behaviour (something we now know to be somewhat optimistic: see Chapter 5). The approach assumed that if we could 'inject' appropriate information into the recipients, this would change their attitudes and in turn influence their behaviour. This approach, led by people such as McGuire (e.g. 1985), suggested that the key to success was to make the information persuasive and for it to come from appropriate sources. Defining each of these elements is not easy. What is persuasive for one person may not be for another. Good sources of information may be an 'expert', 'someone like you', a neutral individual or someone clearly linked to the issue, such as a doctor providing health information. Seeing someone affected by a particular condition or who has achieved significant behavioural change can be a much more potent source of information than a neutral person or even an expert. It is much more powerful to see a 34-year-old man explain how smoking caused his lung cancer, for example, than to have the risks of developing lung cancer explained by a doctor who has not been personally affected by the condition. In one study of this phenomenon, Scollay *et al.* (1992) reported that a lecture to a school audience about the risks of unsafe sex by someone known to be HIV-positive resulted in greater increases in knowledge, less risky attitudes and safer behavioural intentions than a neutral source.

Despite the popularity of media campaigns, a key issue is whether they result in any behavioural change. This cannot be taken for granted – nor can the fact that the target audience even notices the campaign. Isolated health campaigns may have little impact. In one such programme, focusing on attempting to increase levels of exercise in the community, Wimbush *et al.* (1998) assessed the effect of a mass media campaign in Scotland designed to promote walking. Although 70 per cent of those asked about the campaign were aware of its existence, it had no impact on behaviour. Such limited outcomes have led some to argue that media campaigns are best used to raise awareness of health issues rather than as attempts to engender significant behavioural change (Stead *et al.* 2002).

More positively, the cumulative effects of repeated media campaigns may influence attitudes and behaviour. One example of this can be found in US anti-smoking media advertising which has campaigned against smoking consistently over many years. Such advertising has two key goals: first, to be noticed, and second, to influence knowledge, attitudes and behaviour. The programmes seem to have achieved both goals. In Massachusetts, for example, over half the population noticed anti-smoking advertisements at least weekly for a period of three years (Biener McCallum-Keeler and Nyman 2000). Exposure to anti-smoking advertising at this level was associated with increases in the perceived harm of smoking, and stronger intentions not to smoke (Emery *et al.* 2007). It may also impact on smoking rates. McVey and Stapleton (2000) calculated that an 18-month long British anti-smoking advertising campaign resulted in a 1.2 per cent reduction in smoking levels. Even more dramatic results have been reported in programmes specifically targeted at young people. Zucker *et al.* (2000) reported that their 'truth' (anti-tobacco marketing) campaign, which involved 'in-school education, enforcement, a school based youth organisation, community based organisations, and the cornerstone, an aggressive, well funded, counter-advertising programme' resulted in a 19 per cent reduction in smoking among middle-school students, and an 8 per cent reduction among high-school students. It seems that the level of exposure is highly influential in terms of its impact. Hyland *et al.* (2006) found a 10 per cent increase in the likelihood that people would quit smoking for every '5000 units of exposure' to anti-smoking television advertising over a two-year period.

Despite, or perhaps because of, these successes, those involved in using the media to influence behaviour have adopted a number of methods to maximise its effectiveness, including:

- refining communication to maximise its influence on attitudes
- the use of fear messages
- information framing
- specific targeting of interventions.

Refining communication

Different people may be influenced by different types of information or sources of information – they may also be more or less motivated to consider any information they encounter. We considered this issue in relation to working with individuals in our discussion of the stages of change model (Prochaska and di Clemente 1984) in the previous chapter. Media campaigns can also adopt different arguments depending on the stage of change of people in its target audience. They can provide motivating messages, show how to achieve change and even encourage people to plan change. An alternative method of refining communication for those more or less motivated to consider change is provided by a theoretical model known as the elaboration likelihood model (ELM) developed by Petty and Cacioppo (1986; see Figure 7.1). This suggests that attempts to influence people who are not interested in a particular issue by rational argument will not work (nor will they succeed if the arguments for change are weak). Only those individuals with a pre-existing interest in the issue are likely to attend to such information and, perhaps, act on it. In their jargon, individuals are more likely to 'centrally process' messages if they are 'motivated to receive an argument' when:

- it is congruent with their pre-existing beliefs
- it has personal relevance to them
- recipients have the intellectual capacity to understand the message.

Such processing involves evaluation of arguments, assessment of conclusions and their integration into existing belief structures. According to the ELM, any attitude change resulting from such deliberative processes is likely to be enduring and predictive of behaviour. However, given that health promotion is often targeted at individuals who are not interested in an issue and who are not motivated to process messages, how then do we attempt to influence

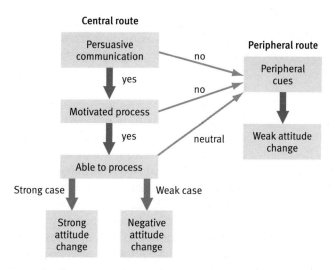

Figure 7.1 The elaboration likelihood model of persuasive communication.

them? According to the ELM, influence here is less reliable but still possible. The model suggests that this can be achieved through what it terms 'peripheral processing'. This is likely to occur when individuals:

- are not motivated to receive an argument
- have low issue involvement
- hold incongruent beliefs.

Peripheral processing involves maximising the credibility and attractiveness of the source of the message using indirect cues and information. Attempts, for example, to influence middle-aged women to take part in exercise may involve a technical message about health gains that can be achieved following exercise (the central route) and also include images associated with exercise that appeal to the target audience, such as making friends while engaging in gentle exercise and wearing attractive clothes in the gym (the peripheral route). Similarly, the importance of a message can be emphasised by a senior person such as a medical professor presenting information. According to the ELM, any attitude change fostered by the peripheral route is likely to be transient and not predictive of behaviour.

A good example of combining the central and peripheral routes with a credible source can be found in a series of UK television advertisements targeted at smokers. These involved real people who had serious smoking-related illnesses – we were told that one person died soon after filming – talking about the adverse outcomes of their smoking. The film was black and white, and the images involved the people sitting in a chair with a very sparse background. The message was that smoking kills, and the peripheral cues associated with the image were downbeat and gloomy. It did not encourage the viewer to take up smoking! Of course, one danger of this negative portrayal is that viewers may find it too depressing and simply disengage from the adverts – either mentally by thinking about something else, or physically by switching the television to another channel (see discussion of fear appeals in the next section). To avoid such an outcome, and in order to find the maximally persuasive approach, it is necessary to develop media campaigns based on sound psychological theory and also to include a testing process, discussing them with their target population – perhaps through the use of focus groups – to fine-tune the finished product.

The ELM has been subject to a number of experimental tests, most of which (e.g. Agostinelli and Grube 2002) suggest that information containing carefully chosen peripheral cues can facilitate attitudinal change in people who are relatively unmotivated to consider particular issues, or that combining central processing with peripheral cues can enhance the effectiveness of some interventions. Kirby *et al.* (1998), for example, showed African American women two health messages about mammography involving both central and peripheral cues. They systematically varied the number of each type of cue over four messages embedded as advertisements in a television talk show. Women who reported a high involvement in the issue reported stronger intentions to seek mammography than those with low involvement, regardless of the presence of central arguments or peripheral cues. By contrast, women with a low involvement in the issue were more likely to report strong intentions to seek mammography if they had been exposed to high levels of favourable peripheral cues than if they had not. Whether these attitudinal changes result in behavioural change is less clear. Drossaert *et al.* (1996) found this not to be the case. Again, in the context of attempts to increase attendance at mammography, they made two versions of a leaflet designed to increase attendance. The main arguments were the same in each leaflet, but one leaflet had low levels of peripheral cues and the other had high levels. Attendance rates of women exposed to the differing leaflets sent out with the invitation to attend did not differ, suggesting that there was little or no benefit from adding peripheral cues to their leaflets. Perhaps this is the real limitation of the ELM and other models of attitude change. They can suggest means of maximising attitudinal change, but many other factors will influence whether any attitudinal change or even behavioural intentions are translated into action (see Chapter 5 for a discussion of the relationship between attitudes and behaviour).

The use of fear

A second potential approach to increasing the influence of mass media communication is through the use of fear messages. This has proven popular among both health promoters and politicians, as well as the recipients of such advertising (Biener *et al.* 2000), who consider fear (and sadness) engendering advertisements to be more effective than humour. Despite this support, high levels of threat have proven relatively ineffective in engendering behavioural change. The problems with this approach can be demonstrated in both the UK and Australian governments' early attempts to change sexual practices in response to the development of HIV/AIDS. Both countries used high-fear messages, including visual images of the chipping of a gravestone with the words AIDS (in the UK) and a celestial bowling alley in which a 'grim reaper' representing HIV bowled down families and children (in Australia). These were associated with portentous messages declaring the need to avoid HIV infection and to use safer sex practices. Both campaigns increased HIV-related anxiety in audiences that saw them, but they did not increase knowledge about HIV/AIDS or trigger any behavioural change (Rigby *et al.* 1989; Sherr

1987). Subsequent fear-based messages have also failed to promote appropriate behavioural change, and may even increase feelings of shame and scepticism relating to the issues being addressed (Slavin *et al.* 2007).

One explanation of this effect may be found in protection motivation theory (Rogers 1983; see Chapter 5). This suggests that individuals will respond to information in either an adaptive or maladaptive manner depending on their appraisal of both threat *and* their own ability to minimise that threat (their self-efficacy judgements). The theory suggests that an individual is most likely to behave in an adaptive manner in response to a fear-arousing health message if they have evidence that engaging in certain behaviour will reduce any threat and they believe they are capable of engaging in it. This approach has been further developed by Witte's (1992) extended parallel process model which states that individuals who are threatened will take one of two courses of action: danger control or fear control. Danger control involves reducing the threat, usually by actively focusing on solutions. Fear control seeks to reduce the perception of the risk, often by avoiding thinking about the threat. For danger control to be selected, a person needs to consider that an effective response is available (response efficacy) and that they are capable of engaging in this response (self-efficacy). If danger control is not selected, then fear control becomes the dominant coping strategy. Both these theories suggest that the most persuasive messages are those that:

- arouse some degree of fear – 'Unsafe sex increases your risk of getting HIV';
- increase the sense of severity if no change is made – 'HIV is a serious condition';
- emphasise the ability of the individual to prevent the feared outcome (efficacy) – 'Here's some simple safer sex practices you can use to reduce your risk of getting HIV'.

These theoretical notions have been reinforced by a number of meta-analyses of the relevant research. Witte and Allen (2000), for example, concluded that high threat fear appeal should be accompanied by an equally high efficacy messages, and that the stronger the levels of fear evoked, the more likely the individual is to produce strong fear defensive responses – the outcome of which is the maintenance of the old behaviour rather than behavioural change. Further cautionary data stem from Earl and Albarracin's (2007) meta-analysis of HIV-specific fear appeals from a sample including 150 treatment groups. These data indicated that receiving fear-inducing arguments increased perceptions of risk but decreased knowledge and condom use. By contrast, resolving fear through HIV counselling and testing both decreased perceptions of risk and increased knowledge and condom use.

Information framing

A less threatening approach to the development of health messages involves 'framing' the message. Health messages can be framed in either positive (stressing positive outcomes associated with action) or negative terms (emphasising negative outcomes associated with failure to act). While some have argued that negative frames are more memorable (Newhagen and Reeves 1987), others have suggested that positive messages enhance information processing. This may particularly be the case when time is short and individuals are not highly motivated to receive a message (Isen 1987). The effectiveness of positive framing is illustrated by a study reported by Detweiler *et al.* (1999), who examined the relative effectiveness of information that either emphasised the positive outcomes of using sunscreen or the negative consequences of not using it. Measures of attitudes and intentions were collected before and after the intervention, and behaviour was assessed via a redeemable voucher for sunscreen. Results showed that messages that emphasised the gains associated with using a sunscreen resulted in significantly higher numbers of requests for sunscreen, stronger intentions to reapply sunscreen at the beach and the use of higher-factor sunscreen than negatively framed threat messages. By contrast, Gerend and Shepherd (2007) found that negatively framed messages were more likely than positively framed messages to increase intentions of young women to have the human *papillomavirus* vaccine – but only among those who had multiple sexual partners and who infrequently used condoms. Finally, Consedine *et al.* (2007) found no effect of type of framing on attendance at breast screening. Overall, these data suggest that we can make no strong *a priori* judgements about what type of framing will affect particular populations – emphasising the need to test out any intervention as a pilot before it is finally aired in public. These conclusions have been supported by a number of meta-analyses which have found non-significant differences in the effectiveness of either loss- or gain-framed approaches in changing behaviours as varied as safer-sex behaviours, skin cancer prevention behaviours, or diet and nutrition behaviours (e.g. O'Keefe and Jensen 2007).

Audience targeting

Early attempts to influence behaviour via the mass media frequently targeted whole populations. This meant that the messages received by the target population were more or less relevant, and the message had to be so broad that it had some potential relevance to all those who received it. As a consequence, health messages were frequently so diluted that they had little relevance to those who received them. Media attempts to influence sexual behaviour illustrate the point. Early media approaches promoting safer sex, as noted above, were based on fear messages, and the same messages were received by all, whether they were elderly, non-sexually active widows and widowers or young sexually active gay men enjoying multiple partners. The outcome of such an approach was the raising of unnecessary fears among a group of people for whom HIV/AIDS had little immediate relevance, while not speaking the language of, or giving relevant advice to, the groups to whom it was most relevant. One way in which any media messages can be made more effective is through more effective targeting of its audience. Now, media messages on sexual behaviour are more carefully targeted and use the language of their differing target audiences, making them much more effective (e.g. Dearing *et al.* 1996).

Audience targeting can be based on a number of factors, including behaviour, age, gender and socio-economic status – each of which is likely to influence the impact of any message (Flynn *et al.* 2007). They may even be developed in part by the target audience. Toroyan and Reddy (2005–6), for

Plate 7.1 An example of a health promotion leaflet targeted at gay men – with a sense of humour – encouraging them to have three vaccinations against hepatitis, produced by the Terrence Higgins Trust.

Source: Terrence Higgins Trust

example, described how young South Africans were involved in the development of photo-comics addressing issues around HIV/AIDS and other sexually transmitted diseases. The Terrence Higgins Trust leaflet in Plate 7.1, would be considered outrageous by many, but it fits the profile of its target audience – young, sexually active, gay men – well.

Audiences may also be segmented along more psychological factors such as their motivation to consider change. A worksite exercise programme reported by Peterson and Aldana (1999), for example, involved attempts to increase levels of participation in exercise among 527 corporate employees who either received written messages tailored to their reported stage of change or general information about exercise. Six weeks after the material was received, participants who received the tailored, staged-based messages increased their activity by 13 per cent and were more likely to shift towards contemplating change (as well as actual change) than those receiving general information. A similar intervention reported a comparable effect one year after the intervention, but only in women (Plotnikoff *et al.* 2007). An interesting study reported by Griffin-Blake and DeJoy (2006) compared a stage-matched intervention and a social cognitive intervention focusing on self-efficacy, outcome expectancies and goal satisfaction (see Chapter 5). Both interventions proved equally effective in increasing physical activity in their target group (college employees).

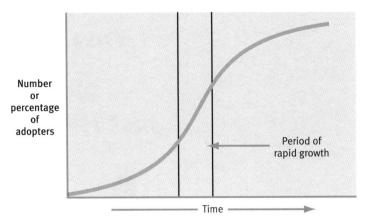

Figure 7.2   The S curve of diffusion, showing the rate of adoption of innovations over time.

Environmental influences on health behaviour

Behaviour and behaviour change do not occur in isolation from the environment in which they occur. The environment may contribute directly to risk of disease (see Chapter 2). It can indirectly affect health, by influencing the ease with which health-promoting or health-damaging behaviour can be conducted. However keen young single mothers may be to exercise, not having someone to look after their child while they are doing so may prevent them from exercising; asking people to eat healthily at work may not be possible unless they are offered healthy choices in the work canteen; and so on. The health belief model (Becker *et al.* 1977; see Chapter 5) provides a simple guide to key environmental factors that can be influenced in order to encourage behavioural change. In particular, the model suggests that an environment that encourages healthy behaviour should:

■ provide cues to action – or remove cues to unhealthy behaviour;
■ enable healthy behaviour by minimising the costs and barriers associated with it;
■ maximise the costs of engaging in health-damaging behaviour.

What do YOU think?

This next section concerns environmental and social issues that can facilitate or inhibit our health-related behaviour. Before considering this in a relatively theoretical way, consider for a moment your own behaviour. What parts of your life increase the possibility of you behaving in a health-enhancing way? What factors prevent this? Do you have easy access to sports or leisure facilities? If you wanted to, would you feel safe cycling or walking around the area where you live? Does your locality offer easy access to good-quality shops, or does accessing them require a car or bus ride? Does this restrict your (or other people's) access to healthy foodstuffs? What about people with fewer resources than you – or with higher demands on their time: single mothers with limited income, for example. How does the environment influence their health choices?

Cues to action

Much of our behaviour is routine, based on habit. Accordingly, we rarely think about change. Cues to action, things that remind us to behave healthily or to change our unhealthy behaviour, can remind us of the need to change our behaviour. Two key areas where this has been used involve health warnings on cigarettes and nutritional information on food. These approaches may be of some benefit, although the evidence suggests that they reinforce existing behaviour rather than prompt consideration of behavioural change. Part of this lack of effect may be due to poor understanding of the issues raised and/or the low visibility of such cues. Cowburn and Stockley (2005) for example, in a review of over a hundred relevant papers, reported that many people in the general public, and particularly those on low incomes, did not understand or were uninterested in the nutritional information on food packaging. One Polish study (Jarosz *et al.* 2003), for example, reported that 23 per cent of those asked did not understand the food information labels even though the majority of respondents valued the information they gained from labelling. Krukowski *et al.* (2006), found that just under half their sample of US college students looked at food labels, or said they would use the information of food labels even if available.

Interestingly, the design of advertising may actually discourage looking at health warnings on tobacco advertisements. A clear delineation between the picture that grabs attention and its associated health warning that is not integrated into it may inhibit reading the warning. Increasing the salience of such cues may therefore increase their effectiveness. Borland (1997) evaluated the effect of the introduction of larger and clearer health warnings on cigarette packets in Australia by comparing self-reported responses to health warnings in two surveys between which the new warnings were introduced. Before the changes were initiated, 37 per cent of respondents reported noticing the health warning. Following increases in its size, 66 per cent reported noticing it. The equivalent figures for refraining from smoking as a result of the warning rose from 7 to 14 per cent. A significant impact can also be obtained by using graphic imagery rather than written text (Thrasher *et al.* 2007; O'Hegarty *et al.* 2006). Cues reminding people to engage in health-promoting behaviours may also be of value. One simple example can be found in posters reminding people to use stairs instead of lifts or escalators. Webb and Eves (2007) found that posters encouraging people to use the stairs instead of a nearby escalator in a shopping centre resulted in a near doubling of stair use. The same research team (Eves *et al.* 2006) found that overweight individuals were more likely to respond to the signs than individuals of more average weight, suggesting this may be a simple but effective way of increasing fitness among this group.

Environmental cues not only act as prompts for healthy behaviour, they can also act as reminders to behave in unhealthy ways. Frequent exposure to relevant advertising, for example, has been shown to increase smoking (Sargent *et al.* 2000) and levels of alcohol consumption (Hurtz *et al.* 2007) among young people. Accordingly, those involved in public health frequently strive to limit and legislate against such things as tobacco and alcohol advertising. The UK government, for example, banned television advertising of tobacco in 1965 and totally banned its advertising from 2003. How effective this approach has been appears to differ across countries. Quentin *et al.* (2007) reported that total bans on advertising of tobacco products were associated with mixed reductions in consumption. Of the 18 studies they reviewed from various countries, only 10 reported a significant reduction in smoking following the ban; 2 studies suggested a partial ban on advertising had little or no effect.

Of course, advertising is not the only media influence on attitudes about health-related behaviour. Many young people consider images in magazines that depict smoking to represent smokers as attractive, reassuring and sociable (MacFadyen *et al.* 2002). These associations affirm and reinforce the positive aspects of smoking among smokers who see them. Similarly, many popular television programmes make verbal or visual references to alcohol and portray its use as an acceptable personal coping strategy (Smith *et al.* 1988). Clearly, the state should not control the content of media images or television programmes. Nevertheless, the potential influence of such images has led some health promoters to work with the producers of television programmes to reduce the overly positive portrayal of alcohol consumption given in some US soap operas (DeFoe and Breed 1989).

Minimising the costs of healthy behaviour

The environment in which we live can either facilitate or inhibit our level of engagement in health-related behaviour. Poor street lighting, busy roads and high levels of pollution may inhibit some inner-city dwellers from taking exercise such as jogging or cycling; shops that sell healthy foods but that are a long way from housing estates may result in more use of local shops that sell less healthy foodstuffs, and so on. Making the environment safe and supportive of healthy activity presents a challenge to town planners and governments. Such an environment should promote safety, provide opportunities for social integration and give the population control over key aspects of their lives.

A number of projects, under the rubric of the 'Healthy Cities movement' (World Health Organization 1988), have attempted to design city environments in ways that promote the mental and physical health of their inhabitants. The movement initially involved cities in industrialised countries, but is now expanding to include cities in industrialising countries such as Bangladesh, Tanzania, Nicaragua and Pakistan. To be a member of the movement, cities have to develop a city health profile and involve citizen and community groups. Priorities for action include attempts to reduce health inequalities as a result of socio-economic factors (see Chapter 2), traffic control, tobacco control, and care of the elderly and those with mental health problems (Kickbusch 2003). Unfortunately, this rather broad set of strategies has proved difficult to translate into measurable and concrete action. Indeed, as recently as 2006, O'Neill and Simard (2006) were still writing discussion papers on how to evaluate the effectiveness of the, by then, twenty-year-old programme. Nevertheless, where appropriate measures have been used and the principles of the healthy cities movement enacted, this does seem to influence health behaviour. Sharpe *et al.* (2004), for example, found that levels of moderate or vigorous exercise were greater in the general population when there was good street lighting, safe areas for jogging or walking, well-maintained pavements, and easy access to exercise facilities than where these did not exist.

More specific studies have shown that environmental manipulations aimed at minimising the costs of engaging in exercise may result in significant change. Linegar *et al.* (1991), for example, took advantage of the closed community of a naval base to manipulate both its physical and organisational environment. They established cycle paths, provided exercise equipment, and organised exercise clubs and competitions within the base. In addition, they gave workers 'release time' from other duties while they participated in exercise. Not surprisingly, perhaps, this combination of interventions resulted in significant increases in exercise, even among people who had not previously exercised. This combination of approaches is rarely possible, but the results indicate what is possible when there is the freedom to manipulate a wide range of environmental factors. A more 'doable' programme, intended to increase levels of exercise among women in a suburb of Sydney, was reported by Wen *et al.* (2002). They targeted women aged between 20 and 50 through a marketing campaign and increasing opportunities for participation in exercise. Their marketing included establishing community walking events, and initiating walking groups and community physical activity classes. Local council members were invited on to the project group to raise the profile of the project with council members and to ensure that the project fitted within the council's social and environmental plans. Pre- and post-project telephone surveys indicated a 6.4 per cent reduction in the proportion of sedentary women in the local population, as well as an increased commitment to promoting physical activity by the local council.

Another area where the costs of healthy behaviour have been considered is that of needle-exchange schemes for injecting drug users. Needle-exchange schemes exchange old for new needles, preventing the need for sharing and reducing the risk of cross-infection of blood-borne viruses, including HIV and hepatitis. Where syringes cannot legally be obtained elsewhere, they are effective (Gibson *et al.* 2001). That said, one important study (Taylor *et al.* 2001) published since Gibson and colleagues' review, showed a reduction in the use of shared needles between 1990 and 1992 in Scotland following the introduction of needle-exchange schemes, but then a gradual increase in sharing in the following years despite their continued provision. These changes mirror some of the changes in risk behaviour in other populations at risk for HIV, where initial changes towards safer behaviour have dwindled, and riskier behaviour has returned over time (e.g. Dodds *et al.* 2004). The reasons for this are unclear but may relate to the relatively low profile given to HIV/AIDS awareness, at least in the UK, and increasing (inappropriate) beliefs that AIDS can be 'cured'.

Increasing the costs of unhealthy behaviour

Making unhealthy behaviour difficult in some way (often through pricing) can act as a barrier to unhealthy behaviour and a facilitator of healthy behaviour. Economic measures related to public health have been largely confined to taxation on tobacco and alcohol. The price of alcohol impacts on levels of consumption, particularly for wines and spirits: beer consumption may be less sensitive to price (Godfrey 1990). These effects may hold not just for 'sensible' drinkers but also for those who have alcohol-related problems (Sales *et al.* 1989). Increases in tobacco taxation may also be the most effective measure in reducing levels of cigarette smoking, with an estimated 4 per cent reduction in consumption for every 10 per cent price rise (Brownson *et al.* 1995). Hu *et al.* (1995) modelled the relative effectiveness of taxation and media campaigns on tobacco consumption in California. They estimated that a 25 per cent tax increase would result in a reduction in sales of 819 million cigarette packs, compared with 232 million packs as a result of media influences. Taxation seems to be a particularly effective deterrent among young people, who are three times more likely to be affected by price rises than older adults (Lewit *et al.* 1981). However, these findings must now be interpreted against attempts to avoid these costs. In the UK, for example, increasing levels of smuggled tobacco and alcohol from the continent (where tax levels are much lower) compete against higher prices in formal outlets.

While prohibition may be seen as a necessary barrier by some, others have called for more modest barriers to availability. Godfrey (1990), for example, has suggested restricting the number of outlets for drugs such as alcohol. This would result in increasing transaction 'costs' as people have to travel further and make more effort to purchase their alcohol, and in reduced cues to consumption from advertising in shop windows and other signs. By contrast, increasing availability – as has occurred relatively recently in Sweden through the Saturday opening of alcohol retail shops – may result in an increase in consumption (Norström and Skog 2005).

A more direct form of control over smoking has been the introduction of smoke-free work and social areas. These clearly reduce smoking in public places – and may impact on smoking elsewhere. Heloma and Jaakalo (2003) found that secondary smoke inhalation levels fell among non-smokers, while smoking prevalence rates at work fell from 30 per cent to 25 per cent following a national smoke-free workplace law. Following a ban on smoking in Norwegian bars and restaurants, Braverman *et al.* (2007) reported significant reductions in the prevalence of daily smoking, daily smoking at work by bar workers, number of cigarettes smoked by continuing smokers, and the number of cigarettes smoked at work by continuing smokers. Restaurants and bars have expressed some concern that smoking bans will reduce their profits. Countering this claim, the US Centers for Disease Control and Prevention (2004) reported the outcome of a ban on smoking in all public work and social outlets, including restaurants and bars, in El Paso, Texas. Breaking the ban would result in a $5,000 fine. There was no reported fall in profits or consumption in any bar or restaurant. Even more encouraging are emerging data suggesting that such bans can positively impact on health. Although they do not provide absolute proof of an association between reduced smoking and reduced disease, a number of studies have now shown reductions in the number of admissions to hospital with myocardial infarction both in the USA (e.g. Juster *et al.* 2007) and Europe (Barone-Adesi *et al.* 2006) since the ban was implemented.

IN THE SPOTLIGHT

The binge drinking epidemic

Despite some reductions in the consumption of alcohol throughout the population, many countries have recently reported significant increases in binge drinking, particularly among young people. This phenomenon has been reported, for example, in the UK, New Zealand, Australia, an area known as the vodka belt (Russia and other countries where vodka is the primary drink), but is less prevalent in South America and southern Europe. The causes of this behaviour are not fully understood, but the availability of cheap alcohol in supermarkets, clubs and pubs – and the culture of drinking while standing – is widely recognised as contributing to the phenomenon. The drinking culture contributes to significant personal harm, as well as having a substantial economic and social impact on the affected communities. Some cities have increased policing in response to the social problems. Some have made bars contribute to the cost of this policing. But one French town took their approach a stage further. They bought the bars! The city of Renne, in Brittany, has bought two bars in the centre of town and converted one into a DVD shop, and one into a restaurant in an attempt to reduce alcohol consumption in its centre. Time will tell whether this impacts on alcohol consumption . . . but you have to admit, it's a pretty bold approach to health promotion!

Health promotion programmes

So far, we have looked at some broad approaches to behavioural change in large populations, and some of the underlying principles that underpin them. The next sections of this chapter examines how these, and some other, approaches have been used in health promotion programmes targeted at whole populations and more specific target groups within them. We consider a number of differing target populations, the approaches that have been used to change their behaviour, the theoretical models that have guided the interventions, and their effectiveness.

Targeting coronary heart disease

Some of the first health promotion programmes targeted at whole towns aimed to reduce the prevalence of key risk factors for CHD – smoking, low levels of exercise, high fat consumption and high blood pressure – across the entire adult population. The first of these, known as the Stanford Three Towns project (Farquhar *et al.* 1977), provided three towns in California with three levels of intervention.

The first town received no intervention. The second received a year-long media campaign targeting CHD-related behaviour. Although the media programme preceded the stages of change model (Prochaska and di Clemente 1984; see Chapter 6) by some years, it followed a programme very similar to that suggested by that model. It started by alerting people to the need to

Plate 7.2 For some, environmental interventions may be far from complex. Simply providing clean water may prevent exposure to a variety of pathogens in dirty water.

Source: © Comic Relief UK, reproduced courtesy of Comic Relief UK

change their behaviour (itself a relatively novel message in the early 1970s). This was followed by a series of programmes modelling behaviour change – for example by broadcasting film of people attending a smoking cessation group or showing cooking skills. These were based on social learning theory (Bandura 1977; see Chapters 5 and 6) and were aimed at teaching skills and increasing recipients' confidence in their ability to change and maintain change of their own behaviour. This phase was followed by further slots reminding people to maintain any behavioural changes they had made, and showing images of people enjoying the benefits of behavioural change such as a family enjoying a healthy picnic (potentially impacting on attitudes and perceived social norms). In the third town, a group of individuals at particularly high levels of risk for CHD and their partners received one-to-one education on risk behaviour change and were asked to disseminate their knowledge through their social networks. This strategy was used to provide another channel for disseminating information – through the use of people given the role of opinion leaders – and increasing motivation in both high-risk people and the general public.

Accordingly, there were three levels of intervention, each of which was expected to result in a step-wise increase in effectiveness (see Table 7.1). The expected outcomes were found. By the end of the one-year programme, scores on a measure of CHD risk status based on factors including blood pressure, smoking and cholesterol level indicated that average risk scores among the general population actually rose in the control town, while they fell significantly among the general population who received the media campaign alone and to an even greater extent among those who lived in the town that received the combined intervention. After a further year, risk scores in the intervention towns were still significantly lower than those of the control town, although because scores in the media-only town continued to improve, there was no difference between the two intervention towns (Farquhar *et al.* 1990a).

Table 7.1 The three levels of intervention in the Stanford Three Towns project

Approach	What it involved	Expected effect
Ongoing health promotion activity	A minimal intervention 'comparison' town	+/−
Year-long media campaign	Phase 1: alerting people to the need to change Phase 2: modelling change Phase 3: modelling continued change	+
Media campaign + high-risk intervention	Media as influence combined with dissemination of knowledge from lay experts	++

The European equivalent of this programme was established in North Karelia in Finland (Puska *et al.* 1985). This five-year programme differed slightly from the Stanford approach in that in addition to a media approach, it also changed environmental factors, encouraging local meat manufacturers and butchers to promote low-fat products, encouraging 'no smoking' restaurants, and so on. It was generally considered to be a success, with reductions in a number of risk factors including blood pressure, cholesterol levels and smoking among men. However, its final summary paper showed that these reductions in risk factors were not consistently better than those in a control area, which received no intervention.

Unfortunately, this apparent lack of success has been repeated in a number of subsequent large-scale interventions. A second study conducted around Stanford, called the Five City project (Farquhar *et al.* 1990b), for example, combined its previous media approach with an increased emphasis on community-initiated education and environmental interventions similar to the Karelia intervention. In a cohort followed for the duration of the intervention, the general population in the intervention area showed improvements in cholesterol levels, fitness and rates of obesity in the early stages of the intervention. However, by its end, the only differences between a comparison area that did not receive the intervention and the intervention areas were on measures of blood pressure and smoking (the latter being perhaps the most important risk behaviour due to its links with so many other diseases). On this criterion, the intervention could be considered a modest success. Unfortunately, on a series of cross-sectional studies comparing control and intervention areas over time, smoking and risk levels for CHD did not differ at any time during the course of the programme – questioning the success of the intervention.

A final US intervention to be considered here used virtually all the approaches so far considered in this and the previous chapter. The Minnesota Heart Health programme (Jacobs *et al.* 1986) used the mass media to promote awareness and to reinforce other educational approaches. In addition, the programme established large-scale screening programmes in primary care settings, as well as a number of other interventions including telephone support, classes in the community and worksite, self-help materials and home correspondence programmes. Environmental interventions included healthy food labelling (low fat, high fibre, etc.), establishing healthy menus in restaurants, smoke-free areas in public and work areas, and increased physical recreation facilities. Despite this complex and sophisticated approach, the programme had surprisingly little impact on health and health behaviour. Levels of smoking in the intervention areas, for example, differed little from those in the control areas, while the average adult weight in both control and intervention areas rose over the course of the study by seven pounds. Similar findings were found for another intervention known as the Community Intervention Trial for Smoking Cessation (COMMIT Research Group 1995), which did not change heavy smokers' behaviour and had only a marginal effect on light smokers.

At first glance, these data appear disappointing. Indeed, they provide little encouragement to suggest that the approaches they used should be continued. However, before they are dismissed, it is important to contextualise their findings. First, apart from the original Stanford study, they occurred at a time when there were significant changes in health behaviour and disease throughout the countries in which the studies were conducted. Rates of CHD fell by 20 per cent over the time they were running (Lefkowitz and Willerson 2001), and there was a general increase in health-promoting behaviour and a concomitant fall in health-damaging behaviour such as smoking. Why did these changes occur, and what implications do they have for interpretation of the results of the large-scale programmes considered above?

Perhaps the experiences of the five-year Heartbeat Wales programme (Tudor-Smith *et al.* 1998) sum up those of all the programmes so far considered. This programme combined health education via the media with health screening and environmental changes designed to promote behavioural change. These included some of the first food labelling (low fat, low sugar, etc.) in the UK, establishing exercise trails in local parks, no-smoking areas in restaurants, the promotion of low-alcohol beers in bars, and so on. It also used doctors and nurses as opinion leaders within their own communities to argue the case for adopting healthy lifestyles. Remember that the interventions in each programme were compared with 'control' areas – areas that did not receive the intervention. However, these were not true 'control' areas in the sense that they received no intervention at all. They received whatever local health education programmes were being conducted at the time. In addition, any innovations conducted by these major research programmes could not be guaranteed to remain only in the intervention area. In the case of Heartbeat Wales, for example, its 'control' area was in the northeast of England, which itself was subject to large-scale heart health programmes conducted in England at the same time as Heartbeat Wales. It was certainly not a 'no intervention' control. In addition, innovations such as food labelling, originally conducted just in Wales, spread through to England via supermarkets such as Tesco over the course of the programme. It is perhaps not surprising, therefore, that although levels of risk factors for CHD fell in Wales over the five-year period of Heartbeat Wales, they did not fall any further than levels in the control area. The research programme essentially compared the effectiveness of two fairly similar interventions. In addition, the majority of health promotion affecting the population with regard to CHD is now probably provided by the mass media as part of its general reporting – through reporting and discussion of healthy diets, issues such as men's health, and so on. It is therefore increasingly difficult for any health promotion programme to add further to this information and result in a meaningful reduction in risk for CHD.

Reducing risk of HIV infection

In contrast to interventions targeted at CHD, those targeted at sexual behaviour in relation to HIV and AIDS appear to have been more successful (Merzel and D'Afflitti 2003). Summing up some of the key data, the US Centers for Disease Control and Prevention (1996) reported significant increases in rates of condom use with main or casual partners in areas that received interventions across a number of US cities in comparison with control areas that had not. In addition, they reported significant increases in the rates of carrying condoms both among those at whom the intervention was targeted and among community members as a whole. In the intervention areas, an average 74 per cent increase in condom carrying was reported. In addition, among injecting drug users, although both intervention and control communities reported a similar rise in the use of bleach to clean their needles and other equipment, those who lived in the intervention areas who were not using bleach were more likely to be considering its use.

Many of these positive outcomes have been achieved using an approach called peer education. In this, opinion leaders and others from specific communities are involved in projects and form a key part of the programme. The approach draws upon social learning theory, as these individuals provide particularly strong role models of change. Using people known and respected within a particular community makes their message salient and shows that appropriate change can be achieved. In one of the first studies using this approach, Kelly et al. (1992) tried to increase levels of safer sexual behaviour among patrons of gay bars in three small southern US cities. They identified and recruited key individuals in these bars and trained them to talk to patrons on issues of risk behaviour change and to distribute relevant health education literature. Following this intervention, levels of high-risk sexual behaviour fell by between 15 and 29 per cent. In a larger community trial conducted by the same team in eight US cities (Kelly et al. 1997), levels of unprotected anal intercourse fell from 32 to 20 per cent among men frequenting gay bars in the intervention group – in contrast to a 2 per cent rise among those in the control cities. The RESEARCH FOCUS below reports in some detail on an attempt to replicate this type of intervention in gay bars in East European countries. In a different approach to reducing risk of AIDS, Asamoah-Adu et al. (1994) engaged prostitutes in Ghana to provide peer education and distribute condoms to their fellow prostitutes, resulting in a significant reduction in unsafe sex. Overall, the women who took part in the intervention were more likely to use a condom than they were prior to the intervention. In addition, three years after the end of the formal programme, women who maintained contact with the project staff were more likely than those who disengaged from them to have continued using them.

Merzel and D'Afflitti (2003) noted that the HIV/AIDS prevention programmes have been markedly more successful than those targeted at CHD. Why this should be the case is unclear. Perhaps the most obvious difference between the interventions was the use of peers by those involved in HIV prevention – working with specific groups of people rather than trying to impose change from without. This may have been a crucial factor. Janz *et al.* (1996), for example, conducted a process evaluation of thirty-seven AIDS prevention programmes and concluded that the use of trained community peers whose life circumstances closely resembled those of the target population was one of the most important factors influencing acceptance of health messages. Similarly, Kelly *et al.* (1993) suggested that the use of peers and role models was an important means of delivering health messages. Merzel and D'Afflitti speculated that a second reason for these differences may lie in the natural history of the diseases that each programme was trying to influence. Coronary heart disease develops over time, and there is no marked increase in risk as a result of particular behaviour – 'One bar of chocolate won't do me any harm'. It is therefore relatively easy to minimise risk and put off behaviour change. By contrast, the risks associated with unsafe sex are highly salient. It can take relatively few unsafe sexual encounters to contract HIV, and the consequences can be catastrophic – so the imperatives of change are much more salient than in CHD.

While the above studies allow comparison of interventions within the same culture, it should not be forgotten that AIDS is a global issue. Given the devastating impact of HIV/AIDS in Africa, interventions here and in other parts of the developing world are of paramount importance. Galavotti *et al.* (2001) described a model known as the Modeling and Reinforcement to Combat HIV (MARCH), which has been developed for use in developing countries. The intervention model has two main components:

1. use of the media
2. local influences of change.

It uses the media to provide role models in 'entertainment that educates'. Interventions include testimonials from people living with HIV/AIDS and peer education similar to that used, for example, in the USA and UK. These provide information on how to change, and model steps to change in sexual behaviour. Serial dramas on television are also used to educate, because they involve the viewer emotionally with the action on the screen, increase its salience and encourage viewing. Interpersonal support involves the creation of small media materials such as flyers depicting role models progressing through stages of behaviour change for key risk behaviour, mobilisation of members of the affected community to distribute media materials and reinforce prevention messages, and the increased availability of condoms and bleacher kits for injecting drug users. In one study of effectiveness of the media elements of this approach (Vaughan *et al.* 2000), Radio Tanzania aired a radio soap opera called *Twende Na Wakati* ('Let's go with the times'). This soap played twice weekly for two years with the intention of promoting reproductive health and family planning, and preventing HIV infection. In comparison with an area of Tanzania that did not receive national radio at the time of the study, people who lived in areas where the radio programme was received reported greater commitment to family planning and higher uptake of safer sex practices. In addition, attendance at family planning clinics increased more in the intervention than control area.

RESEARCH FOCUS

Amirkhanian, Y.A., Kelly, J.A., Kabakchieva, E. *et al.* (2005). A randomized social network HIV prevention trial with young men who have sex with men in Russia and Bulgaria. *AIDS*, 19: 1897–905.

This study describes the outcomes of a social network HIV prevention intervention carried out among young gay men in Russia and Bulgaria. HIV prevention is particularly important in these countries as the prevalence of known HIV cases is increasing dramatically, and the criminalisation of homosexual behaviour in the Soviet era has meant that until recently many gay men remained hidden and received little HIV prevention information.

Method
The study involved a number of stages:

1. Identification of social groups of gay men in bars and nightclubs by ethnographers. Groups were monitored and their leaders identified, approached and invited to take part in the study. Fifty per cent of those approached agreed to participate in the study.

2. Group leaders were asked to identify nine group members – people they most liked to spend time with. These individuals were approached by the research team, and 93 per cent agreed to participate in the study. A total of 52 networks with 276 network members took part in the study. Their mean age was 22.5 years, and 92 per cent of respondents were unmarried, 49 per cent of participants were students, and 52 per cent were employed. Groups were randomly assigned to receive either the social intervention or no intervention.

3. Among those receiving the intervention, all group members completed questionnaires to identify the most influential individuals within each social group. The network member with the highest social status score in each group was invited to attend an educational programme designed to help them teach other members of their group about HIV prevention.

Measures
Measures included the following:

- *Psychosocial scales*: included measures of five AIDS-related issues: knowledge and misconceptions about AIDS, risk behaviour and risk reduction steps, safer-sex peer norms, attitudes towards condom use and safer sex, strength of risk reduction behavioural intentions, and perceived risk reduction self-efficacy.

- *Lifetime, past year, and past 3 months sexual risk behaviour*: Participants reported how many times they had intercourse, and how many of these acts were condom-protected.

- *Communication with friends about AIDS-related topics in the past 3 months*.

Social network leader training intervention
Each social network leader attended a group training programme in which they learned how to communicate HIV prevention messages and personal risk reduction advice to their network members. The intervention involved five weekly group sessions, with four booster sessions over the next 3 months. They were asked to incorporate HIV prevention messages into naturally occurring conversations and to tailor messages to the particular risk issues of each friend.

Results
Network leaders attended an average of eight of the nine group sessions. Talk about AIDS with friends nearly doubled (from a mean of 3.5 times at baseline to 6.1 times at follow-up) among experimental network members but fell among control group members.

continued

Baseline to 3-month follow-up outcomes: the intervention group evidenced significant increases in AIDS risk knowledge, safer-sex peer norms, and risk reduction intentions. Overall, members of experimental networks were less likely to engage in unprotected intercourse with women, but not men. More encouragingly, men with multiple partners in the intervention condition reported lower rates of unprotected intercourse and higher levels of condom use. *Baseline to 12-month maintenance outcomes*: Differences between conditions became attenuated at this time point. Nevertheless, participants in the intervention condition were less likely to engage in unprotected intercourse, although the differences were not as great as at 3-month follow-up. The strongest intervention effects were found among participants who had multiple partners in the previous three months. Those in the intervention group reported less episodes of unprotected sex than those in the control condition.

Discussion

This paper was the first from Eastern Europe to describe the outcomes of a social network intervention aimed at the reduction of risky sexual behaviour. The data showed that the group leaders were willing and able to give AIDS-related prevention information and advice. One year on from the intervention, there was evidence of reduced risky behaviour, particularly among participants who had multiple sexual partners. This provides encouragement to further use this type of intervention – perhaps with a cost–benefit, economic, analysis to determine whether it is not only effective, but also cost effective. One methodological caveat the authors note is that like much sexual behavioural research, this study relied on participants' self-reports of their behaviour, potentially susceptible to recall error and self-presentation bias. Changes in control group networks at final follow-up suggest the possibility that detailed and repeated risk behavioural assessments may have produced reactive effects and also influenced behaviour.

Worksite health promotion

One response to the problems encountered by the large-scale population interventions has been to target smaller, more easily accessible target groups, and the past few decades have seen the development of many impressive health promotion programmes in the workplace. The majority of these have been conducted in the USA, perhaps because enhancing the health of the workforce reduces the cost of workers' health insurance – often paid by the employer – and therefore benefits the company as well as the individuals in it. Worksite programmes have targeted a range of health-related behaviour, including diet, exercise, smoking and stress (generally focusing on risk factors for CHD and cancer). Because the worksite offers a wide possibility of interventions, these have utilised a variety of formats, some extremely innovative. Approaches include:

- screening for risk factors for disease;
- providing health education;
- provision of healthy options, such as healthy food in eating areas;
- providing economic incentives for risk behaviour change;
- manipulating social support to facilitate individual risk behaviour change;
- provision of no-smoking areas (and more recently smoking rooms) in the work environment.

The effectiveness of screening programmes in the worksite does not differ from that offered in other contexts and discussed in the previous chapter. Other programmes have met with mixed success. Perhaps the simplest intervention is simply to provide information on the nutritional and calorific content of the food being provided in the dining areas. Unfortunately, there is no evidence that this simple approach is likely to be successful (Engbers *et al.* 2006). Accordingly, a number of studies have developed more complex interventions. The Well Works programme reported by Sorensen *et al.* (1998) recorded modest improvements in fat and fruit and vegetable consumption following a programme in which they combined health education programmes and provided healthy food options. The prevalence of smoking, a second target of the intervention, did not change. Similarly, the Health Works for Women programme (Campbell *et al.* 2002) targeted blue-collar women employed in small to medium-sized workplaces. They provided information on healthy lifestyle behaviour and suggestions on how to change to it, using information tailored to individual participants' needs, determined by questionnaires completed before the intervention. The programme also worked at developing peer support from social networks among the workforce. Despite these complex interventions, they found no long-term changes in fat intake, smoking or physical activity levels among the intervention group. Their only gain was modest increases in self-reported fruit and vegetable intake.

Acknowledging the potential influence of the home as well as work on diet and health, the Treatwell programme (Sorensen *et al.* 1999) compared two interventions with a minimal intervention control group. An in-work programme involved classes and food demonstrations open to factory workers to teach them about healthy eating, and provided healthy options and food labelling in their worksite eating areas. A second approach combined the in-work programme with a family intervention designed to encourage healthy eating within the home. Total fruit and vegetable intake increased by 19 per cent in the worksite-plus-family group, 7 per cent in the worksite intervention group and zero per cent in the control group.

The worksite provides more than an opportunity for the provision of health education and health food options. It gives the opportunity to exert more influence over behaviour than can be achieved elsewhere. One way that employers can influence their workforce is to provide financial incentives for change – to provide an external reward system for appropriate behavioural change rather than relying on employees' personal motivation. These have proved quite successful. Glasgow *et al.* (1993) offered monthly lottery prizes to people in a factory workforce who quit and maintained their no-smoking status for up to one year: 19 per cent of smokers in the workforce took part in the intervention, 20 per cent of whom remained abstinent by the end of the programme. The study provided no control group, but a 20 per cent abstinence level compares favourably with many more complex interventions (see Chapter 6). By contrast, Jeffery *et al.* (1993) deducted money from participants' pay (on a voluntary basis) and refunded this money for weight loss and smoking cessation – meaning that participants who were unsuccessful lost money. This programme also proved successful for those who took part in it – but participation rates were, perhaps understandably, low.

The worksite can also provide strong social support for those involved in behavioural change. Koffman *et al.* (1998), for example, compared a multi-component smoking cessation programme similar to that described in the previous chapter with a combination of this programme and financial incentives for abstinence and a team competition in which groups supported each other in the weeks and months following cessation. Six months after the initiation of the programme, 23 per cent of those in the multi-component group were abstinent, in comparison with 41 per cent of those who also received the incentive and competition programme. By the one-year follow-up, the equivalent figures were 30 and 37 per cent, respectively.

Preventing people smoking at the worksite will necessarily reduce levels of secondary exposure to cigarette smoke among non-smokers. In addition, the discomfort associated with smoking outside buildings may provide a disincentive for many smokers, which may impact on smoking levels. Longo *et al.* (2001) certainly found such an effect. They studied the smoking habits of employees in hospitals that became smoke-free and those that continued to permit smoking over a period of three years, and found that twice as many smokers in the non-smoking hospitals quit smoking than did in the hospitals that continued to allow smoking. Similar effects were found in an uncontrolled study of the impact of a smoking ban in one hospital, where levels of smoking fell from 22 to 14 per cent following introduction of a no-smoking policy (Hudzinski and Frohlich 1990).

Most worksite interventions have followed a 'traditional' route in attempting to influence the behaviour of employees. A more innovative, and difficult to implement, approach is to change the whole nature of the working environment. One of the few studies to report this approach – in relation to stress at work – was by Maes *et al.* (1990), who combined a health education programme aimed at facilitating CHD risk behaviour change with a series of modifications to the working environment, each of which was intended to reduce the inherent stresses and boredom of assembly work in a large factory. The research team changed employees' job designs to avoid short repetitive tasks and gave them additional control over the organisation of work tasks (see the Karesek model described in the previous chapter). They also facilitated social contact within the working environment. Finally, they trained managers in communication and leadership skills and taught them to recognise and reduce stress in the workforce. Evaluation of the impact of this intervention was limited, with no direct measures of stress taken. However, levels of absenteeism fell and quality of production rose following its implementation. These are often seen as indicators of the quality of work life and suggest some benefit to the workforce. More interventions designed to reduce stress at work are considered in Chapter 13.

School-based interventions

School brings to mind traditional education, and a number of health promotion initiatives have used this type of model. James *et al.* (2007), for example, reported short- but not long-term gains following a series of educational lessons targeted at health nutrition and weight control. It also provides a context in which health professionals can access students and act as agents of change. Pbert *et al.* (2006), for example, found that a smoking cessation intervention involving school nurses working with school students resulted in greater (self-report) abstinence rates than with no intervention.

But the school is not just a place where students congregate and can be subject to educational lessons. Like the worksite, it is a closed community that can provide an over-arching influence on health behaviours and health.

As a consequence, over the past decade there has been a significant development of what has been termed 'the health-promoting school'. These schools prioritise the health of their pupils and develop an integrated approach to enhancing health, preventing uptake of unhealthy behaviour and educating pupils about health-promoting activities. This removes health education from simply being a taught part of the curriculum to something central to the aims of the school, around which the school activities and infrastructure are based. The framework around which schools involved in this sort of programme base themselves was established by the World Health Organization (1996) and now includes:

- school health policies – developing policies for school behaviour, such as a 'no helmet, no bike at school' policy for cycle safety or an Australian 'no hat, no play' policy (to avoid sunburn), as well as more traditional policies such as no smoking on school premises and no tolerance of bullying;
- establishing a safe, healthy physical and social environment;
- teaching health-related skills;
- providing adequate health services within the school;
- providing healthy food;
- school-site health-promotion programmes for staff;
- availability of school counselling or psychology programmes;
- a school physical education programme.

St Leger (1999) summarised the health outcomes of this integrated approach as being generally successful when significant efforts are placed on its successful implementation but having minimal or no effect if only partially implemented. Lee et al. (2006) reported similar conclusions from Hong Kong. They evaluated schools in terms of their success in implementing a health-promoting schools policy, and found that those schools who had most successfully implemented the various elements of the healthy schools evidenced improvements in diet and anti-social behaviour when compared to those who were less successful. This success is not always replicated, however. Schofield, M. et al. (2003) established an intervention involving formal education addressing the health risks associated with smoking, information leaflets and bi-weekly school newsletters for parents, letters to tobacco retailers, smoke-free school policy development, encouragement of non-smoking parents, peers and teachers as role models, peer influence programmes, and incentive programmes. When compared to schools that had not implemented these elements, no differences in smoking rates were found over a period of two years.

What do YOU think?

Effective sex education provides a powerful influence on sexual behaviour. Countries where sex education is central to the curriculum, starts early, and focuses on the social as well as physical aspects of sexual relations have lower unwanted pregnancy rates than countries where the sex education is less central and starts later in the academic curriculum. In the UK, sex education is not compulsory, occurs late in the curriculum, and is often taught in one or two lessons independently of the wider curriculum by teachers lacking in relevant expertise. The UK has one of the highest teenage pregnancy rates in Europe. Are these two factors related? Or is there a third (or fourth) hidden factor that explains this association? How would you teach sex education?

Out-of-school activities

One alternative to school-based programmes is provided by a programme known as Smokebusters. This is a community – deliberately not school-based – intervention aimed at preventing young people smoking. It involves a series of clubs throughout Europe, each of which emphasises the positive aspects of non-smoking rather than the negative aspects of smoking. They are 'fun clubs', where non-smoking is portrayed as the norm and smokers as the minority. The intention is to develop strong social peer groups of non-smokers, intended to assist in self-empowerment and development of rejection skills. Events established by the clubs include discos and outdoor events, and they often provide discount schemes for local shops. Being a non-smoker is often rewarded by free membership of the club. The programme is considered to be more attractive to many smokers, who may reject the authoritarian context of school-based programmes. Bruce and van Teijlingen (1999) summarised the reports of thirty-six Smokebuster clubs throughout the UK. As community-based programmes with no particular research remit, only three had attempted to measure long-term effects of the club on knowledge, attitudes and smoking behaviour. One such study evaluated the effects of a North Yorkshire-based programme. They measured smoking levels, knowledge and attitudes in 866 primary and secondary schoolchildren – only half of whom had subsequent access to the club – before and one year after a local Smokebusters club had been established. Over this time, levels of regular smoking rose in both groups, but less so in the group of young people who had access to the club: an 11 per cent versus 3 per cent rise in smoking prevalence. Similar gains were reported by the two other studies to report smoking prevalence levels (Bruce and van Teijlingen 1999). More disappointingly, intentions to smoke in the future did not differ consistently across the studies: the intervention may have delayed rather than prevented smoking – although some have argued that this is a significant benefit.

Peer education

One final approach to health education in schools involves peer education. As in the social interventions to reduce the spread of HIV described earlier in the chapter, this typically involves training influential pupils in a school about a particular health issue such as smoking, alcohol consumption or HIV education and encouraging them to educate their peers about the issues, hopefully in a way that encourages healthy behaviour. The methods used vary considerably. They may involve teaching whole classes, informal tutoring in unstructured settings, or one-to-one discussion and counselling. In some contexts, peer educators have set up theatre stalls or exhibitions (see Turner and Shepherd 1999). One of the authors (PB) was involved in the evaluation of a peer education programme among schools in South Wales. This adopted an informal approach to peer education and involved a number of stages. In the first, pupils in Year 8 were asked to identify particularly influential people within their social group. From this, the intervention team identified a group of people who were particularly influential among the target population – some of whom may not have been the choice of their form teachers! Volunteers from this group were then taken to a hotel for two days, where they were taught about the nature, costs and benefits of excess alcohol consumption. These 'away days' also involved a number of group exercises to increase support and confidence among the peer education group. Following their training days, the peer educators were then asked to talk to their friends and anyone else they felt appropriate about sensible drinking, sharing information and advice. This model of uncontrolled dissemination contrasts strongly with some of the more formal methods adopted by other programmes.

The strengths of peer education programmes are thought to be a result of peers providing a more credible source of information than standard educational programmes provided by teachers. They may also make health education more acceptable to school pupils than when it is provided by teachers. Peer education also provides an opportunity to empower those involved and for them to act as positive role models. Whether these claims are accurate is not always clear. Pupils may find it hard to teach their peers and adopt the role of teacher either formally or informally. It is also possible that using pupils as channels of legitimised health information actually removes them as a source of genuine influence, or it may result in them pulling back from providing information or advice so as not to appear outside their established peer group and its norms. Even if one accepts the positive principles supporting peer education, evidence of its effectiveness is inconclusive, although it has achieved some benefits. In the field of HIV/AIDS prevention, peer education and support has been shown to reduce risky sexual behaviour in schools in areas of the world as disparate as Mongolia (Cartagena *et al.* 2006), Canada (Caron *et al.* 2004) and South Africa (Visser 2007) when compared to those with no intervention. An Italian study (Borgia *et al.* 2005) found modest differences in knowledge (favouring peer education) and no differences in sexual behaviour when comparing the outcomes of peer and teacher-led educational programmes.

Using the web

The internet provides a simple means of communicating with vast numbers of individuals, and has been eagerly appropriated by many of those involved in health promotion. The early stages of this research and the difficulties in measuring outcomes and conducting randomised controlled trials in this research context means that many papers simply report usage rather than outcomes. McNeill *et al.* (2007), for example, gave access to a site giving nutritional information to fifty-two residents of a multi-ethnic working class area for six weeks. More than half of the participants owned a computer, and 75 per cent of them logged on to the website at least once. Those who visited the site averaged four visits and viewed an average of twenty-five pages on each occasion. Usage declined over the study period, but increased following email reminders. Nearly three-quarters of the participants viewed information on goal setting, 72 per cent viewed information on dietary tracking, and 56 per cent searched for main course recipes.

In a more formal evaluation of outcomes as well as usage, Swartz *et al.* (2006) conducted a randomised controlled trial of the use of an internet-based smoking cessation programme. Participants were engaged from a variety of workplaces and were randomly assigned to receive the programme either immediately or after a period of 90 days. The intervention involved a video-based internet programme that presented current strategies for smoking cessation and motivational materials tailored to the user's ethnicity, sex and age. At follow-up, the cessation rate at 90 days was 24 per cent for the treatment group and 8 per cent for the control group. Winett *et al.* (2007) combined an internet programme designed to improve nutrition and exercise levels alone or in combination with 'live' support. The programme was made available to overweight individuals in a variety of churches. They found a hierarchical effect with the internet condition resulting in significant improvements in reported diet compared to a no-treatment control, but with only the internet plus support resulting in changes in both exercise and diet.

It can be easy for modern health promoters to be attracted by the technology of the internet and ignore more traditional approaches. But does this result in better outcomes? Cook *et al.* (2007) compared the effectiveness of a web- and paper-based intervention designed to improve dietary practices, reduce stress and increase physical activity. The web-based programme was more effective than print materials in producing improvements in the areas of diet and nutrition but was no more effective in reducing stress or increasing physical activity. Marshall *et al.* (2003) found no difference in the effectiveness of written or internet-based programmes designed to increase physical activity, while Marks *et al.* (2006) found that printed materials were more effective than the internet in changing exercise levels. It should be noted, however, that none of these programmes utilised the web and its potential interactivity to its maximum. There was no interaction between the users and the programme and no use of prompts or other strategies that can be used with modern multi-media approaches. Simply emailing reminders to action – easy via the internet but more difficult and expensive to send its paper equivalent – may be sufficient to prompt action among its recipients (Plotnikoff *et al.* 2005).

Summary

This chapter has examined a number of issues related to interventions targeted at improving the health of whole populations. The key targets examined have been those aiming to change incremental risk of disease, in this case CHD, and behaviour that may result in diseases after being enacted on one occasion – those related to safer sex and HIV infection.

The prime method of influence has been use of the media. Three methods of optimising its use were considered:

1. refining communication to maximise their influence on attitudes through the use of differing channels depending on recipients' motivation to consider the information presented;

2. the use of fear messages – and how these may be optimised not only by raising health anxiety but also by providing an easy way of reducing it;

3. more specific targeting of interventions – targeting at groups within society, categorised by such indices as behaviour, social class and prevailing attitudes.

The environment may also be manipulated to make health behaviour more salient, to make it easier to engage in and to reward those who engage in it. In particular, environmental manipulations can:

- provide cues to action – or remove cues to unhealthy behaviour;
- enable health behaviour by minimising the costs and barriers associated with it;
- increase the costs of engaging in health-damaging behaviour.

Interventions using these various principles (and some considered in the previous chapter) have proved reasonably successful at changing behaviour in large and more defined populations such as those in worksites or schools.

Early interventions targeted at changing CHD-related behaviour proved successful, although their very success may have reduced the apparent intervention-specific success of subsequent interventions. By contrast, interventions targeted at safer sex behaviour appear to have been particularly successful.

Interventions in the worksite have had mixed success, although the ability of the worksite to offer financial rewards and to establish peer support makes it a useful arena for influencing public health. Innovative attempts to change working practice may also reduce stress in the workforce.

Schools appear to be the key to establishing health behaviour. 'Healthy schools' appear to benefit the health of children – if their implementation is not half-hearted. Peer education may also have some benefits, although many children may find it difficult to act as health educators, reducing the effectiveness of the approach.

Finally, the internet provides a key medium for future health-promotion programmes, but probably needs to be interactive and engaging to be maximally useful.

Further reading

Acheson, D. (1998). *Independent Inquiry into Inequalities in Health*. Report. London: HMSO.
Looks at some alternative approaches to health promotion, particularly in relation to economic inequalities.

http://www.dh.gov.uk/en/Publicationsandstatistics/Publications/PublicationsPolicy AndGuidance/DH_4094550.
This link takes you to a 'free to download' series of links in which you can access the UK Government's document called 'Choosing health: making healthy choices easier', which examines how health and social policy can influence our lifestyles and health, making healthy behaviours easy to adopt.

Merzel, C. and D'Afflitti, J. (2003). Reconsidering community-based health promotion: promise, performance, and potential. *American Journal of Public Health*, 93: 557–74.
An excellent, readable account of the pros and cons of community-based interventions.

Sangani, P., Rutherford, G., Wilkinson, D. (2004). Population-based interventions for reducing sexually transmitted infections, including HIV infection. *Cochrane Database Systematic Review*, CD001220.
As with all Cochrane reviews it is thorough and up to date.

Naidoo, J. and Wills, J. (2000). *Health Promotion: Foundations for Practice*. London: Bailliere Tindall.
A good review of the practice of health promotion from theoretical and practitioner perspective.

White, J. and Bero, L.A. (2004). Public health under attack: the American Stop Smoking Intervention Study (ASSIST) and the tobacco industry. *American Journal of Public Health*, 94: 240–50.
A reminder that the health promotion agenda is not adopted by all.

http://www.kingsfund.org.uk/health_topics/public_health.html.
The King's Fund is a UK 'think tank' that considers health policy in a number of arenas. This link takes you to their public health webpage, where there is a wealth of information about community and environmental approaches to health promotion.

Katz, D.L., O'Connell, M., Yeh, M.C. *et al.* Task Force on Community Preventive Services (2005). Public health strategies for preventing and controlling overweight and obesity in school and worksite settings: a report on recommendations of the Task Force on Community Preventive Services. *Morbidity and Mortality Weekly Report. Recommendations and Reports*, 54: 1–12.
A thorough review of interventions in both worksite and school, freely available on the web.

van den Berg, M.H., Schoones, J.W. and Vliet Vlieland, T.P. (2007). Internet-based physical activity interventions: a systematic review of the literature. *Journal of Medical Internet Research*, 9: e26.
A good review of internet health-promotion programmes designed to increase exercise levels.

Norman, G.J., Zabinski, M.F., Adams, M.A., *et al.* (2007). A review of eHealth interventions for physical activity and dietary behaviour change. *American Journal of Preventive Medicine*, 33: 336–45.
This one also tackles dietary change.

 Visit the website at **www.pearsoned.co.uk/morrison** for additional resources to help you with your study, including multiple choice questions, weblinks and flashcards.

PART II

Becoming ill

CHAPTER 8

The body in health and illness

Learning outcomes

By the end of this chapter, you should have an understanding of:

- the basic anatomy and function of:
    - specific parts of the brain
    - the autonomic nervous system
    - the immune system and key disorders that can result from immune dysfunction
- the basic anatomy, physiology and disorders of:
    - the digestive system
    - the cardiovascular system
    - the respiratory system

CHAPTER OUTLINE

This chapter provides an introduction to the basic anatomy and physiology of key organ systems within the body. Each section considers the basic anatomy and physiology of each system, and describes some of the disease processes, and their treatment, that may occur within them. These may be diseases that are associated with particular risk behaviours or other psychological processes – usually stress. Others include diseases that present individuals with particular challenges. Later chapters consider how people can prevent or cope with these diseases, and in some cases the psychological interventions that may help them do this. As well as being a chapter to read on its own, it also forms a reference providing basic information on the illnesses and treatments we refer to in other chapters of the book.

We start by examining two systems that influence the whole body:

1. the brain and autonomic nervous system
2. the immune system.

We then go on to examine three other organ systems:

1. the digestive system
2. the cardiovascular system
3. the respiratory system.

The behavioural anatomy of the brain

The brain is an intricately patterned complex of nerve cell bodies. It is divided into four anatomical areas (see Figures 8.1 and 8.2):

1. *Hindbrain*: contains the parts of the brain necessary for life – the medulla oblongata, which controls blood pressure, heart rate and respiration; the reticular formation, which controls alertness and wakefulness; and the pons and cerebellum, which integrate muscular and positional information.

2. *Midbrain*: contains part of the reticular system and both sensory and motor correlation centres, which integrate reflex and automatic responses involving the visual and auditory systems and are involved in the integration of muscle movements.

3. *Forebrain*: contains key structures that influence mood and behaviour, including:

   ■ *Thalamus*: links the basic functions of the hindbrain and midbrain with the higher centres of processing, the cerebral cortex. Regulates attention and contributes to memory functions. The portion that enters the limbic system (see below) is involved in the experience of emotions.

   ■ *Hypothalamus*: regulates appetite, sexual arousal and thirst. Also appears to have some control over emotions.

   ■ *Limbic system*: (Figure 8.3) a series of structures including a linked group of brain areas known as the Circuit of Papez (the hippocampus –fornix–mammillary bodies–thalamus–cingulate cortex–hippocampus). The hippocampus–fornix–mammillary bodies circuit is involved in

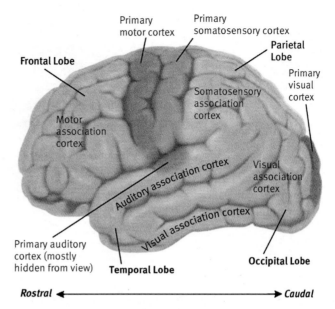

Figure 8.1   A cross-section through the cerebral cortex of the human brain.

Source: Carlson, N. (2005), © 2005, reproduced by permission of Pearson Education, Inc.

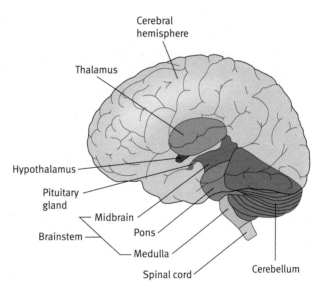

Figure 8.2   A lateral view of the left side of a semi-transparent human brain with the brainstem 'ghosted' in.

Source: Carlson, N. (2005), © 2005, reproduced by permission of Pearson Education, Inc.

memory. The hippocampus is one site of interaction between the perceptual and memory systems. A further part of the system, known as the amygdala, links sensory information to emotionally relevant behaviour, particularly responses to fear and anger. It has been called the 'emotional computer' because of its role in coordinating the process that begins with the evaluation of sensory information for significance (i.e. threat) and then controls the resulting behavioural and autonomic responses (see below).

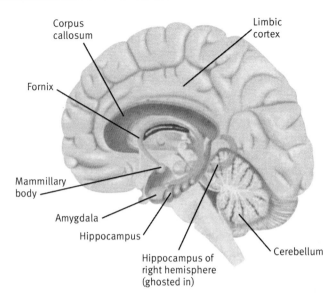

Figure 8.3   The major components of the limbic system. All of the left hemisphere apart from the limbic system has been removed.

Source: Carlson, N. (2005), © 2005, reproduced by permission of Pearson Education, Inc.

4. *Cerebrum*: the most recently evolved part of the brain includes:

 ■ *Basal ganglia*: responsible for complex motor coordination.

 ■ *Cortex*: the convoluted outer layer of grey matter comprising nerve cell bodies and their synaptic connections. It is divided into two functional hemispheres linked by the corpus callosum, a series of interconnecting neural fibres, at its base and is divided into four lobes: frontal, temporal, occipital and parietal:

   ■ The frontal lobe has an 'executive' function, as it coordinates a number of complex processes, including speech, motor coordination and behavioural planning. The frontal lobes also influence motivation. The pre-frontal lobes are connected to the limbic system via the thalamus and motor system within the cortex. Links between the pre-frontal cortex and the limbic system are activated during rewarding behaviour.

   ■ The temporal lobes have a number of functions. In right-handed people, the main language centre is located in the right hemisphere, and visuo-spatial processing is located in the left. In left-handed individuals, there is less localisation within the hemispheres. The temporal lobes are also involved in the systems of smell and hearing. They integrate the visual experience with those of the other senses to make meaningful wholes. The temporal lobes have an important role in memory and contain systems that preserve the record of conscious experience. Finally, they connect to the limbic system and link emotions to events and memories.

   ■ The occipital and parietal lobes are primarily involved in the integration of sensory information. The occipital lobe is primarily involved in visual perception. Links to the cortex permit interpretation of visual stimuli.

The autonomic nervous system

The autonomic nervous system is responsible for control over levels of activity in key organs and organ systems in the body. Many organs have some degree of control over their functioning. The heart, for example, has an intrinsic rhythm of 110 beats per minute. However, this level of activity may not be appropriate at all times. The heart may have to beat more at times of exercise, less at times of rest. The autonomic nervous system overrides local control to provide this higher level of coordinated control across most of the bodily systems in response to the varying demands being placed on the body. Its activity is controlled by a number of brain areas, the most important of which is the hypothalamus. The hypothalamus receives information about the demands being placed on the body from a variety of sources, including:

■ information about skin temperature from the reticular formation in the brainstem;
■ information about light and darkness from the optic nerves;
■ receptors in the hypothalamus itself provide information about the ion balance and temperature of the blood.

The hypothalamus also has links to the cortex and limbic systems of the brain, which are involved in the processing of cognitive and emotional demands. This allows the autonomic system to respond to psychological factors as well as physical demands being placed on the body. Accordingly, the autonomic nervous system can initiate sweating in high temperatures, increase blood pressure and heart rate during exercise, and also make us physiologically responsive at times of stress, distress or excitement (we discuss these responses further in Chapters 11 and 13).

The autonomic nervous system controls these varying levels of activity through two opposing networks of nerves (see Figure 8.4):

1. **the sympathetic nervous system**: involved in activation and arousal – the fight–flight response;
2. the **parasympathetic nervous system**: involved in relaxation – the rest–recover response.

synapse
junction between two neurons or between a neuron and target organ. Nerve impulses cross a synapse through the action of neurotransmitters.

neurotransmitter
a chemical messenger (e.g. adrenaline, acetylcholine) used to communicate between neurons and other neurons and other types of cell.

Both sets of nerves arise in an area in the brainstem known as the medulla oblongata (which is linked to the hypothalamus). From this, they pass down the spinal cord to various **synapses**, where they link to a second series of nerves that are linked to all the key body organs, including the heart, arteries and muscles (Figure 8.4). For the sympathetic arm, the **neurotransmitter** involved at the synapse between the spinal cord nerves and the nerve to the target organ is acetylcholine. Activity at the synapse between this second nerve and the end organ mainly involves a neurotransmitter known as noradrenaline (known alternatively as norepinephrine) and to a lesser extent adrenaline (epinephrine). The parasympathetic system uses acetylcholine at both synapses. The activity in each of the organs depends on the relative activity in the sympathetic and parasympathetic nervous systems. When activity in the sympathetic system dominates, the body is activated: when the parasympathetic system is dominant, the body is resting and relatively inactive, allowing basic functions such as digestion and the production of urine to occur more easily (see Table 8.1).

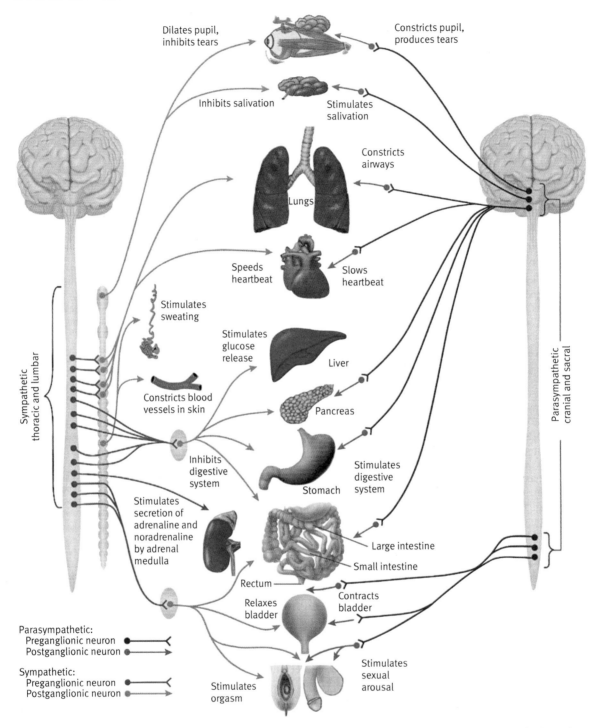

Figure 8.4 The autonomic nervous system, with the target organs and functions served by the sympathetic and parasympathetic branches.

Source: Carlson, N. (2005), © 2005, reproduced by permission of Pearson Education, Inc.

Table 8.1   Summary of responses of the autonomic nervous system to sympathetic and parasympathetic activity

Structure	Sympathetic stimulation	Parasympathetic stimulation
Iris (eye muscle)	Pupil dilation	Pupil constriction
Salivary glands	Salive production reduced	Saliva production increased
Heart	Heart rate and force increased	Heart rate and force decreased
Lung	Bronchial muscle relaxed	Bronchial muscle contracted
Stomach	Peristalsis reduced	Gastric juice secreted; motility increased
Small intestine	Motility reduced	Digestion increased
Large intestine	Motility reduced	Secretions and motility increased
Liver	Increased conversion of glycogen to glucose	
Kidney	Decreased urine secretion	Increased urine secretion
Bladder	Wall relaxed	Wall contracted
	Sphincter closed	Sphincter relaxed

endocrine glands
glands that produce and secrete hormones into the blood or lymph systems. Includes the pituitary and adrenal glands, and the islets of Langerhans in the pancreas. These hormones may affect one organ or tissue, or the entire body.

Endocrine processes

The activity initiated by the sympathetic nervous system is short-lived. A second system is therefore used to provide longer-term arousal. This system uses **endocrine glands**, which communicate with their target organs by releasing hormones into the bloodstream. The endocrine glands that extend the activity of the sympathetic nervous system are the **adrenal glands**, which are situated above the kidneys. These have two functional areas, each of which is activated in different ways:

adrenal glands
endocrine glands, located above each kidney. Comprises the cortex, which secretes several steroid hormones, and the medulla, which secretes noradrenaline.

1. the centre or *adrenal medulla*;
2. the surrounding tissues, known as the *adrenal cortex*.

The adrenal medulla is innervated by the sympathetic nervous system. Activity in this system stimulates the adrenal medulla to release the hormonal equivalent of the neurotransmitter noradrenaline into the bloodstream, in which it is transported to the organs in the body. Receptors in the target organs respond to the hormone and maintain their activation. Because the hormone can be released for a longer period than the neurotransmitter, this extends the period of activation.

corticosteroids
powerful anti-inflammatory hormones (including cortisol) made naturally in the body or synthetically for use as drugs.

cortisol
a stress hormone that increases the availability of energy stores and fats to fuel periods of high physiological activity. It also inhibits inflammation of damaged tissue.

A second activating system involves the pituitary gland, the activity of which is also controlled by the hypothalamus. This lies immediately under the brain (see Figure 8.2), and when stimulated by the hypothalamus, it releases a number of hormones into the bloodstream, the most important of which is adrenocorticotrophic hormone (ACTH). When the ACTH reaches the adrenal cortex, it causes it to release hormones known as **corticosteroids**, the most important of which is **cortisol** – also known as hydrocortisone. Cortisol increases the availability of energy stores and fats to fuel periods of high physiological activity. It also inhibits inflammation of damaged tissue.

The immune system

Components of the immune system

pathogens
a collective name for a variety of challenges to our health and immune system, including bacteria and viruses.

antigens
unique protein found on the surface of a pathogen that enables the immune system to recognise that pathogen as a foreign substance and therefore produce antibodies to fight it.

antibody
immunoglobulins produced in response to an antigen.

lymphocytes
a type of white blood cell. Lymphocytes have a number of roles in the immune system, including the production of antibodies and other substances that fight infection and disease. Includes T and B cells.

phagocytes
an immune system cell that can surround and kill micro-organisms and remove dead cells. Phagocytes include macrophages.

The immune system is very sophisticated and complex, and is designed to help the body to resist disease. It provides a variety of protective mechanisms that respond to attacks from bacteria, viruses, infectious diseases and other sources from outside the body – collectively known as **pathogens** or **antigens**. In this section, we first identify and briefly describe the role of different elements of the immune system. We then go on to look at the links between them and how they combine to combat invading pathogens and the development of cancers.

A number of organs and chemicals form the front line of the system. These include:

- *Physical barriers*: provided by the skin.
- *Mechanical barriers*: cilia (small hairs in the lining of the lungs) propel pathogens out of the lungs and respiratory tract – coughs and sneezes achieve the same goal more dramatically. Tears, saliva and urine also push pathogens out of the body.
- *Chemical barriers*: acid from the stomach provides an obvious chemical barrier against pathogens. Sebum, which coats body hairs, inhibits the growth of bacteria and fungi on the skin. Saliva, tears, sweat and nasal secretions contain lysozyme, which destroys bacteria. Saliva and the walls of the gastrointestinal tract also contain an **antibody** known as immunoglobulin A (IgA).
- '*Harmless pathogens*': a variety of bacteria live within the body and have no harmful effects on us. However, they defend their territory and can destroy other bacteria that invade it.
- *Lymph nodes*: secondary organs at or near possible points of entry for pathogens. This system includes the tonsils, Peyer's patches in the intestines, and the appendix. They have high levels of **lymphocytes** (see below), ready to attack any invading pathogens.

As well as these relatively static defences against attack, there are a number of cells that circulate around the body. This can be through the circulatory system or a parallel system known as the lymphatic system. This carries a fluid called lymph and transports cells important to the destruction of antigens to the sites of cellular damage and the waste products of this destruction away from them.

Two groups of cells in the circulatory and lymphatic systems provide protection against a variety of pathogens. **Phagocytes** (sometimes called white blood cells) circulate within the circulatory system. They are created in the bone marrow and attract, adhere to and then engulf and destroy antigens – a process known as phagocytosis. The immune system has a number of phagocytes, including:

- *Neutrophils* have a short life of a few hours to days. They provide the major defence against bacteria and the initial fight against infection by engulfing and digesting them. They are followed by macrophages about three to four hours later.

- *Macrophages* are long-lived and are best at attacking dead cells and pathogens capable of living within cells. Once a macrophage destroys a cell, it places some of its own proteins on its surface. This allows other immune cells to identify cells as invaders and to attack them.

A second group of cells known as lymphocytes circulate in the blood (where they are also known as white blood cells) and lymph system. These include **T cells** and **B cells**:

- *Cytotoxic T cells* bind on to antigens, including virus-infected cells and tumour cells. They form pores in the target cell's plasma membrane, allowing ions and water to flow into the target cell, making it expand then collapse and die.

- *Helper T cells* trigger or increase an immune response. They identify and bind to antigens, then release chemicals that stimulate the proliferation of cytotoxic T and plasma B cells (see below). Helper T cells are also known as **CD4+ cells** because of their chemical structure.

- *Plasma B cells* destroy antigens by binding to them and making them easier targets for phagocytes. They attack antigens in the blood system before they enter body cells.

- *Memory B cells* live indefinitely in the blood and lymphatic systems. They result from an initial attack by a novel antigen. In their initial response to such attacks, memory B cells 'learn' the chemical nature of such antigens and are able to deal with them more effectively should they encounter them again.

A third group of attacking cells are **natural killer (NK) cells**, which move in the blood and attack cancer cells and virus-infected body cells.

Central nervous system links with the immune system

The immune system is intimately linked to the central nervous system. The influence of these two interacting systems affects the development and activity of the phagocytes, and the B, T and NK cells. Lymphocytes also have adrenal and cortisol receptors, which are affected by hormones from both the adrenal cortex and medulla (see above). The influence of these neurotransmitters and hormones is complex. Increases of adrenaline in response to short-term stress can stimulate the spleen to release phagocytes into the bloodstream and increase NK cell counts, but decrease the number of T cells. Cortisol release decreases the production of helper T cells and ingestion of cells by macrophages. These issues are complex and differ over the time course of stress and the nature of the stressor. However, it is generally recognised that chronic stress significantly impairs the effectiveness of the immune system, leaving us less able to ward off infection.

T cell
a cell that recognises antigens on the surface of a virus-infected cell, binds to that cell and destroys it.

B cell
a form of lymphocyte involved in destruction of antigens. Memory B cells provide long-term immunity against previously encountered pathogens.

CD4+ cells
otherwise known as helper T cells, these are involved in the proliferation of cytotoxic T cells as part of the immune response. HIV infection impairs their ability to provide this function.

natural killer (NK) cells
cells that move in the blood and attack cancer cells and virus-infected body cells.

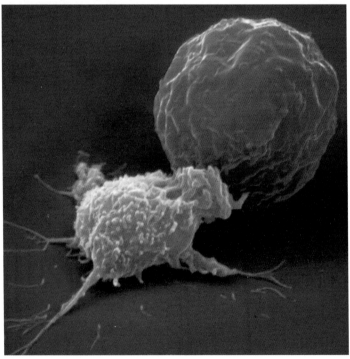

(8.1)

(8.2)

Plates 8.1 and 8.2 Here we see two cells, a virus and cancer cell, being attacked and either engulfed by B cells (8.1) or rendered inert by NK cells (8.2).

Source: Dr Andrejs Liepins/Science Photo Library (8.1) and Eye of Science/Science Photo Library (8.2)

Immune dysfunction

■ Human immunodeficiency virus infection

The human immunodeficiency virus (HIV) is the cause of a potentially fatal condition known as Acquired ImmunoDeficiency Syndrome (AIDS). The virus belongs to a subgroup of viruses known as 'slow viruses', which have a long interval between initial infection and the onset of serious symptoms – potentially up to 10 years and beyond. The virus affects the T helper (CD4+) cells. In response to a virus or other pathogens, healthy CD4+ cells replicate and send messages to B and T cells to also replicate and attack the pathogen. When infected with HIV, CD4+ cells still replicate in response to pathogens, but the replicated CD4+ cells are infected with the virus, are unable to activate their target B and T cells, and eventually die. Initially, the non-infected CD4+ cells still provide an effective response against pathogens. However, over time, proliferation of infected CD4+ cells in response to pathogens results in an increase in infected CD4+ cells in circulation. These will eventually die, but before doing so may bind with healthy CD4+ cells, resulting in their death. In addition, the immune system may recognise the virus-laden cells as invasive, and begin to attack its own CD4+ cells. Together, these processes result in a gradual reduction in the number of circulating CD4+ cells, reducing the immune system's ability to defend itself effectively against viruses, bacteria and some cancers. When the CD4+ cell count falls below $500/mm^3$, approximately half the immune system reserve has been destroyed. At this point minor infection such as cold sores and fungal infections begin to appear. Once the CD4+ cell count falls below $200/mm^3$, life threatening opportunistic infections and cancers typically occur. AIDS, the end point of HIV disease, occurs when the CD4+ cell count is less than $200/mm^3$ or when the individual develops potentially life-threatening infections such as pneumonia or cancers such as **Kaposi's sarcoma**.

Kaposi's sarcoma
a malignant tumour of the connective tissue, often associated with AIDS. The tumours consist of bluish-red or purple lesions on the skin. They often appear first on the feet or ankles, thighs, arms, hands and face.

Treatment for HIV infection involves three classes of drugs.

■ *Reverse transcriptase inhibitors*: HIV uses reverse transcriptase to copy its genetic material and generate new viruses. Reverse transcriptase inhibitors disrupt the process and thereby suppress its growth.

■ *Protease inhibitors*: these interfere with the protease enzyme that HIV uses to produce infectious viral particles.

■ *Fusion inhibitors*: these interfere with the virus's ability to fuse with the cellular membrane of other CD4+ cells, blocking entry into the host cell.

These drugs do not cure HIV infection or AIDS. They can suppress the virus, even to undetectable levels, but are unable to completely eliminate HIV from the body. Accordingly, infected individuals still need to take antiretroviral drugs. In addition, as HIV reproduces itself, different strains of the virus emerge, some of which are resistant to antiretroviral drugs. For this reason, treatment guidelines state that HIV positive individuals take a combination of antiretroviral drugs known as Highly Active Anti-Retroviral Therapy (HAART). This strategy, which typically combines two different classes of antiretroviral drugs, has been shown to effectively suppress the virus when used appropriately. Unfortunately, strict adherence to the HAART regimen presents a significant challenge to the individual taking the medication, both in terms of taking the medication at the correct time and the side-effects that they may experience (see Chapter 10).

Autoimmune conditions

autoimmune conditions
a group of diseases, including type 1 diabetes, Crohn's disease and rheumatoid arthritis, characterised by abnormal functioning of the immune system in which it produces antibodies against its own tissues – it treats 'self' as 'non-self'.

diabetes (type 1 and 2)
a lifelong disease marked by high levels of sugar in the blood and a failure to transfer this to organs that need it. It can be caused by too little insulin (type 1) resistance to insulin (type 2), or both.

type 1 diabetes
see **diabetes**.

pancreas
gland in which the Islets of Langerhans produce insulin. Also produces and secretes digestive enzymes. Located behind the stomach.

type 2 diabetes
see **diabetes**.

The immune system is able to identify cells that are part of the body ('self') and those that are 'non-self': antigens, developing cancers, and so on. On occasion, this process breaks down and the immune system treats cells within the body as non-self and begins to attack them. This can result in a number of **autoimmune conditions**, including diabetes, rheumatoid arthritis and multiple sclerosis.

■ Diabetes

Two types of **diabetes** have been identified. In **type 1 diabetes**, the body does not produce sufficient insulin within the Islets of Langerhans in the **pancreas**. Its onset is frequently triggered by an infection, often by one of the Coxsackie virus family. This virus expresses a protein similar in structure to an enzyme involved in the production of insulin, and the immune response to this virus can also destroy the insulin-producing cells within the pancreas. Insulin normally attaches itself to glucose molecules in the circulatory system, permitting it to be taken up by the various body organs which need it to provide them with energy. Without insulin, these glucose molecules cannot be absorbed, leading to high levels of glucose within the blood which the body cannot use. This can lead to a life-threatening coma known as diabetic ketoacidosis, which requires hospitalisation and immediate treatment to avoid death. Less dramatic symptoms include increased thirst and urination, constant hunger, weight loss, blurred vision and extreme fatigue.

Treatment typically involves between one and four injections of insulin a day, meal planning to avoid sudden peaks of glucose being released into the blood stream, weight control, and exercise. Treatment is a balancing act, aimed at achieving appropriate levels of circulating blood glucose. Too much food and/or too little insulin can result in ketoacidosis. Too little food and/or too much insulin can result in a condition known as hypoglycaemia, characterised by symptoms including a period of confusion and irritability, followed by a fairly rapid loss of consciousness. Immediate treatment is to give oral glucose where possible, or intravenously if the individual has lost consciousness. Good day-to-day control over diabetes reduces but does not obviate long-term complications including poor circulation which can lead to loss of sight, heart disease, skin ulcers, loss of limbs and nerve damage.

A second form of the condition is known as **type 2 diabetes**. In this, the body produces sufficient insulin (or close to sufficient), but the cells that take up the glucose-insulin molecules become 'resistant' to them, and no longer absorb them. Type 2 diabetes often develops later in life, and is associated with obesity – a person's chances of developing Type 2 diabetes increases by 4 per cent for every pound of excess weight. The symptoms of Type 2 diabetes develop gradually, and their onset is not as sudden as in Type 1 diabetes. They may include fatigue or nausea, frequent urination, unusual thirst, weight loss, blurred vision, frequent infections and slow healing of wounds or sores. Some people have no symptoms. First-line treatment involves weight loss and exercise – although many people find it hard to adhere to such regimens

(Vermeire *et al.* 2007). Second-line treatment involves treatment with oral medication designed to variously stimulate the beta cells in the pancreas to release more insulin, decrease the amount of glucose produced by the liver and enhance the effectiveness of naturally produced insulin, and lower glucose levels by blocking the breakdown of starches in the gut.

■ Rheumatoid arthritis

rheumatoid arthritis
a chronic autoimmune disease with inflammation of the joints and marked deformities.

Rheumatoid arthritis (RA) may be triggered by viruses in individuals with a genetic tendency for the disease. It is a systemic disease that affects the entire body (and can impact on internal organs including lungs, heart and eyes) characterised by inflammation of the membrane lining the joints (the synovium). Any joint may be affected, but the hands, feet and wrists are the most frequently involved. It is a chronic, episodic condition, with 'flare-ups' and periods of remission. During flare-ups, people with the condition experience significant pain, stiffness, warmth, redness and swelling in affected joints – as well as fatigue, loss of appetite, fever and loss of energy. Over the long term, inflammatory cells in the synovium release enzymes that digest bone and cartilage, leading to joints losing their shape and alignment, and pain and restricted movement within the joint. Rheumatoid arthritis is more common in women than in men, and affects relatively young people: the age of onset is usually between 25 and 50 years.

There is no known cure for RA. The goal of treatment is to reduce joint inflammation and pain, maximise joint function, and prevent joint destruction and deformity. Treatment involves both medication and self-care: rest, joint strengthening exercises and joint protection. Two types of medications are used in treating rheumatoid arthritis: fast-acting 'first-line drugs' and slow-acting 'second-line drugs'. First-line drugs, such as aspirin and cortisone (corticosteroids), are used to reduce pain and inflammation. Slow-acting second-line drugs, such as gold, methotrexate and hydroxychloroquine promote disease remission and prevent progressive joint destruction. As can be seen in the example of Mrs K, people with RA may also benefit from a number of aids to help them engage in many everyday behaviours. Mrs K recounts a typical day which may not be different to many people's day, but which is characterised by small (and not so small) frustrations due to her condition.

I am a 42-year-old wife and mother of two young children. I have had severe rheumatoid arthritis for nearly 8 years. This has caused deformities in my hands and feet. My fingers are gnarled. My wrists have nearly fused. My toes have bent upwards. My knees and many of the small joints of my knuckles are swollen.

I am usually very stiff when I wake up, so I get up slowly. After sitting at the side of the bed, I stand slowly, then slowly walk to the kitchen to prepare breakfast and school lunches for my children. Because my grip has been impaired with my deformities, I use a knife with an over-sized grip handle to make sandwiches. I use a lid gripper pad to open jars. I take my tablets with my breakfast.

After breakfast, its time for my morning washing routine. I have a raised toilet seat to avoid straining my joints sitting down and getting up. I shower while waiting for the morning tablets to start working. Washing my hair is difficult with my hands and I have adapted a scrubbing brush to help me wash it. I am careful getting in and out of the shower because the instability of my legs puts me at risk of falling.

Getting dressed is not easy. I am too clumsy to use buttons, so most of my shirts are pullover or have velcro attachments. My bra can be fastened in front and reversed or I ask my husband to fasten it for me. Most of my trousers have elastic waistbands and do not require buttoning or zipping. My shoes are especially wide and I usually wear running shoes for comfort. I dress for comfort – not for 'fashion'!

I drive the kids to school. Getting into and out of the car is painful and slow. I have a special key enlarger attachment for my car and house keys, which makes it easier to turn them. I can drive, but it makes my wrists hurt.

I try to exercise every day. I start with stretching exercises, then either ride a stationary bike or go on a walk. Once a week, I go for a swim. Exercise makes me feel good and gives me a sense of control over my body. Housework also always needs doing. I make good use of attachments to the vacuum cleaner that help me get to places that are hard to reach. Our door handles are levers instead of knobs so that it is easier for me to turn them. I can't do the ironing. When I cook, I use special grippers to hold the handles of pots and pans and an electric can opener.

At bedtime, undressing can be as challenging as dressing. My husband frequently assists me with the undressing. My wrists are frequently painful by the evening, so I strap on my wrist splints before reading a few chapters of my novel, and calling it a night.

■ Multiple sclerosis

multiple sclerosis
a disorder of the brain and spinal cord caused by progressive damage to the myelin sheath covering of nerve cells.

Multiple sclerosis (MS) is a neurological condition involving repeated episodes of inflammation of the central nervous system (brain and spinal cord). This results in the slowing or blocking of the transmission of nerve impulses. As this may occur in any part of the brain or spinal cord, symptoms can differ markedly across individuals, and include loss of limb function, loss of bowel and/or bladder control, blindness due to inflammation of the optic nerve and cognitive impairment. Muscular spasticity is a common feature, particularly in the upper limbs. A total of 95 per cent of people with MS experience debilitating fatigue, which can be so severe that about 40 per cent of people with the condition are unable to engage in sustained physical activity: 30 to 50 per cent require walking aids or a wheelchair for mobility. During acute symptomatic episodes, patients may be hospitalised.

The course of MS differs across individuals. Twenty per cent of people with the condition have a benign form of the disease in which symptoms show little or no progression after the initial episode. A few people experience malignant MS, resulting in a swift and relentless decline, with significant disability or even death occurring shortly after disease onset. Onset of this type of MS is usually after the age of 40 years. The majority of people have an episodic condition, known as remitting–relapsing MS, with acute flare-ups followed by periods of remission. Each flare-up, however, is usually followed by a failure to recover to previous levels of function, resulting in a slowly deteriorating condition. Death is usually due to complications of MS including choking, pneumonia and renal failure. As well as physical problems, nearly half the people with MS experience some degree of cognitive impairment and memory problems. In addition, about half the people who develop MS will be clinically depressed at some time during the course of the illness (Siegert and Abernethy 2005). Whether this is a direct result of neuronal damage or a reaction to the experience of the disease is not clear. It may, of course, be both.

One chemical within the immune system, called gamma-interferon, is particularly implicated in MS. This stimulates production of cytotoxic T cells, which are responsible for attacking and destroying diseased or damaged body cells. In MS, the activated cytotoxic T cells wrongly identify the **myelin sheath** of nerve cells within the brain and spinal column as 'non-self', and attempt to destroy it. Viral infections may act as a trigger to the production of gamma-interferon, and the onset of MS may follow a viral infection. One approach to the treatment of MS involves a different type of interferon. Beta interferon appears to inhibit the action of gamma interferon and prevents the T cells attacking the myelin sheath. Unfortunately, interferons have to be regularly injected, and are responsible for the fever, muscle aches, fatigue and headache experienced during illnesses such as influenza. These also form the side-effects of taking them as medication, and as a consequence many patients avoid their use. There is increasing evidence that cannabis can be effective in reducing pain and muscle spasticity associated with MS. But the treatment has to counter the problems of its legal status. It is legally prescribed, for example, in the Netherlands and Canada but is not legally available in the UK or USA. Its status is under review in Australia.

Susan provides an insight into what it feels like to have MS. At the time of our talk (see Bennett 2006) she was taking antidepressants for her depression and, as you will read, was having problems coming to terms with her illness.

myelin sheath
a substance that contains both protein and fat (lipid) and surrounds all nerves outside the brain. It acts as a nerve insulator and helps in the transmission of nerve signals.

I developed MS about four years ago. It was odd to start with. I didn't think I had anything serious, although you do worry about symptoms you don't understand. It started when I had some problems with my sight. I couldn't see as well as I used to be able to – it came on suddenly so I didn't think it was age or anything normal. I think at the time I was also a bit more clumsy than I had been – nothing obvious, but I dropped things a bit more than before. Nothing really that you'd notice unless other things were happening as well. I went to my GP about my eyes and he sent me to see a neurologist. He tried to reassure me that there was nothing too badly wrong and that he wanted to check out a few symptoms. But I began to worry then . . . you don't get sent on to see the hospital doctors unless there is anything really wrong with you. He suggested that he thought it might be MS, which was why he was not sending me to an eye specialist.

I got to see the neurologist pretty quickly and she ran a few tests over a few weeks – testing my muscle strength, coordination, scans and so on . . . sticking needles into me at various times. The upshot of this was that I was diagnosed as having MS. My consultant told me and my husband together, and allowed us to ask questions about things. We also got to speak to a specialist nurse who has helped us over the years. She was able to take the time to tell us more than the doctor about what to expect and what support we could have. Although I think it was nice to hear the diagnosis from the doctor.

I must admit that I found it really hard to deal with things at the beginning – you don't know what to expect and perhaps you expect the worst. You hear all sorts of horror stories about people dying with MS and that. And no one can really reassure you that you won't have problems . . . Over the last few years, I've got to know my body and seen things getting worse. But it happens gradually and a lot of the time there are no changes. So that is reassuring – that things aren't going to collapse too quickly and I won't be left incontinent and unable to feed myself for a long time – hopefully not ever!

The worse thing is the tiredness and clumsiness. My eyes have actually got better, thank goodness. I use sticks to get around the house. Sometimes I can walk a little out of the house. Often I have to take the wheelchair. I just get exhausted too quickly, there isn't a lot of point trying to walk, because I cannot go far . . .

continued

I hate having MS. I used to take part in sports, go out, be lively. Now I can't do any of that. I'm tired . . . down a lot of the time. I think the two often go together. My memory was never that good, but now it seems to be worse than ever. I can hold conversations, but keeping my concentration up for a long time is difficult. So, people find you difficult to deal with. I know my husband feels that way. He married a lively, sporty, slim woman . . . now I'm lethargic, down, putting on weight because I eat and don't exercise – even though they tell me not to, so I can keep mobile and not develop skin problems. I don't go out very much because it's such a hassle in my wheelchair . . . cities were not designed for people in wheelchairs . . . and people don't like people in wheelchairs. You are ignored . . . and just want to say, 'Hey, I'm here. I have a brain you know . . .' I know this sounds sorry for myself. And sometimes I feel more positive. But I find living with uncertainty difficult. Will I have a bad day today? Will I have a flare up – have to go to hospital, take mega-steroids, come out worse than when I went in? I guess you have to live for the day . . . but it can be difficult.

The digestive system

The digestive tract is the system of organs responsible for the ingestion of food, absorption of nutrients from that food, and finally the expulsion of waste products from the body. It comprises a number of connected organs, each with a different role:

- *Mouth*: here, food is masticated by chewing, causing the release of enzymes in the saliva and beginning the process of digestion.
- *Oesophagus*: this transports food from the mouth to the stomach, compressing it in the process.
- *Stomach*: here, food is churned and mixed with acid to decompose it chemically.
- *Small intestine*: this is responsible for mixing the bowel contents with chem-

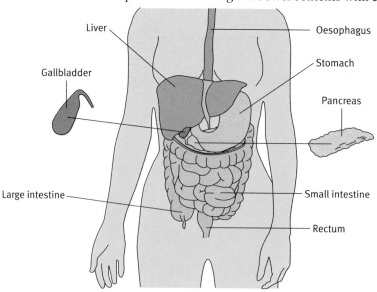

Figure 8.5 The large and small intestine and related organs.

bile
a digestive juice, made in the liver and stored in the gallbladder. Involved in the digestion of fats in the small intestine.

gallbladder
a structure on the underside of the liver on the right side of the abdomen. It stores the bile that is produced in the liver before it is secreted into the intestines. This helps the body to digest fats.

icals to break it into its constituent parts and then absorb them into the bloodstream for transportation to other organs. Chemicals involved in this process include **bile**, which is made by the liver and stored in the **gallbladder** and digests fats, and enzyme-rich juices released from the pancreas.

■ *The large bowel* (colon): this is largely responsible for re-absorption of water from the bowel contents and expulsion of the unused bowel contents. Movement between and along these various organs is controlled by a process known as peristalsis. This involves smooth muscle within the walls of the organs narrowing and the narrow sections moving slowly along the length of the organ in a series of waves, pushing the bowel contents forward with each wave.

Controlling digestion

Each of these digestion processes is controlled by both hormone and nerve regulators. Hormones are produced and released by cells in the mucosa (lining) of the stomach and small intestine at key stages in the digestive process. Among other roles:

■ Gastrin causes the stomach to produce its acid.

■ Secretin causes the pancreas to produce a fluid that is rich in bicarbonate and enzymes to break down food into its constituent proteins, sugars and so on. The bicarbonate is alkaline and prevents the bowel wall from being damaged as the highly acidic stomach contents are released into the small intestine. Secretin also stimulates the liver to produce bile, the acid that aids fat digestion.

■ Cholesystokinin triggers the gallbladder to discharge its bile into the small intestine.

Activity in the digestive system is also controlled by a complex local nervous system known as the enteric nervous system, in which:

■ Sensory neurons receive information from receptors in the mucosa and muscle. Chemoreceptors monitor levels of acid, glucose and amino acids. Sensory receptors respond to stretch and tension within the wall of the gut.

■ Motor neurons, whose key role is to control gastrointestinal motility (including peristalsis and stomach motility) and secretion, control the action on smooth muscle in the wall of the gut.

Key neurotransmitters involved in the activity of the enteric nervous system are noradrenaline and acetylcholine: the former provides an activating role, the second an inhibitory role. The enteric nervous system works independently of the central nervous system. However, the gut also has links to the central nervous system, providing sensory information (such as fullness) to the hypothalamus, and allowing the gut to respond to the various excitatory or inhibitory processes of the autonomic nervous system. In general, sympathetic stimulation inhibits digestive activities, inhibiting gastrointestinal secretion and motor activity, and contracting gastrointestinal sphincters and blood vessels. The latter may be experienced as feelings of 'butterflies in the stomach' – and also some other, perhaps even more obvious, symptoms! Conversely, parasympathetic activity typically stimulates digestive activities.

Disorders of the digestive system

■ Gastric ulcer

Gastric ulcers are ulceration of the lining of the stomach (mucosa), which can result in a number of symptoms, the most common of which is abdominal discomfort or pain. This typically comes and goes for several days or weeks, occurs two to three hours after eating, is relieved by eating, and may be at its worst during the night – when the stomach is empty following a meal. Other symptoms include poor appetite, weight loss, bloating, nausea and vomiting. If the disease process is not treated, the ulcer may erode through the stomach wall, resulting in the potentially fatal outflow of its contents into the abdomen.

Until relatively recently, gastric ulcers were thought to be a consequence of stress, which was thought to increase acid secretion in the stomach. More recent evidence, however, has shown that a bacterium known as *Helicobacter pylori* is responsible for 70 per cent of cases of the disorder. *Helicobacter pylori* infection is thought to weaken the protective mucous coating of the stomach and duodenum, and allow acid to reach the sensitive lining beneath. It may also increase the amount of stomach acid secreted. Both acid and bacteria irritate the stomach lining and cause the ulcer. However, stress may still be implicated in the development and maintenance of gastric ulcers as it may increase risk behaviours such as smoking or alcohol consumption, as well as adversely affecting the immune system's ability to influence levels of *H. pylori* in the gut.

Treatment involves suppressing acid secretion and, if appropriate, eradicating the *H. pylori* bacteria. Various types of drugs may be used to achieve this effect. Reductions in acid production can be achieved by Histamine blockers (e.g. Cimetidine) and drugs known as hydrogen pump antagonists (e.g. Omeprazol). Drugs which eradicate *H. pylori* include antibiotics such as tetracycline or amoxicillin which are frequently given in combination with histamine blockers or hydrogen pump antagonists. Only rarely is surgery used in the treatment of gastric ulcers, and this usually when the ulcer has eroded through the stomach wall and has led to life-threatening haemorrhage.

inflammatory bowel disease
a group of inflammatory conditions of the large intestine and, in some cases, the small intestine. The main forms of IBD are **Crohn's disease** and **ulcerative colitis**.

Crohn's disease
autoimmune disease that can affect any part of the gastrointestinal tract but most commonly occurs in the ileum (the area where the small and large intestine meet).

■ Inflammatory bowel disease

Inflammatory bowel disease (IBD) is a group of inflammatory conditions of the large and, in some cases, small intestine. The main forms of IBD are:

- ■ Crohn's disease
- ■ ulcerative colitis.

Crohn's disease
Crohn's disease can involve any part of the gastrointestinal tract. It is an inflammatory condition characterised by episodes of severe symptoms followed by periods of remission. Its key symptoms are chronic, and occasionally severe, diarrhoea and disrupted digestion. Over time, the inflammation process can result in a thickening of the bowel wall, which may result in the diameter of the bowel becoming so constricted that food cannot pass through these damaged sections. These may require surgical excision. Unfortunately, as the disease tends to recur at these sites, the constriction may reoccur

and require further surgery within a few years. For this reason, surgery is often considered the treatment of last resort. There is some evidence that the condition may have a genetic basis, although a diet high in sugar and fats, smoking and stress have also been implicated in its aetiology. The usual age of onset is between 15 and 30 years of age, with no difference between men and women. Its symptoms include:

fistulas
formation of small passages that connect the intestine with other organs or the skin.

- abdominal pain
- changes in bowel movements – faeces may vary between solid and watery
- periods of mild fever, sometimes with blood in the stools, and pain in the lower right abdomen
- loss of appetite
- unintentional weight loss
- boils and fistulas
- general malaise.

At times of acute symptoms, individuals become severely dehydrated and are unable to digest food and absorb necessary nutrients, resulting in the need for significant medical care. At such times, a number of drugs designed to reduce inflammation and antibiotics may be necessary.

Ulcerative colitis

ulcerative colitis
a chronic inflammatory disease of the large intestine, characterised by recurrent episodes of abdominal pain, fever and severe diarrhoea.

Ulcerative colitis is similar to Crohn's disease, but usually affects the terminal part of the large intestine and rectum. It may develop into cancer after many years of the disease. For this reason, patients have regular check-ups for the beginning of cancer or even have preventive removal of segments of the bowel. This may result in the affected individual needing a **colostomy**. Its severity can be graded as:

- *Mild*: fewer than four stools daily, with or without blood. There may be mild abdominal pain or cramping.

- *Moderate*: more than four stools daily. Patients may be anaemic and have moderate abdominal pain and low grade fever.

tachycardia
high heart rate – usually defined as greater than 100 beats per minute.

- *Severe*: more than six bloody stools a day, and evidence of systemic disease such as fever, **tachycardia**, or anaemia.

- *Fulminant*: ten bowel movements daily, continuous bleeding, abdominal tenderness and distension. Patients will require blood transfusion and their colon may perforate, resulting in the gut content being released into the abdomen. Unless treated, fulminant disease will soon lead to death.

The goals of treatment with medication are to treat acute episodes and to maintain remission once achieved. Treatment is similar to that of Crohn's disease, and involves steroids to reduce inflammation and immunomodulators which suppress the body's immune processes that are contributing to the condition. An interesting fact is that risk of developing ulcerative colitis appears to be higher in non-smokers and in ex-smokers, and some patients may actually improve when treated with nicotine.

irritable bowel syndrome
a disorder of the lower intestinal tract. Symptoms include pain combined with altered bowel habits resulting in diarrhoea, constipation or both. It has no obvious physiological abnormalities, so diagnosis is by the presence and pattern of symptoms.

■ Irritable bowel syndrome

Irritable bowel syndrome (IBS) is a condition of the bowel involving a period of at least three months abdominal discomfort or pain, with two or more of the following features:

■ pain, relieved by defaecation;
■ pain associated with a change in the frequency of bowel movements;
■ change in the form of the stool (loose, watery, or pellet-like).

Also central to a diagnosis of IBS is that these symptoms occur in the absence of any obvious physical pathology. Because of this lack of physical pathology, IBS was at one time considered to be the archetypal psychosomatic disorder. Indeed, Latimer (1981) went so far as to suggest that anxiety and IBS were the same condition, with IBS symptoms reported by people who were unwilling or unable to attribute their symptoms to psychological factors. However, evidence of this link to stress is not as strong as was previously thought, and other factors have now been linked with IBS. These include food hypersensitivities and the presence of bacteria such as *Blastocystis hominis* and *Helicobacter pylori* (see Singh *et al.* 2003). Spence and Moss-Morris (2007) argued that the initial trigger to IBS may be an infection (an episode of gastroenteritis), with the condition maintained in the longer term by high levels of anxiety and/or stress. Whatever its cause, psychological treatment using cognitive-behavioural therapy or a form of relaxation

IN THE SPOTLIGHT

Cancer

Hundreds of genes play a role in the growth and division of cells. Three classes of gene control this process and may contribute to the uncontrolled proliferation of cells, which is cancer:

1. *Oncogenes* control the sequence of events by which a cell enlarges, replicates its DNA, divides and passes a complete set of genes to each daughter cell. When mutated, they can drive excessive proliferation by producing too much – or an overactive form – of a growth-stimulating protein.

2. *Tumour suppressor genes* inhibit cell growth. Loss or inactivation of this gene may produce inappropriate growth by losing this inhibitory control.

cell suicide
a form of cell death in which a controlled sequence of events (or programme) leads to the elimination of cells without releasing harmful substances into the surrounding area.

3. *Checkpoint genes* monitor and repair DNA, which is often damaged prior to reproduction and needs to be repaired before cell division. Without these checking mechanisms, a damaged gene will become replicated as a permanent mutation. One of the most notable checkpoint proteins is known as p53, which prevents replication of damaged DNA in the normal cell and promotes **cell suicide** in cells with abnormal DNA. Faulty p53 allows cells carrying damaged DNA to replicate and survive and has been found to be defective in most human cancers.

Other factors are also important in tumour development. Growing tumours are dependent on a good blood supply. To promote this, local tissues may be transformed into blood vessel cells, allowing the tumour to establish its own blood supply. Some modern treatments of cancer attack this blood supply as well as the tumour mass itself. Tumours also acquire the ability to migrate and invade other tissues, forming tumour masses at different sites in the body. This process is known as metastasis – and in some cases these secondary tumours may be more deadly than the original tumour.

known as autogenic training, in which patients are given specific instructions of visualising and feeling warm and relaxed in the gut appears to be effective forms of treatment (see Chapter 17). Medical treatment involves the use of smooth muscle relaxants to reduce gut motility, adding or reducing fibre to the diet (depending on the level of fibre already in the diet), drugs which 'bulk' up stools to reduce diarrhoea, and on occasion, anxiolytic or anti-depressant drugs. While IBS may be unpleasant, and some people may be restricted by the pain they experience or the fear of not being able to get to a toilet in time if they were to have diarrhoea, it is not a life-threatening condition nor as debilitating as the previously described conditions.

■ Colorectal cancer

Colorectal cancer is the third most common cancer in men and women. Risk for the condition is increased by both biological and behavioural factors, including genetic factors, pre-existing inflammatory conditions including ulcerative colitis, and a diet high in fat and low in fibre. Symptoms of the disorder are often unnoticed because they are relatively mild, and include: bleeding, constipation or diarrhoea, and unformed stool. One early symptom may be a general tiredness and shortness of breath as a consequence of anaemia caused by long-term, but unnoticed, bleeding within the gut. For this reason, the cancer may be quite advanced before people seek medical help. It is nevertheless generally treatable with a combination of surgery to remove the cancer followed by chemotherapy. Radiotherapy is rarely used except in cases of rectal cancer. As with many cancers, the condition can be described in terms of its stages, with the higher stage being more difficult to treat and having a poorer **prognosis**

prognosis
the predicted outcome
of a disease.

- *Stage 1*: the cancer is limited to the inside of the bowel.
- *Stage 2*: the cancer penetrates through the wall of the bowel to the outside layers.
- *Stage 3*: the cancer involves the lymph glands in the abdomen.
- *Stage 4*: the cancer has metastasised to other organs.

The cardiovascular system

The main function of the cardiovascular system is to transport nutrients, immune cells and oxygen to the body's organs and to remove waste products from them. It also moves hormones from their point of production within the body to their site of action. The transport medium used in this process is the blood; the pumping system that pushes the blood around the body involves the heart and various types of blood vessel:

- *Arteries*: transport blood away from the heart. These vessels have a muscular sheath that allows them to contract or expand slightly. This activity is controlled by the autonomic nervous system.
- *Arterioles*: these are small arteries, linking the large arteries to the organs of the body.

■ *Veins*: these transport blood back to the heart once the oxygen and nutrients have been absorbed from it and replaced by carbon dioxide and a variety of waste products. They are thinner than arteries, and because they are so far from the heart have much lower pressures than the arteries. Blood is pushed through them partly by the pressure of the pulse of blood from the heart, partly through the action of the moving muscles. As large muscle groups contract during everyday activities, they push blood through the veins. To prevent back flow of blood they have a series of valves, which allow the blood to flow in only one direction. When the muscles are inactive, blood may no longer flow freely in the veins and may even stagnate and begin to clot – a deep vein thrombosis that may occur after long-haul flights or other periods of inactivity in some susceptible individuals.

The heart

The heart has two separate pumps operating in parallel. The right side of the heart is involved in the transportation of blood to the lungs; the left side pumps blood to the rest of the body (Figure 8.6). Each side of the heart has two chambers (Figure 8.7), known as atria and ventricles. The right atrium takes deoxygenated blood from veins known as the superior and inferior vena cava and pumps it into the right ventricle. Blood is then pumped into the pulmonary artery, taking it to the lungs, where it picks up oxygen in its haemoglobin cells. Oxygen-laden blood then returns to the heart, entering through the left atrium. It is then pumped into the left ventricle, and then into

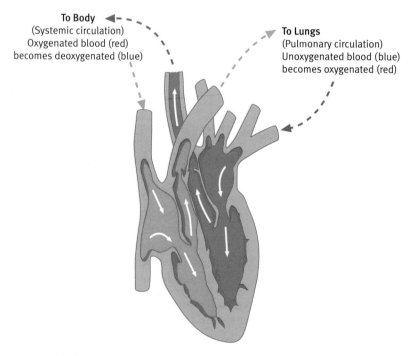

To Body
(Systemic circulation)
Oxygenated blood (red)
becomes deoxygenated (blue)

To Lungs
(Pulmonary circulation)
Unoxygenated blood (blue)
becomes oxygenated (red)

Figure 8.6 The flow of blood through the heart.

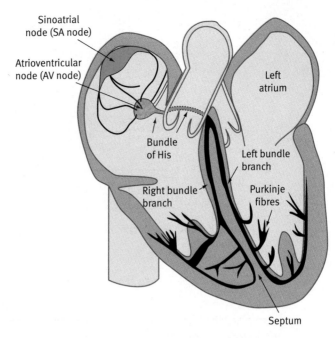

Sinoatrial
node (SA node)

Atrioventricular
node (AV node)

Left
atrium

Bundle
of His

Left bundle
branch

Right bundle
branch

Purkinje
fibres

Septum

Figure 8.7   Electrical conduction and control of the heart rhythm.

aorta
the main trunk of the
systemic arteries,
carrying blood from the
left side of the heart to
the arteries of all limbs
and organs except the
lungs.

the main artery, known as the **aorta**, which carries blood to the rest of the
body.

The rhythm of the heart is controlled by an electrical system. It is initiated
by an electrical impulse generated in a region of the right atrium called the
sinoatrial node. This impulse causes the muscles of both atria to contract. As
the wave of electricity progresses through the heart muscle and nerves, it
reaches an area at the junction of the atria and ventricles known as the atrioventricular node. This second node then fires a further electrical discharge
along a system of nerves including the Bundle of His and Purkinje fibres (see
Figure 8.7), triggering the muscles of both ventricles to contract, completing
the cycle. Although the sinoatrial node has an intrinsic rhythm, its activity is
largely influenced by the autonomic nervous system.

An electrocardiogram (ECG) is used to measure the activity of the heart.
Electrodes are placed over the heart and can detect each of the nodes firing
and recharging. Figure 8.8 shows an ECG of a normal heart, indicating the
electrical activity at each stage of the heart's cycle.

- The P wave indicates the electrical activity of the atria firing – the time
  needed for an electrical impulse from the sinoatrial node to spread
  throughout the atrial musculature.

- The QRS complex represents the electrical activity of the ventricles
  compressing.

- The T wave represents the repolarisation of the ventricles.

defibrillator
a machine that uses an
electric current to stop
any irregular and
dangerous activity of the
heart's muscles. It can
be used when the heart
has stopped (cardiac
arrest) or when it is
beating in a highly
irregular (and
ineffective) manner.

When the heart stops beating or its electrical rhythm is completely irregular and no blood is being pushed around the body, doctors may use a
defibrillator to stimulate a normal (sinusoidal) rhythm.

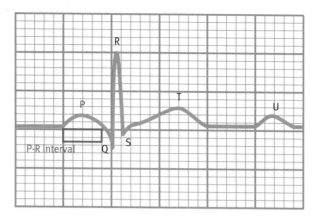

Figure 8.8 An electrocardiograph of the electrical activity of the heart (see text for explanation).

Blood

exogenous
relating to things outside the body.

erythrocyte
a mature blood cell that contains **haemoglobin** to carry oxygen to the bodily tissues.

platelets
tiny bits of protoplasm found in the blood that are essential for blood clotting. These cells bind together to form a clot and prevent bleeding at the site of injury.

The body usually contains about 5 litres of blood. Its constituents include a fluid known as plasma and a variety of cells. As well as the various **exogenous** cells carried in the blood (nutrients, oxygen, etc.), it produces its own cells. These are manufactured by stem cells in the bone marrow. Three different types of cell are produced:

1. **Erythrocytes** (or red blood cells) transport oxygen around the body. In them, oxygen combines with haemoglobin in the lungs and is transported to cells in need of oxygen, where it is released, allowing cell respiration.

2. Phagocytes and lymphocytes (or white blood cells; see above) include the immune system's B cells and T cells described earlier in the chapter.

3. **Platelets** are cells that respond to damage to the circulatory system. They aggregate (form a clot) around the site of any damage and prevent loss of blood from the system. They are also involved in repair to damage within the arteries themselves and contribute to the development of atheroma. We consider this process later in the chapter.

■ Blood pressure

Blood pressure has two components:

1. the degree of pressure imposed on the blood as a result of its constriction within the arteries and veins – known as the diastolic blood pressure (DBP);

2. an additional pressure as the wave of blood pushed out from the heart flows through the system (our pulse) – known as the systolic blood pressure (SBP).

This pressure is measured in millimetres of mercury (mmHg), representing the height of a tube of mercury in millilitres that the pressure can push up (using a now old-fashioned sphygmomanometer). Healthy levels of blood pressure are an SBP below 130–140 mmHg and a DBP below 90 mmHg (written as 130/90 mmHg: see also the discussion of hypertension later in the chapter).

A number of physiological processes are involved in controlling blood pressure. Those of particular interest to psychologists involve the autonomic nervous system. The brainstem receives continuous information from pressure-sensitive nerve endings called **baroreceptors** situated in the **carotid arteries** and aorta. This information is relayed to a centre in the brainstem known as the vasomotor centre, and then on to the hypothalamus. Reductions in blood pressure or physical demands such as exercise that require increased blood pressure causes activation of the sympathetic nervous system. Sympathetic activation results in an increase in the strength and frequency of heart contractions (via the activity of the sinoatrial and atrioventricular nodes) and a contraction of the smooth muscle in the arteries. Together, these actions increase in blood pressure, and allow sustained flow of blood to organs such as the muscles at times of high activity. Parasympathetic activity results in an opposing reaction.

baroreceptors
sensory nerve endings that are stimulated by changes in pressure. Located in the walls of blood vessels such as the carotid sinus.

carotid artery
the main artery that takes blood from the heart via the neck to the brain.

Diseases of the cardiovascular system

■ Hypertension

Hypertension is a condition in which resting blood pressure is significantly above normal levels (see Table 8.2).

Two broad causes of hypertension have been identified:

1. *Secondary hypertension*: here, hypertension is the result of a disease process usually involving the kidneys, adrenal glands or aorta. This type of hypertension accounts for about 5 per cent of cases.

2. *Essential (primary) hypertension*: in the majority of cases, there is no known disease process that causes the problem. It seems to be the 'normal' consequence of a number of risk factors, such as obesity, lack of exercise and a high salt intake. It is a progressive condition, and people with the condition usually experience a gradual rise in blood pressure over a period of years, with no obvious symptoms.

Psychological stress may contribute to the development of essential hypertension. At times of stress, sympathetic activity increases muscle tone in the arteries and the strength of the heart's contractions – both of which contribute to short-term increases in blood pressure, which then falls as parasympathetic activity follows a period of stress. If the stress is sustained or frequent, however, the activity of the sympathetic nervous system begins

Table 8.2   Typical blood pressure readings in normal and hypertensive individuals

	Diastolic (mmHg)	Systolic (mmHg)
Normal	<90	<140
Mild hypertension	90–99	140–159
Hypertension	>100	>160

IN THE SPOTLIGHT

The life and (heroic) death of John Henry

John Henry was born a slave in the USA in the 1840s or 1850s. So what has he got to do with modern-day psychology? Well, legend has it that he was a giant of a man, who rose to any challenge he faced – a characteristic that eventually resulted in his death. He died while working as a labourer on the railroad tunnelling through a mountain in West Virginia. One of his jobs was to pound holes into rock, which were then filled with explosives and used to blast through tunnels. When the railroad owners brought in steam drills to do the same job more quickly and cheaply, he challenged the steam drill to a contest. He won the contest but died of exhaustion soon after. His name has now become synonymous with a process, initially at least, thought to drive hypertension in black males – John Henryism.

Hypertension is particularly prevalent among African Americans. Black people in the USA are up to four times more likely than whites to develop hypertension by the age of 50 (Roberts and Rowland 1981). One of the reasons for this is thought to be that they are more frequently placed in situations in which they have to respond to difficult psychological stressors – poverty, racism, and so on – more than their white counterparts (see Chapter 2). Those people who have strong emotional or behavioural responses to such stressors typically experience sustained increases in heart rate and blood pressure. This overcomes the body's homeostatic processes and pushes the resting blood pressure increasingly up until they develop long-term hypertension. Although initially viewed as an issue for black men, the process is increasingly being seen as the outcome of the stresses associated with low socio-economic position – and may account for some of the health inequalities considered in Chapter 2.

heart failure
a state in which the heart muscle is damaged or weakened and is unable to generate a cardiac output sufficient to meet the demands of the body.

atheroma
fatty deposit in the intima (inner lining) of an artery.

ACE inhibitors
Angiotensin II causes the muscles surrounding blood vessels to contract and thereby narrows the blood vessels. Angiotensin Converting Enzyme (ACE) inhibitors decrease the production of angiotensin II, allowing blood vessels to dilate, and reduce blood pressure.

to dominate and gradually pushes blood pressure up for longer periods until the individual develops chronically raised blood pressure.

Hypertension may be present and remain unnoticed for many years, or even decades. It is usually considered to be a syndrome with few if any symptoms, and many cases of hypertension are detected during routine screening (see Chapter 6). If high blood pressure has no symptoms, why bother treating it? At low levels of high blood pressure – mild hypertension – some have argued that medical treatment may actually be of little benefit, and that the side effects of treatment may outweigh its benefits (although this position is now being challenged as new drugs are used to treat the condition: see Weber and Julius 1998). However, as blood pressure rises, so too does the amount of damage it can do. High blood pressure increases the risk of a heart attack (myocardial infarction; MI – see below), stroke, kidney failure, eye damage and **heart failure**. It also contributes to the development of **atheroma**. Hypertension is usually treated with anti-hypertensive drugs with a variety of actions, including **ACE inhibitors**, **diuretics** and **beta-blockers**, all of which have been proven effective in reducing blood pressure.

Coronary heart disease

Like hypertension, coronary heart disease (CHD) may develop over many years before becoming evident. Indeed, people may have quite significant

diuretics
elevates the rate of bodily urine excretion, reducing the amount of fluid within the cardiovascular system, and reducing pressure within it.

beta-blockers
block the action of epinephrine and norepinephrine on β-adrenergic receptors, which mediate the 'fight or flight' response, within the heart and in muscles surrounding the arteries. In doing so, they reduce increases in blood pressure associated with sympathetic activation.

low-density lipoprotein (LDL)
the main function of LDL seems to be to carry cholesterol to various tissues throughout the body. LDL is sometimes referred to as 'bad' cholesterol because elevated levels of LDL correlate most directly with **coronary heart disease**.

high-density lipoprotein (HDL)
lipoproteins are fat protein complexes in the blood that transport cholesterol, triglycerides and other lipids to various tissues. The main function of HDL appears to be to carry excess cholesterol to the liver for 're-packaging' or excretion in the bile. Higher levels of HDL seem to be protective against CHD, so HDL is sometimes referred to as 'good' cholesterol.

statins
drugs designed to reduce cholesterol levels.

CHD and never be aware of their condition. The long-term, and silent, element of CHD is the development of atheroma in the blood vessels. This may result in more obvious manifestations of CHD, including an MI and angina (see below).

Atherosclerosis

Atherosclerosis is a disease in which atheroma builds up on lining of the arteries. The main constituent of atheroma is cholesterol. This is a waxy substance that is present in blood plasma and in all the body's cells. Without it, cells could not maintain the integrity of their walls, and we would become seriously ill or die. Too much cholesterol, on the other hand, may be harmful. To get to cell walls in order to repair and maintain them, cholesterol must be transported through the body – via the bloodstream. However, it is insoluble in the blood. To allow such transport, it is therefore attached to groups of proteins called lipoproteins. **Low-density lipoproteins** (LDLs) transport cholesterol to the various tissues and body cells, where it is separated from the lipoprotein and is used by the cell. It can also be absorbed into atheroma on the inner surface of the blood vessels. **High-density lipoproteins** (HDLs) transport excess or unused cholesterol from the tissues back to the liver, where it is broken down to bile acids and then excreted. LDLs are therefore characterised as 'harmful' cholesterol: HDLs are considered to be health-protective. Although some cholesterol is absorbed from our food through the gut, about 80 per cent of cholesterol in our bodies is produced by the liver. The development of atherosclerosis involves a series of stages:

- *Early processes*: Atheroma usually occurs at sites of disturbed blood flow, such as bifurcations of the arteries. It forms as part of the repair process to damage of the artery wall caused by the disturbed blood flow. In this process, inflammatory monocytes, which are precursors to macrophages (see the section on the immune system earlier in the chapter), absorb LDL cholesterol from the circulating blood to become what are known as foam cells. These form a coat over the lining of the damaged artery. As the foam cells die, they lose their contents of LDL, resulting in pools of cholesterol forming between the foam cells and the artery wall. The presence of foam cells may trigger the growth of smooth muscle cells from the artery wall to cover them. In this way, the walls of the artery become lined with lipids, foam cells and finally a wall of smooth muscle. This repeated process results in a gradual reduction of the diameter of the artery.

- *Acute events*: At times, more acute events may occur, and clots of cholesterol and foam cells may be pulled out of the artery wall. This may result in a clot blocking an artery in a key organ such as the heart, resulting in a myocardial infarction (MI) (see below).

The distribution of atheroma within the circulatory system is not uniform throughout the body. It is most developed around the junctions of arteries because disturbances in blood flow at such points can facilitate these processes, but the heart arteries are also one of the areas most likely to be affected. High levels of cholesterol may be treated with drugs known as **statins**, if dietary changes are insufficient to lower cholesterol to safe levels. They work by blocking an enzyme (HMG-CoA reductase) the liver needs to make cholesterol. They may also help reabsorb cholesterol that has accumulated in atheroma on the artery walls.

Myocardial infarction

As we noted in the last section, an important end point of CHD is when a clot is pulled off an artery wall and enters the circulating blood. This may prove a harmless event, with no health implications for the individual. However, if the circulating clot has a greater diameter than the blood vessels it is passing through, it will inevitably block the blood vessels and prevent the flow of blood beyond them. This blockage (occlusion) may result in significant health problems if it occurs in the arteries supplying oxygen and nutrients to the heart. Unless rapidly treated, the cells of the heart muscle beyond the occlusion no longer receive their nutrients and oxygen and die – a **myocardial infarction** (MI). The severity of the MI is determined by how large a blood vessel is affected (larger is worse) and which parts of the heart are damaged.

The classic symptoms of an MI include what is often described as 'crushing chest pain'. The affected individual may feel like their chest is trapped in a vice. Other symptoms include shortness of breath, coughing, pain radiating down the left arm, dizziness and/or collapse, nausea or vomiting, and sweating. However, an MI may also be much less dramatic. Indeed, many people delay seeking help for an MI as their symptoms are vague, may be confused with heartburn or indigestion, and the affected individual hopes that the symptoms will go away without treatment. Perhaps the strangest symptom that can rarely be indicative of an MI is toothache – although we would not recommend you visit your local hospital complaining of a heart attack should you be unfortunate enough to develop this problem!

Approximately 45 per cent of people will die of their MI immediately or in the week or so following the event. The majority of people go on to make a good recovery. This may be aided by treatment with drugs known as '**clot busters**'. These drugs dissolve the clot causing the blocked artery and, if given within an hour or so of the infarction, can prevent permanent muscle damage. Longer-term treatment now frequently involves a procedure known as an angioplasty (or its longer formal name, Percutaneous Transluminal Coronary Angioplasty: PTCA) in which a long narrow catheter is inserted into the femoral artery (near the groin) and, guided by X-rays, is pushed along the arteries until it reaches the coronary arteries. After reaching the site of the MI, a small balloon is inflated which pushes against the occluded artery wall, increasing the diameter of the artery and allowing normal blood flow through it. A small wire mesh tube (known as a stent) is then frequently left in position at the site to maintain the patency of the artery. Long-term contributors to CHD, including high cholesterol or blood pressure, are treated with appropriate lifestyle changes (see Chapters 6, 7 and 17) and medication if necessary.

Angina

The key symptom of **angina** is similar to that of an MI. It is a central chest pain that may radiate to the left shoulder, jaw, arm or other areas of the chest. Some patients may confuse arm or shoulder pain with arthritis or indigestion pain. Unlike an MI, however, it is a temporary condition which occurs when the heart muscle needs more oxygen than can be provided by the heart arteries, and stops once these demands are reduced. It is frequently precipitated by exertion or stress, and may result from two underlying causes:

---

myocardial infarction
death of the heart muscle due to a stoppage of the blood supply. More often known as a heart attack.

clot busters
drugs which dissolve clots associated with myocardial infarction and can prevent damage to the heart following such an event. Are best used within one hour of the infarction.

angina
severe pain in the chest associated with a temporary insufficient supply of blood to the heart.

1. atheromatous lesions of the coronary arteries reduce their diameter and limit the blood flow through them;
2. **vasospasm** of the coronary arteries results in a temporary reduction in their diameter;
3. a combination of both.

vasospasm
a situation in which the muscles of artery walls in the heart contract and relax rapidly, resulting in a reduction of the flow of blood through the artery.

Classic angina (or angina pectoris) is associated with high levels of atheroma in the coronary arteries which limits the amount of blood they can carry to the heart muscle. Physical exertion, emotional stress and exposure to cold are among the triggers for this type of angina. In a second type of angina known as unstable angina, people with the condition experience angina symptoms after relatively little effort (such as just taking a few steps) or even when they are resting. It is usually the result of a severe narrowing in a coronary artery, and may lead to an MI if it is not treated. As with an MI, treatment involves interventions to reduce the immediate symptoms of angina and to prevent the underlying disease progress. Symptomatic relief can be achieved through the use of Glyceryl Trinitrate (GTN: otherwise known as nitroglycerin!). This comes as a spray (sprayed into the mouth) or tablets (placed under the tongue) to take when an angina episode starts, and results in an immediate widening of the arteries and relief from symptoms. If the level of disease warrants it, patients with angina may also be given PTCA, or a **coronary artery bypass graft** (CABG), in which blood vessels are taken from the legs or the chest and used to bypass the diseased artery. Treatment of underlying conditions may involve the use of statins or hypertensive medication. In Chapter 17, we describe the case of Mr Jones, whose angina was so severe that on two occasions he believed he was having an MI and went to the emergency department of the local hospital. We also show how we helped him adjust better to his condition.

coronary artery bypass graft
surgical procedure in which veins or arteries from elsewhere in the patient's body are grafted from the aorta to the coronary arteries, bypassing blockages caused by atheroma in the cardiac arteries and improving the blood supply to the heart muscle.

The respiratory system

The respiratory system delivers oxygen to and removes carbon dioxide from the blood. The exchange of oxygen and carbon dioxide occurs in the lungs. The system comprises:

- the *upper respiratory tract*, including the nose, mouth, larynx and trachea;
- the *lower respiratory tract*, including the lungs, bronchi, bronchioles and alveoli. Each lung is divided into upper and lower lobes – the upper lobe of the right lung contains a third subdivision known as the right middle lobe.

The bronchi carry air from the mouth to the lungs. As they enter the lungs, they divide into smaller bronchi, then into smaller tubes called bronchioles (see Figure 8.9). The bronchioles contain minute hairs called cilia, which beat rhythmically to sweep debris out of the lungs towards the pharynx for expulsion and thus form part of the mechanical element of the immune system – see earlier in the chapter. Bronchioles end in air sacs called alveoli – small, thin-walled 'balloons', which are surrounded by tiny blood capillaries. As

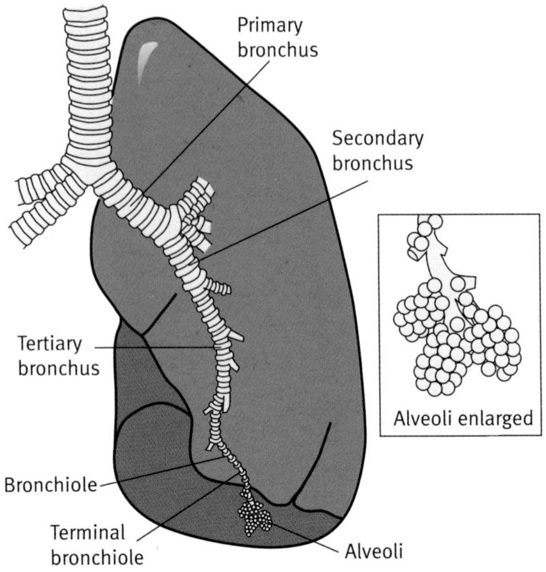

Figure 8.9 Diagram of the lungs, showing the bronchi, bronchioles and alveoli.

we breathe in, the concentration of oxygen is greater in the alveoli than in the haemoglobin in the blood travelling through the capillaries. As a result, oxygen diffuses across the alveolar walls into the haemoglobin. As we breathe out, carbon dioxide concentration in the blood is greater than that in the alveoli, so it passes from the blood into the alveoli and is then exhaled.

Respiration is the act of breathing:

- *Inspiration*: two sets of muscles are involved in inhalation. The main muscle involved is the diaphragm. This is a sheet of muscle that divides the abdomen and is found immediately below the lungs. Contraction of this muscle pulls the lungs down and sucks air into them. The second set of muscles is known as the intercostal muscles. These are found between the ribs and can expand the chest – again pulling air into the lungs.

- *Expiration*: relaxation of the diaphragm and intercostal muscles allows the lungs to contract, decreases lung volume, and pushes air out of them. The air then passively flows out.

The rate of breathing is controlled by respiratory centres in the brainstem. These respond to:

- the concentration of carbon dioxide in the blood (high carbon dioxide concentrations initiate deeper, more rapid breathing);

- air pressure in lung tissue. Expansion of the lungs stimulates nerve receptors to signal the brain to 'turn off' inspiration. When the lungs collapse, the receptors give the 'turn on' signal, known as the Hering–Breuer inspiratory reflex.

Other automatic regulators include increases in blood pressure, which slows down respiration; a fall in blood acidity, which stimulates respiration; and a sudden drop in blood pressure, which increases the rate and depth of respiration.

Diseases of the respiratory system

■ Chronic obstructive airways disease

Chronic obstructive pulmonary disease (COPD) is a group of lung diseases characterised by limited airflow through the airways resulting from damage to the alveoli. Its most common manifestations are **emphysema** and **chronic bronchitis**.

Emphysema

Emphysema results from the destruction of the alveoli, resulting in reduced lung elasticity and reductions in the surface area on which the exchange of oxygen and carbon dioxide can occur. People with the condition experience chronic shortness of breath, an unproductive cough (which produces no phlegm), and a marked reduction in exercise capacity. The condition typically results from exposing the alveoli to irritants, whether as a result of direct or passive smoking or living or working in a polluted environment. About 15 per cent of long-term smokers will develop COPD (Mannino 2003). More rarely, an enzyme deficiency called alpha-1 anti-trypsin deficiency can cause emphysema in non-smokers. Treatment of emphysema involves a number of approaches: drugs known as bronchodilators widen the air passages and relax smooth muscle tissue in the lungs. Some individuals may need continuous oxygen therapy. Finally, as people with emphysema are prone to lung infections, they may require treatment with antibiotics. What is it like to live with emphysema? Well, here is a quote from someone (Gary Bain) with the condition taken from a self-help website (www.emphysema.org):

> *Sit down somewhere and relax a little and when you feel comfortable, take your right or left hand and with your thumb and forefinger, hold your nose shut. While holding your nose shut, cover your mouth tightly with the rest of your hand so you can just barely breathe through your fingers. Now, walk for about 40 steps and turn around and come back while still breathing through your hand. Now, do you see how hard it is to breathe? Especially when you try to walk around? That is what emphysema is . . .*

Chronic bronchitis

Chronic bronchitis results from inflammation and a consequent narrowing of the airways. Bronchitis is considered to be chronic when it persists for three months or more for at least two consecutive years. People with the condition experience shortness of breath and have excessive mucus within the bronchial tree and a 'wet' cough. They may also experience wheezing and fatigue. As with emphysema, it is caused predominantly by smoking and secondhand smoke. Allergies, outdoor and indoor air pollution, and infection may exacerbate the condition. Treatment involves the use of bronchodilators, and for some people, oxygen therapy. Corticosteroids may also be used at times of acute severe episodes of breathing difficulty when other treatments are ineffective.

Self-help for people with COPD

Unfortunately, the way many people cope with their COPD may inadvertently add to their problems. Understandably, people who become out of breath when they exercise stop doing so. It makes sense: breathlessness is

---

emphysema
a late effect of chronic infection or irritation of the bronchial tubes. When the bronchi become irritated, some of the airways may become obstructed or the walls of the tiny air sacs may tear, trapping air in the lung beyond them. As a result, the lungs may become enlarged, at the same time becoming less efficient in exchanging oxygen for carbon dioxide.

chronic bronchitis
an inflammation of the bronchi, the main air passages in the lungs, which persists for a long period or repeatedly recurs. Characterised by excessive bronchial mucus and a cough that produces sputum for three months or more in at least two consecutive years.

both unpleasant and frightening. Unfortunately, this avoidance results in a decrease in lung function and a worsening of symptoms. As patients' contribution to their lung health has become more evident, a number of programmes have now been developed and implemented to teach people how best to cope with COPD. Often referred to as pulmonary rehabilitation, these provide advice on 'lung health' and coping with breathlessness, and a gentle physical exercise programme designed to increase fitness and lung capacity.

■ Lung cancer

Lung cancer is the second most common cancer affecting both sexes. Its symptoms include a dry non-productive cough, shortness of breath, coughing up sputum with signs of blood in it, an ache or pain when breathing, loss of appetite, fatigue and losing weight. The main cause of lung cancer is smoking, and as women have taken up smoking following the Second World War, rates of lung cancer among this group have risen, while those among men have fallen (Tyczynski *et al.* 2004). Other risk factors involve exposure to carcinogens, including asbestos and radon, and scarring from tuberculosis. There is some evidence of a genetic risk also.

Two different types of lung cancer have been identified:

1. Small cell cancer. The main treatment is radiotherapy or chemotherapy. The overall survival rate depends on the stage of the disease. For limited-stage small cell cancer, cure rates may be as high as 25 per cent, while cure rates for extensive-stage disease are less than 5 per cent.
2. Non-small cell cancer (between 70 and 80 per cent of cases). The main treatment for this type of cancer involves removal of the cancer through surgery. Where the tumour is small and has not spread, up to 50 per cent of people with the condition may survive. The prognosis is worse the larger the tumour. Where the tumour has spread and lymph nodes are involved, the disease is almost never cured, and the goals of therapy are to extend life and improve quality of life (Beadsmoore and Screaton 2003).

Summary

This chapter reviewed some of the anatomy and physiology relevant to health psychology and other chapters of this book. In the first section, it briefly described key functions of the brain and their situation within it. Key functional areas include:

■ the medulla oblongata, which controls respiration, blood pressure and heartbeat;

■ the hypothalamus, which controls appetite, sexual arousal and thirst. It also exerts some control over our emotions;

■ the amygdala, which links situations of threat and relevant emotions such as fear or anxiety, and controls the autonomic nervous system response to such threats.

One of the key systems controlled by the brain is the autonomic nervous system. This comprises two parallel sets of nerves:

1. The sympathetic nervous system is responsible for activation of many organs of the body.
2. The parasympathetic nervous system is responsible for rest and recuperation.

The highest level of control of the autonomic nervous system within the brain is the hypothalamus, which coordinates reflexive changes in response to a variety of physical changes, including movement, temperature and blood pressure. It also responds to emotional and cognitive demands, providing a link between physiological systems and psychological stress.

Activation of the sympathetic nervous system involves two neurotransmitters – adrenaline and noradrenaline – which stimulate organs via the sympathetic nerves themselves. Sustained activation is maintained by their hormonal equivalents, released from the adrenal medulla. A second system, controlled by the hypothalamus and pituitary gland, triggers the release of corticosteroids from the adrenal cortex. These increase the energy available to sustain physiological activation and inhibit inflammation of damaged tissue.

The immune system provides a barrier to infection by viruses and other biological threats to our health. Key elements of the system include phagocytes, such as macrophages and neutrophils, which engulf and destroy invading pathogens. A second group of cells, known as lymphocytes, including cytotoxic T cells and B cells, respond particularly to attacks by viruses and developing tumour cells. Both groups of cells can collaborate in the destruction of pathogens through a complex series of chemical reactions.

Slow viruses, including HIV, attack the immune system – by infecting CD4+ cells – and prevent the T and B cell systems from responding effectively. This leaves the body open to attack from viruses and cancers, either of which may result in life-threatening conditions.

The immune system may, itself, cause problems by treating its own cells as external invading agents. This can result in diseases such as multiple sclerosis, rheumatoid arthritis and Type 1 diabetes.

The digestive tract is responsible for the ingestion, absorption and expulsion of food. Activity within it is controlled by the enteric nervous system, which is linked to the autonomic nervous system. Activity in the system is therefore responsive to stress and other psychological states. That said, some conditions thought to be the result of stress are now thought to be the result of physical as well as psychological factors. Gastric ulcers are thought to result from infection by *Helicobacter pylori*, while irritable bowel syndrome is no longer seen as entirely the result of stress but has a multi-factor aetiology of which stress is but one strand.

The cardiovascular system is responsible for carrying oxygen, nutrients and various other materials around the body. Its activity is influenced by the autonomic nervous system. Two long-term 'silent' conditions that may lead to acute illnesses such as myocardial infarction or stroke are hypertension and atheroma. Both involve long-term processes. One way in which long-term hypertension may develop is by repeated short-term increases in blood pressure through the action of the autonomic nervous system in response to stress. Atheroma develops as a result of repair processes to the artery wall. Two obvious outcomes of this process are myocardial infarction, in which an artery supplying the heart muscle is blocked and dies. Angina presents with similar symptoms but is the result of spasm of the arteries and is reversible.

Finally, the respiratory system is responsible for inspiring and carrying oxygen around the body, and the expulsion of carbon dioxide. It is prone to a number of disease processes, including chronic obstructive airways disease and lung cancer, all of which are significantly exacerbated by cigarette smoking.

Further reading

Lovallo, W.R. (1997). *Stress and Health. Biological and Psychological Interactions*. Thousand Oaks, Calif.: Sage.
A relatively easy introduction to the autonomic and immune systems, as well as how stress can influence their activity.

Kumar, P.J. and Clark, K.L. (2002). *Clinical Medicine*. Oxford: W.B. Saunders.
At 1,464 pages, this is not a textbook you may want to buy. But if you want to know more about the development of various diseases, this is an excellent starting point.

Vedhara, K. and Irwin, M. (eds) (2005). *Human Psychoneuroimmunology*. Oxford University Press.
A readable guide to psychoneuroimmunology, written for those people who do not want to plough through £250, 400-page tomes (or so say the editors).

You can also find a wealth of information about illnesses and their treatment from the internet. Three excellent sites are:

http://medlineplus.gov/ It is a free service provided by the US National Library of Medicine and the National Institutes of Health.
http://www.netdoctor.co.uk/ provides similar information and is also free.
http://www.patient.co.uk/ as does this site.

In addition, many sites provide information on specific illnesses, including:

http://www.heartfoundation.org.au/index.htm the Australian Heart Foundation
http://www.ulcerativecolitis.org.uk/ the Ulcerative Colitis Information Centre
http://www.lunguk.org/ the British Lung Foundation

In fact, simply typing in an illness as a search term in any search engine will undoubtedly allow you to access all the information you are likely to need about any illness and its treatment.

Visit the website at **www.pearsoned.co.uk/morrison** for additional resources to help you with your study, including multiple choice questions, weblinks and flashcards.

CHAPTER 9

Symptom perception, interpretation and response

Learning outcomes

By the end of this chapter, you should have an understanding of:

- key theoretical models of symptom perception, interpretation and response
- contextual, cultural and individual influences upon symptom perception
- the core dimensions upon which illness can be represented
- a broad range of influences upon symptom interpretation
- factors that influence delay in seeking healthcare advice for symptoms

CHAPTER OUTLINE

How do we know if we are getting ill? Do we all react in the same way to symptoms? What influences how we perceive and interpret symptoms of illness? Do beliefs about illness differ across the lifespan? Do illness perceptions and their interpretation influence health-care seeking? These types of question are important to our understanding of how people cope with illness and of differentials in health-care-seeking behaviour. They are questions that you need to ask yourself when thinking about the study of health and illness, whether as a future health psychologist or health-care practitioner.

How do we become aware of the sensations of illness?

Illness generates changes in bodily sensations and functions that a person may perceive themselves or perhaps have pointed out to them by another person who says, for example, 'You look pale'. The kind of sign that is likely to be noticed by the individual themselves includes changes in bodily functions (e.g. increased frequency of urination, heartbeat irregularities), emissions (such as blood in one's urine), sensations (e.g. numbness, loss of vision) and unpleasant sensations (e.g. fever, pain, nausea). Other people may not notice these changes but would perhaps notice changes in bodily appearance (weight loss, skin pallor) or function (e.g. paralysis, limping, tremor). Radley (1994) distinguishes between 'bodily signs' and 'symptoms of illness'. The former can be objectively recognised, but the latter requires interpretation; for example, a person has to decide whether a raised temperature (a bodily sign) is symptomatic of illness (e.g. influenza) or simply a sign of physical exertion.

While some diseases have visible symptoms, others do not and instead involve a subjectively sensed component of bodily responses, e.g. feeling sick, feeling tired, being in pain, which cannot be seen *per se*. Many people regularly experience symptoms, but there is huge variability between individuals when it comes to attending to, or reporting, symptoms. Although 70 to 90 per cent of us have, at some time, a condition that could be diagnosed and treated by a health professional, only about one-third will actually seek medical attention. Health psychologists are interested in why this is the case.

As described in Chapter 1, people's views about health are shaped by both their prior experience of illness and their understanding of medical knowledge, whether expert or lay. People therefore learn about health in the same way as they learn about everything else – through experience, either their own or of other people's. People 'fall ill against a background of beliefs about good and poor health' (Radley 1994: 61). Furthermore, Radley notes, people's lives are 'grounded in *activity*', i.e. on the everyday activities or behaviour that depends upon the body, whether they be instrumental activities such as being able to run for a bus or expressive activities like being able to look attractive. Illness can therefore challenge a person at a fundamental level.

Illness or disease?

Cassell (1976) used the word 'illness' to stand for 'what the patient feels when he goes to the doctor', i.e. the experience of not feeling quite right as compared with one's normal state; and 'disease' to stand for 'what he has on the way home from the doctor's office'. Disease, then, is considered as being something of the organ, cell or tissue that suggests a physical disorder or underlying pathology, whereas illness is what the person experiences. People can feel ill without having an identifiable disease (think of a hangover!), and importantly, people can have a disease and not feel ill (for example, well-controlled asthma or diabetes, early stage HIV infection). A routine medical check-up may lead to a person who thought themselves healthy finding out that they are in fact 'officially' ill as indicated by the result of some routine test. By providing a diagnosis, doctors mark the entry of a person into the health-care system.

How does a person know if they are getting ill? This chapter will attempt to answer this by describing the processes underlying three stages of response:

1. perceiving symptoms;
2. interpreting symptoms as illness;
3. planning and taking action.

What do YOU think?

How many of the symptoms below have you experienced in the last two weeks? Of those that you have experienced, how many have you seen a health professional about? Think of the reasons why you did, or did not, seek medical advice about your symptoms.

- fever
- nausea
- headache
- tremor
- joint stiffness
- excessive fatigue
- back pain
- dizziness
- stomach pains
- visual disturbance
- chesty cough
- sore throat
- breathlessness
- chest pain.

Symptom perception

Many different stimuli compete for our attention at any given moment, so why do certain sensations become more salient than others? Why do we seek

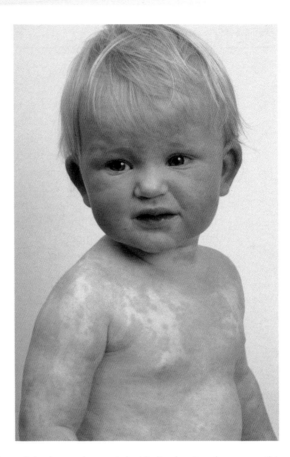

Plate 9.1 This rash looks unpleasant, but is it a heat rash or something more serious?

Source: Alamy Images/Bubbles Photo Library

medical attention for some symptoms when we perceive them and not for others? While an early study of American college students found that they had experienced an average of seventeen different symptoms per month (Pennebaker and Skelton 1981), few will have sought medical attention. This is partly because most symptoms are transient and pass before we think too much about them, but also because people are not necessarily the best judges of whether their own perceived symptoms are in fact signs of illness.

There are several models of symptom perception. The attentional model of Pennebaker (1982) describes how competition for attention between multiple internal or external cues or stimuli leads to the same physical sign or physiological change going unnoticed in some contexts but not in others. The cognitive–perceptual model of Cioffi (1991) focuses more on the processes of interpretation of physical signs and influences upon their attribution as symptoms while also acknowledging the role of selective attention (Cioffi 1991). Overall, research has highlighted an array of biological, psychological and contextual influences upon symptom perception (see Figure 9.1), with bottom–up influences upon perception arising from the physical properties of a bodily sensation, and top-down influences being seen in the influence of attentional processes or mood.

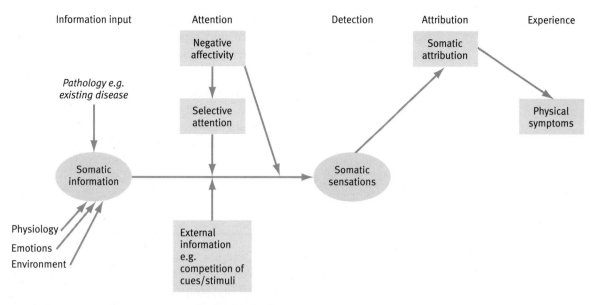

Figure 9.1 A simplified symptom perception model.

Source: adapted from Kolk, Hanewald, Schagen *et al.* (2003)

Characteristics of bodily signs that increase likelihood of symptom perception

subjective
personal, i.e. what a person thinks and reports (e.g. excitement) as opposed to what is **objective**. Subjective is generally related to internal interpretations of events rather than observable features.

objective
i.e. real, visible or systematically measurable (e.g. adrenaline levels). Generally pertains to something that can be seen, or recorded, by others (as opposed to **subjective**).

Bodily signs are physical sensations that may or may not be symptoms of illness: for example, sweating is a bodily sign, but it may not indicate fever if the person has simply been exerting themselves. Signs can be detected and identified for example, blood pressure, whereas symptoms are what is experienced and as such are more **subjective**, e.g. nausea. Symptoms generally result from physiological changes with physical (somatic) properties, but only some will be detected by the individual. Those receiving attention and interpretation as a symptom are likely to be:

- *Painful or disruptive*: if a bodily sign has consequences for the person, e.g. they cannot sit comfortably, vision is impaired, or they can no longer perform a routine activity, then the person is more motivated to perceive this as a symptom (Cacioppo *et al.* 1986, 1989).

- *Novel*: subjective estimates of prevalence have been shown to significantly influence (1) the perceived severity of a symptom and (2) whether the person will seek medical attention (e.g. Ditto and Jemmott 1989; Jemmott *et al.* 1988). Experiencing a 'novel' symptom (new to oneself or believed not to have been experienced by others) is likely to be considered indicative of something rare and serious, whereas experiencing a symptom thought to be common leads to assumptions of lower severity and a reduced likelihood to seek out health information or care. For example, tiredness among students may be normalised and interpreted as a sign of late nights studying or partying, where it may, for some, reflect underlying disease.

- *Persistent*: a bodily sign is more likely to be perceived as a symptom if it persists for longer than is considered usual or if it persists in spite of self-medication.

■ *Pre-existing chronic disease*: having a chronic disease increases the number of other symptoms perceived and reported. Past or current illness experience has a strong influence upon somatisation (i.e. attention to bodily states) (e.g. Epstein *et al.* 1999; Kolk *et al.* 2003).

There are many trivial symptoms which do not require medical attention and which could be self-managed successfully without the costs associated with seeking health care (e.g. most flu episodes), but there are also some illnesses with few initial symptoms, such as cancer; therefore symptoms alone are 'unreliable indicators of the need for medical attention' (Martin *et al.* 2003: 203).

Attentional states and symptom perception

attention
generally refers to the selection of some stimuli over others for internal processing.

Individual differences exist in the amount of **attention** people give to their internal state and external states (Pennebaker and Skelton 1981; Pennebaker 1982, 1992). Pennebaker discovered that somatic sensations are less likely to be noticed when a person's attention is engaged externally than when they are not otherwise distracted. Think, for example, of an athlete going on to win a race in spite of having sustained a leg injury. On the other hand, individuals are more likely to notice tickling sensations in their throats and start coughing towards the end of lectures as attention begins to wane than at the beginning of the lecture or during highly interesting sections. Individuals are limited in their attentional capacity, so internal and external stimuli have to compete for attention; a bodily sign that may be noticed immediately in some contexts may remain undetected in others. (This also points to findings that manipulating attentional focus, through cognitive or behavioural distraction, can be a useful form of symptom management; see Chapter 13.)

A high degree of attention increases a person's sensitivity to new, or different, bodily signs. Consider the effects of well-publicised outbreaks of illnesses, infections or toxins on symptom perception, for example outbreaks of Legionnaire's disease or of *E. coli*, identification of new diseases such as SARS in 2003, or chemical leaks. Attendance at doctors' increases massively at such times and in extreme circumstances can lead to what is called 'mass psychogenic illness'. This response illustrates the powerful effect of anxiety and suggestion on our perceptions and behaviour. Worry about even tenuous links to the source of infection heightens a person's attention to their own bodily signs and can produce the belief that they have contracted the illness. However, many people who seek medical attention at such times will find that there is no organic explanation for their symptoms. Another example of external stimuli altering attention to, and processing of, bodily signs can be seen in what has been described as 'medical students disease' (Mechanic 1962). In this case the increased knowledge about disease-specific symptoms obtained during medical lectures increased the self-reported experience of exactly these symptoms among over two-thirds of the medical students studied!

Social influences on symptom perception

It has been shown that people hold stereotypical notions about 'who gets' certain diseases and that this can interfere with perception and response to

	Production of bodily disturbance	
	High	**Low**
High	Sport	Attending lecture
Low	Giving birth	Watching TV at home

Requirement to contain signs

Figure 9.2 Situational differences in the production and containment of physical symptoms.

Source: adapted from Radley (1994: 69)

initial symptoms. For example, Martin *et al.* (2003) describe studies showing that the general public associate males with vulnerability to heart disease and not females, and that among heart attack patients females less often recognised their initial bodily signs as symptoms of heart disease. The implications for health-care-seeking behaviour are obvious.

Cacioppo *et al.* (1989) pointed to the notion of 'salience' and suggested that our motivation to attend to and detect signs or symptoms of illness will depend on the context at the time the symptom presents itself. As referred to above, people tend not to notice internal sensations when their environment is exciting or absorbing, but a lack of alternative distraction may increase perception of symptoms. Furthermore, situations bring with them varying expectations of physical involvement, as illustrated in Figure 9.2. Bodily signs, for example muscle spasms, when playing sport or giving birth are expected and thus would not generally be taken as symptomatic of illness; however, these two situations differ in the extent to which they would expect a person to suppress the pain caused by the spasms. In contrast, few bodily signs are expected when sitting in lectures or watching TV, and unless the bodily sign (e.g. stiffness) can be attributed to something like posture, then it may be interpreted as a symptom of illness. In terms of suppression or expression, the home and the lecture setting also differ significantly, with suppression of physical discomfort by means of motivated distraction being more likely in the lecture setting (e.g. listening to the lecturer) than pain expression (e.g. moaning out load).

Individual differences affecting symptom perception

The same bodily sign may, or may not, be perceived as a symptom on the basis of individual difference variables such as gender, life stage, emotional state or personality traits, and the effect such factors have on attentional states. Research has tried to identify factors that distinguish between those who frequently seek health care even for trivial symptoms and those who do not seek health care even when faced with potentially serious symptoms.

■ Gender

socialisation

the process by which a person learns – from family, teachers, peers – the rules, norms and moral codes of behaviour that are expected of them.

It is often proposed that gender **socialisation** provides women with a greater readiness to attend to and perceive bodily signs and symptoms; however, the evidence appears to vary according to the symptoms explored (Baum and Grunberg 1991; Macintyre 1993). A recent qualitative study of the symptom perception and reporting behaviour of men with prostate disease found that four themes emerged from interview data: 'living up to the image'; 'normal or illness?' (re symptom interpretation); 'protecting the image'; 'engaging with the system'. These themes encompass men's accounts of learning to ignore symptoms out of a need to be seen to be strong and masculine, point to a lack of understanding about prostate problems being symptoms of illness as opposed to part of ageing, and highlight men's unwillingness or anxiety about taking 'embarrassing' symptoms to a health-care professional (Hale *et al.* 2007). In keeping with this, Gijsbers van Wijk and Kolk (1997) suggest that as male-directed media is less inclined to provide health advice than women's media, this may contribute to less developed illness cognitions in males which reduces the likelihood of perceiving a bodily sign as a 'symptom' and limits reporting behaviour. Hale and colleagues' studies also find evidence of men 'avoiding' information about illness even when they are faced with it in the media. Thus, in considering gender differences in symptom perception, there are many overlapping explanations. It may also be that physiological differences arising from puberty and menstruation influence **pain thresholds** in the first place, or perhaps the evidence that women attend health care more does not reflect so much a gender difference in symptom perception as one in reporting behaviour (see later section). While no full explanation can be expected of such a complex human behaviour (symptom perception), it is generally acknowledged that differences exist in the extent to which males and females are 'allowed' to respond to bodily signs.

pain threshold

the minimum amount of pain intensity that is required before it is detected (individual variation).

■ Life stage

With age comes experience and increasing awareness of one's internal organs and their functions and sensations. While there are age differentials in definitions and perceptions of the meaning of health and illness (Chapter 1), do age differences in whether or not bodily signs are perceived as symptoms of illness contribute to identified differentials in health care-seeking behaviour (Grunfeld *et al.* 2003; Ramirez *et al.* 1999; see Chapter 2)? Ageing populations certainly bear the burden of many chronic or life-threatening diseases, such as heart disease, stroke, arthritis and breast cancer, but does this mean they pay less attention to their bodily states and perceive fewer symptoms? There is little evidence of this. However, it does appear that older adults *interpret* and respond differently to perceived symptoms (see later section).

Children develop a conceptual understanding of illness during the course of their cognitive development and socialisation, but whether children perceive specific symptoms differently to adults is less known, and the limited language of very young children presents challenges to parents, researchers and health professionals alike. Crying, rubbing or other behaviour is relied upon by adults as indicators of symptom experience in the very young, with pain, for example, being exhibited rather than reported. It is likely that symptom perception is influenced by similar attentional, contextual, individual and emotional influences as seen in adults, but that age or developmental stage may have a greater effect upon symptom interpretation and response.

■ Emotions and personality traits

Generally, mood is crucial. People who are in a positive mood have been found to rate themselves as more healthy and indicate fewer symptoms, whereas people in negative moods report more symptoms, are more pessimistic about their ability to act to relieve their symptoms and believe themselves to be more susceptible to illness (Leventhal *et al.* 1996). Negative emotional states, particularly anxiety or depression, may increase symptom perception by means of its effect on attention, as well as by increasing the recall of prior negative health events, which makes it more likely that new bodily signs will be viewed as symptoms of further illness (Cohen *et al.* 1995; Watson and Pennebaker 1989; see Chapter 16). Another emotion associated with symptom perception is that of fear, and it can work in both a positive and a negative direction. For example, fear of pain and fear of recurrence can increase a person's attention and responsiveness to bodily signs, seen among heart attack survivors who often become increasingly vigilant of their internal states in the hope of detecting, at an early stage, signs of possible recurrence. In contrast, fear of being seriously ill can reduce a person's attention to and consideration of possible meanings of their symptoms, such as reported among men with prostate problems who downplayed symptoms out of fear of finding disease (Hale *et al.* 2007).

neuroticism
a personality trait reflected in the tendency to be anxious, feel guilty and experience generally negative thought patterns.

negative affectivity
a dispositional tendency to experience persistent and pervasive negative or low mood and self-concept (related to **neuroticism**).

Neuroticism (N) can be described as a trait-like tendency to experience negative emotional states and is related to the broader construct '**negative affectivity**' (NA). NA can manifest itself either as a state (situation-specific) or a trait (generalised). While state NA can incorporate a range of emotions, including anger, sadness and fear, trait NA, like neuroticism, has been found to affect the perception, interpretation and reporting of symptoms. In terms of perceptual style, neurotics and those high in trait NA are more introspective and attend more negatively to somatic information and thus they perceive more frequent symptoms and are more likely to misattribute them to underlying disease (Williams 2006) and more likely to report them (Bennett *et al.* 1996; Deary *et al.* 1997; Watson and Pennebaker 1989, 1991). It is worth noting that while such traits appear associated with retrospectively reported symptom experience, the support for longitudinal effects of negative affectivity on symptom perception is mixed. For example, trait NA did not predict symptom complaints over time among an elderly sample (e.g. Diefenbach *et al.* 1995; Leventhal *et al.* 1996). Quite often, studies which have studied neuroticism in relation to symptom perception have implied a link between N and hypochondriasis, where there is a preoccupation with having illness based on misattributions and misinterpretations of bodily signs as symptoms (Ferguson 2000). This suggests that the symptom perception is unfounded in terms of actual physical symptoms, yet Williams (2006) in her chapter reviewing this area points to a body of evidence showing that neuroticism is associated with greater physiological reactivity to stress including elevated levels of stress hormones such as cortisol (see Chapter 11). In some circumstances, therefore, there may be a 'real' or objective pathway between this personality trait and increased symptom experience.

■ Cognitions and coping style

type A behaviour (TAB)
a constellation of
characteristics,
mannerisms and
behaviour including
competitiveness, time
urgency, impatience,
easily aroused hostility,
rapid and vigorous
speech patterns and
expressive behaviour.
Extensively studied in
relation to the aetiology
of coronary heart
disease, where hostility
seems central.

repression
a defensive coping style
that serves to protect
the person from negative
memories or anxiety-
producing thoughts by
preventing their gaining
access to
consciousness.

How people characteristically think and respond to external or internal events can also influence symptom perception. For example, there is some evidence that individuals characterised by time urgency, impatience, hostility and competitive drive (i.e. **type A behaviour**: Friedman and Rosenman 1959; Rosenman 1978) are less likely to perceive symptoms, perhaps because they are highly focused on the task in hand or because they avoid paying attention to signs of self-weakness. Their desire for control on the other hand is associated with prompt health-care-seeking behaviour once a severe health threat is acknowledged (Matthews *et al.* 1983). It has also been shown that people who cope with aversive events by using the cognitive defence mechanism of **repression** are less likely to experience symptoms than non-repressors (Ward 1988; Myers 1998), with repression being associated with higher levels of **comparative optimism** regarding controllable health threats such as tooth decay and skin cancer (Myers and Reynolds 2000). Both repressive coping and comparative optimism have previously been related to poor physical health (Weinstein and Klein 1996).

A further distinction has been drawn between monitoring and blunting coping styles (Miller *et al.* 1987). **Monitors** deal with threat by monitoring their situation for threat-relevant information, whereas **blunters** ignore or minimise external and internal stimuli. Where one stands on this dimension will influence symptom perception as well as determine how quickly a person uses health services (see below).

Symptom interpretation

comparative optimism
initially termed
'unrealistic optimism',
this term refers to an
individual's estimate of
their risk of experiencing
a negative event
compared with similar
others (Weinstein and
Klein 1996).

Once a symptom has been perceived, people do not generally consider it in isolation but generally relate it to other aspects of their experience and to their wider concepts of illness. Symptoms are more than labels for the various changes that happen to the body; they not only derive from medical classifications of disease, they can also influence how we think, feel and behave. Culture will influence the meanings that individuals ascribe to symptoms, as will gender, life stage, past experience, illness beliefs and representations. While information about illness and symptoms of illness are increasingly woven into popular television programmes and other media, we know little about how this information is processed by children.

Cultural influences

Our understanding of culture and its influence upon health and illness outcomes is in its relative infancy in terms of research evidence pertaining to the processes through which culture may affect responses to symptoms and to illness. We have heard in earlier chapters about cultural variations in health behaviours and in terms of prevalence of certain diseases (e.g. higher prevalence of diabetes among Asian populations, for example), and it has also been

monitors
a generalised coping style that involves attending to the source of stress or threat and trying to deal with it directly, e.g. through information gathering/ attending to threat-relevant information (as opposed to **blunters**).

blunters
a general coping style that involves minimising or avoiding the source of threat or stress i.e. avoiding threat-relevant information (as opposed to **monitors**).

shown that cultural variation exists in the extent to which individuals show readiness to respond to perceived physical symptoms. For example, among male American pain patients of either Jewish, Italian, Irish or 'old' American origin, it was found that while Jewish and Italian American men expressed pain readily, the two groups differed in the aim of their pain expression. Italian Americans complained about pain discomfort, while Jewish Americans typically expressed worries about what the pain might mean in terms of their underlying and future health. These differences in pain expression and interpretation were associated with group differences in the willingness to accept treatment, with Italian American men more likely to trust the doctor and accept pain medication and Jewish American men more cynical as to the benefits of analgesics. A further difference was found in terms of willingness to complain about pain at home: Italian Americans felt that they lacked the freedom to complain about their pain at home as they wanted to project the image of being the strong 'head of the family', whereas Jewish American men did not see pain expression at home as a sign of weakness. The 'old' Americans differed from both these other groups in that they did not complain or display their feelings but instead reported in a factual way. These men saw emotional expression as pointless in a context where they thought that the doctor's knowledge, skill and efficiency would be effective and would be aided by uncomplaining compliance. At home, the 'old' American men withdrew from other people if their pain got too severe, and even their wives reacted with either embarrassment or grave concern if they saw their husbands express emotional responses to their pain. Irish Americans were found to stoically accept or deny the pain, again reflecting a socialised gender phenomenon. Zborowski (1952) states that such cultural variations are learned during socialisation, where people's ideas about what is acceptable pain to bear and express is shaped. The lengthy illustration above shows that not only do pain perception and expression differ, but they also have a social function in terms of influencing treatment expectations or even the reactions of others (see also Chapter 16). What this illustration also highlights is some of the gendered responses we described in the section on symptom perception.

Individual difference influences

individual differences
aspects of an individual that distinguish them from other individuals or groups (e.g. age, personality).

Some individuals can maintain their everyday activities when experiencing what would be perceived as debilitating symptoms of illness by another person. Why? This is because of **individual differences** in how symptoms are interpreted.

■ Gender

Somatisation disorder, i.e. the experience of multiple unexplained symptoms, is more common in females (Noyes 2001) and thought to overlap with the presence of hypochondriasis, and women tend also to score higher on measures of neuroticism (Williams 2006). For these reasons, and others explored in an earlier section such as general socialisation, it is thought more likely that a woman will interpret a bodily sign as symptomatic of underlying illness than men. Evidence commonly bears this out inasmuch as women are seen to present to health services more frequently. Few studies have explicitly compared men and women matched in terms of other influences on symptom interpretation such as personality, social context and such like, with gender often being controlled for in analysis rather than focused on. Where gender differences are highlighted, such as in some studies of illness perceptions, we have included them.

■ Life stage

It is likely that young children are distinct from adolescents in their cognitive awareness of illness and its implications by virtue of the stage of cognitive development attained (Bibace and Walsh 1980; see Chapter 1) but also by virtue of the difference in life or illness experience and knowledge accumulated (Eiser 1990; Goldman *et al.* 1991). A limited number of studies of the symptom and illness perceptions and interpretations of very young ill children exist, for a variety of reasons, including ethical issues in submitting sick children to the demands of face-to-face interviews, methodological issues such as the limited availability of child-validated assessment tools, or the challenges of limited linguistic and cognitive skills. Young people with diabetes, both pre-adolescent and adolescent, have been described as having 'a basic understanding of the nature, cause and timeline of their illness and treatment recommended' (Standiford *et al.* 1997, cited in Griva *et al.* 2000); however, Paterson *et al.* (1999) believe that there is convincing evidence that children have similar multidimensional illness representations to adults. This is supported in findings drawn from studies of healthy children, for example a study of 5–12-year-olds (Normandeau *et al.* 1998, see RESEARCH FOCUS in Chapter 1) and of healthy pre-school children (Goldman *et al.* 1991) regarding common illnesses such as the common cold. Likewise, multidimensional illness constructs have been reported among children and young adults considering serious and chronic conditions in themselves, such as CFS (Gray and Rutter 2007), asthma and eczema (Walker *et al.* 2006) and in others, such as of their mother's cancer (Forrest *et al.* 2006). In this latter study, children aged 6 to 18 years talked about their mother's breast cancer, and mothers also talked about how they thought their child perceived the cancer and its treatment. Children's ideas about cancer included seeing it as common, as rare, as a killer, as treatable, as something that can be genetic, caused by smoking, worsened by stress; and ideas about treatment included thinking that the more treatment received the worse the cancer, but the less likely it would be to come back. Mothers were not always aware of how much their child understood about the illness and its treatment and, indeed, many found communicating about treatment implications or potential life-threatening consequences of the cancer difficult. When illness is in the family (see Chapter 15), communication and shared understanding of symptoms or treatment is an important factor in aiding adaptive coping with illness, both for the 'ill' person and for those affected by it. Other evidence of differences in parental and child perceptions of a child's illness can be seen in a small-scale study of nine asthmatic children aged 12–15 years, and eleven of their parents (Morrison *et al.* 2000a). While no significant differences emerged in the perceived severity of the illness, parents had higher perceptions of control over the child's asthma than what the children themselves reported. Fuller exploration is needed as to the implications of such differences, for example on adherence or coping behaviours.

■ Personality and experience

As well as influencing symptom perception as described above, personality and emotional characteristics can also influence how symptoms are interpreted. For example, those high in N or NA commonly exhibit heightened symptom perception and although there is some evidence that there may be a physical explanation for this, the consensus view still remains that neurotic or trait NA individuals over-attend to their internal states and exaggerate the meaning and implications of perceived symptoms. As a result of their negative interpretations of symptoms, individuals high in neuroticism are more likely to seek health care than those low in N. However, neuroticism is not all bad: there is evidence that moderate levels of neuroticism can benefit health, for example in terms of better adherence to treatment or quicker presentation to medical services following actual illness events (see Williams 2006 for a fuller discussion).

Prior experience affects interpretation of and response to symptoms in that having a history of particular symptoms or vicarious experience (e.g. experience of illness in others) leads to assumptions about the meaning and implications of some symptoms. (See RESEARCH FOCUS below for a description of the effect of one's own health status on perceptions of cancer). Also, as previously stated, symptoms considered to be rare in either one's own experience, or in that of others, are more likely to be interpreted as serious than a previously experienced or widespread symptom (Croyle and Ditto 1990). Believing symptoms to be 'just a bug that's going round' can mean that people sometimes ignore potentially dangerous 'warning signals'.

A knowledge of which bodily signs are associated with particular behaviour or illnesses (e.g. sweats and flu, sweats and exercise) will enable interpretation and attachment of a meaning to the symptom. These reserves of knowledge are known as 'disease prototypes'.

Disease prototypes and illness perception

Even when a physical sensation is perceived as a 'symptom', what is it that leads a person to believe they are sick? This arises when the symptoms a person is experiencing 'fit' a model of illness retrieved from their memory and it is here that health psychology draws from models dominant in cognitive psychology. People have disease prototypes that help them to organise and evaluate information about physical sensations that might not otherwise be interpretable. Symptoms are placed in the context of a person's past knowledge and experience, which has led to the development of protypical expectations of certain illnesses. Matching or not matching symptoms to a disease prototype (also referred to as cognitive 'schemata') shapes how a person perceives and responds to bodily signs, influences whether bodily signs are perceived to be symptoms of illness or not, and influences how it is then interpreted and responded to.

Illnesses that have clear sign-sets (symptoms) associated with them are more likely to be easily recognised in self-diagnosis; for example, a person experiencing serious abdominal pains may quickly consider appendicitis, and another person experiencing mild chest pain may quickly consider indigestion. It would be easy to assume therefore that a lump found in the breast

Table 9.1 Disease prototypes

	Influenza	AIDS
Identity	runny nose, fever, shivery, sneezing, aching limbs	weight loss, swollen glands, fever, skin lesions, pneumonia
Cause	Virus	Virus
Consequences	rarely long-term or serious (except if new 'strain')	long-term ill-health, death, uncertainty
Timeline	24 hours to a week	Months to years
Cure	time and self-medication	none, multiple treatments to delay progression
Type of person	Anybody	High-risk groups of injecting drug users, increasingly anyone via unprotected sexual intercourse

would, generally, prompt concerns that it may signify cancer and result in health-care seeking, and this is generally the case (see Chapter 4 for a discussion of influences on breast-screening behaviour). However, there are other symptoms of breast cancer, such as breast pain or skin scaling around the nipple, that may not be in a person's 'prototype', and thus such symptoms may go unidentified. This inability to correctly identify various potential breast cancer symptoms predicted help-seeking delay among a general population sample of 546 women (Grunfeld *et al.* 2003). Similarly, Perry *et al.* (2001) report that when heart attack symptoms do not 'match' the existing illness prototype in their severity, delay in seeking medical attention is greatest.

These prototypes have given rise to what is often described as 'common-sense models of illness', examples of which are contained in Table 9.1. A vast amount of health psychology research has developed this thinking into what is often referred to as 'illness representation' research.

■ Illness representations and the 'common-sense model' of illness

illness cognition
the cognitive processes involved in a person's perception or interpretation of symptoms or illness and how they represent it to themselves (or to others) (cf. Croyle and Ditto 1990).

Many different terms are employed, sometimes interchangeably, by authors discussing illness models: for example, cognitive schemata (Pennebaker 1982); **illness cognition** (Croyle and Ditto 1990); common-sense models of illness and illness representations (Lau and Hartman 1983; Lau *et al.* 1989; Leventhal *et al.* 1980; Leventhal *et al.* 1984); personal models (Hampson *et al.* 1990; Lawson *et al.* 2007) and illness perceptions (Weinman *et al.* 1996). One well-known model is the self-regulatory model of illness and illness behaviour proposed by Howard Leventhal and colleagues (see Figure 9.3). In this model, illness cognitions are defined as 'a patient's own implicit common-sense beliefs about their illness' (e.g. Leventhal *et al.* 1980; Leventhal *et al.* 1992). This 'common-sense model' states that mental representations provide a framework for understanding and coping with illness, and help a person to recognise what to look out for. What Leventhal and his colleagues proposed is a dual-processing model, which considers in parallel the objective components of the stimuli: e.g. the symptom is painful (cognitive), and

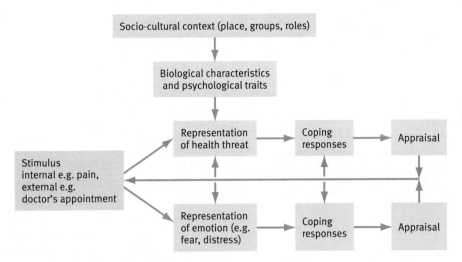

Figure 9.3 The self-regulation model: the 'common-sense model of illness'.
Source: Leventhal, Diefenbach and Leventhal (1992: 147)

the subjective response to that stimulus, e.g. anxiety (emotional). This model suggests that people actively process this information, which then elicits a coping response thought to be appropriate. Coping efforts, if subsequently appraised as being unsuccessful, can be amended, or alternatively the initial representation of the stimuli/health threat can be revisited and amended. For example, if a person experiences a headache that they believe is a hangover, they are unlikely to be too worried about it and may simply self-medicate and wait for the symptoms to pass. If the symptoms persist, however, they may rethink their coping response (e.g. go to bed), or rethink their initial perception (e.g. maybe this isn't a hangover) and thus alter their coping response (e.g. go to the doctor's). The existence of feedback loops from coping to representations and back again contributes to the model being called 'self-regulatory', with self-regulation simply meaning that an individual makes efforts to alter their responses in order to achieve a desired outcome. Feedback loops enable responsiveness to changes in situations, appraisals or coping responses and thus maximise the likelihood of coping in a way that facilitates a return to a state of 'normality' (for that individual).

Mental representations of illness (illness representations – IRs – as they are called by those working within Leventhal's framework) emerge as soon as a person experiences a symptom or receives a diagnostic label. At this point they start a memory search to try to make sense of the current situation by retrieving pre-existing illness schemata with which they can compare (Petrie and Weinman 2003). IRs are acquired through the media, through personal experience and from family and friends and, as prototypes, they can be vague, inaccurate, extensive or detailed. IRs are thought to exist in memory from previous illness experience, generally that of common illness such as a cold or flu, and the new symptom may be matched to a pre-existing model or 'prototype' of illness that the person holds. Obviously, 'matching' chest pain erroneously to previously experienced indigestion could be dangerous if it is in fact a heart attack.

Early work leading to this model asked open-ended questions of people suffering from a range of common conditions, including the common cold (Lau *et al.* 1989), cancer or diabetes (Leventhal *et al.* 1980) and found five consistent themes in the content of IRs reported. These were:

1. *Identity*: variables that identify the presence or absence of the illness. Illnesses are identified by label, concrete signs and concrete symptoms. For example, 'I feel shivery and my joints ache, I think I have flu'.

2. *Consequences*: the perceived effect of illness on life: physical, emotional, social, economic impact or a combination of factors. May be short-term or long-term. For example, 'Because of my illness I won't be able to go to the gym today' or 'Because of my illness I will have to take early retirement'.

3. *Cause*: the perceived cause(s) of illness. May be biological (e.g. germs), emotional (e.g. stress, depression), psychological (e.g. mental attitude, personality), genetic or environmental (e.g. pollution), or as a result of an individual's own behaviour (e.g. overwork, smoking). Some of these causes may overlap, e.g. stress and smoking behaviour, and may overlap with **attributions** of cause made after the onset of illness (e.g. French *et al.* 2001; French *et al.* 2002).

4. *Timeline*: the perceived time-frame for the development and duration of the illness. Can be acute (or short-term, with no long-term consequences), chronic (or long-term) or episodic (or cyclical). For example, 'I think my flu will last only three or four days' or 'My pain comes and goes'.

5. *Curability or controllability*: Lau and Hartmann (1983) added questions to assess the extent to which individuals perceive they, or others, can control, treat or limit progression of their illness. For example, 'If I take this medicine it will help to reduce my symptoms' or 'The doctor will be able to cure this'. As early work was primarily conducted on those with acute, manageable conditions, this fifth dimension may be particularly relevant for those facing chronic disease.

attributions

a person's perceptions of what causes beliefs, feelings, behaviour and actions (based on attribution theory).

The dimensions identified by Leventhal are captured in a quantitative scale developed by John Weinman and colleagues (Weinman *et al.* 1996), the illness perception questionnaire (IPQ), which has been validated across a range of illnesses in a wealth of studies. A child-specific version (CIPQ, Walker *et al.* 2006) has also been developed for children aged 7–12 with asthma and eczema, although in the reported pilot study the cure–control scale did not show acceptable internal consistency, suggesting that perhaps children of this age did not fully understand the concept of personal control or potential for cure. Interestingly, however, it was often this sub-scale that performed less consistently in adult studies and the control/cure items became a main target of IPQ revisions. The new scale, the IPQ-R, distinguished between beliefs about personal control and beliefs about treatment control of the illness (Moss-Morris *et al.* 2002; Moss-Morris and Chalder 2003; see ISSUES below) and also added two further dimensions – emotional representations and illness coherence. These are yet to be tested in a child sample.

There are logical theoretical interrelationships between component IRs: for example, strongly believing that an illness can be controlled or cured is likely to be associated with fewer perceived serious consequences of the illness and a short expected duration. The content and organisation of IRs can vary between individuals and even within the same individual over time, and can be attributed to underlying beliefs about disease. There is also evidence that different illnesses elicit different domains of illness representations. For example, Monique Heijmans and Denise de Ridder in the Netherlands (Heijmans and de Ridder 1998) compared the IRs of patients with either chronic fatigue syndrome (CFS) or Addison's disease (AD), both chronic illnesses with common symptoms of fatigue and weakness. AD is associated with gastrointestinal complaint and responds to medication, whereas CFS is generally very limiting and has no well-established treatment. Results showed that illness perceptions associated with each other similarly in the two disease groups: identity (both frequency and seriousness of symptoms) was positively associated with timeline and consequences, and negatively with control/cure (i.e. those reporting a high number of symptoms perceived more consequences and a longer timeline, and less control over their illness). A chronic timeline was also associated with low perceptions of control or cure and more serious consequences. However, when looking at differences between illness groups, CFS patients viewed their illness more negatively than AD patients, reporting more frequent and serious consequences and less positive future expectation of control or cure. The majority of both CFS and AD patients perceived the cause of their illness to be biological, but many also reported psychological and other causes. This study shows that although IR components are robust across these illnesses in terms of how they relate to each other, illnesses differ in the specific strengths of each component. These kinds of difference should be considered when planning interventions with specific populations or when communicating with patients about their illness.

The influence of self-identity on symptom interpretation

It has been suggested that the medical sociological tradition of assessing lay models of health and illness (e.g. Blaxter's study – see Chapter 1), which takes a broader view of illness beliefs shaped by social factors, and the health psychological model of individual cognitions, should be merged. Levine and Reicher (1996) proposed an account of symptom evaluation based on self-categorisation theory (e.g. Turner *et al.* 1987), which highlights the importance of **social identity**. Most people have several social identities depending on context (e.g. student/partner/daughter), and it is proposed that the interpretation of symptoms differs depending on a person's current salient social identity. For example, they found that female teacher-training students specialising in PE (physical education) evaluated illness and injury scenarios differently depending on whether they were in a condition that identified them by gender or as a PE student. The extent to which the illness scenario details were perceived as threatening their salient identity was important. These findings were explored in two further studies, one involving female secretaries and the other involving rugby-playing males. In the secretary sample, different scenarios (based around threat to attractiveness, occupation or emotionality) elicited different responses depending on whether the women were in the 'gender-identity' group or the 'secretary-identity' group. Perceived illness severity was highest when the scenario posed an attractiveness threat to the gender-identity group, or an occupational performance threat (e.g. hand injury) to the secretary-identity group. The study of male rugby players introduced two hypothetical comparison groups, telling the men that their results would be compared with either females or 'new men'.

social identity
a person's sense of who they are at a group, rather than personal and individual, level (e.g. you are a student, possibly a female).

This allowed the research team to explore the effect of context on symptom representations and self-identity. The scenarios presented threatened physical attractiveness, emotionality or physicality. Attractiveness threat led to greater illness severity perceptions when the comparator group was females, and the threat to emotionality led to less serious perceptions of the illness when compared with 'new men'. There was no difference in the perceived severity of illness when the threat was to physicality.

What this shows is that social identity may alter illness and injury perceptions. This suggests that models of illness representation commonly applied in health psychology research should perhaps expand to consider self and social identity influence. Although participants in Levine's studies were dealing with hypothetical illness/injuries in an artificial experimental setting, the reality is that most people fulfill a variety of social roles, and therefore it is logical to suppose that salient identity may differ in different contexts with potential effects upon symptom perception and interpretation.

RESEARCH FOCUS

Do perceptions of cancer differ according to own health status?

Buick, D. and Petrie, K. (2002). 'I know just how you feel': the validity of healthy women's perceptions of breast cancer patients receiving treatment. *Journal of Applied Social Psychology*, 32: 110–23.

Background
It is a sad fact that most people will encounter cancer at some point in their lives, either personally or through a family member or friend. Buick and Petrie note that cancer is generally a feared disease that can still elicit stigma in the response of others. Previous studies had shown that healthy women differed in the perceived causes of cancer from women with cancer, and that healthy women often had misperceptions about cancer treatments, which could potentially interfere with preventive behaviour or a person's interactions with those diagnosed with cancer. Understanding how and whether the illness perceptions of healthy individuals influence their emotional and behavioural response to that illness in others leads us to consider the wider impact of illness representations. This study therefore aimed to identify and compare cancer perceptions of patients with those of a healthy sample drawn from the community of Auckland, New Zealand.

Method

Participants
Representations about post-surgical treatment of breast cancer were assessed in two groups: seventy-eight post-surgical (partial mastectomy or lumpectomy) breast cancer outpatients receiving either radiation or chemotherapy, and seventy-eight healthy women drawn from the community and matched with patients on age, marital status and level of education. The reason for matching on these criteria is that age may influence perceptions and responses to cancer; level of education may affect knowledge about cancer and its treatment; and marital status may influence social support factors and exposure to others' cancer perceptions. Matching on these variables removes their potential confounding effects. None of the healthy sample had a prior cancer diagnosis; they ranged from 27 to 78 years old (mean 51 years,

s.d. 10.55), almost three-quarters were married, 90 per cent were of European ethnicity, about three-quarters had high school qualifications or above, and slightly over half were employed. Patients had completed either 50 per cent or 95 per cent of their treatment, and were receiving either adjuvant chemotherapy ($n = 26$) or localised radiation ($n = 52$).

Design
The study employed a questionnaire that was administered once, i.e. a cross-sectional study.

Measures
Illness perceptions were assessed using the Illness Perception Questionnaire (IPQ, Weinman *et al.* 1996), based on Leventhal's five illness representation components: identity (participants indicate which of fifteen listed symptoms they feel are part of breast cancer and indicate the frequency with which they are experienced); timeline (e.g. my illness will last a short time); cause (e.g. my breast cancer was caused by stress); consequences (e.g. my illness is a serious condition); and cure–control (e.g. my treatment will be effective in curing my cancer). With the exception of identity, participants rated how much they agreed or disagreed with the statements. Healthy participants responded on the basis of what they thought was true of breast cancer, whereas patients responded from their own experience. The component scales performed well in the study, attaining reliability coefficients (Cronbach's alpha) of between 0.75 and 0.87 (with 1.0 being total consistency). *Emotional distress* was assessed using the Profile of Mood States (POMS; McNair *et al.* 1971). Participants indicated the intensity to which they experienced each of sixty-five adjectives (0 = not at all, 4 = extremely), reflecting moods of tension–anxiety, anger–hostility, vigour–activity, depression–dejection and confusion–bewilderment. Reliability coefficients were good (0.84 to 0.95). All participants were asked to rate the adjectives in accordance with emotions they thought/felt were associated with post-surgical breast cancer treatment. *Coping* (or for healthy participants, imagined coping) was measured using the sixty item Coping Orientation to Problems Experienced scale (COPE; Carver *et al.* 1989) which consists of fifteen distinct scales: mental disengagement; behavioural disengagement; seek instrumental support; seek emotional support; vent emotions; use alcohol or drugs; suppress competing activities; denial; use religion; acceptance; active coping; planning; restraint coping; use humour; positive reinterpretation and growth. Healthy women rated their perception of a 'typical' response of women receiving post-surgical treatment for breast cancer (scored as 0: didn't use at all; 4: used a little; 8: used a medium amount; 12: used a lot). Reliability of sub-scales was good (0.66 to 0.95), and the intercorrelations between sub-scales were not strong, which supports the fifteen sub-scales being treated as conceptually different. Finally, participants rated the perceived health status of breast cancer patients on a single item that asked them to compare their own (or a hypothetical breast cancer patient's) current health status with that of a person in 'excellent health' (between 1 and 7, where 1 is terrible, 4 is fair, and 7 is excellent).

Procedure
Patients were recruited on the basis of physician referral. Healthy women were recruited using a three-stage process: first, a seminar to organisations broadly described the research (but did not mention cancer); second, fliers advertising a study investigating 'attitudes to illness' were placed in worksites and social venues. Those interested were invited to contact the researchers, and if they could be matched to a patient on the criteria listed above, an interview was arranged. Of ninety-seven women initially contacted, seventy-eight took part, which is a highly satisfactory 80 per cent response rate.

continued

Analysis

Between-group differences were examined in terms of mean scores and variances (standard deviations) on key variables, and in terms of their effect sizes (Wilks' lambda produces a coefficient between 0 and 1, where values closer to 0 highlights that means differ between groups, and values closer to 1 do not).

Results

In terms of *perceptions of breast cancer*, healthy women differed significantly from patients. Healthy women rated patient health as poorer, consequences of breast cancer as worse, treatment as offering less of a cure or control over illness, and the illness as having a longer timeline. Healthy women also overestimated the number, severity and frequency of patient symptoms (identity component) and believed more strongly in chance, patient-related, genetic and environmental causes for breast cancer. *Perceptions of coping* also differed, with healthy women thinking that breast cancer patients would focus on the illness and vent emotion, mentally and behaviourally disengage from treatment, plan and suppress competing activities, and use denial, alcohol and drugs, religion and restraint coping to a higher degree than patients themselves reported. Furthermore, healthy women thought that patients were less likely to use positive reappraisal and acceptance than other strategies, yet in reality these were the two most common strategies reported by patients (who also did not report using alcohol or drugs)! The two groups shared perceptions of the use of support seeking (emotional and instrumental), humour and active coping. Given these differences, it was not surprising that healthy women also overestimated the *emotional impact of breast cancer treatment*, rating patient depression, tension, anger, confusion, inertia and, surprisingly, vigour higher than patients did themselves.

Discussion

This study revealed significant discrepancies in the illness/treatment perceptions and responses between healthy women and those undergoing post-surgical treatment for breast cancer. Healthy women imagine breast cancer and its treatment to be significantly worse along most dimensions and, furthermore, believe that patients cope using strategies generally considered to be avoidant in nature. They also attribute cause more internally than do patients, although simultaneously rate environmental and genetic causes highly. A crucial finding is that healthy women misperceive how patients cope with breast cancer and its treatment and differ in terms of where they attribute cause to. If someone believes that an internal controllable cause is behind a person's cancer (e.g. poor diet, smoking), then this may limit their expression or provision of support for that person. Furthermore, if a societal perception of cancer is that patients best cope by denial, then healthy members of that society may think that any attempts to discuss the illness with the affected person would be unhelpful. These mismatched perceptions have obvious implications in terms of social responses and support provision for people with cancer, but they also hold implications for healthy individuals. For example, if social perception is that treatments offer little hope of cure, this may influence preventive health practices such as screening behaviour. If social perception is that breast cancer has severe consequences, this may contribute to fear of receiving a diagnosis, which is a further barrier to the uptake of screening.

Limitations

Some methodological weaknesses are evident and some are noted by the authors. For example, the study is limited to patients who have already experienced surgery, and their perceptions of cancer and its treatment may be shaped by this experience. The fact that some had completed 50 per cent of treatment and others 95 per cent was not considered in the analysis, yet may also have influenced results. Treatment type also differed (chemotherapy versus radiation therapy); chemotherapy patients were significantly younger than women receiving radiation and the form of surgery also varied, with radiation patients most likely to have had a lumpectomy and chemotherapy patients a partial mastectomy. Such differences within the patient sample in terms of what they had experienced may have influenced results: women who have had a lumpectomy (lump removed from breast but conserving the breast) may differ in terms of perceived cure/control and treatment consequences, for example, from those who have had a partial mastectomy (losing some actual breast tissue). While these differences are not central to the aim of the current study, between-patient differences may have obscured the real extent of differences between patients and healthy women.

The method of assessing perceptions of a specific illness from healthy individuals is possibly a bit messy ('Imagine how a breast cancer patient would cope', for example, is asking a person to put themselves into another's shoes – some people are more able to do this than others, depending on their natural qualities of empathy and imagination). The authors suggest that it may be better in future studies to use detailed case scenarios for the healthy participants to rate. However, it has to be said that there is no easy improvement on the methodology used – proxy or hypothetical views are always going to be just that. It is entirely reasonable that researchers wanting to highlight social perceptions of an issue or illness use methods such as those used here. Many currently healthy people will be patients or carers in the future, and it is important that perceptions that may elicit negative attitudes or negative helping behaviour are identified and addressed.

Causal attributions of illness

Attributional models are all about where a person locates the 'cause' of an event, or in the case of this chapter, symptoms and/or illness. We make attributions in order to attempt to make unexpected events more understandable or to try and gain some sense of control – if we know 'why' something has happened we can elicit coping efforts. Of course, attributions can be wrong and thus coping efforts misguided, as we will discuss later.

The majority of attributional research in health psychology has addressed 'ill populations' such as those who have suffered a heart attack (myocardial infarction) (e.g. Affleck *et al.* 1987; Gudmunsdsdottir *et al.* 2001), or those diagnosed with cancer (Lavery and Clarke 1996; Salander 2007). In relation to heart attack, attributions of cause – stress, work, it being in the family, smoking, eating fatty foods – were recorded regardless of whether attributions were *spontaneous* (patients asked to describe what they think about their illness), *elicited* (asked directly about their ideas of what may have caused their heart attack) or *cued* (asked to respond 'yes', 'no' or 'might have' to a list of thirty-four causes) (Gudmundsdottir *et al.* 2001). A review of studies of attributions for heart disease concluded that lifestyle factors and stress were the most common attributions made, with the latter more likely to come from heart attack patients than from healthy individuals, suggesting a form of self-preservation bias (French *et al.* 2001). This bias in perceived cause is also reported in a rare longitudinal study of lung cancer patients (Salander 2007). It is relatively well-established fact that smoking accounts for about 80 per cent of the incidence of lung cancer (see Chapter 3), yet among the 16 smokers interviewed repeatedly (of a sample of 23), the two most common attributions of 'cause of their illness' was 'don't know' and 'environmental toxins/pollution'. Fourteen did not consider smoking as a probable cause, and the author points to this as a defence mechanism or 'disavowal', potentially useful for a sample at a relatively late stage in their illness. Lung cancer patients in other studies have been found to attribute partial cause to their smoking behaviour (e.g. Faller *et al.* 1995) but studies of this patient group are rare and methodologies and timing of sampling generally differ.

When attributions were examined at an earlier stage in illness experience, i.e. at the time of symptom perception, Swartzman and Lees (1996) found that the dimensions of controllability, locus (internal/external causation) and stability described by attributional theorist Weiner (1986), and consistently reported in studies of illness attribution and coping (Roesch and Weiner 2001), were only partially supported. Symptoms addressed primarily reflected physical discomfort and were found to be attributed to either a physical (e.g. age, exertion)–non-physical (e.g. stress, mood) dimension; a high–low personal controllability dimension; and a dimension thought to reflect controllability by health professional/treatable versus stability/not treatable, although this dimension was less clear. Attributions of causes of symptoms (rather than attributions of cause of a confirmed illness) may be an area worth further exploration. Perceiving a cause of discomfort as being non-physical, under high personal control and stable/not treatable may lead to very different interpretation, response and health-care-seeking behaviour than a cause of discomfort with physical, low personal control and treatable attribution.

As seen in RESEARCH FOCUS, attributions of cause can be affected by one's own illness experience and can potentially affect how we respond to illness in others. Attributions of cause also influence how we respond to our own illness, and, unfortunately, attributions of cause can be wrong. For example, a woman may attribute joint pain to over-high heels on her shoes rather than the first signs of arthritis, and she may fail to seek medical advice; or adherence to essential medication could be affected: for example, a study of women with HIV infection found that drug treatment was wrongly attributed as causing their symptoms, leading to reductions in, or cessation of, medication adherence (Siegel and Gorey 1997).

■ Culture and illness perception

Culture influences illness perceptions: for example, there is significant variation in the extent to which members of specific cultures believe in supernatural causes of illness, e.g. evil spirits, divine punishment (Landrine and Klonoff 1992) or in divine or spiritual explanations. In terms of the latter, it has been described how Chinese women made sense of their cancer experiences by attributing their cancer to '*tien-ming*' (the will of Heaven, a concept from the Chinese Confucian and Daoist traditions) and to 'karma' (a Buddhist concept of cause and effect that cannot be changed through human effort) and as a result showed acceptance and 'going with the flow' ('*ping chang xin*') (Leung *et al.* 2007). These findings equate to that reported by non-Eastern research participants explaining the effects of a Buddhism-derived intervention (mindfulness-based cognitive therapy) on their living with cancer (Ingram *et al.* 2008).

Cultural differences have also been reported in terms of other illness representation dimensions. For example, a recent study of perceptions of diabetes held by South Asians, Europeans and Pacific Islanders found that perceived illness identity, timeline beliefs, consequences and emotional representations differed between groups (Bean *et al.* 2007). Pacific Islanders perceived more symptoms of diabetes, greater consequences and were affected more emotionally by the condition, whereas Europeans differed from the other two groups only in terms of perceiving a longer timeline. Illness coherence and personal or treatment control beliefs did not, however, differ. The differences identified were found to relate to poorer metabolic control and aspects of self-care, highlighting a need for health professionals to consistently address illness perceptions when trying to improve a person's self-management of symptoms or health condition such as diabetes, or indeed many other controllable conditions such as hypertension, epilepsy or asthma.

■ Illness representations and outcomes

While proposed in Leventhal's theoretical model to affect illness outcome via effects on coping (i.e. a mediated effect of IRs), illness representations have also been shown to have direct effects on a wide range of outcomes, including, for example:

- seeking and using medical treatment (Leventhal *et al.* 1992; Scharloo *et al.* 1998);
- engagement in self-care behaviour or treatment adherence (Hampson *et al.* 1994; Horne and Weinman 2002);
- illness-related disability and return to work (Lacroix *et al.* 1991; Petrie *et al.* 1996);
- quality of life (QoL; Gray and Rutter 2007).

In terms of predicting attendance at health-care clinics, a recent study (Lawson *et al.* 2007) found that among patients with Type 1 diabetes, perceived treatment effectiveness was a significant predictor along with the coping strategy of seeking instrumental support. In this study, treatment controllability is assessed within a 'personal models' questionnaire which is specific to diabetes but which fits into Leventhal's conceptualisation of illness representations.

The pattern of association reported between illness representations and quality of life outcomes in adults with Chronic Fatigue Syndrome (Heijmans 1998) was recently reported by children and young adults: i.e. low identity beliefs and perceived treatment efficacy was associated with better QoL (Gray and Rutter 2007). Interestingly, there was greater evidence of coping responses mediating the effect of IRs on outcome in this younger sample, than is commonly reported in adult samples, suggesting perhaps that coping plays a greater role in outcomes of younger patients, although why this may be the case needs further exploration.

Unfortunately many studies exploring the role of illness representations in explaining illness outcomes, including the Gray and Rutter study above, are limited by their cross-sectional design, i.e they report only concurrent associations. More recently, efforts have been made to gather longitudinal data, that test associations over a changing illness course. One example is the study of Llewellyn and colleagues (Llewellyn *et al.* 2007) who find that illness and treatment beliefs assessed prior to treatment for head and neck cancer were *not* predictive of health-related QoL, generic QoL or mood, in spite of many associations between IRs and coping at both a 1-month follow-up and at the final 6–8-month follow-up. Timeline beliefs at baseline (that their cancer was chronic) were predictive of depression 6–8 months after treatment, with this being a direct effect (no relationship to the 1-month coping strategies). In predictive analyses, coping and satisfaction with information received pre-treatment are more predictive of these outcomes; however, it is notable that these analyses are limited by a sample size of less than fifty patients and there-fore statistical tests of the effects of change in key variables over time were not possible.

The association between illness representations, coping behaviour and a range of illness outcomes was reviewed in a meta-analysis of forty-five empir-ical studies, many of which were cross-sectional (Hagger and Orbell 2003). Support for the contribution of illness representations to coping and illness outcomes was found. Generally speaking, perceived controllability was asso-ciated with adaptive outcomes including psychological well-being and social functioning, whereas perceptions of high symptom identity, chronicity and serious consequences, were negatively associated with such outcomes.

A further limitation of the vast majority of the empirical evidence-base available to date is that while many confirm statistical associations between the variables specified in the common-sense model of illness (i.e. between ill-ness representations, coping and outcome), they are quantitative in nature and thus commonly limited in the extent to which they develop our under-standing of what lies *within or behind* the representations presented. Consider for example the following quotes from cancer patients, one regard-ing cause and the other regarding consequences:

> *. . . to begin with, it just didn't sink in that I was really sick. I had a lot of difficulty in grasping it, because . . . we have lived pretty – soundly I think . . . outdoors a lot. And that, that I have heart problems also. I just don't really understand that it has turned out like this . . . And just that one should exercise a lot and try to eat properly and I've done that, largely because you don't want to gain weight either, but no – I don't understand it.*
> (woman with lung cancer reflecting on the onset of her condition, Leveälahti *et al.* 2007: 468)

> *I remember sitting in this mound of grass overlooking the bay and just feeling completely in the moment, and completely at peace; this is wonderful, this is one of the best times in my life . . . so in some ways it (the cancer) has given me quite a lot because it's given me that appreciation of living now, living every day . . . I still hold onto that kernel, of this is the only life I've got, today may be the only day I've got, so I think that's a very valuable thing to come from it, a positive thing, and I don't think I've ever had that before, that appreciation.*
> (woman with breast cancer talking about the consequences of her condition, Ingram *et al.* 2008)

The depth of emotion, including positive emotion, seen in these words, would be hard to capture quantitatively (see ISSUES for further discussion of methods of assessing illness representations).

Measuring illness representations

Opinions vary about how best to elicit and assess individuals' privately held illness perceptions and beliefs. The use of open-ended interviews as a method of eliciting illness representations (as used in Leventhal and colleagues' early work) has led to the criticism that questions such as 'To what extent when thinking about your illness do you think about its consequences?' may well be leading. Furthermore, interviews are very time-consuming and generally restrict sample size, although some studies have managed to successfully employ open-ended questioning (using prompts where necessary) (e.g. Forrest *et al.* 2006; Hampson *et al.* 1990; Hampson *et al.* 1994).

While Leventhal's model provides a useful framework on which to base studies of illness perceptions, few studies initially attempted to examine all five constructs (Scharloo and Kaptein 1997), instead assessing specific component beliefs, for example perceived control over illness (e.g. Multidimensional Health Locus of Control Scale, Wallston *et al.* 1978). Addressing these limitations, a team of UK- and New Zealand-based researchers led by Rona Moss-Morris, Keith Petrie and John Weinman developed a quantitative measure, the illness perception questionnaire (IPQ; Weinman *et al.* 1996). A recent meta-analysis of forty-five empirical studies using this tool to assess those with a wide range of health conditions across varying time-spans (Hagger and Orbell 2003) found it to have both construct and predictive validity (although the latter requires further confirmation through more longitudinal studies). This meta-analysis provided support for all IR domains (see earlier description) except for 'cause' representations, because the multitude of overlapping causal attributions made meta-analysis problematic. The authors propose that measurement of this cause dimension requires refinement.

The IPQ was revised in 2002 (IPQ-R) to address concerns over the internal reliability of the original cure/control and timeline sub-scales, and to assess the role of emotions (part of Leventhal's self-regulatory model not well addressed in the original IPQ). The IPQ-R separates personal control over illness from outcome expectancies and from perceived treatment control; strengthens the timeline component by adding items regarding cyclical illnesses as well as acute/chronic timeline items; assesses emotional responses to illness such as fear and anxiety, and finally, examines the extent to which a person feels they understand their condition, defined as illness coherence (Moss-Morris *et al.* 2002).

While Leventhal's framework dominates the study of illness perceptions and outcome within health psychology, other models do exist. For example, the implicit models approach utilises a questionnaire (IMIQ; Turk *et al.* 1986) which, when administered to three groups (diabetic patients, diabetic educators, college students), found four slightly different dimensions to those described by Leventhal: seriousness, personal responsibility, controllability and changeability. However, these results emerged when asking participants to *compare* two diseases, suggesting perhaps that their dimensions are more what discriminates *between* illnesses, rather than domains like Leventhal's, which relate to perceptions of individual illnesses. It may in fact be impossible to have a model or measure to fit all illnesses; for example, the potential for cure or treatment simply does not exist for all conditions and therefore this dimension is likely to lack validity in such situations.

The existence of commonly employed and reasonably well-validated quantitative assessment tools should not detract from the important contribution made by more open-ended

continued

methods of eliciting IRs. Understanding the sources and salience of beliefs and perceptions, and the reasons behind these, could be crucial to the development of targeted interventions. The value of qualitative enquiry can be highlighted by the findings of a recent study conducted in New York (Karasz and McKinley 2007). Cultural differences in illness perceptions were explored using a case vignette of a women suffering from 'fatigue', and responses compared between European American women and South Asian immigrant women. While the women sampled shared some conceptions of fatigue (e.g. perceiving both physical and psychological general causes), there were significant differences. For example, European Americans referred more often to genetic causes, medicalised/somatised the condition more and considered it a chronic condition, whereas South Asian women tended to think fatigue was temporary, caused by something transient and less needing of medical treatment. In exploring reasons for these differences, the qualitative accounts exemplify differing models of illness – a biomedical 'disease' model (European Americans) and a more socially oriented 'depletion' model which also drew on traditional 'humoral' concepts of illness (see Chapter 1). It is worth noting that the similarities and differences between groups may not hold for other symptoms, or indeed for other comparison groups. Culture, these authors note, is more than simply a demographic variable, and only through this type of study can we begin to explore 'the structures, contexts, conditions, ideologies, and processes through which culture shapes illness cognition and illness behaviour' (p. 614). One limitation of this study, however, is that participants were invited to respond to the vignette in a way that addressed predetermined IR dimensions. It would have been interesting to have assessed spontaneous responses to the vignette scenario in order to ascertain whether the dimensions outlined by Leventhal and others were implicit in the models of illness portrayed.

Planning and taking action: responding to symptoms

illness behaviour
behaviour that characterises a person who is sick and who seeks a remedy, e.g. taking medication. Usually precedes formal diagnosis, when behaviour is described as **sick role behaviour**.

lay referral system
an informal network of individuals (e.g. friends, family, colleagues) turned to for advice or information about symptoms and other health-related matters. Often but not solely used prior to seeking a formal medical opinion.

As this chapter has described, the first step towards seeking medical care begins with a person recognising that they have symptoms of an illness, and it may take some time for this step to occur. In many cases, people choose to treat an illness themselves by self-medicating with pharmaceutical, herbal or non-proprietary products, and others will rest or go to bed and wait to see whether they recover naturally. A number of surveys have suggested that less than one-quarter of illnesses are seen by a doctor.

Kasl and Cobb (1966a) refer to the behaviour of those who are experiencing symptoms but who have not yet sought medical advice and received a diagnosis as **illness behaviour**. Illness behaviour includes lying down and resting, self-medication and seeking sympathy, support and informal advice in an attempt to determine one's health status. Many people are reluctant to go to the doctor on the initial experience of a symptom and instead first seek advice from a **lay referral system**, generally including friends, relatives or colleagues (Croyle and Barger 1993). Symptoms are therefore not always sufficient to motivate a visit to the doctor.

Once people recognise a set of symptoms, label them and realise that they could indicate a medical problem, they therefore have the option of:

Plate 9.2   Making screening accessible by means of such mobile screening units outside workplaces or supermarkets may increase the likelihood of screening uptake. How would finding a lump be interpreted?

Source: © Health Screening (UK) Ltd

- ignoring the symptoms and hoping they recede;
- seeking advice from others;
- presenting themselves to a health professional.

Some people will do all three over time.

One might expect that the recognition that one has symptoms would be a sufficient condition for deciding that one is sick, but Radley (1994: 71) suggests that one must question that assumption. Think of your own experience – symptoms do not necessarily precede sickness – sometimes being deemed to be sick (by virtue of receiving a diagnosis) is an important element in appearing symptomatic, and perhaps adopting what is termed **sick role behaviour** (Parsons 1951; Kasl and Cobb 1966b).

Our response even to serious symptoms may still involve some delay to see whether things improve or whether attempts at self-care will improve the situation. A dramatic example of this was reported by Kentsch *et al.* (2002), who found that over 40 per cent of patients who thought they were having a heart attack, *and who considered this to be potentially fatal*, waited over one hour before calling for medical help. This delay would have had a significant impact on the outcome of their illness. Treatment with 'clot-busting' drugs, which dissolve the clot that causes an MI and minimise damage to the heart, are at their most effective when given within an hour of the onset of problems. An example of delay in a more chronic but equally serious condition was reported by Prohaska *et al.* (1990), who found that the first response of over 80 per cent of their sample of patients with colorectal cancer was the use of over-the-counter medication. Patients waited an average of seven months before seeking medical help. Cockburn *et al.* (2003) also found significant evidence of our ability to ignore important symptoms. In a survey of over a

sick role behaviour
the activities undertaken by a person diagnosed as sick in order to try to get well.

thousand adults, they found that 23 per cent of their sample reported having had blood in their stools (a potential symptom of bowel cancer) – but only one-third had ever reported these symptoms to a doctor. Perhaps more encouraging was the reporting of breast lumps by women in a study by Meechan *et al.* (2002). They found that of their sample of women who identified breast lumps following breast self-examination, 40 per cent had seen their doctor within seven days, 52 per cent within fourteen days, 69 per cent within thirty days, and only 14 per cent had waited over ninety days. However, it should be noted that even among this group of health-aware women who took active steps to identify and prevent disease, a significant proportion still delayed significantly in reporting their symptoms to their doctor.

What do YOU think?	Health is one of our most precious attributes. Yet many people who fear they have an illness – in some cases one they think may be fatal – delay in seeking medical help. Interestingly, people who are in the presence of someone else they know when their symptoms occur are more likely to call for help than people who are alone at the time they experience their symptoms. It seems that by talking with this person they are given 'permission' to call for medical aid. Why should this be the case? Are people frightened that their fears, perhaps of having cancer, will be justified, or that the treatment they may receive will be ineffective or too difficult to cope with? Can you think of any factors that might distinguish between those who do seek medical help at the onset of symptoms and those who don't? Think of your own illness experience and that of those close to you.

Delay behaviour

Delay behaviour in this instance refers to an individual's delay in seeking health advice as opposed to delays inherent in the health-care system itself (see IN THE SPOTLIGHT, Chapter 8 for suggestions as to how to reduce such delay in the delivery of treatment for heart attack). Studies of cancer patients have shown that delay in presenting symptoms for medical attention is highly related to outcomes of **morbidity** and mortality (e.g. Andersen *et al.* 1995; Richards *et al.* 1999), and thus it is important to gain an understanding of the factors that influence delay behaviour.

Safer *et al.* (1979) developed a model of delay behaviour, defined as the time between recognising a symptom and seeking help for it. They described three decision-making stages (see Figure 9.4) and point out that a person will enter treatment only after all three stages have been gone through and the questions in each stage have been answered positively.

In the first stage, a person infers that they are ill on the basis of perceiving a symptom or symptoms – the delay in reaching this decision is termed 'appraisal delay'. Next, the person considers whether or not they need medical attention, and the time taken to decide this is termed 'illness delay'. The final stage covers the time taken between deciding one needs medical attention and actually acting on that decision and making an appointment or presenting to a hospital. This is termed 'utilisation delay'.

morbidity
costs associated with illness such as disability, injury.

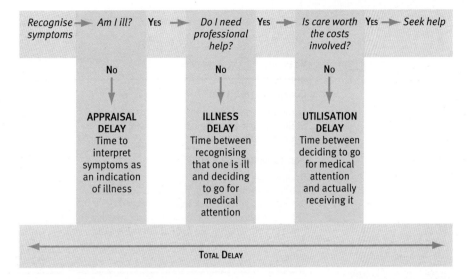

Figure 9.4 The delay behaviour model.

Source: adapted from Safer, Tharps, Jackson and Leventhal (1979)

To illustrate these three stages, let us imagine that on Sunday you wake up with a sore throat (recognise symptoms); by Tuesday you decide you are sick (appraisal delay); on Wednesday you decide to see your doctor (illness delay); on Friday you actually see the doctor (utilisation delay). The latter delay may not be under the individual's control if it includes time to the actual appointment (referred to as a 'scheduling delay'), as opposed to the time taken to *make* the appointment. The length of each delay period is likely to vary for different symptoms and illnesses, with, for example, appraisal delays being long for embarrassing personal symptoms such as rectal bleeding but scheduling delays likely to be short. It becomes obvious therefore that appraisals are crucial in getting the help-seeking process moving along, particularly when symptoms are potentially lethal. It follows therefore that if the potential for the appropriate cognitive appraisal is diminished through intellectual or cognitive impairment, appraisal and illness delays are likely to be exacerbated. There are many other reasons for delaying seeking treatment, including social class and educational level (the lower one's level of education and income, the greater the delay; see Chapter 2), age, gender, ignorance of the meaning of the symptoms, getting used to the symptoms, feeling invulnerable (cf. unrealistic optimism), believing that nothing can be done (relates to treatment perceptions, see below) and, commonly, fear. Earlier sections on influences on symptom perception and interpretation are also relevant here. Table 9.2 presents a summary of reasons that distinguished between seeking and not seeking medical consultation among a sample of 215 Chinese adults suffering from functional dyspepsia – a condition manifested by upper gastrointestinal tract pain and excessive belching, which has no underlying structural or biochemical cause (Cheng 2000). This table highlights many of the reasons for and against health-care-seeking; however, factors *external* to the individual, such as aspects of the condition or of ones' social network, nor reasons *within* the individual, such as demographic characteristics or personality, were explored, and so we address these also.

Table 9.2 Reasons consulters sought, and non-consulters did not seek, a medical consultation

Reason	N	%
Consulters (N = 109)		
Sought information about symptoms	46	42
Sought explanation for causes of symptoms	37	34
Sought advice to cure symptoms	26	24
Non-consulters (N = 106)		
Do not have time	29	27
Think the symptoms will disappear very soon	27	25
Do not want to take sick leave from work	21	20
Think the symptoms are a normal part of busy city life	10	10
Have uncomfortable feelings about hospitals	9	8
Think it is OK or not a problem	6	6
Other	4	4

Source: Cheng, C. (2000) *Psychosomatic Medicine*, 62: 844–52

■ Symptom type, location, perceived prevalence

As described in the Symptom Perception section, symptoms that are visible, painful, disruptive, frequent and persistent generally lead to action. If the symptom is easily visible to oneself and others, for example a rash, then one will delay less in seeking treatment. When people believe that their symptoms are serious (whether or not subsequently confirmed by the doctor), unusual (e.g. no one else seems to have had them) and that they can be controlled or treated through medical intervention, they take action. The effects of symptoms are also important. When symptoms threaten normal relations with friends and family, or when they disrupt regular activity or interaction, people usually seek help (Peay and Peay 1998). However, Grunfeld and colleagues (2003) found that even when a potential symptom of breast cancer had been self-identified, a significant number of women aged 35–54 delayed seeking health care in the belief that seeking help and potentially entering protracted treatment would be disruptive to their lifestyle! Not seeking help for such symptoms could result in an illness and treatment regime significantly more disruptive than presenting to health care early.

The location of the symptom also influences use of a lay referral system and/or going to a doctor: for example, persistent headaches may be discussed with friends and family before seeking medical help, whereas a persistent itch, or detection of a lump in the genital region, may not be – certain parts of the body seem more open to discussion than others. The attributes associated with some diseases may also influence ease of reporting; Hale *et al.* (2007), for example, noted that shame or embarrassment about the likely need for rectal examinations contributed significantly to delayed reporting of symptoms subsequently found to be associated with prostate cancer. This is also one of the reasons that many testicular cancers are diagnosed late, with potentially serious consequences (for cancer screening issues, see Chapter 4).

Furthermore, it has been shown that people make judgements about the prevalence of symptoms and disease that influence their interpretation and whether medical attention is sought. Diseases that a person has experience of have been found to be judged as more prevalent by both students *and* by physicians, and diseases considered prevalent tend to become normalised and viewed as less serious or life-threatening (Jemmott *et al.* 1988). Thankfully, however, it has been shown that presenting with symptoms of a condition that one reports a family history for, predisposes the emergency services to respond in an urgent manner (Hedges *et al.* 1998).

■ Financial reasons for delay

For some, seeking refuge in the sick role following a formal diagnosis might be an attractive option as it can allow a person time out from normal duties and responsibilities. However, some people do not want to be declared sick because of the implications it may have for them socially (If I am sick how can I attend that party?); occupationally (If I am off sick my work will pile up and await my return or will someone else get my job?); or financially (I cannot afford to lose wages or overtime payments by being sick. I cannot afford to pay for tests or medicines). In the USA, some people delay seeking medical care when money for the anticipated treatment is limited; these people are generally among the 16 per cent of American citizens (predominantly Hispanic and black people) who do not have health insurance (USBC 1999). This is not always the case, however – for example, following a heart attack many of those who delayed seeking treatment did have medical insurance (Rahimi *et al.* 2007, see Chapter 2). Luckily, other countries have health-care systems that make personal finance less of a barrier to treatment, for example the National Health Service in the UK.

■ Cultural influences on delay behaviour

Westernised cultures have been found to promote an independent sense of responsibility, i.e. the individual has supreme importance, whereas African cultures (e.g. Chalmers 1996; Morrison *et al.* 1999), and Chinese and Japanese cultures (e.g. Heine and Lehman 1995; Tan and Bishop 1996) have been shown to perceive health and illness more collectively and interdependently, in terms of the effects of health and illness on group function. As a result, different cultures may exhibit broadly different belief systems and different attitudes towards, and responses to, illness. To illustrate this, Bishop and Teng's (1992) study of Singaporean Chinese students found that while severity and contagiousness were commonly used dimensions of illness perception (as found among Western students), an additional dimension existed whereby illness was tied to behaviour and to blocked *qi* – the source of life and energy. These beliefs were associated with the use of traditional and Western health care, where it appeared that when dual health-care systems operate in parallel in a society, they are used differentially depending on the specific illness and illness perceptions (Heine and Lehman 1995; Quah and Bishop 1996; Lim and Bishop 2000). African studies (Chalmers 1996) have shown that the use of traditional medicine such as faith healers remains strong even as Westernised health-care availability increases. These kind of findings suggest that delays in seeking professional medical help may in part result from holding specific cultural beliefs about illness causation that do not 'fit' biomedical views of illness and treatment (Pachter 1994). In these cases, individuals will seek culturally relevant cures, including, for example, herbal or animal-based treatments, acupuncture, faith healing, and so on. In some cases, this may be associated with a parallel seeking of medical help – in others, seeking Westernised medical treatment may be considered only if the condition fails to respond to the more traditional remedies (Chalmers 1996; Heine and Lehman 1995; Lim and Bishop 2000; Quah and Bishop 1996).

Minority status, which includes ethnicity, but also gender, sexuality and so forth, may also contribute to delayed help-seeking where health-care consultations are seen as holding potential for humiliation or discrimination (Wamala *et al.* 2007). A fuller discussion of the influence of ethnicity on health-care-seeking behaviour, and access to services, is covered in Chapter 2.

■ Age and delay behaviour

The young and the elderly use health services more often than other age groups (see Chapter 2). Acute onset of severe symptoms tends to result in quicker seeking of medical attention by everyone, although particularly among the middle-aged. Elderly people generally present to their doctors more quickly regardless of symptom severity and in spite of the fact that many symptoms are commonly attributed initially to ageing (Prohaska *et al.* 1987). The quicker presentation of older individuals to health-care professionals has been interpreted as a need to remove uncertainty, whereas middle-aged individuals may attempt to minimise their problems, often relying on self-medication, until they worsen or fail to disappear naturally (Leventhal and Diefenbach 1991). In terms of a symptomatic child, the responsibility for acting on, interpreting symptoms and subsequently seeking health care (or not) lies often with the parent or guardian, and it may be expected that delay would be minimal. However, this is not inevitable and presenting a child to health care may be subject to similar influences as presenting oneself. For example, a Nepalese study found that even when presenting a child to health care, the speed of seeking health care depended on maternal educational level, family income, and the number and perceived severity of symptoms (Sreeramareddy *et al.* 2006). In late adolescence the decision to attend moves away from some parents and these young people can become reluctant to seek medical attention, particularly if their symptoms are something they wish to conceal from their parents. For example Meyer-Weitz *et al.* (2000) interviewed 292 South African adolescent and young adults (aged under 20 years) about the influences on their seeking health care for a sexually transmitted disease. The majority presented within 6 days of symptoms (56 per cent), 23 per cent waited 7–10 days, and 21 per cent waited more than 10 days. The reasons given for those seeking health care early were perceived seriousness of the symptoms, absence of any self treatments and positive attitudes to autonomy, and perhaps surprisingly, to condoms. Adolescents may also delay in seeking health care out of a sense of invulnerability and a resulting optimism about susceptibility to health problems (see Chapter 3).

■ Gender and delay behaviour

Women generally use health services more than men and we have already explored whether this may reflect greater attention being paid to internal states and bodily signals or gender socialisation. Perhaps women make better use of their social support and lay referral networks, which promote health care-seeking behaviour (Krantz and Orth 2000). However, a study conducted in France (Melchior *et al.* 2003) found that occupational status, and not gender, influenced social support usage, with those with low social status reporting better support. This contradicts American and British findings (Marmot *et al.* 1998; Stansfeld *et al.* 1998), where low socio-economic status was associated with less social support. The interaction between gender, socio-economic status, social support and health-care use is not yet fully understood (see Chapter 2) and any explanation is likely to be multifaceted, given the range of potential influences described in this section.

Gender differences in seeking medical help may occur as a result of different meanings given to health-related behaviour by the two sexes (Courtenay 2000). The differences, they propose, reflect issues of masculinity, femininity and power. Men show their masculinity and power by engaging in health-risking behaviour and not showing signs of weakness – even when ill. Women, conversely, experience no such issues and are more willing to seek medical help. It may be that women are more willing to confront the implications of any symptoms than men; this can be seen in the context of testicular, bowel and prostate cancer, for example, where women are often highly influential in encouraging their male partners to attend for doctor consultations (e.g. Hale *et al.* 2007; Gascoigne *et al.* 1999).

Finally, parenthood (motherhood has been studied more extensively to date than fatherhood) may also influence seeking help. Perhaps surprisingly, it has been shown that self-help or medical aid may be sought more willingly for symptoms perceived as minor than for those perceived as serious, perhaps suggesting avoidance of diagnoses that may interfere with the parenting role (Timko and Janoff-Bulman 1985).

■ Influence of others on delay behaviour

People often take action only when they are encouraged to do so by others in their lay referral network or when they realise that others with the same problem sought help in the past. It appears that many people look for 'permission' to call for help from their friends or family members – and are more reluctant to call for help in its absence (Finnegan *et al.* 2000; Kentsch *et al.* 2002). Related to this are delays as a result of 'not wanting to bother anybody'.

Discussing symptoms with others can be helpful. For example, Turk *et al.* (1985) found that discovering the presence of a family history of the symptoms currently being experienced led to health-care contact being made. Such disclosures of family history or of others' illness experiences are a likely outcome of conversations within a lay referral network, and having a family history is associated with seeking health care (Petrie and Weinman 1997). However, not all social networks are helpful: some people consulted may distrust doctors after negative experiences of their own; others may believe in alternative treatment or therapies rather than traditional medical routes; yet others may decide that the symptoms reflect something else going on, their friend/relative being stressed for example (Leventhal and Crouch 1997). The use of lay referral networks can therefore work for or against delays in the seeking of health care.

■ **Treatment beliefs and delay behaviour**

Horne (Horne 1999; Horne and Weinman 1999) suggests an extension to Leventhal's self-regulation model (described earlier in the chapter) whereby, in addition to illness perceptions predicting illness responses, the perceived benefits that an individual foresees of any treatments they may obtain as a result of seeking medical help are also predictive. For example, believing that one has a serious illness but that it can be cured with treatment is more likely to result in seeking medical help than the opposite cluster of beliefs. The identification of treatment representations (Horne and Weinman 1999) highlights perceptions of medicines as restorative, as symptom relievers, or as disruptive, harmful or addictive. Representations of medication and knowledge about treatment rationale have been associated with treatment adherence among adult populations (e.g. McElnay and McCallion 1998; Horne and Weinman 1999, 2002), and this is a growing area of research. A further effect of beliefs about treatment might be an effect on decisions to seek or not seek health professional advice for a symptom.

Perhaps due to growing concerns about some traditional medical treatments (e.g. antiobiotics, steroids, HRT – hormone replacement therapy), an increasing number of individuals are utilising what are known as complementary therapies involving both physical and non-traditional pharmaceutical interventions, such as acupuncture, chiropractice, homeopathy and traditional Chinese herbal medicine. Interestingly, those who use such treatments tend to be among the more highly educated and more economically well-off groups in society (Astin 1998).

■ **Emotions, traits and delay behaviour**

Fear and anxiety have been inconsistently associated with delay in seeking health care. O'Carroll *et al.* (2001), for example, found that people who had relatively high scores on a measure of dispositional anxiety were more likely to seek help quickly following the onset of symptoms than their less anxious counterparts. While fear of doctors, treatment procedures or medical environments can delay health-care-seeking, and trait anxiety, neuroticism and negative affectivity generally increase health-care utilisation, illness-specific anxiety appears to be less influential. For example, delay in seeking medical care was not significantly associated with anxiety among a study of individuals with head and neck cancer (Tromp *et al.* 2004).

Emotion itself may be insufficient to determine health-care-seeking behaviour, given the previously described importance of illness prototypes, symptom perception and interpretations and treatment beliefs, all of which act together to shape a person's response to a health threat. For example, a person who is highly anxious about a symptom and believes it signifies a terminal illness for which there is no treatment is less likely to seek medical attention quickly than someone who is equally anxious but believes that the symptom may be an early warning sign of a condition for which preventive or curative treatment is available.

One further response to health threats is that of denial. It has been shown that people who engage in denial generally show reduced symptom perception and report, and greater delay in seeking help (Jones 1990; Zervas *et al.* 1993). Unrealistically optimistic beliefs about health status or illness outcomes were thought to reduce symptom report and preventive health behaviour by means of increasing the presence of denial. However, neither of these relationships was upheld in a recent study of symptom report among those with either multiple sclerosis or insulin-dependent diabetes (de Ridder *et al.* 2004). Aspinwall and Brunhart (1996) have pointed out that optimism is not necessarily unrealistic and maladaptive, but that optimistic beliefs may actually benefit symptom report by enabling people to attend to symptoms without perceiving them as a threat. Tromp *et al.* (2004) offer support for this from a study of predictors of delay among patients with head and neck cancer, where delay was found to be greater (>3 months) in those scoring low on optimism, as well as low on active coping, the use of social support and low **health hardiness**.

health hardiness
the extent to which a person is committed to and involved in health-relevant activities, perceives control over their health and responds to health stressors as challenges or opportunities for growth.

There is a limited literature examining the influence of personality traits on health-care-seeking behaviour (Williams 2006), and what there is tends to focus on optimism, as discussed above, or neuroticism. Neurotic individuals, as described earlier, tend to over-attend to internal bodily signs and over-interpret and over-report symptoms; this means that they generally exhibit shorter delays in seeking help than those less neurotic individuals (O'Carroll *et al.* 2001). However, it has been suggested that their consulting style, of elaborate symptom description, for example, works against them being seen as credible and potentially undermines the medical care they receive (Ellington and Wiebe 1999).

Finally, following diagnosis, Kasl and Cobb describe how people engage in sick role behaviour, as the symptoms have been validated (and may increase once a label has been attached to them; Kasl and Cobb 1966b). People are then working towards getting better or preserving health such as avoiding activity or further injury. Seeking health care does not inevitably lead a person into the sick role, however, as effective treatment may be provided that rids them of their symptoms and enables them to carry on as usual.

Summary

This chapter has described the various processes that people go through before deciding that they might be getting ill. We have described how people may or may not become aware of certain bodily signs depending upon the context in which they are experienced or upon individual characteristics such as neuroticism. Both internal and external factors influence the extent to which a person attends to their bodily states, and how they subsequently interpret bodily signs as symptoms. We have described how, upon interpreting bodily signs as symptoms of some underlying illness, a person compares them with pre-existing illness prototypes derived from their personal experience or from external sources of information. People's beliefs about illness have commonly been found to cluster around five domains: perceived identity (label), timeline, consequences, cure–control and cause. These ways of thinking about illness are relatively stable across various patient groups, but specific beliefs can differ from that of a healthy person. Finally, we have described a range of personal, social and emotional factors that influence whether a person responds to their symptoms by seeking the advice of a health-care professional. The journey from a bodily sign perceived as a symptom to the doctor's door is often a long one, and delay in seeking health care can itself be damaging to one's health. Health psychology therefore has an important role to play in identifying the factors that contribute to this journey in order to maximise the likelihood of positive health outcomes for patients. How people communicate with health professionals and engage in their treatment is discussed in the following chapter.

Further reading

Buick, D. and Petrie, K. (2002). 'I know just how you feel': the validity of healthy women's perceptions of breast cancer patients receiving treatment. *Journal of Applied Social Psychology*, 32: 110–23.
This paper highlights the fact that personal experience shapes one's perceptions of a particular illness in terms of its causes, consequences and treatment outcomes. Discrepant perceptions between lay and 'patient' populations has implications for societal and carer responses.

Hale, S., Grogan, S. and Willott, S. (2007). Patterns of self-referral in men with symptoms of prostate disease. *British Journal of Health Psychology*, 12: 403–19.
An interesting qualitative study which highlights the influence of masculine identity on symptom perception and interpretation, and thus potentially illness outcome.

Martin, R., Rothrock, N., Leventhal, H. and Leventhal, E. (2003). Common sense models of illness: implications for symptom perception and health-related behaviours. In J. Suls and K.A. Wallston (eds), *Social Psychological Foundations of Health and Illness* (pp. 199–225). Oxford: Blackwell.
This chapter, contained in an excellent and well-resourced text, provides a clear and comprehensive overview of common-sense models of how ordinary people interpret and act upon symptoms (addresses the role of attention, cognition and illness representations, mood, social context and culture).

Williams, P.G. (2006). Personality and illness behaviour. In M.E. Vollrath (ed.), *Handbook of Personality and Health* (pp. 157–73). Chichester: John Wiley & Sons.
This chapter provides an up-to-date overview of evidence regarding the role of personality in illness behaviour, from symptom perception to health-care-seeking behaviour. It also highlights key gaps in current knowledge and highlights why personality research offers exciting opportunities to develop our theoretical models of illness behaviour.

 Visit the website at **www.pearsoned.co.uk/morrison** for additional resources to help you with your study, including multiple choice questions, weblinks and flashcards.

CHAPTER 10

The consultation and beyond

Learning outcomes

By the end of the chapter, you should have an understanding of:

- the process of the medical consultation
- the movement towards 'shared decision making' and the issues it creates
- factors that contribute to effective and ineffective consultations with health professionals
- issues related to 'breaking bad news'
- issues in medical decision making
- factors that influence adherence to medical treatments
- interventions to improve adherence in patients and health professionals

Image: Alamy/Image Source

CHAPTER OUTLINE

Conversations between health-care providers and patients are one of the most important means through which both groups give and receive information relevant to medical decisions, treatment and self-care. As such, the consultation remains one of the most important aspects of medical care. Good communication enhances the effectiveness of care; poor communication can lead doctors to make poor diagnoses and treatment decisions and leave patients feeling dissatisfied and unwilling or unable to engage appropriately in their own treatment. This chapter considers a number of factors that contribute to the quality of the consultation, and how doctors and patients act on information gained from it. It starts by examining the process of the consultation – what makes a 'good' or a 'bad' consultation. It then considers how doctors utilise the information given in the consultation to inform their diagnostic decisions. Finally, the chapter considers how factors in the consultation and beyond influence whether and how much patients follow medical treatments recommended in it.

The medical consultation

The nature of the encounter

Consultations are a time in which doctors and other health professionals gain information to inform their diagnostic and treatment decisions. They can monitor progress and change their treatment accordingly. They can also provide a time for the patient to discuss issues relevant to them and gain information about their condition and its treatment. As Ong *et al.* (1995) noted, the key goals of the consultation are:

- developing a good relationship between health-care provider and patient;
- exchanging relevant information;
- making relevant decisions.

The process through which these goals are achieved has been mapped by a number of researchers. One of the first such analyses was conducted by Byrne and Long (1976), who identified five phases within the typical medical consultation:

1. The doctor establishes a relationship with the patient.
2. The doctor attempts to discover the reason for the patient's attendance.
3. The doctor conducts a verbal or physical examination or both.
4. The doctor, or the doctor and the patient, or the patient (in that order of probability) consider the condition.
5. The doctor, and occasionally the patient, consider further treatment or further investigation.

These phases appear to hold for most consultations – although as we shall see later, what happens within each 'stage' can vary significantly. Another way of exploring this process is to consider the key elements that make for a successful interview. Ford *et al.* (2003) identified six factors considered to be important to a 'good' medical consultation by a variety of informants including general practitioners, hospital doctors, nurses and lay people:

1. having a good knowledge of research or medical information and being able to communicate this to the patient;
2. achieving a good relationship with the patient;
3. establishing the nature of the patient's medical problem;
4. gaining an understanding of the patient's understanding of their problem and its ramifications;
5. engaging the patient in any decision-making process – treatment choices, for example, are discussed with the patient;
6. managing time so that the consultation does not appear rushed.

Who has the power?

The consultation involves both patient and health professional: and both can contribute to its outcome. The nature of the meeting, however, means that the health professional usually has more power over the consultation than the patient. This power differential can be exacerbated by the patient's behaviour and expectations within the consultation. They may often defer to the professional and be reluctant to ask clarifying questions or challenge any conclusions the professional may make. Such behaviour is more likely to occur in consultations with doctors than with other health professionals, such as nurses. Nevertheless, all health professionals have significant responsibility for determining the style and outcome of the consultation. This can result in approaches differing from 'doctor knows best', the professional-centred approach identified by Byrne and Long (1976), to a more patient-centred approach advocated by people such as Pendleton (1983).

Characteristics of the professional-centred approach include:

- The health professional keeps control over the interview.
- They ask questions in order to gain information. These are direct, closed (allow yes/no answers), and refer to medical or other relevant facts.
- The health professional makes the decision.
- The patient passively accepts this decision.

Characteristics of the patient-centred approach include:

- The professional identifies and works with the patient's agenda as well as their own.
- The health professional actively listens to the patient and responds appropriately.
- The communication is characterised by the professional encouraging engagement and seeking the patient's ideas about what is wrong with them and how their condition may be treated.
- The patient is an active participant in the process.

Over the past decade, there has been a gradual shift from the professional-centred model to the patient-centred approach. Increasingly, both health

lumpectomy
a surgical procedure in which only the tumour and a small area of surrounding tissue are removed. Contrasts with mastectomy in which the whole breast is removed.

professionals and patients are seen as collaborators in decisions concerning patient health care. This is perhaps expressed in a movement among health professionals towards what is often referred to as 'shared decision making' (Elwyn *et al.* 2000), in which the patient and health professional have an equal share (and responsibility) in any treatment decision. Its advocates note that it is not relevant to all medical encounters, and may only truly occur where there is no dominant choice of treatment – a situation referred to as equipoise. This may occur in very important areas – such as a woman with breast cancer deciding whether or not to conserve a breast with a **lumpectomy** or to have more radical surgery and remove the whole affected breast. Here, there is no differential medical benefit from either approach (i.e. equipoise), and the choice may be more determined by factors such as the patient's concerns over their appearance or their desire to minimise the risk of recurrence. Although the health professional may provide information to inform patient choice, or even offer an opinion about that choice, the final decision should be reached jointly. Where equipoise does not exist, for example, in the case of a request for antibiotics for the treatment of a viral condition (where they will be of no benefit), the health professional may educate the patient to accept their choice of treatment, and so arrive at a 'joint decision', but not a truly shared decision.

These issues are taken into account in Elwyn *et al.*'s (2000) shared decision-making approach which involves the following steps:

1. Explore the patient's ideas about the nature of the problem and potential treatments.
2. Identify how much information the patient would prefer, and tailor information to meet these needs.
3. Check the patient's understanding of ideas, fears and expectations of potential treatment options.
4. Assess the patient's decision-making preference (joint, doctor, or patient-led) – and adopt their preferred mode.
5. Make, discuss or defer decisions.
6. Arrange follow-up.

This approach to the consultation is being advocated by the British National Health Service (NHS) which calls for 'active partnerships' between health professionals and patients (NHS Executive 1996). Despite this enthusiasm, there are often power differentials between high status health professionals (particularly doctors) and patients within the consultation. Accordingly, some have argued that while the idea that the health professional should provide or disclose information to the patient encourages equality within the decision-making process, it also implicitly accepts that the health professional has more relevant knowledge than the patient. The appearance of equality can therefore be an illusion and not reality, and both health professionals and patients may find it difficult to move away from this implicit power structure. Indeed, many patients prefer this asymmetry and resist moves to 'empower' them into a decision-making role. Some patients may be distressed and worried if a health-care professional admits that there is no clear evidence about the best choice of intervention, or that the evidence is mixed or premised on poor methodology. By contrast, being prescribed a particular treatment by an expert health professional may confer certainty and reassurance in the treatment of disease that cannot be found when the patient is asked to make choices about a number of uncertain treatment options.

Empirical research confirms some of these cautions. Lee *et al.* (2002) asked over 1,000 patients with either breast cancer or who were receiving **stem cell transplants** to identify their preferred consultation style. Only a minority of individuals opted for the shared decision-making approach:

Physician makes treatment decisions	10 per cent
Physician makes decisions following discussion with patient	21 per cent
Shared decision making	42 per cent
Patient makes decision following discussion with doctor	22 per cent
Patient makes decision	5 per cent

stem cell transplants procedure in which stem cells are replaced within the bone marrow following radiotherapy or chemotherapy or diseases such as leukaemia where they may be damaged.

Unfortunately, patients' preferences may not always be met. Keating *et al.* (2002) found that most patients (64 per cent) in their sample of over a thousand women with breast cancer desired a collaborative role in decision making, but only 33 per cent reported actually having such a role when they discussed treatments with their surgeons. Overall, 49 per cent of women reported an actual role that matched their desired role, 25 per cent had a less active role than desired, and 26 per cent had a more active role. Engagement may also not result in the desired treatment outcome. Vogel *et al.* (2008) found that of their sample of German women with breast cancer, only 64 per cent were able to have the treatment they asked for. Women, older people, those with an active coping style, and people with more education and who have a severe health problem are most likely to want to be engaged in the decision-making process (Arora and McHorney 2000). Interestingly, Arora and McHorney also found that people who placed the highest value on their health were least likely to want to be engaged in the decision-making process – perhaps because they considered this to be such an important issue that they did not want to question the expert opinion of the doctor.

RESEARCH FOCUS

Bensing, J.M., Tromp, F., van Dulmen, S. *et al.* (2006). Shifts in doctor–patient communication between 1986 and 2002: a study of videotaped general practice consultations with hypertension patients. *BMC Family Practice*, 25: 62.

Introduction
The authors note that there have been major changes in doctor–patient relationships, reflected in emerging concepts such as 'patient empowerment' and 'shared decision making'. However, there is also evidence that the reality of everyday practice is somewhat less 'advanced', partly because many patients do not wish to be active participants in decision making, partly because doctors experience a tension between providing 'patient-centred' care and more biomedically oriented health care, based on protocols and guidelines. The extent to which these two approaches have influenced the communication process in day-to-day care by ordinary physicians is not clear. This study aimed to provide relevant evidence, comparing the nature of consultations between a sample of Dutch general practitioners and their patients over a 16-year period in relation to the treatment of hypertension.

continued

Method

The study was a secondary analysis of two data sets containing videotaped primary care medical consultations collected in 1986 and 2002 in the Netherlands. In both instances, a sample of approximately 100 consultations with hypertensive patients were drawn from larger data sets. The first wave comprised consultations by 27 general practitioners. The second wave involved recordings of 108 GPs.

Sample

In both samples, the majority of doctors had more than 5 years' experience. In 1986, all were white males. In 2002, 74 per cent were white males. Patients in both samples did not differ on measures of age or gender. Their mean age was 60 years, and 64 per cent of the samples were female. There were no data available on patients' SES.

Measures included:

- The total *visit length*
- *Communication patterns*, measured using the Roter Interaction Analysis System (RIAS). In this, every doctor and patient utterance is coded into categories. All coders were extensively trained using the manual and material provided by Roter. Inter-observer reliability of RIAS ranged from 0.72 to 0.99.

Results

Visit length was slightly, but not significantly, longer in the more recent consultations (9 versus 10 minutes). The amount of talk by doctors did not significantly differ between 1986 and 2002, but patients talked less in 2002 (139 versus 109 utterances). They asked fewer medical questions, reported less concerns or worries, and had fewer process-oriented interventions (e.g. asking for clarification, or partnership-building). Doctors in 2002 asked fewer biomedical questions, made fewer process-oriented interventions, and expressed concern about the patients' medical condition less frequently than in 1986. By contrast, they gave significantly more medical information. The lower levels of patient talk in 2002 was attributed to silences due to the doctors' computerised record keeping. In 1986 none of the physicians had a computer on their desks: by 2002, all of them did. On average nearly 2 minutes were spent on computerised administrative work.

Discussion

Despite the widely reported philosophical move towards patient involvement in consultations, this study suggests that the day-to-day reality of medical consultations is far removed from this ideal. The general practitioners in the 2002-sample were more task-oriented than the GPs from 1986, who asked more questions and sought more interaction with their patients. In keeping with this, the 2002 patients made a substantially smaller contribution to the consultation than their 1986-counterparts: they asked fewer biomedical questions and engaged less in partnership-building with their doctor.

Several explanations are possible for this finding. In the first place, it can be argued that patients who visit their general practitioner with hypertension are usually older and don't fit into the model of the 'autonomous patient'. While this could explain why patient contribution in the medical consultation was low, it does *not* explain why patients' level of activity was lower than that of sixteen years previously. The main shift in doctor communication behaviour that they found was a shift from process-oriented towards task-oriented communication – mainly biomedical information giving. The study shows that Dutch GPs have increased their information giving, but might have lost some of their former capacity to let patients talk along the way.

Consultations which involve patients in decision making can result in increased patient satisfaction, greater confidence in health-care recommendations, improvements in self-care and wellbeing, and, on occasion, fewer drug prescriptions and less demand for inappropriate surgical treatments. They also appear to have similar medical outcomes to more traditional consultation approaches (see Ford *et al.* 2003; Edwards *et al.* 2004). However, medical outcomes may not always be optimal. Kinmonth *et al.* (1998), for example, found that patients who were given a patient-centred approach to the treatment of their Type 2 diabetes expressed higher levels of satisfaction with their communication with health professionals, greater treatment satisfaction, and greater wellbeing than patients who received a standard health-professional-led consultation. However, they were less careful in sticking to the calorie controlled diet necessary to maximise control over their condition. This may not be a bad outcome, of course. Rather, it implies that patients have knowingly opted to have a higher day-to-day quality of life rather than one constrained by medical 'necessities'. Ultimately, it is their life, and fully informed decisions such as this need to be supported.

Compliance, adherence and concordance

A specific form of decision making involves decisions concerning treatment – and in particular, drug and behavioural treatments to follow in the weeks and months after a consultation. Initially, research into this issue focused on what was termed treatment compliance, which implied a doctor- or health-professional-led process in which the patient was expected to comply with whatever instructions they were given. After several years, the more politically correct term of adherence was introduced, implying that patients were more involved in the decision-making process – although how this increase in patient independence was achieved was not always clear. More recently still, the term concordance has been introduced reflecting a further development in this process. Here, both doctor and patient reach a jointly determined agreement concerning the treatment regimen. This joint decision requires a patient to be fully informed of the benefits and costs (in terms of side-effects, treatment benefits, etc.) of following a particular treatment regimen. Full concordance between health professional and patient is assumed to increase the likelihood of patients following a treatment plan – although patients may of course change their decision or not follow the agreed treatment for a number of other reasons. We consider some of these later in the chapter.

Factors that influence the process of consultation

Health professional factors

A variety of factors may influence the behaviour of health professionals. Some may have strong beliefs in the type of consultation they wish to have with their patients. But more subtle factors may also influence their behaviour. Gerbert (1984), for example, found that health professionals give more information to patients that they liked than those they disliked. Encounters may also be influenced by the time available, the type of problem being dealt with, and so on. Patients and health professionals may also hold different agendas and expectations of the consultation. Patients are frequently concerned about issues such as pain and how the illness may interfere with their everyday lives. Heath professionals are often more concerned with understanding the severity of the patient's condition and developing their treatment plan. These differing agendas may mean that health professionals and patient fail to appreciate important aspects of information given and received. They may also impact on the outcome of the consultation. The findings of Zachariae *et al.* (2003) typify the outcomes frequently found in studies of this phenomenon. They examined the relationship between the quality of doctors' interactions with patients who had cancer and the patients' satisfaction with the consultation and confidence in their ability to cope with their condition. They rated various aspects of the doctors' communication style, including some related to the decision-making process, and others concerning more subtle aspects of the interview, including:

- whether the doctor attempted to gain an understanding of the patient's viewpoint;
- how well patients considered the physician to understand their feelings during the consultation;
- patients' satisfaction with the doctor's ability to handle medical aspects of their care;
- the quality of the contact with the doctor.

Plate 10.1   Being a friendly face and expressing empathy can help patients cope with bad news. Here an occupational therapist discusses therapy options with someone with a progressive muscular disorder in a completely informal and 'non-medical' manner.

Their results indicated that higher scores on all measures were associated with patients reporting higher levels of satisfaction with the interview, more confidence in their ability to cope with the illness, and lower levels of emotional distress. Of note also was that doctors who evidenced poor communication skills were least aware of the patients' responses and level of satisfaction with the interview.

The type of health professional

As well as these subtle differences in skills and personal characteristics, more obvious factors may also influence the style of the encounter. It is often suggested that the style of interaction differs across professions. Nurses, for example, are generally seen as more nurturing, easier to talk to and better listeners than doctors. Their role often involves exploring psychosocial issues more than, say, doctors. These different roles were highlighted by Nichols (1993) who suggested that doctors may find it difficult to become emotionally involved or to know their patients as people when they are involved in life and death decisions or actions such as surgery. With this in mind, he suggested that nurses should provide the main 'caring' role and be more involved in holistic care of the individual. For this reason, it may not be surprising that nurses typically do address more psychosocial concerns than doctors, and have different styles of talking to patients. Collins (2005), for example, found that nurses' communication frequently involved responding to patients' contributions; doctors' communication involved leading the consultation and addressing matters important to them. In addition, nurses' explanations began from the viewpoint of patients' responsibilities and behaviour; doctors' explanations began from the viewpoint of biomedical intervention.

Gender of the health professional

The gender of the health professional may also influence the nature of the consultation. Hall and Roter (2002), for example, concluded from their meta-analysis of seven relevant studies that patients spoke to female physicians more than male physicians, reported more medical and personal information, and made more positive statements. Patients also appeared more assertive and interrupted more when being interviewed by female doctors than by their male counterparts. Interestingly, perhaps, the gender of the doctor did not influence the degree to which emotional issues, such as concern, worries and personal feelings, were discussed. Some of these differences may be a consequence of the doctors' behaviour: female physicians tend to ask more questions and make more active efforts to build a relationship with their patients than male physicians – behaviours that would lead to higher levels of disclosure than would otherwise occur. These gender specific styles are not universal, however, and some research has shown no gender differences in doctor behaviour during consultations (Bensing *et al.* 2006). What may also be important is the concordance or lack of concordance between the gender of health professionals and patients. Beran *et al.* (2007), for example, found that both men and women were more likely to report not being treated with respect by doctors of the opposite gender than when they saw someone of the same gender.

Culture and language

Culture and language are inextricably linked in the context of the consultation, and there is clear evidence that people from differing cultures and languages will experience differing styles of consultation (see also Chapter 2). Neal *et al.* (2006), for example, found that in the UK, South Asians fluent in English had the shortest consultations with their general practitioners; South Asians non-fluent in English had the longest. White patients discussed more emotional problems than the South Asian patients, and were more active during the consultations than either of the Asian groups. Similarly, a Dutch research group (Meeuwesen *et al.* 2006) found that consultations with immigrant patients (especially those from Turkey and Morocco) were significantly briefer, and the power distance between them and their doctor was greater than those with Dutch patients. Doctors invested more effort in trying to understand the immigrant patients, while they showed more involvement and empathy with Dutch patients. Problems in communication may result in doctors experiencing difficulties in reaching appropriate diagnoses (e.g. Okelo *et al.* 2007) and patients misunderstanding information given in the consultation (e.g. Jones *et al.* 2007). The likelihood of these communication errors may be increased as a consequence of many health professionals' overestimation of the level of language understanding these patients have (Kelly and Haidet 2007), and may be exacerbated further by health professionals' expectations of how patients expect to be treated. Fagerli *et al.* (2007), for example, found that their sample of Norwegian health professionals thought that Pakistani-born patients preferred an authoritarian health-worker style. In fact, they preferred empathy and care. This disparity resulted in a lack of trust between patients and professionals.

Perhaps the most difficult communication issue health professionals face is when they do not speak the same language as that of their patients – a frequent issue with asylum seekers as well as others. In such cases, interpreters may be used to facilitate communication. This brings inevitable problems, as the communication is now between three people, and the risk of mistranslation is high. As Greenhalgh *et al.* (2006) noted, the interpreter's presence makes a dyadic interaction into a triad, adding considerable complexity to the social situation and generating operational and technical challenges. The interpreter occupies multiple social roles, including translator, interpersonal mediator, system mediator, educator, advocate and social worker – all of which may result in significant mistranslations and misunderstandings by all involved.

The type of information and the way it is given

One obvious factor that can influence the degree to which patients understand what is said in a consultation is the language used within it. Technical or medical language can be confusing unless appropriately explained. Lobb *et al.* (1999), for example, found significant misunderstandings of information given to women diagnosed with breast cancer. Not surprisingly, 73 per cent of their sample did not understand the term 'median survival' – nor did the term 'good prognosis' carry a clear meaning. Even much simpler terms may not be understood by many patients. Words such as arthritis, jaundice, anti-emetic, dilated and haemorrhoids are not understood by nearly half the population (Ley 1997). In a study of patients' understandings of words used to describe 'lumps', Chadha and Repanos (2006) found that a majority of patients were unaware of the meaning of words such as 'sarcoma' and 'lipoma'. While this confusion may be expected, 19 per cent of patients thought that a 'benign' lump was a malignant cancer – a serious misunderstanding. Not surprisingly, the use of jargon may result in significant anxiety. Abramsky and Fletcher (2002), for example, found that the words rare, abnormal, syndrome, disorder, anomaly and high risk in the context of genetic screening were particularly worrying to patients. They also found that risk for developing a disorder expressed as '1 in X' evoked more worry than when the same information was expressed as a percentage. These subtle uses of language show how careful health-care professionals need to be in talking to patients.

The way information is given within consultations is also important. Of particular importance may be the way in which information is framed in a positive or negative way. Edwards *et al.* (2001) noted the 'paucity of evidence' relating to the effects of framing of information and health behaviour. However, what evidence there is points to framing as an important influence on patient and even health professional behaviour. McNeil *et al.* (1982), for example, found that when given various probabilities for the outcome of treatment of a hypothetical case of lung cancer, patients, medical students and even surgeons were more likely to opt for surgery when the same risks for surgery were presented framed in terms of the probability of the individual surviving rather than dying. That is, they were more likely to choose surgery if the risk was presented as a 40 per cent likelihood of survival than if it was presented as a 60 per cent risk of dying. Similarly, Marteau (1989) reported that medical students were more likely to recommend surgery to hypothetical patients when they had previously been provided with information on survival rates following surgery rather than mortality rates.

Patient factors

Patient factors will also significantly influence the consultation. High levels of anxiety or distress during the interview, a lack of familiarity with the information discussed, a failure to actively engage with the interview, and not having considered issues to be discussed within the consultation may minimise patients' level of engagement. Patients may not think through what information they want, or realise only after the interview what they could have asked. They may also be reluctant to ask questions of doctors and other health professionals who are still frequently seen as of a higher status than them (Schouten *et al.* 2003). Perhaps for these reasons, people who are well educated and of high socio-economic status tend to gain more information and to have longer consultations than people with low levels of education and less economic status (Stirling *et al.* 2001).

Breaking bad news

One type of consultation for which the necessary skills have received particular attention is called the 'bad news' interview. As its name implies, these interactions are typically those in which patients and/or their partners are told that they have a serious illness or that they may die of their illness. Clearly, such interviews are stressful for both patients and health-care professionals. Historically, information about the likelihood of dying has frequently been withheld from patients – although their relatives were frequently told, placing a significant burden of knowledge on these people. However, this is no longer considered ethical – patients are now considered to have the right to be told their prognosis.

There is consistent evidence that the way in which bad news is given will impact on patient well-being (Schofield, P. *et al.* 2003). Unfortunately, there is little evidence about the best methods of doing so, and most guidelines are based on opinion and basic principles of good communication. Buckman (1992) suggested a six-step protocol for the process:

1. Give the news in person, in private, with enough time and without interruptions.
2. Find out what the patient knows about their diagnosis.
3. Find out what the patient wants to know.
4. Share the information: start with a 'warning shot' and then a small amount of information in simple language at a pace the patient can cope with.
5. Respond to the patient's feelings, including acknowledging and validating their emotional reaction to the news.
6. Plan and follow-through: includes planning next steps, summarising what has been said, identifying sources of support, and making an early follow-up appointment.

When these, or similar, guidelines are followed, patients appear to benefit. Schofield, M. *et al.* (2003), for example, asked patients to recall a bad news interview in which they received information about a 'life threatening' **melanoma**. They were asked questions about how their diagnosis was given, whether they received as much information as they wanted about their diagnosis, its treatment options, and its prognosis, and how the interview was conducted. They examined the relationship between their responses and levels of anxiety and depression at the time of diagnosis, and 4 and 13 months later. Factors associated with low levels of anxiety included the health professional preparing the patient for their diagnosis, giving as much information as required, providing written information, talking about the patient's feelings, being reassuring, and the presence of other (supportive) people while being given the diagnosis. Practices associated with low levels of depression included encouraging the patient to be involved in treatment-related decisions and discussing the severity of the diagnosis and how it may affect other aspects of their life. The importance of non-specific factors within the interview was highlighted by the findings of Roberts *et al.* (1994), who found that the physician's caring attitude was more important in aiding psychological adjustment to a diagnosis of breast cancer than the information given during the interview.

melanoma
a form of skin cancer. Usually begins in a mole and has a poor prognosis unless treated early.

What do YOU think?

Many doctors considered it a kindness not to tell patients when they were dying – a belief that also obviated *their* need to go through this painful process (see below). Indeed, so common was this practice that a rule of thirds was often cited as relevant to this situation. That is, two-thirds of patients were assumed to wish to know their prognosis – and two-thirds of doctors did not want to tell them. It is now considered a patient's right to know they are dying, and the practice of telling the relatives and not the patient is no longer acceptable – and many patients know they are dying without being told.

Patients may be upset, or even distraught, when given such information. However, knowledge of a poor prognosis can allow patients to prepare for death – from the most prosaic preparation such as making sure bills are paid to dealing with relationship issues and other important aspects of their lives. When death is not immediate, patients may prepare life goals that they wish to achieve before they die, and so on. So there are both positive and negative issues to be considered. Do the benefits outweigh the costs? Perhaps this decision can only be made on an individual basis. But on what grounds? Or perhaps all patients should be told whatever their circumstances?

Having identified 'best practice', a number of studies have examined how well physicians actually give bad news. Farber *et al.* (2002) found that over half their sample of junior doctors reported always or frequently performing 10 of 11 emotionally supportive items (e.g. ask about patients' worries, fears and concerns) and six of the nine environmental support items (e.g. ensure that the patient has a support person present). Similarly, Chadha and Repanos (2006) found that 64 per cent of their sample of surgeons felt confident in their ability to break bad news (compared to 91 per cent who felt confident in gaining consent to surgery and 40 per cent who felt confident in discussing 'do not resuscitate' decisions). These optimistic self-ratings may be contrasted with the findings of Ford *et al.* (1996), who used audiotapes of consultations to analyse cancer specialists' bad news interviews with their patients and found that the majority of time in their interviews was spent giving biomedical information with relatively little emphasis on empathic responses or acknowledgment of distress. In addition, the doctors exerted significant levels of control over the interview, moving away from the patient-led interview that the guidelines indicate as being optimal. Another observational study by the same group (Fallowfield *et al.* 1990) found that surgeons did not detect 70 per cent of instances of emotional distress in women being diagnosed with breast cancer.

These findings indicate the need for training in breaking bad news – a process that may result in significant improvements in this skill. Back *et al.* (2007), for example, measured bad news skills in what they termed standardised patient encounters, which involved the use of actors playing patients. They found that physicians made significant gains in their ability to give bad news following a four-day workshop. Most changes were substantial: for example, 16 per cent of participants used the word 'cancer' when giving bad news before the workshop; 54 per cent used it after the workshop. However, it is not clear how these skills translated to their day-to-day work. In a similar study, Alexander *et al.* (2006) found similar gains in skills, including information giving, responding to emotional cues, discussing probability and presenting clinical scenarios.

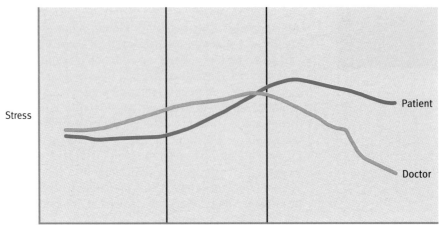

Figure 10.1   The timescale of stress experienced by health-care professionals and patients in relation to the bad news interview.

Source: adapted from Ptacek and Eberhardt (1996)

Before ending this section, it should be acknowledged that the bad news interview is stressful for both patients and health professionals. Ptacek and Eberhardt (1996) mapped out patient and doctor stress in relation to the interview (see Figure 10.1), suggesting that doctors experience significant anticipatory stress before the consultation, peaking during the 'clinical encounter', while patients' levels of stress typically peak following the interview. However, even for physicians the stress associated with giving bad news can last as long as three days or more (Ptacek *et al.* 2001), and can be sufficient to result in significant increases in blood pressure and impaired immune (NK cell) response (Cohen *et al.* 2003).

Moving beyond the consultation

A key goal of the consultation is for health-care professionals and patients to receive and provide information relevant to medical decision making and treatment. The next part of the chapter considers two outcomes of this process: one involving the health-care professional, and one involving the patient.

Medical decision making

Health-care decisions do not happen in a neutral context – and may be influenced by a wide variety of factors. They may be biased by health-care professionals' expectations of their patients, their fellow professionals, and the sheer pressure of making decisions in a short time – often without all the information necessary to make a fully informed decision. Doctors' own views about the nature of health care may also influence their decisions. Some doctors, for example, may only be willing to treat patients who are willing to be actively involved in their own health. Such doctors may refuse to provide expensive curative treatment for smoking-related diseases in patients who are unwilling to give up smoking. Other biases may be less conscious, or may be motivated by non-health related issues. Mitchell *et al.* (2000), for example, found that, even after adjusting for demographic factors, the presence of other serious diseases and ability to pay, African American patients with **transient ischaemic attacks** were significantly less likely to receive specialist diagnostic tests or to see a specialist doctor than white patients (see also Chapter 2 for an extended discussion of this issue). Gender differences may also influence the care people receive in hospital. Nurses are more likely to offer pain medication to women than to men, at least in casualty departments (Raftery *et al.* 1995). By contrast, more men than women are likely to be offered a place on cardiac rehabilitation programmes following an MI (Allen *et al.* 2004; Halm *et al.* 1999).

A key area of medical decision making involves diagnosing the illness with which patient present. Elstein and Schwarz (2002) identified a number of ways that doctors achieve this:

- *hypothesis testing*: the so-called 'gold star' level of decision making. This involves a logical sequencing of establishing and testing hypotheses about the nature of the diagnosis. Hypotheses are established, tested, and when they fail are replaced by further hypotheses until a final 'correct' hypothesis is established.

- *pattern recognition*: compared patterns of symptoms with disease prototypes. Perhaps a good way of reaching easy diagnoses, with the hypothesis-testing approach being utilised for more complex decisions.

- *opinion revision or 'heuristics and biases'*: perhaps the least reliable approach to making diagnoses: involves making decisions based on partial evidence as a result of using rules of thumb or heuristics.

Clearly, most of the diagnoses assigned by doctors are accurate. However, their decision making may be prone to error, particularly when the third of these approaches is used. This may sometimes be inevitable in the context of medical decision making where rapid decisions without optimal information may need to be made. Such situations may push doctors towards the use of diagnostic short-cuts. But the use of these short-cuts may happen in other, less demanding, situations as well. Tversky and Kahneman (1981) suggested that because we can only handle limited amounts of information when making decisions, we often take short-cuts known as heuristics or 'rules of thumb'. Those that are most useful for medicine may be 'fast and frugal' (Elstein and Schwarz 2002): that is, they aid quick decision making on the basis of minimal information. They allow doctors to make decisions at times of uncertainty and when information is lacking, but may lead to errors because they are based on assumptions which may or may not be relevant to particular situations. André *et al.* (2002) identified two differing types of heuristic frequently used by doctors in primary care. One doctor stated, for example, that she was so used to forty-year-olds presenting with chest pain having had an MI that she no longer tested for alternative diagnoses (as is recommended practice). Another doctor stated that if he thought a condition was psychosomatic, 'I begin to try to tie down the idea right away. I won't start with physical examination before talking about the possibility that it could be something emotional . . .' – a process that may miss a physical disease process.

transient ischaemic attacks
short periods of reduced blood flow to the brain resulting in symptoms including short periods of confusion, weakness and other minor neurological symptoms.

A key problem with the use of heuristics is that they limit thinking through the full diagnostic possibilities, and may be biased by a number of factors (Elstein and Schwarz 2002). These include:

■ *availability*: Diseases that receive considerable media attention are frequently thought to be more common than they actually are, even by doctors. Assuming a high probability of finding a condition may lead to it being diagnosed in error. A similar factor may occur if the diagnosing doctor has knowledge of previous diagnoses given by colleagues.

■ *representativeness*: Here, errors can occur because a set of symptoms is compared to a prototype set of symptoms and matched to one of two conditions without taking into account the likelihood of each of the two conditions being present. If these vary in prevalence within the population, the likelihood is that the condition being diagnosed will be the more pre-valent disease. Heuristics that do not take this aspect into account may result in the physician not challenging their initial diagnosis through strict hypothesis testing.

■ *potential 'pay off' of differing diagnoses*: If a diagnosis is unclear, the diagnosis assigned may be the one that carries the least cost and most benefit for the individual. When doctors are presented with a young child complaining of abdominal pain of no obvious origin, for example, a dia-gnosis of appendicitis and treatment of appendicectomy may be made, as treating the appendicitis successfully may be considered to outweigh the risks of an unnecessary operation.

In essence, heuristics reduce the cognitive load involved in making decisions at the cost of fully exploring all the potential issues that could be considered. These processes perhaps link to the findings of Ely *et al.* (1995) who asked fifty-three family doctors to describe their most memorable errors and their perceived causes. The errors they described were generally very serious: 47 per cent led to a patient death – in only 26 per cent of cases was there no adverse outcome. Only 10 per cent of those who were asked to take part could not remember making any such errors. The key factors identified included a number related to the use of inappropriate heuristics in medical practice:

■ *physician stressors*: including being hurried or distracted;
■ *process-of-care factors*: including premature closure of the diagnostic process;
■ *patient factors*: including misleading normal findings;
■ *physician factors*: including lack of knowledge.

One method of improving decision making may involve the use of com-puterised programmes that support doctors in their decision making. One web-based programme was evaluated by Ramnarayan *et al.* (2006). The programme was a 'diagnostic reminder system that provided rapid advice with free text data entry' that participants could access if they were unsure of a diagnosis. To evaluate its impact, trainee doctors who used the system to diagnose children with acute disorders noted the diagnosis they initially arrived at without the programme and then following its use over a five-month period. These diagnoses were compared to the diagnosis the child was finally given prior to discharge from hospital. Participants attempted to access the diagnostic aid on 595 occasions during the study period (8.6 per cent of all medical assessments). Prior to using the programme, 45 per cent of diagnoses were considered 'unsafe'; following its use 33 per cent were considered unsafe. In an analogue study of a similar programme, using simulated patients, the same team (Ramnarayan *et al.* 2006) found that the diagnostic accuracy of all grades of doctors, including experienced hospital consultants, improved following the use of such a system.

IN THE SPOTLIGHT

More heads make worse decisions

Decisions may be affected by a number of factors beyond the consultation. Christensen *et al.* (2000) examined the effect of group diagnostic decision making involving small teams of junior doctors and medical students. Information given to the groups was manipulated by asking the physicians to individually watch videos of actors acting as patients, offering the same information to all those in the group, and some information unique to each viewer, including one viewer who was given information crucial to making a correct diagnosis.

Their results were interesting in that, once convened, the groups discussed the information common to all those involved more than they discussed the unique information held by each group member. As a result they actually made *more* diagnostic errors than a control group of individual doctors given the same information. These data are particularly pertinent to making difficult diagnoses that may involve discussion by several doctors with information gleaned from a variety of different consultations or some medical specialties (particularly those involved in mental health) where information from many sources may be used to arrive at a diagnosis.

Plate 10.2   Some decision-making contexts are more difficult than others. Joint decisions, particularly if led by a powerful consultant, may not always be correct.

Source: Rex Features/TM & 20th Centery Fox/Everett

Taking the tablets

Effective treatment of many medical conditions frequently requires patients to take an active role within any treatment programme. In this chapter we focus on a relatively simple behaviour – taking medication. We examine interventions designed to facilitate more complex behavioural change in Chapters 6 and 17. In this context, the most frequent requirement placed on patients involves taking prescribed medication at times and in sufficient quantities to provide a therapeutic dose. This may not be a simple task. Taking HIV antiretroviral medication known as HAART (Highly Active AntiRetroviral Therapy: see Chapter 8), for example, is an extremely import-ant and complex issue. People taking this medication not only have to take tablets on a daily basis, but they also have to take them within very tight time limits during the day. HAART medications may require different dosing schedules – some at twelve-, eight-, six-, or four-hour intervals. Some tablets need to be taken with food, some with fatty foods, some with non-fatty foods and some on an empty stomach. Many result in serious side-effects that require taking further medication, and other medications may be required to treat secondary opportunistic infections. Not only is the required regimen for taking HAART complex, but it may also take place in the absence of symptoms – indeed, it may cause more short-term symptoms than it appears to prevent. Failure to keep to this regime, however, can result in the virus mutating – with serious implications for both the individual involved and any person to whom they may pass the mutated virus. Patterson *et al.* (1999) found that 81 per cent of HIV-positive individuals who take 95 or more per cent of their required medication showed complete viral suppression, whereas only 64 per cent of those who adhered to the medical recommenda-tions for between 90–95 per cent of the time did so, as did only 50 per cent of those with 80–90 per cent adherence. Only 30 per cent of those people with 80 per cent adherence showed viral suppression. Despite these dire health consequences, many people prescribed this type of medication do not follow the drug regimen sufficiently for it to be effective. Malow *et al.* (1998), for example, found that only 17 per cent of their sample of inner-city living HIV-positive men were fully adherent to their antiretroviral medication.

The complexity of taking the anti-HIV regimen perhaps makes this a spe-cial case. However, the percentage of people to follow the optimal medical regimen required in many chronic illnesses can be quite low. It has been estimated that, on average, only half of those who are prescribed pharma-cological therapies take sufficient medication to experience a therapeutic benefit (e.g. Haynes *et al.* 1996), a factor that results in about 10 per cent of hospital admissions (Schlenk *et al.* 2004). Looking at more specific disorders, Cramer (2004) reported that between 36 and 93 per cent of patients with Type 2 diabetes followed the recommended regimen of **oral hypoglycaemic agents** for between 6 and 24 months. Between 50 to 70 per cent of people are thought to take all their anti-hypertensive medication (Caro *et al.* 1999). Krigsman *et al.* (2007) reported that 42 per cent of their sample were under-using their asthma medication, while 23 per cent were overusing it. Similarly, Bernal *et al.* (2006) reported that 43 per cent of patients with inflam-matory bowel disease admitted to missing medication; 20 per cent of patients admitted to self-medicating.

oral hypoglycaemic agents
various drug types, all of which reduce circulating blood glucose levels.

Given the importance of taking these medications, one may wonder why people fail to take them appropriately. One simple explanation is that many people simply forget to take their medication or find their treatment regimen too complicated to cope with effectively. This may be particularly pertinent in the complex medical regime associated with the treatment of HIV. Maggiolo *et al.* (2002) found that 60 per cent of failures to follow the recommended medical regimen were associated with forgetfulness, 50 per cent with being away from home, while 38 per cent of failures were associated with problems with the drug schedule. A wide range of other factors have also been found to predict suboptimal use of medication (e.g. Chesney 2003) including:

- *social factors*: including low levels of education, unemployment, concomitant drug use, low levels of social support;
- *psychological factors*: including high levels of anxiety and depression, use of emotion-focused coping strategies such as denial, a belief that continued use of a drug will reduce its effectiveness, taking drug holidays to prevent 'harm' as a consequence of long-term drug use;
- *Treatment factors*: including misunderstandings regarding treatment, complexity of the treatment regimen, high numbers of side-effects, little obvious benefit from taking medication, poor relationship between patient and health-care provider, poor health professional–patient communication.

Another contextual factor that may affect adherence with medical regimens, particularly in children, are family systems. Tubiana-Rufi *et al.* (1998) found that diabetic children from families characterised as rigid, with low levels of cooperation and communication between family members, were more than six times less likely to adhere to their insulin regimes than children from families with more positive dynamics. Similar family dynamics have been associated with poor adherence to medication and dietary requirements associated with renal failure (Boyer *et al.* 1990). Some people have argued that older people are less adherent to recommended treatment regimens than younger people. However, any age issues may be more apparent than real (Edelmann 1999). As older people tend to have more chronic diseases than younger people, any differences in following medical recommendations may reflect the problems of taking multiple prescriptions rather than being an age-related phenomenon. Mills *et al.* (2006) failed to find any cross-cultural issues that influenced adherence to HAART medication. Summarising data from studies conducted in industrialised and developing countries, they found a consistent group of variables that influenced adherence across them all. Important barriers included fear of disclosure, concomitant substance abuse, forgetfulness, suspicions of treatment, regimens that were too complicated, number of pills required, decreased quality of life, work and family responsibilities, falling asleep and access to medication.

A more theoretical perspective on adherence to medication is provided by an extension of the health belief model (see Chapter 5). Horne (1997) has developed a model of adherence based on the health belief model used in combination with the illness representations model (Leventhal *et al.* 1992: see Chapter 9) to explain medication adherence. According to Horne's model, adherence is predicated upon a combination of patients' beliefs about the nature of their illness and the treatment they are being given to treat it. Illness beliefs include understandings of the nature of the illness, its severity, cause, time-frame, likely prognosis, and its 'treatability'. Illnesses that are seen as minor, short-term and likely to self-remit may result in less use of active treatments than conditions which are seen as long-term and likely to benefit from treatment. The second arm of this deliberation involves an evaluation of the costs and benefits of taking any medication. These include consideration of how likely the treatment is to cure the condition and how 'costly' this is likely to be. Cost here includes, but is not limited to, consideration of the likely side-effects of the medication. Applying this model to a condition such as hypertension may explain why adherence to antihypertensive medication is frequently so low (Mallion *et al.* 1998). Many people believe hypertension to be a short-term condition. It is symptom-free, so it is not clear to the patient that it is present for much of the time. Accordingly, people prescribed such medication may not see the necessity to take any medication over a long period of time. Add in a number of side-effects associated with this type of medication, such as dizziness or light-headedness, dry mouth, constipation, drowsiness, headache and impotence, and the result is a scenario that involves patients taking medication for a condition they are not aware of having, which provides no obvious benefit, and which brings with it some unpleasant side-effects. Little wonder that adherence to such medication can be so low. Even in severe conditions such as HIV infection, these issues also hold. Siegel *et al.* (1999) found that HIV-positive men and women stopped taking their antiretroviral medication if they considered it either made them sicker than their condition itself or carried greater risks than benefits. However, these assumptions may not hold in all circumstances – sometimes resulting in seemingly contradictory results. When a medical condition is severe, patients may in some cases actually welcome a treatment that brings high levels of side-effects. Leventhal *et al.* (1986) found that some women who received chemotherapy for the treatment of breast cancer found the *absence* of side-effects distressing: their expectation was that treatment of serious illnesses involved serious side-effects, and the lack of them implied that the drug used was not sufficiently potent to cure their condition. Other factors may be quite idiosyncratic to the individual. Gamble *et al.* (2007), for example, found that as Horne and others would predict, adherence to asthma medication was largely influenced by the fear of side-effects such as weight gain, anxiety, irritability and depression. However, participants also described feelings of 'not being themselves' and personality changes, resulting in a loss of their role within relationships when taking the medication. These feelings resulted in a reluctance to adhere fully to the recommended medication regimen.

■ Maximising appropriate use of medication

Maximising the appropriate use of medication involves, (i) maximising factors within the consultation that improve concordance and ensure the patient is willing and able to take the prescribed medication, and (ii) preventing errors and other factors beyond the consultation leading to less than optimal adherence.

Maximising concordance

The discussion of shared decision making earlier in this chapter provided an outline of the steps within the consultation that will lead to a shared decision/concordance between doctor and patient. A number of processes that enhance this process can also be identified from the previous discussion, including the doctor providing relevant information in a language understandable to the patient, and the doctor listening and responding to the patient in ways that encourage engagement in the decision-making process. Other factors that contribute to achieving concordance include having sufficient time in the consultation to fully discuss relevant issues, and seeing the same health professional on repeat visits. Concordance is unlikely to be achieved by health professionals who adopt a strong biomedical stance within the consultation and who pay little regard for the social and emotional concerns that patients may bring to the consultation.

Maximising understanding

One obvious method of increasing patients' understanding of the consultation process is to use language that they understand. However, there are other ways of doing so. One involves ensuring patients leave the consultation with all the information they need to make an appropriate decision. Many people leave a consultation without the information they want – and any decisions are therefore not fully concordant. This may be for a variety of reasons. Health professionals may lead the interview and, perhaps without realising it, inhibit the patient from asking questions. Alternatively, patients may not think through what information they want, or realise only after the interview what they could have asked. They may also be reluctant to ask questions of doctors who are still frequently seen as being of higher status than them. To avoid such lapses, a number of studies have examined whether preparing patients before a consultation can help them to ask questions necessary to elicit information they want within the consultation. Bruera *et al.* (2003) compared the effectiveness of giving a 'prompt sheet' providing suggested questions with a general information sheet normally given to women with breast cancer attending their first out-patient consultation with a consultant. The prompt sheet was rated as more helpful than the information sheet, but the women in this condition asked no more questions than those in the information-only condition. In a later, more thorough, evaluation of the value of prompts, Clayton *et al.* (2007) randomly allocated patients with advanced cancer to either a standard consultation or a consultation augmented by a prompt sheet. They evaluated the programme by examining audiotapes of the consultation as well as by patient-completed questionnaires. There results were impressive. Patients given the prompt sheet asked more than twice as many questions than patients in the control group. In addition, they discussed 23 per cent more issues, asked more prognostic questions and discussed more end-of-life issues. Their consultations with the doctors were longer, and they left the consultation with less unmet-information needs. These and other data suggest that encouraging patients to be actively involved in the consultation by prompting them to voice opinions or to ask clarifying questions will result in them achieving a greater understanding of their health problems and how these may best be treated. Advice given to people by the University of Michigan to maximise the effectiveness of their consultations with their medical services (www.mcare.org/healthathome/doctorpa.cfm) summarise the key issues well:

- Plan what you will say about your problem ahead of time.
- Repeat in your own words what the health professional has told you. Use simple phrases like, 'Do I hear you say that . . .?' or 'My understanding of the problem is . . .'

- Take notes on what is wrong and what you need to do.

- If you are confused by medical terms, ask for simple definitions. There is no need to be embarrassed by this. When a medication is prescribed, ask about its possible side-effects, its effectiveness, and how long it must be taken. If your health professional discusses surgery, ask about alternatives, risks and a second opinion.

- Be frank with the health professional if any part of the office visit is annoying, such as lengthy waiting time or discourteous staff. Be tactful but honest.

- Don't be afraid to voice your fears about what you've heard. The health professional may be able to clarify any misconceptions.

Maximising memory

Memory for information given in consultations is often surprisingly poor. Ley (1997) summarised the relevant data which suggested that half the information given in a consultation is almost immediately forgotten. The more information given in a consultation, the less it is likely to be remembered. Ley (1997) suggested a simple 'rule of thumb', suggesting that 75 per cent of information given in four statements is likely to be retained – only 50 per cent of information given in ten statements will be. In time, patients may even forget even their own actions. Montgomery *et al.* (1999), for example, reported that nearly a quarter of patients undergoing radiotherapy for the treatment of cancer could not recall having signed a consent form to permit the treatment – despite there being clear evidence that they had. Of those who did remember providing consent, a quarter could not remember being told about the side-effects of the treatment, while half could not remember its most frequent side-effect of feelings of exhaustion. Such poor outcomes are not always found, though. In a study of this phenomenon in the African country of Benin, Kelly *et al.* (2007) reported very high retention of information given during consultations, even when the amount of information given was high and the majority of the recipients were illiterate. People in the study were given an average of 39 points of information designed to improve their management of their child's illness. Immediately following the consultation, they were able to accurately recall an average of 90 per cent of the information points given. One day later, this had fallen to 82 per cent of the information points.

Despite this optimistic finding, many people do forget what happens in consultations, and there is a need for health professionals to help maximise patients' memories of what has occurred. One simple strategy involves giving information in a structured manner (Ley 1998), using language and terms the patient can understand. The most important information should be given early or late in the flow of information to maximise primacy and recency effects and its importance should be emphasised. Further strategies include repetition and the use of specific rather than general statements. To paraphrase part of Ley's advice: 'Tell them what you're going to tell them, tell them, and then tell them what you've told them . . .'. This may be augmented by asking patients to repeat key messages during the consultation to ensure understanding and increase memory consolidation.

A second strategy involves providing some form of permanent record of key information. This may involve pre-prepared information or a record of the information given during a consultation. In one examination of the latter approach, Tattersall *et al.* (1994) compared the impact of an audiotape of a consultation with that of individualised summary letters sent to patients after their first consultation with a cancer specialist. Patients listened to the tape an average of 2.3 times and read the letter 2.8 times over the following month. Ninety per cent shared the contents of the tape or letter with a friend, relative, or health professional. Both methods impacted equally on measures of recall, as well as on anxiety and depression. However, the audiotape proved the more popular method: when asked to rank six communication options, 46 per cent of patients gave the highest rank to the tape and 21 per cent to the letter.

Where information is given in written form, many people read it: Nathan *et al.* (2007), for example, found that 70 per cent of patients read patient-information leaflets when given new medication. Of course, written information should take into account the same issues as those that relate to spoken information – it needs to be clear, jargon-free, and not so complex that readers will be unable to understand it. Unfortunately, this requirement is not always met. Alexander (2000) reviewed a number of US dental educational leaflets, and found that 42 per cent of them were written at a more complex level than could be understood by the majority of patients – many required a university-level education to understand them. Similarly, Freda (2005) found that 41 of 74 patient-education brochures produced by the American Academy of Pediatrics had readability levels beyond the majority of their readers. At the other end of the scale, some innovative methods have been used to increase the readability of leaflets. One approach has involved the use of pictograms in addition to text to help people with limited literacy skills. This has proven surprisingly difficult to do. Knapp *et al.* (2005), for example, found that only 30 per cent of pictograms used in medication leaflets were understood by 85 per cent of the population.

Maintaining behavioural change

Whatever transpires within the consultation, patients have to be motivated and remember to take their medication or follow other advice in the hurly-burly of their everyday life. Any intervention designed to maximise adherence has to take these contextual issues into account. McDonald *et al.* (2002) examined the effectiveness of thirty-nine interventions which did so and were designed to enhance adherence to medication in a variety of chronic health problems including CHD, hypertension, asthma, COPD, HIV infection, rheumatoid arthritis and epilepsy. They concluded that the most effective interventions were generally complex and involved combinations of:

- convenient timing of drug taking;
- providing relevant information;
- reminders to take medications;
- self-monitoring (i.e. noting down when and where medication is taken);
- reinforcement of appropriate use of medication;
- family therapy.

They also noted that even the most effective interventions had 'modest' effects. The simplest methods involve ensuring that the prescribed medical regimen places as little demand on memory as possible. Orrell *et al.* (2003), for example, found that South African HIV-positive patients given a relatively simple antiretroviral drug regimen, involving three daily doses, were three times more likely to be fully adherent than those on a more complex schedule. Other approaches involve helping patients to select contextual cues to help them remember to take medication (take with food or other daily routines) or placing medicine in plastic medication boxes with compartments that are filled with the tablets to be taken at each time during the week. These are often used by older people, and can be filled by health-care professionals or family members. More complex procedures involve the use of reminders. In a study of this method, Chatkin *et al.* (2006) found that 74 per cent of people with asthma followed the recommended treatment regimen while receiving bi-weekly reminders; 52 per cent of those in a standard treatment (no reminders) group achieved the same level of adherence. Puccio *et al.* (2006) contacted newly diagnosed young people who were HIV-positive when their medication was required by telephone. While the calls continued, adherence remained high. However, as the calls were tapered and then stopped over a period of several weeks, so did levels of adherence, and levels of viral suppression decreased. It seems that once initiated, prompting needs to continue in the long term. This may be because a dependency on prompts has been established; it may reflect a lack of carry-over effect following cessation. One hi-tech approach has been to include microelectronic devices in tablet containers that prompt users to take their medication, and measures whether the container is moved or opened (e.g. Wu *et al.* 2006). Failure to do so within certain time limits can result in electronic notification of health-care providers and contacting the patient to remind them of the need to take their medication.

A second group of interventions involves self-management programmes similar to those discussed in Chapter 17. Here we consider self-management programmes specifically developed to increase adherence to medication regimens, focusing on one of the more complex regimens – HAART medication. Safren *et al.* (2001) compared two different interventions in this context. The first intervention involved self-monitoring and use of a pill diary to record when each tablet was taken, combined with visits to the clinic to provide feedback on medication usage. A more active intervention, known as Life-Steps, involved a single-session intervention involving an educational video, motivational interview (see Chapter 6), training in planning medication schedules, cues to pill taking, and the use of imagery of successful adherence in response to daily cues. This may seem an overly complex process. However, it should be remembered that taking HAART medication can involve planning different types of meals and being in particular places at set times. Patients may even be taught skills to take pills surreptitiously so that no one knows they are taking them. With this in mind, this sort of training programme may not seem so excessive. Adherence was measured at two and twelve weeks following the intervention. The researchers also examined a number of personal and social predictors of adherence. Both interventions led to improvements in adherence. However, among people with low levels of adherence, the Life-Steps programme achieved these more quickly than the self-monitoring condition. It also appeared to improve adherence more than the self-monitoring programme in those people who were depressed – a particularly important finding, as depression was the one person-factor they found to be independently associated with non-adherence.

In contrast to these positive results, a warning that some people can be particularly difficult to influence was provided by Martin *et al.* (2001). They compared the effect of an educational plus counselling intervention with counselling alone to enhance adherence to HAART therapy. Seventy-four per cent of those approached (many of whom were injecting drug users) refused to take part in the programme. Fifty-nine per cent of those who refused to take part did so for 'personal reasons', while 33 per cent did so because of trouble in their jobs. Those who were poor adherers to their HAART were most likely not to want to take part in the programme. Similar null effects have been reported elsewhere, including a report by Simoni *et al.* (2007) in an intervention involving peer support to a group largely comprising 'indigent' men and women from the Bronx. Despite the dire effects of non-adherence, there are many societal groups who find it difficult to follow recommended treatment programmes, and who are not helped by even quite substantial and sophisticated interventions.

Summary

The chapter has reviewed a number of issues related to how health professionals interact with patients, and how this can influence the outcome of any treatment they may recommend.

In the first section we considered the shift from the paternal 'doctor knows best' type of consultation to more patient-centred approaches, and the ultimate outcome of this shift – shared decision making. It was noted that while this has many benefits, many patients are cautious in adopting it, as it raises concerns over the apparent expertise of health professionals and may place a responsibility on patients for their treatment that they are unwilling to carry.

We went on to consider some other elements of the consultation that may influence its outcome, including:

- the gender of the health professional – women appear more empathic and caring, factors usually associated with greater satisfaction with the interview;
- the 'spin' given to information;
- the input of the patient: people who ask more questions tend to gain more information from the consultation.

Breaking bad news involves telling patients that they have a serious illness, and that they may die from it. It is a stressful process for both patient and health professional. Key factors in optimising this process include:

- Give the news in person, in private, with enough time and without interruptions.
- Find out what the patient knows about their diagnosis.
- Find out what the patient wants to know.
- Share the information, starting with a 'warning shot'.
- Respond to the patient's feelings.
- Plan and follow-through.

Medical decision making can be influenced by a number of factors. Doctors often employ heuristics to help them arrive at a diagnosis. This can speed the process up, but increases the risk of diagnostic errors. Typical errors are those of:

- availability
- representativeness
- differing pay-offs of differing diagnoses.

Adherence to recommended medical treatments is influenced by a number of factors, including:

- social factors
- psychological factors
- treatment factors
- family dynamics
- beliefs about the nature of the illness and its treatment regimen.

Adherence may be enhanced by:

- the use of patient-centred approaches and shared decision making;
- maximising satisfaction with the process of treatment;
- maximising understanding of the condition and its treatment;
- maximising memory for information given.

Beyond the consultation, these factors may be added to be a number of strategies, including:

- convenient timing of drug taking;
- relevant information;
- reminders to take medications;
- self-monitoring (i.e. noting down when and where medication is taken);
- reinforcement of appropriate use of medication.

Finally, consideration has to be given to the use of strategies to increase health professionals' adherence to professional issues, including the use of standardised medical treatment protocols. Just like their patients, some health professionals' behaviour may prove difficult to influence.

Further reading

Here are a number of reviews of issues dealt with in the chapter. Most of them are 'as its says on the tin', in that the title shows the content of the paper.

Brédart, A., Bouleuc, C. and Dolbeault, S. (2005). Doctor–patient communication and satisfaction with care in oncology. *Current Opinions in Oncology*, 17: 351–4.

Coderre, S., Mandin, H., Harasym, P.H. *et al.* (2003). Diagnostic reasoning strategies and diagnostic success. *Medical Education*, 37: 695–703.

Elstein, A.S. and Schwarz, A. (2002). Clinical problem solving and diagnostic decision making: selective review of the cognitive literature. *British Medical Journal*, 324: 729–32.
A useful insight into medical decision making.

Elwyn, G., Edwards, A., Kinnersley, P. and Grol, R. (2000). Shared decision making and the concept of equipoise: the competences of involving patients in healthcare choices. *British Journal of General Practice*, 50: 892–9.
A paper on the process of shared decision making by the leading UK research group.

Grime, J., Blenkinsopp, A., Raynor, D.K. *et al.* (2007). The role and value of written information for patients about individual medicines: a systematic review. *Health Expectations*, 10: 286–98.

Mast, M.S. (2007). On the importance of nonverbal communication in the physician–patient interaction. *Patient Education and Counseling*, 67: 315–18.
Tackles an important issue not looked at in the chapter – the role of non-verbal behaviour during the doctor consultation.

Siminoff, L.A. and Step, M.M. (2005). A communication model of shared decision making: accounting for cancer treatment decisions. *Health Psychology*, 24: S99–S105.

Teutsch, C. (2003). Patient–doctor communication. *Medical Clinics of North America*, 87: 1115–45.
A substantial review of a variety of issues relating to communication with patients.

van Dulmen, S., Sluijs, E., van Dijk, L. *et al.* (2007). Patient adherence to medical treatment: a review of reviews. *BMC Health Service Research*, 7: 55.
Free on the internet, and a good review to boot.

Visit the website at **www.pearsoned.co.uk/morrison** for additional resources to help you with your study, including multiple choice questions, weblinks and flashcards.

CHAPTER 11

Stress, health and illness: theory

Learning outcomes

By the end of this chapter, you should have an understanding of:

- stress as a stimulus (stressors)
- stress as a result of an interaction between an event and an individual
- the critical role of cognitive appraisal
- the nature of acute and chronic stress
- physiological processes invoked by the stress experience
- how stress manifests itself in various diseases

CHAPTER OUTLINE

The beginning of this chapter outlines the main thinking about stress in terms of nature and definition and highlights three main ways in which stress is studied: as a stimulus, as a transaction between a stimulus event and an individual's appraisal of it, and as a biological and physiological response. The second of these reflects a psychological model of stress proposed by Richard Lazarus and his colleagues and is described in detail to illustrate the central role of cognitive appraisal. This is done by examining how stress impacts upon us all in our living and working lives, and by examining acute and chronic stressors. The final part of the chapter provides evidence as to the physiological processes by which stress and our responses to it exert an influence on physical health, focusing particularly, but not solely, on cancer, CHD and HIV. By the end of the chapter, the nature of stress and the processes by which it may impact on illness should be clear.

Concepts of stress

The term 'stress' is used very widely and with several meanings: everyone probably thinks they know what the term means, but few people define it in exactly the same way.

What do YOU think?

What does stress mean to you? What causes you to feel stressed? How do you respond?

Think of some recent events that you have experienced as stressful. Why was this? Reflect on your answers to these questions as the chapter progresses.

Stress has generally been examined in one of three ways: as a stimulus or event external to the individual; as a psychological transaction between the stimulus event and the cognitive and emotional characteristics of the individual; or as a physical or biological reaction. Each of these perspectives and their accompanying methodologies have their own strengths and weaknesses, which are outlined in the forthcoming sections.

Stress as a stimulus

In thinking of stress as a stimulus, researchers focus on stressful events themselves and on the external environment; i.e. a person will attribute their tension to an event or events such as moving house or getting married. The event and its properties are considered amenable to objective definition and measurement: for example, the event can be labelled (e.g. wedding) and aspects of it such as its proximity (e.g. next week, next year) can be assessed.

Researchers taking this approach have studied the impact of a wide variety of stressors on individuals or groups, including *catastrophic events* such as earthquakes, floods or plane crashes, and more commonly, *major life events* such as losing one's job or starting a new job, getting married or divorced, giving birth, being bereaved, or even going on holiday. Life events such as these are considered to require significant adjustment on the part of the person experiencing them, and can include both positive and negative events.

■ Life events theory

life events
a term used to describe occurrences in a person's life which may be viewed positively or negatively but which inherently require some adjustment on the part of the person (e.g. marriage, loss of job). Such events are implicated in the experience of stress.

The major proponents of this approach were Holmes and Rahe, who in 1967 proposed their **life events** theory. They proposed that naturally occurring life events did not simply have unitary consequences for a person but cumulative effects; in other words, the more life events one experienced, for example within the past year, the greater the likelihood of physical health problems. Furthermore, they claimed that specific kinds of event could be weighted against each other. To make these claims, Holmes and Rahe had carried out a series of interesting studies. First, they invited over 5,000 participants to generate a list of events that they found most stressful; from this, they generated a representative list of forty-three commonly mentioned events, including positive, negative, frequent and rare events. Holmes and Rahe then asked a new sample of almost 400 people to rank the listed events in order of the degree of disruption the event, if experienced, had caused them. Furthermore, they asked participants to rate each event against marriage, which had arbitrarily been given a value of 500 by the researchers. For example, if divorce was considered by a respondent as requiring twice as much adjustment as marriage, it was given a value of 1,000. By averaging the ratings received for each event item and then ranking them, Holmes and Rahe were able to produce a scale known as the social readjustment rating scale (SRRS; Holmes and Rahe 1967; see Table 11.1), with values scaled out of 100 (maximum of 100 assigned to death of a spouse, which averaged out as the event requiring greatest adjustment). The values were called life change units (LCU). Social readjustment was defined as 'the intensity and length of time necessary to accommodate to a life event, *regardless of the desirability of this event*' (Holmes and Masuda 1974: 49), highlighting the fact that both positive events (e.g. marriage) and negative events (e.g. redundancy) would require some adjustment on the part of the individual. A subsequent study of eighty-eight physicians (Rahe 1974) found that the greater the LCU score the higher the risk of ill-health. Of the ninety-six major health changes reported by the participants, eighty-nine took place in individuals scoring over 150 LCUs; and when scores were greater than 300, over 70 per cent of the physicians reported subsequent ill-health. Those individuals scoring less than 150 LCUs tended to report good health. Holmes and Masuda (1974) defined a *mild life crisis* as scoring between 150 and 199 LCUs, a *moderate life crisis* as scoring between 200 and 299 and a *major life crisis* as scoring over 300; they drew not only on their own work but also on that of other researchers of the time to support their hypothesis that life change could cause ill-health.

Limitations of life events measurement

The evidence of the associations between LCUs and ill-health (physical and/or mental) was soon questioned (e.g. Dohrenwend and Dohrenwend

Table 11.1 Representative life event items from the social readjustment rating scale and their LCUs

Event	LCU rating (1–100)
Death of a spouse	100
Divorce	75
Death of a close family member	63
Personal injury or illness	53
Marriage	50
Being fired from work	47
Retirement	45
Sex difficulties	39
Death of a close friend	37
Change to a different job	36
Foreclosure of mortgage or loan	30
Son or daughter leaving home	29
Outstanding personal achievement	28
Begin or end school	26
Trouble with boss	23
Change in residence	20
Change in social activities	18
Vacation	13
Christmas	12

Source: Holmes and Rahe (1967)

1982), as a result of various methodological or sampling limitations. For example, many studies reporting moderate to strong associations between LCU's, health and illness (including many of Holmes and colleagues'), relied on retrospective assessment: i.e. participants who were already ill were asked to report whether or not they had experienced any life events prior to the onset of illness. In contrast, studies employing prospective designs found much weaker or non-existent relationships. Other weaknesses exist in terms of the items included in the scale. For example, depending on your age, many of the listed events may not be applicable (divorce, childbirth, etc.). Some of the listed events may simply not occur with sufficient frequency to enable many individuals to report them or for their effects on health to be experienced (e.g. moving house, going to jail), and others may be intertwined and may cancel out, or enhance the effects of one another (for example, marriage requiring positive adjustments but coinciding with a negatively perceived house move). Other events listed are vague and ambiguous: for example, reporting a 'change in social activities' could mean many things brought about for many different reasons. Finally, and perhaps most importantly for psychologists, allocating LCUs to events assumes that all people rank events in a similar way. However, think of divorce. For some people this will be a positive event reflecting the end of an unsatisfactory relationship, while for others it will be a devastating and possibly unexpected blow. The life events approach to stress therefore fails to systematically address the many factors (internal and external) that may moderate the relationship between stressful events and illness events. Psychological theories of stress illustrated in this chapter highlight the importance of such factors (which are then described in Chapter 12).

In spite of many limitations, this body of work shows that major life events need to be considered; for example, prospective longitudinal studies often assess the life event experience of those studied on the basis that it may influence other variables of interest: for example, adjustment to an illness may be undermined by the occurrence of other major life changes.

Life hassles

In addition to major and often rare life events, research has highlighted the stressful nature of daily *hassles*. Kanner *et al.* (1981: 3) defined hassles as 'irritating, frustrating, distressing demands that to some degree characterize everyday transactions with the environment' and measured such things as not having enough money for food or clothing, losing things, being over-loaded with responsibilities, making silly practical mistakes, or having a row with a partner. Unlike major life events, hassles do not generally require major adjustment on the part of the person experiencing them but their impact was thought to be particularly evident if they were frequent, chronic or repeated over a particular period of time. To test this proposal, Kanner and colleagues developed a tool to assess daily hassles and found that they strongly associated with negative mental and physical outcomes even when controlling for major life events. Positively rated events, described as 'uplifts' (e.g. getting away with something, completing a task, getting or giving a compliment, having a laugh) were acknowledged more thoroughly in this theory than in life events theory. Kanner studied three groups of people – middle-aged, professionals and students – and found that these groups differed in the importance they attached to particular events, in particular the importance they attached to economic concerns, work and time pressures, and social hassles. In terms of uplifts, the groups differed in their weighting of having good health, spending time with family, and hedonistic items such as social-ising and having fun. This raises the important question of *how* events are perceived and appraised, and the influence that life stage or role can have upon perceptions of potential stressors. Kanner also reports a curious gender difference whereby women experienced psychological symptoms following uplifts as well as hassles, whereas men were unaffected by uplifts, suggesting perhaps that women are affected by 'change' in either a positive or negative direction. These findings highlight that two people could experience the same number of events and weight them equally but experience very different health outcomes. Why could this be? This question moves us away from con-sidering stress simply in terms of the stimulus and is an issue we return to later and also in Chapter 12 where moderators of the stress experience are discussed.

It has also been suggested that only negatively rated events or hassles lead to adverse outcomes and that positive events or uplifts may 'moderate' the impact of negative events (e.g. Thoits 1995), but the evidence for this is inconclusive as few studies explore the prospective interactions between positive and negative events.

If health outcomes are indeed affected by major events or an accumulation of minor events, what are the processes (psychophysiological or behavioural) by which this occurs? The stress-as-a-stimulus approach has proved attrac-tive to many epidemiologists, who aim to identify significant stressful events and to calculate their effect on adverse health outcomes, for example studies of the effects of unemployment on morbidity and mortality (e.g. House *et al.*

1982). However, such studies do not tell us *how* unemployment affects illness or even death rates, or *why* it may in some people but not others (Marmot and Madge 1987). To answer the 'how' question leads us to consider physiological theories of stress (stress manifest in biological responses), whereas to answer the 'why' question requires consideration of sociological explanations (see in part, Chapter 2's discussion of social inequalities in health) and psychological theories of stress (involving cognitive appraisal and emotion). We turn here to the psychological explanations.

Stress as a transaction

distancing response
taking a detached view, often a scientific view, of an event or stimulus in order to reduce emotional activation.

denial response
taking a view that denies any negative implications of an event or stimulus. If subconscious, it is considered a defence mechanism.

appraisals
interpretations of situations, events or behaviour that a person makes.

According to psychological theory, stress is a subjective experience, an internal state of being that may or may not be considered by an outside observer as being appropriate to the situation that evoked the response. As John Milton (1608–74) put it when he wrote *Paradise Lost*: 'The mind is its own place, and in itself can make a heaven of hell, a hell of heaven'. This points to what has become the central tenet of psychological theories of stress: that appraisal is central to whether or not an event is deemed to be a stressor or not. The key figure in this domain is Richard Lazarus, who with colleagues (e.g. Lazarus and Launier 1978; Lazarus and Folkman 1984) proposed what is called a cognitive transactional model of stress. Evidence of the importance of psychological processes was drawn from early experimental studies of Lazarus and colleagues (e.g. Speisman *et al.* 1964), which quite simply exposed student participants to stressful films while monitoring self-reported stress levels and physiological arousal (i.e. heart rate and skin conductance). One example included a gruesome video about tribal initiation rites that included genital surgery. Before the film, participants were divided into four experimental conditions, each of which received different introductions and soundtracks. One group heard an intellectual description of the rites from a cultural perspective (to mimic a **distancing response**); another heard a lecture that de-emphasised the pain the 'willing' initiates were experiencing and emphasised the excitement they were feeling (to mimic a **denial response**); another heard a narrative that emphasised the pain and trauma the initiates were undergoing (to emphasise the perceived threat); and a control group received no information or soundtrack. Results showed quite clearly that the introductions influenced the way in which the film was seen, reflected in both self-reported stress and skin conductance, with the first and second groups (distancing and denial) showing significantly less stress than group 3. While these studies were initially intended to address the idea of 'ego defences' (i.e. what people do to protect themselves from threat), Lazarus realised that appraisal processes were mediating stress responses, and hence his subsequent work developed a theory of stress that is today one of the most influential in health psychology.

According to Lazarus, stress is a result of an interaction between an individual's characteristics and appraisals, the external or internal event (stressor) environment, and the internal or external resources a person has available to them. Motivational and cognitive variables are considered central. Lazarus's initial model maintained that when individuals confront a new or changing environment they engage in a process of **appraisal**, which is of two types: primary and secondary.

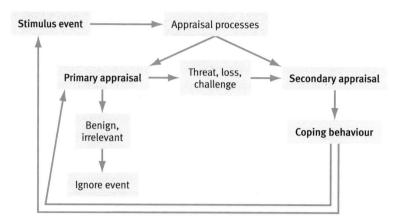

Figure 11.1 Lazarus's early transactional model of stress.
Source: adapted from Lovallo (1997: 77)

■ Primary appraisal processes

In primary appraisal, a person considers the quality and nature of the stimulus event. Lazarus distinguished three kinds of possible stressor: those that pose harm, those that threaten and those that set a challenge. Harm is considered as damage that has already been done, i.e. a loss or failure; threat is the expectation of future harm; and challenge results from demands that are appraised as opportunities for personal growth or opportunities that a person is confident about dealing with. Events that are not appraised as either harm, threat or challenge are considered to be benign events that require no further action. The questions asked of oneself are along the lines of 'Is this event something I have to deal with?', 'Is it relevant to me?', 'If so, what is at stake?', 'Is it a positive, negative or neutral event? If potentially or actually negative, then is it posing me harm/threat or challenge?' Simultaneously to making these appraisals, emotions may arise that elicit various physiological responses, as we shall describe later.

■ Secondary appraisal processes

At the same time as carrying out primary appraisals, Lazarus proposed that secondary appraisals are initiated whereby one assesses one's resources and abilities to cope with the stressor (coping potential). The questions asked of oneself at this stage are of the type: 'How am I going to deal with this?', 'What can I use or call upon to help me?' Resources can be either internal (e.g. strength, determination) or external (e.g. social support, money).

Using forthcoming exams as an example, various appraisal judgements may be made, for example:

■ There is no way I can possibly deal with this. I simply know I will fail (threat + no resources = stress).
■ This will be really hard. I just am not as clever as the other students (threat + limited internal resources = stress).
■ Maybe I can manage this if I revise really hard (challenge + possible internal resources = less stress).

- I could perhaps do it if I get some help from my friends (challenge + external resources = less stress).
- This isn't a problem. I know the material really well (benign).
- I managed to pass the last time, I'll be okay this time (benign).

Lazarus's early work maintained that stress would be experienced when perceived harm or threat was high but perceived coping ability was low, whereas when perceived coping ability was appraised to be high (i.e. resources were considered to be available to deal with the threat), then stress was likely to be minimal. In other words, stress arose from a mismatch between perceived demands and resources, both of which could change over time. It is important that stress is viewed as a dynamic process.

■ Developments in Lazarus's framework

In the 1990s, Lazarus increasingly considered the stress process as part of the wider domain of emotions and modified his cognitive appraisal theory of stress accordingly (Lazarus 1991a). He also collaborated with an eminent colleague at this time (Smith and Lazarus 1993), although the two academics differed slightly in the components of appraisal proposed. Smith proposed that primary appraisal consists of two sequential assessments: one of *motivational relevance*, i.e. the extent to which the event is considered relevant to one's current goals or commitments; the other of *motivational congruence*, i.e. the extent to which the situation is perceived to be congruent with current goals. Stress was likely in situations where relevance was high and congruence was low. This is illustrated below:

APPRAISAL	
motivational relevance	motivational congruence
'The proposed class test is important to my studies'	*'I would prefer to party'*
High relevance	low congruence

Lazarus included in primary appraisal an appraisal of *ego involvement*, whereby appraisals of threat to one's sense of self or social esteem would elicit anger, events violating one's moral codes would result in guilt, and any existential threat would create anxiety.

Removing threat/challenge and harm/loss appraisals from the core cognitive definition of primary appraisal and instead attaching them to emotion types is important to how we think about stress. Prior to this, it had often been overlooked that appraisals associate with emotions, yet it makes intuitive sense. For example, appraising an event as a threat is likely to precede the emotion of fear, whereas a loss appraisal is likely to precede the emotion of sadness (Smith and Lazarus 1993). Less well articulated are the appraisals associated with positive emotions, but positive appraisals such as that of benefit, gain or challenge may precede emotions such as joy or hope. An early stress researcher, Hans Selye (1974), generally known for his work on physiological responses to stressful stimuli (see later section), had distinguished between good and bad stress; between 'eustress', i.e. good stress associated with positive feelings or healthy states, and 'distress', i.e. the bad kind of

Plate 11.1 Queueing as a potential stressor.
Source: Alamy Images/Imagebroker

Table 11.2 Appraisal-related emotions (Lazarus 1993a)

- *Loss/harm*: sadness, depression, despair, hopelessness
- *Threat*: anxiety, fear, anger, jealousy
- *Challenge*: worry, hope, confidence

---

stress associated with negative feelings and disturbed bodily states. Although he did not detail how these two types of stress differed in terms of physiological response, their distinction remains an important one, and research attempts such as those examining the emotions attached to different forms of stress appraisal go some way towards addressing this distinction.

Also in working with Smith, secondary appraisal became more complex, consisting of four assessments (Smith) or three (Lazarus):

1. *Internal/external accountability ('blame/credit', Lazarus)*: concerned with attributing responsibility for the event; is seen to distinguish between emotions of anger (other-blame) and guilt (self-blame). Credit is less often studied but may associate with emotions such as pride.

2. *Problem-focused coping potential*: considers the extent to which the situation is perceived as changeable by instrumental (practical, problem-focused) coping options. If not perceived as changeable, the emotions of fear and anxiety will be elicited.

3. *Emotion-focused coping potential*: concerned with perceiving an ability to cope emotionally with the situation. Perceptions of not being able to cope are associated with fear, anxiety or sadness.

4. *Future expectancy concerning situational change*: refers to perceived possibilities of the situation being changeable. Sadness is associated with perceptions of unchangeability.

Lazarus merged the second and third assessment, referring simply to 'coping potential'.

The important factor to hold on to from these developments in Lazarus's theory is that the role of emotions is being addressed as well as the cognitions, with both aspects interlinked in an ongoing and dynamic transaction. Furthermore, this theory proposes that emotional impressions of events are stored in memory and will influence how we appraise the same event in any future encounters.

■ Criticism of Lazarus's framework

There appear to be many advantages of the transactional approach and its cognitive appraisal theory; it is compatible with both biological and social models, acknowledging as it does the role of the stimulus, of emotional and behavioural responses, of individual differences and of the external environment. Certainly, in the psychological literature there is a large body of supporting empirical evidence, and few studies of coping with stress or illness are conducted without acknowledging the central role of individual difference variables and appraisals. This will become quite evident in the subsequent chapter. However, no model or theory escapes without criticism, as this is one way in which academic understanding is advanced. Some have criticised Lazarus's framework for its circularity. For example, limited research has attempted to examine the nature of interaction between primary and secondary appraisals, i.e. between perceived demands and perceived coping resources. Demand and coping capacity are not defined separately, leading to claims of the model being tautological (Hobfoll 1989) – put simply, this means that whether an event is demanding or not depends on perceived coping capacity, and whether coping capacity is perceived as adequate or not is dependent on perceived demand! Furthermore, it is unclear whether both primary and secondary appraisal are necessary; for example, Zohar and Dayan (1999) found positive mood outcomes in their sample to be affected mainly by coping potential variables and not by primary appraisal variables. Additionally, they found that stress arose and increased as the stakes or motivational relevance of an event increased, even in situations where coping potential was not restricted. They noted that any slight uncertainty about coping potential modified the effect of 'stakes' (primary appraisal) on stress. Imagine, for example, a situation where a person believes that their forthcoming mid-term examination is a 'mock' and does not count towards their final grade, but on turning up to the exam they are told that it is not a 'mock' but a 'real' exam. In spite of having revised the exam subject seriously and having no major concerns about the topic and their ability to answer the questions, this new situation is likely to be appraised differently because its value has changed (raised stakes), and the stress experience will therefore also change (increase), even though their resources (secondary appraisals of coping potential) have not. Such findings point to a need for further research investigating the interaction between primary and secondary appraisals, and whether the assumption that demands need to outweigh resources in order for stress to be experienced can be upheld.

What do YOU Think?

Which do you think comes first – the thought (appraisal) or the emotion? Is it possible to order them? Think of a recent event that you were happy about – what thoughts were 'attached' to that happiness? Did your feelings about the event change over time and if so, did your thoughts also change? What about an event that made you unhappy – WHY did it make you unhappy? Consider the thought processes. Does Lazarus's model make sense to you?

■ What factors influence appraisal?

While the nature of stimulus events/potential stressors varies hugely, from, for example, receiving a final demand for an unpaid bill to being a victim of a natural disaster, from having a head cold to receiving a diagnosis of a life-threatening illness, certain features of all events have been found to increase the likelihood of their being appraised as stressful:

- events that are *imminent* (e.g. medical results due the next day; driving test that afternoon);
- events that occur at an *unexpected time* in life (e.g. being widowed in one's 40s compared with when in one's 70s; the death of a child);
- events that are *unpredictable* in nature (e.g. being made redundant; sudden bereavement);
- events that are *ambiguous* in terms of
  - personal role (e.g. starting a new job);
  - potential risk or harm involved (e.g. undergoing surgery, taking new medication);
- events that are *undesirable* (e.g. having to move house because of financial loss);
- events over which the individual perceives *no control* (behavioural or cognitive, e.g. noisy neighbours);
- events that elicit high amounts of *life change* (e.g. childbirth, relocation).

Further distinction has been drawn (e.g. Sapolsky 1994: 5) between acute physical stressors, which demand immediate physiological adaptation (e.g. being attacked); chronic physical stressors (e.g. being ill or surviving in a hostile environment); long-term physiological demands that we are not so good at dealing with, such as pain; and psychosocial stressors, which involve our cognitions, emotions and behavioural responses as well as the physiological arousal that will be triggered. Many psychologists would argue that all these are in fact psychosocial as they involve more than simply the event or stimulus. Chapter 12 will deal with the personal and interpersonal influences on appraisals and stress responses.

Lay theories of stress

Before moving on to describing types and potential sources of stress, it is worth stopping to reflect on what has been made clear in the above review of scientific study of stress. Stress is the subject of significant scientific enquiry yet as a subjective construct it is hard to define. As was discussed in Chapter 9 in relation to symptom perception and interpretation and the importance of lay models of illness in the process between perception and response, similarly in relation to stress we are perhaps none the wiser about what the layperson considers to be the causes and consequences of stress even though stress as a concept exists not only in scientific study but in our everyday language. Several authors have studied these understandings in relation to work stress (e.g. Furnham 1997; Rystedt *et al.* 2004; Kinman and Jones 2005) and some have studied understanding of stress in relation to specific illnesses, such as heart attack (e.g. Clark 2003). In a study of fourteen Scottish heart attack survivors, while the understanding of social, personal and situational influences on what was considered to be 'stress' varied significantly between individuals, there was a common view that the stress was a more salient cause of their heart attack than even smoking or diet. This type of understanding and attribution could of course be self-serving! In relation to work stress, lay theories were similarly multifaceted and variable. Interestingly in Kinman and Jones's (2005) study, we find an example of rank or position in a company making a difference (see later discussion of police stress). In this instance it is seen in the differential understanding of the impact of stress – lower-level workers considered the impact of occupational stress to be more personal and requiring of joint efforts by themselves and the organisation if stress were to be managed, whereas managerial workers considered that the responsibility for stress management lay at the feet of the individual workers. This is in spite of agreement that many of the causes of stress were organisational! Such lay beliefs are important given that there is evidence of their longitudinal effects on worker stress, including mental strain (Rystedt *et al.* 2004) and certainly lay theorising about why stress has occurred and what its likely consequences are holds implications for stress management interventions (see Chapter 13).

Now we turn our attention to potential sources of stress – 'potential' sources because, as described above, the role of appraisal is brought to bear on the stimulus and it is this situation – person interaction that determines whether stress as a response, results.

Types of stress

Stress and resource loss

Hobfoll (1989) proposed a 'conservation of resources' model of stress whereby individuals are assumed to work to conserve or protect their valued resources (e.g. objects, roles, personal characteristics such as self-esteem, energy, time, money, skills). Hobfoll suggests that stress will result when there is actual or threatened loss of resources or a lack of gain after investing resources. Resources are thought to be quantifiable and 'real' and therefore 'mean' the same to all people when they are lost. This therefore de-emphasises the role of individual appraisal, central to Lazarus's model. Hobfoll states that the more resources are lost, the more difficult it becomes to replace them, and the greater the resulting stress. This quantification of resources fits with the kind of evidence discussed in Chapter 2, i.e. that of socio-economic deprivation, unemployment and poverty, all of which are found to associate with illness, independent of the individual's appraisals. By focusing on loss of quantifiable entities rather than appraisals, this model avoids any difficulties in distinguishing appraisals from responses. However, Marks *et al.* (2000) point out that the loss and resource constructs are not particularly well defined or easy to measure, and that many questions remain unanswered by this model. For example, how permanent must loss be for a person to experience stress? Does the speed and extent of resource loss matter? Is resource gain never stressful? (Some lottery winners would perhaps challenge this.)

Hobfoll (1991) found that rapid and extensive depletion of valued resources, such as that experienced following a natural disaster, was associated with traumatic stress responses. Natural disasters are generally acute-onset stressors, but many may have long-term consequences. Examples of other acute stressors are given below.

Acute stress

Studies of acute-onset stress generally distinguish between stimulus events that are rare but cataclysmic and more common acute stressors, such as exams.

■ Cataclysmic events

Earthquakes, hurricanes and air disasters are rare events that allow a person little or no preparation time. Natural catastrophes, such as the Asian tsunami in 2004, Hurricane Katrina in 2005, and technological disasters such as the nuclear meltdown at Chernobyl in 1986, produce intense physical and psychosocial suffering for victims and for the 'worried well', i.e. those not actually in the disaster but affected by it in that it raises issues for them about their own personal safety and future. Environmental stress theory (Fisher *et al.* 1984; Baum 1990) considers stress to be a combined psychological and physiological response to demands, and support for this can be found in the many psychological and physical symptoms reported in survivors of a natural calamity. These include:

■ initial panic
■ anxiety
■ phobic fear
■ vulnerability
■ guilt (survivor guilt)
■ isolation
■ withdrawal (including some suicide attempts)
■ anger and frustration
■ interpersonal and marital problems
■ disorientation
■ lack of attachment
■ loss of sense of security
■ sleep disturbances
■ eating disturbances.

Plate 11.2   Environmental events, such as the Asian tsunami, have devastating short-term effects, as shown above, but also have serious long-term effects on survivors, some of whom will experience post-traumatic stress disorder (PTSD).

Source: Rex Features/Cameron Laird

The severity and duration of these effects seem to depend on the magnitude of the loss. In addition to this long list of possible outcomes, some people continuously relive the event in distressing dreams and/or suffer from 'flashbacks'. Such symptoms may lead to the individual being diagnosed as suffering from post-traumatic stress disorder (PTSD; see Chapter 13).

Hobfoll's 'conservation of resources' model of stress was applied in a study of lost resources or 'losses' among 135 individuals assessed following Hurricane Andrew in the United States (Benight *et al.* 1999). This study also investigated the extent to which **coping self-efficacy** (cf. Bandura 1986) determined stress responses and the ability of individuals to recover from their losses by employing their remaining coping resources. Coping self-efficacy was specific to the ability to meet needs following the hurricane, and losses were focused on loss of material resources rather than psychological resources, although both were assessed. Overall, the results confirmed a positive association between loss of resource, coping self-efficacy and subsequent distress. Resource loss was positively associated with long-term distress, with active coping efforts mediating this relationship and reducing the distress experienced.

This study highlights that quantifiable resource loss is in itself distressing, but that appraisals related to coping ability also play a significant role: thus the conservation of resources model has to extend to consider such factors. It is clear that acute-onset stressors can have chronic effects on a person's psychological wellbeing and interventions to minimise distress therefore need to be targeted appropriately. For example, in the case of hurricane survivors, interventions may maximise their effectiveness if they target both the lost resources (e.g. restoration of housing, water, clothing) and the emotions and

coping self-efficacy
the belief that one can carry out a particular coping response in a given set of circumstances.

cognitions (e.g. self-efficacy) of the victims. Stress management and coping-based interventions are discussed fully in Chapter 13.

■ Exam stress

Cohen *et al.* (1986) found that high levels of perceived stress can impair people's memory and attention during cognitive activities. For example, many students report the experience of having the answer to questions on the tip of their tongue, and even memories of revising it the night before, but being unable to remember it once in the exam setting. Others will misread and misinterpret clearly written questions. It has been found that there is an optimum level of arousal necessary to maintain attention and memory, but that too little arousal, or too much, can be detrimental to one's performance. This is known as the Yerkes–Dodson law, first described in 1908 (see Figure 11.2). An exam in a subject where the result is desired and valued will generally elicit more arousal than an exam that is not valued, and the key to good performance lies in not becoming over-aroused so that all the learning goes to waste and the mind empties in the exam room!

Exams have been found to influence healthy and unhealthy behaviour such as smoking, snacking, alcohol consumption and exercise (e.g. Ogden and Mtandabari 1997), and stress arising from both educational factors and family factors predicted smoking among adolescent girls only (Byrne and Mazanov 2003). This association between stress and behaviour is an indirect route by which stress can be considered to influence illness status. Exam stress has also been found to affect bodily responses, such as blood pressure, which was found to increase among medical students on the day of their exams (Sausen *et al.* 1992). This kind of study is required to continuously assess physical indices of **stress reactivity** (such as blood pressure) in order to achieve multiple baselines against which to assess increases and decreases in blood pressure over time and during different activities. To obtain such data, Sausen and colleagues employed ambulatory monitoring techniques whereby

stress reactivity
the physiological arousal, such as increased heart rate or blood pressure, experienced during a potentially stressful encounter.

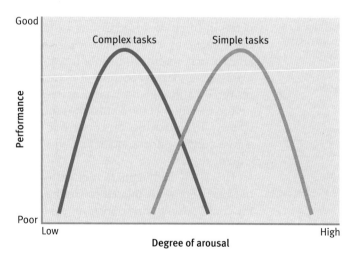

Figure 11.2   The Yerkes–Dodson law.
Source: Rice (1992: 5)

devices attached to individual participants activated at set and regular intervals to read blood pressure.

A link between acute stressors such as exams and actual illness (rather than focusing on physiological reactivity, which is generally short-lived and poses no danger to the individual) has been proposed following findings that students exhibit increased prevalence of infections at exam periods compared with during non-assessment periods. These studies often include blood sampling and have examined immunological markers that have led to the conclusion that for many individuals, exams appear to be sufficiently stressful to increase susceptibility to illness, via immunosuppressant effects (e.g. Kiecolt-Glaser *et al.* 2002. See also the later section on stress as a physiological response).

Chronic stress

■ Occupational stress

The workplace is a good environment in which to study the chronic effects of stress, although many other environmental situations have been studied, for example traffic jams and road rage, noise pollution and overcrowding on public transport (Fisher *et al.* 1984; Topf 1989). Loss of control in these situations appears to play a crucial role in the stress experienced (for discussion of this construct see Chapter 12). Most working individuals will experience workplace stress at some point, and while for many it is short-lived or manageable, for others it is chronic and damaging, being accompanied, for example, by changes in eating or sleep patterns, fatigue or relationship strain. Occupational stress has also been associated with 'burn-out' (Maslach 1982, 1997). Burn-out is considered to be the outcome of chronic long-lasting job stress and is similar to the final stage of Selye's general adaptation syndrome: i.e. exhaustion, both mental and physical (see later section on stress response). Maslach (1997) defined burn-out as a three-part syndrome of emotional exhaustion, depersonalisation and reduced personal accomplishment that occurs among individuals who work with people in some capacity, and which can be associated with both physical and mental ill-health. Related to burn-out is the concept of carer strain or carer burden, identified among many individuals who provide care for dependent relatives (due to chronic illness or disability). Carer strain is discussed in Chapter 15, where we explore the impact of illness on family and friends. Burn-out can also be experienced among professional carers; for example, among nurses burn-out is found to be at moderate to high levels (Barnard *et al.* 2006; Jones and Johnston 2000; Payne 2001; and see RESEARCH FOCUS below).

What is it about some jobs that makes them so stressful? One possible explanation for stress in the work environment is offered by person–environment fit theories (cf. French *et al.* 1982), or the 'goodness-of-fit' approach described by Lazarus (1991b). Such approaches suggest that stress arises because of a mismatch between environmental variables (demands) and person variables (resources). 'Fit' is considered as dynamic rather than static, in that demands and resources can change over time. Early work focused more on environmental features of the workplace than on individual difference variables, a primary example of this being the job demand–control

Table 11.3 Examples of items to assess work-related stress

	Never	Rarely	Sometimes	Often	Most times
Demand					
■ My workload is never-ending					
■ Job deadlines are constant					
■ My job is very exciting					
Control					
■ I have autonomy in carrying out my duties					
■ There are too many bosses					
Predictability					
■ My job consists of responding to emergencies					
■ I am never sure what will be expected of me					
Ambiguity					
■ My job is not very well defined					
■ I am not sure about what is expected of me					

Source: adapted from Rice (1992: 188–2).

(JDC) model of occupational stress, or job strain, put forward by Karasek and colleagues (1979, 1981, 1990). The job features identified as leading to stress included:

■ demand
■ controllability
■ predictability
■ ambiguity.

Each of these broad features can be assessed with specific questions, as illustrated in Table 11.3. Chronic ongoing stressors such as permanently excessive workload demands are thought to create stress in employees, as are sudden, unexpected requests or interruptions, being pushed to make a decision, or being unclear as to what is expected of one. Interestingly, underload, as well as overload, has been found stressful, with frustration and boredom proving as stressful for some employees as overload. This highlights a point central to the study of stress: it is subjective and each individual will construct their own definition of what is stressful 'for them'. This is seen in the findings of an idiographic study of the meaning of stress to five health professionals (neurological consultant – NC, ophthalmology assistant – OA, paediatrician – P, psychiatrist – PS and theatre nurse – TN) where aspects listed as most stressful included work environment factors such as monotonous tasks (NC), maintaining cleanliness (TN), time pressures (NC, TN), full waiting room (P), overload (NC), poor pay or conditions (OA) as well as external factors such as family pressure (PS, P) (Kirkcaldy *et al.* 2000).

Karasek's model proposed that a combination of demand and control would determine whether or not the employee experienced stress (high demand and low control contributing to higher stress–strain than would situations of high demand and high control) (Karasek and Theorell 1990). Karasek's model has been tested and proven useful in many studies. However, while it was initially thought that perceived or actual control acted as a moderator of demand (in other words, that control 'buffered' the negative effects of demands), reviews of studies using the JDC model between

1979 and 1997 (van der Doef and Maes 1998, 1999) found only minimal evidence that control moderated the negative impact of high work demands upon wellbeing, or upon burn-out (Rafferty *et al.* 2001). It appears that demand and control have independent and direct effects on stress outcomes.

Critics suggested that the control component needed to be specified better and that social support, or lack of it, needed to be added to the model (see Searle *et al.* 2001; Van der Doef and Maes 1999 for reviews). This led to an expanded model known as the job demand–control–support model (JDCS) which has since been tested in over a hundred studies. Increasing attention is being paid to aspects of the individual that are potentially more amenable to intervention, such as skills, self-belief or the use of social support. Addressing such factors are several studies carried out among staff in the police force (in a range of countries, e.g. Germany: Kirkcaldy and Cooper 1992; Britain: Brown *et al.* 1996; Wales: Morrison, V. *et al.* 2002; New Zealand: Stephens *et al.* 1997; Scotland: Biggam *et al.* 1997; the Netherlands: Kop *et al.* 1999), an occupation considered to be inherently stressful due to operational, bureaucratic and interpersonal demands. Morrison *et al.*, investigated the personal and occupational sources of stress among 699 police officers and 230 support personnel in North Wales, and explored whether personal resource variables of self-efficacy and optimism and home- and workplace-based support moderated perceived stress and emotional distress. They found that perceived stress and emotional distress were significantly associated with low levels of dispositional optimism, low self-efficacy and low levels of social support at home and in the workplace. Levels of stress and distress were high in both support staff and police officers with those employed in mid-high ranks, such as sergeants and above, reporting higher stress than junior-ranked constables. Rank was also significantly correlated with levels of support used in the workplace, with higher ranks reporting lower levels of access to, and use of, workplace support. Home support was associated with lower stress among support staff, whereas work-based and home support were important to reduced stress among police staff. The personal resources of self-efficacy and optimism were found to moderate stress levels, with females benefiting particularly from high self-efficacy (although as a group females had lower self-efficacy than male colleagues). Support staff generally had lower levels of self-efficacy beliefs than police staff. Occupational stressors were generally identified as being bureaucracy-associated (increased paperwork, poor communication with managers) among mid-low ranked staff and additionally job-overload related in terms of increasing levels of unpaid overtime and the need to take work home among higher-ranked personnel.

The above findings show quite complex effects of rank on the personal resources of self-efficacy and social-support use and on the stress experienced. While rank may not be so explicit in all occupations, the implicit hierarchy that exists in most workforces and its effects upon interactions between personnel is a factor that needs considering in any studies of occupational stress. Illustrating this, conflict with or harassment by other colleagues has been associated with a significant level of staff absenteeism, to the stage where the Royal College of Nursing (RCN 2002) has acknowledged a need to improve interprofessional and intraprofessional communication and management style. Workplace-based interventions targeting both the work environment as well as individuals stress responses have shown considerable success in enhancing physical and emotional wellbeing and also productivity – outcomes of importance to both employee and employer (e.g. Brabantia Work Health Program, Maes and van der Doef 2004). Some models of occupational stress have therefore succeeded in integrating what the individual brings to the workplace in terms of personal characteristics, cognitions and support resources with the environmental features, with different occupations producing different results and hence differing opportunities for intervention (see RESEARCH FOCUS, and Chapter 13).

Attempts to challenge or resolve issues of overload, underload or ambiguity of role are not always easy or feasible in many workplaces, and coping behaviour has been found to include health-damaging behaviour, for example excessive alcohol consumption and absenteeism (e.g. among Scottish police officers, Alexander and Walker 1994). These responses also carry huge costs for employers in terms of loss of productivity, staffing shortages and accidents in the workplace (Cooper and Payne 1988).

RESEARCH FOCUS

Stressful occupation, coping and mood disturbance in a nursing sample

Healy, C.M. and McKay, M.F. (2000). Nursing stress: the effects of coping strategies and job satisfaction in a sample of Australian nurses. *Journal of Advanced Nursing*, 31: 681–8.

Background

The transactional model of Lazarus and colleagues (e.g. Lazarus and Folkman 1984; Lazarus 1991b) proposes that events and how they are appraised, and the emotional reactions elicited, influence coping, and hence various outcomes including self-reported stress, distress, and other more objective indicators as described in this chapter. Previous studies of nursing stress have found positive associations between work stress and subjective reports of mental distress, including incidences of stress-related burn-out and emotional disorder (for a review see McVicar 2003). However, the nursing environment, as perhaps with other professional environments where involvement with the public is central, such as the police force, has strong internal sanctions operating against 'showing symptoms of stress'. In order to cope with these constraints, it has been suggested that nurses may be using avoidant forms of coping, and humour, neither of which may be adaptive in the long term.

Aims

This study aims to explore the relationship between stress, coping, job satisfaction and mood disturbance where a positive association was hypothesised between higher perceived stress, avoidance coping and mood disturbance, and a negative association between approach coping (problem solving), humour, job satisfaction and mood disturbance.

Methods used

A total of 129 registered nurses from Melbourne metropolitan and Victoria regional hospitals in Australia volunteered to complete a survey comprising of open-ended questions and the following standardised questionnaires: the Nursing Stress Scale (NSS, Gray-Toft and Anderson 1981), the Ways of Coping questionnaire (WOCQ, Folkman and Lazarus 1988) the Coping Humour Scale (CHS, Martin and Lefcourt 1983), the Job Satisfaction Scale of the Nurse Stress Index (Harris 1989) and a shortened version of the Profile of Mood States (Shacham 1983).

Results

Results for the NSS indicated that 'workload' was the highest perceived stressor, with items in this sub-scale tapping into issues arising from the actual physical environment, such as actual workload, inadequate staffing levels and insufficient time to complete nursing tasks. As hypothesised, higher scores on the NSS were concurrently and significantly associated with more negative mood and less job satisfaction. Contrary to hypotheses, coping-humour scores were not associated with stress or mood scores, whereas escape-avoidance coping was significantly and positively related. Regression analyses were conducted in an attempt to 'predict' mood as assessed by the POMS (NB: This is, however, a cross-sectional study). Escape-avoidance coping of an emotion-focused type was predictive of poorer mood, and surprisingly, humour also appeared to predict greater, not less, mood disturbance. Humour did not mediate the effects of stress on mood disturbance.

Conclusions

The finding that higher levels of perceived nursing stress, particularly related to workload, was associated with negative mood states, is not unexpected. Heavy physical work and demanding workloads in the face of continuing staff shortages are well-documented and acknowledged sources of stress. However, it is worth noting (Healy and McKay do not) that not all studies have found this association: for example, workload was not associated with burn-out among a sample of female hospice nurses (Payne 2001, and see McVicar 2003 for a review). One of the reasons for such differences between study findings is likely to lie in the sample or setting differences (e.g. registered general nurses vs. palliative or hospice nurses), although another likely factor which Healy and Mckay's findings highlight is that of coping (see Chapter 12 for a full discussion of coping). Although avoidance coping was reported as being the least used coping strategy, when it was used it was associated with greater mood disturbance. The negative finding for humour is considered by the authors as possibly resulting from the fact that humour is used to release tension after the stressor event has passed rather than at the time of it – however, this is not testable in the current study.

Given that stress specifically related to workload factors was found to explain more variance in mood disturbance than nurses' coping responses, this study would appear to point to organisational interventions aimed at reducing workload as being more appropriate and of more potential benefit to staff than interventions targeting the individuals themselves in terms of their coping strategies. This contrasts with the conclusion of McVicar following his review of 21 studies, where he states (p. 640) that 'Development of preventative strategies will be hindered until employers enable individualized coping strategies, and research enables understanding of personal and workplace interactions and provides a means of assessing the intensity of distress experienced by individuals.' This conclusion concurs with the potential intervention targets highlighted in the study of police stress described earlier where perceived stress and emotional distress were significantly associated with aspects of the individual, i.e. low levels of dispositional optimism and self-efficacy and aspects of their home as well as work environment in terms of perceived levels of social support (Morrison, V. *et al.* 2002).

Therefore, the paper selected for review here highlights the fact that stress is subjective and influenced by individual as well as environmental features. While the focus has been on occupational stress in this section, the reader is directed to Chapters 14 and 15 for a discussion of illness and caring for someone with illness as other potential life stressors.

We have thus far established that stress responses arise from events and from appraisals of these events, but we have not yet described what happens following these cognitive or emotional processes. Lazarus's transactional model of stress posits that appraisals and their attached emotions lead to cognitive and behavioural coping efforts, and in Chapter 12 coping theory and the role of coping in moderating stress outcomes is discussed fully. However, in addition to psychological stress responses, there are also biological and physiological responses, and it is to this growing area of research that we now turn our attention.

Stress as a physiological response

Thinking of stress as a response takes us into the domain of seeking biological or physiological explanations of how stress affects the body and potentially illness; the assumption here is that stressors place demands on the person that are manifested in some response; in physics, this response would be termed 'strain'. Proponents of the 'response' model of stress describe how individuals react to danger or potentially harmful situations or even pleasant demands with a coordinated physiological and behavioural response (e.g. Cassel 1974, cited in Leventhal and Tomarken 1987). Initially, an event has to be appraised, and this involves the **central nervous system** (CNS). The sensory information and the appraisal of the event combine to initiate autonomic and endocrine responses, which feed back to the cortex and limbic system, which in turn links with the hypothalamus and brainstem. It has been found that, for example, appraising an event as *unpredictable* in nature affects various aspects of physiological activation (Zakowski 1995).

These processes are summarised below, although Chapter 8 provides greater physiological definition and detail.

central nervous system
that part of the nervous system consisting of the brain and spinal cord.

Early work on the stress response

An early researcher, Walter Cannon (1932), outlined the role of catecholamines (adrenaline and noradrenaline), which, when released from the adrenal glands of the **sympathetic nervous system** as hormones, heighten arousal in order to facilitate the 'fight or flight' response. When faced with imminent danger or a high level of threat (such as when being charged at by an angry dog), the typical response is one of physical arousal – dry mouth, increased heart rate, rapid breathing. It is this arousal that signifies the release of adrenaline, a hormone that enlarges the autonomic responses and facilitates the release of stored fuels for energy, which enables the rapid response of either running away or fighting the threat. This 'fight or flight syndrome', Cannon reasoned, was *adaptive* because it enabled quick responses to threat but also *harmful* because it disrupted emotional and physiological functioning and if prolonged could contribute to many medical problems (early animal work confirmed this, with dogs and monkeys exposed to prolonged periods of stress producing excessive hydrochloric acid in the stomach,

sympathetic nervous system
the part of the autonomic nervous system involved in mobilising energy to activate and maintain arousal (e.g. increased heart rate).

contributory to ulcer formation). In other words, in situations of chronic or ongoing stress, this fight–flight response would not be adaptive.

Subsequent to Cannon another physiologist, Hans Selye (1956), discovered (quite accidentally while conducting animal research into the sex hormones), that a triad of responses commonly followed the unpleasant injecting procedures used – the adrenal glands enlarged, the thymus gland shrank and ulcers developed in the digestive tract. He followed up his early findings with over forty years of research using different aversive stimuli (injections, heat, cold, exercise), and came to the conclusion that there were universal and non-specific responses to stress: i.e. the same physiological responses followed a range of stimuli, whether pleasant or unpleasant, and that the 'fight–flight' response was only the first stage of response to stress (e.g. Selye 1974). Selye's model of stress is known as the **general adaptation syndrome**. The response to stress was seen to be an innate drive of living organisms to maintain internal balance, i.e. homeostasis, and he proposed that it did so in a three-stage process:

general adaptation syndrome
a sequence of physiological responses to prolonged stress, from the alarm stage through the resistance stage to exhaustion.

1. *Alarm reaction*: the awareness of a stressor is the initial response that can cause a downturn in bodily defences, and blood pressure and heart rate may initially decrease before rising to higher than normal levels. Selye stated that this arousal could not be maintained for long periods. He attributed his stress response to activitation of the anterior–pituitary–adrenal cortex system, although exact physiological processes only became clear some years later (Pinel 2003; Selye 1991; and see later section).

2. *Stage of resistance*: the next stage is where the body tries to adapt to a stressor that has not subsided in spite of resistance efforts made during the acute/alarm stage. Arousal decreases from that seen in the alarm stage but is still higher than normal, and Selye noted that this stage of mobilisation of bodily defences could not last indefinitely without the organism becoming vulnerable to illness.

3. *Stage of exhaustion*: exhaustion would occur if the resistance stage lasts too long, resulting in a depletion of bodily resources and energy. At this stage, the ability to resist the stress declines, and Selye proposed the increased likelihood of 'diseases of adaptation' such as cardiovascular disease, arthritis and asthma.

Later work on stress responses

Cannon's and Selye's work stimulated a huge amount of research into the physiology of stress. Much of it has not confirmed Selye's proposed 'non-specific response', as different physiological responses have been found to be associated with different kinds of stressor. Evidence for this comes from consistent findings of experimental studies carried out in the 1980s; for example, an experimental study that exposed participants to different types of challenge (mental or physical) and took continuous blood samples during exposure found that blood levels of adrenaline were increased during mental stress, whereas noradrenaline increased during physical stress (Ward *et al.* 1983, cited in Rice 1992).

However, there is a large and growing body of evidence that shows that adverse events (and positive events) produce physiological changes. Typical stress responses (e.g. rapid and deeper breathing, increased heart rate, sweating or shaking) result not just from activation of the anterior–pituitary–adrenal cortex system as Selye thought but also from increased activity of the sympathetic branch of the autonomic nervous system (ANS). The ANS can be divided into two connected systems – the sympathetic nervous system (SNS) and the parasympathetic nervous system (PNS) – which 'exist in a state of dynamic but antagonistic tension' (Rice 1992: 126). The SNS is involved in arousal and expenditure of energy (such as during a 'fight–flight' response), whereas the PNS is involved in reducing arousal and in restoring and conserving the body's energy stores (such as during rest) (see Chapter 8). Both systems control the actions of many internal organs, such as the heart and skeletal muscles, with their activity initially mediated by the neurotransmitter acetylcholine. Acetylcholine links the neurons of the spinal synapse to the brainstem, where the nerves then act on their target organs. Mediation in the sympathetic branch is provided by noradrenaline (adrenergic fibres) and, to a lesser degree, adrenaline; whereas in the parasympathetic branch, acetylcholine (cholinergic fibres) makes this final link.

The stress response is maintained following short-lived sympathetic arousal by neuroendocrine responses resulting from activation of the sympathetic–adrenomedullary system (SAM) and release of the catecholamines adrenaline (epinephrine) and noradrenaline (norepinephrine), those in brackets being the US terms, from the adrenal glands. This activation of the adrenal medullary system, in conjunction with the more crucial action of the hypothalamus in activating the pituitary–adrenal cortex (the hypothalamic–pituitary–adrenocortical (HPA) system), enables our bodily organs to alter their usual function to facilitate an adaptive stress response even in situations of prolonged stress.

The HPA system originates in the hypothalamus, which releases its own hormone, corticotrophin-releasing factor (CRF), which controls the anterior pituitary gland in its secreting of ACTH (adrenocorticotrophic hormone). ACTH then travels to the adrenal gland, where the hormones adrenaline and noradrenaline are released, as well as stimulating glucocorticoid secretion from the adrenal cortex, in particular the hormone cortisol. While Cannon's early model described the role of adrenaline, Selye was more interested in adrenocortical responses. We now know that circulating glucocorticoids provide energy for the 'alarm phase' as the release of glucocorticoids into the bloodstream regulates the levels of glucose in the blood from which energy can be drawn. Almost every cell in the human body contains glucocorticoid receptors, and hormones such as cortisol affect every major organ system in the body. For example, cortisol inhibits glucose and fat uptake by tissue cells so that more can be drawn on for immediate energy, it increases blood flow, it suppresses immune function by inhibiting the action of phagocytes and lymphocytes, and it inhibits inflammation of any damaged tissue (e.g. Antoni 1987; Dantzer and Kelly 1989). The suppression of the immune system caused by increased blood-circulating cortisol (serum or s-cortisol) can make a person vulnerable to infection. However, it has been noted following a review of evidence relating to endocrine responses in stressful situations, that cortisol activity undergoes extinction when exposed to chronic stress or to repeated acute stressors (Rose 1980, cited in Kasl 1996; Nicolson and van Diest 2000).

HPA activation also elevates the production of growth hormones and pro-lactin, beta endorphins and encephalin, which are also found in the brain in response to stress and are thought to play a role in immune-related disease and in problems such as depression. Beta endorphins have a useful analgesic (pain-killing) function and as such may explain why people can endure high levels of pain until they succeed in escaping stressful situations or completing demanding tasks: for example, soldiers with extreme injuries have been known to crawl long distances to receive help, and athletes can complete races in spite of damaged muscles (e.g. Wall 1979).

These responses within the autonomic nervous system and the endocrine (hormonal) system work together to prepare our bodies to meet the demands of our environment. Our autonomic nervous system may work 'behind the scenes', but its functions are essential to basic human responses. The duration of some of the stress responses, such as the release of cortisol, influences whether the responses are beneficial to the organism or not. As previously noted, cortisol production over long periods of time can actually damage immunity, as seen in animal research where long-term exposure to such glucocorticoids was found to damage neurons in the hippocampal formation (Antoni 1987; Sapolsky 1986; Sapolsky 1996). This area of the brain is crucial to learning and memory, with a link being proposed with ageing (Sapolsky *et al.* 1986), although human research is required to address this further. Prolonged release of adrenaline and noradrenaline is also known to have negative effects, including suppressed cellular immune function, increases in heart rate and blood pressure, heartbeat irregularities (arrhythmia) and, potentially, hypertension and heart disease (Fredrickson and Matthews 1990).

The need for combined psychological and physiological understanding of stress can be seen in the subsequent sections where evidence of an association between stress and physiological pathways is considered and then explored in relation to various illness conditions.

Stress and immune function dysregulation

Declines or alterations in immune function have frequently been associated with the experience of stressful life events (e.g. Ader 2001; Dantzer and Kelley 1989; Glaser and Kiecolt-Glaser 2005; Salovey *et al.* 2000). The immune system, as described in Chapter 8, is the body's defence against disease. It operates by producing certain types of cell that operate against foreign organisms (e.g. bacteria, poisons, viruses, parasites) and abnormal cells (e.g. cancer cells) in the blood and lymphatic systems. These potential threats to the body are known as antigens, and their threat can be met by either a general first line of defence, or a more specifically targeted defence. Immune cells are white blood cells of two major types, lymphocytes and phagocytes, which can be found in the lymphatic system, in the lymph nodes, spleen and in the blood circulation. The second of these, phagocytes, are attracted to sites of infection due to tissue releasing chemical messengers, and when they reach their destination they destroy abnormal cells or antigens by engulfing and consuming them. They provide what is known as 'non-specific immunity' in that they offer a first general line of defence. Lymphocytes on the other hand offer 'specific immunity'. This involves 'cell-mediated immunity' via lymphocyte action (triggered by a subtype of phagocytes, a macrophage) where lymphocytes consist of T cells made in the thymus (CD4+ T cells or helper T cells, and CD8+ cells or cytoxic T cells) and also 'humoral-mediated immunity' involving B cells (memory and plasma cells). B cells label invading antigens in order to identify them for destruction and also 'remember' the antigen to enable early detection of future attacks. Their plasma produces antibodies, which remain in the blood circulation until the germ or disease is no longer present.

Natural killer (NK) cells also occur in body plasma and slow down the growth of abnormal cells (in cancer, for example) so that other immune responses can form an attack. As with phagocyte action, the NK cells provide non-specific immunity in that they defend against a wide variety of antigens, whereas the specific immunity provided by B and T cells is to specific antigens that they have been sensitised to (see Table 11.4 for a summary of T and B cell roles). Each type of cell, NK, B and T, interact and help one another in the fight against infection or the growth of abnormal cells (see Chapter 8 for further details of the action of each of these cell types, and also for a discussion of specific conditions associated with 'faulty' immune system function i.e. diabetes, rheumatoid arthritis, multiple sclerosis).

The immune system is also affected by the workings of the sympathetic nervous system and the endocrine responses described earlier; for example, the HPA system causes the release of hormones such as cortisol from the adrenal glands, and these hormones are thought to stimulate the immune system. Unfortunately, cortisol appears to damage T and B cells and increase a person's susceptibility to infection, not decrease it (see Chapter 8). It is now generally accepted that there is communication both within and between the neuroendocrine and immune systems, with the brain providing an immunoregulatory role (e.g. Blalock 1994).

What is important to health psychologists is that studies have found a link between the proliferation of B, T and NK cells and the subjective experience of stress; in other words, they have shown that psychological stress interferes with the workings of our body. One early study by Kiecolt-Glaser *et al.* (1984) found a significant reduction in NK cell activity among students prior to important end-of-term exams compared with those tested in mid-term. In addition, those students who reported feelings of loneliness plus a high number of recent stressful life events showed significantly less NK cell activity at

Table 11.4 Specific immunity and cell types

Humoral immunity: B cells	Cell-mediated immunity: T cells
Operate in the bloodstream	Operate at level of the cell
Work by releasing antibodies, which then destroy the antigen	Include memory, killer, helper (CD4+) and suppressor T cells
Include memory cells	Mature in the thymus and not the bone marrow as other white blood cells do

both times than those students who were low in life events and low in loneliness. This evidence was simultaneously being confirmed elsewhere, but it took a long time for the findings of such experimental studies to be accepted, because these findings necessitated a paradigm shift from where the body was thought to operate independently of the mind to acceptance of the fact that psychological factors could influence immuno-competence (i.e. the degree to which our immune system functions effectively). Since the late 1970s, work in the area of psychoneuroimmunology (the study of how psychosocial factors interact with the central and peripheral nervous system and the immune system) has gone from strength to strength, with improvements in technologies leading to even greater developments in the twenty-first century (compare the classic reviews of Herbert and Cohen 1993 and Cohen and Herbert 1996, with more recent work, e.g. Vedhara *et al.* 2001; reviews, e.g. Vingerhoets and Perski 2000, and textbooks, e.g. Ader 2007).

■ Age and immune function

It is generally accepted that immune function declines with age. This is sometimes referred to as 'immunosenescence' whereby the innate system of an immediate immune response to invading germs, and also the slower-acting immune resistance response, declines (Gomez *et al.* 2005). There is evidence, from animal and human studies, suggesting that NK cell function becomes less efficient even though they are increased in number in older people, and that pro-inflammatory cytokine activity is also increased. The importance of these findings lies in the fact that they place older people at greater risk of severe reactions to infections, as seen in the figures for deaths from influenza for example, or in the complications of inflammation following wounds or surgery and slower healing. Additionally, Graham *et al.* (2006), following a review of the current evidence, have suggested that in young adults stress can mimic the effects of aging, and in older adults, stress can exaggerate the effects of aging on immune competence. While this is a relatively underresearched area as yet, studies of caregivers are certainly pointing to significant associations (see Chapter 15).

Stress and cardiovascular reactivity

There is also a reasonably consistent body of psychobiological evidence showing that stress can cause alterations in physiological responses, in some people more than others. This 'reactivity hypothesis' first proposed by Krantz and Manuck (1984) describes how genetic or environmental factors combine to influence a person's vulnerability to a physiological response following stress and negative emotion that is likely to be detrimental to their health, particularly their arterial health implicated in heart disease. Reactivity, for example periods of elevated heart rate or blood pressure, is seen in both laboratory settings where individuals are exposed to acute or repeated stress, such as mental arithmetic tasks or public speaking, and in real-life settings where people face occupational challenge or marital conflict, for example. Whether or not this CVR (cardiovascular reactivity) is related to the development of disease, or indeed disease progression, is something of great interest to psychobiologists and psychologists alike (e.g. Johnston 2007; Linden *et al.* 2003) although evidence is mixed, as seen in a subsequent section where we review the role of stress in cardiovascular disease.

Evidence of the influence of psychological stress upon immune function, or upon cardiovascular reactivity has provided scientists with the opportunity to assess 'objective' indices of the stress response alongside, and in relation to, subjective stress reports. For example, Burns, V. *et al.* (2003) examined the effects of minor and major life events on the antibody response to influenza vaccination among a sample of undergraduate students. Students were followed up over five months and results found that participants with low antibody levels at five months reported having experienced significantly more life events in the intervening time following vaccination. Although a relatively small-scale study, if replicated in larger studies, such findings would have implications for the long-term success of vaccination programmes. Evidence of physiological correlates of occupational stress have also been reported, for example Clays *et al.* (2007) found that the ambulatory blood pressure at work, home and even while asleep, was significantly higher in workers with high job strain than in those with lower strain. Students are often used as participants in this area of research due to the 'occupational hazard' of exposure to potentially stressful patterns of assessment and examinations. Chandrashekara *et al.* (2007), for example, found that medical students with high anxiety and poorer emotional adaptability about end-of-term exams showed lower levels of an inflammatory cytokine (tumor necrosis factor alpha – TNF-a) than students with lower anxiety and greater emotional adaptability. The effect was not seen for mid-term exams, similar to that reported in the 1984 study of Kiecolt-Glaser *et al.* mentioned above. Such situation-specific responses contrasts with other findings where exposure to non-academic stressors contributed to a delayed *increase* in circulating cytokine levels (Steptoe *et al.* 2001). More research on these responses is warranted, particularly studies which contrast stressor types and contexts, as well as consider other individual difference variables that may contribute to stress reactivity (see Chapter 12). In terms of the implications of such findings for psychological intervention, there is some evidence that immune conditioning effects can be achieved (see Miller and Cohen 2001 for a meta-analytic review of 85 studies of psychological interventions and immune functioning) whereby individuals can be 'trained' using classical or operant conditioning procedures to alter immune response to threat. However further work, including better controlled studies that also address potential mediators of any shown effects, is needed.

It should therefore have become clear during the course of this chapter that stress is not a unitary process but a highly complex one. The experience of stress is, to varying degrees, dependent on stimulus events (acute or chronic, physical or psychological), on internal representations of events, including a person's appraisals and emotional responses, and on the nature and extent of physiological and behavioural activation that follows. Stress indisputably has a strong psychological component, and furthermore stress responses change over time as a person adjusts (or not) to their situation. Given all the evidence reviewed above, it is hardly surprising that measuring stress is complex, and some of these complexities are described in ISSUES below.

Can stress be measured?

As with any concept, the manner in which it is defined will influence how it is measured or assessed. We have described three broad ways of thinking about stress – as a stimulus, as the result of cognitive appraisal and as a physiological response – and each of these views leads to different forms of assessment.

Measuring stress as a stimulus is problematic, given what was described earlier as weaknesses in the life events approach to stress – if many of the life events are irrelevant to the responder because of their age or life stage, does this mean that they are less stressed because their potential total scores are reduced? Additionally, people generally search for explanations for how they feel or for events that have happened to them – it is common, for example, for people to report many life events in the lead up to a heart attack – so measuring retrospective accounts of life events or even smaller 'hassles' may in this instance lead to inflated estimates of the role that stress plays in illness.

Stress is based upon appraisal, which involves stimulus, cognition and emotion, and therefore it is necessary to measure people's appraisals of the stimulus event, their emotions, their perceived resources and their perceived coping potential. Stress appraisals tend to be assessed by simply asking people how they feel or getting them to complete a standardised psychometric assessment. One commonly employed example is the Perceived Stress Scale, which assesses the degree to which life situations are appraised as stressful (Cohen *et al.* 1983). Examples include 'In the last month, how often have you been upset because of something that happened unexpectedly?' and 'In the last month, how often have you found that you could not cope with all the things you had to do?' (scored as 0 = never; 1 = almost never; 2 = sometimes; 3 = fairly often; 4 = very often). Higher scores are indicative of greater perceived stress. The stressor, or the event being considered is not specified in the standard wording of this scale, thus general appraisals are assessed only. Some studies, however, reword the PSS to record event-specific stress appraisals, e.g. 'In the last weeks since receiving your diagnosis . . .'

In order to assess secondary appraisal processes central to Lazarus's model, research studies also commonly employ measures of personal resource, such as self-efficacy or perceived social support, which are thought to moderate, mediate or 'buffer' the stress–outcome relationship (see Chapter 12). Regardless of the number of assessment tools used, however, there are inherent limitations in assessing an experience as subjective as stress. For example, distress is likely to bias the answers one gives to questions regarding the nature of the stressor, or regarding the number of recent life events experienced. Being anxious or depressed is also likely to influence the resources one considers to have available. There is substantial evidence pointing to the fact that aspects of the stress experience interact, and therefore it is necessary for research studies to disentangle precursors of a stress response from the stress response itself.

In terms of assessing individual responses considered to be indicative of stress, many studies will include a measure of distress or more specific mood states (e.g. anger, depression or anxiety). One commonly used instrument is the general health questionnaire (GHQ; Goldberg and Williams 1988). There are various GHQs, which vary in the number of items included. The twenty-eight item version measures a combination of emotional states (anxiety, insomnia, social dysfunction, severe depression and somatic symptoms), whereas the commonly employed twelve-item version does not distinguish between each of these, although it has still proved a sensitive measure of psychiatric disorder. Respondents indicate whether

continued

they have experienced a particular symptom or behaviour 'less than usual', 'no more than usual', 'rather more than usual' or 'much more than usual', and example items include 'have you recently . . . been able to concentrate on whatever you're doing? . . . been feeling unhappy and depressed? . . . felt constantly under strain?' This scale and other measures of mood or distress are most commonly used as measures of stress outcome.

Stress as a response can be measured using physiological and physical indices such as heart rate, blood pressure, galvanic skin response, levels of adrenaline, noradrenaline and cortisol levels in the blood or saliva, other indicators of increased cortisol levels such as reflected decreases in salivary secretory immunoglobulins (Sig-A), or other immune responses such as described earlier in relation to helper T cells, B or NK cell activity. Measurement of these aspects of the stress experience require specific skills and expertise in their collection, storage, analysis and interpretation (see Vedhara *et al.* 2001). However, even such so-called 'objective' measures of stress are open to question, as some people are quite simply more 'stress-responsive' or 'stress-reactive' than others (Felsten 2004; Johnston 2007). For example, the level of heart-rate or blood-pressure increase seen in response to threat is not universal, as a result of genetic differences, variations in central nervous system activity (Lovallo 1997) and other individual differences such as personality (e.g. neuroticism, hostility), appraisals and past experience (Lazarus 1999) (see Chapter 12 for a review of such factors).

In spite of challenges of measurement, a vast amount of research is conducted in this field that acknowledges that since stress is a subjective experience, measuring it cannot expect to be an exact science. As Kasl (1996: 21) states: 'What we have, at best, are indirect and partial indicators of the stress process, and these indicators tend to measure both too much and not enough'. As an illustration of this, he refers to the perceived stress scale, which measures 'too much' in that it correlates significantly with depression and measures 'not enough' in that it does not assess secondary appraisal processes, emotions or indicators of physiological re-activity. As this chapter has hopefully indicated, stress is by its very essence complex, and you will discover through your wider reading that many empirical research studies have acknow-ledged this by adopting multiple methods of assessment.

The final challenge in the domain of stress research is that of establishing causality between stressful events and illness, ideally via immune or other physiological pathways. The concluding section of this chapter therefore describes some of the evidence that stress is associated with the development of illness.

The stress and illness link

In Chapter 8, the workings of the nervous, respiratory, digestive, cardio-vascular and immunological systems were described in some detail and the reader was introduced to common diseases associated with these bodily sys-tems. This final section takes a closer look at the role of stress in activating these systems with resulting implications for the development of illness. First, however, it is worth knowing that there are different ways of viewing the relationship between stress and illness.

The direct route

As described above, stress can produce physiological changes that may lead to the development of illness, particularly in instances where the stress is chronic rather than brief (Cacioppo *et al.* 1998; Johnston 2007; Smith *et al.* 2003). However, there is so much individual variation in responding to stressors that the direct route is complex (e.g. Esterling *et al.* 1996; Vedhara *et al.* 1999). The mixed evidence for direct effects of stress on the development of specific diseases is reviewed below.

The indirect routes

- People, by virtue of their behavioural responses to stress such as smoking, eating habits and drinking, predispose themselves to disease (see Chapter 3). Such behaviour may serve coping functions (see Chapter 5).
- People, by virtue of certain personality traits, predispose themselves to disease by the manner in which they respond to stress (see Chapter 12).
- People experiencing stress are more likely to use health services than people who are not under stress. Stress can produce symptoms such as anxiety, fatigue, insomnia and shakiness, which people seek treatment for but which are not in themselves illnesses (see Chapter 12).

However, we should bear in mind a quote of Sapolsky's throughout the reading of the next sections: 'everything bad in human health now is not caused by stress, nor is it in our power to cure ourselves of our worst medical nightmares merely by reducing stress and thinking healthy thoughts full of courage and spirit and love. Would it were so. And shame on those who sell this view' (1994).

There is a moderate relationship between stress and illness and this is best illustrated by selectively reviewing the evidence, as we do below. We can of course only address a selected few of the many illnesses that have been found to have an association with stress. Psychosocial influences upon, or moderators of, the stress response are discussed in Chapter 12.

Stress and the common cold

Cohen and his colleagues (Cohen *et al.* 1993a, 1993b; Cohen *et al.* 1998) have conducted a series of experiments where volunteers submitted themselves to artificial exposure to respiratory rhinoviruses of the common cold (using nasal drops mainly). Participants then remained in a controlled environment for varying lengths of time while researchers waited to see whether colds or infections develop more often among those who received viral drops than among the control subjects, who received saline drops. Volunteers who had reported more chronic negative life events, perceived stress, negative affect and poor coping responses prior to the experiment were more likely to develop signs of respiratory infection and subsequent colds than both control subjects and experimental subjects with low-level life stress. Perceived stress and negative affect predicted infection rates, whereas negative life events did not predict infection itself but predicted the probability of illness among those who became infected. These associations persisted when health behaviour such as smoking and alcohol consumption or personality variable such as self-esteem and introversion–extroversion were controlled for. Similarly, Stone *et al.* (1993) found a similar dose–response relationship between the number of stressful life events experienced prior to the introduction of a rhinovirus and the subsequent presentation of cold symptoms.

Although the results relating to stress and susceptibility to influenza have been inconsistent and predominantly lab-based using artificially induced viruses, the work of Cohen's research group, summarised in their 1998 paper, provides convincing evidence of a relationship between chronic stress (as opposed to severity) and the common cold. They controlled for other potential influences such as mood and smoking behaviour and hoped to identify a physiological or immunological pathway that mediated the stress–colds relationship, but they failed to find one despite taking many careful neuroendocrine and immune function measures (Leventhal *et al.* 1998). More recent work has, however, supported chronic stress–immune response – cold and influenza association (Marsland *et al.* 2002; Takkouche *et al.* 2001). This latter study importantly also considered the naturally acquired common cold. They carried out a one-year prospective cohort study among the faculty and staff of a Spanish university (N = 1,149) and found that the occurrence of stressful life events, perceived stress, positive and negative affect were all related to the occurrence of common cold.

There is still some way to go before full understanding of how stress operates and, in particular, how it operates in real-life environments. This has been achieved to some extent in studies of real-life stress and cardiovascular reactivity, although reactivity in itself is not 'disease', but a risk factor (Johnston 2007). We return to this work in the next section.

Prospective studies with clinical populations facing 'natural' stressors will inevitably improve our understanding of the stress–immune function–illness link. While some evidence exists that stress-mediated physiological changes play a role in the initial onset of disease among healthy individuals (such as coronary heart disease), there is more evidence that stress experienced by 'ill' individuals can affect further progression of their symptoms or disease. We review some of this evidence below.

Stress and coronary heart disease

cardiovascular
pertaining to the heart and blood vessels.

Coronary heart disease (CHD) is a disease of the **cardiovascular** system that develops over time in response to a range of factors, such as family history and lifestyle factors (e.g. smoking and diet; see Chapter 3). As described in Chapter 8, the cause of CHD is a gradual narrowing of blood vessels that supply the heart. In situations of acute stress, activation of the sympathetic nervous system causes increased cardiac output and the blood vessels to constrict, thus restricting blood flow, so blood pressure increases. This can cause damage to the artery walls, a process that is contributed to further by stress-induced adrenaline and noradrenaline output. If blood pressure remains raised for prolonged periods of time, a person is said to have hypertension, a contributory factor in CHD.

Repeated or chronic stress also activates the sympathetic nervous system's release of fatty acids into the bloodstream, which, if not utilised for energy expenditure, are metabolised by the liver into cholesterol. A build-up of cholesterol is highly implicated in the 'furring up' of arteries or atheroma (the laying down of fatty plaques on artery walls), and a key feature of heart disease is this atherosclerosis. Furthermore, the release of catecholamines during the stress process also increases the stickiness of blood platelets (thrombocytes), which elevates the risk of a clot forming or thrombosis as they adhere to the artery walls with the fatty plaques, thus making the 'passageway' narrower for blood to flow through. Inflammatory processes, involving proinflammatory cytokines such as IL-6 (interleukin-6), are also implicated in this process (see Chapter 12 in relation to hostility). If reduced blood flow causes a clot to form, it could then travel through a person's arteries until it becomes so big as to form a blockage (occlusion) and depending on whether it blocks an artery to the brain or to the heart, this will lead to either a stroke or a heart attack – both major causes of mortality worldwide. (Chapter 8 also discusses these processes.)

In terms of CHD, stress does appear to contribute to various related conditions, such as hypertension, elevated serum lipids (fats in the blood) and smoking behaviour, an acknowledged risk factor (e.g. Ming *et al.* 2004). Cardiovascular reactivity during acute stress (i.e. the extent to which a stressor produces cardiac arousal such as increased heart rate or blood pressure) has been implicated in various disease processes, such as the extent and progression of carotid artery atherosclerosis, and the emergence of coronary heart disease itself (Smith *et al.* 2003). Experimental studies of reactivity in response to aversive or rewarding stimuli have speculated that the individuals who responded to aversive tasks with sizeable heart-rate and blood-pressure increases (high reactives) but who showed no difference from controls in subjective ratings of the tasks, had greater activation of the hypothalamic system and neuroendocrine responses such as those described earlier. Indeed, high-reactive participants showed larger noradrenaline increases in response to both types of task than low-reactive participants and larger cortisol increases to the aversive task but not to the reward task (Lovallo *et al.* 1990). This highlights the importance of considering the type of task. Also important is finding whether effects persist outwith the artificial laboratory setting. This has been achieved, for example, by Johnston and colleagues (Johnston 2007) who found that laboratory-based reactivity was reflected in similar increases in heart rate reactivity when individuals were exposed to the real-life stressor of public speaking.

What this section points to is a need to distinguish between chronic stress and its role in potentiating certain risk behaviours which provide the 'indirect' link with chronic manifestations of CHD, e.g. smoking and arterial disease; and acute stress events which appear implicated in the potentiating of acute coronary events, such as heart attacks (Johnston 2002, 2007; Strike and Steptoe 2005).

Speculation as to the role of stress in the development of actual disease has abounded for many years; for example, Rosch (1994), in an editorial in the journal *Stress Medicine*, pointed to the importance of distinguishing between causal factors and contributing factors when considering disease, arguing that the 'true cause' of any disease is biomedical and that behavioural or social factors such as smoking or stress are not 'true' causes but contributors. This conclusion seems to have been challenged through research developments over the past decade or more, in that the evidence of causality in relation to acute coronary events and to CHD does seem to implicate stress reactivity and also negative emotions (depression primarily). We know from many years of research that the mind and body interact, and if into this we add individual 'risk' or 'protective' behaviours (see Chapters 3–4), we can begin to understand the complexity of influences upon disease processes such as those subsumed under the broad heading of 'heart disease'.

Finally, just as reactivity can be considered as a 'psychophysiological trait' that is stable within any given individual across time and events, it can also be considered as a moderator, in that evidence suggests that being reactive or not will moderate any effect of stress upon disease risk: in other words, stress poses a greater threat to the health of high-reactive individuals than it does low-reactive individuals (Segerstrom and Smith 2006). Furthermore, as discussed in Chapter 12, stress reactivity can itself be influenced by other traits, such as anger, and therefore reactivity is considered within a broader personological model. However reactivity is considered, it is a factor that seems unwise to ignore.

Stress and cancer

Cancer, like heart disease, develops slowly and begins with mutation of cells and the development of generally undetectable neoplasms, which eventually develop into spreadable tumours (i.e. the cells metastasise). Forms of cancer vary hugely in terms of rates of growth, spread and prognosis; in terms of their sensitivity to neuroendocrine or immune system changes (Greer 1999), and in terms of available treatment options. Accordingly, it is perhaps unwise to expect stress to exert uniform effects, if any, on different forms of cancer. There has also been caution in adopting a biopsychosocial perspective on this group of diseases because of concerns about overstating the role of the individual and their cognitions, emotions and stress or coping responses in cancer progression (Spiegel 1992). Stress may, however, affect tumour cell mutation by slowing down the cell repair process, possibly by virtue of its effects on hormonal activation and the release of glucocorticoids, or by influences on the immune system's production of lymphocytes (see Rosch 1996 for a review of both animal and human research).

A meta-analysis of forty-six studies investigating the association between psychosocial factors, including life event stress, and the development of breast cancer concluded that breast cancer could not be explained by life events, but it could by a combination of risk factors and psychosocial factors (McKenna *et al.* 1999). This is consistent with findings of another meta-analysis specifically examining the predictive role of life events in breast cancer development (Petticrew *et al.* 1999). The general consensus is that there is no clear link in terms of cancer aetiology, although there is mixed evidence in terms of stress and cancer progression or recurrence. For example, a recent review of 24 studies reported that 19 studies showed an association between depression and faster breast cancer progression (Spiegel and Giese-Davis 2003). In terms of life events and progression, Palesh *et al.* (2007) presented data from 94 women with metastatic or recurrent breast cancer tumours and found that those with no retrospective reports of traumatic life events, or lesser stressful events, had a significantly longer disease-free interval than women with experience of traumatic events, or of stressful events (median of 62 months as compared to median of 31 months). Women who had experienced traumatic events, or lesser stressful events, did not differ from women reporting no stress events, in terms of current age, age at diagnosis, medical history, relationship status, cortisol levels, site of metastases, and disease status indicators that may have offered alternative explanations for the findings. It is worth noting, however, that the reported events had not necessarily occurred in the intervening time period (i.e. between first diagnosis and recurrence) and therefore some had potentially played a role in the initial cancer. The authors had hypothesised that the mechanisms through which stress exerted any effect on recurrence was likely to relate to HPA function, yet cortisol did not differ between groups. However, this study is limited by its retrospective nature and in fact a five-year prospective study of women diagnosed with breast cancer found that recurrence was not increased in those who had experienced one or more extremely stressful events in the year prior to diagnosis or in the five years subsequently (Graham *et al.* 2002). This finding is perhaps more robust, given that their study involves a larger sample of women, is prospective in nature, and more clearly controls for biological prognostic indicators such as tumour size and the extent to which the cancer involved the lymph nodes.

In addition to exploring the relationship of stressful events to cancer outcomes, many other studies have explored whether personality, coping style (particularly one that is passive and indicative of helplessness and hopelessness) and mood affect cancer outcome (Walker *et al.* 1999; and see Spiegel 2001 for a brief discussion of the literature). These issues have provoked some controversy and are addressed more fully in Chapter 12.

Stress and bowel disease

Two diseases of the bowel have been investigated in terms of their association with the experience of stress. In both, stress is examined as an exacerbating factor rather than one involved in the aetiology of the condition (see also Chapter 8). First, *irritable bowel syndrome* is a disorder of the lower large intestine characterised by abdominal pain and prolonged periods of either diarrhoea or constipation, although no organic disease is identifiable. Naliboff *et al.* (1998) note that during stressful episodes, the reactivity of the gut is greater and symptoms such as bloatedness, pain or diarrhoea increase. A second bowel disease is *inflammatory bowel disease* (IBD), which can be subdivided into Crohn's disease (CD) and ulcerative colitis (UC). These diseases are both typified by pain and diarrhoea, which worsen and improve in an alternating and disruptive manner. UC is typified by inflammation of the lower colon, whereas CD can occur anywhere in the gastrointestinal tract and is seen as inflammation of the outer intestinal wall (see Chapter 8). Both diseases, as with IBS, were originally thought to be psychosomatic; however, evidence that stress plays a role in their aetiology is limited, although stress may exacerbate the condition, being associated with symptom 'flare-ups' (Searle and Bennett 2001). This is also reported by Duffy *et al.* (1991) who examined exposure to stressful events among 124 individuals and found that over a period of six months, those exposed to stress showed a two- to fourfold increase in clinical disease episodes compared with those participants who did not report stressful incidents. When the authors distinguished between disease-related and disease-unrelated events (on the basis of patient report), the relationship between stress and illness was clearest when the reported events were health-related but not necessarily IBD-specific. When the authors examined the issue of time lag between event and disease activity (i.e. a stressful event preceding disease activity), they found instead that concurrent relationships were strongest. Furthermore, their results showed that disease activity was predictive of subsequent levels of stress. Such bidirectional relationships between variables makes the disentangling of issues of cause and effect difficult.

In addition, individual variation in stress-responsivity/reactivity may explain mixed research findings. Illustrating this point, Dancey *et al.* (1998) used repeated measures of daily stress and daily symptomatology obtained from thirty-one IBS patients to examine the associations between stress and symptoms over time and found that only in half of the sample was an association evident between stress and the onset or exacerbation of symptoms. As described in Chapter 9, symptom perception and reactivity can also be influenced by personal characteristics of somatisation and attention to internal organs, often features associated with neuroticism.

Stress and HIV/AIDS

Over the past twenty or so years, AIDS has spread throughout the world to become a major cause of death in Africa and a leading cause of death elsewhere (see Chapter 3). AIDS (acquired immune deficiency syndrome) is a syndrome characterised by opportunistic infections and other malignant diseases, and until the HIV (human immunodeficiency virus) was identified in 1984, the cause of such immunosuppression was unclear. The nature of the HIV virus and how it infiltrates the body is described in Chapter 8, but crucially, in terms of potential stress for the sufferer, as a lentivirus (i.e. slow-acting) it can be many years before an HIV-infected individual develops AIDS. As well as being life-threatening, the disease label itself can be psychologically stressful due to the continued social stigma attached to the disease (due primarily to its early associations with homosexuality, drug abuse and sexual promiscuity). Petrak *et al.* (2001) found that self-disclosure of HIV status to family (53 per cent of sample had told their family) and to friends (79 per cent had told close friends) was significantly influenced by wanting to protect others from distress and out of fear of discrimination. Living with this illness is inherently stressful, and although there is only limited suggestion that stress influences the likelihood of infection when exposed to the virus (Marks *et al.* 2000), there is evidence that stress plays an influential role in disease progression. Evidence is particularly strong when moderating variables such as depression, social support and coping responses are taken into consideration. For example, a meta-analysis (Zorrilla *et al.* 1996) suggested that depressive symptoms, but not stress experience, were associated with increased speed of symptom onset in HIV-positive individuals, and that stress, but not depressive symptoms, was associated with reduced NK cell count. Similarly, progression to AIDS was found to be quicker in those experiencing a build-up of stressful life events, depressive symptoms and low social support (Leserman *et al.* 1999). Other studies have also reported associations between baseline depression and a CD4+ cell decline (Burack *et al.* 1993) and in the same sample nine years later, faster progression to AIDS (Page-Shafer *et al.* 1996).

Within this disease group, a sad reality is that many individuals will face the loss of a partner through AIDS, which itself has been found to impact upon disease progression over subsequent years (Kemeny *et al.* 1994). Social support, or lack or loss of it, is discussed in Chapter 12, however, social support in the form of providing care to a loved one is considered in the final section of this chapter, as the demands of the carer role have been shown to impact upon carer health.

Stress and carer health

The nature, intensity, duration and frequency of stressor events have been found to influence the nature and extent of immune change in a dynamic manner in part dependent on the state of the immune system at the time the stressor event occurs (Dantzer and Kelley 1989). One population that has been relatively frequently studied in this regard is carers of those with chronic disease, for example those caring for elderly relatives with Alzheimer's disease. Ongoing mental, physical and social demands of caring have been found to cause stress among many elderly carers, stress that has been found to manifest itself immunologically, for example in terms of reduced wound healing (Kiecolt-Glaser *et al.* 1995); see also IN THE SPOTLIGHT), increased illness episodes compared with healthy controls (Kiecolt-Glaser *et al.* 1991) and reduced antibody build-up following vaccination (Kiecolt-Glaser *et al.* 1996), although studies of younger carers have not consistently supported such findings (e.g. Vedhara *et al.* 2002). For a fuller discussion of the effects of caring, see Chapter 15. Most research into the physical consequences of carer stress have examined the increased vulnerability to disease resulting from immune changes rather than actual disease development, for example raised levels of the pro-inflamatory cytokine Interleukin-6 found among caregivers is at a level considered a risk factor for cardiovascular disease (Kiecolt-Glaser *et al.* 2003).

IN THE SPOTLIGHT

Can stress prevent your wounds healing?

Janice Kiecolt-Glaser and Ronald Glaser have spent many years researching the mind–body relationship, in particular the relationship between the experience of stress and immune function. While this chapter has presented evidence of the physiological pathways underlying stress responses, you may not have stopped to consider how stress might affect you, not just in terms of potentially increasing your risk of diseases such as heart disease but in terms of more day-to-day health challenges, such as wounds received while participating in sporting activities. The Glasers have shown in many studies of elderly carers of people with Alzheimer's disease that healing of experimentally induced tissue wounds took significantly longer among carers than among healthy age-matched control participants. However, this may in part be due to coexisting ageing processes, so further studies have explored whether similar effects can be found in younger samples. Vedhara and colleagues in Bristol (2003) examined the healing rates of foot ulcers among sixty adults with Type 2 diabetes. They found that healing was reduced in those who had shown high anxiety, depression or stress. Importantly, similar effects of stress have been found on the healing rates of otherwise healthy students who are given a small experimental skin wound at two different times, one during

continued

the summer holiday, the other prior to sitting exams. The wound inflicted before exams took on average three days longer to heal, and this was reflected by decreases in immunological status (Marucha *et al.* 1998). Broadbent *et al.* (2003) have confirmed the impairing effects of high stress and worry levels on wound healing where wounds were not experimental but real, i.e. participants were recovering from hernia surgery.

Why do all these findings matter? Think of your own stress levels; think of your likelihood of becoming wounded in sport or other activity; or of the potential to be facing surgery in the future. Think of current concern about MRSA (methicillin-resistant *Staphylococcus aureus*) and *C difficile* infections in hospitals and in the community. Effectively dealing with your own stress is important, not only in keeping you healthy but also in helping you to heal and recover when and if you become ill or injured or require surgery.

Summary

This chapter set out to provide a definition of stress and has shown that there is no such thing as a simple definition of this phenomenon. Stress is generally examined in one of three ways: as a stimulus that focuses on the external event (stressors); as a transaction between the external event and the individual experiencing it; and as an array of physiological responses that are manifested when an individual faces demanding events. The transactional psychological model of stress highlighted the crucial role of appraisal and points to the importance of considering the individual in the stress experience. Many different events may be appraised as stressful, and stressor events can be acute or chronic in their manifestation and in the responses they require. Examples of these were presented, with particular emphasis on occupational stress, something that most of us will experience at some time. The physiological pathways by which stress has been shown to affect health status were examined, and these processes were explored further in relation to evidence (or not) of their direct role in diseases such as coronary heart disease and cancer. While some evidence of a direct effect of stress on the development of illness exists, many of stress's effects are either indirect, for example via an influence on behaviour, or are more evident during the illness experience, when individual differences in personality, cognitions and social resources become important to outcome. These moderating variables are the focus of the next chapter.

Further reading

Key texts
Rice, P.L. (1992). *Stress and Health*. California: Brooks/Cole.
Although dated in terms of the empirical material reviewed, this book is a good starting point for clearly written and well-resourced coverage of the stress process, from theory to intervention, including biological, cognitive and social explanations.

Sapolsky, R.M. (1994). *Why Zebras Don't Get Ulcers*. New York: Freeman.
Another well-written and engaging book on the subject of stress with excellent coverage of both physiological and psychological theories. You will, however, need to supplement reading of this book with reading of up-to-date empirical studies such as those referred to in this chapter!

Ader, R. (2007). *Psychoneuroimmunology*, 4th edition. New York: Academic Press.
This text book is written for an interdisciplinary audience including behavioural scientists, psychobiologists, neuroscientists and immunologists. The book covers key topics in PNI research and provides up-to-date and expert commentary on the processes, mechanisms and effects of behavioural, neural, endocrine and immune responses.

Key articles

Lazarus, R.S. (1993). From psychological stress to the emotions: a history of changing outlooks. *Annual Review of Psychology*, 44: 1–21.
This article provides a useful account of the transactional model of stress and the developments in thinking about appraisal in terms of relations with emotions.

Johnston, D.W. (2002). Acute and chronic psychological processes in cardiovascular disease. In K.W. Schaie, H. Leventhal and S.L. Willis (eds), *Effective Health Behavior in Older Adults*, New York: Springer (pp. 55–64).
This article provides a clear and comprehensive overview of the empirical evidence pertaining to the contribution of acute and chronic stress and related negative emotions to heart disease.

McVicar, A. (2003). Workplace stress in nursing: a literature review. *Journal of Advanced Nursing*, 44: 633–42.
This article describes the psychological and physiological indicators distinguishing between positive stress (eustress), distress (e.g. depression. anger, fatigue) and severe distress (e.g. burn-out) in a well-written review of papers published between 1985 and 2003. Many of the findings are relevant to other occupations.

Graham, J.E., Christian, L.M. and Kiecolt-Glaser, J.K. (2006). Stress, age and immune function: toward a lifespan approach. *Journal of Behavioral Medicine*, 29: 389–400.
This well-written paper catalogues the key findings relating to the relationship between age and immune function, stress and immune function (considering both acute and chronic stressors), and the interaction between stress, age and the immune function, with a particular, but not exclusive, focus on older adults.

The International Labour Organization website:
http://www.ilo.org/public/english/protection/safework/stress/nursing.htm
Provides access to a wealth of global materials regarding occupational stress. The link above takes you specifically to details of a manual on stress prevention which was commissioned by the ILO specifically to consider nursing stress. The full report can be ordered via this website and is referenced below.

Cox, T., Griffith, A. and Cox, S. (1996). Work-related stress in nursing: Controlling the risk to health. (CONDIT/T/WP 4/1996), available from ILO as detailed above.

 Visit the website at **www.pearsoned.co.uk/morrison** for additional resources to help you with your study, including multiple choice questions, weblinks and flashcards.

CHAPTER 12

Stress and illness moderators

Learning outcomes

By the end of this chapter, you should have an understanding of:

- coping theory, definitions and the distinction between coping styles and coping strategies
- coping functions and goals
- how coping responses influence the manner in which stress may affect health outcomes
- aspects of personality, such as neuroticism, hostility and optimism, which influence stress appraisal, coping response and illness outcomes
- aspects of individual cognitions, such as personal control, efficacy and hope, which influence stress appraisal, coping response and illness outcomes
- aspects of emotion, such as depression and emotional expression, which influence stress appraisal, coping response and illness outcomes
- the nature and function of social support and how it influences stress appraisal, coping responses and illness outcomes

CHAPTER OUTLINE

The preceding chapter established that stress can be considered as both an objective and subjective experience, and evidence was provided as to physiological and immunological pathways by which stress may influence health and illness status. However, not all people will become ill when exposed to stressful events, and this raises questions of great fascination to health psychologists. What aspects of the individual, their stress responses, or their stress-coping resources moderate or influence the negative impact of stress on health? This chapter will present evidence showing that psychosocial factors are crucial to stress appraisals, responses and outcomes. Individual differences in personality, cognitions and emotions (both positive and negative) have direct and indirect effects on stress outcomes. Indirectly, such factors affect outcome via their influence upon cognitive and behavioural responses to stressful demands placed on us – these efforts are known as coping. In addition, aspects of social relationships and social support act as external resource variables, which directly and indirectly influence the negative impact of stress. Evidence as to the direct and/or moderating role of such variables will be presented and their importance examined. By the end of the chapter, the complexities of the relationship between stress, health and illness should be clear.

In Chapter 11 we described stress theories, acute and chronic stressors and the broad theoretical links between stress and disease. We also presented evidence relating to direct pathways by which physiological and immune processes affect the stress–disease relationship. As there is so much individual variation in responding to stressors, this chapter focuses more on the indirect routes introduced in Chapter 11, i.e. how different personalities, beliefs and emotions influence the stress–illness relationship, either directly, or via an effect on cognitive and behavioural coping responses.

It is unlikely that anyone can avoid stress, and certainly, as indicated previously, some stress is good for us (eustress); but negative appraisals and negative emotions generally elicit a desire to reduce such thoughts and feelings in order to restore a sense of harmony or balance in our lives. Lazarus's transactional model of stress and coping (Lazarus 1966; Lazarus and Folkman 1984) was introduced in the previous chapter and highlights the crucial role of appraisal of events. Individual differences in appraisal in turn influences the cognitive, emotional and behavioural response to them, i.e. the coping response. What exactly do we mean by coping?

Coping defined

Although over thirty definitions of coping exist, Lazarus's transactional model (see Figure 11.1) has had the most profound impact on the conceptualisation of coping (cf. Lazarus 1993a, 1993b; Lazarus and Folkman 1984). According to this model, psychological stress results from an unfavourable person–environment fit: in other words when there is a perceived mismatch between demands and resources as perceived by an individual in a specific situation (Lazarus and Folkman 1984; Lazarus 1993a). Individuals are required to alter either the stressor or how it is interpreted in order to make it appear more favourable. This effort is called coping.

Coping is viewed as a dynamic process involving a constellation of cognitions and behaviour that arise from the primary and secondary appraisals of events, and the emotions attached to them (see Chapter 11). Coping is *anything* a person does to reduce the impact of a perceived or actual stressor, and because appraisals elicit emotions, coping can operate to either alter or reduce the negative emotions, or it can directly target the 'objective' stressor. Coping does not inevitably succeed in eliminating the stressor, but it may manage the stressor by various means, for example through mastering new skills to deal with it, tolerating it, reappraising it or minimising it. Coping is concerned therefore with trying to achieve adaptation.

Cohen and Lazarus (1979) described five main coping functions, each of which contribute to successful adaptation to a stressor:

1. reducing harmful external conditions;
2. tolerating or adjusting to negative events;
3. maintaining a positive self-image;
4. maintaining emotional equilibrium and decreasing emotional stress;
5. maintaining a satisfactory relationship with the environment or with others.

Coping responses may succeed in one or more of these tasks, but adaptation may not necessarily be long-lived, depending upon the context and the nature of the stressor. It is unlikely that any person would cope with flu in the same way as they would a diagnosis of cancer, or would cope with failing a driving test the second time in the same way as they coped with failing the first time.

Coping can be cognitive or behavioural, active or passive, with many different, often overlapping, terms being used in the coping literature. Two of the main coping taxonomies are summarised in Table 12.1: firstly those which differentiate between problem-focused and emotion-focused coping (cf. Folkman and Lazarus 1980, 1985); and secondly those which distinguish between approach-oriented coping and avoidance (cf. Roth and Cohen 1986; Suls and Fletcher 1985). Within each of the broad dimensions described in Table 12.1 are a variety of coping sub-scales, generally derived from factor analysis of a large number of coping items in an attempt to identify statistically meaningful 'clusters' of items that can then be used in a new measurement scale. Folkman and Lazarus (1988), in the popular Ways of Coping scale, distinguish eight sub-scales that address the two dimensions of problem-focused and emotion-focused coping: confrontive coping, distancing, self-controlling, seeking social support, accepting responsibility, escape–avoidance, planned problem solving and positive reappraisal. Carver and colleagues (1989) distinguish thirteen, and latterly fifteen, sub-scales: planning, active coping, suppressing competing activities, acceptance, turning to religion, venting emotions, seeking instrumental support, seeking emotional support, humour, positive reinterpretation, restraint coping, denial, mental disengagement, behavioural disengagement, alcohol or drug use (COPE scale). In contrast, Endler and colleagues (Endler and Parker 1993; Endler *et al.* 1998) assess across three dimensions: *emotion-oriented* (person-oriented strategies such as daydreaming, emotional response or self-preoccupation); *task-oriented* (strategies to solve, minimise or reconceptualise

Table 12.1 Coping dimensions

1. **Problem-focused coping (problem-solving function)** i.e. instrumental coping efforts (cognitive and/or behavioural) directed at the stressor in order to either reduce the demands of it or increase one's resources. Strategies include: planning how to change the stressor or how to behave in order to control it; suppressing competing activities in order to focus on ways of dealing with the stressor; seeking practical or informational support in order to alter the stressor; confronting the source of stress; or showing restraint.

   Versus

   Emotion-focused coping (emotion-regulating function) i.e. mainly, but not solely, cognitive coping efforts directed at managing the emotional response to the stressor; for example, positively reappraising the stressor in order to see it in a more positive light; acceptance; seeking emotional support; venting anger; praying.

2. **Attentional/approach, monitoring, vigilant, active**, i.e. concerned with attending to the source of stress and trying to deal with the problem by, for example, seeking information about it, or making active cognitive or behavioural efforts to manage the stressor (see also coping styles).

   Versus

   Avoidant, blunting, passive, i.e. concerned with avoiding or minimising the threat of the stressor; sometimes emotion-focused, sometimes involves avoiding the actual situation; for example, distraction by thinking of pleasant thoughts or distraction by engaging in other activities to keep one's mind off the stressor; disengagement through substance use.

the problem) and *avoidance-oriented* (includes distraction or social diversion (CISS scale). Krohne (1993) described vigilance and cognitive avoidance as two coping 'superstrategies' which he considered were orthogonal dimensions of attention orientation and likely to reflect underlying personality, therefore being indicative of a coping 'style'.

Coping styles or strategies

Coping styles are generally considered as unrelated to the context or to the stressor stimulus; instead, they are trait-like forms of coping that people have a tendency to adopt when facing a potentially difficult situation. If you think about your own behaviour you will probably know whether you tend to duck and avoid stressors or whether you face them head-on! One example of a coping style dimension is that of 'monitoring versus blunting' (Miller 1987; Miller *et al.* 1987). Monitoring reflects an approach style of coping, where threat-relevant information is sought out and processed, for example asking about treatments and side-effects, or seeking information about forthcoming exam content. Blunting reflects a general tendency to avoid or distract one-self from threat-relevant information, such as by sleeping or daydreaming, or engaging in other activities. Van Zuuren and Dooper (1999) examined the relationship between monitoring and blunting coping styles and engagement in disease detection (e.g. attending doctor if frequently feeling tired, having blood pressure checked) and preventive behaviour (e.g. eating low-fat diet, exercising regularly). Monitoring was modestly, but significantly, associated with both detection and preventive behaviour, and individuals with a dominant blunting style were less likely to engage in protective behaviour than those where blunting was less dominant. In contrast, among a sample of women with cancer, monitoring was associated with negative responses of increased feelings of vulnerability and elevated distress, and the authors propose that this tendency to scan for and amplify threatening cues can be counter-productive (Miller *et al.* 1999). The conflicting outcomes of a monitoring style of coping shown by these two studies highlights the importance of context – a persons' coping style may not 'fit' the situation and as a result may be counter-adaptive. This is where the adoption of situation-specific coping strategies is important.

Coping strategies (see Table 12.1 for examples of commonly employed coping sub-scales) derive from an approach that considers stress and coping as a dynamic process that varies according to context, event and the person's personal resources, mood, and so on. Coping at any one time might include a range of seemingly oppositional strategies. For example, Lowe *et al.* (2000) found that in the months following a heart attack, people used both passive coping (e.g. acceptance, positive reappraisal) and active, problem-focused coping simultaneously. In a similar vein, Macrodimitris and Endler (2001) found that a combination of instrumental and distraction coping strategies were employed by people with diabetes. There is some evidence that individual differences in aspects of personality influence the extent to which people are flexible in their choice of coping strategy (see later section).

While coping research in the field of health psychology more commonly assesses coping strategies than styles, the two approaches can be addressed simultaneously. For example, studies adopting repeated assessment periods can examine the nature and consistency of coping strategies over time, with consistent use of specific strategies suggesting a 'style' of coping (e.g. Tennen *et al.* 2000). Other studies can explore explicit associations between aspects of personality and specific coping responses (for example, the effects of neuroticism and extroversion (see Watson, D. *et al.* 1999) or of optimism (e.g. Carver and Scheier 2005) on coping). These issues are addressed later in this chapter.

What is adaptive coping?

Lazarus's model of coping suggests that it is hard to predict which coping strategies will be effective in which situations, as both problem-focused and emotion-focused strategies are interdependent and work together to create the overall coping response in any situation (Lazarus 1993b). Tennen *et al.* (2000) confirmed this in an impressive longitudinal study of pain patients where daily measures of coping were taken. They found that emotion-focused coping strategies were 4.4 times more likely to be used on a day when problem-focused strategies were also used than on days where problem-focused strategies were not used. They also report that day-to-day pain symptomatology influenced the coping strategies used on a daily basis; for example, 'an increase in pain over yesterday's pain increased the likelihood that problem-focused coping yesterday would be followed by emotion-focused coping today' (p. 632). This highlights the role of appraisal and reappraisal of coping efforts: modifications are made depending on whether previous coping efforts are thought to have been successful or not.

Coping is highly contextual – to be effective it has to be amenable to change (see Figure 11.1 in the previous chapter, where there are arrows

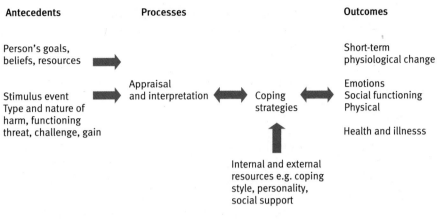

Figure 12.1   The coping process.
Source: adapted from Lazarus (1999: 198)

feeding back from coping to (re)appraisal, and also Figure 12.1). If the stressor event is starting a new job and this is eliciting anxiety, coping can either deal with the 'job' (make contacts with new colleagues, research the company and its products), or it can deal with the anxiety (talk with a friend, get drunk). It should not be assumed, however, that coping in a way which addresses the problem directly (researching the new role) is inherently more adaptive than coping which does not (getting drunk); there are some situations where emotion-focused coping, or even avoidant coping, is adaptive.

Generally, it is considered that problem-focused or attentional coping is more likely to be adaptive when there is something that can be done to alter or control the stressor event. Focusing one's thoughts on aspects of the situation and planning how to deal with each would be an example of a cognitive problem-focused coping strategy, whereas seeking helpful information about the event would be a behavioural problem-focused coping strategy. On the other hand, emotion-focused or avoidant coping is more likely to be adaptive where the individual has little control over the event or if their resources to deal with it are low. Cognitive emotion-focused coping would be reflected in a person exhibiting denial or attending to other thoughts as a means of distraction, whereas behavioural examples of this form of coping could include venting and displaying emotion, or seeking emotional support.

Individuals who are typically problem-focused, vigilant or attentional in their coping with stress may find that in some circumstances this is counterproductive. When facing life-changing surgery for example, or on receipt of a diagnosis of a life-threatening illness, avoidant coping may be more adaptive. For example, denial has been shown to be an effective coping response among women with a recent breast cancer diagnosis (Carver *et al.* 1993; Greer *et al.* 1990); however, among Greer's sample, ongoing denial was associated with poorer fifteen-year survival outcomes, as were coping responses reflecting stoic acceptance, anxious preoccupation with the illness and helplessness/hopelessness.

One psychological coping response known as 'fighting spirit' (e.g. 'I am determined to beat this disease') was associated, in early studies of this construct, with improved outcomes and long-term survival among breast cancer patients (Greer *et al.* 1979; Greer *et al.* 1990). In contrast, feelings of hope-lessness and helplessness (e.g. 'I feel there is nothing I can do to help myself') were associated with poorer survival among this same population (Watson, M. *et al.* 1999a) and among stroke patients (Lewis *et al.* 2001). These coping responses of fighting spirit and helplessness differentially associate with either active, problem-focused or passive, avoidant coping behaviour. Fighting spirit reflects a kind of realistic optimism and determination, with people high in fighting spirit tending to face the illness head-on rather than avoid it (Spiegel 2001). Findings such as these elicited hope for interventions that could enhance disease outcomes by targeting such attitudes and coping responses, for example increasing fighting spirit while decreasing feelings of helplessness. However, some authors have questioned these findings; for example, a review of twenty-six studies investigating the coping styles of fighting spirit or hopelessness/helplessness and cancer survival or recurrence concluded that many of the reported predictive associations between such variables were limited by restricted sample sizes or poor methodological quality of the studies (Petticrew *et al.* 2002). Furthermore, recent studies have failed to replicate long-term predictive associations. In particular, a ten-year follow-up of 578 women with early-stage breast cancer whose coping and mood status had been assessed at baseline following diagnosis, found that while helpless/hopelessness remained predictive of survival outcome, the relationship between fighting spirit and outcome did not (Watson *et al.* 2005).

Finally, in relation to coping and adaptation, Stanton *et al.* (2000) have pointed out that emotions can have adaptive coping functions rather than disruptive functions as implied in the emotion-focused coping distinction. In a series of studies, they examined 'emotional-approach coping' and distin-guished between 'emotional processing' (active attempts to understand the emotions experienced) and 'emotional expression'. Both forms of coping associated with indicators of positive psychological adjustment (see later section on emotional expression).

The RESEARCH FOCUS below highlights that maintaining distinctions between emotion-focused and problem-focused coping is sometimes difficult, as movement between them is ever-present.

RESEARCH FOCUS

Coping strategies of young adults with cancer

Miedema, B., Hamilton, R. and Easley, J. (2007). From 'invincibility' to 'normalcy': coping strategies of young adults during the cancer journey. *Palliative and Supportive Care*, 5: 41–9.

There is a relatively large literature on middle-aged and older adult coping responses – to diagnosis, to treatment, to later stages of the disease – and there is a steadily growing body of work addressing those diagnosed in childhood, but there is limited work addressing those diagnosed in early adulthood (17–20 through to 44 years generally speaking, although stud-ies vary in the cut-offs used). This is a stage of life which, according to Erikson (see Chapter 1) is considered as one of intimacy, work and relationship commitment and self-reliance, leading up to mid-adulthood generativity. Receiving a diagnosis of a potentially life-threatening disease is therefore generally one which had not been anticipated 'yet', and one which places demands on the individual that require coping with. The majority of coping research uses quantitative methods of assessment using questionnaires which ascertain the nature and frequency of use of a range of listed coping strategies, some of which are described in this chapter. However, there is a body of work which takes a qualitative approach, seeking to understand (rather than only describe) the experiences of those with cancer. This study set out to do this through interviews with young adults with cancer and three central phenomena emerged in the interviews – delayed diagnosis, support issues and coping strategies. The current paper addresses the latter of these.

Method

Participants
Face-to-face interviews were carried out with 15 young adults, aged between 21 and 43 years who had been diagnosed with cancer when aged between 20 and 35 (the definition of young adulthood adopted in this study). Of these individuals 9 were considered as 'survivors' in that they had completed treatment, although it is not clear which of the sample are those who had had cancer twice (n = 4, 3 of whom had had a recurrence, one had a new primary cancer). The sample is therefore mixed in terms of their cancer stage and history.

In this study interviewers were gender-matched; the male researcher interviewing the 6 male participants and one of the two female researchers interviewing the 9 female participants. This was done on the assumption that participants 'might be more comfortable discussing intimate details' with a same-sex interviewer.

Method of analysis
The chosen method applied to the tape-recorded and transcribed interview data was Grounded Theory, whereby the verbatim accounts are read in turn and the codes (themes) generated are compared to those arising from previous interviews, until no new codes emerge (this is known as saturation point). Codes were discussed within the research team and memoed in terms of their categories and properties; using an iterative process, subsequent interviews follow a trail suggested in a previous interview. In this way the theory is developed, and 'grounded' in participants' own accounts, while also being confirmed in discussions with the research group. Cross-coding and categorising the data ensures 'fittingness'. For this paper the focus is on the 'strategies and intervening conditions that influenced participants' coping approaches', and the authors apply Folkman and Lazarus's theory of coping (see this chapter) as a framework for interpretation of their findings.

Results
The coping strategies described span from the time 'before cancer' through time of diagnosis, treatment and treatment outcomes, and the authors present a 'model' of the young adults' coping strategies.

The coping strategies were seen to be rooted in their 'pre-cancer' lives but to have developed as they received information, endured physical hardship, interacted with others involved in the cancer experience (family, friends, health professionals), and reflected on their experience. The 'goals' were firstly to survive the illness and its treatment, and secondly, to get back to 'normalcy'. The strategies used included: information, interactions, and perceptions at the point of diagnosis, taking action, seeking control, and adapting over the treatment phase and

continued

into the subsequent phase (which could be simply post-treatment, being in remission, or for some, reaching a palliative stage where treatment could not offer success) where situating 'self' was important. These themes reflect aspects of coping that interacted with each other. In the pre-cancer life accounts, feelings of having been 'invincible' were seen, where home and work life had been taken for granted. Participants thought that they had their lives ahead of them, then came the diagnosis of cancer:

> 'Cause at that age, you think that nothing's going to touch you, nothing is going to go wrong, and that [being diagnosed] completely shatters everything you believe.

The crucial importance of having existing support networks was acknowledged as they started the cancer 'journey'. Cancer brings with it a new language and new experiences; not having support was thought to hinder effective coping.

> I've never forgiven them for not being there when I had my surgery
> > (34-year-old female, only child, talking of parents)

After diagnosis participants talked of accessing information, often via the internet (which sometimes was too much for them to deal with); and of looking at their relationships – some adult participants found it hard to deal with thoughts of their illness being somehow out of turn, i.e. facing a life-threatening illness before their parents. Some participants felt they needed to shield their parents from their illness. In terms of the relationship participants had 'with' their illness, there were many differences, from those who saw the cancer as an 'opponent' that had to be beaten or a 'game' to be won, to illness as being a part of them (personification) or not 'This is not really me, it is not really attached'. These beliefs were thought to influence the coping responses made, although the authors could have illustrated these links more fully. Waiting for treatment was stressful for participants and their families – with a perceived need to get it going. Coping with this included behavioural strategies such as doing relaxation exercises or focusing efforts on staying healthy through diet and exercise, and many used cognitive strategies such as positive self-talk or goal setting. Such actions can be considered to constitute problem-focused coping, i.e. gaining control over aspects of one's illness or treatment. Loss of control is a common experience following diagnosis and in this young-adult group several found that renewed dependency on parents or family could be compensated for by trying to do things for oneself. Adaptation to the reality of being sick was considered important and this was achieved in a variety of ways that helped get them through treatment. Towards the end of treatment participants coped by reflecting on their experiences and that of others they had met; they 'situated' themselves by these comparisons. Most saw the cancer experience as life-changing in terms of changed philosophy of life and the primary goal became one of returning to some level of 'normalcy', albeit with a changed, more mature perspective on life.

Discussion

The authors note that this is not a study of young-adult coping strategies (that intends generalisability) but rather an exploration of the experience of those interviewed during which it emerged that ways of coping were important to each person's journey. Coping strategies are seen to evolve and change over time from diagnosis to post-treatment, and individuals not only differed from one another in their approaches but also drew on different strategies at differing time points as different goals of coping were sought. The authors contend that their findings fit the complex and interacting model presented and, while illustrating the use of many problem-focused and emotion-focused coping strategies, note that the distinctions were unclear in some instances. They do not illustrate this but I can add that both functions can be served by some coping strategies, for example seeking support. They contend that their findings may help service providers target resources and interventions more effectively towards young cancer patients.

The authors do not consider the limitations of their study, nor try and 'place' their findings within the larger literature – do the themes emerging from this sample differ from coping strategies of cancer patients assessed quantitatively, or do the themes seen here differ from those grounded in accounts of those coping with other illnesses, or even of an older population of cancer patients? In not doing this the authors perhaps fail to answer some of the questions that it usefully could have, but nonetheless it makes an interesting contribution to our understanding of the impact of cancer.

Coping goals

As inferred by the findings described in the study reported in RESEARCH FOCUS, coping intentions or goals (cf. Laux and Weber 1991) are likely to influence the coping strategies employed in any given situation and their likely success. Few studies have addressed goals (such as a desire to return to 'normalcy' after a trauma or illness) in relation to the specific strategies which are selected in an attempt to achieve that goal.

Why do people choose to cope in the way that they do? The reason for selecting one (or more) strategy to deal with a perceived stressor is related to past experience with that coping response, but more importantly it is related to the anticipated outcomes of that coping response, i.e. coping is a purposeful or motivational process (Lazarus 1993b). The general purpose or goal of coping, i.e. to manage a situation so as to make it less distressing, brings with it an inherent need to maintain one's self-esteem and self-image, and to maintain good relations with others. To illustrate this, a study of arguments between married couples found that anger and attack coping responses arose when one or other party felt that their self-esteem was under threat and their coping goal was therefore one of self-defence. In contrast, when couples were in a situation where there was a shared anxiety about some external event, anger was more often suppressed and supportive forms of coping used instead, as the goal in such instances was that of resolving shared concerns (Laux and Weber 1991).

As Coyne and Racioppo note (2000: 658) 'Coping checklist research has paid scant attention to differences in goals and agendas across situations and persons, and coping effectiveness cannot be evaluated without attention to these considerations.' In other words, unless we know 'why' a person choses to cope in a particular way in terms of what they hoped to achieve – reduced distress, more support, more interaction, less pain etc. etc. – we cannot tell whether or not that particular coping strategy has been effective. People use different coping strategies, often simultaneously, perhaps because each one is aiming for a different goal and some goals may be short-term (e.g. reduce pain) and others may be longer-term (e.g. to manage to walk independently). More research needs to assess coping goals if we are to progress our understanding of coping and how and why it changes over time. Furthermore, if coping interventions are to succeed, the practitioners need to know what the participants' coping goals are in order that the intervention can be appropriately targeted.

Everyone experiences stress at some point in their lives. Think of a recent stressful experience you have faced. How did you cope with it? Think of any different strategies you adopted in order to deal with this event. What were you hoping to achieve through the use of these strategies? Did different strategies have different intended goals? Which were effective, and which were not?

In revisiting that experience, can you think of anything in your personal background, your character or outlook on life that influenced how you responded to that event? There are many influences on how we appraise events and how we respond to them. Keep the experience you have just been thinking about in mind as you read the next sections of this chapter and consider whether any of the influences on stress and coping that we describe are relevant to how you deal with stress.

Stress, personality and illness

What is personality? Personality can be defined as the 'dynamic organization within the individual of those psychophysical systems that determine his characteristic behavior and thought' (Allport 1961: 28). This definition reflects a trait approach to personality, which considers a person's personality profile in terms of stable and enduring dimensions such as sensitivity, conscientiousness or neuroticism. Trait views dominated research until the late 1960s, but when traits failed to explain observed behaviour sufficiently well, attention turned to the role of external or situational variables and the existence of state-like characteristics (e.g. anxiety specific to a situation). Personality traits are constructs that provide a helpful means for us to typify behaviour patterns, with clusters of traits often providing 'typologies'; for example, an extroverted 'type' of person will generally exhibit sociable, adventurous and impulsive traits, while a psychotic 'type' will exhibit egocentric, aggressive, cold and impulsive characteristics (Eysenck 1982). Note that impulsivity features in both 'types', yet overall the two types differ in terms of clustered traits.

There are various possible models of association between personality variables and health and illness, with differing degrees of 'directness':

- Personality may promote unhealthy behaviour predictive of disease (e.g. smoking) thereby having an indirect effect on disease risk (see Chapter 3).
- General aspects of personality may influence the manner in which an individual copes with stress or illness events (e.g. pessimistic individuals may not use social support effectively) thereby having an indirect effect on illness progression or outcomes.

- Personality may be predictive of disease onset (e.g. Friedman and Booth-Kewley 1987). This is the notion of a generic 'disease-prone personality' which underpins the psychosomatic tradition.
- Specific clusters of personality traits may predispose to specific illnesses (e.g. Type A behaviour pattern and heart disease, Type C and cancer, see later section). One likely route of such effects is physiological (see Chapter 11) although influence is seen in the encountering of stress and subsequent appraisal and coping responses. Thus this route is also indirect.

To examine some of the evidence that general trait aspects of one's character indirectly influence one's health via an effect on the response to stress, we need to introduce the 'Big 5'.

The 'Big Five' personality dimensions

One current and popular way of conceptualising and assessing personality uses five dimensions (Costa and McCrae 1992a, 1992b):

- agreeableness, i.e. cooperative
- conscientiousness, i.e. responsible
- extroversion, i.e. sociable
- neuroticism, i.e. tense, anxious
- openness, i.e. imaginative, open to new experiences.

Each of these factors has been considered as a set of traits that enable both individuals and groups to adapt to demands of life. Studies employing five-factor models have found that each has differential associations with health behaviour (e.g. Booth-Kewley and Vickers 1994; Friedman *et al.* 1995), symptom perception (Feldman *et al.* 1999), coping (e.g. David and Suls 1996) and illness behaviour (e.g. Korotkov and Hannah 2004).

Of the Big Five the aspect that has received the most research attention in relation to illness is that of neuroticism.

■ Neuroticism

Neuroticism was one of the three personality dimensions identified by Eysenck (1982), and is one of the 'Big Five'. Neuroticism is considered a trait which is relatively unchangeable and is a broad dimension characterised by the tendency to experience negative emotions and to exhibit associated beliefs and behaviours (Costa and McCrae 1987; McCrae 1990). Individuals high on neuroticism often display anxious beliefs and behaviour disproportionate to the situation (Suls and Martin 2005, and see also Chapter 9 in terms of attention to internal states and increased somatic complaints). In trying to explain this, it has been suggested that neurotics by virtue of their character become exposed to more negative stressors (Suls and Martin 2005). It is hard to address this and to disentangle actual events from subjective reports of events as most studies rely on self-report; it may in fact be an appraisal or reporting bias of those high in neuroticism. In terms of responding to events appraised as stressful, research has suggested that neurotic individuals employ more different types of coping strategies (perhaps searching for one that works) and that these tend to be maladaptive and emotion-focused coping strategies (see Semmer 2006).

Negative affectivity

Watson and Clark (1984) proposed that a related construct, a pervasive trait known as negative affectivity (NA), would also play a central role in the stress–health relationship. High-NA individuals are characterised by a generalised negative outlook, greater introspection, low affect (mood) and low self-concept. In studies of a range of adult samples, NA was also found to be associated with lower self-rated health, greater health complaints, but generally not with objective ill-health indicators (Cohen *et al.* 1995; Watson and Pennebaker 1989; Evers *et al.* 2003). In the absence of consistent evidence of an association with actual illness events, NA is described as a 'nuisance factor' (Watson and Pennebaker 1989: 248) that makes it necessary for researchers to interpret with caution self-reported outcomes of health complaints and self-reported predictors of stress or distress, as the relationship 'found' between stress and illness may be inflated by reporting bias of participants high in NA. In spite of only weak longitudinal or predictive associations between NA and objective indicators of illness, studies have still sought to identify a mechanism of action, with some suggestion that NA is associated with raised cortisol levels, which causes immune function to be suppressed (e.g. van Eck *et al.* 1996).

Of the other 'Big 5' personality traits, perhaps Agreeableness and Extraversion have received most attention, with Agreeableness generally considered adaptive in terms of response to stressors, and Extraversion positive in some regards, e.g. appraisal and coping, but less so in relation to exposure to health-risk behaviours. The interested reader is referred to Semmer (2006) for a useful, more detailed review of personality, stress and coping.

So far, we have presented personality concepts associated often with negative outcomes, but other personality traits have been identified that have 'general' positive effects on stress responses and health, and we turn attention now to these 'personal resource' variables.

■ Optimism

One 'protective' resource is that of dispositional optimism, i.e. having a generally positive outlook and positive outcome expectations. Scheier and colleagues (Scheier *et al.* 1986; Scheier and Carver 1992) proposed that dispositional optimists are predisposed towards believing that desired outcomes are possible, and that this motivates optimistic individuals to cope more effectively and persistently with stress or illness events, thus reducing their risk of negative outcomes. Dispositionally optimistic persons are less likely to make internal ('It is my fault'), stable ('It is an aspect of my personality that I cannot change') and global attributions for negative events; i.e. they are more likely to appraise stress as changeable and specific and coming from external sources that are potentially more changeable or ignorable than internal ones. Pessimism, on the other hand, is a generalised negative outlook associated with denial and distancing responses to stress. Pessimism among cancer patients, for example, was found to have independent effects to optimism and was associated with mortality among younger patients even when controlling for the related construct of depression (Schulz *et al.* 1996).

Table 12.2   Measuring optimism: the life orientation test

Please be as honest and accurate as you can be throughout. Try not to let your response to one statement influence your responses to other statements. There are no 'correct' or 'incorrect' answers. Answer according to your *own* feelings rather than how you think 'most people' would answer. Using the scale below, write the appropriate letter in the box beside each statement.

A	B	C	D	E
I agree a lot	I agree a little	I neither agree nor disagree	I disagree a little	I disagree a lot

1. In uncertain times, I usually expect the best ☐
2. It's easy for me to relax* ☐
3. If something can go wrong for me, it will ☐
4. I always look on the bright side ☐
5. I'm always optimistic about my future ☐
6. I enjoy my friends a lot* ☐
7. It's important for me to keep busy* ☐
8. I hardly ever expect things to go my way ☐
9. Things never work out the way I want them to ☐
10. I don't get upset easily* ☐
11. I'm a believer in the idea that 'every cloud has a silver lining' ☐
12. I rarely count on good things happening to me* ☐

*These are 'filter' items, which have the function of disguising the focus of the test

In a meta-analysis of studies using the life orientation test (the measure of optimism developed by Scheier and Carver 1985; see Table 12.2) Andersson (1996) reports that optimism was significantly associated with coping, with reduced symptom reporting and with reduced negative mood or depression, with this latter relationship being strongest. Of the studies reviewed by Andersson, examples include Aspinwall and Taylor's (1992) findings that optimism predicted active coping responses among students during times of stress; and, among a clinical sample, Taylor *et al.*'s (1992) findings that optimism predicted better psychological and physical functioning in HIV-positive men. Optimism has therefore had reported benefits for both healthy populations dealing with stressful events and patient populations dealing with various aspects of their illness.

Optimism seems to lead to better functioning and outcomes because optimistic people appraise events in a way that makes it more likely that they will employ problem-focused coping strategies (Taylor and Armor 1996). For example, a study of law students found that optimistic students exhibited less avoidance coping and lower perceived stress than non-optimistic students, although the authors (Segerstrom *et al.* 1998) do point out that situational rather than dispositional optimism was associated with the lowered stress appraisals. This distinction between different types of optimism is important, particularly given that the different measures of optimism predicted different outcomes – situational optimism predicted elevated mood and immune function, where dispositional optimism did not.

Such beneficial effects of optimism as have been relatively consistently reported in the literature raises the question of the feasibility of interventions to enhance optimistic beliefs. If optimism is stable, how could this be achieved? Folkman and Moskowitz (2000) have suggested that optimistic

Plate 12.1 How optimistic are you? Is this glass half-empty or half-full?
Source: Alamy/Steve Hamblin

beliefs can be maintained by successful coping outcomes. This leads to a consideration of whether coping-skills training and positive feedback on successful efforts may build optimism. If so, optimism would then become closer to what is termed self-efficacy, i.e. a belief that one has the capacity to do what is required in a given situation (see Chapter 5, and also the later section on control beliefs in this chapter). Another construct related to dispositional optimism is that of unrealistic optimism, i.e. the view that unpleasant events are more likely to happen to others than to oneself, and that pleasant events are more likely to happen to oneself than to others (Weinstein 1982; see Chapter 5). Sometimes referred to as 'defensive optimism' (Schwarzer 1994), this way of thinking may operate as an emotional buffer against the recognition or acceptance of possible negative outcomes, i.e. it may protect people from a depressing reality.

How is dispositional optimism related to the two constructs of unrealistic optimism and self-efficacy, and do they each have independent effects on adaptation to illness? The relationship between these three related constructs has been addressed by Fournier *et al.* (2002), who examined predictors of self-care in people with either insulin-dependent diabetes or multiple sclerosis (MS). They hypothesised that people with diabetes – a disease generally controllable by self-management – would have better mood and self-care if they were high on positive **efficacy** and dispositional optimism, as this would lead to better self-care strategies, perceived positive benefits to

efficacy
Bandura's technical term analogous to confidence.

their condition and thus lower levels of anxiety and depression. In contrast, positive efficacy expectations in the MS patients were thought to be less important to self-care, as this disease is less controllable. In MS patients, it was hypothesised that unrealistic optimism would instead benefit mood, because these beliefs were maintained in the face of health deterioration, and therefore the individual is not facing negative feedback from unrealistically optimistic expectations and attempts to control their illness. Both hypotheses were confirmed by their data, highlighting the fact that optimistic beliefs work in different ways, depending on context and the controllability of the disease. They also report that dispositional optimism and self-efficacy beliefs remained relatively stable over the twelve-month follow-up period in comparison with unrealistic optimism, which decreased over time. Stable, dispositional variables such as optimism may offer more limited opportunity for intervention than do cognitions, such as situational and unrealistic optimism or perceptions of control (see later section).

Hardiness

The concept of hardiness was identified and tested by Kobasa (1979) when searching for factors that might differentiate those who respond to stress by becoming ill from those who stay healthy. Hardiness can be considered more perhaps as a belief system than part of personality, given that it was defined as an aspect of a person arising from having experienced rich, varied and rewarding experiences in childhood, and manifest in feelings of:

- *Commitment*: a person's sense of purpose or involvement in events, activities and with people in their lives. Committed individuals would view potentially stressful situations as meaningful and interesting.
- *Control*: a person's belief that they can influence events in their lives. Individuals high on control were thought to view stressors as potentially changeable.
- *Challenge*: a person's tendency to view change as a normal aspect of life and as something that can be positive. Individuals scoring high on the challenge dimension would view change as an opportunity for growth rather than as a threat to security.

Rather than exerting a direct effect on health experience, it is thought that by possessing each of these characteristics, a hardy person was equipped with characteristics which would buffer them against the experience of stress, thus enabling them to remain healthy. Kobasa's first study reported correlations between the scores of male executives on the Holmes and Rahe's social readjustment rating scale (see Chapter 11) and their self-reported checklist of symptoms and illness events. Correlational findings were upheld in subsequent longitudinal prospective studies (Kobasa *et al.* 1982), and the buffering effects are presented in Figure 12.2, where it is evident that hardiness has more effect in situations of high stress than in situations of low stress, i.e. a 'buffering' effect. This was supported by findings of Beasley *et al.* (2003) in a study of 187 university students who retrospectively reported life stress. In addition to finding a direct relationship between hardiness and reduced distress, hardiness buffered the effects of negative life events on the psychological health of female participants, i.e. the effects of negative life events

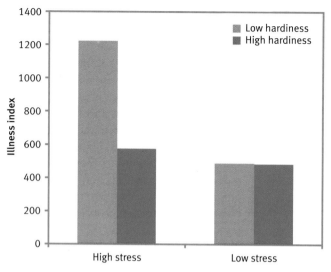

Figure 12.2 The buffering effects of hardiness.
Source: adapted from Kobasa *et al.* (1982)

were less for females higher in hardiness. For both genders, the negative effect of emotion-oriented coping on distress was less in those scoring high on the hardiness measure. However, this study was cross-sectional and, in fact, several prospective studies have failed to find evidence of buffering effects of hardiness. Some have concluded that a lack of hardiness is important, rather than the presence of it, in terms of how this might affect appraisals. This has led to suggestions that non-hardiness may reflect underlying trait neuroticism (Funk 1992) and certainly there is a relationship between the two (see review by Semmer 2006).

As well as the above broad personality traits, research has produced a wealth of findings pertaining to specific personality characteristics and specific illness risk and these are described next.

Type A behaviour and personality

Coronary heart disease (CHD), and its outcomes (heart attack, angina, cardiac death) have been studied extensively in relation to personality variables and to emotion (see later section). The search for a coronary-prone personality led to the discovery of a constellation of behaviour labelled Type A behaviour (TAB) (Friedman and Rosenman 1959, 1974; Rosenman 1978). TAB is a multidimensional concept combining action and emotion and is manifest in individuals showing the following:

- competitiveness
- time-urgent behaviour (trying to do too much in too little time)
- easily annoyed/aroused hostility and anger
- impatience
- achievement-oriented behaviour
- a vigorous speech pattern.

In the 1960s and 1970s, TAB was found to modestly but consistently increase the risk of CHD and MI (heart attack) mortality when compared with persons showing a Type B behaviour pattern (the converse of Type A, i.e. relaxed with little aggressive drive) (e.g. the Western Collaborative Group study (WCGS) – Rosenman *et al.* 1976; and the Framingham heart study – Haynes *et al.* 1980). Yet most subsequent research, including longer-term (twenty-two years) follow-up of the WCGS participants, failed to confirm these early associations (e.g. Hollis *et al.* 1990; Orth-Gomér and Undén 1990; Ragland and Brand 1988; see Booth-Kewley and Friedman 1987 for a review). In fact, some of these studies found very different results to what was expected; for example, Ragland and Brand's twenty-two-year follow-up of the WCGS cohort found that Type B's with prior CHD experienced a second heart attack sooner than Type A's with prior CHD, and healthy Type A's were no more likely than healthy Type B's to have experienced a fatal heart attack. Some of these contradictory findings may be explained by differences in the methods of assessment of TAB (for example, structured face-to-face interviews versus self-completed questionnaires), differences in the heart disease outcome assessed (e.g. heart attack event, heart attack death, angina, arterial disease) or in sampling differences. For example, some studies used healthy samples, others used heart attack survivors or those with other risk factors, such as smoking (see Miller *et al.* 1991 for a review of explanations for contradictory findings from Type A behaviour research).

While evidence of a TAB–coronary illness link may be controversial, there is some evidence suggesting that Type As respond more quickly and in a stronger emotional manner to stress, and that they exhibit a greater need for control than non-Type A individuals (Furnham 1990). These features of Type A may actually increase the person's likelihood of encountering stress, as they are likely to influence their interactions with others (Smith 1994) and result in the individual experiencing a more 'stressful' environment. Type As also show greater physiological reactivity than Type Bs, although this appears to be task-dependent and evident when tasks are competitive or challenging rather than in tasks that are irrelevant to the TAB character, such as simple perceptuo-motor tasks (e.g. Krantz *et al.* 1982). As described in the previous chapter, cardiovascular reactivity during stress has been implicated in various disease processes, such as the extent and progression of carotid artery atherosclerosis and the emergence of coronary heart disease (Smith *et al.* 2003), and therefore it is this reactivity that may provide the mechanism by which personality or Type A characteristics influence disease. Part of Type A therefore is a behavioural response to provocative situations. The core component appears to be antagonistic or hostile attitudes and behaviour, considered to be a trait. This became evident in the review by Booth-Kewley and Friedman (1987), where the collapsing of findings across 83 different studies of the links between Type A and CHD found small but consistently significant correlations between the hostility component and total CHD outcomes, and in fact this was the only aspect of TAB that showed this, although anger showed some associations with subcategories of outcomes. A review almost a decade later confirmed this conclusion (Miller *et al.* 1996)

■ Hostility and anger

Hostility is defined as a trait made up of emotional, cognitive and behavioural components. Trait anger is thought to be a central emotional component that is both experienced by the individual and manifested in aggressive or antagonistic actions or expressions. Cognitive components of hostility include having a cynical view of the world, a negative general attitude and negative expectations (cynicism, mistrust and denigration) about the motives of others. Behaviourally, hostile individuals may appear overtly aggressive or angry.

Hostility emerged as an important predictor of illness from various large-scale studies (e.g. the MRFIT study – Houston *et al.* 1992; the Western Collaborative Group study – Dembrowski *et al.* 1989; and see Miller *et al.* 1996 for a meta-analysis of the findings of 45 studies). While links were being established, so too were investigations of the pathways through which hostility might be having its effects on health status, and several possible mechanisms have been explored.

First, hostile individuals have been found to engage in health-risk behaviour which may itself be risk factors for illnesses such as heart disease, for example excessive smoking or alcohol intake (e.g. Lipkus *et al.* 1994; Whiteman *et al.* 1997). Vögele (1998) has also found that anger is associated with increased intake of alcohol and cigarettes (see Figure 12.3). It is therefore essential that studies investigating the hostility–disease link control for such risk factors, so that the actual extent to which hostility independently contributes to disease outcomes becomes clear.

Second, hostile individuals have been found to have a lower capacity to benefit from psychosocial resources or interpersonal support and thus they are less 'buffered' against the negative effects of stressful or challenging events (Miller *et al.* 1996). This has been termed a 'psychosocial vulnerability hypothesis', whereby hostility is considered to be a moderator of the relationship between stressful environmental characteristics and health problems (Kivimäki *et al.* 2003). Their large-scale study of Finnish adults found that, for men only, hostility influenced the relationship between unemployment and ill-health, with hostile men having a high prevalence of health problems regardless of employment status, whereas non-hostile men had better health if employed. This paper also highlights a commonly reported, but unsatisfactorily explored, gender difference in the associations between hostility and

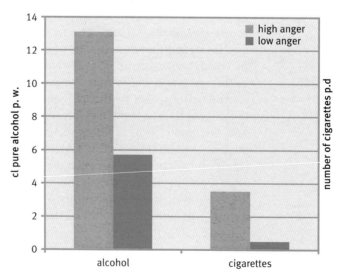

Figure 12.3 Anger and health behaviour.
Source: Vögele (1998)

health outcomes (although at least studies conducted in the 1990s onwards tend to include women as well as men, where many earlier studies did not).

Third, experimental studies have shown that hostile individuals are generally more stress-reactive than non-hostile individuals. Reduced 'buffers' plus a tendency to greater stress reactivity among hostile individuals makes them vulnerable to coronary heart disease, and even acute events such as heart attack (Strike and Steptoe 2005). For example, in a series of experimental studies, Suarez and colleagues (e.g. Suarez and Williams 1989; Suarez *et al.* 1998) found that persons scoring high in cynical hostility on the Cook–Medley hostility scale produced larger blood-pressure responses and greater neuroendocrine responses (e.g. raised cortisol levels) than non-hostile participants did when performing a task either during or immediately after an encounter with a rude and harassing laboratory assistant. Similar evidence from Everson *et al.* (1995) showed that individuals scoring high in hostility had increased cardiovascular activation during a task performed after a staged interruption, and that, furthermore, hostile individuals differed in their evaluations of the experiment and the person who interrupted them than did low-hostility participants (e.g. they manifest more irritation and anger, and feelings of being personally insulted). As described in Chapter 11, prolonged or repeated episodes of elevated blood pressure may cause damage to the walls of vessels carrying blood to the heart (the coronary arteries).

Enough evidence has been amassed from systematic reviews and meta-analyses to conclude that hostility is a likely risk factor for development of CHD (see Whiteman 2006 for a review), with several authors suggesting that the association is most evident in younger samples (aged 60 or under) (Kop and Krantz 1997; Miller *et al.* 1996; Smith *et al.* 2003). Some authors suggest that risk 'characteristics' such as hostility may be created by certain social contexts that undermine an individual's ability to attain goals or financial security, and that hostility may be less of a trait than a coping response (e.g. Taylor *et al.* 1997). This view raises the question of whether hostility is also indirectly associated with disease by virtue of a relationship with social deprivation (see Chapter 2).

Finally, investigations of the pathways through which hostility affected health status have highlighted one of its core features – trait anger. Studies of psychosocial factors in blood pressure and hypertension have consistently identified associations with both inhibited anger (anger-in) and anger expression (anger-out). Some studies have reported an increased CHD risk among participants with high anger expression (e.g. Rosenman 1996; Suls *et al.* 1995; Williams *et al.* 2000), with anger inhibition or suppression more associated with hypertension risk (Vögele and Steptoe 1993; Vögele *et al.* 1997), although a UK-based study, the Caerphilly study, found that low anger expression and suppressed anger significantly increased CHD risk (Gallacher *et al.* 1999). Such mixed findings are likely to be due to differences in measures used.

Type C personality

The search for a disease-prone personality in relation to CHD which led to identification and examination of type A and hostility, stimulated research into whether or not there was a cancer-prone personality type. Earlier work that considered the existence of disease-prone personality types (e.g. Eysenck 1985; Grossarth-Maticek *et al.* 1985) identified four personality 'types'. Their 'cancer-prone personality', type 1, was characterised by suppression of emotion and inability to cope with interpersonal stress, leading to feelings of hopelessness, helplessness and finally depression, whereas a CHD-prone personality, type 2, was characterised by strong reactions of frustration, anger, hostility and emotional arousal (similar to TAB described above). Eysenck and Grossarth-Maticek (1989), following a large-scale community survey in Yugoslavia, reported evidence to show that type 1 increased individual risk of cancer by 120 times and type 2 increased CHD risk 25 times. These figures obviously suggest that phenomenal amounts of risk can be conferred on personality variables, for example greater risk than that elicited even by smoking. Their claims inevitably led to much scrutiny of their work, and the survey and its findings have now been heavily criticised on the grounds of inappropriate analyses, insufficient methodological detail being provided in their paper, and a general inability of others to replicate their findings in either CHD studies or cancer studies (Amelang and Schmidt-Rathjens 1996; Pelosi and Appleby 1992, 1993; Smedslund and Rundmo 1999).

In contrast, Temoshok's typology (Temoshok and Fox 1984; Temoshok 1987), following a fifteen-year follow-up of women with breast cancer, did generate a robust finding of an association between passive and helpless coping style and poor disease prognosis. They described a **type C personality** as having the following characteristics:

type C personality
a cluster of personality characteristics manifested in stoic, passive and non-emotionally expressive coping responses. Thought to be associated with an elevated cancer risk.

- cooperative and appeasing
- compliant and passive
- stoic
- unassertive and self-sacrificing
- tendency to inhibit or repress negative emotions, particularly anger.

Several early studies offered support for the Type C typology and elevated cancer risk. For example, Shaffer *et al.* (1987) conducted a thirty-year prospective study of 972 physicians and found that participants who exhibited high levels of emotional expression and 'acting out' had less than a 1 per cent risk of developing cancer, whereas those who inhibited emotional expression were sixteen times more likely than this group to develop cancer. However, recent reviews of the role of Type C characteristics and cancer onset suggest that effects are limited (e.g. Garssen 2004).

Personality as a factor that influences appraisal of, and response to cancer, has also been explored in terms of outcomes such as recurrence and survival. Generally, support for the predictiveness of characteristics of Type C is limited (Garssen 2004), and this is true also of studies examining effects of other personality characteristics such as neuroticism or extroversion (e.g. Canada *et al.* 2005). There is mixed evidence of survival benefits of aspects of personality best described as 'coping styles', for example of 'fighting spirit' (see 'What is adaptive coping?' above), and of helplessness–hopelessness.

Type D personality

More recent than research into elevated CHD risk through Type A behaviour and hostility is the notion of a **type D personality**, considered to be

type D personality
a personality type
characterised by high
negative affectivity
and social inhibition.

detrimental to cardiovascular disease prognosis and outcomes (Denollet and Potter 1992; Denollet *et al.* 1996; Denollet 1998). This personality type is best described as a 'distressed' personality, with individuals scoring highly on negative affectivity (NA) and social inhibition (SI, defined as 'the avoidance of potential dangers involved in social interaction such as disapproval or nonreward by others', Denollet 1998: 209). Type D individuals therefore are thought to experience negative emotions but inhibit them while also avoiding social contact. There is evidence from a few small-scale studies that these characteristics associated with increased mortality following a heart attack or other cardiac event, even when controlling for other biomedical risk factors (e.g. Denollet *et al.* 1996). The effect was found in both women and men who had pre-existing heart disease.

In an attempt to identify physiological correlates of Type D personality, Habra *et al.* (2003) examined cardiovascular reactivity (blood pressure, heart rate, salivary cortisol levels) of undergraduate students completing a mental arithmetic task while being harassed. Socially inhibited males showed heightened blood pressure reactivity; negative affectivity was associated with dampened heart-rate changes during the task in males; and salivary cortisol levels were positively associated with both Type D dimensions (but not in final, more stringent analyses). However, unlike Denollet's studies, where NA and SI were only predictive jointly, Habra's findings suggested that NA and SI operated independently. These differences may be due to clear differences in the samples (older adults with CHD versus healthy undergraduate students).

Stress and cognitions

Perceived control

Early work on the construct of control considered it to be a personality trait. Locus of control, derived from Rotter's social learning theory, proposed LoC as a generalised belief that would influence behaviour as greater reinforcements (e.g. rewarding outcomes) were expected when responsibility for events was placed internally rather than externally (Rotter 1966). Furthermore, internal locus of control beliefs would only predict behaviour in situations where the rewards/outcomes were valued. LoC therefore refers to the trait-like expectation that personal actions will be effective in controlling or mastering the environment, with individuals falling on the side of either internality or externality. An 'internal' individual would take responsibility for what happens to them; for example, they would attribute successes to their own efforts and their failures to their own laziness. An 'external' individual would be more likely to believe that outside forces or chance circumstances control their lives, and both success and failures would be likely to be attributed to luck or chance. These beliefs would therefore influence a person's behaviour. It is considered that internal individuals have more efficient cognitive systems and that they expend energy on obtaining information that will enable them to influence events of personal importance. In other words, internally oriented individuals would engage in more problem-focused coping efforts when faced with personal or social stressors.

There is a large body of evidence relating locus of control to physical and psychological health, and much of it has employed a scale developed by Kenneth Wallston and colleagues (e.g. Wallston *et al.* 1978). They described a health locus of control construct assessed using a scale which they called the multidimensional health locus of control scale. The MHLC assesses the extent to which a person believes that they themselves, external factors or 'powerful others' (e.g. friends, health professionals) are responsible for their health and health outcomes. This measure therefore has three sub-scales and includes items such as:

- 'I am in control of my health' – internal;
- 'No matter what I do, if I am going to get sick I will get sick' – external;
- 'Regarding my health, I can only do what my doctor tells me to do' – powerful others.

Scores on these sub-scales have been found to be associated with a range of coping, emotional and behavioural outcomes (including health behaviour itself). For example, among two longitudinal studies of patients with lower back pain, internal HLC was associated with reduced physical disability at follow-up, and patients with stronger internal control beliefs gained more from their treatment and exercised more often (distress was associated with poorer exercise behaviour) (Fisher and Johnston 1998; Härkäpää *et al.* 1991). Using an HLC measure specific to recovery from disability (the recovery locus of control scale; Partridge and Johnston 1989), Johnston *et al.* (1999) also found that perceptions of internal control predicted better recovery from disability six months after an acute stroke. However, when attempting to reveal how perceived control may have influenced physical recovery (measured in terms of the ability to perform a range of activities such as walking, dressing and toileting), the authors did not find that internal PC led to an increase in exercise behaviour, as reported by the Finnish study (Härkäpää *et al.* 1991). Importantly, these authors reassessed this group of stroke survivors at three years following their stroke to examine whether the beneficial effects of PC persisted long term, and results confirmed that perceived-control beliefs, as assessed at baseline (10–20 days post-stroke onset) were significantly predictive of long-term physical recovery but not emotional recovery in terms of reduced distress (Johnston *et al.* 2004; Morrison *et al.* 2005).

The importance of this type of finding is that, unlike neurological impairment or age (both predictors of outcome following stroke), control beliefs can be modified. For example, Fisher and Johnston (1996) showed how a simple letter-based intervention increased internal control beliefs and reduced pain reports in a chronic-pain sample. Such findings suggest that enhancing internal control beliefs is a useful intervention approach when the outcome concerned is physical. However, few studies have found perceived control to be predictive of disease course, for example cancer relapse or survival (DeBoer *et al.* 1999).

Furthermore, there is evidence that internal control is not always adaptive in that it can lead to optimistic biases such as unrealistic optimism, although the direction of causality is unclear (do optimists perceive control, or does perceiving control make you optimistic? e.g. Klein and Helweg-Larsen

2002). Furthermore, maintaining beliefs in internal control in situations where such beliefs are unrealistic (e.g. severe and permanent disability following traumatic brain injury), may lead to problem-focused coping efforts that fail. This perceived failure could in turn contribute to feelings of depression and helplessness, whereas accepting the reality of having no control may lead to more adaptive emotion-focused coping responses (Folkman 1984; Thompson 1981).

One important question to be asked in this regard is 'Control over what?' Various types of control have been described:

■ *Behavioural*: the belief that one can perform behaviours likely to reduce the negative impact of a stressor, e.g. using controlled breathing techniques prior to and during a painful dental procedure.

■ *Cognitive*: the belief that one has certain thought processes or strategies available that would reduce the negative impact of a stressor, e.g. distracting oneself from surgical pain by focusing on pleasant thoughts of a forthcoming holiday.

■ *Decisional*: having the opportunity to choose between options, e.g. having a local anaesthetic prior to a tooth extraction (bearing in mind that the after-effects can last for hours!) or having the tooth removed without anaesthetic.

■ *Informational*: having the opportunity to find out about the stressor; i.e. the what, why, when, where, likely outcomes, possibilities, etc. Information allows preparation (see Chapter 13).

■ *Retrospective*: attributions of cause or control of an event made after it happens: i.e. searching for the meaning of an event can give some sense of order in life; e.g. blaming a birth defect on a defective gene (internal) may be more adaptive than attributing blame externally, although this is not clear-cut.

Each of these types of control can reduce the stressfulness of an event by altering the appraisal a person makes of the stressor, by reducing emotional arousal or by influencing the coping responses adopted. Thompson *et al.* (1993), in a study of 71 adult cancer patients, showed that, even in generally uncontrollable circumstances in terms of disease progression, perceiving control over day-to-day emotions and physical symptoms significantly reduced distress, and that these perceptions of control remained associated with adjustment even in those with poorer physical functioning. This highlights that while control over outcome may not be realistic, control over aspects of the event or responses to it remain beneficial to adjustment.

Self-efficacy and perceived locus of control are the two main control concepts used in health psychology, and they could be considered as spanning different phases of the coping process; for example, locus of control is an appraisal of the extent to which an individual believes they can control outcomes, whereas self-efficacy addresses appraisal of the resources and skills an individual believes they can use in order to achieve desired outcomes. Also related to control beliefs are **causal attributions**. In a review of 64 data sets exploring associations between attributions of cause in a wide range of conditions (including arthritis, cancer, heart disease, burns, AIDS, infertility, stroke and pregnancy loss) and adjustment (Hall and Marteau 2003), 80 per cent of studies reported no association between internal (behavioural

causal attribution
where a person attributes the cause of an event, feeling or action to themselves, to others, to chance or to some other causal agent.

self-blame) attributions or external (other-blame) attributions and adjustment. In fact, no particular attribution was strongly associated with achieving a better outcome. Characterological self-blame (e.g. It is something in my nature that I can't change that caused me to become ill) was most often associated with poorer outcomes. This type of self-blame has been associated with negative emotions such as depression.

Importantly, there is evidence that social class influences the extent of an individual's belief in personal control (see also Chapter 2). Examining two control-related constructs in a large sample of adults aged 25–75 years, Lachmann and Weaver (1998) found that personal mastery beliefs (e.g. 'I can do just about anything I really set my mind to') and perceptions of constraints in one's life (e.g. 'Other people determine most of what I can and cannot do') differed according to their indice of social class–household income. Mastery was lower and constraints higher among those with lower incomes, but when lowest-income participants reported a high sense of control, their health and wellbeing became comparable with the higher-income groups. Control therefore moderated the effect of low income on both physical (self-rated health, functional limitations) and psychological (life satisfaction, depressed mood) outcomes.

What do YOU think?	While findings such as those described above make general conclusions, there are obviously individuals who differ from the mean (in other words, some people of low SES will report high mastery, and some of high SES will report low mastery). However, thinking of the overall picture, stop and ask yourself why many people of a lower socio-economic status have a lower sense of control and greater perceptions of constraints in their lives than people of higher socio-economic status. Do you think they are right in having such views, i.e. might such beliefs be adaptive in certain circumstances? Refer back to Chapter 2 when thinking about these issues.

■ Hope

Snyder (1989) introduced 'hope theory' to the study of cognitive–motivational processes involved in explaining human behaviour. Relevant to the study of stress and coping, hope is defined as 'a positive motivational state that is based on an interactively derived sense of successful (a) agency (goal-directed energy) and (b) pathways (planning to meet goals)' (Snyder *et al.* 1991: 287). Hope therefore is the person's belief that they can set, plan and attain goals – it is about goal-directed thinking and is believed to have both trait and state-like aspects.

It has been pointed out that there is conceptual overlap between the hope construct and other constructs in this domain of 'positive psychology' such as, dispositional optimism and self-efficacy. As seen already in this chapter, both these constructs have been associated with positive physical and emotional wellbeing. Snyder *et al.* (2006) acknowledge this and attribute overlap to the fact that all three constructs focus on individual 'resources', but point out that hope is about the motivation (agency) and route (pathway) to achieving goals (outcomes), whereas optimism is about generalised positive outcome expectancies that are not founded solely on agency and pathway thinking, and self-efficacy is less a generalised belief than a situation and goal-specific belief that depends on various contingencies (i.e. I can do 'a' even if the situation is 'b'). This is questionable perhaps as self-efficacy theories do also propose a more generalised construct. Snyder supports his argument that the three constructs differ by describing how a hope-based intervention would differ from an optimism or a self-efficacy-based intervention; however, the differences have not been fully tested.

The construct of hope is hard to disentangle from these other, more commonly investigated constructs, and there is a clear need for empirical studies to establish whether hope adds any 'unique' explanation in terms of health outcomes, than that offered by assessment of optimism and self-efficacy.

The constructs reviewed in this section are often referred to within a field of study known as 'positive psychology', i.e. where a person's strengths, resources and abilities are focused on and harnessed rather than their pathology, limitations or negative cognitions and emotions. The next section addresses emotions found to be associated with stress responses and outcomes.

Stress and emotions

Depression and anxiety

The role of depression in increasing the incidence/likelihood of disease experience is controversial and depends on the disease concerned. The Alameda County study discussed in Chapter 3 (where we listed the seven types of 'healthy behaviour') did not find any effect of depressed mood upon CHD incidence; however, other studies have associated depression with hypertension, even when taking other risk factors into consideration. For example, the Framingham Heart Study found that depression, as well as anxiety, predicted twenty-year incidence of hypertension even controlling for age, smoking and obesity (Markovitz *et al.* 1993). In relation to cancer, a major study showed that recurrent major depression among an elderly sample predicted a higher incidence of breast cancer (Penninx *et al.* 1998).

Booth-Kewley and Friedman (1987), in their meta-analysis of studies exploring the psychological predictors of heart disease, highlighted several studies that found a significant association between depression and CHD outcomes (heart attack, angina, cardiac death, as well as global CHD). More recently, a review by Hemingway and Marmot (1999) found that eleven out of eleven longitudinal prospective studies in healthy populations presented results supportive of a role of depression and/or anxiety in the aetiology (development) of CHD, and that six out of six prospective studies among CHD patients reported a significant prognostic role for depression.

A significant association between depressed mood and mortality from heart attack (myocardial infarction, MI) has also been reported. For example, Frasure-Smith *et al.* (1995) found that depression was more predictive of death than was either the degree of heart damage or having had a previous heart attack. Subsequent work has confirmed such findings; for example, an impressive longitudinal study of 237 healthy men (Vaillant 1998) found that

45 per cent of those with a depressive episode at or before the baseline assessment were dead by the time of follow-up – a massive fifty-five years later – compared with only 5 per cent of those who had not experienced such an episode. Neither depression nor anxiety were predictive of (non-) survival in two longitudinal studies of stroke patients carried out in Scotland (Johnston *et al.* 2004; Lewis *et al.* 2001; Morrison *et al.* 2005), although other studies with longer follow-ups have found a significant relationship (Morris *et al.* 1993).

Depressed mood may reflect an underlying state of negative affectivity (see earlier section on personality), which is what has been suggested through the work of Denollet and his colleagues (Denollet and dePotter 1992; Denollet 1998). These researchers have found that cardiovascular disease outcomes (recovery, death, further heart attacks) can be partially explained by high NA scores combined with social inhibition ('type D' personality; see earlier section). It is likely that for some individuals, psychosocial risk factors cluster together, for example, stress plus hostility plus depression plus social isolation would confer compounded risk.

Research has also attempted to identify emotions associated with increased cancer risk. One such study is the Western Electric study (WES; Persky *et al.* 1987), which conducted seventeen- and twenty-year follow-ups and found that those participants who initially scored highly on the global depression sub-scale of the MMPI (Minnesota multiphasic personality inventory) had a greater incidence of cancer at follow-up. However, this was later attributed to environmental factors. Another large-scale longitudinal study – the Alameda County study – did not replicate these findings (Kaplan and Reynolds 1988). Although there is some suggestion that feelings of hopelessness and helplessness associated with depression are implicated in cancer onset (Everson *et al.* 1996), the evidence appears to be, as with CHD, more strongly in support of depression influencing outcomes rather than aetiology (Petticrew *et al.* 2002). The subject of depression as an outcome itself is addressed in Chapter 14.

When considering pathways by which depression may affect health outcomes, there are, as with personality, various possible routes.

Firstly, depression and anxiety have been shown to influence the appraisals that individuals make when facing stressful events (appraisals of threat, as opposed to appraisals of challenge), thus influencing the coping actions a person engages in. For example, Lowe *et al.* (2003), drawing from the stress–emotion–coping framework of Smith and Lazarus (1993; see Chapter 11 for theoretical explanation) examined whether the emotion of depression was attached to secondary appraisals of low problem-focused coping potential and pessimistic future expectations, and whether anxiety was attached to appraisals of low emotion-focused coping potential. Results from 148 women with suspected breast cancer confirmed expectations in relation to stress appraisals and also found that confrontation coping, avoidance coping and acceptance–resignation coping were all positively associated with anxiety, whereas depression was negatively associated with confrontation and not related to the other two coping responses.

The second route is also indirect, i.e. via a person's behaviour. Depression is seen to reduce the likelihood of healthy behaviour or cessation of unhealthy behaviour. For example, people who had experienced a heart attack (MI) and who exhibited subsequent depression had lower rates of smoking cessation than those who did not show signs of depression five months after the MI (Huijbrechts *et al.* 1996). Depressed individuals were also less likely to attend cardiac rehabilitation classes than non-depressed individuals (Lane *et al.* 2001), and generally research findings suggest that adherence to therapeutic interventions or treatments such as exercise or medication is lower among depressed individuals than those who are not depressed (e.g. DiMatteo *et al.* 2000; Wing *et al.* 2002). Such non-adherent behaviour can expose individuals to adverse health outcomes, such as future illness, poorer recovery from illness, or even mortality (McDermott *et al.* 1997).

Depression may also interfere with a person's ability to seek, or benefit from, social support and supportive interactions (see later section on support).

IN THE SPOTLIGHT below highlights the fact that coping with stress is not all about negative emotions and that there is a growing body of research pointing to the importance of thinking and acting positively.

Emotional disclosure

One possible moderator of coping receiving increased attentions in recent years is that of emotional disclosure – the opposite of emotional suppression, or repressive coping, commonly found to be detrimental to health (see earlier

IN THE SPOTLIGHT

Positivity and meaningful lives

There has been a growth in studies in what is being called 'positive psychology' (Folkman and Moskowitz 2000: Seligman and Csikszentmihalyi 2000; Snyder and Lopez 2005). Basically, what these authors, among others, are suggesting is that we need to move away from a focus on the negatives (inability as a result of illness pathology, lack of resources, negative thoughts and emotions) and turn more attention towards the benefits to health and wellbeing offered by thinking and acting positively. For example, in addition to optimism and hope, which we have discussed in this chapter, happiness and joy are thought to contribute to what Seligman, in a special edition on positive psychology in *The Psychologist* (2003), calls desirable lives: the pleasant life, the good life and the meaningful life. A pleasant life arises from one that pursues positive emotions about present, past and future experiences and involves the simple pleasures and gratifications or rewards that we get out of life. A good life arises from 'being' as well as 'doing' and by being involved in life and all its activities, one is thought to get the best out of it. A meaningful life is when we use our strengths and skills to benefit more than just ourselves.

To feel that life is pleasant, good or meaningful would imply that a person would therefore be happy, but little research has actually addressed happiness in relation to health outcomes, more often than not assessing subjective 'wellbeing', which may not be quite the same. Veenhoven (2003) states that happiness can be defined and measured and that by simply asking people about their levels of happiness we could explore questions such as: is quality of life associated with happiness or can we have a quality of life without it? What makes a good life?

Think about your own life and what makes you happy – it may help you live longer!

expressed emotion
the disclosure of emotional experiences as a means of reducing stress; often achieved by describing the experience in writing.

congestive heart failure
a disorder in which the heart loses its ability to pump blood efficiently. As a consequence, many organs do not receive enough oxygen and nutrients, leading to the potential for them to become damaged and, therefore, not work effectively.

'Type C personality' section). A leading figure in this area is Pennebaker (e.g. Pennebaker *et al.* 1988; Pennebaker 1993), who with various colleagues has developed a paradigm whereby writing about one's recent trauma is found to have long-term benefits in terms of immune functioning (Pennebaker *et al.* 1988; Petrie *et al.* 1995), and health-care use (Pennebaker and Beall 1986).

Disclosure of emotional experiences is not to be confused with work on **expressed emotion** (EE; can include the venting of negative as well as positive emotion), which although studied using a similar expressive writing paradigm, has been associated with poorer prognosis among psychiatric populations and is showing contradictory findings among the physically ill (interested readers can see the recent meta-analysis by Panagopoulou *et al.* 2002). It is thought that venting negative emotion may maintain the emotion by virtue of increasing the attention paid to it; it can also interfere with the potential to receive social support (Semmer 2006). For example, Coyne and colleagues (2003) found that EE among couples where one had experienced **congestive heart failure** was associated with poorer marital quality and increased distress. Other authors suggest that EE assists in emotional self-regulation by allowing the person carer to develop greater mental control over the stressor and a coherent narrative of events in their head, which facilitates 'closure' and reduces distress (Niederhoffer and Pennebaker 2005). There is evidence that the style of expression (antagonistic vs. constructive expression of anger) influences whether the outcome of expression is positive or not (e.g. Davidson *et al.* 2000). However, the evidence on the benefits and 'dis-benefits' of emotional writing, disclosure and emotional expression remain mixed and further research enquiry is warranted.

Social support and stress

The final topic in this chapter is that of social support, a potential resource available to most (but not all) of us that has been shown to be strongly associated with health and illness outcomes. Social support is also discussed in a later chapter when we consider the impact of illness upon individuals and their family members.

Evidence exists that people who have strong (in both size and usage) networks of social support are healthier and live longer than the socially isolated, but what actually is meant by 'social support'?

Definition, types and functions of social support

Social support can be actual or perceived. People with social support believe they are loved and cared for, esteemed and valued, and part of a social network of communication and mutual obligation, such as that often shared with family, friends or members of a social organisation. The social network facilitates the provision of goods, services and mutual defence in times of need or danger (Cobb 1976). Social support is generally considered in terms

Table 12.3   Types and functions of social support

	Provider	Recipient
Emotional support	empathy caring concern	reassurance sense of comfort and belongingness
Esteem support	positive regard encouraging person positively comparing	builds self-worth sense of competence being valued
Tangible/instrumental support	direct assistance financial/practical aid	reduces strain/worry
Informational support	advice, suggestions feedback	communication self-efficacy/self-worth
Network support	welcoming shared experiences	sense of belonging affiliation

of two interacting components – its structure (i.e. type of supports) and the functions they serve (Uchino 2006). Table 12.3 presents examples of types of social support and their functions in terms of what the social support provider provides and in terms of what is received by the recipient. Five basic types have been described, although some authors only distinguish between instrumental, emotional and informational, and most studies do not attempt to record what the recipient actually 'gets' from the support but instead assume that it is all helpful. (Chapter 15 challenges this assumption when carer and patient relationships are examined).

Social support is considered within Lazarus's stress and coping framework as a resource variable that when perceived as being available will affect how individuals appraise and respond to events. Individuals who perceive support levels as high are likely to appraise events as less stressful than individuals who do not perceive they have any support (i.e. social support acts as a 'buffer' against stress). The next sections review evidence of the association between social support and health outcomes, following which we consider some of the likely mechanisms of action.

Social support and mortality

Many years have been spent trying to establish whether social support is causally implicated in mortality. Early support was obtained from the Alameda County study (Berkman and Syme 1979), even when health status and self-reported health-risk behaviour were controlled for; and social isolation (low levels of social support and social activity) was associated with heart disease mortality among middle-aged men followed up for ten years (Orth-Gomér *et al.* 1988). An impressive fifteen-year follow-up of 2,603 adults (Vogt *et al.* 1992) concluded that social 'networks' (assessed by size, number of supportive domains (scope) and frequency of use) strongly predicted mortality from ischaemic heart disease, cancer and stroke.

Social support and disease

Evidence of a relationship between life stress and health status has pointed to social support as a moderator. For example, Rosengren *et al.* (1993) found that among middle-aged men, the association between an accumulation of critical life changes and subsequent heart attack was moderated by the quality of social support. Among individuals suffering from rheumatoid arthritis, social support in terms of a limited social network was predictive of disease activity three years later, even when coping behaviour was controlled for (Evers *et al.* 2003); even among healthy samples, for example a large sample of French employees (Melchior *et al.* 2003), a lack of social support and dissatisfaction with social relationships predicted poor health status.

It has been suggested that social relationships are particularly important in diseases where physical dependence on others, and decreased social activity resulting from the disease, are present (Penninx *et al.* 1999). Furthermore, social support may buffer the impact of depression on mortality following a heart attack (Frasure-Smith *et al.* 2000).

How does social support influence health status?

We all need support. There is ample evidence that social support effectively reduces distress during times of stress, and furthermore the lack of social support during times of need can itself be very stressful, particularly for people with high needs for social support but insufficient opportunities to obtain it, e.g. the elderly, the recently widowed and other victims of sudden, severe or uncontrollable life events (e.g. Balaswamy *et al.* 2004; Penninx *et al.* 1999; Stroebe *et al.* 2005). Although there is more evidence for the benefit of social support in reducing stress and distress during illness than there is on actually preventing it occurring, Greenwood *et al.* (1996), following a review of empirical studies, also concluded that poor social support had a stronger effect on CHD incidence than did stressful life events.

Two broad theories as to how social support might operate have been proposed (Cohen 1988):

1. *Direct effects hypothesis*: social support is beneficial regardless of the amount of stress people experience, and a lack of social support is detrimental to health even in the absence of stress. High levels of social support provide a greater sense of belonging and self-esteem than low levels, thus producing a positive outlook and healthier lifestyles. Alternatively, social support has a physiological route to health by virtue of either reduced blood pressure reactivity, thought to arise from positive stress appraisals and emotions, or possibly via enhanced endocrine or immune system functions, although there are less consistent findings in this area. (For a comprehensive review, see Uchino 2006).

2. *Buffering hypothesis*: social support protects the person against negative effects of high stress. Social support acts as a buffer by either (a) influencing the person's *cognitive appraisals* of a situation so they perceive their resources as being greater to meet threat; or (b) modifying the person's *coping response* to a stressor after it has been appraised as stressful (i.e. they do not cope alone) (Cohen and Wills 1985; Schwarzer and Leppin 1991).

Plate 12.2 From an early age, social support is a powerful moderator of stress response.

Evidence for direct effect of social support

In terms of direct effects on healthy behaviour, there is reasonably consistent evidence that social support facilitates healthy behaviours such as not smoking and adhering to medication, although as discussed in Chapter 5 social influence can also be negative. Here we consider more the direct effects of social support on physiological rather than behavioural processes.

Uchino (2006) reviews the evidence regarding physiological pathways affected by social support, and highlights both reduced stress reactivity seen in typical measures of cardiovascular reactivity (see Chapter 11) and also some evidence of neuroendocrine and immune responses, the latter particularly important among older samples. Turner-Cobb *et al.* (2000) found that breast cancer patients who assessed social support as being present and helpful had lower morning cortisol levels than those who did not assess social support in this way, suggesting a physiological route by which social support may enact its benefits. As described in Chapter 8 and Chapter 11 cortisol has been implicated in immune down-regulation and is perhaps implicated in tumour growth. Cognitive-behavioural interventions that have provided breast cancer patients with group support have also reported reduced cortisol levels (e.g. Creuss *et al.* 2000).

Evidence for indirect or 'buffering' effect of social support

The effect of perceived and actual social support on the appraisal of stressful events has not perhaps been rigorously studied to date, although there is some evidence that perceiving social support as being available contributes to more positive outcome expectancies and appraisals of control over the event. Furthermore, perceptions of control in relation to illness outcomes were positively associated with seeking social support in a meta-analysis of forty-five empirical studies, albeit not as strongly as might have been expected (Hagger and Orbell 2003). The authors consider that this may in part be due to social support being assessed as part of a generic measure of coping, as opposed to more specific assessment of the different types and function of social support.

Generally speaking, seeking social support is considered an active coping strategy, whether the support is sought for informational and practical reasons or with the goal of emotional support. For example, Kyngaes *et al.* (2001) examined the coping strategies of young people within two months of developing cancer and found that they engaged in emotion-, appraisal- and problem-focused coping strategies, and accessing social support was one of the most common strategies. Different 'functions' of support were seen in that they sought information about their disease and its treatment from health professionals, and emotional support from their families.

Stroebe and colleagues tested the widely held assumption that social support acts as a buffer against the impact of loss following bereavement in their study of 1,532 recently widowed adults aged over 65 years (Stroebe *et al.* 2005). They found limited evidence of support acting as a buffer against loss, or that it facilitated general 'recovery', when assessing participants at 6, 18 and 48 months after bereavement. What they did find, however, is that social support had a beneficial effect on depression levels.

■ Can social support be bad for you?

It is worth noting that there are some instances where high levels of social support can be detrimental. For example, among pain patients it was found that high social support in terms of providing practical assistance with everyday tasks caused poor adaptation through operant conditioning (e.g. Gil *et al.* 1987). Over-caring can cause the care recipient to become overly dependent on the carer and overly passive in terms of their own recovery (see Chapter 15). In addition, the type of social support provided may not always be received as supportive, or, more importantly, the help offered may not match the needs of the patient: e.g. instrumental support is helpful if aspects of the event are controllable; emotional support may be more helpful when things are uncontrollable, e.g. after a death (e.g. Cutrona and Russell 1990).

Finally, there is a caveat in social support research. Given the subjectivity of the construct in that it is defined in terms of 'How much social support do you perceive?', studies have to rely on self-report. As noted elsewhere, there are inherent biases in gathering self-report data, and it is likely that individual difference variables, such as neuroticism, may influence not only an individual's perceptions of the nature and level of social support they have received but also their satisfaction with it. Additionally, personality or emotional state might interfere with social resources and in effect prevent or enhance a person's ability to access support, or gain from it (see discussion of hostility or depression).

Summary

The evidence reviewed in Chapter 11 suggested that stress can increase the risk of artery damage, which in turn encourages the development of CHD. This is a direct effect proposal, which implies that simply reducing stress exposure would reduce the likelihood of that disease. However, this chapter has shown this to be overly simplistic. Many factors moderate the impact of stress on health, or the impact of stressful illness upon longer-term outcomes such as disability, distress and survival. This chapter has described how factors attributed to a person's personality, beliefs, emotions and use of social support can affect stress responses and outcomes. Such variables can be studied in terms of the direct relationships they have with stress outcomes, or as variables that need to be controlled for when examining other predictors. For example, one study might examine whether trait neuroticism predicts psychological distress following surgery, where another study might control for neuroticism in examining the effects of a pre-surgical information sheet on patient distress following surgery. Whatever the research question, it has become increasingly clear that many variables influence the relationship between a stressful event and its outcomes, and that biological, psychological and social factors work together in the stress–illness experience.

Further reading

Adler, N.E. and Matthews, K.A. (1994). Health psychology: why do some people get sick and some stay well? *Annual Review of Psychology*, 45: 229–59.
A useful overview of many of the moderating variables discussed in this chapter which is useful conceptually, although you will need to supplement your reading of this with reading of more recent empirical papers!

Rice, P.L. (1992). *Stress and Health*. California: Brooks/Cole.
A clearly written book addressing most if not all of the topics discussed in this chapter.
Again, you should supplement reading of this with reading of the burgeoning empirical papers on stress and its effects on health, illness and immune function.

Snyder, C. and Lopez, S.J. (2005). *Handbook of Positive Psychology*. New edition, USA: Oxford University Press.
A comprehensive collection of chapters from eminent research academics such as Martin Seligman (positive psychology), Ed Diener (science of happiness), Howard Tennen and Glenn Affleck (benefit-finding). The chapters address the cognitive, emotional, interpersonal, behavioural and biological aspects of positive strengths such as seen in appraisals, coping or social support mechanisms.

Key papers
Uchino, B.N. (2006). Social support and health: a review of physiological processes potentially underlying links to disease outcomes. *Journal of Behavioral Medicine*, 29: 377–87.

A well-presented review of social support and its effects on cardiovascular, endocrine and immune system functioning. Very useful summaries are provided of key studies.

Semmer, N.K. (2006) Personality, stress, and coping. In M.E. Vollrath (ed.) *Handbook of Personality and Health*. London: John Wiley & Sons (pp. 73–113). A clear account of the various processes and mechanisms through which personality may influence stress and coping responses and disease risk, progression or other outcomes.

Watson, M., Homewood, J., Haviland, J. and Bliss, J.M. (2005). Influence of psychological response on breast cancer survival: 10-year follow-up of a population-based cohort. *European Journal of Cancer*, 41: 1710–14. A rare long-term follow-up study exploring psychological predictors of the key outcome of survival. Discusses helplessness–hopelessness and fighting spirit, both constructs which have received a lot of attention in both the scientific and popular literature; and findings highlight the fact that predictors of short-term outcome do not necessarily remain predictive in the longer term.

Tennen, H., Affleck, G., Armeli, S. *et al.* (2000). A daily process approach to coping: linking theory, research, and practice. *American Psychologist*, 55: 620–5. An impressive longitudinal study of pain patients where daily measures of coping were taken. While a time-consuming methodology, daily measurement is an excellent way of illustrating dynamic processes such as coping.

Visit the website at **www.pearsoned.co.uk/morrison** for additional resources to help you with your study, including multiple choice questions, weblinks and flashcards.

CHAPTER 13

Managing stress

Learning outcomes

By the end of this chapter, you should have an understanding of:

■ ways of intervening at a population or organisational level to reduce work stress

■ the elements of a cognitive-behavioural approach to stress management

■ the nature and treatment of post-traumatic stress disorder in response to the onset of illness

■ interventions of value in helping people to cope with the stress associated with a surgical operation

Image: Alamy/David Sanger

CHAPTER OUTLINE

Stress, they say, is all around us. Indeed, one of the most frequently reported problems in general practitioners' surgeries is tiredness – often as a symptom of stress. Other chapters in this book comment on the role of stress in the development of illness (Chapter 11), or how learning to manage stress effectively can enhance mood, improve the outcome of a number of diseases and reduce the experience of pain (Chapters 16, 17). What they do not consider in any detail is how such changes can be achieved. This chapter addresses this issue from a number of perspectives. First, it considers approaches used to minimise stress in healthy individuals, both in the public at large and in the workplace. In this, it complements Chapters 5 and 6 and their consideration of health-promotion strategies. The chapter then considers the nature of stress management interventions used when working with individuals who are experiencing stress. This section builds on Chapters 11 and 12, which examined the relationship between stress, coping and illness and will prepare you for Chapters 16 and 17, which include sections on how stress management can help people to cope with illness and pain. The chapter then examines how we treat an extreme response – known as post-traumatic stress – that can occur in response to the onset of illness. Finally, we consider how stress may be minimised when people face a specific stressor – in this case a surgical intervention – in hospital, using relatively simple interventions. This flow of the chapter moves us from discussion of stress management in preventive settings to those where an individual is coping with the stress of having a disease or its treatment. It also moves from highly complex systemic interventions involving whole organisations to much simpler interventions that can be conducted by nursing and other health professionals in general conversations with patients.

Stress theory: a quick review

stress management training
a generic term for interventions designed to teach participants how to cope with stress.

In this first section, we examine some of the components of a set of interventions collectively referred to as **stress management training**. They are based on cognitive-behavioural theories of stress, which consider stress to be the outcome of a variety of environmental and cognitive processes. Stress is seen as a negative emotional and physiological state resulting from our cognitive responses to events that occur around us: that is, stress can be seen as a process rather than an outcome. We discussed appraisal and transactional theories of stress in Chapter 11. Stress management approaches are in part based on these theories and in part based on more clinical theories, the two most prominent of which are those of Aaron Beck (1976) and Albert Ellis (1977). Both assumed that our cognitive response to events – not the events themselves – determines our mood, and that feelings of distress or other negative emotional states are a consequence of 'faulty' or 'irrational' thinking (see Figure 13.1). That is, they considered stress to be the result of *misinterpretations* of environmental events or cognitions that exaggerate the negative elements within them and lose focus on any positive aspects of the situation.

Beck referred to the thoughts that drive negative emotions as automatic negative assumptions. They come to mind automatically as the individual's first response to a particular situation and are without logic or grounding in reality. Despite this, their very automaticity means they are unchallenged and

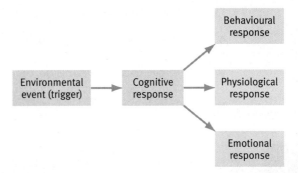

Figure 13.1 A simplified representation of the event–stress process suggested by Beck and other cognitive therapists.

taken as true. He identified two levels of cognition. Surface cognitions are those we are aware of. We can access them and report them relatively easily. Underlying them are a set of unconscious beliefs about ourselves and the world, known as **cognitive schemata** (singular, schema) which influence our surface cognitions and, in turn, influence our emotions, behaviour and physiological arousal. Stress-evoking thoughts, for example, result in an increase in sympathetic nervous system arousal (see Chapter 8), behaviour that may be more or less helpful in resolving the problem an individual is facing, and feelings of anxiety. Beck identified a number of categories of thought that lead to negative emotions, including:

- *Catastrophic thinking*: considering an event as completely negative, and potentially disastrous: 'That's it – I've had a heart attack. I'm bound to lose my job, and I won't be able to earn enough to pay the mortgage'.

- *Over-generalisation*: drawing a general (negative) conclusion on the basis of a single incident: 'That's it – my pain stopped me going to the cinema – that's something else I can't do'.

- *Arbitrary inference*: drawing a conclusion without sufficient evidence to support it: 'The pain means I have a tumour. I just know it'.

- *Selective abstraction*: focusing on a detail taken out of context: 'OK, I know I was able to cope with going out, but my joints ached all the time, and I know that will stop me going out in future'.

A good example of how long-term schemata drive very stressful ways of responding to external events is provided by Price's (1988) cognitive model of type A behaviour (see Chapter 12). From her clinical work with type A men, she concluded that the schemata underlying type A behaviour were low self-esteem and a belief that one can gain the esteem of others only by continually proving oneself as an 'achiever' and a capable individual. These underlying beliefs underpinned more conscious competitive, time-urgent or hostile thoughts.

Surface cognitions associated with type A behaviour include:

- *Time-urgent thoughts*: 'Come on – we haven't got all day – I'm going to be late! Why is he so slow? Am I the only person who gets things done around here?'

- *Hostile thoughts*: 'That person cut me up deliberately! I'll sort him out. Why is everyone else so incompetent – they really are pretty stupid'.

cognitive schemata
set of unconscious beliefs about the world and ourselves that shape more conscious cognitive responses to events that impinge on us.

Deeper (unconscious) schemata include:

- 'I can't say no to her request or I will look incompetent and I will lose her respect'.
- 'I must get to the meeting on time – whatever the cost – or people will think I'm incompetent and I will lose their respect'.
- 'People only respect you for what you do for them – not for who you are'.

What do YOU think?	The cognitive-behavioural model of stress assumes that stress lies within the individual. Stress arises from the misinterpretation of events that happen to us. But is this really true? It is possible to argue that while some stress may be the result of faulty thinking, stress can also be triggered by truly stressful circumstances. Most people would consider having a surgical operation, for example, to be a stressful event. Theorists such as Hobfoll have argued that many more general factors, such as being a single mother or holding down a demanding job, are universally stressful events. Arguments that socio-economic status influences health through psychological processes discussed in Chapter 2 also implicitly suggest that there are broad differences in the degree of stress experienced across different social groups.

If these assertions are true, then, at least in some cases, stress truly does result from environmental circumstances and not from an individual's interpretation of a situation. Such arguments may lead us to question how relevant stress management techniques based on the cognitive-behavioural models described above can be in these contexts.

The argument that cognitive-behavioural therapists would marshal against this critique is that even acknowledging that there are environmental factors that influence stress, some people cope with them better than others. There is individual variability in our ability to cope with similar demands placed on us. The role of stress management is not to deny the role of the environment but to help people to cope with the stressful circumstances they face as effectively as they can and with the least possible emotional distress. This seems to be a reasonable argument, but it leaves a number of questions for health psychologists. One particularly pertinent issue is how much effort we should put into changing the sources of stress and how much into changing people's responses to potentially stressful environments. Should we put our emphasis on reducing social inequalities by changing the environment, or on helping people to cope better with the demands of their environment here and now? Should we help some people to cope better with operations, or try to make the processes before and after an operation less stressful for all? Often, teaching people to cope better with stressful situations is easier and cheaper than changing the causes of stress. But is it the best approach?

Stress management training

The model of the stress response described above suggests a series of factors that can be changed in order to reduce an individual's stress. These include:

- environmental events that trigger the stress response – or series of triggers to longer-term stress;
- inappropriate behavioural, physiological or cognitive responses that occur in response to this event.

Most stress management programmes focus on changing people's reactions to events that happen around them or to them. Many simply teach relaxation to minimise the high levels of arousal associated with stress (see Chapter 11). More complex interventions try to change participants' cognitive (and therefore emotional) reactions to these events. Few address the factors that trigger the stress response in the first place. This can be considered a serious limitation – the most effective way of reducing stress is to prevent it occurring in the first place. Accordingly, we incorporate into our overview of stress management training a process of both identifying and changing triggers to stress as well as strategies for dealing with stressful thoughts, feelings, emotions and behaviour once initiated:

cognitive restructuring a reconsideration of automatic negative or catastrophic thoughts to make them more in line with reality.

- Triggers can be identified and modified using problem-solving strategies.
- Cognitive distortions can be identified and changed through a number of cognitive techniques, such as **cognitive restructuring** (see below).
- High levels of muscular tension and other signs of high arousal can be reduced through relaxation techniques.
- 'Stressed' behaviour can be changed through consideration and rehearsal of alternative behavioural responses.

Changing triggers

This is an often neglected part of stress management training, perhaps because there is no standard intervention that can be applied. The triggers to each person's stress necessarily differ, as will any strategies they develop to reduce their frequency. Changing them involves first identifying situations that add to an individual's stress and then either changing their nature or reducing the frequency with which they occur. A simple strategy to reduce an individual's level of stress or anger while driving to work, for example, may be to start the journey earlier than previously so they feel less pressure during the journey.

One of the most frequently used approaches to identifying and changing triggers to stress was developed by Gerard Egan (1998). His model of problem-focused counselling introduced in Chapter 6 can be adapted to coping with stress, so stress triggers are dealt with in three stages:

1. *Problem exploration and clarification*: what are the triggers to stress?
2. *Goal setting*: which stress triggers does the individual want to change?
3. *Facilitating action*: how do they set about changing these stress triggers?

Stress may have multiple sources, and some areas of stress may be easier to change than others. It can be helpful to change relatively easy triggers at the beginning of any attempt at change before working towards more serious or difficult-to-change triggers as the individual gains skills or confidence in their ability to change. Some changes can be achieved using the personal resources already available to the individual – once they have planned how they will achieve them, they feel confident in their ability to put the plan into action. Others may require the individual to learn new skills in order to manage their stress more effectively. They may benefit, for example, from learning to relax or reducing the frequency or type of any stress-provoking thoughts that contribute to their stress. It is to these taught skills that we now turn.

Relaxation training

The goal of teaching relaxation skills is to enable the individual to relax as much as is possible and appropriate both throughout the day and at times of particular stress. This contrasts with procedures such as meditation, which generally provide a period of deep relaxation and 'time out' as sufficient in themselves. As well as the physical benefits, effective use of relaxation techniques can lead to an increase in actual and perceived control over the stress response. This can be a valuable outcome in itself. Relaxation may also increase access to calm and constructive thought processes, although this is a relatively weak effect, reflecting the reciprocity between each of the different stress components. Relaxation skills are best learned through three phases:

1. learning basic relaxation skills
2. monitoring tension in daily life
3. using relaxation at times of stress.

■ Learning relaxation skills

The first stage involves learning to relax under optimal conditions – a comfortable chair in a quiet room. Ideally, a trained practitioner should teach the process of deep relaxation. This can then be added to by continued practice at home, typically using taped instructions. Regular practice over a period of days, and sometimes weeks, is important at this stage, as the skills need to be well practised and relatively automatic before they can be used effectively in 'real life' contexts.

The relaxation process most commonly taught is based on Jacobson's (1938) deep muscle relaxation technique. This involves alternately tensing and relaxing muscle groups throughout the body in an ordered sequence. Over time, the emphasis of practice shifts towards relaxation without prior tension, or relaxing specific muscle groups while using others, to mimic the use of relaxation in the 'real world'. The order in which the muscles are relaxed varies, but a typical exercise may involve the following stages (the tensing procedure is described in brackets):

- hands and forearms (making a fist);
- upper arms (touching fingers to shoulder);
- shoulders and lower neck (pulling up shoulders);
- back of neck (touching chin to chest);
- lips (pushing them together);
- forehead (frowning);
- abdomen/chest (holding deep breath);
- abdomen (tensing stomach muscles);
- legs and feet (push heel away, pull toes to point at head: not lifting leg).

Time	Situation	Tension	Behaviours	Thoughts
8.32	Driving to work – late!	62	Tense – gripping steering wheel Cutting up other drivers Cursing at traffic lights	Late again!! . . . the boss is bound to notice . . . Come on – hurry up – I haven't got all day! Why do these bloody traffic lights always take so long to change?!
10.00	Presenting work to colleagues	75	Spoke too quickly Rushed	I'm not looking good here . . . why can I never do this properly? They must think I'm a fool! I feel a wreck!

Figure 13.2 Excerpt from a stress diary noting stress triggers, levels of tension and related behaviours and thoughts

At the same time as practising relaxation skills, individuals can begin to monitor their levels of physical tension throughout the day. Initially, this serves as a learning process, helping them to identify how tense they are at particular times and what triggered any excessive tension. This process may also help to identify likely future triggers to stress and provide clues as to when the relaxation procedures may be particularly useful. This frequently involves the use of a 'tension diary', in which the individual records their level of tension on some form of numerical scale (0 = no tension, 100 = the highest tension possible) at regular intervals throughout the day or at times of particular stress. As a prelude to cognitive or behavioural interventions, such diaries may also focus on the thoughts, emotions or behaviour experienced at such times. Figure 13.2 provides an excerpt from a typical stress diary. As the individual begins to use additional strategies to combat their stress, they may add columns measuring their level of tension after the use of relaxation, the thoughts they used to deal with their stressful thoughts, and so on.

After a period of learning relaxation techniques and monitoring tension, individuals can begin to integrate relaxation into their daily lives. At this stage, relaxation involves reducing tension to appropriate levels while engaging in everyday activities. Initially, this may involve trying to keep as relaxed as possible and appropriate at times of relatively low stress and then, as the individual becomes more skilled, using relaxation at times of increasing stress. The goal of relaxation at these times is not to escape from the cause of stress but to remain as relaxed as possible while dealing with the particular stressor. An alternative strategy involves relaxing at regular intervals (such as coffee breaks) throughout the day.

Cognitive interventions

self-talk
talking to oneself (internally). Can be negative and thus add to stress. Therapeutically, individuals are taught to use self-talk in a way that helps them to keep calm.

Two strategies for changing cognitions are frequently employed. The simplest, known as self-instruction training, was developed by Meichenbaum (1985) and is targeted at surface cognitions. It involves interrupting the flow of stressogenic (stress-provoking) thoughts and replacing them with pre-rehearsed stress reducing or 'coping' thoughts – so-called 'positive **self-talk**'. These typically fall into one of two categories. The first are reminders to use any stress-coping techniques the person has learned ('You're winding yourself up here – come on, take it easy, remember to relax, deep breathe, relax your muscles'). The second form of self-instruction acts as a form of reassurance, reminding the individual that they have previously coped effectively with their feelings of distress and will be able to now ('Come on, you've dealt with this before – you should be able to again – keep calm – things will not get out of control'). To make sure these are relevant to the individual, and to help to actually evoke these thoughts at times of stress, Meichenbaum suggested that particular coping thoughts should be rehearsed, wherever possible, before the stressful events occur – whether in a therapy session or minutes before an anticipated stressor is likely to occur. At a minimum, such thoughts interrupt the flow of stressful thoughts; at best, they actively reduce an individual's levels of stress.

A more complex intervention, known as cognitive restructuring, involves first identifying and then challenging the accuracy of stressogenic thoughts. It asks the individual to consider them as hypotheses, not facts, and to assess their validity without bias. This process may involve consideration of both surface cognitions and cognitive schemata – although the latter require significant insight and may best be achieved in the context of therapy. To teach the skill, the therapist typically uses a process known as the Socratic method or 'guided discovery' (Beck 1976), in which the client identifies a number of thoughts, and then challenges their accuracy under the guidance of their therapist. They may challenge their stressful assumptions by asking key questions such as:

- What evidence is there that supports or denies my assumption?
- Are there any other ways I can think about this situation?
- Could I be making a mistake in the way I am thinking?

Once the individual can engage in this process within the therapy session, they are encouraged to use the Socratic process at times when they experience stress in their daily lives (see also the discussion of the downward-arrow technique in Chapter 6).

■ Meditation

It may seem odd to place meditation within the cognitive strategies section of this chapter. But, meditation is a very cognitive process. At its most fundamental, meditation can be described as a state of concentrated attention on some 'object of thought or awareness'. Two sorts of mediation are fairly well known. Transcendental Meditation (TM) was introduced to the West by the Maharishi Mahesh Yogi. It is typically practised twice daily and involves resting quietly for a short period then repeating a mantra chosen for about twenty minutes. A second form of meditation that is becoming increasingly popular is known as mindfulness (Kabat-Zinn 2001). Based on Buddhist teachings, the technique teaches people to live 'in the moment' (whether in the process of meditation or simply going about one's day-to-day business). It involves being aware and attentive to the present, and not focusing on worries about the future or the past. Thoughts are seen as potential truths rather than actual truths (as in the cognitive model described earlier in the chapter). The skill of mindfulness is to be aware of any thoughts or worries one may have, but to disengage from them and focus on other elements of the individual's experiences in the here and now. This can be achieved through meditation or engaging in this focus throughout the day. Practitioners often use triggers such as a chiming clock or red traffic light to trigger this process, even if this involves a simple procedure such as focusing on three successive breaths. This approach is particularly helpful when it is difficult to establish a regular meditation practice.

Behavioural interventions

The goal of behavioural change is to help the individual respond to any stress triggers in ways that maximise their effectiveness in dealing with the trigger and cause them minimal stress. Some behaviour can be relatively simple. Behaviour that reduces the stress of driving may involve driving within the speed limits, putting the handbrake on when stopped at traffic lights and taking time to relax, not cutting in front of other cars, and so on. Others may take practice – a person who becomes excessively angry, for example, may role-play assertive responses in therapy sessions to prepare them for doing the same in 'real life'. Still others may have to be thought through at the time of the stress. Here, the goal of stress management training may be to teach the individual to plan their response to any potential stressor to be one that minimises their personal stress. A simple rule of thumb that can be useful here is to encourage individuals to stop and plan what they are going to do – even if this takes a few seconds – rather than to jump into action without thought, as this typically leads to more rather than less stress.

Stress inoculation training

stress inoculation training
a form of stress-reducing intervention in which participants are taught to control stress by rehearsing prior to going into stressful situations. Participants are taught to relax and use calming self-talk. The approach was developed by Donald Meichenbaum.

In his approach called **stress inoculation training**, Meichenbaum (1985) suggested that the various strands of cognitive therapy described above could be combined so that when an individual is facing a stressor, they concentrate on:

■ checking that their behaviour is appropriate to the circumstances;
■ maintaining relaxation;
■ giving themselves appropriate self-talk.

In addition, he suggested that where a particular stressor can be anticipated, the opportunity should be taken to rehearse these actions before the event itself. Once in the situation, the planned strategies should be enacted. Finally, after the situation has occurred, time should be given to review what occurred and successes or failures learned from – rather than treated as triumphs or disasters that should be soon forgotten.

Preventing stress

Teaching stress management strategies

Perhaps the simplest way that we can help to minimise stress among the general population is to teach them stress management techniques. These can be taught in night school or even at health fairs using the approach adopted by Brown, J.S. *et al.* (2000). They ran eight free full- or half-day stress management workshops in a leisure centre following a publicity drive as part of the 'Healthy Birmingham 2000' programme. These workshops taught attenders relaxation and other strategies for controlling their stress. Their comparison groups comprised people who took part in a day-long programme focusing on sessions on healthy eating, alcohol awareness and physical exercise, and a group of people on a waiting list for future workshops. The event proved very popular and attracted both people who had already seen a health professional, usually their general practitioner, about stress-related problems and those who had not. The intervention also proved successful. Compared with baseline levels, participants in the full-day workshops reported significantly greater reductions in stress and anxiety three months following the workshop than those in the comparison groups – an impressive result, given the relative brevity of the intervention and the wide range of people attending. More rigorous studies of the impact of stress management programmes have shown them to consistently impact on perceived stress. In addition, there is good evidence that they impact on a variety of biological processes known to be affected by stress. Both, Storch *et al.* (2007) and Hammerfald *et al.* (2006), for example, found differing stress management programmes to be effective in reducing both perceived stress and levels of the stress hormone, cortisol. We consider the impact of stress management on wellbeing and biological processes in people with health problems in more detail in Chapter 17. The next sections, however, examine stress management interventions conducted with healthy individuals in a specific context – the workplace.

Stress management in the workplace

Stress management interventions clearly have the potential to provide significant benefit to those who take part – but only a very small proportion of the public who have the potential to benefit are likely to take the time and trouble to attend workshops or other training programmes. Health psychologists and others have therefore turned to other methods of attempting to reduce the stress of significant parts of the general population. One of the most important approaches they have adopted is to develop strategies for reducing stress in more 'captive audiences', the most important of which has been people at work.

There is significant and rising pressure on employers to provide staff with the skills to manage stress effectively. In the UK, this has become increasingly important as the Health and Safety Executive, which determines safety standards in the workplace, gives employers a legal obligation to protect the emotional as well as physical wellbeing of their employees. Their reasons for this policy include data from their own sources (e.g. Jones *et al.* 2003), which indicated that:

- In 2002, over half a million individuals in Britain reported experiencing work-related stress at a level that was making them ill, while nearly one in five thought their job was very or extremely stressful.
- Work-related stress, depression or anxiety accounts for an estimated 13.5 million lost working days per year in Britain.

- Levels of work stress are rising.
- Teachers and nurses have particularly high prevalence of work-related stress.

Most published attempts to reduce stress in the workplace have involved running stress management training at the workplace using similar methods to those of Brown and colleagues described above: that is, they have tried to help attenders to cope more effectively with the demands placed upon them. These appear to be effective. Summarising the relevant data, Richardson and Rothstein (2008) reported a consistent significant benefit to those attending stress management programmes based on the principles outlined earlier in the chapter. In one such study, Eriksen *et al.* (2002) randomly allocated a large group of employees to one of three intervention conditions: physical exercise, stress management training, or an integrated health programme involving physical exercise and health information. None of the interventions influenced health complaints, sick leave or job stress. However, each of the interventions did appear to impact on its target. Participants in the physical activity intervention showed improvements in general health and physical fitness, while the stress management group reported reductions in their levels of general stress. A similar result was reported by Mino *et al.* (2006) who found improvements in general mood following a stress management programme, but little effect on the specific stress associated with work.

There have been a number of criticisms of individually targeted stress management programmes within the workplace. Oldenburg and Harris (1996), for example, noted that this type of programme usually attracts only between 10 and 40 per cent of the workforce – and even less if it is not given a 'high profile' in the workplace. In addition, the majority of people who do attend seem to have relatively few stress-related problems, while many anxious individuals do not attend, perhaps because they feel that they will gain little from such courses or do not want to air their problems in front of their colleagues. Noblet and Lamontagne (2006) had more philosophical concerns, as they suggested that the approach can be seen as labelling those with high stress as somehow not coping, and avoids employers having to modify any work-related causes of stress. The failure of Eriksen *et al.* and Mino *et al.* to influence either work-related stress or levels of sick leave highlights the need to influence these issues more directly – by addressing the *causes* of stress.

Identifying organisational causes of stress is more complex than providing stress management classes and has more significant implications for an organisation. Table 13.1 indicates the variety of potential stressors that may influence the stress of people working in a hospital, some of which are common to many work situations, some of which are unique to working in health-care settings.

Changing any of these factors may impact on the stress of hospital workers, and working out where and how to intervene at an organisational level is not easy. However, the process used by one of the authors (PB) to reduce stress in a group of hospitals provides an example of how this might be done. The process involved:

- identifying causes of stress in the working environment;
- identifying solutions to this stress from those most involved;
- developing a process of change to address the issues raised.

Plate 13.1 The London Stock Exchange typifies an environment that encourages stress and high levels of aggressive behaviour and adrenaline.

Source: Alamy/The Hoberman Collection

Table 13.1 Some of the sources of stress for hospital workers

Professional issues	Patient issues	Work issues
Over-promotion	Distressed patients or relatives	Shift work
Under-promotion	'Difficult' patients or relatives	Poor working conditions
Interactions with colleagues	Dying patients	Too high a workload
Interactions with management	Complaints made against staff	Work intruding on home time
Working beyond knowledge level		Lack of social support
Lack of management support		Inadequate equipment

The first two stages of the intervention involved running a series of focus groups with different staff throughout the organisation. These were led by a health psychologist, who worked with the management of the hospital but who was not part of the management team. Many focus groups were run with key hospital staff, including cleaners and porters, nurses, managers, clerical workers, and people from the paramedical professions such as occupational therapists and physiotherapists. In each of these meetings, comprising about six people, attenders were invited to identify factors in their working environments that adversely affected their 'quality of life' at work. If problems were identified – and they inevitably were – they were also asked to identify any solutions to those problems. These meetings were intended to last up to one hour but often went on longer, and they were extremely productive.

Each of the issues and solutions put forward in the groups were then arranged into a set of common problems (and perhaps solutions) in a document that formed the basis of the next phase of the intervention. Problems raised included major systemic problems, such as:

- a poor computer network system;
- poor timing of the hospital bus provision (it did not fit in with shift times);
- very poor parking facilities, making transport to and from work difficult;
- inadequate crèche facilities;
- the organisation of various groups of wards in the hospital into competing rather than cooperating units;
- a working culture among management that punished people who did not work significant overtime.

Interestingly, the solutions that some workers had used to manage their stress impacted on other workers by increasing their dissatisfaction and stress. One example of this was that the management team in one hospital had moved its offices away from the wards to avoid what they thought of as too much day-to-day contact with the ward staff and to allow them to concentrate on more long-term planning. As a result, the management group felt less stressed and more able to get on with their job effectively. By contrast, and unbeknown to the management team, the ward nurses were angry and disillusioned as they felt this was an example of management blocking off contact they felt vital to their effective running of the wards.

Once the problems and solutions were documented, these were taken to a small committee of senior managers, which formed a response to the needs. It did so by grouping the issues raised into three broad categories:

1. those likely to have minimal effect, but relatively easy to instigate;
2. those likely to have a significant effect, but more difficult to instigate;
3. those likely to have a significant effect, but impossible to instigate.

Clearly, the interventions focused on the first two of these categories. Changes made included increasing the size of the crèche and lengthening its opening hours so that it was more useful for shift workers, changing the times of the hospital buses to make them more user-friendly, and initiating a new hospital computer system – over a number of years. However, any interventions need not necessarily be on such a large scale. One example of this was provided by a nurse manager, who noted that her staff often arrived late or very close to the time of their morning shift. When she asked them why, she found that these were predominantly single mothers who had to leave their child with a childminder on their way to work. Because childminders would only take children from a time close to the beginning of the shift, this put these nurses under significant time pressure. If the traffic was good between the childminder and hospital, they got to work on time; if the traffic was busy or delayed, they were late to work. The simple solution to the problem was to start the shift fifteen minutes later.

■ Do organisational interventions work?

There have been relatively few empirical studies of the effectiveness of this type of intervention. However, those that have been reported suggest they may be of benefit. Maes *et al.* (1990), for example, changed the nature of the working environment by redesigning jobs to avoid short and repetitive performance tasks, giving workers some control over the organisation of work, and enhanced social contact. They also trained managers in communication and leadership skills and encouraged them to develop strategies for reducing stress in their area of work. This intervention resulted in an increase in work quality and lower absenteeism rates in comparison with the control sites, which received no intervention.

A second intervention to use such an approach was reported by Mikkelsen and Saksvik (1999). They intervened in two offices in the Norwegian Post Office. The intention of their intervention was to increase employees' learning opportunities and decision-making authority in order to improve the work environment and health. In order to decide what changes to make, they ran discussion groups with the workers, which 'diagnosed' any problems, then planned and enacted changes to the working environment to remedy them. They reported that work conditions in the larger organisation actually deteriorated over the course of the study, a process that was reversed in one but not both intervention offices. They attribute the failure of the latter to organisational restructuring and turbulence interfering with potential benefits of the intervention. A third, and much simpler, intervention was reported by Dababneh *et al.* (2001). They evaluated the impact of short rest breaks on productivity and wellbeing in a meat processing factory. In one condition, workers were given thirty-six minutes of extra breaks by adding to their present breaks – one by adding four nine-minute break schedules distributed evenly throughout the day, the other by adding twelve three-minute breaks. Neither additional break lowered production, but both resulted in significant reductions in psychological discomfort. Workers preferred the nine-minute rest interval.

IN THE SPOTLIGHT

Ban football . . . save a life!

There may be one stress management approach not detailed in the chapter that could save many lives. Ban football! Or at least, ban watching football. There is now accumulating evidence that high levels of excitement and stress associated with important games of football can trigger a heart attack in vulnerable individuals. Wilbert-Lampen and colleagues (2008), for example, reported in the *New England Journal of Medicine* that three times as many German men had an MI on the days that Germany was playing in the 2008 World Cup than on days they were not playing. Women were also at increased risk, but slightly less so than men. The peak admission time was in the first two hours after the beginning of each match. But this is not an isolated finding . . . and it is not restricted to German fans. Similar findings were reported by Carroll and colleagues (2002) for English fans during the 1998 World Cup. They found that the risk of admission to hospital with an MI increased by 25 per cent on 30 June 1998 – the day England lost to Argentina in a penalty shoot-out – and the following two days. Dutch, Australian and other fans have also been similarly affected. The moral of the story? If banning football can save one life, it has to be considered!

Helping people to cope with trauma

Post-traumatic stress disorder

post-traumatic stress disorder
a disorder that forms a response to experiencing a traumatic event. The key elements are unwanted repetitive memories of the event, often in the form of flashbacks, attempts at avoidance of such memories, and a generally raised level of arousal.

The American Psychiatric Association (American Psychiatric Association 2000) states that for a person to be given a diagnosis of **post-traumatic stress disorder** (PTSD) they must have experienced or witnessed an event that involved actual or threatened death or serious injury, or a threat to the physical integrity of self or others, and that their immediate response involved intense fear, helplessness or horror. In the longer term, the individual must have experienced three clusters of symptoms lasting one month or more:

1. *Intrusive memories*: the trauma is re-experienced through intrusive thoughts, flashbacks or nightmares. Flashbacks often feel as real as the event but may be fragmentary or partial. Emotions and sensations associated with the trauma may be relived with similar intensity to those felt at the time. Images are often described as if being in a film of the incident. Initially, the person may feel that they are actually 'in' the film: as they recover, their perspective may shift to that of outside observer watching a film. That is, they begin, almost literally, to feel more detached from the trauma.

2. *Avoidance*: this may involve mental defence mechanisms such as being unable to recall aspects of the trauma, emotional numbness or detachment from others, as well as physically avoiding reminders of the trauma.

3. *Arousal*: persistent feelings of over-arousal that may be evidenced by irritability, being easily startled or hyper-vigilant, suffering insomnia, or having difficulty concentrating.

Many health workers may witness other people at times of either threatened or actual death. Emergency ambulance workers, for example, are frequently involved in incidents involving serious trauma, death and high levels of personal distress. For this reason, the prevalence of PTSD in this group is alarmingly high. Bennett *et al.* (2004), for example, found that 21 per cent of their sample of working emergency ambulance personnel were experiencing some degree of PTSD. Many patients also experience PTSD as a consequence of events that led them to hospital or which occurred in hospital, although the exact prevalence of PTSD among such people is difficult to determine, as some studies use much stricter criteria for a 'diagnosis' of PTSD than others. Among cancer patients, for example, two studies using very rigorous criteria for the diagnosis of PTSD have reported a 3 per cent prevalence among women with breast cancer (Green *et al.* 1998) and 5 per cent of people undergoing bone marrow transplant in the treatment of cancer (Widows *et al.* 2000). Using less rigid criteria, Meeske *et al.* (2001) reported that 20 per cent of their sample of adults who had been treated successfully for cancer an average of eleven years previously still met the full criteria for PTSD. A small percentage of people may have residual symptoms of PTSD twenty years after diagnosis and treatment (Kornblith *et al.* 2003). About 10 per cent of people who have had a myocardial infarction may also experience PTSD (e.g. Bennett *et al.* 2002).

Post-traumatic stress may not just affect those with the condition. High rates of PTSD have also been found among the parents of children diagnosed as having cancer. Landolt *et al.* (2003), for example, found that 16 per cent of the fathers and 24 per cent of the mothers of children diagnosed with either cancer or diabetes met the diagnostic criteria for PTSD five–six weeks after the diagnosis was given.

■ Preventing PTSD: psychological debriefing

psychological debriefing
a procedure in which people who have been through a particular trauma talk through the trauma in a structured way with a counsellor.

Because of the serious impact that PTSD can have on an individual, much research and clinical work has been conducted to try to prevent PTSD occurring following traumatic incidents. The most frequently used approach is called **psychological debriefing**. Many emergency services such as the ambulance and police services regularly use psychological debriefing to help staff to cope following traumatic incidents (Smith and Roberts 2003). This usually comprises a single-session interview conducted close to the time of a traumatic event during which the individual talks about the event and their emotional reactions to it in a detailed and systematic manner. The therapist leads the person through the event in a very structured manner, asking them to talk about the events that have occurred and their emotional, cognitive and behavioural responses to those events. It is hoped that this procedure helps the individual to come to terms with any emotional trauma they have experienced and prevent the development of PTSD.

The procedure is at least partly justified by theorists such as Brewin and Holmes (2003), who have suggested that the symptoms of PTSD result from traumatic memories remaining isolated from the general memory system, with flashbacks and other unwanted recall of events being the result of cognitive attempts to integrate isolated traumatic memories into general memory. Once such memories are fully integrated into the memory system, they lose their emotional charge and are no more salient than other more general memories. This process of integration is facilitated by thinking and rethinking about the memories until full integration has been achieved. Debriefing may encourage the integration of memories into general memory from the outset and prevent them becoming isolated and emotionally distressing.

How effective psychological debriefing is in achieving its goals is, unfortunately, somewhat questionable. In a meta-analysis of trials using debriefing, Rose *et al.* (2001) concluded that it may not only be ineffective in preventing PTSD, it may actually *increase* risk for the disorder. None of the studies they analysed found that debriefing lowered risk for PTSD in the three–four months following a traumatic incident. More worrying were the results of the two studies that reported longer-term findings. Both found that those who received debriefing were at nearly twice the risk of developing PTSD than those who did not receive the intervention. That is, debriefing seemed to inhibit long-term recovery from psychological trauma. A number of explanations have been proposed for these findings:

- ■ 'Secondary traumatisation' may occur as a result of further exposure to a traumatic incident within a short time of the event.
- ■ Debriefing may 'medicalise' normal distress and increase the expectancy of developing psychological symptoms in those who would otherwise not have done so.

■ Debriefing may prevent the potentially protective responses of denial and distancing that may occur in the immediate aftermath of a traumatic incident.

These findings seem particularly worrying, given the continued widespread use of debriefing. It may well be that in the immediate aftermath of a trauma, the person may benefit from some degree of avoidance of thinking about the trauma, only allowing themselves to think about it and deal with it over a longer period.

■ Treating PTSD

Following a traumatic incident, many people experience PTSD-like symptoms for a limited period. Many will also recover from them in the weeks following the incident. However, where these are persistent and distressing (for at least one month), people may be diagnosed as having PTSD. In such cases, the optimum treatment seems to be very similar to debriefing, as it involves repeated exposure to memories of the event. This may take place over a period of several sessions, until integration of isolated memories into general memory is achieved and the symptoms no longer occur. This type of intervention, known as **exposure therapy**, may lead to an initial increase in distress as upsetting images, previously avoided where possible, are deliberately recollected. To minimise this distress, Leskin *et al.* (1998) recommended a graded exposure process in which the individual initially recalls and talks about particular elements of a traumatic event at a level of detail they choose over several occasions until they no longer find them upsetting. Any new and potentially more distressing memories remain the focus of the next stages of the intervention.

Reactivation of memories by this procedure involves describing the experience in detail, focusing on what happened, the thoughts and emotions experienced at the time, and any memories that the incident triggered. This approach can be augmented by a variety of cognitive-behavioural techniques, including relaxation training and cognitive restructuring. Relaxation helps the individual to control their arousal when recalling distressing events, or at other times in the day when they are feeling tense or on edge. Cognitive restructuring can help them to change any distorted cognitions they had in response to the event and make them less threatening ('I'm going to die!' to 'It felt like I was going to die, but actually most people survive a diagnosis of . . .').

A number of studies have found exposure-based therapy to be superior to no treatment and interventions such as supportive counselling and relaxation therapy without exposure. Foa *et al.* (1991), for example, compared the effectiveness of a waiting-list control condition, self-instruction training as developed by Meichenbaum (see above), supportive counselling, and an exposure programme. Participants in each of the active interventions experienced more improvements than those in the waiting-list condition. However, by the three-month follow-up, people in the exposure programme reported the least intrusive memories and arousal.

The most recent treatment for PTSD is known as **eye movement desensitisation and reprocessing** (EMDR). This approach was discovered by chance by Shapiro (1995). In a now famous story of how the approach was initially

---

exposure therapy
a form of therapy involving exposure to traumatic memories, based on the theoretical assumption that continued exposure will result in a gradual reduction in the level of fear associated with such memories.

eye movement desensitisation and reprocessing (EMDR)
a form of therapy for post-traumatic stress disorder involving exposure to traumatic memories while repeatedly moving the eyes. Its method of working is not clear. However, the most popular theory is that when the eyes move back and forth this creates brain activity similar to that which occurs during REM (rapid eye movement) sleep. This may help the brain to process the 'stuck' material, enabling the person to arrive at an adaptive resolution.

developed, she noticed that while walking in the woods her disturbing thoughts began to disappear and were less upsetting than before. She linked this change to her eyes spontaneously moving rapidly backwards and forwards in an upward diagonal while walking. Since then, the procedure has been developed into a standardised intervention, and its effectiveness has been evaluated in a number of clinical trials. The intervention involves recall of trauma memories as visual images. The participant is then asked to link these images with a negative cognition associated with the memory but framed in the present tense ('I am terrified'). The individual rates the strength of emotion evoked by this process on a scale of 0–100. They are then asked to track the therapist's finger as it is moved increasingly quickly across their line of vision. After twenty-four such movements, the patient is instructed to 'blank it out' or 'let it go' and asked to rate their level of emotion. This procedure is repeated until the patient experiences minimal distress to the presence of the image and negative cognition. If no changes occur, the direction of eye movements is changed.

RESEARCH FOCUS

Donahue, S.A., Jackson, C.T., Shear, K.M. *et al.* (2006). Outcomes of enhanced counseling services provided to adults through Project Liberty. *Psychiatric Services*, 57: 1298–303.

Disasters, such as the terrorist attacks on the World Trade Centre (WTC), can have significant detrimental consequences for the mental health of those involved. This study evaluated the effectiveness of a programme established in New York following the September 11th attack on the WTC to minimise its effect on the population of New York. It is not a well-controlled randomised controlled trial. Instead, it attempted to provide a realistic assessment of the effectiveness of the interventions provided in the years following the attack, when the researchers and clinicians were grappling with a very real health problem.

Immediately following the attack on the WTC, the Federal Emergency Management Agency (FEMA) implemented Project Liberty to provide crisis counselling and public education services for residents of New York City and surrounding counties. Individual crisis counselling services were provided to 687,848 people, and approximately 550,000 received public education. More than a year after the attacks, reports from Project Liberty providers indicated that additional services were needed for some individuals still struggling with serious disaster-related problems. In response to this, FEMA funded an additional 'enhanced services' programme of counselling for individuals who remained significantly affected by the attacks. To select people into the programme, individuals who needed three or more sessions of counselling were screened for presence of depression, PTSD, or an abnormal grief reaction. Where these conditions were found, individuals were offered the enhanced services. These comprised cognitive-behavioural intervention for depression or PTSD and/or a grief intervention that included strategies for dealing with loss and re-engaging in satisfying life activities and techniques for working with problem emotions (guilt and anger). Both interventions were designed to last between ten and twelve sessions.

Participants and procedure

Over the period of the study, 214 individuals who only received crisis counselling agreed to be contacted, and 153 (71 per cent) completed a telephone interview. Of the 119 people who received enhanced services over this time, 102 agreed to be interviewed and 93 (91 per cent) completed the same telephone interview. A total of 76 (75 per cent) completed a second telephone interview approximately forty days later.

Telephone interview

The telephone interview assessed participants' experiences during the attacks, their reasons for contacting Project Liberty, demographic characteristics, extent of symptoms, functional impairment and interventions received. In addition, they measured:

- *Depression and PTSD symptoms.* Respondents reported whether they had experienced a series of symptoms consistent with depression or PTSD for two weeks or longer during the previous month.

- *Complicated grief.* If respondents indicated that someone they knew died during the attacks, they were asked to respond to five questions measuring complicated grief (e.g. How much does your grief still interfere with your life?). A score of 8 or more indicated probable complicated grief.

- *Daily functioning.* Respondents rated their current functioning in five domains using 4-point Likert scales: job or school, maintaining relationships with family and friends, handling daily household activities, ability to take care of physical health, and staying involved in community activities.

Findings

Comparisons between counselling groups

The crisis counselling and enhanced services samples did not differ in age or gender composition. There was no significant difference in respondents' assessment of being in immediate danger during the attacks, but a significantly greater proportion of enhanced-services recipients reported knowing someone who died as a result of the attacks, having been involved in rescue efforts, or having lost their job because of them. At the time of the first interview, the enhanced-services recipients reported significantly more symptoms of depression and PTSD, more intense grief, and were more likely to be defined as 'cases' of depression or PTSD. Forty-two per cent of the enhanced-services sample met the criteria for a major depressive disorder, and 39 per cent met the criteria for PTSD. Enhanced-services recipients were also significantly more impaired in all domains of their daily functioning.

Changes over time

Enhanced-services recipients reported a significant reduction in the number of depressive symptoms from the first to the second interview (mean score time 1 = 4.2; time 2 = 2.8), significantly reduced intensity of grief (mean 7.4 versus 4.8), and significantly improved daily functioning in three of five life domains (job and school, personal relationships and household activities). The number of PTSD symptoms was also notably reduced (6.1 versus 5.1). These scores were similar to those of the crisis-counselling recipients about one year earlier.

Discussion

This investigation has several limitations, and findings should be considered preliminary. Perhaps the greatest methodological weakness was the lack of randomisation into treated and untreated individuals. The changes in the enhanced service could have occurred naturally over time, and not be a result of the enhanced intervention. Accordingly, while the study suggests that individuals with severe and enduring problems following the September 11th attacks benefited from the interventions, this cannot be stated definitively. The authors can be forgiven this weakness – they placed the wellbeing of those involved over methodological rigour.

EMDR incorporates exposure to elements of the trauma stimulus. It is therefore important to determine whether the addition of the eye movements enhances the effect of exposure. This does not seem to be the case. While EMDR is certainly more effective than no treatment, it may be no more effective than standard exposure methods. Reviewing the evidence, Davidson and Parker (2001) used meta-analysis to compare the effectiveness of EMDR with no treatment, non-specific treatments and the exposure methods described above. While their analyses indicated a benefit for EMDR when compared with no treatment or non-specific treatments, its benefits were similar to or less than those resulting from exposure approaches.

Minimising stress in hospital settings

Pre-operational preparation

Having an operation is a stressful event, whether it is a small operation conducted under local anaesthetic or a larger one involving a period of unconsciousness and a significant period of recovery. It should not be surprising, therefore, that levels of anxiety can be high both before and after an operation. This anxiety is both unpleasant for the individual concerned and can add to the complications they experience. It may increase the amount of painkilling medication they take, the degree to which they need reassurance both before and after the operation, and even the time necessary for them to stay in hospital (Johnston and Vogele 1993). As a consequence, a number of researchers have attempted to identify ways of minimising this distress. While the stress management approaches described above may be appropriate under such circumstances, health-care staff and patients rarely have the time (or the inclination) to teach or learn these strategies (although hypnosis has been used with some effect with children; Liossi *et al.* 2006). Accordingly, a very different approach has been taken to help people to cope with this specific type of stress.

Many studies have shown that we feel less anxiety when faced with potentially stressful circumstances if we can be given some degree of control over them (e.g. Lok and Bishop 1999). These findings have led health psychologists to examine whether giving patients undergoing surgery some degree of control over their situation will reduce the amount of stress they experience. Clearly, patients cannot have much control over their anaesthetics or surgery – such things really should be left to the experts! So, in this case, 'giving control' has been interpreted as 'keeping people informed about what is happening to them'. This is thought to reduce anxiety by minimising the fear of the unknown. If patients know what to expect, they may understand better and be less alarmed by any experiences they have. If patients are told, for example, that they will experience some pain after their surgery they will be less alarmed and less likely to think that things have gone wrong if they do experience any pain. A number of studies have examined the effectiveness of providing two sorts of information to patients prior to them having surgery:

Plate 13.2 The calming presence of a parent can help children to relax and cope better with any concerns they may have about their operation.

Source: John Cole/Science Photo Library

1. *Procedural information*: telling patients about the events that will occur before and after surgery; having a pre-medication injection, waking in the recovery room and having a drip in their arm, and so on.

2. *Sensory information*: telling patients what they will feel before and after surgery; that it is normal to feel some pain following surgery, they may feel confused when they come round from the anaesthetic, and so on.

The overall picture is that these interventions usually work (Johnston and Vogele 1993), although not always. Luck *et al.* (1999), for example, found that showing a video about the procedure a week before patients were given a **colonoscopy** reduced anxiety in the period leading up to the procedure. In a subsequent study of the same procedure, however, they found no such benefit (Pearson *et al.* 2005).

colonoscopy
a minor surgical procedure in which a small piece of bowel wall is cut from the colon. This can then be tested for the presence of malignant cells.

■ Matching patient needs

One explanation for these mixed findings is that the effect of the intervention is relatively weak, and may not always be found. Another explanation could be that the intervention works for some people, and not others. What may be as important as the type of intervention is matching it to the characteristics of the patients receiving it. Patients who typically cope with stress by using avoidant coping strategies may benefit, for example, from receiving less information than those who typically cope through the use of problem-focused strategies (see Chapter 11), and vice-versa. This hypothesis was tested by Morgan *et al.* (1998), who gave people identified as primarily 'information seekers' or 'avoiders' either sensory information about the nature of a forthcoming colonoscopy or no information. Patients who were given information congruent with their coping style (i.e. no information for 'avoiders'; information for 'seekers') reported less anxiety prior to the procedure than those who were given incongruent information. They also scored lower on a measure of 'pain behaviour' made by nursing staff during the procedure, although participants did not report any differences in pain during the procedure, or differ in their use of sedative drugs. These data suggest that:

■ People who usually cope using problem-focused strategies benefit from information that helps them to understand their experience and to actively interpret their experience in relation to information they are given.

■ People who usually cope using avoidant, emotion-focused, strategies benefit most from not being told what to expect, and perhaps being helped to develop strategies that help them distract from the situation.

Levels of anxiety may also influence the impact of pre-operative preparation. Hathaway (1986), for example, concluded from a meta-analysis that patients with low levels of anxiety benefited most from the provision of procedural information, while those with high levels of anxiety gained most from unstructured discussion. Anxiety inhibits new learning, partly because people who are anxious may not attend to whatever they are being told, partly as a direct inhibition of memory processes. It is possible, therefore, that anxious patients may benefit most when they are given relatively little information, but the information they are given matches their needs.

Studies of the effects of teaching relaxation to anxious patients have reported mixed results. Wilson (1981) found that patients who had relatively low levels of anxiety seemed to benefit most from learning relaxation skills. By contrast, those patients with particularly high levels of anxiety did not benefit from being taught relaxation – perhaps because their anxiety prevented them learning and implementing their relaxation skills sufficiently well.

More complex interventions have taught people cognitive restructuring techniques (see above) to help to minimise anxiety-provoking thoughts both before and after surgery. Ridgeway and Mathews (1982), for example, assigned women having gynaecological surgery to one of three conditions: a placebo condition in which they received general information about the hospital ward; procedural and sensory information; and training in cognitive restructuring methods. Following surgery, there were no differences between the groups on measures of pain, nausea or sleep duration. However, participants in the cognitive restructuring condition used less analgesia while in hospital and reported less pain following discharge from hospital than either of the other groups. Despite the success of the cognitive intervention, the simplicity of the informational-based interventions makes them more likely to be carried out in the 'real world' of a busy ward.

■ Working with children and parents

Much of the recent work in preparing people for surgery has focused on helping children and their parents. Studies that have focused on children have shown that a variety of techniques may be of benefit. Mahajan *et al.* (1998), for example, randomly allocated young people aged between 6 and 19 years to one of two conditions prior to gastrointestinal endoscopy. The first received routine preparation. The second received procedural preparation, involving a demonstration of materials that would be used during the endoscopy and the use of a doll or a book of photographs showing the procedure. Compared with the no-preparation condition, participants in the procedural information condition reported less anxiety both before and during the procedure, used less anaesthetic and had lower heart rates, suggesting that they were more relaxed. Hatava *et al.* (2000) randomly assigned children and parents to one of two interventions designed to reduce anxiety before an ear, nose or throat (ENT) operation. In the first condition, they were given written or verbal information by a nurse two weeks prior to surgery. This included information about general hospital rules, routines and the date of the operation. This acted as a form of placebo intervention as there is little here that would have been expected to reduce anxiety other than meeting the nurse that may be involved in their care. The second group were given a more complex intervention comprising the same information two weeks prior to the operation followed by a visit to the ENT department the day before surgery. During this visit, each child and parent met the anaesthetist who would be at the operation and took part in a group session led by a nurse in which they were shown the operating theatre and lay on the operating table. They were also shown the equipment that would be used during anaesthesia and were encouraged to play with it in order to minimise its threat and increase familiarity. They were then shown the procedure that would occur on the day through role-play using a doll. This complex intervention resulted in significant benefits – particularly for the youngest children in the programme, those under five years old. Both younger and older children reported less fear and anxiety prior to the surgery. In addition, their parents reported more satisfaction and less anxiety than those who did not receive the intervention.

Jay *et al.* (1995) provided an unusual comparison between medical and psychological methods of reducing distress in children undergoing **bone marrow biopsy** – an excruciatingly painful procedure. It can also be distressing for both the children and parents involved. They compared two approaches to minimising this distress in a sample of children aged between 3 and 12 years. The first was simply to fully anaesthetise the children. While this approach evokes some degree of anxiety, they reasoned that it may be less distressing than experiencing the process while under local anaesthetic. They compared this approach with conducting the procedure under local anaesthetic after teaching the children both relaxation and cognitive restructuring as a means of controlling their distress. One can only imagine that this was taught at a very simple level, particularly to the younger children. Perhaps not surprisingly, the children who received training in stress management methods experienced more distress than those who were anaesthetised at the beginning of the procedure. However, their parents' ratings suggested that they were the least distressed in the following days. Interestingly, neither the children nor their parents showed any preference for either intervention.

Interventions that target parents may benefit both parent and child. Campbell *et al.* (1992), for example, prepared mothers of pre-school age children having a cardiac operation during which their child would be conscious in one of three ways: supportive counselling, education about the hospital and procedure, and relaxation and positive self-talk (stress management). The latter interventions proved most effective. Mothers and children who

bone marrow biopsy usually performed under local anaesthetic by making a small incision into the skin. A biopsy needle is then pushed through the bone and takes a sample of marrow from the centre of the bone. Marrow contains platelets, phagocytes and lymphocytes.

received the stress management training coped better with the procedure itself, and their children adapted more positively at home following discharge from hospital than those in the other conditions. The women who received the educational intervention reported less anxiety and tension during the procedure than those in the other conditions. Again, it seems that a combination of interventions including education and teaching coping strategies may provide the optimal intervention.

Summary

This chapter has examined a variety of approaches to stress management and contexts in which it has been conducted. Systemic interventions that target whole organisations can be used as a preventive approach. More individual approaches based around specific therapeutic approaches may benefit people experiencing mild to highly traumatic stress. Finally, simple procedural information may benefit people facing the stress of an operation where there is little time (or need) to use these more complex interventions.

We noted that while stress management 'classes' provide a potentially useful and effective way of reaching the public, attendance is likely to be limited, and health psychologists and others have targeted larger and more 'captive audiences' in organisations.

Managing stress at this level can involve a variety of approaches depending on the organisational causes of stress. Stress management interventions should follow an audit of stressors and target environmental issues that both contribute to stress and can realistically be changed in the context of the particular workplace.

Cognitive-behavioural interventions targeted at reducing stress involve changing:

- triggers to stress, using, for example, the problem-focused approach of Egan;
- the cognitive precursors to stress, using the self-instruction and cognitive restructuring approaches of Beck, Meichenbaum and Ellis;
- the physiological response to stress using relaxation methods, including the modified Jacobsen technique;
- the behavioural reactions to stressful situations using Meichenbaum's stress inoculation and role-play techniques.

Treatments of trauma include those that are thought to be preventive and those that help people to cope with longer-term conditions such as PTSD.

- Clinical debriefing close to the time of the incident does not appear to be preventive.
- Exposure-based interventions seem to be effective in the treatment of established PTSD.
- EMDR seems to provide no additional benefit to these approaches.

Finally, providing relevant information to help people to understand and cope with the stress of hospital procedures such as operations may reduce distress and pain and facilitate rehabilitation following surgery. However, its benefits vary according to individual differences in coping style.

- Patients who are typically problem solvers benefit most from the provision of information.
- Patients who typically cope with stress using avoidant strategies may be helped best by teaching them distraction techniques.

Further reading

Elkin, A. (1999). *Stress Management for Dummies*. New York: Wiley.
A fairly irreverent but useful guide to managing your own stress.

Goulston, G. (2007). *Post-traumatic Stress Disorder for Dummies*. New York: Wiley.
A similar approach to treating PTSD.

Meichenbaum, D. (1985). *Stress Inoculation Training*. Longman Higher Education.
A more academic clinical consideration of stress management techniques for working with individuals. It's a bit old now, but it remains one of the best introductory texts there is.

Carlson, R. (1998). *Don't Sweat the Small Stuff . . . and It's All Small Stuff*. London: Hodder Mobius.
Multiple five-star ratings on Amazon; recommended by clients dealing with stress and anger. What better recommendations can you have? It's a self-help book, not an academic text, but it gives good insight into cognitive and other elements of stress management. I certainly found it useful!

Williams, S. and Cooper, L. (2002). *Managing Workplace Stress*. Chichester: Wiley.
A good and practical review of stress management issues at an organisational level. It was sponsored by the 'bosses' (the Confederation of British Industry), so they should know what they are talking about.

Jones, M.C. and Johnston D.W. (2000). Reducing distress in first level and student nurses: a review of the applied stress management literature. *Journal of Advanced Nursing*, 32: 66–74.
It's a little old now, but still the most up-to-date and good review of a variety of systemic and individual interventions to reduce stress among student nurses.

Lamontagne, A.D., Keegel, T., Louie, A.M. *et al.* (2007). A systematic review of the job-stress intervention evaluation literature, 1990–2005. *International Journal of Occupational and Environmental Health*, 13: 268–80.
A good up-to-date review.

Jain, S., Shapiro, S.L., Swanick, S. *et al.* (2007). A randomized controlled trial of mindfulness meditation versus relaxation training: effects on distress, positive states of mind, rumination, and distraction. *Annals of Behavioral Medicine*, 33: 11–21.
An interesting study showing a specific effect of meditation on levels of intrusive worries.

Takao, S., Tsutsumi, A., Nishiuchi, K. *et al.* (2006). Effects of the job stress education for supervisors on psychological distress and job performance among their immediate subordinates: a supervisor-based randomized controlled trial. *Journal of Occupational Health*, 48: 494–503.
Interesting Japanese study looking at the impact of training supervisors in stress management and its effect on the people they are supervising. Free off the web.

Type in stress management (training) into any search engine, and you will get thousands of hits. Few are useful resources though, as most are links to commercial sites who want your money before you can access information. You could try this site, though (although no promises!):
http://www.mindtools.com/smpage.html

Visit the website at **www.pearsoned.co.uk/morrison** for additional resources to help you with your study, including multiple choice questions, weblinks and flashcards.

PART III

Being ill

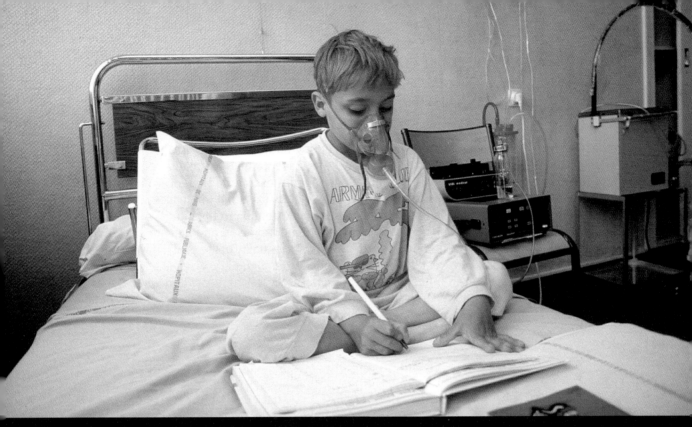

CHAPTER 14

The impact of illness on quality of life

Learning outcomes

By the end of this chapter, you should have an understanding of:

- quality of life as a multidimensional, dynamic and subjective construct
- demographic, clinical and psychosocial influences on perceptions of quality of life
- benefits and disadvantages of common methods of assessing quality of life
- the need to consider specific populations when developing measurement tools

CHAPTER OUTLINE

Illness is a dynamic process, beginning with perception of symptoms or a diagnosis and continuing or changing over time as a function of the disease pathology, treatment possibilities and the responses to illness by the person affected and those around them. We have shown in previous chapters that many individual and social factors exist that influence the responses to a stressful experience, and in this chapter we turn our attention to the impact of illness. We address the impact of illness on an individual's emotional wellbeing and adjustment, on their global and health-related functioning – in other words, their quality of life (QoL). It is first necessary to define this broad construct, before exploring how demographic, disease and treatment, and psychosocial factors can influence perceptions of QoL. Having described what QoL is (if that is fully possible, given the subjectivity of the concept), we turn attention to issues of how to measure this multidimensional, dynamic and subjective concept.

Illness and quality of life

While the primary goal of medicine and health care is to improve health and/or treat and cure illness and its symptoms, there is a need to address more global outcomes of health-care treatments and services, such as patient wellbeing. While clinical outcomes can be assessed in an objective manner (such as observing improved physical functioning or reduced symptomatology), assessing patient wellbeing requires that the view of the patient be sought. For example, in clinical trials (such as those conducted to test the efficacy of a new drug) and intervention studies (psychological or clinical), it is important to evaluate clinical outcomes such as symptom reduction but also the individual's own perceptions of how the treatment or intervention has influenced their illness experience and their general psychosocial functioning. Quality of life (QoL) research has become a major area of multidisciplinary research for a variety of reasons. One likely reason is that because technological advances in medicine can effectively treat more conditions that in previous generations people would have died from, for example major strokes, heart attacks and many forms of cancer, people are living longer, often with some dependency needs or with some aspect of their life restricted. A consequence of this is growing acceptance, primarily within the medical domain, of the importance of knowing about and understanding the psychosocial as well as the clinical outcomes of treatments or interventions. Having this fuller knowledge has implications for future care, treatment and service provision. As Boini *et al.* (2004: 4) succinctly put it, 'physicians now have the opportunity to add life to years, as well as adding years to life'. Furthermore, patients may derive great benefit from certain treatments or interventions in terms of enhanced quality of life, even though these same treatments or interventions may not extend survival or quantity of life (see IN THE SPOTLIGHT below).

To illustrate the growth of QoL research in both the psychological and medical literature, Garratt *et al.* (2002) published a review in the *British*

Medical Journal, where it was revealed that between 1990 and 1999 there were over 23,000 QoL records in the literature engines searched, 4,000 of which were specifically about scale development and testing. What is this construct that has received so much research attention?

What do YOU think?

How would you define quality of life? Think about you 'now' compared perhaps with your parents and your friends. Do you think you see 'quality of life' differently to them? Consider why this may be. Consider what you see as being important to your quality of life in the future.

What is quality of life?

In general terms, quality of life (QoL) can be referred to as an individual's evaluation of their overall life experience at a given time (global quality of life), with the term 'health-related QoL' emerging to refer to evaluations of life experience and how they are affected by symptoms, disease, accidents or treatments. A health-related quality of life (HRQoL) is therefore associated with 'optimal levels of mental, physical, role (e.g. work, parent, carer) and social functioning, including relationships, and perceptions of health, fitness, life satisfaction and well-being. It should also include some assessment of the patient's level of satisfaction with treatment, outcome and health status and with future prospects' (Bowling 1995a: 3).

According to the World Health Organization Quality of Life (WHOQOL) working group (1993, 1994), QoL is a person's perceptions of their position in life in relation to their cultural context and the value systems of that context in relation to their own goals, standards and expectations. Quality of life is considered to be a broad concept affected by an individual's physical and mental health, level of independence, quality of social relationships, social integration and, added subsequently (WHOQOL 1998), their personal, religious and spiritual beliefs. This working group has produced a generic and cross-culturally valid assessment tool (WHOQOL-100), which addresses twenty-five different facets of QoL grouped into one of six domains:

1. *physical health*: pain and discomfort; energy and fatigue; sleep and rest;
2. *psychological*: positive feelings; self-esteem; thinking, memory, learning and concentration; bodily image and appearance; negative feelings;
3. *level of independence*: activities of daily living (e.g. self-care); mobility; medication and treatment dependence; work capacity;
4. *social relationships*: personal relationships; practical social support; sexual activity;
5. *relation to environment*: physical safety and security; financial resources; home environment; availability and quality of health/social care; learning opportunities; leisure participation and opportunities; transport; physical environment;
6. *Spirituality, religion and personal beliefs.*

This generic tool provides core items for use across all conditions, with disease- and population-specific versions being developed subsequently (see later section on measuring quality of life). Most of the QoL measures available to researchers or clinicians address the multiple dimensions described above, and certainly if you asked someone nowadays what their 'quality of life' was, their answer would reflect many differing aspects of life. However, early studies tended to focus more keenly on physical function as if QoL was reflected fundamentally in this. Certainly one of the aims of assessing QoL is to ascertain the impact of disease on an individual's functioning, and many studies use measures of disease or symptom severity, disability or physical functioning as outcome measures considered to be indicative of quality of life. However, the WHO model of impairment, disability and handicap (see Chapter 1; WHO 1980) described how illness had more than just physical consequences, by defining handicap as disadvantages and limitations in performing social roles that resulted directly from impairment and/or disability. Johnston and Pollard (2001), in testing the WHO model, further concluded that the linear relationship between impairment, disability and handicap was not inevitable but depended on psychological and social factors. Further support for this comes from studies of individuals suffering from rheumatoid arthritis, where the link between pathophysiology and disability outcomes is often found to be indirect and moderated by psychosocial and environmental factors (see Walker *et al.* 2004 for a review).

Rather than considering disease, disability and handicap as indicative *of* quality of life, they could therefore be considered as potential influences *upon* it (McKenna *et al.* 2000; McKenna 2004) that may or may not affect a person's perceived QoL, depending on the extent to which that individual rates them as important to that judgement (e.g. Cox 2003). For some individuals, the inability to perform valued activities as a result of impairment or disability may be considered a 'fate worse than death' (e.g. Ditto *et al.* 1996); however, for others they will continue to find meaning and purpose in life in spite of disablement. IN THE SPOTLIGHT (below) raises the question of whether the outcomes important to the person concerned are the same as the outcomes valued by the health profession or, in particular, health economists.

What influences quality of life?

Many factors influence QoL:

- demographics: e.g. age, culture;
- the condition itself: e.g. symptoms, presence or absence of pain, functional disability, neurological damage with associated motor, emotional or cognitive impairment, sensory or communicative impairment;
- treatment: e.g. its availability, nature, extent, toxicity, side-effects, etc.;
- psychosocial factors: e.g. emotions (anxiety, depression), coping, social context, goals and support.

IN THE SPOTLIGHT

Which health outcomes are important to whom?

For most people, the choice between a treatment without major side-effects and a treatment with major side-effects would be an easy decision, i.e. that without the side-effects. However, the decision becomes more complex if the choice is now between a treatment without major side-effects but with only moderate proven success in eradicating or controlling the illness concerned, and a treatment with significant side-effects but with excellent success rates. Which would you choose? These types of decision are faced daily by many cancer patients, who are fighting for survival but facing often toxic treatments in terms of their side-effects. The quantity of life may be added to by these treatments, but what about life quality? These questions raise the issue of which outcomes are best for the individual being treated.

If economics also enters the debate, as it increasingly does in terms of treatment costs, costs of hospital stays, costs of follow-up care, etc., then decisions about which treatment outcomes are best often fall into the hands of doctors and hospital managers who are responsible for spending. The outcome of mortality has little health-care cost, whereas prolonged morbidity does and therefore treatment efficacy is central to these decisions. The ideal outcome from a medical standpoint is likely to be optimal functioning, but few treatments come with that guarantee, and if they do, then they are likely to be very expensive! Decisions are generally made in terms of weighing up the costs of treatment (e.g. financial costs, costs to the person in terms of side-effects) against the objective benefits of treatment (e.g. financial savings from reduced further treatment needs, projected quantity of life gain for the individual).

Time trade-off techniques used by health economists can examine the utility (importance) attached to health states. Patients can be asked to imagine living with a certain condition for a couple of years, compared with living in better health for a shorter length of time if given a certain treatment, although they may die or be very ill after this time. The actual periods in normal health are adjusted until the person can no longer choose between the states. For example, if you were indifferent to whether you lived in poor health for six months or in optimal health for three months with treatment, then this would indicate the utility of that treatment for that individual. Basically, these kinds of judgement require individuals to consider how much time in terms of current QoL they would be willing to trade for post-treatment QoL; for example, how many days of treatment would you willingly trade for how many months of improved health? (See Bowling 1995a: 12–14 for a fuller discussion of the complexities of such techniques).

There is evidence that health professionals differ in their ability to communicate about such issues, and furthermore, that they may underestimate patients HRQoL (Detmar *et al.* 2000). This illustrates the point that such decisions, and the values placed on outcomes such as pain, disability, distress and even death, are subjective: i.e. different individuals value different aspects of life. As this chapter will also show, what is valued may change over the lifespan. For example, will a 75-year-old cancer patient consider the treatment options such as six three-weekly doses of chemotherapy, the anticipated benefits in terms of extended lifespan, and the likely side-effects (nausea, achey limbs, hair loss, etc.) in the same way as a 35–45-year-old parent? This is why it is so important to assess individuals' perceptions of what makes their life 'quality'.

■ Age and quality of life

Age has been shown to influence the aspects of life considered to be important to people. While studies of QoL in child populations remains relatively limited and focused on chronic, rather than generally life-threatening illness (e.g. asthma and epilepsy), Matza and colleagues (Matza *et al.* 2004) noted in their review of conceptual, methodological and regulatory issues relevant to HRQoL in children that 'researchers are becoming aware of the unique challenges of assessing pediatric health outcomes, including health-related quality of life' (p. 79). They point to the different contexts which may mediate the impact of illness and its treatments on the child. For example, cancer treatments commonly impact upon school attendance and participation in school activities important to a child's social development (Eiser 2004); childhood epilepsy can impede social functioning, independence and relationships with peers as well as, in some cases, self-esteem and mood (McEwan *et al.* 2004).

Jirojanakul *et al.* (2003) note that understanding childhood QoL is important because any effects of impaired QoL may be cumulative and affect later development. Given that QoL judgements are made by assessing present lifestyle relative to one's expectations (Eiser and Morse 2001), a fruitful avenue of work might therefore examine whether children with chronic disease modify their future life expectations as a result of QoL being compromised in their childhood. To date, we are unaware of any such studies. Logically, however, we might expect consequences, given the evidence that negative experiences such as social rejection in childhood (a possible consequence of the non-participation some physical illnesses may create) can have long-term effects.

While the majority of studies have relied on parental 'proxy' reports of their child's QoL (see the section on measuring quality of life, below), several interesting studies have employed qualitative methods to elicit domains of importance in QoL and factors that influence it, for example by carrying out focus group discussions with the children themselves. Cramer *et al.* (1999, cited in McEwan *et al.* 2004) conducted focus groups with adolescents with epilepsy and identified eight sub-scales that related to the health-related QoL:

1. general epilepsy impact
2. memory/concentration problems
3. attitudes towards epilepsy
4. physical functioning
5. stigma
6. social support
7. school behaviour
8. general health perceptions.

These findings reflect a broad range of influences on the QoL of young people (aged 11–17), and quantitative results from the same study found that seizure severity was the main predictor of health-related quality of life, independent of age of onset of the illness. In other words, length of time that the illness had been present did not appear to reduce the impact of severe seizures on QoL. In another focus-group study that examined health-related QoL and its relation to distress among children with epilepsy aged 6–12, distress was mainly associated with loss of independence and restrictions in daily activities, concern about the reactions of others to their illness and seizures, treatment by peers, and concerns about the side-effects of medication (Ronen *et al.* 1999, as cited in McEwan *et al.* 2004).

An unusual study of children aged 5–8 either attending school or working alongside construction worker parents in Thailand, found, perhaps surprisingly, that generic QoL (as opposed to HRQoL) was less affected by health states (chronic, acute or severe illness) than by socio-economic factors (Jirojanakul *et al.* 2003). Social background variables such as parental income, education and occupational status, type of housing and extent of child's extracurricular activities significantly explained QoL (assessed with a child-friendly form as well as by proxy), whereas health status did not. While this study was conducted in Thailand, and among predominantly healthy children, the findings are considered consistent with studies in Western child populations, where current life circumstances (and the expectations they bring with them) are important to QoL (e.g. Eiser and Morse 2001).

The effect of age on QoL ratings is not inevitable. For example, age was not predictive of quality of life in a one-year longitudinal study of stroke survivors ranging from 32 to 90 years old, where other factors, such as physical disability, depressed mood and gender (females had poorer QoL) were (Carod-Artal *et al.* 2000). It may be that age is less important than 'life stage': i.e. the impact of illness on QoL might vary according to whether or not it occurs at a time in life when a person is still professionally or reproductively active. Among younger people who have suffered an acute stroke, being unable to return to work has been associated with reduced life satisfaction and subjective wellbeing (e.g. Vestling *et al.* 2003), whereas this would not concern the majority of stroke patients who are post-retirement age. Referred to as the 'third age' the period of life after retirement can continue to be full of enjoyment and opportunity whereas the 'fourth age' is when illness and disability present challenges to an older persons' independence (Woods 2008). Maintaining QoL and promoting healthy, positive and successful ageing has become increasingly important, given the ageing population of most societies (Baltes and Baltes 1990; Grundy and Bowling 1999). The goal of healthy ageing approaches is to minimise dependency (physical and/or emotional), which, in turn, it is hoped, will reduce the 'costs' to society of healthcare provision for an increasingly ageing population. Studies of older people have found the life domains of importance to be good physical functioning, having relationships with others, and maintaining health and social activity. Compared with younger samples, older people are more likely to mention independence, or the fear of losing it and becoming dependent (Bowling 1995b). Blane *et al.* (2004) examined influences on QoL in over three hundred individuals aged between 65 and 75 and found that serious and limiting health problems were most strongly predictive of QoL, whereas non-limiting chronic disease did not affect QoL. They also found housing security, receipt of welfare or non-pension income and (for men only) years out of work to be predictive. When a limiting illness is involved, the domains of importance in terms of judging one's own QoL become more focused on physical functioning and activity, social support and social contact, although illness type appears less important than the level of resultant physical disability.

**What do
YOU think?**

Have you ever experienced something which has challenged your quality of life? If so, in what way did it challenge it, and how did you deal with it? Did you find that one domain of QoL took on greater importance than it had previously? Why was this the case? Have the 'weightings' you attach to the different domains returned to their pre-challenge levels or has the event had a long-lasting impact on how you evaluate life and opportunities?

If you are lucky enough not to have experienced any major challenges to your QoL, consider how the loss of some aspect of health seems to have impacted on someone you know. Consider whether you would respond in the same way were you to lose that same aspect of health.

While being limited in terms of one's activities or roles is commonly a predictor of poorer mental and physical QoL, this is not always the case. Over half of the older people surveyed by Evandrou (2006) who had long-standing limiting illness self-rated their health as good or fairly good, highlighting the fact that quality of life is about more than just physical health and physical function. While a key global aim of interventions to enhance QoL, regardless of disease type, is the improvement and maintenance of physical and role functioning, in old age as at all ages QoL continues to be multidimensional. Even among the 'oldest old' (i.e. 85 or older), QoL encompasses psychological, social and environmental wellbeing (Grundy and Bowling 1999). ISSUES (below) addresses the question of whether or not QoL is attainable at the end of life, as a result of either ageing or terminal illness.

Plate 14.1   Social isolation increases the risk a reduced quality of life.
Source: Jerry Cooke/Corbis

End-of-life QoL

While the majority of deaths take place in hospitals, the care of the dying more often takes place in patients' homes, until the point is reached where some home carers can no longer provide the necessary care or medication, and hospitalisation in nursing homes or hospices ensues. Among others, Elizabeth Kubler-Ross (1969) highlighted the psychological and emotional aspects of dying and the need to 'listen to the dying patient'. The hospice movement developed in the late 1960s out of recognition that traditional hospitals with their routines, emphasis on treatment and depersonalised atmosphere were not best placed to provide care to the dying (Saunders and Baines 1983). The hospice movement aimed to provide care that facilitated an optimal QoL for both patients and their families as death approaches. This requires that patients are pain-free, experience little distress, maintain some dignity and control, and can maintain relationships with loved ones in a caring and compassionate environment. A good QoL at the end of life has also been found to encompass patients' need to remain as independent as possible so as not to 'burden' (see later section) their carer (e.g. Gill *et al.* 2003). It is also important for carers' needs to be supported in order that they are able to provide the patient with whatever support is needed during the final days and weeks of their life (World Health Organization Expert Committee 1990). Hospices therefore provide this kind of environment, although hospice beds remain predominantly for cancer patients (Seale 1991). However, do hospices make a difference?

Carers of patients who had died in hospices reported that 'their' patients were more aware that they were dying than did carers of those who had died in hospital, perhaps reflecting the ethos of openness encouraged in hospices (*ibid.*). This openness regarding dying may enable greater preparation for death and bereavement among patients and spouse carers, which has, in turn, been associated with reduced levels of emotional distress (e.g. Chochinov *et al.* 2000). The positive differences attributed to hospice care are not consistently reported, however; for example, Seale and Kelly (1997) did not find a difference between hospice and hospital care in terms of the care and support provided to spouses. Thinking positively, this may reflect the changing nature of hospital care towards more holistic, psychosocial care, or thinking less positively, perhaps a growing medicalisation of hospices (Crossley and Small 1998). With specialist nurses in hospitals, at least in terms of cancer services, and in the UK, we can perhaps infer that hospital care has become more holistic. Certainly, within England and Wales the National Institute for Clinical Excellence (NICE) guidance on Improving Supportive and Palliative Care for Adults with Cancer (2004) recommends that 'assessment and discussion of patients' needs for physical, psychological, social, spiritual and financial support should be undertaken at key points (such as at diagnosis; at commencement, during, and at the end of treatment; at relapse; and when death is approaching)' (Key recommendation 2).

Whenever a person is facing death as a result of a long-standing illness, whether cancer or not, issues such as 'a good death' and 'dying with dignity' become salient and bring with them many ethical and moral debates. Research has consistently shown that older people do not fear death itself, as younger people do, but are more concerned about the process of dying and the fear of dying in pain or without dignity and self-control (e.g. Chochinov *et al.* 2002; McKiernan 1996; Strang and Strang 2002). Questions are many, and the answers are not simple. When should treatment be stopped? How much pain can a person endure, and for how long? Should a dying person who has been experiencing great pain be resuscitated if they

continued

become unconscious? Should a person facing a terminal illness and inevitable decline towards death (such as the highly publicised case of Diane Petty, who faced full physical paralysis while remaining mentally intact as a result of motor neurone disease) be allowed to invite assisted suicide? How, and even where, an ill person chooses to die is inevitably a personal decision. Choosing 'when' to die is altogether more contentious. 'Advance directives' are becoming increasingly common, whereby people indicate their wishes for medical intervention (or not) when and if the time comes that they are unable to communicate their wishes. The practice of non-treatment of a dying person – passive euthanasia – is generally acknowledged as an inevitable part of medicine; however, active euthanasia in terms of carrying out an action that effectively ends that life (such as administering a fatal dose of adrenaline) is much less common. Van der Heide *et al.* (2003), in a study of end-of-life decision-making practices in six European countries, found that the explicit hastening of death varied from less than 1 per cent in Denmark, Italy, Sweden and Switzerland, through to 1.82 per cent in Belgium and 3.4 per cent in The Netherlands. The legality of assisted suicide or euthanasia also varies from being fully prohibited (e.g. Italy) to prohibited except in specific circumstances (e.g. Belgium, The Netherlands). In The Netherlands, GPs have been able to carry out these practices since 1991 (Onwuteaka-Phillipsen *et al.* 2003). Other countries, however, have yet to make policy on this issue. For example, a study conducted in Wales (Pasterfield *et al.* 2006) asked GPs this question 'Do you think that the law on intentional killing should be changed to allow (a) physician-assisted suicide and (b) voluntary euthanasia? Of the 1025 doctors who responded (a very reasonable 65 per cent of those invited into the study), 62.4 per cent did not favour a change in law regarding (a), and 55.8 per cent similarly did not favour a change of law regarding (b). In the face of such findings, it is likely to be some time before this contentious issue is resolved in terms of any legislation, at least in the UK, although public support is reported to be high in the case of those suffering from painful, terminal illness (House of Lords 2005).

Human rights legislation, the desire for control over our lives and the fact that the world is facing an ageing population, many of whom will live many years with chronic ill health, suggests that issues regarding euthanasia are going to remain, and possibly grow.

Have your own personal experiences of death, if you have experienced any, influenced your thoughts on how you would choose to die, if that choice were available? What do you think would provide 'quality of life' at the end of life?

■ Culture and quality of life

Chapter 1 described how health itself is viewed slightly differently in Western and non-Western cultures, with individualistic Western views and more collectivist Eastern views of health being identified. Yan and Sellick (2004) point out that culture influences many factors relevant to quality of life judgements, such as responses to pain, attitudes towards and use of traditional versus Western medicines and treatments, concepts of dependency, and the culture of communication. While their longitudinal study of Chinese cancer patients revealed many of the same physical, psychosocial and emotional responses to gastrointestinal cancer reported in Western studies, the authors note that their sample differed from Western samples in their emphasis on family support, and in the patients' indirect indication of distress through symptom report rather than through direct interpersonal communication. The role of culture and the underlying values and beliefs about health, illness and QoL must therefore be considered in terms of their influence on self-reported QoL. As Bullinger (1997: 816) observed: 'If disease, as anthropological research suggests, is so very much culture-bound, how could quality of life be culture free?' Conceptually, the meaning of health and illness has been shown to be affected by cultural norms and experiences of health, illness and health care, as well as by different belief systems, such as the Chinese belief in the need to maintain a balance between *yin* and *yang*, or as in some tribal beliefs in the supernatural. We described many such different beliefs in the opening chapter. Cultural differences also affect how QoL can be assessed (see the section on measuring quality of life, below).

■ Aspects of the illness and quality of life

It is quite common for QoL not to be predicted by objectively determined severity of illness and associated symptoms. Furthermore, among carers, it has also been shown that the severity of symptoms or disability of the cared-for does not inevitably reduce carer QoL. We return to this issue in Chapter 15. The finding that symptom severity or extent of disability does not consistently predict QoL highlights the subjective nature of this concept, and it should come as no surprise to readers that QoL judgements, as with stress and illness discussed in previous chapters, are influenced by individual differences in the appraisal of, and subsequent coping with, ill health. It also highlights the fact that QoL is by definition about the things that people value in life, and that illness or physical disability may or may not change such perceptions. Most available measures assume that illness will disrupt many domains of QoL, yet, as noted by Carr and Higginson (2001: 1,359): 'if they [standardised measures] do not cover domains that are important to individual patients they may not be valid measures for those patients'.

In many instances, however, illness does affect QoL. For example, pervasive and persistent pain and disability are generally found to be associated with a lower QoL, for example as reflected in depression levels, disability and use of health care (see Chapter 16). Ferrucci *et al.* (2000) investigated the extent to which disease severity in stroke, Parkinson's disease or coronary heart disease patients was associated with their health-related QoL. They found that the relationship between disease severity and health-related QoL was non-linear in the stroke and CHD patients, and that only in the least severe stroke and most severe CHD cases was QoL in fact associated. In Parkinson's disease, however, there was a linear relationship reported whereby severe PD associated with lower health-related QoL. In other words, severity of illness is not inevitably or consistently associated with lower health-related QoL, and disease-specific relationships need to be explored.

In those with neurological illnesses such as Parkinson's disease, cognitive dysfunction such as memory impairment or attentional deficits can disrupt key QoL domains such as physical and psychosocial functioning. Furthermore, memory deficits can make it hard for some individuals to evaluate their current status against their former status in order to make meaningful QoL judgements (Murrell 2001). Perhaps for this reason, patients with cognitive impairments have been the subject of less research attention (see also the section on measuring quality of life, below).

■ Aspects of treatment and quality of life

Treatment itself also influences QoL. Most studies that examine the effects of treatment on QoL do so in order to either determine its impact on specific populations or to compare which of several treatment alternatives is associated with the greatest QoL outcomes. In cancer, for example, scores on the POQOLS (pediatric oncology (child cancer) QoL scale; Goodwin *et al.* 1994) differed across groups receiving different treatments; for example, children undergoing intensive treatment showed poorer QoL than those in remission (Bijttebier *et al.* 2001).

Many treatment evaluations carried out as part of randomised controlled trials of new or comparable treatments include some indicator of QoL such as symptomatology, physical functioning or return to work. However, few as yet have adopted 'patient-centred' measures, which invite patients to describe outcomes important to them in terms of their QoL (Carr and Higginson 2001). However, this is an area of research and evaluation that is becoming more widespread, particularly in studies of cancer or pain. For example, several studies have been carried out to ascertain the impact of bone marrow transplantation in leukaemia patients. In a UK study, Watson *et al.* (2004) examined the QoL outcomes of a large number (481) of patients who had participated in a randomised trial of one of two types of bone marrow transplantation (BMT) (both preceded by intensive chemotherapy) compared with a course of intensive chemotherapy alone. On following participants up after one year, those patients who received BMT reported greater fatigue, more problems in sexual and social relationships, and disruptions to work and leisure activities. In addition, having BMT from a related sibling had a greater negative impact on the QoL indices than either unrelated donor transplantation or the chemotherapy group. A Dutch study of psychological functioning and QoL following BMT found that a quarter of patients still experienced significant functional limitations when followed up after three years, although almost 90 per cent of the total sample (thus including many of those with functional limitations) reported their quality of life to be good to excellent (Broers *et al.* 2000). Although effects of BMT on quality of life appear from these data to be long-lasting, another study of Dutch patients by Helder *et al.* (2004) found that the majority of QoL domain scores in young adults who had been children (an average age of 11) at the time of their BMT were not significantly lower than that found in a comparison group of healthy young adults. For example, those who had undergone childhood BMT between six and twelve years previously did not score lower in terms of physical or role functioning, pain or vitality, mental health, social and emotional functioning than the healthy participants, although their general health was rated lower (using the SF36 measure – see below). These findings would suggest that the childhood experience of a serious illness requiring intensive treatment and a prolonged period of adjustment does not have long-lasting effects into adulthood, although such conclusions have to be tempered by the fact that the study involved a relatively small sample, was cross-sectional and did not assess a number of other factors that may have contributed to the QoL of BMT survivors, such as social support resources.

■ Psychosocial influences on quality of life

Among physically healthy populations, the presence of anxiety symptoms or disorder has been associated with poor QoL (e.g. Mendlowicz and Stein 2001). Among those with physical illness, emotional responses have also been shown to impact upon quality of life. For example, both depression and anxiety symptoms measured within fifteen days of a heart attack were found to predict low QoL at four months, although depression was the strongest predictor (Lane *et al.* 2000). Similarly, among 568 cancer patients, anxiety and depression were both related to the QoL dimensions of emotional, physical and social functioning, pain, fatigue (depression only), and global QoL, although as in Lane's study, depression was more strongly associated (Skarstein *et al.* 2000).

Studies of the impact of pain on patient wellbeing may offer some explanation as to why depression is commonly associated with QoL, as pain is strongly associated with depressed mood (see Chapter 16). One study that examined both pain and depression is that of Rosenfeld *et al.* (1996) who conducted a prospective survey of over four hundred AIDS patients in New York; 63 per cent of participants reported frequent or persistent pain in the preceding two weeks. Comparing scores across a range of QoL indices between those who were and those who were not currently experiencing pain revealed significant differences between the groups in terms of psychological distress, depression, feelings of hopelessness and global QoL. The analyses controlled for other possible influences on the QoL indices, such as age or gender, and social support (which itself was an independent predictor of distress). These results are consistent with many pain studies, showing that pain affects a broad range of psychosocial functioning. Also of importance is the finding that race was significantly related to QoL and distress, with non-white patients reporting poorer QoL and more distress. The authors consider whether this may be due to differences in access to pain management, or whether it reflects other factors not considered in their study, such as socio-economic or life stress, which may be detrimental to the QoL evaluations these individuals made. These findings highlight that several factors need to be taken into account when attempting to establish what 'predicts' QoL: the presence or absence of pain; the presence or absence of depressed mood; levels of social support, ethnicity and other background stressors that may be happening independently of the disease process under study.

In terms of coping response, Carver *et al.* (1992) point out that avoidant coping is likely to be beneficial to QoL in situations where a person is unable to exert control, and they suggest that approach coping in these situations could lead to frustration when control is not forthcoming. Others suggest that maintaining a good QoL in relatively unalterable situations, such as that faced by individuals with chronic pain, may require individuals to cope by means of acceptance coping or positive reinterpretation (McCracken 1998). For example, McCracken and Eccleston (2003), in a study of 230 adults with chronic pain, found that coping was weakly related to pain acceptance and unreliably associated with adjustment, but that among those who did show acceptance of their pain, many QoL indicators were higher, including reduced pain symptomatology and disability, less depression and pain-related anxiety, a higher amount of time per day spent up and about, and a greater likelihood to be working. Such findings underscore the fact that, as discussed in Chapter 12, there is no one coping strategy that is inherently better than another and coping will change over time and place depending on the demands and resources available to the person.

In terms of resources upon which individuals may draw when faced with stress or the demands of illness, previous chapters have highlighted the crucial role of social support. Perceived social support is generally considered important to personal wellbeing, and many positive relationships between perceived social support, coping and adjustment to chronic disease have been reported. However, the direction of causality between variables is not always clear. For example, in a study of 210 outpatients receiving treatment for epilepsy, results of regression analyses found that, independently of current physical health status, psychological distress, loneliness, adjustment and coping and stigma perception, contributed most significantly to the measures of QoL (Suurmeijer *et al.* 2001). However, disentangling the direction of relationships between mood, resources (or lack of resource if considering loneliness) or coping variables and illness outcomes such as QoL requires studies with several waves of data collection, where change in the levels of support and adjustment, changes in coping responses, etc. can be assessed. In an attempt to do this, Burgoyne and Renwick (2004) assessed forty-one Canadian adults with HIV three times over a four-year period and examined whether changes or stability in social support was associated with changes or stability in QoL. Although having a relatively small sample size, this well-designed study considers the dynamic associations between disease symptomatology, social support and QoL and explores the direction of causality between these factors; for example, do changes in social support lead to changes in QoL, or do changes in QoL lead to changes in social support? Slightly contrary to expectations, analyses revealed that both social support and QoL remained relatively stable over the four-year period, although social support did decrease significantly for 40 per cent of the sample (a finding such as this, if obtained in a larger sample, would have warranted further exploration to try and ascertain 'who' these 40 per cent were, i.e. did they differ from those for whom social support remained stable in terms of any personal or illness characteristics?). Poorer mental functioning QoL scores tended to predict subsequent lower perceived emotional and informational support, but the directional relationship between physical functioning QoL and social support was unclear. Importantly, results did not show any strong longitudinal association between social support and subsequent QoL. Furthermore, results did not reveal that changes in either QoL or social support were linked in the longer term (i.e. from year 1 to year 4), although there was evidence of a link between the first and second year. Certainly the two measures were associated within each time point, with positive or negative changes in social support corresponding to positive or negative changes in QoL domains; however, the disappointing longitudinal predictive results means that social support and its effects on QoL, at least in this disease group, remains open to debate and in need of a similarly designed study to be conducted with a much larger sample.

■ Goals and QoL

QoL research has sometimes been criticised for the absence of a theoretical model around which to develop and test the QoL concept. One attempt to

coronary angioplasty
a procedure where a small balloon is inserted into the blocked coronary artery of a person with **atheroma**.

bring theory to bear has employed Scheier and Carver's self-regulation theory (see Chapter 9), which describes a process of goal attainment in the face of a disturbance such as illness (1992). It is proposed that the disturbance of personal goal attainment caused by chronic illness and its consequences is likely to influence a person's perceived QoL (e.g. Echteld *et al.* 1998). Within the self-regulatory framework, event appraisal, appraisals of goal disturbance, outcome expectancies, appraisals of resources and coping processes all combine to influence QoL (e.g. Maes *et al.* 1996). Echteld *et al.* (2003), for example, found that among 158 patients who had undergone **coronary angioplasty**, disease-specific quality of life and positive affect three months after surgery were predicted by pre-surgery QoL, low stress appraisals and avoidant coping. Goal disturbance predicted disease-specific QoL and negative affect. Boersma *et al.* (2005) also found that disturbance in 'higher-order' goals such as fulfilling duties to others, or having fun, following a heart attack was associated with anxiety, depression and a lower health-related quality of life. It may be that goals indirectly influence QoL outcomes by altering the 'meaning' a person attaches to their illness (Taylor 1983; theory of cognitive adaptation to illness, see below). The 'meaning' of illness has been defined as 'an individual's understanding of the implications an illness has on self, relationships with others, priorities, and future goals', and as such has been shown to influence wellbeing and adjustment, for example among those with cancer (e.g. Fife 1995, cited in Walker *et al.* 2004: 467). Examining personal goals (both day-to-day and higher-order goals) and their attainment or non-attainment as a result of ill-health is therefore important if we are to better understand why people rate their QoL in the way that they do when given standardised QoL assessment tools.

What do YOU think?

While we have shown that age, illness and culture might affect how we perceive QoL, where you live may also influence the extent to which a 'good' QoL can be achieved. A survey of the economies of 183 countries found that while Britain had the fifth biggest economy in the world, it ranked seventeenth for quality of life (based on *PocketWorld in Figures*, 2008, published by The Economist)

1. Norway
2. Iceland
3. Australia
4. Ireland
5. Sweden
6. Canada
7. Japan
8. USA
9. Finland, Netherlands, Switzerland
12. Belgium, Luxemborg
14. Austria
15. Denmark
16. France
17. Italy, United Kingdom

continued

19. Spain
20. New Zealand

Is your own country in the Top 20? Who is above it and who is below? Why do you think The Netherlands does so much 'better' than the UK?

Why do you think Norway and Iceland are top (the weather?)?

If you are living in Britain, it may please you to know that Britain tops the table for attracting foreign investment, although any pleasure at this is short-lived if you then consider the rankings for child wellbeing – Britain came twenty-first, where Holland came first!

The rankings were actually based on environmental indicators such as traffic, pollution, the housing market, and on social statistics regarding leisure activities, consumer-good ownership, crime, educational attainment and unemployment, as well as health indicators, and as such provide an 'objective' estimate of 'quality of life'. Whatever you think of league tables generally (for example, Good University guides, school A-level league tables), in the domain of quality of life they are perhaps misleading, given how we have shown in this chapter that qualty of life is a subjective construct. Should we pay much attention to these rankings? Do they make any difference to how you lead your life? Are they there purely to feed the media with buckshot to fire at our politicians? Or do they raise real concerns about the health and social care systems and environmental policies of your country?

Measuring quality of life

Several main reasons have been suggested as to why QoL assessment is a useful clinical practice (e.g. Higginson and Carr 2001). These include:

■ *Measure to inform*: to increase understanding about the multidimensional impact of illness and factors that moderate impact, in order to (a) inform interventions and best practice, and (b) inform patients about treatment outcomes or possible side-effects in order that they are mentally 'prepared' for them, or, so that supportive resources can be put in place. Descriptive data from QoL studies can also be used to inform patients and their families about likely treatment experiences so that treatment choices can be made. For example, Cocquyt *et al.* (2003) found that there is no definite evidence that breast-sparing procedures have more favourable QoL and psychosocial outcomes than mastectomy (although some studies do find better body image and sexual functioning in those with breast-conserving therapy). This information can be presented by health-care providers to aid patient decision making.

■ *Measure to evaluate alternatives*: QoL measures may be used as a form of clinical 'audit' to identify which interventions have the 'best' outcomes – for the patient, but also often in relation to costs. In medicine (and health economics), a related concept has emerged, called quality-adjusted life years, or QALYs. Different treatments may be considered as increasing length of life and QoL to varying degrees, and if weightings are attached to certain treatments and assessed against the actual cost of the treatment, QALYs can be used to inform medical treatment decisions. For example, two cancer treatments may offer the same survival benefits, but QoL and QALYs may be poorer during and after one treatment than the other; or one treatment may be cheaper than the other where both have the same effect on improved QoL. Brewster *et al.* (2006) surveyed the influences upon health professionals and general public attitudes towards treating cancer in the elderly and found that hypothetical decisions to offer treatment were most commonly influenced by life gain, followed by quality of life gain, severity of side-effects and finally patient age. The financial cost of treatment was not examined in this study.

■ *Measure to promote communication*: while this is unlikely to be the primary motive for conducting a QoL assessment in a clinical setting, engaging patients in QoL assessment may require health professionals to address areas that they may not otherwise have done, for example about treatment satisfaction, family interactions, hobbies or sexual functioning. This will provide health professionals with a more holistic view of the impact that illness or treatment has had upon their patient and may help future treatment decision making or health care.

Whatever the motive for assessing QoL, a major issue faced by researchers or clinicians is which instrument or method of assessment to use. If we accept that QoL is a multidimensional, dynamic and subjective construct, measurement is inevitably going to face many challenges!

Leventhal and Colman (1997) state that QoL should be considered not only in terms of outcomes but also as a process that is influenced by individuals' perceptions of various domains of their lives, including their perceptions of any illness and its treatment (see Chapter 9), and the weightings or importance they attach to their perceptions at any given point in time (see also the discussion of 'response-shift' below). They do not argue that QoL should be assessed separately from all its possible component parts, e.g. physical, emotional and social functioning, but that each should be seen as separate factors, as possible determinants of QoL. Changes in any of these determinants will influence changes in QoL (see Figure 14.1). This process model has generally been accepted in psychological research studies where multiple measures of determinants are used, as well as generic or specific QoL measures, as will be seen in the discussion of measures below.

Generic versus specific QoL measures

The global domains of QoL described by the WHOQOL group and outlined earlier in the chapter have been supported in many empirical studies; however, a question remains as to whether to adopt a generic, or global, measure of QoL which assesses concepts relevant to all illness groups or to adopt a measure specific to the illness being studied. Commonly employed generic measures include the Medical Outcome study short form 36, usually referred to as the SF36 (Stewart and Ware 1992); the Nottingham Health Profile (NHP; Hunt *et al.* 1986); and the EUROQOL (Euroqol group 1990). In terms of disease-specific measures an increasing number are available, such

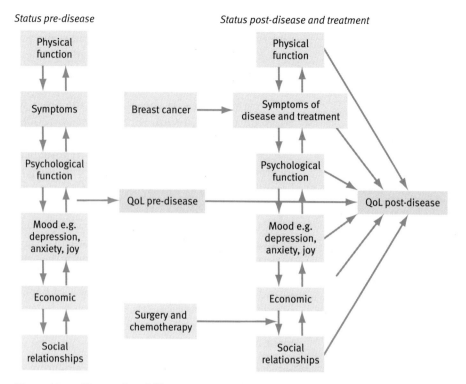

Status pre-disease   *Status post-disease and treatment*

Figure 14.1 The quality-of-life process prior to and subsequent to breast cancer. Baseline QoL is changed by the impact of the disease and treatment upon each of the domains. Changes in functioning post-disease are weighted and will lead to changes in post-disease onset QoL.

Source: Leventhal and Coleman (1997: 759)

as those developed for people with cancer (e.g. EORTC QLQ-C30; Aaronson *et al.* 1993, or the FACT-G, Cella *et al.* 1993; Holzner *et al.* 2004), asthma (e.g. Hyland *et al.* 1996), arthritis (e.g. AIMS-1, 2; Meenan and Mason 1990) or Parkinson's disease (see review by Marinus *et al.* 2002).

There are disadvantages and advantages to both types of measure. Generic measures, while allowing for comparison between different illness groups, often fail to address some of the unique QoL issues for that illness. In cancer, for example, the European Organisation for Research and Treatment of Cancer (EORTC) developed a cancer-specific tool (EORTC QLQ-C30) to assess not only quality of life issues relevant to most people but also including cancer-specific issues such as fears of recurrence or of treatment side-effects (Aaronson *et al.* 1993). In HIV infection and AIDS issues such as HIV testing and the results process, concern with symptoms, and disclosure of a positive diagnosis to others, are addressed in a tool developed out of the previously mentioned WHOQOL (the WHOQOL-HIV) (O'Connell *et al.* on behalf of WHOQOL-HIV group 2003).

Disease-specific measures therefore have 'added value', but they do not allow for the same amount of between-illness comparability. This comparability enables questions such as 'Is the quality of life reduced more by cancer than by heart disease?' to be asked – a question of interest perhaps to those considering research funding allocations or developing community support resources, for example.

Individualised QoL measures

Another option available to health researchers is to use individualised measures of QoL. Individual QoL instruments abandon the dimensions of many generic and disease-specific instruments and allow respondents to choose the dimensions and concerns relevant and of value to them (see RESEARCH FOCUS). This 'idiographic' approach can be seen in the schedule for the evaluation of individual quality of life (SEIQoL; O'Boyle *et al.* 1993; Joyce *et al.* 2003), which invites individuals to identify five aspects of life that are important to them (i.e. 'What are the five most important areas of your life at present – the things that make your life a relatively happy or sad one at the moment . . . the things that you feel determine your quality of life?'). Individuals then rate their current level of functioning on each, attach a weighting of importance to each aspect and rate how satisfied they are currently with that aspect of life. The aspects of life mentioned most often by the hip replacement patients in the original study were family, leisure activities, independence, happiness, finances and religion; with control subjects being very similar, although nominating health more often than patients. Perhaps it was important to the healthy participants to retain health and therefore these participants mentioned it, whereas it featured less strongly in the patient sample perhaps because they had had to readjust their life goals and values and no longer rated health as one of the most important domains in their lives, although this was not explored in the study.

RESEARCH FOCUS

Generating individualised QoL beliefs

Stenner, P. H. D., Cooper, D. and Skevington, S. (2003). Putting the Q into quality of life: the identification of subjective constructions of health-related quality of life using Q methodology. *Social Science and Medicine*, 57: 2161–72.

Background aims

Measures of QoL need to tap into individual patients' points of view. This makes 'standardisation' of measurement a difficult goal, as the factors that make up perceived quality of life for one person may be very different to the factors that make up the same 'level' of quality of life for another. This issue has been addressed in an interesting study by Stenner *et al.* (2003), who employed an idiographic technique, i.e. one where each participant identifies aspects of QoL important to them.

Method

The specific technique adopted was 'Q' methodology, whereby participants sort a collection of fifty-two statements about QoL (developed from WHOQOL and other sources) into piles according to their importance to them (least important, neutral, most important), and then return to the three piles and sort each item within the piles on a scale ranging from −5 least important, through 0 neutral, to +5 extremely important. In this way, ninety healthy participants produced what is known as their own Q sort. They then examine their Q sort and

continued

discuss why they ranked some items as more important than others, and whether they believe it is an accurate reflection of their personal view about QoL.

Results

When analysed statistically, eight significant factors emerged that were interpreted as reflecting distinct constructs of the meaning and personal relevance of QoL:

1. *Happy families* (fifteen participants): the factor on to which the Q sorts of older (mean 49 years), married individuals (thirteen) fell. Relationships within and support from the family were crucial to these individuals, with relationships and support from non-family members being considered less important. Family relationships and support were considered important to good health, contentment and QoL, as were, to a lesser degree, financial concerns. These individuals valued physical health and independence more than either psychological wellbeing or spiritual concerns.

2. *Stand on my own two feet*: this factor included fourteen participants of a younger mean age (34.4 years) with a mix of married, single and cohabiting individuals. For these individuals, psychological wellbeing was central, with aspects of QoL that maintain independence rated highly. A need to feel in control was important, in terms of life and work issues, and financial issues following from work success related to feelings of self-worth, life satisfaction and control. Although relationships with friends and family were considered important, independence and personal control over achievements were more important. Physical states such as pain were not highly important to the perceived QoL of this group, although physical independence was.

3. *Emotional independence*: ten participants (mean age 30.5 years, majority (six) single, five were university educated) loaded on to this factor, exemplified by a need for mental wellbeing and stability and for physical functioning not to be interfered with by negative emotions. Spiritual calmness and inner peace were considered important to wellbeing, although not religion *per se*. This inner peace and happiness was thought to come from oneself, and from self-control of negative feelings, rather than from reliance on relationships with others, or from physical states.

4. *Just do it*: nine participants loaded on this factor (similar age to the previous group, 30.4 years, majority (five) single, and majority (six) university-educated). This group placed high importance on being active and having a meaningful life, which was brought about by 'doing' things considered to be important to them, e.g. being active, engaging in leisure activities, having a good sex life. Friends were more central to this group than family. Personal beliefs rather than religion were important to overall wellbeing, with self-esteem being derived from self-control and action.

5. *Life as a positive challenge*: five participants (mean age 22.8 years, three single, all educated to university level) on this factor highlighted learning and knowledge as important, whereas money was considered less important. Negative emotions functioned as a means of enabling a person to experience life, and for these individuals meaningfulness in life was more important than personal control. Relationships with others, friends and family, were rated more important than both health and overall QoL, although health became important if it impacted on daily functioning (NB: this relates nicely to the surveys of health perceptions reported in Chapter 1, where health becomes more important when ill-health is experienced).

6. *In God we trust*: four participants loaded on to this factor, all of whom were young females (mean age 25.3 years) who reported practising religion. For these individuals, the dominant

theme was that life is controlled by 'something' or 'someone' else and that faith in this is crucial. Personal beliefs and meaningfulness in life were also important, with the next most important aspect being supportive relationships with others. Health and overall QoL were not ranked highly by this group.

7. *Staying healthy enough to bring home the bacon*: four participants loaded on to this factor, three of whom were male (mean age 44, three married, one separated, none university educated). For these individuals, physical health was crucial, as was sex and mobility, treatment for health problems, and external appearance. Good health was considered functional and central to a sense of pride, although money was important to providing for home and family.

8. *You can't choose your family*: three participants (mean age 23 years, two undergraduate, one postgraduate). Similar to the 'life as a positive challenge' group in terms of age and educational level, this group differed in that they placed high importance on relationships and the support of friends, whereas family lacked importance. Importance was attached to not experiencing negative feelings or letting them interfere with daily functioning. Self-esteem and satisfaction were important, with mental health, rather than physical health, crucial to this.

Discussion

This study was selected for attention because results such as these highlight that while there are certain commonalities in what people think is important in their lives (such as the importance of relationships, control and independence), many differences exist (e.g. the extent to which spirituality is a self-belief or based on a religion; the extent to which friends and/or family support is valued; the extent to which mental wellbeing is valued in comparison to physical health; and the extent to which control is considered to be an internal or external resource). These findings also highlight that the different strands of QoL interact and causal sequencing seems likely; in other words, psychological aspects may influence the reported social, financial and physical aspects, and vice versa. Interesting differences are suggested for age, gender and educational status, although this study is limited by not including participants over the age of 64, anyone who was unemployed, or anyone not of white English origin. (The influence of ageing on perceived QoL was addressed earlier in the chapter.) Gender, age and educational attainment differences may influence an individual's current and future life goals, and it has been suggested that goal direction and attainment may be important influences upon a person's QoL. The role of goals and QoL has been addressed in several studies working within the self-regulation framework of Carver and Scheier (e.g. Carver and Scheier, 1981; Carver *et al*. 1992).

While individualised methods of assessment acknowledge the subjectivity of QoL, such methods are time-consuming and relatively complex processes that critics suggest may exclude their use in certain populations. Addressing this point, Jenkinson *et al.* (2001) adopted technology to make QoL assessment quicker, portable and possibly more adaptable to clinical situations. They describe a method of assessment known as the dynamic health assessment (DYNHA) system (see www.qualitymetric.co) which is a short computer-based instrument. Items for assessment are selected from a pool, dependent upon participants' earlier responses to global questions, and currently on offer are assessments for generic Qol based on the SF36, as well as specific measures of the impact of headache, arthritis, pain and pediatric asthma. The benefit of this method is that assessment is more adapted to uniquely individual problems, while the use of SF36 items still enables comparison with other groups assessed with SF36. More studies are required using this method, but results from Jenkinson's study with neurological populations are encouraging.

Practicality of measures

Where assessment circumstances allow, most studies use multiple measures, and as well as assessing generic and/or illness-specific multidimensional QoL will generally also include unidimensional outcome measures such as assessments of mood, pain or disability that address only one specific aspect of QoL. There is a natural limit to how many questionnaires can be 'inflicted' on an ill individual, and it is important for researchers to be sensitive to this. A good research tool may not be an appropriate tool to administer in a clinical setting. For example, the functional limitations profile (Patrick and Peach 1989) (or its American precursor the sickness impact profile; Bergner et al. 1981) while a well-validated and commonly employed outcome measure, has 136 items assessing twelve domains of potential illness impact (e.g. self-care, mobility, social functioning, communication and emotion), and it takes twenty–thirty minutes to complete, which is potentially impossible in many clinical settings!

In addition, certain conditions make it difficult to carry out assessments of subjective perceptions, such as QoL. Illnesses that elicit a communication deficit, such as the receptive and expressive aphasias that are common following a stroke, often results in such patients being excluded from self-report studies (e.g. Morrison et al. 2005) and the use of proxy measures often results, the limitations of which are described below.

Overall, there has been a proliferation of QoL measures and assessment methods available to researchers in this area, and the choice of which to use will be determined by the aims of the study and by the practicalities offered by the research situation and the population to be studied. This makes it quite difficult to compare across studies, and quite difficult to translate research findings into clinical practice. While the growth of the WHOQOL group measures may go some way towards achieving consistency in measurement, the standardisation of quantitative measures and methods bring with them the risk of losing information as to the very personal and individualised meaning of QoL (see RESEARCH FOCUS above).

Response shift

Some authors have found individuals with limiting illness to rate their QoL higher than do healthy people (e.g. in diabetes; Hart et al. 2003). In trying to interpret this counter-intuitive finding we can either consider simply that it reflects the subjectivity of QoL, or that illnesses do not inevitably limit a person's perceived quality of life. More recently, researchers have begun to consider the idea that illness can bring about changes that create what is

response shift
changes in subjective
reports that may result
from a reprioritisation
of life expectations or
recalibration of internal
standards so that the
construct being
assessed is
reconceptualised.

described as a **response shift**, i.e. the meaning of the concept being assessed changes in the view of an individual because perhaps their illness causes them to recalibrate their internal standards, or reprioritise expectations and life values (Schwartz *et al.* 2004). Yardley and Dibb (2007) nicely illustrated response shift recently in a longitudinal study of 301 individuals with Meniere's disease, a chronic although not life-threatening condition characterised by severe and disabling vertigo, tinnitus and progressive hearing loss. They found that when the scores obtained on the SF36 quality of life measure obtained at the first study time point were compared with the score given when participants were asked ten months later to look back to that first time point and score their quality of life 'then', there was a significant reduction in the reported level of general health, mental health, role-physical, and role-emotional attributed to the first time point. In other words, when looking back, these participants attributed poorer QoL across all SF36 sub-scales except the 'physical health' one, to 'then' than they had reported at the time. The 'then test' was significant whereas the difference between the first time point and the second time point was not, i.e. the ten-month follow-up scores themselves did not differ from the baseline scores. This is response shift and is worth bearing in mind when conducting longitudinal studies. Yardley offers some explanation for this response shift by also showing that scores on a measure of goal orientation relevant to five broad domains of QoL DID change over time with an improvement in participants' approach. If we are to better understand 'change' over the course of illness the use of the 'then-test' is likely to be seen in many more studies in future. Qualitative findings have commonly pointed to changes in life expectations, meanings, goals and priorities following or during illness (e.g. Ingram *et al.* 2008) and therefore we should not be surprised to find that such 'shifts' in perspective affects how questionnaire items are interpreted and scored at different time points.

Two final factors that warrant consideration in the development of new measures or in the choice made from existing instruments (see Bowling 1995a for coverage of many QoL instruments) is that of participant age and culture.

■ Culture

Measures of health-related QoL have been developed predominantly in the English language, meaning that for use in non-English-speaking countries, measures have to be translated. Bowden and Fox-Rushby (2003) reviewed the process of translating measures, generally developed in English, in twenty-three countries across Africa, Asia, Eastern Europe, the Middle East and South America. These authors concluded that in the process of translation the meaning of items may be lost, and that using measures that have been generated predominantly from samples of Western populations assumes that words and concepts have equivalent meaning in different cultures, and that domains have equal salience. Furthermore, the nature of disease varies considerably between countries, with, for example, the authors citing evidence that in Europe only 6 per cent of mortality is attributable to communicable diseases (such as HIV, TB), whereas in Africa and South-east Asia communicable diseases account for 71 and 39 per cent of deaths, respectively. Differences in disease experience such as these are likely to have an effect on illness and QoL expectations. The WHOQOL group is addressing these culturally relevant questions in its many studies.

In relation to cancer, the commonly employed health-related QoL measure, the FACT-G (Cella *et al.* 1993), has also received cross-cultural validation within a sample of Korean women with breast cancer (Lee *et al.* 2004). While perceptions of illness and health-care-seeking behaviour have been shown to vary between Western and non-Western populations (see Chapter 9), few studies have addressed specific differences in understanding of QoL. Lee *et al.* find that the FACT-G and its physical, emotional and functional wellbeing dimensions had good construct validity when the items were entered into factor analysis, but that the social/family wellbeing sub-scale was problematic in that items did not load together onto a coherent factor. This sub-scale assesses closeness to friends and partners, seeking of emotional support from family or friends, family communication, accepting illness on the part of the family, and sex life. The authors interpret these findings as evidence that the Korean women separated out family from friends in terms of what they offered to their wellbeing, with family communication and closeness fundamental, whereas the cancer was often kept from friends. Such findings have been reported within other Asian cultures and need to be borne in mind when pooling the data obtained from multidimensional measures used within mixed cultural samples. Cultural differences are likely to affect statistical findings and thus the conclusions drawn from the data.

■ Age

McEwan *et al.* (2004: 4) point out that adapting an adult questionnaire into a child version 'fails to acknowledge important aspects of child and adolescent development and functioning'. The young child may, for example, have cognitive limitations that make it difficult for them to understand abstract questions such as those concerning life satisfaction or global wellbeing. Developmentally, and consistent with Piagetian thinking (see Chapter 1), the understanding of the more concrete domains of QoL (such as pain) may emerge as early as between 4 and 6 years of age, for example the Childhood Asthma Questionnaire Form A (French *et al.* 1994), whereas the more abstract domains (such as feelings) emerge from around age 7.

Although some measures have been developed specifically to assess QoL in child populations not many have been validated, and this fact, alongside a common assumption of cognitive limitation in children, has led to many studies using parents to complete questionnaires on behalf of their children (e.g. Bijttebier *et al.* 2001). This is known as proxy measurement. However, parental 'proxy' reports in effect go against the principle of QoL being a personal subjective belief, as a parent may not share the same views as their child (Matza *et al.* 2004). This point was well illustrated by Eiser and Morse (2001) when they reviewed studies of chronically ill samples where both child reports and parental proxy reports were generated. Parent–child agreement was greater for observable aspects of QoL such as physical functioning but less for emotional or perceived social functioning. In Bijttebier *et al.*'s (2001) study of QoL among young cancer patients (using parental proxy reports), predominantly observable aspects of QoL were assessed in relation to:

■ *physical restriction*: e.g. my child has been able to perform as usual;
■ *emotional distress*: e.g. my child has anger outbursts;
■ *discomfort from medical treatment*: e.g. my child complained of pain after a medical procedure.

As such, the data on child QoL obtained in this study may be more reliable than if 'non-behavioural' aspects of QoL had been assessed; however, whole domains of QoL are not examined.

As further illustration of possible discrepancies between proxy and 'real' reports, a study of 100 children with congenital heart disease and their parents found that while both parents and children reported reduced child motor functioning and autonomy when compared with healthy children, the children reported lower levels of emotional QoL than did their parents. Overall, parents reported that more problems were faced by their children than the children themselves reported (Krol *et al.* 2003). Healthy children, by contrast, have been reported to show less agreement with their parents regarding their physical status than they do in other domains (e.g. Theunissen *et al.* 1998).

Additionally, it has been shown following a review of findings of six studies where two sets of ratings were obtained, that significant discrepancies exist in the perceptions of patient wellbeing and QoL during the course of long-term (primarily cancer) treatment reported by their physicians and that reported by the patients themselves, or in the case of children, parental perceptions (Janse *et al.* 2004).

The findings reviewed here highlight that parent–child dyads may converge and diverge in terms of their beliefs, depending on various factors including the child's current health status. In the context of a child with illness, parental over- or underestimation of a child's problem areas can have implications for parental caring behaviour (see Chapter 15). Furthermore, we have presented evidence that patient (or parent) ratings often diverge from health professionals' ratings of that patient's QoL, and this could lead to misunderstandings about treatment or its usefulness in terms of QoL gain, which may, as Janse *et al.* note, have implications for non-adherence. Given the above evidence of divergence in reports, it is unclear who researchers should direct their questions to: it may be that assessing both the 'patient' and a significant other will in fact give a more complete picture.

In addition to who the questions are directed to, consideration needs to be given to the content of the questions. As Matza and colleagues note in their very useful review in this area (Matza *et al.* 2004): 'When designing a pediatric HRQoL instrument, it is important to ensure that items correspond to experiences, activities, and contexts that are directly relevant to the age of the sample' (p. 80). There is little to be gained from asking children about the impact of illness on general functioning where a distinction between school, play, at home, and with peers is likely to be needed.

Finally, consideration needs to be given about when and how often HRQoL is assessed, and by whom. This chapter has shown that QoL is an important outcome of illness and treatment and has noted that increasingly medical professionals are recognising the scientific evidence regarding the importance of psychosocial outcomes. The potential to take the research evidence back into practice is illustrated in the findings of a recent randomised controlled trial comparing the effects of computerised real-time feedback of patient HRQoL results to physicians (experimental group), versus no feedback (control group), on the HRQoL scores, patient satisfaction and consultation behaviours of 162 liver disease patients (Gutteling *et al.* 2008). While no direct effect of the experiment was found in terms of overall patient QoL (similar to reports from some earlier studies), several interesting interaction effects emerged from more detailed analyses. Older patients who were in the experimental group had a better disease-specific QoL than controls; and both older patients, and males of any age, in the experimental group had better mental QoL than control group patients. In addition, the physicians themselves were seen to have benefited in that those in the experimental group altered their patient management practices in terms of time spent discussing psychosocial issues. While a relatively small study and a poor response rate, this kind of study is immensely valuable in that it begins to demonstrate how we, as health psychologists, can put our years of studying QoL and how to assess it to good use in clinical practice.

Summary

This chapter has provided evidence that QoL is an important concept that encompasses a person's subjective belief about the quality of various life domains of importance to them. The domains generally considered in quality of life research include:

■ physical functioning
■ role functioning
■ emotional functioning
■ social functioning
■ environmental aspects, and, increasingly,
■ spiritual functioning.

We have described a range of influences on the experience of quality of life, including aspects of the disease and its treatment, as well as aspects of the individual such as their age, ethnicity, mood or levels of social support. We have also shown that, in spite of difficulties in clearly defining and measuring QoL, there is a growing recognition of the need to do so, and for research and practice to look beyond traditionally clinical outcomes of illness, such as disability, symptomatology and mortality, to more holistic psychosocial outcomes.

While there is increasing evidence of the inclusion of QoL assessment in clinical trials of treatments or in psychosocial interventions, the debate as to whether it is best assessed objectively or subjectively, generically or specifically remains. There is also the need to be sensitive to the needs of specific populations, for example children, and to address cultural variation in the understanding of QoL. We have described various methods of assessing this subjective construct including:

■ self-report interview
■ self-report questionnaire completion
■ proxy report (either interview or questionnaire).

As with beauty, quality of life is in 'the eye of the beholder' and therefore this presents challenges to interventions based on identified predictors of quality of life, as it is unlikely that 'one size will fit all'. However, this chapter has, it is hoped, presented some of the general influences and is a starting point from which to develop interventions.

Further reading

Bowling, A. (1991). *Measuring Health: A Review of Quality of Life*. Buckingham: Open University Press.

Bowling, A. (1997). *Measuring Disease: A Review of Disease-specific Quality of Life Measurement Scales*. Second edition. Buckingham: Open University Press.
Although getting old now, these two well-written books still provide the reader with a comprehensive overview of issues in both health- and illness-related quality of life. Additionally, many of the available QoL scales are outlined and useful examples provided. While many new scales appear, such as the WHOQOL, these books provide essential background reading.

Carr, A.J. and Higginson, I.J. (2001). Are quality of life measures patient centred? *British Medical Journal*, 32: 1357–60.
This brief paper addresses the crucial issues of how to measure QoL, and who should take the measurements – doctors, patients or other proxy reporters? The fact that this paper was published in the *British Medical Journal* is encouraging testimony to the fact that QoL is on the medical profession's agenda.

Eiser, C. and Morse, R. (2001). The measurement of quality of life in children: past and future perspectives. *Journal of Developmental and Behavioral Pediatrics*, 22: 248–56.
An important and clearly written paper considering the specific issues of QoL in children.

Matza, L.S., Swensen, A.R., Flood, E.M. *et al.* (2004). Assessment of health-related quality of life in children: A review of conceptual, methodological, and regulatory issues. *Value in Health*, 7: 79–92.
For anyone considering a research project involving assessment of children, this paper is a must, whether you are assessing QoL or some other construct. Matza and colleagues clearly describe issues regarding the timing, content and scoring of QoL measures in children and debate the issues of proxy measurement and response bias. They also provide a useful table of selected child QoL measures.

Type in 'QUALITY OF LIFE' into Google and you will get thousands of hits, some from health-professional pages, some from academia, and others will be papers from economists, policy-makers and even governmental bodies. It is clear to see that QoL is a term being used in many domains outside psychology!

 Visit the website at **www.pearsoned.co.uk/morrison** for additional resources to help you with your study, including multiple choice questions, weblinks and flashcards.

CHAPTER 15

The impact of illness on patients and their families

Learning outcomes

By the end of this chapter, you should have an understanding of:

- typical models of adjustment to illness
- the negative emotional consequences of physical illness, for both the person with illness and those around them
- the evidence that benefits can be derived from being ill or providing care to an ill relative or friend
- the diverse nature of coping responses in the face of illness or caregiving
- how some forms of caregiving can be detrimental to the recipient
- why research should consider the perceptions and responses of the ill person and their informal caregivers when trying to predict psychosocial outcomes

CHAPTER OUTLINE

In previous chapters, although describing many individual and social factors that influence the responses to a stressful experience such as illness, the focus has predominantly been on the person experiencing the stress or suffering the illness. In this chapter, we spend equal attention to the impact of illness on the wellbeing and quality of life of family members, many of whom act as informal caregivers.

In the first part of the chapter we focus on the person with an illness and describe the potential impact of illness and treatments on them, primarily in relation to their emotional wellbeing and quality of life. We highlight the multidimensionality of adjustment and that illness-specific, personal, psychological and social factors play a role. Next we present evidence of benefit-finding in the illness experience and consider how positive appraisals, emotions and possibly culture may influence the perception of gain. Coping is addressed next in terms of the kinds of coping responses seen in individuals facing the crisis of various illnesses.

As we saw in earlier chapters, one resource for coping with stress, including illness, is that of social support, and so in the second part of the chapter we turn attention to those providing that support and ask what impact caregiving has on them. We address similar questions but in relation to the informal caregivers who are predominantly family members, and describe the evidence pointing to significant negative consequences of caregiving. Positive outcomes are again possible and so we end the chapter by exploring factors which have potential to improve positive experiences in illness and caregiving by focusing on the dyad, on shared perceptions and experiences, and on the value of matched support.

Illness, emotions and adjustment

The impact of illness

Illness presents individuals with many challenges and issues that change over time, depending upon the illness, the treatment, the individual's cognitive, behavioural and emotional responses, and the social and cultural context in which the illness occurs. Illness is a complex process, illustrated by Morse and Johnson (1991) in their generic model of the emotional and coping responses from the onset of symptoms through to living with a chronic illness. Individuals facing illness are considered as having to deal with:

1. *Uncertainty*: this is a period in which the individual tries to understand the meaning and severity of the first symptoms.
2. *Disruption*: this occurs when it becomes evident to the individual that they have a significant illness. At this time, they experience a crisis characterised by intense stress and a high level of dependence on health professionals and/or other people who are emotionally close to the individual.
3. *Striving for recovery*: this period is typified by the individual attempting to gain some form of control over their illness by means of active coping.

4. *Restoration of wellbeing*: in this phase, the individual achieves a new emotional equilibrium based on an acceptance of the illness and its consequences.

In relation to cancer, a similar series of stages of response to diagnosis has been proposed (Holland and Gooen-Piels 2000):

1. *Initial response*: can include a range of responses, including disbelief, denial and shock. Some people may challenge the diagnosis or the ability of the health professional. At this stage, individuals try to defend themselves from the implications of the diagnosis and may not process information clearly.

2. *Dysphoria*: this phase may last one–two weeks and involves individuals gradually coming to terms with the reality of their diagnosis. Simultaneously, they may experience significant distress and related symptoms such as insomnia, reduced appetite, poor concentration, anxiety and depression. As information about treatment is gradually presented and processed, hope and optimism may emerge to compete with the more distressing thoughts.

3. *Adaptation*: this period may last for weeks, or months, and involves the person adapting more positively to their diagnosis and developing long-term coping strategies in order to maintain equilibrium.

Although these models propose a staged adaptive process, not all individuals will move through the stages smoothly and achieve emotional equilibrium or a stage of acceptance and adaptation. It is likely that elements from different 'stages' may co-occur: for example, a person may experience significant distress even when actively coping with their illness. Individuals may also move backwards and forwards between stages and reactions, for example shifting their focus from one of cure to one of 'healing', in which they try to resolve life issues and achieve some completion of their life's achievements. They may still maintain hope at this time, but rather than hope for a cure they may shift towards hope for a 'good' or pain-free death (Little and Sayers 2004). Religion and spirituality are frequently important factors in maintaining this type of hope (see IN THE SPOTLIGHT later in this chapter).

Several authors have criticised 'staged' approaches for the manner in which they categorise patients and create expectations of responses to serious illness events (e.g. Hale 1996; Crossley 2000), whereas people's experiences and reactions vary hugely and are unique, as we shall see in the discussion of coping below. However, such theories can be considered a useful starting point for those working with the ill or the dying, on the understanding that individuals may not neatly fit into any one of the defined stages and that caring responses therefore need to be individually tailored.

■ Models of adjustment

Adjustment or adaptation in fact means different things depending on the perspective taken. For example: adaptation from a medical viewpoint will consider pathology, symptom reduction or physical adjustment; from a psychological viewpoint it may well consider emotional wellbeing or lack of distress, cognitive adaptation (see below) or psychiatric morbidity; and from a biopsychosocial perspective (that adopted by health psychology as outlined in Chapter 1) adaptation is likely to consider pathology, emotions, cognitions and coping responses, and also the nature and extent of social adjustment or functioning. Walker *et al.* (2004) review these three approaches or paradigms in relation to adjustment to rheumatoid arthritis, which has a clear pathology and is a typically painful and disabling chronic inflammatory disease of the joints with significant repercussions for both the sufferer and their families. All three models of adjustment have relevance to this condition. However, following an informed review and critique, Walker and colleagues conclude that the biopsychosocial approach best 'fits' the chronic disease experience (not just of rheumatoid arthritis), given evidence of the critical role of personal characteristics (e.g. optimism), appraisals (e.g. of control), mood (e.g. anxiety) and coping responses in predicting symptom experience and disease outcomes. Support for this biopsychosocial approach can be seen in a study of the disabling conditions of stroke and chronic idiopathic axonal polyneuropathy (CIAP) where the extent of disease impairment explained variance in control beliefs, and activity limitations explained variance in mood and in control beliefs, suggesting that outcome may be best explained by a combination of disease factors and psychological factors (Schröder *et al.* 2007).

A well-cited example of a psychological model of adjustment was provided by Shelley Taylor (1983), who argued that the process of adjustment to threatening events, whether illness or not, centre around three themes:

- Searching for meaning in the experience
- Attempting to gain a sense of control or mastery over the experience
- Making efforts to restore self esteem.

This is known as a cognitive adaptational model in that, following a stressful event (challenge or threat), a person is motivated to face the challenges of their illness and be proactive in finding ways to deal with them in order to restore equilibrium in one's life. Unlike the stage models of response to illness described earlier, Taylor does not impose any sequencing on these three themes of adjustment, although it is likely that finding meaning in the experience will facilitate attempts to gain some control or enhance self-esteem. Finding meaning implies a degree of acceptance of the situation, but not to the extent that it produces passivity, but rather to the extent that it promotes adjustments being made (to expectations and goals, to behaviours) that enable life to carry on. Gaining a realistic sense of control need not mean actual control over the illness, but may simply mean control over some aspects of that illness, for example, over symptom medications or over dietary change. In fact Taylor describes how the meaning, sense of control and restoring self-esteem may be 'illusions' which are nonetheless essential if adjustment is to take place.

Negative emotional reactions to illness

■ Reactions to diagnosis

Many studies have been conducted with patients with cancer, from diagnosis through active treatment to terminal stages, or to survival (e.g. Kornblith 1998). Most studies find that reactions to a cancer diagnosis are frequently catastrophic and highly emotional, with some individuals describing themselves quite literally as 'fighting for their life' (Landmark and Wahl 2002). This qualitative study reports how one woman, recently diagnosed with breast cancer, described herself as standing 'with one foot in the grave, the other on the edge' (p. 115). In the early stages of cancer, Montgomery *et al.* (2003) found moderate to severe or severe levels of depression in 51 per cent of their sample of people with leukaemia and lymphoma, with 14 per cent reporting similarly high levels of anxiety. Burgess *et al.* (2005) found that almost 50 per cent of early stage breast cancer patients had depression, anxiety or both in the first year following diagnosis, but that incidence dropped to 25 per cent at 2-, 3- and 4-year follow-ups, and further to 15 per cent at a 5-year follow-up. It is not of course only cancer diagnosis that is seen to cause distress; negative emotional reactions are also common among many other conditions, including, for example, those with sudden-onset heart disease (e.g. Lane *et al.* 2002b), stroke (e.g. Astrom 1996; Robinson 1998), or following a positive HIV diagnosis (Valente 2003).

■ Emotional reactions to illness or its treatment

It would be impossible to address reactions to all illnesses, or even all chronic illnesses, so what follows is a representative selection of common and potentially life-changing illnesses: cancer, diabetes, HIV, heart attack and stroke.

While initial levels of distress among cancer patients generally fall to levels comparable with healthy populations (e.g. Burgess *et al.* 2005), they are seen to become elevated at certain points during treatment, or when awaiting test results, and when end-stage illness is reached and treatment ended with no further hope for a cure. During the active treatment phase of their illness, cancer patients may have to cope with a variety of stressors, including significant side-effects such as potentially debilitating and distressing nausea, fatigue and weight loss. Distress at this time is complex; individuals may weigh up the unwanted effects of treatment against the benefits of symptom reduction and survival gains, and patient perceptions and expectancies of the treatment as well as the perceived severity of symptoms play a role (Thuné-Boyle *et al.* 2006). While the majority of individuals choose to continue with treatment, a small minority do opt to withdraw from treatment. Even when *at risk* of illness, not everyone will opt for treatment when it is offered. For example, Lovegrove *et al.* (2000) found that half of the 106 women at high familial risk of breast cancer attending a breast care clinic, and who were asked to take part in a trial of tamoxifen (a synthetic, non-steroidal agent with tumour-limiting benefits in an unaffected breast), refused to participate. Those refusing tended to be younger, found the information about tamoxifen as a potential preventive treatment harder to understand than those who took part, knew more about lifestyle risk factors, and saw fewer benefits of the drug.

For those living with diabetes, a chronic, controllable, but potentially life-threatening illness, daily self-management behaviours are required including controlling diet, taking insulin, and testing glucose levels by daily urine sampling. Emotional distress is prevalent, as shown by a systematic review of studies with a combined population of over two-and-a-half thousand adults with diabetes and almost one-and-a-half thousand control participants.

Authors report a 14 per cent prevalence of generalised anxiety disorder among those with diabetes, compared with population norms of around 3–4 per cent, and elevated anxiety symptoms in 40 per cent (Grigsby *et al.* 2002). Anderson *et al.* (2001) report that depression is twice as likely in adults with diabetes than in those without.

In terms of living with a disease for which a certain degree of stigma is still attached, studies of those with HIV infection and AIDS point to even higher levels of distress. Perhaps unique to those with HIV infection, the presence of what have been identified as 'punishment beliefs' (i.e. where HIV infection is considered by the individual to be a 'punishment' for 'inappropriate' behaviour) have been associated with relatively high levels of depression and relatively low self-esteem (Safren *et al.* 2002). Such beliefs reflect possible internalisation of early beliefs or prejudices about HIV and likely routes of infection, such as injecting drug use or unprotected homosexual sex. Valente (2003) concluded from a summary of existing data that between 20 and 30 per cent of people with HIV are clinically depressed at some stage in their illness, and among women with HIV, Morrison, M. *et al.* (2002) reported depression levels four times higher than that expected among age-matched control subjects. However, among this female-only sample, anxiety levels were not raised significantly, although other studies of both genders have reported 70 per cent having moderate to high anxiety (Cohen *et al.* 2002). As with depression among physically healthy individuals, high levels of background stress, low levels of personal resources and social support, and poor coping skills all contribute to depression (e.g. Catz *et al.* 2002).

In terms of two of the major killers in Western society, heart disease and heart attack, it has been estimated that one-third or more of sufferers will experience levels of depression above cut-offs indicating clinical disorder. Depression and anxiety often persist for up to a year following hospital discharge (Lane *et al.* 2002b). Among stroke patients the figures have been reported as anywhere between 10 and 40 per cent, with variation depending on whether samples are assessed while in hospital or once home in the community (Robinson 1998). For many stroke patients, the significant levels of emotional distress (anxiety and/or depression) persist for many months, with an estimated 22 per cent expected to experience major depression at some point (Robinson, 1998). It has been shown that psychosocial factors in addition to disease features predict long-term outcome of stroke; for example, patient satisfaction with health care and confidence in recovery predicted depression at six months and three years following acute stroke (Morrison *et al.* 2000b; Morrison *et al.* 2005).

As well as or often tied up with distress, chronic illness can also bring about a sense of 'loss of self' (Charmaz 1983, 1991) to the sufferer, a condition exacerbated by the necessity of living a restricted life due to symptoms, or by social isolation due to physical limitations or fears of others' response to their 'new state'. Negative responses of others can sometimes lead to perceptions of the self being discredited, or to perceiving oneself as being a burden on others by being unable to fulfil one's 'normal' social roles and tasks. As Radley (1994: 148) notes: 'The problems of chronic illness are to do with retention and loss, not just of "self" but of a way of life'. Illness often forces the person to redefine themselves, from a 'healthy' person to one with limitations, and this can reduce feelings of self-worth or self-esteem. There is evidence that enabling a person to hold on to their pre-illness sense of identity rather than having an identity consumed by a serious or chronic illness can be beneficial. Aujoulat *et al.* (2008) interviewed forty chronically ill patients in Belgium and Italy and describe a process of patient empowerment which requires two processes, one of being able to 'hold on' to earlier ideas of 'self' (identity and worth, different roles) and learning to control the illness as something separate to these, and the other process of 'letting go' where patients accept that they cannot control everything and that they have boundaries, and in effect this requires them accommodating the illness. In engaging in both processes, the authors suggest, patients will experience greater adjustment and ability to value oneself. Research is needed which follows up on this important distinction as it has implications for those working with patients with a view to enhancing control – there are aspects to hold on to, and others to let go, and as stated previously in this textbook, perceived control beliefs have to be realistic if they are to be most helpful.

■ Reactions at the end of treatment

In the immediate period following treatment, cancer patients and their families may experience a degree of emotional ambivalence: on the one hand, the treatment and its side-effects have stopped, but on the other hand, a sense of vulnerability and of being abandoned can result from decreased contact with the health professional staff, with whom relationships have inevitably built up during treatment. This feeling of 'abandonment' following treatment discharge has been reported in other patient groups, for example, stroke patients (e.g. Pound *et al.* 1994). However, Wiles *et al.*'s (2004) qualitative study of stroke patients' experience on discharge from physiotherapy noted that where discharge is 'managed well', disappointment can be contained to disappointment at cessation of physiotherapy but not disappointment in terms of a loss of expectation of further potential recovery.

A transition from curative to palliative treatment, if the former is unsuccessful, can be extremely distressing for patients. Overall, the rates of anxiety and/or depression are high among people who are dying, although this is by no means universal (e.g. Heaven and Maguire (1998) reported only 17 per cent prevalence of clinical levels of distress in their sample). The certainty of death commonly brings with it emotional and existential crises alongside concerns about the process of dying and about pain control (Strang and Strang 2002), and fears about a loss of dignity, which can raise distress and even lower the will to live (Chochinov *et al.* 2002). Kubler-Ross (1969) described a staged reactive process to dying, with initial shock and numbness following a terminal diagnosis being followed by a stage of denial and feelings of isolation, at which point individuals may become angry, blame others or even attempt to 'bargain' for goals they wish to meet before dying. Kubler-Ross describes the final stage as one of acceptance. However, acceptance is not always reached, highlighting as we have previously, that the proposed 'stages' do not hold for all cases. For example, among cancer patients, some will enter the terminal phase still 'in denial' of their impending death. Hinton (1999) found that by the time of their death, only half of the people followed in their study were 'accepting' of death, and 18 per cent of patients and 24 per cent of relatives actually became less accepting of death as they moved towards it.

■ The effect of negative emotional reactions to illness

Unfortunately, the presence of depression and anxiety can impede engagement in treatment or rehabilitation efforts. Depressed people, for example, are less likely to attend cardiac rehabilitation classes than non-depressed ones (Lane *et al.* 2001), and anxiety is often associated with poor control of blood glucose levels among those with diabetes (e.g. Niemcryk *et al.* 1990). Depression and anxiety have also been shown to impede behavioural change. For example, Huijbrechts *et al.* (1996) reported lower rates of smoking cessation following a heart attack in people who were depressed or anxious than among those who reported no distress five months after the event; and among HIV-positive homosexual males, depression was associated with more than twice the rate of engagement in unprotected anal sex with partners than that reported by non-depressed HIV-positive homosexual males (Rogers *et al.* 2003).

Depression also exerts a significant influence on whether such patients resume pre-illness functioning, particularly in terms of return to work and social activities, and this may in part be due to the symptom inflation commonly witnessed among depressed people (see Chapter 9). It is clear therefore that depressive illness is a significant cause of morbidity and disability (and even reduced survival among the physically ill, e.g. Morris *et al.* 1993; Peveler *et al.* 2002, although this association has not been found in all studies).

Positive responses to illness

Although studies of positive responses to illness remain relatively rare when contrasted with those that address the negative responses, there is consistent evidence that positive dispositional characteristics and positive appraisals, can influence outcomes either directly or indirectly, and that illness itself can bring about positive changes. We review some of this evidence below.

■ Positive appraisals

Having a positive or optimistic outlook has been consistently associated either directly wth positive outcomes, or indirectly via effects on coping responses thought to be 'more adaptive' (as indicated by improved outcomes such as lowered distress, greater reported QoL). For example, Kurtz *et al.* (2008) have recently shown that being optimistic and having higher mastery beliefs was associated with less severe pain and reduced fatigue among patients with cancer followed up from receiving chemotherapy for ten weeks. Conversely, pessimists have been shown to endorse more maladaptive coping strategies, which are then predictive of greater emotional morbidity, for example as found by Schou and colleagues (Schou *et al.* 2004) among patients followed for a year after having breast cancer surgery.

■ Positive emotions

Fredrickson (1998, 2001) has summarised the key benefits of maintaining positive emotions:

■ the promotion of psychological resilience and more effective problem solving;

■ the dispelling of negative emotions;

■ the triggering of an upward spiral of positive feelings.

Illustrating the benefits of positive emotions, Fredman and colleagues (Fredman *et al.* 2006) found that elderly patients with a hip fracture who had high levels of positive affect at baseline (during initial hospitalisation for the fracture) had better functional recovery as seen in standing and walking speeds at 2-, 6-, 12-, 18- and 24-month follow-up, than those with low levels of positive affect. Those with consistently high levels, i.e. high positive affect at each time point, had the best recovery in function. However, maintaining positive emotions form only part of a person's response to illness: the coping strategies that a person adopts to help them to cope with the disease and its consequences are also important in determining illness outcomes (see below, but also Chapters 9, 11 and 12 for a discussion of Leventhal's self-regulation model of illness and Lazarus's stress-coping theory).

■ Finding benefit

A growing number of studies are reporting that those facing significant health or life stressors often report gains from their experience. Commonly referred to as benefit-finding, studies of this phenomenon fit within a larger framework described as 'post-traumatic growth', whereby individuals experience positive psychological change as a result of a struggle with stressful life circumstance(s) (Tedeschi and Calhoun 2004; and see the handbook of Calhoun and Tedeschi 2007 for a discussion of post-traumatic growth following a range of stressors).

Five domains of positive change as a result of stress or trauma have generally been identified:

1. Enhanced personal relationships
2. Greater appreciation for life
3. A sense of increased personal strength
4. Greater spirituality
5. A valued change in life priorities and goals.

The strength of these possible dimensions of growth vary across studies depending on the event under consideration, but there is reasonable consistency from quantitative studies (e.g. Park *et al.* 1996 – general stress; Fromm *et al.* 1996 – bone marrow transplant; Petrie *et al.* 1999 – heart attack and breast cancer; Tomich and Helgeson 2004 – breast cancer), and from qualitative studies (e.g. Gall and Cornblatt 2002; Ingram *et al.* 2008 (both cancer)). Importantly, Carver and Antoni (2004) report long-term advantage to benefit-finding in that women who found benefit in the first year following a breast cancer diagnosis showed improved psychological adjustment 5–8 years after treatment compared to those who did not find benefit. Park and Lechner (2007) point to the importance of including control groups, however, when assessing 'post-traumatic growth' as growth may be an integral part of 'normal' life experiences rather than specific to particular challenges.

IN THE SPOTLIGHT

Religiosity, finding meaning and hope in the illness experience

A recent Gallup survey found that 83 per cent of Americans felt that a God was important in their lives, whereas in Western and Eastern Europe this figure reduced to 49 per cent (Gallup International online millenium survey, 2000). In the UK, 12 per cent of the population attend a place of worship in contrast to 47 per cent of North Americans. Does this really matter and what has this to do with health psychology?

Increasing interest is being paid to the effects of religiosity and, in many cases, spirituality, on the event appraisals and coping methods employed by people when faced with stressful events, including illness, and the subsequent effects this has on outcome (Harrison *et al.* 2001; Thuné-Boyle *et al.* 2006). In terms of adjustment to illness, Thuné-Boyle *et al.* (2006) reviewed 17 studies addressing this question in relation to cancer adjustment. They found that 7 studies found benefits of religious coping for reduced distress and increased adjustment (3 found benefits only for specific subgroups according to race, extent of 'hope'), 7 studies found no beneficial effects, and 3 studies in fact found religious coping to be harmful (one example of this was an increase in anxiety seen among women given a same-day diagnosis of symptomatic breast problems, Harcourt *et al.* 1999). In terms of general stress, Park (2006) found that religiousness was associated with higher perceived challenge appraisals, greater meaning-making (positive appraisals of events, personal growth), and better emotional and physical adjustment among older adults followed up one month later. Indeed, the findings of several studies point to an association between religiosity and optimism (e.g. long-term adjustment to breast cancer, Gall *et al.* 2000), positive affect (e.g. adjustment and reduced negative affect in those with rheumatoid arthritis, van de Creek *et al.* 2004), and hope (religious coping effects on distress found to be mediated by hope among cardiac surgery patients, Ai *et al.* 2007).

Measures of religious coping have been developed to specifically identify the cognitive and behavioural coping strategies and functions involved and distinctions have been drawn between positive, negative, active and passive religious coping (RC). Positive RC is where God is seen as supportive and comforting, for example; negative RC is where a less secure relationship exists with a more distant and punishing God (e.g. the RCOPE, Pargament *et al.* 2000). Where religious coping may often be considered as passive, it is clear that it is not necessarily so: consider, for example, attending prayer groups as a form of seeking intimacy or support from like-minded others, or of setting out to help others (Harrison *et al.* 2001).

These examples have been provided in order to highlight a growing area of interest in health psychology. Snyder *et al.* (1991) described two aspects of hope: one is the individual's belief in the possibility of favourable outcomes (related to optimism), and the other being the ability to visualise how to obtain the favourable outcome. It may be that, as well as having faith or confidence in one's own ability to deal with illness, related treatments, and their consequences, that having faith in a God may also be beneficial. From the brief overview here, it appears likely that religiosity effects outcomes via its influence upon appraisals of meaning, in maintaining hope, or on coping responses, but there is clearly a need for further research if we are to gain better understanding of the role religiosity plays in adjustment to illness.

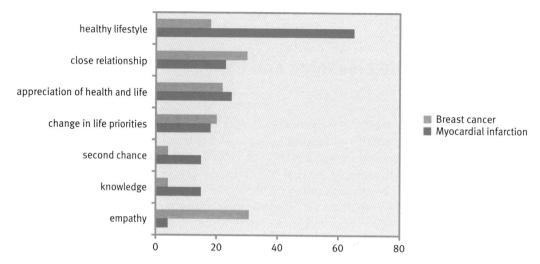

Figure 15.1   Perceived gains following breast cancer or a heart attack.

Source: Petrie, Buick, Weinman and Booth (1999)

So, how common is benefit-finding and what form does it take? Petrie *et al.* (1999) found that 60 per cent of those who had had a heart attack or had developed breast cancer reported some personal gains over the first three months following illness onset, and 58 per cent reported specific positive effects of their illness (see Figure 15.1). The most commonly endorsed benefits were improved close relationships, increased empathy among women with breast cancer, and a healthier lifestyle for men following a heart attack. In a qualitative study of women with breast cancer Gall and Cornblatt (2002) revealed a spiritual aspect to growth, with women reporting an increased inner strength, spirituality and sense of peace, a sense of becoming a better person and being more thoughtful, compassionate, understanding and accepting, and increased confidence. Improved relationships with significant others is a commonly reported 'benefit' of illness, and it has been suggested (de Vellis *et al.* 2003) that good relationships between couples may work towards the creation and maintenance of positive emotions (in patients and/or caregivers), which may benefit adjustment. Becoming more accepting of things in life or having closer relationships with family or friends, may in fact lead to reported QoL levels higher than those reported by healthy individuals (as reported by Tempelaar *et al.* 1989, cited in Schulz and Mohamed 2004).

Benefit-finding can be considered as a potential predictor of outcomes such as improved mood, better adjustment or QoL, but it has also been considered by some as an outcome in its own right. In these instances, as with studies of predictors of negative consequences of illness, the experiencing of benefits is influenced by personal characteristics and psychosocial resources including coping responses. Stanton *et al.* (2007) notes that in terms of demographic correlates of benefit-finding, younger age is commonly associated, lower socio-economic status and ethnicity effects are variable but gender tends not to exert a significant effect. In terms of psychosocial predictors, Schulz and Mohamed (2004) carried out a prospective study of 105 cancer patients, interviewed at one, six and twelve months following tumour

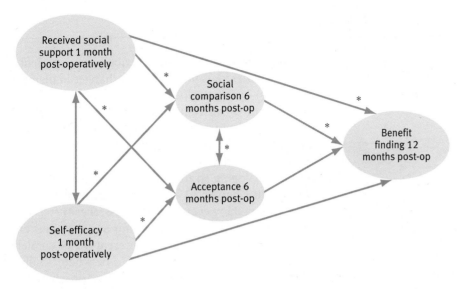

Figure 15.2 The direct and indirect effects of internal (self-efficacy) and external (social support) resources upon benefit finding in the twelve months following cancer surgery.

Source: adapted from Schulz and Mohamed (2004: 659)

acceptance coping
accepting the reality of a situation and that it cannot easily be changed.

social comparison
the process by which a person or group of people compare themselves (their behaviour or characteristics) with others.

surgery and found that finding benefit at twelve months was directly predicted by levels of self-efficacy (a personal resource) and social resources (amount of social support received) at one month. However, as can be seen in Figure 15.2 (in which the arrowed lines with asterisks reflect significant associations), when examining whether coping mediated the relationship between these internal and external resources and benefit-finding, individuals with high social support resources exhibited greater benefit-finding regardless of whether **acceptance coping** or **social comparison** coping was used, whereas the beneficial effect of self-efficacy appeared to be mediated by coping (as the direct association between self-efficacy and finding benefit was insignificant). These findings are based on a prospective study but it is worth noting that studies of benefit-finding and personal growth often assess these variables retrospectively and, as Stanton *et al.* (2007) points out in his review of this area, time since the event is likely to influence the extent to which growth is reported. People often reconstruct past experiences in order to make them more congruent with current experience.

The final point worth considering in relation to this relatively new field of study is that cultural variations may exist in the nature of personal growth or benefit-finding experienced. Ho *et al.* (2004) suggest that individuals from Asian cultures which are more 'collectivist' in approach to health and illness (see Chapter 1), may not make changes to one's personal outlook, goals or priorities to the same extent as individuals from more 'individualistic' cultures. However, Rapp and Chao (2000) found that the reported benefits of caregiving for a spouse or parent with dementia were greater in their small sample of black caregivers than their larger sample of white caregivers. These findings may be an artefact of sample size differences, however, and therefore these questions warrant further research attention.

Coping with illness

Moos and Schaefer (1984) described the experience of illness as a 'crisis', whereby individuals face potential changes in identity (healthy person to sick person, for example), location (home to hospital or nursing home), role (e.g. independent breadwinner to dependant), and changes to aspects of social support (e.g. from socially integrated to socially isolated). The coping strategies used to cope with illness do not differ from those used to cope with any other problem that an individual faces; in other words, illness does not trigger unique coping strategies, and as such the theory and concepts of coping outlined in Chapter 11 are as relevant here as they are to consideration of stress coping. However, as with stress, there needs to be a distinction between acute illness events (e.g. flu, minor surgery) and chronic illnesses, as these present the individual with a different set of challenges. The accepted 'cut-off' for becoming 'chronic' tends to be where an illness and its symptoms or effects last for greater than six months, or where there may be no potential for cure. Some, but not all, chronic diseases are progressive, for example asthma is not, whereas many forms of cancer or arthritis are.

Moos and Schaefer (1984) identified three processes that resulted from the crisis of illness:

1. *Cognitive appraisal*: the individual appraises the implications of the illness for their lives.

2. *Adaptive tasks*: the individual is required to perform illness-specific tasks such as dealing with symptoms, and general tasks such as preserving emotional balance, or relationships with others (see below).

3. *Coping skills*: the individual engages in coping strategies defined as either appraisal-focused (e.g. denial or minimising, positive reappraisal, mental preparation/planning); problem-focused (e.g. information and support-seeking, taking direct action to deal with a problem, identifying alternative goals and rewards); and emotion-focused coping (e.g. mood regulation, emotional discharge such as venting anger, or passive and resigned acceptance).

Full discussion of symptom and illness appraisal and stress appraisals can be found in Chapters 9 and 11. Here we explore further the second and third processes outlined by Moos and Schaefer. The adaptive tasks required as a result of chronic illness include:

- dealing with the symptoms of the disease and the possibility of pain;
- maintaining control over illness, including aspects of symptom management, treatment, or prevention of progression;
- managing communicative relationships with health professionals;
- facing and preparing for an uncertain future;
- preserving self-image and possibly self-esteem when challenged (e.g. by altered appearance or function);
- maintaining control and emotional balance over health and life in general;
- dealing with changes in relationships with family and friends.

Although the challenges are generic to many different conditions, aspects may vary in strength and salience depending on the condition (Stanton *et al.* 2001), for example dealing with treatments may present greater challenges to adaptation in those with cancer than among those with asthma. How a person chooses to deal with these challenges may vary, as discussed in Chapters 11 and 12 in relation to a range of stressors including illness, and as we now describe in the discussion of coping below.

■ Coping by denial or avoidance

Of the many studies conducted in relation to coping, a common initial response to diagnosis or illness onset is either conscious or unconscious denial of its occurrence. Denial appears to be adaptive in the short term as it enables the individual to cope with the distress felt. In the longer term, however, denial and the related strategy of avoidance tend to interfere with active coping efforts and are associated with increased long-term distress. Many, but not all, studies report negative outcomes of avoidant coping and denial; for example:

■ Avoidant coping and emotion-focused strategies were associated with greater depression than problem-focused coping among a sample of HIV-positive homosexual men (Safren *et al.* 2002).

■ Cognitive avoidance coping including passive acceptance and resignation among women with breast cancer was associated with a significant risk of poor long-term psychological adjustment at a three-year follow-up (Hack and Degner 2004).

■ Among adolescents with chronic disease (asthma, juvenile arthritis, cystic fibrosis, eczema), positive adjustment was predicted by seeking social support and confrontational coping; negative adjustment was predicted by depressive coping (e.g. passivity), but avoidance coping was not a strong predictor (Meijer *et al.* 2002).

■ Among patients with rheumatoid arthritis, scoring highly on the avoidance/denial sub-scale of the Vanderbilt multidimensional pain coping inventory, was positively correlated with active coping and positive outcomes (Smith *et al.* 1997). This unusual finding is thought to reflect the specific context of coping with pain (see Chapter 16).

■ Problem-focused and acceptance coping

Generally speaking, after the initial period following illness onset or diagnosis has passed, problem-focused coping, such as making use of social support resources or planning how to deal with the problems faced, and acceptance coping are associated with more positive adaptation. Lowe *et al.* (2000) examined levels of distress six months following a heart attack in relation to the coping and emotions reported in hospital and at two months. Acceptance-focused coping (e.g. accepting things as they are, reinterpreting things in a positive light) was the most prevalent form of coping, followed by problem-focused, emotion-focused and, least of all, avoidance coping. Acceptance coping was associated with lower levels of distress, problem-focused coping was associated with high levels of positive mood, and emotion-focused coping was associated with low mood. Longitudinal analyses confirmed a prospective relationship between problem-focused coping and improved health outcomes, suggesting that effort directed to changeable

aspects of the situation resulted in improved health outcomes (either perceived or actual).

People engage in all sorts of coping efforts and do not generally use
strategies defined as only emotion-focused, only problem-focused or only
avoidant. This is because situations are generally dynamic and multidimensional, and therefore responses also need to be dynamic and multidimensional. As evidence of this, a study of young people within two months
of developing cancer (Kyngaes *et al.* 2001) found that emotion-focused,
appraisal-focused and problem-focused strategies were employed. The strategies most frequently used were accessing social support (seeking information
from health professionals as well as emotional support from families), believing in recovery and returning to 'normal' life (positive reframing). Some
authors point to a 'time *X* strategy interaction' whereby different strategies
are adopted at different periods in the illness 'crisis'. For example, Heim *et al.*
(1987) suggested that cancer patients use more active and problem-focused
strategies earlier in the disease, with a shift to more passive and avoidant
strategies as the disease progresses. This shift may be highly functional.
Stanton *et al.* (2002a) reported a complex relationship between positive
future expectancies, coping and outcomes of women with early-stage breast
cancer. Active acceptance at the time of diagnosis predicted better adjustment
in terms of mood and reduced fear of recurrence than did avoidant strategies.
Pessimism about the future was associated with coping by turning to religion,
whereas those women who retained high amounts of hope for the future
generally benefited from the use of more active coping strategies.

The nature of coping responses to illness may also be influenced by culture, as suggested by Roy *et al.* (2005) when their study of an ethnically
diverse British cancer population revealed that UK Asians who were more
depressed than the Caucasian sample endorsed helplessness and hopelessness
and a greater fatalistic attitude to coping.

The coping responses of people facing illness are therefore individual and
influenced by many factors. They are also dynamic and, reflecting Lazarus's
transactional model of stress and coping (see Chapter 11), change over time
as a result of changing demands and resources and of coping appraisal (what
seems to work best for the person). The factors that moderate this relationship may also change over time: for example, social support may fluctuate.
The crisis theory of Moos and Schaefer (1984) mentioned earlier assumes
that individuals cope out of a motivation to restore equilibrium and normality to their lives. One of the key resources that most individuals have to aid
in that process is that of family support, yet, as we describe in the next section, illness also impacts on these individuals, which can have additional
effects on the adjustment of the individual facing the illness.

Illness: a family affair

People do not get ill in a vacuum: their illness exists within their immediate
personal context and within their larger social network and culture. Not
surprisingly, many of the wide-ranging effects of illness on the 'sufferer'
described earlier in this chapter can also be experienced by those closest to

the ill person. The growing trend towards home care and day treatments places further pressures on families.

Family systems

The families of people who develop an illness also need to adapt to changes that an illness brings. The diagnosis of serious illness and subsequent tests and/or treatments can have a significant impact on family coping and on their levels of certainty for the future, and life goals (Sherman and Simonton 2001). As described at the start of this chapter, theories of patient adjustment to illness (e.g. Morse and Johnson 1991) generally posit a staged approach towards adjustment. Relative to family members, McCubbin and Patterson (1982) note that stress in the family is a pressure that can disrupt or change the 'family system', and they also suggested stages in a continuum of adaptation:

1. *Stage of resistance*: where family members try to deny or avoid the reality of what has happened.
2. *Stage of restructuring*: where family members begin to acknowledge reality and start to reorganise their lives around the notion of a changed family.
3. *Stage of consolidation*: where newly adopted roles may have to become permanent, for example if recovery is not forthcoming; and where new ways of thinking (about life/health/behaviour) may emerge.

Relevant to this continuum of adaptation are the three integrated dimensions of family system functioning highlighted by Olson and Stewart (1991): cohesion, adaptability and communication. Olson provided evidence that families who were balanced on these dimensions (i.e. they work together and are affiliated and emotionally bonded with each other; they adapt roles and rules in face of new situations, and they communicate effectively) showed better adaptation to life stressors, including illness. These broad dimensions can be seen in a study by McCubbin and Patterson (1983) of parental coping in relation to having a child with cystic fibrosis, where three specific factors within parental coping strategies were identified, each of which held different implications for family functioning:

1. coping by maintaining and focusing on family life and the relationships therein;
2. coping by trying to maintain wellbeing through the use of social relationships;
3. coping by having relationships with medical staff and parents of other ill children.

The influence of context, in terms of the length of time since the onset of illness, upon parental coping is highlighted in RESEARCH FOCUS below. Reviewing family systems in relation to the impact of a disabling stroke, Palmer and Glass (2003) identify the need for families to adjust to new patterns of relationship, roles and communication styles and 'to accommodate the stroke survivor's functional and social losses while continuing to meet the psychosocial needs of the entire family' (p. 256). Their review highlights the fact that the process of recovery from stroke, from a family systems perspective, is about support and collaboration from and between family members, and that the absence of these can have detrimental effects on both the wellbeing of the stroke sufferer and on the family members.

How do parents cope with cancer in their child?

Norberg, A.L., Lindblad, F. and Boman, K.K. (2005). Coping strategies in parents of children with cancer. *Social Science and Medicine*, 60: 965–75.

Background

Receiving a diagnosis at any point in one's life can be inherently stressful. In spite of advances in treatment, many forms of cancer remain life-threatening, and where treatment is available it is generally intensive, intrusive on one's life, and can bring with it undesirable side-effects. It is difficult to imagine any family that would not be affected by any member receiving such a diagnosis; however it is probably even more distressing when the diagnosis is received by a child. Watching a child suffer and dealing with the reactions of others pose many challenges for parents in terms of their own coping and in terms of helping their child to cope.

Aims of study

This paper addresses the impact of childhood cancer on parental coping where children are dealing with various types of cancer at various stages following diagnosis. It also examines whether the parents of children with cancer coped with general life stresses any differently than parents of a healthy child.

Methods

A total of 395 parents (224 mothers and 171 fathers) of children either undergoing (44.3 per cent) or having completed cancer treatment (55.2 per cent) were recruited from two Swedish paediatric oncology units. The overall response rate for study participation was an excellent 73 per cent, reflecting the interest that parents had in being provided with an opportunity to talk about their experience. A total of 59 per cent of non-responders were fathers, which is similar to that found previously, and points to an area in need of further investigation. The average total number of children in responding families was 2.5.

In terms of cancer type, the two largest diagnostic groups were leukaemia (44 per cent) and brain tumours (14.9 per cent). Parents were excluded from the study if their child had an incurable diagnosis or if their child was currently receiving palliative treatment. In terms of time since diagnosis, there was a wide range from 0 months to 21 years, but for analysis purposes, only three groups were compared: 1–8 weeks (86 parents); 18–30 months (72 parents) and 60–120 months (60 parents). A third of the children had been diagnosed while under 3 years of age; 23 per cent had been 3–6 years old; 13.9 per cent 6–9 years old; 18.5 per cent 9–15 years old; and 10.6 per cent 15–21 years old.

A comparison group of 184 parents of healthy children aged 0–16 (58 per cent mothers) was also recruited from the same geographical area. The average total number of children per control family was 2.2. Questionnaires included the Utrecht coping list, and as measures of outcome, state anxiety using Spielberger's state–trait anxiety scale and the Zung self-rating depression scale. The coping measure required parents to respond in relation to general stressful events on seven sub-scales of coping strategies: *active problem focusing* (e.g. goal-oriented, sorting things out); *palliative reaction pattern* (e.g. behavioural distraction, relaxation); *avoidance behaviour* (e.g. withdrawing from difficult situations); *social support seeking*; *passive reaction pattern* (isolating self from others, fantasy escape); *expression of emotion* (annoyance and anger); and *comforting cognition* (looking on bright side, positive comparison).

Results

Both state anxiety and state depression were higher among parents of children with cancer (PCC) than among parents of healthy children (PHC). Mothers of both healthy children and those with cancer reported significantly higher levels of anxiety and depression than did the fathers. Overall, coping, perhaps surprisingly, was not found to differ between PCC and PHC, although PCC showed a significant tendency towards the use of passive reaction coping.

When coping was compared across the two main cancer sites, no significant differences in coping strategies emerged, and furthermore no coping differences were seen between the three groupings according to length of time since diagnosis. Neither did whether the child was currently undergoing treatment, or had completed it, affect coping responses or the levels of anxiety and depression in PCC.

Given the lack of between-group differences in coping, the authors then explored the within-group associations; in other words, they examined which coping strategies were correlated with greater anxiety or depression. Among both PCC and PHC, more frequent use of active problem focusing and less use of avoidance and passive reaction coping was associated with lower levels of anxiety and depression. Given the gender differences found in anxiety and depression, analyses were rerun controlling for gender (partial correlations), and the negative effects of these coping strategies persisted.

Finally, the relationship between coping and anxiety and depression was examined according to length of time since diagnosis, and in terms of the two main diagnostic groupings. These factors were found to make some significant differences. For example, active problem focusing was associated with less emotional distress in parents of children with leukaemia, but not those with brain tumours; and avoidance behaviour was not related to anxiety or depression in the recently diagnosed group (1–8 weeks), whereas in parents of those diagnosed 60–120 months previously, it related to both anxiety and depression.

Discussion

This is a fascinating study, which although cross-sectional, manages to address questions related to illness stage and parental coping through the use of different 'cohorts' of parents, i.e. different lengths of time since the child was diagnosed. Perhaps surprisingly, PCC did not differ in terms of how they coped with general stress from PHC, even though they were experiencing greater distress. This may in part be because coping was assessed in terms of general stress, whereas mood measures reflected current mood. In addition, while coping strategies were differentially related to anxiety and depression in each disease group, disease group did not itself affect the coping strategies reported. Among both sets of parents the patterns of association between coping, anxiety and depression reflected that which is reported in the wider literature: i.e. active, problem-focused forms of coping appear to be more effective in dealing with stress than passive or emotion-focused responses.

In conclusion, results highlight the value of subgroup analysis where sample size allows this. One crucial finding, which reflects what has been said in Chapter 14 regarding the use of avoidance coping, is that it appears less beneficial when being used by parents who are further removed in time from the cancer diagnosis than when it is reported by parents who have recently received their child's diagnosis. Ideally, to address questions raised by this study more fully would inevitably require a prospective longitudinal study of parents and children from as soon as possible following diagnosis.

Caring

While family members are generally involved in providing support to a family member if they become ill, some also become that person's primary (main) caregiver: i.e. they are required to provide assistance above and beyond that which is 'normal' for their role (preparing a meal for a partner may be usual, whereas helping them to bathe may not be) (e.g. Schulz and Quittner 1998). There are approximately 5.7 million UK-based informal (unpaid, non-professional) caregivers, aged predominantly between 45 and 64, 3.3 million of whom are female (Department of Health 1999a). The 'problems' caregivers are providing care for are predominantly those of chronic diseases (approximately 40 per cent), with significant proportions caring for problems relating to ageing: dementia, problems of mobility, and mental, emotional or neurological problems. As noted by Kalra *et al.* (2004: 1,099) in relation to stroke management: 'Although the physical, psychological, emotional, and social consequences of care-giving and its economic benefit to society are well recognised, care-givers' needs are often given low priority'. These authors go on to present positive effects of caregiver training in providing physical care to the stroke survivor, in terms of reduced caregiver burden, reduced anxiety and depression, and improved QoL for both the caregivers and their patients. Addressing caregiver issues is therefore crucial to both patient and caregiver outcomes, and therefore the remainder of this chapter is dedicated to their experience or their relationship with the person they care for.

What do YOU think?

We live in an ageing society, but increasing life expectancy brings with it increasing needs for care of the elderly. We also live in a society where chronic diseases are of growing prevalence due to medical successes. This means that disability and dependence is increasing, not only among those considered 'elderly' but also in those in late middle age who may live for a further ten, twenty or thirty years in a dependent condition. More and more societies seem to be turning to families as sources of care. Although the gender imbalance in terms of who provides care has shifted away from being predominantly female towards being more balanced, gender roles have generally changed hugely over past decades. Ask your mother or your grandmother about their views on staying at home to care for a sick or dependent relative, and then consider your own situation. Are you already, or likely to be facing in the future, the need to provide informal and unpaid care for a relative? How does this make you feel? How do you imagine you will balance your various life roles if you take on an additional caring role? Are your projected life goals likely to be constrained by anticipated caring needs? Do you already worry about what will happen to your parents if they become chronically ill or develop dementia?

Questions such as these need to be asked, and answers need to be found. Are family members, particularly women, due to societal change in employment and social status, less willing to care for a dependent, possibly ageing, family member than previous generations? If so, what are the likely consequences for their mental and physical wellbeing if providing care becomes a necessity? What are the implications for health and social care policy? Such questions require wider social and political answers, but they have significant psychological implications.

Supportive relationships

There is a clear need to evaluate the effects of supportive relationships, because, as Evans and Bishop (1990) noted in relation to acute stroke outcomes, 'the patient's support system 1) is ultimately responsible for long-term care and 2) may influence poststroke psychosocial outcomes dramatically' (p. 48). As described in Chapter 12, there is consistent evidence as to the benefits of being part of a functional supportive network as opposed to being socially isolated (lack of support can increase stress levels, for example following bereavement; Balaswamy *et al.* 2004; Stroebe *et al.* 2005).

Benefits of social support include:

- increased adherence to treatment and self-care (e.g. Lo 1999; Toljamo and Hentinen 2001);
- less distress/better emotional adjustment and coping with stressful events (e.g. Hallaråker *et al.* 2001; Stroebe *et al.* 2005);
- better physiological functioning (e.g. Taylor *et al.* 2003; Uchino 2006);
- reduced mortality or increased survival (e.g. Greenwood *et al.* 1996; Vogt *et al.* 1992).

Consensus exists that it is not simply the absolute number of supports a person has available to them (structural) but the perceived quality and function of these supports (functional) and satisfaction with the support provided that is critical in predicting such outcomes (e.g. Quick *et al.* 1996; Vogt *et al.* 1992). However, social support is not always helpful, even if intended as such by the caregiver.

■ Helpful and unhelpful caring

Studies of caring for people with a range of illnesses, such as AIDS, diabetes and cancer, have found that there are common caring actions that are perceived as helpful, such as practical assistance and expressions of love, concern and understanding, and relative consistency in terms of actions considered to be unhelpful, for example minimising the situation, being unrealistically cheerful, underestimating the illness effects on the patient, or being critical or over-demanding. Patients who perceived their caregivers' actions as unhelpful have been found to have more negative perceptions of themselves and their spouses, and greater depression (Clark and Stephens 1996). Although helpful actions have generally been shown to occur more frequently than unhelpful actions, unhelpful actions appear to have a more strongly negative effect on wellbeing than helpful actions have a positive effect (e.g. Norris *et al.* 1990). Additionally, over-caring or being overly helpful and solicitous (e.g. taking over a person's chores, encouraging them to rest) can act as a form of operant conditioning in which patients are rewarded for exhibiting 'sick role' behaviour (see Chapter 1). For example, among a sample of 119 patients with chronic fatigue syndrome and their significant other, 'over-helped' care recipients exhibited greater fatigue and pain than those receiving punishing (e.g. caregiver expresses irritation at patient) or distracting (e.g. caregiver involves patient in activities) caregiver responses (Schmaling *et al.* 2000). Over-protected patients may also experience reduced perceptions of self-efficacy, self-esteem and recovery motivation, and elevated depression (e.g. Thompson and Pitts 1992) and, among pain patients, increased disability (e.g. Williamson *et al.* 1997).

Several studies have identified social interactions that are unsupportive and detrimental to the care receiver's wellbeing. For example, a study of 271 individuals living with HIV identified four types of unsupportive interaction:

1. insensitivity
2. disconnecting or disengaging behaviour
3. blaming or fault-finding
4. forced optimism.

The first three of these interaction types were significantly predictive of patient depression, above and beyond the prediction offered by patient physical functioning and positive social support (Ingram *et al.* 1999). Similarly, Kerns *et al.* (1990) found that what they termed 'punishing' spousal responses (such as ignoring the patient or expressing impatience or anger with them) was predictive of increased distress and depressive symptoms. These types of findings highlight the need to assess positively perceived support separately from negatively perceived support rather than assessing on a continuum of overall support without addressing how that support is evaluated. Given the evidence as to the presence of helpful and unhelpful caring actions, it is not perhaps surprising that when initially faced with a caring role, care providers ask themselves questions such as 'What is "good" care?' 'Am I suitably equipped to deal with the demands of the person I am caring for?' It may be that gender offers part of an answer to these questions.

In an interesting study, Neff and Karney (2005) explore the widely held assumption that women are better at providing support than men, a conclusion drawn in part from findings that married men benefited more from their wives' support during times of stress than married women seemed to benefit from husband support (e.g. Cutrona 1996). Using both observational data and seven-day diaries obtained from 169 newly married couples without children (within six months of marriage), the authors reached the conclusion that it is not that men and women differ in the skills of giving support to their partner, or even in the amount of support provided day to day, but that women are more responsive to the changing needs of their husbands as indicated in their stress-indicative behaviours and therefore provided better and more positive support at times of greater need.

The act of caring for a person with a chronic illness presents many challenges to caregivers, and not surprisingly research attention has increasingly turned to the examination of the impact of caring on the caregivers themselves.

Consequences of caring

Many different terms have been used to describe caregiver outcomes of providing care, and just as many different outcome measures are used, some of which assess mental health, some physical health and some global psychosocial wellbeing. A commonly employed term is that of 'caregiver burden', defined as the objective and subjective 'costs' of caring to the caregiver (e.g. Zarit *et al.* 1980). This term covers a broad-based outcome of caring that encompasses physical, psychological, financial and social costs of caring, and many studies have explored burden as an outcome, rather than focusing solely on emotional distress or physical outcomes (e.g. Scholte op Reimer *et al.* 1998; Schulz *et al.* 1995).

■ Emotional impact of caring

Research has suggested that up to three-quarters of caregivers experience clinically significant distress, a level significantly higher than that found in age-matched controls. Similarly, caregivers' physical health and life satisfaction are generally found to be lower than in non-caregivers. Feelings of loss, anxiety or depression are common among partners of those who have had a heart attack (e.g. Arefjord *et al.* 1998); and among those caring for a relative following a stroke, levels of depression have been shown to be two to three times that found in a comparable group of non-caregivers (Scholte op Reimer *et al.* 1998). It is not just spouses or partners that experience the distress of caring but also the parents of ill children, or children providing care for a dependent relative (see RESEARCH FOCUS below). Parental caregiving was considered in an earlier RESEARCH FOCUS, but other studies confirm what was reported there; for example, parents of children with cancer showed relatively stable but high levels of distress, with 51 per cent of mothers and 39 per cent of fathers exhibiting levels above the cut-off for emotional disorder, and distress remained high even after treatment had been completed, reflecting parental fears of recurrence (Sloper 2000).

RESEARCH FOCUS

Can teenagers cope with caregiving?

Bolas, H., Van Wersch, A.S. and Flynn, D. (2007). The well-being of young people who care for a dependent relative: an interpretative phenomenological analysis. *Psychology and Health*, 22: 829–50.

Background
As described elsewhere in this chapter informal family caregiving has increased and will continue to increase in societies where the population is ageing and people are surviving longer with chronic disease than they are likely to have in previous generations. Health and social care policy in most European countries has acknowledged this and has begun to address how to meet carer needs. However, much of this policy attention and much of the available service provision is directed at adult caregivers. In the UK alone it is estimated that there are between 19,000 and 51,000 informal caregivers under the age of 18 and, given informal mechanisms of identifying such carers, this figure may well be higher. Little is known about the impact of caregiving on these child caregivers, in terms of their emotional, social, educational and physical wellbeing.

Aims and method
This qualitative study addresses a hugely neglected area and sets out to explore the experiences of caregiving and the meanings attached to it, as identified in semi-structured interviews

continued

with three female (aged 14, 14, 18) and two male caregivers (aged 14 and 16). These young caregivers attended a young carer's support group as a result of educational or social service referral; hence it is acknowledged that they may not be representative of all young carers. They provide examples of the caregiving experience that have their own value. Interviews lasted approximately 45 minutes and were audio-recorded and transcribed verbatim before being analysed using IPA-interpretative phenomenonlogical analysis. As explained elsewhere in this text, IPA requires that each transcript is read and reread, emergent themes recorded and interrelationships between themes identified along with the superordinate themes. New themes are tested against other transcripts in order to identify shared themes.

Results

Three superordinate themes emerged from the data:

1. *what caring means*, i.e. the lived experience

   The participants stated that they had 'no choice' in taking up this role and so feelings about it were often ambivalent, e.g. '*I don't know, I feel like it's something that I've got to do and I haven't got a choice really. I cannot not do it cos I'm not like that, I cannot watch, sit and watch the telly or play to by meself knowing that Leon is working me Nana, I cannot do that. I've got to help her if I know she's stresses, she gets stressed really a lot, really lots.*'

   Participants felt the role was demanding and admitted they would prefer not to have to do it, but for some it was seen as inescapable. One young man caring for his Mum said '*Really you're a carer from when you wake up in the morning to when you go to sleep at night. Even if you're not in the house you're having still basically thinking about what've got to do when I get home, well really what I've got to do so it never really leaves me mind.*'

   Sometimes providing care was overwhelming, with participants describing how getting upset, angry and frustrated sometimes led to them directing frustration at the care recipient, which they felt was unacceptable.

2. *isolation and distancing from others*: changes in social relationships

   When talking about their experiences the isolation and distance from others became apparent, whether this was due to their trying to conceal their family member's condition from others (one girl cared for her brother who had ADHD) or because they didn't want to be seen as 'different'. For some the concern of others acted as a reminder of their situation and so they avoided social situations, for others they felt they were stigmatised and that people did not understand. '*It's a lot to cope with most of the time but . . . when you go out to the shops or something and there's people in the shops that take the mick out of your parents and all that. If it's like, me mam, I'll take offence very bad . . .*'. Day-to-day events could highlight their 'difference' such as being unable to easily go out with friends, as could the fact that for some of the families going out socially, or going on holiday, had become a thing of the past. For some they felt that their future wouldn't be a proper life.

3. *integrating caring*: the young peoples' reflections on their experiences of caregiving and their efforts to integrate this role into their self-concept.

   In spite of feeling different to others by virtue of their role, in some ways this enhanced their self-regard and self-esteem. Pride was taken in performing caregiving tasks and feeling useful, and caring became an important part of the identity of many of the participants, even if that identity was sometimes considered similar to that of a slave or servant. For some, the skills learnt as a caregiver were seen as useful to life beyond the here and now '*Well, I think it it's good because, I know it's hard work but when I grow up I could like look after children like, say I could work as a carer . . .*'.

Discussion

It is impossible in this RESEARCH FOCUS section to do justice to the richness of material produced in these interviews but the selection above should give a flavour of the experience of these young carers.

Themes cross over in some regard, with the lack of understanding of others (theme 2) highlighting that many people simply did not appreciate the enormity of the tasks these young people were undertaking (theme 1). However, we see how this can be exacerbated by the caregivers' reluctance to share their experience with others, and by their withdrawal. These young caregivers are without doubt experiencing burden; some are overwhelmed by what they see as inescapable; some described clearly the emotions that build up inside, and yet many chose not to trust the wider social world and got embroiled in secrecy both about their role and about the care recipient's condition for fear of rejection or stigmatisation. This isolation has clear implications for the wellbeing of these caregivers. Even if participants are seen to integrate their caring role into a sense of self that they are proud of, we need to question whether this is sufficient to buffer against inevitable stress. The authors discuss their findings in relation to theories of adaptation such as already addressed in this chapter, for example a search for meaning, a search for mastery. In spite of some limitations to the sample in terms of where they were recruited from, the diversity of relations and conditions they were caring for, this study offers a moving insight into the experiences and needs of young carers, that policymakers should acknowledge to a greater extent than perhaps is currently the case. To answer the question posed in the title of this RESEARCH FOCUS, the answer is 'Yes, but at what cost?'.

Studies suggest that emotional distress is most marked among women caregivers (e.g. Pinquart and Sörensen 2003; van den Heuvel et al. 2001), although some of the reported gender differences may be confounded by the fact that about 70 per cent of caregivers are women, which is reflected in study samples. Gender bias in the caring role may be a result of the greater life expectancies for women, as well as perhaps a questionable societal expectation of caring being a 'natural' role for women, who are 'expected' to find it fulfilling, even in the absence of financial reward (e.g. Lee 2001; Yee and Schulz 2000). Studies of motivations or willingness to care have shown that the relationship between the potential caregiver and recipient, and intrinsic motivations to care (e.g. principles, caring nature) as opposed to extrinsic motivations (e.g. out of guilt or expectation) are crucial to caregiver wellbeing (Cahill 1999; Lyonette and Yardley 2003; Wells 1999). This small body of evidence point to some key differences, however. Wells found a gender effect whereby men reported greater hypothetical willingness to care than women, and also, perhaps unrealistically, expected less burden to result from caregiving than did the women interviewed. Lyonette and Yardlet find an effect of relationship quality, and Cahill further distinguishes between relationship type, i.e between wives, daughters and daughters-in-law as she found that daughters and daughters-in-law in this qualitative study of Australian caregivers reported more extrinsic motivations such as kinship obligations. This is consistent with findings from studies with ethnic minority caregivers (African-American, Hispanic and Asian-American caregivers) where a greater emphasis on collectivism, including familism and filial responsibility is seen in the ethnic minority groups than in white caregivers (Pinquart and Sörensen, 2005).

■ Physical effects of caring

The stress of caring may also impact on some, but perhaps not all, people's physical health. Among cancer caregivers, for example, female caregivers experienced a decline in their own physical health in the six months following their partner's diagnosis of colorectal cancer, whereas male caregivers did not (Nijboer *et al.* 2001), perhaps relating to the higher levels of distress or lower levels of caregiver-perceived efficacy reported among women caregivers in other studies, although this study did not explore these issues. Interestingly, an extremely large study of the physical health, psychological wellbeing and quality of life of over eleven thousand Australian women aged from 70 to 75 (Lee 2001) did not find a significant difference in physical health between the 10 per cent identified as caregivers and the majority of the elderly sample. However, the caregivers did differ significantly in terms of their emotional wellbeing and perceived stress levels, supporting the reasonably consistent findings as to the emotional impact of caring.

■ Immunological effects of caring

There is a large body of evidence that points to immunosuppressant effects of chronic stressors such as long-term caring, and the effects can be exacerbated in older adults (Graham *et al.* 2006, and see Chapter 12). In relation to caregiving stress, while immune effects are seen consistently in studies of older caregivers, several studies among younger populations report inconsistent effects of chronic caring on immune function and resistance to infection. For example, elderly caregivers of a spouse with Alzheimer's disease had lower immune function and reported more days of illness over the previous year than similarly aged healthy control subjects (Kiecolt-Glaser *et al.* 1994), and the immunocompromising effects of caring for a person with Alzheimer's has generally been confirmed (e.g. reviews by Bourgeois *et al.* 1996; Schulz *et al.* 1995; Kiecolt-Glaser *et al.* 2002). With regard to reduced immune responses following influenza vaccination, an age difference has been suggested by findings that vary by population. For example, Kiecolt-Glaser *et al.* (1996) conducted a study where caregivers were given an influenza vaccination, and showed less appropriate immune responses to the vaccination than did the well-matched control participants, and the differences were particularly evident when comparing those aged over 70 years (23.3 per cent of caregivers responded to the vaccine, compared to 60 per cent of controls when aged over 70 years; when younger than 70 years, 53.8 per cent of the caregivers responded compared to 70 per cent of the control subjects). Further supporting that older caregivers are further immunocompromised than younger caregivers, Vedhara *et al.* (2002) did not find that caregivers of a spouse with multiple sclerosis differed in their immune responses following an influenza vaccination from non-caregivers. Multiple sclerosis is a condition equally as chronic as Alzheimer's but affecting a younger population, thus spousal caregivers are generally younger than spousal caregivers in the dementias. Vedhara's sample of younger caregivers did, however, appear to be less distressed about their caring than that reported among other caregiver groups, which may in part explain their 'preserved' immune responses following vaccination.

Finally, the damaging effects of caring on caregiver immune function are not confined to those individuals caring for spouses with chronic and degenerative conditions such as Alzheimer's disease or multiple sclerosis. Just as we know from studies of responses to acute stress such as examinations that immune changes are provoked such as reduced NK cell activity or slowed wound healing (see Chapter 11), studies of those experiencing acute pain or undergoing surgery have reported immune changes of a similar nature (see review by Graham *et al.* 2006).

■ Positive aspects of the caring role

In spite of the negative aspects of caring considered above, many studies have identified positive aspects of the caring role. Orbell *et al.* (1993) noted that caring 'may be appraised by the caregiver as negative, benign or positive. Caring may be appraised as an intrusion on personal lifeplans, but may also be appraised as positive, to the extent that it provides affirmation of valued aspects of the self' (p. 153). For example, studies have identified caring satisfaction such as feeling a sense of fulfilment, feeling useful, increased feelings of closeness or increased day-to-day interactions as a result of patients and caregivers spending more leisure time together (e.g. Kinney *et al.* 1995; Kramer 1997). Kinney *et al.* (1995) investigated the daily hassles and uplifts (stresses and satisfactions) reported by seventy-eight family caregivers of stroke patients and found that caregivers generally reported more uplifts (such as the care recipient cooperating with them, having pleasant interactions with care recipient) on a day-to-day basis than they did hassles (such as care recipient complaining or criticising, care recipient being unresponsive).

Plate 15.1   Having more time to spend with a partner as a result of illness can lead to a sharing of activities previously lost to the other demands of life. Spending 'quality time' together can strengthen some relationships.

Source: © Reg Charity/Corbis

However, this did vary depending on the care recipient's level of impairment, with care recipients who had greater impairment generally having caregivers who reported more hassles. While hassles were strong predictors of poor caregiver wellbeing, when the overall number of uplifts outweighed the number of hassles reported, caregivers were less depressed and had better social relations than when hassles outweighed uplifts. Such protective or buffering effects of uplifts, even in the face of concurrent hassles, highlights the need for studies to assess both negative and positive aspects of caring and to examine the interaction between them in order to further understanding of the effects of such counterbalancing on caregiver wellbeing. Rapp and Chao (2000) did exactly that in their study of dementia caregivers and they concluded from regression analyses that appraisals of strain and appraisals of gain exerted independent effects on negative affect (strain positively associated with NA, gain negatively associated). Interestingly, neither gain nor strain was associated with positive affect, which points to the fact that many factors influence caregiver affect, not only their appraisals of gain or strain. We explore some of these factors in the next section.

Influences on caring outcomes

■ Features of the illness or of the cared-for

The illness or behavioural features of the care recipients have important but complex influences on caregiver outcome. Studies of caregivers of people with Alzheimer's disease, for example, have shown that distress is more clearly associated with demanding or disruptive behaviour than with the level of physical impairment or disability of the care recipient (e.g. Gaughler *et al.* 2000; Morrison 1999). Caregiver distress is subject to further fluctuations dependent on the care recipient's physical and mental wellbeing at any point in time (e.g. Beach *et al.* 2000).

Among caregivers of stroke survivors, while the severity of stroke impairment during the acute phase (i.e. approximately ten days post-stroke) predicted their future expectancies, it was their appraisals of the consequences of the illness and of their coping resources that predicted their psychological wellbeing (Forsberg-Wärleby *et al.* 2001). Subjective appraisals of the situation made by the caregiver therefore differ from objective features of the illness, such as disability, in the extent to which they determine caregiver outcomes. To illustrate this further, again among those caring for stroke survivors, depression at six months was predicted primarily by an increase in negative characteristics of the care recipient (such as demanding behaviour), by reductions in caregivers perceiving that they had a reciprocal confiding relationship with the person they cared for, by the age and health of the care recipient (but not the caregiver's own age and health), and by income and a change in living standards. In contrast, caregiver burden was explained by the age of the caregiver (older caregivers were less burdened), a decline in the positive characteristics of the care recipient, reduced satisfaction with their own social contacts, and increased concern for future care (Schulz *et al.* 1988). This study, while somewhat dated, remains important because it examined changes in objective and subjective predictor variables over time, reflecting how the demands of caring are dynamic and fluctuating. It is worth

Table 15.1   Potential causes of caregiver distress

- The financial drain of caring caused by caring interference with employment
- The emotional demands of providing long-term care for a relative who often provides little in return
- The physically tiring nature of some caring roles
- The inability to replenish personal resources due to social isolation or poor utilisation of support resources and leisure time

or more deep-seated, even unacknowledged sources of stress:

- Feelings of anger (e.g. with the person for becoming ill, for them being born handicapped)
- Feelings of guilt (e.g. that they may have directly/indirectly contributed to the situation)
- Feelings of grief (e.g. that they have 'lost' who they used to have)

These latter are indicative of extremely complex feelings that are difficult to voice, but if they are suppressed they can cause increased stress and distress.

noting that an increase in negative characteristics of the care recipient predicted caregiver depression, whereas a decrease in their positive characteristics predicted caregiver perceived burden. This reflects that burden is not equivalent to depression (as some studies imply) but is perhaps more tied up with the relationship between the caregiver and care recipient. It is increasingly evident that adjustment on the part of the caregiver (as well as the patient's own adjustment) is influenced by interpersonal processes and in the case of couples where one has an illness, the emotional, cognitive and behavioural responses of both parties to the situation. We address such dyadic factors in a later section.

The influence of caregiver characteristics and responses

Caregiver appraisals

It is generally accepted that the underlying source of caregiver distress or strain appears to result from subjective appraisals of an imbalance between the demands of caring and the resources perceived to be available to the caregiver (e.g. Orbell and Gillies 1993), which may include what Wallander and Varni (1998) refer to as 'resistance factors'. Resistance factors include intrapersonal factors such as personality and motivation, socio-ecological factors such as the caregiver's family environment and support resources, and stress-processing factors, which include an individual's cognitive appraisals of a situation and their coping responses (akin to Lazarus's theory, Chapter 11).

The role of caregiver appraisal in predicting caregiver stress was highlighted in one of the few prospective studies of caregiver health carried out with 122 family caregivers of persons with Alzheimer's disease: in this sample, improvements in caregiver physical or mental health were not directly associated with a reduction in caring demands but with the caregiver's appraisal of the stressors as benign, with approach rather than avoidant coping, and with greater levels of the personal resource of social support (Goode *et al.* 1998). Cross-sectional support for the role of appraisal comes from a rare study of parent and spouse caregivers of individuals with traumatic brain injury (primarily following a vehicle accident) (Chronister and Chan 2006). They found that caregiver quality of life could be best explained by perceived burden (negative) and perceived mastery (positive). They did not, however, find any association between the third appraisal assessed, that of perceived caregiving satisfaction and caregiver QoL, and they propose that QoL is perhaps mediated by factors such as coping strategies (satisfaction was positively associated with emotion-focused coping and negatively associated with avoidant coping, and the appraisals of burden and mastery also had strong links with coping). Perceptions of the illness itself, rather than of caregiving, also play a role as shown by McClenahan and Weinman (1998) where caregivers who had a chronic perceived timeline for the illness showed greater caregiver distress (see Chapter 9 for full discussion of illness perceptions).

Hagedoorn *et al.* (2002), in a comparison of male and female caregivers of a partner with cancer, found that elevated distress among female caregivers was found only in those who reported low levels of caregiver efficacy (not believing in one's ability to care effectively) and perceived challenges to their role identity resulting from a perception of not 'caring well'.

Use of social support

Shewchuck *et al.* (1998) found that adjustment to caring for a person with a spinal cord injury varied significantly over the first caring year and was influenced by patient and caregiver characteristics, such as age, the caregiver's own health, and also by the caregiver's behaviour in terms of their use of support. Using social support as a coping strategy has emerged as an important predictor of caregiver outcomes. For example, in a study of male heart attack patients and their spouses, Bennett and Connell (1999) found that the primary causes of caregiver anxiety were the perceived consequences of the heart attack, with many wives becoming hyper-vigilant, watching for signs that their partner may have a further MI, and that the lack of a confidant with whom they could discuss these concerns was an important factor in maintaining anxiety. Perceived social support, or the lack of it, also played a central role in the stress process model predicting QoL or burden in caregiving for a family member with traumatic brain injury (Chronister and Chan 2006).

Protective buffering

Other caregiver behaviour, such as that made in response to the patient's situation, may also influence their emotional wellbeing; for example, spousal caregivers have been found to inhibit, deny or conceal negative information, thoughts or feelings, and yield to partners, in order to 'protect' their partners, although in doing so they may increase their own distress and even that of the patient partner (e.g. wives of heart attack patients, Coyne and Smith 1991; spouses of cancer patients, Langer *et al.* 2007; Manne *et al.* 2007). There is some evidence that 'protective buffering' is associated with lower marital satisfaction, although the directionality of this relationship remains unclear. It may be that caregivers are dissatisfied with the relationship and therefore avoid engaging in discussions of emotions, for example; or it may be that their inhibition of expression creates dissatisfaction, or it may be that there is bidirectional flow! Manne *et al.*'s (2007) longitudinal study assessed the protective buffering behaviours of both patients and spouses, and their distress and relationship satisfaction at three time points over an eighteen-month period following diagnosis of early stage breast cancer. Buffering on the part of both patients and caregivers was found to decrease over time, whereas the high levels of relationship satisfaction remained relatively stable, suggesting that they are independent; however, buffering by either the patient or the partner contributed to patient distress and if buffering increased, so did distress.

Other relationship factors may also influence caregiver outcome and so we return to such issues in the next section.

Personality

Finally, other studies have highlighted the role of caregiver personality variables such as optimism (generally a positive resource) and neuroticism (generally a negative characteristic), showing that these characteristics had direct effects on caregiver mental health, as well as indirect effects via their influence on perceived stress, and on the perceptions and appraisals of the care recipient's level of impairment (e.g. Hooker *et al.* 1992; Shifren and Hooker 1995).

■ The relationship between caregiver and patient

Many studies have examined spousal caregivers, where the relationship is characterised by being full-time, interdependent and intimate (cf. Coyne and Fiske 1992) and thus uniquely supportive. Other studies have shown less control over the caregiver 'types' recruited to the study and have included informal caregivers with varying degrees of association – mothers, fathers, siblings, daughters, friends. Pinquart and Sörensen (2003) hypothesised that differences in psychological and physical health would be greater among spousal caregivers than non-spousal caregivers, for female rather than male caregivers, and for older rather than younger caregivers. While a study of caring for an older adult only, their results did support these hypotheses. What is becoming increasingly clear is that as well as the nature of the caregiver–patient relationship, the quality of the relationship between these individuals influences the outcomes of caring for both parties.

Relationship quality

DeVellis *et al.* (2003) consider that increased research into the nature and processes in dyadic relationships will benefit our understanding of adjustment to illness. They note that social support research does not necessarily explore the relationship between those studied in terms of the nature and quality of the interaction, and that more studies are required that address the reciprocal and interdependent relationships that people engage in. This reciprocity is represented in Figure 15.3, where the relationship depicted is that of a marriage.

Banthia *et al.* (2003) reported that the quality of a relationship may moderate the effects of individual coping. They measured coping and dyadic adjustment in couples where the male had prostate cancer and found that while low patient mood was generally associated with avoidant coping and high levels of intrusive thinking, patients in strong relationships experienced less distress than those in less strong relationships, even when they engaged

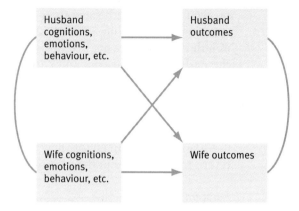

Figure 15.3 The interdependence model of couple adjustment.
Source: DeVellis, Lewis and Sterba (2003: 263)

in these maladaptive coping strategies. The quality of the spousal relationship was also an important determinant of the effects of caring on caregiver functioning in a cross-sectional study of seventy-five caregivers of cancer patients (Williamson *et al.* 1998). In this study, a distinction was drawn between depressed caregivers and resentful caregivers: depressed caregivers reported close, communal and intimate relationships with the patient, and this closeness created the restrictions on their own activities (i.e. they wanted to be with the person they cared for), whereas resentful caregivers reported less close relationships and reported their activity restriction to be predicted by severity of patient symptoms (they were restricted out of the necessity to provide care). This important, but subtle, distinction between depressed and resentful caregivers may help to explain differences in longer-term caregiver outcomes. Thompson *et al.* (2002) also found that resentful caregivers tend to provide overly controlling and over-protective care, and they suggest that such caring styles may undermine patient autonomy and progress. More research that explores the causes of caregiver resentment is required as it may offer potential opportunites for intervention, to the benefit of both parties. Relationship quality is also likely to interact with motivations to commence, and to continue to provide care (see Lyonette and Yardley 2003).

Couple identity
Another aspect that may mediate the stress of caregiving for a spouse is that of 'couple identity' whereby the relationship takes on its own identity, rather than being seen as two separate individuals. In a relatively new field of enquiry, Badr and colleagues (Badr *et al.* 2007) found that the extent to which a healthy spouse saw their relationship with their ill spouse as part of their self-concept (reflecting the importance to them of being part of a couple) partially mediated the effects of perceived overload, relational changes, and loss of independence and loss of 'self' on mental health scores. Although cross-sectional, and involving relatively established caregivers (average of over 5 years), it is likely that this study will stimulate more research into this construct.

<table>
<tr><td>**What do YOU think?**</td><td>If you are in a relationship, what does it mean to you? Do your close personal relationships offer an implicit extension to how you see yourself? While research seems to suggest that couple identity is a positive factor when examining the mental health of members of the couple, can you think of any situations where there are possible risks to having a strong 'couple identity', perhaps at the expense of a strong sense of self? What about when the couple separates or one of the couple is widowed? What implications may there be then for wellbeing?</td></tr>
</table>

■ Dyadic perceptions, shared and discrepant beliefs

Given the individual nature of health and illness beliefs, stress appraisal and coping responses, it cannot be assumed that caregivers and those they care for will exhibit similar beliefs and responses. A growing avenue of research is exploring whether differences in the beliefs and responses of informal caregivers and their partners influence illness outcomes (e.g. Coyne and Fiske 1992; Heijmans *et al.* 1999; Morrison 2001). Caregivers provide support to their ill partner, primarily because they think it is needed. However, this does not mean that care recipients will perceive the care and social support received as positive or helpful. This discrepancy is important: e.g. differences in perceived care needs between the caregiver and the patient may exist. Sarason *et al.* (1990) have shown that caregiver and patient perceptions often do not correlate, with caregivers perceiving that they are giving more than the patients feel they are receiving. This has inevitable consequences for caregiver distress (see earlier).

In addition to divergent perception of patient needs, individuals in caring dyads may hold different and diverging beliefs about the illness itself. For example, the illness representations (see Chapter 9) of identity, timeline, causes, consequences and control/cure may also differ between patients, caregiver spouses and significant others. In a recent longitudinal study Weinman *et al.* (2000) found that following a heart attack, participation in rehabilitation exercises could be predicted more from spousal beliefs, particularly where the spouse attributed the heart attack to the patient's poor health habits (internal cause) than by the patient's own attributions. Figueiras and Weinman (2003) further examined the illness representations of seventy patient–partner dyads following a heart attack and distinguished between couples who shared 'similar positive' perceptions, 'similar negative' perceptions or 'conflicting' perceptions. The most negative perceptions and conflicting perceptions emerged in relation to perceptions of control/cure, with shared positive perceptions more evident in relation to the identity, timeline and consequences dimensions. Dyads with shared positive perceptions fared better in terms of lower disability, fewer sexual functioning difficulties, less health-related distress, greater vitality and better global adjustment than dyads with negative or conflicting perceptions. In a similar vein, Heijmans *et al.* (1999) compared the illness representations of married couples in chronic fatigue syndrome (CFS) and Addison's disease (AD) and found that couples in both disease groups differed in terms of perceived consequences and timeline of the disease (AD caregivers perceived greater and longer-lasting consequences than patients; CFS patients perceived greater consequences but a shorter timeline than caregivers). Perceptions of identity and cause of the illnesses were relatively similar within couples. Although this cross-sectional study reported only minimal association between discrepant illness perceptions and coping behaviour, consistent relationships were found between discrepancies and the patient outcomes of physical and social functioning, psychological adjustment, and vitality. Spousal minimisation of CFS and its consequences was predictive of poorer patient outcomes, and perhaps surprisingly, spousal pessimism about timeline was associated with better outcomes in AD.

It is not just spouses' perceptions that may influence patient outcomes; for example, a recent study (Urquhart-Law 2002) of thirty adolescents with Type 1 diabetes and their mothers showed that illness representations of severe and negative consequences and emotional representations were greater in the mothers than in the adolescents. However, analysis showed that this 'maximising' (as opposed to 'minimising' found in the CFS study reported above) on the part of the mothers was not associated with adolescent wellbeing. However, this was a small-scale study that also suffered from being cross-sectional.

Reviewing the available evidence would lead to a conclusion that both maximising and minimising on the part of caregivers can have adverse consequences, whereas shared perceptions are more adaptive; but there remains a need for further study within both adult and parent–child dyads to address the prospective impact (positive and negative) of such discrepancies on patient outcomes, and on the psychosocial outcomes of the caregivers.

Summary

This chapter has described two broad areas where illness has an impact: on the emotional wellbeing and the QoL of the patient; and on emotional and physical wellbeing of informal caregivers. It should have become clear that physical illness has potentially many and varied consequences, and that this complexity of influence places many challenges in front of a researcher or practitioner wishing to assess illness outcomes. We have described a large evidence base as to the effects of caring for a sick relative or friend. Acknowledging and identifying the consequences of caring enables interventions to be implemented for the benefit of caregivers and those they care for, as well as potentially for society in terms of reduced social and health-care costs of caring for caregivers who themselves experience significant stress, burden or ill health.

Importantly, we have highlighted that caring, or being ill, does not bring with it inevitable negative consequences. We have also addressed a new and important area of research that highlights that perceptions of illness and its consequences can vary in couples living with illness, and how such discrepancies and the interdependence in relationships can influence a range of outcomes. It is intended that the breadth of consequences and moderating factors described in this chapter provide the reader with a strong foundation on which to study the psychology of illness.

Further reading

Suls, J. and Wallston, K.A. (eds) (2003). *Social Psychological Foundations of Health and Illness*. Malden, Mass., Blackwell.

This comprehensive text presents material that is central to many chapters in our textbook. For the current chapter, you could look particularly at Chapters 16–19, where psychological, social and relationship influences on adjustment to illness are described.

Stanton, A.L., Bower, J.E. and Low, C.A. (2007). Post-traumatic growth after cancer. In Calhoun, L.G. and Tedeschi, R.G. (eds) (2007). *Handbook of Post-traumatic Growth: Research and Practice* (pp. 138–75). London: Lawrence Erlbaum Associates.

This excellent handbook contains many chapters relevant to topics addressed in this textbook but for this chapter I recommend you look at Stanton and colleagues' chapter for an up-to-date account of how some good can come from what is often perceived as all bad.

Walker, J.G., Jackson, H.J. and Littlejohn, G.O. (2004). Models of adjustment to chronic illness: using the example of rheumatoid arthritis. *Clinical Psychology Review*, 24: 461–88.

A useful paper reviewing and critiquing the biomedical, psychological and bio-psychosocial perspectives on adjustment to chronic disease. Even though rheumatoid arthritis is used as the exemplar, much of the discussion of both theory, and empirical findings, is directly relevant to other chronic illnesses.

Palmer, S. and Glass, T.A. (2003). Family function and stroke recovery: a review. *Rehabilitation Psychology*, 48: 255–65.

This paper provides a clear overview of the value of taking a family-systems approach to the consideration of illness, in this case, stroke. The evidence of impact on family functioning highlights the need for interventions to be at the level of the family, rather than at the individual.

Pinquart, M. and Sörensen, S. (2003). Differences between caregivers and non-caregivers in psychological health and physical health: a meta-analysis. *Psychology and Aging*, 18: 250–67.

This paper reviews the data from many key studies of the relationship between caring and health outcomes and is a valuable source of referenced information should you wish to pursue this topic further.

Pinquart, M. and Sörensen, S. (2005). Ethnic differences in stressors, resources, and psychological outcomes of family caregiving: a meta-analysis. *The Gerontologist*, 45: 90–106.

This paper integrates the findings of 116 studies which have explored ethnicity in relation to caregiver demographics, filial obligation beliefs, coping and social support processes, and health outcomes. While the majority of studies compare African-American caregivers with white caregivers, interesting findings are also gathered from Hispanic, Asian and Native Americans.

Lee, C. (1999). Health, stress and coping among women caregivers: a review. *Journal of Health Psychology*, 4: 27–40.

This review paper describes and discusses some of the gendered issues in caring, and takes a useful historical look at the changing pattern of our workforce and implications that may have for women taking up a caring role in the future.

 Visit the website at **www.pearsoned.co.uk/morrison** for additional resources to help you with your study, including multiple choice questions, weblinks and flashcards.

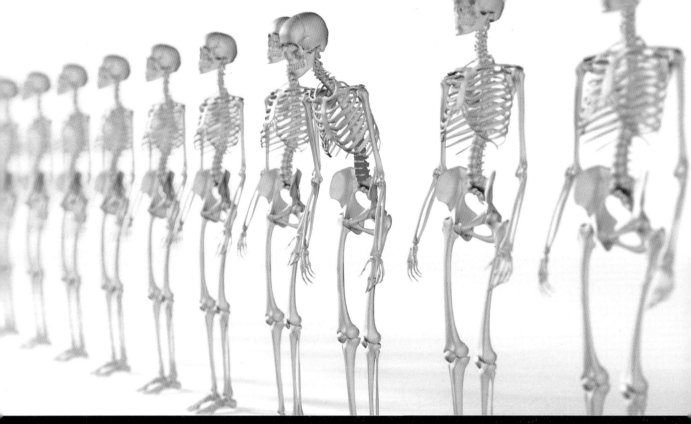

CHAPTER 16

Pain

Learning outcomes

By the end of this chapter, you should have an understanding of:

- different types of pain
- the prevalence of chronic pain
- psychological factors that influence the experience of pain
- the gate theory of pain
- the neuromatrix theory of pain
- behavioural and cognitive-behavioural treatments of acute and chronic pain

Image: David Mack/Science Photo Library

CHAPTER OUTLINE

Pain occurs in a variety of medical conditions, and sometimes in the absence of any physical problems. So prevalent is this experience that we have taken an entire chapter to examine its aetiology and treatment. This chapter examines a number of physiological and psychological explanations for our differing experiences of pain. It first examines the experience of pain: how various types of pain are defined, how prevalent they are, and how we respond to acute and chronic pain. It then considers the role of emotion, cognitions and attention in mediating the experience of pain. The next section describes the gate theory of pain developed by Melzack and Wall, which explains how both biological and psychological factors combine to create our experience of pain. Finally, the chapter goes on to consider a number of psychological interventions used in the treatment of both acute and chronic pain. Additional or alternative treatments for many of these conditions are considered in Chapter 17, which may usefully be read in conjunction with this chapter if you are reading about the totality of psychological treatments that patients may encounter.

The experience of pain

Pain is a familiar sensation for most of us. It is functional. It is unpleasant, and it warns us of potential damage to the body. A reflex action when we feel pain is to pull away from its cause or to try to reduce it in some way. Pain may also signal the onset of disease – and is the symptom most likely to lead an individual to seeking medical help. The value of pain as a warning indicator is shown by the disadvantages experienced by those who feel no pain. People with a condition known as congenital universal insensitivity to pain (CUIP) usually die at a young age because they fail to respond to illnesses of which the main symptom is pain (such as appendicitis) or to avoid situations that risk their health (Nagasako *et al.* 2003). They could, for example, receive extensive burns by sitting too close to a hot fire without experiencing the warning signs that most of us take for granted.

Despite its survival benefits, when pain lasts for a long time, it feels destructive and problematic. It can be so difficult to ignore that it takes over our lives. Chronic pain may be the result of long-term conditions such as rheumatoid arthritis. It may endure long after the time of any physical damage, or even be experienced in areas of the body that no longer exist. Many people who have had an arm or leg amputated go on to experience **phantom limb pain**, in which they feel pain in their non-existent limb – sometimes for many years. Accordingly, pain can also be maladaptive and contribute to long-term problems for an affected individual.

phantom limb pain
a phenomenon that occurs following amputation of a limb, in which the individual feels like they still have their limb, and the limb is in pain.

Types of pain

Medical definitions have categorised various types of pain, including:

- *Acute pain*: despite most people's experience of acute pain as lasting only a few minutes, acute pain is defined as pain lasting less than three to six

migraine
a headache with symptoms including nausea, vomiting or sensitivity to light. Associated with changes in vascular flow within the brain.

trigeminal neuralgia
a painful inflammation of the trigeminal nerve that causes sharp and severe facial pain.

months. Some episodes of acute pain, usually involving some form of injury, may occur only once, and generally the pain disappears once the damaged tissue has healed. Examples include toothache and childbirth. However, acute pain may be recurrent. Conditions such as **migraine**, headaches or **trigeminal neuralgia** may involve repeated episodes of pain, each one of which can be defined as 'acute' but which are also part of a longer-term condition.

■ *Chronic pain*: this is pain that continues for more than three to six months. Chronic pain generally begins with an episode of acute pain that fails to improve over time. In this category, there are two broad types of pain: (1) pain with an identifiable cause such as rheumatoid arthritis or a back injury, and (2) pain with no identifiable cause. The latter is not unusual – 85 per cent of cases of back pain have no known physical cause (Deyo 1991). Chronic pain can, itself, be divided into two types:

1. *Chronic benign pain*: in which long-term pain is experienced to a similar degree over time. An example of this may be lower back pain.

2. *Chronic progressive pain*: here, the pain becomes progressively worse over time due to the progression of a disease such as rheumatoid arthritis.

Another way of thinking about types of pain is to think about the nature of the pain. Here, three dimensions of experience are frequently used:

1. *the type of pain*: including stabbing, shooting, throbbing, aching, piercing, sharp and hot;
2. *the severity of pain*: from mild discomfort to excruciating;
3. *the pattern of pain*: including brief, continuous and intermittent.

The prevalence of pain

It would be difficult to find many people who had not experienced some degree of acute pain in the last month or so, but chronic pain is also remarkably common. Blyth *et al.* (2003) found that 21 per cent of a large community sample reported some degree of chronic pain. The most frequently reported causes were injury (38 per cent), sports injury (13 per cent) and a 'health problem' (29 per cent). Nearly 80 per cent of those who reported having chronic pain had consulted a doctor about it in the six months before the survey. Eriksen *et al.* (2003) reported similar prevalence levels: 19 per cent of their community sample had some degree of chronic pain. Older people were more likely to report pain than younger people. Divorced or separated people were more likely to report having pain than married people. Not surprisingly, perhaps, people with jobs that involved 'high physical strain' were more likely to report chronic pain than those in more sedentary jobs. These high levels of pain appear to be a universal finding. Across Africa, 50 per cent of adults are likely to complain of lower back pain in any one year (Louw *et al.* 2007). Perhaps more alarming is the large numbers of young people that experience some degree of debilitating pain. Skoffer (2007) for example, examined a sample of Danish schoolchildren aged between 15 and 16 years. More than half their sample reported pain or discomfort in their lower back; a quarter experienced a decreased function as a consequence of this pain. The pain appears to have been caused mainly by carrying a heavy satchel over one shoulder. Another way of looking at the prevalence of pain is to examine the use of analgesics within the general population. A Finnish study gives us some relevant data. Turunen *et al.* (2005) found that in a population sample of people aged 15–74 years old, 8.5 per cent used over-the-counter analgesics daily, and 13.6 per cent used analgesics at least several times a week.

Pain is a primary reason for visiting a doctor. Mantyselka *et al.* (2001), for example, reported that 40 per cent of primary care visits were the result of pain; 21 per cent of their sample who attended their doctor with a primary symptom of pain had experienced pain for more than six months, and 80 per cent reported limited physical function as a consequence of their pain. The most common areas of pain were in the lower back, abdomen and head. Among particular patient groups, levels of pain can be even higher. Potter *et al.* (2003), for example, reported that 64 per cent of people receiving care from a hospice, the majority of whom had a diagnosis of terminal cancer, reported pain as one of their primary symptoms. The cost of pain is not only physical and psychological, but also economic. Maniadakis and Gray (2000) estimated the direct costs to the British health service of treating back pain in 1998 to be £1,632 million. The *indirect* costs of back pain to the economy in terms of days off sick, production losses in industry, the costs of 'informal' care of people with back pain, and so on, were even greater – an estimated £10,668 million.

Living with pain

To say that chronic pain is unpleasant is understating its potential effects. Pain can have a profound effect on an affected individual and those close to them, so much so that many people with chronic pain organise their day around their pain. They may be prevented from engaging in physical, social and even work activities. Some may even find looking after themselves on a day-to-day basis difficult. It may affect social and marital relationships, resulting in conflict between couples – which may itself exacerbate the pain (Lang *et al.* 1996). It may also affect an individual's financial situation, as they may lose their job because of pain-related disability. It is noteworthy that people who have physically demanding jobs are more likely to experience pain than those in sedentary jobs – and most likely to lose them due to any physical limitations caused by pain (Eriksen *et al.* 2003).

Not surprisingly, levels of depression are high among people with chronic pain (Lépine and Briley 2004). However, the direction of association between depression and pain is not always clear. It is possible that some people who are depressed focus on bodily symptoms or minor aches and pains and are more likely to perceive them as painful 'symptoms' of disease than people who are not depressed. That is, depression may lead to high levels of reporting of pain symptoms. In other cases, the strain of living with pain and the restrictions on life that it imposes may lead to depression. There may indeed be a *reciprocal* relationship between depression and pain. People who are depressed may feel unable to cope with their pain and thus limit their activity to minimise any pain they experience. This lack of activity may lead to a stiffening of joints and muscles, which results in increased pain when they do attempt activities. This, in turn, may restrict their activity further and increase their depression. And so the cycle continues. The case of Mrs B provides an example of this.

I have a headache all the time. Some days are worse than others. When it's bad, its pounding and I cannot escape it. When I have a good day, I can feel it, but it is not so dominating. When I have a bad day, I don't want to do anything. I struggle to go to work as I do not want to lose my job. But I take 10 hours to do 5 hours' work. I can't concentrate, everything feels bad. I just want to lie down and not move. I don't want to do things at the weekend, but I know I must. But it really gets me down. I do things, but I'm not really all there . . . I don't enjoy them really. So, even when I do things I should enjoy I don't enjoy them like I used to . . . and knowing this makes me feel depressed, as I cannot see an end to the pain . . .

A further factor that may influence how people respond to pain comes from their interactions with their social environment. Pain brings a number of costs – it may also bring a number of (often unconscious) benefits to both the person in pain and those around them. Bokan *et al.* (1981) identified three kinds of 'gain' or reward associated with pain:

1. *primary (intrapersonal) gain*: occurs when expressions of pain (wincing, clutching painful areas, and so on) results in the cessation or reduction of an aversive consequence – for example, someone taking over a household chore that causes pain;

2. *secondary (interpersonal) gain*: occurs when pain behaviour results in a positive outcome, such as expressions of sympathy or care;

3. *tertiary gain*: involves feelings of pleasure or satisfaction that someone other than the individual in pain may experience when they help them.

A further type of gain may stem from an individual's beliefs about their pain. If they believe that when they do certain things the pain they experience indicates they are causing themselves physical harm, the relief gained from avoiding that activity may also reinforce inaction and lack of activity.

These various reward systems can lead to considerable problems. If an individual in pain experiences an environment in which their expressions of pain are rewarded by outcomes that they desire and that those around them gain satisfaction from providing, this may result in them doing less and less to help themselves, leading to increasing inactivity, muscle stiffness and wastage, which exacerbate any problems they may have.

Take the case of Mr Jones, who had chronic backache for a number of months. Over this time, he found that certain activities increased his pain. Activities such as standing while raising his hands and lifting proved particularly difficult. Unfortunately, these activities corresponded to those involved in washing the dishes following a meal. Because of this, he worried that any pain he experienced was because of the position he was adopting while washing up. As a result, although he did not complain about doing the washing-up, he showed his pain through winces and an awkward stance at the sink. His wife, alert to his non-verbal behaviour and not wishing her husband to be in pain, offered to do the washing-up for him on a couple of occasions, and soon he stopped doing it altogether. As a result, Mr Jones felt better because he was avoiding his worries and a boring task, and Mrs Jones felt better because she cared about her husband and wanted to do the best she could for him. It seems like a win–win situation. However, both parties may eventually lose as a result of this process: Mr Jones because his increasing inactivity will lead to further back problems; Mrs Jones because she will potentially become overburdened and resentful of her role as a 'carer'.

Brena and Chapman (1983) described the so-called 'five Ds' that may result from such an environment:

1. dramatisation of complaints;
2. disuse through inactivity;
3. drug misuse as a result of over-medication in response to pain behaviour;
4. dependency on others due to learned helplessness and impaired use of personal coping skills;
5. disability due to inactivity.

By contrast, many people cope well with chronic pain for significant periods of time without encountering such problems, and many environments will encourage activity and minimise the pain experience. Evers *et al.* (2003), for example, found that patients with rheumatoid arthritis who had good social support reported less pain and better physical functioning than those who were less well supported. This may be the result of a number of factors. People who are well supported may be encouraged by friends to take part in activities which maintain function and prevent joint stiffening and other factors that contribute to pain. The emotional support that such people provide may also influence the experience of pain. Interestingly, patients with pain express similar levels of satisfaction with their partners whether they are too supportive or encourage independence and more positive coping strategies (Holtzman *et al.* 2004).

IN THE SPOTLIGHT

Ethnicity and pain

An anaesthetist who had worked in a variety of countries was describing the amount of anaesthetic he had to give to people having the same operation in different countries across Europe and the USA. He suggested that if the UK acted as a sort of 'baseline' against which to compare other countries, then people in the USA liked to be knocked out completely and not to experience any pain at all – so they needed more anaesthetic than people in the UK. By contrast, he suggested that people from Scandinavian countries expected to experience a reasonable amount of pain following surgery, so they needed less anaesthetic than people from the UK. Whether his story is true or not, it raises issues about whether there are differences in pain expectations and tolerance across countries and cultures.

A number of studies have examined similar issues, studying ethnic differences in the experience of both acute and chronic pain in the USA. Sheffield *et al.* (2000), for example, found that African American participants in their study rated a series of thermal stimuli as more unpleasant and showed a tendency to rate their pain as more intense than whites. Incidentally, women also showed a tendency to rate the stimuli as more unpleasant and more intense than men. Similarly, Riley *et al.* (2002) found that African American patients experiencing chronic pain reported significantly higher levels of pain unpleasantness, emotional response to pain and pain behaviour, but not pain intensity, than their white counterparts. In a similar study, Green *et al.* (2003) reported that African Americans with chronic pain reported more pain, sleep disturbance and depression than their white counterparts.

continued

These data evoke a number of questions. The first question that has to be asked is why are we interested in this type of issue? Why should we expect such differences, and what if anything do they tell us? Are any differences biological or genetic? Are they the result of socio-cultural factors? Are they cognitively mediated? Are they the results of biased reporting of results – are there studies out there that have found no differences in pain experiences and responses between different social and ethnic groups that do not get reported? The data tell us very little about the origins of any between-group differences – and lead to dangers of negative stereotyping.

Ironically, these emerging stereotypes conflict with at least some health professionals' beliefs about ethnic differences in pain thresholds. What evidence there is suggests that African Americans are likely to be offered less analgesic than their white counterparts, at least in some US hospitals (see Chapter 2). But stereotypes do seem to influence our expectations of different social groups and how they are treated. Morris (1999), for example, noted that the least powerful groups within any culture are the most likely to experience disregard for their pain – and the most powerful are likely to have access to good pain relief should it be required. He cited historical examples of the disregard of pain among insane people in the eighteenth century, and black American women in the nineteenth century. One interesting belief noted by Morris, was that in the eighteenth and nineteenth century labourers were thought to have 'coarse' nerves that freed them from pain while undertaking hard manual work, while upper-class men and women were thought to have 'refined' nervous systems that would not allow them to engage in such labour without harm. Care should be taken not to establish more racial or ethnic stereotypes.

Biological models of pain

Perhaps the simplest biological theory of pain is that there are 'pain receptors' in the skin and elsewhere in the body that when activated transmit information to a centre in the brain that processes pain-related information. Once activated, this 'pain centre' produces the sensory experience of pain. This type of theory, known as a specificity theory, was first proposed in the third century BC by Epicurus and was taken up later by Descartes and others in the seventeenth century. Von Frey (1894; see Norrsell *et al.* 1999) added to this theory by suggesting that our skin includes three different types of nerve, each of which responds to touch, warmth or pain. These theories were further elaborated by Goldscheider (1884; see Norrsell *et al.* 1999), whose pattern theory of pain suggested that pain sensations occurred only when the degree of nerve stimulation crossed a certain threshold. These basic biological models of pain, with some elaboration, remained dominant until the 1960s. They were supported by the identification of nerves that were sensitive to different types of pain, and nerve tracts that led from the skin to the spine, where they linked with other nerves before leading to the brain (see below).

These theories have one common tenet: that the sensation of pain is a direct representation of the degree of physical damage or sensation sustained by the individual. This tenet has the benefit of simplicity. Unfortunately, it can easily be shown to be wrong. We have already hinted at a number of factors that influence our experience of pain. Three other sets of evidence have been used to challenge these simple biological theories of pain:

1. pain in the absence of pain receptors;
2. 'pain receptors' that do not transmit pain;
3. the influence of psychological factors on the experience of pain.

Pain in the absence of pain receptors

Perhaps the most obvious evidence to counter these simple biological models is the evidence that many people experience pain in the absence of any nerve pain receptors. The most dramatic example of this phenomenon is known as 'phantom limb pain', which involves sensations, sometimes extremely painful, that feel located in a patient's missing limb following amputation. Up to 70 per cent of amputees report phantom limb pain a week after amputation, and over half of these people continue to experience phantom limb pain for many months or even years after their surgery (Dijkstra *et al.* 2002). Two years following amputation, nearly a third of patients who initially experienced phantom limb pain still experience significant pain despite using strong opiate medication (Mishra *et al.* 2007). Interestingly, people who have their upper limb amputated are far less likely to experience phantom limb pain than those who have had a leg amputated. Similar experiences are reported by people with spinal cord injuries and paralysis. Unfortunately, phantom limb pain is difficult to treat and can have a significant negative impact on those with the condition.

'Pain receptors' that do not transmit pain

A second physical phenomenon that presents problems for these early theories stems from the experiences of people with CUIP referred to above. Individuals with this condition may experience painless bone fractures and ulceration to their hands and feet, which may go unnoticed. They may also fail to identify pain as a symptom of severe disease and sustain dramatic injuries as a result of a failure to respond to danger signals. Some people with CUIP may even experience ulceration of the cornea of the eye as they fail to protect against strong sunlight (Nagasako *et al.* 2003). Individuals with CUIP appear to have intact pain pathways, so they present the opposite problem to that posed by phantom limbs: a failure to perceive pain in the presence of an apparently intact pain pathway.

Psychological influences on pain

A number of psychological factors have been found to influence the experience of pain. Three of the key ones are:

1. *Mood*: anxiety and depression reduce pain tolerance and increase the reporting of pain.

2. *Attention*: focusing on pain increases the experience of pain.
3. *Cognitions*: expectations of increases or reductions in pain can be self-fulfilling.

■ Mood and pain

Mood influences the perception of pain – and pain influences mood. Evidence of the influence of mood on the experience of pain can be found in studies in which participants are asked to rate or tolerate pain until their discomfort is too great to tolerate it any further. These have shown that depressed or anxious participants report the equivalent pain stimulus as more painful than people without any mood disorder (e.g. Mel'nikova 1993) and tolerate pain for significantly less time (Pinerua-Shuhaibar *et al.* 1999).

Short-term mood states may also affect the experience of pain. Fisher and Johnston (1996b), for example, gave patients with lower back pain a simple mood induction procedure in which they were asked either about upsetting aspects of their condition or to report more positive aspects of their condition and how they were coping with it. Before and after this procedure, participants were given a plastic bag into which were placed as many packets of rice as they felt able to tolerate and then held the bag until it felt uncomfortable. In comparison with their performance at baseline, participants who reported the upsetting issues (and were therefore assumed to be more depressed) performed less well. By contrast, those whose mood was improved were able to hold the same weights for a longer period than baseline. This was an important study, as it used real patients faced with a task similar to their everyday activities.

Evidence of a reciprocal relationship between pain and mood has also been reported in a number of studies. Magni *et al.* (1994), for example, followed over two thousand participants for a period of eight years. They found that participants who reported chronic pain at the beginning of the study were nearly three times more likely to become depressed over the follow-up period than those without this problem. By contrast, another group of people who were depressed and free of pain at the beginning of the study were over twice as likely to report having had a significant period of pain over the follow-up period. The authors speculated that depression may predict some 'pain conditions' while some 'pain conditions' may predict depression, although the nature of these two conditions was not clear. Suffice it to say that there is an interaction between pain and mood that can operate in both directions.

■ Attention and pain

One of the ways that mood may influence our perception of pain is by influencing the attention we pay to any pain sensations. Depressed or anxious people may pay more attention to pain sensations than other people, and this focus may significantly influence their experience of pain. Focusing on pain seems to increase its impact: focusing on other things seems to reduce it. Many people who experience injuries while playing sports requiring effort and concentration, for example, do not notice the extent of any injuries until after the game has finished. Less anecdotally, there is evidence that fewer

Plate 16.1   The experience of pain differs according to context. Terry Butcher (in photograph) probably experienced no pain when clearly injured while playing football for England. After the match, it may have been a different story.

Source: David Cannon/Allsport/Getty

people experience pain following physical trauma at times of intense stress, such as being on the battlefield, than when similar levels of injury are sustained in less stressful situations (Beecher 1946). This may be because of attentional factors – in the battlefield there are many important distractions from one's own pain. However, other factors may also have been involved. It is possible, for example, that the soldiers were simply pleased to be alive following battle and thought that their injury would result in them being sent away from the battlefield. Civilians would be more likely to view their injuries as unwelcome and likely to interfere with their day-to-day activities. The issue here, therefore, may be the meaning ascribed to the injury and pain as much as the degree of attention paid to it.

Despite these alternative explanations, more controlled evaluations of the relationship between attention and pain have shown that the use of distraction can reduce pain, while experimental manipulations that increase attention to painful stimuli result in increased reporting of pain. James and Hardardottir (2002), for example, asked patients to place their lower arm in

cold pressor test
procedure in which participants place their arm in a mixture of water and ice maintaining the water temperature at between 0 and 3°C.

freezing cold water (an excruciatingly painful procedure known as the **cold pressor test**) and to either concentrate on a computer-based task or the pain sensations. Those who focused on the pain were least able to tolerate it and pulled their arm out of the water significantly earlier than those in the distraction task.

Attentional bias may also explain why some people with acute pain go on to develop chronic pain, while others do not. Vlaeyen *et al.* (1995) suggested that people who develop chronic pain in the absence of any clear physical injury or inflammation may respond to acute pain with a degree of fear, worry about its consequences and begin to check themselves for any pain sensations. Because they are now paying attention to a variety of aches and pains that may pass unnoticed in other people, they label their pain as symptomatic of an underlying problem. They may also stop engaging in activities that could trigger an episode of pain. In an experimental study that relates to this process, Nouwen *et al.* (2006) asked patients with chronic pain and individuals with no such problem to focus on the pain experienced during a cold pressor task (and therefore not related to the medical cause of their pain). Patients with chronic pain reported more pain and withdrew their hand from the water earlier than those in the control group. Further evidence of this process is provided by Dehghani *et al.* (2003). Their study, which used the dot probe task to explore attentional bias towards pain-related stimuli, found that people with chronic pain were more attentive to words describing the sensory experience of pain than neutral words or words describing its emotional or behavioural consequences. Their results also indicated that people with high levels of fear of pain both attended to relevant words more quickly and then had difficulty in focusing their attention away from them. Both results support the attentional hypothesis of chronic pain.

■ Cognition and pain

Mood may influence pain by influencing our thoughts about the nature and consequences of any pain. The types of thought that may influence the pain experience include:

■ attributions concerning the cause of pain;
■ beliefs about the ability to tolerate pain;
■ beliefs about the ability to control pain;
■ expectations of pain relief – the placebo effect.

sciatica
pain down the leg, which is caused by irritation of the main nerve into the leg, the sciatic nerve. This pain tends to be caused where the nerves pass through and emerge from the lower bones of the spine (lumbar vertebrae).

A simple example of how attributions concerning the cause of pain may influence the pain experience was described by Cassell (1982) in a case report in which one patient's pain was easily controlled with codeine when they attributed it to **sciatica** but required strong opiate analgesia when they attributed the same pain to having cancer. Walsh and Radcliffe (2002) found that the beliefs of people with chronic back pain influenced their willingness to take part in an exercise programme. Those people who believed their pain was the result of physical damage to their spine were more reluctant to engage in exercise than those who attributed it to 'psychological' factors – because they were afraid that exercise would exacerbate their damaged back and increase their pain. Similarly, Murphy *et al.* (1997) found that the activities of people with lower back pain were more restricted by their expectations of pain than by the actual pain they experienced. They were most restricted when the pain they experienced exceeded the level of pain they expected – presumably because they considered this additional pain to indicate some physical damage as a result of their exercise. One particular cognitive response to pain, known as catastrophising (e.g. 'This pain means something is seriously wrong!') is consistently associated with poor outcomes in relation to pain, including reports of pre-operative pain (Roth *et al.* 2007), pain following physiotherapy (Hill *et al.* 2007), and restrictions in activity as a consequence of pain (Voerman *et al.* 2007). The RESEARCH FOCUS below considers the role of catastrophising in relation to a particularly painful condition – sickle cell disease.

People who feel able to tolerate or manage their pain are less restricted by their pain. Maly *et al.* (2007) found that patients with osteoarthritis of the knee with high levels of belief in their ability to manage their pain walked more than those with less strong beliefs. Similarly, fit cyclists who believed in their ability to control or manage their pain allowed themselves to experience more painful exercise than those with lower control beliefs (Motl *et al.* 2007). Individuals with high control beliefs may also experience less pain. Jensen *et al.* (2001), for example, found that among a group of patients with chronic pain involved in a pain management programme, increased perceptions of control over pain accompanied reductions in reported pain. Experimental studies also provide support. In one such study, van den Hout *et al.* (2000) randomly assigned healthy participants to one of three preparatory conditions before they were given a cold pressor task. The preparatory conditions involved a task during which participants were given feedback indicating high levels of control over the task, low levels of control, or no feedback. Despite the fact that the initial task was not pain-related, it seemed to have some carry-over to the cold pressor task. In this, participants who received the high control feedback tolerated the cold pressor task for significantly longer than those who received low control feedback. Perceived control may also influence pain-related behaviour in patient populations. In a partial replication of their study of the effect of mood on pain behaviour described above, Fisher and Johnston (1996) allocated patients with chronic pain to conditions in which their perceptions of control over their pain were experimentally increased or decreased. Control was increased by asking patients to talk about times when they had been in control of their pain and decreased by asking them to recount periods when their control was low. Patients in the increased control condition performed their lifting task for longer than those in the decreased control condition.

■ Expectations of pain relief: the placebo response

One of the most fascinating phenomena associated with pain is known as the placebo response. If you were to give an inert tablet with no biochemical effects to people experiencing some degree of pain, *tell* them that it will have no effect, a percentage of those individuals (and probably quite a significant percentage) would report some relief from pain as a result of being given the 'tablet'. Red 'tablets' are more effective than blue 'tablets' in this context (Huskisson 1974). There appears to be some benefit to simply being given what appears to be treatment, whether this is a tablet, injection or more culturally diverse form of treatment. This phenomenon is known as the placebo effect.

A placebo (from the Latin, 'I please') is an inert preparation that has no pharmacological effects. Two of hundreds of studies provide examples of its impact. Verdugo and Ochoa (1994) examined the placebo response to an injection of saline (salt water) close to the area of maximum pain in patients with neuropathic pain – that is, pain that seems to be generated by the nerves themselves – which can be difficult to treat with conventional analgesia. Following this simple intervention, nearly two-thirds of the patients reported a 50 per cent or greater reduction in pain. In a similar study, Fine *et al.* (1994) tested a placebo injected into patients with chronic lower back pain. All participants in the study reported significant reductions in pain beginning between fifteen minutes and one hour after the injection and lasting up to several days. These are not unusual findings. Across a range of studies, the percentage of individuals to report at least a 50 per cent reduction in pain following being given a placebo ranges from a lowly 7 per cent to nearly 50 per cent across a variety of conditions and periods of time (McQuay and Moore 2005). Its effect is not limited to pain. The placebo effect can be found in inflammation, the speed of wound healing, immune responses to infection, and the treatment of conditions as diverse as angina, asthma and depression (Humphrey 2002). If a placebo is given following treatment with an active drug, the patient may not only show the degree of benefit in symptom reduction experienced during the active treatment, they may also experience the same side-effects as they did while on the active drug (Suchman and Ader 1992).

Two key mechanisms through which placebo is assumed to work have been posited. The first involves a classical conditioned response, which has been implicated in immune and respiratory responses. A second process, particularly relevant to pain, involves our expectations of pain or pain relief (Price *et al.* 2008). We experience a reduction in pain because we expect a reduction in pain. The logic of this theory (and consistent with explanations of pain experiences described earlier in the chapter), is that if we can somehow change expectations about the efficacy or otherwise of a particular placebo treatment, then the effectiveness of that placebo treatment will also vary. In one of the few studies to attempt this, Fedele *et al.* (1989) found that repeated use of a placebo over several menstrual cycles in women suffering from painful periods resulted in a lowering of the placebo's success in controlling pain. Although they did not directly measure the beliefs and expectations of these women, such a finding is consistent with a gradual change of expectations in the effectiveness of the treatment leading to a reduction in placebo response. Of course, just as positive expectations can lead to a reduction in pain, negative expectations can lead to increases in pain – the nocebo response. Patients recently diagnosed as having a serious illness or patients who distrust their therapy, for example, are likely to report more pain than others (Benedetti *et al.* 2007).

On a slightly tangential note, the placebo effect is considered so important and pervasive that the best trials of the effectiveness of a new intervention involve a comparison with a placebo version of the intervention, for which trial participants have an equal expectation of effectiveness. To simply compare an intervention with no-treatment condition is no longer considered a good test of the effectiveness of an intervention. It must fare significantly better than a placebo to be considered an effective treatment. Medical placebos are relatively easy to construct – usually a tablet or injection identical to the real intervention. Psychological placebos are more difficult to construct, but typically involve as a minimum the same amount of time spent with the participants in some apparently 'psychological' act (e.g. a non-specific discussion of a problem) as the active therapy.

RESEARCH FOCUS

Citeroa, V. de A., Levenson, J.L., McClish, D.K. *et al.* (2007). The role of catastrophizing in sickle cell disease: The PiSCES project. *Pain*, 133: 39–46

Sickle cell disease (SCD) is an inherited disease found mainly in populations of African descent. People with this disorder have atypical haemoglobin molecules which can, on occasion, distort the red blood cells into a sickle, or crescent, shape. These 'sickled' cells can block small blood vessels throughout the body, resulting in acute debilitating pain – referred to here as SCD-crisis. The condition may also result in chronic pain as a result of the destruction of bones, joints and visceral organs that occur during these crises. Treatment is aimed at minimising symptoms, but is not curative. Patients with SCD may experience low self-esteem, anxiety, depression, and impairment of day-to-day activities.

The authors noted there is consistent evidence that our emotional and behavioural reaction to pain is influenced by our cognitive response to the pain. In this paper, the authors examined the role of one type of cognitive response, catastrophising, in relation to depression, quality of life, crisis and non-crisis SCD-related pain, and responses to pain in patients with SCD. They hypothesised that high catastrophisers would report greater intensity of pain, distress, interference in everyday activities, and visit their doctor more frequently than low catastrophisers both during and between SCD-crises.

Method
Three hundred and eight patients with SCD were enrolled into the study. Two hundred and twenty completed a baseline survey, provided blood samples for laboratory testing, and a daily pain diary for up to 188 days. Participants were predominantly female (61 per cent), single (63 per cent), with an average age of 34 years. They were in pain for 63 per cent of the diary days, and experienced an SCD-crisis on 20 per cent of the diary days.

Measures
The following measures were taken at baseline:

■ *Catastrophising sub-scale of the Coping Strategy Questionnaire* (CAT): rated how much participants catastrophised in response to their pain.

■ *Patient Health Questionnaire* (PHQ): assessed the presence of a number of psychiatric diagnoses, including major depressive disorder, panic disorder and bulimia.

■ *Medical Outcome Study 36 item Short Form* (SF-36): measured quality of life on 8 scales: physical functioning, physical limitation, emotional limitation, vitality, bodily pain, social functioning, mental health, general health.

In addition, all participants completed a daily pain diary.

■ *Pain diary*: each day, participants rated their worst perceived SCD-pain intensity, its level of interference with everyday living, distress, and their response to pain including use of health care resources. Participants also reported whether or not they were in a SCD-crisis.

continued

Findings
CAT scores were

- negatively correlated with SF-36 scores: (general health: $r = -0.47$; mental health: $r = -0.45$; emotional limitation: $r = -0.41$; vitality: $r = -0.39$; bodily pain: $r = -0.36$; physical limitation: $r = -0.34$; social functioning: $r = -0.31$; physical functioning: $r = -0.24$)
- positively correlated with depression scores ($r = .48$)

CAT scores were *not* associated with

- intensity of pain, distress and interference, unscheduled visits to the doctor, emergency room visits, hospitalisation, or use of any other health-care service on crisis days.

Regression analyses showed CAT scores to be predicted by measures of pain ($\beta = 0.14$, $p = 0.04$), distress ($\beta = 0.19$, $p = 0.01$) and interference ($\beta = 0.19$, $p = 0.01$) on non-crisis days, but these relationships disappeared after controlling for depression severity.

Discussion
The mean CAT score in this study was higher than that found in other populations, including patients with rheumatoid arthritis, spinal cord injury and osteoarthritis. Despite this, and in contrast to a number of other studies, catastrophising was not independently associated with any measure of pain. By contrast, catastrophising was associated with depression and low quality of life. The direction of these associations cannot be fully determined due to the cross-sectional nature of the study. However, it is a reasonable assumption that catastrophising impacted in a negative way on key psychological and emotional variables including social functioning, vitality and mental health. Accordingly, despite it not moderating participants' direct response to their pain, it still appears to be an important moderator of their mental and physical well-being.

The authors had some suggestions for the lack of association between catastrophising and any measure of pain. They suggested that the chronicity of the participants' condition may have reduced the impact of catastrophising on their responses to their pain. SCD begins in early childhood, and the people in this study would have had many years' experience of it, and modified their response according to a variety of experiences, including the responses of others (including the health-care providers) to their pain. Accordingly, catastrophising was no longer a dominant contributor to their response to the pain they experienced during crisis.

A psycho-biological theory of pain

gate control theory of pain
a theory of pain developed by Melzack and Wall in which a 'gate' is used as a metaphor for the chemicals, including endorphins, that mitigate the experience of pain.

The evidence considered previously suggests that two sets of processes are involved in the experience of pain: one involving sensory information from the site of the painful stimulation, the other involving emotional and cognitive processes. The **gate control theory of pain** proposed by Melzack and Wall (e.g. 1965) takes both processes into account and is generally recognised as the best theoretical account of pain we now have. Melzack and Wall used the analogy of a gate to explain the pain experience. The essence of their gate control theory of pain is that the degree of pain we experience is the result of two sets of processes:

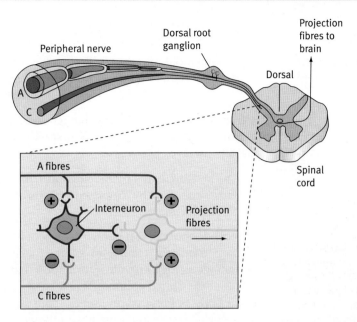

Figure 16.1   The transmission of information along the A and C fibres to the gelatinosa substantia in the spinal cord and upwards to the brain.

Source: adapted from Rosenzweig, Leiman and Breedlove (1996: 272)

1. Pain receptors in the skin and organs transmit information about physical damage to a series of 'gates' in the spinal column (see Figure 16.1). Within the gates, these nerves link to other nerves along the spinal column that transmit information up to pain centres in the brain.

2. At the same time as we experience physical damage, we also experience related cognitions and emotions – fear, alarm, and so on. This information results in the activation of nerve fibres taking information from the brain down the spinal column to the gate at which the incoming pain signals enter the spinal column.

The degree of pain we experience is a result of differing levels of activation in these two systems. Activation of the sensory nerves from the site of the pain to the spinal column 'opens' the gate. This activates the nerves leading to the pain centres and is recognised as pain – that is the essence of the biological theories of pain described above. However, the downward pathways activated by emotional and cognitive factors can also influence the position of the gate. Anxious thoughts or focusing attention on pain 'open' the gate and increase our experience of pain; calming or distracting thoughts 'close' the gate. This, in effect, prevents neural impulses travelling up through the spinal cord to the brain and reduces the experience of pain. The intensity of pain we experience at any time will be a function of these two sometimes competing and sometimes complementary processes.

Pain sensations are transmitted from the site of an injury to the spinal gate by nerves known as nociceptors, three types of which have been identified:

- A delta fibres (types I and II):
  - respond to light touch, mechanical and thermal stimuli. Carry information about brief sharp pain;

- very strong noxious stimuli related to potential or actual damage to tissues. The experience is short-lasting.
- C polymodal fibres:
  - slow conducting; carry information about dull, throbbing, pain – which is experienced for a longer period than that from the A delta fibres.

Perhaps the most important characteristic of these different fibres is that they transmit information at different speeds. As a result, our response to injury usually involves two phases:

1. The first, mediated by A delta fibres, involves the experience of sharp pain.
2. This is followed by a more chronic throbbing pain mediated by the C polymodal fibres.

A second set of nerves, known as A beta fibres, also transmit tactile information, particularly related to gentle touch. These fibres can work to our advantage as they provide information that competes with the A delta and C fibres at the spinal column. When we receive an injury, activation of the A delta fibres is initiated and sends 'pain signals' via the spinal column to the brain. The first instinct we have following such an injury is to rub the site of the injury. This simple act reduces the amount of pain we experience. This occurs because rubbing the site of injury activates A beta fibres. Because they transmit information more quickly than C fibres, this information also reaches the brain more quickly and reduces the degree of activation that would have been triggered by the C fibres alone. Thus, in the terms of Melzack and Wall, activation of A beta fibres to touch and gentle stimuli can close the pain gate. Activation of A delta and C fibres to painful stimuli opens the gate.

The A and C fibres transmit information to areas in the spinal cord known as the substantia gelatinosa. These lie within the dorsal horn of each part of the spinal column (see Figure 16.1). Nerve impulses here trigger the release of a chemical known as substance P into the substantia gelatinosa. This, in turn, activates nerve fibres known as T(ransmitter) fibres, which transmit the sensation of pain to the brain:

- Information from A fibres is taken to the **thalamus** and on to the cortex, where the individual can plan and initiate action to remove them from the source of the pain.
- Information from the C fibres follows a pathway to the **limbic system, hypothalamus** and autonomic nervous system (see Chapter 8). Activity within the limbic system adds an emotional content, such as fear or alarm, to the experience of pain. The hypothalamus controls activity within the autonomic nervous system (see Chapter 8), which allows us to respond quickly to remove ourselves from harm.

The results of this neural activity are transmitted *down* the spinal column through nerve pathways known as reticulospinal fibres to the spinal gate mechanism (see Figure 16.2). These may trigger the release of a variety of chemicals into the 'soup' of chemicals in the substantia gelatinosa (and brain), the most important of which are naturally occurring opiate-like substances called **endorphins**. These 'close' the gate and moderate the degree of pain experienced. Activity in this system is mediated by a number of factors, each of which influences the release of endorphins. These include:

thalamus
area of the brain that links the basic functions of the hindbrain and midbrain with the higher centres of processing, the cerebral cortex. Regulates attention and contributes to memory functions. The portion that enters the limbic system is involved in the experience of emotions.

limbic system
a series of structures in the brain, often referred to as the 'emotional computer' because of its role in coordinating emotions. It links sensory information to emotionally relevant behaviour, in particular responses to fear and anger.

hypothalamus
area of the brain that regulates appetite, sexual arousal and thirst. Also appears to have some control over emotions.

endorphins
naturally occurring opiate-like chemicals released in the brain and spinal cord. They reduce the experience of pain and can induce feelings of relaxation or pleasure. Associated with the so-called 'runner's high'.

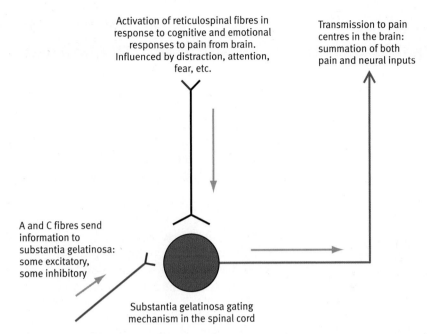

Activation of reticulospinal fibres in response to cognitive and emotional responses to pain from brain. Influenced by distraction, attention, fear, etc.

Transmission to pain centres in the brain: summation of both pain and neural inputs

A and C fibres send information to substantia gelatinosa: some excitatory, some inhibitory

Substantia gelatinosa gating mechanism in the spinal cord

Figure 16.2   A schematic view of the gate control mechanism postulated by Melzack and Wall.

catastrophising
the act of constructing **catastrophic thoughts**.

- *Focusing on the pain*: worrying, or **catastrophising**, reduces the amount of endorphins released and opens the gate.

- *Emotional and cognitive factors*: feeling optimistic and unconcerned about the 'meaning' of the pain increases endorphin release and closes the gate – anxiety, worry, anger or depression opens the gate.

- *Physical factors*: relaxation increases endorphin release and lessens the experience of pain.

Pain medication will also 'close' the pain gate.

What do YOU think?

We have already identified a number of factors that influence our experience of pain. Think how *you* react to pain. Do these factors reflect your own experience of pain? And how do we come to respond to pain in the way we do? Do you rub yourself if you are bruised to ease the pain? If so, why? Did you learn to do it as a response to previous pain experiences – or were you told to do so by a parent or friend? Are you stoic in the face of pain? If so, is this a result of how others have expected you to respond? 'Big boys don't cry': cultural and childhood experiences may encourage different ways of expressing both emotional and physical pain in men and women. Do they affect how you respond to pain? Or do you respond in ways determined by your personality? People who are generally anxious may be more prone to respond to pain with catastrophic thinking, anxiety and high levels of physiological arousal – resulting in a relatively high experience of pain (and other labelling of bodily sensations as 'symptoms' of disease: see Chapter 9). People who are more relaxed and optimistic may have a less emotional response to pain and experience relatively less pain. Is this the case for you?

Future understandings of pain: the neuromatrix

Despite the success of the gate theory of pain, it has still struggled to account for one important type of pain – phantom limb pain. The theory cannot account for pain in the absence of stimulation by the A and C fibres. In response to these limitations, Melzack (2005) has developed a more complex theory of the mechanisms of pain that attempts to explain this mysterious phenomenon. His model has three key assumptions:

1. The same neural processes that are involved in pain perception in the intact body are involved in pain perception in the phantom limb.
2. All the qualities that we normally feel from the body, including pain, can be felt in the absence of inputs from the body.
3. The body is perceived as a unity and is identified as the 'self', distinct from other people and the surrounding world.

Melzack contended that the anatomical substrate of the 'body-self' is a large, widespread network of neurons linking the thalamus, cortex and limbic system in the brain. He termed this system the 'neuromatrix'. We process and integrate pain-related information within the neuromatrix. Related information about a pain experience (physical elements of the injury, emotional reactions to the injury, and so on) combine to form a 'neurosignature' or network of information about the nature and emotional reaction to a pain stimulus. Neurosignatures have two components:

1. *the body-self matrix*: processes and integrates incoming sensory and emotional information;
2. *the action neuromatrix*: develops behavioural responses in response to these networks.

Behavioural responses to pain can only occur after information about the nature of the pain, its cause, and physical and emotional consequences have been, at least, partially processed and integrated. We do not move away from a hot object, for example, until we realise that it is the cause of pain and that continuing to be near it will cause further pain and potential injury. We only become consciously aware of pain after this integrated network of information is then projected to what Melzack terms the 'sentient neural hub': the seat of consciousness. Here, the stream of nerve impulses is converted into a continually changing stream of awareness.

So far, Melzack's new theory does not explain the experience of phantom limb pain. This moves us from an explanation of how we feel pain from external sources to one explaining how we feel pain generated by the body itself. Melzack suggested that the neuromatrix is pre-wired to 'assume' that the limbs can move. Accordingly, in people who have had limbs removed, the body still sends signals to try to move them. When they do not move in response to these signals, stronger and more frequent messages may be sent to the muscles, and these are perceived as pain. Melzack's theory of pain is still relatively new and has only recently been subjected to empirical research. However, what data there are provide broad support for the existence of a neuromatrix, but we have yet to locate it within any particular brain area (Derbyshire 2000).

Helping people to cope with pain

The first-line treatment for *acute* pain is generally some form of pharmacological treatment – varying in strength from aspirin to some form of opium derivative such as pethidine. Psychological interventions generally form a second-level intervention. The American Agency for Health Care Policy (1992), for example, suggested that these should be used for those who find this type of intervention 'appealing', where patients may benefit from reducing or avoiding pharmacological treatment, have high levels of anxiety, would need prolonged pain relief and/or who have incomplete pain relief following pharmacological intervention. By contrast, increasing numbers of patients with *chronic* pain resulting from conditions as varied as rheumatoid arthritis and lower back pain are being taught to manage their pain using psychological approaches in order to minimise the amount of painkilling medication they need to take and to maintain or improve their quality of life. It is important that the effectiveness of these interventions is evaluated as part of the day-to-day care of patients as well as in research studies. So, before we look at some of the approaches used to treat both acute and chronic pain, we examine some simple, and not so simple, ways of measuring pain.

Measuring pain

The simplest measure of pain involves the use of a simple linear visual analogue or numerical rating scales – typically varying from a score of 0, registering no pain, to 100, rating the most pain you could imagine. This type of measure is quick to administer and score and is frequently used in clinical settings. A limitation of the approach is that patients often find it quite difficult to consider pain in numerical terms. Another simple approach involves patients rating their pain on a series of adjectives denoting increasing pain: mild, distressing, excruciating, and so on. This has the advantage of being more easily comprehensible to patients than numeric scales – it uses concepts patients are more familiar with. However, this approach has its disadvantages, as many patients tend to rate themselves somewhere in the middle of such scales, making them less sensitive to subtle differences in pain than analogue scales.

One important limitation of these measures is that they simply measure the sensation of pain. However, we have already noted that the experience of pain is multidimensional. It involves emotional, cognitive and behavioural responses as well as sensory experiences. A number of measures have tried to address these inadequacies. Perhaps the best known of these is the McGill pain questionnaire (e.g. Melzack 1975). This is more complicated to administer and interpret than the simple scales described above. However, it provides a multidimensional understanding of the nature of the pain that an individual is experiencing. In its various forms, it measures:

- *the type of pain*: including throbbing, shooting, stabbing, cramping, gnawing, hot and tender, using a four-point scale from 'none' to 'severe';
- *the emotional response to the pain*: including tiring, exhausting, fearful and punishing;
- *the intensity of the pain*: on a scale from 'no pain' to 'worst possible pain';
- *the timing of pain*: whether it is brief, continuous or intermittent.

While this measure extends our assessment of pain, it does not address all the responses to it. It does not, for example, measure pain in relation to movement or measure an individual's behavioural response to pain. How much does it restrict their daily life? Can they walk up stairs, or lift heavy weights? These may all have to be measured separately. Turk and Okifuji (1999) suggested that one can also measure the pain behaviour in which an individual engages. They suggested measuring:

- *verbal/vocalisations*: sighs, moans, complaints
- *motor behaviour*: facial grimacing, distorted gait (limping), rigid or unstable posture, excessively slow or laboured movement, seek help/pain reducing behaviour
- *treatment behaviours*: taking medication, use of protective device (e.g. cane, cervical collar), visit doctor
- *functional limitations*: resting, reduced activity.

Each of these may become a target for some of the interventions discussed below.

Acute pain

A number of approaches have been used to help people to cope with acute pain. Any procedures used need to be relatively easy to learn and use. Accordingly, most approaches to acute pain control have focused on:

- increasing patients' sense of control over the pain experience and medical procedures that may be causing the pain;
- teaching coping skills, including distraction techniques and relaxation;
- hypnosis.

Some of these are discussed further in the context of preparing people for the experience of surgery in Chapter 10. Here, we address other ways of achieving these goals.

■ Increasing control: patient-controlled anaesthesia

The experience of pain following trauma or surgical operations can be made worse by patients' fears that they cannot control their pain. They may be frightened that when they are in significant pain the nurses may be too busy to give them painkillers, that the pain will be so bad that it will not be controlled by the type of painkiller they will be given, and so on. To alleviate such fears, patients may exaggerate reports of pain or pester health-care professionals to give them painkillers in order to avoid periods of inadequate analgesia. This may result in them experiencing unnecessary anxiety and using more medication than necessary.

One way that each of these issues can be addressed is through the use of **patient-controlled analgesia** (PCA). Using this method, the patient controls how much analgesic drug they receive through an intravenous drip – albeit with some controls built into the delivery system so they cannot exceed a specified dosage. It is assumed that because patients can control the timing of their pain relief, they will be less anxious about the control of their pain, be more satisfied with their analgesia and use less analgesic. Systematic reviews of this approach, summarised in *Bandolier* (2003), suggest that this is the case. The majority of studies that have compared levels of satisfaction with PCA against health-care professional-controlled analgesia have found higher levels of satisfaction with PCA. There is also consistent evidence that PCA may result in less use of analgesics than when health professionals have control over pain control. Van der Vyver *et al.* (2002), for example, reported a systematic review of the use of analgesia and pain control during childbirth. In all cases of comparison between PCA and doctor-controlled analgesia, they found that women used less analgesia. Children can also use PCA systems. Birmingham *et al.* (2003) reported data from over a hundred children for whom PCA was used for acute post-operative pain control. Satisfactory analgesia was obtained in 90 per cent of cases, with no evidence of toxicity or serious adverse effects. It therefore seems a safe, beneficial form of treatment for a wide range of people.

patient-controlled analgesia (PCA)
a technique through which small doses of analgesic drugs, usually opioids, are administered (usually by an intravenous drip and controlled by a pump) by patients themselves. It is mostly used for the control of post-operative pain.

■ Teaching coping skills

Distraction

We have already noted in the chapter that focusing on pain tends to increase the experience of pain, while distraction decreases it. Given the apparent simplicity of teaching distraction techniques, these would seem to be sensible strategies to teach patients who are in acute pain or who have to undergo painful procedures. The procedure seems to work. Callaghan and Li (2002), for example, taught women undergoing a hysterectomy to distract themselves from worrisome thoughts prior to their operation. Compared with women only given information about the procedure, they reported less pain and evidenced less distress after the operation. Fauerbach *et al.* (2002) also reported success after teaching distraction skills – but only if patients actively focused on something other than the pain experience rather than simply trying not to think of the pain. Their study involved a comparison of an intervention designed to reduce the negative emotional aspects of a painful procedure and one designed to distract completely from the procedure – both of which should reduce the intensity of any pain (see above). In their study, patients receiving regular, extremely painful, dressing changes to burns were randomly assigned to an emotional control or distraction condition. In the first condition, participants were asked to focus on the sensory experience of their dressing change 'while noticing subtle variations in the sensory experience and the ebb and flow of pain sensations', to focus on the present and not to anticipate or dwell on future and past pain, limiting thoughts to those about the sensory experience and not its implications or other potentially

catastrophic thoughts
automatic thoughts that
exaggerate the negative
aspects of any situation.

catastrophic thoughts. In the distraction condition, participants were given a choice of music to listen to and taught to focus on the melody, style or emotional tone, different instruments and lyrics. Their analyses focused on the degree of tension the patients experienced during the dressing change and the number of intrusive and catastrophic thoughts they had during and after the procedures. The distraction procedure resulted in fewer intrusive thoughts and less tension during the procedure than the emotion-focusing procedure. However, patients who did not focus on the tasks assigned, but tried to ignore the sensations without this focus, experienced the most intrusive thoughts and tension during the dressing change. It seems that having a focused concentration on something other than the pain is beneficial – but unfocused attempts simply to ignore it are less so.

Relaxation

A second relatively simple approach that can be taught to patients is the use of relaxation. This involves teaching people to relax the muscles throughout their body, particularly those close to the site of the pain (see Chapter 13). This has a number of advantages. First, it can be used to reduce any muscular tension that can contribute to the experience of pain. Second, because relaxation instructions may explicitly involve thinking about pleasant images or at least images inconsistent with the painful situation, it may act as a form of distraction. The concentration involved in relaxing may also distract from pain sensations. Finally, there is evidence that relaxation promotes endorphin release and thus has a direct impact on the pain experience. There is ample evidence that relaxation procedures can help reduce levels of pain and distress associated with post-operative pain. Renzi *et al.* (2000), for example, reported that patients undergoing major bowel surgery who used relaxation experienced less pain, less distress and better sleep following surgery than a control group receiving 'standard care'. Similarly, Friesner *et al.* (2007) found that relaxation combined with the use of opiate drugs was superior to opiate drugs alone during a short but painful surgical procedure involving removal of a tube inserted into the chest during coronary artery bypass surgery. The evidence in support of relaxation is so consistent that the American National Institutes of Health consensus panel (National Institutes of Health Technology Assessment Panel 1996) concluded that relaxation procedures should be adopted for general use.

■ Hypnosis

Hypnosis is a procedure during which a health professional suggests that a patient experience changes in sensations, perceptions, thoughts or behaviour. The hypnotic context is generally established by an induction procedure. Although there are many different hypnotic inductions, most include suggestions for relaxation, calmness and wellbeing. Instructions to imagine or think about pleasant experiences are also commonly included in hypnotic inductions. It has been shown to have a reliable and significant effect on acute pain. Lang *et al.* (2006), for example, found self-hypnosis to reduce both pain and anxiety associated with having a needle breast biopsy. Not only can hypnosis reduce pain, but it may also aid patients' physical recovery. Ginandes *et al.* (2003) examined the effects of hypnosis on pain and wound healing following breast surgery. They allocated women to three interventions following surgery: usual care (normal analgesia); sessions with a counsellor providing unstructured support; and hypnosis, in which they focused on relaxation and 'accelerated wound healing' as part of the instructions ('Imagine your wound healing well'). They measured the women's pain and level of wound healing one week and seven weeks following the interventions and found that the wounds of the women in the hypnosis condition healed significantly more quickly than those in the others. They also experienced less pain over the course of their recovery. The benefits of self-hypnosis need not be restricted to adults: Liossi *et al.* (2006) found self-hypnosis combined with local anaesthetic to be more effective than anaesthetic alone in young people aged between 6 and 16 years receiving a lumbar puncture. Of note also was that the benefits of hypnosis varied according to the hypnotisability of individual participants.

Treating chronic pain

■ Transcutaneous electrical nerve stimulation (TENS)

Before examining psychological interventions to reduce pain, we first consider a popular method of pain control, based on the electrical stimulation of A beta fibres in order to compete with the pain signals of pain-related nerves (see discussion earlier in the chapter) and stimulate C fibres to result in endorphin release. Transcutaneous electrical nerve stimulation (TENS) involves the use of a small electrical device, about the size of a personal stereo, that is connected by wires to electrodes, placed on the skin in the area of the pain. This allows a small, low-intensity electric charge to be passed across the area. Such stimulation devices are typically used for between fifteen to twenty minutes, several times a day, and are controlled by the user. Search the internet using the acronym TENS, and you will find a multiplicity of websites selling TENS machines, many of which claim it to be an effective form of treatment. A Canadian review (Reeve *et al.* 1996) in which the authors surveyed TENS use across Canada, was broadly supportive of this use. They surveyed 50 hospitals with 200 or more beds, and estimated that over 450,000 uses of TENS take place in Canadian hospitals each year with widespread use in the treatment of acute pain (used by 93 per cent of hospitals), pain associated with labour and delivery (43 per cent), and chronic pain (96 per cent).

Unfortunately, a series of subsequent reviews and empirical studies suggest this use is largely inappropriate. Khadilkar *et al.* (2005), for example, in conducting a Cochrane review of the area found only two studies that were of sufficient methodological rigour to provide a meaningful test of the approach's effectiveness. One study (Cheing and Hui-Chan 1999) found some short-term benefits compared to placebo; another (Deyo *et al.* 1990) found no such benefit. In a review of studies of post-operative pain, Carroll *et al.* (1996b) concluded that TENS was no better than placebo in 15 out of 17 of them. Other reviews have come to similar conclusions. Unfortunately, studies into the effectiveness of TENS are frequently small or uncontrolled. Al-Smadi *et al.* (2003) found, for example, that TENS was no better than TENS placebo in the treatment of low back pain in people with multiple sclerosis. However, they randomly allocated only 5 people to each treatment group – making any statistically significant treatment effect almost impossible to find. With this lack of high quality of evidence in mind, *Bandolier* (www.jr2.ox.ac.uk/bandolier/band37/b37-3.html) argued that better evidence in still needed, but in the meantime 'those of you who see full-page adverts in the national newspapers full of happy souls extolling the virtues of TENS might like to refer the Advertising Standards Authority to these reviews.'

■ Behavioural interventions

The first modern psychological intervention for pain involved behavioural interventions, based on operant conditioning processes. The treatment model, initially developed by Fordyce (1976), is based on the premise that we cannot truly understand the pain experience of others; all we can do is observe 'pain behaviour'. Fordyce argued that this behaviour should, therefore, form the target of any intervention, not the unobservable inner experience. Operant theory states that pain behaviour may be established and controlled not only by the experience of pain but also by how others respond to expressions of pain. Pain behaviour may be as subtle as gentle winces or as obvious as lying down unable to move as a result of apparently unbearable pain. It may be reinforced by expressions of sympathy, being 'let off' tasks about the home, given analgesia, and so on (see Bokan *et al.* 1981, earlier in the chapter).

The aim of behavioural interventions is to reduce disability by changing the environmental contingencies that influence pain behaviour – to remove the individual from any reinforcement of their pain behaviour. Instead, non-pain-related, adaptive behaviour is reinforced. The methods used include:

■ reinforcement of adaptive behaviour such as appropriate levels of exercise;
■ withdrawal of attention or other rewards that were previous responses to pain behaviour;
■ providing analgesic medication at set times rather than in response to behaviour.

In this way, new forms of behaviour are encouraged through appropriate reinforcement, and older maladaptive behaviour is extinguished through non-reinforcement. The approach may involve both health professionals and others with whom the patient interacts, including their partner or even friends.

Depending on the nature of the presenting problem, these processes may be added to by other interventions. In the case of lower back pain, for example, where disuse may have resulted in a weakening of the back muscles, patients may take part in exercise programmes. In these, patients will typically engage in a number of exercise trials to identify their tolerance for various lifting activities and movements. The programme will then advance them through a series of progressively more difficult steps towards full mobility and strength. Success at each stage of the intervention is positively rewarded by the healthcare professionals involved in the treatment programme.

Early studies of this approach were often case histories, as the approaches used to treat individual cases were necessarily quite different. Fordyce (1976), for example, reported a case in which they moved a hospital patient who was engaging in excessive pain behaviour into a single room, the door of which could be closed if necessary. This prevented the patient trying to attract the attention of nurses in the ward. Rewards for non-pain behaviour and 'punishments' for pain-related behaviour were achieved by entering and leaving the room if the patient inappropriately demanded pain medication or staying for social chat if they did not do so. These various case reports indicated the potential for this type of treatment. More recently, the development of standardised behavioural programmes in the treatment of a variety of disorders, including back pain, has meant that their effectiveness can be assessed using group designs.

Back pain is frequently treated using behavioural methods, possibly because it is a common disorder that often has no obvious pathology but which can cause significant impairment. They are also very effective in treating the disorder. Van Tulder *et al.* (2003), for example, reported a meta-analysis of the effects of behavioural programmes on lower back pain, and concluded that there was strong evidence that behavioural treatments were of significant benefit on measures of reported pain, improvements in mobility and lifting capacity, and on behaviour away from the clinic.

■ Cognitive-behavioural interventions

Behavioural interventions clearly work by changing behaviour, but these changes may also influence other parts of the pain experience. Active engagement in activities may distract patients from negative cognitive and emotional responses to pain. Re-engaging in activities previously stopped may increase self-efficacy beliefs and optimism ('Wow – I didn't think I was going to be able to do that. Perhaps I can do some other things I've stopped doing'). That is, behavioural programmes may *indirectly* change pain-related cognitions, and these changes may contribute to any improvements that patients make. Cognitive-behavioural approaches tackle these issues more directly. They focus on the cognitions mediating our emotional and behavioural responses to pain. Cognitions are seen as central to our experience of pain, and our reactions to it. As such, the model does not contradict the model of pain provided by the gate control model – it focuses on one group of variables that influence the gate. The goals of cognitive-behavioural therapy for pain are threefold:

1. To help patients alter their beliefs that their problems are unmanageable. To help them to become 'resourceful problem solvers' and move away from feeling unable to cope with their pain.
2. To help patients identify the relationship between their thoughts, emotions and behaviour, and in particular how catastrophic or other negatively biased thoughts can lead to increased perceptions of pain, emotional distress and psychosocial difficulties.
3. To provide patients with strategies to manage their pain, emotional distress and psychosocial difficulties, and in particular to help them to develop effective and adaptive ways of thinking, feeling and behaving.

Cognitive-behavioural interventions can take the form of both individual and group interventions. Cognitive change is brought about in a number of stages (see also the discussion of stress management skill in Chapter 13). In these, patients are helped to identify any maladaptive thoughts that are increasing their experience of pain or their disability. This can be achieved by discussion in therapy sessions in which patients reflect back on periods of pain or when they have been frightened to engage in particular behaviour. Any thoughts that occurred at such times are identified and discussed. Patients may also be asked to monitor their thoughts during their day-to-day activities by completing a diary in which they record their level of pain, accompanying thoughts and mood.

Once patients have begun to identify how their thoughts influence the level of pain they experience, their behaviour and their mood, they are taught to change the nature of their thoughts to more adaptive ones. This may involve two types of cognitive intervention. The first is known as self-instruction training. In this, patients are taught to change the commentary in their head at times of worry or concern about their pain or activities to a more positive commentary. This can be pre-rehearsed and thought through with the therapist. Such thoughts include reassuring commentaries, such as *'I've had pain like this before and it didn't do me any harm in the long run'* or *'The pain only means I'm extending myself, not doing myself any damage'*. Other thoughts may involve reminders to use other strategies to help to control the pain: *'OK! When the pain starts, remember to relax so I don't add to it with tension'*, and so on.

A more complex cognitive process involves trying to identify the thoughts that are driving any emotional distress or inhibiting behaviour and challenging them. This involves treating them not as truths but as hypotheses, and challenging the hypotheses by looking for contrary evidence. In practice, these types of challenge may not be that different to the self-instructions, but they may be more targeted at particular worries or concerns:

> *Oh no! My back's beginning to hurt again. I know that means I'm going to be in pain for hours – I'd better stop now and take it easy. Hang on! Remember the last time this happened; I didn't feel that bad, particularly after relaxing and slowing down a bit. So take it easy – keep going . . . I'll feel better in myself for trying.*

These cognitive interventions are often accompanied by a programme of gradually increasing exercise. This may have a number of advantages. First, and most obviously, it will increase fitness and minimise restriction of activities. In addition, it allows patients to learn from their own experience that they will not be harmed by exercising – and therefore confirm some of the new beliefs that the cognitive therapy is trying to instil.

Other interventions may also be provided. One frequently used intervention involves teaching people to relax their muscles throughout their body and, particularly, close to the site of the pain (see above in the case of acute pain). Hanson and Gerber (1990) summarised a number of strategies for coping with periods of particularly intense pain that can be taught in a cognitive-behavioural programme, including:

- stop and ask myself if I can identify the pain trigger or learn anything from this pain;
- begin slow, deep breathing and remind myself to keep calm; review my alternatives;
- identify some distracting activities – a conversation with my partner about anything but the pain, a crossword puzzle, baking biscuits, etc.;
- take a long, hot shower;
- listen to relaxation or self-hypnosis tape;
- use positive self-talk – *'The pain won't last. I can handle this on my own'*;
- use pain-modification imagery – *'Imagine a block of ice resting on my back, see my endorphins working to counter the pain'*, and so on.

Cognitive-behavioural interventions have proved very effective in the treatment of chronic pain. Morley and Williams (1999), for example, found twenty-five trials suitable for meta-analysis that examined their effectiveness in the treatment of pain resulting from medical conditions, including back problems, arthritis and musculo-skeletal problems but excluding head-aches. Overall, cognitive-behavioural treatments proved more effective than no treatment on measures of reported pain, mood, cognitive coping and appraisals, behavioural activity and social engagement. They proved more effective than pharmacological, educational and occupational therapy inter-ventions on measures of reported pain, cognitive coping and appraisal, and in reducing the frequency of pain-related behaviour. Perhaps surprisingly, however, cognitive-behavioural interventions were no more effective than the others in reducing negative, fearful or catastrophic thoughts. Nor were they more effective in changing mood. This may be because the most import-ant therapeutic process in these interventions was that patients engaged in higher levels of activity than they previously had. As we suggested earlier in the chapter, this may change their beliefs about their ability to exercise, to control their pain while doing so, and their mood.

Whatever the cause, there is mounting evidence that cognitive change is an important mediator of change in therapy. In a relatively early study of this phenomenon, Burns *et al.* (2003) found that the cognitive changes patients made in the early stages of a cognitive-behavioural programme were strongly predictive of pain outcomes later in therapy. They took measures of cata-strophising and pain at the beginning, end and middle of a four-week cognitive-behavioural pain management programme. Early changes on the measure of catastrophising were predictive of pain measures taken at the end of therapy. By contrast, early changes in pain did not predict changes in catastrophising. Turner *et al.* (2007) came to similar conclusions using data from patients with **temporomandibular disorder pain**. In this group, changes in pain beliefs (control over pain, disability and pain signals harm), cata-strophising and self-efficacy for managing pain mediated the effects of CBT on pain, activity interference and jaw use limitations at one year.

temporomandibular disorder pain
a variety of conditions that cause tenderness and pain in the temporomandibular joint (hinge joint of the jaw).

One of the difficulties many patients who are referred for cognitive-behavioural therapy experience is that it presents a very different model of pain and its treatment to that which they are used to. Often because patients are frequently offered cognitive-behavioural therapy at the end of a long chain of medical or surgical treatments – most of which have failed – but which have emphasised the medical rather than psychological aspects of their condition:

I [Mr Brown] came to this clinic [for cognitive-behavioural therapy] after years of looking for a treatment for my back pain. The doc sends you here, there, everywhere looking for the answer. I've had pain killers, TENS, physiotherapy, manipulation . . . and then surgery. Every time you go to the next treatment, you have that little ray of hope that this will provide the cure! I've even gone to the alternative people in the hope that they would help. The weirdest thing I have had was something called cranial manipulation . . . supposed to relieve the nerves or something. But every one you hope the pain will go . . . even if you don't believe it quite as strongly with different treatments! But this has been different. Rather than trying to take the pain away, the course has focused on helping me cope with the pain. That was the first shock on the course – and it was disappointing. I expected that you could get rid of it, not keep it . . . and let me cope better! I was quite depressed for a few days when I learned this . . . but I guess I had to stick it out. I don't have much choice. But I must admit, as the course has gone on, it has helped. The relaxation really helps me. I can take myself away from the pain for a while if I imagine stuff. And at least I know I can cope with the pain, and won't let it stop me doing things like I used to . . .

■ Relaxation and biofeedback

Relaxation can be used to relax the whole body or to relax specific muscle groups such as those on the forehead or back, which contribute to headaches and back pain, respectively. The latter may be of particular benefit in some patients. Turk (1986), for example, noted that many patients taught general relaxation for the treatment of back pain generally reported reductions in pain. However, one small subgroup of individuals reported either no benefit or even an increase in pain following the intervention. Closer assessment revealed that while many people in this group had been able to relax most of their muscles, they had been unable to relax the particular muscles in their back that were contributing to their pain. To do this, they needed guidance on relaxing these specific muscles. This can be achieved through the use of **biofeedback** techniques, including electromyographic biofeedback, galvanic skin response and thermal biofeedback:

- *Electromyographic (EMG) biofeedback*: measures the small amount of electrical current in the muscles. The voltage equates with muscle tension: higher voltage = higher tension. Uses electrodes stuck to the skin over specific muscles that contribute to pain.
- *Galvanic skin response (GSR)*: measures general tension in the body by measuring subtle changes in the moisture (sweat) typically of the hand. Increased sweat relates to increased general muscle tension – although the relationship is far from one to one.
- *Thermal biofeedback*: based on a theory that warming the skin can reduce the pain of headaches. Skin temperature is measured by a thermistor, often placed on the back of the fingers to avoid sweat and to provide a more accurate gauge of body temperature.

Whatever the mode of measurement, biofeedback helps patients to make changes (relax, increase finger temperature) guided by auditory or visual feedback of any physiological changes they produce. In the case of auditory feedback, for example, a tone may become lower as the person relaxes their muscles. Visual feedback may involve moving an indicator along a scale as they do the same. In this way, changes in physiology that the patient may not recognise are made apparent and the patient can learn how to change their muscle tension.

One area in which biofeedback has been used with some success is in the treatment of chronic headaches. Rains *et al.* (2005), for example, reported that biofeedback interventions resulted in between 35 per cent and 55 per cent improvements in migraine and tension-type headaches. These improvements are about three times as large as any gains following some form of placebo intervention, and the equivalent to gains achieved by medication (Andrasik 2007). However, while biofeedback may be an effective intervention in other forms of pain, it is generally no more effective than relaxation alone. As relaxation is both simpler and cheaper to implement, this should perhaps be the first-line treatment rather than biofeedback.

If relaxation techniques are to be augmented, it may be better to do so using strategies that address other aspects of the pain experience than the physiological ones. More complex cognitive-behavioural interventions, for example, may add to the benefits of relaxation in the treatment of tension headaches, particularly where an individual is facing significant stresses in

biofeedback
technique of using monitoring devices to provide information regarding an autonomic bodily function, such as heart rate or blood pressure. Used in an attempt to gain some voluntary control over that function.

Plate 16.2   Biofeedback has proven to be an excellent treatment for specific pain due to muscle tension. However, in many cases, simple relaxation may prove as effective.

Source: Will & Deni Mcintyre/Science Photo Library

their lives which add to their overall stress or inhibit their use of simple relaxation strategies.

An alternative strategy has been to combine relaxation with antidepressant medication. No one has fully explained why antidepressant medication helps to reduce pain, but it has consistently been shown to do so. With this in mind, Holroyd *et al.* (2001) compared treatment with antidepressant medication, training in relaxation techniques, a combination of the two, and a placebo drug therapy. The results were encouraging for both interventions. Both antidepressant and cognitive-behavioural techniques proved to be more effective than the placebo on measures including the frequency of headaches, analgesic medication use and restrictions in activity as a result of the headache. Although both single active interventions were equally effective, patients who received the pharmacological medication experienced these changes more quickly than those in the cognitive-behavioural intervention. Despite these gains, the combined therapy proved the most effective. This resulted in clinically significant reductions on a combined index of headache severity in 64 per cent of participants in this condition. This compared with 38 per cent of those in the antidepressant condition, 35 per cent of those receiving stress management, and 29 per cent of those in the placebo condition.

Pain management clinics

So far, we have considered treatments for pain in isolation, without considering who provides the treatment or where patients may go for treatment.

Nowadays, many hospitals provide services specifically for people with chronic pain – of whatever origin. These services will involve a number of people. Doctors, usually anaesthetists, provide expertise in the pharmacological and even surgical treatment of pain. Physiotherapists work with patients to develop exercise programmes that they can realistically expect to be able to engage in. Occupational therapists may work with patients to consider how they can improve their day-to-day activities around the home if their mobility is restricted. Specialist nurses may work with patients to develop pain management plans for individuals or groups of individuals. Psychologists may also contribute to and develop such programmes. Table 16.1 shows the outline of a typical outpatient pain management programme – conducted at the Gloucester Royal Hospital in the UK.

Table 16.1 Outline of a typical pain management programme, in this case run at the Gloucester Royal Hospital in the UK

WEEK 1	Welcome, introduction and housekeeping Pain management philosophy What is chronic pain? – questions answered Introduction to exercise – sitting and standing Pacing everyday activities The stress response and introduction to diaphragmatic breathing
WEEK 2	Recap pacing Goal setting and action plans Introduction to exercise – lying Sitting and chairs Introduction to stretch and relax Video patients doing exercises for comparison at end of group
WEEK 3	How pain works: the gate control theory of pain How pain works: pain pathways Thoughts and feelings about pain Exercises Stretch and relax Action plans
WEEK 4	Recommended use of medication for chronic pain Communication and relationships Pain management graduate perspective talk Exercises Introduction to relaxing your mind Action plans
WEEK 5	Lifting and bending Managing everyday activities Sexual relationships The benefits of exercise Exercise Relaxing your mind Action plans
WEEK 6	Introduction to fitness and fitness equipment Doctor's talk: medication, treatments and surgery for chronic pain, sleeping and beds/positions to ease pain Action plans Relaxation
WEEK 7	Flare-ups and setbacks Helpful sleep habits Video exercises and compare with the beginning of the course Introduction to brief relaxation techniques Reviewing progress, and setting goals for the follow-up sessions

Summary

Pain is a widely prevalent phenomenon. Over 20 per cent of the general population are experiencing chronic pain at any one time, and the personal and social consequences of chronic pain are significant. Various types of pain have been identified:

- *acute*: lasting up to between three and six months;
- *chronic*: lasting more than three to six months; can be further categorised as chronic benign and chronic progressive pain.

Pain can also be defined in terms of its nature: its type, severity and pattern.

The experience of pain is moderated by a variety of physical and psychological factors, including:

- the degree of attention paid to the pain;
- the mood of the individual;
- the person's beliefs about the nature of the pain, including its cause and controllability.

Early specificity and pattern theories that did not take account of these psychological factors proved to be unsuccessful in explaining the various ways in which pain can be experienced. A more complex model developed by Melzack and Wall, known as the gate theory of pain, has superseded these models of pain. This suggests that pain is the outcome of a number of complementary or competing processes. Any model of pain has to take into account how psychological factors affect the perception of pain. The gate theory of pain suggests that:

- Afferent nerves carry pain messages up to the substantia gelatinosa and then through the spinal gate mechanism to the brain.
- At the same time, psychological processes influence the activity of nerves leading from the brain to the spinal gate.
- Activation of both systems results in a variety of chemicals being produced within the gate (substantia gelatinosa), some of which 'open' the pain gate, some of which 'close' it. The main chemicals involved in reducing pain sensations in the substantia gelatinosa are endorphins.

Melzack has developed a more complex neurological model of pain, known as the neuromatrix, which accounts for phenomena previously difficult to account for by the gate theory (including phantom limb pain).

TENS is a physiological intervention based on the gate control theory of pain. Unfortunately, consistent evidence of its effectiveness is lacking.

Both behavioural and cognitive-behavioural interventions have proved to be effective in the treatment of both acute and more chronic pain. Cognitive changes appear to mediate changes in the experience of pain.

Biofeedback interventions can help to reduce pain, but their overall effectiveness is no greater than more general relaxation procedures. They may be best used when there are individual muscle groups contributing to the pain that are not relaxed following more general relaxation instructions, or for the treatment of headaches.

Psychological interventions may be combined (at least in some cases) with antidepressant medication to provide maximal benefit.

Further reading

Melzack, R. and Wall, P.D. (1996). *The Challenge of Pain*. Penguin.
A classic. The most up-to-date text by the originators of the gate control theory – and over £200 cheaper than the more recent *Wall and Melzack's Textbook of Pain*. Written in a non-technical way for the interested 'lay' reader.

Three papers from the pain research centre at Bath University are worth a read:
Morley, S., Eccleston, C. and Williams, A. (1999). Systematic review and meta-analysis of randomized controlled trials of cognitive-behavioural therapy and behaviour therapy for chronic pain in adults, excluding headache. *Pain*, 80: 1–13.
A relatively up-to-date review of intervention studies to treat pain.

Crombez, G., Eccleston, C., De Vlieger, P. *et al.* (2008). Is it better to have controlled and lost than never to have controlled at all? An experimental investigation of control over pain. *Pain*, 137: 631–9.
An experimental study of what happens when you first provide control over pain, and then take it away.

Vowles, K.E., McCracken, L.M. and Eccleston, C. (2007). Processes of change in treatment for chronic pain: the contributions of pain, acceptance, and catastrophizing. *European Journal of Pain*, 11: 779–87.
Another paper examining the mediating effects of changed cognitions on the experience of pain.

Morris, D.B. (1999). Sociocultural and religious meanings of pain. In R.J. Gatchel and D.C. Turk (eds), *Psychosocial Factors in Pain*. New York: Guilford Press.
Extends the discussion from psychology to other perspectives on pain.

Meredith, P., Ownsworth, T. and Strong, J. (2008). A review of the evidence linking adult attachment theory and chronic pain: presenting a conceptual model. *Clinical Psychology Review*, 28: 407–29.
A very different model of chronic pain to those discussed here.

A number of websites may also provide useful information:
http://www.jr2.ox.ac.uk/bandolier/booth/painpag/
http://www.painrelieffoundation.org.uk/
http://www.nlm.nih.gov/medlineplus/pain.html
http://www.psychnet-ukk.com/clinical_psychology/clinical_psychology_pain_management.htm

Visit the website at **www.pearsoned.co.uk/morrison** for additional resources to help you with your study, including multiple choice questions, weblinks and flashcards.

CHAPTER 17

Improving health and quality of life

Learning outcomes

By the end of this chapter, you should have an understanding of a number of psychological interventions that aim to:

- *reduce distress*: focusing on information provision, stress management training and providing social support
- *improve disease management*: focusing on information provision, self-management training, stress management training, facilitating family and social support, and the use of written emotional expression
- *reduce the risk of future disease or disease progression*: focusing on counselling, stress management and providing social support

CHAPTER OUTLINE

This chapter focuses on a number of psychological interventions used to help people to cope with and manage serious illnesses. These interventions have a number of goals. Some seek to reduce the distress associated with having a serious illness. Others aim to help people to manage their illness as effectively as possible and to minimise its impact on their daily life. Yet others are designed to prevent the progression of an illness and minimise the risk of further health problems in the future. This chapter considers a number of interventions designed to achieve these goals in the context of a number of chronic diseases, such as cancer, coronary heart disease and arthritis.

Coping with chronic illness

The onset of a serious illness has many implications for both the individual concerned and those around them (see also the discussion in Chapter 12). Following the onset of symptoms, the person with the illness may experience the anxiety of waiting for and being given a serious diagnosis, the possibility of having to come into hospital, with its associated discomfort and disruption of normal life, and so on. In the longer term, they may have to come to terms with restrictions or handicaps associated with their condition and the possibility of a gradual decline in health. They may have to learn how to manage their condition or take action to prevent their health deteriorating further. Having a chronic illness presents the individual with a number of 'tasks'. People who are HIV-positive have to take many drugs each day at carefully determined times; people with arthritis may benefit from engaging in a variety of exercises to maintain joint mobility; and so on. Other diseases, such as coronary heart disease (CHD), may or may not be apparent on a day-by-day basis. However, changing risk factors such as diet or smoking may help to prevent the disease progressing further. A third issue that patients often have to deal with is the significant emotional distress that may accompany a diagnosis of severe or chronic disease.

The interventions considered in this chapter aim to help people to cope with each of these challenges. This chapter examines the effectiveness of a number of approaches used to help people to reduce any distress they experience, to manage their disease and to prevent it developing further. The therapeutic approaches we consider include:

- providing relevant information
- stress management training
- the use of social support
- self-management training
- enhancing social support
- the use of written emotional expression.

Each type of intervention may have multiple benefits. Improvements in mood, for example, may increase the likelihood of cardiac patients participating in an exercise programme, and therefore impact on both their wellbeing and their physical health. Conversely, taking part in an exercise programme may reduce depression or anxiety as the individual feels they are gaining control over their illness and their life. Stress management training may simultaneously reduce the distress associated with being HIV-positive and improve its prognosis through its positive impact on immune function. So, separating the specific outcomes of the various interventions is a little artificial. Nevertheless, we try to tease out each of these multiple end points and consider how well each intervention achieves each of these separate goals.

Reducing distress

Information provision

Many people with serious illness experience significant levels of distress. They may have concerns about their prognosis and treatment, the potential effects of their illness on their quality of life, and so on. Levels of distress are perhaps highest in the early stages of an illness or at times when the nature of an illness changes. We discuss these issues in more detail in Chapter 12. However, as examples of the level of distress many patients experience, about a third of patients with cancer and a quarter of those who have had a myocardial infarction (MI) report clinically significant levels of distress at some time in the course of their illness (e.g. Lane *et al.* 2002b). This can be reduced by various types of information, including information about:

- the nature of a disease and/or its treatment;
- how to cope with disease and/or its treatment;
- how to change behaviour in order to reduce risk of disease or disease progression.

Perhaps the simplest form of information provision involves keeping patients informed about the progress of their condition and its treatment. Uncertainty can increase distress – providing information can reduce it. Wells *et al.* (1995), for example, found that giving information to people with cancer about their chemotherapy, showing them around the clinic in which they were to receive the treatment, and giving them the opportunity to ask questions to a specialist counsellor was highly effective in reducing their levels of distress.

More complex interventions may also be relevant at the beginning of a serious illness. One particular issue that needs to be dealt with particularly sensitively is telling patients and relatives when they have a disease with a poor or fatal prognosis – a process often known as 'breaking bad news'. The way that this information is given at this time may have important implications for how people cope and come to terms with their prognosis. Clearly, the communication skills of the person giving the bad news are important in the success of this process – we discuss these issues in more detail in Chapter 10. However, a simple informational strategy may also facilitate this process. Hogbin and Fallowfield (1989) gave patients an audiotape of the consultation in which they were given their 'bad news'. They were encouraged to play the tape in their own time to help them to recall the information given. This simple procedure helped them to recall more information than a control group who did not receive the tape, and to be more confident about telling their family and friends about their illness and prognosis. In a different context, Cope *et al.* (2003) compared the effectiveness of a variety of communication strategies with women having a scan for a potential foetal abnormality. Two weeks after their consultation, women who received an audiotape or letter summarising the information given in the session reported less anxiety than the control group without this information. The groups did not differ on recall of information. Despite these encouraging findings, it should be noted that not all patients may benefit from this approach. McHugh *et al.* (1995) found that patients with a particularly poor prognosis who were given a tape recording of their bad news consultation were more likely to be depressed than those not given a tape.

Providing people with information about how to cope emotionally with medical procedures can add to the benefits of providing information about their illness or the nature of any medical procedures they will experience (see also discussion of pre-operative information discussed in Chapter 10). Marteau *et al.* (1996), for example, considered the effectiveness of two booklets given to women referred for **colposcopy** following an abnormal **cervical smear**:

1. A coping booklet provided brief information about the procedure they were about to experience, information on the likely outcomes of the procedure, and instructions on relaxation and distraction techniques (see Chapter 13) they could use to help them to cope before and during the procedure.
2. A medical information booklet provided more details on the nature of cervical abnormalities, the procedure and its likely outcomes than the standard information booklet. However, it did not suggest any coping strategies that the women might use.

The results suggested a specific effect of each aspect of the information given. All patients who received the booklets knew more about issues around the colposcopy than a group of patients who received the standard level of information. However, the women who received the medical booklet did not experience any reductions in anxiety as a consequence. By contrast, those patients given the coping booklet were less anxious when they attended the hospital for their operation than those who either received the medical or no booklet.

Educational programmes whose primary intention is to help people to manage a disease or reduce risk of further disease may also impact on mood. Why this should happen is not clear. It is possible that such interventions provide patients with a sense of control over their illness and reduce anxieties about their long-term health. They may also encourage participants not to overly restrict their lives as a result of their disease. Each may result in improved mood. The first of these studies was an influential UK study of rehabilitation of people following an MI. In this, Lewin *et al.* (1992) compared the effectiveness of a six-week home-based education package known as the 'Heart Manual' with a placebo package of information and informal

colposcopy
a method used to identify cells that may develop into cancer of the cervix. Sometimes follows a cervical smear if abnormalities are found. A colposcope is a low-power microscope.

cervical smear
smear of cells taken from the cervix to examine for the presence of cell changes indicating risk of cancer.

counselling. The Heart Manual focused on guiding patients through a progressive change of risk factors for CHD, including changes in diet, exercise and relaxation techniques. Patients followed the manual at home for a period of six weeks. Over this time, they also received three telephone calls from expert nurses to discuss their progress and any problems they were experiencing. Over the following year, participants who received the Heart Manual reported lower levels of anxiety and depression than those in the control group. They were also less likely than people in the control group to go to their doctor with concerns about their heart condition in the first six months following their discharge. In a similar type of programme, Hartford *et al.* (2002) used a telephone contact programme for patients who had had a **coronary artery bypass graft** and their partners. The programme provided information on a number of issues to aid recovery, including a graded activity and exercise plan, coping with pain, and dealing with psychosocial problems, diet and medication use. The programme began with a meeting between a specialist nurse and the patient and their partner on the day of discharge, when they were provided with information about medication for pain, distances to walk, rest stops on the way home, the nurse's 24-hour telephone number, and a time when they would phone again. This was followed by six telephone calls at increasing intervals over the next seven weeks, during which problems were assessed and relevant information provided. Despite its emphasis on changing behaviour, it also proved effective in reducing both patient and partner levels of anxiety. New technologies may also be used to help the provision of information. Rawl *et al.* (2002) evaluated the effect of a computer-based intervention providing women newly diagnosed with breast cancer with information on the disease, its treatment and strategies for symptom management. This was combined with support from a nurse specialising in the care of people with cancer. Following the intervention, participants reported less depression and anxiety than those who did not receive the intervention, although combining the two elements of the intervention makes it difficult to work out which aspect of the intervention proved the more effective.

coronary artery bypass graft
surgical procedure in which veins or arteries from elsewhere in the patient's body are grafted from the aorta to the coronary arteries, bypassing blockages caused by atheroma in the cardiac arteries and improving the blood supply to the heart muscle.

Stress management training

Stress management training involves teaching individuals directly how to cope with stress, using strategies including:

- *problem-solving*: to prevent or minimise external problems that contribute to stress;
- *cognitive restructuring*: to identify and challenge stress-provoking thoughts which may initiate or exacerbate the stress response;
- *relaxation*: to reduce the physiological arousal that forms part of the stress response.

We discuss these approaches in more detail in Chapter 13. Given that these strategies are directly targeted at reducing distress, one would hope that they are effective in doing so – and this does seem to be the case. A meta-analysis of forty-five studies involving some form of stress management procedure (Meyer and Mark 1995) concluded that the average person was up to 60 per cent better off than those not receiving the intervention. The approach has proven effective at various stages in the process of care, including:

- waiting for a diagnosis;
- during treatment;
- coping with the emotional stress of living with a long-term illness.

Here, we consider examples of the effectiveness of stress management procedures in the context of HIV/AIDS, cancer and heart disease.

Living with HIV is not easy. People with the virus have to regularly take tablets that remind them of their illness and its prognosis. They may experience distressing symptoms or side-effects of their medication, isolation and so on. The stress engendered by these and other factors not only impacts at a psychological level but may also impact adversely on their health, and ultimately how long they live (see Chapter 8). Minimising distress should therefore form an important part of any HIV treatment package. Accumulating evidence suggests that stress management interventions achieve this goal. In a series of studies conducted by researchers at the University of Miami, group stress management interventions have been shown to improve cognitive functioning and reduce distress in women with AIDS (Lechner *et al.* 2003), reduce depression in HIV-positive homosexual men (Carrico *et al.* 2005), as well as influencing physiological correlates of stress including cortisol levels (Antoni *et al.* 2000). Using a slightly different approach to managing distress, Chesney *et al.* (1996) compared a three-month programme of **coping effectiveness training** (see Chapter 13) with an education-only group and a waiting-list control group in reducing distress in HIV-positive individuals. The intervention proved effective, with people in the active-intervention group reporting significantly greater reductions in stress and increases in self-efficacy than those in either of the other conditions. However, not all stress management interventions need to be so complex. Bormann *et al.* (2006) found a simple meditation course proved effective in reducing distress: use of a mantra was inversely associated with non-HIV related intrusive thoughts and positively associated with quality of life, total existential spiritual wellbeing, meaning/peace and spiritual faith. The carers of people who are HIV-positive may also experience significant stress and may benefit from being taught stress management techniques. But is it better to work with such people individually, or as part of a couple and include the cared-for person in the intervention? Pakenham *et al.* (2002) addressed this issue, comparing a stress management intervention targeted at carers individually or as a dyad. The intervention included strategies to help the resolution of problems through problem-solving techniques as well as strategies to help participants cope with any distress they experienced. Although working with individuals proved better than no intervention, the most effective intervention involved working with both members of the couple in the programme.

A second group of patients for whom stress management has proven effective is people with a diagnosis of cancer. One early study in this population was reported by Fawzy *et al.* (1993), who compared a stress management programme with usual care in a group of patients with **malignant melanoma** whose tumours had been surgically excised. Only the active-intervention group reported any improvements in mood both immediately after the intervention and at six-month follow-up. More recently, Antoni *et al.* (2001) found that a stress management programme was more effective than a one-day

coping effectiveness training
a specialist form of stress management in which participants are taught to alter the nature of their coping efforts to suit the particular type of demands they are facing: using emotion-focused coping where the situation cannot be changed and problem-focused coping where it can.

malignant melanoma
a rare but potentially lethal form of skin cancer.

benefit finding
a process of finding beneficial outcomes as a consequence of what is normally seen as a negative event, such as developing cancer or being infected with the HIV.

educational seminar in improving measures of depression and 'benefit finding' among women with early stage breast cancer. Typical benefits included:

- a greater enthusiasm to live life to the full;
- making positive life choices as a result of illness;
- a greater appreciation of being alive;
- improved relationships with partner.

Similar gains have been made among men following medical treatment of prostate cancer (Penedo *et al.* 2006) and men and women during a course of radiotherapy (Krischer *et al.* 2007).

A third group in which we consider the effectiveness of stress management programmes is cardiac patients. Most of these interventions have targeted levels of anxiety, usually with significant effect (Rees *et al.* 2004). A second potentially beneficial area for stress management interventions involves the treatment of heart arrhythmias through the use of Implantable Cardioverter Defibrillators (ICDs). These are small instruments placed in patients' abdomens with leads leading to the heart. They monitor the heart for potentially fatal changes in heart rhythm, which they correct firstly by 'pacing' the heart and, if necessary, shocking the heart. Pacing involves increasing the heart rate for a short time. The shock is similar to that from an external defibrillator. Patients may not notice the pacing, although many do. They certainly notice the shock, which has been described as similar to being punched hard in the chest. Although most patients never actually experience a shock, they are all aware that it can occur. As a consequence, many people avoid situations that they think may lead to an arrhythmia, such as engaging in exercise or potentially stressful situations. Those that have experienced a shock may experience classically conditioned fear in situations where this has occurred or those similar to it. ICDs are a relatively new technology, but are now being increasingly used, and studies helping people cope with them are now emerging. One such pilot study tested a stress management programme. Sears *et al.* (2007) compared two active stress management programmes following ICD implantation, one lasting a full day, the other involving six, weekly, sessions. Both interventions were associated with short-term reductions in anxiety and cortisol levels – although the lack of no treatment control group allows the possibility that these changes would have occurred naturally as patients adapted to having the ICD.

RESEARCH FOCUS

Pradhan, E.K., Baumgarten, M., Langenberg, P. *et al.* (2007) Effect of mindfulness-based stress reduction in rheumatoid arthritis patients. *Arthritis and Rheumatism*, 57: 1134–42.

The authors note that meditation has been found to be effective in helping people cope with a number of medical conditions, but that data on its effectiveness with patients who have arthritis is lacking, despite the condition having a significant impact on patients' psychological and physical wellbeing. Their study examined whether a mindfulness meditation intervention would improve the wellbeing of patients with rheumatoid arthritis, as well as improve measures of disease activity.

continued

Method

Participants

Participants were adults aged 18 or more years, with active rheumatoid arthritis. They were recruited through a variety of means, including advertisements in local newspapers, presentations at community health fairs, and informational flyers sent to self-help groups. Exclusion criteria included having a major mental health problem or drug or alcohol dependency. All participants continued their usual treatment during the study.

Interventions

Participants were randomly assigned to either mindfulness meditation or a waiting-list control group by a researcher who had no direct contact with participants. The mindfulness meditation condition involved participating in eight weekly training sessions, followed by three follow-up 'refresher sessions' over the next four months. Participants in the waiting-list control group were offered the same course at the end of the study.

Assessments and method

All measures were taken at baseline, two-month, and six-month assessment points. Participants could send in questionnaires through the post if they were unable to attend assessment visits, but the physical evaluation required them to attend the hospital.

Outcome measures

- The *Symptom Checklist-90-Revised* (SCL-90-R) was used to evaluate depressive symptoms and psychological distress.
- The *Disease Activity Score in 28 joints* (DAS-28) measured disease status. This index is based on a combination of scores reflecting the number of tender and swollen joints, blood measures of inflammation, and patients' assessment of their disease activity on a 10 cm visual analog scale.
- *Psychological Well-Being Scales* (PWBS) measured wellbeing: these scales combine to provide a total score reflecting 'positive affect associated with successful life experience in the face of difficult circumstances'.
- The *Mindfulness Attention Awareness Scale* (MAAS) assessed the state of mindfulness by evaluating one of its core characteristics: attention to what is taking place in the present.

Results

Three hundred and thirty-two people responded to the advertisements. However, 58 did not have active rheumatoid arthritis, 78 did not respond to contact by the researchers or attend the baseline measures, 100 had 'scheduling problems', and 33 had a major illness. A total of 63 people were therefore eligible for the study, and randomised to either mindfulness meditation (n = 31) or to the control group (n = 32); 5 participants did not complete the study. Most of the participants were female, white, married, with a mean age of fifty-four years. Participants in the control group were more likely to have had a history of depression and had experienced rheumatoid arthritis for marginally longer than those in the intervention group. These differences were taken into account in the analyses conducted.

- *Two-month outcome*: There were no significant differences between the groups on any of the measures.
- *Six-month outcome*: By this time, participants in the mindful meditation condition had made statistically significant improvements on the measure of wellbeing relative to the control group, and marginally greater improvements on measures of depression and mindfulness. The intervention had no impact on disease activity.

At two-month follow-up, there was a small but significant relationship between improvements on the measures of depression and wellbeing and higher levels of use of meditation. This effect was no longer evident at six-month assessment. Of note also, was that the outcome of one of the three teachers used in the study was significantly better than that of the other two, suggesting a significant therapist effect.

Discussion

The researchers noted some disappointment with their findings. Although the levels of adherence to the intervention were high, they found only modest effects on mood. They noted that these results are atypical of mindfulness meditation interventions, which usually report much better results, and speculated that this may have been a result of their final sample having relatively low levels of depression, and therefore having little to gain from the study. Despite this, participants in the meditation group achieved a 35 per cent reduction in psychological distress. There was no impact of the meditation on disease activity. The authors note that this is consistent with a number of other studies of stress management in this condition, which have usually shown no impact on disease activity, and may represent a limit to the benefits of psychological interventions in this condition.

This study had limitations, particularly its small sample – despite the large initial sample size and widespread efforts at recruitment – which may have limited the significance of any between-condition effects. That many people did not finally enter the study, despite having shown initial interest in it, also suggests that the final sample may have been biased towards a specific group of people with time and willingness to engage in this type of therapy. Many others may not, and the applicability of the intervention may be limited. Despite the limited findings, and perhaps generalisability of the results, the study does indicate that at least some people with rheumatoid arthritis may benefit psychologically from the use of meditation, if not in terms of symptom reduction.

Enhancing social support

We discussed in Chapter 12 how social support can improve or maintain both mental and physical health. With this in mind, a number of studies have evaluated the impact of support groups designed to provide social support from people experiencing similar health problems. Many of these have been led by professionals and include an element of group therapy or working towards group goals. One of the first studies to evaluate the effectiveness of this approach was reported by Spiegel *et al.* (1989). They randomly assigned women with breast cancer to either a usual treatment control or weekly support groups led by health professionals. These focused on a number of issues, including:

- building strong, supportive bonds;
- expressing emotions;
- dealing directly with fears of dying;
- improving relationships within the family;
- active involvement in decisions concerning treatment.

Only those in the active intervention evidenced any improvements on measures of depression and anxiety.

radical prostatectomy
otherwise known as a
total prostatectomy, this
involves using surgery
to remove all of the
prostate as a cure for
prostate cancer.

Subsequently, Classen *et al.* (2001) reported on the effectiveness of a year-long series of weekly support groups in which patients with breast cancer were encouraged to explore their emotional reactions to their illness and to gain support from the group. Compared with participants in a control group provided with educational materials, participants in the active intervention reported significantly greater reductions in traumatic stress symptoms and better mood in the long term. In a later report by the same research team, Giese-Davis *et al.* (2002) reported that women who went through the groups reported less suppression of negative moods while also showing less aggressive, inconsiderate, impulsive and irresponsible behaviour in comparison with the no-treatment group. They therefore concluded that this form of intervention can help women to become more expressive of their emotions without becoming more hostile. Supportive interventions appear to be of benefit to women across a variety of cultures, including Iranian (Montazeri *et al.* (2001) and Japanese (Fukui *et al.* 2000) women. Men may also benefit from peer support. Weber *et al.* (2007) found that men who had experienced **radical prostatectomy** benefited more than a control group from meeting with a fellow patient once a week for eight weeks to discuss any concerns they had and coping strategies they could use, on measures of depression and self-efficacy.

Patients may also benefit from therapists working with family members to increase the support given them within the family. Northouse *et al.* (2005) found gains on measures of hopelessness and negative appraisal of illness among patients with recurrent breast cancer, and their caregivers reported a significantly less negative appraisal of caregiving three months (but not six months) following such an intervention. In a second study in men with prostate cancer (Northouse *et al.* 2007), the same group reported that at four-month follow-up, intervention patients reported less uncertainty and better communication with their partners than control patients. Intervention partners reported higher quality of life, higher self-efficacy, better communication, and less negative appraisal of care-giving, uncertainty, hopelessness, and symptom distress at four months compared with controls. Comparing new-age and traditional approaches to support, Targ and Levine (2002) investigated the effects of a twelve-week course in complementary and alternative medicine including the use of meditation, affirmation, imagery and ritual with attendance at a breast cancer support group. The group support included teaching cognitive-behavioural stress management skills as well as providing social support. Both intervention approaches proved effective in improving outcomes such as anxiety, helplessness/hopelessness, depression and confusion. However, the complementary-intervention group made gains on a measure of 'spiritual wellbeing' not found in the cognitive-behavioural support group.

Before leaving this issue, it is important to note that although socially based interventions have proven effective, they are not for all. Pollock *et al.* (2007) found that many patients preferred to turn to friends and families for support, and did not wish to attend more professionally organised support groups.

Managing illness

A second set of interventions can be used to help people to gain the skills and motivation to manage the symptoms of an illness as effectively as possible: to maintain an exercise and mobility programme in rheumatoid arthritis, an insulin regimen in Type 2 diabetes, and so on. The goal of the intervention here is not to prevent the development of a disease but to minimise its negative impact on the affected individual.

Information provision

There is a significant body of evidence showing that patient education programmes can enhance knowledge about a condition or its management, at least in the short term (e.g. Gibson *et al.* 2000; van den Arend *et al.* 2000). However, even where increases in knowledge are achieved, they may not always impact on behaviour or symptom control. Indeed, a number of studies have found only a marginal relationship between educational programmes and behavioural change. In a systematic review of eleven educational programmes for people with asthma, for example, Gibson *et al.* (2000) concluded that while such programmes increased knowledge, there was no evidence that they impacted on measures of medication use, doctor visits, hospitalisation and lung function.

The internet now provides a key source of information for many patients. This provides both formal 'official' sites and 'unofficial' sites, many of which advocate the use of a variety of treatment approaches or condemn them as dangerous and unacceptable. Given the plethora of, often contradictory, information on the internet, access to this information can both benefit patients and carry the potential for confusion and even harm. It also presents significant challenges for doctors when giving information about a particular condition. Witness one anecdotal story in which a UK doctor prescribed tamoxifen, a drug treatment known to significantly reduce the risk of cancer recurrence in women that have had breast cancer (see Buzdar 2004). In the consultation, he described both the benefits and the common side-effects and health risks of taking the drug to one patient. With this knowledge, she decided to take the drug on a preventive basis. The next day she telephoned the doctor to say that she was no longer willing to take the drug as she had searched a number of US websites, and their descriptions of the health risks associated with the drug made her decide against its use. While in one way this may be seen as the power of truly informed consent, what had frightened this woman was reading a list of diseases that had occurred in women taking the drug. What she did not have was the data to contextualise this list, which included many conditions that may have occurred in only a very small percentage of those taking the drug, or which may not even have been the result of taking it.

Health-care providers are now responding to this sort of challenge by providing their own web-based information that patients can easily access and that can provide appropriate information. One of many web-based health information sites is provided by the American Heart Association (Yancy

2002). Heart Profilers (www.americanheart.org/profilers) provides a web-based interactive tool through which patients can obtain a personalised report of 'scientifically accurate' treatment options, a list of questions to ask their doctor on their next visit (which has been shown to improve doctor–patient communication and patient satisfaction – see Chapter 10), and key information they need to participate in their treatment. In the site, menus lead to information related to heart failure and CHD, hypertension, high cholesterol and **atrial fibrillation**. The effectiveness of this type of intervention is difficult to assess. However, people who access health- and illness-related websites are generally more knowledgeable than those who do not (Kalichman *et al.* 2003), although this may be the result of better-informed people being more likely to access internet sites relevant to their illness. Nevertheless, these data suggest that the internet may prove a useful resource for people with many chronic conditions, and as we shall show later, can prove an effective medium of change.

atrial fibrillation

a heart rhythm disorder (arrhythmia). It involves a very rapid heart rate, in which the atria (upper chambers of the heart) contract in a very rapid and disorganised manner and fail to pump blood effectively through the heart.

Self-management training

Perhaps the best-known approach to helping patients to gain control over their illness is known as self-management training (Lorig 1996), and those who undertake this form of training are often referred to as 'expert patients'. The approach involves teaching affected individuals how to manage their illness in a way that maximises control over their symptoms and quality of life. It is based on social cognition theory (e.g. Bandura 2001), which suggests that patients can learn self-management skills from practice and watching others, and that success in achieving control leads, in turn, to increased confidence and continued application of new skills. Accordingly, the core of self-management training is a structured, progressive, skills-training programme that ensures success at each stage before progression to the next. Self-management programmes are usually, but not uniquely, run as group interventions, facilitating the process of learning from observation of others. The approach is specifically targeted at the effective management of disease. It does not focus on the emotional sequelae of disease; nor is it intended to be a preventive intervention. Self-management programmes began by focusing on helping people cope with arthritis, typically addressing issues such as:

- exercising with arthritis
- managing pain
- eating healthily
- preventing fatigue
- protecting joints
- taking arthritis medication
- dealing with stress and depression
- working with the doctor and health-care team
- evaluating alternative treatments
- outsmarting arthritis: problem solving.

These programmes proved extremely effective. A review by SuperioCabuslay *et al.* (1996), for example, reported gains in excess of drug treatment alone of:

- 20 to 30 per cent on measures of pain relief;
- 40 per cent in functional ability;
- 60 to 80 per cent in the reduction in tender joint counts.

The original self-management programmes addressed all issues with all people. However, it is possible that some issues were more relevant than others. As a result, a number of programmes have now moved from a 'one size fits all' approach to tailored programmes that provide a number of modules that participants can select according to their particular needs. Evers *et al.* (2002) evaluated the effectiveness of one such programme targeted at people with rheumatoid arthritis. Modules included those targeted at helping people to cope with fatigue, negative mood and pain, and to maintain or improve social relationships. The programme resulted in mid- to long-term gains on a number of psychological measures, including the use of active coping strategies, mood, fatigue and helplessness in comparison with a no-treatment condition. Gains were also reported in an Australian study reported by Osborne *et al.* (2007) using the same approach. This study found significant reductions in pain and health distress, as well as increases in self-efficacy and exercise – changes which were sustained for at least two years. Adding an exercise component to a specific programme for people with osteoarthritic knee pain led Yip *et al.* (2007) to report significant gains in comparison to a no-treatment control group on measures of arthritis pain, fatigue, duration of weekly light exercise practice and knee flexion.

Following their success with arthritis, self-management programmes are now used to help people to manage a number of long-term conditions. Gifford *et al.* (1998), for example, randomly assigned men with symptomatic HIV or AIDS to either a seven-session group self-management programme or usual care. The intervention used interactive methods to provide information about living with HIV/AIDS and a number of disease self-management skills, including symptom assessment and management, medication use (see Chapter 10), physical exercise and relaxation skills. Over the course of the study, participants who did not enter the programme reported increases in the number of 'troubling symptoms' they experienced and an increased feeling of loss of control over their health. By contrast, participants in the self-management condition reported more control over their health and fewer 'troubling symptoms'. One other programme (Inouye *et al.* 2001) reported short-term gains on measures of mood, including anger, and increases in perceived control over their condition following an HIV self-management intervention compared with a waiting-list control group.

A further example of self-management programmes involves the control of blood sugar levels in diabetes. Langewitz *et al.* (1997) reported a particularly interesting study of the effectiveness of what they termed intensified functional insulin therapy. Not only did their intervention involve an educational component, but it also taught participants how factors such as additional exercise and eating meals with varying levels of carbohydrate may influence their blood sugar levels by allowing them to experience, and then cope with, these situations within the programme. This approach should provide more realistic learning than conventional approaches and therefore provide more benefit should problems arise. In comparison with baseline measures, participants in the intervention evidenced significant improvements in blood sugar levels and a reduction in the frequency with which they experienced **hypoglycaemic episodes** in the following year.

Self-management programmes need not be delivered live. There are now several examples of graduated skills-based programmes that have translated the key elements of the self-management process into written or computer-based form. The Heart Manual, which we described earlier in this chapter,

hypoglycaemic episode occurs when the body's glucose level is too low. It frequently occurs when too much insulin or oral diabetic medication is taken, not enough food is eaten, or following exercise without appropriate food intake. Symptoms include excessive sweating, paleness, fainting and eventually loss of consciousness.

provides a good example of this. The latest evaluation of this approach was reported by Jolly *et al.* (2007). They randomly allocated participants who had experienced an MI from inner-city, ethnically diverse, socially deprived areas of the West Midlands of England to receive either a hospital-based cardiac rehabilitation programme or the Heart Manual used at home. Both involved programmes including exercise, relaxation, education and lifestyle counselling. The Heart Manual followed the developmental approach of gradual change and skills learning suggested by Lorig. Significant improvements in total cholesterol, smoking prevalence, anxiety scores, self-reported physical activity and diet were seen in both conditions between baseline and the six-month follow-up. However, no clinically or statistically significant differences were seen between the home- and centre-based groups, suggesting the home intervention is a viable and effective intervention. In a similar study, Lewin *et al.* (2002) evaluated a written intervention to help patients manage their angina. They compared a standard educational package providing information but no strategies of change with a written behavioural programme showing participants how best to manage their angina and encouraging them to plan new activities and to limit the impact of angina on their lives. Six months after the end of the intervention, patients in the self-management intervention reported lower levels of angina, used drugs to control their angina less frequently, and reported fewer physical restrictions on their activities than patients in the control group.

Self-management programmes can be implemented simply and cheaply using the internet or interactive programmes on computers. It is important to note, though, that such interventions may appeal to specific groups within the population. Several studies, for example, have shown younger people to enjoy and benefit from the use of such technology in managing illnesses such as diabetes (Chan *et al.* 2007) and asthma (e.g. van der Meer *et al.* 2007). But not all patient populations will feel comfortable with such an approach. In an ethnically diverse Californian sample, Sarkar *et al.* (2007), for example, found that 69 per cent of their respondents reported interest in telephone support, 55 per cent wanted group medical visits, while only 42 per cent would use the internet. Unsurprisingly, people who reported themselves as having poor literacy were more likely to be interested in telephone support than the alternative approaches.

Stress management training

atopic dermatitis
a number of conditions, including eczema, involving an inflammatory response of the skin.

A number of interventions have focused on teaching stress management procedures in an effort to control the symptoms of disorders as diverse as rheumatoid arthritis and **atopic dermatitis**. Some of the relevant literature is reviewed below, focusing on the treatment of irritable bowel syndrome (IBS), angina and diabetes.

Although the role attributable to stress in the aetiology of IBS has been downplayed recently (see Chapter 8), a number of interventions using stress management techniques have been evaluated, and they seem to be reasonably effective – achieving similar outcomes to medical interventions (Spiller *et al.* 2007).

Taking the issue one step further, Kennedy *et al.* (2005) reported a study in which they examined whether stress management could add to the effectiveness of a drug that slows down the gut's activity and is generally used to treat IBS. All the people in the study were first given the drug treatment. Those who continued to have IBS symptoms six weeks later were either entered into a stress management programme or continued on their drug regimen in the hope that additional time on the drug would improve their symptoms. Patients in the cognitive-behavioural programme fared best, reporting significant improvements on a variety of measures of IBS symptoms as well as reductions in measures of emotional distress.

Episodes of angina may be triggered by emotional as well as by physical stresses (see Chapter 8). Accordingly, a number of studies have explored the potential benefits of stress management procedures in people with this condition. One of the first was reported by Bundy *et al.* (1994), who found that patients who took part in a stress management programme reported greater reductions in the frequency of angina symptoms, were less reliant on medication and performed better on a standardised exercise known as a **treadmill test** than a control group who did not receive the intervention. A much larger study, involving hundreds of participants, was reported by Gallacher *et al.* (1997), who compared a less intensive intervention, involving a stress management programme delivered in booklet form and three group meetings, with a no-treatment control condition. At six-month follow-up, patients in the intervention condition reported significantly fewer episodes of angina triggered by stress, but not exercise – a finding consistent with the intervention impacting directly on the stress mechanisms that led to the episodes of angina.

treadmill test
a test of cardiovascular fitness in which participants gradually increase the level of exercise on a treadmill while having their heart monitored with an electrocardiogram.

Alan Jones provides an interesting case involving the use of stress management and angina. His problems began when he was admitted to hospital following an MI. As with most patients, he spent two days in the coronary care unit before being transferred to a medical ward, and was discharged a few days later following an uneventful time on that ward. Unfortunately, when he went home he developed the symptoms of angina, which on occasion mimicked the symptoms Mr Jones had experienced at the time of his initial infarction: chest pain, shortness of breath and feeling dizzy. The second of these episodes occurred following a major sale (he was a sales representative) leading to him feeling very excited, after which he walked out of a building into a freezing cold night to go to his car to drive home. The combination of adrenalin-fuelled excitement and sudden exposure to cold air triggered a significant episode of angina. Unfortunately, he found these symptoms extremely frightening and interpreted them as indicating he was having a further MI. This resulted in him hyperventilating, exacerbating his physical symptoms, having a 'full-blown' panic attack, and then calling out an ambulance to be admitted to the same hospital. As on the first occasion, he was discharged from hospital the following day after being told that he had 'only' had an episode of angina.

In an attempt to stop this happening again, he was referred to a clinical psychologist. The challenges of therapy were to help Mr Jones distinguish (and then control) any panic symptoms from those of his heart disease, and to be able to distinguish any symptoms of angina from symptoms of a true MI. A mistake at any stage in this process could prove, literally, fatal. The intervention proved relatively simple, as Mr Jones was keen to adopt a psychological approach to managing his problems. The first stage involved working out exactly what was contributing to his feelings of panic. The key issue here was panicky thoughts, in particular thoughts that his heart disease was out of control and that he could die unless he got medical help. This led to increased sympathetic arousal, ironically placing more strain on his heart and increasing his angina, and hyperventilation which added to his feelings of being out of control, and dizziness.

continued

The goal of therapy was to break this circle. This initially involved Mr Jones learning to relax and to use some simple breathing techniques he could use to slow his breathing when he became anxious. He practised these skills regularly until they became relatively easy to implement. Then, working with the psychologist, he developed a strategy to use if he experienced any angina symptoms. These were:

- *Assume that the symptoms were angina, not a heart attack. Use positive self-talk to remind himself that he had experienced the symptoms before and they were not a sign of impending death, that he could control them, and if he used his gtn [glyceryl trinitrate] spray (see Chapter 8) they would soon go.*

- *Use relaxation and breathing exercises to bring his symptoms under control.*

- *Wait 5–10 minutes, to see whether the symptoms reduced as a result of these procedures.*

- *If they did not, to call an ambulance and seek medical help.*

He talked this action plan through during a therapy session, and planned on its use at key times during the day. He used it twice, successfully, in the month following its development. In the next month, he did not experience any panic attacks, and was discharged from the psychology services. Another successful case!

The potential benefits of stress management for the control of diabetes are perhaps less obvious than those related to angina. Nevertheless, there are reasons to presume that they could form an effective element in any programme of diabetes control. Stress often precedes periods of reduced adherence to self-care behaviour and may be associated with inappropriate changes in eating patterns (Viner *et al.* 1996). In addition, high levels of stress hormones such as cortisol reduce the body's sensitivity to insulin and may be accompanied by elevations in blood sugar (Surwit and Schneider 1993). As a consequence, some studies have found relaxation to be an effective intervention in keeping blood sugar levels within the optimum range. Attari *et al.* (2006), for example, reported an Iranian study comparing the effectiveness of stress management versus no intervention in the long-term control of high blood sugar levels in people with type 1 diabetes. Their main outcome measure was a substance known as HbA(1c), which indicates levels of blood sugar over the previous three months. Over the course of the three-month intervention, participants in the stress management group had lower levels of HbA(1c) than those in the no-intervention group. Similar gains have also been reported in people with type 2 diabetes (Surwit *et al.* 2002). Interestingly, Aikens *et al.* (1997) found that those people who reported the most stress and who felt that their levels of insulin were most susceptible to changes in stress levels were, paradoxically, least likely to use the relaxation methods they were taught. However, those who did practise relaxation did benefit in terms of diabetic control.

Perhaps the best interventions are those that combine teaching stress management techniques with other strategies to help to control diabetes. Grey *et al.* (2000), for example, compared an intensive diabetes management programme combined with a stress management programme with the diabetes management programme alone in young people with diabetes. By one-year follow-up, participants in the combined intervention had lower blood sugar levels and a higher belief in their ability to control diabetes and general health than those in the single condition. In addition, participants in the combined

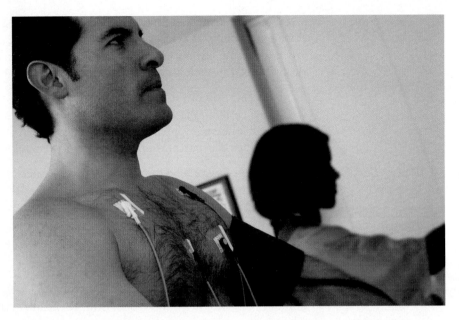

Plate 17.1 The treadmill can provide a good test of cardiac fitness while in the safety of a medical setting.

intervention were less likely to gain weight than those in the diabetes management programme, and women in this condition were least likely to report hypoglycaemic episodes.

Enhancing social and family support

Despite the widely acknowledged impact that family and friends of people with chronic illnesses may have on their behaviour and emotional wellbeing (see Chapter 12), relatively few interventions have targeted such individuals. Those that have, have had generally positive results – although among them are also some cautionary findings.

Some programmes have involved peers to help patients cope with chronic conditions. These usually involve peer experts showing how best to manage a particular condition. In one such programme, Lorig *et al.* (2003) reported the outcomes of this type of programme among a Hispanic community, with peers teaching strategies for managing a variety of chronic conditions – CHD, lung disease and type 2 diabetes. The intervention proved successful, with attenders reporting better health status, health behaviours and more confidence in their ability to manage their condition than controls who did not attend the sessions for up to one year after the end of the programme. Another project, described by Greco *et al.* (2001), reported outcomes of an intervention in which young people with diabetes and their best friends took part in a group intervention aimed at increasing diabetes-related knowledge in both participants and increasing the friend's support of the patient's diabetes care behaviour. The intervention achieved these goals. In addition, the young people's wider groups of friends understood more about diabetes, and parents reported less diabetes-related conflict.

Involving partners in any intervention may also be of value – and may be done quite simply. Taylor *et al.* (1985), for example, compared the effects of wives' differing levels of involvement in testing the exercise tolerance of cardiac patients. In their study, wives were allocated to one of three conditions:

1. no observation of the test;
2. observing their partners taking part in a treadmill test to assess their cardiac fitness;
3. observing their partners take the test and also taking part in it themselves;

All the women were fully informed of their partners' level of fitness in a counselling session. The key measure in the study was the wives' ratings of their partners' physical and cardiac efficiency. Partners who both observed and took part in the treadmill exercise were more reassured of their husbands' ability to exercise than women in either of the other groups. Although we do not know from the results of this study, it is hoped that this confidence would result in the women being less restrictive of their levels of exercise and less anxious when they did so. However, involving partners in educational programmes may not always be successful. Riemsma *et al.* (2003) reported that when both patients and their partners attended a cardiac group education programme, participants reported *decreases* in self-efficacy and increased fatigue. By contrast, patients participating in group education without partners showed *increases* in self-efficacy and decreased fatigue.

More complex family interventions have also proven of benefit in helping young people manage chronic illnesses. Wysocki *et al.* (2007), for example, reported on the outcomes of a programme involving working with whole families to help young people cope with their diabetes. The intervention both changed the family dynamics, for example, by reducing family conflict, and also changed condition-specific factors, such as improving adherence and long-term HbA(1c) levels. Similar benefits have been found in the treatment of other conditions that require young people to be actively involved in the management of their condition, such as asthma (Yorke and Shuldham 2005) and cystic fibrosis (Duff 2001).

Emotional expression

Perhaps the most unexpected therapeutic approach now being developed for people with physical health problems is variously termed narrative or written emotional expression. The work stems from the findings by Pennebaker in the 1980s (see Pennebaker *et al.* 1990) of the psychological effects of a writing task in which healthy participants, usually students, wrote about an event or issue from the past that had caused them upset or distress in a way that explored their emotional reaction to that event for about fifteen–twenty minutes on three consecutive days. Typical instructions for this exercise were:

1. Find a place where you will not be disturbed. You can write by hand or on a computer – whatever you are most comfortable with. If you don't want to write, you can also talk into a tape recorder.
2. Plan on your writing for a minimum of three days and a minimum of 15 minutes a day. The only rule is that you write continuously. If you run out of things to say, simply repeat what you have already written.

3. Instructions: really let go and write about your very deepest thoughts and feelings about X. How does X relate to other parts of your life? For example, how do they tie into issues associated with your childhood, your relationship with your family and friends, and the life you have now. How might they be related to your future, your past, or who you are now? Why are you feeling the way you are and what other issues are being brought up by this?

4. You can write about the same general topic every day or a different one each day. Don't worry about spelling or grammar. Your writing is for you and you alone. Many people throw away their writing samples as soon as they are finished. Others keep them and even edit them.

5. Be your own experimenter. Try writing in different ways. If you find that you are getting too upset in your writing, then back off and change directions. Your goal here is to better understand your thoughts and feelings associated with X. See which approach to writing works best for you.

Following this process, participants typically reported short-term increases in depression or distress, but in the mid- to long-term experienced better mood, and importantly in this context, seemed to have better physical health as measured by immune function and the frequency of visiting a doctor (see Esterling *et al.* 1999). It took some time for this approach to be tested in patient populations. However, the interventions that have been conducted appear to show benefits. Smyth *et al.* (1999), for example, compared the effects of written expressed emotion and a neutral writing task in patients with rheumatoid arthritis and asthma. Those in the intervention condition were asked to write about the 'most stressful experience they had ever undergone'; those in the control group were asked to write about time-management issues as an exercise to reduce stress. Both types of patient in the intervention group fared better than their equivalents in the control group at four-month follow-up: patients with asthma showed improvements in lung function, while patients with rheumatoid arthritis showed improvements on a combined index measuring physician-rated factors such as disease activity, joint swelling and tenderness, and the presence and severity of joint deformities as well as patient reports of any constraints on daily living tasks. Accordingly, the gains reported cannot simply be attributed to changes in self-report of symptoms as a function of improved mood following the intervention: they appear to be 'objective' gains in disease activity. Warner *et al.* (2006) reported similar benefits for young people with asthma, and began to explore what elements of the writing task appeared to mediate the improvements they found. By analysing the content of the participants' writing, they noted that the greatest improvements in asthma were associated with improved insight into the issue the participants were writing about, and the expression of more negative emotions.

In another study examining who benefits most from this approach, Stanton *et al.* (2002b) assigned participants, all of whom were in the early stages of breast cancer, to write about either: (a) their deepest thoughts and feelings regarding breast cancer (the emotional expression condition), (b) positive thoughts and feelings regarding breast cancer, or (c) facts about their experience of having breast cancer (the neutral task). Once again, the emotional expression seemed to be of benefit. In comparison with the neutral task, participants in the emotional expression condition reported fewer somatic symptoms and fewer visits to the doctor with worries about cancer or related medical conditions. Of interest was that women who typically did not use avoidant coping strategies appeared to benefit most from the emotional expression condition. The positive emotional expression task appeared to benefit those women who were typically avoidant, presumably because it did not force them to confront their fears and other issues raised by their disease. A subsequent paper, with data taken from this study (Low *et al.* 2006) replicated the findings of Warner *et al.* above, as the expression of negative emotions was significantly associated with an improvement in symptoms.

Despite these positive results, it should be acknowledged that not all interventions involving written expression are effective. Harris *et al.* (2005), for example, found it did not benefit adults with asthma. Similarly, there may be some contexts in which the expression of emotions is actually counterproductive. Panagopoulou *et al.* (2006) found that women who were emotionally expressive were less likely to become pregnant while undergoing *in vitro* fertilisation than those who contained their emotions. The goal of the next phase of research into the written emotional expression is to find out with whom and in what context the approach works best (see the special section of the *British Journal of Health Psychology*, volume 13, part 1, 2008 for a series of papers that address this issue).

What do YOU think?

The premise of the emotional expression paradigm is that it can be useful to think about, and somehow process, emotional issues. This has proved effective in a number of settings, but are there times when this may not be an optimal, or even a desirable approach? It has been suggested that there may be times when the opposite approach may be of benefit. It was reasoned that people waiting for medical information – some of which may have powerful implications for the individual, such as their HIV status or a diagnosis of cancer – may benefit more by being distracted from any worries they may have than dwelling on them. At this time, they have no information to process emotionally – rather, they are lacking any relevant information. At such times, it may be best to distract from any intrusive worries rather than focus on them using the Pennebaker approach. This finding raises a frequently raised issue concerning the targeting of interventions at appropriate times and at individuals most likely to benefit from them. So what sort of conditions, situations or individuals may be best helped by emotional expression? Are there situations where this approach should be avoided, and other approaches considered?

Preventing disease progression

Counselling

One particular form of counselling has been used with cardiac patients in an attempt to prevent disease progression – with somewhat mixed results.

The Life Stress Monitoring Program (LSMP: Frasure-Smith and Prince 1985) targeted middle-aged men who had experienced an MI and who were struggling to cope in the year following their infarction. In the study, over four hundred and fifty patients were allocated into either a no-intervention control group or a low-contact 'counselling' intervention. In this, they received monthly telephone contact from a nurse for a period of one year, during which they completed a measure of psychological distress. If they scored above a criterion score, indicating significant stress, they were offered a home visit by the nurse. The action taken by this nurse could vary according to the circumstances they encountered: the majority of contacts involving teaching and providing reassurance by supplying information, but the intervention could involve changes in medication and referral to a cardiologist if necessary.

Half the participants in the intervention condition were visited by the nursing team over the period of the intervention, with an average of six hours contact per patient. By the end of the intervention, the total death rate in the control group was 9 per cent, while that of the intervention group was 5 per cent – a significant difference. Four years following baseline, although a similar percentage of patients in the intervention and control groups had a further MI, patients in the intervention group were less likely to have died from their MI, suggesting a smaller but still significant benefit from having taken part in the counselling intervention. Unfortunately this finding may not be as exciting as it first appears. The proportion of white-collar workers in the intervention group was significantly greater than that in the control group. Accordingly, many of those in the intervention group may have been at less risk of re-infarction than those in the control group simply as a consequence of socio-economic differences (see Chapter 2). As a consequence of methodological constraints, these differences could not be statistically partialled out in their analyses, and the interpretation of the results must therefore be considered with some caution.

Such caution may be justified by the results of a later attempt to replicate these findings by the same team (Frasure-Smith *et al.* 1997). The Montreal heart attack readjustment trial (M-HART) study evaluated the same form of intervention, this time including interventions with women and an older population. Unfortunately, the intervention resulted in no benefits for men – re-infarction rates in the first year were 2.4 per cent in the intervention group and 2.5 per cent in the control group. Worse, women in the intervention group proved to be *more* at risk of re-infarction than those in the control group, with re-infarction rates of 10.3 per cent and 5.4 per cent, respectively – an effect maintained up to five-year follow-up (Frasure-Smith *et al.* 2002). In retrospect, these findings may have been a consequence of inadequately trained nurses attempting to cope with extremely distressed individuals and thus perhaps exacerbating rather than moderating their problems.

Stress management training

The impact of more traditional cardiac rehabilitation programmes that provide some form of intervention to all patients has been reviewed by Dusseldorp

exercise programme
a key element of most cardiac rehabilitation, including a progressive increase in exercise usually starting in a gym, sometimes developing into exercise in the home and beyond.

et al. (1999) and Linden *et al.* (1996), who conducted meta-analyses of the effect of 'psychosocial' and 'psycho-educational' interventions on twenty-three and thirty-seven programmes, respectively. These interventions typically combined some form of **exercise programme** involving graded increases in activity with an educational programme about risk factor change, medication and other issues relevant to patients being discharged home following an MI. Both reviews came to some positive conclusions. Linden and colleagues, for example, reported that patients who did not enter a psychosocial programme were significantly more likely to experience a death or have further cardiac problems in the two years following their infarction than those who did. After this, any protective effect was weaker. Dusseldorp *et al.* similarly reported that psycho-educational interventions resulted in a 34 per cent reduction in cardiac mortality, a 29 per cent reduction in recurrence of MI, and significant positive effects on blood pressure, cholesterol, body weight, cigarette smoking, physical exercise and eating habits. However, both reviews did not separate the effects of different psychosocial interventions such as counselling, risk behaviour education and what they term 'stress management trials'.

type A behaviour (TAB)
a constellation of characteristics, mannerisms and behaviour including competititiveness, time urgency, impatience, easily aroused hostility, rapid and vigorous speech patterns and expressive behaviour. Extensively studied in relation to the aetiology of coronary heart disease, where hostility seems central.

Perhaps the strongest evaluation of the effectiveness of stress management in the context of cardiac disease was provided by Friedman *et al.* (1986), who reported on a trial known as the Recurrent Coronary Prevention Program. This targeted men high on a measure of **type A behaviour** who had experienced an MI. Participants were allocated to one of three groups: cardiac rehabilitation, cardiac rehabilitation plus type A management, and a usual care control. The rehabilitation programme involved small group meetings over a period of four-and-half years, in which participants received information on medication, exercise and diet, as well as social support from the group. The type A management group received the same information in addition to engaging in a sustained programme of behavioural change involving training in relaxation, cognitive techniques and specific behavioural change plans in which they reduced the frequency of their type A behaviour. Evidence of the effectiveness of this process was compelling. Over the four-and-a-half years of the intervention, those in the type A management programme were at half the risk of further infarction than those in the traditional rehabilitation programme, with total infarction rates over this time of 6 and 12 per cent in each group, respectively. This remains one of the most convincing studies of the effectiveness of stress management on survival following an MI (Schneiderman *et al.* 2001), although whether most healthcare services could provide such an expensive long-term intervention is debatable.

Smaller studies have also shown positive gains following stress management interventions targeted at more general responses to stress. Blumenthal *et al.* (1997) assigned cardiac patients to either a 'usual care' group involving regular out-patient appointments with a cardiologist, a four-month programme of exercise, or a programme of stress management training. Those in the stress management group were least likely to have a cardiac event over the following year. In a second study examining these issues, the same team (Blumenthal *et al.* 2005) found both stress management and exercise to be equally effective in changing a number of psychological and physiological markers of disease. More specifically, meditation may prove an effective intervention for people with CHD. Castillo-Richmond *et al.* (2000), for example, found evidence of a slowing in the development (and even perhaps a modest decrease) in the thickness of atherosclerosis in the carotid artery of hypertensive African Americans who were taught meditation compared to controls who were not.

Depression substantially increases risk of infarction or re-infarction (see Frasure-Smith *et al.* 1995). Such a relationship suggests that interventions that reduce depression should reduce the risk of re-infarction. However, evidence in support of this hypothesis is still lacking. In one of the first studies to examine this issue, Black *et al.* (1998) allocated MI patients found to be experiencing significant distress to either usual care or to one to seven sessions of behavioural therapy. They found that 35 per cent of participants in the active intervention were hospitalised with cardiac symptoms in the following year, in comparison with 48 per cent of those in the usual care group. However, whether this difference was a consequence of physiological or psychological changes such as less anxiety over cardiac symptoms is not clear.

Unfortunately, evidence from the largest trial of any form of cardiac rehabilitation, known as the ENRICHD study (Berkman *et al.* 2003) suggests that interventions targeted at depression may not prove as effective as this early study suggested. The ENRICHD study was a large multicentre study involving 2,481 patients, providing an intervention lasting up to one year for people identified as depressed immediately following their MI. All participants in the active intervention arm received two or three treatment components, each aimed at improving their emotional state:

- group cognitive-behavioural therapy;
- social support enhanced by training participants in the social skills needed to develop their social support network;
- antidepressant medication for people who did not evidence any improvement in mood received.

A comparison group received the usual care provided by the institutions in which the study took place. Unfortunately, the results of the study were disappointing. Although the ENRICHD intervention did result in lower levels of depression than those achieved in the usual care condition, there were no differences in survival between the two groups over the two years following infarction. These data have led some to claim that there are no benefits to treating depression in MI patients – and they certainly seem to indicate this to be the case. However, the sheer size of the study meant that the investigators had limited control over the interventions received by patients in both arms of the study. This meant that the usual care received by some people in the control condition was, in fact, very similar to that provided by the ENRICHD study. In addition, attendance at the ENRICHD intervention was less than optimal, with most patients attending about eleven sessions – an attendance not that different to many of the control group interventions. Perhaps because of these factors, the differences in levels of depression between the two groups, although statistically significant, were not that great. Accordingly, it remains possible that the reductions in depression in the ENRICHD condition relative to the control condition were not sufficiently large to bring about reductions in risk for further MI.

IN THE SPOTLIGHT

Reading the report of the ENRICHD study, which was published in the prestigious *Journal of the American Medical Association*, it is clear that the readers of this journal had one interest. Did treating depression save lives? This is a question that has excited many health psychologists as well as medical doctors – and it is very important. But because it did not save lives, many psychologists consider the ENRICHD study to be a failure. But was it? Yes, from a biomedical stance, the results of the ENRICHD study were disappointing. But what about a more psychological perspective?

Depression is a potentially disabling condition that has significant implications for the quality of life and rehabilitation outcomes of both patients and the people involved with them. While psychologists should be involved in the questions of the impact of disease on physiological processes, they should also be careful not to lose sight of other psychological questions and adopting too strong a biomedical stance in the questions they address. Changes in depression are an important outcome in themselves – not just a vehicle to reduce mortality. From this perspective, the ENRICHD intervention proved a costly one that fared moderately better than the care usually provided. As such, it provides a wealth of information about how to identify and treat depression in cardiac patients, with potentially significant benefits to future patients. We should be careful not to throw out the 'psychological baby' when we throw out the 'medical bath water'.

If treating depression does not appear to result in health gains in cardiac patients, treating anxiety in patients with immune-system-mediated diseases does. One condition in which this issue has been explored is that of HIV/AIDS. Antoni *et al.* (2002), for example, followed the immunological outcomes in twenty-five HIV-positive men randomly allocated to either a ten-week stress management intervention or a waiting-list control condition. Their measures particularly focused on the impact of the intervention on CD4+ cells (see Chapter 8). Immediately following the intervention, those who took part had higher CD4+ cell counts than those in the control group, despite there being no pre-treatment differences, suggesting that stress management may slow down the disease progress and reduce the risk of opportunistic infections.

A second set of studies has examined whether stress management procedures can influence the health outcomes of people with cancer. There is evidence that stress management can improve immune function in the short term in people with cancer (e.g. McGregor *et al.* 2004). The key question that then follows is whether these immune changes translate into health gains. The outcomes following the intervention conducted by Fawzy *et al.* (1993) described earlier in the chapter were impressive. In a series of studies, they reported the percentage of people in a stress management group and a no-treatment control group to show progression of malignant melanoma six months, five–six years, and ten years after the intervention. At the first of the long-term follow-up periods, participants were significantly less likely to have died of cancer than those in the control group and were marginally more likely to have had a longer period free of disease. By the ten-year follow-up (Fawzy *et al.* 2003), these differential effects remained. By this time, eleven of the thirty-four people in the control group had had recurrences and had died of cancer: three others had had non-fatal recurrences. In the stress management group, nine of thirty-four had died of cancer, and two had survived recurrences. Overall, these differences were not significantly different between the groups. However, after statistically controlling for differences in the severity of the presenting melanoma, more participants who took part in the stress management intervention survived up to ten years after their initial diagnosis than those in the control group. Similar gains following stress management training or similar interventions have been found in two large studies of patients with gastrointestinal cancer (Kuchler *et al.* 1999) and a mixture of cancers (McCorkle *et al.* 2000), although some smaller studies have reported null findings. However, Ross *et al.* (2002) pointed out that the effects of these interventions may have been stronger if patients had been selected for any of the studies as a result of their having some distress to ameliorate rather than simply having a diagnosis of cancer.

Enhancing social support

One of the earliest studies to examine the impact of increasing social support on disease outcomes was reported by Spiegel *et al.* (1981). In a study designed to improve the quality of life in cancer patients, they randomly assigned women with breast cancer to either an active treatment programme or a no-treatment control. The active intervention involved weekly support groups that emphasised building strong supportive bonds, expressing emotions, dealing directly with fears of dying, improving relationships within the family and active involvement in decisions concerning treatment. To the

Plate 17.2   Social support can help you keep healthy. Sometimes by just having someone to talk to. Sometimes by supporting healthy behaviours – even in difficult circumstances!

surprise of the investigators, women in this group lived an average of eighteen months longer than those in the no-treatment control, despite being well matched for disease status at the beginning of the trial. These findings generated a great deal of excitement in the research and clinical community when published. Unfortunately, attempts at replication, including a study conducted by Spiegel himself (Spiegel *et al.* 2007), have failed to replicate this finding, and social support has yet to be convincingly shown to impact on illness outcomes in patients with cancer.

Summary

The chapter considered psychological interventions designed to achieve three interacting goals in patients with serious chronic diseases:

■ to reduce distress
■ to improve disease management
■ to reduce risk of future disease or disease progression.

A number of approaches have been successfully used in each case. Reductions in distress have been achieved by the use of:

■ appropriate information (including information about a condition or coping strategies to minimise distress or improve control over the condition);

■ stress management training while waiting for a diagnosis, during treatment and while coping with the emotional stress of living with a long-term illness;

■ providing social support – often in the guise of professionally run support groups.

Improvements in the management of illness have been achieved by:

■ providing information – particularly information that provides a structure to achieve symptom control rather than simply providing information about a condition or its treatment;

■ training in self-management programmes, with emphasis shifting from the provision of general 'one size fits all' programmes to more bespoke programmes specifically developed to suit participants' needs;

■ stress management training in conditions in which stress is involved in their aetiology (e.g. irritable bowel syndrome) or may exacerbate symptoms (e.g. angina, diabetes);

■ improving social and family support;

■ written emotional expression.

Finally, a number of interventions may impact on longer-term health:

■ Counselling may be of benefit in cardiac patients, but results of the M-HART study have made people cautious in adopting this model.

■ Stress management appears to be of benefit in improving health in a number of conditions, including CHD and HIV/AIDS.

■ Treatment of depression in cardiac patients may impact on prognosis, although the ENRICHD study suggests that this approach should be viewed with caution.

■ Social support may be of benefit, although the promise of some early studies has not been repeated in later studies.

Overall, there is significant evidence that psychological interventions can be of great value in helping people to come to terms with the emotional consequences of having a serious chronic illness. They may also be of benefit in aiding day-to-day symptoms and even longer-term prognoses in a more limited set of conditions.

Further reading

The entire volume of the *Journal of Consulting and Clinical Psychology* for June 2002 (volume 70, part 3) provides an excellent overview of the types of psychological intervention that may be used with a variety of health conditions. It's a little dated now, but still worth a read.

A section of the February 2008 *British Journal of Health Psychology* considers new evidence in relation to the written emotional expression approach. Edited by two of the leaders in the field (Pennebaker and Smyth); well worth a read.

Berkman, L.F., Blumenthal, J., Burg, M. *et al.* (2003). Effects of treating depression and low perceived social support on clinical events after myocardial infarction: the Enhancing Recovery in Coronary Heart Disease Patients (ENRICHD) randomized trial. *Journal of the American Medical Association*, 289: 3106–16.
An important study, although a disappointing one, certainly from the perspective of the authors.

Fekete, E.M., Antoni, M.H. and Schneiderman, N. (2007). Psychosocial and behavioral interventions for chronic medical conditions. *Current Opinion in Psychiatry*, 20: 152–7.
An up-to-date review of recent evidence by leading researchers in the area.

Newbould, J., Taylor, D. and Bury, M. (2006). Lay-led self-management in chronic illness: a review of the evidence. *Chronic Illnesses*, 2: 249–61.
One of the most recent reviews of the expert patient (Lorig) approach to self-management of chronic disease.

Kennedy, P. and Llewlyn, S. (2006). *The Essentials of Clinical Health Psychology*. Chichester: Wiley.
An interesting edited text, with key chapters covering many of the issues discussed in the chapter written by experts in each area. This is a selection of chapters from a larger text (*The Handbook of Clinical Health Psychology*) which may be worth looking at.

Friedman, M., Thoresen, C., Gill, M. *et al.* (1984). Alteration of type A behaviour and reduction in cardiac recurrences in post-myocardial infarction patients. *American Heart Journal*, 108: 237–48.
Twenty years old. One of the first studies to show that psychological interventions can reduce mortality.

Fann, J.R., Thomas-Rich, A.M., Katon, W.J. *et al.* (2008). Major depression after breast cancer: a review of epidemiology and treatment. *General Hospital Psychiatry*, 30: 112–26.
Up-to-date review of an important issue.

Anderson, A.S. and Klemm, P. (2008). The Internet: friend or foe when providing patient education? *Clinical Journal of Oncology Nursing*, 12: 55–63.
Interesting paper considering the pros and cons of the internet as a means of providing patient education.

There are many expert patient websites. Some, such as the Stanford site, focus on research and payment is required to access self-help materials. Others, such as the expert patient programme or the British Heart Foundation offer a little more. The cardiac psychology site is particularly helpful.
http://www.expertpatients.co.uk/public/default.aspx?load=PublicHome
http://patienteducation.stanford.edu/
http://www.bhf.org.uk/
http://www.cardiacpsychology.com/page/page/4176374.htm

 Visit the website at **www.pearsoned.co.uk/morrison** for additional resources to help you with your study, including multiple choice questions, weblinks and flashcards.

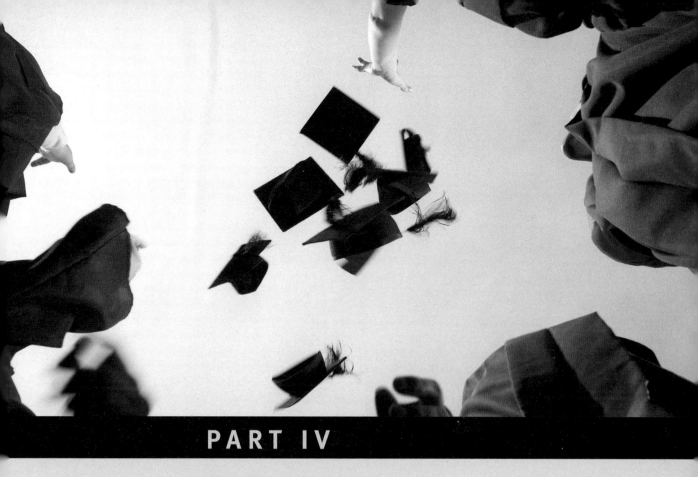

PART IV

Futures

CHAPTER 18

Futures

Learning outcomes

By the end of this chapter, you should have an understanding of:

- the need for theory-led practice
- how psychologists may influence practice, and some of the barriers to the effective development of practice
- the role and training of health psychologists in differing parts of the world
- influences on the uptake (or not) of recommended treatment approaches

CHAPTER OUTLINE

This chapter draws together a number of the strands of research and the practice of health psychology. It starts with a reminder of the need for health psychologists not only to develop the practice of health psychology, but also to develop and utilise theory in our practice of health psychology. It provides some examples of how theory may inform practice, before examining who may come to actually use interventions based on health psychology theory. The chapter considers some of the barriers to the dissemination of good health-care practice, whether based on health psychology or input from other disciplines. It also considers the development of health psychology as a health-care profession across a number of health-care settings.

The need for theory-driven practice

This book has outlined a wide range of contemporary evidence showing the importance of psychological and psychosocial factors in explaining health, health-related behaviour, and the outcomes of interventions to affect both. Key variables that influence behaviour have been integrated into coherent theories such as the theory of planned behaviour, social cognitive theory, and so on. More complex models, such as the health action process, have further integrated these theories into second-order theories of behavioural acquisition and change. These theories are not only of academic benefit to researchers and other psychologists but should also be of importance to a range of health-care practitioners, because they help identify which, out of the vast range of potential factors, are most likely to influence behaviour. They can help us construct interventions that are most likely to be effective in a variety of contexts. An example of this can be found in work on smoking cessation. Ask many health professionals how to help someone stop smoking, and they will probably say that the best way is to scare them into behavioural change. Empirical evidence suggests that such an approach will work for some, but not the majority of smokers. Psychological theory provides a series of alternative factors that may be more influential:

- The *health belief model* suggests that not only do we need to convince smokers that smoking will result in serious illness and that they are at significant risk of developing such illnesses, but we also have to convince them that the benefits of stopping smoking (health, cost, fitness, etc.) outweigh the benefits of continued smoking (avoidance of withdrawal symptoms, loss of social camaraderie, 'it can't happen to me' etc.).

- The *theory of planned behaviour* further emphasises the role of attitudes and beliefs in behaviour change. It also indicates the potential role of peers and other important others in developing personal strategies in stopping smoking. It, and the *health action process*, also clearly indicates the benefit of planning behavioural change, not simply acting on impulse.

- *Social cognition theory* suggests that before people are motivated to stop smoking and/or to continue in any efforts to remain stopped they have to believe they have the ability to do so. The principle of vicarious learning suggests we gain both skills and self-efficacy from observation of coping models – and these should form an integral part of smoking cessation programmes. The theory also suggests that although health may be a long-term gain following smoking cessation, we are largely influenced by shorter-term benefits. Accordingly, smoking cessation programmes should highlight the short-term benefits of stopping smoking as well as the long-term health gains.

Finally, the emphasis of theory on the role of environmental triggers to behaviours such as smoking indicates the benefit of modifying the environment in the early days of smoking cessation to either minimise the number of cues to smoking a person may experience, or plan specific strategies on how to deal with any urges to smoke as a consequence of such cues should they occur.

These factors have not designed an intervention programme, but they provide a good framework, based on first principles, on which to base any smoking cessation programme. We now consider how two theories may inform our understanding of an individual's response to a set of symptoms and how they can determine the types of intervention we conduct.

Some of the first theoretically driven interventions involved changing patients' inappropriate responses to their illness – and in particular the pain they were experiencing (see also Chapter 16). Seminal work by Fordyce (1982) was influenced by learning theory and used operant conditioning techniques to influence patients' pain-related behaviour. Fordyce argued that our response to pain is determined by both internal sensations of pain and the environmental contingencies any pain-related behaviour provokes. He noted that some individuals responded to pain with either an exaggerated response (groans of pain, winces, and so on) or an absence of behaviour (avoidance of behaviours that may result in pain). Both of these responses may result in poor outcomes. Exaggerated responses may result in over-medication, as carers and health professionals respond to these pain behaviours; avoidance behaviours may result in a reduction in physical capacity. Fordyce argued that rather than treat the pain, which we cannot see and evaluate, we should instead manage the pain-related behaviours by either administering pain relief on a regular basis, ignoring (not reinforcing) pain behaviours, and/or rewarding (reinforcing) appropriate behaviours such as engagement in physical activity. He showed in a series of elegant case reports how these simple interventions could significantly alter quite marked inappropriate use of pain medication.

More recent influences on the practice of health-care practitioners have been based on more cognitive models of how we respond to and cope with serious illnesses. Leventhal's self-regulation theory (see Chapter 9), for example, suggests we generate a set of beliefs, or more technically we appraise the nature of our symptoms in terms of what illness they are associated with, its consequences, curability and so on. As in broader theories of emotion, this appraisal determines our emotional reaction to the illness. Although Leventhal does not specify the appraisal–emotion links, other theories (e.g. Lazarus 1999) make the links for us. Appraisals of an illness as serious and out of our control may be associated with the emotions of anxiety and depression. Appraisals of an illness as serious but controllable may be associated with some anxiety, but also optimism and hope. Appraisals also determine our behavioural response to the illness. Appraisals that an illness is long-term and untreatable, for example, may result in different behaviours to appraisals that the illness will quickly go and is easily treatable. Self-regulation theory also suggests that coping is elicited by our emotional response to a situation – and in particular a negative emotional response. The coping strategies we adopt, whether emotion- or problem-focused, are designed to moderate negative emotions. Accordingly, someone who has had a myocardial infarction may choose to exercise or stop smoking – acts that will both help reduce risk for disease progression and reduce anxieties associated with such risk. Another individual may avoid exercise as the sensations they experience while doing so remind them of their illness and the threat it carries to their health. The actions we take at this time are triggered by our emotional response, but guided by our cognitive appraisal of the illness. As we have seen in Chapter 11, where the coping responses match the reality of the situation, they are likely to be effective and appropriate. Where there is a mismatch between appraisals and reality, inappropriate coping strategies may be evoked. Worse, inappropriate coping may lead to poor emotional and health states, and lead to a downward cycle of negative expectations and responses to illness. We need to know more about these various steps. However, the basic framework enables effective theoretically driven interventions. For example, we know that any intervention designed to optimise patients' responses to the onset of illness may benefit from a number of elements, including:

- Identification of illness beliefs and attempts to change them if they are either inadequate or incorrect – see for example, the work of Petrie *et al.* with cardiac patients described in Chapter 17. The intervention may involve the use of cognitive restructuring techniques described in Chapter 13.

- Teaching coping skills to help people cope more effectively with the stress of living with a serious illness. Encourage the use of problem-focused coping as appropriate in order to facilitate active attempts to enhance control over the illness, and emotion-focused coping to provide ways of reducing any emotional distress the individual may experience.

- Behavioural hypothesis testing (see Chapter 13) to disconfirm any inappropriate beliefs an individual may hold.

Again, the theory does not provide an individualised intervention, but it does provide a structure around which such an intervention may be designed.

The wider social and psychological environment may also be invaluable in facilitating and maintaining behavioural change. Such interventions draw on models of family dynamics, and argue for a less individualised approach to behaviour change than is usually the case. These models may be particularly pertinent in the context of changing young people's behaviour, although we would argue that similar issues could usefully be considered in many interventions to change older people's behaviour. DiMatteo (2004), for example, highlighted the following factors that should be considered when attempting to do so:

- building trust between health professional, young patient and parent through supportive and sensitive interactions and discussion of perspectives on treatment needs and goals;

- the consideration of specific beliefs and attitudes about treatment needs and goals, including areas of discrepancy between young person and parent, and in particular identifying the young person's health beliefs;

- identification and discussion of norms and expectations in relation to the desired behaviour that the young person is exposed to: for example, parental adherence behaviour and treatment anxieties, cultural and social norms of treatment adherence;

- gaining and encouraging family commitment to treatment and within-family communication if problems with treatment arise by providing social support, possibly via illness-specific support groups;

- working together to overcome barriers and increase belief in the ability of the young person to make any required behavioural changes (self-efficacy);

- tailoring wherever possible the treatment regime to the lifestyles of the family unit.

After reading this text, you may think that the issues raised here are obvious, and surely must be taken into account when health professionals develop their interventions in the 'real world'. But this is far from the case, as we highlight in IN THE SPOTLIGHT and in the following section. Thus, a key future issue for health psychology is to continue developing relevant theories and interventions based upon them – particularly interventions that are 'doable' within the context of busy health professionals (we return to this issue later) – and also to consider ways in which the implementation of these interventions can be encouraged. We turn to this issue in the next section.

IN THE SPOTLIGHT

Who uses research?

As we discuss in the text, one of the key issues in health psychology is how to link theory to practice. This is a particularly salient issue in public health initiatives as relatively few health psychologists work directly in health promotion. Furthermore, much of the research reported by health psychologists is in the journals they read. How much these journals are read by others, such as health promotion practitioners – and how much of what they read is translated into actual practice – is questionable.

This issue was highlighted in a paper published by Abraham *et al.* (2002), who performed a content analysis on safer-sex promotion leaflets used in the UK and Germany. They first identified the types of information that we know from theory and/or empirical data are likely to influence behaviour. They then examined the frequency with which these types of information were presented in their sample of safer-sex leaflets. Of the twenty categories of information they identified as influencing behaviour, only one-quarter of the leaflets used text that referred to more than ten. Two-thirds of the leaflets used two or less of these information categories. These data highlight a key issue facing health psychology – how to influence people involved in the health-care system, whether in prevention or treatment of illness. Without this influence, our research is of little or no benefit to health professionals and those they seek to care for.

Getting evidence into practice

Having considered how psychological theory can guide the development of clinical and preventive interventions, we now consider how health psychologists and others may facilitate the application of these interventions with relevant client groups. Nowadays, clinicians of all types do not have the luxury of trying out or using interventions that they 'like' or 'feel' may be effective. Increasingly, we are constrained by guidelines and limits of acceptable interventions. All clinicians working within modern health-care systems necessarily engage in what is known as evidence-based practice. We use, or at least we should use, interventions or techniques for which there is good evidence of effectiveness. The intervention studies reported in this book have contributed to the knowledge upon which this evidence is based. But simply doing and reporting the research may not be sufficient for psychologists and others to make a contribution to health care. One key issue that all researchers need to address is how our research can effectively influence the process of health care.

The role of health psychologists

In the light of the significant research conducted by health psychologists, it would seem reasonable that health psychologists should be able to apply their theoretical and practical knowledge within the health-care system. Certainly the British Psychological Society (BPS) thought so when it facilitated the development of the profession of health psychologists by first stimulating and then evaluating and accrediting training programmes in this emerging discipline. The BPS Division of Health Psychology identifies the key roles of health psychologists as people who apply psychological research and methods to:

- the promotion and maintenance of health;
- the prevention and management of illness;
- the identification of psychological factors contributing to physical illness;
- the improvement of the health-care system;
- the formulation of health policy.

They also note that the types of questions addressed by health psychologists include:

- How do people adapt to chronic illness?
- What factors influence healthy eating?
- How is stress linked to heart disease?
- Why do patients often not take their medication as prescribed?

Health psychologists work as applied psychologists, teachers, consultants and researchers within a variety of settings such as the NHS, higher education, health promotion, schools or industry. 'Prospects', the official UK graduate careers website, states that the typical work activities of health psychologists include:

Plate 18.1 Psychologists have a lot to offer in terms of healthy eating programmes for young children.

Source: University of Wales Bangor

- using psychological theories and interventions for primary prevention and health-related behaviour change in community and workplace settings to reduce health-damaging behaviour;
- encouraging the uptake of health-enhancing behaviour and psychological approaches to health promotion, improving communication between health-care professionals and patients;
- investigating cognitive processes, which mediate and determine health and illness behaviours;
- looking at the psychological impact of acute and chronic illness on individuals and their families to improve quality of life and reduce disability.

They also note that there has been a significant increase in the number of lectureships in health psychology, and growth in research into social and behavioural factors in health and health care. To gain a more detailed perspective on the role and type of job conducted by members of the Division of Health Psychology, the division conducted a survey of all its members – of whom roughly one-quarter responded. A total of 58 per cent of the survey responders were chartered (i.e. professionally qualified), and one-quarter were also chartered to another discipline of psychology. Just over half the respondents were currently working within the university sector, while 9 per cent were in the NHS in secondary health-care services (usually hospitals) and clinical (direct patient contact) posts. A further 6 per cent of respondents were working in areas such as the prison service, charities, the civil service, research councils and self-employment. Of those working in the NHS, 37 per cent were consultant psychologists (of whom many were consultant *clinical* psychologists), 20 per cent were lower grade qualified psychologists, while 12 per cent were trainees and 4 per cent were psychology assistants. The types of work individuals engaged in differed, of course, according to work setting and grade. Of those in the NHS, over two-thirds conducted a clinical service, mostly in chronic illness management, while others worked in health promotion, consultancy, education and training, health service research, public health and non-physical health-related practice (e.g. mental health, counselling, learning disabilities). Academics were largely involved in research and teaching. Many of the more senior individuals in the NHS were probably clinical psychologists with joint membership of the divisions of clinical and health psychology. As the profession matures, the number of individuals with a solely health psychology qualification is likely to increase. The following case studies are examples of job descriptions of health psychologists provided by the Division of Health Psychology.

CASE STUDY 1

National health service, consultant health psychologist

Location of job: Gloucestershire Hospitals NHS Foundation Trust

Job title: Consultant Health Psychologist

Main roles: Responsible for developing, leading, managing and providing the psychology service to Cardiac Medicine and Renal Medicine. Responsible for the coordination and management of the Health Psychology Department's (HPD) Clinical Governance agenda. Provides highly specialist psychological care (including individual and group interventions, consultative advice and supervision for colleagues, education of colleagues and service-based research) for patients with renal disease and coronary heart disease as part of the multi-disciplinary teams. Provides supervision, teaching and training and consultation to other health-care staff and organisations. Supervises doctoral trainees and newly qualified Clinical and Health psychologists. Member of the HPD Management Team which provides strategic and operational management of Health Psychology Services. Line-manages staff within the Renal and Cardiac Rehabilitation services (currently one Grade A Clinical Psychologist)

Participates in budgetary planning for the Renal and Cardiac Rehabilitation services.

CASE STUDY 2

Chartered health psychologist

Location of job: Working within the Public Health Directorate of an NHS Primary Care Trust.

Job title: Head of Stop Smoking Services.

Main roles: Managing and developing a stop smoking service. Applying research into practice. Determining levels of stop smoking treatment required according to local demand. Managing service budget. Ensuring that there is appropriate training available for health professionals and others regarding smoking cessation. Ensuring that trained staff receive appropriate ongoing professional development. Evaluating existing services and applying changes as necessary. Chairing the Primary Care Trust steering group for smoking cessation. Managing multi-disciplinary team of stop smoking advisers. Providing a health psychology input for other public health initiatives. Providing treatment services to people expressing an interest in stopping smoking. Liaising with other services within the Health Authority and Region to ensure exchange of information and coordinated service provision. Coordinating Continuing Professional Development provision for stop smoking staff within the Health Authority. Working on Pan-London initiatives to promote stop smoking services.

The Australian Psychology Society (APS) division of health psychology has a similar training and work type as in the UK – but, interestingly, they include clinical work as a core element of their work (in the UK, clinical skills are seen as an additional rather than a core skill of the profession). The APS notes that health psychologists have knowledge and skills in the following areas:

- the interaction between the physical systems of the body, psychological make-up and social networks of friends and family and how they influence health and illness;

- the amount and type of health problems experienced by various groups in Australia;

- the way that people behave, or the underlying attitudes that put their health at risk and how they might change these behaviours to prevent illness and promote health;

- strategies that people can learn to help them cope with illness or associated problems and how they can involve their friends and family to help them in their recovery; and

- the psychological impact of illness.

They identify the areas of specialism of health psychologists as:

- Health promotion
  - development and provision of programmes that assist in the prevention of illnesses such as heart attacks, stroke, cancer, sexually transmitted diseases, smoking-related illness and dietary-related problems;
  - linking up with other health professionals to understand what behaviours might be contributing to illness and how they might be changed, e.g. understanding why some people overeat or eat a high-fat diet;
  - identifying how behaviour is linked with the development of disease and injury;
  - designing public health education programmes in areas such as exercise and alcohol, cigarette and drug consumption;
  - determining the distribution of disease and the health needs of differing communities;
  - working with community members to improve their health.

- Clinical health
  - developing therapy and education programmes to help people cope with health issues such as weight management, cancer and heart health;
  - using psychological treatment for problems that often accompany ill health and injury, such as anxiety, depression, pain, addiction, sleep and eating problems;
  - understanding how psychological factors such as stress, depression and anxiety might be contributing to illness;
  - helping people with the self-management of chronic illness;
  - understanding how people cope with diagnosis and medical treatment of acute health problems and how they obtain medical care;
  - understanding how people cope with terminal illness, including the impact of grief, bereavement, death and dying;

- identifying how the relationship between health professionals, such as doctors, nurses and psychologists, and their patients can influence how well they recover from illness and injury;

- helping people cope with trauma, disability and rehabilitation.

Other countries have less developed professional roles for health psychologists. The Netherlands, for example, despite having a significant number of academic health psychologists does not have a training programme for health psychologists – they have a two-year training programme for generic health professionals who may be involved in some of the work that health psychologists do in other countries.

Other people also 'do' psychology

Despite the developing profession of health psychologists within a number of health-care systems, all of whom will clearly utilise psychological theory and practice, there are still far too few qualified health psychologists (or other types of psychologist) to provide a service to all patients that may benefit from their work. In addition, there is a clear need for all health-care professionals to adopt psychologically sophisticated ways of working with patients. Accordingly, the application of the principles of care derived from health psychology research is very much in the hands of health professionals with no immediate alliance to psychology. In the absence of health psychologists, how can one ensure that the research conducted by health psychologists is taken into practice in the wider health-care system?

A key role of health psychologists employed within any health-care system is to teach other professions about the principles of health psychology, so their practice can be influenced by such knowledge. But how else can this information be disseminated? Unfortunately, at the present time, the answer to this question has to be 'With difficulty'. One acknowledged problem in influencing health professionals (including psychologists!) is the communication gap between researchers and practitioners – something that psychological research may particularly suffer from. Most health-care practitioners and managers rarely read journals which provide cutting-edge research on the delivery of health care – even within their own discipline. But for psychology, the communication problem may be even more acute. Nurses tend to read nursing journals, doctors read medical journals, and so on. Walk through

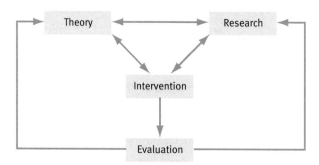

Figure 18.1 From theory to practice and back again.

most hospital libraries and you will not see a psychology journal. Yet most psychological research is published in psychology journals – not medical journals, and not nursing journals. As Richard Lazarus (2000: 667) noted, 'The lack of collaboration and communication between researcher and clinician . . . is a familiar and painful topic for most psychologists'. He went on to say that 'It is disheartening that so few researchers accept the responsibility of making the relevance of their research clear to the practitioner, and so few clinicians pay attention to such research even when it has implications for clinical practice'. Although Lazarus was referring primarily to the situation in the USA, his comments also reflect the situation elsewhere in the world.

If reaching and influencing individual health-care professionals is difficult, how *can* psychology influence health care? One way is to publish in relevant journals. Another is through its influence on higher integrative policies. Health-care professionals provide care. But the type of care they provide is constrained by a number of bodies external to them. A number of national psychology and other professional bodies have produced guidelines on psychological care, mostly (it must be admitted) in the treatment of mental health problems or more general therapy issues (working with young people, professional standards, and so on), but some of which may be relevant to the care of people with physical health problems. Even more influential than these, though, may be guidelines for care produced by governments and government-sponsored organisations (to which we provide some useful internet links at the end of the chapter). In the United Kingdom, for example, the National Institute for Health and Clinical Excellence (NICE) is responsible for producing treatment guidelines for a variety of health conditions treated within the National Health Service. Still other bodies are responsible for ensuring that these guidelines are followed. These guidelines are the strongest influence on the nature of health care, and can be extremely detailed, noting the types of drugs and dosages that can be given, the types of psychological therapy that are considered effective and should be used (and for how long any form of therapy should last), and so on. Some of these guidelines have a strong focus on the treatment of psychological problems, such as anxiety, depression and PTSD or medical problems where there is an acknowledged role for psychological interventions such as patients with cardiac disorders. Others deal with clearly medical issues such as anaemia in chronic kidney disease and caesarean section. However, even here psychological factors are acknowledged. The first page of text of the NICE guidelines for the 'treatment of acutely ill patients in hospital' runs as follows:

- 'This guideline offers best practice advice on the care of adult patients within the acute hospital setting. Treatment and care should take into account patients' needs and preferences. People with an acute illness should, if appropriate, have the opportunity to make informed decisions about their care and treatment, in partnership with their healthcare professionals . . .

- Good communication between healthcare professionals and patients is essential. It should be supported by evidence-based written information tailored to the patient's needs. Treatment and care, and the information patients are given about it, should be culturally appropriate. It should also be accessible to people with additional needs such as physical, sensory or learning disabilities, and to people who do not speak or read English.

■ If the patient agrees, carers and relatives should have the opportunity to be involved in decisions about treatment and care. Carers and relatives should also be given the information and support they need.'

The research reported in Chapter 10 has clearly contributed to this emphasis on good communication between health professionals and their patients. Clearly, health psychology has made a contribution, and an acknowledged contribution, to the care of critically ill patients through its influence on care guidelines. It has also contributed to more specific guidelines including re-habilitation following myocardial infarction and the implantation of ICDs (see Chapter 17). As guidelines develop for the care of patients with a variety of disorders, we can confidently expect psychological care and interventions to be integrated into them. But despite this optimism, our contribution may be far from optimal. And there is even evidence to show that inclusion within guidelines does not guarantee the implementation of any form of care.

Implementing (or not) clinical guidelines

bronchiolitis
inflammation of the bronchioles, the smallest air passages of the lungs. It is a common childhood disorder.

Unfortunately, even when a fully informed evidence base and written guide-lines of best practice exist, and therefore the gap between research and practice has theoretically been bridged, there is no guarantee that they will actually be implemented by the health professions concerned. Touzet *et al.* (2007), for example, reported on the impact of new guidelines for French doctors on the primary care of **bronchiolitis**. This study showed only a slight increase in adherence to the guidelines for the use of non-validated drugs (6.6 per cent adherence before and 14.3 per cent after), provision of general advice (29.0 per cent adherence before and 57.1 per cent after) and physical therapy (91.9 per cent adherence before and 98.8 per cent after). This finding is by no means unique – even asking staff to engage in relatively simple tasks such as hand-washing following patient contact has proven extremely difficult. The NHS Centre for Reviews and Dissemination report, *Effective Health Care: Getting Evidence into Practice* (1999) noted that 'Unless research-based evidence and guidance is incorporated into practice, efforts to improve the quality of care will be wasted. Implementing evidence may require health professionals to change long-held patterns of behaviour' (NHS Centre for Reviews and Dissemination 1999: 1). They highlighted the following factors that may reduce the uptake of clinical guidelines:

■ weaknesses in communicating the evidence base to practitioners;

■ conflicting sources of information and opinion being available to practitioners (such as patient preferences, which can contradict global recommendations);

■ a tendency to individually tailor responses and make decisions that may not always adhere to guidelines[1];

[1] An interesting example of this can be found in the clinical work of a Professor of General Practice known by one of the authors who has written several articles arguing that General Practitioners should not prescribe antibiotics to people with a cold, as there is no infection to treat, and the cause is a virus. He nevertheless does occasionally prescribe antibiotics at such a time 'just to be sure', despite no evidence of infection.

■ difficulties in getting the right people to work together to implement change (for example, to involve a health promotion adviser in a general practice making changes aimed at improving smoking cessation);

■ resistance to change, which is amplified by health professionals' stress levels.

Other factors include:

■ *Personal attitudes and beliefs* regarding the *target behaviour* (their own and/or the patients' behaviour), the *treatment* (for example, attitudes towards HRT (hormone replacement therapy), chemotherapy, child immunisation, abortion) and the *condition* (e.g. obesity, drug use, heart disease, AIDS, chronic fatigue syndrome);

■ *Personal characteristics of the professional*: age, gender, culture and ethnic values or norms may all impact on the willingness to make any required changes;

■ *Information content*: any changes will not be implemented if they are not seen as credible or applicable to health professionals, patients or patient groups;

■ *Information transfer*: deficient communication of information due to the problems of communication within a large and complex organisation such as a hospital or health-care system;

■ *Transferability*: staff may argue that 'what works in research may not work in practice';

■ *Environmental/organisational issues*: staff may consider there not to be enough time, staff, or support in making any changes to their practice. They may also consider the changes to be too expensive.

Given these broad-ranging potential weaknesses in the system, it is not surprising that efforts are being made to try to address this situation. However, simply providing research information alone has been shown to be insufficient to alter an individual practitioner's health practice. Oxman *et al.* (1995), for example, reviewed 102 studies of interventions to improve health-care delivery, and found that interventions in which information on 'what to do' was distributed passively to health professionals showed little evidence that the health professionals had adopted the recommended changes to their practice. Unfortunately, even following what they termed 'targeted education' in an attempt to increase adherence to guidelines, Vikman *et al.* (2004) reported only modest increases in adherence to guidelines for the treatment of high-risk cardiac patients. Nevertheless, the changes that were made did result in improved survival rates. Even more complex interventions, including training in the new approach combined with feedback on practice may have only moderate effects on behaviour. Furthermore, these multifaceted interventions tend to cost more, which is a further barrier to change, and one that needs to be overcome by politicians and funders (Chaillet *et al.* 2006).

The need for health psychologists to engage politically

Despite this rather pessimistic take on the likelihood of uptake of new types of care, health psychologists do need to engage in appropriate dissemination

Plate 18.2 To make an increasing difference to the health of our nations, health psychologists need to disseminate their findings to a wide audience, including health professionals, educators and policy makers.

Source: Bananastock/Photolibrary.com

to health-care practitioners and, ideally, to policy makers – and need to become better at it. Having greater professional 'status', as implied in the British example of stage 2 professional recognition for example (see companion website), and the increasing presence of health psychology 'practitioners' in health-care settings, will go some way towards making health psychology voices 'heard'. However, there is some concern that psychologists are reluctant to use their carefully collected evidence to provide 'guidelines' for practice. Johnson (1999) suggested that this wariness is, in part, due to psychologists' training in being critically aware of limitations in a knowledge base; for example, we typically encourage students (and subsequently researchers) to become increasingly critical in their thinking and in their interpretation of research methodologies and evidence. Johnson concluded that: 'I sometimes think we spend more time criticizing each other than we do promoting our accomplishments. In the meantime, other health professionals are more than willing to write practice guidelines and identify standards of care in areas where psychology has greater expertise' (p. 330). To 'sell' our findings to practitioners and policy makers, we need to have confidence in both our findings and ourselves.

In addition to learning how to better 'sell' the findings of health psychology research to health professions and policy makers, Murray and Campbell (2003) argued that health psychologists need to engage more effectively at a socio-political level. To do so, they argued, health psychology needs to broaden its approaches to encompass sociocultural, economic and political aspects of health and health care. (This book has acknowledged this need in a whole chapter addressing social inequalities in health, and integrated elsewhere in the book are many of the criticisms targeted at mainstream health psychologists by critical health psychologists.) The perception of psychology, and by default, health psychology, is that we develop and test our theories and methods at an individual level. This traditional narrowness of focus has, Murray and Campbell noted, held back the effectiveness of strategies to improve health on a large scale (such as reducing HIV infection in sub-Saharan Africa, promoting healthier diets in the West), because salient aspects of the micro and macro socio-economic and political environment that act to maintain inequalities in health are ignored. Health psychology, Murray and Campbell proposed, needs to engage in some reflection in order to move forward in a more 'actionable' manner. Schwarz and Carpenter (1999, cited in Davey-Smith *et al.* 2001) also noted that focusing on individual-level determinants of health instead of macro-level determinants (such as income or poverty levels), leads to individualised interventions that fail to address the question, or the solution, appropriately.

What do YOU think?	So, what do you think? How *should* psychology and psychologist attempt to influence key players both in health care and other spheres? What can individuals do to disseminate good psychological practice? And what should learned and professional bodies do to promote the discipline? Who are the key players psychologists should influence? Should they seek allies in other health professions such as nurses or occupational therapists, disciplines for which psychology is a core element of their work? Should we influence politicians, leaders of health services, or others? Who would you target as people or positions to influence, and how would you set about this?

Keep it simple

One key element that has only briefly been touched upon in this chapter is that interventions are more likely to be implemented by both health professionals and their clients if they are relatively simple and easy to implement. One of the authors of this book (PB) was made acutely aware of this in a discussion with colleagues in an academic department of General Practice in which he was working at the time. He was thinking of researching a group intervention targeted at depressed cardiac patients to see whether it would reduce both depression and the incidence of recurrent myocardial infarction (see Chapter 17). The discussion revolved around whether it would be better to run the groups in the weeks immediately after the intervention (and therefore be able to prevent any depression becoming chronic, but also risk treating people who would naturally recover without any intervention) or wait for six months and treat people whose depression had become chronic (and potentially harder to treat). Unfortunately, the debate was rather cut short when one of the GPs noted that even if such an intervention were to work, there are so few psychologists who would be able to run such groups (and no likely funding within the NHS), that no GP would be able to send their patients to it! As a result of this discussion, PB went on to develop a one-page written intervention, based around active distraction, designed to reduce distress in women undergoing genetic risk assessment (Bennett *et al.* 2007).

Whatever the impact of this discussion on PB's career, the discussion held a key truth. Psychologists and others can develop many and complex interventions, but unless they are implementable within the context of a busy, and tightly resourced health-care service (as they all are), they will not be taken up by health-care professionals, and managers will not fund them. Interventions such as the Recurrent Coronary Prevention Program (which worked) and the ENRICHD study (which didn't) described in Chapter 17 may show the potential impact of complex and extended psychological interventions on health. But even if both had proved enormously successful, neither would be implemented in most existing health services. Interventions such as establishing implementation intentions or using simple distraction techniques to reduce worry may be less glamorous than these hugely expensive multifactorial studies, but they may ultimately be of more benefit. Health psychologists may usefully concentrate on this type of intervention if they want their interventions to be of value in the health-care system.

RESEARCH FOCUS

Skevington, S.M., Day, R., Chisholm, A. and Trueman, P. (2005). How much do doctors use quality of life information in primary care? Testing the trans-theoretical model of behaviour change. *Quality of Life Research,* 14: 911–22.

The authors note that many quality of life (QoL) scales have been developed in recent years for general (i.e. measuring QoL across a number of health conditions) and specific (measuring QoL for one specific condition) use, and that QoL is acknowledged as an important outcome measure in health care. However, there is little empirical evidence showing whether doctors are actually measuring and using this information in clinical practice. The authors identify three benefits of doctors using generic QoL scales: (i) they can use the same scale over a variety of conditions, (ii) they enable comparisons between groups of patients with many different diagnoses, and can be used for audit purposes, and (iii) norms are available for 'well' people, giving them additional baseline information about the quality of their patients' life. The present study aimed to measure how and why general practitioners (family doctors) used, or did not use, measures of QoL.

Method

Procedure and sample
The study comprised a cross-sectional national postal survey of 800 British GPs using names taken from the UK Medical Directory. A pilot questionnaire was tested on 200 doctors, and then the main sample (n = 600) was derived by taking the first doctor's name on every seventh page of this document. The questionnaire was mailed to each GP, with a stamped addressed envelope in which to return the completed questionnaire. A reminder phone call was made if this was not returned within two weeks. A second reminder was sent in the post two weeks later, if necessary.

Questionnaire
The GP's were asked the following questions:

- the stage of change they were in in relation to the use of QoL measures (pre-contemplation, contemplation, planning, action, maintenance);

■ whether they had ever used QoL information (either 'general unrecorded discussion', 'informal note taking' or 'use of formal standardised questionnaires') in daily practice and if so, why (or why not);

■ their sources of knowledge about QoL, and the formal measures of QoL they had used or were aware of;

■ what difficulties they experienced in using QoL information.

Findings

The final sample achieved a 38 per cent response rate (n = 280), of which 39 per cent were women, with an overall median age of between 36 and 50 years. The authors suggest that this made the sample reasonably representative of GPs (in fact, this was a good response rate for a questionnaire sent to GPs, although less than optimal in an absolute sense).

Responses to the stages of change question, showed that 2 per cent of the sample did not intend to use QoL information; 22 per cent had not thought, or barely thought, about using it; 18 per cent had thought about it but were unlikely to use it; 7 per cent planned to use it, and 36 per cent did use it but only irregularly. Only 15 per cent said they used it regularly. The majority of GPs (59 per cent) said they made informal records about QoL. A further 28 per cent assessed it through general discussion but without recording the outcome. Only 11 per cent reported using formal standardised QoL questionnaires.

More than half the GP's (59 per cent) had not seen any evidence about the use of QoL measures. A total of 52 per cent were not aware of any formal measures of QoL. Of those that were aware of them, relatively few knew about well-validated and widely used measures of QoL, including the Short Form-36 (14 per cent), WHOQOL (12 per cent), Nottingham Health Profile (9 per cent), Sickness Impact Profile (7 per cent), SF-12 (6 per cent) or Euroqol (5 per cent). Only 1 per cent knew about QALYs, which is the most popular method used in the NHS.

One hundred and seventeen GPs gave reasons for why they did not use QoL measures in daily practice.

Do not understand how QoL information would be used	51
Do not fully understand the evidence	19
Do not know what QoL is	8
No access to QoL information	7
No evidence available	5
No resources or time	4
Have not seen any benefits from using QoL information	4
Do not trust the evidence	1
The evidence is not relevant to GPs	1

GPs were asked whether there were any practical difficulties in using QoL information: 65 per cent of GPs replied. They reported that the greatest barrier to using QoL information was time (68 per cent). This included time taken to complete questionnaires, the need for longer consultations, and to record and interpret data. 'Added burden' was also an important theme, involving both burden to GPs (13 per cent), to patients (5 per cent), and the burden of acquiring new skills or formal training (6 per cent). Shortage of knowledge, lack of expertise about QoL measurement and being unable to gain access to recent information about scales presented additional difficulties. There were also concerns about using QoL data effectively.

continued

Discussion

The authors considered that these results indicated considerable interest in QoL information among the GPs who responded to the survey and many believe that QoL is important. However, there was little evidence that GPs were using QoL questionnaires and most of those who obtain QoL information do so in a relatively unstructured way within the clinical interview. This may be because they are very busy and short of time, short of relevant and accurate information, are not paid to do this work and do not know how to integrate it into their routine. This finding strongly suggests that knowledge about how to evaluate medical and health interventions in an evidence-based manner has had a small and limited impact in primary care. There is also a widespread misunderstanding about what QoL is, and scepticism about whether it can really be measured.

Perhaps the key message is that unless changes to practice are seen as useful to both doctor (in this case) and patient, and can be easily assimilated into daily practice, they are unlikely to be integrated into health care.

. . . and finally, be positive

While this textbook has highlighted many of the challenges faced by our discipline (such as definitional clarity, choice of assessment techniques and tools, inclusion and consideration of sociocultural influences on health and illness), it has highlighted the many domains in which health psychology has contributed significantly to understanding (e.g. health behaviour and behaviour change, stress and coping, illness processes and outcomes, psychosocial interventions). There is a lot to be positive about, but clearly not complacent, and many questions remain. For example, do implementation intentions work in clinical samples? Do stage-based activity interventions work in the long term? Does coping really make a difference? Perhaps we should also take note of other areas in psychology. Much of health psychology tends to focus on problems – preventing illness, coping with illness and so on. As well as being optimistic in ourselves, we can also learn from developments in the field of 'positive psychology' (e.g. Seligman and Csikszentmihalyi 2000), which bring with them many other opportunities for health psychology to strengthen its evidence base. Research in the 'positive psychology' tradition has shown that out of many potentially negative situations come positives (for example, reaffirmed love, or the discovery of unknown personal strengths, caused by entering a spousal caring role), and that positive affect and the finding of 'meaning' in stressful situations can be adaptational (e.g Folkman and Moscowitz 2000). Underlying many psychosocial interventions to improve adjustment or behavioural change has been the assumption that certain stressors (e.g. illness, caring) inevitably elicit negative affect and cognition, and that these need to be reduced in order to improve outcome. In contrast, positive psychology encourages thinking to turn to enhancement of positive affect (particularly that which is congruent with one's current situation), such as hope or optimism in a situation where goals are attainable, humour or positive reappraisal where goals are not so easily reached. Furthermore, in the area of preventive health, health psychology research has identified 'protective' factors for health as well as risk factors for morbidity. For example, think of the research supporting positive associations between social support, or optimism, and positive adjustment to stressful events. Such findings provide opportunities for interventions that are quite different in emphasis from those offered by the findings of negative associations between hostility, stress responses and coronary heart disease. We must not fall into the trap of assuming that we can only advise on 'what not to do'.

Health psychology will not stand still. Its contribution to the health of society is likely to grow as our knowledge base and our confidence in it grows, and as external bodies grow in confidence as to the important role psychology has to play in relation to health. Keep in touch via our website. New developments in the professional and academic practice of this discipline will be highlighted and updated annually on the companion website to this text: www.pearsoned.co.uk/morrison.

Summary

This final chapter has attempted to draw together much of the work described in this book and to give the reader a picture of the ways in which health psychology research can contribute to health practice. Although health psychology is a theory-led discipline, its goals are applied, and we have attempted in this chapter to make the links between theory and practice evident. In addition, we have noted that there is a need for health psychologists to engage more politically and to 'sell' themselves and their (cost-effective) 'goods' more effectively to policy makers and health practitioners. In doing so, we would hope to maximise the impact of health psychology as a discipline upon health psychology as a practice. Our final aim should be to strengthen the links between health psychology and health professional practice in order to benefit all of us who will at some point in their lives enter the health-care system.

Further reading

Norman, P., Abraham, C. and Conner, M. (2000). *Understanding and Changing Health Behaviour: From Health Beliefs to Self-Regulation*. Psychology Press.
This book focuses on a range of key social cognitive factors involved in behavioural change, using examples from a number of applied settings that include smoking cessation, condom use and breast examination.

Rutter, D. and Quine, L. (2002). *Changing Health Behaviour*. Buckingham: Open University Press.
This well-written text highlights many areas of intervention in which health and social psychologists have been at the forefront. Chapters describe specific theory-

based interventions including those directed at safer sex practices, smoking cessation, reduced fat intake, uptake of screening for colorectal or cervical cancer, the use of cycling helmets by schoolchildren and pedestrian safety. It also includes a useful chapter by Steve Sutton that raises some of the difficulties in turning research findings into effective interventions.

The Improved Clinical Effectiveness through Behavioural Research Group (ICEBeRG) (2006). Designing theoretically-informed implementation interventions. *Implementation Science*, 1: 4.
A freely accessible paper examining issues in the translation of psychological theory to psychological practice.

Eccles, M., Grimshaw, J., Walker, A., Johnston, M. and Pitts, N. (2005). Changing the behavior of healthcare professionals: the use of theory in promoting the uptake of research findings. *Journal of Clinical Epidemiology*, 58, 107-112.
Another paper examining how to translate theory to practice in the context of health professional behaviour.

In addition to these static texts, it may be interesting to go to websites describing developments in the profession of health psychology. Some examples of such sites (extant in 2007) are:

The Australian Psychological Society:
http://www.psychology.org.au/community/specialist/health
The site provides a description of the role of health psychologists, as seen by the APS.

The British Psychological Society:
http://www.bps.org.uk/careers/accredited-courses/accredited-courses.cfm?action=postgrad
This takes you to a description of a variety of post-graduate courses, including training in health psychology.

http://www.bps.org.uk/careers/areas/health.cfm
The site provides a description of the role of health psychologists, as seen by the BPS.

http://www.health-psychology.org.uk/menuItems/HPUpdate.php Health Psychology Update
This is the newsletter of the BPS Division of Health Psychology.One step back and you are in the main site of the British Division of Health Psychology, which may be worth keeping up with.

The European Health Psychology Society
http://www.ehps.net/800/index.html
This introductory page to EHPS, leads to information about access to conferences and other potentially relevant information. Of particular note is that it also allows access to the EHPS's newsletter, *The European Health Psychologist*, which regularly presents updates on the professional developments in health psychology within Europe.

The New Zealand Psychology Society
http://www.psychology.org.nz/psychinnz/careers.html
There is no mention of health psychology on this site at the moment; but watch this space.

The International Society of Behavioural Medicine
http://www.isbm.info

According to the ISBM, 'Behavioral Medicine is the interdisciplinary field concerned with the development and integration of behavioral, psychosocial, and biomedical science knowledge and techniques relevant to the understanding of health and illness, and the application of this knowledge and these techniques to prevention, diagnosis, treatment and rehabilitation.' As such, it has much in common with the applied end of health psychology (and much that is different). The website may be of interest.

Some sources of published clinical guidelines. These are central government resourced guideline resources. Other guidelines may be produced by (usually) specific medical organisations involved in the treatment of specific disorders. Psychology guidelines tend to be more general, and not specific to conditions or types of intervention:

http://www.nhmrc.gov.au/publications/subjects/clinical.htm (Australia)
http://www.nice.org.uk/ (England)
http://www.sign.ac.uk/guidelines/published/index.html (Scotland)
http://www.guideline.gov/ (USA)

Visit the website at **www.pearsoned.co.uk/morrison** for additional resources to help you with your study, including multiple choice questions, weblinks and flashcards.

GLOSSARY

A   **acceptance coping:** accepting the reality of a situation and that it cannot easily be changed.

ACE inhibitors: angiotensin II causes the muscles surrounding blood vessels to contract and thereby narrows the blood vessels. Angiotension Converting Enzyme (ACE) inhibitors decrease the production of angiotensin II, allowing blood vessels to dilate, and reduce blood pressure.

acetylcholine: a white crystalline derivative of choline that is released at the ends of nerve fibres in the parasympathetic nervous system and is involved in the transmission of nerve impulses in the body.

adrenal glands: endocrine glands, located above each kidney. Comprises the cortex, which secretes several steroid hormones, and the medulla, which secretes noradrenaline.

adrenaline: a neurotransmitter and hormone secreted by the adrenal medulla that increases physiological activity in the body, including stimulation of heart action and an increase in blood pressure and metabolic rate. Also known as epinephrine.

aetiology (etiology): the cause of disease.

affective: to do with affect or mood and emotions.

age-specific mortality: typically presented as the number of deaths per 100,000, per annum, according to certain age groups, for example comparing rates of death from cancer in 2001 between those aged 45–54 with those aged 55–64.

agonist: a drug that simulates the effects of neurotransmitters, such as the serotonin agonist fluoxetine, which induces satiety (reduces hunger).

Alcoholics Anonymous: a worldwide self-help organisation for people with alcohol-related problems. Based on the belief that alcoholism is a physical, psychological and spiritual illness and can be controlled by abstinence. The twelve steps provide a framework for achieving this.

ambivalence: the simultaneous existence of both positive and negative evaluations of an attitude object, which could be both cognitive and emotional.

ambulatory blood pressure: blood pressure measured over a period of time using an automatic blood pressure monitor which can measure blood pressure while the individual wearing it engages in their everyday activities.

angina: severe pain in the chest associated with a temporary insufficient supply of blood to the heart.

antibodies: immunoglobulins produced in response to an antigen.

antigen: unique protein found on the surface of a pathogen that enables the immune system to recognise that pathogen as a foreign substance and therefore produce antibodies to fight it. Vaccinations introduce specially prepared viruses or bacteria into a body, and these have antigens.

antioxidant: oxidation of low-density lipoprotein (LDL or 'bad') cholesterol has been shown to be important in the development of fatty deposits in the arteries; anti-oxidants are chemical properties (polyphenols) of some substances (e.g. red wine) thought to inhibit the process of oxidation.

anti-retroviral drugs: drugs that prevent the reproduction of a type of virus known as a retrovirus. Most well known in the treatment of the HIV.

aorta: the main trunk of the systemic arteries, carrying blood from the left side of the heart to the arteries of all limbs and organs except the lungs.

appraisals: interpretations of situations, events or behaviour that a person makes.

arteriosclerosis: loss of elasticity and hardening of the arteries.

atherosclerosis: formation of fatty plaque in the arteries.

atheroma: fatty deposit in the intima (inner lining) of an artery.

atopic dermatitis: a number of conditions, including eczema, involving an inflammatory response of the skin.

atrial fibrillation: a heart rhythm disorder (arrhythmia). It involves a very rapid heart rate, in which the atria (upper chambers of the heart) contract in a very rapid and disorganised manner and fail to pump blood effectively through the heart.

attention: generally refers to the selection of some stimuli over others for internal processing.

attributions: a person's perceptions of what causes beliefs, feelings, behaviour and actions (based on attribution theory).

autoimmune condition: a group of diseases, including type 1 diabetes, Crohn's disease and rheumatoid arthritis, characterised by abnormal functioning of the immune system in which it produces antibodies against its own tissues – it treats 'self' as 'non-self'.

avoidant coping: a style of coping that involves emotional regulation by avoiding confrontation with a stressful situation. Analogous to emotion-focused coping.

B

bad news (interview): conversation between health professional (usually a doctor) and patient in which they are told 'bad news', usually that their illness has a very poor prognosis and they may die.

baroreceptors: sensory nerve endings that are stimulated by changes in pressure. Located in the walls of blood vessels such as the carotid sinus.

basal ganglia: area of the brain responsible for complex motor coordination.

B cell: a form of lymphocyte involved in destruction of antigens. Memory B cells provide long-term immunity against previously encountered pathogens.

behavioural immunogen: a behavioural practice considered to be health-protective, e.g. exercise.

behavioural pathogen: a behavioural practice thought to be damaging to health, e.g. smoking.

behaviourism: the belief that psychology is the study of observables and therefore that behaviour, not mental processes, is central.

benefit finding: a process of finding beneficial outcomes as a consequence of what is normally seen as a negative event, such as developing cancer or being infected with the HIV.

benign (tumour): tumour that cannot spread by invasion or metastasis. It does not carry the risk to health that a malignant tumour carries.

beta-blockers: block the action of epinephrine and norepinephrine on β-adrenergic receptors, which mediate the 'fight or flight' response, within the heart and in muscles surrounding the arteries. In doing so, they reduce increases in blood pressure associated with sympathetic activation.

β-blocker medication: a form of medication that acts to slow down and strengthen the heart contractions. Acts on the adrenergic receptors within the heart muscle.

bile: a digestive juice, made in the liver and stored in the gallbladder. Involved in the digestion of fats in the small intestine.

biofeedback: technique of using monitoring devices to provide information regarding an autonomic bodily function, such as heart rate or blood pressure. Used in an attempt to gain some voluntary control over that function.

biomedical model: a view that diseases and symptoms have an underlying physiological explanation.

biopsy: the removal of a small piece of tissue for microscopic examination and/or culture, usually to help to make a diagnosis.

biopsychosocial: a view that diseases and symptoms can be explained by a combination of physical, social, cultural and psychological factors (cf. Engel 1977).

blunters: a general coping style that involves minimising or avoiding the source of threat or stress, i.e. avoiding threat-relevant information (as opposed to **monitors**).

body mass index: a measurement of the relative percentages of fat and muscle mass in the human body, in which weight in kilograms is divided by height in metres and the result used as an index of obesity.

bone marrow biopsy: usually performed under local anaesthetic by making a small incision into the skin. A biopsy needle is then pushed through the bone and takes a sample of marrow from the centre of the bone. Marrow contains platelets, phagocytes and lymphocytes.

bronchiolitis: inflammation of the bronchioles, the smallest air passages of the lungs. It is a common childhood disorder.

C

carcinogenesis: the process by which normal cells become cancer cells (i.e. carcinoma).

cardiac arrest: situation in which the heart ceases to beat.

cardiac event: generic term for a variety of end-points of coronary heart disease, including a myocardial infarction, angina and cardiac arrest.

cardiovascular: pertaining to the heart and blood vessels.

carotid artery: the main artery that takes blood from the heart via the neck to the brain.

catastrophic thoughts: automatic thoughts that exaggerate the negative aspects of any situation.

catastrophising: the act of constructing **catastrophic thoughts**.

catecholamines: these chemical substances are brain neurotransmitters and include adrenaline and noradrenaline.

causal attribution: where a person attributes the cause of an event, feeling or action to themselves, to others, to chance or to some other causal agent.

CD4+ cells: otherwise known as helper T cells, these are involved in the proliferation of cytotoxic T cells as part of the immune response. HIV infection impairs their ability to provide this function.

cell suicide: a type of cell death in which the cell uses specialised cellular machinery to kill itself.

central nervous system: that part of the nervous system consisting of the brain and spinal cord.

cervical smear: smear of cells taken from the cervix to examine for the presence of cell changes indicating risk of cancer.

chronic bronchitis: an inflammation of the bronchi, the main air passages in the lungs, which persists for a long period or repeatedly recurs. Characterised by excessive bronchial mucus and a cough that produces sputum for three months or more in at least two consecutive years.

chronic obstructive airways disease: a persistent airway obstruction associated with combinations of chronic bronchitis, small airways disease, asthma and emphysema.

clot busters: drugs which dissolve clots associated with myocardial infarction and can prevent damage to the heart following such an event. Are best used within one hour of the infarction.

cognitive dissonance: a state in which conflicting or inconsistent cognitions produce a state of tension or discomfort (dissonance). People are motivated to reduce the dissonance, often by rejecting one set of beliefs in favour of the other.

cognitive restructuring: a reconsideration of automatic negative or catastrophic thoughts to make them more in line with reality.

cognitive schema (schemata): set of unconscious beliefs about the world and ourselves that shape more conscious cognitive responses to events that impinge on us.

cold pressor test: procedure in which participants place their arm in a mixture of water and ice maintaining the water temperature at between 0 and 3°C.

collectivist: a cultural philosophy that emphasises the individual as part of a wider unit and places emphasis on actions motivated by collective, rather than individual, needs and wants.

colonoscopy: a minor surgical procedure in which a small piece of bowel wall is cut from the colon. This can then be tested for the presence of malignant cells.

colostomy: a surgical procedure that creates an opening (stoma) in the abdomen for the drainage of stool from the large intestine (colon). It may be temporary or permanent.

colposcopy: a method used to identify cells that may develop into cancer of the cervix. Sometimes follows a cervical smear if abnormalities are found. A colposcope is a low-power microscope.

comparative optimism: initially termed 'unrealistic optimism', this term refers to an individual's estimate of their risk of experiencing a negative event compared with similar others (Weinstein and Klein 1996).

congestive heart failure: a disorder in which the heart loses its ability to pump blood efficiently. As a consequence, many organs do not receive enough oxygen and nutrients, leading to the potential for them to become damaged and, therefore, not work effectively.

coping effectiveness training: a specialist form of stress management in which participants are taught to alter the nature of their coping efforts to suit the particular type of demands they are facing: using emotion-focused coping where the situation cannot be changed and problem-focused coping where it can.

coping self-efficacy: the belief that one can carry out a particular coping response in a given set of circumstances.

coronary angioplasty: a procedure where a small balloon is inserted into the blocked coronary artery of a person with **atheroma**.

coronary artery bypass graft: surgical procedure in which veins or arteries from elsewhere in the patient's body are grafted from the aorta to the coronary arteries, bypassing blockages caused by atheroma in the cardiac arteries and improving the blood supply to the heart muscle.

coronary heart disease: a narrowing of the blood vessels that supply blood and oxygen to the heart. Results from a build-up of fatty material and plaque (**atherosclerosis**). Can result in **angina** or **myocardial infarction**.

corticosteroids: powerful anti-inflammatory hormones (including cortisol) made naturally in the body or synthetically for use as drugs.

cortisol: a stress hormone that increases the availability of energy stores and fats to fuel periods of high physiological activity. It also inhibits inflammation of damaged tissue.

Crohn's disease: autoimmune disease that can affect any part of the gastrointestinal tract but most commonly occurs in the ileum (the area where the small and large intestine meet).

cross-sectional design: a study that collects data from a sample on one occasion only. Ideally, the sample should be selected to be representative of the population under study.

D

decisional balance: where the costs of behaviour are weighed up against the benefits of that behaviour.

defibrillator: a machine that uses an electric current to stop any irregular and dangerous activity of the heart's muscles. It can be used when the heart has stopped (**cardiac arrest**) or when it is beating in a highly irregular (and ineffective) manner.

denial response: taking a view that denies any negative implications of an event or stimulus. If subconscious, it is considered a defence mechanism.

diabetes (type 1 and 2): a lifelong disease marked by high levels of sugar in the blood and a failure to transfer this to organs that need it. It can be caused by too little insulin (type 1) resistance to insulin (type 2), or both.

diastolic blood pressure: the minimum pressure of the blood on the walls of the arteries between heart beats (measured in relation to **systolic blood pressure**).

dispositional pessimism: having a generally negative outlook on life and a tendency to anticipate negative outcomes (as opposed to dispositional optimism).

distancing response: taking a detached view, often a scientific view, of an event or stimulus in order to reduce emotional activation.

diuretics: elevates the rate of bodily urine excretion, reducing the amount of fluid within the cardiovascular system, and reducing pressure within it.

drug abuse: involves use of a drug that results in significant social or work-related problems.

drug dependence: usually a progression from drug abuse. Involves dependence on the drug to achieve a desired psychological state, withdrawal symptoms in the absence of the drug, and social and work-related problems.

dualism: the idea that the mind and body are separate entities (cf. Descartes).

E

efficacy: Bandura's technical term analogous to confidence.

egocentric: self-centred, such as in the pre-operational stage (age 2–7) of children, when they see things only from their own perspective (cf. Piaget).

empathy: an understanding of the situation from the individual's viewpoint.

emphysema: a late effect of chronic infection or irritation of the bronchial tubes. When the bronchi become irritated, some of the airways may be obstructed or the walls of the tiny air spaces may tear, trapping air in the lung beyond them. As a result, the lungs may become enlarged, at the same time becoming less efficient in exchanging oxygen for carbon dioxide.

empiricism: arising from a school of thought that all knowledge can be obtained through experience.

endocrine glands: glands that produce and secrete hormones into the blood or lymph systems. Includes the pituitary and adrenal glands, and the islets of Langerhans in the pancreas. These hormones may affect one organ or tissue, or the entire body.

endorphins: naturally occurring opiate-like chemicals released in the brain and spinal cord. They reduce the experience of pain and can induce feelings of relaxation or pleasure. Associated with the so-called 'runner's high'.

endoscopy: the use of a thin, lighted tube (called an endoscope) to examine the inside of the body.

epidemiology: the study of patterns of disease in various populations and the association with other factors such as lifestyle factors. Key concepts include mortality, morbidity, prevalence, incidence, absolute risk and relative risk. Type of question: Who gets this disease? How common is it?

erythrocyte: a mature blood cell that contains **haemoglobin** to carry oxygen to the bodily tissues.

exercise programme: a key element of most cardiac rehabilitation, including a progressive increase in exercise usually starting in a gym, sometimes developing into exercise in the home and beyond.

exogenous: relating to things outside the body.

exposure therapy: a form of therapy involving exposure to traumatic memories, based on the theoretical assumption that continued exposure will result in a gradual reduction in the level of fear associated with such memories.

expressed emotion: the disclosure of emotional experiences as a means of reducing stress; often achieved by describing the experience in writing.

eye movement desensitisation and reprocessing: a form of therapy for post-traumatic stress disorder involving exposure to traumatic memories while repeatedly moving the eyes. Its method of working is not clear. However, the most popular theory is that when the eyes move back and forth this creates brain activity similar to that which occurs during REM (rapid eye movement) sleep. This may help the brain to process the 'stuck' material, enabling the person to arrive at an adaptive resolution.

F

false positive result: a situation in which an individual is told that they may have a disease or are at risk of disease, but subsequent tests show that they are not at risk or do not have the disease.

fine needle aspiration: entails placing a very thin needle into a mass within the breast and extracting cells for microscopic evaluation. It takes seconds, and the discomfort is comparable with that of a blood test.

fistulas: formation of small passages that connect the intestine with other organs or the skin.

G

gallbladder: a structure on the underside of the liver on the right side of the abdomen. It stores the bile that is produced in the liver before it is secreted into the intestines. This helps the body to digest fats.

gate control theory of pain: a theory of pain developed by Melzack and Wall in which a 'gate' is used as a metaphor for the chemicals, including **endorphins**, that mitigate the experience of pain.

general adaptation syndrome: a sequence of physiological responses to prolonged stress, from the alarm stage through the resistance stage to exhaustion.

H   **haemoglobin:** the main substance of the red blood cell. When oxygenated in the lungs, it is converted to oxyhaemoglobin, thus allowing the red blood cells to carry oxygen from the air in our lungs to all parts of the body.

health behaviour: behaviour performed by an individual, regardless of their health status, as a means of protecting, promoting or maintaining health, e.g. diet.

health differential: a term used to denote differences in health status and life expectancy across different groups.

health hardiness: the extent to which a person is committed to and involved in health-relevant activities, perceives control over their health and responds to health stressors as challenges or opportunities for growth.

health locus of control: the perception that one's health is under personal control; controlled by powerful others such as health professionals; or under the control of external factors such as fate or luck.

heart failure: a state in which the heart muscle is damaged or weakened and is unable to generate a cardiac output sufficient to meet the demands of the body.

high-density lipoprotein (HDL): lipoproteins are fat protein complexes in the blood that transport cholesterol, triglycerides and other lipids to various tissues. The main function of HDL appears to be to carry excess cholesterol to the liver for 're-packaging' or excretion in the bile. Higher levels of HDL seem to be protective against CHD, so HDL is sometimes referred to as 'good' cholesterol.

holistic: root word 'wholeness', holistic approaches are concerned with the whole being and its wellbeing, rather than addressing the purely physical or observable.

Human papillomavirus (HPV): a family of over 100 viruses, of which 30 types can cause genital warts and be transmitted by sexual contact. While most genital HPV come and go over the course of a few years, some HPV infections may markedly elevate the risk for cancer of the cervix.

hypertension: a condition in which blood pressure is significantly above normal levels.

hypoglycaemic episode: occurs when the body's glucose level is too low. It frequently occurs when too much insulin or oral diabetic medication is taken, not enough food is eaten, or following exercise without appropriate food intake. Symptoms include excessive sweating, paleness, fainting and eventually loss of consciousness.

hypothalamus: area of the brain that regulates appetite, sexual arousal and thirst. Also appears to have some control over emotions.

I   **illness behaviour:** behaviour that characterises a person who is sick and who seeks a remedy, e.g. taking medication. Usually precedes formal diagnosis, when behaviour is described as **sick role behaviour**.

illness cognition: the cognitive processes involved in a person's perception or interpretation of symptoms or illness and how they represent it to themselves (or to others) (cf. Croyle and Ditto 1990).

illness representations: beliefs about a particular illness and state of ill health – commonly ascribed to the five domains described by Leventhal: identity, timeline, cause, consequences and control/cure.

incidence: the number of new cases of disease occurring during a defined time interval – not to be confused with prevalence, which refers to the number of established cases of a disease in a population at any one time.

individual differences: aspects of an individual that distinguish them from other individuals or groups (e.g. age, personality).

individualistic: a cultural philosophy that places responsibility at the feet of the individual; thus behaviour is often driven by individual needs and wants rather than by community needs or wants.

inflammatory bowel disease: a group of inflammatory conditions of the large intestine and, in some cases, the small intestine. The main forms of IBD are **Crohn's disease** and **ulcerative colitis**.

irritable bowel syndrome: a disorder of the lower intestinal tract. Symptoms include pain combined with altered bowel habits resulting in diarrhoea, constipation or both. It has no obvious physiological abnormalities, so diagnosis is by the presence and pattern of symptoms.

ischaemic heart disease: a heart disease caused by a restriction of blood flow to the heart.

K

Kaposi's sarcoma: a malignant tumour of the connective tissue, often associated with AIDS. The tumours consist of bluish-red or purple lesions on the skin. They often appear first on the feet or ankles, thighs, arms, hands and face.

L

lay referral system: an informal network of individuals (e.g. friends, family, colleagues) turned to for advice or information about symptoms and other health-related matters. Often but not solely used prior to seeking a formal medical opinion.

life events: a term used to describe occurrences in a person's life which may be viewed positively or negatively but which inherently require some adjustment on the part of the person (e.g. marriage, loss of job). Such events are implicated in the experience of stress.

limbic system: a series of structures in the brain, often referred to as the 'emotional computer' because of its role in coordinating emotions. It links sensory information to emotionally relevant behaviour, in particular responses to fear and anger.

locus of control: a personality trait thought to distinguish between those who attribute responsibility for events to themselves (i.e. internal LoC) or to external factors (external LoC).

longitudinal (design): responses assessed in a study that have been taken on more than one occasion over time, either prospectively (future-oriented) or retrospectively (based on recall of past events). Prospective longitudinal studies are more powerful, and such methods are important to studies where assessment of change is important.

low-density lipoprotein (LDL): the main function of LDLs seems to be to carry cholesterol to various tissues throughout the body. LDLs are sometimes referred to as 'bad' cholesterol because elevated levels of LDL correlate most directly with **coronary heart disease**.

lower respiratory tract infection: infection of the parts of the respiratory system including the larynx, trachea, bronchi and lungs.

lumpectomy: a surgical procedure in which only the tumour and a small area of surrounding tissue are removed. Contrasts with mastectomy, in which the whole breast is removed.

lymphocyte: a type of white blood cell. Lymphocytes have a number of roles in the immune system, including the production of antibodies and other substances that fight infection and disease. Includes T and B cells.

M

malignant melanoma: a rare but potentially lethal form of skin cancer.

mammography: a low-dose X-ray procedure that creates an image of the breast. The X-ray image can be used to identify early stages of tumours.

mechanistic: a reductionist approach that reduces behaviour to the level of the organ or physical function. Associated with the **biomedical** model.

mediate/mediator: some variables may mediate the effects of others upon an outcome: for example, individual beliefs may mediate the effects of gender upon behaviour, thus gender effects would be said to be indirect, rather than direct, and beliefs would be mediator variables.

melanoma: a form of skin cancer. Usually begins in a mole and has a poor prognosis unless treated early.

meta-analysis: a review and re-analysis of pre-existing quantitative datasets that combines the analysis so as to provide large samples and high statistical power from which to draw reliable conclusions about specific effects.

migraine: differs from other headaches because it involves symptoms such as nausea, vomiting or sensitivity to light. Their exact cause is not known. However, they appear to be related to problems with blood flow through parts of the brain. At the start of a migraine, blood vessels in certain areas of the brain constrict, leading to symptoms including visual disturbances, difficulty in speaking, weakness or numbness. Minutes to hours later, the blood vessels dilate, leading to increased blood flow in the brain and a severe headache.

monitors: a generalised coping style that involves attending to the source of stress or threat and trying to deal with it directly, e.g. through information gathering/attending to threat-relevant information (as opposed to **blunters**).

morbidity: costs associated with illness such as disability, injury.

mortality: death. Generally presented as mortality statistics, i.e. the number of deaths in a given population and/or in a given year ascribed to a given condition (e.g. number of cancer deaths among women in 2000).

motivation: memories, thoughts, experiences, needs and preferences that act together to influence (drive) the type, strength and persistence of our actions.

motivational interview: developed by Miller and Rollnick, a set of procedures designed to increase motivation to change behaviour.

multiple sclerosis: a disorder of the brain and spinal cord caused by progressive damage to the myelin sheath covering of nerve cells. This results in decreased nerve functioning, which can lead to a variety of symptoms, including weakness, paralysis, tremor, pain, tingling, numbness and decreased coordination.

myelin sheath: a substance that contains both protein and fat (lipid) and surrounds all nerves outside the brain. It acts as a nerve insulator and helps in the transmission of nerve signals.

myocardial infarction: death of the heart muscle due to a stoppage of the blood supply. More often known as a heart attack.

N **natural killer (NK) cells:** cells move in the blood and attack cancer cells and virus-infected body cells.

negative affectivity: a dispositional tendency to experience persistent and pervasive negative or low mood and self concept (related to **neuroticism**).

neophobia: a persistent and chronic fear of anything new (places, events, people, objects).

neuroticism: a personality trait reflected in the tendency to be anxious, feel guilty and experience generally negative thought patterns.

neurotransmitter: a chemical messenger (e.g. adrenaline, acetylcholine) used to communicate between neurons and other neurons and other types of cell.

nicotine replacement therapy (NRT): replacement of nicotine to minimise withdrawal symptoms following the cessation of smoking. Delivered in a variety of ways, including a transdermal patch placed against the skin, which produces a measured dose of nicotine over time.

noradrenaline: this **catecholamine** is a neurotransmitter found in the brain and in the **sympathetic nervous system**. Also known as norepinephrine.

O **objective:** i.e. real, visible or systematically measurable (e.g. adrenaline levels). Generally pertains to something outside the body that can be seen by others (as opposed to **subjective**).

operant conditioning: attributed to Skinner, this theory is based on the assumption that behaviour is directly influenced by its consequences (e.g. rewards, punishments, avoidance of negative outcomes).

oral hypoglycaemic agents: various drug types, all of which reduce circulating blood sugar.

outcome expectancies: the outcome that is expected to result from behaviour, e.g. exercise will make me fitter.

P **pain threshold:** the minimum amount of pain intensity that is required before it is detected (individual variation).

pancreas: gland in which the islets of Langerhans produce insulin. Also produces and secretes digestive enzymes. Located behind the stomach.

parasympathetic nervous system: arm of the autonomic nervous system that is responsible for rest and recuperation.

pathogen: a collective name for a variety of challenges to our health and immune system, including bacteria and viruses.

patient-controlled analgesia (PCA): a technique through which small doses of analgesic drugs, usually opioids, are administered (usually by an intravenous drip and controlled by a pump) by patients themselves. It is mostly used for the control of post-operative pain.

perceived behavioural control: one's belief in personal control over a certain specific action or behaviour.

phagocyte: an immune system cell that can surround and kill micro-organisms and remove dead cells. Phagocytes include macrophages.

phantom limb pain: a phenomenon that occurs following amputation of a limb, in which the individual feels like they still have their limb, and the limb is in pain.

placebo intervention: an intervention designed to simulate a psychological intervention but not believed to be a specific therapy for the target condition.

platelets: tiny bits of protoplasm found in the blood that are essential for blood clotting. These cells bind together to form a clot and prevent bleeding at the site of injury.

post-traumatic stress disorder: a disorder that forms a response to experiencing a traumatic event. The key elements are unwanted repetitive memories of the event, often in the form of flashbacks, attempts at avoidance of such memories, and a generally raised level of arousal.

predisposing factors: factors that increase the likelihood of a person engaging in a particular behaviour, such as genetic influences on alcohol consumption.

premature mortality: death before the age it is normally expected. Usually set at deaths under the age of 75.

prevalence: the number of established cases of a disease in a population at any one time. Often described as a percentage of the overall population or cases per 100,000 people.

primary prevention: intervention aimed at changing risk factors prior to disease development.

problem-focused coping: a style of coping that involves active planning and dealing with any source of stress.

problem-focused counselling: a counselling approach developed by Gerard Egan that attempts to foster a collaborative and structured approach between counsellor and client to solving life problems.

procedural information: telling patients about the events that will occur before and after surgery, such as having a pre-medication injection, waking in the recovery room, and having a drip in their arm.

prognosis: the predicted outcome of a disease.

prosocial behaviour: behavioural acts that are positively valued by society and that may elicit positive social consequences, e.g. offering sympathy, helping others.

psychological debriefing: a procedure in which people who have been through a particular trauma talk through the trauma in a structured way with a counsellor.

psychosocial: an approach that seeks to merge a psychological (more micro- and individually oriented) approach with a social approach (macro-, more community- and interaction-oriented), for example to health.

Q **qualitative methodologies:** qualitative methods are concerned with describing (qualifying) the experience, beliefs and behaviour of a particular group of people. Data elicited is non-numerical, may or may not be generalisable to the wider population, but may generate themes of response that can be examined in further samples. The depth of material gained through qualitative work is great and allows insight into the meaning behind people's responses. Methods may include open-ended interviews, focus group discussions, taped transactions and conversations. Samples are generally small given the time demands of data collection and analysis.

quantitative methodologies: unlike **qualitative** methods, quantitative methods are concerned with counting (quantifying), i.e. data describes the frequency with which a set of beliefs are held or behaviour actioned and means of scores can be obtained and compared statistically. Larger and more representative samples can be obtained, as the method of data collection is predominantly paper-based questionnaires that are self-completed (or can be completed in the presence of a researcher). Criticised for reducing data to numerical categories at the expense of breadth of illustrative meaning.

R **radical prostatectomy:** otherwise known as a total prostatectomy, this involves using surgery to remove all of the prostate as a cure for prostate cancer.

reinforcers: factors that reward or provide a positive response following a particular behaviour or set of behaviours (positive reinforcer); or enable the removal or avoidance of an undesired state or response (negative reinforcer).

relapse prevention: a set of skills taught to people needing to achieve long-term behavioural change that prepare them to resist temptation and how to minimise the impact of any relapse should it occur. Often used with people taking addictive drugs.

repression: a defensive coping style that serves to protect the person from negative memories or anxiety-producing thoughts by preventing their gaining access to consciousness.

response shift: changes in subjective reports that may result from a reprioritisation of life expectations or recalibration of internal standards so that the construct being assessed is reconceptualised.

rheumatoid arthritis: a chronic autoimmune disease with inflammation of the joints and marked deformities. Something (possibly a virus) triggers an attack of the synovium in the joint by the immune system, which stimulates an inflammatory reaction that can lead to destruction of the joint.

risk ratio: a way of comparing whether the probability of a certain event is the same for two groups. A risk ratio of 1 implies that the event is equally likely in both groups. A risk ratio greater than 1 implies that the event is more likely in the first group. A risk ratio of less than 1 implies that the event is less likely in the first group.

S **salience:** strength and importance.

sciatica: pain down the leg, which is caused by irritation of the main nerve into the leg, the sciatic nerve. This pain tends to be caused where the nerves pass through and emerge from the lower bones of the spine (lumbar vertebrae).

self-concept: those conscious thoughts and beliefs about yourself that allow you to feel are distinct from others and that you exist as a separate person.

self-efficacy: the belief that one can perform particular behaviour in a given set of circumstances.

self-regulation: the process by which individuals monitor and adjust their behaviour, thoughts and emotions in order to maintain a balance or a sense of normal function.

self-talk: talking to oneself (internally). Can be negative and thus add to stress. Therapeutically, individuals are taught to use self-talk in a way that helps them to keep calm.

sensitivity (of a test): the probability that a test is correctly positive or correctly negative; for example, a sensitive test may have 95 percent success in detecting a disease among patients known to have that disease, and 95 percent success in not detecting a disease among disease-free individuals.

seropositive: the presence of the HIV in the bloodstream.

sick role behaviour: the activities undertaken by a person diagnosed as sick in order to try to get well.

social capital: feelings of social cohesion, solidarity and trust in one's neighbours.

social cognition: a model of social knowledge and behaviour that highlights the explanatory role of cognitive factors (e.g. beliefs and attitudes).

social comparison: the process by which a person or group of people compare themselves (their behaviour or characteristics) with others.

social desirability bias: the tendency to answer questions about oneself or one's behaviour in a way that is thought likely to meet with social (or interviewer) approval.

social identity: a person's sense of who they are at a group, rather than personal and individual, level (e.g. you are a student, possibly a female).

socialisation: the process by which a person learns – from family, teachers, peers – the rules, norms and moral codes of behaviour that are expected of them.

social learning theory: a theory that has at its core the belief that a combination of outcome expectancy and outcome value will shape subsequent behaviour. Reinforcement is an important predictor of future behaviour.

socio-economic status: a measure of the social class of an individual. Different measures use different indicators, including income, job type or years of education. Higher status implies a higher salary or higher job status.

Socratic dialogue: exploration of an individual's beliefs, encouraging them to question their validity.

specificity (of a test): the likelihood that a test will produce a few false positive results and a few false negatives; i.e. does not produce a positive result for a negative case, and vice versa.

stages of change model: developed by Prochaska and di Clemente, this identifies five stages through which an individual passes when considering behavioural change: pre-contemplation, contemplation, preparation, change and maintenance/ relapse.

statins: drugs designed to reduce cholesterol levels.

stem cell: a 'generic' cell that can make exact copies of itself indefinitely. In addition, such cells have the ability to produce specialised cells for various tissues in the body, including blood, heart muscle, brain and liver tissue. Found in the bone marrow.

stem cell transplant: procedure in which stem cells are replaced within the bone marrow following radiotherapy or chemotherapy or diseases such as leukaemia where they may be damaged.

stress inoculation training: a form of stress-reducing intervention in which participants are taught to control stress by rehearsing prior to going into stressful situations. Participants are taught to relax and use calming self-talk. The approach was developed by Donald Meichenbaum.

stress management training: a generic term for interventions designed to teach participants how to cope with stress.

stress reactivity: the physiological arousal, such as increased heart rate or blood pressure, experienced during a potentially stressful encounter.

stroke: damage to the brain either as a result of a bleed into the brain tissue or a blockage in an artery, which prevents oxygen and other nutrients reaching parts of the brain. More scientifically known as a cerebro-vascular accident (CVA).

subjective: personal, i.e. what a person thinks and reports (e.g excitement) as opposed to what is **objective**. Subjective is generally related to internal interpretations of events rather than observable features.

subjective expected utility (seu) theory: a decision-making model where an individual evaluates the expected utility (cf. desirability) of certain actions and their outcomes and selects the action with the highest seu.

subjective norm: a person's beliefs regarding whether important others (referents) would think that they should or should not carry out a particular action. An index of social pressure, weighted generally by the individual's motivation to comply with the wishes of others (see theory of planned behaviour).

sympathetic nervous system: the part of the autonomic nervous system involved in mobilising energy to activate and maintain arousal (e.g. increased heart rate).

synapse: junction between two neurons or between a neuron and target organ. Nerve impulses cross a synapse through the action of neurotransmitters.

systolic blood pressure: the maximum pressure of blood on the artery walls, which occurs at the end of the left ventricle output/contraction (measured in relation to **diastolic blood pressure**).

T

tachycardia: high heart rate – usually defined as greater than 100 beats per minute.

T cell: a cell that recognises antigens on the surface of a virus-infected cell, binds to that cell and destroys it.

temporomandibular disorder pain: a variety of conditions that cause tenderness and pain in temporomandibular joint (hinge joint of the jaw).

thalamus: area of the brain that links the basic functions of the hindbrain and midbrain with the higher centres of processing, the cerebral cortex. Regulates attention and contributes to memory functions. The portion that enters the limbic system is involved in the experience of emotions.

theory: a general belief or beliefs about some aspect of the world we live in or those in it, which may or may not be supported by evidence. For example, women are worse drivers than men.

transdermal patch: a method of delivering a drug in a slow release form. The drug is impregnated into a patch, which is stuck to the skin and gradually absorbed into the body.

transient ischaemic attacks: short periods of reduced blood flow to the brain, resulting in symptoms including short periods of confusion, weakness and other minor neurological symptoms.

treadmill test: a test of cardiovascular fitness in which participants gradually increase the level of exercise on a treadmill while having their heart monitored with an electrocardiogram.

trigeminal neuralgia: a painful inflammation of the trigeminal nerve that causes sharp and severe facial pain.

type A behaviour (TAB): a constellation of characteristics, mannerisms and behaviour including competitiveness, time urgency, impatience, easily aroused hostility, rapid and vigorous speech patterns and expressive behaviour. Extensively studied in relation to the aetiology of coronary heart disease, where hostility seems central.

type C personality: a cluster of personality characteristics manifested in stoic, passive and non-emotionally expressive coping responses. Thought to be associated with an elevated cancer risk.

type D personality: a personality type characterised by high negative affectivity and social inhibition.

type 1 diabetes: see **diabetes**.

type 2 diabetes: see **diabetes**.

U

ulcerative colitis: a chronic inflammatory disease of the large intestine, characterised by recurrent episodes of abdominal pain, fever and severe diarrhoea.

ultrasound: the use of ultra high-frequency sound waves to create images of organs and systems in the body.

unrealistic optimism: also known as 'optimistic bias', whereby a person considers themselves as being less likely than comparable others to develop an illness or experience a negative event.

V

variable: (noun). Something that can be measured or is reported and recorded as data, such as age, mood, smoking frequency or physical functioning.

vasospasm: a situation in which the muscles of artery walls in the heart contract and relax rapidly, resulting in a reduction of the flow of blood through the artery.

vicarious learning: learning from observation of others.

volition: action or doing (the post-intentional stage highlighted in the HAPA model of health behaviour change).

W

written emotional expression: a writing technique in which participants write about upsetting incidents either in their past or related to specific issues.

REFERENCES

Aaronson, N.K., Ahmedzai, S., Bergman, B. *et al.* (1993). The European Organisation for Research and Treatment of Cancer QLQ-C30: A quality of life instrument for use in international clinical trials in oncology. *Journal of the National Cancer Institute*, 85: 365–76.

Aarts, H. (2007). Health and goal-directed behavior: The nonconscious regulation and motivation of goals and their pursuit. *Health Psychology Review*, 1: 53–82.

Abbott, S. (1988). Talking about AIDS. Report for AIDS Action Council, Canberra. *National Bulletin*, August, 24–7.

Abraham, C., Krahé, B., Dominic, R. *et al.* (2002). Do health promotion messages target cognitive and behavioural correlates of condom use? A content analysis of safer sex promotion leaflets in two countries. *British Journal of Health Psychology*, 7: 227–46.

Abraham, S.C.S., Sheeran, P., Abrams, D. *et al.* (1996). Health beliefs and teenage condom use: a prospective study. *Psychology and Health*, 11: 641–55.

Abramsky, L. and Fletcher, O. (2002). Interpreting information: what is said, what is heard – a questionnaire study of health professionals and members of the public. *Prenatal Diagnosis*, 22: 1188–94.

Absetz, P., Aro, A.R. and Sutton, S.R. (2003). Experience with breast cancer, pre-screening perceived susceptibility and the psychological impact of screening. *Psycho-Oncology*, 12: 305–18.

Achat, H., Kawachi, I., Byrne, C. *et al.* (2000). Prospective study of job strain and risk of breast cancer. *International Journal of Epidemiology*, 29: 622–8.

Acheson, D. (1998). *Independent Inquiry into Inequalities in Health*. Report. London: HMSO.

Adams, J. and White, M. (2005). Why don't stage-based activity promotion interventions work? *Health Education Research*, 20: 237–43.

Ader, R. (2001). Psychoneuroimmunology. *Current Directions in Psychological Science*, 10: 94–8.

Ader, R. (2007). *Psychoneuroimmunology* (4th edition). New York: Academic Press.

Ader, R. and Cohen, N. (1993). Psychoneuroimmunology: conditioning and stress. *Annual Review of Psychology*, 44: 53–85.

Adler, N.E. and Matthews, K.A. (1994). Health psychology: why do some people get sick and some stay well? *Annual Review of Psychology*, 45: 229–59.

Affleck, G., Tennen, H., Croog, S. *et al.* (1987). Causal attributions, perceived benefits, and morbidity after a heart attack: an 8-year study. *Journal of Consulting and Clinical Psychology*, 55: 29–35.

Agency for Health Care Policy and Research (1992). *Acute Pain Management, Clinical Practice Guideline*. Silver Spring, Md: AHCPR.

Ager, A., Carr, S., Maclachlan, M. *et al.* (1996). Perceptions of tropical health risks in Mponda, Malawi: attributions of cause, suggested means of risk reduction and preferred treatment. *Psychology and Health*, 12: 23–31.

Agostinelli, G. and Grube, J.W. (2002). Alcohol counter-advertising and the media. A review of recent research. *Alcohol Research and Health*, 26: 15–21.

Ahmad, W. (2000) (ed.). *Ethnicity, Disability and Chronic Illness*. Buckingham: Open University Press.

Ai, A.L., Park, C.L., Huang, B. *et al.* (2007). Psychosocial mediators of religious coping styles: a study of short-term distress following cardiac surgery. *Personality & Social Psychology Bulletin*, 33: 867–82.

Aitken, J.F., Youl, P.H., Janda, M. *et al.* (2006). Increases in skin cancer screening during a community-based randomized intervention trial. *International Journal of Cancer*, 118: 1110–16.

Aikens, J.E., Kiolbasa, T.A. and Sobel, R. (1997). Psychological predictors of glycemic change with relaxation training in non-insulin-dependent diabetes mellitus. *Psychotherapy and Psychosomatics*, 66: 302–6.

Ajzen, I. (1985). From intentions to actions: a theory of planned behavior. In J. Kuhl and J. Beckman (eds), *Action-control: From Cognition to Behavior*. Heidelberg: Springer Verlag.

Ajzen, I. (1991). The theory of planned behaviour. *Organizational Behavior and Human Decision Processes*, 50: 179–211.

Ajzen, I. and Fishbein, M. (1970). The prediction of behavior from attitudinal and normative beliefs. *Journal of Personality and Social Psychology*, 6: 466–87.

Ajzen, I. and Madden, T.J. (1986). Prediction of goal-directed behavior: attitudes, intentions, and perceived behavioral control. *Journal of Experimental Social Psychology*, 22: 453–74.

Alaranta, H., Rytokoski, U., Rissanen, A. *et al.* (1994). Intensive physical and psychosocial training program for patients with chronic low back pain. *Spine*, 19: 1339–49.

Alcohol Concern (2002) *Alcohol & Teenage Pregnancy*. Drug & Alcohol Education and Prevention Team, London: Alcohol Concern.

Alexander, D.A. and Walker, L.G. (1994). A study of methods used by Scottish police officers to cope with work-induced stress. *Stress Medicine*, 10: 131–8.

Alexander, F. (1950). *Psychosomatic Medicine: Its Principles and Application*. New York: W.W. Norton.

Alexander, R.E. (2000). Readability of published dental educational materials. *Journal of the American Dental Association*, 131: 937–42.

Alexander, S.C., Keitz, S.A., Sloane, R. *et al.* (2006). A controlled trial of a short course to improve residents' communication with patients at the end of life. *Academic Medicine*, 81: 1008–12.

Alfredsson, L., Spetz, C.-L. and Theorell, T. (1985). Type of occupational and near-future hospitalization for myocardial infarction and some other diagnoses. *International Journal of Epidemiology*, 4: 378–88.

Allen, J.D., Stoddard, A.M., Mays, J. *et al.* (2001). Promoting breast and cervical cancer screening at the workplace: results from the Woman to Woman study. *American Journal of Public Health*, 91: 584–90.

Allen, J.K., Scott, L.B., Stewart, K.J. *et al.* (2004). Disparities in women's referral to and enrollment in outpatient cardiac rehabilitation. *Journal of General Internal Medicine*, 19: 747–53.

Allied Dunbar National Fitness Survey (1992). *A Report on Activity Patterns and Fitness Levels*. London: Sports Council and Health Education Authority.

Allport, G.W. (1920). The influence of the group upon association and thought. *Journal of Experimental Psychology*, 3: 159–82.

Allport, G.W. (1935). Attitudes. In C. Murchison (ed.), *Handbook of Social Psychology*, Worcester, Mass.: Clark University Press.

Allport, G.W. (1961). *Pattern and Growth in Personality*. New York: Holt, Rinehart & Winston.

Allport, G.W. (1966). Traits revisited. *American Psychologist*, 21: 1–10.

Aloise-Young, P.A., Hennigan, K.M. and Graham, J.W. (1996). Role of self-image and smoker stereotype in smoking onset during early adolescence: a longitudinal study. *Health Psychology*, 15: 494–7.

Al-Smadi J., Warke K., Wilson I. *et al.* (2003). A pilot investigation of the hypoalgesic effects of transcutaneous electrical nerve stimulation upon low back pain in people with multiple sclerosis. *Clinical Rehabilitation*, 17: 742–9.

Amelang, M. and Schmidt-Rathjens, C. (1996). Personality, cancer and coronary heart disease: further evidence on a controversial issue. *British Journal of Health Psychology*, 1: 191–205.

American Agency for Health Care Policy (1992). *Acute Pain Management: Operative or Medical Procedures and Trauma. Clinical Practice Guideline No. 1*. AAHCP: Washington, DC.

American Heart Association (1995). *Heart and Stroke Facts: 1995 Statistical Supplement*. American Heart Association, Dallas.

American Psychiatric Association (2000). *Diagnostic and Statistical Manual of Mental Disorders*, 4th edn with revised text. Washington.

Ames, G.M. and Janes, C.R. (1987). Heavy and problem drinking in an American blue-collar population: implications for prevention. *Social Science and Medicine*, 25: 949–60.

Andersen, B.L., Cacioppo, J.T. and Roberts, D.C. (1995). Delay in seeking a cancer diagnosis: delay stages and psychophysiological comparison processes. *British Journal of Social Psychology*, 34: 33–52.

Andersen, R. and Newman, F. (1973). Societal and individual determinants of medical care utilization in the United States. *Millbank Memorial Fund Quarterly*, 51: 95–107.

Anderson, R.J., Friedland, K.E., Clouse, R.E. *et al.* (2001). The prevalence of comorbid depression in adults with diabetes: a meta-analysis. *Diabetes Care*, 24: 1069–78.

Andersson, G. (1996). The benefits of optimism: a meta-analytic review of the Life Orientation Test. *Personality and Individual Differences*, 21: 719–25.

Andrasik, F. (2007). What does the evidence show? Efficacy of behavioural treatments for recurrent headaches in adults. *Neurological Sciences*, 28: S70–7.

André, M., Borgquist, L. and Molstad, S. (2002). Asking for 'rules of thumb': a way to discover tacit knowledge in general practice. *Family Practice*, 19: 617–22.

Andreasson, S., Holder, H.D., Norström, T. *et al.* (2006). Estimates of harm associated with changes in Swedish alcohol policy: results from past and present estimates. *Addiction*, 101:1096–105.

Ansari, M., Shlipak, M.G., Heidenreich, P.A. *et al.* (2003). Improving guideline adherence: a randomized trial evaluating strategies to increase beta-blocker use in heart failure. *Circulation*, 107: 2799–804.

Antoni, M.H. (1987). Neuroendocrine influences in psychoimmunology and neoplasia: a review. *Psychology and Health*, 1: 3–24.

Antoni, M.H., Baggett, L., Ironson, G. *et al.* (1991). Cognitive behavioral stress management intervention buffers distress responses and immunological changes following notification of HIV-1 seropositivity. *Journal of Consulting and Clinical Psychology*, 59: 906–15.

Antoni, M.H., Cruess, S., Cruess, D.G. *et al.* (2000). Cognitive-behavioral stress management reduces distress and 24-hour urinary free cortisol output among symptomatic HIV-infected gay men. *Annals of Behavioral Medicine*, 22: 29–37.

Antoni, M.H., Cruess, D.G., Klimas, N. *et al.* (2002). Stress management and immune system reconstitution in symptomatic HIV-infected gay men over time: effects on transitional naive T-cells (CD4+CD45RA+CD29+). *American Journal of Psychiatry*, 159: 143–5.

Antoni, M.H., Lehman, J., Kilbourn, K. *et al.* (2001). Cognitive-behavioral stress management intervention decreases depression and enhances optimism and the sense of positive contributions among women under treatment for early-stage breast cancer. *Health Psychology*, 20: 20–32.

Antonovsky, A. (1987). *Unravelling the Mystery of Health: How People Manage Stress and Stay Well.* San Francisco: Jossey-Bass.

Appels, A., Bar, F., Lasker, J. *et al.* (1997). The effect of a psychological intervention program on the risk of a new coronary event after angioplasty: a feasibility study. *Journal of Psychosomatic Medicine*, 43: 209–17.

Arefjord, K., Hallarakeri, E., Havik, O.E. *et al.* (1998). Myocardial infarction: emotional consequences for the wife. *Psychology and Health*, 13: 135–46.

Armitage, C. and Conner, M. (1998). Extending the theory of planned behaviour: a review and avenues for further research. *Journal of Applied Social Psychology*, 28: 1429–64.

Armitage, C.J. (2003). The relationship between multi-dimensional health locus of control and perceived behavioural control: how are distal perceptions of control related to proximal perceptions of control? *Psychology and Health*, 18: 723–38.

Armitage, C.J. (2007). Efficacy of a brief worksite intervention to reduce smoking: the roles of behavioral and implementation intentions. *Journal of Occupational Health Psychology*, 12: 376–90.

Armitage, C.J. and Conner, M. (2002). Reducing fat intake: interventions based on the theory of planned behaviour. In D. Rutter and L. Quine (eds), *Changing Health Behaviour*. Buckingham: Open University Press.

Armitage, C.J., Conner, M., Loach, J. *et al.* (1999). Different perceptions of control: applying an extended theory of planned behaviour to legal and illegal drug use. *Basic and Applied Social Psychology*, 21: 301–16.

Arora, N.K. and McHorney, C.A. (2000). Patient preferences for medical decision making: who really wants to participate? *Medical Care*, 38: 335–41.

Asamoah-Adu, A., Weir, S., Pappoe, M. *et al.* (1994). Evaluation of a targeted AIDS prevention intervention to increase condom use among prostitutes in Ghana. *AIDS*, 8: 239–46.

Ashton, L., Karnilowicz, W. and Fooks, D. (2001). The incidence and belief structures associated with breast self examination. *Social Behavior and Personality*, 29: 223–9.

Aspinwall, L.G. and Brunhart, S.M. (1996). Distinguishing optimism from denial: optimistic beliefs predict attention to health threats. *Personality and Social Psychology Bulletin*, 22: 993–1003.

Aspinwall, L.G. and Taylor, S.E. (1992). Modeling cognitive adaptation: a longitudinal investigation of the impact of individual differences and coping on college adjustment and performance. *Journal of Personality and Social Psychology*, 61: 755–65.

Astin, J.A. (1998). Why patients use alternative medicine: results of a national study. *Journal of the American Medical Association*, 279: 1548–53.

Astrom, M. (1996). Generalized anxiety disorder in stroke patients: a 3-year longitudinal study. *Stroke*, 17: 270–5.

Atkinson, R.M. (1994). Late onset problem drinking in older adults. *International Journal of Geriatric Psychiatry*, 9: 321–6.

Attari, A., Sartippour, M., Amini, M. *et al.* (2006). Effect of stress management training on glycemic control in patients with type 1 diabetes. *Diabetes Research and Clinical Practice*, 73: 23–8.

Audrain, J., Boyd, N.R., Roth, J. *et al.* (1997). Genetic susceptibility testing in smoking-cessation treatment: one-year outcomes of a randomized trial. *Addictive Behaviors*, 22: 741–51.

Aujoulat, I., Marcolongo, R., Bonadiman, L. *et al.* (2008). Reconsidering patient empowerment in chronic illness: a critique of models of self efficacy and bodily control. *Social Science & Medicine*, 66: 1228–39.

Austoker, J. (1994). Screening for ovarian, prostrate and testicular cancers. *British Medical Journal*, 309: 315–20.

Australian Bureau of Statistics (2005). *The Health and Welfare of Australia's Aboriginal and Torres Strait Islander Peoples*. Canberra: Australian Bureau of Statistics.

Avendano, M., Kawachi, I., van Lenthe, F. *et al.* (2006). Socioeconomic status and stroke incidence in the US elderly. *Stroke*, 37: 1368–76.

Ayanian, J.Z., Cleary P.D., Weissman J.S. *et al.* (1999). The effect of patients' preferences on racial differences in access to renal transplantation. *New England Journal of Medicine*, 341: 1661–9.

Bacharach, S.B., Bamberger, P.A., Sonnenstuhl, W.J. *et al.* (2004). Retirement, risky alcohol consumption and drinking problems among blue-collar workers. *Journal of Studies in Alcohol*, 65: 537–45.

Bachiocco, V., Scesi, M., Morselli, A.M. *et al.* (1993). Individual pain history and familial pain tolerance models: relationships to post-surgical pain. *Clinical Journal of Pain*, 9: 266–71.

Back, A.L., Arnold, R.M., Baile, W.F. *et al.* (2007). Efficacy of communication skills training for giving bad news and discussing transitions to palliative care. *Archives of Internal Medicine*, 167: 453–60.

Badr, H., Acitelli, L.K. and Carmack Taylor, C.L. (2007). Does couple identity mediate the stress experienced by caregiving spouses? *Psychology & Health*, 22: 211–30.

Bagozzi, R.P. (1993). On the neglect of volition in consumer research: a critique and proposal. *Psychology and Marketing*, 10: 215–37.

Baider, L., Andritsch, E., Uziely, B. *et al.* (2003). Effects of age on coping and psychological distress in women diagnosed with breast cancer: review of literature and analysis of two different geographical settings. *Critical Reviews in Oncology/Hematology*, 46: 5–16.

Bair, M.J., Robinson, R.L., Katon, W. *et al.* (2003). Depression and pain comorbidity: a literature review. *Archives of Internal Medicine*, 163: 2433–45.

Bajekal, M., Primatesta, P. and Prior, G. (2003). *Health Survey for England 2001: Fruit and Vegetable Consumption*. London: Stationery Office.

Baker, A.H. and Wardle, J. (2003). Sex differences in fruit and vegetable intake in older adults. *Appetite*, 40: 269–75.

Balarajan, R. and Raleigh, V. (1993). *Ethnicity and Health in England*. London: HMSO.

Balaswamy, S., Richardson, V. and Price, C.A. (2004). Investigating patterns of social support used by widowers during bereavement. *The Journal of Men's Studies*, 13: 67–84.

Balldin, J., Berglund, M., Borg, S. *et al.* (2003). A 6-month controlled naltrexone study: combined effect with cognitive behavioral therapy in outpatient treatment of alcohol dependence. *Alcoholism Clinical and Experimental Research*, 27: 1142–9.

Baltes, P.B. and Baltes, M.M. (1990). *Successful Aging: Perspectives from the Behavioral Sciences*. New York: Cambridge University Press.

Bandolier (1999). Transcutaneous electrical nerve stimulation (TENS) in postoperative pain. *Bandolier*, July. Available from www.bandolier.com.

Bandolier (2003). Acute pain. *Bandolier* extra, February. Available from www.ebandolier.com.

Bandura, A. (1977). Self-efficacy: toward a unifying theory of behavioral change. *Psychological Review*, 84: 191–215.

Bandura, A. (1986). *Social Foundations of Thought and Action*. New Jersey: Prentice Hall.

Bandura, A. (1997). *Self-Efficacy: The Exercise of Control*. New York: W.H. Freeman.

Bandura, A. (2001). Social cognitive theory: an agentic perspective. *Annual Review of Psychology*, 52: 1–26.

Banks, S.M., Salovey, P., Greener, S. *et al.* (1995). The effects of message framing on mammography utilization. *Health Psychology*, 14: 178–84.

Banthia, R., Malcarne, V.L., Varni, J.W. *et al.* (2003). The effects of dyadic strength and coping styles on psychological distress in couples faced with prostate cancer. *Journal of Behavioral Medicine*, 26: 31–52.

Barefoot, J.C., Dahlstrom, G. and Williams, R.B. (1983). Hostility, CHD incidence, and total mortality: a 25-year follow-up study of 255 physicians. *Psychosomatic Medicine*, 45: 59–63.

Barlow, J., Turner, A.P. and Wright, C.C. (2000). A randomised controlled study of the Arthritis Self-Management Programme in the UK. *Health Education Research Theory and Practice*, 15: 665–80.

Barlow, J.H., Wright, C., Sheasby, J. *et al.* (2002). Self-management approaches for people with chronic conditions: a review. *Patient Education and Counselling*, 48: 177–87.

Barnard, D., Street, A., Love, D.W. *et al.* (2006). Relationships between stressors, work support and burnout among cancer nurses. *Cancer Nursing*, 29: 338–45.

Baron-Epel, O. and Kaplan, G. (2001). General subjective health status or age-related subjective health status: does it make a difference? *Social Science and Medicine*, 53: 1373–81.

Barone-Adesi, F., Vizzini, L., Merletti, F. *et al.* (2006). Short-term effects of Italian smoking regulation on rates of hospital admission for acute myocardial infarction. *European Heart Journal*, 27: 2468–72.

Bartley, M., Sacker, A. and Clarke, P. (2004). Employment status, employment conditions, and limiting illness: prospective evidence from the British household panel survey 1991–2001. *Journal of Epidemiology and Community Health*, 58: 501–6.

Barton, M.B., Morley, D.S. and Moore, S. (2004). Decreasing women's anxieties after abnormal mammograms: a controlled trial. *Journal of the National Cancer Institute*, 96: 529–38.

Bashir, S.A. (2002). Home is where the harm is: inadequate housing as a public health crisis. *American Journal of Public Health*, 92: 733–8.

Baum, A. (1990). Stress, intrusive imagery and chronic distress. *Health Psychology*, 9: 665–75.

Baum, A., Garofalo, J.P. and Yali, A.M. (1999). Socioeconomic status and chronic stress. Does stress account for SES effects on health? *Annals of the New York Academy of Science*, 896: 131–44.

Baum, A., Gatchel, R.J. and Krantz, D.S. (1997). *An Introduction to Health Psychology*, 3rd edition, New York: McGraw-Hill.

Baum, A. and Grunberg, N.E. (1991). Gender, stress and health. *Health Psychology*, 10: 80–5.

Bauman, B. (1961). Diversities in conceptions of health and fitness. *Journal of Health and Human Behavior*, 2: 39–46.

Beach, S.R., Schulz, R., Lee, J.L. *et al.* (2000). Negative and positive health effects of caring for a disabled spouse: longitudinal findings from the Caregiver Health Effects study. *Psychology and Aging*, 15: 259–71.

Beadsmoore, C.J. and Screaton, N.J. (2003). Classification, staging and prognosis of lung cancer. *European Journal of Radiology*, 45: 8–17.

Bean, D., Cundy, T. and Petrie, K. (2007). Ethnic differences in illness perceptions, self-efficacy and diabetes self-care. *Psychology & Health*, 22: 787–811.

Beasley, M., Thompson, T. and Davidson, J. (2003). Resilience in response to life stress: the effects of coping style and cognitive hardiness. *Personality and Individual Differences*, 34: 77–95.

Beaver, K., Bogg, J. and Luker, K.A. (1999). Decision-making role preferences and information needs: a comparison of colorectal and breast cancer. *Health Expectations*, 2: 266–76.

Beaver, K., Luker, K.A., Owens, R.G. *et al.* (1996). Treatment decision making in women newly diagnosed with breast cancer. *Cancer Nursing*, 19: 8–19.

Beck, A. (1977). *Cognitive Therapy of Depression*. New York: Guilford Press.

Beck, A.T. (1976). *Cognitive Therapy and the Emotional Disorders*. New York: International Universities Press.

Beck, A.T., Ward, C.H., Mendelson, M. *et al.* (1962). Reliability of psychiatric diagnoses: 2. A study of consistency of clinical judgements and ratings. *American Journal of Psychiatry*, 119: 351–7.

Beck, A.T., Wight, F.D., Newman, C.F. *et al.* (1993). *Cognitive Therapy for Substance Abuse*. New York: Guilford Press.

Becker, M.H. (ed.) (1974). The health belief model and personal health behavior, *Health Education Monographs*, 2: 324–508.

Becker, M.H. and Maiman, L.A. (1975). Socio-behavioral determinants of compliance with health and medical care recommendations. *Medical Care*, 13: 10–14.

Becker, M.H., Haefner, D.P. and Maiman, L.A. (1977). The health belief model in the prediction of dietary compliance: a field experiment. *Journal of Health and Social Behavior*, 18: 348–66.

Becker, M.H. and Rosenstock, I.M. (1987). Comparing social learning theory and the health belief model. In W.B. Ward (ed.), *Advances in Health Education and Promotion*. Greenwich, Conn.: JAI Press.

Beecher, H.K. (1946). Pain in men wounded in battle. *Annals of Surgery*, 123: 96–105.

Bell, D.E. (1982). Regret in decision-making under uncertainty. *Operations Research*, 21: 961–81.

Bellaby, P. (2003). Communication and miscommunication of risk: understanding UK parents' attitudes to combined MMR vaccination. *British Medical Journal*, 327: 725–8.

Belloc, N.B. and Breslow, L. (1972). Relationship between physical health status and health practices. *Preventive Medicine*, 1: 409–21.

Benedetti, F., Lanotte, M., Lopiano, L. *et al.* (2007). When words are painful: unraveling the mechanisms of the nocebo effect. *Neuroscience*, 147: 260–71.

Benight, C.C., Ironson, G., Klebe, K. *et al.* (1999). Conservation of resources and coping self-efficacy predicting distress following a natural disaster: a causal model analysis where the environment meets the mind. *Anxiety, Stress and Coping*, 12: 107–26.

Bennett, P. (2000). *Introduction to Clinical Health Psychology*. Oxford: Oxford University Press.

Bennett, P. (2003). *Abnormal and Clinical Psychology: An Introductory Text*. Buckingham: Open University Press.

Bennett, P. (2005a). Gastric and duodenal ulcers. In S. Ayers, A. Baum, C. McManus, S. Newman, K. Wallston, J. Weinman and R. West (eds) *Cambridge Handbook of Psychology, Health and Medicine* (2nd Edition). Cambridge: Cambridge University Press.

Bennett, P. (2005b). Irritable Bowel Syndrome. In S. Ayers, A. Baum, C. McManus, S. Newman, K. Wallston, J. Weinman and R. West (eds) *Cambridge Handbook of Psychology, Health and Medicine* (2nd Edition). Cambridge: Cambridge University Press.

Bennett, P. (2006). *Abnormal and Clinical Psychology: An Introductory Text*. 2nd edition. Buckingham: Open University Press.

Bennett, P., Ahmed, A. and Lowe, R. (in revision). Linking appraisals, emotions and coping in response to work-related stress. *British Journal of Clinical Psychology*.

Bennett, P. and Connell, H. (1999) Dyadic responses to myocardial infarction. *Psychology, Health and Medicine*, 4: 45–55.

Bennett, P. and Murphy, S. (1997). *Psychology and Health Promotion*. Buckingham: Open University Press.

Bennett, P. and Smith, C. (1992). Parents' attitudinal and social influences on childhood vaccination. *Health Education Research: Theory and Practice*, 73: 341–8.

Bennett, P., Owen, R.L., Koutsakis, S. *et al.* (2002). Personality, social context and cognitive predictors of post-traumatic stress disorder in myocardial infarction patients. *Psychology and Health*, 17: 489–500.

Bennett, P., Phelps, C., Brain, K. *et al.* (2007). A randomised controlled trial of a brief self-help coping intervention designed to reduce distress when awaiting genetic risk information. *Journal of Psychosomatic Research*, 63: 59–64.

Bennett, P., Smith, P. and Gallacher, J.E.J. (1996). Vital exhaustion, neuroticism and symptom report-ing in cardiac and non-cardiac patients. *British Journal of Health Psychology*, 1: 309–13.

Bennett, P., Wilkinson, C., Turner, J. *et al.* (2008) Psychological factors associated with emotional responses to receiving genetic risk information. *Journal of Genetic Counseling*. Published on line, 8th February.

Bennett, P., Williams, Y., Page, N. *et al.* (2004). Levels of mental health problems among UK emergency ambulance personnel. *Emergency Medical Journal*, 21: 235–6.

Bensing, J.M., Tromp, F., van Dulmen, S. *et al.* (2006). Shifts in doctor–patient communication between 1986 and 2002: a study of videotaped general practice consultations with hypertension patients. *BMC Family Practice*, 7: 62.

Benyamini, Y., Leventhal, E.A. and Leventhal, H. (2003). Elderly people's ratings of the importance of health-related factors to their self-assessments of health. *Social Science and Medicine*, 56: 1661–7.

Beran, M.S., Cunningham, W., Landon, B.E. *et al.* (2007). Clinician gender is more important than gender concordance in quality of HIV care. *Gender Medicine*, 4: 72–84.

Bergner, M., Bobbitt, R.A., Carter, W.B. *et al.* (1981). The sickness impact profile: development and final revision of a health status measure. *Medical Care*, 19: 787–805.

Berkman, L.F. (1984). Assessing the physical health effects of social networks and social support. *Annual Review of Public Health*, 5: 413–32.

Berkman, L.F. and Syme, S.L. (1979). Social networks, lost resistance and mortality: a nine-year follow-up of Alameda County residents. *American Journal of Epidemiology*, 109: 186–204.

Berkman, L.F., Blumenthal, J., Burg, M. *et al.* (2003). Effects of treating depression and low perceived social support on clinical events after myocardial infarction: the Enhancing Recovery in Coronary Heart Disease (ENRICHD) patients randomized trial. *Journal of the American Medical Association*, 289: 3106–16.

Bernal, I., Domènech, E., Garcia-Planella, E. *et al.* (2006). Medication-taking behavior in a cohort of patients with inflammatory bowel disease. *Digestive Diseases and Sciences*, 51: 2165–9.

Bhopal, R., Hayes, L., White, M. *et al.* (2002). Ethnic and socio-economic inequalities in coronary heart disease, diabetes and risk factors in Europeans and South Asians. *Journal of Public Health Medicine*, 24: 95–105.

Bhopal, R., Unwin, N., White, M. *et al.* (1999). Heterogeneity of coronary heart disease risk factors in Indian, Pakistani, Bangladeshi, and European origin populations: cross-sectional study. *British Medical Journal*, 319: 215–20.

Bibace, R., Schmidt, L.R. and Walsh, M.E. (1994). Children's perceptions of illness. In G.N. Penny, P. Bennett and M. Herbert (eds), *Health Psychology: A Lifespan Perspective*. Switzerland: Harwood Academic Publishers.

Bibace, R. and Walsh, M.E. (1980). Development of children's conceptions of illness, *Pediatrics*, 66: 912–17.

Biddle, S. (1995). Exercise and psychosocial health. *Research Quarterly for Exercise and Sport*, 66: 292–7.

Biddle, S. and Murtrie, N. (1991). *Psychology of Physical Activity: A Health Related Perspective*. London: Springer Verlag.

Biddle, S., Fox, K. and Boutcher, S. (2000). *Physical Activity and Psychological Wellbeing*. London: Routledge.

Biener, L., McCallum-Keeler, G. and Nyman, A.L. (2000). Adults' response to Massachusetts anti-tobacco television advertisements: impact of viewer and advertisement characteristics. *Tobacco Control*, 9: 401–7.

Biggam, F.H., Power, K.G., MacDonald, R.R. *et al.* (1997). Self-perceived occupational stress and distress in a Scottish police force. *Work and Stress*, 11: 118–33.

Biglan, A., Duncan, T.E., Ary, D.A. and Smolkovski, K. (1995). Peer and parental influences on adolescent tobacco use. *Journal of Behavioural Medicine*, 18: 315–30.

Bijttebier, P., Vercruysse, T., Vertommen, H. *et al.* (2001). New evidence on the reliability and validity of the pediatric oncology quality of life scale. *Psychology and Health*, 16: 461–9.

Billings, A.G. and Moos, R.H. (1981). The role of coping responses and social resources in attenuating the stress of life events. *Journal of Behavioural Medicine*, 4: 139–57.

Billings, A.G. and Moos, R.H. (1984). Coping, stress, and resources among adults with unipolar depression. *Journal of Personality and Social Psychology*, 46: 877–91.

Bird, J.E. and Podmore, V.N. (1990). Children's understanding of health and illness. *Psychology and Health*, 4: 175–85.

Birmingham Health Authority (1995). *Birmingham Annual Public Health Report: Closing the Gap*. Birmingham: Birmingham Health Authority.

Birmingham, P.K., Wheeler, M., Suresh, S. *et al.* (2003). Patient-controlled epidural analgesia in children: can they do it? *Anesthesia and Analgesia*, 96: 686–91.

Bishop, G.D. and Teng, C.B. (1992). Cognitive organization of disease information in young Chinese Singaporeans. Paper presented at First Asian Conference in Psychology, Singapore.

Bjordal, J.M., Johnson, M.I. and Ljunggreen, A.E. (2002). Transcutaneous electrical nerve stimulation (TENS) can reduce postoperative analgesic consumption. A meta-analysis with assessment of optimal treatment parameters for postoperative pain. *European Journal of Pain*, 7: 181–8.

Black, J.L., Allison, T.G., Williams, D.E. *et al.* (1998). Effect of intervention for psychological distress on rehospitalization rates in cardiac rehabilitation patients. *Psychosomatics*, 39: 134–43.

Blair, S. and Brodney, S. (1999). Effects of physical inactivity and obesity on morbidity and mortality: current evidence and research issues. *Medicine and Science in Sports and Exercise*, 31 (suppl.): S646–62.

Blalock, J.E. (1994). The syntax of immune-neuroendocrine communication. *Immunology Today*, 15: 504–11.

Blane, D., Higgs, P., Hyde, M. *et al.* (2004). Life course influences on quality of life in early old age. *Social Science and Medicine*, 58: 2171–9.

Blaxter, M. (1987). Evidence on inequality in health from a national survey, *The Lancet*, ii: 30–3.

Blaxter, M. (1990). *Health and Lifestyles*. London: Routledge.

Blenkinsop, S., Boreham, R. and McManus, S. (NFER) (2003). *Smoking, Drinking and Drug Use among Young People in England in 2002*. London: Stationery Office.

Block, G., Patterson, B. and Subar, A. (1992). Fruit, vegetables and cancer prevention: a review of the epidemiological evidence. *Nutrition and Cancer*, 18: 1–29.

Blumenthal, J.A., Jiang, W., Babyak, M.A. *et al.* (1997). Stress management and exercise training in cardiac patients with myocardial ischemia. *Archives of Internal Medicine*, 157: 2213–17.

Blumenthal, J.A., Sherwood, A., Babyak, M.A. *et al.* (2005). Effects of exercise and stress management training on markers of cardiovascular risk in patients with ischemic heart disease: a randomized controlled trial. *Journal of the American Medical Association*, 293: 1626–34.

Blyth, F.M., March, L.M. and Cousins, M.J. (2003). Chronic pain-related disability and use of analgesia and health services in a Sydney community. *Medical Journal of Australia*, 179: 84–7.

Boersma, S., Maes, S. and Joekes, K. (2005). Goal disturbance in relation to anxiety, depression, and health-related quality of life after myocardial infarction. *Quality of Life Research*, 14: 2265–75.

Boersma, S.N., Maes, S. and Joekes, K. (in press). Goal disturbance in relation to anxiety, depression, and health-related quality of life after myocardial infarction. *Quality of Life Research*

Boersma, S.N., Maes, S. and van Elderen, T.M.T. (in press). Goal disturbance predicts health-related quality of life and depression four months after myocardial infarction. *British Journal of Health Psychology*

Bogg, T. and Roberts, B.W. (2004). Conscientiousness and health-related behaviors: a meta-analysis of the leading behavioural contributors to mortality. *Psychological Bulletin*, 130: 887–919.

Boini, S., Briançon, S., Guillemin, F. *et al.* (2004). Impact of cancer occurrence on health-related quality of life: a longitudinal pre-post assessment. *Health and Quality of Life Outcomes*, 2: 4–19.

Bokan, J.A., Ries, R.K. and Katon, W.J. (1981). Tertiary gain and chronic pain. *Pain*, 10: 331–5.

Bolas, H., van Wersch, A. and Flynn, D. (2007). The well-being of young people who care for a dependent relative: an interpretative phenomenonological analysis. *Psychology & Health*, 22: 829–50.

Booth-Kewley, S. and Friedman, H.S. (1987). Psychological predictors of heart disease: a quantitative review. *Psychological Bulletin*, 101: 343–62.

Booth-Kewley, S. and Vickers, R.R., Jr (1994). Associations between major domains of personality and health behaviour. *Journal of Personality*, 62: 281–98.

Boreham, R. and Shaw, A. (2001). *Smoking, Drinking and Drug Use Among Young People in England in 2000*. London: Stationery Office.

Borgia, P., Marinacci, C., Schifano, P. *et al.* (2005) Is peer education the best approach for HIV prevention in schools? Findings from a randomized controlled trial. *Journal of Adolescent Health*, 36: 508–16.

Borland, R. (1997). Tobacco health warnings and smoking related cognitions and behaviours. *Addiction*, 92(11): 1427–35.

Bormann, J.E., Gifford, A.L., Shively, M. *et al.* (2006). Effects of spiritual mantram repetition on HIV outcomes: a randomized controlled trial. *Journal of Behavioral Medicine*, 29: 359–76.

Bourdeaudhuij, I.D. (1997). Family food rules and healthy eating in adolescents. *Journal of Health Psychology*, 2: 45–56.

Bourdeaudhuij, I. de. and Van Oost, P. (1998) Family characteristics and health behaviours of adolescents and families. *Psychology and Health*, 13: 785–804.

Bourgeois, M., Schulz, R. and Burgio, L. (1996). Interventions for caregivers of patients with Alzheimer's disease: a review and analysis of content, process and outcomes. *International Journal of Aging and Human Development*, 43: 35–92.

Bowden, A. and Fox-Rushby, J.A. (2003). A systematic and critical review of the process of translation and adaptation of generic health-related quality of life measures in Africa, Asia, Eastern Europe, the Middle East, South America. *Social Science and Medicine*, 57: 1289–306.

Bowland, L., Cockburn, J., Cawson, J. *et al.* (2003). Counselling interventions to address the psychological consequences of screening mammography: a randomised trial. *Patient Education and Counseling*, 49: 189–98.

Bowling, A. (1991). *Measuring Health: A Review of Quality of Life*. Buckingham: Open University Press.

Bowling, A. (1995a). *Measuring Disease: A Review of Disease-specific Quality of Life Measurement Scales*. Buckingham: Open University Press.

Bowling, A. (1995b). The most important things in life. Comparisons between older and younger population age groups by gender. Results from a national survey of the public's judgements. *International Journal of Health Sciences*, 6: 169–75.

Bowling, A. and Iliffe, S. (2006). Which model of successful ageing should be used? Baseline findings from a British longitudinal survey of ageing. *Age and Ageing*, 35: 607–14.

Boyer, C.B., Friend, R., Chlouverakis, G. *et al.* (1990). Social support and demographic factors influencing compliance of hemodialysis patients. *Journal of Applied Social Psychology*, 20: 1902–18.

Brabin, L., Roberts, S.A., Farzaneh, F. *et al.* (2006). Future acceptance of adolescent human papillomavirus vaccination: A survey of parental attitudes. *Vaccine*, 24: 3087–94.

Bracken, P. and Thomas, P. (2002). Time to move beyond the mind–body split (editorial). *British Medical Journal*, 325: 1433–4.

Brain, K., Gray, J., Norman, P. *et al.* (2000). Randomized trial of a specialist genetic assessment service for familial breast cancer. *Journal of the National Cancer Institute*, 92: 1345–51.

Braithwaite, D., Sutton, S. and Steggles, N. (2002). Intention to participate in predictive genetic testing for hereditary cancer: the role of attitude toward uncertainty. *Psychology and Health*, 17: 761–72.

Bratzler, D.W., Oehlert, W.H. *et al.* (2002). Smoking in the elderly – It's never too late to quit. *Journal of the Oklahoma State Medical Association*, 95: 185–91.

Braverman, M.T., Aarø, L.E. and Hetland, J. (2007). Changes in smoking among restaurant and bar employees following Norway's comprehensive smoking ban. *Health Promotion International*, 23: 5–15.

Brawley, O.W. and Freeman, H.P. (1999). Race and outcomes: is this the end of the beginning for minority health research? *Journal of the National Cancer Institute*, 91: 1908–9.

Brena, S.F. and Chapman, S.L. (1983). *Management of Patients with Chronic Pain*. Great Neck, NY: PMA Publications.

Breslow, L. (1983). The potential of health promotion. In D. Mechanic (ed.), *Handbook of Health, Health*

Care and the Health Professions. New York: Free Press.

Brett, J. and Austoker, J. (2001). Women who are recalled for further investigation for breast screening: psychological consequences 3 years after recall and factors affecting re-attendance. *Journal of Public Health Medicine*, 23: 292–300.

Brewer, B.W., Manos, T.M., McDevitt, A.V. *et al.* (2000). The effect of adding lower intensity work on the perceived aversiveness of exercise. *Journal of Sport and Exercise Psychology*, 22: 118–30.

Brewer, N.T., Salz, T. and Lillie, S.E. (2007). Systematic review: the long-term effects of false-positive mammograms. *Annals of Internal Medicine*, 146: 502–10.

Brewin, C., Dalgleish, T. and Joseph, S. (1996). A dual representation theory of post-traumatic stress disorder. *Psychological Review*, 103: 670–86.

Brewin, C.R. and Holmes, E.A. (2003). Psychological theories of posttraumatic stress disorder. *Clinical Psychology Review*, 23: 339–76.

Brewster, A.E., Hackett, P., Morrison, V. *et al.* (under review). Attitudes of the general public and professional health care staff towards cancer treatment in the elderly.

Brewster, A.E., Morrison, V., Hackett, P. *et al.* (2006). Attitudes of the general public and professional health care staff towards cancer treatment: the influence of age, quality of life, survival and side effects. *British Geriatric Society*, Spring meeting.

British Medical Association (2003a). *Adolescent Health*. British Medical Association, Board of Science and Education: BMA Publications Unit.

British Medical Association (2003b). *Childhood Immunisation: A Guide for Healthcare Professionals*. British Medical Association, Board of Science and Education: BMA Publications Unit.

British Thoracic Society (1997). Guidelines for the management of chronic obstructive pulmonary disease. *Thorax*, 52 (suppl. 5): 1–26.

Briviba, K., Pan, L. and Rechkemmer, G. (2002). Red wine polyphenols inhibit the growth of colon carcinoma cells and modulate the activation pattern of mitogen-activated protein kinases. *Journal of Nutrition*, 132: 2814–18.

Broadbent, E., Petrie, K.J., Alley, P.G. *et al.* (2003). Psychological stress impairs early wound repair following surgery. *Psychosomatic Medicine*, 65: 865–9.

Brodaty, H., Thomson, C., Thompson, C. *et al.* (2005). Why caregivers of people with dementia and memory loss don't use services. *International Journal of Geriatric Psychiatry*, 20: 537–546.

Broers, S., Kaptein, A.A., Le Cessie, S. *et al.* (2000). Psychological functioning and quality of life following bone marrow transplantation: a 3-year follow-up study. *Journal of Psychosomatic Research*, 48: 11–21.

Brosschot, J.F. and Thayer, J.F. (1998). Anger inhibition, cardiovascular recovery, and vagal function: a model of the link between hostility and cardiovascular disease. *Annals of Behavioral Medicine*, 20: 326–32.

Brown, J., Cooper, C. and Kirkcaldy, B. (1996). Occupational stress among senior police officers. *British Journal of Psychology*, 87: 31–41.

Brown, J.E., Brown, R.F., Miller, R.M. *et al.* (2000). Coping with metastatic melanoma: the last year of life. *Psycho-Oncology*, 9: 283–92.

Brown, J.S.L., Cochrane, R. and Hancox, T. (2000). Large-scale health promotion stress workshops for the general public: a controlled evaluation. *Behavioural and Cognitive Psychotherapy*, 28: 139–51.

Brownson, R., Koffman, D., Novotny, T. *et al.* (1995). Environmental and policy interventions to control tobacco use and prevent cardiovascular disease. *Health Education Quarterly*, 22: 478–98.

Bruce, J. and van Teijlingen, E. (1999). A review of the effectiveness of Smokebusters: community-based smoking prevention for young people. *Health Education Research*, 14: 109–20.

Bruera, E., Sweeney, C., Willey, J. *et al.* (2003). Breast cancer patient perception of the helpfulness of a prompt sheet versus a general information sheet during outpatient consultation: a randomized, controlled trial. *Journal of Pain and Symptom Management*, 25: 412–19.

Brug, J., Conner, M., Harre, N. *et al.* (2005). The transtheoretical model and stages of a change: a critique. Observations by five commentators on the paper by Adams, J. and White, M. Why don't stage-based activity promotion interventions work? *Health Education Research*, 20: 244–58.

Brunton, G., Harden, A., Rees, R. *et al.* (2003). *Children and Physical Activity: A Systematic Review of Barriers and Facilitators*. London: EPPI-Centre, Social Science Research Unit, Institute of Education, University of London.

Bryan, A.D., Aiken, L.S. and West, S.G. (1996). Increasing condom use: evaluation of a theory-based intervention to prevent sexually transmitted diseases in young women. *Health Psychology*, 15: 371–82.

Bryan, A.D., Aiken, L.S. and West, S.G. (1997). Young women's condom use: the influence of acceptance of sexuality, control over the sexual encounter, and perceived susceptibility to common STDs. *Health Psychology*, 16: 468–79.

Bryon, M. (1998). Adherence to treatment in children. In L.B. Myers and K. Midence (eds), *Adherence to*

Treatment in Medical Conditions, Netherlands: Harwood Academic Publishers.

Buckman, R. (1992). Who's for CPR? *Journal of the Royal College of Physicians of London*, 26: 461–2.

Budd, R. and Rollnick, S. (1996). The structure of the readiness to change questionnaire: a test of Prochaska and di Clemente's transtheoretical model. *Health Psychology*, 15: 365–76.

Budd, R.J. (1987). Response bias and the theory of reasoned action. *Social Cognition*, 5: 95–107.

Buick, D. and Petrie, K. (2002). 'I know just how you feel': the validity of healthy women's perceptions of breast cancer patients receiving treatment. *Journal of Applied Social Psychology*, 32: 110–23.

Bullinger, M. (1997). The challenge of cross-cultural quality of life assessment. *Psychology and Health*, 12: 815–26.

Bundy, C., Carroll, D., Wallace, L. *et al.* (1994). Psychological treatment of chronic stable angina pectoris. *Psychology and Health*, 10: 69–77.

Burack, J.H., Barrett, D.C., Stall, R.D. *et al.* (1993). Depressive symptoms and CD4 lymphocyte decline among HIV infected men. *JAMA*, 270(21): 2568–73.

Burell, G. (1996). Group psychotherapy in project New Life: treatment of coronary-prone behaviors for patients who had coronary bypass graft surgery. In S. Scheidt and R. Allan (eds), *Heart and Mind*. American Psychological Association.

Burgess, C., Cornelius, V., Love, S. *et al.* (2005). Depression and anxiety in women with early breast cancer: five-year observational cohort study. *British Medical Journal*, 330: 702–5.

Burgoyne, R. and Renwick, R. (2004). Social support and quality of life over time among adults living with HIV in the HAART era. *Social Science and Medicine*, 58: 1353–66.

Burns, J.W., Kubilus, A., Bruehl, S. *et al.* (2003). Do changes in cognitive factors influence outcome following multidisciplinary treatment for chronic pain? A cross-lagged panel analysis. *Journal of Consulting and Clinical Psychology*, 71: 81–91.

Burns, V.E., Carroll, D., Drayson, M. *et al.* (2003). Life events, perceived stress and antibody response to influenza vaccination in young, healthy adults. *Journal of Psychosomatic Research*, 55: 569–72.

Bury, J., Morrison, V. and MacLachlan, S. (1992). *Working with Women and AIDS: Medical, Social and Counselling Issues*. London: Routledge.

Buzdar, A.U. (2004). Hormonal therapy in early and advanced breast cancer. *Breast Journal*, 10 (suppl. 1): S19–21.

Byrne, D.G. and Mazanov, J. (2001). Self-esteem, stress and cigarette smoking in adolescents. *Stress and Health*, 17: 105–110.

Byrne, D.G. and Mazanov, J. (2003). Adolescent stress and future smoking behaviour: a prospective investigation. *Journal of Psychosomatic Research*, 54: 313–21.

Byrne, P. and Long, B. (1976). *Doctors Talking to Patients: A Study of the Verbal Behaviour of General Practitioners Consulting in their Surgeries*. London: HMSO.

Cacioppo, J.T., Andersen, B.L., Turnquist, D.C. *et al.* (1986). Psychophysiological comparison processes: interpreting cancer symptoms. In B.L. Andersen (ed.), *Women with Cancer: Psychosocial Perspectives*. New York: Springer Verlag.

Cacioppo, J.T., Andersen, B.L., Turnquist, D.C. *et al.* (1989). Psychophysiological comparison theory: on the experience, description and assessment of signs and symptoms. *Patient Education and Counselling*, 13: 257–70.

Cacioppo, J.T., Poehlmann, K.M., Kiecolt-Glaser, J.K. *et al.* (1998). Cellular immune responses to acute stress in female caregivers of dementia patients and matched controls. *Health Psychology*, 17: 182–9.

Cahill, S.M. (1999). Caring in families: what motivates wives daughter, and daughters-in law to provide dementia care? *Journal of Family Studies*, 5: 235–47.

Calhoun, L.G. and Tedeschi, R.G. (eds) (2007). *Handbook of Post-traumatic Growth: Research and Practice*. London: Lawrence Erlbaum Associates.

California Department of Health Services (2003). *Alcohol Use During Pregnancy*. Sacramento CA: CDHS.

Callaghan, P. and Li, H.C. (2002). The effect of pre-operative psychological interventions on post-operative outcomes in Chinese women having an elective hysterectomy. *British Journal of Health Psychology*, 7: 247–52.

Calnan, M. (1987). *Health and Illness: The Lay Perspective*. London: Tavistock.

Cameron, L. (2008). Illness risk representations and motivations to engage in protective behavior: the case of skin cancer risk. *Psychology & Health*, 23: 91–112.

Camp, D.E., Klesges, R.C. and Relyea, G. (1993). The relationship between bodyweight concerns and adolescent smoking. *Health Psychology*, 12: 24–32.

Campbell, J.D., Mauksch, H.O., Neikirk, H.J. *et al.* (1990). Collaborative practice and provider styles in delivering health care. *Social Science and Medicine*, 30: 1359–65.

Campbell, L.A., Kirkpatrick, S.E., Berry, C.C. *et al.* (1992). Psychological preparation of mothers of pre-school children undergoing cardiac catheterization. *Psychology and Health*, 7: 175–85.

Campbell, M.K., Tessaro, I., DeVellis, B. *et al.* (2002). Effects of a tailored health promotion program for female blue-collar workers: health works for women. *Preventive Medicine*, 4: 313–23.

Canada, A., Fawzy, N. and Fawzy, F. (2005). Personality and disease outcome in malignant melanoma. *Journal of Psychosomatic Research*, 58: 19–27.

Cannon, W.B. (1932). *The Wisdom of the Body*. New York: W.W. Norton.

Cardano, M., Costa, G. and Demaria, M. (2004). Social mobility and health in the Turin longitudinal study. *Social Science and Medicine*, 58: 1563–74.

Carels, R.A., Darby, L., Cacciapaglia, H.M. *et al.* (2007). Using motivational interviewing as a supplement to obesity treatment: a stepped-care approach. *Health Psychology*, 26: 369–74

Carlson, L.E., Taenzer, P., Koopmans, J. *et al.* (2003). Predictive value of aspects of the transtheoretical model on smoking cessation in a community-based, large-group cognitive behavioral program. *Addictive Behaviors*, 28: 725–40.

Carlson, N. (2003) *Physiology of Behaviour*, 8th edition, Boston MA: Allyn and Bacon.

Caro, J.J., Speckman, J.L., Salas, M. *et al.* (1999). Effect of initial drug choice on persistence with antihypertensive therapy: the importance of actual practice data. *Canadian Medical Association Journal*, 160: 41–6.

Carod-Artal, J., Egido, J.A., González, J.L. *et al.* (2000). Quality of life among stroke survivors evaluated 1 year after stroke. *Stroke*, 31: 2995–3005.

Caron, F., Godin, G., Otis, J. *et al.* (2004). Evaluation of a theoretically based AIDS/STD peer education program on postponing sexual intercourse and on condom use among adolescents attending high school. *Health Education and Research*, 19: 185–97.

Carr, A.J. and Higginson, I.J. (2001). Are quality of life measures patient centred? *British Medical Journal*, 32: 1357–60.

Carr, D. (2003). A 'good death' for whom? Quality of spouse's death and psychological distress among older widowed persons. *Journal of Health and Social Behavior*, 44: 215–32.

Carrico, A.W., Antoni, M.H., Weaver, K.E. *et al.* (2005). Cognitive-behavioural stress management with HIV-positive homosexual men: mechanisms of sustained reductions in depressive symptoms. *Chronic Illness*, 1: 207–15.

Carroll, D., Davey-Smith, G. and Bennett, P. (1996a). Some observations on health and socioeconomic status. *Journal of Health Psychology*, 1: 1–17.

Carroll, D., Ebrahim, S., Tilling, K. *et al.* (2002). Admissions for myocardial infarction and World Cup football: database survey. *British Medical Journal*, 325: 1439–42.

Carroll, D., Moore, R.A., McQuay, H.J. *et al.* (2001). Transcutaneous electrical nerve stimulation (TENS) for chronic pain. In *The Cochrane Library*, issue 4. Oxford: Update Software.

Carroll, D., Tramèr M., McQuay H. *et al.* (1996b). Randomization is important in studies with pain outcomes: systematic review of transcutaneous electrical nerve stimulation in acute postoperative pain. *British Journal of Anaesthesia*, 77: 798–803.

Carroll, K.M., Libby, B., Sheehan, J. *et al.* (2001). Motivational interviewing to enhance treatment initiation in substance abusers: an effectiveness study. *American Journal of Addiction*, 10: 35–9.

Cartagena, R.G., Veugelers, P.J., Kipp, W. *et al.* (2006). Effectiveness of an HIV prevention program for secondary school students in Mongolia. *Journal of Adolescent Health*, 39: 9–16.

Carver, C.S. and Antoni, M.H. (2004). Finding benefit in breast cancer during the year after diagnosis predicts better adjustment 5–8 years after diagnosis. *Health Psychology* 26: 595–8.

Carver, C.S., Pozo, C., Harris, S.D. *et al.* (1993). How coping mediates the effect of optimism on distress: a study of women with early stage breast cancer. *Journal of Personality and Social Psychology*, 65: 375–90.

Carver, C.S. and Scheier, M.F. (1981). *Attention and Self-Regulation: A Control Theory Approach to Human Behavior*. New York: Springer.

Carver, C.S. and Scheier, M.F. (1998) *On the Self-regulation of Behaviour*. New York: Cambridge University Press.

Carver, C.S. and Scheier, M.F. (2005). Optimism. In C.R. Snyder and S.J. Lopez (eds), *Handbook of Positive Psychology* (pp. 231–43). Oxford: Oxford University Press.

Carver, C.S., Scheier, M.F. and Pozo, C. (1992). Conceptualizing the process of coping with health problems. In H.S. Friedman (ed.), *Hostility, Coping and Health*. Washington: American Psychological Association.

Carver, C.S., Scheier, M.F. and Weintraub, J.K. (1989). Assessing coping strategies: a theoretically based approach. *Journal of Personality and Social Psychology*, 56: 267–83.

Cassel, J. (1974). An epidemiological perspective of psychosocial factors in disease etiology. *American Journal of Public Health*, 64: 1040–3.

Cassell, E.J. (1976). Disease as an 'it': concepts of disease revealed by patients' presentation of symptoms. *Social Science and Medicine*, 10: 143–6.

Cassell, E.J. (1982). Paracetamol plus supplementary doses of codeine. An analgesic study of repeated doses. *European Journal of Clinical Pharmacology*, 23: 315–19.

Cassell, J.A., Mercer, C.H., Imriel, J. *et al.* (2006). Who uses condoms with whom? Evidence from national probability sample surveys. *Sexually Transmitted Infections*, 82: 467–73.

Cassileth, B.R., Lusk, E.J., Brown, L.L. *et al.* (1985). Psychosocial status of cancer patients and next of kin: normative data from the profile of mood states. *Journal of Psychosocial Oncology*, 3: 99–105.

Castillo-Richmond, A., Schneider, R.H., Alexander, C.N. *et al.* (2000). Effects of stress reduction on carotid atherosclerosis in hypertensive African Americans. *Stroke*, 31: 568–73.

Catz, S.L., Gore-Felton, C. and McClure, J.B. (2002). Psychological distress among minority and low-income women living with HIV. *Behavioral Medicine*, 28: 53–60.

Cavelaars, A.E.J.M., Kunst, A.E. and Mackenbach, J.P. (1997). Socio-economic differences in risk factors for morbidity and mortality in the European Community. *Journal of Health Psychology*, 2: 353–72.

Cella, D.F., Tulsky, D.S., Gray, G., *et al.* (1993). The Functional Assessment of Cancer Therapy scale: development and validation of the general measure. *Journal of Clinical Oncology*, 11: 570–9.

Chacham, A.S., Maia, M.B., Greco, M. *et al.* (2007). Autonomy and susceptibility to HIV/AIDS among young women living in a slum in Belo Horizonte, Brazil. *AIDS Care*, 19 Suppl 1: S12–22.

Chadha, N.K. and Repanos, C. (2004). How much do healthcare professionals know about informed consent? A Bristol experience. *Surgeon*, 2: 328–33, 360.

Chadha, N.K. and Repanos, C. (2006). Patients' understanding of words used to describe lumps: a cross-sectional study. *Journal of Laryngology and Otology*, 120: 125–8.

Chaillet, N., Dubé, E., Dugas, M. *et al.* (2006). Evidence-based strategies for implementing guidelines in obstetrics: a systematic review. *Obstetrics and Gynaecology*, 108: 1234–45.

Chaix, B., Rosvall, M. and Merlo, J. (2007). Neighborhood socioeconomic deprivation and residential instability: effects on incidence of ischemic heart disease and survival after myocardial infarction. *Epidemiology*, 18: 104–11.

Chalmers, B. (1996). Western and African conceptualisations of health. *Psychology and Health*, 12: 1–10.

Champion, V.L. (1990). Breast self-examination in women 35 and older: a prospective study. *Journal of Behavioural Medicine*, 13: 523–38.

Champion, V.L. and Miller, T.K. (1992). Variables related to breast self-examination. *Psychology of Women Quarterly*, 16: 81–96.

Chan, D.S. and Fishbein, M. (1993). Determinants of women's intentions to tell their partner to use condoms. *Journal of Applied Social Psychology*, 23: 1455–70.

Chan, D.S., Callahan, C.W., Hatch-Pigott, V.B., *et al.* (2007). Internet-based home monitoring and education of children with asthma is comparable to ideal office-based care: results of a 1-year asthma in-home monitoring trial. *Pediatrics*, 119: 569–78.

Chandrashekara, S., Jayashree, K., Veeranna, H.B. *et al.* (2007). Effects of anxiety on TNF-a levels during psychological stress. *Journal of Psychosomatic Research*, 63: 65–9.

Charmaz, K. (1983). Loss of self: a fundamental form of suffering in the chronically ill. *Sociology of Health and Illness*, 5: 168–95.

Charmaz, K. (1991). *Good Days, Bad Days: The Self in Chronic Illness and Time*. New Brunswick, NJ: Rutgers University Press.

Charmaz, K. (1994). Identity dilemmas of chronically ill men. *Sociological Quarterly*, 35: 269–88.

Chassin, C., Presson, C.C., Rose, J.S. *et al.* (1996). The natural history of cigarettes from adolescence to adulthood: demographic predictors of continuity and change. *Health Psychology*, 15: 478–84.

Chatkin, J.M., Blanco, D.C., Scaglia, N. *et al.* (2006). Impact of a low-cost and simple intervention in enhancing treatment adherence in a Brazilian asthma sample. *Journal of Asthma*, 43: 263–6.

Cheing, G.L. and Hui-Chan, C.W. (1999). Transcutaneous electrical nerve stimulation: nonparallel antinociceptive effects on chronic clinical pain and acute experimental pain. *Archives of Physical Medicine and Rehabiltation*, 80: 305–12.

Cheing, G.L., Tsui, A.Y., Lo, S.K. *et al.* (2003). Optimal stimulation duration of TENS in the management of osteoarthritic knee pain. *Journal of Rehabilitation Medicine*, 35: 62–8.

Chen, S.Y., Gibson, S., Katz, M.H. *et al.* (2002). Continuing increases in sexual risk behavior and sexually transmitted diseases among men who have sex with men: San Francisco, Calif., 1999–2001. *American Journal of Public Health*, 92: 1387–8.

Cheng, C. (2000). Seeking medical consultation: perceptual and behavioural characteristics distinguishing consulters and nonconsulters with functional dyspepsia. *Psychosomatic Medicine*, 62: 844–52.

Cheng, T.L., Savageau, J.A., Sattler, A.L. *et al.* (1993). Confidentiality in health care: a survey of knowledge, perceptions, and attitudes among high school students. *Journal of the American Medical Association*, 269: 1404–7.

Chesney, M.A. (2003). Adherence to HAART regimes. *AIDS Patient Care and STDs*, 17: 169–77.

Chesney, M.A., Folkman, S. and Chambers, D. (1996). Coping effectiveness training for men living with HIV: preliminary findings. *International Journal of STDs and AIDS*, suppl. 2: 75–82.

Cho, H. and Salmon, C.T. (2006). Fear appeals for individuals in different stages of change: intended and unintended effects and implications on public health campaigns. *Health Communication*, 20: 91–9.

Chochinov, H.M., Hack, T., Hassard, T. *et al.* (2002). Dignity in the terminally ill: a cross-sectional, cohort study. *The Lancet*, 360: 2026–30.

Chochinov, H.M., Tataryn, D.J., Wilson, K.G., *et al.* (2000). Prognostic awareness and the terminally ill. *Psychosomatics*, 41: 500–4.

Choi, W.S., Harris, K.J., Okuyemi, K. *et al.* (2003). Predictors of smoking initiation among college-bound high school students. *Annals of Behavioral Medicine*, 26: 69–74.

Choinière, R., Lafontaine, P., Edwards, A.C. (2000). Distribution of cardiovascular disease risk factors by socioeconomic status among Canadian adults. *Canadian Medical Association Journal*, 162 (9 Suppl): S13–24.

Christensen, A.J., Edwards, D.L., Wiebe, J.S. *et al.* (1996). Effect of verbal self-disclosure on natural killer cell activity: moderating influence of cynical hostility. *Psychosomatic Medicine*, 58: 150–5.

Christensen, C., Larson, J.R., Jr, Abbott, A. *et al.* (2000). Decision making of clinical teams: communication patterns and diagnostic error. *Medical Decision Making*, 20: 45–50.

Chronister, J. and Chan, F. (2006). A stress process model of caregiving for individuals with traumatic brain injury. *Rehabilitation Psychology*, 51: 190–201.

Cioffi, D. (1991). Beyond attentional strategies: a cognitive-perceptual model of somatic interpretation. *Psychological Bulletin*, 109: 25–41.

Clark, R. and Gochett, P. (2006). Interactive effects of perceived racism and coping responses predict a school-based assessment of blood pressure in black youth. *Annals of Behavioral Medicine*, 32: 1–9.

Clark, A. (2003). 'It's like an explosion in your life . . .' Lay perspectives on stress and myocardial infarction. *Journal of Clinical Nursing*, 12: 544–53.

Clark, D.B. and Sayette, M.A. (1993). Anxiety and the development of alcoholism: clinical and scientific issues. *American Journal on Addictions*, 2: 59–76.

Clark, S.L. and Stephens, M.A.P. (1996). Stroke patients' well-being as a function of caregiving spouses' helpful and unhelpful actions. *Personal Relationships*, 3: 171–84.

Clark-Carter, D. (2003). Effect sizes; the missing piece in the jigsaw. *The Psychologist*, 16: 636–8.

Clarke, R. (2000). Perceptions of interethnic group racism predict increased vascular reactivity to a laboratory challenge in college women. *Annals of Behavioral Medicine*, 22: 214–22.

Classen, C., Butler, L.D., Koopman, C. *et al.* (2001). Supportive–expressive group therapy and distress in patients with metastatic breast cancer: a randomized clinical intervention trial. *Archives of General Psychiatry*, 58: 494–501.

Clays, E., Leynen, F., De Bacquer, D. *et al.* (2007). High job strain and ambulatory blood pressure in middle-aged men and women from the Belgian job stress study. *Journal of Occupational and Environmental Medicine*, 49: 360–7.

Clayton, J.M., Butow, P.N., Tattersall, M.H. *et al.* (2007). Randomized controlled trial of a prompt list to help advanced cancer patients and their caregivers to ask questions about prognosis and end-of-life care. *Journal of Clinical Oncology*, 25: 715–23.

Clifford, S., Barber, N. and Horne, R. (2008). Understanding different beliefs held by adherers, unintentional nonadherers, and intentional non-adherers: application of the Necessity-Concerns Framework. *Journal of Psychosomatic Research*, 64: 41–6.

Coates, T.J., McKusick, L., Kuno, R. *et al.* (1989). Stress management training reduced numbers of sexual partners but did not improve immune function in men infected with HIV. *American Journal of Public Health*, 79: 885–7.

Cobb, S. (1976). Social support as a moderator of life stress. *Psychosomatic Medicine*, 38: 300–14.

Cockburn, J., Paul, C., Tzelepis, F. *et al.* (2003). Delay in seeking advice for symptoms that potentially indicate bowel cancer. *American Journal of Health Behavior*, 27: 401–7.

Cocquyt, V.F., Blondeel, P.N., Depypere, H.T. *et al.* (2003). Better cosmetic results and comparable quality of life after skin-sparing mastectomy and immediate autologous breast reconstruction compared to breast conservative treatment. *The British Association of Plastic Surgeons*, 56: 462–70.

Cohen, F. and Lazarus, R. (1979). Coping with the stresses of illness. In G.C. Stone, F. Cohen and N.E. Adler (eds), *Health Psychology: A Handbook*. San Francisco: Jossey-Bass.

Cohen, H.J., Pieper, C.F., Harris, T. *et al.* (1997). The association of plasma IL-6 levels with functional disability in community-dwelling elderly. *Journal of Gerontology. A: Biological Science and Medical Science*, 52: M201–8.

Cohen, L.A. (1987). Diet and cancer. *Scientific American*, 102: 42–8.

Cohen, L., Baile, W.F. and Henninger, E. (2003). Physiological and psychological effects of delivering medical news using a simulated physician–patient scenario. *Journal of Behavioral Medicine*, 26: 459–71.

Cohen, M., Hoffman, R.G., Cromwell, C. *et al.* (2002). The prevalence of distress in persons with human immunodeficiency virus infection. *Psychosomatics*, 43: 10–15.

Cohen, S. (1988). Psychosocial models of the role of social support in the etiology of physical disease. *Health Psychology*, 7: 269–97.

Cohen, S. and Herbert, T.B. (1996). Health psychology: psychological factors and physical disease from the perspective of human psychoneuroimmunology. *Annual Review of Psychology*, 47: 113–42.

Cohen, S. and Hoberman, H. (1983). Positive events and social support as buffers of life change stress. *Journal of Applied Social Psychology*, 13: 99–125.

Cohen, S. and Williamson, G.M. (1991). Stress and infectious disease in humans. *Psychological Bulletin*, 109: 5–24.

Cohen, S. and Wills, T.A. (1985). Stress, social support and the buffering hypothesis. *Psychological Bulletin*, 98: 310–57.

Cohen, S., Doyle, M.J., Skoner, D.P. *et al.* (1995). State and trait negative affect as predictors of objective and subjective symptoms of respiratory viral infections. *Journal of Personality and Social Psychology*, 68: 159–69.

Cohen, S., Evans, G.W., Stokols, D. *et al.* (1986). *Behavior, Health and Environmental Stress*. New York: Plenum.

Cohen, S., Frank, E., Doyle, W.J. *et al.* (1998). Types of stressors that increase susceptibility to the common cold in healthy adults. *Health Psychology*, 17: 214–23.

Cohen, S., Kamarck, T. and Mermelstein, R. (1983). A global measure of perceived stress. *Journal of Health and Social Behaviour*, 24: 385–96.

Cohen, S., Tyrell, D.A. and Smith, A.P. (1993a). Life events, perceived stress, negative affect and susceptibility to the common cold. *Journal of Personality and Social Psychology*, 64: 131–40.

Cohen, S., Tyrell, D.A. and Smith, A.P. (1993b). Psychological stress and susceptibility to the common cold. *New England Journal of Medicine*, 325: 606–12.

Cole, S.W., Kemeny, M.E., Taylor, S.E. *et al.* (1996). Elevated physical health risk among gay men who conceal their homosexual identity. *Health Psychology*, 15: 23–51.

Coleman, D.L. (1979). Obesity genes: beneficial effects in heterozygous mice. *Science*, 203: 663–5.

Coleman, P.G. (1999). Identity management in later life. In R.T. Woods (ed.), *Psychological Problems of Ageing: Assessment, Treatment and Care*. Chichester: Wiley.

Collins, S. (2005). Explanations in consultations: the combined effectiveness of doctors' and nurses' communication with patients. *Medical Education*, 39: 785–6.

COMMIT (1995). Community intervention trial for smoking cessation (COMMIT): II. Changes in adult cigarette smoking prevalence. *American Journal of Public Health*, 85: 193–200.

Committee on Understanding and Eliminating Racial and Ethnic Disparities in Health Care, Institute of Medicine, National Academy of Sciences, Smedley, B.D., Stith, A.Y. and Nelson, A.R. (eds) (2002). *Unequal Treatment: Confronting Racial and Ethnic Disparities in Health Care*. National Academy Press.

Compas, B.E., Stoll, M.F., Thomsen, A.H. *et al.* (1999). Adjustment to breast cancer: age-related differences in coping and emotional distress. *Breast Cancer Research and Treatment*, 54: 195–203.

Conard, M.A. and Matthews, R.A. (2008). Modeling the stress process: Personality eclipses dysfunctional cognitions and workload in predicting stress. *Personality & Individual Differences*, 44: 171–181.

Conner, M. and Armitage, C.J. (1998). Extending the theory of planned behaviour: a review and avenues for further research. *Journal of Applied Social Psychology*, 28: 1429–64.

Conner, M. and Norman, P. (1996). *Predicting Health Behaviour: Research and Practice with Social Cognition Models*. Buckingham: Open University Press.

Considine, N.S., Horton, D., Magai, C. *et al.* (2007). Breast screening in response to gain, loss, and empowerment framed messages among diverse, low-income women. *Journal of Health Care for the Poor and Underserved*, 18: 550–66.

Constans, J.I., Mathews, A., Brantley, P.J. *et al.* (1999). Attentional reactions to an MI: the impact of mood state, worry, and coping style. *Journal of Psychosomatic Research*, 46: 415–23.

Cook, R.F., Billings, D.W., Hersch, R. *et al.* (2007). A field test of a web-based workplace health promotion program to improve dietary practices, reduce stress, and increase physical activity: randomized controlled trial. *Journal of Medical Internet Research*, 9: e17.

Cooper, C.L. and Payne, R. (eds), (1988). *Causes, Coping and Consequences of Stress at Work*. Chichester: Wiley.

Cope, C.D., Lyons, A.C., Donovan, V. *et al.* (2003). Providing letters and audiotapes to supplement a prenatal diagnostic consultation: effects on later distress and recall. *Prenatal Diagnosis*, 23: 1060–7.

Cordova, M., Andrykowski, M., Kenady, D. *et al.* (1995). Frequency and correlates of posttraumatic-stress-disorder-like symptoms after treatment for breast cancer. *Journal of Consulting and Clinical Psychology*, 63: 981–6.

Costa, P.T., Jr and McCrae, R.R. (1987). Neuroticism, somatic complaints and disease: is the bark worse than the bite? *Journal of Personality*, 55: 299–316.

Costa, P.T. and McCrae, R.R. (1992a). Four ways five factors are basic. *Personality and Individual Differences*, 13: 653–65.

Costa, P.T. and McCrae, R.R. (1992b). *Revised NEO Personality Inventory (NEO PI-R) and NEO five-factor inventory (NEO FFI) professional manual*. Odessa, Fla: Psychological Assessment Resources.

Cotman, C.W. and Engesser-Cesar, C. (2002). Exercise enhances and protects brain function. *Exercise Sport Science Reviews*, 30: 75–9.

Courtenay, W.H. (2000). Constructions of masculinity and their influence on men's well-being: a theory of gender and health. *Social Science and Medicine*, 50: 1385–1401.

Cowburn, G. and Stockley, L. (2005). Consumer understanding and use of nutrition labelling: a systematic review. *Public Health Nutr.* 8: 21–8.

Cowburn, G. and Stockley, L. (2006). Consumer understanding and use of nutrition labelling: a systematic review. *Journal of the American Dietetic Association*, 106: 917–20.

Cox, K. (2003). Assessing the quality of life of patients in phase I and II anti-cancer drug trials: interviews versus questionnaires. *Social Science and Medicine*, 56: 921–34.

Cox, K.L., Gorely, T.J., Puddey, I.B. *et al.* (2003). Exercise behaviour change in 40- to 65-year-old women: the SWEAT study (Sedentary Women Exercise Adherence Trial). *British Journal of Health Psychology*, 8: 477–95.

Cox, W.M. and Klinger, E. (2004). A motivational model of alcohol use: determinants of use and change. In W.M. Cox and E. Klinger (eds), *Handbook of Motivational Counselling: Concepts, Approaches, and Assessments* (pp. 121–38). Chichester: John Wiley.

Coyne, J. and Fiske, V. (1992). Couples coping with chronic and catastrophic illness. In T.J. Akamatsu, M.A.P. Stephens, S.E. Hobfoll and J.H. Crowther (eds), *Family Health Psychology*. Washington: Hemisphere Publishing.

Coyne, J.C. and Racioppo, M.W. (2000). Never the twain shall meet? Closing the gap between coping research and clinical intervention research. *American Psychologist*, 55: 655–64.

Coyne, J.C. and Smith, D.A.F (1991). Couples coping with a myocardial infarction: a contextual perspective on wive's distress. *Journal of Personality and Social Psychology*, 61: 404–12.

Coyne, J.C., Benazon, N.R., Rohrbaugh, M.J. *et al.* (2003). Patient and spousal attitude in couples living with chronic heart failure. Symposium paper presented at the 17th Conference of the European Health Psychology Society, September, Kos.

Cramer, J.A. (1998). Enhancing patient compliance in the elderly. Role of packaging aids and monitoring. *Drugs and Aging*, 12: 7–15.

Cramer, J.A. (2004). A systematic review of adherence with medications for diabetes. *Diabetes Care*, 27: 1218–24.

Creuss, D.G., Antoni, M.H., McGregor, B.A. *et al.* (2000). Cognitive-behavioral stress management reduces serum cortisol by enhancing benefit finding among women being treated for early stage breast cancer. *Psychosomatic Medicine*, 62: 304–8.

Crisp, A., Sedgwick, P., Halek, C. *et al.* (1999). Why may teenage girls persist in smoking? *Journal of Adolescence*, 22: 657–72.

Crombez, G., Eccleston, C., De Vlieger, P. *et al.* (2008). Is it better to have controlled and lost than never to have controlled at all? An experimental investigation of control over pain. *Pain*, 137: 631–9.

Crossley, M.L. (2000). *Rethinking Health Psychology*. Buckingham: Open University Press.

Crossley, M.L. and Small, N. (1998). Evaluation of HIV/AIDS education training services provided by London Lighthouse at St. Ann's Hospice. Stockport Health Authority.

Crowe, F.L., Key, T.J., Appleby, P. N. *et al.* (2008). Dietary fat intake and risk of prostate cancer in the European: prospective investigation into cancer and nutrition. *American Journal of Clinical Nutrition*, 87: 1405–13.

Croyle, R.T. and Barger, S.D. (1993). Illness cognition. In S. Maes, H. Leventhal and M. Johnston (eds), *International Review of Health Psychology*, Vol. II. Chichester: Wiley.

Croyle, R.T. and Ditto, P.M. (1990). Illness cognition and behavior: an experimental approach. *Journal of Behavioral Medicine*, 13: 31–52.

Cummings, J.H. and Bingham, S.A. (1998). Diet and the prevention of cancer. *British Medical Journal*, 317: 1636–40.

Curbow, B., Somerfield, M.R., Baker, F. *et al.* (1993). Personal changes, dispositional optimism, and psychological adjustment to bone marrow transplantation. *Journal of Behavioral Medicine*, 16: 423–43.

Curry, S.J. and Emmons, K.M. (1994). Theoretical models for predicting and improving compliance with breast cancer screening. Mini-series: advances in behavioural medicine research on breast cancer. *Annals of Behavioral Medicine*, 16: 302–16.

Cutrona, C.E. (1996). *Social Support in Couples*. Thousand Oaks, CA: Sage.

Cutrona, C.E. and Russell, D.W. (1987). The provision of social relationships and adaptation to stress. In W.H. Jones and D. Perlman (eds), *Advances in Personal Relationships*, Vol. 1. Greenwich, Conn.: JAI Press.

Cutrona, C.E. and Russell, D.W. (1990). Type of social support and specific stress: toward a theory of optimal matching. In B.A. Sarason, I.G. Sarason and

G.R. Pierce (eds), *Social Support: An Interactional View*. New York: Wiley.

Dababneh, A.J., Swanson, N. and Shell, R.L. (2001). Impact of added rest breaks on the productivity and well being of workers. *Ergonomics*, 44: 164–74.

Dalton, S.O., Boesen, E.H., Ross, L. *et al.* (2002). Mind and cancer: do psychological factors cause cancer? *European Journal of Cancer*, 38: 1313–23.

Dancey, C.P., Taghavi, M., Fox, R.J. (1998). The relationship between daily stress and symptoms of irritable bowel: a time-series approach. *Journal of Psychosomatic Research*, 44: 537–45.

Dantzer, R. and Kelley, K.W. (1989). Stress and immunity: an integrated view of relationships between the brain and the immune system. *Life Sciences*, 44: 1995–2008.

Darnley, S.E., Kennedy, T., Jones, R. *et al.* (2002). A randomised controlled trial of the addition of cognitive behavioural therapy (CBT) to antispasmodic therapy for irritable bowel syndrome (IBS) in primary care. *Gastroenterology*, 122: A–69.

Davey-Smith, G. and Philips, A.N. (1991). Socio-economic conditions in childhood and ischaemic heart disease in middle age. *British Medical Journal*, 302: 113–14.

Davey-Smith, G., Ebrahim, S. and Frankel, S. (2001). How policy informs the evidence: 'evidence-based' thinking can lead to debased policy making (editorial). *British Medical Journal*, 322: 184–5.

Davey-Smith, G., Wentworth, D., Neaton, J.D *et al.* (1996). Socio-economic differentials in mortality risk among men screened for the Multiple Risk Factor Intervention Trial, 2: black men. *American Journal of Public Health*, 86: 497–504.

David, J.P. and Suls, J. (1996). Coping efforts in daily life: role of big five traits and problem appraisals. *Journal of Personality*, 67: 265–94.

Davidson, K.W., MacGregor, M.E., Stuhr, J. *et al.* (2000). Constructive anger verbal behaviour predicts blood pressure in a population-based sample. *Health Psychology*, 19: 55–64.

Davidson, P.R. and Parker, K.C.H. (2001). Eye movement desensitization and reprocessing (EMDR): a meta-analysis. *Journal of Consulting and Clinical Psychology*, 69: 305–16.

Davies, J.B. and Baker, R. (1987). The impact of self-presentation and interviewer bias on self-reported heroin use. *British Journal of Addiction*, 82: 907–12.

Dearing, J.W., Rogers, E.M., Meyer, G. *et al.* (1996). Social marketing and diffusion-based strategies for communicating with unique populations: HIV prevention in San Francisco. *Journal of Health Communication*, 1: 343–63.

Deary, I.J., Clyde, Z. and Frier, B.M. (1997). Constructs and models in health psychology: the case of

personality and illness reporting in diabetes mellitus. *British Journal of Health Psychology*, 2: 35–54.

DeBoer, M.F., Ryckman, R.M., Pruyn, J.F. *et al.* (1999). Psychosocial correlates of cancer relapse and survival: a literature review. *Patient Education and Counselling*, 37: 215–30.

Deci, E.L. and Ryan, R.M. (2000). The 'what' and 'why' of goal pursuits: human needs and the self-determination of behavior. *Psychological Inquiry*, 11: 227–68.

DeFoe, J.R. and Breed, W. (1989). Consulting to change media contents: two cases in alcohol education. *International Quarterly of Community Health Education*, 4: 257–72.

DeFriese, G. and Woomert, A. (1983). Self-care among the US elderly. *Research on Aging*, 5: 3–23.

De Haes, H. and Koedoot, N. (2003). Patient centered decision making in palliative cancer treatment: a world of paradoxes. *Patient Education and Counselling*, 50: 43–9.

Dehghani, M., Sharpe, L. and Nicholas, M.K. (2003). Selective attention to pain-related information in chronic musculoskeletal pain patients. *Pain*, 105: 37–46.

de Lange, A.H., Taris, T.W., Kompier, M.A. *et al.* (2003). 'The very best of the millennium': longitudinal research and the demand–control–(support) model. *Journal of Occupational Health Psychology*, 8: 282–305.

Dembrowski, T.M., MacDougall, J.M., Costa, P.T. *et al.* (1989). Components of hostility as predictors of sudden death and myocardial infarction in the Multiple Risk Factor Intervention Trial. *Psychosomatic Medicine*, 51: 514–22.

De Moor, C., Sterner, J., Hall, M. *et al.* (2002). A pilot study of the effects of expressive writing on psychological and behavioral adjustment in patients enrolled in a phase II trial of vaccine therapy for metastatic renal cell carcinoma. *Health Psychology*, 21: 615–19.

Denollet, J. (1998). Personality and coronary heart disease: the type-D scale-16 (DS16). *Annals of Behavioral Medicine*, 20: 209–15.

Denollet, J. and dePotter, B. (1992). Coping subtypes for men with coronary heart disease: relationship to well-being, stress and type-A behavior. *Psychological Medicine*, 22: 667–84.

Denollet, J., Sys, S.U., Stroobant, N. *et al.* (1996). Personality as an independent predictor of long-term mortality in patients with coronary heart disease. *The Lancet*, 347: 417–21.

de Nooijer, J., de Vet, E, Brug, J. and de Vries, N.K. (2006). Do implementation intentions help to turn good intentions into higher fruit intakes? *Journal of Nutrition Education and Behavior*, 38: 25–9.

de Nooijer, J., Lechner, L. and de Vries, H.A. (2001). Qualitative study on detecting cancer symptoms and seeking medical help; an application of Andersen's model of total patient delay. *Patient Education and Counseling*, 42: 145–57.

Denscombe, M. (2001). Peer group pressure, young people and smoking: new developments and policy implications. *Drugs: Education, Prevention and Policy*, 8: 7–32.

Department of Health (1991). *The Health of the Nation*. London: HMSO.

Department of Health (1992). *The Health of the Nation: A Strategy for Health in England*. London: HMSO.

Department of Health (1995). *Obesity: Reversing the Increasing Problem of Obesity in England*. Report from the Nutrition and Physical Activity Task Forces. London: HMSO.

Department of Health (1998a). *Health Survey for England: The Health of Young People 1995–1997*. London: Department of Health.

Department of Health (1998). *Report of the Scientific Committee on Tobacco and Health*. London: Department of Health.

Department of Health (1999a). *Caring about Carers: A National Strategy for Carers*. London: Department of Health.

Department of Health (1999b). *Saving Lives: Our Healthier Nation*. London: Department of Health.

Department of Health (2000). Statistics on Smoking: England 1978 onwards. *Statistical Bulletin* 200/17. London: Department of Health.

Department of Health (2000a). *Health Survey for England*. London: National Centre for Social Research & the National Foundation for Educational Research.

Department of Health (2001a). *The 2000 Health Survey for England: The Health of Older People (aged 65+)*. London: Department of Health.

Department of Health (2001b). *The Expert Patient: A New Approach to Chronic Disease Management for the 21st Century*. London: Department of Health.

Department of Health (2001c). *Involving Patients and the Public in Healthcare*, www.dh.gov.uk/Policy AndGuidance/OrganisationPolicy/PatientAnd PublicInvolvement/InvolvingPatientsPublic Healthcare/ fs/en.

Department of Health (2003). *Teenage Mothers and their Children: Factors Affecting their Health and Development*. London: Department of Health.

Department of Health (2004). *At least five a week: Evidence of the impact of physical activity and its relationship with health – a report from the Chief Medical Officer*. London UK: Department of Health.

Department of Health and Human Services (1996). Report of final mortality statistics, 1994. *Monthly Vital Statistics Report*, 45 (3 suppl.). Hyattsville, Md: Public Health Service.

Department of Health and Human Services (1998). *Health, United States, 1998: Socio-economic Status and Health Chartbook*. Hyattsville, Md: National Centre for Health Statistics.

Derbyshire, S.W. (2000). Exploring the pain 'neuro-matrix'. *Current Reviews of Pain*, 4: 467–77.

De Ridder, D. and Schreurs, K. (2001). Developing interventions for chronically ill patients: Is coping a helpful concept? *Clinical Psychology Review*, 21: 205–40.

De Ridder, D., Fournier, M. and Bensing, J. (2004). Does optimism affect symptom report in chronic disease? What are its consequences for self-care behaviour and physical functioning? *Journal of Psychosomatic Research*, 56: 341–50.

Descartes, R. (1664). *Traite de l'homme*. Paris: Angot.

Detmar, S.B., Aaronson, N.K., Wever, L.D. *et al.* (2000). How are you feeling? Who wants to know? Patients' and oncologists preferences for discussing halth-related quality of life issues. *Journal of Clinical Oncology*, 18: 3295–301.

Detweiler, J.B., Bedell, B.T., Salovey, P. *et al.* (1999). Message framing and sunscreen use: gain framed messages motivate beachgoers. *Health Psychology*, 18: 189–96.

Devanesen, D. (2000). Traditional Aboriginal medicine practice in the Northern Territory. In *International Symposium on Traditional Medicine*, Awaji Islands, Japan. Available from: www.nt.gov.au/health/ comm_health/abhealth_strategy?Traditional% 20Aboriginal%20Medicine%20- %20Japan%20Paper.pdf

DeVellis, R.F., Lewis, M.A. and Sterba, K.R. (2003). Interpersonal emotional processes in adjustment to chronic illness. In J. Suls and K.A. Wallston (eds), *Social Psychological Foundations of Health and Illness*. Malden, Mass.: Blackwell.

Devine, C.M., Jastran, M., Jabs, J. *et al.* (2006). 'A lot of sacrifices:' work–family spillover and the food choice coping strategies of low-wage employed parents. *Social Science and Medicine*, 63: 2591–603.

Dey, P., Bundred, N., Gibbs, A. *et al.* (2002). Costs and benefits of a one stop clinic compared with a dedicated breast clinic: randomised controlled trial. *British Medical Journal*, 324: 507.

Deyo, R.A. (1986). Early diagnostic evaluation of lower back pain. *Journal of General Internal Medicine*, 1: 328–38.

Deyo, R.A. (1991). Fads in the treatment of low back pain. *New England Journal of Medicine*, 325: 1039–40.

Deyo, R.A., Walsh, N.E., Martin, D.C. *et al.* (1990). A controlled trial of transcutaneous electrical nerve stimulation (TENS) and exercise for chronic low back pain. *New England Journal of Medicine*, 322: 1627–34.

di Clemente, C.C. and Prochaska, J.O. (1982). Self-change and therapy change of smoking behavior: a comparison of processes of change in cessation and maintenance. *Addictive Behaviours*, 7: 133–42.

di Clemente, C.C. and Velicer, W.F. (1997). The trans-theoretical model of health behavior change. *American Journal of Health Promotion*, 12: 11–12.

di Clemente, C.C., Prochaska, J.O., Fairhurst, S.K. *et al.* (1991). The process of smoking cessation: an analysis of precontemplation, contemplation, and preparation stages of change. *Journal of Consulting and Clinical Psychology*, 59: 295–304.

Didlake, R.H., Dreyfus, K., Kerman, R.H. *et al.* (1988). Patient noncompliance: a major cause of late graft failure in cyclosporine-treated renal transplants. *Transplant Proceedings*, 20: 63–9.

Diefenbach, M.A., Leventhal, E.A., Leventhal, H. *et al.* (1995). Negative affect relates to cross-sectional but not longitudinal symptom reporting: data from elderly adults. *Health Psychology*, 15: 282–8.

Digiusto, E. and Bird, K.D. (1995). Matching smokers to treatment: self-control versus social support. *Journal of Consulting and Clinical Psychology*, 63: 290–295.

Dijkstra, P.U., Geertzen, J.H., Stewart, R. *et al.* (2002). Phantom pain and risk factors: a multivariate analysis. *Journal of Pain Symptom Management*, 24: 578–85.

Dillay, J.W., McFarland, W., Woods, W.J. *et al.* (2002). Thoughts associated with unprotected anal intercourse among men at high risk in San Francisco 1997–1999. *Psychology and Health*, 17: 235–46.

DiMatteo, R. (2004). The role of effective communication with children and their families in fostering adherence to pediatric regimes. *Patient Education and Counselling*, 55: 339–44.

DiMatteo, R.M., Lepper, H.D. and Croghan, T.W. (2000). Depression is a risk factor for non-compliance with medical treatment: meta-analysis of the effects of anxiety and depression on patient adherence. *Archives of Internal Medicine*, 160: 2101–7.

Dimigen, G. and Ferguson, K. (1993). An investigation into the relationship of children's cognitive development and their concepts of illness. *Psychologia*, 36: 97–102.

Ditto, P.H., Druley, J.A., Moore, K.A. *et al.* (1996). Fates worse than death: the role of valued life activities in health state evaluations. *Health Psychology*, 15: 332–43.

Ditto, T.T. and Jemmott, J.B., III (1989). From rarity to evaluative extremity: effects of prevalence information on evaluations of positive and negative characteristics. *Journal of Personality and Social Psychology*, 57: 16–26.

Dodds, J. and Mercey, D. (2002). *London Gay Men's Survey: 2001 Results*. London: Department of STDs, Royal Free and University College Medical School.

Dodds, J.P., Mercey, D.E., Parry, J.V. *et al.* (2004). Increasing risk behaviour and high levels of un-diagnosed HIV infection in a community sample of homosexual men. *Sexually Transmitted Infections*, 80: 236–40.

Dohrenwend, B.S. and Dohrenwend, B.P. (1982). Some issues in research on stressful life events. In T. Millon, C. Green and R. Meagher (eds), *Handbook of Clinical Health Psychology*, New York: Plenum.

Doll, R. and Hill, A.B. (1954). The mortality of doctors in relation to their smoking habits: a preliminary report. *British Medical Journal*, 1: 1451–5.

Doll, R. and Peto, R. (1981). *The Cause of Human Cancer*. Oxford: Oxford University Press.

Doll, R., Peto, R., Hall, E. *et al.* (1994). Mortality in relation to consumption of alcohol: 13 years observation on male British doctors. *British Medical Journal*, 309: 911–18.

Dooley, D., Fielding, J. and Levi, L. (1996). Health and unemployment. *Annual Review of Public Health*, 17: 449–65.

Doyal, L. (2001). Sex, gender, and health: the need for a new approach. *British Medical Journal*, 323: 1061–3.

Dragano, N., Verde, P.E. and Siegrist, J. (2005). Organisational downsizing and work stress: testing synergistic health effects in employed men and women. *Journal of Epidemiology and Community Health*, 59: 694–9.

Droomers, M., Schrijvers, C.T.M. and Mackenbach, J.P. (2002). Why do lower educated people continue smoking? Explanations from the longitudinal GLOBE study. *Health Psychology*, 21: 263–72.

Drossaert, C.H., Boer, H. and Seydel, E.R. (1996). Health education to improve repeat participation in the Dutch breast cancer screening programme: evaluation of a leaflet tailored to previous participants. *Patient Education and Counselling*, 8: 121–31.

Duff, A.J. (2001). Psychological interventions in cystic fibrosis and asthma. *Paediatric Respiratory Reviews*, 2: 350–7.

Duffy, L.C., Zielezny, M.A., Marshall, J.R. *et al.* (1991). Relevance of major stress events as an indicator of disease activity prevalence in inflammatory bowel disease. *Behavioral Medicine*, fall: 101–10.

Duncan, S., Strycker, L. and Duncan, T. (1999). Exploring associations in developmental trends of adolescent substance use and risky sexual behaviour in a high risk population, *Journal of Behavioral Medicine*, 22: 21–34.

Dundas, R., Morgan, M. and Redfern, J. (2001). Ethnic differences in behavioural risk factors for stroke: implications for health promotion. *Ethnicity and Health*, 6: 95–103.

Dunbar-Jacob, J., Burke, L.E. and Pucznski, S. (1995). Clinical assessment and management of adherence to medication regimens. In P.M. Nicassio and T.W. Smith (eds), *Managing Chronic Illness: A Biopsychosocial Perspective*. Washington: American Psychological Association.

Dunn, D.S. and Dougherty, S.B. (2005). Prospects for a positive psychology of rehabilitation. *Rehabilitation Psychology*, 50: 305–311.

Dutta-Bergman, M.J. (2003). A descriptive narrative of healthy eating: a social marketing approach using psychographics in conjunction with interpersonal, community, mass media and new media activities. *Health Marketing Quarterly*, 20: 81–101.

Dusseldorp, E., van Elderen, T., Maes, S. *et al.* (1999). A meta-analysis of psycho-educational programs for coronary heart disease patients. *Health Psychology*, 18: 506–19.

Dzewaltowski, D.A. (1989). Toward a model of exercise motivation. *Journal of Sport and Exercise Psychology*, 11: 251–69.

Eagly, A.H. and Chaiken, S. (1993). *The Psychology of Attitudes*. Orlando, Fla: Harcourt Brace Jovanovich.

Earl, A. and Albarracín, D. (2007). Nature, decay, and spiraling of the effects of fear-inducing arguments and HIV counseling and testing: a meta-analysis of the short- and long-term outcomes of HIV-prevention interventions. *Health Psychology*, 26: 496–506.

Echabe, A.E., Guillen, C.S. and Ozamiz, J.A. (1992). Representations of health, illness and medicines: coping strategies and health promoting behaviour. *British Journal of Clinical Psychology*, 31: 339–49.

Echteld, M.A., Maes, S. and van Elderen, T.M.T. (1998). Predictors of quality of life in PTCA* patients: avoiding stressors increases quality of life. In R. Schwarzer (ed.), *Advances in Health Psychology Research*. Berlin: Berlin Free University. [*percutaneous transluminal coronary angioplasty]

Echteld, M.A., van Elderen, T.M.T. and van der Kamp, L.J.T. (2001). How goal disturbance, coping and chest pain relate to quality of life: a study among patients waiting for PTCA. *Quality of Life Research*, 10: 487–501.

Edelmann, R. (1999). *Psychosocial Aspects of the Health Care Process*. Harlow: Prentice Hall.

Edwards, A., Elwyn, G., Covey, J. *et al.* (2001). Presenting risk information – a review of the effects of 'framing' and other manipulations on patient outcomes. *Journal of Health Communication*, 6: 61–82.

Edwards, A., Elwyn, G., Hood, K. *et al.* (2004). Patient-based outcome results from a cluster randomized trial of shared decision-making skill development and use of risk communication aids in general practice. *Family Practice*, 21: 347–54.

Edwards, G., Anderson, P., Babor, T. *et al.* (1994). *Alcohol Policy and the Public Good*. Oxford: Oxford University Press.

Edwards, W. (1954). The theory of decision making. *Psychological Bulletin*, 51: 380–417.

Egan, G. (1998). *The Skilled Helper: Models, Skills, and Methods for Effective Helping*. Monterey, Calif.: Brooks/Cole.

Egan, G. (2006). *The Skilled Helper: A Problem-management and Opportunity Development Approach to Helping*. Belmont, Calif.: Wadsworth.

Eiser, C. (1985). *The Psychology of Childhood Illness*. New York: Springer Verlag.

Eiser, C. (1990). *Chronic Childhood Disease: An Introduction to Psychological Theory and Research*. Cambridge: Cambridge University Press.

Eiser, C. (2004). *Children with Cancer. Their Quality of Life*. NJ: Lawrence Erlbaum.

Eiser, C. and Havermans, T. (1992). Mothers' and fathers' coping with chronic childhood disease. *Psychology and Health*, 7: 249–57.

Eiser, C. and Morse, R. (2001). The measurement of quality of life in children: past and future perspectives. *Journal of Developmental and Behavioral Pediatrics*, 22: 248–56.

Eiser, C., Patterson, D. and Tripp, J.H. (1984). Diabetes and developing knowledge of the body. *Archives of Disease in Childhood*, 59: 167–9.

Eiser, J.R. (1996). Reconnecting the individual and the social in health psychology. *Psychology and Health*, 11: 605–18.

Eiser, J.R., Eiser, C. and Pauwels, C. (1993). Skin cancer: assessing perceived risk and behavioral attitudes. *Psychology and Health*, 8: 393–404.

Ellington, L. and Wiebe, D.J. (1999). Neuroticism, symptom presentation, and medical decision making. *Health Psychology*, 18: 634–43.

Ellis, A. (1977). The basic clinical theory of rational–emotive therapy. In A. Ellis and R. Grieger (eds), *Handbook of Rational–Emotive Therapy*. New York: Springer Verlag.

Elmer, P.J., Grimm, R., Jr, Laing, B. *et al.* (1995). Lifestyle intervention: results of the Treatment of Mild Hypertension Study (TOMHS). *Preventive Medicine*, 24: 378–88.

Elstein, A.S. and Schwarz, A. (2002). Clinical problem solving and diagnostic decision making: selective review of the cognitive literature. *British Medical Journal*, 324: 729–32.

Elwyn, G., Edwards, A., Kinnersley, P. *et al.* (2000). Shared decision making and the concept of equipoise: the competences of involving patients in healthcare choices. *British Journal of General Practice*, 50: 892–9.

Ely, J.W., Levinson, W., Elder, N.C. *et al.* (1995). Perceived causes of family physicians' errors. *Journal of Family Practice*, 40: 337–44.

Emery, S., Wakefield, M.A., Terry-McElrath, Y. *et al.* (2007a). Televised state-sponsored antitobacco advertising and youth smoking beliefs and behavior in the United States, 1999–2000. *Archives of Pediatric and Adolescent Medicine*, 159: 639–45.

Emery, S., Wakefield, M.A., Terry-McElrath, Y. *et al.* (2007b). Using message framing to promote acceptance of the human papillomavirus vaccine. *Health Psychology*, 26: 745–52.

Emler, N. (1984). Delinquency and reputation. *Progress in Experimental Personality Research*, 13: 174–230.

Endler, N.S. and Parker, J.D.A. (1993). The multidimensional assessment of coping: concepts, issues, measurement. In G.L. Van Heck, P. Bonaiuto, I.J. Deary and W. Nowack (eds), *Personality Psychology in Europe*, Vol. 4. Netherlands: Tilburg University Press.

Endler, N.S., Parker, J.D.A. and Summerfeldt, L.J. (1998). Coping with health problems: developing a reliable and valid multidimensional measure. *Psychological Assessment*, 10: 195–205.

Eng, J.J. and Martin-Ginis, K.A. (2007). Using the Theory of Planned Behaviour to predict leisure time physical activity among people with chronic kidney disease. *Rehabilitation Psychology*, 52: 435–442.

Engbers, L.H., van Poppel, M.N., Chin, A. *et al.* (2006). The effects of a controlled worksite environmental intervention on determinants of dietary behavior and self-reported fruit, vegetable and fat intake. *BMC Public Health*, 6: 253.

Engel, G.L. (1977). The need for a new medical model: a challenge for biomedicine. *Science*, 196: 129–36.

Engel, G.L. (1980). The clinical application of the bio-psychosocial model. *American Journal of Psychiatry*, 137: 535–44.

Epstein, R.M., Quill, T.E. and McWhinney, I.R. (1999). Somatization reconsidered: incorporating the patient's experience of illness. *Archives of Internal Medicine*, 159: 215–22.

Erens, B., McManus, S., Prescott, A. *et al.* (2003). *National Survey of Sexual Attitudes and Lifestyles II: Reference Tables and Summary Report*. London: National Centre for Social Research.

Eriksen, H.R., Ihlebaek, C., Mikkelsen, A. *et al.* (2002). Improving subjective health at the worksite: a randomized controlled trial of stress management training, physical exercise and an integrated health programme. *Occupational Medicine*, 52: 383–91.

Eriksen, J., Jensen, M.K., Sjogren, P. *et al.* (2003). Epidemiology of chronic non-malignant pain in Denmark. *Pain*, 106: 221–8.

Erikson, E.H. (1959). Identity and the life cycle. *Psychological Issues*, 1: 1–171.

Erikson, E.H. (1980). *Identity and the Life Cycle: A Reissue*. New York: W.W. Norton.

Erikson, E.H., Erikson, J.M. and Kivnick, H.Q. (1986). *Vital Involvement in Old Age: The Experience of Old Age in Our Time*. New York: W.W. Norton.

Esterling, B.A., Kiecolt-Glaser, J.K. and Glaser, R. (1996). Psychosocial modulation of cytokine induced natural killer cell activity in older adults. *Psychosomatic Medicine*, 58: 264–72.

Esterling, B.A., L'Abate, L., Murray, E.J. *et al.* (1999). Empirical foundations for writing in prevention and psychotherapy: mental and physical health outcomes. *Clinical Psychology Review*, 19: 79–96.

European Commission (1999). *A Pan-EU Survey of Consumer Attitudes to Physical Activity, Body Weight and Health*. Luxembourg: EC. DGV/F.3.

Euroqol Group (1990). Euroqol: a new facility for the measurement of health related quality of life. *Health Policy*, 16: 199–208.

Evandrou, M. (2006). Inequalities among older people in London: the challenge of diversity. In V.R. Rodwin and M.K. Gusmano (eds), *Growing Older in World Cities: New York, London, Paris and Tokyo*. Nashville: Vanderbilt University Press, pp. 173–98.

Evans, D. and Norman, P. (2002). Improving pedestrian road safety among adolescents: an application of the theory of planned behaviour. In D. Rutter and L. Quine (eds), *Changing Health Behaviour*. Buckingham: Open University Press.

Evans, R.L. and Bishop, D.S. (1990). Psychosocial outcomes in stroke survivors. *Stroke*, 21 (suppl. II): II-48–II-49.

Evans, S., Fishman, B., Spielman, L. and Haley, A. (2003). Randomized trial of cognitive behaviour therapy versus supportive psychotherapy for HIV-related peripheral neuropathic pain. *Psychosomatics*, 44: 44–50.

Evers, A.W., Kraaimaat, F.W., Geenen, R. *et al.* (2003). Pain coping and social support as predictors of long-term functional disability and pain in early rheumatoid arthritis. *Behaviour Research and Therapy*, 41: 1295–310.

Evers, A.W., Kraaimaat, F.W., van Riel, P.L. *et al.* (2002). Tailored cognitive-behavioral therapy in early rheumatoid arthritis for patients at risk: a randomized controlled trial. *Pain*, 100: 141–53.

Everson, S.A., Goldberg, D.E., Kaplan, G.A. *et al.* (1996). Hopelessness and risk of mortality and incidence of myocardial infarction and cancer. *Psychosomatic Medicine*, 58: 113–24.

Everson, S.A., McKey, B.S. and Lovallo, W.R. (1995). Effects of trait hostility on cardiovascular responses to harassment in young men. *International Journal of Behavioral Medicine*, 2: 172–91.

Eves, F.F., Webb, O.J. and Mutrie, N. (2006). A work-place intervention to promote stair climbing: greater effects in the overweight. *Obesity (Silver Spring)*, 14: 2210–6.

Expert Group (2004). Research in the behavioural and social sciences to improve cancer control and care: a strategy for development. *European Journal of Cancer*, 40: 316–25.

Eysenck, H.J. (1970). *The Structure of Human Personality*, 3rd edn. London: Methuen.

Eysenck, H.J. (1982). *Personality, Genetics and Behaviour*. New York: Praeger.

Eysenck, H.J. (1985). Personality, cancer and cardio-vascular disease: a causal analysis. *Personality and Individual Differences*, 6: 535–56.

Eysenck, H.J. (1991). Dimensions of personality: 16, 5, or 3? Criteria for a taxonomic paradigm. *Personality and Individual Differences*, 12: 773–90.

Eysenck, H.J. and Grossarth-Maticek, R. (1989). Prevention of cancer and coronary heart disease and the reduction in the cost of the National Health Service. *Journal of Social, Political and Economic Studies*, 14: 25–47.

Fagerli, R.A., Lien, M.E. and Wandel, M. (2007). Health worker style and trustworthiness as perceived by Pakistani-born persons with type 2 diabetes in Oslo, Norway. *Health (London)*, 11: 109–29.

Faller, H. and Bülzebruck, H. (2002). Coping and survival in lung cancer: a 10-year follow-up. *American Journal of Psychiatry*, 159: 2105–7.

Faller, H., Schilleing, S. and Lang, H. (1995). Causal attribution and life threatening disease. *Journal of Psychosomatic Research* 39: 619–627.

Fallowfield, L.J., Hall, A., Maguire, G.P. *et al.* (1990). Psychological outcomes of different treatment policies in women with early breast cancer outside a clinical trial. *British Medical Journal*, 301: 575–80.

Fallowfield, L., Jenkins, V., Farewell, V. *et al.* (2002). Efficacy of a Cancer Research UK communication skills training model for oncologists: a randomised controlled trial. *The Lancet*, 359: 650–6.

Family Heart Study Group (1994). Randomised controlled trial evaluating cardiovascular screening and intervention in general practice: principal results of British family heart study. *British Medical Journal*, 308: 313–20.

Farber, N.J., Urban, S.Y., Collier, V.U. *et al.* (2002). The good news about giving bad news to patients. *Journal of General Internal Medicine*, 17: 914–22.

Farooqi, I.S., Jebb, S.A., Langmack, G. *et al.* (1999). Effects of recombinant leptin therapy in a child with congenital leptin deficiency. *New England Journal of Medicine*, 341: 879–84.

Farquhar, J., Fortmann, S., Flora, J. *et al.* (1990a). Effects of community-wide education on cardiovascular disease risk factors. *Journal of the American Medical Association*, 264: 359–65.

Farquhar, J., Maccoby, N. and Wood, P. (1977). Community education for cardiovascular disease. *The Lancet*, 1: 1192–5.

Farquhar, J.W., Fortmann, S.P., Flora, J.A. *et al.* (1990b). Effects of community-wide education on cardiovascular disease risk factors. The Stanford Five-City Project. *Journal of the American Medical Association*, 264: 359–65.

Faulkner, A. (1998). *When the News is Bad*. Cheltenham: Stanley Thorne.

Faulkner, A., Argent, J., Jones, A. *et al.* (1995). Improving the skills of doctors in giving distressing information. *Medical Education*, 29: 303–7.

Fauerbach, J.A., Lawrence, J.W., Haythornthwaite, J.A. *et al.* (2002). Coping with the stress of a painful medical procedure. *Behaviour Research and Therapy*, 40: 1003–15.

Fawzy, F.I. and Fawzy, N.W. (1998). Psychoeducational interventions. In J. Holland (ed.), *Textbook of Psycho-Oncology*. New York: Oxford University Press.

Fawzy, F.I., Canada, A.L. and Fawzy, N.W. (2003). Malignant melanoma: effects of a brief, structured psychiatric intervention on survival and recurrence at 10-year follow-up. *Archives of General Psychiatry*, 60: 100–3.

Fawzy, F.I., Fawzy, N.W., Hyun, C.S. *et al.* (1993). Malignant melanoma: effects of an early structured psychiatric intervention, coping, and affective state on recurrence and survival 6 years later. *Archives of General Psychiatry*, 50: 681–9.

Fedele, L., Marchini, M., Acaia, B. *et al.* (1989). Dynamics and significance of placebo response in primary dysmenorrhea. *Pain*, 36: 43–7.

Feldman, P.J., Cohen, S., Doyle, W.J. *et al.* (1999). The impact of personality on the reporting of unfounded symptoms and illness. *Journal of Personality and Social Psychology*, 77: 370–8.

Felsten, G. (2004). Stress reactivity and vulnerability to depressed mood in college students. *Personality and Individual Differences*, 36: 789–800.

Fenton, K.A., Korovessis, C., Johnson, A.M. *et al.* (2001). Sexual behaviour in Britain: reported sexually transmitted infections and prevalence of genital *Chlamydia trachomatir* infection. *The Lancet*, 358: 1851–4.

Ferguson, E. (2000). Hypochondriacal concerns and the five factor model of personality. *Journal of Personality*, 68: 705–24.

Ferrie, J.E., Martikainen, P., Shipley, M.J. *et al.* (2001). Employment status and health after privatisation in white collar civil servants: prospective cohort study. *British Medical Journal*, 322: 647.

Ferro, J.M. and Crespo, M. (1994). Prognosis after transient ischemic attack and ischemic stroke in young adults. *Stroke*, 25: 1611–16.

Ferrucci, L., Baldasseroni, S., Bandinelli, D. *et al.* (2000). Disease severity and health-related quality of life across different chronic conditions, *Journal of the American Geriatrics Society*, 48: 1490–95.

Festinger, L. (1957). *A Theory of Cognitive Dissonance*. Stanford, Calif.: Stanford University Press.

Figueiras, M.J. and Weinman, J. (2003). Do similar patient and spouse perceptions of myocardial infarction predict recovery? *Psychology and Health*, 18: 201–16.

Filakti, H. and Fox, J. (1995). Differences in mortality by housing tenure and by car access from the OPCS Longitudinal Study. *Population Trends*, 81: 27–30.

Fine, P.G., Roberts, W.J., Gillette, R.G. *et al.* (1994). Slowly developing placebo responses confound tests of intravenous phentolamine to determine mechanisms underlying idiopathic chronic low back pain. *Pain*, 56: 235–42.

Finkelstein, D.M., Kubzansky, L.D., Capitman, J. *et al.* (2007). Socioeconomic differences in adolescent stress: the role of psychological resources. *Journal of Adolescent Health*, 40: 127–34.

Finnegan, J.R. Jr, Meischke, H., Zapka, J.G. *et al.* (2000). Patient delay in seeking care for heart attack symptoms: findings from focus groups conducted in five U.S. regions. *Preventive Medicine*, 31: 205–13.

Finney, L.J. and Iannotti, R.J. (2002). Message framing and mammography screening: a theory-driven intervention. *Behavioral Medicine*, 28: 5–14.

Fishbein, M. (1967). Attitude and the prediction of behavior. In M. Fishbein (ed.), *Readings in Attitude Theory and Measurement*. New York: Wiley.

Fishbein, M. and Ajzen, I. (1985). *Belief, Attitude, Intention and Behavior: An Introduction to Theory and Research*. Reading, Mass.: Addison-Wesley.

Fisher, J.D., Bell, P.A. and Baum, A. (1984). *Environmental Psychology*, 2nd edn. New York: Holt, Rinehart & Winston.

Fisher, K. and Johnston, M. (1996). Emotional distress as a mediator of the relationship between pain and disability: an experimental study. *British Journal of Health Psychology*, 1: 207–18.

Fisher, K. and Johnston, M. (1996b). Experimental manipulation of perceived control and its effect on disability. *Psychology and Health*, 11: 657–69.

Fisher, K. and Johnston, M. (1998). Emotional distress and control cognitions as mediators of the impact of chronic pain on disability. *British Journal of Health Psychology*, 3: 225–36.

Fiske, S.T. and Taylor, S.E. (1991). *Social Cognition*, 2nd edn. New York: McGraw-Hill.

Fleishman, J.A., Sherbourne, C.D., Cleary, P.D. *et al.* (2003). Patterns of coping among persons with HIV infection: configurations, correlates, and change. *American Journal of Community Psychology*, 32: 187–204.

Fletcher, S.W., Black, W., Harris, R. *et al.* (1993). Report of the international workshop on screening for breast cancer. *Journal of the National Cancer Institute*, 85: 1644–56.

Fletcher, S.W., Harris, R.P., Gonzalez, J.J. *et al.* (1993). Increasing mammography utilization: a controlled study. *Journal of the National Cancer Institute*, 20: 112–20.

Flor, H., Breitenstein, C., Birbaumer, N. and Fuerst, M. (1995). A psychophysiological analysis of spouse solicitousness towards pain behaviours, spouse interaction and physical consequences. *Behavior Therapy*, 26: 255–72.

Flynn, B.S., Worden, J.K., Bunn, J.Y. *et al.* (2007). Youth audience segmentation strategies for smoking-prevention mass media campaigns based on message appeal. *Health Education and Behavior*, 34: 578–93.

Foa, E.B., Rothbaum, B.O., Riggs, D.S. *et al.* (1991). Treatment of posttraumatic stress disorder in rape victims: a comparison between cognitive and behavioural procedures and counselling. *Journal of Consulting and Clinical Psychology*, 59: 715–23.

Folkman, S. (1984). Personal control and stress and coping processes: a theoretical analysis. *Journal of Personality and Social Psychology*, 46: 839–52.

Folkman, S. and Chesney, M. (1995). Coping with HIV infection. In M. Stain and A. Baum (eds), *Chronic Diseases. Perspectives in Behavioral Medicine*. Hillsdale, NJ: Lawrence Erlbaum.

Folkman, S. and Lazarus, R.S. (1980). An analysis of coping in a middle-aged community sample. *Journal of Health and Social Behavior*, 21: 219–39.

Folkman, S. and Lazarus, R.S. (1985). If it changes it must be a process: study of emotion and coping during three stages of a college examination. *Journal of Personality and Social Psychology*, 48: 150–70.

Folkman, S. and Lazarus, R.S. (1988). *Manual for the Ways of Coping Questionnaire*. Palo Alto, Calif.: Consulting Psychologists Press.

Folkman, S.K. and Moskowitz, J.T. (2000). Positive affect and the other side of coping. *American Psychologist*, 55: 647–54.

Food Standards Agency (2000). *National Diet and Nutrition Survey: Young People Aged 4–18 Years*. London: Stationery Office.

Ford, S., Fallowfield, L. and Lewis, S. (1996). Doctor–patient interactions in oncology. *Social Science and Medicine*, 42: 1511–19.

Ford, S., Schofield, T. and Hope, T. (2003). What are the ingredients for a successful evidence-based patient choice consultation? A qualitative study. *Social Science and Medicine*, 56: 589–602.

Fordyce, W.E. (1976). *Behavioural Methods for Chronic Pain and Illness*. St Louis: Mosby.

Fordyce, W.E. (1982). The modification of avoidance learning in pain behaviors. *Journal of Behavioral Medicine*, 5: 405–14.

Fordyce, W.E. (1986). Learning processes in pain. In R.A. Sternbach (ed.), *The Psychology of Pain*, 2nd edn. New York: Raven Press.

Forrest, G., Plumb, C., Ziebland, S. *et al.* (2006). Breast cancer in the family-children's perceptions of their mother's cancer and its initial treatment: Qualitative study. *British Medical Journal*, 332: 998–1003.

Forsberg-Wärleby, G., Möller, A. and Blomstrand, C. (2001). Spouses of first-ever stroke patients: psychological well-being in the first phase after stroke. *Stroke*, 32: 1646–56.

Forwell, G.D. (1993). *Glasgow's Health: Old Problems – New Opportunities*. A report by the Director of Public Health. Glasgow: Department of Public Health.

Fournier, M., de Ridder, D. and Bensing, J. (2002). Optimism and adaptation to chronic disease: the role of optimism in relation to self-care options in type 1 diabetes mellitus, rheumatoid arthritis and multiple sclerosis. *British Journal of Health Psychology*, 7: 409–32.

Franzkowiak, P. (1987). Risk taking and adolescent development. *Health Promotion*, 2: 51–60.

Frasure-Smith, N. (1991). In-hospital symptoms of psychological stress as predictors of long-term outcome after acute myocardial infarction in men. *American Journal of Cardiology*, 67: 121–7.

Frasure-Smith, N. and Prince, R. (1985). The ischemic heart disease life stress monitoring program: impact on mortality. *Psychosomatic Medicine*, 47: 431–45.

Frasure-Smith, N., Lespérance, F., Gravel, G. *et al.* (2000). Social support, depression, and mortality during the first year after myocardial infarction. *Circulation*, 101: 1919–24.

Frasure-Smith, N., Lespérance, F., Gravel, G. *et al.* (2002). Long-term survival differences among low-anxious, high-anxious and repressive copers enrolled in the Montreal heart attack re-adjustment trial. *Psychosomatic Medicine*, 64: 571–9.

Frasure-Smith, N., Lespérance, F., Prince, R.H. *et al.* (1997). Randomised trial of home-based psycho-social nursing intervention for patients recovering from myocardial infarction. *The Lancet*, 350: 473–9.

Frasure-Smith, N., Lespérance, F. and Talajic, M.E. (1995). Coronary heart disease/myocardial infarction: depression and 18-month prognosis after myocardial infarction. *Circulation*, 91: 999–1005.

Freda, M.C. (2005). The readability of American Academy of Pediatrics patient education brochures. *Journal of Pediatric Health Care*, 19: 151–6.

Fredman, L., Hawkes, W.G., Black, S. *et al.* (2006). Elderly patients with hip fracture with positive affect have better functional recovery over 2 years. *Journal of the American Geriatric Society*, 54: 1074–81.

Fredrickson, B.L. (1998). What good are positive emotions? *Review of General Psychology*, 2: 300–19.

Fredrickson, B.L. (2001). The role of positive emotions in positive psychology: the broaden-and-build theory of positive emotions. *American Psychologist*, 56: 218–26.

Fredrickson, M. and Matthews, K.A. (1990). Cardiovascular responses to behavioral stress and hypertension: a meta-analytic review. *Annals of Behavioral Medicine*, 12: 30–9.

Freedland, K.E., Carney, R.M., Hance, M.L. *et al.* (1996). Cognitive therapy for depression in patients with coronary artery disease. *Psychosomatic Medicine*, 58: 93.

Freidson, E. (1961). *Patients' Views of Medical Practice*. New York: Russell Sage Foundation.

French, D.J., Christie, M.J., Sowden, A.J. (1994). The reproducibility of the Childhood Asthma Questionnaires: measures of quality of life for children with asthma aged 4–16 years. *Quality of Life Research*, 3: 215–24.

French, D.P., Marteau, T., Senior, V. *et al.* (2002). The structure of beliefs about the causes of heart attack: a network analysis. *British Journal of Health Psychology*, 7: 463–79.

French, D.P., Senior, V., Weinman, J. *et al.* (2001). Causal attributions for heart disease. *Psychology and Health*, 16: 77–98.

French, J.R.P. Jr, Caplan, R.D. and Van Harrison, R. (1982). *The Mechanisms of Job Stress and Strain*. Chichester: Wiley.

French, S.A., Perry, C.L., Leon, G.R. and Fulkerson, J.A. (1994). Weight concerns, dieting behaviour, and smoking initiation among adolescents: a prospective study. *American Journal of Public Health*, 84: 1–3.

Freud, S. and Breuer, J. (1895). Studies on hysteria. In J. Strachey (ed.), *The Standard Edition of the Complete Psychological Works of Sigmund Freud.* London: Hogarth Press.

Friedman, H.S. (2003). Healthy life-style across the life-span: the heck with the Surgeon General! In J. Suls and K.A. Wallston (eds), *Social Psychological Foundations of Health and Illness.* Malden, Mass.: Blackwell.

Friedman, H.S. and Booth-Kewley, S. (1987). The 'disease-prone personality'. A meta-analytic view of the construct. *American Psychologist*, 42: 539–55.

Friedman, H.S., Tucker, J.S., Schwartz, J.E. *et al.* (1995). Childhood conscientiousness and longevity: health behaviors and cause of death. *Journal of Personality and Social Psychology*, 68: 696–703.

Friedman, M. and Rosenman, R.H. (1959). Association of specific overt behavior pattern with blood and cardiovascular findings. *Journal of American Medical Association*, 169: 1286–97.

Friedman, M. and Rosenman, R.H. (1974). *Type A Behavior and Your Heart.* New York: A.A. Knopf.

Friedman, M., Thoresen, C.E., Gill, J.J. *et al.* (1986). Alteration of Type A behavior and its effect on cardiac recurrences in post myocardial infarction patients: summary results of the Recurrent Coronary Prevention Project. *American Heart Journal*, 112: 653–65.

Friesner, S., Curry, D. and Moddeman, G. (2007). Comparison of two pain-management strategies during chest tube removal: relaxation exercise with opioids and opioids alone. *Acute Pain*, 8: 188–188.

Fromm, K., Andrykowski, M.A. and Hunt, J. (1996). Positive and negative psychosocial sequelae of bone marrow transplantation: implications for quality of life assessment. *Journal of Behavioral Medicine*, 19: 221–40.

Fukui, S., Kugaya, A., Okamura, H. *et al.* (2000). A psychosocial group intervention for Japanese women with primary breast carcinoma. *Cancer*, 89: 1026–36.

Funk, S.C. (1992). Hardiness: a review of theory and research. *Health Psychology*, 11: 335–45.

Furnham, A. (1990). The Type A behaviour pattern and perception of self. *Personality and Individual Differences*, 11: 841–51.

Furnham, A. (1997). Lay theories of work stress. *Work & Stress*, 11: 68–78.

Gadsby, J.G. and Flowerdew, M.W. (2000). Transcutaneous nerve stimulation and acupuncture-like transcutaneous nerve stimulation for chronic low back pain. In *The Cochrane Library*, issue 2. Oxford: Update Software.

Galavotti, C., Pappas-DeLuca, K.A. and Lansky, A. (2001). Modeling and reinforcement to combat HIV: the MARCH approach to behavior change. *American Journal of Public Health*, 91: 1602–7.

Gall, T.L. and Cornblatt, M.W. (2002). Breast cancer survivors give voice: a qualitative analysis of spiritual factors in long-term adjustment. *Psycho-Oncology*, 11: 524–35.

Gall, T.L., Miguez de Renart, R.M. and Boonstra, B. (2000). Religious resources in long-term adjustment to breast cancer. *Journal of Psychosocial Oncology*, 18: 21–37.

Gallacher, J.E.J., Hopkinson, C.A., Bennett, P. *et al.* (1997). Effect of stress management on angina. *Psychology and Health*, 12: 523–32.

Gallacher, J.E.J., Yarnell, J.W.G., Sweetnam, P.M. *et al.* (1999). Anger and incident heart disease in the Caerphilly study. *Psychosomatic Medicine*, 61: 446–53.

Gamble, J., Fitzsimons, D., Lynes, D. *et al.* (2007). Difficult asthma: people's perspectives on taking corticosteroid therapy. *Journal of Clinical Nursing*, 16: 59–67.

Gander, P.H., Merry, A., Millar, M.M. *et al.* (2000). Hours of work and fatigue-related error: a survey of New Zealand anaesthetists. *Anaesthetics and Intensive Care*, 28: 178–83.

Garnefski, N. and Kraaij, V. (2006). Cognitive emotion regulation questionnaire-development of a short 18-item version (CERQ-short). *Personality and Individual Differences*, 41: 1045–53.

Garratt, A., Schmidt, L., Mackintosh, A.M. *et al.* (2002). Quality of life measurement: bibliographic study of patient assessed health outcome measures. *British Medical Journal*, 324: 1417–21.

Garssen, B. (2004). Psychological factors and cancer development: evidence after 30 years of research. *Clinical Psychology Review*, 24: 315–38.

Gascoigne, P., Mason, M.D. and Roberts, E. (1999). Factors affecting presentation and delay in patients with testicular cancer: results of a qualitative study. *Psycho-Oncology*, 8: 144–54.

Gauce, A.M., Comer, J.P. and Schwartz, D. (1987). Long-term effect of a systems orientated school prevention program. *American Journal of Orthopsychiatry*, 57: 127–31.

Gaughler, J.E., Davey, A., Pearlin, L.I. *et al.* (2000). Modeling caregiver adaptation over time: the longitudinal impact of behaviour problems. *Psychology and Aging*, 15: 437–50.

Gawande, A.A., Zinner, M.J., Studdert, D.M. *et al.* (2003). Analysis of errors reported by surgeons at three teaching hospitals. *Surgery*, 133: 614–21.

Geirdal, A.Ø., Reichelt, J.G., Dahl, A.A. *et al.* (2005). Psychological distress in women at risk of hereditary breast/ovarian or HNPCC cancers in the absence of demonstrated mutations. *Family Cancer*, 4: 121–6.

Gellert, G., Maxwell, R.M. and Siegel, B.S. (1993). Survival of breast cancer patients receiving adjunctive psychosocial support therapy: A 10-year follow-up study. *Journal of Clinical Oncology*, 11: 66–9.

General Medical Council (2002). *Tomorrow's Doctors, Recommendations on Undergraduate Medical Education*. London: General Medical Council.

Gerbert, B. (1984). Perceived likeability and competence of simulated patients: influence on physician's management plans. *Social Science and Medicine*, 18: 1053–60.

Gerend, M.A. and Shepherd, J.E. (2007) Using message framing to promote acceptance of the human papillomavirus vaccine. *Health Psychology*, 26: 745–52.

Gerend, M.A., Aiken, L.S. and West, S.G. (2004). Personality factors in older women's perceived susceptibility to diseases of aging. *Journal of Personality*, 72: 243–70.

German, J.B. and Walzem, R.L. (2000). The health benefits of wine. *Annual Review of Nutrition*, 20: 561–93.

Gibson, D.R., Flynn, N.M. and Perales, D. (2001). Effectiveness of syringe exchange programs in reducing HIV risk behavior and HIV seroconversion among injecting drug users. *AIDS*, 15: 1329–41.

Gibson, P.G., Coughlan, J., Wilson, A.J. *et al.* (2000). Limited (information only) patient education programs for adults with asthma. *Cochrane Database Systematic Review*, 2: CD001005.

Giese-Davis, J., Koopman, C., Butler, L.D. *et al.* (2002). Change in emotion-regulation strategy for women with metastatic breast cancer following supportive–expressive group therapy. *Journal of Consulting and Clinical Psychology*, 70: 916–25.

Gifford, A.L., Laurent, D.D., Gonzales, V.M. *et al.* (1998). Pilot randomized trial of education to improve self-management skills of men with symptomatic HIV/AIDS. *Retrovirology*, 18: 136–44.

Gijsbers van Wijk, C.M.T. and Kolk, A.M. (1997). Sex differences in physical symptoms: the contribution of symptom perception theory. *Social Science & Medicine*, 45: 231–46.

Gil, K.M., Keefe, F.J., Crisson, J.E. *et al.* (1987). Social support and pain behavior. *Pain*, 29: 209–17.

Gil, K.M., Williams, D.A., Keefe, F.J. *et al.* (1990). The relationship of negative thoughts to pain and psychological distress. *Behavior Therapy*, 21: 349–62.

Gill, P., Kaur, J.S., Rummans, T. *et al.* (2003). The hospice patient's primary caregiver. What is their quality of life? *Journal of Psychosomatic Research*, 55: 445–51.

Gillam, S., Jarman, B., White, P. *et al.* (1989). Ethnic differences in consultation rates in urban general practice. *British Medical Journal*, 299: 953–7.

Gillies, P.A. (1991). HIV infection, alcohol and illicit drugs. *Current Opinion in Psychiatry*, 4: 448–53.

Ginandes, C., Brooks, P., Sando, W. *et al.* (2003). Can medical hypnosis accelerate post-surgical wound healing? Results of a clinical trial. *American Journal of Clinical Hypnosis*, 45: 333–51.

Glanz, K., Grove, J., Lerman, C. *et al.* (1999). Correlates of intentions to obtain genetic counseling and colorectal cancer gene testing among at-risk relatives from three ethnic groups. *Cancer Epidemiology Biomarkers and Prevention*, 8: 329–36.

Glanz, K., Lankenau, B., Foerster, S. *et al.* (1995). Environmental and policy approaches to cardiovascular disease prevention through nutrition: opportunities for state and local action. *Health Education Quarterly*, 22: 512–27.

Glaser, R. and Kiecolt-Glaser, J.K. (2005). Stress-induced immune dysfunction: implications for health. *National Reviews in Immunology*, 5: 243–51.

Glaser, R., Rice, J., Sheridan, J. *et al.* (1987). Stress-related immune suppression: health implications. *Brain, Behavior and Immunity*, 1: 7–20.

Glasgow, R.E., Boles, S.M., McKay, H.G. *et al.* (2003). The D-Net diabetes self-management program: long-term implementation, outcomes, and generalization results. *Preventive Medicine*, 36: 410–19.

Glasgow, R.E., Hollis, J.F., Ary, D.V. *et al.* (1993). Results of a year-long incentives based worksite smoking cessation program. *Addictive Behaviors*, 18: 209–16.

Glasgow, R.E., Toobert, D.J. and Hampson, S.E. (1996). Effects of a brief office-based intervention to facilitate diabetes dietary self-management. *Diabetes Care*, 19: 835–42.

Glenister, D. (1996). Exercise and mental health: a review. *Journal of the Royal Society of Health*, 116: 7–13.

Glenton, C. (2002). Developing patient-centred information for back pain sufferers. *Health Expectations*, 5: 319–29.

Goddard, M. and Smith, P. (1998). *Equity of Access to Health Care*. York: University of York.

Godfrey, C. (1990). Modelling demand. In A. Maynard and P. Tether (eds), *Preventing Alcohol and Tobacco Problems. 1*. Avebury: ESRC.

Godin, G. and Kok, G. (1996). The theory of planned behavior: a review of its applications to health-related behaviours. *American Journal of Health Promotion*, 11: 87–98.

Godin, G. and Shephard, R.J. (1986). Normative beliefs of school children concerning regular exercise. *Journal of School Health*, 54: 443–5.

Godin, G., Gagné, C., Maziade, J. *et al.* (2001). Breast cancer: the intention to have a mammography and a clinical breast examination – application of the theory of planned behavior. *Psychology and Health*, 16: 423–41.

Godin, G., Lambert, L.-D., Owen, N. *et al.* (2004). Stages of motivational readiness for physical activity: a comparison of different algorithms of classification. *British Journal of Health Psychology*, 9: 253–67.

Godin, G., Valois, P., Lepage, L. *et al.* (1992). Predictors of smoking behaviour – an application of Ajzen's theory of planned behaviour. *British Journal of Addiction*, 87: 1335–43.

Goldberg, D. (1997). *General Health Questionnaire (GHQ–12)*. Windsor: NFER-Nelson.

Goldberg, D. and Williams, P. (1988). *A User's Guide to the General Health Questionnaire*. Windsor: NFER-Nelson.

Goldberg, L.R. and Strycker, L.A. (2002). Personality traits and eating habits: the assessment of food preferences in a large community sample. *Personality and Individual Differences*, 32: 49–65.

Goldberg, R.J., Steg, P.G., Sadiq, I. *et al.* (2002). Extent of, and factors associated with, delay to hospital presentation in patients with acute coronary disease (the GRACE registry). *American Journal of Cardiology*, 89: 791–6.

Goldman, S.L., Whitney-Saltiel, D., Granger, J. *et al.* (1991). Children's representations of 'everyday' aspects of health and illness. *Journal of Pediatric Psychology*, 16: 747–66.

Gollwitzer, P.M. (1993). Goal achievements: the role of intentions. In E.T. Higgins and R.M. Sorrentino (eds), *Handbook of Motivation and Cognition: Foundations of Social Behaviour*, Vol. 2. New York: Guilford Press.

Gollwitzer, P.M. (1999). Implementation intentions: strong effects of simple plans. *American Psychologist*, 54: 493–503.

Gollwitzer, P.M. and Brandstätter, V. (1997). Implementation intentions and effective goal pursuit. *Journal of Personality and Social Psychology*, 73: 186–99.

Gollwitzer, P.M. and Oettingen, G. (1998). The emergence and implementation of health goals. *Psychology and Health*, 13: 687–715.

Gollwitzer, P.M. and Oettingen, G. (2000). The emergence and implementation of health goals. In P. Norman and C. Abraham (eds), *Understanding and Changing Health Behaviour: From Health Beliefs to Self Regulation* (229–60). Amsterdam: Harwood Academic Press.

Gollwitzer, P.M. and Schaal, B. (1998). Metacognition in action: the importance of implementation intentions. *Personality and Social Psychology Review*, 2: 124–36.

Gomel, M., Oldenburg, B., Simpson, J.M. *et al.* (1993). Work-site cardiovascular risk reduction: a randomized trial of health risk assessment, education, counseling, and incentives. *American Journal of Public Health*, 83: 1231–8.

Gomez, C.R., Boehmer, E.D. and Kovacs, E.J. (2005). The aging innate immune system. *Current Opinions in Immunology*, 17: 457–62.

Goode, K.T., Haley, W.E., Roth, D.L. *et al.* (1998). Predicting longitudinal changes in caregiver physical and mental health: a stress process model. *Health Psychology*, 17: 190–8.

Goodkin, K., Feaster, D.J., Asthana, D. *et al.* (1998). A bereavement support group intervention is longitudinally associated with salutary effects on the CD4 cell count and number of physician visits. *Clinical and Diagnostic Laboratory Immunology*, 5: 382–91.

Goodkin, K., Baldewicz, T.T., Asthana, D. *et al.* (2001). A bereavement support group intervention affects plasma burden of human immunodeficiency virus type 1. Report of a randomized controlled trial. *Journal of Human Virology*, 4: 44–54.

Goodwin, D., Boggs, S. and Graham-Pole, J. (1994). Development and validation of the Pediatric Oncology Quality of Life Scale. *Psychological Assessment*, 6: 321–8.

Goodwin, P.J., Leszcz, M., Ennis, M. *et al.* (2001). The effect of group psychosocial support on survival in metastatic breast cancer. *New England Journal of Medicine*, 345: 1719–26.

Goyder, E.C., McNally, P.G. and Botha, J.L. (2000). Inequalities in access to diabetes care: evidence from a historical cohort study. *Quality in Health Care*, 9: 85–9.

Graham, H. (1994). Gender and class as dimensions of smoking behaviour in Britain: insights from a survey of mothers. *Social Science and Medicine*, 38: 691–8.

Graham, J.E., Christian, L.M. and Kiecolt-Glaser, J.K. (2006). Stress, age and immune function: toward a lifespan approach. *Journal of Behavioral Medicine*, 29: 389–400.

Graham, J., Ramirez, A., Love, S. *et al.* (2002). Stressful life experiences and risk of relapse of breast cancer: observational cohort study. *British Medical Journal*, 324: 1420–3.

Gratton, L., Povey, R. and Clark-Carter, D. (2007). Promoting children's fruit and vegetable consumption: interventions using the Theory of Planned Behaviour as a framework. *British Journal of Health Psychology*, 12: 39–50.

Gray, S.E. and Rutter, D.R. (2007). Illness representations in young people with Chronic Fatigue Syndrome. *Psychology and Health*, 22: 159–74.

Gray-Toft, P. and Anderson, J.G. (1981). The Nursing Stress Scale: development of an instrument. *Journal of Psychopathology and Behavioral Assessment*, 3: 11–23.

Greco, P., Pendley, J.S., McDonell, K. *et al.* (2001). A peer group intervention for adolescents with type 1 diabetes and their best friends. *Journal of Pediatric Psychology*, 26: 485–90.

Green, B.L., Rowland, J.H., Krupnick, J.L. *et al.* (1998). Prevalence of posttraumatic stress disorder in women with breast cancer. *Psychosomatics*, 39: 102–11.

Green, C.R., Baker, T.A., Sato, Y. *et al.* (2003). Race and chronic pain: a comparative study of young black and white Americans presenting for management. *Journal of Pain*, 4: 176–83.

Greenhalgh, T., Robb, N. and Scambler, G. (2006). Communicative and strategic action in interpreted consultations in primary health care: a Habermasian perspective. *Social Science and Medicine*, 63: 1170–87.

Greenwood, C.R., Carta, J.J. and Kamps, D. (1990). Teacher versus peer-mediated instruction: a review of educational advantages and disadvantages. In H. Foot, M. Morgan and R. Shute (eds), *Children Helping Children*. Chichester: Wiley.

Greenwood, D.C., Muir, K.R., Packham, C.J. *et al.* (1996). Coronary heart disease: a review of the role of psychosocial stress and social support. *Journal of Public Health Medicine*, 18: 221–31.

Greer, S. (1999). Mind–body research in psycho-oncology. *Advances in Mind–Body Medicine*, 15: 236–81.

Greer, S., Morris, T. and Pettingale, K. (1979). Psychological responses to breast cancer: effect on outcome. *The Lancet*, 2: 940–9.

Greer, S., Morris, T., Pettingale, K. *et al.* (1990). Psychological response to breast cancer and 15 year outcome. *The Lancet*, 335: 49–50.

Grey, M., Boland, E.A., Davidson, M. *et al.* (2000). Coping skills training for youths with diabetes mellitus has long-lasting effects on metabolic control and quality of life. *Journal of Pediatrics*, 137: 107–13.

Griffin-Blake, C.S. and DeJoy, D.M. (2006). Evaluation of social-cognitive versus stage-matched, self-help physical activity interventions at the workplace. *American Journal of Health Promotion*, 20: 200–9.

Griffith, G.L., Morrison, V., Williams, J.M.G. *et al.* (in press 2008). Can we assume that research participants are utility maximisers? *European Journal of Health Economics*.

Grigsby, A.B., Anderson, R.J., Freedland, K.E. *et al.* (2002). Prevalence of anxiety in adults with diabetes. A systematic review. *Journal of Psychosomatic Research*, 53: 1053–60.

Griva, K., Myers, L.B. and Newman, S. (2000). Illness perceptions and self-efficacy beliefs in adolescents and young adults with insulin dependent diabetes mellitus. *Psychology and Health*, 15: 733–50.

Grodstein, F., Chen, J. and Willett, W.C. (2003). High-dose antoxidant supplements and cognitive function in community-dwelling elderly women. *American Journal of Clinical Nutrition*, 77: 975–84.

Grossarth-Maticek, R., Bastiaans, J. and Kanazin, D.T. (1985). Psychosocial factors as strong predictors of mortality from cancer, ischemic heart disease and stroke: the Yugoslav prospective study. *Journal of Psychosomatic Research*, 29: 167–76.

Grundy, E. and Bowling, A. (1999). Enhancing the quality of extended life years. Identification of the oldest old with a very good and very poor quality of life. *Aging and Mental Health*, 3: 199–212.

Grunfeld, E.A., Hunter, M.S., Ramirez, A.J. *et al.* (2003). Perceptions of breast cancer across the lifespan. *Journal of Psychosomatic Research*, 54: 141–6.

Gudbergsson, S.B., Fosså, S.D., Sanne, B. *et al.* (2007). A controlled study of job strain in primary-treated cancer patients without metastases. *Acta Oncologica*, 46: 534–44.

Gudmunsdottir, H., Johnston, M., Johnston, D. *et al.* (2001). Spontaneous, elicited and cued causal attributions in the year following a first myocardial infarction. *British Journal of Health Psychology*, 6: 81–96.

Gulland, A. (2002). BMA steps up call for ban on smoking in public places. *British Medical Journal*, 325: 1058.

Guthrie, R.M. (2001). The effects of postal and telephone reminders on compliance with pravastatin therapy in a national registry: results of the first myocardial infarction risk reduction program. *Clinical Therapeutics*, 23: 970–80.

Gutteling, J.J., Darlington, A-S.E., Janssen, H.L.A. *et al.* (2008). Effectiveness of health-related quality of life measurement in clinical practice: a prospective, randomized controlled trial in patients with chronic liver disease and their physicians. *Quality of Life Research*, 17: 195–205.

Haan, M.H. (2003). Can vitamin supplements prevent cognitive decline and dementia in old age? (editorial). *American Journal of Clinical Nutrition*, 77: 762–3.

Haan, M.N. and Kaplan, G.A. (1985). The contribution of socio-economic position to minority health. In M. Heckler (ed.), *Report of the Secretary's Task Force on Black and Minority Health: Crosscutting*

Issues in Health and Human Services. Washington: US DHHS.

Haberman, D. and Bloomfield, D.S.F. (1988). Social class differences in mortality in Great Britain around 1981. *Journal of the Institute of Actuaries,* 115: 495–517.

Habra, M.E., Linden, W., Anderson, J.C. *et al.* (2003). Type D personality is related to cardiovascular and neuroendocrine reactivity to acute stress. *Journal of Psychosomatic Research,* 55: 235–45.

Hack, T.F. and Degner, L.F. (2004). Coping responses following breast cancer diagnosis predicts psychological adjustment 3 years later. *Psycho-Oncology,* 13: 235–47.

Hagedoorn, M., Sandermann, R., Buunk, B.P. *et al.* (2002). Failing in spousal caregiving: the 'identity-relevant stress' hypothesis to explain sex differences in caregiver distress. *British Journal of Health Psychology,* 7: 481–94.

Hagger, M., Chatzisarantis, N.L.D. and Bidle, S.J.H. (2002). A meta-analytic review of the theories of reasoned action and planned behavior in physical activity: Predictive validity and the contribution of additional variables. *Journal of Sport and Exercise Psychology,* 24: 3–32.

Hagger, M., Chatzisarantis, N., Biddle, S.J.H. *et al.* (2001). Antecedents of children's physical activity intentions and behaviour: predictive validity and longitudinal effects. *Psychology and Health,* 16: 391–407.

Hagger, M.S. and Orbell, S. (2003). A meta-analytic review of the common-sense model of illness representations. *Psychology and Health,* 18: 141–84.

Hakim, A.A., Petrovitch, H., Burchfield, C.M. *et al.* (1998). Effects of walking on mortality among non-smoking retired men. *New England Journal of Medicine,* 338: 94–9.

Hale, G. (1996). The social construction of grief. In N. Cooper, C. Stevenson and G. Hale (eds), *Integrating Perspectives on Health.* Buckingham: Open University Press.

Hale, S., Grogan, S. and Willott, S. (2007). Patterns of self-referral in men with symptoms of prostate disease. *British Journal of Health Psychology,* 12: 403–19.

Halford, J.C.G. and Blundell, J.E. (2000). Serotonin drugs and the treatment of obesity. In T.G. Heffner and D.H. Lockwood (eds), *Obesity: Pathology and Therapy.* Berlin: Springer Verlag.

Hall, E.E., Ekkekakis, P. and Petruzzello, S.J. (2002). The affective beneficence of vigorous exercise revisited. *British Journal of Health Psychology,* 7: 47–66.

Hall, J.A. and Roter, D.L. (2002). Do patients talk differently to male and female physicians? A meta-analytic review. *Patient Education and Counseling,* 48: 217–24.

Hall, J.A., Roter, D.L. and Katz, N.R. (1988). Meta-analysis of correlates of provider behavior in medical encounters. *Medical Care,* 26: 657–75.

Hall, S. and Marteau, T.M. (2003). Causal attributions following serious unexpected negative events: a systematic review. *Journal of Social and Clinical Psychology,* 22: 515–36.

Hall, S.M., Tunstall, C., Rugg, D. *et al.* (1985). Nicotine gum and behavioral treatment in smoking cessation. *Journal of Consulting and Clinical Psychology,* 53: 256–8.

Hallal, P.C., Victora, C.G., Azevedo, M.R. *et al.* (2006). Adolescent physical activity and health: a systematic review. *Sports Medicine,* 36: 1019–30.

Hallaråker, E., Arefjord, K., Havik, O.E. *et al.* (2001). Social support and emotional adjustment during and after a severe life event: a study of wives of myocardial infarction patients. *Psychology and Health,* 16: 343–56.

Halm, M., Penque, S., Doll, N. *et al.* (1999). Women and cardiac rehabilitation: referral and compliance patterns. *Journal of Cardiovascular Nursing,* 13: 83–92.

Halstead, M.T. and Fernsler, J.I. (1994). Coping strategies of long-term cancer patients. *Cancer Nursing,* 17: 94–100.

Hammerfald, K., Eberle, C., Grau, M. *et al.* (2006). Persistent effects of cognitive-behavioral stress management on cortisol responses to acute stress in healthy subjects – a randomized controlled trial. *Psychoneuroendocrinology,* 31: 333–9.

Hampson, S.E., Glasgow, R.E. and Toobert, D.J. (1990). Personal models of diabetes and their relation to self-care activities. *Health Psychology,* 9: 632–46.

Hampson, S.E., Glasgow, R.E. and Zeiss, A. (1994). Personal models of osteoarthritis and their relation to self-management activities and quality of life. *Journal of Behavioural Medicine,* 17: 143–58.

Han, K.S. (2002). The effect of an integrated stress management program on the psychologic and physiologic stress reactions of peptic ulcer in Korea. *International Journal of Nursing Studies,* 39: 539–48.

Hanson, R.W. and Gerber, K.E. (1990). *Coping with Chronic Pain. A Guide to Patient Self-management.* New York: Guilford Press.

Harburg, E.J.C., Chape, C., Erfurt, J.C. *et al.* (1973). Socio-ecological stressor areas and black and white blood pressure: Detroit. *Journal of Chronic Disease,* 26: 595–611.

Harcourt, D., Ambler, N., Rumsey, N. *et al.* (1998). Evaluation of a one-stop breast lump clinic: a randomised controlled trial. *The Breast,* 7: 314–19.

Harcourt, D., Rumsey, N. and Ambler, N. (1999). Same-day diagnosis of symptomatic breast problems: psychological impact and coping strategies. *Psychology, Health & Medicine*, 4: 57–71.

Harding, S. and Maxwell, R. (1997). Differences in mortality of migrants. In F. Drever and M. Whitehead (eds), *Health Inequalities: Decennial Supplement*. London: HMSO.

Härkäpää, K., Järvikoski, A., Mellin, G. *et al.* (1991). Health locus of control beliefs and psychological distress as predictors for treatment outcome in low-back pain patients: results of a 3-month follow-up of a controlled intervention study. *Pain*, 46: 35–41.

Harland, J., White, M., Drinkwater, C. *et al.* (1999). The Newcastle exercise project: a randomised controlled trial of methods to promote physical activity in primary care. *British Medical Journal*, 319: 828–32.

Harris, A.H., Thoresen, C.E., Humphreys, K. *et al.* (2005). Does writing affect asthma? A randomized trial. *Psychosomatic Medicine*, 67: 130–6.

Harris, D.M. and Guten, S. (1979). Health-protective behaviour: an exploratory study. *Journal of Health and Social Behavior*, 20: 17–29.

Harris, P. and Middleton, W. (1994). The illusion of control and optimism about health: on being less at risk but no more in control than others. *British Journal of Social Psychology*, 33: 369–86.

Harris, P.E. (1989). The nurse stress index. *Work & Stress*, 3: 335–46.

Harris, T., Ferrucci, L., Tracy, R. *et al.* (1999). Associations of elevated interleukin-6 and C-reactive protein levels with mortality and the elderly. *American Journal of Medicine*, 106: 506–12.

Harrison, J.A., Mullen, P.D. and Green, L.W. (1992). A meta-analysis of studies of the health belief model with adults. *Health Education Research, Theory and Practice*, 7: 107–16.

Harrison, M.O., Koenig, H.G., Hays, J.C. *et al.* (2001). The epidemiology of religious coping: a review of recent literature. *International Reviews in Psychiatry*, 13: 86–93.

Hart, C.L., Davey-Smith, G., Hole, D.J. *et al.* (1999). Alcohol consumption and mortality from all causes, coronary disease, and stroke: results from a prospective cohort study of Scottish men with 21 years of follow-up. *British Medical Journal*, 318: 133–40.

Hart, H., Bilo, H., Redekop, W. *et al.* (2003). Quality of life in patients with type 1 diabetes mellitus. *Quality of Life Research*, 12: 1089–97.

Hartford, K., Wong, C. and Zakaria, D. (2002). Randomized controlled trial of a telephone intervention by nurses to provide information and support to patients and their partners after elective coronary artery bypass graft surgery: effects of anxiety. *Heart and Lung*, 31: 199–206.

Haste, H. (2004). *My Body, My Self: Young People's Values and Motives about Healthy Living*, Report 2. London: Nestlé Social Research Programme.

Hatava, P., Olsson, G.L. and Lagerkranser, M. (2000). Preoperative psychological preparation for children undergoing ENT operations: a comparison of two methods. *Paediatric Anaesthesia*, 10: 477–86.

Hathaway, D. (1986). Effect of preoperative instruction on postoperative outcomes: a meta-analysis. *Nursing Research*, 35: 269–75.

Hausenblas, H.A. and Symons Downs, D. (2002). How much is too much? The development and validation of the Exercise Dependence Scale. *Psychology and Health*, 17: 387–404.

Havik, O.E. and Maeland, J.G. (1988). Changes in smoking behavior after a myocardial infarction. *Health Psychology*, 7: 403–20.

Hayes, J. and Morrison, V. (under review). Attitudes towards breaking bad news among junior doctors.

Hayes, L., White, M., Unwin, N. *et al.* (2002). Patterns of physical activity and relationship with risk markers for cardiovascular disease and diabetes in Indian, Pakistani, Bangladeshi and European adults in a UK population. *Journal of Public Health Medicine*, 24: 170–8.

Haynes, B. and Haines, A. (1998). Barriers and bridges to evidence-based clinical practice. *British Medical Journal*, 317: 273–6.

Haynes, G. and Feinleib, M. (1980). Women, work, and coronary heart disease: prospective findings from the Framingham heart study. *American Journal of Public Health*, 70: 133–41.

Haynes, R.B., McKibbon, A. and Kanani, R. (1996). Systematic review of randomized trials of interventions to assist patients to follow prescriptions for medications. *The Lancet*, 384: 383–5.

Haynes, S.G., Feinleib, M. and Kannel, W.B. (1980). The relationship of psychosocial factors to coronary heart disease in the Framingham study. III. Eight year incidence of coronary heart disease. *American Journal of Epidemiology*, 111: 37–58.

Health Development Agency Magazine (2005). *Smoking Out Pregnant Teenagers*, Issue 25, Feb/March.

Health Education Authority (1997). *Guidelines: Promoting Physical Activity with Black and Minority Ethnic Groups*. London: Health Education Authority.

Health Education Authority (1998). *Young and Active? Policy Framework for Young People and Health – Enhancing Physical Activity*. London: Health Education Authority.

Health Promotion Authority for Wales (1996). *Lifestyle Changes in Wales. Health in Wales Survey*

1996, Technical Report no. 27. Cardiff: Health Promotion Authority for Wales.

Health Survey for England (2005). *The Health of Older People: Summary of Key Findings*. The Information Centre, Leeds, available from: www.ic.nhs.uk.

Health Survey for England (2006). http://www.ic.nhs.uk/statistics-and-data-collections/healthand-lifestyles-related-surveys/health-survey-for-england/health-survey-for-england-2006-latest-trends.

Health Survey for England (2007). Leeds: Health and Social Care Information Centre (2008), available from www.ic.nhs.uk.

Health Utilisation Research Alliance (2006). Ethnicity, socioeconomic deprivation and consultation rates in New Zealand general practice. *Journal of Health Service Research and Policy*, 11: 141–9.

Healy, C.M. and McKay, M.F. (2000). Nursing stress: the effects of coping strategies and job satisfaction in a sample of Australian nurses. *Journal of Advanced Nursing*, 31: 681–8.

Heather, N. and Robertson, I. (1997). *Problem Drinking*. Oxford: Oxford University Press.

Heaven, C.M. and Maguire, P. (1998). The relationship between patients' concerns and psychological distress in a hospice setting. *Psycho-Oncology*, 7: 502–7.

Heckhausen, H. (1991). *Motivation and Action*. Berlin: Springer Verlag.

Hedges, J.R., Mann, N.C., Meischke, H. *et al.* (1998). Assessment of chest pain onset and out-of-hospital delay using standardised interview questions: the REACT pilot study. *Academic Emergency Medicine*, 5: 773–80.

Heijmans, M. (1998). Coping and adaptive outcome in chronic fatigue syndrome: importance of illness cognitions. *Journal of Psychosomatic Research*, 45: 39–51.

Heijmans, M. and de Ridder, D. (1998). Structure and determinants of illness representation in chronic disease: a comparison of Addison's disease and chronic fatigue syndrome. *Journal of Health Psychology*, 3: 523–37.

Heijmans, M., de Ridder, D. and Bensing, J. (1999). Dissimilarity in patients' and spouses' representations of chronic illness: explorations of relations to patient adaptation. *Psychology and Health*, 14: 451–66.

Heim, E., Augustiny, K., Blaser, A. *et al.* (1987). Coping with breast cancer: a longitudinal prospective study. *Psychotherapy and Psychosomatics*, 48: 44–59.

Hein, H.O., Suadicani, P. and Gyntelberg, F. (1992). Ischaemic heart disease incidence by social class and form of smoking: the Copenhagen male study – 17 years follow-up. *Journal of Internal Medicine*, 231: 477–83.

Heine, S.J. and Lehman, D.R. (1995). Cultural variation in unrealistic optimism: does the West feel more invulnerable than the East? *Journal of Personality and Social Psychology*, 68: 595–607.

Helder, D.I., Bakker, B., deHeer, P. *et al.* (2004). Quality of life in adults following bone marrow transplantation during childhood. *Bone Marrow Transplantation*, 33: 329–36.

Helman, C. (1978). Feed a cold starve a fever – folk models of infection in an English suburban community and their relation to medical treatment. *Culture, Medicine and Psychiatry*, 2: 107–37.

Heloma, A. and Jaakola, M.S. (2003). Four-year follow-up of smoke exposure, attitudes and smoking behaviour following enactment of Finland's national smoke-free work-place law. *Addiction*, 98: 1111–17.

Hemingway, H. and Marmot, M. (1999). Psychosocial factors in the aetiology and prognosis of coronary heart disease: systematic review of prospective cohort studies. *British Medical Journal*, 318: 1460–7.

Henderson, L., Gregory, J. and Swan, G. (2002). *The National Diet and Nutrition Survey: Adults Aged 19 to 64 years*. London: HMSO.

Hendry, L.B. and Kloep, M. (2002). *Lifespan Development: Resources, Challenges, Risks*. London: Thomson Learning.

Hennessy, D.A., Lanni-Manley, E. and Maiorana, N. (2006). The effects of fatal vision goggles on drinking and driving intentions in college students. *Journal of Drug Education*, 36: 59–72.

Henoch, I., Bergman, B., Gustafsson, M. *et al.* (2007). The impact of symptoms, coping capacity, and social support on quality of life experience over time in patients with lung cancer. *Journal of Pain and Symptom Management*, 34: 37–39.

Herbert, T.B. and Cohen, S. (1993). Stress and immunity in humans: a meta-analytic review. *Psychosomatic Medicine*, 55: 364–79.

Herzlich, C. (1973). *Health and Illness: A Social Psychological Analysis*. London: Academic Press.

Hewitt, D., McDonald, M., Portenoy, R. *et al.* (1997). Pain syndromes and etiologies in ambulatory AIDS patients. *Pain*, 70: 117–23.

Higginson, I.J. and Carr, A.J. (2001). Using quality of life measures in the clinical setting. *British Medical Journal*, 322: 1297–300.

Hill, J.C., Lewis, M., Sim, J. *et al.* (2007). Predictors of poor outcome in patients with neck pain treated by physical therapy. *Clinical Journal of Pain*, 23: 683–90.

Hingson, R.M., Heeren, T., Winter, M.R. and Wechsler, H. (2003). Early age of first drunkenness as a factor in college students' unplanned and unprotected sex attributable to drinking. *Pediatrics*, 111: 34–41.

Hinton, J. (1999). The progress of awareness and acceptance of dying assessed in cancer patients and their caring relatives. *Palliative Medicine*, 13: 19–35.

Ho, S.M.Y., Chan, C.L.W. and Ho, R.T.H. (2004). Post-traumatic growth in Chinese cancer survivors. *Psycho-Oncology*, 13: 377–89.

Hobfoll, S. (1991). Traumatic stress: a theory based on rapid loss of resources. *Anxiety Research*, 4: 187–97.

Hobfoll, S.E. (1989). Conservation of resources: a new attempt at conceptualizing stress. *American Psychologist*, 44: 513–24.

Hobfoll, S.E. (2001). The influence of culture, community, and the nested-self in the stress processes: advancing conservation of resources theory. *Applied Psychology: An International Review*, 50: 337–421.

Hobfoll, S.E., Jackson, A.P., Lavin, J. *et al.* (1994). Women's barriers to safer sex. *Psychology and Health*, 9: 233–52.

Hobfoll, S.E. and Lilly, R.S. (1993). Conservation of resources; a new attempt at conceptualising stress. *American Psychologist*, 44: 513–24.

Hodgson, S. and Maher, E. (1999). *A Practical Guide to Human Cancer Genetics*. Cambridge: Cambridge University Press.

Hogbin, B. and Fallowfield, L. (1989). Getting it taped: the 'bad news' consultation with cancer patients. *British Journal of Hospital Medicine*, 41: 330–3.

Holland, J.C. and Gooen-Piels, J. (2000). Principles of psycho-oncology. In J.C. Holland and E. Frei (eds), *Psychological Care of the Patient with Cancer*. New York: Oxford University Press.

Hollis, J.F., Connett, J.E., Stevens, V.J. *et al.* (1990). Stressful life events, Type A behaviour, and the prediction of cardiovascular disease and total mortality over six years. *Journal of Behavioral Medicine*, 13: 263–81.

Holmes, T.H. and Masuda, M. (1974). Life change and illness susceptibility. In B.S. Dohrenwend and B.P. Dohrenwend (eds), *Stressful Life Events: Their Nature and Effects*. New York: Wiley.

Holmes, T.H. and Rahe, R.H. (1967). The social readjustment rating scale. *Journal of Psychosomatic Research*, 11: 213–18.

Holroyd, K.A. and Lipchik, G.L. (1999). Psychological management of recurrent headache disorders: progress and prospects. In R.J. Gatchel and D.C. Turk (eds), *Psychosocial Factors in Pain*. New York: Guilford Press.

Holroyd, K.A., O'Donnell, F.J., Stensland, M. *et al.* (2001). Management of chronic tension-type headache with tricyclic antidepressant medication, stress management therapy, and their combination. *Journal of the American Medical Association*, 285: 2208–15.

Holtzman, S., Newth, S. and DeLongis, A. (2004). The role of social support in coping with daily pain among patients with Rheumatoid Arthritis. *Journal of Health Psychology*, 9: 749–67.

Holzner, B., Kemmler, G., Cella, D. *et al.* (2004). Normative data for functional assessment of cancer therapy: general scale and its use for the interpretation of quality of life scores in cancer survivors. *Acta Oncologica*, 43: 153–60.

Hooker, K., Monahan, D., Shifren, K. *et al.* (1992). Mental and physical health of spouse caregivers: the role of personality. *Psychology and Aging*, 7: 367–75.

Hooper, L., Bartlett, C., Davey-Smith, G. *et al.* (2002). Systematic review of long-term effects of advice to reduce dietary salt in adults. *British Medical Journal*, 325: 628–32.

Hoorens, V. and Buunk, B.P. (1993). Social comparisons of health risks: locus of control, the person-positivity bias, and unrealistic optimism. *Journal of Applied Social Psychology*, 23: 291–302.

Hopwood, P. (1997). Psychological issues in cancer genetics: current research and future priorities. *Patient Education and Counselling*, 32: 19–31.

Horgan, R.P. and Kenny, L.C. (2007). Management of teenage pregnancy. *The Obstetrician and Gynaecologist*, 9: 153–8.

Horne, P.J., Tapper, K., Lowe, C.F. *et al.* (2004). Increasing children's fruit and vegetable consumption: a peer modelling and rewards-based intervention. *European Journal of Clinical Nutrition*, 58: 1649–60.

Horne, R. (1997). Representations of medication and treatment: advances in theory and measurement. In K.J. Petrie and J. Weinman (eds) *Perceptions of health and illness*. Chur: Harwood.

Horne, R. (1999). Patients' beliefs about treatment: the hidden determinant of treatment outcome? *Journal of Psychosomatic Research*, 47: 491–5.

Horne, R. and Weinman, J. (1999). Patients' beliefs about prescribed medicines and their role in adherence to treatment in chronic physical illness. *Journal of Psychosomatic Research*, 47: 555–67.

Horne, R. and Weinman, J. (2002). Self-regulation and self-management in asthma: exploring the role of illness perceptions and treatment beliefs in explaining non-adherence to preventer medication. *Psychology and Health*, 17: 17–32.

Hosking, S.G., Marsh, N.V. and Friedman, P.J. (1996). Post-stroke depression: prevalence, course and associated factors. *Neuropsychological Review*, 6: 107–33.

House, A., Dennis, M., Mogridge, L. *et al.* (1991). Mood disorders in the year after first stroke. *British Journal of Psychiatry*, 2: 211–21.

House, J.S. (1987). Chronic stress and chronic disease in life and work: conceptual and methodological issues. *Work and Stress*, 1: 129–34.

House, J.S., Kessler, R., Herzog, A.R. *et al.* (1991). Social stratification, age, and health. In K.W. Scheie, D. Blazer and J.S. House (eds), *Aging, Health Behaviours, and Health Outcomes*. Hillsdale, NJ: Lawrence Erlbaum.

House, J.S., Robbins, C. and Metzner, H.L. (1982). The association of social relationships and activities with mortality: prospective evidence from the Tecumseh Community Health Study. *American Journal of Epidemiology*, 116: 123–40.

House of Lords Select Committee on the Assisted Dying for the Terminally Ill Bill (HL). *Report on the assisted dying for the terminally ill bill, Vol 1: Appendix 7*. London: Stationery Office.

Houston, B.K., Chesney, M.A., Black, G.W. *et al.* (1992). Behavioral clusters and coronary heart disease. *Psychosomatic Medicine*, 54: 447–61.

Houston, M. (2004). Commissioner denies plans for a Europe-wide smoking ban. *British Medical Journal*, 328: 544.

Hu, F.B., Willett, W.C., Colditz, G.A. *et al.* (1999). Prospective study of snoring and risk of hypertension in women. *American Journal of Epidemiology*, 150: 806–16.

Hu, F.B., Willett, W.C., Manson, J.E. *et al.* (2000). Snoring and risk of cardiovascular disease in women. *Journal of the American College of Cardiology*, 35: 308–13.

Hu, T.-W., Sung, H.-Y. and Keeler, T.E. (1995). Reducing cigarette consumption in California: tobacco taxes vs. an anti-smoking media campaign. *American Journal of Public Health*, 85: 1218–22.

Hudzinski, L.G. and Frohlich, E.D. (1990). One-year longitudinal study of a no-smoking policy in a medical institution. *Chest*, 97: 1198–202.

Hughes, B.M. and Callinan, S. (2007). Trait dominance and cardiovascular reactivity to social and non-social stressors: Gender-specific implications. *Psychology and Health*, 22: 457–472.

Hughes G., Bennett, K.M. and Hetherington, M. (2004). Old and alone: barriers to healthy eating in older men living on their own. *Appetite*, 43: 269–276.

Huijbrechts, P., Duivenvoorden, H.J., Deckers, J.W. *et al.* (1996). Modification of smoking habits five months after myocardial infarction: relationship with personality characteristics. *Journal of Psychosomatic Research*, 40: 369–78.

Hulse, G.K. and Tait, R.J. (2002). Six-month outcomes associated with a brief alcohol intervention for adult in-patients with psychiatric disorders. *Drug and Alcohol Review*, 21: 105–12.

Humphrey, N. (2002). Great expectations: the evolutionary psychology of faith-healing and the placebo effect. In *Psychology at the Turn of the Millennium, Vol. 2: Social, Developmental, and Clinical Perspectives*, C. von Hofsten and L. Bäckman (eds). Hove: Psychology Press.

Hunt, S.M. and Martin, C.J. (1988). Health related behaviour change – a test of a new model. *Psychology and Health*, 2: 209–30.

Hunt, S.M., McEwan, J. and McKenna, S.P. (1986). *Measuring Health Status*. Beckenham: Croom Helm.

Hunter, M.S., Grunfeld, E.A. and Ramirez, A.J. (2003). Help-seeking intentions for breast-cancer symptoms: a comparison of self-regulation model and the theory of planned behaviour. *British Journal of Health Psychology*, 8: 319–34.

Hurtz, S.Q., Henriksen, L., Wang, Y. *et al.* (2007). The relationship between exposure to alcohol advertising in stores, owning alcohol promotional items, and adolescent alcohol use. *Alcohol and Alcoholism*, 42: 143–9.

Huskisson, E.C. (1974). Measurement of pain. *Lancet*, Nov 9; 2(7889): 1127–31.

Hyland, A., Wakefield, M., Higbee, C. *et al.* (2006). Anti-tobacco television advertising and indicators of smoking cessation in adults: a cohort study. *Health Education Research*, 21: 296–302.

Hyland, M.E., Bellesis, M., Thompson, P.J. *et al.* (1996). The constructs of asthma quality of life: psychometric, experimental and correlational evidence. *Psychology and Health*, 12: 101–21.

Illinois Racial and Ethnic Health Disparities Council: http://app.idph.state.il.us/iphi/docs/DraftFinal.pdf

Ingledew, D.K. and Ferguson, E. (2007). Personality and riskier sexual behaviour: motivational mediators. *Psychology & Health*, 22: 291–315.

Ingledew, D.K. and McDonagh, G. (1998). What coping functions are served when health behaviours are used as coping strategies? *Journal of Health Psychology*, 3: 195–213.

Ingram, K.M., Jones, D.A., Fass, R.J. *et al.* (1999). Social support and unsupportive social interactions: their association with depression among people living with HIV. *AIDS Care*, 11: 313–29.

Ingram, L., Morrison, V., Soulsby, J. *et al.* (2008 in review). Mindfulness-based cognitive therapy for oncology outpatients and their family carers: a qualitative evaluation.

Inoue, S., Saeki, T., Mantani, T. *et al.* (2003). Factors related to patients' mental adjustment to breast cancer: patient characteristics and family functioning. *Support Care Cancer*, 11: 178–84.

Inoyue, J., Flannelly, L. and Flannelly, K.J. (2001). The effectiveness of self-management training for individuals with HIV/AIDS. *Journal of the Association of Nurses in AIDS Care*, 12: 71–82.

International Center for Alcohol Policies (ICAP) (1998). *Report 5*. Washington: ICAP.

International Obesity Taskforce and European Association for the Study of Obesity (2002). *Obesity in Europe: The Case for Action*. London: International Obesity Taskforce.

Isen, A.M. (1987). Positive affect, cognitive processes, and social behaviour. In L. Berkowitz (ed.), *Advances in Experimental Social Psychology 20*. New York: Academic Press.

Iwasaki, M., Otani, T., Sunaga, R. *et al.* (2002). Social networks and mortality based on the Komo-Ise cohort study in Japan. *International Journal of Epidemiology*, 31: 1208–18.

Jackson, R., Scragg, R. and Beaglehole, R. (1991). Alcohol consumption and risk of coronary heart disease. *British Medical Journal*, 303: 211–16.

Jacobs, D.R. Jr, Luepker, R.V., Mittelmark, M.B. *et al.* (1986). Community-wide prevention strategies: evaluation design of the Minnesota Heart Health Program. *Journal of Chronic Diseases*, 39: 775–88.

Jacobsen, P.B. and Hahn, D.M. (1998). Cognitive behavioral programmes. In J. Holland (ed.), *Textbook of Psycho-Oncology*. New York: Oxford University Press.

Jacobson, E. (1938). *Progressive Relaxation*. Chicago: University of Chicago Press.

Jaffe, H. (1997). Dying for dollars. *Men's Health*, 12: 132–7.

Jaffe, L., Lutter, J.M., Rex, J. *et al.* (1999). Incentives and barriers to physical activity for working women. *American Journal of Health Promotion*, 13(4): 215–18.

James, J., Thomas P. and Kerr D. (2007). Preventing childhood obesity: two year follow-up results from the Christchurch obesity prevention programme in schools (CHOPPS). *British Medical Journal*, 335: 841.

James, J.E. (2004). Critical review of dietary caffeine and blood pressure: a relationship that should be taken more seriously. *Psychosomatic Medicine*, 66: 63–71.

James, J.E. and Hardardottir, D. (2002). Influence of attention focus and trait anxiety on tolerance of acute pain. *British Journal of Health Psychology*, 7: 149–62.

James, S.A., LaCroix, A.Z., Kleinbaum, D.G. *et al.* (1984). John Henryism and blood pressure differences among black men. II. The role of occupational stressors. *Journal of Behavioral Medicine*, 7: 259–75.

Janlert, U., Asplund, K. and Weinehall, L. (1992). Unemployment and cardiovascular risk indicators. Data from the MONICA survey in northern Sweden. *Journal of Social Medicine*, 20: 14–18.

Janse, A.J., Gemke, R.J.B.J., Uiterwaal, C.S.P.M. *et al.* (2004). Quality of life: patients and doctors don't always agree. *Journal of Clinical Epidemiology*, 57: 653–61.

Janz, N.K. and Becker, M.H. (1984). The health belief model: a decade later. *Health Education Quarterly*, 11: 1–17.

Janz, N.K., Zimmerman, M.A., Wren, P.A. *et al.* (1996). Evaluation of 37 AIDS prevention projects: successful approaches and barriers to program effectiveness. *Health Education Quarterly*, 23: 80–97.

Janzon, E., Hedblad, B., Berglund, G. *et al.* (2004). Changes in blood pressure and body weight following smoking cessation in women. *Journal of Internal Medicine*, 255: 266–72.

Jarosz, A., Kozłowska-Wojciechowska, M. and Uramowska-Zyto, B. (2003). [Expectations regarding nutrition information on food product packages] *Roczniki Państwowego Zakładu Higieny*, 54: 231–9.

Jarvis, M.J. (2004). Why people smoke. *British Medical Journal*, 328: 277–9.

Jay, S.M., Elliott, C.H. and Fitzgibbons, I. (1995). A comparative study of cognitive behavior therapy versus general anaesthesia for painful medical procedures in children. *Pain*, 62: 3–9.

Jeffery, R.W., Forster, J.L., French, S.A. *et al.* (1993). The Healthy Worker Project: A work-site intervention for weight control and smoking cessation. *American Journal of Public Health*, 83: 395–401.

Jellinek, E.M. (1960). *The Disease Concept of Alcoholism*. New Haven, Conn.: Hillhouse Press.

Jemmott, J.B., Croyle, R.T. and Ditto, P.H. (1988). Commonsense epidemiology: self-based judgements from laypersons and physicians. *Health Psychology*, 7(1): 55–73.

Jenkins, P.R., Jenkins, R.A., Nannis, E.D. *et al.* (2000). Reducing risk of sexually transmitted disease (STD) and human immunodeficiency virus infection in a military STD clinic: evaluation of a randomized preventive intervention trial. *Clinical Infectious Diseases*, 30: 730–5.

Jenkins, R.L., Lewis, G. and Bebbington, P. (1997). The National Psychiatric Morbidity Surveys of Great Britain: initial findings from the household survey. *Psychology and Medicine*, 27: 775–89.

Jenkinson, C., Fitzpatrick, R., Garrat, A. *et al.* (2001). Can item response theory reduce patient burden when measuring health status in neurological disorders? Results from Rasch analysis of the SF36 physical functioning scale (PF-10). *Journal of Neurology, Neurosurgery and Psychiatry*, 71: 220–4.

Jensen, M.P., Turner, J.A. and Romano, J.M. (2001). Changes in beliefs, catastrophizing, and coping are associated with improvement in multidisciplinary pain treatment. *Journal of Consulting and Clinical Psychology*, 69: 655–62.

Jerram, K.L. and Coleman, P.G. (1999). The big five personality traits and reporting of health behaviours and health problems in old age. *British Journal of Health Psychology*, 4: 181–92.

Jerusalem, M. and Schwarzer, R. (1992). Self-efficacy as a resource factor in stress appraisal process. In R. Schwarzer (ed.), *Self Efficacy: Thought Control of Action*. Washington: Hemisphere.

Jessor, R. and Jessor, S.L. (1977). *Problem Behavior and Psychosocial Development: A Longitudinal Study of Youth*. New York: Academic Press.

Jewell, J. and Hupp, S.D. (2005). Examining the effects of fatal vision goggles on changing attitudes and behaviors related to drinking and driving. *Journal of Primary Prevention*, 26: 553–65.

Jirojanakul, P., Skevington, S.M. and Hudson, J. (2003). Predicting young children's quality of life. *Social Science and Medicine*, 57: 1277–88.

Johnson, J.V., Hall, E.M. and Theorell, T. (1989). Combined effects of job strain and social isolation on cardiovascular disease morbidity and mortality in a random sample of the Swedish male working population. *Scandinavian Journal of Work, Environment, and Health*, 15: 271–9.

Johnson, M.I. (2001). Transcutaneous electrical nerve stimulation (TENS) and TENS-like devices: do they provide pain relief? *Pain Reviews*, 8: 121–58.

Johnson, S.B. (1999). Commentary: psychologists' resistance to showcasing the profession's accomplishments: What is all the fuss about? *Journal of Pediatric Psychology*, 24: 329–30.

Johnsson, K.O. and Berglund, M. (2003). Education of key personnel in student pubs leads to a decrease in alcohol consumption among patrons: a randomized controlled trial. *Addiction*, 98: 627–33.

Johnston, D.W. (2002). Acute and chronic psychological processes in cardiovascular disease. In K.W. Schaie, H. Leventhal and S.L. Willis (eds), *Effective Health Behavior in Older Adults*. New York: Springer (pp. 55–64).

Johnston, D.W. (2007). Emotions and the heart: psychological risk factors for cardiovascular disease. *European Health Psychologist*, 1: 9–11.

Johnston, M. and Kennedy, P. (1998). Editorial: special issue on clinical health psychology in chronic conditions. *Clinical Psychology and Psychotherapy*, 5: 59–61.

Johnston, M. and Pollard, B. (2001). Consequences of disease: testing the WHO International Classification of Impairments, Disability and Handicap (ICIDH) model. *Social Science and Medicine*, 53: 1261–73.

Johnston, M. and Vogele, K. (1993). Benefits of psychological preparation for surgery: a meta-analysis. *Annals of Behavioral Medicine*, 15: 245–56.

Johnston, M., Morrison, V., MacWalter, R. and Partridge, C. (1999). Perceived control, coping and recovery from disability following stroke, *Psychology and Health*, 14: 181–92.

Johnston, M., Pollard, B., Morrison, V. *et al.* (2004). Functional limitations and survival following stroke: psychological and clinical predictors of 3 year outcome. *International Journal of Behavioral Medicine*, 11: 187–96.

Joint Health Surveys Unit (2001). *Health Survey for England: The Health of Minority Ethnic Groups 1999*. London: HMSO.

Jolly, K., Taylor, R., Lip, G.Y. *et al.* (2007). The Birmingham Rehabilitation Uptake Maximisation Study (BRUM). Home-based compared with hospital-based cardiac rehabilitation in a multiethnic population: cost-effectiveness and patient adherence. *Health Technology Assessment*, 11: 111–18.

Jonas, B.S. and Mussolino, M.E. (2000). Symptoms of depression as a prospective risk factor for stroke. *Psychosomatic Medicine*, 62: 463–71.

Jones, B.A., Reams, K., Calvocoressi, L. *et al.* (2007). Adequacy of communicating results from screening mammograms to African American and White women. *American Journal of Public Health*, 97: 531–8.

Jones, E. and Morrison, V. (2004). Patient–carer interactions following stroke: the effect on distress. BPS Division of Health Psychology Annual Conference, Edinburgh, September.

Jones, J.R., Huxtable, C.S., Hodgson, J.T. *et al.* (2003). *Self-reported Illness in 2001/02: Results from a Household Survey*. London: Health and Safety Executive.

Jones, M.A. and Johnston, D.W. (2000). A critical review of the relationship between perception of the work environment, coping and mental health in trained nurses, and patient outcomes. *Clinical Effectiveness in Nursing*, 4: 74–85.

Jones, R.A. (1990). Expectations and delay in seeking medical care. *Journal of Social Issues*, 46: 81–95.

Jones, R., Pearson, J., McGregor, S. *et al.* (2002). Does writing a list help cancer patients ask relevant questions? *Patient Education and Counseling*, 47: 369–71.

Jørgensen, K.J. and Gøtzsche, P.C. (2004). Presentation on websites of possible benefits and harm from screening for breast cancer: a cross-sectional study. *British Medical Journal*, 328: 148–53.

Jousilahti, P., Vartiainen, E., Tuomilehto, J., Pekkenen, J. and Puska, P. (1995). Effect of risk factors and changes in risk factors on coronary mortality in three cohorts of middle aged people in eastern Finland. *American Journal of Epidemiology*, 141: 50–60.

Joyce, C., Hickey, H., McGee, H. *et al.* (2003). A theory-based method for the evaluation of individual quality of life: the SEIQoL. *Quality of Life Research*, 12: 275–80.

Julien, R.M. (1996). *A Primer of Drug Action: A Concise, Nontechnical Guide to the Actions, Uses and Side Effects of Psychoactive Drugs*, 7th edn. New York: W.H. Freeman.

Juster, H.R., Loomis, B.R., Hinman, T.M. *et al.* (2007). Declines in hospital admissions for acute myocardial infarction in New York state after implementation of a comprehensive smoking ban. *American Journal of Public Health*, 97: 2035–9.

Kabat-Zinn, J. (2001). *Full Catastrophe Living: How to Cope with Stress, Pain and Illness Using Mindfulness Meditation*. Piatkus Books.

Kahn, K.L., Pearson, M.L., Harrison, E.R. *et al.* (1994). Health care for black and poor hospitalized Medicare patients. *Journal of the American Medical Association*, 271: 1169–74.

Kalichman, S.C., Benotsch, E.G., Weinhardt, L. *et al.* (2003). Health-related internet use, coping, social support, and health indicators in people living with HIV/AIDS: preliminary results from a community survey. *Health Psychology*, 22: 111–16.

Kalichman, S.C., Cherry, C. and Browne-Sperling, F. (1999). Effectiveness of a video-based motivational skills-building HIV risk-reduction intervention for inner-city African American men. *Journal of Consulting and Clinical Psychology*, 67: 959–66.

Kalnins, I.H.C., Ballantyne, P. and Quartaro, G. (1994). School based community development as a health promotion strategy for children. *Health Promotion International*, 9: 269–79.

Kalra, L., Evans, A., Perez, I. *et al.* (2004). Training carers of stroke patients: randomised controlled trial. *British Medical Journal*, 328: 1099–104.

Kanner, A.D., Coyne, J.C., Schaefer, C. *et al.* (1981). Comparison of two models of stress management: daily hassles and uplifts versus major life events. *Journal of Behavioral Medicine*, 4: 1–39.

Kaplan, G. and Baron-Epel, O. (2003). What lies behind the subjective evaluation of health status? *Social Science and Medicine*, 56: 1669–76.

Kaplan, G.A. and Reynolds, P. (1988). Depression and cancer mortality and morbidity: prospective evidence from the Alameda County study. *Journal of Behavioral Medicine*, 11: 1–14.

Karasek, R. (1996). Lower health risk with increased job control among white collar workers. *Journal of Organizational Behavior*, 11: 171–85.

Karasek, R.A. (1979). Job demands, job decision latitude and mental strain: implications for job redesign. *Administrative Science Quarterly*, 24: 285–308.

Karasek, R.A. and Theorell, T. (1990). *Healthy Work: Stress, Productivity and the Reconstruction of Working Life*. New York: Basic Books.

Karasek, R.A., Baker, D., Marxer, F. *et al.* (1981). Job decision latitude, job demands and cardiovascular disease: a prospective study of Swedish men. *American Journal of Public Health*, 71: 694–705.

Karasz, A. and McKinley, P.S. (2007). Cultural differences in conceptual models of fatigue. *Journal of Health Psychology*, 12: 613–26.

Kasl, S.V. (1996). Theory of stress and health. In C.L. Cooper (ed.), *Handbook of Stress, Medicine and Health*. London: CRC Press.

Kasl, S.V. and Cobb, S. (1966a). Health behavior, illness behavior, and sick role behavior. I. Health and illness behavior. *Archives of Environmental Health*, 12: 246–66.

Kasl, S.V. and Cobb, S. (1966b). Health behavior, illness behavior, and sick role behavior. II. Sick role behavior. *Archives of Environmental Health*, 12: 531–41.

Katbamna, S., Bhakta, P. and Parker, G. (2000) Perceptions of disability and care-giving relationships in South Asian communities. In W.I.U. Ahmad (ed.), *Ethnicity, Disability and Chronic Illness*. Buckingham: Open University Press (pp. 12–27).

Katz, M.H. (1997). AIDS epidemic in San Francisco among men who report sex with men: successes and challenges of HIV prevention. *Journal of Acquired Immune Deficiency Syndrome and Human Retrovirology*, 14: S38–S46.

Kauff, N.D., Satagopan, J.M., Robson, M.E. *et al.* (2002). Risk-reducing Salpingo-oophorectomy in women with a BRCA1 or BRCA2 mutation. *New England Journal of Medicine*, 346: 1609–15.

Kawachi, I., Kennedy, B.P., Lochner, K. *et al.* (1997). Social capital, income inequality, and mortality. *American Journal of Public Health*, 87: 1491–8.

Keating, N.L., Guadagnoli, E., Landrum, M.B. *et al.* (2002). Treatment decision making in early-stage breast cancer: should surgeons match patients' desired level of involvement? *Journal of Clinical Oncology*, 20: 1473–9.

Keats, M.R., Culos-Reed, S.N., Courneya, K.S. *et al.* (2007). Understanding physical activity in adolescent cancer survivors: an application of the theory of planned behavior. *Psycho-Oncology*, 16: 448–57.

Keefe, F.J., Caldwell, D.S., Williams, D.A. *et al.* (1990). Pain coping skills training in the management of osteoarthritic knee pain – II: Follow-up results. *Behavior Therapy*, 21: 435–47.

Keinan, G., Carmil, D. and Rieck, M. (1991). Predicting women's delay in seeking medical care after discovery of a lump in the breast: the role of personality and behaviour patterns. *Behavioral Medicine*, 17: 177–83.

Kelly, J.A., Murphy, D.A., Sikkema, K.J. *et al.* (1993). Psychological interventions to prevent HIV infection are urgently needed. *American Psychologist*, 48: 1023–34.

Kelly, J.A., Murphy, D.A., Sikkema, K.J. *et al.* (1997). Randomised, controlled, community-level HIV-prevention intervention for sexual-risk behaviour among homosexual men in US cities. *The Lancet*, 350: 1500–5.

Kelly, J.A., Murphy, D.A., Washington, C.D. *et al.* (1994). The effects of HIV/AIDS intervention groups for high-risk women in urban clinics. *American Journal of Public Health*, 84: 225–37.

Kelly, J.A., St Lawrence, J.S., Stevenson, L.Y. *et al.* (1992). Community AIDS/HIV risk reduction: the effects of endorsements by popular people in three cities. *American Journal of Public Health*, 82: 1483–9.

Kelly, J.M., Rowe, A.K., Onikpo, F. *et al.* (2007). Care takers' recall of Integrated Management of Childhood Illness counselling messages in Benin. *Tropical Doctor*, 37: 75–9.

Kelly, P.A. and Haidet, P. (2007) Physician overestimation of patient literacy: a potential source of health care disparities. *Patient Education and Counseling*, 66: 119–22.

Kemeny, M.E., Weiner, H., Taylor, S.E. *et al.* (1994). Repeated bereavement, depressed mood, and immune parameters in HIV seropositive and seronegative homosexual men. *Health Psychology*, 13: 14–24.

Kennedy, T., Jones, R., Darnley, S. *et al.* (2005). Cognitive behaviour therapy in addition to antispasmodic treatment for irritable bowel syndrome in primary care: randomised controlled trial. *British Medical Journal*, 331: 435.

Kentsch, M., Rodemerk, U., Muller-Esch, G. *et al.* (2002). Emotional attitudes toward symptoms and inadequate coping strategies are major determinants of patient delay in acute myocardial infarction. *Zeitschrift zu Kardiologie*, 91: 147–55.

Kerns, R.D., Haythornwaite, J., Southwick, S. *et al.* (1990). The role of marital interaction in chronic pain and depressive symptom severity. *Journal of Psychosomatic Research*, 34: 401–8.

Key, T.J., Fraser, G.E., Thorogood, M. *et al.* (1998). Mortality in vegetarians and non-vegetarians: a collaborative analysis of 8,300 deaths among 76,000 men and women in five prospective studies. *Public Health Nutrition*, 1: 33–41.

Khadilkar A., Milne S., Brosseau L. *et al.* (2005). Transcutaneous electrical nerve stimulation (TENS) for chronic low-back pain. *Cochrane Database of Systematic Reviews*. 3: CD003008.

Khantzian, E.J. (2003). Understanding addictive vulnerability: an evolving psychodynamic perspective. *Neuro-psychoanalysis*, 5: 3–35.

Khatbamna, S., Bhakta, P. and Parker G. (2000). Perceptions of disability and care-giving relationships in South Asian Communities. In Ahmad, W. (2000) (ed.), *Ethnicity, Disability and Chronic Illness*. Buckingham: Open University Press (pp. 12–27).

Kickbusch, I. (2003). The contribution of the World Health Organization to a new public health and health promotion. *American Journal of Public Health*, 93: 383–8.

Kiechl, S., Egger, G., Mayr, M. *et al.* (2001). Chronic infections and the risk of carotid atherosclerosis: prospective results from a large population study. *Circulation*, 103: 1064–70.

Kiecolt-Glaser, J.K., Dura, J.R., Speicher, C.E. *et al.* (1991). Spousal caregivers of dementia victims: longitudinal changes in immunity and health. *Psychosomatic Medicine*, 53: 345–62.

Kiecolt-Glaser, J.K., Garner, W., Speicher, C. *et al.* (1984). Psycho-social modifiers of immunocompetence in medical students. *Psychosomatic Medicine*, 46: 7–14.

Kiecolt-Glaser, J.K. and Glaser, R. (1995). Psychological influences on immunity. *Psychosomatics*, 27: 621–4.

Kiecolt-Glaser, J.K. and Glaser, R. (1999). Psychoneuroimmunology and cancer: fact or fiction? *European Journal of Cancer*, 35: 1603–7.

Kiecolt-Glaser, J.K., Glaser, R., Gravenstein, S. *et al.* (1996). Chronic stress alters the immune response to influenza virus vaccination in older adults. *Proceedings of the National Academy of Science USA*, 93: 3043–7.

Kiecolt-Glaser, J.K., Glaser, R., Williger, D. *et al.* (1985). Psychosocial enhancement of immunocompetence in a geriatric population. *Health Psychology*, 4: 25–41.

Kiecolt-Glaser, J.K., Malarkey, W.B., Cacioppo, J.T. *et al.* (1994). Stressful personal relationships: immune and endocrine function. In R. Glaser and J.K. Kiecolt-Glaser (eds), *Handbook of Human Stress and Immunity*. San Diego, Calif.: Academic Press.

Kiecolt-Glaser, J.K., Marucha, P.T., Malarkey, W.B. *et al.* (1995). Slowing wound healing by psychosocial stress. *The Lancet*, 4: 1194–6.

Kiecolt-Glaser, J.K., McGuire, L., Robles, T.F. *et al.* (2002). Psychoneuroimmunology: psychological influences on immune function and health. *Journal of Consulting and Clinical Psychology*, 70: 537–47.

Kiecolt-Glaser, J.K., Preacher, K.J., MacCallum, R.C. *et al.* (2003). Chronic stress and age-related increases in the pro-inflammatory cytokine IL-6. *Proceedings of the National Academy of Science*, 10: 9090–95.

Kiernan, P.J. and Isaacs, J.B. (1981). Use of drugs by the elderly. *Journal of the Royal Society of Medicine*, 74: 196–200.

Kinman, G. and Jones, F. (2005). Lay representations of work stress: what do people really mean when they say they are stressed? *Work & Stress*, 19: 101–20.

Kinmonth, A.L., Woodcock, A., Griffin, S. *et al.* (1998). Randomised controlled trial of patient-centred care of diabetes in general practice: impact on current wellbeing and future disease risk. The Diabetes Care from Diagnosis Research Team. *British Medical Journal*, 317: 1202–8.

Kinney, J.M., Stephens, M.A.P., Franks, M.M. *et al.* (1995). Stresses and satisfactions of family care-givers to older stroke patients. *The Journal of Applied Gerontology*, 14: 3–21.

Kirby, S.D., Ureda, J.R., Rose, R.L. *et al.* (1998). Peripheral cues and involvement level: influences on acceptance of a mammography message. *Journal of Health Communication*, 3: 19–35.

Kirkcaldy, B.D. and Cooper, C.L. (1992). Managing the stress of change: occupational stress among senior police officers in Berlin. *Stress Medicine*, 8: 219–31.

Kirkcaldy, B.D., Athanasou, J.A. and Trimpop, R. (2000). The idiosyncratic construction of stress: examples from medical work settings. *Stress Medicine*, 16: 315–26.

Kittleson, M.M., Meoni, L.A., Wang, N.Y. *et al.* (2006). Association of childhood socioeconomic status with subsequent coronary heart disease in physicians. *Archives of Internal Medicine*, 166: 2356–61.

Kivimäki, M., Elovainio, M., Kokko, K. *et al.* (2003). Hostility, unemployment and health status: testing three theoretical models. *Social Science and Medicine*, 56: 2139–52.

Kivimäki, M., Lawlor, D.A., Davey Smith, G. *et al.* (2007). Socioeconomic position, co-occurrence of behavior-related risk factors, and coronary heart disease: the Finnish Public Sector study. *American Journal of Public Health*, 97: 874–9.

Kivimäki, M., Vahtera, J., Kosekenvuo, M. *et al.* (1998). Response of hostile individuals to stressful changes in their working lives: test of a psychosocial vulnerability model. *Psychological Medicine*, 28: 903–13.

Kiviruusu, O., Huurre, T. and Aro, H. (2007). Psychosocial resources and depression among chronically ill young adults: Are males more vulnerable? *Social Science & Medicine*, 65: 173–186.

Klein, C.T.F. and Helweg-Larsen, M. (2002). Perceived control and the optimistic bias: a meta-analytic review. *Psychology and Health*, 17: 437–46.

Kline, K.N. and Mattson, M. (2000). Breast self-examination pamphlets. A content analysis grounded in fear appeals research. *Health Communication*, 12: 1–21.

Kline, P. (1993). *Personality – the Psychometric View*. London: Routledge.

Klonoff, E.A. and Landrine, H. (1994). Culture and gender diversity in commonsense beliefs about the causes of six illnesses. *Journal of Behavioral Medicine*, 17: 407–18.

Knapp, P., Raynor, D.K. and Jebar, A.H. *et al.* (2005). Interpretation of medication pictograms by adults in the UK. *Annals of Pharmacotherapy*, 39: 1227–33.

Knowler, W.C., Barrett-Connor, E., Fowler, S.E. *et al.* (2002). Reduction in the incidence of type 2 diabetes with lifestyle intervention or metformin. *New England Journal of Medicine*, 346: 393–403.

Kobasa, S.C. (1979). Stressful life events, personality and health: an inquiry into hardiness. *Journal of Personality and Social Psychology*, 37: 1–11.

Kobasa, S.C., Maddi, S. and Kahn, S. (1982). Hardiness and health: a prospective study. *Journal of Personality and Social Psychology*, 42: 168–77.

Koffman, D.M., Lee, J.W., Hopp, J.W. *et al.* (1998). The impact of including incentives and competition in a workplace smoking cessation program on quit rates. *American Journal of Health Promotion*, 13: 105–11.

Kohl, H.W. (2001). Physical activity and cardiovascular disease: evidence for a dose–response. *Medicine and Science in Sports and Exercise*, 33: S472–S487.

Koikkalainen, M., Lappalainen, R. and Mykkanen, H. (1996). Why cardiac patients do not follow the nutritionist's advice: barriers in nutritional advice perceived in rehabilitation. *Disability and Rehabilitation*, 13: 619–23.

Kok, G. and Schaalma, H. (1998). Theory-based and data-based health education intervention programmes. *Psychology and Health*, 13: 747–51.

Kole-Snijders, A.M.J., Vlaeyen, J.W.S. and Goossens, M.E.J. *et al.* (1999). Chronic low back pain: what does cognitive coping skills training add to operant behavioural treatment? Results of a randomized trial. *Journal of Consulting and Clinical Psychology*, 67: 931–44.

Kolk, A.M., Hanewald, G.J.F.P., Schagen, S. *et al.* (2003). A symptom perception approach to common physical symptoms. *Social Science and Medicine*, 57: 2343–54.

Kop, N., Euwema, M. and Schaufeli, W. (1999). Burnout, job stress and violent behaviour among Dutch police officers. *Work and Stress*, 13: 3226–340.

Kop, W.J. and Krantz, D.S. (1997). Type A behaviour, hostility and coronary artery disease. In A. Baum,

S. Newman, J. Weinman *et al.* (eds), *Cambridge Handbook of Psychology, Health and Medicine*. Cambridge: Cambridge University Press.

Korfage, J., Essink-Bot, M-L., Daamen, R. *et al.* (2008). Women show mixed intentions regarding the uptake of HPV vaccinations in pre-adolescents: A questionnaire study. *European Journal of Cancer*, 44: 1186–92.

Kornblith, A.B. (1998). *Psychosocial Adaptation of Cancer Survivors*. In J.C. Holland, W. Breibart and P.B. Jacobsen (eds), *Psycho-Oncology*. New York: Oxford University Press.

Kornblith, A.B., Herndon, J.E. II, Weiss, R.B. *et al.* (2003). Long-term adjustment of survivors of early-stage breast carcinoma, 20 years after adjuvant chemotherapy. *Cancer*, 98: 679–89.

Korotkov, D. and Hannah, T.E. (2004). The five factor model of personality: strengths and limitations in predicting health status, sick role and illness behaviour. *Personality and Individual Differences*, 36: 187–99.

Kraft, P., Sutton, S. and McCreath-Reynolds, H. (1999). The transtheoretical model of behaviour change: are the stages qualitatively different? *Psychology and Health*, 14: 433–50.

Kramer, B.J. (1997). Gain in the caregiving experience. Where are we? What next? *The Gerontologist*, 37: 218–32.

Krantz, D.S. and Manuck, S.B. (1984). Acute psychophysiological reactivity and risk of cardiovascular disease: a review and methodological critique. *Psychological Bulletin*, 96: 435–64.

Krantz, D.S., Glass, D.C., Shaeffer, M.A. *et al.* (1982). Behavior patterns and coronary disease: a critical evaluation. In J.T. Cacioppo and R.E. Petty (eds), *Perspectives in Cardiovascular Psycho-physiology*. New York: Guilford Press.

Krantz, G. and Lundberg, U. (2006). Workload, work stress, and sickness absence in Swedish male and female white-collar employees. *Scandinavian Journal of Public Health*, 34: 238–46.

Krantz, G. and Orth, P. (2000). Common symptoms in middle-aged women: their relation to employment status, psychosocial work conditions and social support in a Swedish setting. *Journal of Epidemiology and Community Health*, 54: 192–9.

Krause, N.M. and Jay, G.M. (1994). What do global self-rated health items measure? *Medical Care*, 32: 930–42.

Krieger, N., Queensbury, C. and Peng, T. (1999). Social class, race/ethnicity, and incidence of breast, cervix, colon, lung, and prostate cancer among Asian, black, Hispanic, and white residents of the San Francisco Bay area. *Cancer Causes Control*, 10: 525–37.

Krigsman, K., Nilsson, J.L. and Ring, L. (2007). Adherence to multiple drug therapies: refill adherence to concomitant use of diabetes and asthma/COPD medication. *Pharmacoepidemiology and Drug Safety*, 16: 1120–8.

Krischer, M.M., Xu, P., Meade, C.D. *et al.* (2007). Self-administered stress management training in patients undergoing radiotherapy. *Journal of Clinical Oncology*, 25: 4657–62.

Kriska, A. (2003). Can a physically active lifestyle prevent type 2 diabetes? *Exercise and Sport Science Review*, 31: 132–7.

Kristensen, T.S. (1995). The demand–control–support model: methodological challenges for future research. *Stress Medicine*, 11: 17–26.

Krohne, H.W. (1993). Vigilance and cognitive avoidance as concepts in coping research. In H.W. Krohne (ed.), *Attention and Avoidance: Strategies in Coping with Aversiveness*. Seattle: Hogrefe and Huber.

Krol, Y., Grootenhuis, M.A., Destrée-Vonk, A. *et al.* (2003). Health-related quality of life in children with congenital heart disease. *Psychology and Health*, 18: 251–60.

Krukowski, R.A., Harvey-Berino, J. and Kolodinsky, J. (2006). Consumers may not use or understand calorie labeling in restaurants. *Journal of the American Dietetic Association*, 107: 33–4.

Kubler-Ross, E. (1969). *On Death and Dying*. New York: Macmillan.

Kuchler, T., Henne-Bruns, D., Rappat, S. *et al.* (1999). Impact of psychotherapeutic support on gastrointestinal cancer patients undergoing surgery: survival results of a trial. *Hepato-gastroenterology*, 46: 322–35.

Kuntzleman, C.T. (1985). Enhancing cardiovascular fitness of children and youth: the Feelin' Good Program. In J.E. Zins, D.I. Wagner and C.A. Maher (eds), *Health Promotion in the Schools: Innovative Approaches to Facilitating Physical and Emotional Well-being*. New York: Hawthorn Press.

Kurtz, M.E., Kurtz, J.C., Given, C.W. *et al.* (2008). Patient optimism and mastery – do they play a role in cancer patients' management of pain and fatigue? *Journal of Pain & Symptom Management*, 36: 1–10.

Kurtz, S. and Silverman, J. (1996). The Calgary–Cambridge observation guides: an aid to defining the curriculum and organising the teaching in communication training programmes. *Medical Education*, 30: 83–9.

Kylmä, J. and Juvakka, T. (2007). Hope in parents of adolescents with cancer-factors endangering and engendering parental hope. *European Journal of Oncology Nursing*, 11: 262–71.

Kyngaes, H., Mikkonen, R., Nousiainen, E.M. *et al.* (2001). Coping with the onset of cancer. Coping strategies and resources of young people with cancer. *European Journal of Cancer Care*, 10: 6–11.

Lachman, M.E. and Weaver, S.L. (1998). The sense of control as a moderator of social class differences in health and well-being. *Journal of Personality and Social Psychology*, 74: 763–73.

Lacroix, J.M., Martin, B., Avendano, M. *et al.* (1991). Symptom schemata in chronic respiratory patients. *Health Psychology*, 10: 268–73.

Lahelma, E., Martikainen, P., Rahkonen, O. *et al.* (1999). Gender differences in ill-health in Finland: patterns, magnitude and change. *Social Science and Medicine*, 48: 7–19.

Lancaster, T., Silagy, C., Fowler, G. *et al.* (1999). Training health professionals in smoking cessation. In *The Cochrane Library*, issue 1. Oxford: Update Software.

Landmark, B.T. and Wahl, A. (2002). Living with newly diagnosed breast cancer: a qualitative study of 10 women with newly diagnosed breast cancer. *Journal of Advanced Nursing*, 49: 112–21.

Landolt, M.A., Vollrath, M., Ribi, K. *et al.* (2003). Incidence and associations of parental and child posttraumatic stress symptoms in pediatric patients. *Journal of Child Psychology and Psychiatry*, 44: 1199–207.

Landrine, H. and Klonoff, E.A. (1992). Culture and health-related schema: a review and proposal for interdisciplinary integration. *Health Psychology*, 11: 267–76.

Landrine, H. and Klonoff, E.A. (1994). Cultural diversity in causal attributions for illness: the role of the supernatural. *Journal of Behavioral Medicine*, 17: 181–93.

Lane, D., Beevers, D.G. and Lip, G.Y. (2002). Ethnic differences in blood pressure and the prevalence of hypertension in England. *Journal of Human Hypertension*, 16: 267–73.

Lane, D., Carroll, D., Ring, C. *et al.* (2000). Effects of depression and anxiety on mortality and quality-of-life 4 months after myocardial infarction. *Journal of Psychosomatic Research*, 49: 229–38.

Lane, D., Carroll, D., Ring, C. *et al.* (2001). Predictors of attendance at cardiac rehabilitation after myocardial infarction. *Journal of Psychosomatic Research*, 51: 497–501.

Lane, D., Carroll, D., Ring, C. *et al.* (2002). The prevalence and persistence of depression and anxiety following myocardial infarction. *British Journal of Health Psychology*, 7: 11–21.

Lang, E.V., Berbaum, K.S., Faintuch S. *et al.* (2006). Adjunctive self-hypnotic relaxation for outpatient medical procedures: a prospective randomized trial with women undergoing large core breast biopsy. *Pain*, 126: 155–64.

Lang, E.V., Joyce, J.S., Spiegel, D. *et al.* (1996). The role of pain behaviors in the modulation of marital conflict in chronic pain couples. *Pain*, 65: 227–33.

Lang, T., Nicaud, V., Slama, K. *et al.* (2000). Smoking cessation at the workplace. Results of a randomised controlled intervention study. Worksite physicians from the AIREL group. *Journal of Epidemiology and Community Health*, 54: 349–54.

Langer, S.L., Rudd, M.E. and Syrjala, K.L. (2007). Protective buffering and emotional desynchrony among spousal caregivers of cancer patients. *Health Psychology* 26: 635–43.

Langewitz, W., Wossmer, B., Iseli, J. *et al.* (1997). Psychological and metabolic improvement after an outpatient teaching program for functional intensified insulin therapy. *Diabetes Research and Clinical Practice*, 37: 157–64.

Larsen, R.J. and Kasimatis, M. (1991). Day-to-day physical symptoms: individual differences in the occurrence, duration, and emotional concomitants of minor daily illnesses. *Journal of Personality*, 59: 387–423.

Larson, J. (1999). The conceptualization of health. *Medical Care and Review*, 56: 123–236.

Latimer, P. (1981). Irritable bowel syndrome: a behavioral model. *Behaviour Research and Therapy*, 19: 475–83.

Latimer, P., Sarna, S., Campbell, D. *et al.* (1981). Colonic motor and myoelectric activity: a comparative study of normal subjects, psychoneurotic patients and patients with the irritable bowel syndrome. *Gastro-enterology*, 80: 893–901.

Lau, R.R. and Hartman, K.A. (1983). Common sense representations of common illnesses. *Health Psychology*, 2: 167–85.

Lau, R.R., Bernard, T.M. and Hartman, K.A. (1989). Further explorations of common sense representations of common illnesses. *Health Psychology*, 8(2): 195–219.

Lauby, J.L., Smith, P.J., Stark, M. *et al.* (2000). A community-level HIV prevention intervention for inner-city women: results of the Women and Infants Demonstration Projects. *American Journal of Public Health*, 90: 216–22.

Laugesen, M. and Meads, C. (1991). Tobacco restrictions, price, income and tobacco consumption in OECD countries, 1960–1986. *British Journal of Addiction*, 86: 1343–54.

Laux, L. and Weber, H. (1991). Presentation of self in coping with anger and anxiety: an intentional approach. *Anxiety Research*, 3: 233–55.

Lavery, J.F. and Clarke, V.A. (1996). Causal attributions, coping strategies and adjustment to breast cancer. *Cancer Nursing*, 19: 20–8.

Law, M.R., Frost, C.D. and Wald, N.J. (1991). By how much does dietary salt lower blood pressure? I – Analysis of observational data among populations. *British Medical Journal*, 302: 811–15.

Law, M.R., Wald, N.J. and Thompson, S.G. (1994). By how much and how quickly does reduction in serum cholesterol concentration lower risk of ischemic heart disease? *British Medical Journal*, 308: 367–72.

Lawlor, D.A., Ebrahim, S. and Davey Smith, G. (2002). Role of endogenous oestrogen in aetiology of coronary heart disease: analysis of age related trends in coronary heart disease and breast cancer in England and Wales and Japan. *British Medical Journal*, 325: 311–2.

Lawrence, D., Fagan, P., Backinger, C.L. *et al.* (2007). Cigarette smoking patterns among young adults ages 18–24 in the U.S. *Nicotine & Tobacco Research*, 9: 687–97.

Lawson, V.L., Lyne, P.A., Bundy, C. *et al.* (2007). The role of illness perceptions, coping and evaluation in care-seeking among people with type 1 diabetes. *Psychology and Health*, 22: 175–91.

Lazarus, R.S. (1966). *Psychological Stress and the Coping Process*. New York: McGraw-Hill.

Lazarus, R.S. (1991a). *Emotion and Adaptation*. New York: Oxford University Press.

Lazarus, R.S. (1991b). Psychological stress in the workplace. In P. Perrewe (ed.), *Handbook on Job Stress*. Special issue of *Journal of Social Behavior and Personality*, 6: 1–13.

Lazarus, R.S. (1993a). From psychological stress to the emotions: a history of changing outlooks. *Annual Review of Psychology*, 44: 1–21.

Lazarus, R.S. (1993b). Coping theory and research: past, present and future. *Psychosomatic Medicine*, 55: 234–47.

Lazarus, R.S. (1999). *Stress and Emotion: A New Synthesis*. New York: Springer Verlag.

Lazarus, R.S. (2000). Toward better research on stress and coping. *American Psychologist*, 55: 665–73.

Lazarus, R.S. and Folkman, S. (1984). *Stress, Appraisal, and Coping*. New York: Springer Verlag.

Lazarus, R.S. and Launier, R. (1978). Stress related transactions between person and environment. In L.A. Pervin and M. Lewis (eds), *Perspectives in International Psychology*, New York: Plenum.

Lechner, S.C., Antoni, M.H., Lydston, D. *et al.* (2003). Cognitive-behavioral interventions improve quality of life in women with AIDS. *Journal of Psychosomatic Research*, 54: 253–61.

Lee, A., Cheng, F.F., Fung, Y. *et al.* (2006). Can Health Promoting Schools contribute to the better health and wellbeing of young people? The Hong Kong experience. *Journal of Epidemiology and Community Health*, 60: 530–6.

Lee, C. (1999). Health, stress and coping among women caregivers: a review. *Journal of Health Psychology*, 4: 27–40.

Lee, C. (2001). Experiences of family caregiving among older Australian women. *Journal of Health Psychology*, 6: 393–404.

Lee, E-H., Chun, M., Kang, S. *et al.* (2004). Validation of the Functional Assessment of Cancer Therapy-General (FACT-G) scale for measuring the health-related quality of life in Korean women with breast cancer. *Japanese Journal of Clinical Oncology*, 34: 393–9.

Lee, I.-M., Rexrode, K.M., Cook, N.R. *et al.* (2001). Physical activity and coronary heart disease in women: is 'no pain, no gain' passé? *Journal of the American Medical Association*, 285: 1447–54.

Lee, S.J., Back, A.L., Block, S.D. *et al.* (2002). Enhancing physician–patient communication. *Hematology*, 464–83.

Lefkowitz, R.J. and Willerson, J.T. (2001). Prospects for cardiovascular research. *Journal of the American Medical Association*, 285: 581–7.

Leon, D.A. and McCambridge, J. (2006). Liver cirrhosis mortality rates in Britain from 1950 to 2002: an analysis of routine data. *The Lancet*, 367: 52–56.

Lépine, J.P. and Briley, M. (2004). The epidemiology of pain in depression. *Human Psychopharmacology*, 19: S3–7.

Lerman, C. and Croyle, R. (1994). Psychological issues in genetic testing for breast cancer susceptibility. *Archives of Internal Medicine*, 154: 609–16.

Lerman, C., Hughes, C., Croyle, R.T. *et al.* (2000). Prophylactic surgery and surveillance practices one year following BRCA1/2 genetic testing. *Preventative Medicine*, 1: 75–80.

Lerman, C., Marshall, J. and Caminerio, A. (1996). Genetic testing for colon cancer susceptibility: anticipated reactions of patients and challenges to providers. *International Journal of Cancer*, 69: 58–61.

Leserman, J., Jackson, E.D., Petitto, J.M. *et al.* (1999). Progression to AIDS: The effects of stress, depressive symptoms, and social support. *Psychosomatic Medicine*, 61: 397–406.

Leskin, G.A., Kaloupek, D.G. and Keane, T.M. (1998). Treatment for traumatic memories: review and recommendations. *Clinical Psychology Review*, 18: 983–1002.

Letherman, C., Blackburn, D. and Davidhizar, R. (1990). How postpartum women explain their lack of obtaining adequate prenatal care. *Journal of Advanced Nursing*, 15: 256–67.

Leung, P.Y., Chan, C.L.W. and Ng, S.M. (2007). Tranquil acceptance coping: Eastern cultural beliefs as a source of strength among Chinese women with breast cancer. Paper presented at the International Psycho-Oncology Society (IPOS) conference, London, September 2007.

Leveälahti, H., Tishelman, C. and Öhlén, J. (2007). Framing the onset of lung cancer biographically: Narratives of continuity and disruption. *Psycho-Oncology*, 16: 466–73.

Leventhal, E.A. and Crouch, M. (1997). Are there differences in perceptions of illness across the lifespan? In K.J. Petrie and J. Weinman (eds), *Perceptions of Health and Illness*. Amsterdam: Harwood Academic (pp. 77–102).

Leventhal, E.A. and Prohaska, T.R. (1986). Age, symptom interpretation and health behavior. *Journal of the American Geriatric Society*, 34: 185–91.

Leventhal, E.A., Hansell, S., Diefenbach, M. *et al.* (1996). Negative affect and self-report of physical symptoms: two longitudinal studies of older adults. *Health Psychology*, 15: 193–9.

Leventhal, H. and Coleman, S. (1997). Quality of life: a process view. *Psychology and Health*, 12: 753–67.

Leventhal, H. and Diefenbach, M. (1991). The active side of illness cognition. In J.A. Skelton and R.T. Croyle (eds), *Mental Representations in Health and Illness*. New York: Springer Verlag.

Leventhal, H. and Tomarken, A. (1987). Stress and illness: perspectives from health psychology. In S.V. Kasl and C.L. Cooper (eds), *Research Methods in Stress and Health Psychology*. London: Wiley.

Leventhal, H., Diefenbach, M. and Leventhal, E. (1992). Illness cognition: using common sense to understand treatment adherence and effect cognitive interactions. *Cognitive Therapy and Research*, 16(2): 143–63.

Leventhal, H., Easterling, D.V., Coons, H. *et al.* (1986). Adaptation to chemotherapy treatments. In B. Anderson (ed.), *Women with Cancer*. New York: Springer Verlag.

Leventhal, H., Meyer, D. and Nerenz, D. (1980). The common sense model of illness danger. In S. Rachman (ed.), *Medical Psychology*, Vol. 2. New York: Pergamon.

Leventhal, H., Nerenz, D.R. and Steele, D.J. (1984). Illness representations and coping with health threats. In A. Baum, S.E. Taylor and J.E. Singer (eds), *Handbook of Psychology and Health: Social Psychological Aspects of Health*, Vol. 4. Hillsdale, NJ: Lawrence Erlbaum.

Leventhal, H., Patrick-Miller, L. and Leventhal, E.A. (1998). It's long-term stressors that take a toll: comment on Cohen *et al.* (1998). *Health Psychology*, 17: 211–13.

Levinson, D.J., Darrow, C.N., Klein, E.B., Levinson, M.H. and McKee, B. (1978). *The Seasons of a Man's Life*. New York: A.A. Knopf.

Levine, R.M. and Reicher, S. (1996). Making sense of symptoms: self categorization and the meaning of illness/injury. *British Journal of Social Psychology*, 35: 245–56.

Levy, L., Patterson, R.E., Kristal, A.R. *et al.* (2000). How well do consumers understand percentage daily value of food labels? *American Journal of Health Promotion*, 14: 157–60.

Lewin, B., Robertson, I.H., Irving, J.B. *et al.* (1992). Effects of self-help post-myocardial-infarction rehabilitation on psychological adjustment and use of health services. *The Lancet*, 339: 1036–40.

Lewin, R.J., Furze, G., Robinson, J. *et al.* (2002). A randomised controlled trial of a self-management plan for patients with newly diagnosed angina. *British Journal of General Practice*, 52: 194–6, 199–201.

Lewis, C.L. and Brown, S.C. (2002). Coping strategies of female adolescents with HIV/AIDS. *The Association of Black Nursing Faculty*, 13: 72–7.

Lewis, G., Bebbington, P., Brugha, T. *et al.* (1998). Socioeconomic status, standard of living, and neurotic disorder. *The Lancet*, 352: 605–9.

Lewis, S.C., Dennis, M.D., O'Rourke, S.J. *et al.* (2001). Negative attitudes among short-term stroke survivors predict worse long-term survival. *Stroke*, 32: 1640–45.

Lewit, E., Coates, D. and Grossman, M. (1981). The effects of governmental regulation on teenage smoking. *Journal of Law and Economics*, 24: 545–69.

Ley, P. (1988). *Communicating with Patients. Improving Communication, Satisfaction, and Compliance*. London: Chapman Hall.

Ley, P. (1997). Compliance among patients. In A. Baum, S. Newman, J. Weinman, R. West and C. McManus (eds), *Cambridge Handbook of Psychology, Health and Medicine*. Cambridge: Cambridge University Press.

Lichtenstein, P. and Pedersen, N.L. (1995). Social relationships, stressful life events, and self-reported physical health: genetic and environmental influences. *Psychology and Health*, 10: 295–319.

Lim, A.S.H. and Bishop, G.D. (2000). The role of attitudes and beliefs in differential health care utilisation among Chinese in Singapore. *Psychology and Health*, 14: 965–77.

Linden, W., Gerin, W. and Davidson, K. (2003). Cardiovascular reactivity: status quo and a research agenda for the new millennium. *Psychosomatic Medicine*, 65: 5–8.

Linden, W., Stossel, C. and Maurice, J. (1996). Psychosocial treatment for cardiac patients: a meta-analysis. *Archives of Internal Medicine*, 156: 745–62.

Linegar, J., Chesson, C. and Nice, D. (1991). Physical fitness gains following simple environmental change. *American Journal of Preventive Medicine*, 7: 298–310.

Linn, S., Carroll, M., Johnson, C. *et al.* (1993). High density lipoprotein cholesterol and alcohol consumption in US white and black adults: data from NHANES II. *American Journal of Public Health*, 83: 811–16.

Liossi, C., White, P. and Hatira, P. (2006). Randomised clinical trial of a local anaesthetic versus a combination of self-hypnosis with a local anaesthetic in the management of paediatric procedure-related pain. *Health Psychology*, 25: 307–15.

Liossi, C., White, P., Franck, L. *et al.* (2007). Parental pain expectancy as a mediator between child expected and experienced procedure-related pain intensity during painful medical procedures. *The Clinical Journal of Pain*, 23: 392–99.

Lipkus, I.M., Barefoot, J.C., Williams, R.B. *et al.* (1994). Personality measures as predictors of smoking initiation and cessation in the UNC Alumni heart study. *Health Psychology*, 13: 149–55.

Lipton, A.A. and Simon, F.S. (1985). Psychiatric diagnosis in a state hospital: Manhattan state revisited. *Hospital and Community Psychiatry*, 36: 368–73.

Litt, M.D., Nye, C. and Shafer, D. (1995). Preparation for oral surgery: evaluating elements of coping. *Journal of Behavioral Medicine*, 18: 435–59.

Little, M. and Sayers, E-J. (2004). While there's life . . . hope and the experience of cancer. *Social Science and Medicine*, 59: 1329–37.

Livingston, G. and Hinchliffe, A.C. (1993). The epidemiology of psychiatric disorders in the elderly. *International Review of Psychiatry*, 5: 317–29.

Llewellyn, C.D., McGurk, M. and Weinman, J. (2007). Illness and treatment beliefs in head and neck cancer: Is Leventhal's common sense model a useful framework for determining changes in outcomes over time? *Journal of Psychosomatic Research*, 63: 17–26.

Lo, B. (2006) HPV vaccine and adolescents' sexual activity. *British Medical Journal*, 332: 1106–7.

Lo, B. (2007) Human papillomavirus vaccination programmes. *British Medical Journal*, 335: 357–8.

Lo, R. (1999). Correlates of expected success at adherence to health regimen of people with IDDM. *Journal of Advanced Nursing*, 30: 418–24.

Lobb, E.A., Butow, P.N., Kenny, D.T. *et al.* (1999). Communicating prognosis in early breast cancer: Do women understand the language used? *Medical Journal of Australia*, 171: 290–94.

Lobchuk, M.M. and Vorauer, J.D. (2003). Family care-giving, perspective-taking, and accuracy in estimating cancer patient symptom experiences. *Social Science and Medicine*, 57: 2379–84.

Locke, E.A. and Latham, G.P. (2002). Building a practically useful theory of goal setting and task motivation: a 35-year odyssey. *American Psychologist*, 57: 705–17.

Locke, G.R. III, Weaver, A.L., Melton, L.J. III *et al.* (2004). Psychosocial factors are linked to functional gastrointestinal disorders: a population based nested case-control study. *American Journal of Gastroenterology*, 99: 350–7.

Lodder, L., Frets, P.G., Trijsburg, R.W. *et al.* (2001). Psychological impact of receiving a BRCA1/BRCA2 test result. *American Journal of Medical Genetics*, 98: 15–24.

Löf, M., Sardin, S. Lagiou, P. *et al.* (2007). Dietary fat and breast cancer risk in the Swedish women's lifestyle and health cohort. *British Journal of Cancer*, 97: 1570–76.

Logan, T.K., Cole, J. and Leukefeld, C. (2002). Women, sex, and HIV: social and contextual factors, meta-analysis of published interventions, and implications for practice and research. *Psychological Bulletin*, 128: 851–85.

Lok, C.F. and Bishop, G.D. (1999). Emotion control, stress, and health. *Psychology and Health*, 14: 813–27.

Lomas, J. (1991). Words without action? The production, dissemination, and impact of consensus recommendations. *Annual Reviews in Public Health*, 12: 41–65.

Longabaugh, R. and Morgenstern, J. (1999). Cognitive-behavioural coping-skills therapy for alcohol dependence. *Alcohol Research and Health*, 23: 78–85.

Longo, D.R., Johnson, J.C., Kruse, R.L. *et al.* (2001). A prospective investigation of the impact of smoking bans on tobacco cessation and relapse. *Tobacco Control*, 10: 267–72.

Lorig, K. (1996). *Patient Education: A Practical Approach*. Newbury Park, Calif.: Sage.

Lorig, K. and Holman, H. (1989). Long-term outcomes of an arthritis self-management study: effects of reinforcement efforts. *Social Science and Medicine*, 29: 221–4.

Lorig, K.R., Ritter, P.L. and Gonzalez, V.M. (2003). Hispanic chronic disease self-management: a randomized community-based outcome trial. *Nursing Research*, 52: 361–9.

Lorig, K., Sobel, D.S., Stewart, A.L. *et al.* (1999). Evidence suggesting that a chronic disease self-management program can improve health status while reducing hospitalisation. *Medical Care*, 37: 5–14.

Louria, D. (1988). Some concerns about educational approaches in AIDS prevention. In R. Schinazi and A. Nahmias (eds), *AIDS children, adolescents and heterosexual adults*. New York: Elsevier Science.

Louw, Q.A., Morris, L.D. and Grimmer-Somers, K. (2007). The prevalence of low back pain in Africa: a systematic review. *BMC Musculoskeletal Disorders*, 8: 105.

Lovallo, W.R. (1997). *Stress and Health: Biological and Psychological Interactions*. Newbury Park, Calif.: Sage.

Lovallo, W.R., Pincomb, G.A., Brackett, D.J. *et al.* (1990). Heart rate reactivity as a predictor of neuroendocrine responses to aversive and appetitive challenges. *Psychosomatic Medicine*, 52: 17–26.

Lovegrove, E., Rumsey, N., Harcourt, D. *et al.* (2000). Factors implicated in the decision whether or not to join the tamoxifen trial in women at high familial risk of breast cancer. *Psycho-Oncology*, 9: 193–202.

Low, C.A., Stanton, A.L. and Danoff-Burg, S. (2006). Expressive disclosure and benefit finding among breast cancer patients: mechanisms for positive health effects. *Health Psychology*, 25: 181–9.

Lowe, C.F., Horne, P.J., Tapper, K. *et al.* (2004). Effects of a peer-modelling and rewards based intervention to increase fruit and vegetable consumption in children. *European Journal of Clinical Nutrition*, 58: 510–22.

Lowe, R., Norman, P. and Bennett, P. (2000). Coping, emotion and perceived health following myocardial infarction. *British Journal of Health Psychology*, 5: 337–50.

Lowe, R., Vedhara, K., Bennett, P. *et al.* (2003). Emotion-related primary and secondary appraisals, adjustment and coping associations in women awaiting breast disease diagnosis. *British Journal of Health Psychology*, 8: 377–91.

Lowes, J. and Tiggemann, M. (2003). Body dissatisfaction and dieting awareness in young children. *British Journal of Health Psychology*, 8: 135–47.

Lox, C.L., Martin Ginis, K.A. and Petruzzello, S.J. (2006). *The Psychology of Exercise: Integrating Theory and Practice* (2nd edition). Scottsdale Ariz.: Holcomb Hathaway.

Luck, A., Pearson, S., Maddern, G. *et al.* (1999). Effects of video information on pre-colonoscopy anxiety and knowledge: a randomised trial. *Lancet*, 354: 2032–5.

Lundberg, U., de Chateau, P., Winberg, J. *et al.* (1981). Catecholamine and cortisol excretion patterns in three year old children and their parents. *Journal of Human Stress*, 7: 3–11.

Luszczynska, A. and Schwarzer, R. (2003). Planning and self-efficacy in the adoption and maintenance of breast self-examination: a longitudinal study on self-regulatory cognitions. *Psychology and Health*, 18: 93–108.

Luszczynska, A., Diehl, M., Gutiérrez-Doña, B. *et al.* (2004). Measuring one component of dispositional self-regulation: attention control in goal pursuit. *Personality and Individual Differences*, 37: 555–66.

Luszczynska, A., Sobczyk, A. and Abraham, C. (2007). Planning to lose weight: randomized controlled trial of an implementation intention prompt to enhance weight reduction among overweight and obese women. *Health Psychology*, 26: 507–12.

Lyonette, C. and Yardley, L. (2003). The influence on carer wellbeing of motivations to care for older people and the relationship with the care recipient. *Ageing & Society* 23: 487–506.

MacFadyen, L., Amos, A., Hastings, G. *et al.* (2002). They look like my kind of people – perceptions of smoking images in youth magazines. *Social Science and Medicine*, 56: 491–9.

Macintyre, S. (1986). The patterning of health by social position in contemporary Britain: directions for sociological research. *Social Science and Medicine*, 23: 393–415.

Macintyre, S. (1993). Gender differences in the perceptions of common cold symptoms. *Social Science and Medicine*, 36: 15–20.

Macintyre, S. and Ellaway, A. (1998). *Ecological Approaches: Rediscovering the Role of the Physical and Social Environment*. Oxford: Oxford University Press.

MacNee, W. (2004). Guidelines for chronic obstructive pulmonary disease (editorial). *British Medical Journal*, 329: 361–3.

MacNicol, S.A.M., Murray, S.M. and Austin, E.J. (2003). Relationships between personality, attitudes and dietary behaviour in a group of Scottish adolescents. *Personality and Individual Differences*, 35: 1753–64.

Macrodimitris, D. and Endler, N.S. (2001). Coping, control, and adjustment in Type 2 diabetes. *Health Psychology*, 20: 208–16.

Maes, S. and van der Doef, M. (2004). Worksite health promotion. In A. Kaptein and J. Weinman (eds), *Health Psychology*. Oxford: BPS Blackwell (pp. 358–83).

Maes, S., Leventhal, H. and de Ridder, D.T. (1996). Coping with chronic disease. In M. Zeidner and N.S. Endler (eds), *Handbook of Coping*. New York: Wiley.

Maes, S., Kittel, F., Scholten, H. *et al.* (1990). Effects of the Brabantia project, a Dutch wellness-health programme at the worksite. *American Journal of Public Health*, 88: 1037–41.

Magar, E.C.E., Phillips, L.H. and Hosie, J.A. (2008). Self-regulation and risk-taking. *Personality & Individual Differences*, 45: 153–9.

Magarey, A., Daniels, L., Boulton, T. *et al.* (2003). Predicting obesity in early adulthood from childhood and parental obesity. *International Journal of Obesity*, 27: 505–13.

Magarey, A., Daniels, L.A. and Smith, A. (2001). Fruit and vegetable intakes of Australians aged 2–18 years: an evaluation of the 1995 National Nutrition Survey data. *Australian and New Zealand Journal of Public Health*, 25: 155–61.

Mager, W.M. and Andrykowski, M.A. (2002). Communication in the cancer 'bad news' consultation: patient perceptions and psychological adjustment. *Psycho-Oncology*, 11: 35–46.

Maggiolo, F., Ripamonti, D., Arici, C. *et al.* (2002). Simpler regimens may enhance adherence to antiretrovirals in HIV-infected patients. *HIV Clinical Trials*, 3: 371–8.

Magni, G., Moreschi, C., Rigatti-Luchini, S. *et al.* (1994). Prospective study on the relationship between depressive symptoms and chronic musculoskeletal pain. *Pain*, 56: 289–97.

Magnusson, J.E. and Becker, W.J. (2003). Migraine frequency and intensity: relationship with disability and psychological factors. *Headache*, 43: 1049–59.

Maguire, P. and Faulkner, A. (1988). How to improve the counselling skills of doctors and nurses in cancer care. *British Medical Journal*, 297: 847–9.

Maguire, P. and Pitceathly, C. (2002). Key communication skills and how to acquire them. *British Medical Journal*, 325: 697–700.

Mahajan, L., Wyllie, R., Steffen, R. *et al.* (1998). The effects of a psychological preparation program on anxiety in children and adolescents undergoing gastrointestinal endoscopy. *Journal of Pediatric Gastroenterology and Nutrition*, 27: 161–5.

Mahalik, J.R., Burns, S.M. and Syzdek, M. (2007). Masculinity and perceived normative health behaviors as predictors of men's health behaviors. *Social Science & Medicine*, 64: 2201–9.

Maisto, S.A. and Connors, G.J. (1992). Using subject and collateral reports to measure alcohol consumption. In R.Z. Litten and J.P. Allen (eds), *Measuring Alcohol Consumption: Psychosocial and Biochemical Methods*. New Jersey: Humana Press.

Malfetti, J. (1985). Public information and education sections of the report of the Presidential Commission on Drunk Driving: a critique and a discussion of research implication. *Accident Analysis and Prevention*, 17: 347–53.

Maliski, S.L., Heilemann, M.V. and McCorkle, R. (2002). From 'death sentence' to 'good cancer': couples' transformation of a prostate cancer diagnosis. *Nursing Research*, 51: 391–7.

Malkin, C.J., Pugh, P.J., Jones, R.D. *et al.* (2003). Testosterone as a protective factor against atherosclerosis – immunomodulation and influence upon plaque development and stability. *Journal of Endocrinology*, 178: 373–80.

Mallion, J.M., Baguet, J.P., Siche, J.P. *et al.* (1998). Compliance, electronic monitoring and antihypertensive drugs. *Journal of Hypertension*, (suppl.)16: S75–9.

Malow, R.M., Baker, S.M., Klimas, N. *et al.* (1998). Adherence to complex combination antiretroviral therapies by HIV-positive drug abusers. *Psychiatric Services*, 49: 1021–2.

Maly, M.R., Costigan, P.A. and Olney, S.J. (2007). Self-efficacy mediates walking performance in older adults with knee osteoarthritis. *Journal of Gerontology A: Biological Sciences and Medical Sciences*, 62: 1142–6.

Mandelblatt, J. and Kanesky, P.A. (1995). Effectiveness of interventions to enhance physician screening for breast cancer. *Journal of Family Practice*, 40: 162–71.

Maniadakis, N. and Gray, A. (2000). The economic burden of back pain in the UK. *Pain*, 84: 95–103.

Manne, S.L., Norton, T.R., Ostroff, J.S. *et al.* (2007). Protective buffering and psychological distress among couples coping with breast cancer: the moderating role of relationship satisfaction. *Journal of Family Psychology* 21: 380–88.

Manning, P.K. and Fabrega, H. (1973). The experience of self and body: health and illness in the Chiapas Highlands. In G. Psathas (ed.), *Phenomenological Sociology: Issues and Applications*. New York: Wiley.

Mannino, D.M. (2003). Chronic obstructive pulmonary disease: definition and epidemiology. *Respiratory Care*, 48: 1185–91.

Manson, J.E., Greenland, P., LaCroix, A.Z. *et al.* (2002). Walking compared with vigorous exercise for prevention of cardiovascular events in women. *New England Journal of Medicine*, 347: 716–25.

Manstead, A.S.R. (2000). The role of moral norm in the attitude–behavior relationship. In D.J. Terry and M.A. Hogg (eds), *Attitudes, Behavior and Social Context: The Role of Norms and Group Membership*. Mahwah, NJ: Lawrence Erlbaum.

Mantyselka, P., Kumpusalo, E., Ahonen, R. *et al.* (2001). Pain as a reason to visit the doctor: a study in Finnish primary health care. *Pain*, 89: 175–80.

Marcell, A.V., Ford, C.A., Pleck, J.H. *et al.* (2007). Masculine beliefs, parental communication, and male adolescents' health care use. *Pediatrics*, 119: 966–75.

Marcus, B.H., Rakowski, W. and Rossi, J.S. (1992). Assessing motivational readiness and decision-making for exercise. *Health Psychology*, 22: 3–16.

Marcus, B.H., Selby, V.C., Niaura, R.S. and Rossi, J.S. (1992). Self-efficacy and the stages of exercise behaviour change. *Research Quarterly in Exercise and Sport*, 63: 60–6.

Marinus, J., Ramaker, C., van Hilten, J.J. *et al.* (2002). Health related quality of life in Parkinson's disease: a systematic review of disease specific instruments. *Journal of Neurology, Neurosurgery and Psychiatry*, 72: 241–8.

Markovitz, J.H., Matthews, K.A., Kannel, W.B. *et al.* (1993). Psychological predictors of hypertension in the Framingham Study: is there tension in hypertension? *Journal of the American Medical Association*, 270: 2439–43.

Marks, D.F. (ed.) (2002). *The Health Psychology Reader*. London: Sage Publications.

Marks, D.F., Murray, M., Evans, B. and Willig, C. (2000). *Health Psychology: Theory, Research and Practice*. London: Sage.

Marks, I., Lovell, K., Noshirvani, H. *et al.* (1998). Treatment of post-traumatic stress disorder by exposure and/or cognition restructuring. *Archives of General Psychiatry*, 55: 317–25.

Marks, J.T., Campbell, M.K., Ward, D.S. *et al.* (2006). A comparison of Web and print media for physical activity promotion among adolescent girls. *Journal of Adolescent Health*, 39: 96–104.

Marlatt, G.A., Baer, J.S., Donovan, D.M. *et al.* (1986). Addictive behaviors: etiology and treatment. *Annual Review of Psychology*, 39: 223–52.

Marmot, M.G. and Madge, N. (1987). An epidemiological perspective on stress and health. In S.V. Kasl and C.L. Cooper (eds), *Research Methods in Stress and Health Psychology*, London: Wiley.

Marmot, M.G., Davey-Smith, G. and Stansfield, S. (1991). Health inequalities among British civil servants: the Whitehall study II. *The Lancet*, 337: 1387–93.

Marmot, M.G., Fuhrer, R., Ettner, S.L. *et al.* (1998). Contribution of psychosocial factors to socioeconomic differences in health. *The Milbank Quarterly*, 76: 403–48.

Marmot, M., Ryff, C.D., Bumpass, L.L. *et al.* (1997). Social inequalities in health: next questions and converging evidence. *Social Science and Medicine*, 44: 901–10.

Marmot, M.G., Shipley, M.J. and Rose, G. (1984). Inequalities in health – specific explanations of a general pattern? *The Lancet*, i, 1003–6.

Marshall, A.L., Leslie, E.R., Bauman, A.E. *et al.* (2003). Print versus website physical activity programs: a randomized trial. *American Journal of Preventive Medicine*, 25: 88–94.

Marsland, A.L., Bachen, E.A., Cohen, S. *et al.* (2002). Stress, immune reactivity and susceptibility to infectious diseases. *Physiology & Behaviour*, 77: 711–16.

Marteau, T.M. (1989). Framing of information: its influence upon decisions of doctors and patients. *British Journal of Social Psychology*, 28: 89–94.

Marteau, T.M. and Kinmouth, A.L. (2002). Screening for cardiovascular risk: public health imperative or matter for individual informed choice? *British Medical Journal*, 325: 78–80.

Marteau, T.M., Kidd, J., Cuddeford, L. and Walker, P. (1996). Reducing anxiety in women referred for colposcopy using an information booklet. *British Journal of Health Psychology*, 1: 181–9.

Martin, J., Sabugal, G.M., Rubio, R. *et al.* (2001). Outcomes of a health education intervention in a sample of patients infected by HIV, most of them injection drug users: possibilities and limitations. *AIDS Care*, 13: 467–73.

Martin, L.M., Calle, E.E., Wingo, P.A. *et al.* (1996). Comparison of mammography and Pap test use from the 1987 and 1992 National Health Interview Surveys: are we closing the gaps? *American Journal Preventive Medicine*, 12: 82–90.

Martin, R., Rothrock, N., Leventhal, H. *et al.* (2003). Common sense models of illness: implications for symptom perception and health-related behaviours. In J. Suls and K.A. Wallston (eds), *Social Psychological Foundations of Health and Illness*. Oxford: Blackwell.

Martin, R.A. and Lefcourt, H.M. (1983). Sense of humor as a moderator of the relation between stressors and moods. *Journal of Personality & Social Psychology*, 45: 1313–24.

Martin Ginis, K.A., Burke, S.M. and Gauvin, L. (2007). Exercising with others exacerbates the negative effects of mirrored environments on sedentary women's feeling states. *Psychology & Health*, 22: 945–62.

Marucha, P.T., Kiecolt-Glaser, J.K. and Favgehi, M. (1998). Mucosal wound healing is impaired by examination stress. *Psychosomatic Medicine*, 60: 362–5.

Maslach, C. (1982). *Burnout: The Cost of Caring*. Englewood Cliffs, NJ: Prentice Hall.

Maslach, C. (1997). Burnout in health professionals. In A. Baum, S. Newman, J. Weinman *et al.* (eds), *Cambridge Handbook of Psychology, Health and Medicine*. Cambridge: Cambridge University Press.

Matano, R.A., Futa, K.T., Wanat, S.F. *et al.* (2000). The Employee Stress and Alcohol Project: the development of a computer-based alcohol abuse prevention program for employees. *Journal of Behavioral Health Services Research*, 27: 152–65.

Matarazzo, J.D. (1982). Behavioral health's challenge to academic, scientific and professional psychology. *American Psychologist*, 37: 1–14.

Matarazzo, J.D. (1984). Behavioral health: a 1990 challenge for the health sciences professions. In J.D. Matarazzo, N.E. Miller, S.M. Weiss *et al.* (eds), *Behavioral Health: A Handbook of Health Enhancement and Disease Prevention*. New York: Wiley.

Mathews, C., Guttmacher, S.J., Coetzee, N. *et al.* (2002). Evaluation of a video based health education strategy to improve sexually transmitted disease partner notification in South Africa. *Sexually Transmitted Infections*, 78: 53–7.

Mathieu, E., Barratt, A., Davey, H.M. *et al.* (2007). Informed choice in mammography screening: a randomized trial of a decision aid for 70-year-old women. *Archives of Internal Medicine*, 167: 2039–46.

Matthews, K.A., Siegel, J.M., Kuller, L.H. *et al.* (1983). Determinants of decision to seek medical treatment by patients with acute myocardial infarction symptoms. *Journal of Personality and Social Psychology*, 44: 1144–56.

Mattocks, C., Ness, A., Deere, K. *et al.* (2008). Early life determinants of physical activity in 11 to 12 year olds: cohort study. *British Medical Journal*, 336: 26–9.

Matza, L.S., Swensen, A.R., Flood, E.M. *et al.* (2004). Assessment of health-related quality of life in children: a review of conceptual, methodological, and regulatory issues. *Value in Health*, 7: 79–92.

McCann, B.S., Retzlaff, B.M., Dowdy, A.A., Walden, C.E. and Knopp, R.H. (1990). Promoting adherence to low-fat, low-cholesterol diets: review and recommendations. *Journal of the American Dietetic Association*, 90: 1408–14.

McCann, J., Stockton, D. and Goddard, S. (2002). Impact of false-positive mammography on subsequent screening attendance and risk of cancer. *Breast Cancer Research*, 4: R11.

McCarron, P., Davey-Smith, G. and Wormsley, J. (1994). Deprivation and mortality in Glasgow: changes from 1980 to 1992. *British Medical Journal*, 309: 1481–2.

McCarthy, W.H. and Shaw, H.M. (1989). Skin cancer in Australia, *Medical Journal of Australia*, 150: 469–70.

McClenahan, R. and Weinman, J. (1998). Determinants of carer distress in non-acute stroke. *International Journal of Language and Communication Disorders*, 33: 138–43.

McCorkle, R., Strumpf, N., Nuamah, I. *et al.* (2000). A specialized home care intervention improves survival among older post-surgical cancer patients. *Journal of the American Geriatric Society*, 48: 1707–13.

McCracken, L. (1998). Learning to live with the pain: acceptance of pain predicts adjustment in persons with chronic pain. *Pain*, 74: 21–7.

McCracken, L.M. and Eccleston, C. (2003). Coping or acceptance: what to do about chronic pain? *Pain*, 105: 197–204.

McCrae, R.E. and Costa, P.T. (1987). Validation of the five-factor model of personality across instruments and observers. *Journal of Personality and Social Psychology*, 52: 81–90.

McCrae, R.E. and Costa, P.T. (1990). *Personality in Adulthood*. New York: Guilford Press.

McCrae, R.E., Costa, P.T., Ostendorf, F. *et al.* (2000). Nature over nurture: temperament, personality and life-span development. *Journal of Personality and Social Psychology*, 78: 173–86.

McCrae, R.R. (1990). Controlling neuroticism in the measurement of stress. *Stress Medicine*, 6: 237–40.

McCubbin, H.I. and Patterson, J.M. (1982). Family adaptations to crisis. In H.I. McCubbin, A. Cauble and J. Patterson (eds), *Family Stress, Coping and Social Support*. Springfield, Ill.: Charles Thomas.

McCubbin, H.I. and Patterson, J.M. (1983). The family stress process: the double ABCX model of adjustment and adaptation. In H.I. McCubbin, M.B. Sussman and J.M. Patterson (eds), *Social Stress and the Family: Advances and Developments in Family Stress Theory and Research*. New York: Haworth Press.

McDermott, M.M., Schmitt, B. and Wallner, E. (1997). Impact of medication non-adherence on coronary heart disease outcomes. *Archives of Internal Medicine*, 157: 1921–9.

McDonald, H.P., Garg, A.X. and Haynes, R.B. (2002). Interventions to enhance patient adherence to medication prescriptions: scientific review. *Journal of the American Medical Association*, 288: 2868–79.

McElnay, J. and McCallion, C.R. (1998). Adherence and the elderly. In L.B. Myers and K. Midence (eds), *Adherence to Treatment in Medical Conditions*. Amsterdam: Harwood Academic.

McEwan, M.J., Espie, C.A. and Metcalfe, J. (2004). A systematic review of the contribution of qualitative research to the study of quality of life in children and adolescents with epilepsy. *Seizure*, 13: 3–14.

McGill, H.C. and Stern, M.P. (1979). Sex and atherosclerosis. *Atherosclerosis Review*, 4: 157–248.

McGregor, B.A., Antoni, M.H., Boyers, A. *et al.* (2004). Cognitive-behavioral stress management increases benefit finding and immune function among women with early-stage breast cancer. *Journal of Psychosomatic Research*, 56: 1–8.

McGuire, W. (1985). Attitudes and attitude change. In G. Lindzey and E. Aronson (eds), *Handbook of Social Psychology*, Vol. 2. New York: Random House.

McHugh, P., Lewis, S., Ford, S. *et al.* (1995). The efficacy of audiotapes in promoting psychological well-being in cancer patients: a randomised, controlled trial. *British Journal of Cancer*, 71: 388–92.

McKenna, M.C., Zevon, M.A., Corn, B. *et al.* (1999). Psychosocial factors and the development of breast cancer: a meta-analysis. *Health Psychology*, 18: 520–31.

McKenna, S.P. (2004). Assessing the quality of life in phases I and II anti-cancer drug trials: interviews versus questionnaires by Cox K (letter to the editor). *Social Science and Medicine*, 58: 659–60.

McKenna, S.P., Whalley, D. and Doward, L.C. (2000). Which outcomes are important in schizophrenia trials? *International Journal of Methods in Psychiatric Research*, 9 (suppl. 1): S58–67.

McKiernan, F.M. (1996). Bereavement and attitudes to death. In R.T. Woods (ed.), *Handbook of the Clinical Psychology of Ageing*. Chichester: Wiley.

McLeod, J.D. and Kessler, R.C. (1990). Socioeconomic status differences in vulnerability to undesirable life events. *Journal of Health and Social Behaviour*, 31: 162–72.

McNair, D., Lorr, M. and Droppelman, L. (1971). *Manual for the Profile of Mood States*. San Diego, Calif.: Educational and Industrial Testing Service.

McNeil, B.J., Pauker, S.G., Sox, H.C. Jr *et al.* (1982). On the elicitation of preferences for alternative therapies. *New England Journal of Medicine*, 306: 1259–62.

McNeill, L.H., Viswanath, K., Bennett, G.G. *et al.* (2007). Feasibility of using a web-based nutrition intervention among residents of multiethnic working-class neighborhoods. *Preventing Chronic Disease*, 4: A55.

McPherson, K.M., McNaughton, H. and Pentland, B. (2000). Information needs of families when one member of the family has a severe brain injury. *International Journal of Rehabilitation Research*, 23: 295–301.

McQuay, H.J. and Moore, R.A. (2005). Placebo. *Postgraduate Medical Journal*, 81: 155–60.

McVey, D. and Stapleton, J. (2000). Can anti-smoking television advertising affect smoking behaviour? Controlled trial of the Health Education Authority for England's anti-smoking TV campaign. *Tobacco Control*, 9: 273–82.

McVicar, A. (2003). Workplace stress in nursing: a literature review. *Journal of Advanced Nursing*, 44: 633–42.

Mechanic, D. (1962). The concept of illness behavior. *Journal of Chronic Disease*, 15: 189–94.

Mechanic, D. (1972). Social psychological factors affecting the presentation of bodily complaints. *New England Journal of Medicine*, 286: 1132–9.

Mechanic, D. (1978). *Medical Sociology*, 2nd edn. New York: Free Press.

Meechan, G., Collins, J. and Petrie, K. (2002). Delay in seeking medical care for self-detected breast symptoms in New Zealand women. *New Zealand Medical Journal*, 115: U257.

Meenan, R.F. and Mason, J.H. (1990). *AIMS2 Users Guide*. Boston University School of Medicine, Department of Public Health.

Meeske, K.A., Ruccione, K. and Globe, D.R. (2001). Posttraumatic stress, quality of life, and psychological distress in young adult survivors of childhood cancer. *Oncology Nursing Forum*, 28: 481–9.

Meeuwesen, L., Harmsen, J.A., Bernsen, R.M. *et al.* (2006). Do Dutch doctors communicate differently with immigrant patients than with Dutch patients? *Social Science and Medicine*, 63: 2407–17.

Meichenbaum, D. (1985). *Stress Inoculation Training*. New York: Pergamon Press.

Meijer, S.A., Sinnema, G., Bijstra, J.O. *et al.* (2002). Coping style and locus of control as predictors for psychological adjustment of adolescents with a chronic illness. *Social Science and Medicine*, 54: 1453–61.

Melchior, M., Berkman, L.F., Niedhammer, I. *et al.* (2003). Social relations and self-reported health: a prospective analysis of the French Gazel cohort. *Social Science and Medicine*, 56: 1817–30.

Mel'nikova, T.S. (1993). Thresholds of pain responses to electrical stimuli in patients with endogenous depression. *Patologichskaia Fiziologiia I Eksperimentalnaia Terapiia*, 4: 19–21.

Melzack, R. (1973). *The Puzzle of Pain*. London: Penguin Education.

Melzack, R. (1975). The McGill pain questionnaire: major properties and scoring methods. *Pain*, 1: 277–99.

Melzack, R. (1999). From the gate to the neuromatrix. *Pain*, suppl. 6: S121–6.

Melzack, R. (2005). Evolution of the neuromatrix theory of pain. The Prithvi Raj Lecture: presented at the third World Congress of World Institute of Pain, Barcelona 2004. *Pain Practice*, 5: 85–94.

Melzack, R. and Wall, P.D. (1965). Pain mechanisms: a new theory. *Science*, 50: 971–9.

Mendlowicz, M.V. and Stein, M.B. (2001). Quality of life in individuals with anxiety disorders. *American Journal of Psychiatry*, 157: 669–82.

Merritt, M.M., Bennett, G.G., Williams, R.B. *et al.* (2004). Low educational attainment, John Henryism, and cardiovascular reactivity to and recovery from personally relevant stress. *Psychosomatic Medicine*, 66: 49–55.

Merzel, C. and D'Aflitti, J. (2003). Reconsidering community-based health promotion: promise, performance, and potential. *American Journal of Public Health*, 93: 557–74.

Meyer, J.M. and Stunkard, A.J. (1993). Genetics and human obesity. In A.J. Stunkard and T.A. Wadden (eds), *Obesity: Theory and Therapy*. New York: Raven Press.

Meyer, T.J. and Mark, M.M. (1995). Effects of psychosocial interventions with adult cancer patients: a meta-analysis of randomized experiments. *Health Psychology*, 12: 101–8.

Meyer-Weitz, A., Reddy, P., Van Den Borne, H.W. *et al.* (2000). The determinants of health care seeking behaviour of adolescents attending STD clinics in South Africa. *Journal of Adolescence*, 23: 741–52.

Michell, L. and Amos, A. (1997). Girls, pecking order, and smoking. *Social Science and Medicine*, 44: 1861–9.

Michie, S., Dormandy, E. and Marteau, T.M. (2004). Increasing screening uptake among those intending to be screened: the use of action plans. *Patient Education and Counselling*, 55: 218–22.

Michie, S., Miles, J. and Weinman, J. (2003). Patient-centredness in chronic illness: what is it and does it matter? *Patient Education and Counselling*, 51: 197–206.

Michie, S., Rothman, A.J. and Sheeran, P. (2007). Editorial: Current issues and new directions in Psychology and Health: advancing the science of behaviour change. *Psychology & Health*, 22: 249–54.

Miedema, B., Hamilton, R. and Easley, J. (2007). From 'invincibility' to 'normalcy': coping strategies of young adults during the cancer journey. *Palliative and Supportive Care*, 5: 41–9.

Mikkelsen, A. and Saksvik, P.O. (1999). Impact of a participatory organizational intervention on job characteristics and job stress. *International Journal of Health Services Research*, 29: 871–93.

Miller, G.E. and Cohen, S. (2001). Psychological interventions and the immune system: a meta-analytic review and critique. *Health Psychology*, 20: 47–63.

Miller, S.M. (1987). Monitoring and blunting: validation of a questionnaire to assess styles of information seeking under threat. *Journal of Personality and Social Psychology*, 52: 345–53.

Miller, S.M., Brody, D.S. and Summerton, J. (1987). Styles of coping with threat: implications for health. *Journal of Personality and Social Psychology*, 54: 142–8.

Miller, S.M., Fang, C.Y., Manne, S.L. *et al.* (1999). Decision making about prophylactic oophorectomy among at-risk women: psychological influences and implications. *Gynaecological Oncology*, 75: 406–12.

Miller, S.M., Rodoletz, M., Mangan, C.E. *et al.* (1996). Applications of the monitoring process model to coping with severe long-term medical threats. *Health Psychology*, 15: 216–25.

Miller, T.Q., Smith, T.W., Turner, C.W. *et al.* (1996). A meta-analytic review of research on hostility and physical health. *Psychological Bulletin*, 119: 322–48.

Miller, T.Q., Turner, C.W., Tindale, R.S. *et al.* (1991). Reasons for the trend towards null findings in research on Type A behavior. *Psychological Bulletin*, 110: 469–85.

Miller, W. and Rollnick, S. (2002). *Motivational Interviewing: Preparing People to Change Addictive Behaviour*. New York: Guilford Press.

Milne, S., Welch, V., Brosseau, L. *et al.* (2001). Transcutaneous electrical nerve stimulation (TENS) for chronic low back pain. In *The Cochrane Library*, issue 4. Oxford: Update Software.

Mills, E.J., Nachega, J.B., Bangsberg, D.R. *et al.* (2006). Adherence to HAART: a systematic review of developed and developing nation patient-reported barriers and facilitators. *PLoS Medicine*, 3: e438.

Ming, E.E., Adler, G.K., Kessler, R.C. *et al.* (2004). Cardiovascular reactivity to work stress predicts subsequent onset of hypertension: the Air Traffic Controller Health Change Study. *Psychosomatic Medicine*, 66: 459–65.

Mino, Y., Babazono, A., Tsuda, T. *et al.* (2006). Can stress management at the workplace prevent depression? A randomized controlled trial. *Psychotherapy and Psychosomatics*, 7: 177–82.

Mishra, S., Bhatnagar, S., Gupta, D. *et al.* (2007). Incidence and management of phantom limb pain according to World Health Organization analgesic ladder in amputees of malignant origin. *American Journal of Hospice and Palliative Care*, 24: 455–62.

Misra, R., Crist, M. and Burant, C.J. (2003). Relationships among life stress, social support, academic stressors, and reactions to stressors of international students in the United States. *International Journal of Stress Management*, 10: 137–57.

Mitchell, A.J. and Kumar, M. (2002). Influence of psychological coping on survival – review is not systematic (letter to the editor). *British Medical Journal*, 326: 598.

Mitchell, J.B., Ballard, D.J., Matchar, D.B. *et al.* (2000). Racial variation in treatment for transient ischemic attacks: impact of participation by neurologists. *Health Services Research*, 34: 1413–28.

Mittag, W. and Schwarzer, R. (1993). Interaction of employment status and self-efficacy on alcohol consumption: a two-wave study on stressful life transitions. *Psychology and Health*, 8: 7–87.

Moens, V., Baruch, G. and Fearon, P. (2003). Opportunistic screening for Chlamydia at a community based contraceptive service for young people. *British Medical Journal*, 326: 1252–5.

Moldofsky, H. and Chester, W.J. (1970). Pain and mood patterns in patients with rheumatoid arthritis. A prospective study. *Psychosomatic Medicine*, 32: 309–18.

Molyneux, A., Lewis, S., Leivers, U. *et al.* (2003). Clinical trial comparing nicotine replacement therapy (NRT) plus brief counselling, brief counselling alone, and minimal intervention on smoking cessation in hospital inpatients. *Thorax*, 58: 484–8.

Montazeri, A., Jarvandi, S., Haghighat, S. *et al.* (2001). Anxiety and depression in breast cancer patients before and after participation in a cancer support group. *Patient Education and Counseling*, 45: 195–8.

Montgomery, C., Lydon, A. and Lloyd, K. (1999). Psychological distress among cancer patients and informed consent. *Journal of Psychosomatic Research*, 46: 241–5.

Montgomery, C., Pocock, M., Titley, K. *et al.* (2003). Predicting psychological distress in patients with leukaemia and lymphoma. *Journal of Psychosomatic Research*, 54: 289–92.

Moore, L. (2001). Are fruit tuck shops in primary schools effective in increasing pupils' fruit consumption? A randomised controlled trial. Abstract available from http://www.cf.ac.uk/socsi/whoswho/moore-tuckshop.html

Moore, L., Paisly, C.M. and Dennehy, A. (2000). Are fruit tuck shops in primary schools effective in increasing pupils' fruit consumption? A randomised controlled trial. *Nutrition and Food Science*, 30: 35–8.

Moore, S. and Rosenthal, D. (1993). *Sexuality in Adolescence*. London: Routledge.

Moore, S.M., Barling, N.R. and Hood, B. (1998). Predicting testicular and breast self-examination behaviour: a test of the theory of reasoned action. *Behaviour Change*, 15: 41–9.

Moorey, S. and Greer, S. (1994). Adjuvant psychological therapy for patients with cancer: outcome at one year. *Psycho-Oncology*, 3: 39–46.

Moorey, S., Greer, S., Bliss, J. *et al.* (1998). A comparison of adjuvant psychological therapy and supportive counselling in patients with cancer. *Psycho-Oncology*, 7: 218–28.

Moorey, S., Greer, S., Watson, M. *et al.* (1994). Adjuvant psychological therapy for patients with cancer: outcome at one year. *Psycho-oncology*, 3: 39–46.

Moos, R.H. and Schaefer, A. (1984). The crisis of physical illness: an overview and conceptual approach. In R.H. Moos (ed.), *Coping with Physical Illness: New Perspectives*, Vol. 2. New York: Plenum.

Mor, V., Malin, M. and Allen, S. (1994). Age differences in the psychosocial problems encountered by breast cancer patients. *Journal of the National Cancer Institute Monographs*, 16: 191–7.

Morgan, J., Roufeil, L., Kaushik, S. *et al.* (1998). Influence of coping style and precolonoscopy information on pain and anxiety of colonoscopy. *Gastrointestinal Endoscopy*, 48: 119–27.

Morley, S., Eccleston, C. and Williams, A. (1999). Systematic review and meta-analysis of randomized controlled trials of cognitive behaviour therapy and behaviour therapy for chronic pain in adults, excluding headache. *Pain*, 80: 1–13.

Morris, C.D. and Carson, S. (2003). Routine vitamin supplementation to prevent cardiovascular disease: a summary of the evidence for the U.S. Preventive Services Task Force. *Annals of Internal Medicine*, 139: 56–70.

Morris, D.B. (1999). Sociocultural and religious meanings of pain. In R.J. Gatchel and D.C. Turk (eds), *Psychosocial Factors in Pain*. New York: Guilford Press.

Morris, J.N., Clayton, D.G., Everitt, M.G. *et al.* (1990). Exercise in leisure time: coronary attack and death rates. *British Heart Journal*, 63: 325–34.

Morris, P.L.P., Robinson, R.G., Andrzejewski, P. *et al.* (1993). Association of depression with 10-year poststroke mortality. *American Journal of Psychiatry*, 150: 124–9.

Morrison, M.F., Petitto, J.M., Ten Have, T. *et al.* (2002). Depressive and anxiety disorders in women with HIV infection. *American Journal of Psychiatry*, 159: 789–96.

Morrison, V. (1988). Observation and snowballing: useful tools for research into illicit drug use? *Social Pharmacology*, 2: 247–71.

Morrison, V. (1999). Predictors of carer distress following a stroke. *Reviews in Clinical Gerontology*, 9: 265–71.

Morrison, V. (2001). The need to explore discrepant illness cognitions when predicting patient outcomes. *Health Psychology Update*, 10: 9–13.

Morrison, V. (2003). Furthering the socio-cognitive explanation of addiction. *Neuro-Psychoanalysis*, 5: 39–42.

Morrison, V. (2008). Ageing and physical health. In: Woods, R. and Clare, L. (eds). *Handbook of the Clinical Psycholog of Ageing*, (2nd edition). London: John Wiley & Sons (pp. 57–74).

Morrison, V. and Plant, M.A. (1991). Licit and illicit drug initiations and alcohol related problems among illicit drug users in Edinburgh. *Drug and Alcohol Dependence*, 27: 19–27.

Morrison, V., Ager, A. and Willock, J. (1999). Perceived risk of tropical diseases in Malawi: evidence of unrealistic pessimism and the irrelevance of beliefs of personal control? *Psychology, Health and Medicine*, 4: 361–8.

Morrison, V., Cottrell, L., Dawson, J. *et al.* (2002). Police force stress: psychological and job feature characteristics. Paper presented at the *Annual Conference of the European Health Psychology Society*, September.

Morrison, V., Griffith, G., Henderson, B.J. *et al.* (2008 in review). Can information modify people's intentions to undergo genetic testing: an experimental study.

Morrison, V., Hutchinson, A. and McCarthy, M. (2000a). Illness perceptions, perceived control and adherence in child asthmatics: are child–parent beliefs discrepant? Poster presentation at European Health Psychology Society annual conference, Leiden, The Netherlands.

Morrison, V., Johnston, M. and MacWalter, R. (2000b). Predictors of distress following an acute stroke: disability, control cognitions and satisfaction with care. *Psychology and Health*, 15: 395–407.

Morrison, V., Pollard, B., Johnston, M. *et al.* (2005) Anxiety and depression 3 years following stroke: demographic, clinical and psychological predictors. *Journal of Psychosomatic Research*, 59: 209–13.

Morrison, V.L. (1991a). The impact of HIV upon injecting drug users: a longitudinal study. *AIDS Care*, 3: 197–205.

Morrison, V.L. (1991b). Starting, switching, stopping: users' explanations of illicit drug use. *Drug and Alcohol Dependence*, 27: 213–17.

Morse, J.M. and Johnson, J.L. (1991). Towards a theory of illness. The illness constellation model. In J.M. Morse and J.L. Johnson (eds), *The Illness Experience: Dimensions of Suffering*. Newbury Park, Calif.: Sage.

Morse, S.R. and Fife, B. (1998). Coping with a partner's cancer: adjustment at four stages of the illness trajectory. *Oncology Nursing Forum*, 25: 751–60.

Moss, S., Thomas, I., Evans, A. *et al.* (2005) Randomised controlled trial of mammographic screening in women from age 40: predicted mortality based on surrogate outcome measures. *British Journal of Cancer*, 92: 955–60.

Moss-Morris, R. and Chalder, T. (2003). Illness perceptions and levels of disability in patients with chronic fatigue syndrome and rheumatoid arthritis. *Journal of Psychosomatic Research*, 55: 305–8.

Moss-Morris, R., Weinman, J., Petrie, K.J. *et al.* (2002). The revised Illness Perception Questionnaire (IPQ-R). *Psychology and Health*, 17: 1–16.

Motl, R.W., Gliottoni, R.C. and Scott, J.A. (2007). Self-efficacy correlates with leg muscle pain during maximal and submaximal cycling exercise. *Journal of Pain*, 8: 583–7.

Murgraff, V., McDermott, M.R., White, D. *et al.* (1999). Regret is what you get: the effects of manipulating anticipated affect and time perspective on risky single occasion drinking. *Alcohol and Alcoholism*, 34: 590–600.

Murphy, D., Lindsay, S. and Williams, A.C. de C. (1997). Chronic low back pain: predictions of pain and relationship to anxiety and avoidance. *Behaviour Research and Therapy*, 35: 231–8.

Murray, C.J.L. and Lopez, A.D. (1997). Alternative projections of mortality and disability by cause 1990–2020: Global Burden of Disease Study. *The Lancet*, 349: 1498–504.

Murray, D.F., Marks, M., Evans, B. and Willig, C. (2000). *Health Psychology: Theory, Research and Practice*. London: Sage.

Murray, M. (1997). A narrative approach to health psychology: background and potential. *Journal of Health Psychology*, 2: 9–20.

Murray, M. and Campbell, C. (2003). Beyond the sidelines: towards a more politically engaged health psychology. *Health Psychology Update*, 12: 12–17.

Murrell, R. (2001). Assessing the quality of life of individuals with neurological illness. *Health Psychology Update*, 10.

Myers, J., Froelicher, V., Do, D. *et al.* (2002). Exercise capacity and mortality among men referred for exercise testing. *New England Journal of Medicine*, 346: 793–801.

Myers, L.B. (1998). Repressive coping, trait anxiety and reported avoidance of negative thoughts. *Personality and Individual Differences*, 24: 299–303.

Myers, L.B. and Reynolds, D. (2000). How optimistic are repressors? The relationship between repressive coping, controllability, self-esteem and comparative optimism for health-related events. *Psychology and Health*, 15: 677–87.

Nagasako, E.M., Oaklander, A.L. and Dworkin, R.H. (2003). Congenital insensitivity to pain: an update. *Pain*, 101: 213–19.

Naish, J., Brown, J. and Denton, B. (1994). Intercultural consultations: investigation of factors that deter non-English speaking women from attending their general practitioners for cervical screening. *British Medical Journal*, 309: 1126–8.

Naliboff, B.D., Munakata, J., Chang, L. *et al.* (1998). Toward a biobehavioral model of visceral hypersensitivity in irritable bowel syndrome. *Journal of Psychosomatic Research*, 45: 485–93.

Narevic, E. and Schoenberg, N.E. (2002). Lay explanations for Kentucky's 'Coronary Valley'. *Journal of Community Health*, 27: 53–62.

Nathan, J.P., Zerilli, T., Cicero, L.A. *et al.* (2007). Patients' use and perception of medication information leaflets. *Annals of Pharmacotherapy*, 41: 777–82.

National Collaborating Centre for Chronic Conditions (2004). Chronic obstructive pulmonary disease. National clinical guidelines on management of chronic obstructive pulmonary disease in adults in primary and secondary care. *Thorax*, 59 (suppl. 1): 1–232.

National Diet and Nutrition Survey: Adults aged 19–64, Vol 1. (2000) Carried out in 2000 on behalf of the Food Standards Agency and Department of Health by the Social Survey Division of the Office for National Statistics and Medical Research Council Human Nutrition Research. London: Stationery Office.

National Institute for Clinical Excellence (2004). *Guidance on Cancer Services: Improving Supportive and Palliative Care for Adults with Cancer.* London: NICE.

National Institutes of Health Technology Assessment Panel (1996). Integration of behavioral and relaxation approaches into the treatment of chronic pain and insomnia. *Journal of the American Medical Association*, 276: 313–18.

Navas-Nacher, E.L., Colangelo, L., Beam, C. *et al.* (2001). Risk factors for coronary heart disease in men 18 to 39 years of age. *Annals of Internal Medicine*, 134: 433–9.

Nazroo, J. (1997). *The Health of Britain's Ethnic Minorities: Findings from a National Survey.* London: Policy Studies Institute.

Nazroo, J.Y. (1998). *Genetic, Cultural or Socioeconomic Vulnerability? Explaining Ethnic Inequalities in Health.* Oxford: Blackwell.

Neal, R.D., Ali, N., Atkin, K. *et al.* (2006). Communication between South Asian patients and GPs: comparative study using the Roter Interactional Analysis System. *British Journal of General Practice*, 56: 869–75.

Neaton, J.D., Blackburn, H., Jacobs, D. *et al.* (1992). Serum cholesterol and mortality findings for men screened in the Multiple Risk Factor Intervention Trial. *Archives of Internal Medicine*, 152: 1490–500.

Neff, L.A. and Karney, B.R. (2005). Gender differences in social support: a question of skill or responsiveness? *Journal of Personality & Social Psychology*, 88: 79–90.

Nelson, D.V., Baer, P.E. and Cleveland, S.E. (1998). Family stress management following acute myocardial infarction: an educational and skills training intervention program. *Patient Education and Counseling*, 34: 135–45.

Ness, A., Hooper, L., Egger, M. *et al.* (2003). Fruit and vegetables for cardiovascular disease. In *The Cochrane Library*, issue 1. Oxford: Update Software.

Ness, A.R. and Powles, J.W. (1997). Fruit and vegetables, and cardiovascular disease: a review. *International Journal of Epidemiology*, 26: 1–13.

Ness, A.R., Frankel, S.J., Gunnell, D.J. *et al.* (1999). Are we really dying for a tan? *British Medical Journal*, 319: 114–16.

Nestle, M. (1997). Alcohol guidelines for chronic disease prevention: from prohibition to moderation. *Nutrition Today*, 32: 86–92.

New, S.J. and Senior, M. (1991). 'I don't believe in needles': qualitative aspects of a study into the uptake of infant immunisation in two English health authorities. *Social Science and Medicine*, 33: 509–18.

Newhagen, J. and Reeves, B. (1987). Emotion and memory responses for negative political advertising: a study of television commercials used in the 1988 presidential campaign. In F. Biocca (ed.), *Television and Political Advertising*, Vol. 1. Hillsdale, NJ: Lawrence Erlbaum.

Newton, T.L., Watters, C.A., Philhower, C.L. *et al.* (2005). Cardiovascular reactivity during dyadic social interaction: the roles of gender and dominance. *International Journal of Psychophysiology*, 57: 219–28.

Ng, B., Dimsdale, J.E., Rollnick, J.D. and Shapiro, H. (1996). The effect of ethnicity on prescriptions for patient-controlled anaesthesia for post-operative pain. *Pain*, 66: 9–12.

NHS Centre for Reviews and Dissemination (1999). *Effective healthcare: getting evidence into practice.* NHS CRD, Vol. 5, No. 1. London: Royal Society of Medicine Press.

NHS Executive (1996). *Patient Partnership: Building a Collaborative Strategy.* Leeds: NHS Executive.

Nichols, K. (1993). *Psychological Care in Physical Illness.* Nelson Thornes.

Nicholson, N., Soane, E., Fenton-O'Creevy, M. *et al.* (2005). Personality and domain-specific risk-taking. *Journal of Risk Research*, 8: 157–76.

Nicolson, N.A. and van Diest, R. (2000). Salivary cortisol levels in vital exhaustion. *Journal of Psychosomatic Research*, 49: 335–42.

Niederhoffer, K.G. and Pennebaker, J.W. (2005). Sharing one's story: on the benefits of writing or talking about emotional experience. In C. Snyder and S.J. Lopez (2005). *Handbook of Positive Psychology.* New edition, USA: Oxford University Press.

Niemcryk, S.J., Speer, M.A., Travis, L.B. *et al.* (1990). Psychosocial correlates of haemoglobin A1c in young adults with type I diabetes. *Journal of Psychosomatic Research*, 34: 617–27.

Niemi, M., Laaksonen, R., Kotila, M. and Waltimo, O. (1988). Quality of life 4 years after stroke. *Stroke*, 19: 1101–7.

Nijboer, C., Tempelaar, R., Triemstra, M. *et al.* (2001). Dynamics in cancer caregiver's health over time: gender-specific patterns and determinants. *Psychology and Health*, 16: 471–88.

Noble, L.M. (1998). Doctor–patient communication and adherence to treatment. In L.B. Myers and K. Midence (eds), *Adherence to Treatment in Medical Conditions*. Amsterdam: Harwood Academic.

Noblet, A.J. and LaMontagne, A. (2006). The role of workplace health promotion in addressing job stress. *Health Promotion International*, 21: 346–53.

Noguchi, K., Albarracín, D., Durantini, M.R. *et al.* (2007). Who participates in which health promotion programs? A meta-analysis of motivations underlying enrolment and retention in HIV-prevention interventions. *Psychological Bulletin*, 133: 955–75.

Norberg, A.L., Lindblad, F. and Boman, K.K. (2005). Coping strategies in parents of children with cancer. *Social Science and Medicine*, 60: 965–75.

Nordstrom, C.K., Dwyer, K.M., Merz, C.N. *et al.* (2001). Work-related stress and early atherosclerosis. *Epidemiology*, 12: 180–5.

Norman, P. and Bennett, P. (1996). Health locus of control. In M. Conner and P. Norman (eds), *Predicting Health Behaviour*. Buckingham: Open University Press.

Norman, P. and Smith, L. (1995). The theory of planned behaviour and exercise: an investigation into the role of prior behaviour, behavioural intentions and attitude variability. *European Journal of Social Psychology*, 25: 403–15.

Norman, P., Bennett, P., Smith, C. *et al.* (1998). Health locus of control and health behaviour. *Journal of Health Psychology*, 3: 171–80.

Norman, P., Conner, M. and Bell, S. (1999). The theory of planned behaviour and smoking cessation. *Health Psychology*, 18: 89–94.

Normandeau, S., Kalnins, I., Jutras, S. *et al.* (1998). A description of 5 to 12 year old children's conception of health within the context of their daily life. *Psychology and Health*, 135: 883–96.

Norris, V.K., Stephens, M.A. and Kinney, J.M. (1990). The influence of family interactions on recovery from stroke: help or hindrance? *The Gerontologist*, 30: 535–42.

Norrsell, U., Finger, S. and Lajonchere, C. (1999). Cutaneous sensory spots and the 'law of specific nerve energies': history and development of ideas. *Brain Research Bulletin*, 48: 457–65.

Norström. T. and Skog, O.J. (2005). Saturday opening of alcohol retail shops in Sweden: an experiment in two phases. *Addiction*, 100: 767–76.

Northouse, L., Kershaw, T., Mood, D. *et al.* (2005). Effects of a family intervention on the quality of life of women with recurrent breast cancer and their family caregivers. *Psycho-oncology*, 14: 478–91.

Northouse, L.L., Mood, D.W., Schafenacker, A. *et al.* (2007). Randomized clinical trial of a family intervention for prostate cancer patients and their spouses. *Cancer*, 110, 2809–18.

Nouwen, A., Cloutier, C., Kappas, A. *et al.* (2006). The effects of focusing and distraction on cold-pressor induced pain in chronic back pain patients and controls. *Journal of Pain*, 7: 62–71.

Noyes, R., Jr (2001). Hypochondriasis: boundaries and comorbidities. In G.J.G. Asmundson, S. Taylor and B.J. Cox (eds), *Health Anxiety: Clinical and Research Perspectives on Hyponchondriasis and Related Conditions* (pp. 132–60). New York: John Wiley & Sons.

Nutbeam, D., Smith, C., Moore, L. *et al.* (1993). Warning! Schools can damage your health: alienation from school and its impact on child behaviour. *Journal of Paediatrics and Child Health*, 29 (suppl. 1): S25–30.

O'Boyle, C.A., McGee, H., Hickey, A. *et al.* (1992). Individual quality of life in patients undergoing hip replacement. *The Lancet*, 339: 1088–91.

O'Boyle, C.A., McGee, H., Hickey, A. *et al.* (1993). *The Schedule for the Evaluation of Individual Quality of Life (SEIQoL): Administration Manual*. Dublin: Department of Psychology, Royal College of Surgeons.

O'Brien, M.K., Petrie, K. and Raeburn, J. (1992). Adherence to medication regimens: updating a complex medical issue. *Medical Care Review*, 49: 435–54.

O'Carroll, R.E., Smith, K.B., Grubb, N.R. *et al.* (2001). Psychological factors associated with delay in attending hospital following a myocardial infarction. *Journal of Psychosomatic Research*, 51: 611–14.

O'Cleirigh, C., Ironson, G., Antoni, M. *et al.* (2003). Emotional expression and depth processing of trauma and their relation to long-term survival in patients with HIV/AIDS. *Journal of Psychosomatic Research*, 54: 225–35.

O'Connell, K., Skevington, S. and Saxena, S. *et al.* (2003). Preliminary development of the World Health Organization's Quality of Life HIV instrument (WHOQOL-HIV): analysis of the pilot version. *Social Science and Medicine*, 57: 1259–75.

O'Connor, A.P., Wicker, C.A. and Germino, B.B. (1990). Understanding the cancer patient's search for meaning. *Cancer Nursing*, 13: 167–75.

Odgers, P., Houghton, S. and Douglas, G. (1996). Reputation Enhancement Theory and adolescent substance use. *Journal of Child Psychology, Psychiatry and Allied Disciplines*, 37: 1015–22.

O'Donnell, C.R., O'Donnell, L., San Doval, A. *et al.* (1998). Reductions in STD infections subsequent to an STD clinic visit. Using video-based patient education to supplement provider interactions. *Sexually Transmitted Diseases*, 25: 161–8.

O'Donnell, L., San Doval, A., Duran, R. and O'Donnell, C.R. (1995). The effectiveness of video-based interventions in promoting condom acquisition among STD clinic patients. *Sexually Transmitted Diseases*, 22: 97–103.

O'Farrell, T.J. and Fals-Stewart, W. (2000). Behavioral couples therapy for alcoholism and drug abuse. *Journal of Substance Abuse Treatment*, 18: 51–4.

Office for National Statistics (1997). *Smoking among Secondary School Children in 1996: England.* London: Stationery Office.

Office for National Statistics (1998). *1996 Mortality Statistics: Cause*, Series DH2, 23. London: The Stationery Office.

Office for National Statistics (1999). *Social Trends 29.* London: Stationery Office.

Office for National Statistics (2000). *Results from the 1998 General Household Survey.* London: Stationery Office.

Office for National Statistics (2001) *Smoking Related Behaviour and Attitudes.* Series OS No.17, London: ONS.

Office for National Statistics (2008). *Deaths Registered in 2006: Review of the Registrar General or dealths in England and Wales, 2006.* Newport: Office for National Statistics.

Ogden, J. (2003). Some problems with social cognition models: a pragmatic and conceptual analysis. *Health Psychology*, 22: 424–8.

Ogden, J., Fuks, K., Gardner, M. *et al.* (2002). Doctors' expressions of uncertainty and patient confidence. *Patient Education and Counselling*, 48: 171–6.

Ogden, J. and Mtandabari, T. (1997). Examination stress and changes in mood and health related behaviours. *Psychology and Health*, 12: 288–99.

Ogden, J., Veale, D. and Summers, Z. (1997). The development and validation of the Exercise Dependence Questionnaire. *Addiction Research*, 5: 343–56.

Ohayon, M.M., Guilleminault, C., Priest, R.G. *et al.* (2000). Is sleep-disordered breathing an independent risk factor for hypertension in the general population (13,057 subjects)? *Journal of Psychosomatic Research*, 48: 593–601.

O'Hegarty, M., Pederson, L.L., Nelson, D.E. *et al.* (2006). Reactions of young adult smokers to warning labels on cigarette packages. *American Journal of Preventive Medicine*, 30: 467–73.

Okamoto, K. (2006). Life expectancy at the age of 65 years and environmental factors: an ecological study in Japan. *Archives of Gerontology and Geriatrics*, 43: 85–91.

O'Keefe, D.J. and Jensen, J.D. (2007). The relative persuasiveness of gain-framed and loss-framed messages for encouraging disease prevention behaviors: a meta-analytic review. *Journal of Health Communication*, 12: 623–44.

Okelo, S.O., Wu, A.W., Merriman, B. *et al.* (2007). Are physician estimates of asthma severity less accurate in black than in white patients? *Journal of General Internal Medicine*, 22: 976–81.

Oldenburg, B. and Harris, D. (1996). The workplace as a setting for promoting health and preventing disease. *Homeostasis*, 37: 226–32.

Oldenburg, B., Glanz, K. and French, M. (1999). The application of staging models to the understanding of health behaviour change and the promotion of health. *Psychology and Health*, 14: 503–16.

Olson, D.H. and Stewart, K.L. (1991). Family systems and health behaviours. In H.E. Schroeder (ed.), *New Directions in Health Psychology Assessment.* New York: Hemisphere.

O'Malley, P.M., Johnston, L.D., Chaloupka, F.J. *et al.* (2005). Televised state-sponsored antitobacco advertising and youth smoking beliefs and behavior in the United States, 1999–2000. *Archives of Pediatric and Adolescent Medicine*, 159: 639–45.

O'Neill, M. and Simard, P. (2006). Choosing indicators to evaluate Healthy Cities projects: a political task? *Health Promotion International*, 21: 145–52.

Ong, L.M.L., de Haes, J.C.J.M., Hoos, A.M. *et al.* (1995). Doctor–patient communication: a review of the literature. *Social Science and Medicine*, 40: 903–18.

Onwuanyi, A.E., Clarke, A. and Vanderbush, E. (2003). Cardiovascular disease mortality. *Journal of the National Medical Association*, 95: 1146–51.

Onwuteaka-Phillipsen, B., van der Heide, A., Koper, D., *et al.* (2003). Euthanasia and other end-of-life decisions in The Netherlands in 1990, 1995 and 2001. *The Lancet*, 362: 395–9.

Orbell, S. and Gillies, B. (1993). What's stressful about caring? *Journal of Applied Social Psychology*, 23: 272–90.

Orbell, S., Hodgkins, S. and Sheeran, P. (1997). Implementation intentions and the theory of planned behaviour. *Personality and Social Psychology*, 23: 945–54.

Orbell, S., Hopkins, N. and Gillies, B. (1993). Measuring the impact of informal caregiving.

Journal of Community and Applied Social Psychology, 3: 149–63.

Orbell, S. and Sheeran, P. (2002). Changing health behaviours: the role of implementation intentions. In D. Rutter and L. Quine (eds), *Changing Health Behaviour*. Buckingham: Open University Press.

Orford, J. (2001). *Excessive Appetites: A Psychological View of Addictions*, 2nd edn. Chichester: Wiley.

Orrell, C., Bangsberg, D.R., Badri, M. *et al.* (2003). Adherence is not a barrier to successful antiretroviral therapy in South Africa. *AIDS*, 1369–75.

Orth-Gomér, K. and Undén, A.-L. (1990). Type A behaviour, social support, and coronary risk: interaction and significance for mortality in cardiac patients. *Psychosomatic Medicine*, 52: 59–72.

Orth-Gomér, K., Undén, A.-L. and Edwards, M.-E. (1988). Social isolation and mortality in ischemic heart disease. *Acta Medica Scandinavica*, 224: 205–15.

Osborne, R.H., Wilson, T., Lorig, K.R. *et al.* (2007). Does self-management lead to sustainable health benefits in people with arthritis? A 2-year transition study of 452 Australians. *Journal of Rheumatology*, 34: 1112–7.

Osse, B.H.P., Myrra, J.F.J., Vernooj-Dassen, E.S. *et al.* (2002). Problems to discuss with cancer patients in palliative care: a comprehensive approach. *Patient Education and Counseling*, 47: 195–204.

OXCHECK Study Group (1994). Effectiveness of health checks conducted by nurses in primary care: results of the OXCHECK study after one year. Imperial Cancer Research Fund OXCHECK Study Group. *British Medical Journal*, 308: 308–12.

OXCHECK Study Group (1995). Effectiveness of health checks conducted by nurses in primary care: final results of the OXCHECK study. Imperial Cancer Research Fund OXCHECK Study Group. *British Medical Journal*, 310: 1099–104.

Oxman, A.D., Davis, D., Haynes, R.B. *et al.* (1995). No magic bullets: a systematic review of 102 trials of interventions to improve professional practice. *Canadian Medical Association Journal*, 153: 1423–31.

Oyebode, J. (2003). Assessment of carers' psychological needs. *Advances in Psychiatric Treatment*, 9: 45–53.

Pachter, L.M. (1994). Culture and clinical care: folk illness beliefs and behaviours and their implications for health care delivery. *Journal of the American Medical Association*, 7: 690–4.

Paffenbarger, R.S., Hyde, J.T., Wing, A.L. *et al.* (1986). Physical activity, all-cause mortality, and longevity of college alumni. *New England Journal of Medicine*, 314: 605–12.

Page-Shafer, K.A., Satariano, W.A., Winkelstein, W., Jr, *et al.* (1996) Comorbidity and HIV disease progression in homosexual/bisexual men. The San Francisco Men's Health Study. *Annals of Epidemiology 1996*, 6: 420–30.

Pakenham, K.I., Dadds, M.R. and Lennon, H.V. (2002). The efficacy of a psychosocial intervention for HIV/AIDS caregiving dyads and individual caregivers: a controlled treatment outcome study. *AIDS Care*, 14: 731–50.

Pakenham, K.I., Pruss, M. and Clutton, S. (2000). The utility of sociodemographics, knowledge and health belief model variables in predicting reattendance for mammography screening: a brief report. *Psychology and Health*, 15: 585–91.

Palesh, O., Butler, L.D., Koopman, C. *et al.* (2007). Stress history and breast cancer recurrence. *Journal of Psychosomatic Research*, 63: 233–9.

Palmer, S. and Glass, T.A. (2003). Family function and stroke recovery: a review. *Rehabilitation Psychology*, 48: 255–65.

Panagopoulou, E., Kersbergen, B. and Maes, S. (2002). The effects of emotional (non-) expression in (chronic) disease: a meta-analytic review. *Psychology and Health*, 17: 529–45.

Panagopoulou, E., Vedhara, K., Gaintarzti, C. *et al.* (2006). Emotionally expressive coping reduces pregnancy rates in patients undergoing in vitro fertilization. *Fertility and Sterility*, 86: 672–7.

Papanicolaou, D.A., Wilder, R.L., Manolagas, S.C. and Chrousos, G.P. (1998). The pathophysiologic roles of interleukin-6 in human disease. *Archives of Internal Medicine*, 128: 127–37.

Paris, W., Muchmore, J., Pribil, A. *et al.* (1994). Study of the relative incidences of psychosocial factors before and after heart transplantation and the influence of posttransplantation psychosocial factors on heart transplantation outcome. *Journal of Heart Lung Transplantation*, 13: 424–30.

Pargament, K.I., Koenig, H.G. and Perez, L.M. (2000). The many methods in religious coping: Development and initial validation of the RCOPE. *Journal of Clinical Psychology*, 56: 519–43.

Park, C.L. (2006). Exploring relations among religiousness, meaning, and adjustment to lifetime and current stressful encounters in later life. *Anxiety, Stress, and Coping*, 19: 33–45.

Park, C.L., Cohen, L.H. and Murch, R. (1996). Assessment and prediction of stress-related growth. *Journal of Personality*, 64: 71–105.

Park, C.L. and Lechner, S.C. (2007). Measurement issues in assessing growth following stressful life experiences. In L.G. Calhoun and R.G. Tedeschi (eds) (2007). *Handbook of Post-traumatic Growth: Research and Practice*. London: Lawrence Erlbaum Associates, pp. 47–67.

Park, D.C., Morrell, R.W., Frieske, D. *et al.* (1992). Medication adherence behaviors in older adults:

effects of external cognitive supports. *Psychology and Aging*, 7: 252–6.

Parkes, K. (1984). Locus of control, cognitive appraisal, coping appraisal and coping in stressful episodes. *Journal of Personality and Social Psychology*, 46: 655–68.

Parle, M., Maguire, P. and Heaven, C. (1997). The development of a training model to improve health professionals' skills, self-efficacy and outcome expectancies when communicating with cancer patients. *Social Science and Medicine*, 44: 231–40.

Parsons, T. (1951). *The Social System*. New York: Free Press.

Partridge, C. and Johnston, M. (1989). Perceived control of recovery from physical disability: measurement and prediction. *British Journal of Clinical Psychology*, 28: 53–9.

Pasterfield, D., Wilkinson, C., Finlay, I.G. *et al.* (2006). GPs' views on changing the law on physician-assisted suicide and euthanasia, and willingness to prescribe or inject lethal drugs: a survey from Wales. *British Journal of General Practice*, 56: 450–52.

Pate, R.R., Pratt, M., Blair, S.N. *et al.* (1995). Physical activity and public health: a recommendation from the Centers for Disease Control and the American College of Sports Medicine. *Journal of the American Medical Association*, 273: 402–7.

Paterson, J., Moss-Morris, R. and Butler, S.J. (1999). The effect of illness experience and demographic factors on children's illness representations. *Psychology and Health*, 14: 117–29.

Paton, A. (1999). Reflections on alcohol and the young. Invited commentary. *Alcohol and Alcoholism*, 34: 502–5.

Patrick, D.L. and Peach, H. (1989). *Disablement in the Community*. Oxford: Oxford University Press.

Patterson, B.K., Carlo, D.J., Kaplan, M.H. *et al.* (1999). Cell-associated HIV-1 messenger RNA and DNA in T-helper cell and monocytes in asymptomatic HIV-1-infected subjects on HAART plus an inactivated HIV-1 immunogen. *AIDS*, 13: 1607–11.

Patterson, D.R. and Jensen, M.P. (2003). Hypnosis and clinical pain. *Psychological Bulletin*, 129: 495–521.

Patton, G.C., Johnson-Sabine, E., Wood, K. *et al.* (1990). Abnormal attitudes in London schoolgirls – a prospective epidemiological study: outcome at twelve month follow-up. *Psychological Medicine*, 20: 383–94.

Payne, N. (2001). Occupational stressors and coping as determinants of burnout in female hospice nurses. *Journal of Advanced Nursing*, 33: 396–405.

Pbert L., Osganian S.K., Gorak D. *et al.* (2006). A school nurse-delivered adolescent smoking cessation intervention: a randomized controlled trial. *Preventive Medicine*, 43: 312–20.

Pearlin, L.I. (1983). Role strains and personal stress. In H.B. Kaplan (ed.), *Psychosocial Stress: Trends in Theory and Research*. New York: Academic Press.

Pearlin, L.I. and Mullan, J.T. (1992). Loss and stress in ageing. In M.L. Wykle, E. Kahara and J. Kowal (eds), *Stress and Health among the Elderly*. New York: Springer Verlag.

Pearson, S., Maddern, G. and Hewett, P. (2005). Interacting effects of pre-operative information and patient choice in adaptation to colonoscopy: a randomised trial. *Diseases of the Colon and Rectum*, 48: 2047–54.

Peay, M.Y. and Peay, E.R. (1998). The evaluation of medical symptoms by patients and doctors. *Journal of Behavioral Medicine*, 21: 57–81.

Pelosi, A.J. and Appleby, L. (1992). Psychological influences on cancer and ischaemic heart disease (for debate). *British Medical Journal*, 304: 1295–8.

Pelosi, A.J. and Appleby, L. (1993). Personality and fatal diseases. *British Medical Journal*, 306: 1666–7.

Peltola, H., Patja, A., Leinikkii, P. *et al.* (1998). No evidence for measles, mumps and rubella vaccine-associated inflammatory bowel disease or autism in a 14-year prospective study. *The Lancet*, 351: 1327–8.

Pendleton, D.A. (1983). Doctor–patient communication: a review. In D. Pendleton and J. Hasler (eds), *Doctor–Patient Communication*. London: Academic Press.

Pendleton, D., Schofield, T., Tate, P., Havelock, P. *et al.* (1984). *The Consultation: An Approach to Learning and Teaching*. Oxford: Oxford University Press.

Penedo, F.J., Molton, I., Dahn, J.R. *et al.* (2006). Randomized clinical trial of group-based cognitive-behavioral stress management in localized prostate cancer: development of stress management skills improves quality of life and benefit finding. *Annals of Behavioral Medicine*, 31: 261–70.

Pennebaker, J.W. (1982). Social and perceptual factors affecting symptom reporting and mass psychogenic illness. In M.J. Colligan, J.W. Pennebaker and L.R. Murphy (eds), *Mass Psychogenic Illness: A Social Psychological Analysis*. Hillsdale, NJ: Lawrence Erlbaum.

Pennebaker, J.W. (1992). *The Psychology of Physical Symptoms*. New York: Springer Verlag.

Pennebaker, J.W. (1993). Putting stress into words: health, linguistic and therapeutic implications. *Behavioral Research Therapy*, 31: 539–48.

Pennebaker, J.W. and Beall, S. (1986). Confronting a traumatic event: toward an understanding of inhibition and disease. *Journal of Abnormal Psychology*, 95: 274–81.

Pennebaker, J.W. and Skelton, J.A. (1981). Selective monitoring of bodily sensations. *Journal of Personality and Social Behaviour*, 35: 167–74.

Pennebaker, J.W., Colder, M. and Sharp, L.K. (1990). Accelerating the coping process. *Journal of Personality and Social Psychology*, 58: 528–37.

Pennebaker, J.W., Kiecolt-Glaser, J. and Glaser, R. (1988). Disclosure of trauma and immune function: health implications for psychotherapy. *Journal of Consulting and Clinical Psychology*, 56: 239–45.

Penninx, B., Guralnik, J.M., Pahor, M. *et al.* (1998). Chronically depressed mood and cancer risk in older persons. *Journal of the National Cancer Institute*, 90: 1888–93.

Penninx, B.W.J.H., van Tilburg, T., Kriegsman, D.M.W. *et al.* (1999). Social network, social support, and loneliness in older persons with different chronic diseases. *Journal of Ageing and Health*, 11: 151–68.

Penny, G.N., Bennett, P. and Herbert, M. (eds) (1994). *Health Psychology: A Lifespan Perspective*. Switzerland: Harwood Academic.

Perloff, L.S. and Fetzer, B.K. (1986). Self–other judgements and perceived vulnerability to victimization. *Journal of Personality and Social Psychology*, 50: 502–10.

Perry, C.L. and Grant, M. (1988). Comparing peer-led to teacher-led youth alcohol education in four countries. (Australia, Chile, Norway and Swaziland). *Alcohol Health and Research World*, 12: 322–6.

Perry, K., Petrie, K.J., Ellis, C.J. *et al.* (2001). Symptom expectations and delay in acute myocardial infarction patients. *Heart*, 86: 91–2.

Persky, V.W., Kempthorne-Rawson, J. and Shekelle, R.B. (1987). Personality and risk of cancer: 20 year follow-up of the Western Electric study. *Psychosomatic Medicine*, 49: 435–49.

Perugini, M. and Bagozzi, R.P. (2001). The role of desires and anticipated emotions in goal-directed behaviours: broadening and deepening the theory of planned behaviour. *British Journal of Social Psychology*, 40: 79–98.

Peterson, T.R. and Aldana, S.G. (1999). Improving exercise behaviour: an application of the stages of change model in a worksite setting. *American Journal of Health Promotion*, 13: 229–32.

Peto, R. and Lopez, A.D. (1990). Worldwide mortality from current smoking patterns. In B. Durston and K. Jamrozik (eds), *Tobacco and Health 1990: The Global War*. Proceedings of the 7th World Conference on Tobacco and Health. Perth: Health Department of Western Australia.

Peto, R., Darby, S., Deo, H. *et al.* (2000). Smoking, smoking cessation, and lung cancer in the UK since 1950: combination of national statistics with two case-control studies. *British Medical Journal*, 321: 323–9.

Peto, R., Lopez, A.D., Borehan, J. *et al.* (1994). *Mortality from Smoking in Developed Countries 1950–2000*. Oxford: Oxford University Press.

Petrak, J.A., Doyle, A.-M., Smith, A. *et al.* (2001). Factors associated with self-disclosure of HIV serostatus to significant others. *British Journal of Health Psychology*, 6: 69–79.

Petrie, K. and Weinman J. (1997). Illness representations and recovery from myocardial infarction. In K.J. Petrie and J. Weinman (eds), *Perceptions of Health and Illness*. Amsterdam: Harwood Academic, pp. 441–62.

Petrie, K.J. and Weinman, J. (2003). More focus needed on symptom appraisal (editorial). *Journal of Psychosomatic Research*, 54: 401–3.

Petrie, K.J., Booth, R.J., Pennebaker, J.W. *et al.* (1995). Disclosure of trauma and immune response to hepatitis B vaccination program. *Journal of Consulting and Clinical Psychology*, 63: 787–92.

Petrie, K.J., Buick, D.L., Weinman, J. *et al.* (1999). Positive effects of illness reported by myocardial infarction and breast cancer patients. *Journal of Psychosomatic Research*, 47: 537–43.

Petrie, K.J., Weinman, J., Sharpe, N. *et al.* (1996). Role of patients' view of their illness in predicting return to work and functioning after a myocardial infarction. *British Medical Journal*, 312: 1191–4.

Petruzzello, S.J., Jones, A.C. and Tate, A.K. (1997). Affective responses to acute exercise: a test of opponent-process theory. *Journal of Sports Medicine and Physical Fitness*, 37: 205–11.

Petticrew, A., Fraser, J. and Regan, M. (1999). Adverse life events and risk of breast cancer: a meta-analysis. *British Journal of Health Psychology*, 4: 1–17.

Petticrew, M., Bell, R. and Hunter, D. (2002). Influence of psychological coping on survival and recurrence in people with cancer: a systematic review. *British Medical Journal*, 325: 1066.

Petty, R. and Cacioppo, J. (1986). The elaboration likelihood model of persuasion. In L. Berkowitz (ed.), *Advances in Experimental Social Psychology*, Vol. 19. Orlando, Fla: Academic Press.

Petty, R.E. and Cacioppo, J.T. (1996). *Attitudes and Persuasion: Classic and Contemporary Approaches*. Boulder, Colo.: Westview Press.

Peveler, R., Carson, A. and Rodin, G. (2002). Depression in medical patients. *British Medical Journal*, 325: 149–52.

PHLS Communicable Disease Surveillance Centre (2002). *HIV and AIDS in the United Kingdom 2001. An Update: November 2002*. London: PHLS, ICH (London) and SCIEH.

Piaget, J. (1930). *The Child's Conception of Physical Causality*. London: Routledge and Kegan Paul.

Piaget, J. (1970). Piaget's theory. In P.H. Mussen (ed.), *Carmichael's Manual of Child Psychology*, 3rd edn, Vol. 1. New York: Wiley.

Piette, J.D., Weinberger, M. and McPhee, S.J. (2000). The effect of automated calls with telephone nurse follow-up on patient-centered outcomes of diabetes care: a randomized controlled trial. *Medical Care*, 38: 218–30.

Pinel, J.P.J. (2003). *Biopsychology*, (5th edn). Boston: Allyn and Bacon.

Pinerua-Shuhaibar, L., Prieto-Rincon, D., Ferrer, A. *et al.* (1999). Reduced tolerance and cardiovascular responses to ischemic pain in minor depression. *Journal of Affective Disorders*, 56: 119–26.

Pinquart, M. and Sörensen, S. (2003). Differences between caregivers and noncaregivers in psychological health and physical health: a meta-analysis. *Psychology and Aging*, 18: 250–67.

Pinquart, M. and Sörensen, S. (2005). Ethnic differences in stressors, resources, and psychological outcomes of family caregiving: a meta-analysis. *The Gerontologist*, 45: 90–106.

Pirozzo, S., Summerbell, C., Cameron, C. *et al.* (2003). Advice on low-fat diets for obesity. In *The Cochrane Library*, issue 1. Oxford: Update Software.

Plante, T.G. and Rodin, J. (1990). Physical fitness and enhanced psychological health. *Current Psychology Research and Reviews*, 9: 3–24.

Plotnikoff, R.C., Brunet, S., Courneya, K.S. *et al.* (2007). The efficacy of stage-matched and standard public health materials for promoting physical activity in the workplace: the Physical Activity Workplace Study (PAWS). *American Journal of Health Promotion*, 21: 501–9.

Plotnikoff, R.C., McCargar, L.J, Wilson, P.M. *et al.* (2005). Efficacy of an e-mail intervention for the promotion of physical activity and nutrition behavior in the workplace context. *American Journal of Health Promotion*, 19: 422–9.

Pollock, K., Wilson, E., Porock, D. *et al.* (2007). Evaluating the impact of a cancer supportive care project in the community: patient and professional configurations of need. *Health and Social Care in the Community*, 15: 520–9.

Potter, J., Hami, F., Bryan, T. *et al.* (2003). Symptoms in 400 patients referred to palliative care services: prevalence and patterns. *Palliative Medicine*, 17: 310–14.

Potter, J.D., Slattery, M.L., Bostick, R.M. *et al.* (1993). Colon cancer: a review of the epidemiology. *Epidemiological Review*, 15: 499–545.

Pound, P., Bury, M., Gompertz, P. *et al.* (1994). Views of survivors of stroke on the benefits of physiotherapy. *Quality in Health Care*, 3: 69–74.

Powell-Griner, E., Anderson, J.E. and Murphy, W. (1997). State and sex-specific prevalence of selected characteristics behavioural risk factor surveillance system, 1994 and 1995. *Morbidity and Mortality Weekly Report*, Centres for Disease Control, surveillance summaries, 46: 1–31.

Power, R., Koopman, C., Volk, J. *et al.* (2003). Social support, substance use, and denial in relationship to antiretroviral treatment adherence among HIV-infected persons. *AIDS Patient Care and STDs*, 17: 245–52.

Prentice, A.M. and Jebb, S.A. (1995). Obesity in Britain: gluttony or sloth. *British Medical Journal*, 311: 437–9.

Prescott-Clarke, P. and Primatesta, P. (1998). *Health survey for England: the health of young people 1995–97*. London: The Stationery Office.

Price, D.D., Finniss, D.G. and Benedetti, F. (2008) A comprehensive review of the placebo effect: recent advances and current thought. *Annual Review of Psychology*, 59: 565–90.

Price, R.A. and Gottesman, I.I. (1991). Body fat in identical twins reared apart: roles for genes and environment. *Behavioral Genetics*, 21: 1–7.

Price, V.A. (1988). Research and clinical issues in treating Type A behavior. In B.K. Houston and C.R. Snyder (eds), *Type A Behavior Pattern: Research, Theory, and Practice*. New York: Wiley.

Prochaska, J.O. (1994). Strong and weak principles for progressing from precontemplation to action based on twelve problem behaviours. *Health Psychology*, 13: 47–51.

Prochaska, J.O. and di Clemente, C.C. (1984). *The Transtheoretical Approach: Crossing Traditional Boundaries of Therapy*. Homewood Ill.: Dow Jones Irwin.

Prochaska, J.O. and di Clemente, C.C. (1986). Towards a comprehensive model of change. In B.K. Houston and N. Heather (eds), *Treating Addictive Behaviours: Processes of Change*. New York: Plenum.

Prochaska, J.O. and Marcus, B.H. (1994). The transtheoretical model: applications to exercise. In R.K. Dishman (ed.), *Advances in Exercise Adherence*. Champaign, Ill.: Human Kinetics.

Prochaska, J.O., Norcross, J.C., Fowler, J.L. *et al.* (1992). Attendance and outcome in a worksite weight control program: processes and stages of change as process and predictor variables. *Addictive Behaviors*, 17: 35–45.

Prochaska, J.O., Velicer, W.F., Rossi, J.S. *et al.* (1994). Stages of change and decisional balance for 12 problem behaviours. *Health Psychology*, 13: 39–46.

Prohaska, T.R., Funch, D. and Blesch, K.S. (1990). Age patterns in symptom perception and illness behaviour among colorectal cancer patients. *Behavior, Health and Aging*, 1: 27–39.

Prohaska, T.R., Keller, M.L., Leventhal, E.A. *et al.* (1987). Impact of symptoms and aging attribution on emotions and coping. *Health Psychology*, 6: 495–514.

Project MATCH Research Group (1998). Matching alcoholism treatments to client heterogeneity: Project MATCH three-year drinking outcomes. *Alcoholism: Clinical and Experimental Research*, 22: 1300–11.

Ptacek, J.T.P. and Eberhardt, T.L. (1996). Breaking bad news: a review of the literature. *Journal of the American Medical Association*, 276: 496–502.

Ptacek, J.T., Ptacek, J.J. and Ellison, H. (2001). 'I'm sorry to tell you' – physicians' reports of breaking bad news. *Journal of Behavioral Medicine*, 24: 205–17.

Puccio, J.A., Belzer, M., Olson, J. *et al.* (2006). The use of cell phone reminder calls for assisting HIV-infected adolescents and young adults to adhere to highly active antiretroviral therapy: a pilot study. *AIDS Patient Care and STDS*, 20: 438–44.

Puska, P., Tuomilehto, J., Nissinen, A. *et al.* (1985). *The North Karelia Project: 20 Year Results and Experiences*. Helsinki: National Public Health Institutem.

Quah, S.-H. and Bishop, G.D. (1996). Seeking help for illness: the roles of cultural orientation and illness cognition. *Journal of Health Psychology*, 1: 209–22.

Quentin, W., Neubauer, S., Leidl, R. *et al.* (2007). Advertising bans as a means of tobacco control policy: a systematic literature review of time-series analyses. *International Journal of Public Health*, 52: 295–307.

Quick, J.D., Nelson, D.L., Matuszek, P.A.C. *et al.* (1996). Social support, secure attachments and health. In C.L. Cooper (ed.), *Handbook of Stress, Medicine and Health*. London: CRC Press.

Qureshi, M., Thacker, H.L., Litaker, D.G. *et al.* (2000). Differences in breast cancer screening rates: an issue of ethnicity or socioeconomics? *Journal of Women's Health and Gender Based Medicine*, 9: 1025–31.

Radley, A. (1994). *Making Sense of Illness: The Social Psychology of Health and Disease*. London: Sage.

Radley, A. (1996). Social psychology and health: framing the relationship. *Psychology and Health*, 11: 629–34.

Rafferty, Y., Friend, R. and Landsbergis, P.A. (2001). The association between job skill discretion, decision authority and burnout. *Work and Stress*, 15: 73–85.

Raftery, K.A., Smith-Coggins, R. and Chen, A.H. (1995). Gender-associated differences in emergency department pain management. *Annals of Emergency Medicine*, 26: 414–21.

Ragland, D.R. and Brand, R.J. (1988). Type A behaviour and mortality from coronary heart disease. *New England Journal of Medicine*, 318: 65–9.

Rahe, R. (1974). Life change and subsequent illness reports. In E.K.E. Gunderson and R. Rahe (eds), *Life Stress and Illness*. Springfield, Ill.: Charles Thomas.

Rahimi, A.R., Spertus, J.A., Reid, K.J. *et al.* (2007). Financial barriers to health care and outcomes after acute myocardial infarction. *Journal of the American Medical Association*, 297: 1063–72.

Rains, J.C., Penzien, D.B., McCrory, D.C. *et al.* (2005). Behavioral headache treatment: history, review of the empirical literature, and methodological critique. *Headache*, 45: S91–S108.

Ramirez, A., Craig, T., Watson, J. *et al.* (1989). Stress and relapse of breast cancer. *British Medical Journal*, 298: 291–3.

Ramirez, A.J., Westcombe, A.M., Burgess, C.C. *et al.* (1999). Factors predicting delayed presentation of symptomatic breast cancer: a systematic review. *The Lancet*, 353: 1119–26.

Ramnarayan, P., Roberts, G.C., Coren, M. *et al.* (2006). Assessment of the potential impact of a reminder system on the reduction of diagnostic errors: a quasi-experimental study. *BMC Medical Informatics and Decision Making*, 6: 22.

Rand, C.S. and Wise, R.A. (1994). Measuring adherence to asthma medication regimens. *American Journal of Respiratory and Critical Care Medicine*, 149 (suppl.): 69–76.

Rapp, S.R. and Chao, D. (2000). Appraisals of strain and of gain: effects on psychological wellbeing of caregivers of dementia patients. *Aging & Mental Health*, 4: 142–7.

Rasulo, D., Bajekal, M. and Yar, M. (2007). Inequalities in health expectancies in England and Wales – small area analysis from the 2001 Census. *Health Statistics Quarterly*, 34: 35–45.

Rawl, S.M., Given, B.A., Given, C.W. *et al.* (2002). Intervention to improve psychological functioning for newly diagnosed patients with cancer. *Oncology Nursing Forum*, 29: 967–75.

RCN (2002). Royal College of Nursing Congress 2002 Report summaries. *Nursing Standard*, 16: 4–9.

Reddy, D.M., Fleming, R. and Adesso, V.J. (1992). Gender and health. In S. Maes, H. Leventhal and M. Johnston (eds), *International Review of Health Psychology*, Vol. 1. Chichester: Wiley.

Rees, K., Bennett, P., Vedhara, K. *et al.* (2004). Stress management for coronary heart disease. *The Cochrane Library*. Issue 2. Chichester: John Wiley & Sons.

Reeve J., Menon, D. and Corabian, P. (1996). Transcutaneous electrical nerve stimulation (TENS): a technology assessment. *International Journal of Technology Assessment in Health Care*, 12: 299–324.

Rennemark, M. and Hagberg, B. (1999). What makes old people perceive symptoms of illness? The impact of psychological and social factors. *Aging & Mental Health*, 3: 79–87.

Renner, B. and Schwarzer, R. (2003). Social-cognitive factors in health behaviour change. In J. Suls and K. Wallston (eds), *Social Foundations of Health and Illness*. Oxford: Blackwell.

Renzi, C., Peticca, L. and Pescatori, M. (2000). The use of relaxation techniques in the perioperative management of proctological patients: preliminary results. *International Journal of Colorectal Diseases*, 15: 313–16.

Resnicow, K., Jackson, A., Wang, T. *et al.* (2001). Motivational interviewing intervention to increase fruit and vegetable intake through black churches: results of the Eat for Life trial. *American Journal of Public Health*, 91: 1686–93.

Rhodes, F. and Wolitski, B. (1990). Perceived effectiveness of fear appeals in AIDS education: relationship to ethnicity, gender, age and group membership. *AIDS Education and Prevention*, 2: 1–11.

Rhodewalt, F. and Zone, J.B. (1989). Appraisal of life change, depression, and illness in hardy and non-hardy women. *Journal of Personality and Social Psychology*, 56: 81–8.

Ricciardelli, L.A. and McCabe, M.P. (2001). Children's body image concerns and eating disturbance: a review of the literature. *Clinical Psychology Review*, 21: 325–44.

Rice, P.L. (1992). *Stress and Health*. California, Brooks/Cole.

Richard, R., van der Pligt, J. and de Vries, N. (1996). Anticipated regret and time perspective: changing sexual risk-taking behaviour. *Journal of Behavioural Decision Making*, 9: 185–99.

Richards, J., Fisher, P. and Conner, F. (1989). The warnings on cigarette packages are ineffective. *Journal of the American Medical Association*, 261: 45.

Richards, M.A., Westcombe, A.M., Love, S.B. *et al.* (1999). Influence of delay on survival in patients with breast cancer: a systematic review. *The Lancet*, 353: 1119–26.

Richardson, J. (2000). The use of randomised control trials in complementary therapies: exploring the issues. *Journal of Advanced Nursing*, 32: 398–406.

Richardson, K.M. and Rothstein, H.R. (2008). Effects of occupational stress management intervention programs: a meta-analysis. *Journal of Occupational Health Psychology*, 13: 69–93.

Richmond, R.L., Kehoe, L. and de Almeida Neto, A.C. (1997). Effectiveness of a 24-hour transdermal nicotine patch in conjunction with a cognitive behavi-oural programme: one year outcome. *Addiction*, 92: 27–31.

Ridgeway, V. and Mathews, A. (1982). Psychological preparation for surgery: a comparison of methods. *British Journal of Clinical Psychology*, 21: 271–80.

Riemsma, R.P., Taal, E. and Rasker, J.J. (2003). Group education for patients with rheumatoid arthritis and their partners. *Arthritis and Rheumatism*, 49: 556–66.

Rigby, K., Brown, M., Anagnostou, P. *et al.* (1989). Shock tactics to counter AIDS: the Australian experience. *Psychology and Health*, 3: 145–59.

Riley, J.L. III, Wade, J.B., Myers, C.D. *et al.* (2002). Racial/ethnic differences in the experience of chronic pain. *Pain*, 100: 291–8.

Rivis, A. and Sheeran, P. (2003). Social influences and the theory of planned behaviour: evidence for a direct relationship between prototypes and young people's exercise behaviour. *Psychology and Health*, 18: 567–83.

Roberts, C.S., Cox, C.E., Reintgen, D.S. *et al.* (1994). Influence of physician communication on newly diagnosed breast patients' psychologic adjustment and decision-making. *Cancer*, 74: 336–41.

Roberts, J. and Rowland, M. (1981). *Hypertension in Adults 25–74 years of age, United States, 1971–1975*. Hyattsville, Md: National Center for Health Statistics (Vital and Health Statistics, Series II: Data from the National Health Survey, No. 221). DHHS publication No. 81–1671.

Robinson, R.G. (1998). *The Clinical Neuropsychiatry of Stroke*. Cambridge: Cambridge University Press.

Roesch, S.C. and Weiner, B. (2001). A meta-analytic review of coping with illness: do causal attributions matter? *Journal of Psychosomatic Research*, 50: 205–19.

Rogers, C.R. (1961). *On Becoming a Person*. Boston: Houghton Mifflin.

Rogers, E. (1983). *Diffusion of Innovations*. New York: Free Press.

Rogers, G., Curry, M., Oddy, J. *et al.* (2003). Depressive disorders and unprotected casual anal sex among Australian homosexually active men in primary care. *HIV Medicine*, 4: 271–5.

Rogers, R.W. (1983). Cognitive and physiological responses to fear appeals and attitude change: a revised theory of protection motivation. In J.T. Cacioppo and R.E. Petty (eds), *Social Psychophysiology: A Source Book*. New York: Guilford Press.

Romelsjö, A. and Branting, M. (2000). Consumption of illegal alcohol among adolescents in Stockholm county. *Contemporary Drug Problems*, 27: 315–33.

Rosch, P.J. (1994). Can stress cause coronary heart disease? (editorial). *Stress Medicine*, 10: 207–10.

Rosch, P.J. (1996) Stress and sleep: some startling and sobering statistics. *Stress Medicine*, 12: 207–10.

Rose, J.S., Chassin, L., Presson, C.C. *et al.* (1996). Prospective predictors of quit attempts and smoking cessation in young adults. *Health Psychology*, 15: 261–8.

Rose, S., Bisson, J. and Wessely, S. (2001). Psychological debriefing for preventing post traumatic stress disorder (PTSD). *Cochrane Database Systematic Review*, 3.

Rosenfeld, B., Breitbart, W., McDonald, M.V. *et al.* (1996). Pain in ambulatory AIDS patients II: impact of pain on psychological functioning and quality of life. *Pain*, 68: 323–8.

Rosengren, A., Orth-Gomér, K., Wedel, H. *et al.* (1993). Stressful life events, social support, and mortality in men born in 1933. *British Medical Journal*, 307: 1102–5.

Rosenman, R.H. (1978). Role of Type A pattern in the pathogenesis of ischaemic heart disease and modification for prevention. *Advances in Cardiology*, 25: 34–46.

Rosenman, R.H. (1996). Personality, behavior patterns, and heart disease. In C. Cooper (ed.), *Handbook of Stress, Medicine and Health*. Florida: CRC Press.

Rosenman, R.H., Brand, R.J., Jenkins, C.D. *et al.* (1975). Coronary heart disease in the Western Collaborative Group study; follow-up experience after 8 and a half years. *Journal of the American Medical Association*, 233: 872–7.

Rosenman, R.H., Brand, R.J., Sholtz, R.I. *et al.* (1976). Multivariate prediction of coronary heart disease during 8.5 year follow-up in the Western Collaborative Group study. *The American Journal of Cardiology*, 37: 903–10.

Rosenstock, I.M. (1966). Why people use health services. *Milbank Memorial Fund Quarterly*, 44: 94–124.

Rosenstock, I.M. (1974). The health belief model and preventive health behaviour. *Health Education Monographs*, 2: 354–86.

Rosenzweig, M.R., Leiman, A.L. and Breedlove, S.M. (1996). *Biological Psychology: An Introduction to Behavioural, Cognitive, and Clinical Neuroscience*. Harlow, Essex: Pearson Education/Prentice Hall.

Ross, L., Boesen, E.H., Dalton, S.O. and Johansen, C. (2002). Mind and cancer: does psychosocial intervention improve survival and psychological well-being? *European Journal of Cancer*, 38: 1447–57.

Roth, M.L., Tripp, D.A., Harrison, M.H. *et al.* (2007). Demographic and psychosocial predictors of acute perioperative pain for total knee arthroplasty. *Pain Research and Management*, 12: 185–94.

Roth, S. and Cohen, L.J. (1986). Approach, avoidance, and coping with stress. *American Psychologist*, 41: 813–19.

Rotter, J.B. (1966). Generalized expectancies for the internal versus external control of reinforcement. *Psychological Monographs*, 90: 1–28.

Roy, R., Symonds, R.P., Kymar, D.M. *et al.* (2005). The use of denial in an ethnically diverse British cancer population: a cross-sectional study. *British Journal of Cancer*, 91: 1–5.

Rovelli, M., Palmeri, D., Vossler, E. *et al.* (1989). Noncompliance in organ transplant recipients. *Transplant Proceedings*, 21: 833–4.

Royal College of Physicians (1995). *Alcohol and the Public Health*. London: Macmillan.

Roye, C., Perlmutter Silverman, P. & Krauss B. (2007). A brief, low-cost, theory-based intervention to promote dual method use by black and Latina female adolescents: a randomized clinical trial. *Health Education and Behavior*, 34: 608–21.

Ruberman, W., Weinblatt, E., Goldberg, J.D. *et al.* (1984). Psychosocial resilience and protective mechanisms. *American Journal of Orthopsychiatry*, 57: 316–30.

Rudat, K. (1994). *Black and Minority Ethnic Groups in England: Health and Lifestyles*. London: Health Education Authority.

Russell, M.A., Wilson, C. and Baker, C.D. (1979). Effect of general practitioners' advice against smoking. *British Medical Journal*, 2: 231–5.

Rutter, D.R. (2000). Attendance and reattendance for breast cancer screening: a prospective 3-year test of the theory of planned behaviour. *British Journal of Health Psychology*, 2: 199–216.

Rutter, D. and Quine, L. (2002). *Changing Health Behaviour*. Buckingham: Open University Press.

Rutter, D.R., Steadman, L. and Quine, L. (2006). An implementation intentions intervention to increase uptake of mammography. *Annals of Behavioral Medicine*, 32: 127–34.

Rystedt, L.W., Devereux, J. and Furnham, A.F. (2004). Are lay theories of work stress related to distress? A longitudinal study in the British workforce. *Work & Stress*, 18: 245–54.

Safer, M.A., Tharps, Q.J., Jackson, T.C. *et al.* (1979). Determinants of three stages of delay in seeking care at a medical setting. *Medical Care*, 7: 11–29.

Safren, S.A., Otto, M.W. and Worth, J.L. (2001). Two strategies to increase adherence to HIV antiretroviral medication: Life-Steps and medication monitoring. *Behaviour Research and Therapy*, 39: 1151–62.

Safren, S.A., Radomsky, A.S., Otto, M.W. *et al.* (2002). Predictors of psychological well-being in a diverse sample of HIV-positive patients receiving highly active antiretroviral therapy. *Psychosomatics*, 43: 478–84.

Salander, P. (2007). Attributions of lung cancer: my own illness is hardly caused by smoking. *Psycho-Oncology*, 16: 587–92.

Sales, J., Duffy, J., Plant, M. *et al.* (1989). Alcohol consumption, cigarette sales and mortality in the United Kingdom: an analysis of the period 1970–1985. *Drug and Alcohol Dependence*, 24: 155–60.

Salovey, P., Rothman, A.J., Detweiler, J.B. *et al.* (2000). Emotional states and physical health. *American Psychologist*, 55: 110–21.

Samkoff, J.S. and Jacques, C.H. (1991). A review of studies concerning effects of sleep deprivation and fatigue on residents' performance. *Academic Medicine*, 66: 687–93.

Sanders, S.H., Brena, S.F., Spier, C.J. *et al.* (1992). Chronic low back pain patients around the world: cross-cultural similarities and differences. *Journal of Clinical Pain*, 8: 317–23.

Sanderson, C. and Jemmott, J. (1996). Moderation and mediation of HIV-prevention interventions: relationship status, intentions, and condom use among college students. *Journal of Applied Social Psychology*, 26: 2076–99.

Sanderson, C.A. and Yopyk, D.J. (2007). Improving condom use intentions and behavior by changing perceived partner norms: an evaluation of condom promotion videos for college students. *Health Psychology*, 26: 481–7.

Sapolsky, R. (1986). Glucocorticoid toxicity in the hippocampus: reversal by supplementation with brain fuels. *Journal of Neuroscience*, 6: 2240–4.

Sapolsky, R.M. (1994). *Why Zebras Don't Get Ulcers*. New York: W.H. Freeman.

Sapolsky, R.M. (1996). Why stress is bad for your brain. *Science*, 273: 749–50.

Sapolsky, R.M., Krey, L.C. and McEwan, B.S. (1986). The neuroendocrinology of stress and ageing: the glucocorticoid cascade hypothesis. *Endocrine Reviews*, 7: 284–301.

Sarason, B.R., Sarason, I.G. and Pierce, G.R. (1990). Traditional views of social support and their impact on assessment. In B.R. Sarason, I.G. Sarason and G.R. Pierce (eds), *Social Support: An Interactional View*. New York: Wiley.

Saremi, A., Hanson, R.L., Tulloch-Reid, M. *et al.* (2004). Alcohol consumption predicts hypertension but not diabetes. *Journal of Studies of Alcohol*, 65: 184–90.

Sargent, J.D., Dalton, M. and Beach, M. (2000). Exposure to cigarette promotions and smoking uptake in adolescents: evidence of a dose-response relation. *Tobacco Control*, 9: 163–8.

Sarkar, U., Piette, J.D., Gonzales, R. *et al.* (2007). Preferences for self-management support: findings from a survey of diabetes patients in safety-net health systems. *Patient Education and Counseling*, 70: 102–10.

Sarkeala, T., Heinavaara, S. and Anttila, A. (2008). Organised mammography screening reduces breast cancer mortality: a cohort study from Finland. *International Journal of Cancer*, 122: 614–9.

Sarkisian, C.A., Liu, H.H., Ensrud, K.E. *et al.* (2001). Correlates of attribution of new disability to 'old age'. *Journal of the American Geriatric Society*, 49: 134–41.

Saunders, C. and Baines, M. (1983). *Living with Dying: The Management of Terminal Disease*. Oxford: Oxford University Press.

Saunders, R.P., Pate, R.R., Felton, G. *et al.* (1997). Development of questionnaires to measure psychosocial influences on children's physical activity. *Preventive Medicine*, 26: 241–7.

Sausen, K.P., Lovallo, W.R., Pincomb, G.A. *et al.* (1992). Cardiovascular responses to occupational stress in medical students: a paradigm for ambulatory monitoring studies. *Health Psychology*, 11: 55–60.

Savage, R. and Armstrong, D. (1990). Effect of a general practitioner's consulting style on patients' satisfaction: a controlled study. *British Medical Journal*, 301: 968–70.

Savage, S.A. and Clarke, V.A. (1996). Factors associated with screening mammography and breast self-examination intentions. *Health Education Research*, 11: 409–21.

Scharloo, M. and Kaptein, A. (1997). Measurement of illness perceptions in patients with chronic somatic illness: a review of the literature. In K.J. Petrie and J. Weinman (eds), *Perceptions of Health and Illness: Current Research and Applications*. London: Harwood Academic.

Scharloo, M., Kaptein, A.A., Weinman, J. *et al.* (1998). Illness perceptions, coping and functioning in patients with rheumatoid arthritis, chronic obstructive pulmonary disease, and psoriasis. *Journal of Psychosomatic Research*, 44: 573–85.

Scheier, M.F. and Carver, C.S. (1985). Optimism, coping and health: assessment and implications of generalized outcome expectancies. *Health Psychology*, 4: 219–47.

Scheier, M.F. and Carver, C.S. (1992). Effects of optimism on psychological and physical well-being: theoretical overview and empirical update. *Cognitive Therapy Research*, 16: 201–28.

Scheier, M.F., Weintraub, J.K. and Carver, C.S. (1986). Coping with stress: divergent strategies of optimists and pessimists. *Journal of Personality and Social Psychology*, 51: 1257–1264.

Scherwitz, L., Perkins, L., Chesney, M. *et al.* (1992). Hostility and health behaviours in young adults: the CARDIA study. *American Journal of Epidemiology*, 136: 136–45.

Schiaffino, K.M. and Cea, C.D. (1995). Assessing chronic illness representations: the implicit models of illness questionnaire. *Journal of Behavioral Medicine*, 18: 531–48.

Schlenk, E.A., Dunbar-Jacob, J. and Engberg, S. (2004). Medication non-adherence among older adults: a review of strategies and interventions for improvement. *Journal of Gerontological Nursing*, 30: 33–43.

Schmaling, K.B., Smith, W.R. and Buchwald, D.S. (2000). Significant other responses are associated with fatigue and functional status among patients with chronic fatigue syndrome. *Psychosomatic Medicine*, 62: 444–50.

Schneider, R.J., Casey, J. and Kohn, R. (2000). Motivational versus confrontational interviewing: a comparison of substance abuse assessment practices at employee assistance programs. *Journal of Behavioral Health Service Research*, 27: 60–74.

Schneiderman, N., Antoni, M.H. and Saab, P.G. (2001). Health psychology: psychosocial and bio-behavioral aspects of chronic disease management. *Annual Review of Psychology*, 52: 555–80.

Schofield, M.J., Lynagh, M. and Mishra, G. (2003). Evaluation of a Health Promoting Schools program to reduce smoking in Australian secondary schools. *Health Education and Research*, 18: 678–92.

Schofield, P.E., Butow, P.N., Thompson, J.F. *et al.* (2003). Psychological responses of patients receiving a diagnosis of cancer. *Annals of Oncology*, 14: 48–56.

Scholte op Reimer, J., de Haan, R.J., Rijners, P.T. *et al.* (1998). The burden of caregiving in partners of long-term stroke survivors. *Stroke*, 29: 1605–11.

Schou, I., Ekeberg, O., Rulan, C.M. *et al.* (2004). Pessimism as a predictor of emotional morbidity one year following breast cancer surgery. *Psycho-Oncology*, 13: 309–20.

Schouten, B.C., Hoogstraten, J. and Eijkman, M.A. (2003). Patient participation during dental consultations: the influence of patients' characteristics and dentists' behavior. *Community and Dental Oral Epidemiology*, 31: 368–77.

Schröder, C., Johnston, M., Morrison, V. *et al.* (2007). Health condition, impairment, activity limitations: Relationship with emotions and control cognitions in people with disabling conditions. *Rehabilitation Psychology*, 52: 280–89.

Schulz, R. and Quittner, A.L. (1998). Caregiving for children and adults with chronic conditions: introduction to the special issue. *Health Psychology*, 17: 107–11.

Schulz, R., Bookwala, J., Knapp, J.E. *et al.* (1996). Pessimism, age, and cancer mortality. *Psychology and Aging*, 11: 304–9.

Schulz, R., O'Brien, A., Bookwala, J. *et al.* (1995). Psychiatric and physical morbidity effects of dementia caregiving: prevalence, correlates and causes. *The Gerontologist*, 35: 771–91.

Schulz, R., Tompkins, C.A. and Rau, M.T. (1988). A longitudinal study of the psychosocial impact of stroke on primary support persons. *Psychology and Aging*, 3: 131–41.

Schulz, U. and Mohamed, N.E. (2004). Turning the tide: benefit finding after cancer surgery. *Social Science and Medicine*, 59: 653–62.

Schur, E.A., Sanders, M. and Steiner, H. (2000). Body dissatisfaction and dieting in young children. *International Journal of Eating Disorders*, 27: 74–82.

Schwartz, C., Sprangers, M., Carey, A. *et al.* (2004). Exploring response shift in longitudinal data. *Psychology & Health*, 9: 161–80.

Schwartz, G.E. and Weiss, S. (1977). What is behavioral medicine? *Psychosomatic Medicine*, 36: 377–81.

Schwartz, B.S., Stewart, W.F., Simon, D. *et al.* (1998). Epidemiology of tension-type headache. *Journal of the American Medical Association*, 279: 381–3.

Schwarzer, R. (1992). Self efficacy in the adoption and maintenance of health behaviours: theoretical approaches and a new model. In R. Schwarzer (ed.), *Self Efficacy: Thought Control of Action*. Washington: Hemisphere.

Schwarzer, R. (1994). Optimism, vulnerability, and self-beliefs as health-related cognitions: a systematic overview. *Psychology and Health*, 9: 161–80.

Schwarzer, R. (2001). Social-cognitive factors in changing health-related behavior. *Current Directions in Psychological Science*, 10: 47–51.

Schwarzer, R. and Leppin, A. (1991). Social support and health: a theoretical and empirical overview. *Journal of Social and Personal Relationships*, 8: 99–127.

Schwarzer, R. and Renner, B. (2000). Social-cognitive predictors of health behavior: action self-efficacy and coping self-efficacy. *Health Psychology*, 19: 487–95.

Scollay, P., Doucett, M., Perry, M. *et al.* (1992). AIDS education of college students: the effect of an HIV-positive lecturer. *AIDS Education and Prevention*, 4: 160–71.

Scott, N.W., Fayers, P.M., Aaronson, N.K. *et al.* (2008). The relationship between overall quality of life and its subdimensions was influenced by culture: analysis of an international database. *Journal of Clinical Epidemiology*, 61: 788–95.

Scottish Executive (1999). *Fair Shares for All*. Report of the National Review of Resource Allocation for the NHS in Scotland, chaired by Professor Sir John Arbuthnott, principal and vice-chancellor of Strathclyde University. Edinburgh: HMSO.

Seale, C. (1991). A comparison of hospice and conventional care. *Social Science and Medicine*, 32: 147–52.

Seale, C. and Kelly, M. (1997). A comparison of hospice and hospital care for the spouses of people who die. *Palliative Care*, 11: 101–6.

Searle, A. and Bennett, P. (2001). Psychological factors and inflammatory bowel disease: a review of a decade of literature. *Psychology, Health and Medicine*, 6: 121–35.

Searle, B., Bright, J.E.H. and Bochner, S. (2001). Helping people to sort it out: the role of social support in the Job Strain Model. *Work and Stress*, 15: 328–46.

Sears, S.F., Sowell, L.D., Kuhl, E.A. *et al.* (2007). The ICD shock and stress management program: a randomized trial of psychosocial treatment to optimize quality of life in ICD patients. *Pacing and Clinical Electrophysiology*, 30: 858–64.

Segan, C.J., Borland, R. and Greenwood, K.M. (2002). Do transtheoretical model measures predict the transition from preparation to action in smoking cessation? *Psychology and Health*, 17: 417–35.

Segerstrom, S.C. and Smith, T.W. (2006). Physiological pathways from personality to health: the cardiovascular and immune systems. In M.E. Vollrath (ed.), *Handbook of Personality and Health*. Chichester: John Wiley & Sons (pp. 175–94).

Segerstrom, S.C., Taylor, S.E., Kemeny, M.E. *et al.* (1998). Optimism is associated with mood, coping, and immune change in response to stress. *Journal of Personality and Social Psychology*, 74: 1646–55.

Seidman, D.F. and Covey, L.S. (eds) (1999). *Helping the Hard-core Smoker. A Clinician's Guide*. Mahwah, NJ: Lawrence Erlbaum.

Seligman, M.E.P. (2003). Positive psychology: fundamental assumptions. *The Psychologist*, 16: 126–7.

Seligman, M.E.P. and Csikszentmihalyi, M. (2000). Positive psychology: an introduction. *American Psychologist*, 55: 5–14.

Selye, H. (1956). *The Stress of Life*. New York: McGraw-Hill.

Selye, H. (1974). *Stress without Distress*. Philadelphia: Lipincott.

Selye, H. (1991). History and present status of the stress concept. In A. Monat and R.S. Lazarus (eds), *Stress and Coping*. New York: Columbia University Press.

Semmer, N.K. (2006) Personality, stress, and coping. In M.E. Vollrath (ed.) *Handbook of Personality and Health*. London: John Wiley & Sons (pp. 73–113).

Shacham, S. (1983). A shortened version of the Profile of Mood States. *Journal of Personality Assessment*, 47: 305–6.

Shaffer, J.W., Graves, P.L., Swank, R.T. and Pearson, T.A. (1987). Clustering of personality traits in youth and the subsequent development of cancer among physicians. *Journal of Behavioral Medicine*, 10: 441–7.

Shakeshaft, A.P., Bowman, J.A. and Sanson-Fisher, R.W. (1999). A comparison of two retrospective measures of weekly alcohol consumption: diary and quantity/frequency index. *Alcohol and Alcoholism*, 34: 636–45.

Shaper, A.G., Wannamethee, G. and Walker, M. (1994). Alcohol and coronary heart disease: a perspective from the British Regional Heart Study. *International Journal of Epidemiology*, 23: 482–94.

Shapiro, F. (1995). *Eye Movement Desensitisation and Reprocessing: Basic Principles*. New York: Guilford Press.

Sharp, T.J. (2001). Chronic pain: a reformulation of the cognitive-behavioural model. *Behaviour Research and Therapy*, 39: 787–800.

Sharpe, P.A., Granner, M.L., Hutto, B. *et al.* (2004). Association of environmental factors to meeting physical activity recommendations in two South Carolina counties. *American Journal of Health Promotion*, 18: 251–7.

Sheeran, P. (2002). Intention–behaviour relations: a conceptual and empirical review. In M. Hewstone and W. Stroebe (eds), *European Review of Social Psychology*, Vol. 11. Chichester: Wiley.

Sheeran, P. and Abraham, C. (1996). The health belief model. In M. Conner and P. Norman (eds), *Predicting Health Behaviour*. Buckingham: Open University Press.

Sheeran, P. and Orbell, S. (1996). How confidently can we infer health beliefs from questionnaire responses? *Psychology and Health*, 11: 273–90.

Sheeran, P. and Orbell, S. (1998). Do intentions predict condom use? Meta-analysis and examination of six moderator variables. *British Journal of Social Psychology*, 37: 231–50.

Sheeran, P. and Orbell, S. (1999). Implementation intentions and repeated behaviour: augmenting the predictive validity of the theory of planned behaviour. *European Journal of Social Psychology*, 29: 349–69.

Sheeran, P. and Orbell, S. (2000). Using implementation intentions to increase attendance for cervical cancer screening. *Health Psychology*, 19: 283–9.

Sheeran, P., Abraham, C.S. and Orbell, S. (1999). Psychosocial correlates of heterosexual condom use: a meta-analysis. *Psychological Bulletin*, 125: 90–132.

Sheffield, D., Biles, P.L., Orom, H. *et al.* (2000). Race and sex differences in cutaneous pain perception. *Psychosomatic Medicine*, 62: 517–23.

Sheppard, B.H., Hartwick, J. and Warshaw, P.R. (1988). The theory of reasoned action: a meta-analysis of past research with recommendations for modifications and future research. *Journal of Consumer Research*, 15: 325–43.

Sherbourne, C.D., Hays, R.D., Ordway, L. *et al.* (1992). Antecedents of adherence to medical recommendations: results from the Medical Outcomes Study. *Journal of Behavioral Medicine*, 15: 447–68.

Sherman, A.C. and Simonton, S. (2001). Coping with cancer in the family. *The Family Journal: Counselling and Therapy for Couples and Families*, 9: 193–200.

Sherr, L. (1987). An evaluation of the UK government health education campaign on AIDS, *Psychology and Health*, 1: 61–72.

Sherwood, A. and Turner, J.R. (1992). A conceptual and methodological overview of cardiovascular reactivity research. In J.R. Turner, A. Sherwood and K.C. Light (eds), *Individual Differences in Cardiovascular Responses to Stress*. New York, Plenum.

Shewchuck, R.M., Richards, J.S. and Elliott, T.R. (1998). Dynamic processes in health outcomes among caregivers of patients with spinal cord injuries. *Health Psychology*, 17: 125–9.

Shifren, K. and Hooker, K. (1995). Stability and change in optimism: a study among spouse caregivers. *Experimental Aging Research*, 21: 59–76.

Shilts, R. (2000). *And the Band Played on: Politics, People and the AIDS Epidemic*. London: Penguin.

Shinar, D., Schechtman, E. and Compton, R. (1999). Trends in safe driving behaviors and in relation to trends in health maintenance behaviors in the USA: 1985–1995. *Accident Analysis and Prevention*, 31: 497–503.

Shorey, H.S., Little, T.D., Snyder, C.R. *et al.* (2007). Hope and personal growth initiative: A comparison of positive, future-oriented constructs. *Personality and Individual Differences*, 43: 1917–1926.

Siegel, K. and Gorey, E. (1997). HIV infected women: Barriers to AZT use. *Social Science and Medicine*, 45: 15–22.

Siegel, K., Karus, D.G., Raveis, V.H. *et al.* (1996). Depressive distress among the spouses of terminally ill cancer patients. *Cancer Practice*, 4: 25–30.

Siegel, K., Scrimshaw, E.W. and Dean, L. (1999). Symptom interpretation and medication adherence among late middle-age and older HIV-infected adults. *Journal of Health Psychology*, 4: 247–57.

Siegert, R.J. and Abernethy, D.A. (2005). Depression in multiple sclerosis: a review. *Journal of Neurology, Neurosurgery and Psychiatry*, 76: 469–75.

Siegrist, J., Peter, R., Junge, A. *et al.* (1990). Low status control, high effort at work and ischemic heart disease: prospective evidence from blue collar men. *Social Science and Medicine*, 35: 1127–34.

Sieverding, M., Weidner, G., von Volkmann, B. *et al.* (2005). Cardiovascular reactivity in a simulated job interview: the role of gender role self-concept. *International Journal of Behavioral Medicine*, 12: 1–10.

Sikkema, K.J., Kelly, J.A., Winett, R.A. *et al.* (2000). Outcomes of a randomized community-level HIV-prevention intervention for women living in 18 low-income housing developments. *American Journal of Public Health*, 90: 53–7.

Silverman, D. (1987). *Communication and Medical Practice: Social Relations and the Clinic*. London: Sage.

Simon, J.A., Carmody, T.P., Hudes, E.S. *et al.* (2003). Intensive smoking cessation counseling versus minimal counseling among hospitalized smokers treated with transdermal nicotine replacement: a randomized trial. *American Journal of Medicine*, 114: 555–62.

Simoni, J.M., Pantalone, D.W., Plummer, M.D. *et al.* (2007). A randomized controlled trial of a peer support intervention targeting antiretroviral medication adherence and depressive symptomatology in HIV-positive men and women. *Health Psychology*, 26: 488–95.

Singh, R.B., Sharma, J.P., Rastogi V. *et al.* (1997). Prevalence of coronary artery disease and coronary risk factors in rural and urban populations of north India. *European Heart Journal*, 18: 1728–35.

Singh, R.K., Panday, H.P. and Singh, R.H. (2003). Irritable bowel syndrome: challenges ahead. *Current Science*, 84: 1525–33.

Skarstein, J., Aass, N., Fossa, S.D. *et al.* (2000). Anxiety and depression in cancer patients: relation between the Hospital Anxiety and Depression Scale and the European Organization for Research and Treatment of Cancer Core Quality of Life Questionnaire. *Journal of Psychosomatic Research*, 49: 27–34.

Skelton, D.A., Young, A., Walker, A. *et al.* (1999). *Physical Activity in Later Life: Further Analysis of the Allied Dunbar National Fitness Survey and the Health Education Authority National Survey of Activity and Health*. London: Health Education Authority.

Skevington, S.M. (1990). A standardised scale to measure beliefs about controlling pain (BPCQ): a preliminary study. *Psychology & Health*, 4: 221–32.

Skoffer, B. (2007). Low back pain in 15- to 16-year-old children in relation to school furniture and carrying of the school bag. *Spine*, 32: E713–7.

Slavin, S., Batrouney, C. and Murphy, D. (2007). Fear appeals and treatment side-effects: an effective combination for HIV prevention? *AIDS Care*, 19: 130–7.

Sloper, P. (2000). Predictors of distress in parents of children with cancer: a prospective study. *Journal of Pediatric Psychology*, 25: 79–92.

Smedslund, G. and Rundmo, T. (1999). Is Grossarth-Maticek's coronary prone type II an independent predictor of myocardial infarction? *Personality and Individual Differences*, 27: 1231–42.

Smee, C., Parsonage, M., Anderson, R. *et al.* (1992). *Effects of tobacco advertising on tobacco consumption: a discussion document reviewing the evidence.* London: Department of Health.

Smith, A. and Roberts, K. (2003). Interventions for post-traumatic stress disorder and psychological distress in emergency ambulance personnel: a review of the literature. *Emergency Medical Journal*, 20: 75–8.

Smith, C., Roberts, J.L. and Pendelton, L.L. (1988). Booze on the box. The portrayal of alcohol on British television: a content analysis. *Health Education Research*, 3: 267–72.

Smith, C.A. and Lazarus, R.S. (1993). Appraisal components, core relational themes, and the emotions. *Cognition and Emotion*, 7: 233–69.

Smith, C.A., Wallston, K.A., Dwyer, K.A. *et al.* (1997). Beyond good or bad coping: a multi-dimensional examination of coping with pain in persons with rheumatoid arthritis. *Annals of Behavioral Medicine*, 19: 11–21.

Smith, H., Gooding, S., Brown, R. *et al.* (1998). Evaluation of readability and accuracy of information leaflets in general practices for patients with asthma. *British Medical Journal*, 317: 264–5.

Smith, M.Y., Redd, W.H., Peyer, C. *et al.* (1999). Post-traumatic stress disorder in cancer: a review. *Psycho-Oncology*, 8: 521–37.

Smith, T.W. (1994). Concepts and methods on the study of anger, hostility and health. In A.W. Siegman and T.W. Smith (eds), *Anger, Hostility and the Heart*. Hillsdale, NJ: Lawrence Erlbaum.

Smith, T.W., Gallo, L.C. and Ruiz, J.M. (2003). Toward a social psychophysiology of cardiovascular reactivity: interpersonal concepts and methods in the study of stress and coronary disease. In J. Suls and K. Wallston (eds), *Social Psychological Foundations of Health and Illness*. Oxford: Blackwell.

Smyth, J.M., Stone, A.A., Hurewitz, A. *et al.* (1999). Effects of writing about stressful experiences on symptom reduction in patients with asthma or rheumatoid arthritis: a randomized trial. *Journal of the American Medical Association*, 281: 1304–9.

Snell, J.L. and Buck, E.L. (1996). Increasing cancer screening: a meta analysis. *Preventive Medicine*, 25: 702–7.

Snow, P.C. and Bruce, D.D. (2003). Cigarette smoking in teenage girls: exploring the role of peer reputations, self concept and coping. *Health Education Research*, 18: 439–52.

Snyder, C.R. (1989). Reality negotiation: from excuses to hope and beyond. *Journal of Social and Clinical Psychology*, 8: 130–57.

Snyder, C. and Lopez, S.J. (2005). *Handbook of Positive Psychology*. New edition, USA: Oxford University Press

Snyder, C.R., Irving, L.M. and Anderson, J.R. (1991). Hope and health. In D.R. Forsyth and C.R. Snyder (eds), *Handbook of Social and Clinical Psychology: The Health Perspective* (pp. 285–305). Elmsford, NY: Pergamon Press.

Snyder, C.R., Lehman, K.A., Kluck, B. *et al.* (2006). Hope for rehabilitation and vice versa. *Rehabilitation Psychology*, 51: 89–112.

Soames-Job, R.F. (1988). Effective and ineffective use of fear in health promotion campaigns. *American Journal of Public Health*, 78: 163–7.

Solmes, M. and Turnbull, O.H. (2002). *The Brain and the Inner Mind: An Introduction to the Neuroscience of Subjective Wellbeing*. New York: Other Press/Karnac.

Solomon, R.L. (1977). Addiction: an opponent-process theory of acquired motivation. The affective dynamics of addiction. In J.D. Maser (ed.), *Psychopathology: Experimental Models*. San Francisco: W.H. Freeman.

Sorensen, G., Morris, D.M., Hunt, M.K. *et al.* (1992). Work-site nutrition intervention and employees' dietary habits: the Treatwell program. *American Journal of Public Health*, 82: 877–80.

Sorensen, G., Stoddard, A., Hunt, M.K. *et al.* (1998). The effects of a health promotion–health protection intervention on behavior change: the WellWorks Study. *American Journal of Public Health*, 88: 1685–90.

Sorensen, G., Stoddard, A., Peterson, K. *et al.* (1999). Increasing fruit and vegetable consumption through worksites and families in the Treatwell 5-a-day study. *American Journal of Public Health*, 89: 54–60.

Soria, R., Legido, A., Escolano, C. *et al.* (2006). A randomised controlled trial of motivational interviewing for smoking cessation. *British Journal of General Practice*, 56: 768–74.

Sorlie, P.D., Backlund, E. and Keller, J.B. (1995). US mortality by economic, demographic, and social characteristics: the National Longitudinal Mortality Study. *American Journal of Public Health*, 85: 949–56.

Sparks, P. and Shepherd, R. (1992). Self-identity and the theory of planned behaviour: assessing the role of identification with green consumerism. *Social Psychology Quarterly*, 55: 388–99.

Sparks, P., Conner, M., James, R. *et al.* (2001). Ambivalence about health-related behaviours: an exploration in the domain of food choice. *British Journal of Health Psychology*, 6: 53–68.

Speca, M., Carlson, L.E., Goodey, E. *et al.* (2000). A randomized wait-list controlled clinical trial: the effect of mindfulness meditation-based stress reduction program on mood and symptoms of stress in cancer patients. *Psychosomatic Medicine*, 62: 613–22.

Speisman, J.C., Lazarus, R.S., Mordkoff, A. *et al.* (1964). Experimental reduction of stress based on ego defense theory. *Journal of Abnormal and Social Psychology*, 68: 367–80.

Spence, M.J. and Moss-Morris, R. (2007). The cognitive behavioural model of irritable bowel syndrome: a prospective investigation of patients with gastroenteritis. *Gut*, 56: 1066–71.

Spiegel, D. (1992). Effects of psychosocial support on patients with metastatic breast cancer. *Journal of Psychosocial Oncology*, 10: 113–20.

Spiegel, D. (2001). Mind matters. Coping and cancer progression. *Journal of Psychosomatic Research*, 50: 287–90.

Spiegel, D. and Giese-Davis, J. (2003). Depression and cancer: mechanisms and disease progression. *Biological Psychiatry*, 54: 269–82.

Spiegel, D., Butler, L.D., Giese-Davis, J. *et al.* (2007). Effects of supportive–expressive group therapy on survival of patients with metastatic breast cancer: a randomized prospective trial. *Cancer*, 110: 1130–8.

Spiegel, D., Bloom, J.R. and Yalom, I. (1981). Group support for patients with metastatic cancer. A randomized outcome study. *Archives of General Psychiatry*, 38: 527–33.

Spiegel, D., Bloom, J.R., Kraemer, H.C. *et al.* (1989). Effect of psychosocial treatment on survival of patients with metastatic breast cancer. *The Lancet*, 14(2): 888–91.

Spiller, R., Aziz, Q., Creed, F. *et al.* (2007). Clinical Services Committee of The British Society of Gastroenterology. Guidelines on the irritable bowel syndrome: mechanisms and practical management. *Gut*, 56: 1770–98.

Sreeramareddy, C.T., Shankar, R.P., Sreekumaran, B.V. *et al.* (2006). Care seeking behaviour for childhood illness: a questionnaire survey in western Nepal. *BMC Int Health Hum Rights*, 6: 7. Published online 2006 May 23. doi: 10.1186/1472-698X-6-7.

Stansfeld, S.A., Bosma, H., Hemingway, H. *et al.* (1998). Psychosocial work characteristics and social support as predictors of SF-36 health functioning: the Whitehall II study. *Psychosomatic Medicine*, 60: 247–55.

Stanton, A.L., Bower, J.E. and Low, C.A. (2007). Post-traumatic growth after cancer. In L.G. Calhoun and R.G. Tedeschi (eds) (2007). *Handbook of Post-traumatic Growth: Research and Practice* (pp. 138–75). London: Lawrence Erlbaum Associates.

Stanton, A.L., Collins, C.A. and Sworowski, L.A. (2001). Adjustment to chronic illness: theory and research. In A. Baum, T.A. Revenson and J.E. Singer (eds.), *Handbook of Health Psychology*. Maah NJ: Lawrence Erlbaum, pp. 387–403.

Stanton, A.L., Danoff-Burg, S. and Huggins, M.E. (2002). The first year after breast cancer diagnosis: hope and coping strategies as predictors of adjustment. *Psycho-Oncology*, 11: 93–102.

Stanton, A.L., Danoff-Burg, S., Sworowski, L.A. *et al.* (2002). Randomized, controlled trial of written emotional expression and benefit finding in breast cancer patients. *Journal of Clinical Oncology*, 20: 4160–8.

Stanton, A.L., Kirk, K.B., Cameron, C.L. *et al.* (2000). Coping through emotional approach: scale construction and validation. *Journal of Personality and Social Psychology*, 78: 1150–69.

Stanton, A.L. and Snider, P.R. (1993). Coping with a breast cancer diagnosis: a prospective study. *Health Psychology*, 12: 16.

Starace, F., Bartoli, L., Aloisi, M.S. *et al.* (2000). Cognitive and affective disorders associated to HIV infection in the HAART era: findings from the NeuroICONA study. Cognitive impairment and depression in HIV/AIDS. *Acta Psychiatria Scandinavica*, 106: 20–6.

Stead, M., Hastings, G. and Eadie, D. (2002). The challenge of evaluating complex interventions: a framework for evaluating media advocacy. *Health Education Research*, 17: 351–64.

Steadman, L. and Quine, L. (2004). Encouraging young males to perform testicular self-examination: a simple, but effective, implementations intervention. *British Journal of Health Psychology*, 9: 479–88.

Steadman, L., Rutter, D.R. and Field, S. (2002). Individually elicited versus modal normative beliefs in predicting attendance at breast screening: examining the role of belief salience in the theory of planned behaviour. *British Journal of Health Psychology*, 7: 317–30.

Steffen, L.M., Arnett, D.K. and Blackburn, H. (2006). Population trends in leisure-time physical activity: Minnesota Heart Survey, 1980–2000. *Medicine and Science in Sports and Exercise*, 38: 1716–23.

Steinbrook, R. (2006). The potential of human papillomavirus vaccines. *New England Journal of Medicine*, 354: 1109–12.

Stenner, P.H.D., Cooper, D. and Skevington, S. (2003). Putting the Q into quality of life: the identification of subjective constructions of health-related quality of life using Q methodology. *Social Science and Medicine*, 57: 2161–72.

Stephens, C., Long, N. and Miller, N. (1997). The impact of trauma and social support on post traumatic stress disorder: a study of New Zealand police officers. *Journal of Criminal Justice*, 25: 303–14.

Stephenson, J., Bauman, A., Armstrong, T. *et al.* (2000). *The Costs of Illness Attributable to Physical Inactivity in Australia: A Preliminary Study*. Canberra: Commonwealth Government of Australia.

Steptoe, A., Doherty, S., Rink, E. *et al.* (1999). Behavioural counselling in general practice for the promotion of healthy behaviour among adults at increased risk of coronary heart disease: randomised trial. *British Journal of Medicine*, 319: 943–7.

Steptoe, A., Pollard, T. and Wardle, J. (1995). Development of a measure of the motives underlying the selection of food: the food choice questionnaire. *Appetite 1995*, 25: 267–84.

Steptoe, A., Wardle, J., Fuller, R. *et al.* (1997). Leisure-time physical exercise: prevalence, attitudinal correlates and behavioural correlates among young Europeans from 21 countries. *Preventive Medicine*, 26: 845–54.

Steptoe, A., Willemsen, G., Owen, N. *et al.* (2001). Acute mental stress elicits delayed increases in circulating inflammatory cytokines. *Clinical Science* (London), 101: 185–92.

Sterne, J.A.C. and Davey-Smith, G. (2001). Sifting the evidence – what's wrong with significance tests? *British Medical Journal*, 322: 226–31.

Stevenson, M., Palamara, P., Rooke, M. *et al.* (2001). Drink and drug driving: what's the skipper up to? *Australia and New Zealand Journal of Public Health*, 25: 511–13.

Stewart, A.L. and Ware, J.E. (eds) (1992). *Measuring Functioning and Well-being: The Medical Outcomes Study Approach*. Durham, NC: Duke University Press.

Stewart, M., Davidson, K., Meade, D. *et al.* (2000). Myocardial infarction: survivors' and spouses' stress, coping, and support. *Journal of Advanced Nursing*, 31: 1351–60.

Stirling, A.M., Wilson, P. and McConnachie, A. (2001). Deprivation, psychological distress, and consultation length in general practice. *British Journal of General Practice*, 51: 456–60.

St Leger, L.H. (1999). The opportunities and effectiveness of the health-promoting school in improving child health – a review of the claims and evidence. *Health Education Research*, 14: 51–69.

Stoate, H.G. (1989). Can health screening damage your health? *Journal of the Royal College of General Practitioners*, 39: 193–5.

Stocks, N.P., Ryan, P., McElroy, H. *et al.* (2004). Statin prescribing in Australia: socioeconomic and sex differences. A cross-sectional study. *Medical Journal of Australia*, 180: 229–31.

Stokols, D. (1992). Establishing and maintaining health environments. *American Psychologist*, 47: 6–22.

Stone, A.A., Bovbjerg, D.H., Neale, J.M. *et al.* (1993). Development of common cold symptoms following experimental rhinovirus infection is related to prior stressful life events. *Behavioral Medicine*, 8: 115–20.

Stone, D.H. and Stewart, S. (1996). Screening and the new genetics: a public health perspective on the ethical debate. *Journal of Public Health Medicine*, 18: 3–5.

Stone, G.C. (1979). Health and the health system: a historical overview and conceptual framework. In G.C. Stone, F. Cohen and N.E. Adler (eds), *Health Psychology: A Handbook*. San Francisco: Jossey-Bass.

Storch, M., Gaab, J., Küttel, Y. *et al.* (2007). Psychoneuroendocrine effects of resource-activating stress management training. *Health Psychology*, 26: 456–63.

Stoudemire, A. and Hales, R.E. (1991). Psychological and behavioral factors affecting medical conditions and DSM-IV: an overview. *Psychosomatics*, 32: 5–12.

Strang, S. and Strang, P. (2002). Questions posed to hospital chaplains by palliative care patients. *Journal of Palliative Medicine*, 5: 857–64.

Strauss, R.S. (2000). Childhood obesity and self esteem. *Pediatrics*, 105: e15.

Strecher, V.J. and Rosenstock, I.M. (1997). The health belief model. In A. Baum, S. Newman, J. Weinman *et al.* (eds), *Cambridge Hand-book of Psychology, Health and Medicine*. Cambridge: Cambridge University Press.

Strecher, V.J., Champion, V.L. and Rosenstock, I.M. (1997). The health belief model and health behaviour. In D.S. Gochman (ed.), *Handbook of Health Behavior Research I: Personal and Social Determinants*. New York: Plenum.

Strike P.C. and Steptoe, A. (2005). Behavioral and emotional triggers of acute coronary syndromes: a systematic review and critique. *Psychosomatic Medicine*, 67: 179–86.

Stroebe, W., Zech, E., Stroebe, M.S. *et al.* (2005). Does social support help in bereavement? *Journal of Social and Clinical Psychology*, 24: 1030–50.

Stronks, K., VandeMheen, H., VandenBos, J. *et al.* (1997). The interrelationship between income, health and employment status. *International Journal of Epidemiology*, 16: 592–600.

Stuckey, S.J., Jacobs, A. and Goldfarb, J. (1986). EMG biofeedback training, relaxation training, and placebo for the relief of chronic back pain. *Perceptual and Motor Skills*, 63: 1023–36.

Stunkard, A.J. and Wadden, T. (1993). *Obesity: Theory and Therapy*, 2nd edn. New York: Raven Press.

Suarez, E.C. and Williams, R.B. (1989). Situational determinants of cardiovascular and emotional reactivity in high and low hostile men. *Psychosomatic Medicine*, 51: 404–18.

Suarez, E.C., Kuhn, C.M., Schanberg, S.M. *et al.* (1998). Neuro-endocrine, cardiovascular, and emotional responses of hostile men: the role of interpersonal challenge. *Psychosomatic Medicine*, 60: 78–88.

Suchman, A.L. and Ader, R. (1992). Classic conditioning and *placebo* effects in crossover studies. *Clinical Pharmacology and Therapeutics*, 52: 372–7.

Suchman, C.A. (1965). Stages of illness and medical care. *Journal of Health and Social Behavior*, 6: 114–28.

Suitor, J.J. and Pillemer, K. (1996). Sources of support and interpersonal stress in the networks of married caregiving daughters: findings from a 2-year longitudinal study. *Journal of Gerontology Series B: Psychological Sciences & Social Science*, 51: S297–S306.

Sullivan, M.J.L., Rodgers, W.M. and Kirsch, I. (2001). Catastrophizing, depression and expectancies for pain and emotional distress. *Pain*, 91: 147–54.

Suls, J. and Fletcher, B. (1985). The relative efficacy of avoidant and nonavoidant coping strategies: a meta-analysis. *Health Psychology*, 4: 249–88.

Suls, J. and Martin, R. (2005). The daily life of the garden-variety neurotic: reactivity, stressors exposure, mood spillover, and maladaptive coping. *Journal of Personality*, 73: 1–25.

Suls, J. and Rittenhouse, J.D. (eds) (1987). Personality and Physical Health (Special Issue). *Journal of Personality*, 55: 155–393.

Suls, J., Wan, C.K. and Costa, P.T. Jr (1995). Relationship of trait anger to resting blood pressure: a meta-analysis. *Health Psychology*, 14: 444–56.

SuperioCabuslay, E., Ward, M.M. and Lorig, K.R. (1996). Patient education interventions in osteoarthritis and rheumatoid arthritis: a meta-analytic comparison with nonsteroidal antiinflammatory drug treatment. *Arthritis Care and Research*, 9: 292–301.

Surwit, R.S. and Schneider, M.S. (1993). Role of stress in the etiology and treatment of diabetes mellitus. *Psychosomatic Medicine*, 55: 380–93.

Surwit, R.S., van Tilburg, M.A., Zucker, N. *et al.* (2002). Stress management improves long-term glycemic control in type 2 diabetes. *Diabetes Care*, 25: 30–4.

Suter, P.B. (2002). Employment and litigation: improved by work, assisted by verdict. *Pain*, 100: 249–57.

Sutherland, I. and Shepherd, J.P. (2001). Social dimensions of adolescent substance use. *Addiction*, 96: 445–58.

Sutton, S. (1996). Can 'stages of change' provide guidance in the treatment of addictions? A critical examination of Prochaska and DiClemente's model. In G.E. Edwards and C. Dare (eds), *Psychotherapy, Psychological Treatments and the Addictions*. Cambridge: Cambridge University Press.

Sutton, S. (1998). Predicting and explaining intentions and behaviour: how well are we doing? *Journal of Applied Social Psychology*, 28: 1317–38.

Sutton, S. (2000). A critical review of the transtheoretical model applied to smoking cessation. In P. Norman, C. Abraham and M. Conner (eds), *Understanding and Changing Health Behaviour*. Amsterdam: Harwood Academic.

Sutton, S. (2001). Back to the drawing board? A review of applications of the transtheoretical model to substance use. *Addiction*, 96: 175–86.

Sutton, S. (2002). Using social cognition models to develop health behaviour interventions: problems and assumptions. In D. Rutter and L. Quine (eds), *Changing Health Behaviour*. Buckingham: Open University Press.

Sutton, S., McVey, D. and Glanz, A. (1999). A comparative test of the theory of reasoned action and the theory of planned behaviour in the prediction of condom use intentions in a national sample of English young people. *Health Psychology*, 18: 72–81.

Suurmeijer, T.P.B.M., Reuvekamp, M.F. and Aldenkamp, B.P. (2001). Social functioning, psychological functioning, and quality of life in epilepsy. *Epilepsia*, 42: 1160–8.

Swartz, L.H., Noell, J.W., Schroeder, S.W. *et al.* (2006). A randomised control study of a fully automated internet based smoking cessation programme. *Tobacco Control*, 15: 7–12.

Swartzman, L.C. and Lees, M.C. (1996). Causal dimensions of college students' perceptions of physical symptoms. *Journal of Behavioral Medicine*, 19: 85–110.

Taaffe, D.R., Harris, T.B., Ferrucci, L. *et al.* (2000). Cross-sectional and prospective relationships of interleukin-6 and C-reactive protein with physical performance in elderly persons: MacArthur Studies of Successful Aging. *Journal of Gerontology. A:*

Biological Science and Medical Science, 55: M709–15.

Takeuchi, D.T., Leaf, P.J. and Kuo, H. (1988). Ethnic differences in the perception of barriers to help-seeking. *Social Psychiatry & Psychiatric Epidemiology*, 23: 273–80.

Takkouche, B., Regueira, C., Gestal-Otero, J.J. and Jesus, J. (2001). A cohort study of stress and the common cold. *Epidemiology*, 12: 345–9.

Tan, P.E.H. and Bishop, G.D. (1996). Disease representations and related behavioural intentions among Chinese Singaporeans. *Psychology and Health*, 11: 671–83.

Tang, P.C. and Newcomb, C. (1998). Informing patients: a guide for providing patient health information. *Journal of the American Medical Informatics Association*, 5: 563–70.

Tapper, K., Horne, P. and Lowe, C.F. (2003). The Food Dudes to the rescue! *The Psychologist*, 16: 18–21.

Targ, E.F. and Levine, E.G. (2002). The efficacy of a mind–body–spirit group for women with breast cancer: a randomized controlled trial. *General Hospital Psychiatry*, 24: 238–48.

Tattersall, M.H., Butow, P.N., Griffin, A.-M. *et al.* (1994). The take-home message: patients prefer consultation audiotapes to summary letters. *Journal of Clinical Oncology*, 12: 1305–11.

Taylor, A., Goldberg, D., Hutchinson, S. *et al.* (2001). High risk injecting behaviour among injectors from Glasgow: cross sectional community wide surveys 1990–1999. *Journal of Epidemiology and Community Health*, 55: 766–7.

Taylor, B., Miller, E., Farrington, C.P. *et al.* (1999). Autism and measles, mumps and rubella vaccine: no epidemiological evidence for a causal association. *The Lancet*, 453: 2026–9.

Taylor, B., Miller, E., Lingam, R. *et al.* (2002). Measles, mumps and rubella vaccination and bowel problems or developmental regression in children with autism: population study. *British Medical Journal*, 324: 393–6.

Taylor, C.B., Bandura, A., Ewart, C.K. *et al.* (1985). Exercise testing to enhance wives' confidence in their husbands' cardiac capability soon after clinically uncomplicated acute myocardial infarction. *American Journal of Cardiology*, 55: 635–8.

Taylor, S. (1983). Adjustment to threatening events: a theory of cognitive adaptation. *American Psychologist*, 38: 1161–73.

Taylor, S.E. and Armor, D.A. (1996). Positive illusions and coping with adversity. *Journal of Personality*, 64: 873–98.

Taylor, S.E. and Seeman, T.E. (1999). Psychosocial resources and the SES–health relationship. *Annals of the New York Academy of Science*, 896: 210–25.

Taylor, S.E., Kemeny, M.E., Aspinwall, L.G. *et al.* (1992). Optimism, coping, psychological distress, and high-risk sexual behaviour among men at risk for acquired immunodeficiency syndrome (AIDS). *Journal of Personality and Social Psychology*, 63: 460–73.

Taylor, S.E., Klein, L.C., Grunewald, T.L. *et al.* (2003). Affiliation, social support, and biobehavioral responses to stress. In J. Suls and K.A. Wallston (eds), *Social Psychological Foundations of Health and Illness*. Oxford: Blackwell.

Taylor, S.E., Repetti, R.L. and Seeman, T. (1997). Health psychology: what is an unhealthy environment and how does it get under the skin? *Annual Reviews in Psychology*, 48: 411–47.

Tedeschi, R.G. and Calhoun, L.G. (2004). Post-traumatic growth: conceptual foundations and empirical evidence. *Psychological Enquiry*, 15: 1–18.

Temoshok, L. (1987). Personality, coping style, emotion and cancer: towards an integrative model. *Social Science and Medicine*, 20: 833–40.

Temoshok, L. and Dreher, H. (1993). *The Type C connection: The Behavioral Links to Cancer and Your Health*. New York: Penguin.

Temoshok, L. and Fox, B.H. (1984). Coping styles and other psychosocial factors related to medical status and to prognosis in patients with cutaneous malignant melanoma. In B.H. Fox and B. Newberry (eds), *Impact of Psychoendocrine Systems in Cancer and Immunity*. Toronto: C.J. Hogrefe.

Tennen, H., Affleck, G., Armeli, S. *et al.* (2000). A daily process approach to coping: linking theory, research, and practice. *American Psychologist*, 55: 620–5.

Terry, D.J. (1992). Stress, coping and coping resources as correlates of adaptation in myocardial infarction patients. *British Journal of Clinical Psychology*, 31: 215–25.

Theisen, M.E., MacNeill, S.E., Lumley, M.A. *et al.* (1995). Psychosocial factors related to unrecognized acute myocardial infarction. *American Journal of Cardiology*, 75: 1211–13.

Theorell, T. and Karasek, R.A. (1996). Current issues relating to psychosocial job strain and cardiovascular disease research. *Journal of Occupational Health Psychology*, 1: 9–26.

Theunissen, N.C.M., de Ridder, D.T.D., Bensing, J.M. *et al.* (2003). Manipulation of patient–provider interaction: discussing illness representations or action plans concerning adherence. *Patient Education and Counselling*, 51: 247–58.

Theunissen, N.C.M., Vogels, T.G.C., Koopman, H.M. *et al.* (1998). The proxy problem: child report versus parent report in health-related quality of life research. *Quality of Life Research*, 7: 387–97.

Thoits, P.A. (1995). Stress, coping and social support processes. Where are we? What next? *Journal of Health and Social Behavior* (extra issue), 36: 53–79.

Thomas, D.B., Gao, D.L., Ray, R.M. *et al.* (2002). Randomized trial of breast self-examination in Shanghai – final results. *Journal of the National Cancer Institute*, 94: 1445–57.

Thomas, M., Walker, A., Wilmot, A. *et al.* (1998). *Living in Britain: Results from the 1996 General Household Survey*. London: Stationery Office.

Thompson, S.C. (1981). Will it hurt less if I can control it? A complex answer to a simple question. *Psychological Bulletin*, 90: 89–101.

Thompson, S.C. and Pitts, J.C. (1992). In sickness and in health: chronic illness, marriage and spousal caregiving. In S. Spacapan and S. Oskamp (eds), *Helping and Being Helped: Naturalistic Studies*. Newbury Park, Calif.: Sage.

Thompson, S.C., Galbraith, M., Thomas, C. *et al.* (2002). Caregivers of stroke patient family members: behavioural and attitudinal indicators of overprotective care. *Psychology & Health*, 17: 297–312.

Thompson, S.C., Sobolew-Shubin, A., Galbraith, M.E. *et al.* (1993). Maintaining perceptions of control: finding perceived control in low-control circumstances. *Journal of Personality and Social Psychology*, 64: 293–304.

Thompson, W.G., Longstreth, G. and Drossman, D.A. (2000). Functional bowel disorders and functional abdominal pain. In D.A. Drossman, E. Corazziari, N. Talley *et al.* (eds), *Rome II: The Functional Gastrointestinal Disorders*, 2nd edn. McLean, Va: Degnon Associates.

Thrasher, J.F., Hammond, D., Fong, G.T. *et al.* (2007). Smokers' reactions to cigarette package warnings with graphic imagery and with only text: a comparison between Mexico and Canada. *Salud Publica Mexico*, 49 Suppl 2: S233–40.

Thuné-Boyle, I.C.V., Myers, L., Newman, S.P. (2006). The role of illness beliefs, treatment beliefs and perceived severity of symptoms in explaining distress in cancer patients during chemotherapy treatment. *Behavioral Medicine*, 32: 19–29.

Thuné-Boyle, I.C.V., Stygall, J., Keshtgar, M.R.S. *et al.* (2006). Do religious/spiritual coping strategies affect illness adjustment? A systematic review of the literature. *Social Science & Medicine*, 63: 151–64.

Thurstone, L.L. (1928). Attitudes can be measured. *American Journal of Sociology*, 33: 529–44.

Timko, C. and Janoff-Bulman, R. (1985). Attributions, vulnerability and psychological adjustment: the case of breast cancer. *Health Psychology*, 4: 521–44.

Tobias, M. and Yeh, L.C. (2006). Do all ethnic groups in New Zealand exhibit socio-economic mortality gradients? *Australian and New Zealand Journal of Public Health*, 30: 343–9.

Tobin, D.L., Holroyd, K.A., Baker, A. *et al.* (1988). Development and clinical trial of a minimal contact, cognitive-behavioral treatment for tension headache. *Cognitive Therapy and Research*, 12: 325–39.

Toljamo, M. and Hentinen, M. (2001). Adherence to self care and social support. *Journal of Clinical Nursing*, 10: 618–27.

Tomich, P.L. and Helgeson, V.S. (2004). Is finding something good in the bad always good? Benefit-finding among women with breast cancer. *Health Psychology*, 23: 16–23.

Topf, M. (1989). Sensitivity to noise, personality hardiness, and noise-induced stress in critical care nurses. *Environment and Behaviour*, 21: 717–33.

Toroyan, T. and Reddy, P.S. (2005–2006). Participation of South African youth in the design and development of AIDS photocomics. 1997–98. *International Quarterly of Community Health Education*, 25: 149–63.

Touzet, S., Réfabert, L., Letrilliart, L. *et al.* (2007). Impact of consensus development conference guidelines on primary care of bronchiolitis: are national guidelines being followed? *Journal of Evaluation of Clinical Practice*, 13: 651–6.

Triandis, H.C. (1977). *Interpersonal Behavior*. Monterey, Calif.: Brooks/Cole.

Tromp, D.M., Brouha, X.D.R., DeLeeuw, J.R.J. *et al.* (2004). Psychological factors and patient delay in patients with head and neck cancer. *European Journal of Cancer*, 40: 1509–16.

Tschuschke, V., Hertenstein, B., Arnold, R. *et al.* (2001). Associations between coping and survival time of adult leukaemia patients receiving allogenic bone marrow transplantation. Results of a prospective study. *Journal of Psychosomatic Research*, 50: 277–85.

Tubiana-Rufi, N., Moret, L., Czernichow, P. *et al.* (1998). The association of poor adherence and acute metabolic disorders with low levels of cohesion and adaptability in families with diabetic children. The PEDIAB Collaborative Group. *Acta Paediatrica*, 87: 741–6.

Tudor-Smith, C., Nutbeam, D., Moore, L. *et al.* (1998). Effects of the Heartbeat Wales programme over five years on behavioural risks for cardiovascular disease: quasi-experimental comparison of results from Wales and a matched reference area. *British Medical Journal*, 316: 818–22.

Turk, D.C. (1986). Workshop on pain management. Birmingham, UK.

Turk, D.C. and Okifuji, A. (1999). Assessment of patients' reporting of pain: an integrated perspective. *The Lancet*, 353: 1784–8.

Turk, D.C., Litt, M.D., Salovey, P. *et al.* (1985). Seeking urgent pediatric treatment: factors contributing to frequency, delay and appropriateness. *Health Psychology*, 4: 43–59.

Turk, D.C., Rudy, T.E. and Salovey, P. (1986). Implicit models of illness. *Journal of Behavioral Medicine*, 9: 453–74.

Turner, G. and Shepherd, J. (1999). A method in search of a theory: peer education and health promotion. *Health Education Research*, 14: 235–47.

Turner, J. (2001). Medically unexplained symptoms in secondary care. *British Medical Journal*, 322: 745–6.

Turner, J., Page-Shafer, K., Chin, D.P. *et al.* (2001). Adverse impact of cigarette smoking on dimensions of health-related quality of life in persons with HIV infection. *AIDS Patient Care and STDs*, 15: 615–24.

Turner, J.A. and Clancy, S. (1988). Comparison of operant behavioral and cognitive-behavioral group treatment for chronic low back pain. *Journal of Consulting and Clinical Psychology*, 56: 261–6.

Turner, J.A., Holtzman, S. and Mancl, L. (2007). Mediators, moderators, and predictors of therapeutic change in cognitive-behavioral therapy for chronic pain. *Pain*, 127: 276–86.

Turner, J.C., Hogg, M.A., Oakes, P.J. *et al.* (1987). *Rediscovering the Social Group: A Self-categorization Theory*. Oxford: Blackwell.

Turner-Cobb, J.M., Gore-Felton, C., Marouf, F. *et al.* (2002). Coping, social adjustment, and attachment style as psychosocial correlates of adjustment in men and women with HIV/AIDS. *Journal of Behavioral Medicine*, 25: 337–53.

Turner-Cobb, J.M., Sephton, S.E., Koopman, C. *et al.* (2000). Social support and salivary cortisol in women with metastatic breast cancer. *Psychosomatic Medicine*, 62: 337–45.

Turunen, J.H., Mäntyselkä, P.T., Kumpusalo, E.A. *et al.* (2005). Frequent analgesic use at population level: prevalence and patterns of use. *Pain*, 115: 374–81.

Tversky, A. and Kahneman, D. (1981). The framing of decisions and the psychology of choice. *Science*, 211: 453–8.

Tyas, S.L. and Pederson, L.L. (1998). Psychological factors related to adolescent smoking: a critical review of the literature. *Tobacco Control*, 7: 409–20.

Tyczynski, J.E., Bray, F., Aareleid, T. *et al.* (2004). Lung cancer mortality patterns in selected Central, Eastern and Southern European countries. *International Journal of Cancer*, 109: 598–610.

Uchino, B.N. (2006). Social support and health: a review of physiological processes potentially underlying links to disease outcomes. *Journal of Behavioral Medicine*, 29: 377–87.

Uchino, B.N., Cacioppo, J.T. and Kiecolt-Glaser, J.K. (1996). The relationship between social support and physiological processes: a review with emphasis on underlying mechanisms and implications for health. *Psychological Bulletin*, 119: 488–533.

UK Central Statistics Office (1980). A change in revenue from an indirect tax change. *Economic Trend*, March, 97–107.

UK Health Education Authority and UK Sports Council (1992). *Allied Dunbar National Fitness Survey*. London: Allied Dunbar, Health Education Authority and Sports Council.

UNAIDS 2008: http://www.unaids.org/en/

Ungar, W.J., Mirabelli, C., Cousins, M. *et al.* (2006). A qualitative analysis of a dyad approach to health-related quality of life measurement in children with asthma. *Social Science & Medicine*, 63: 2354–66.

United Nations (2006). *World Population Prospects: The 2006 Revision and World Urbanization Prospects: The 2005 Revision, Population Division of the Department of Economic and Social Affairs of the United Nations Secretariat*. Available from http://esa.un.org/unpp (accessed 12 December, 2007).

United Nations Secretariat (2002). The ageing of the world's population. Population Division, Department of Economic and Social Affairs, United Nations Secretariat. http://www.un.org/esa/socdev/ageing/agewpop.htm

Unrod, M., Smith, M., Spring, B. *et al.* (2007). Randomized controlled trial of a computer-based, tailored intervention to increase smoking cessation counseling by primary care physicians. *Journal of General Internal Medicine*, 22: 478–84.

Urquhart-Law, G. (2002). Dissimilarity in adolescent and maternal representations of type 1 diabetes: exploration of relations to adolescent well-being. *Child Health Care and Development*, 28: 369–78.

US Bureau of the Census (1999). *Statistical Abstracts of the United States: 1998* (118th edn). Retrieved (2.10.2002) from http://www.census.gov

US Centers for Disease Control and Prevention (1996). Community-level prevention of human immunodeficiency virus infection among high-risk populations: the AIDS Community Demonstration Projects. *MMWR Morbidity and Mortality Weekly Reports*, 45 (RR-6): 1–24.

US Centers for Disease Control and Prevention (2004). Impact of a smoking ban on restaurant and bar revenues – El Paso, Texas. *MMWR Morbidity and Mortality Weekly Reports*, 53: 150–1.

US Department of Health and Human Services (1996). *Physical Activity and Health: A Report of the Surgeon General*. US Department of Health and

Human Services, Centers for Disease Control and Prevention, National Center for Chronic Disease Prevention and Health Promotion, Atlanta.

US Department of Health and Human Services (1997). *Ninth Special Report to the U.S. Congress on Alcohol and Health, June 1997*. US Department of Health and Human Services, NIH, NIAAA.

US Department of Health and Human Services (2000). *Healthy People 2010*. Washington DC: US Department of Health and Human Services.

United States Preventive Services Task Force (USPSTF) (2003). Routine vitamin supplementation to prevent cancer and cardiovascular disease: recommendations and rationale. *Annals of Internal Medicine*, 139: 51–5.

Vaillant, G.E. (1998). Natural history of male psychological health XIV: relationship of mood disorder, vulnerability and physical health. *American Journal of Psychiatry*, 155: 184–91.

Valente, S.M. (2003). Depression and HIV disease. *Journal of Association of Nurses in AIDS Care*, 14: 41–51.

Van de Creek, L., Paget, S., Horton, R. *et al.* (2004). Religious and non-religious coping methods among persons with rheumatoid arthritis. *Arthritis and Rheumatology* 51: 49–55.

van den Arend, I.J., Stolk, R.P., Rutter, G.E. and Schrijvers, G.J. (2000). Education integrated into structured general practice care for Type 2 diabetic patients results in sustained improvement of illness knowledge and self-care. *Diabetes Medicine*, 17: 190–7.

van den Heuvel, E.T.P., de Witte, L.P., Schure, L.M. *et al.* (2001). Risk factors for burn-out in caregivers of stroke patients, and possibilities for intervention. *Clinical Rehabilitation*, 15: 669–77.

van den Hout, J.H.C., Vlaeyen, J.W.S., Peters, M.L. *et al.* (2000). Does failure hurt? The effects of failure feedback on pain report, pain tolerance and pain avoidance. *European Journal of Pain*, 4: 335–46.

van der Doef, M. and Maes, S. (1998). The job demand–control(–support) model and physical health outcomes: a review of the strain and buffer hypotheses. *Psychology and Health*, 13: 909–36.

van der Doef, M. and Maes, S. (1999). The job demand–control(–support) model and psychological well-being: a review of 20 years empirical research. *Work and Stress*, 13: 87–114.

van der Geest, S. and Whyte, S. (1989). The charm of medicines: metaphors and metonyms. *Medical Anthropology Quarterly*, 3: 345–67.

van der Heide, A., Deliens, L., Faisst, K. *et al.* (2003). End-of-life decision-making in six European countries: descriptive study. *The Lancet*, 361: 345–50.

van der Meer, V., van Stel, H.F., Detmar, S.B. *et al.* (2007). Internet-based self-management offers an opportunity to achieve better asthma control in adolescents. *Chest*, 132: 112–9.

van der Pligt, J. and de Vries, N.K. (1998). Expectancy-value models of health behaviour: the role of salience and anticipated affect. *Psychology and Health*, 13: 289–305.

van der Pligt, J., Otten, W., Richard, R. *et al.* (1993). Perceived risk of AIDS: unrealistic optimism and self-protective action. In J.B. Prior and G.D. Reeder (eds), *The Social Psychology of HIV Infection*. Hillsdale, NJ: Lawrence Erlbaum.

van der Velde, F.W., Hooykaas, C. and van der Pligt, J. (1992). Risk perception and behaviour: pessimism, realism and optimism about AIDS-related health behaviour. *Psychology and Health*, 6: 23–38.

van der Vyver, M., Halpern, S. and Joseph, G. (2002). Patient-controlled epidural analgesia versus continuous infusion for labour analgesia: a meta-analysis. *British Journal of Anaesthesia*, 89: 459–65.

van Eck, M., Berkhof, H., Nicolson, N. *et al.* (1996). The effects of perceived stress, traits, mood states, and stressful daily events on salivary cortisol. *Psychosomatic Medicine*, 58: 508–14.

van Tulder, M.W., Ostelo, R.W.J., Vlaeyen, J.W.S. *et al.* (2003). Behavioural treatment for chronic low back pain. In *The Cochrane Library*, issue 1. Oxford: Update Software.

van Zuuren, F.J. and Dooper, R. (1999). Coping style and self-reported health promotion and disease detection behaviour. *British Journal of Health Psychology*, 4: 81–9.

Vaughan, P.W., Rogers, E.M., Singhal, A. *et al.* (2000). Entertainment-education and HIV/AIDS prevention: a field experiment in Tanzania. *Journal of Health Communication*, 5: 81–100.

Vedhara, K., Cox, N.K.M., Wilcock, G.K. *et al.* (1999). Chronic stress in elderly carers of dementia patients and antibody responses to influenza vaccination. *The Lancet*, 353: 627–31.

Vedhara, K., McDermott, M.P., Evans, T.G. *et al.* (2002). Chronic stress in nonelderly caregivers. Psychological, endocrine and immune implications. *Journal of Psychosomatic Research*, 53: 1153–61.

Vedhara, K., Shanks, N., Anderson, S. *et al.* (2000). The role of stressors and psychosocial variables in the stress process: a study of chronic caregiver stress. *Psychosomatic Medicine*, 62: 374–85.

Vedhara, K., Tallon, D., Gale, L. *et al.* (2003). Psychological determinants of wound healing in diabetic patients with foot ulceration. Paper presented at the European Health Psychology conference, Kos, August 2003.

Vedhara, K., Wang, E.C.Y., Fox, J.D. *et al.* (2001). The measurement of stress-related immune dysfunction in humans: an introduction to psychoneuroimmunology. In A.J.J.M. Vingerhoets and K. Orth-Gomer (eds), *Psychology in Medicine.* Houten: Wolters Kluwer International (pp. 34–49).

Veenhoven, R. (2003). Happiness. *The Psychologist,* 16: 128–9.

Verbrugge, L.M. and Steiner, R.P. (1985). Prescribing drugs to men and women. *Health Psychology,* 4: 79–98.

Verdugo, R.J. and Ochoa, J.L. (1994). Sympathetically maintained pain. I. Phentolamine block questions the concept. *Neurology,* 44: 1003–10.

Vermeire, E., Hearnshaw, H., Rätsep, A. *et al.* (2007). Obstacles to adherence in living with type-2 diabetes: an international qualitative study using meta-ethnography (EUROBSTACLE). *Primary Care Diabetes,* 1: 25–33.

Vestling, M., Tfvesson, B. and Iwarsson, S. (2003). Indicators for return to work after stroke and the importance of work for subjective well-being and life satisfaction. *Journal of Rehabilitation Medicine,* 35: 127–31.

Vikman, S., Airaksinen, K.E., Tierala, I. *et al.* (2004). Improved adherence to practice guidelines yields better outcome in high-risk patients with acute coronary syndrome without ST elevation: findings from nationwide FINACS studies. *Journal of Internal Medicine,* 256: 316–23.

Viner, R., McGrath, M. and Trudinger, P. (1996). Family stress and metabolic control in diabetes. *Archives of Diseases of Childhood,* 74: 418–21.

Vingerhoets, A.J.J.M. and Perski, A. (2000). The psychobiology of stress. In A.A. Kaptein, A.W.P.M. Appels and K. Orth-Gomér (eds) *Psychology in Medicine.* Houten: Wolters Kluwer International, pp. 34–49.

Visser, de R.O. and Smith, J.A. (2007). Alcohol consumpton and masculine identity among young men. *Psychology & Health,* 22: 595–614.

Visser, M.J. (2007). HIV/AIDS prevention through peer education and support in secondary schools in South Africa. *Sahara Journal,* 4: 678–94.

Visser-Meily, A., van Heugten, C., Post, M. *et al.* (2005). Intervention studies for caregivers of stroke survivors: a critical review. *Patient Education and Counselling,* 56: 257–67.

Vlaeyen, J.W., Kole-Snijders, A.M., Boeren, R.G. *et al.* (1995). Fear of movement/(re)injury in chronic low back pain and its relation to behavioral performance. *Pain,* 62: 363–72.

Vogel, B.A., Helmes, A.W. and Hasenburg, A. (2008). Concordance between patients' desired and actual decision-making roles in breast cancer care. *Psychooncology,* 17: 182–9.

Voerman, G.E., Sandsjö, L., Vollenbroek-Hutten, M.M. *et al.* (2007). Changes in cognitive-behavioral factors and muscle activation patterns after interventions for work-related neck–shoulder complaints: relations with discomfort and disability. *Journal of Occupational Rehabilitation,* 17: 593–609.

Vögele, C. (1998). Serum lipid concentrations, hostility and cardiovascular reactions to mental stress. *International Journal of Psycophysiology,* 28: 167–79.

Vögele, C. and Steptoe, A. (1993). Anger inhibition and family history as moderators of cardiovascular responses to mental stress in adolescent boys. *Journal of Psychosomatic Research,* 37: 503–14.

Vögele, C., Jarvis, A. and Cheeseman, K. (1997). Anger suppression, reactivity, and hypertension risk: gender makes a difference. *Annals of Behavioral Medicine,* 19: 61–9.

Vogt, T.M., Mullooly, J.P., Ernst, D. *et al.* (1992). Social networks as predictors of ischemic heart disease, cancer, stroke and hypertension: incidence, survival and mortality. *Journal of Clinical Epidemiology,* 45: 659–66.

Vosvick, M., Koopman, C., Gore-Felton, C. *et al.* (2003). Relationship of functional quality of life to strategies for coping with the stress of living with HIV/AIDS. *Psychosomatics,* 44: 51–8.

Wade, D.T. and Halligan, P.W. (2004). Do biomedical models of illness make for good healthcare systems? *British Medical Journal,* 329: 1398–401.

Wakefield, A.J., Murch, S.H., Anthony, A. *et al.* (1998). Ileal-lymphoid nodular hyperplasia, non-specific colitis and pervasive developmental disorder in children. *The Lancet,* 351: 637–41.

Wakefield, M.A., Chaloupka, F.J., Kaufman, N.J. *et al.* (2000). Effect of restrictions on smoking at home, at school, and in public places on teenage smoking: Cross-sectional study. *British Medical Journal,* 321: 333–7.

Walker, C., Papadopoulos, L., Lipton, M. *et al.* (2006). The importance of children's illness beliefs: the Children's Illness Perception Questionnaire (CIPQ) as a reliable assessment tool for eczema and asthma. *Psychology, Health & Medicine,* 11: 100–7.

Walker, J.G., Jackson, H.J. and Littlejohn, G.O. (2004). Models of adjustment to chronic illness: using the example of rheumatoid arthritis. *Clinical Psychology Review,* 24: 461–88.

Walker, L.G., Heys, S.D. and Eremin, O. (1999). Surviving cancer: do psychosocial factors count? *Journal of Psychosomatic Research,* 47: 497–503.

Walker, Z.A.K. and Townsend, J. (1999). The role of general practice in promoting teenage health: a review of the literature. *Family Practice*, 16: 164–72.

Wall, P.D. (1979). On the relation of injury to pain. The John J. Bonica Lecture. *Pain*, 6: 253–64.

Wallander, J.L. and Varni, J.W. (1998). Effects of pediatric chronic physical disorders on child and family adjustment. *Journal of Child Psychology and Psychiatry*, 39: 29–46.

Wallston, K.A. (1991). The importance of placing measures of health locus of control beliefs in a theoretical context. *Health Education Research*, 6: 251–2.

Wallston, K.A. and Smith, M.S. (1994). Issues of control and health: the action is in the interaction. In G. Penny, P. Bennett and M. Herbert (eds), *Health Psychology: A Lifespan Perspective*. London: Harwood Academic.

Wallston, K.A., Wallston, B.S. and deVellis, R. (1978). Development of the multidimensional health locus of control (MHLC) scale. *Health Education Monographs*, 6: 160–70.

Walsh, D.A. and Radcliffe, J.C. (2002). Pain beliefs and perceived physical disability of patients with chronic low back pain. *Pain*, 97: 23–31.

Walton, K.G., Schneider, R.H. and Nidich, S. (2004). Review of controlled research on the transcendental meditation program and cardiovascular disease. Risk factors, morbidity, and mortality. *Cardiology Review*, 12: 262–6.

Wamala, S., Merlo, J., Bostrom, G. *et al.* (2007). Socioeconomic disadvantage and primary non-adherence with medication in Sweden. *International Journal for Quality in Health Care*, 19: 134–40.

Warburton, D.M., Revell, A.D. and Thompson, D.H. (1991). Smokers of the future. Special issue: Future directions in tobacco research. *British Journal of Addiction*, 86: 621–5.

Ward, M.M., Mefford, I.N., Parker, S.D. *et al.* (1983). Epinephrine and norepinephrine responses in continuously collected human plasma to a series of stressors. *Psychosomatic Medicine*, 45: 471–86.

Ward, S.E., Leventhal, H. and Love, R. (1988). Repression revisited: tactics used in coping with a severe health threat. *Personality and Social Psychology Bulletin*, 14: 735–46.

Wardle, J., Cooke, L.J., Gibson, E.L. *et al.* (in press). Increasing children's acceptance of vegetables; a randomized trial of parent-led exposure. *Appetite*, 40: 155–62.

Wardle, J. and Steptoe, A. (2003). Socioeconomic differences in attitudes and beliefs about healthy lifestyles. *Journal of Epidemiology and Community Health*, 57: 440–3.

Warner, L.J., Lumley, M.A., Casey, R.J. *et al.* (2006). Health effects of written emotional disclosure in adolescents with asthma: a randomized, controlled trial. *Journal of Pediatric Psychology*, 31: 557–68.

Warren, L. and Hixenbaugh, P. (1998). Adherence and diabetes. In L. Myers and K. Midence (eds), *Adherence to Treatment in Medical Conditions*. The Netherlands: Harwood Academic.

Watson, D. and Clark, L.A. (1984). Negative affectivity: the disposition to experience aversive emotional states. *Psychological Bulletin*, 96: 465–90.

Watson, D. and Pennebaker, J.W. (1989). Health complaints, stress and distress: exploring the central role of negative affectivity. *Psychological Review*, 96: 234–54.

Watson, D. and Pennebaker, J.W. (1991). Situational, dispositional and genetic bases of symptom reporting. In J.A. Skelton and R.T. Croyle (eds), *Mental Representation in Health and Illness*. New York: Springer Verlag.

Watson, D., David, J.P. and Suls, J. (1999). Personality, affectivity, and coping. In C.R. Snyder (ed.), *Coping: The Psychology of What Works* (pp. 119–40). Oxford: Oxford University Press.

Watson, M., Buck, G., Wheatley, K. *et al.* (2004). Adverse impact of bone marrow transplantation on quality of life in acute myeloid leukaemia patients: analysis of the UK Medical Research Council AML 10 Trial. *European Journal of Cancer*, 40: 971–8.

Watson, M., Davidson-Homewood, J., Haviland, J. *et al.* (2002). Influence of psychological coping on survival and recurrence: a response to the systematic review (letter to the editor). *British Medical Journal*, 325: 598.

Watson, M., Foster, C., Eeles, R. *et al.* (2004). Psychosocial impact of breast/ovarian (BRCA1/2) cancer-predictive genetic testing in a UK multi-centre clinical cohort. *British Journal of Cancer*, 91: 1787–94

Watson, M., Haviland, J.S., Greer, S. *et al.* (1999). Influence of psychological response on survival in breast cancer: a population-based cohort study. *The Lancet*, 9187: 1331–6.

Watson, M., Homewood, J., Haviland, J. *et al.* (2005). Influence of psychological response on breast cancer survival: 10-year follow-up of a population-based cohort. *European Journal of Cancer*, 41: 1710–14.

Watson, M., Lloyd, S., Davidson, J. *et al.* (1999). The impact of genetic counselling on risk perception and mental health in women with a family history of breast cancer. *British Journal of Cancer*, 79: 868–74.

Webb, O.J. and Eves, F.F. (2007). Effects of environmental changes in a stair climbing intervention:

generalization to stair descent. *American Journal of Health Promotion*, 22: 38–44.

Weber, A. and Lehnert, G. (1997). Unemployment and cardiovascular diseases: a causal relationship? *International Archives of Occupational and Environmental Health*, 70: 153–60.

Weber, B.A., Roberts, B.L., Yarandi, H. *et al.* (2007). The impact of dyadic social support on self-efficacy and depression after radical prostatectomy. *Journal of Aging and Health*, 19: 630–45.

Weber, M.A. and Julius, S. (1998). The challenge of very mild hypertension: should treatment be sooner or later? *American Journal of Hypertension*, 11: 1495–6.

Weiner, B. (1986). *An Attributional Theory of Motivation and Emotion*. New York: Springer.

Weinman, J. and Petrie, K.J. (1997). Illness perceptions: a new paradigm for psychosomatics? (editorial). *Journal of Psychosomatic Research*, 42: 113–16.

Weinman, J., Petrie, K.J., Moss-Morris, R. *et al.* (1996). The Illness Perception Questionnaire: a new method for assessing the cognitive representation of illness. *Psychology and Health*, 11: 431–55.

Weinman, J., Petrie, K.J., Sharpe, N. *et al.* (2000). Causal attributions in patients and spouses following first-time myocardial infarction and subsequent life changes. *British Journal of Health Psychology*, 5: 263–74.

Weinstein, N. (1984). Why it won't happen to me: perceptions of risk factors and susceptibility. *Health Psychology*, 3: 431–57.

Weinstein, N. (1987). Unrealistic optimism about illness susceptibility: conclusions from a community-wide sample. *Journal of Behavioral Medicine*, 10: 481–500.

Weinstein, N.D. (1982). Unrealistic optimism about susceptibility to health problems. *Journal of Behavioral Medicine*, 2: 125–40.

Weinstein, N.D. (1988). The precaution adoption process. *Health Psychology*, 7: 355–86.

Weinstein, N.D. (2003). Exploring the links between risk perception and preventive health behaviour. In J. Suls and K.A. Wallston (eds), *Social Psychological Foundations of Health and Illness*. Malden, Mass.: Blackwell.

Weinstein, N.D. and Klein, W.M. (1996). Unrealistic optimism: present and future. *Journal of Social and Clinical Psychology*, 15: 1–8.

Weinstein, N.D. and Sandman, P.M. (1992). A model of the precaution adoption process: evidence from home radon testing. *Health Psychology*, 11: 170–80.

Weinstein, N. and Sandman, P.M. (2002). Reducing the risk of exposure to radon gas: an application of the Precaution Adoption Process model. In D. Rutter and L. Quine (eds), *Changing Health Behaviour* (pp. 66–86). Buckingham: Open University Press.

Weinstein, N.D., Rothman, A.J. and Sutton, S.R. (1998). Stage theories of health behavior: conceptual and methodological issues. *Health Psychology*, 17: 290–9.

Weisenberg, M., Raz, T. and Hener, T. (1998). The influence of film-induced mood on pain perceptions. *Pain*, 76: 365–75.

Weisse, C.S., Turbiasz, A.A. and Whitney, D.J. (1995). Behavioral training and AIDS risk reduction: overcoming barriers to condom use. *AIDS Education and Prevention*, 7: 50–9.

Weller, D. (2004). Behavioural and social science research in cancer: time for action (editorial comment). *European Journal of Cancer*, 40: 314–15.

Wellings, K., Field, S., Johnson, A.M. *et al.* (1994). Studying sexual lifestyles. In K. Wellings, S. Field, A.M. Johnson and J. Wadsworth (eds), *Sexual Behaviour in Britain*. London: Penguin.

Wellings, K., Nanchahal, K., Macdowall, W. *et al.* (2001). Sexual behaviour in Britain: early heterosexual experience. *The Lancet*, 358/9296: 1843–50.

Wells, M.E., McQuellon, R.P., Hinkle, J.S. *et al.* (1995). Reducing anxiety in newly diagnosed cancer patients: a pilot program. *Cancer Practice*, 3: 100–4.

Wells, Y.D. (1999). Intentions to care for a spouse: gender differences in anticipated willingness to care and expected burden. *Journal of Family Studies*, 5: 220–34.

Wen, L.M., Thomas, M., Jones, H. *et al.* (2002). Promoting physical activity in women: evaluation of a 2-year community-based intervention in Sydney, Australia. *Health Promotion International*, 17: 127–37.

Wessely, S., Rose S. and Bisson, J. (1999). A systematic review of brief psychological interventions ('debriefing') for the treatment of immediate trauma related symptoms and the prevention of post-traumatic stress disorder. In *The Cochrane Library*. Oxford: Update Software.

West, R. (1992). Nicotine addiction: a re-analysis of the arguments. *Psychopharmacology*, 108: 408–10.

West, R., Edwards, M. and Hajek, P.A. (1998). Randomized controlled trial of a 'buddy' system to improve success at giving up smoking in general practice. *Addiction*, 93: 1007–11.

Westman, M., Eden, D. and Shirom, A. (1985). Job stress, cigarette smoking and cessation: conditioning effects of peer support. *Social Science and Medicine*, 20: 637–44.

Whelan, E.M. (1988). The truth about Americans' health. In R. Yarian (ed.), *Annual Editions: Health* (9th edition), pp. 25–9.

White, A., Nicolaas, G., Foster, K. *et al.* (1993). *Health Survey for England 1991*. London: HMSO.

Whitehead, M., Townsend, P. and Davidson, N. (eds) (1992). *Inequalities in Health: The Black Report/ The Health Divide*. London: Penguin Social Sciences.

Whiteman, M.C. (2006). Personality, cardiovascular disease and public health. In M.E. Vollrath (ed.), *Handbook of Personality and Health*. Chichester: John Wiley & Sons (pp. 13–34).

Whiteman, M.C., Fowkes, F.G.R., Deary, I.J. *et al.* (1997). Hostility, smoking, and alcohol consumption in the general population. *Social Science & Medicine*, 44: 1089–96.

WHO 2007: http://www.who.int/healthinfo/statistics/indhale/en/

WHO 2008: http://www.who.int/whosis/database/life_tables/life_tables.cfm

WHOQOL Group (1993). Study protocol for the World Health Organization project to develop a quality of life assessment instrument (WHOQOL). *Quality of Life Research*, 2: 153–9.

WHOQOL Group (1994). Development of the WHO-QOL: rationale and current status. Monograph on quality of life assessment: cross-cultural issues 2. *International Journal of Mental Health*, 23: 24–56.

WHOQOL Group (1998). The World Health Organization Quality of Life Assessment (WHO-QOL): development and psychometric properties. *Social Science and Medicine*, 46: 1569–85.

Widows, M.R., Jacobsen, P.B. and Fields, K.K. (2000). Relation of psychological vulnerability factors to posttraumatic stress disorder symptomatology in bone marrow transplant recipients. *Psychosomatic Medicine*, 62: 873–82.

Wilbert-Lampen, U., Leistner, D., Greven, S. *et al.* (2008) Cardiovascular events during World Cup soccer. *New England Journal of Medicine*, 358: 475–83.

Wild, S. and McKeigue, P. (1997). Cross sectional analysis of mortality by country of birth in England and Wales, 1970–92. *British Medical Journal*, 314: 705–10.

Wiles, R., Ashburn, A., Payne, S. *et al.* (2004). Discharge from physiotherapy following stroke: the management of disappointment. *Social Science and Medicine*, 59: 1263–73.

Wilkinson, M. (1992). Income distribution and life expectancy. *British Medical Journal*, 304: 165–8.

Wilkinson, R.G. (1990). Income distribution and mortality: a 'natural' experiment. *Sociology of Health and Illness*, 12: 391–412.

Williams, J., Wake, M., Hesketh, K. *et al.* (2005). Health-related quality of life of overweight and obese children. *Journal of the American Medical Association*, 293: 1–5.

Williams, J.E., Paton, C.C., Siegler, I.C. *et al.* (2000). Anger proneness predicts coronary heart disease risk: prospective analysis from Atherosclerosis Risk in Communities (ARIC) study. *Circulation*, 1010: 2034–9.

Williams, P.G. (2006). Personality and illness behaviour. In M.E. Vollrath (ed.), *Handbook of Personality and Health* (pp. 157–173). Chichester: John Wiley & Sons.

Williamson, D., Robinson, M.E. and Melamed, B. (1997). Pain behaviour, spouse responsiveness, and marital satisfaction in patients with rheumatoid arthritis. *Behavioral Modification*, 21: 97–118.

Williamson, G.M., Shaffer, D.R. and Schulz, R. (1998). Activity restriction and prior relationship history as contributors to mental health outcomes among middle-aged and older spousal caregivers. *Health Psychology*, 17: 152–62.

Williamson, S. and Wardle, J. (2002). Increasing participation with colorectal cancer screening: the development of a psychoeducational intervention. In D. Rutter and L. Quine (eds), *Changing Health Behaviour*. Buckingham: Open University Press.

Wilson, J.F. (1981). Behavioral preparation for surgery: benefit or harm? *Journal of Behavioral Medicine*, 4: 79–102.

Wilson, J.F., Moore, R.W., Randolph, S. and Hanson, B.J. (1982). Behavioral preparation of patients for gastrointestinal endoscopy: information, relaxation and coping style. *Journal of Human Stress*, 8: 13–23.

Wilson, P.W.F., D'Agostino, R.B., Sullivan, L. *et al.* (2002). Overweight and obesity as determinants of cardiovascular risk, *Archives of Internal Medicine*, 162: 1867–72.

Wimbush, E., MacGregor, A. and Fraser, E. (1998). Impact of a national mass media campaign on walking in Scotland. *Health Promotion International*, 13: 45–53.

Winett, R.A., Anderson, E.S., Wojcik, J.R. *et al.* (2007). Guide to health: nutrition and physical activity outcomes of a group-randomized trial of an Internet-based intervention in churches. *Annals of Behavioral Medicine*, 33: 251–61.

Wing, R.R., Phelan, S. and Tate, D. (2002). The role of adherence in mediating the relationship between depression and health outcomes. *Journal of Psychosomatic Research*, 53: 877–81.

Winkleby, M., Fortmann, S. and Barrett, D. (1990). Social class disparities in risk factors for disease: eight year prevalence patterns by level of education. *Preventive Medicine*, 19: 1–12.

Wise, R.A. (1998). Drug activation of brain reward pathways. *Drug and Alcohol Dependence*, 51: 13–22.

Witte, K. (1992). Putting the fear back into fear appeals: the extended parallel process model. *Communication Monographs*, 59: 329–49.

Witte, K. and Allen, M. (2000). A meta-analysis of fear appeals: implications for effective public health campaigns. *Health Education and Behavior*, 27: 591–615.

Wollin, S.D. and Jones, P.J. (2001). Alcohol, red wine and cardiovascular disease. *Journal of Nutrition*, 131: 1401–4.

Woods, R. (2008). Introduction. In R. Woods and L. Clare (eds), *Handbook of the Clinical Psychology of Ageing*, (2nd edition). London: John Wiley & Sons (pp. 1–16).

Woods, R.T. (ed.) (1999). *Psychological Problems of Ageing: Assessment, Treatment and Care*. Chichester: Wiley.

Woodward, M., Oliphant, J., Lowe, G. *et al.* (2003). Contribution of contemporaneous risk factors to social inequality in coronary heart disease and all causes mortality. *Preventive Medicine*, 36: 561–8.

Woolf, S.H. (1996). Immunizations. In S.H. Woolf, S. Jonas and R.S. Lawrence (eds), *Health Promotion and Disease Prevention in Clinical Practice*. Baltimore: Williams & Wilkins.

World Cancer Research Fund (1997). *Food Nutrition and the Prevention of Cancer: A Global Perspective*. Washington: American Institute for Cancer Research.

World Health Organization (1947). *Constitution of the World Health Organization*. Geneva: WHO.

World Health Organization (1980). *International Classification of Impairments, Disabilities and Handicaps (ICIDH). A Manual of Classification Relating to the Consequences of Disease*. Geneva: WHO.

World Health Organization (1981). *Global Strategy for Health for All by the Year 2000*. Geneva: WHO.

World Health Organization (1988). *Healthy Cities Project: Five Year Planning Framework*. Copenhagen: WHO Regional Office for Europe.

World Health Organization (1995). *World Health Report*. Geneva: WHO.

World Health Organization (1996). *Health Promoting Schools. Report of a WHO Expert Committee on Comprehensive School Health Education and Promotion*. Geneva: WHO.

World Health Organization (1999). *Health 21: Health for All in the 21st Century*. Copenhagen: WHO Regional Office for Europe.

World Health Organization (2002). *The World Health Report: Reducing Risks, Promoting Healthy Life*. Copenhagen: WHO Regional Office for Europe.

World Health Organization (2003). *Diet, nutrition and the prevention of chronic diseases: Report of a joint WHO/FAO expert consultation*. Geneva: World Health Organization.

World Health Organization (2003). *Global Alcohol Database*. Available from www.who.int/ncd_surveillance/infobase/web/InfoBaseCommon/ (accessed 12 January 2008).

World Health Organization (2004). *Young People's Health in Context: Health Behaviour in School-aged Children (HBSC) Study:* International report from the 2001/2002 survey. C. Currie, C. Roberts, A. Morgan *et al.* (eds). www.euro.who.int

World Health Organization Expert Committee (1990). *Cancer Pain Relief and Palliative Care*, Technical Report Series No. 84. Geneva: WHO.

World Health report (2008). http://www.who.int/research/en/

Wortley, P. and Fleming, P. (1997). AIDS in women in the United States: recent trends. *Journal of the American Medical Association*, 278: 911–16.

Wu, A.W., Snyder, C.F., Huang, I.C. *et al.* (2006). A randomized trial of the impact of a programmable medication reminder device on quality of life in patients with AIDS. *AIDS Patient Care and STDS*, 20: 773–81.

Wysocki, T., Harris, M.A., Buckloh, L.M. *et al.* (2007). Randomized trial of behavioral family systems therapy for diabetes: maintenance of effects on diabetes outcomes in adolescents. *Diabetes Care*, 30: 555–60.

Yan, H. and Sellick, K. (2004). Quality of life of Chinese patients newly diagnosed with gastrointestinal cancer: a longitudinal study. *International Journal of Nursing Studies*, 41: 309–19.

Yancy, C. (2002). Online program aids heart patients and their doctors. *Circulation*, 106: 2299.

Yardley, L. and Dibb, B. (2007). Assessing subjective change in chronic illness: an examination of response shift in health-related and goal-oriented subjective status. *Psychology & Health*, 22: 813–28.

Yee, J.L. and Schulz, R. (2000). Gender differences in psychiatric morbidity among family caregivers: a review and analysis. *The Gerontologist*, 40: 147–64.

Yip, Y.B., Sit, J.W., Fung, K.K. *et al.* (2007). Impact of an Arthritis Self-Management Programme with an added exercise component for osteoarthritic knee sufferers on improving pain, functional outcomes, and use of health care services: an experimental study. *Patient Education and Counseling*, 65: 113–21.

Yorke, J. and Shuldham, C. (2005). Family therapy for chronic asthma in children. *Cochrane Database Systematic Review* (2): CD000089.

Young, J.M., D'Este, C. and Ward, J.E. (2002). Improving family physicians' use of evidence-based smoking cessation strategies: a cluster randomization trial. *Preventive Medicine*, 35: 572–83.

Yzer, M.C., Fisher, J.D., Bakker, A.B. *et al.* (1998). The effects of information about AIDS risk and self-efficacy on women's intentions to engage in AIDS preventive behavior. *Journal of Applied Social Psychology*, 28: 1837–52.

Yzer, M.C., Siero, F.W. and Buunk, B.P. (2001). Bringing up condom use and using condoms with new sexual partners: intention or habitual? *Psychology and Health*, 16: 409–21.

Zabora, J., BrintzenhofeSzoc, K., Curbow, B. *et al.* (2001). The prevalence of psychological distress by cancer site. *Psycho-Oncology*, 10: 19–28.

Zachariae, R., Pedersen, C.G., Jensen, A.B. *et al.* (2003). Association of perceived physician communication style with patient satisfaction, distress, cancer-related self-efficacy, and perceived control over the disease. *British Journal of Cancer*, 88: 658–65.

Zakowski, S. (1995). The effects of stressor predictability on lymphocyte proliferation in humans. *Psychology & Health*, 10: 409–25.

Zakowski, S.G., McAllister, C.G., Deal, M. *et al.* (1992). Stress, reactivity, and immune function in healthy men. *Health Psychology*, 11: 223–32.

Zarit, S., Reever, K. and Bach-Peterson, J. (1980). Relatives of the impaired elderly: correlates of feelings of burden. *The Gerontologist*, 20: 649–55.

Zaza, C. and Baine, N. (2002). Cancer pain and psychosocial factors: a critical review of the literature. *Journal of Pain and Symptom Management*, 24: 526–42.

Zborowski, M. (1952). Cultural components in response to pain. *Journal of Social Issues*, 8: 16–30.

Zeidner, M. and Saklofske, D. (1996). Adaptive and maladaptive coping. In M. Zeidner and N. Endler (eds), *Handbook of Coping: Theory, Research, Application*. New York: Wiley.

Zelter, L. and LeBaron, S. (1982). Hypnosis and non-hypnotic techniques for reduction of pain and anxiety during painful procedures in children and adolescents with cancer. *Journal of Pediatrics*, 101: 1032–5.

Zervas, I.M., Augustine, A. and Fricchione, G.L. (1993). Patient delay in cancer. A view for the crisis model. *General Hospital Psychiatry*, 15: 9–13.

Zhang, Y., Proenca, R., Maffie, M. *et al.* (1994). Positional cloning of the mouse obese gene and its human homologue. *Nature*, 372: 425–32.

Zimmers, E., Privette, G., Lowe, R.H. *et al.* (1999). Increasing use of the female condom through video instruction. *Perceptual and Motor Skills*, 88: 1071–7.

Zinovieff, F., Morrison, V., Coles, A. *et al.* (2005). Are the needs of cancer patients and their carers generic? Paper presented to the European Health Psychology Society annual conference, Galway, September.

Zohar, D. and Dayan, I. (1999). Must coping options be severely limited during stressful events: testing the interaction between primary and secondary appraisals. *Anxiety, Stress and Coping*, 12: 191–216.

Zola, I.K. (1973). Pathways to the doctor – from person to patient. *Social Science and Medicine*, 7: 677–89.

Zorrilla, E.P., McKay, J.R., Luborsky, L. *et al.* (1996). Relation of stressors and depressive symptoms to clinical progression of Viral Illness. *American Journal of Psychiatry*, May, 1996. 153(5): 626–35.

Zucker, D., Hopkins, R.S., Sly, D.F. *et al.* (2000). Florida's 'truth' campaign: a counter-marketing, anti-tobacco media campaign. *Journal of Public Health Management Practice*, 6: 1–6.

Zuckerman, M. (1979). *Sensation Seeking: Beyond the Optimal Level of Arousal*. Hillsdale, NJ: Lawrence Erlbaum.

Zuckerman, M. (1984). Sensation seeking: a comparative approach to a human trait. *Behavioral and Brain Sciences*, 7: 413–17.

INDEX